Creo Parametric 11.0 Basics

Tutorial Books

Contact us at online.books999@gmail.com for resource files and technical support.

Contents

Introduction

Welcome to the *Creo Parametric 11.0 Basics* book. This book is written to assist students, designers, and engineering professionals. It covers the important features and functionalities of Creo Parametric using relevant examples and exercises.

This book is written for new users, who can use it as a self-study resource to learn Creo Parametric. In addition, it can also be used as a reference for experienced users. The focus of this book is part modeling, assembly modeling, drawings, sheet metal, and surface design.

Topics covered in this Book

Chapter 1, "Getting Started with Creo Parametric 11.0", introduces Creo Parametric. The user interface and terminology are discussed in this chapter.

Chapter 2, "Sketching", explores the sketching commands in Creo Parametric. You will learn to create parametric sketches.

Chapter 3, "Basic features", teaches you to create basic 3D geometry using the Extrude and Revolve commands. You will also learn to create datum features, which will act as supporting geometry.

Chapter 4, "Holes and Placed Features", covers the features, which can be created without using sketches.

Chapter 5, "Patterned Geometry", explores the commands to create patterned and mirrored geometry.

Chapter 6, "Sweep Features", teaches you to create basic and complex features by sweeping a profile along a path.

Chapter 7, "Blend Features", teaches you to create features by using different cross-sections.

Chapter 8, "Modifying Parts", explores the commands and techniques to modify the part geometry.

Chapter 9, "Assemblies", explains you to create assemblies using the bottom-up and top-down design approaches.

Chapter 10, "Drawings", covers how to create 2D drawings from 3D parts and assemblies.

Chapter 11, "Sheet Metal Design", covers how to create sheet metal parts and flat patterns.

Chapter 12, "Surface Design", covers how to create complex shapes using surface design commands.

Chapter 1: Getting Started with Creo Parametric 11.0

Introduction to Creo Parametric 11.0

Creo Parametric 11.0 is a parametric and feature-based system that allows you to create 3D parts, assemblies, and 2D drawings. The design process in Creo Parametric is shown below.

Environments in Creo Parametric 11.0

Creo Parametric offers many environments to carry out different types of operations. For example, Creo Parametric provides you with the **Part** environment to design a part. Likewise, there are many environments to perform advanced operations, such as manufacturing processes, process diagrams, and assemblies. However, in this book, we cover the basic environments such as **Part**, **Assembly**, and **Drawing**. A brief introduction to these environments is given next.

Part environment

The **Part** environment provides you with commands to create parametric solid models. You can start a document in this environment by clicking the **New** icon and selecting **Type > Part** on the **New** dialog. To create solid models, you must draw parametric sketches in the **Sketch** environment and then convert them into solids.

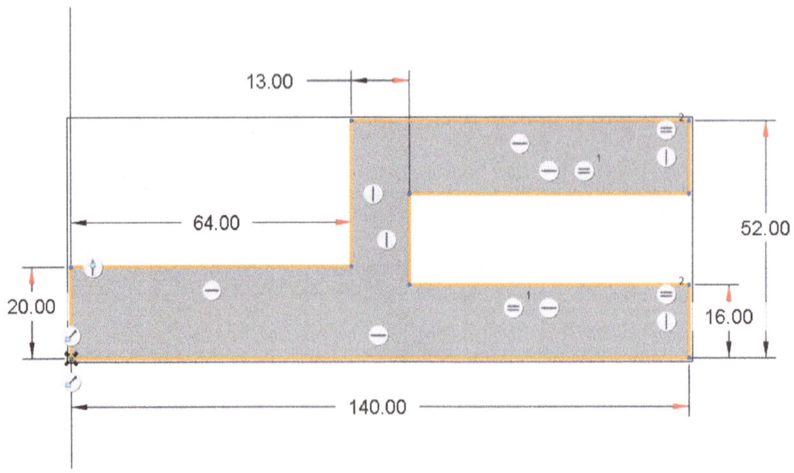

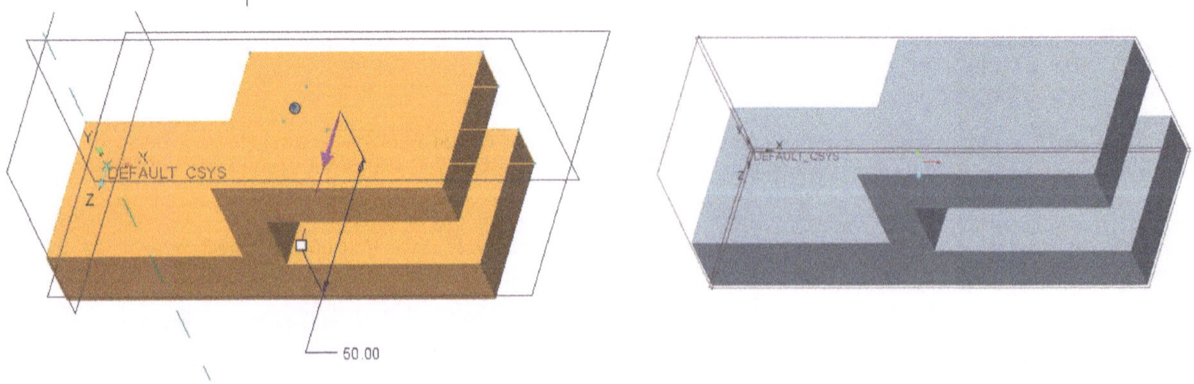

However, you can add some additional features to the solid models, which do not require sketches.

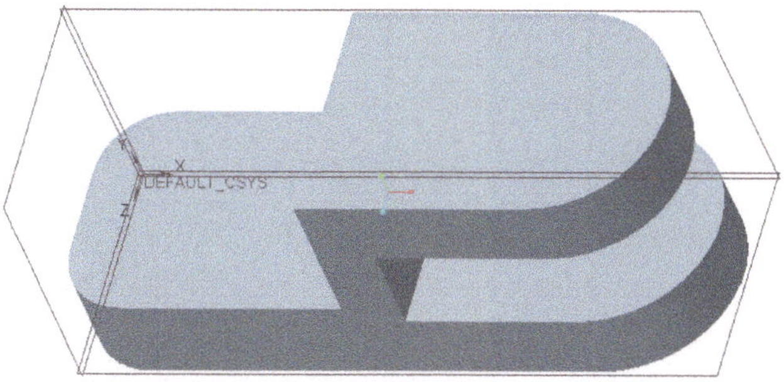

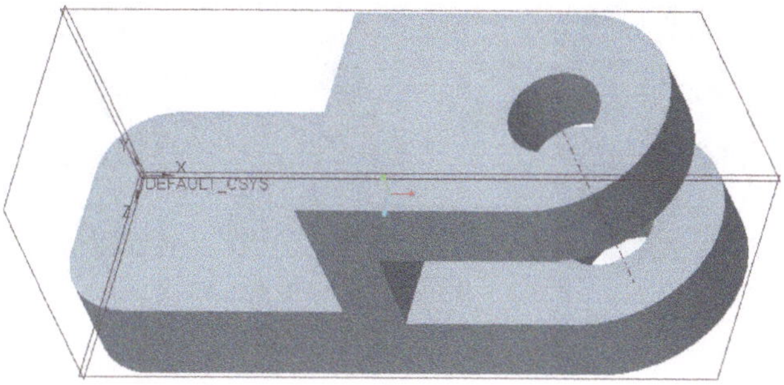

Assembly

The **Assembly** environment (click **Type > Assembly** on the **New** dialog) has commands to combine individual parts in an assembly. There are two ways to create an assembly. The first way is to create individual parts and assemble them in the **Assembly** environment (Bottom-up assembly design). The second way is to start an assembly file and create individual parts (Top-down assembly design).

Drawing

The **Drawing** environment (click **Type > Drawing** on the **New** dialog) has commands to create 2D drawings, which can be used for the manufacturing process. There are two ways to create drawings. The first way is to generate the standard views of a 3D component or assembly. The second way is to sketch the drawings manually.

Sheetmetal

The **Sheetmetal** environment (click **Type > Part** and click **Subtype > Sheetmetal** on the **New** dialog) has commands to create sheet metal models. You can create a sheet metal model either by building features systematically or by converting a part geometry into sheet metal.

Parametric Modeling

In Creo Parametric, parameters, dimensions, or constraints control everything. For example, if you want to change the hole's position shown in the figure, you need to change the dimension or constraint that controls its position.

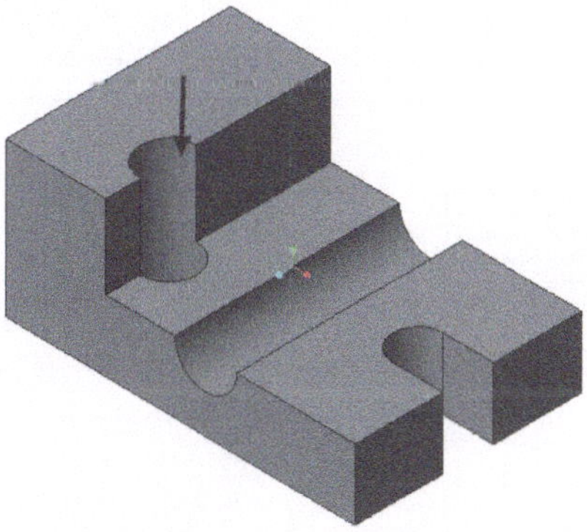

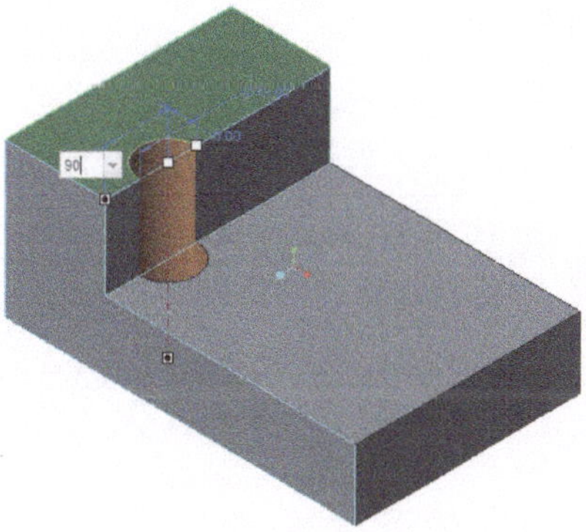

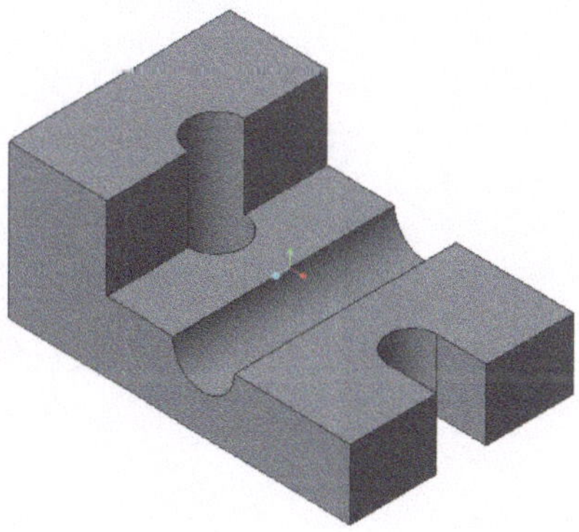

Associativity

The other big advantage of Creo Parametric is the associativity between parts, assemblies, and drawings. When you make changes to a part's design, the changes will occur in all linked assemblies. Also, the 2D drawing will update automatically.

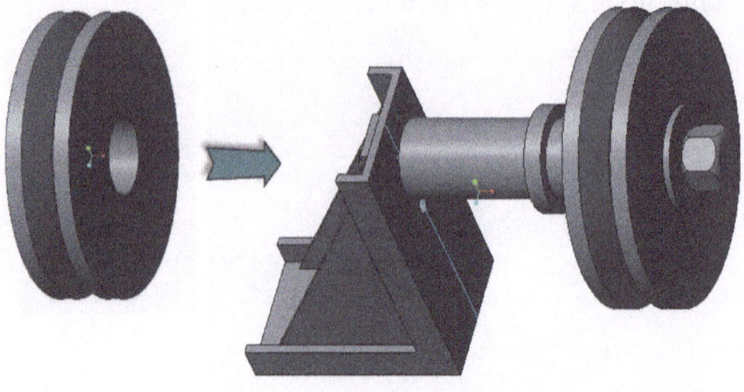

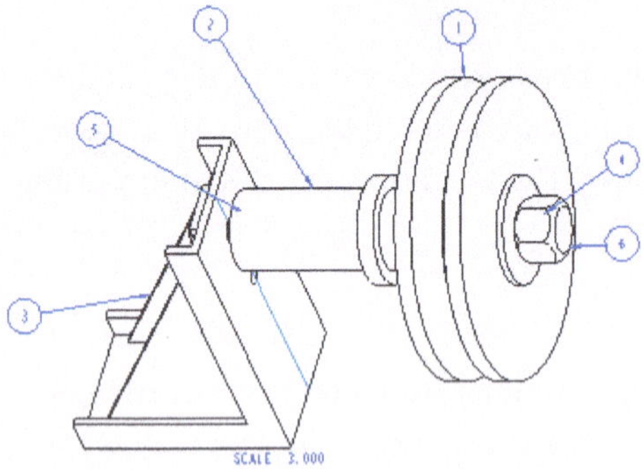

1	1	1	prt0001 prt	
2	2	1	prt0002 prt	
3	3	1	prt0003 prt	
4	4	1	4 prt	
5	5	2	prt0005 prt	
6	6	1	6 prt	

Modified Part

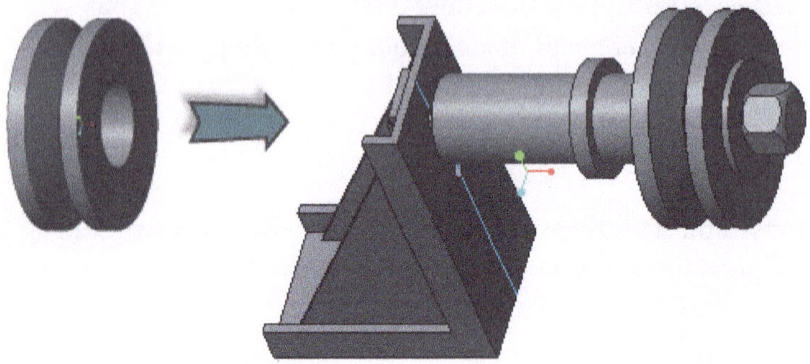

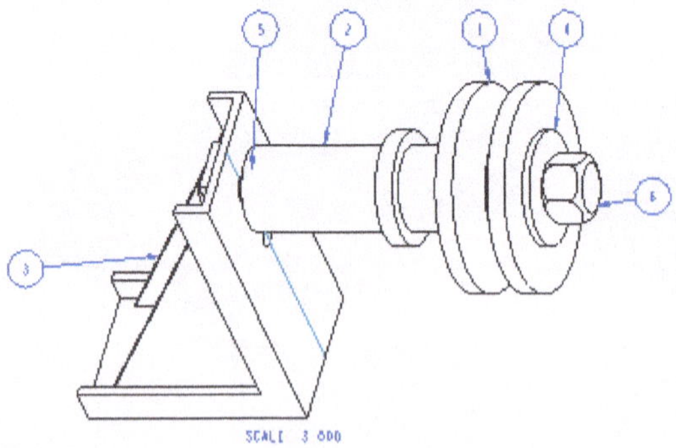

1	1	1	pi 10001.pi 1	
2	2	1	pi 10002.pi 1	
3	3	1	pi 10003.pi 1	
4	4	1	4.pi 1	
5	5	2	pi 10005.pi 1	
6	6	1	6.pi 1	

File Types in Creo Parametric

Creo Parametric offers three main file types:

.prt: This type of file has a geometry of the individual part. The files created in **Part** and **Sheetmetal** environments will have this extension.

.asm: This type of file is an assembly of one or more parts. It is a link between one or more parts.

.drw: The files created in the Drawing environment have this extension.

Starting Creo Parametric 11.0

To start **PTC Creo Parametric 11.0**, click the **PTC Creo Parametric 11.0** icon on your computer screen (or) click **Start > PTC > Creo Parametric 11.0**.

User Interface

The following image shows the **Creo Parametric 11.0** application window.

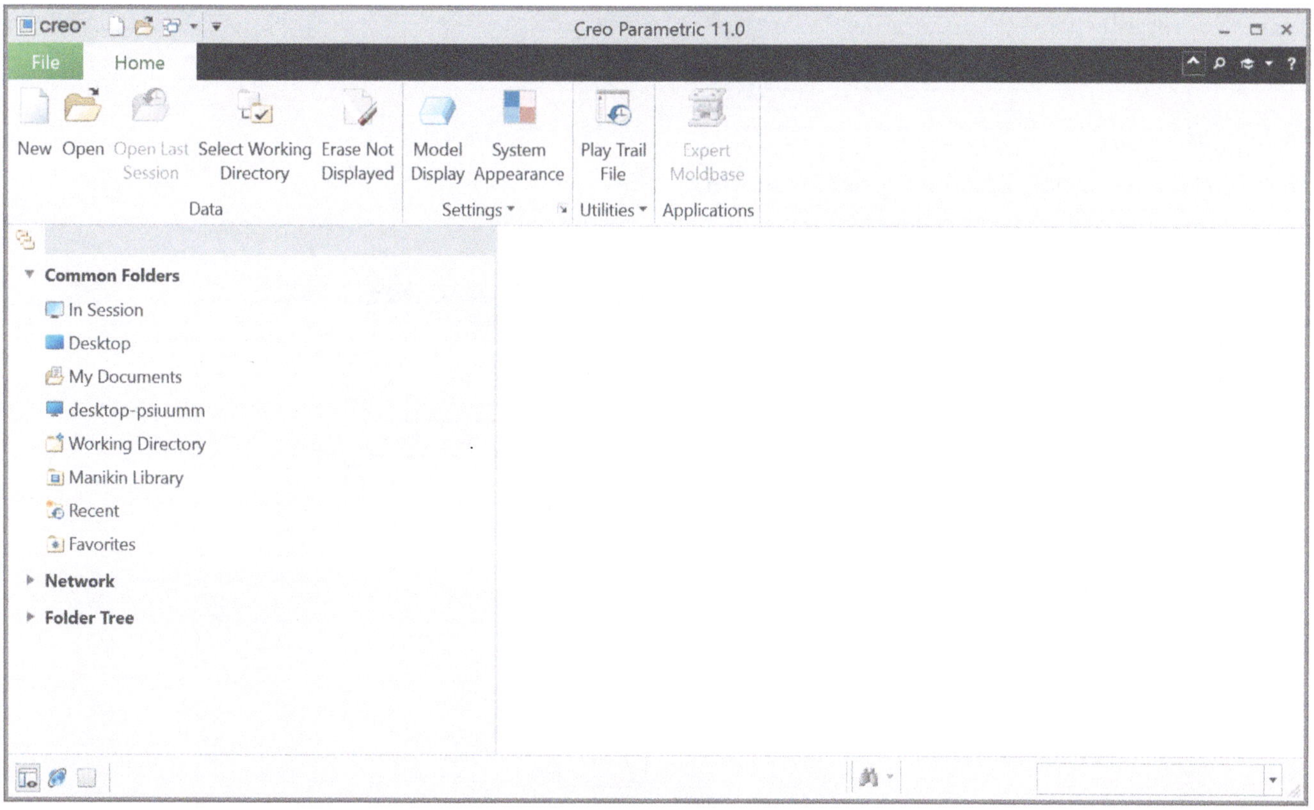

1. On the **Home** tab of the ribbon, click the **New** icon.
2. On the **New** dialog, select **Type > Part**.
3. Type-in the name of the part file in the **Name** box.
4. Click **OK**.

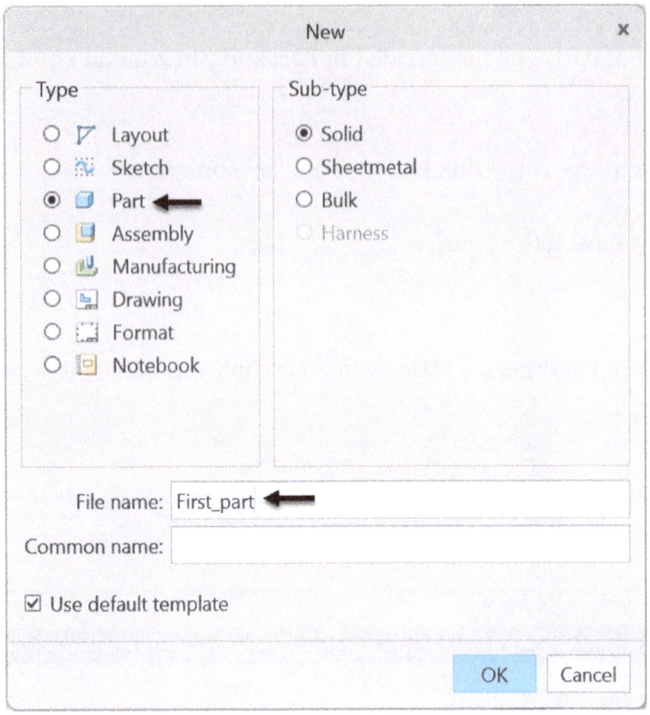

The Creo Parametric part window appears, as shown.

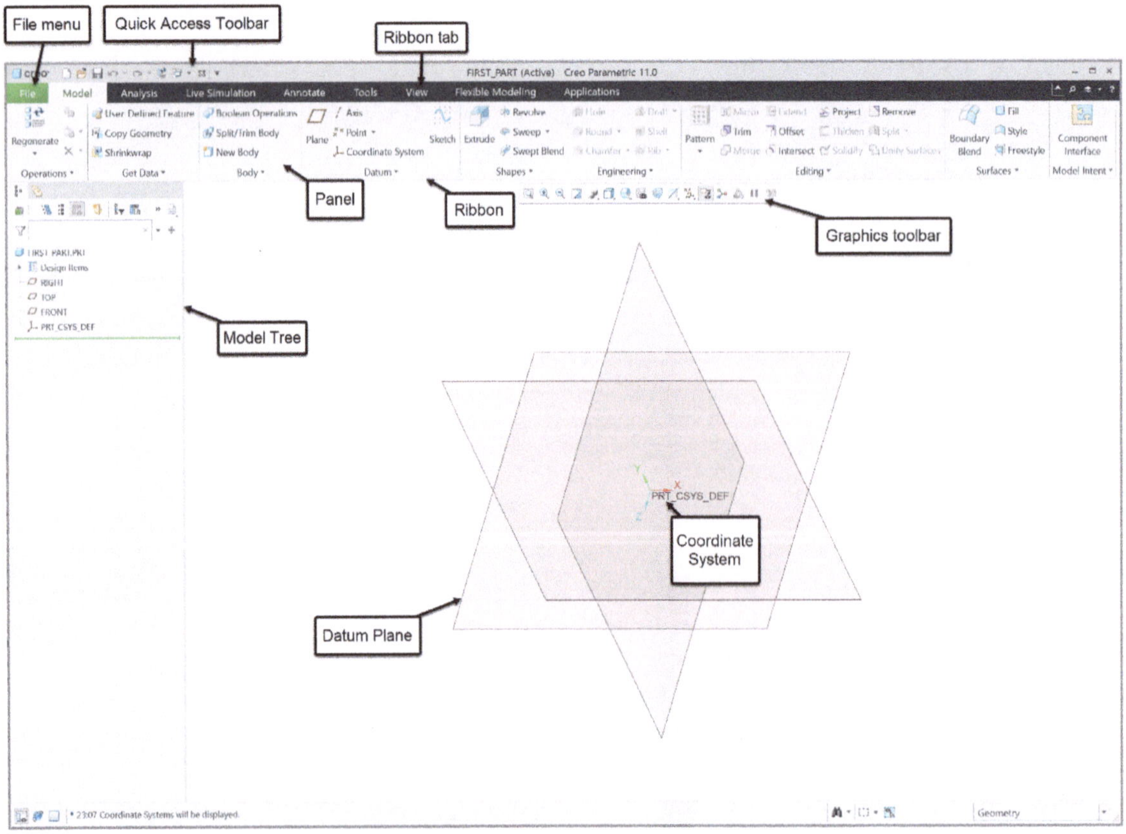

Various components of the user interface are:

Quick Access Toolbar

The **Quick Access Toolbar** has some commonly used commands such as **New, Open, Save, Undo, Redo, Regenerate,** and so on. You can add more commands to the **Quick Access Toolbar** by clicking on the down-arrow next to it and then selecting commands from the drop-down menu. If the required command is not available in the drop-down menu, then select the **More Commands** options; the **Creo Parametric Options** dialog pops up on the screen. On this dialog, select the required command from the commands list available on the left side, and click **Add selected item to the ribbon** ➡ icon. Next, click **OK**.

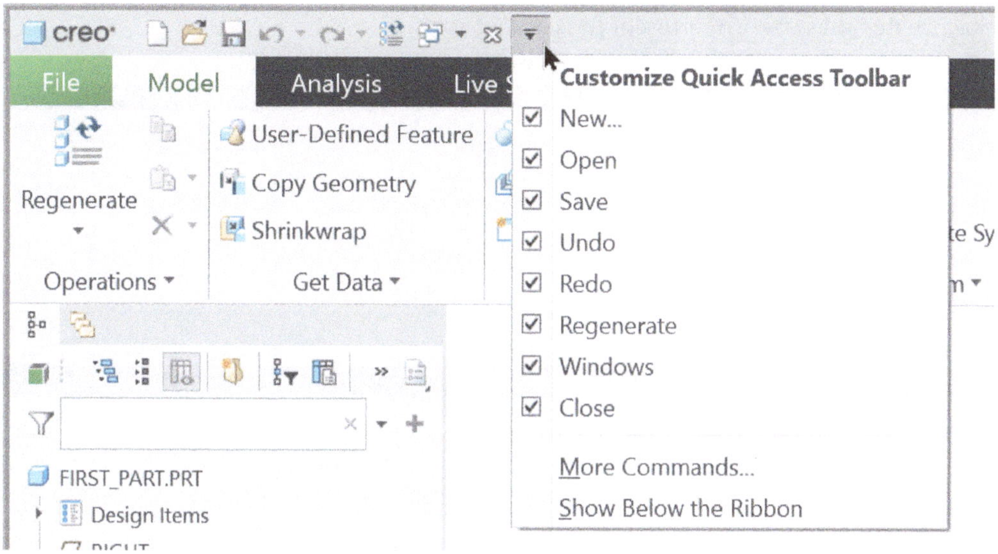

File Menu

The **File Menu** appears when you click on the **File** button located at the top left corner of the window. The **File Menu** has a list of self-explanatory menus. You can see a list of recently opened documents in the **Recent Files** menu.

Ribbon

The ribbon is located at the top of the window. It has various tabs. When you click on a tab, various panels appear. These panels have commands.

Various ribbons available in different environments are given next.

Part environment

Sketch tab

The **Sketch** tab has commands to create and edit sketches. This tab is activated while creating sketches.

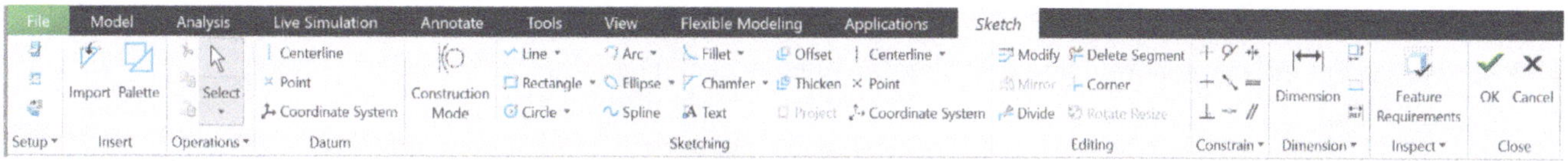

Model tab

This tab has commands to create and edit solid/surface geometry.

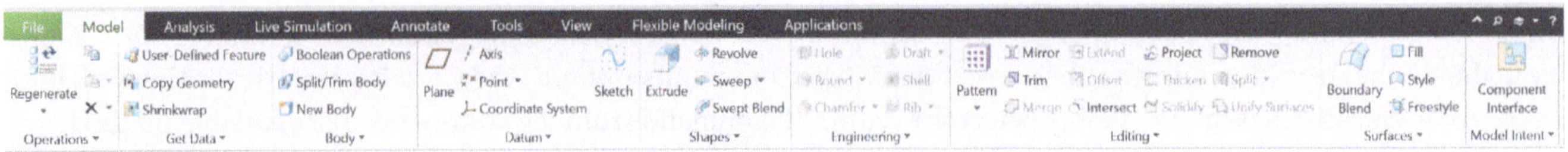

Analysis tab

This tab has commands to measure the physical properties of the geometry.

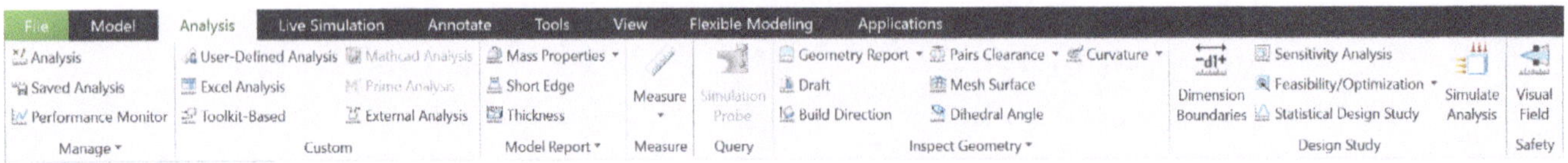

View tab

This tab has commands to zoom, pan, rotate, or change a 3D model's view.

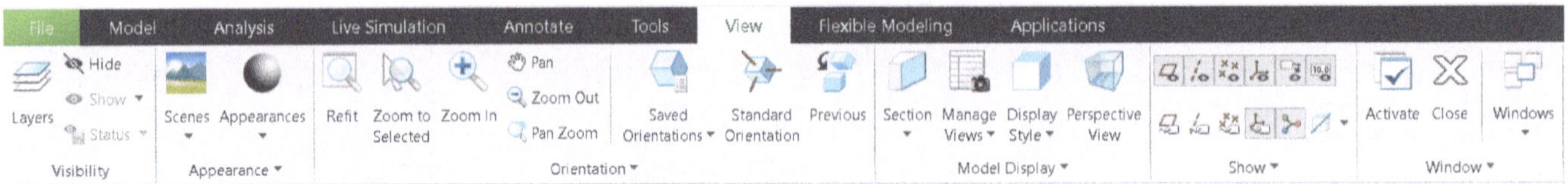

Assembly environment

The **Model** tab has commands to create components or insert existing components into an assembly.

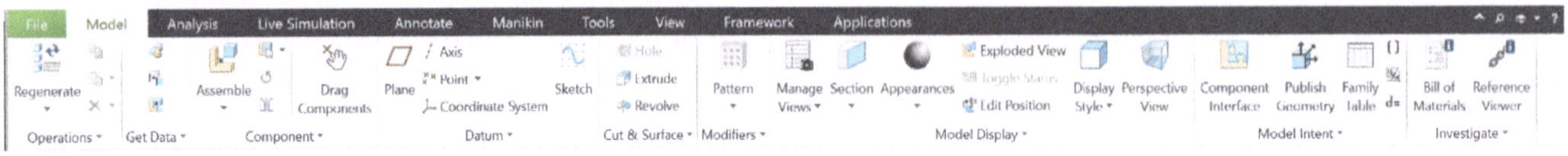

Sheetmetal environment

The **Model** tab has commands to create sheet metal parts.

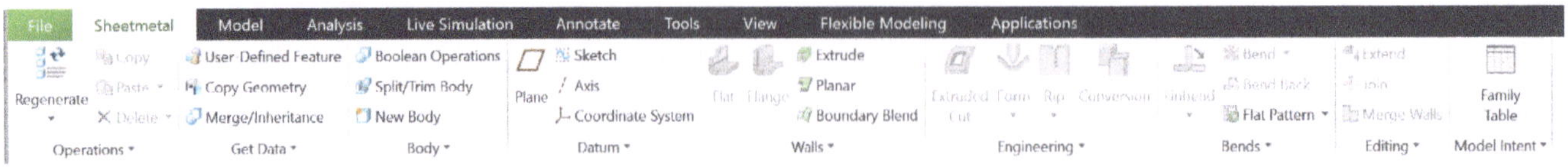

Drawing environment

Layout tab

This tab has commands to generate and edit standard views of a 3D geometry.

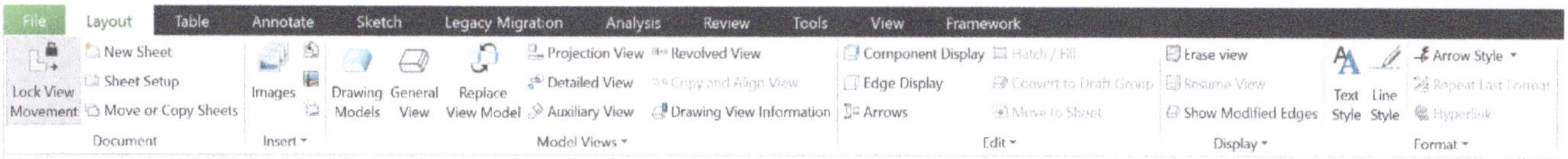

Table tab

This tab commands to insert tables, balloons, and other data into the drawing.

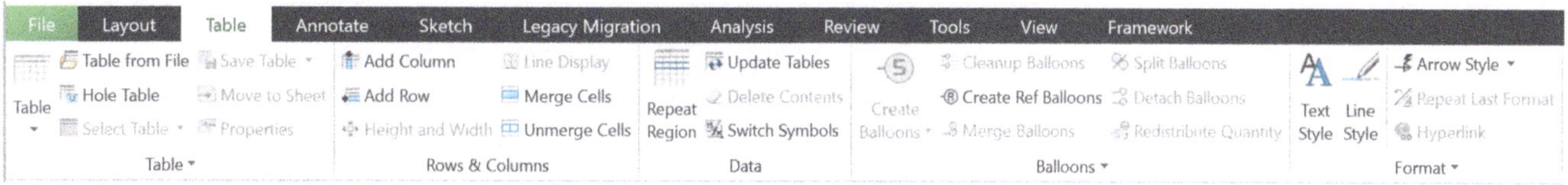

Annotate tab

This tab has commands to add dimensions and other annotations to the drawing.

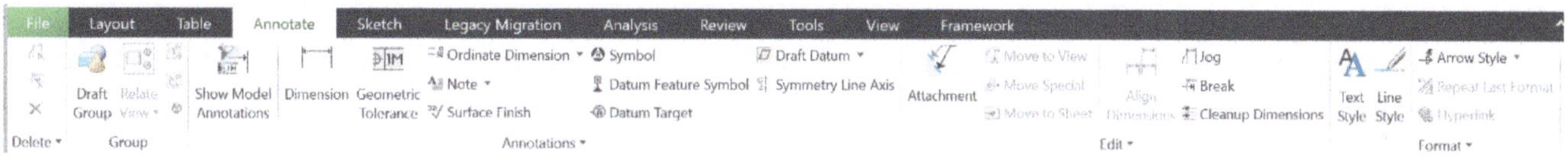

Status bar

The status bar is available below the graphics window. It shows the prompts while using the commands.

Command Search

The **Command Search** bar is used to search for any command. On the top right corner of the window, click the **Command Search** icon to display the **Command Search** bar. You can type any keyword in the **Command Search** bar and find a list of commands related to it.

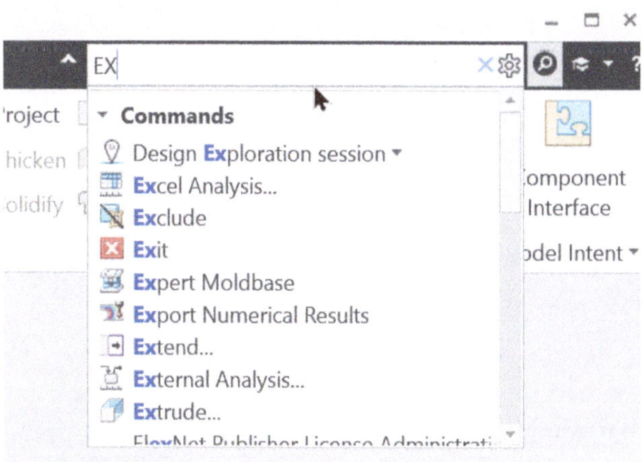

Model Tree

It contains the list of operations carried while constructing a part.

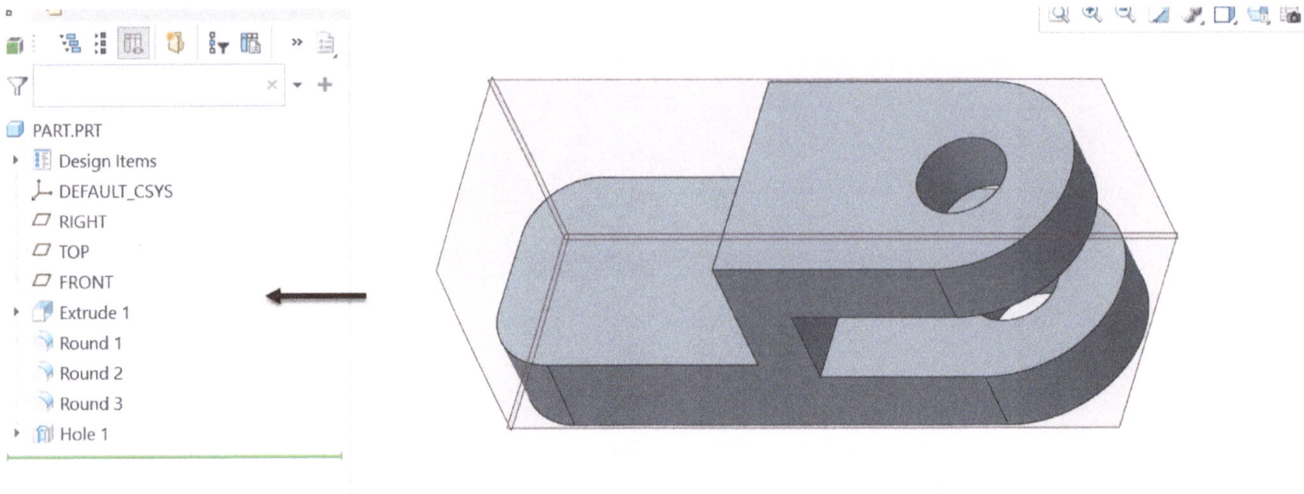

Dashboard

When you execute any command in Creo Parametric, the dashboard related to it appears. A dashboard has various options. The following figure shows various components of a dashboard.

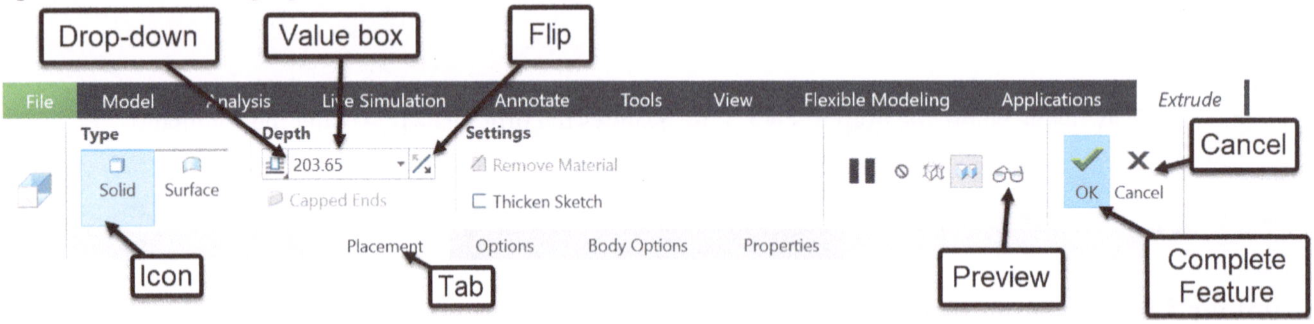

This textbook uses the default options on the dashboard.

Mouse Functions

Various functions of the mouse buttons are:

Left Mouse button (MB1)

When you double-click the left mouse button (MB1) on a feature, the dimensions related to it would appear. You can edit the parameters of the feature.

Middle Mouse button (MB2)

Press the middle mouse and drag the mouse to rotate the view.

Right Mouse button (MB3)

Select an object and click this button to open the shortcut menu related to it.

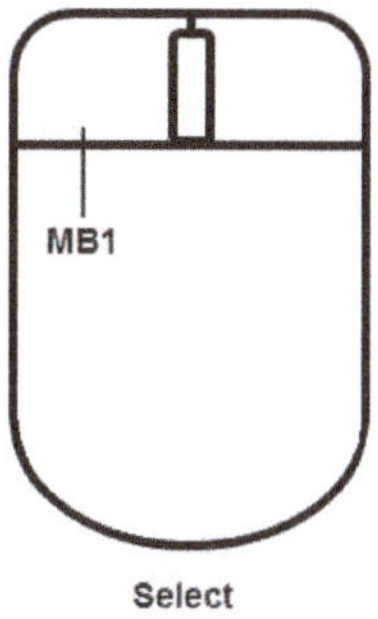

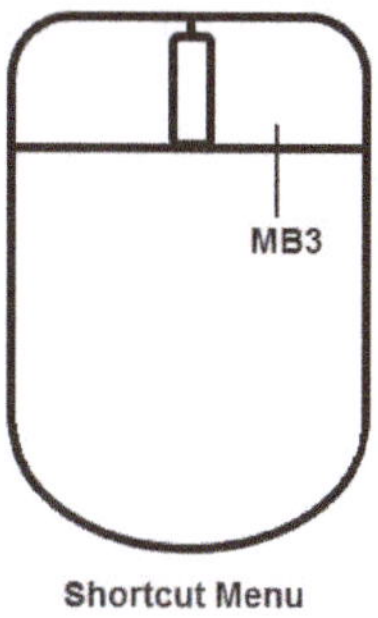

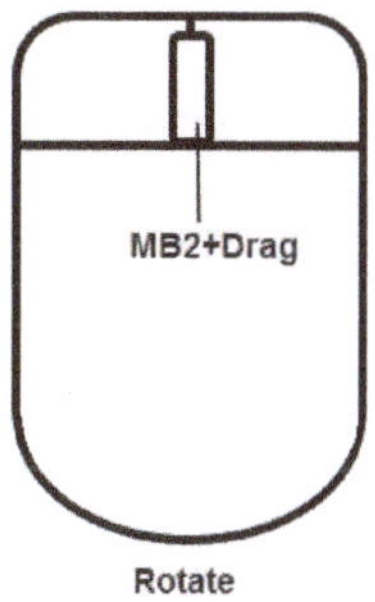

Background

To change the background color of the window, click **File > Options**. On the **PTC Creo Parametric Options** dialog, click **System Appearance** on the left side. Set the **System Colors** and click **OK**.

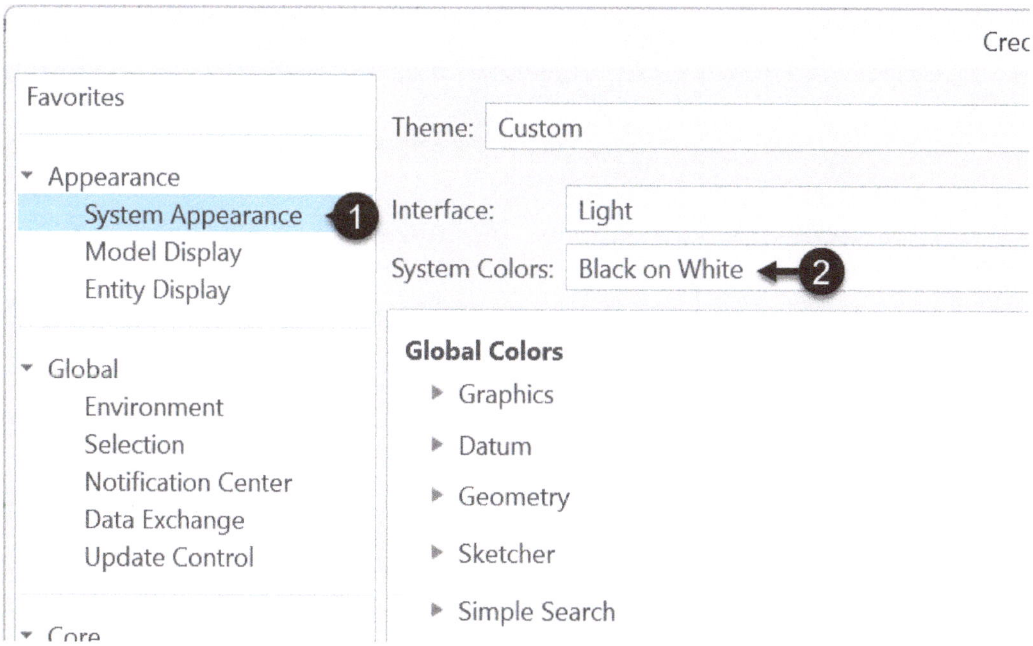

Shortcut Keys

CTRL+Z	Undo
CTRL+Y	Redo

CTRL+S	Save
F1	Creo Parametric Help
CTRL+N	New File
CTRL+O	Open File
CTRL+P	Print
Ctrl+F	Search
Ctrl+C	Copy
Ctrl+V	Paste
Delete	Delete
Ctrl+R	Repaint
Ctrl+D	Switch to the default view orientation

Chapter 2: Sketching

This chapter covers the methods and commands to create sketches used in the Part environment. In Creo Parametric, you can create sketches in the Sketch environment. You will learn to create sketches in this environment.

In Creo Parametric, you create a rough sketch and then apply dimensional and geometric constraints that define its shape and size. The dimensions define the length, size, and angle of a sketch element, whereas geometric constraints define the relations between sketch elements.

The topics covered in this chapter are:

- Sketching in the Sketch environment
- Using constraints and dimensions
- Learn sketching commands
- Learn commands and options that help you to create sketches easily

Sketching in the Sketch environment

Creating sketches in the Sketch environment is very easy. You have to activate the **Sketch** command and then define a plane on which you want to create the sketch.

1. On the ribbon, click the **Model** tab > **Datum** panel > **Sketch** icon.

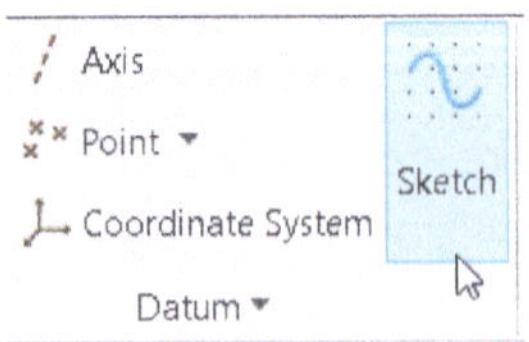

2. Click on the top datum plane located at the center of the graphics window.

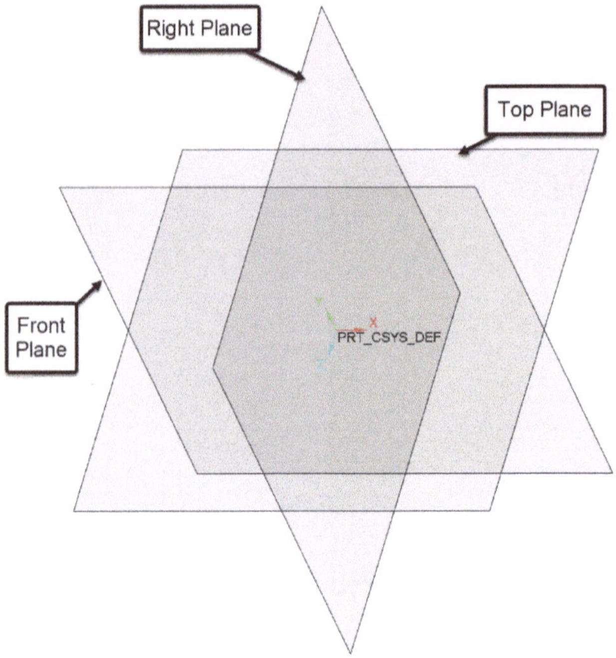

Now, you need to define the reference plane. The sketch will be constrained to the reference plane. When you select the top datum plane, the right and top planes are selected as the reference. However, you change the reference as per your requirement.

3. On the **Sketch** dialog, click in the **Reference** box and select a reference plane.

Now, you can define the viewing direction of the sketch. By default, the view direction is from the top. You can reverse it by clicking the **Flip** button.

4. On the **Sketch** dialog, click the **Properties** tab and type-in the name of the sketch.
5. Click the **Sketch** button to start the sketch.
6. On the ribbon, click **Sketch** tab > **Setup** panel > **Sketch View** icon. This option changes the view orientation parallel to the screen.

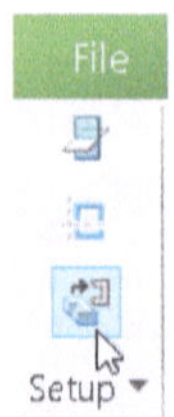

7. You can now start drawing sketches on the selected plane.

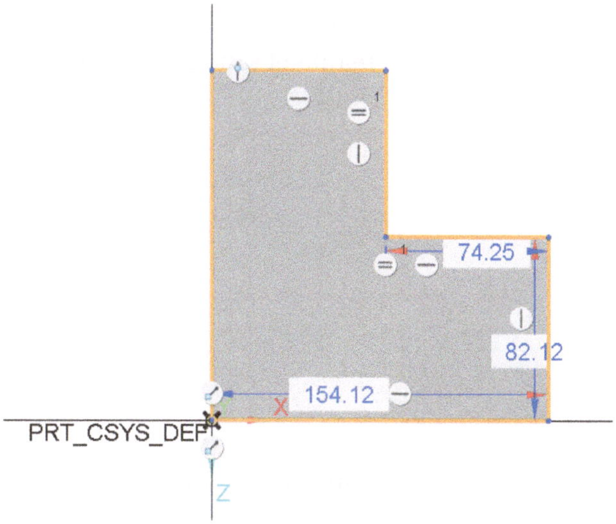

8. After creating the sketch, click **Sketch** tab > **Close** panel > **OK** icon to exit the sketch.

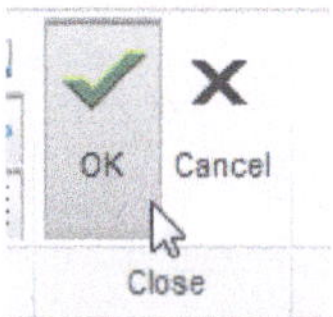

Sketching Commands

Creo Parametric provides you with a set of commands to create sketches. These commands are located on the **Sketch** ribbon tab.

 The Line Chain command

The **Line Chain** command is the most commonly used while creating a sketch.

1. To activate this command, click **Sketch** tab > **Sketching** panel > **Line** icon on the ribbon.
2. To create a line, click in the graphics window, move the pointer and click again. After clicking for the second time, you can see that an endpoint is added, and another line segment is started. It is a convenient way to create a chain of lines.

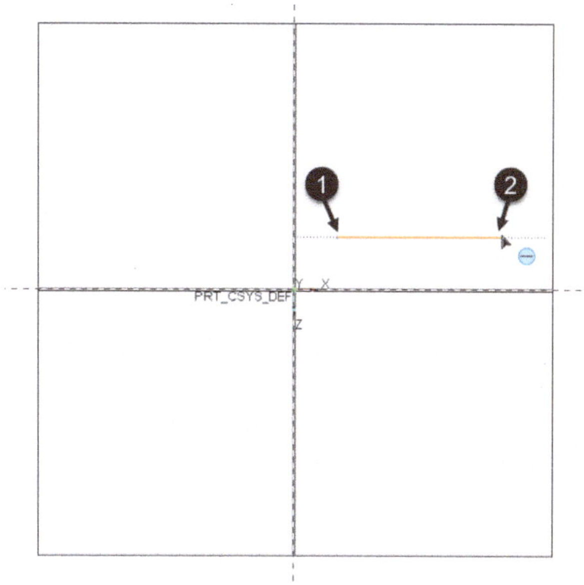

3. Continue to click to add more line segments.

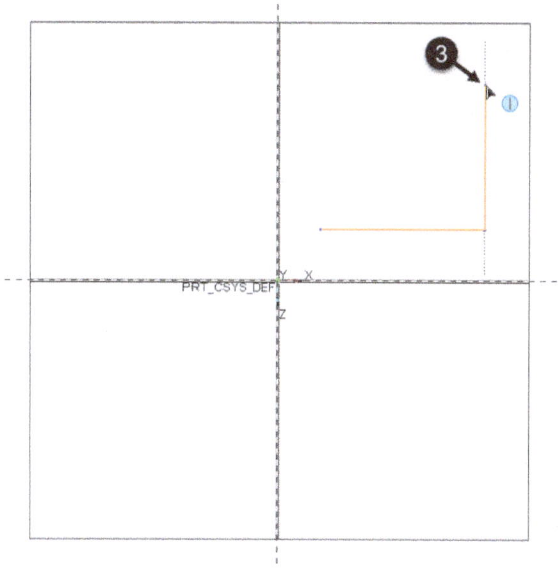

While creating lines, you will notice some symbols. For example, when you click and move the pointer horizontally, the Horizontal symbol appears. It indicates that you are drawing a horizontal line. Now, when you click the right mouse button, the constraint will be locked.

When you move the pointer vertically, the Vertical symbol appears. It indicates a vertical line.

If the Equal symbol appears on two different lines, the two lines' lengths will be equal.

If the endpoint of the line is collinear with another point, the vertical symbol appears. Also, a vertical dotted line appears between the points. It indicates that the points are aligned vertically.

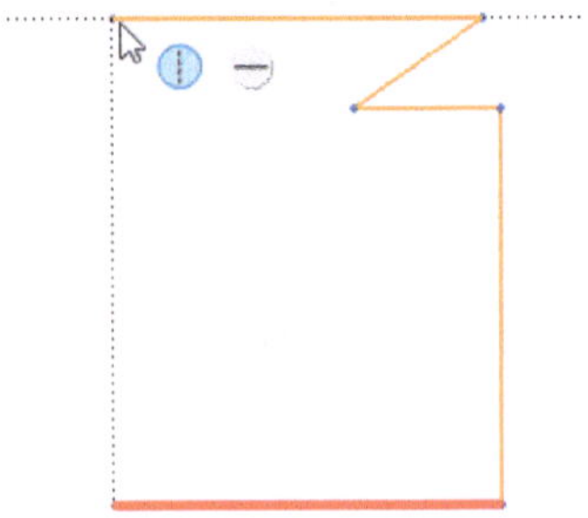

If you want to draw a line parallel to another line, then move the pointer until the parallel symbol appears.

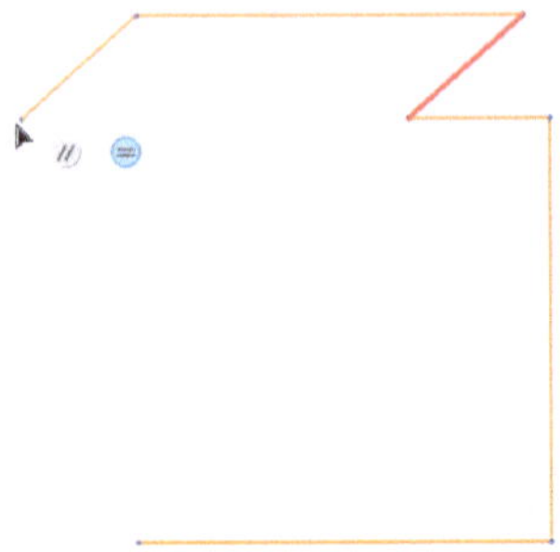

Likewise, you can draw perpendicular lines using the perpendicular symbol.

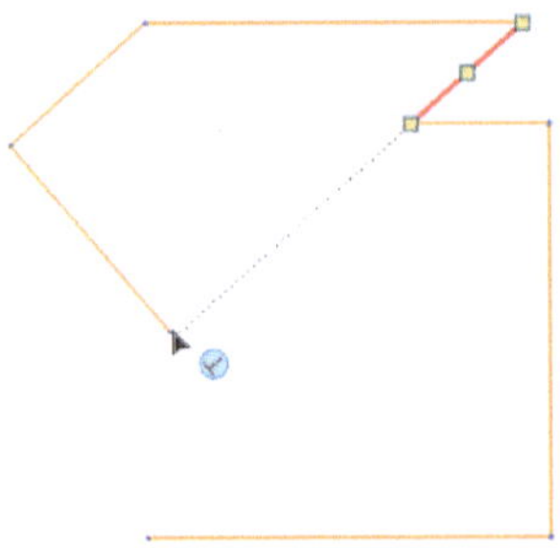

If you want to click on the midpoint of a line, move the pointer until the midpoint symbol appears.

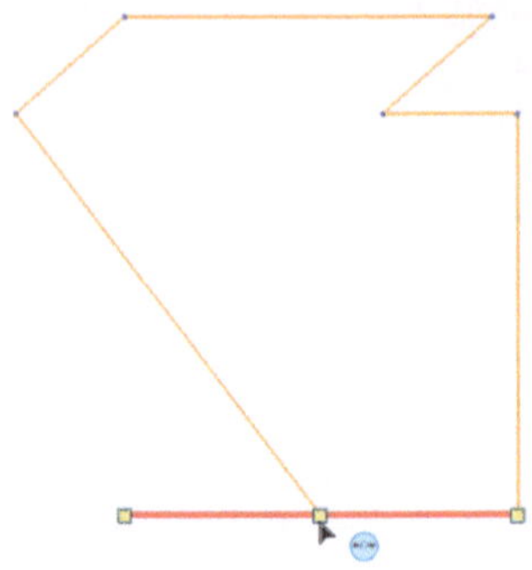

Likewise, select the start point of the sketch to close it.

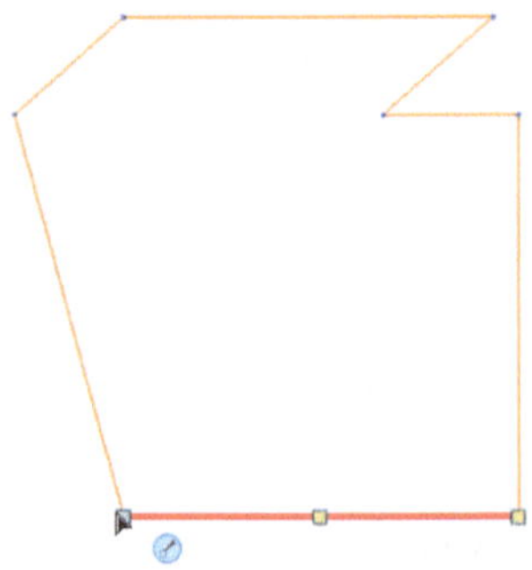

You will notice that another line is attached to the pointer even after closing the sketch loop. On the ribbon, click **Sketch** tab **> Operations** panel **> Select** icon to deactivate any sketch command.

After creating the sketch, you will notice that the dimensions are added to it automatically. However, these dimensions will not constraint the sketch fully. When you drag the elements of the sketch, the dimension values will change automatically. Also, some dimensions may not be required. You will learn more about how to add and modify dimensions later in this chapter.

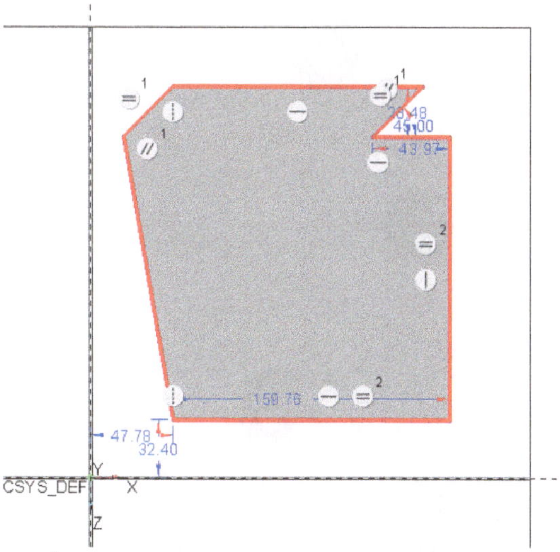

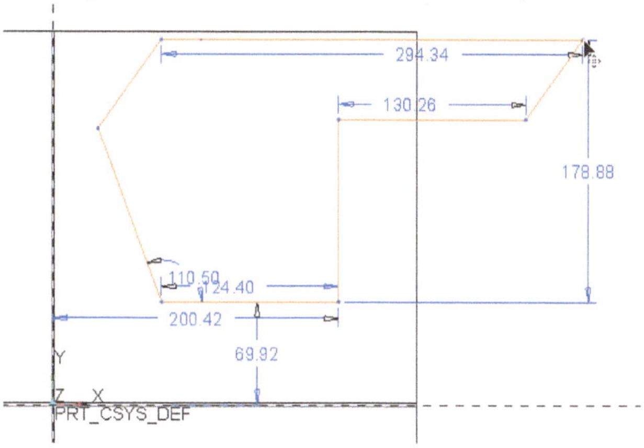

To delete a line, select it and press the **Delete** key. To select more than one line, press the Ctrl key and click on multiple line segments; the lines will be highlighted. You can also select multiple lines by dragging a box from left to right. Press and hold the left mouse button and drag a box from left to right; the lines inside the box boundary will be selected.

3-Point/Tangent End

This command creates an arc by clicking three points in the graphic window. You can also use this command to create an arc tangent to another sketch element.

1. On the ribbon, click **Sketch** tab > **Sketching** panel > **Arc** drop-down > **3-Point/Tangent End**.

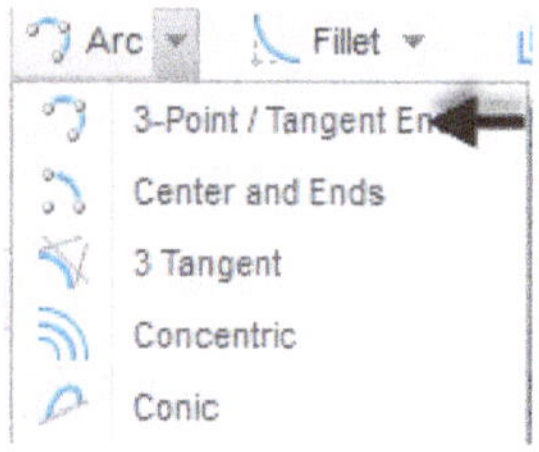

2. Click to define the start point of the arc.
3. Move the pointer and click to define the endpoint of the arc.
4. Move the pointer and click to define a point on the periphery of the arc.

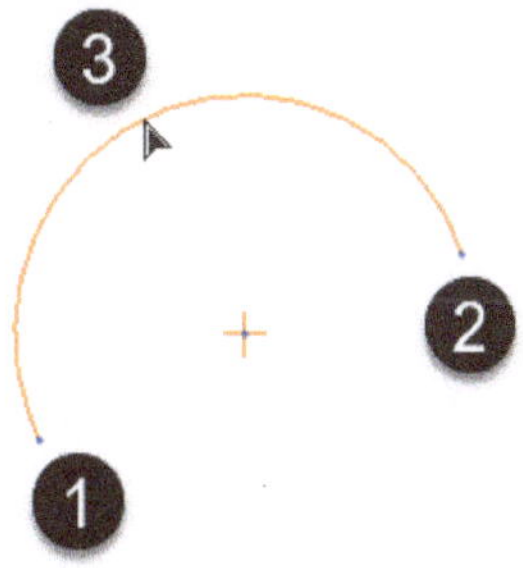

To create an arc tangent to a sketch element, activate the **3-Point/Tangent End** command and select the sketch element's endpoint.

You will notice that a tangent arc appears along with a four-segment circle at the selected endpoint.

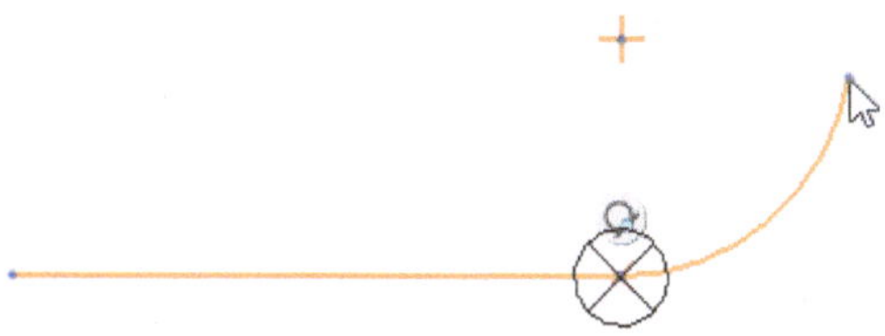

If you do not want to create a tangent arc, take the pointer to the sketch element's endpoint and move it in the direction perpendicular to it.

Define the endpoint and limiting point.

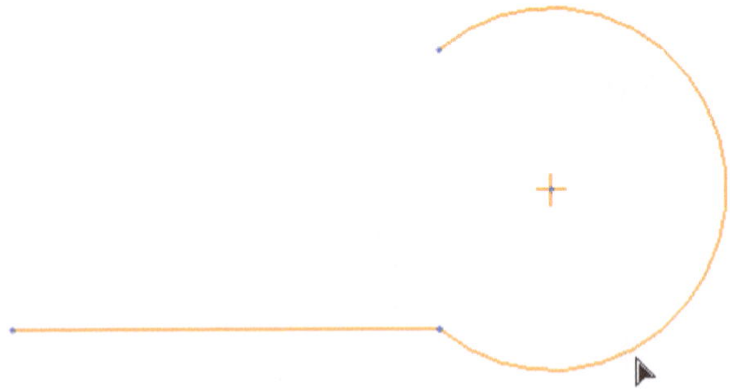

Center and Ends

This command creates an arc by defining its center, start, and end.

1. On the ribbon, click **Sketch** tab **>** **Sketching** panel **> Arc** drop-down > **Center and Ends**.
2. Click to define the center point.
3. Next, move the pointer, and you will notice that a circle appears attached to the pointer. It defines the radius of the arc.
4. Now, click to define the start point of the arc and move the pointer; you will notice that an arc is drawn from the start point.
5. Once the arc appears the way you want, click to define its endpoint.

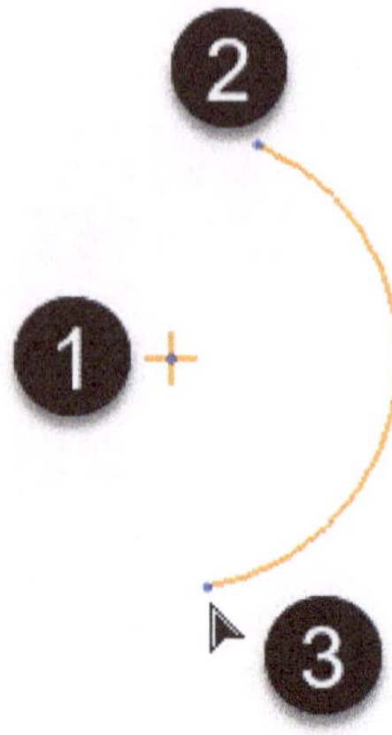

3 Tangent

This command creates an arc tangent to three lines.

1. On the ribbon, click **Sketch** tab **> Sketching** panel **> Arc** drop-down > **3 Tangent**.
2. Select three lines, arcs, or circles. It creates an arc tangent to selected lines.

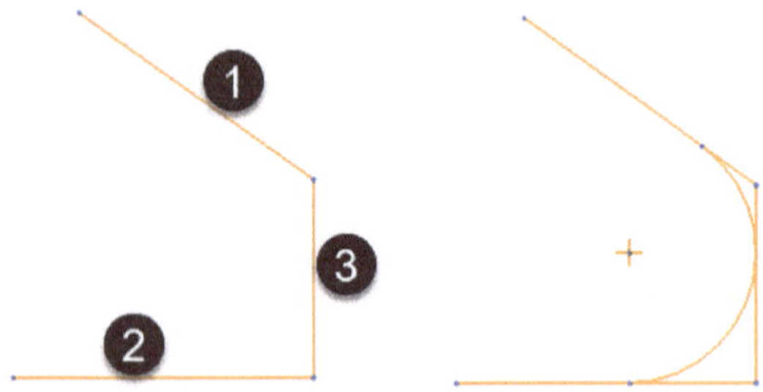

Concentric

This command creates an arc concentric to another arc or circle.

1. On the ribbon, click **Sketch** tab **> Sketching** panel **> Arc** drop-down > **Concentric**.
2. Click on an arc/circle or its center point.
3. Move the pointer and click to define the radius and start point of the arc.
4. Move the pointer and click to define the endpoint.

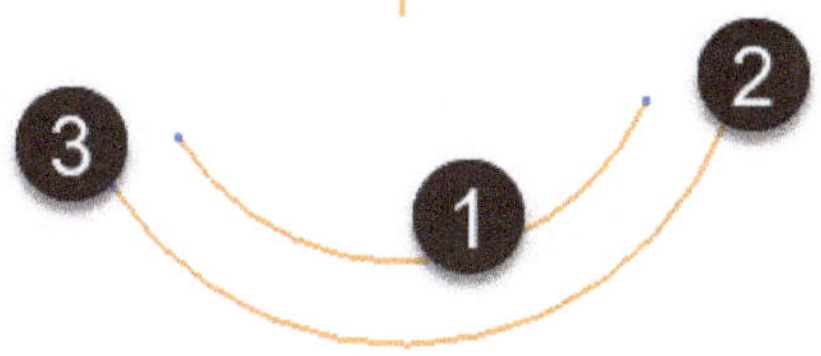

5. Likewise, you can create multiple concentric arcs.
6. On the ribbon, click **Sketch** tab **> Operations** panel **> Select** icon to deactivate the command.

Conic

The **Conic** tool is used to create a conic curve. You can use a conic curve to connect two open sketch entities.

1. Create a line and arc, as shown.

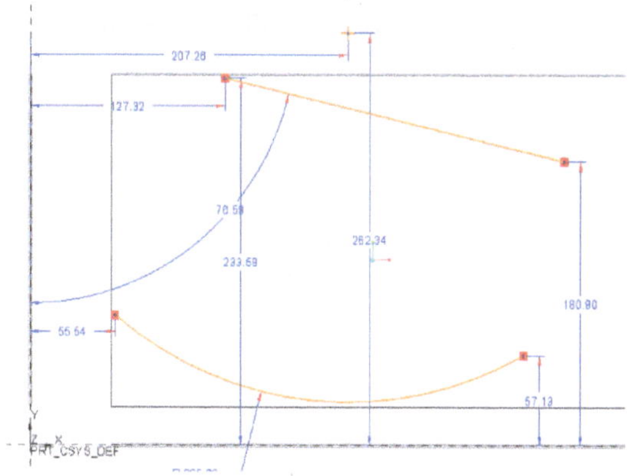

2. On the **Sketch** tab of the ribbon, click **Sketching** panel > **Arc** drop-down **> Conic**.

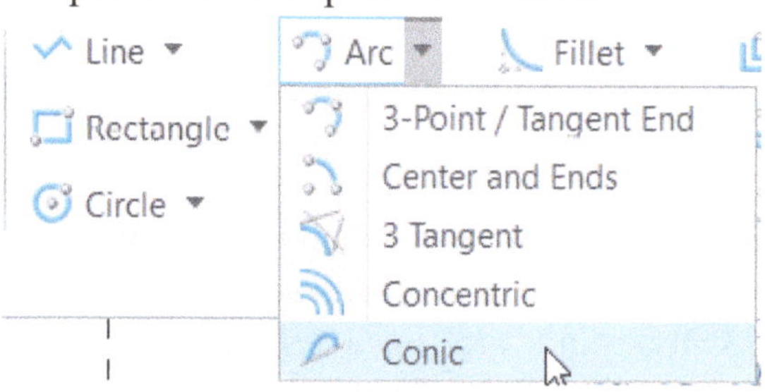

3. Select the endpoints of the line and arc.
4. Move the pointer and click.

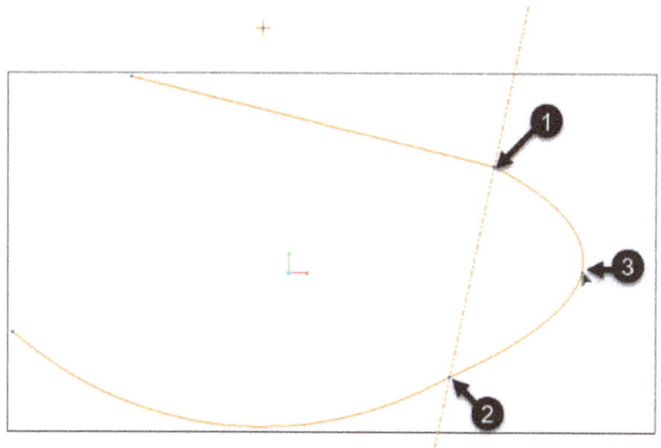

5. Press ESC.
6. On the **Sketch** tab of the ribbon, click **Constrain** panel > **Tangent**.
7. Select the conic and the arc.
8. Select the conic and the line. The conic is made tangent to the arc and the line.
9. Press ESC.

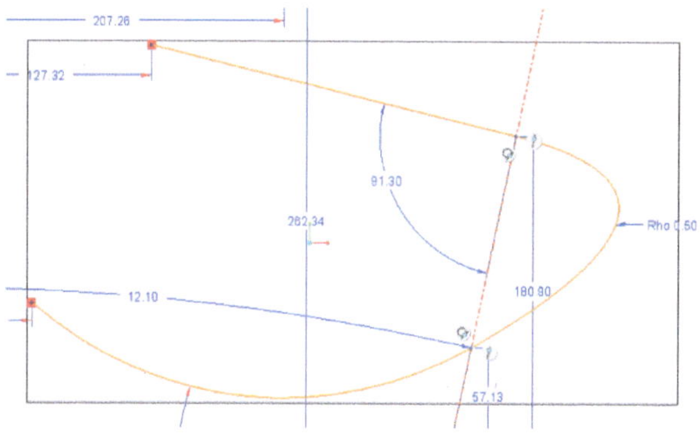

Now, you have to specify the Rho value.

Rho value = $A/(A+B)$

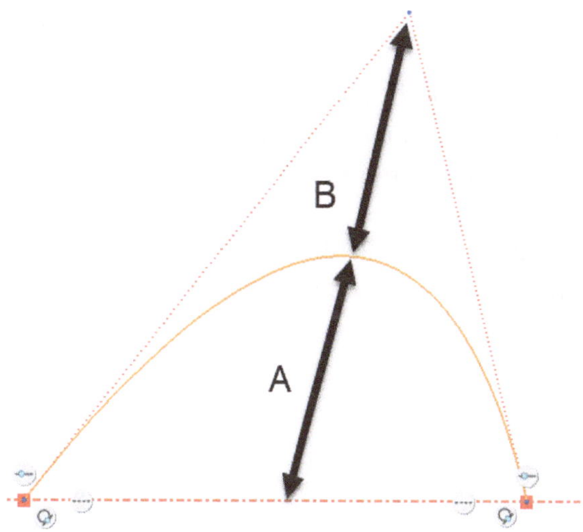

The Rho value varies from 0.05 to 0.95.

If the Rho value is 0.5, then it results in a parabola.

If the Rho value is less than 0.5, then it results in an ellipse.

If the Rho value is greater than 0.5, then it results in a hyperbola.

10. Double-click on the Rho value dimension.

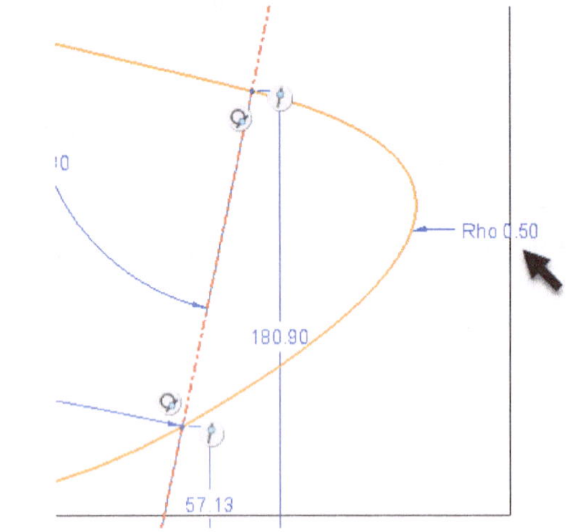

11. Type 0.6 and press ENTER.

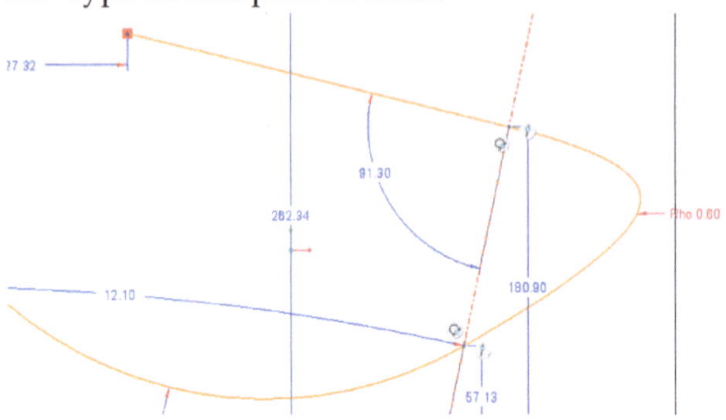

Center and Point

The **Center and Point** command is the most commonly used to draw a circle.

1. On the ribbon, click **Sketch** tab > **Sketching** panel > **Circle** drop-down > **Center and Point**.

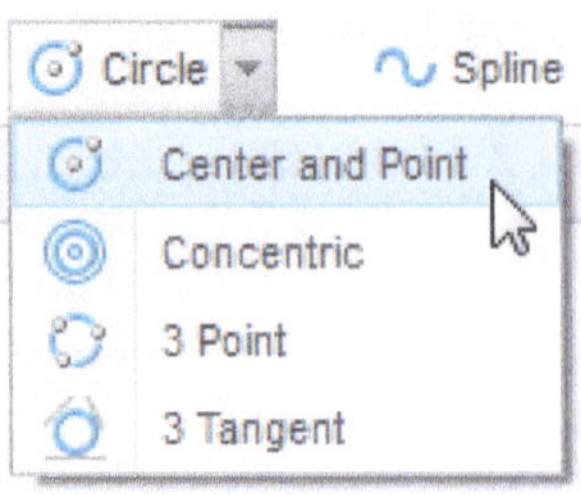

2. Click to define the center point of the circle.
3. Drag the pointer, and then click again to define the diameter of the circle.

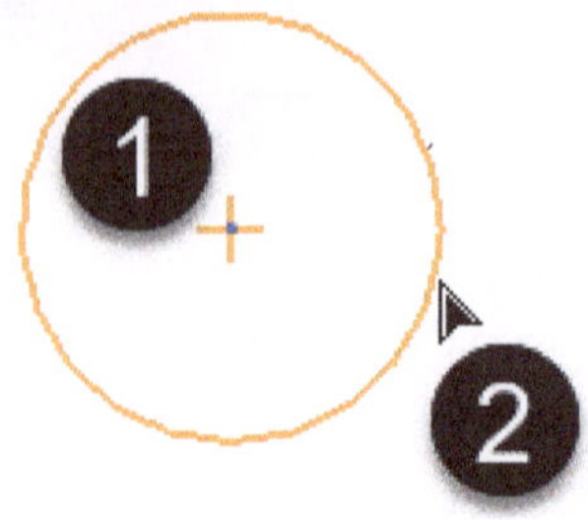

3 Point

This command creates a circle by using three points.

1. On the ribbon, click **Sketch** tab **> Sketching** panel **> Circle** drop-down > **3 Point**.
2. Select three points from the graphics window. You can also select existing points from the sketch geometry. The first two points define the location of the circle, and the third point defines its diameter.

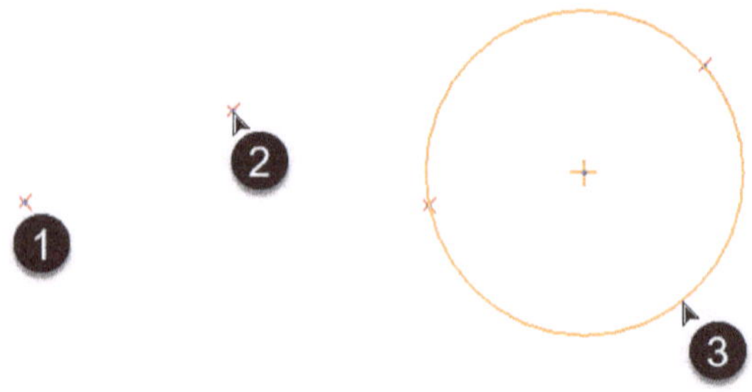

3 Tangent

This command creates a circle tangent to three lines, arcs, or circles.

1. On the ribbon, click **Sketch** tab **> Sketching** panel **> Circle** drop-down > **3 Tangent**.
2. Select three lines, arcs, or circles. It creates a circle tangent to the selected elements.

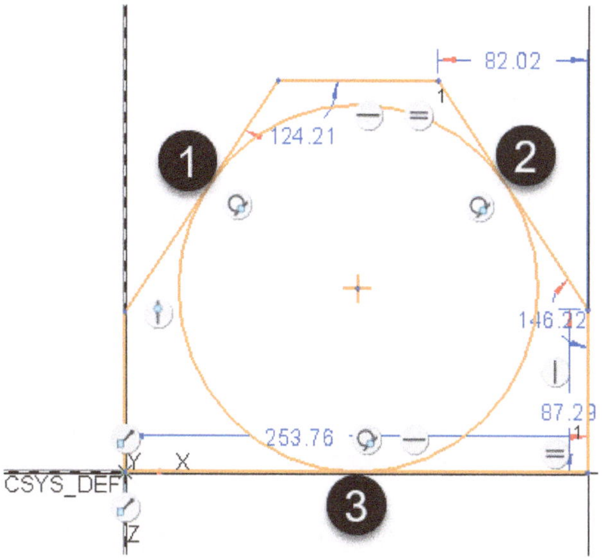

Concentric

This command creates a circle concentric to another circle or arc.

1. On the ribbon, click **Sketch** tab **> Sketching** panel **> Circle** drop-down > **Concentric**.
2. Select the circle center point of the circle.
3. Move the pointer and click to create the circle.

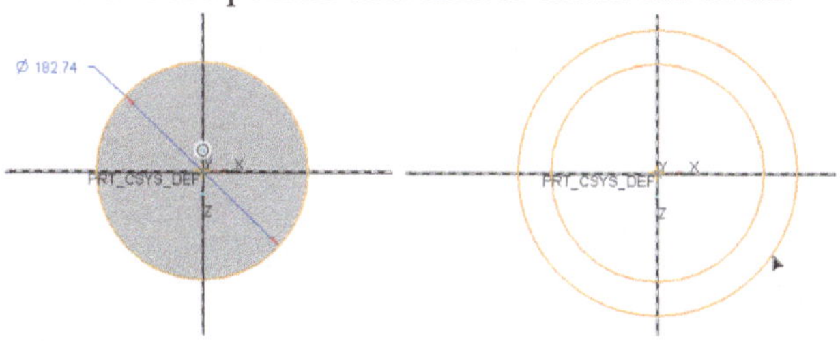

Corner Rectangle

This command creates a rectangle by defining its diagonal corners.

1. On the ribbon, click **Sketch** tab **> Sketching** panel **> Rectangle** drop-down > **Corner Rectangle.**

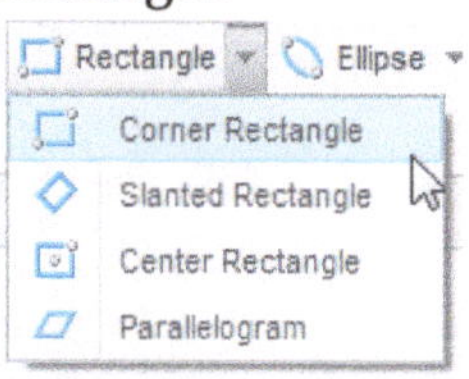

2. Click to define the first corner.
3. Drag the pointer and click to define the second corner.

Slanted Rectangle

This command creates a slanted rectangle. The first two points define the width and inclination angle of the rectangle. The third point defines its height. You can activate this command by clicking **Sketch** tab > **Sketching** panel > **Rectangle** drop-down > **Slanted Rectangle**.

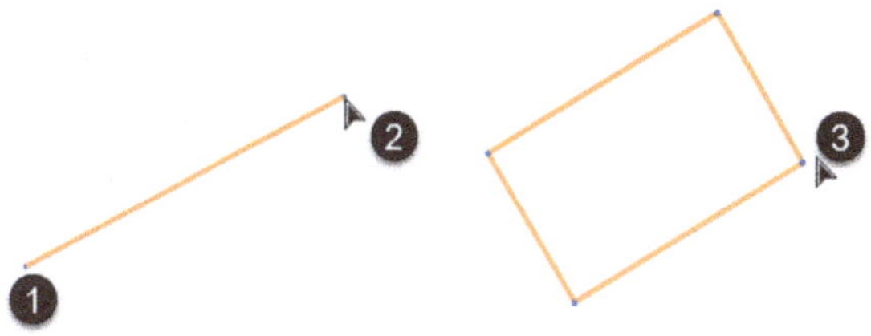

Center Rectangle

This command creates a rectangle by defining two points: the center of the rectangle and its corner.

1. On the ribbon, click **Sketch** tab **> Sketching** panel **> Rectangle** drop-down **> Center Rectangle**.
2. Click to define the center of the rectangle.
3. Move the pointer and click again to define the corner point.

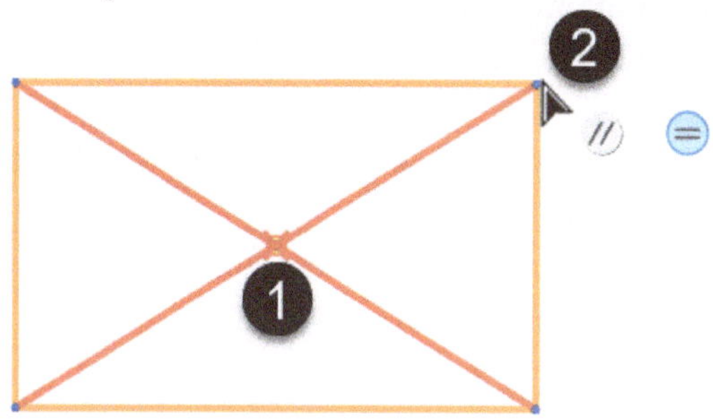

Parallelogram

This command creates a parallelogram by using three points that you specify.

1. On the ribbon, click **Sketch** tab **>** **Sketching** panel **>** **Rectangle** drop-down **>** **Parallelogram**.
2. Select two points to define the width of the parallelogram.
3. Drag the pointer and click to define the height of the parallelogram.

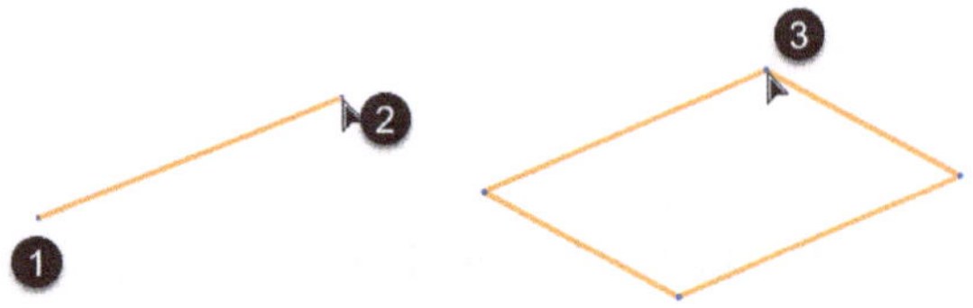

Line Tangent

This command creates a line tangent to two circles or arcs.

1. On the ribbon, click **Sketch** tab **>** **Sketching** panel **>** **Line** drop-down **>** **Line Tangent**.
2. Select two circles or arcs. A line tangent to the selected elements is created.

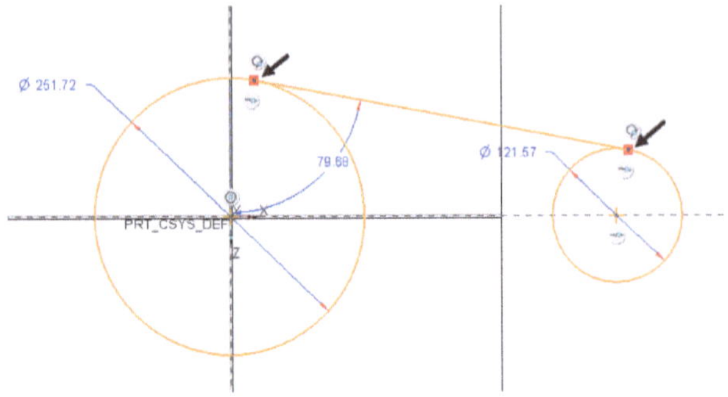

Centerline

This command creates a centerline, which can be used while creating the revolved feature.

1. On the ribbon, click **Sketch** tab > **Sketching** panel > **Centerline**.
2. Click to define the start point.
3. Move the pointer and click to define the endpoint of the centerline.

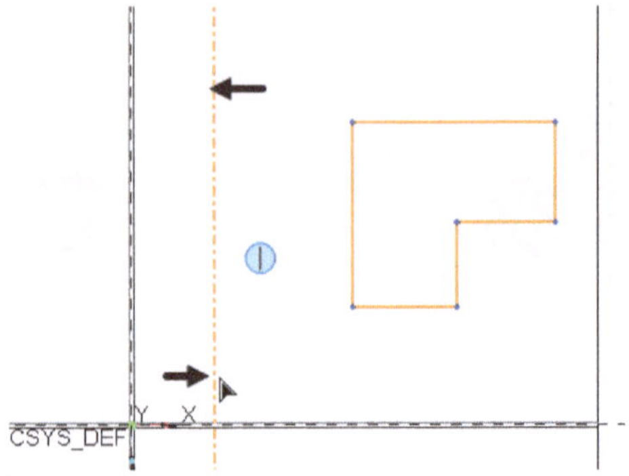

Axis Ends Ellipse

This command creates an ellipse using the endpoints of the major and minor axes.

1. On the ribbon, click **Sketch** tab > **Sketching** panel > **Ellipse** drop-down > **Axis Ends Ellipse**.
2. Define the endpoints of the first axis.
3. Drag the pointer and click to define the second axis.

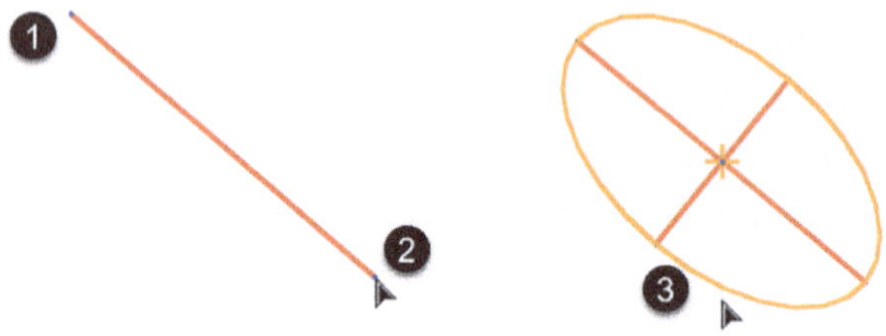

4. On the ribbon, click **Sketch** tab > **Dimension** panel > **Dimension**.
5. Select the ellipse and click the Middle mouse button.
6. Select the Major axis option and click the Accept button.
7. Type 40 and press ENTER.
8. Select the ellipse and click the Middle mouse button.
9. Type 15 and press ENTER.
10. Select the major axis and the vertical reference line.

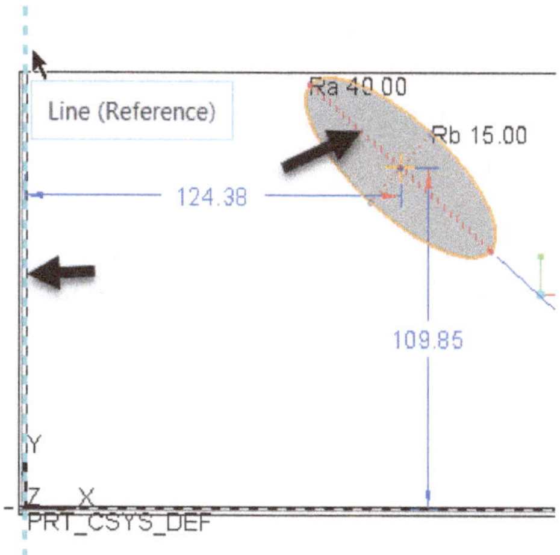

11. Click the middle mouse button.
12. Type 45 and press ENTER.

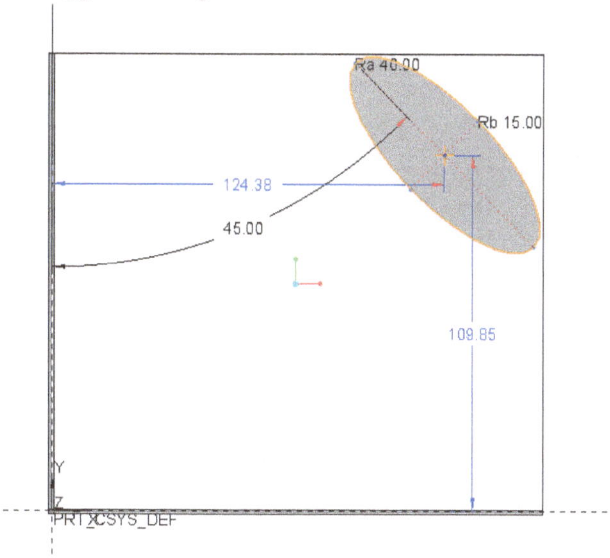

Center and Axis Ellipse

This command creates an ellipse using a center point and major and minor axes.

1. On the ribbon, click **Sketch** tab > **Sketching** panel > **Ellipse** drop-down > **Center and Axis Ellipse**.
2. Click to define the center of the ellipse.
3. Drag the pointer and click to define the major axis and orientation of the ellipse.
4. Drag the pointer and click again to define the minor axis.

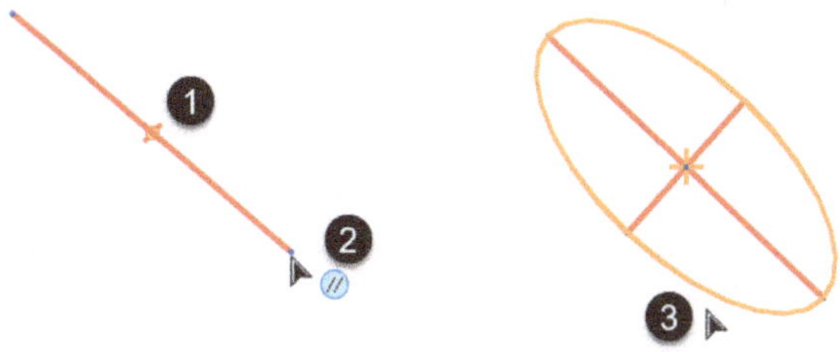

Point

This command creates points as you click in the graphics window.

1. On the ribbon, click **Sketch** tab > **Sketching** panel > **Point**.
2. Click in the graphics window to create points.

Spline

This command creates a smooth B-spline curve passing through the points you select.

1. On the ribbon, click **Sketch** tab **> Sketching** panel **> Spline**.
2. Click to define points in the graphics window. A spline is created passing through the selected points.

If you want to create a closed spline, click the start point of the spline.

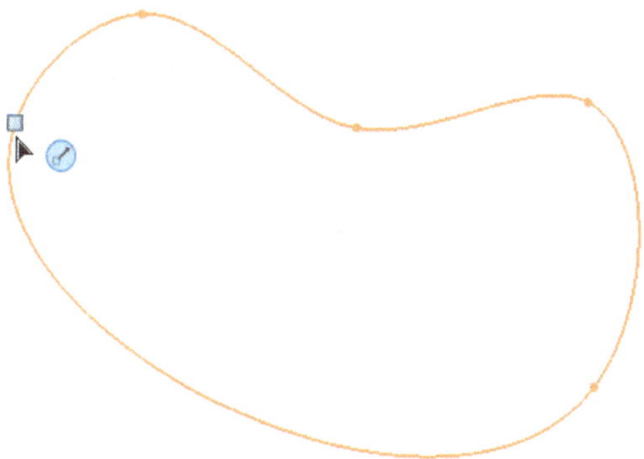

Dimensions

It is generally considered good practice to ensure that every sketch you create is fully defined before moving on to creating features. The term 'fully-defined' means that the sketch has a definite shape and size. You can fully-define a sketch by using dimensions and constraints. As you create sketches in Creo Parametric, some dimensions are added to the sketch elements. These dimensions are called Weak dimensions, and they do not have any control over the sketch geometry. If you want these dimensions to control the sketch geometry's shape and size, you must lock these dimensions.

You can lock a weak dimension by using the **Lock** option. Select the weak dimension and click the right mouse button. Select the **Lock** option from the menu and type-in a new value of the dimension. Press Enter to create the locked dimension. You can modify the dimension value by double-clicking on it and entering a new value.

If you want to lock the modified dimensions and user-defined dimensions, then follow the step given next.

1. Click **File** tab > **Options**.
2. Select the **Sketcher** option from the tree located on the left side.
3. Under **Dimensions** section, check the **Lock modified dimensions**, and **Lock user defined dimensions** options.
4. Click **OK** and **Yes**.
5. Enter the configuration file name and click **OK** on the **Save As** dialog.

The Dimension command

You can add dimensions to a sketch by using the **Dimension** command. You can use this command to add all dimensions such as length, angle, and diameter. This command creates a dimension based on the geometry that you select. For instance, to dimension a circle, activate the **Dimension** command (On the ribbon, click **Sketch** > **Dimension** > **Dimension**), and then click on the circle. Next, move the pointer and click the Middle mouse button to position the dimension. Notice that a box pops up. Type-in a value in this box, and then press Enter to update the dimension.

If you click a line, this command creates a linear dimension. Move the pointer and middle-click to position the dimension.

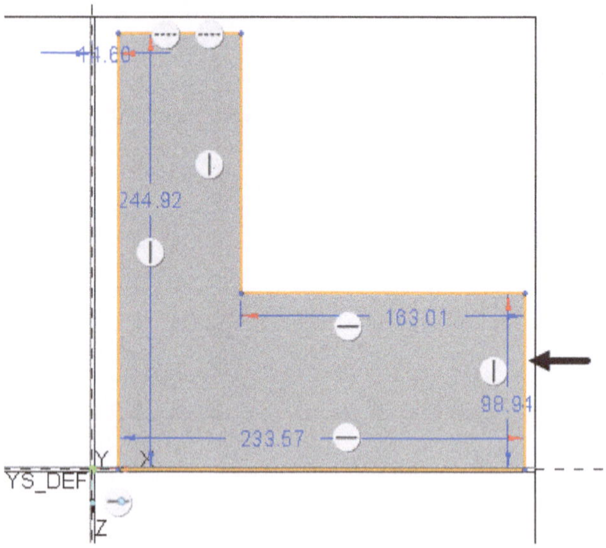

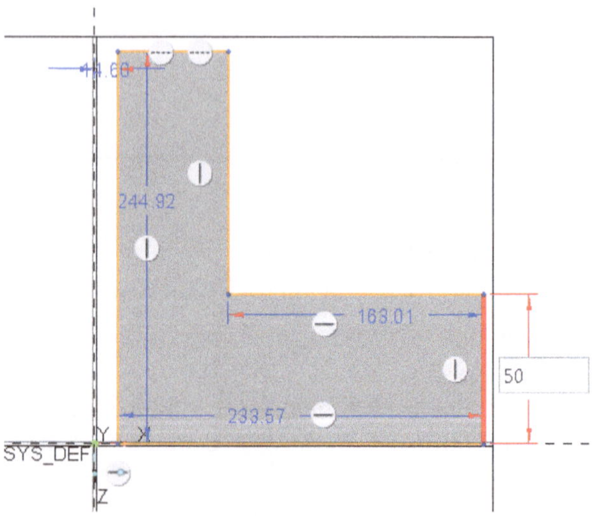

If you click on an inclined line, this command creates a dimension parallel to the line.

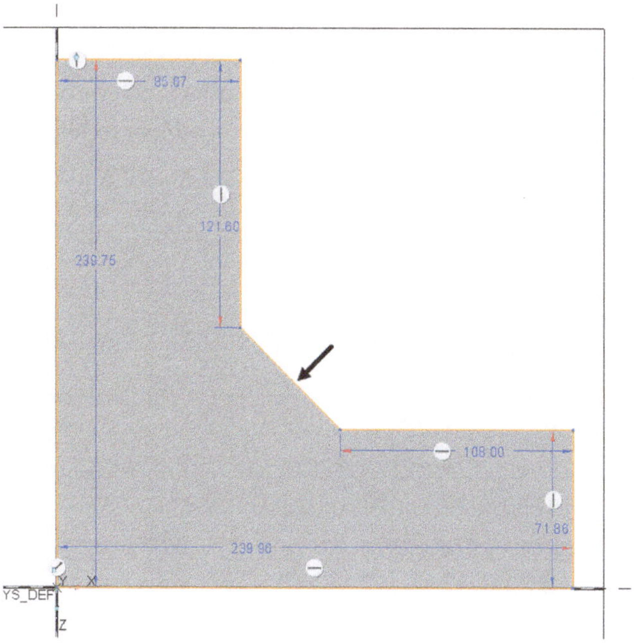

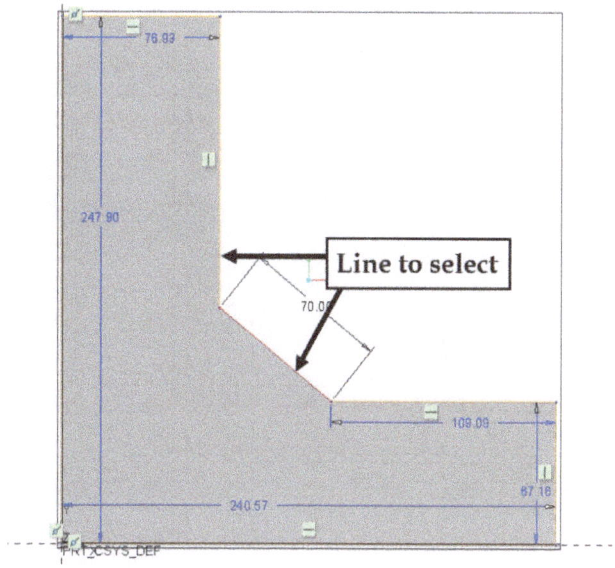

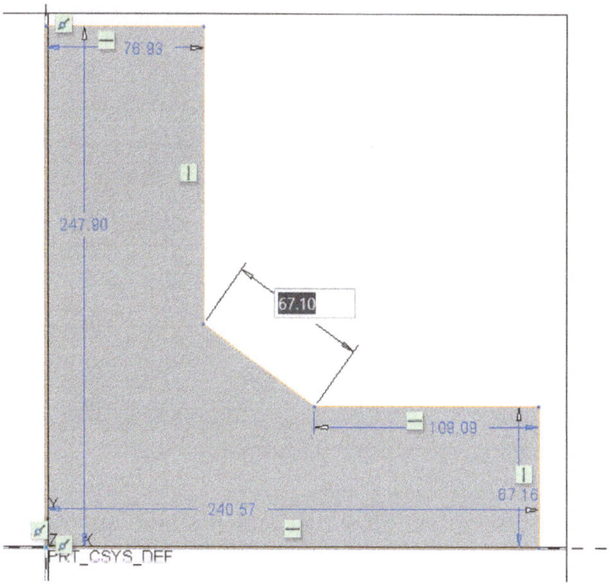

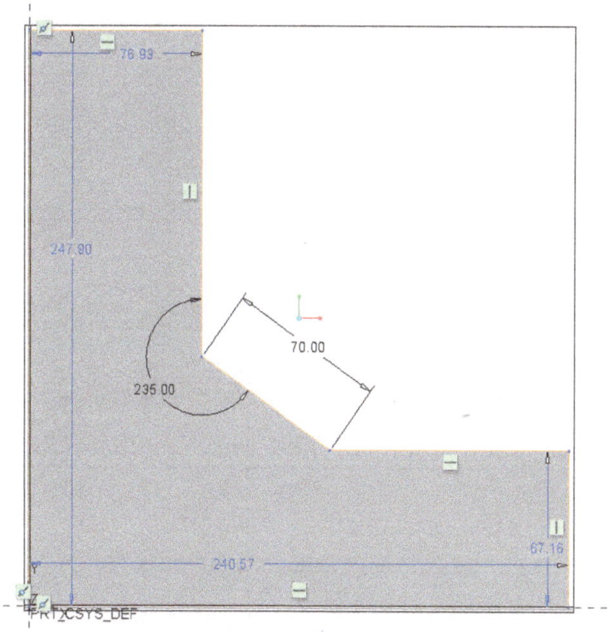

If you want to create an angle dimension between two elements, activate the **Dimension** command and select the elements. Next, move the pointer and click the middle mouse button to position the dimension. Type-in the angle value and press Enter.

Resolve Sketch

When creating sketches for a part, Creo Parametric will not allow you to over-constrain the geometry. The term 'over-constrain' means adding more dimensions than required. The following figure shows a fully constrained sketch. If you add another dimension to this sketch (e.g., diagonal dimension), the **Resolve sketch** dialog appears.

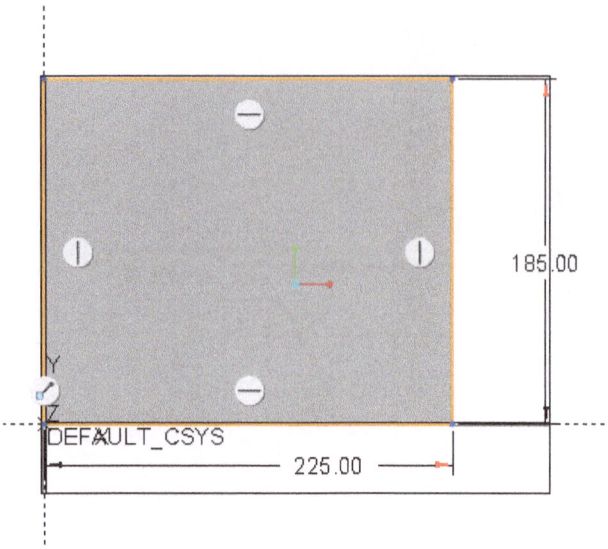

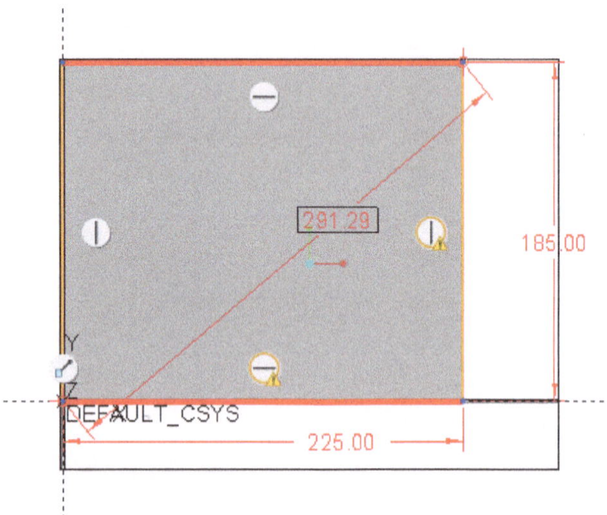

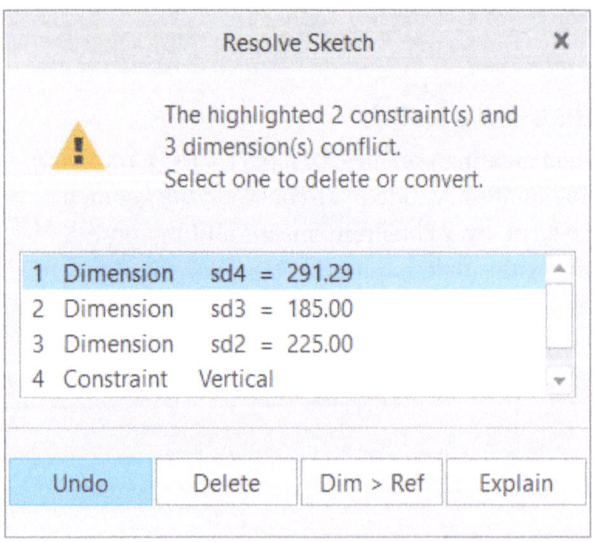

You have to delete one of the dimensions (or) convert the new dimension into reference. Click the **Dim > Ref** button to convert the dimension into reference. The reference dimension will be in blue, and **REF** will be added to it.

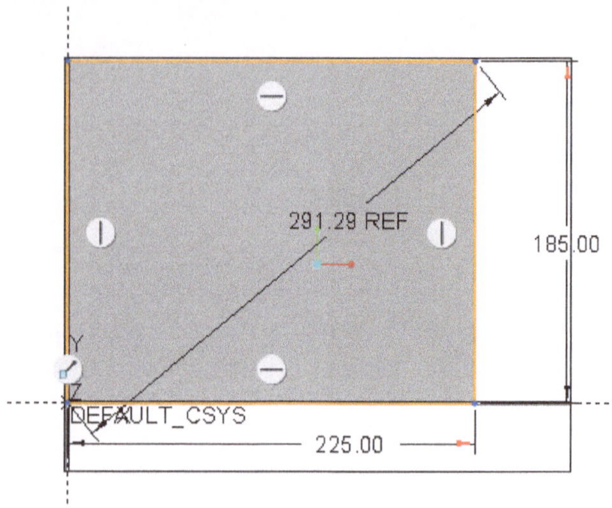

If you change the width's value, the reference dimension along the diagonal updates automatically. Also, note that the dimensions, which are initially created, will be driving dimensions, whereas the dimensions created after fully defining the sketch are over constraining dimensions.

Modify

This command modifies all the dimensions in a sketch using the **Modify Dimensions** dialog.

1. On the ribbon, click the **Sketch > Editing > Modify**.
2. Select the dimension as shown.

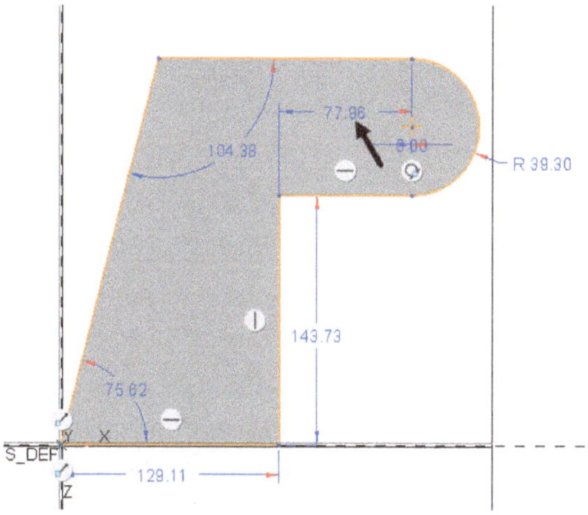

3. On the **Modify Dimensions** dialog, type-in a value in the box.

You can also use the dimension dragger located next to the dimension box to modify the value. The dimension value changes as you drag the dimension dragger. You can set the sensitivity of the dimension dragger by using the **Sensitivity** scroll bar.

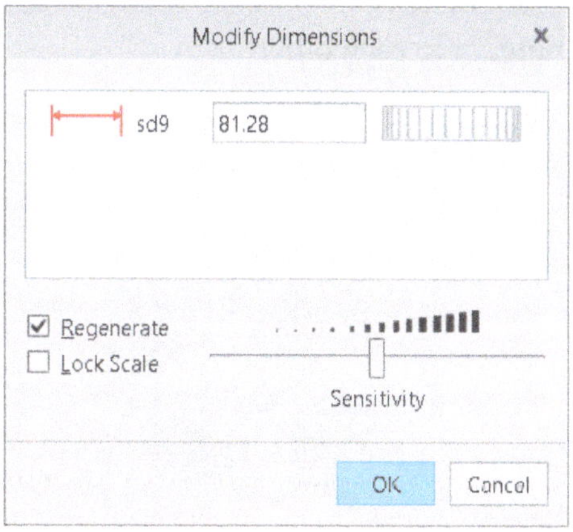

4. Check the **Regenerate** option to regenerate the sketch after clicking **OK**.
5. Click **OK** on the dialog.
6. Drag a box around the sketch to select all its dimensions.
7. Activate the **Modify** command.
8. On the **Modify Dimension** dialog, click on the dimension boxes one-by-one and enter new values.

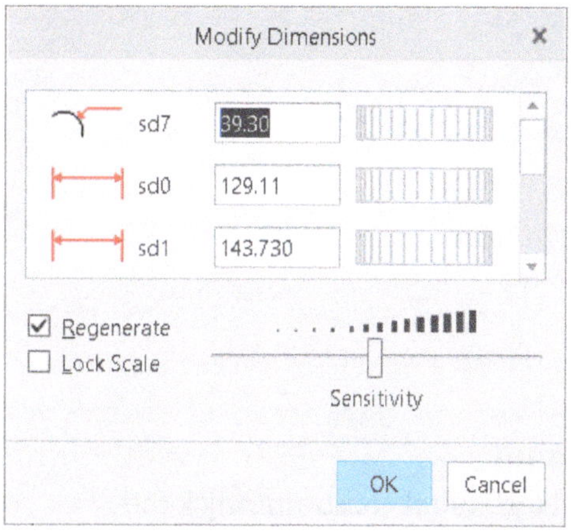

9. Click **OK** to update the dimension.

Constraints

Constraints are used to control the shape of a sketch by establishing relationships between the sketch elements. These constraints are available on the **Constrain** panel of the **Sketch** tab and are explained next.

Coincident

This constraint connects a point to another point.

1. On the **Constrain** panel of the ribbon, click **Coincident** .
2. Select two points. The selected points will be connected.

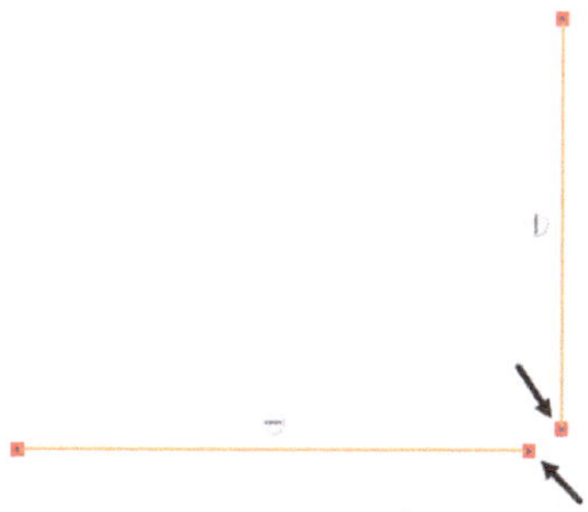

Horizontal

To apply the **Horizontal** constraint, click the **Horizontal** icon on the **Constrain** panel, and select a line.

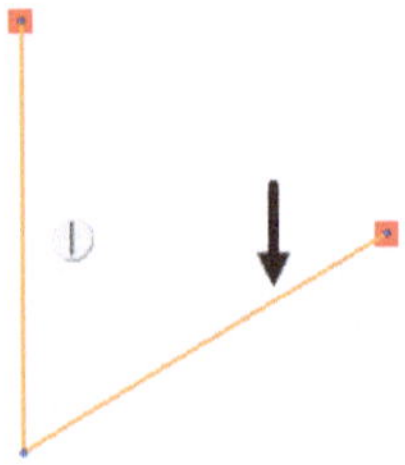

You can also align two points or vertices horizontally.

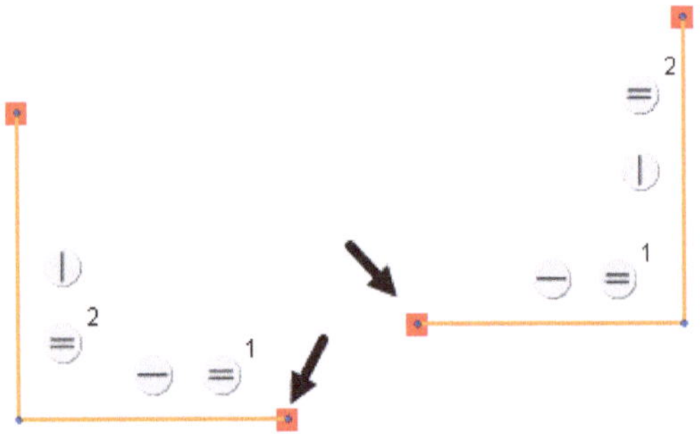

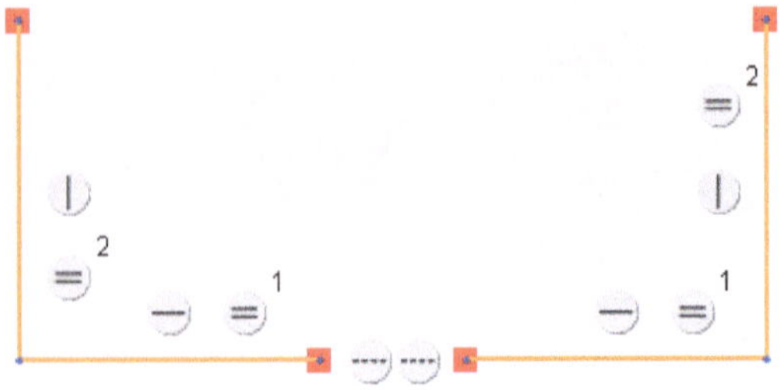

Vertical

Use the **Vertical** command to make a line vertical. You can also align two vertices vertically by using this command.

Tangent

This command makes an arc, circle, or line tangent to another arc or circle. On the **Constrain** panel, click the **Tangent** icon and select a circle, arc, or line. Select another circle, arc, or line. The two elements will be tangent to each other.

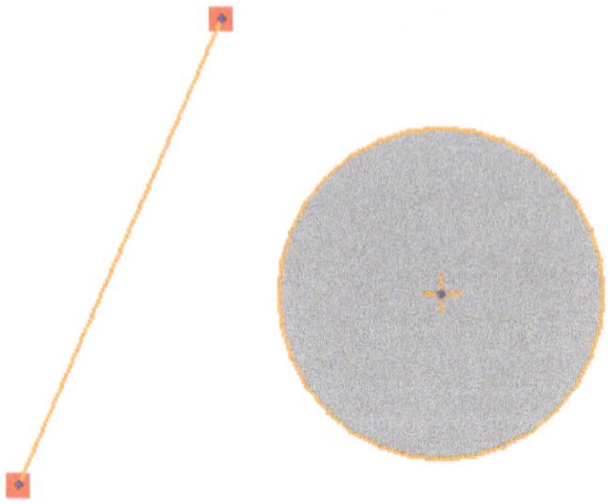

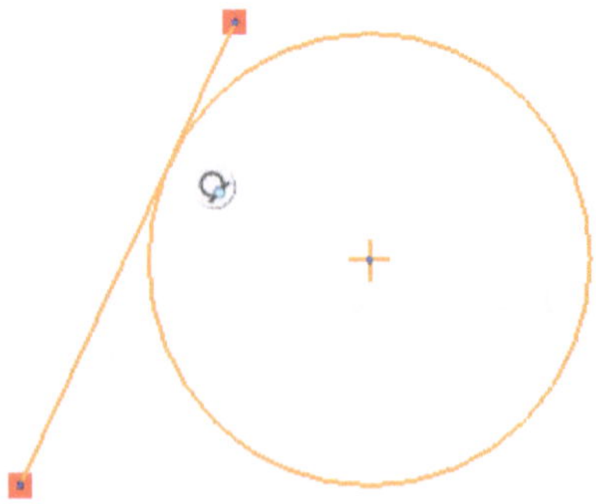

// Parallel

Use the **Parallel** command to make two lines parallel to each other.

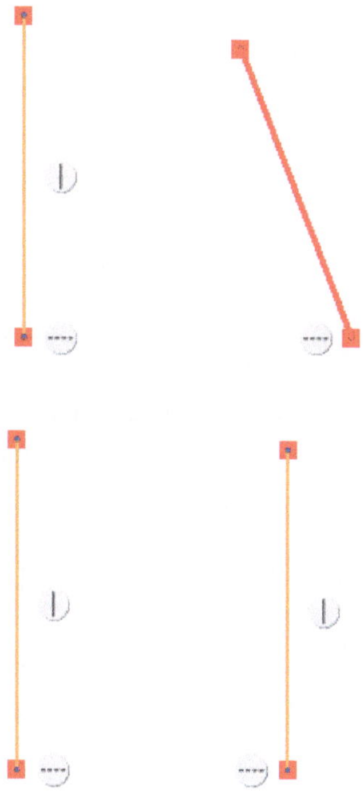

Perpendicular

Use the **Perpendicular** command to make two entities perpendicular to each other.

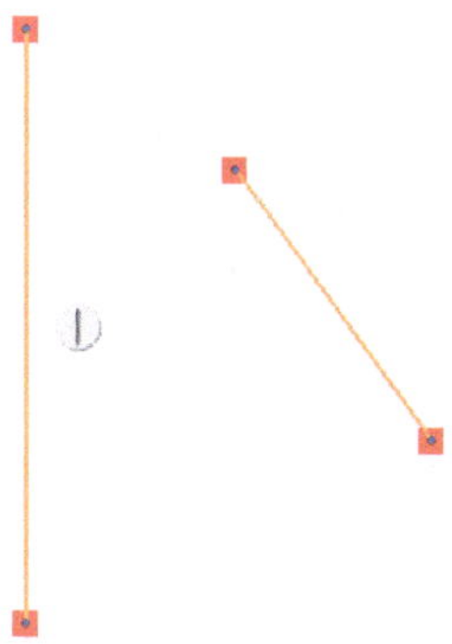

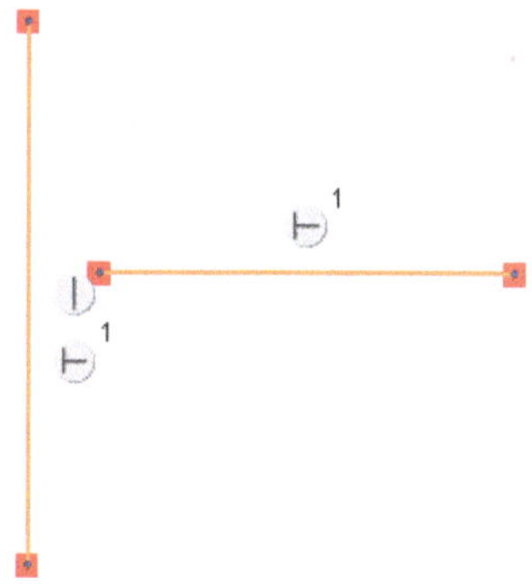

Midpoint

Use the **Midpoint** command to make a point coincide with the midpoint of a line or arc.

1. On the **Constrain** panel, click the **Midpoint** icon.
2. Select and line/arc and a point.

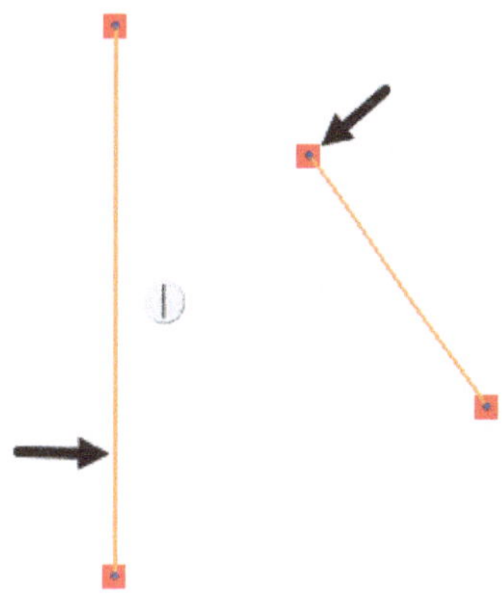

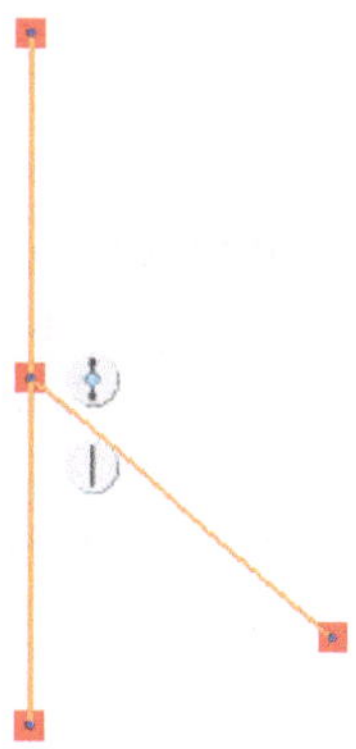

Symmetric

Use the **Symmetric** command to make two points or vertices symmetric about a centerline.

1. On the **Constrain** panel, click the **Symmetric** icon.
2. Click on the symmetric line.
3. Click on two points to be made symmetric.

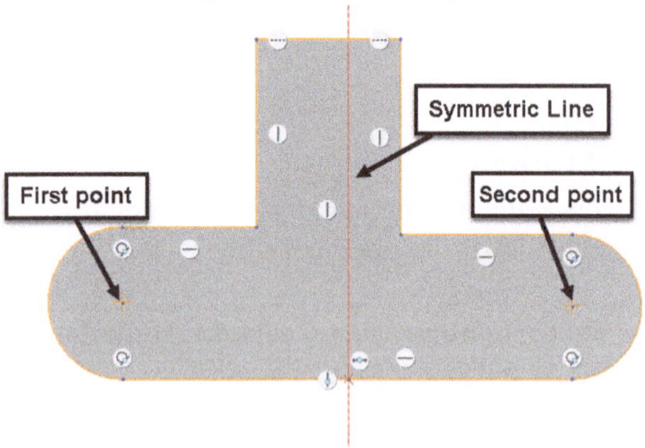

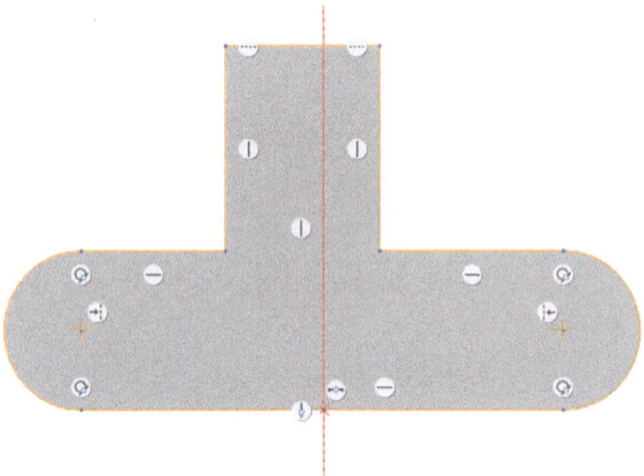

Turning ON/OFF Dimensions and Constraints

As dimensions and constraints are created, they can be shown or hidden using the **Sketcher Display Filter** drop-down on the **Graphics** toolbar. When dealing with complicated sketches involving numerous constraints, you can deactivate this drop-down options to turn off the display of all dimensions, constraints, grid, and vertices.

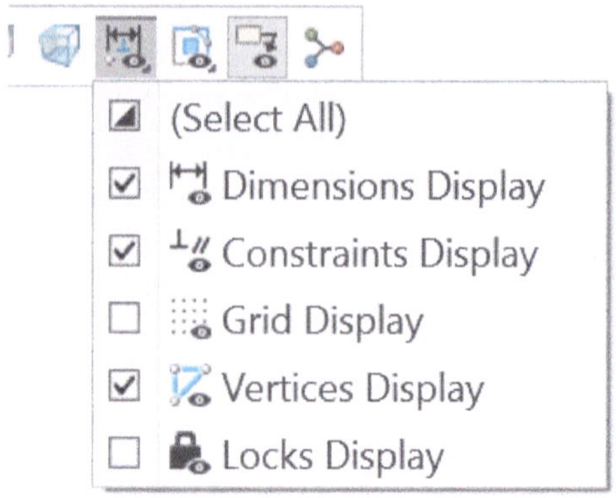

Construction Mode

This command allows you to create construction elements. They support you to create a sketch of the desired shape and size.

1. On the ribbon, click **Sketch** tab > **Sketching** panel > **Construction** Mode.
2. Activate any sketching command and create construction elements.

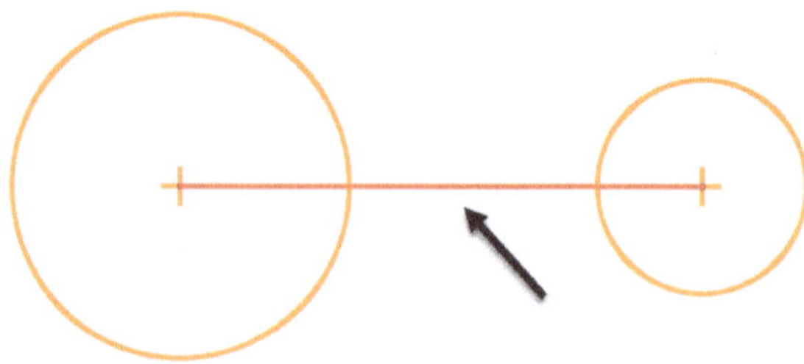

You can also convert a sketch element into a construction element. To do this, select the sketch element, and then click the right mouse button. Select **Construction** from the shortcut menu that appears.

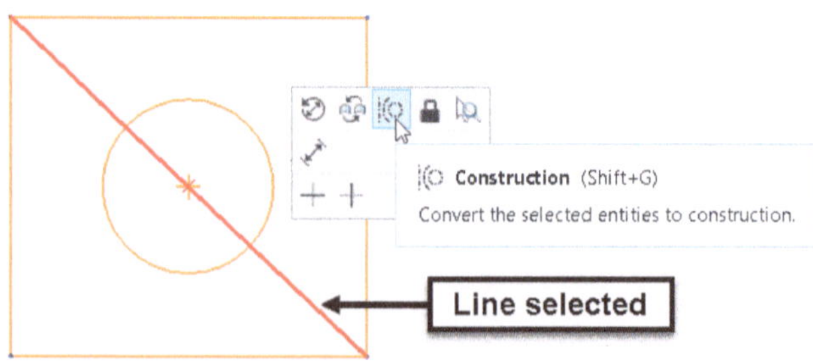

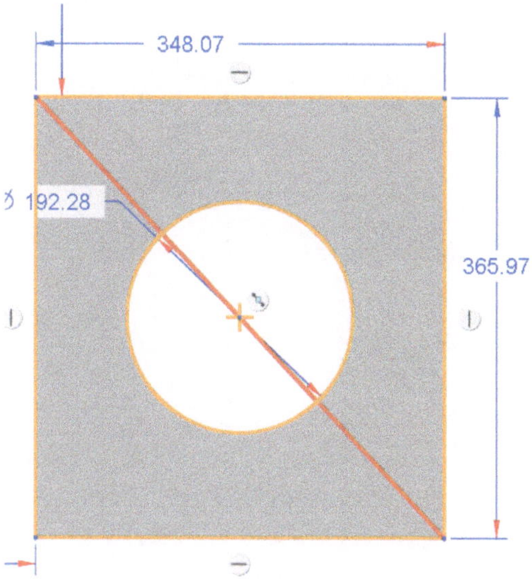

You can also convert the construction element back to a standard sketch element. To do this, click the right mouse button and select **Geometry** from the shortcut menu.

The Circular Trim command

1. On the ribbon, click **Sketch > Sketching > Fillet > Circular Trim**.
2. Select the intersecting elements to add a fillet.

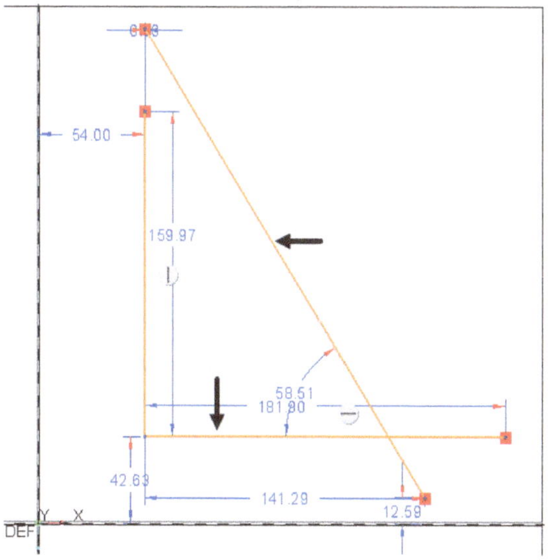

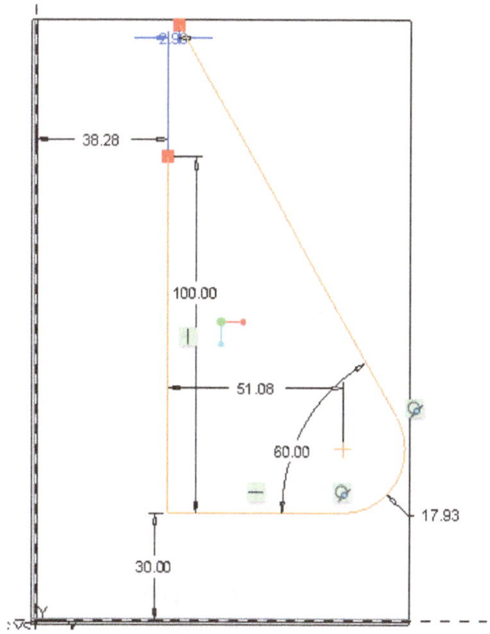

You can modify the fillet size by changing its dimension value.

The elements to be cornered are not required to touch each other.

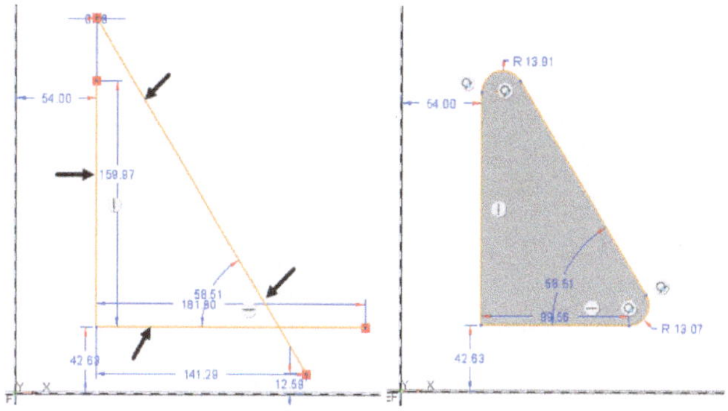

The Circular command

The **Circular Trim** command creates a fillet by trimming/extending the intersecting elements automatically. Whereas, the **Circular** command (On the ribbon, click **Sketch > Sketching > Fillet > Circular**) creates a fillet and converts the intersecting elements in the construction elements.

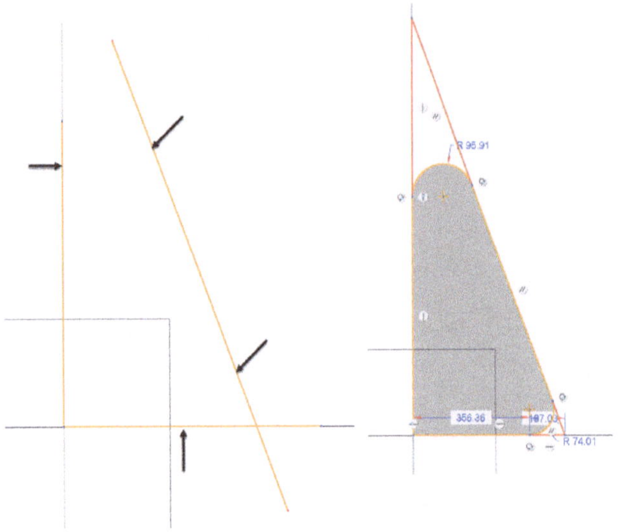

The Chamfer Trim command

This command replaces a sharp corner with an angled line.

1. On the ribbon, click **Sketch > Sketching > Chamfer > Chamfer Trim**.
2. Select the elements' ends to be chamfered.

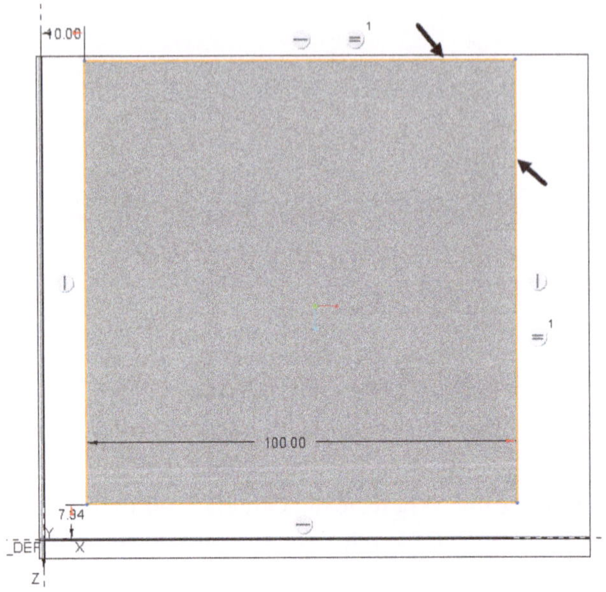

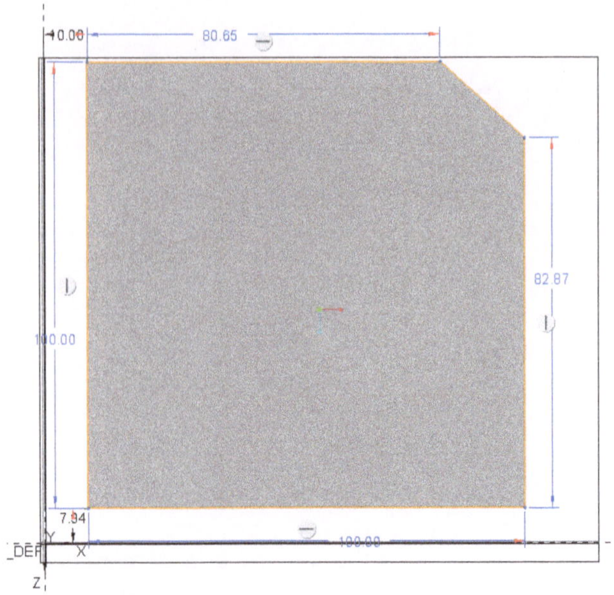

The Elliptical command

This command creates an elliptical fillet at a sharp corner created by the intersection of two lines, arcs, circles, and rectangle or polygon vertices.

1. Create a sketch, as shown.

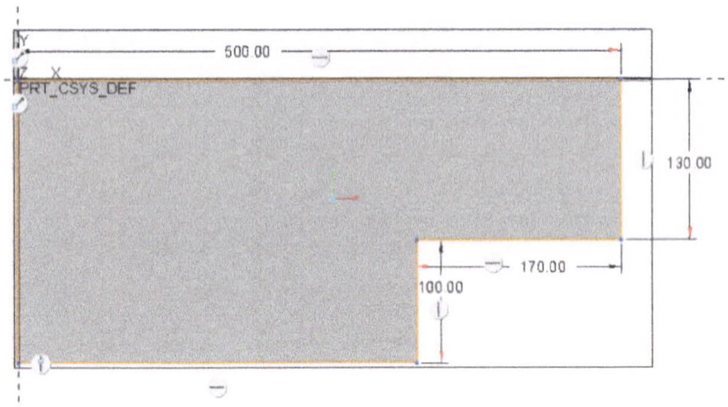

2. On the ribbon, click **Sketch** tab > **Sketching** panel > **Fillet** drop-down > **Elliptical**.

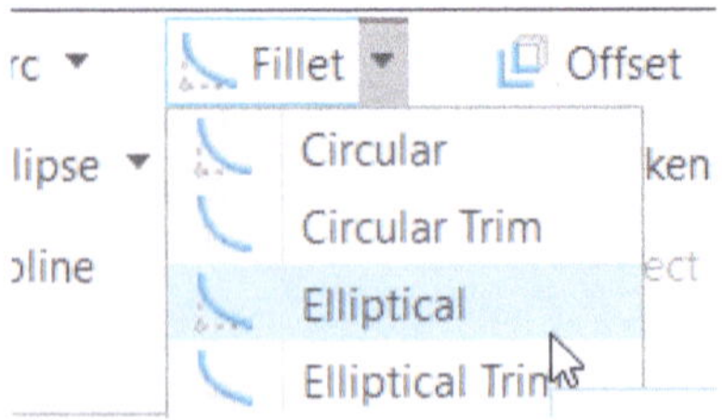

3. Select the lines forming a corner, as shown.

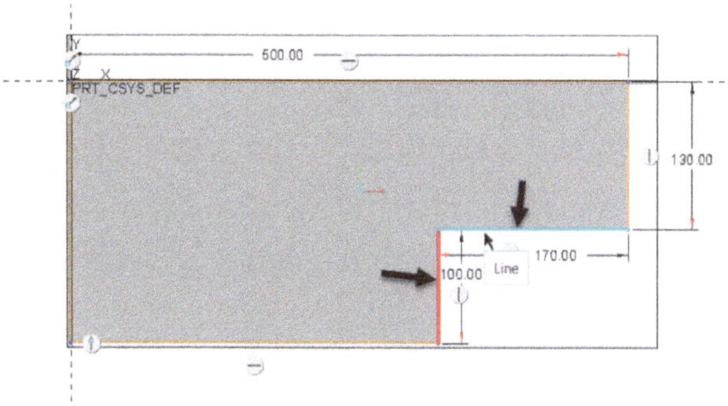

4. On the **Sketch** tab of the ribbon, click **Constrain > Vertical**.
5. Select the construction line, as shown.

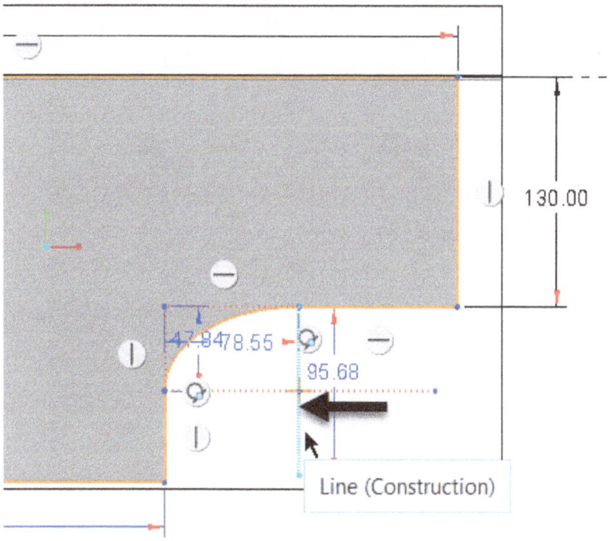

6. On the **Sketch** tab of the ribbon, click **Dimensions > Dimension**.
7. Select the elliptical fillet and click the middle mouse button.
8. Select the **Major Axis** option from the **Ellipse Radius** dialog, and then click **Accept**.
9. Type 60 and press ENTER.
10. Again, select the elliptical fillet and click the middle mouse button.
11. Select the **Minor Axis** option from the **Ellipse Radius** dialog, and then click **Accept**.
12. Type 40 and press ENTER.

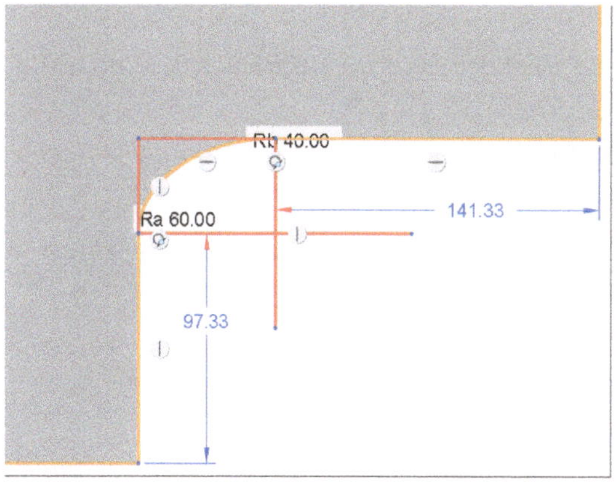

The Elliptical Trim command

This command creates an elliptical fillet the sharp corners and trims the excess elements.

1. On the ribbon, click **Sketch** tab > **Sketching** panel > **Fillet** drop-down > **Elliptical Trim**.

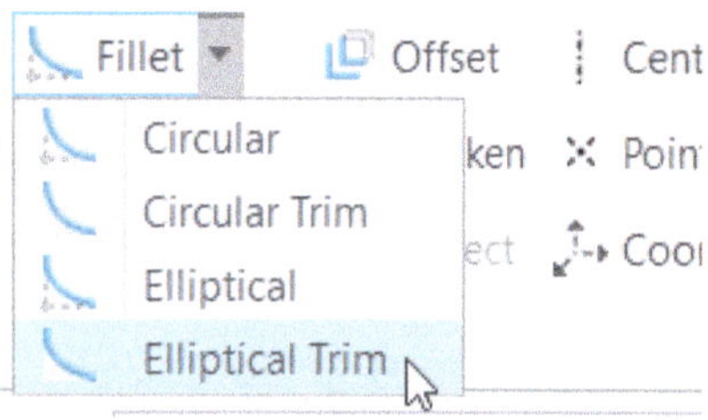

2. Select the elements, as shown.

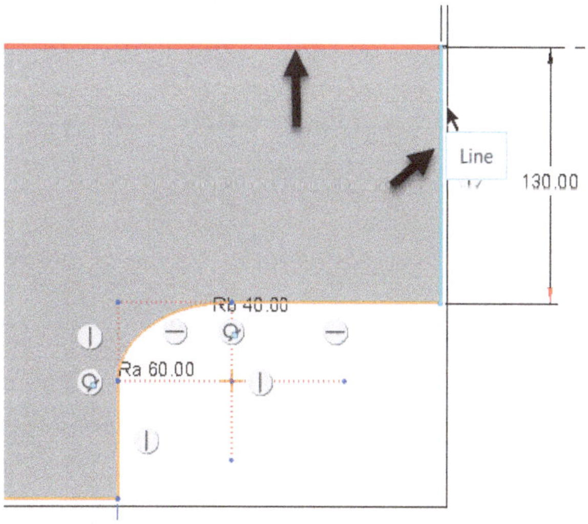

3. On the **Sketch** tab of the ribbon, click **Dimensions > Dimension**.
4. Select the Major axis and click.
5. Type 60 and press ENTER.
6. Select the Minor axis and press ENTER.

7. Type 40 and press ENTER.
8. On the **Sketch** tab of the ribbon, click **Constrain > Horizontal**.
9. Select the minor axis.

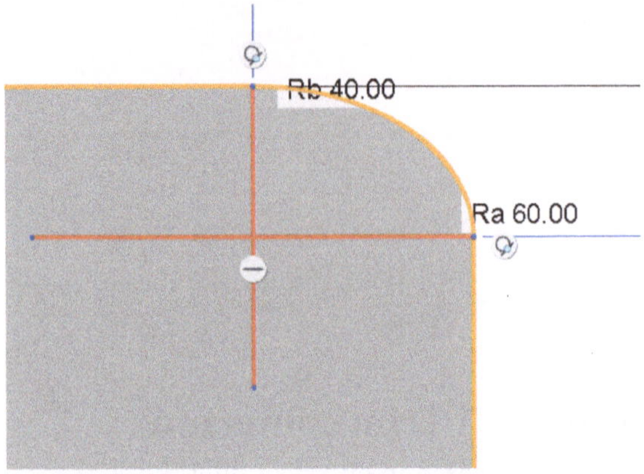

The Delete Segment command

This command trims the end of an element back to the intersection of another element.

1. On the ribbon, click **Sketch** tab > **Editing** panel > **Delete Segment**.
2. Click on the element to trim.

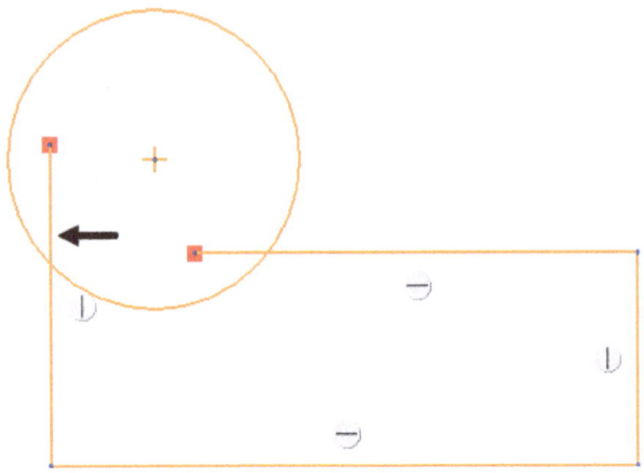

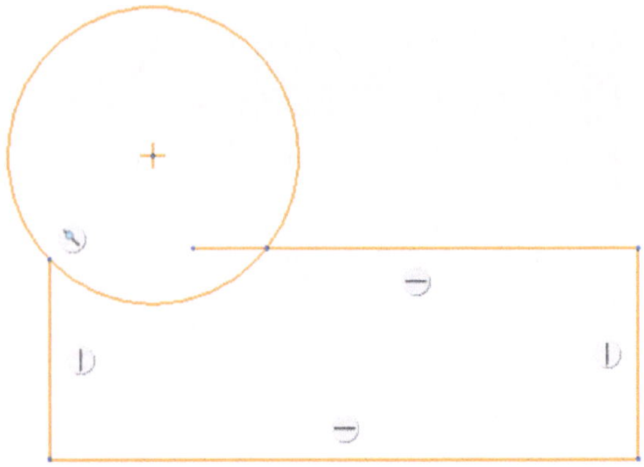

You can also trim the elements by pressing the left mouse button and dragging the pointer.

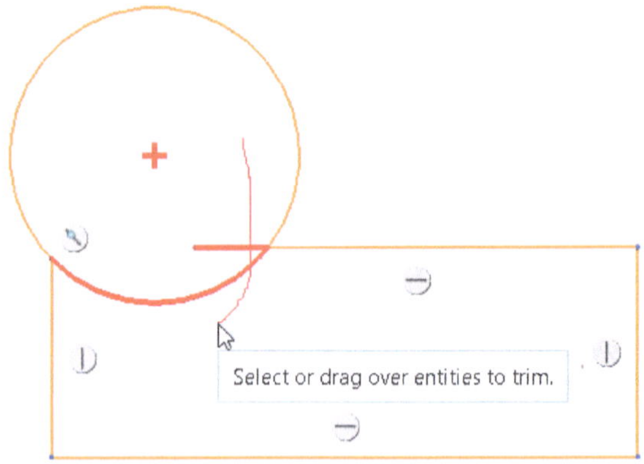

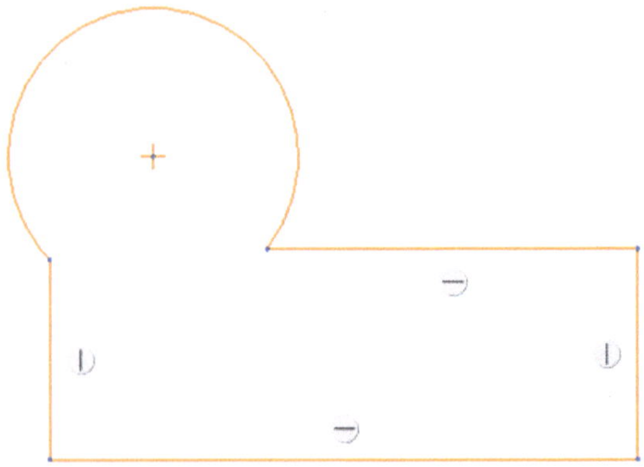

The Divide command

This command breaks a sketch element at a selected point.

1. On the ribbon, click **Sketch** tab > **Editing** panel > **Divide**.

2. Click on the sketch element to define the breaking point.

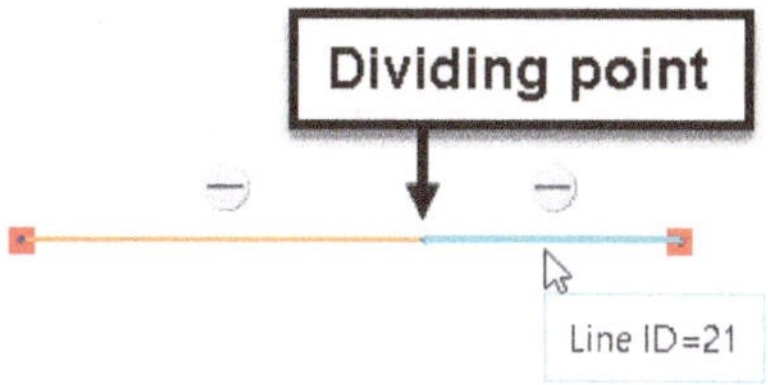

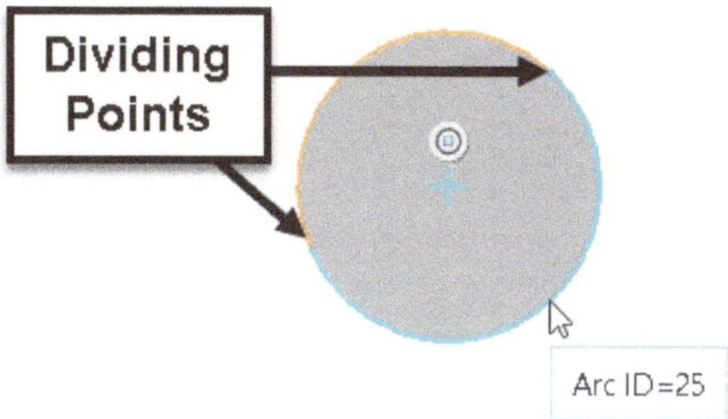

The Corner command

This command trims and extends elements to form a corner.

1. On the ribbon, click **Sketch** tab > **Editing** panel > **Corner**.
2. Select two intersecting elements. The elements will be trimmed and extended to form a closed corner.

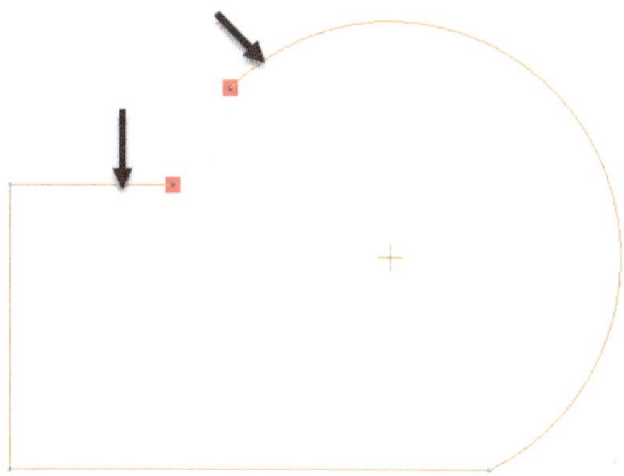

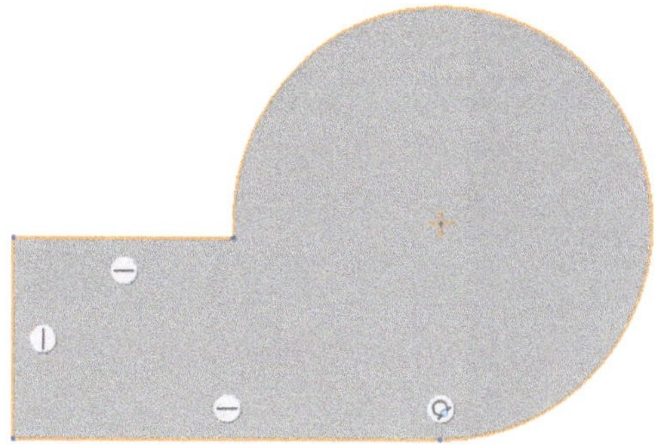

The Mirror command

This command creates a mirror copy of selected sketch elements.

1. Drag a selection box and select the elements to mirror.

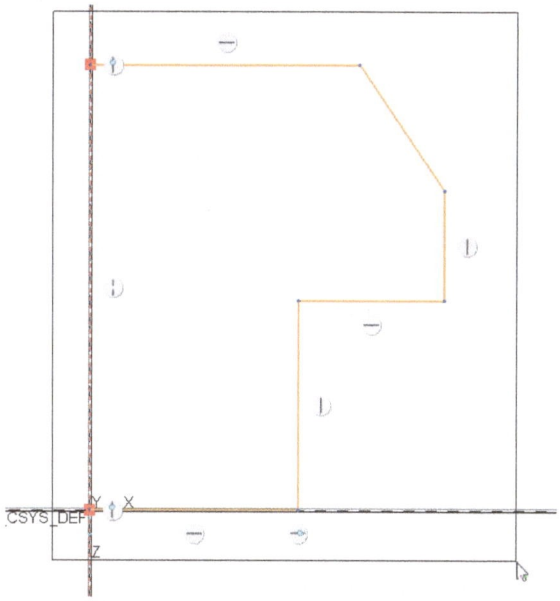

2. On the ribbon, click **Sketch** tab > **Editing** panel > **Mirror**.
3. Click on a line or centerline to define the mirror line.

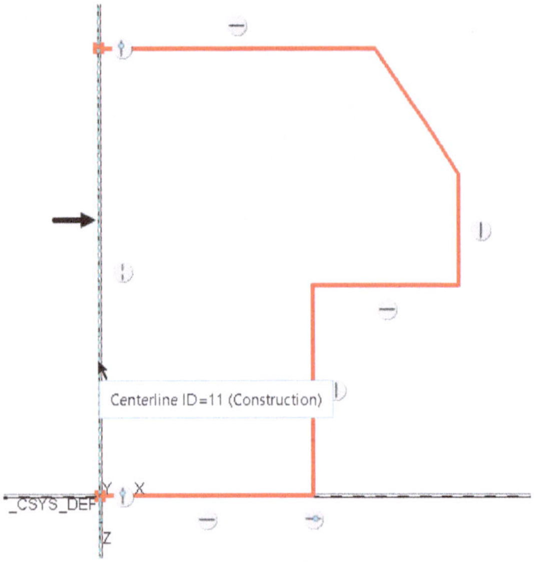

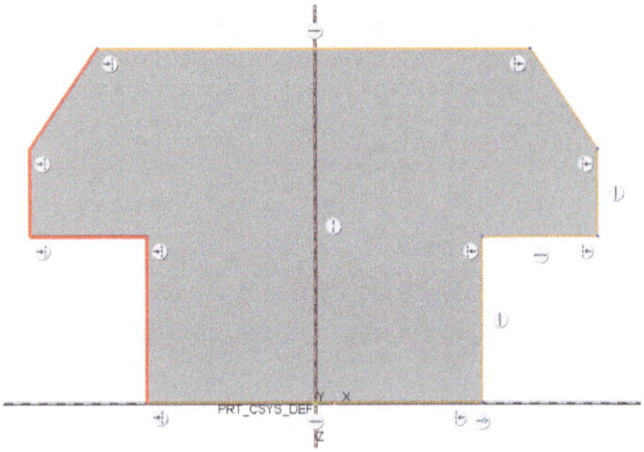

The Rotate Resize command

This command can be used to rotate or resize the selected elements.

1. Select the elements to rotate.

2. On the ribbon, click **Sketch** tab > **Editing** panel > **Rotate Resize**.

You will notice that the rotate and resize handles appear on the selected elements. Click and drag the rotate handle to rotate the selected elements.

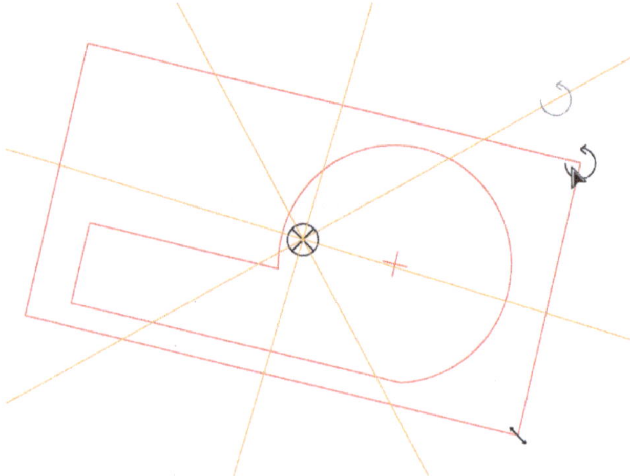

While rotating the element, you can define the center of rotation by clicking in the **Enter reference to rotate entity** box on the ribbon and selecting a point.

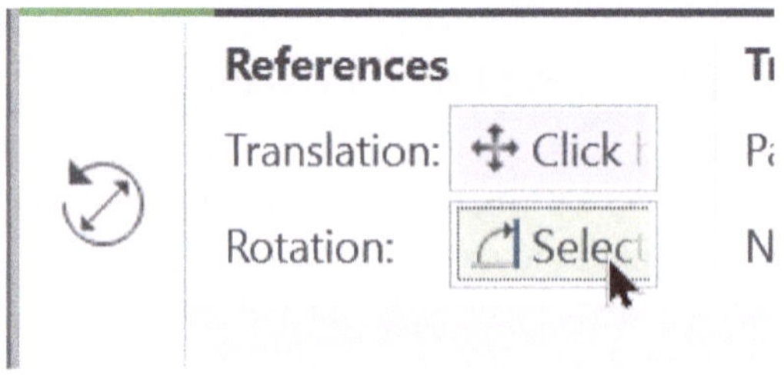

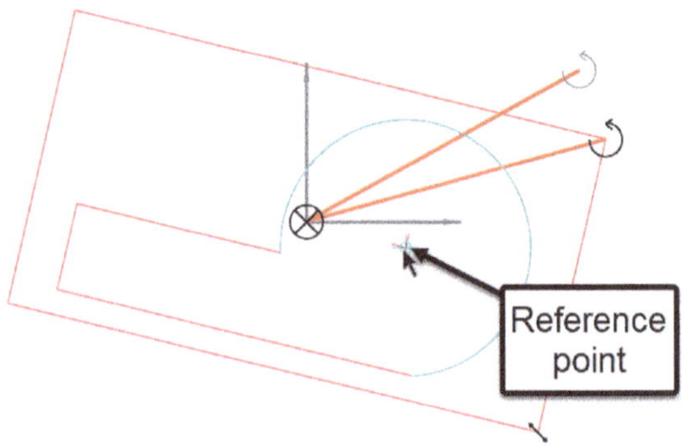

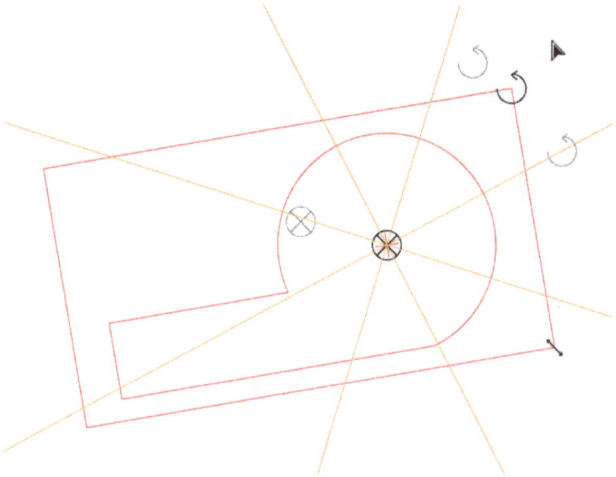

Likewise, use the resize handle to change the size of the elements.

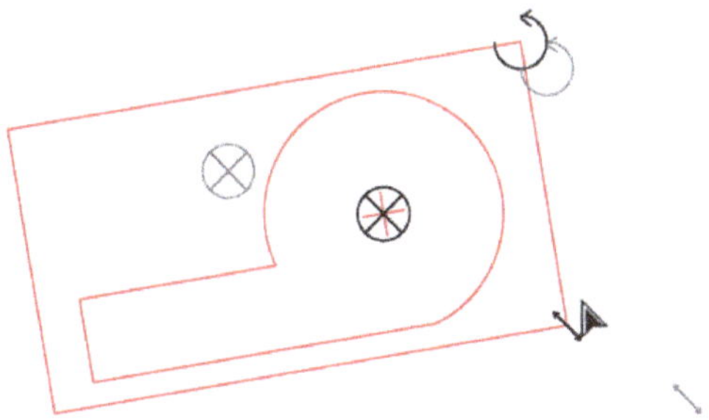

After rotating/resizing the elements, click the green check on the ribbon.

The Offset command

This command creates a parallel copy of a selected element or chain or closed loop of elements.

1. On the ribbon, click **Sketch** tab > **Sketching** panel > **Offset**.

A toolbar appears on the screen. It displays a tip to help you in selecting the entities to offset. You can select single, chain, or loop of entities.

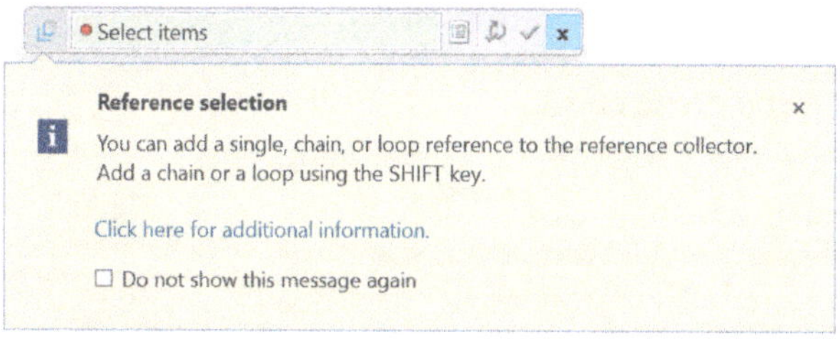

2. Select a single entity from the graphics window.

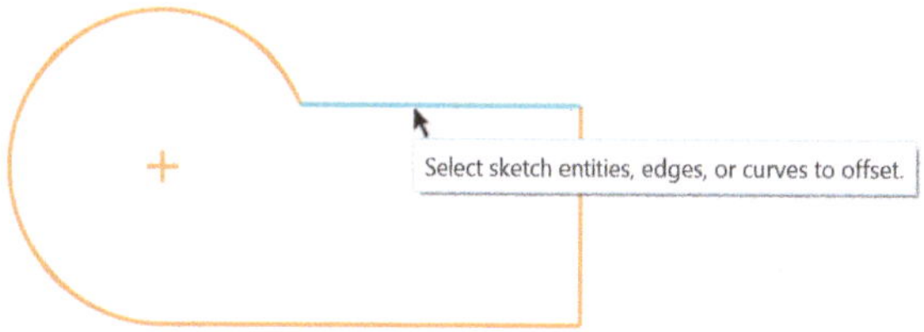

3. Press and hold the SHIFT key and select another entity of the sketch; the chain of entities is selected.
4. Click the **Review and edit chain properties** icon on the toolbar.

5. On the **Chain** dialog, select **Rule-based** option. Notice that the **Partial Loop** option is selected y default.
6. Click the **Flip** button to change the portion of the loop selected.

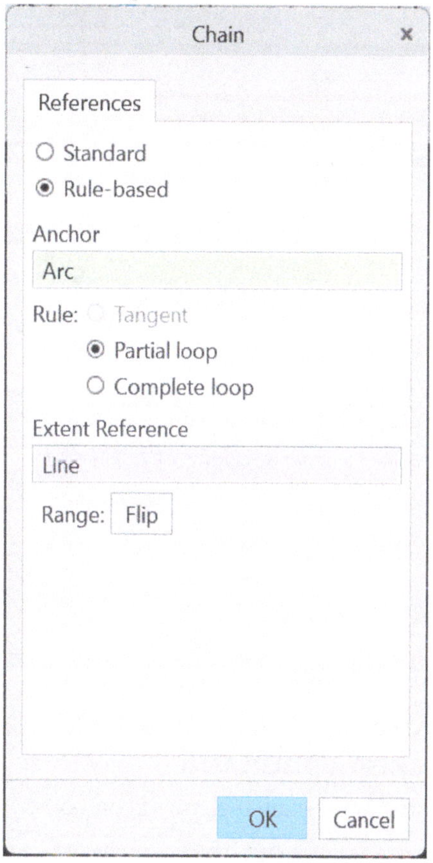

7. Select the **Complete Loop** option to select a closed loop

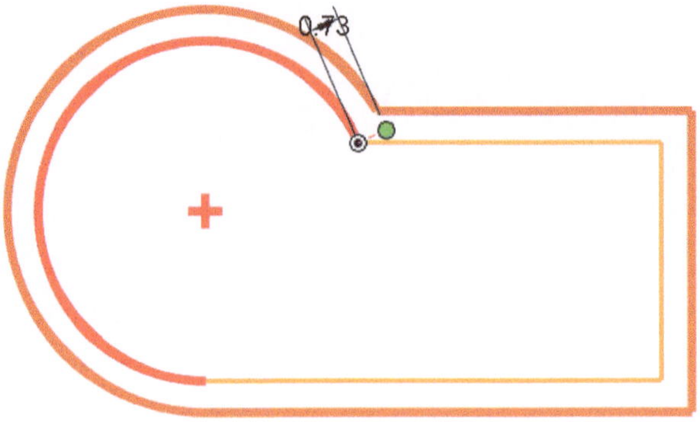

8. Click **OK** on the **Chain** dialog.
9. Type-in the offset distance value in the value box attached to the selected entities.

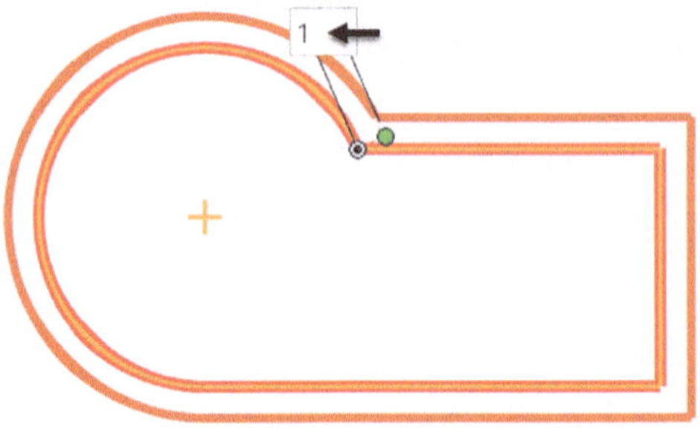

10. Click the green check.

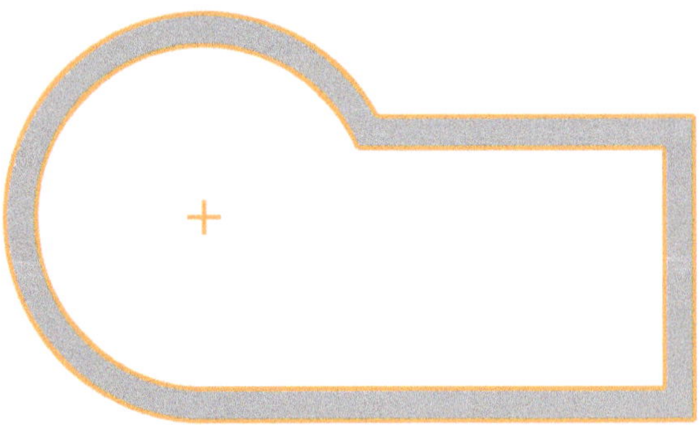

The Thicken command

This command offsets the sketch elements on both sides.

1. On the ribbon, click **Sketch** tab > **Sketching** panel > **Thicken**.
2. On the **Type** dialog, select an option from the **Select Thicken Edge** section.
3. Select an option from the **End caps** section.

The **Open** option creates an offset with open ends.

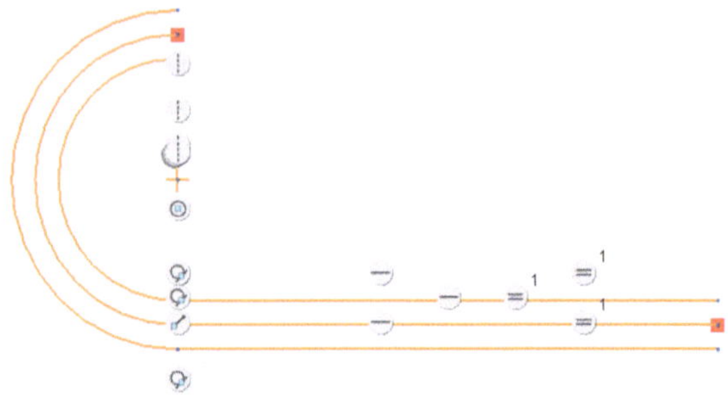

The **Flat** option closes the ends with a line.

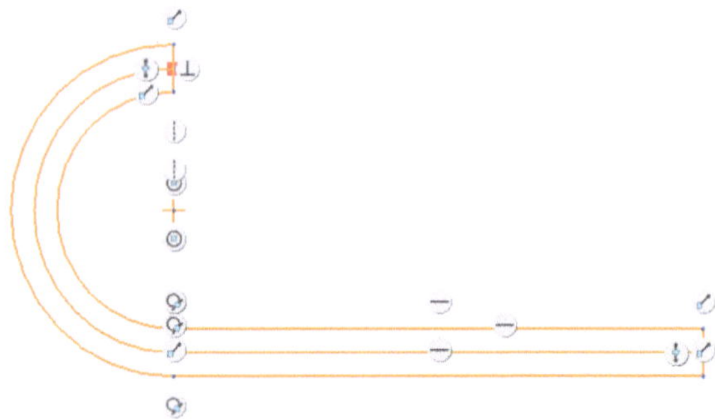

The **Circular** option closes the ends with an arc.

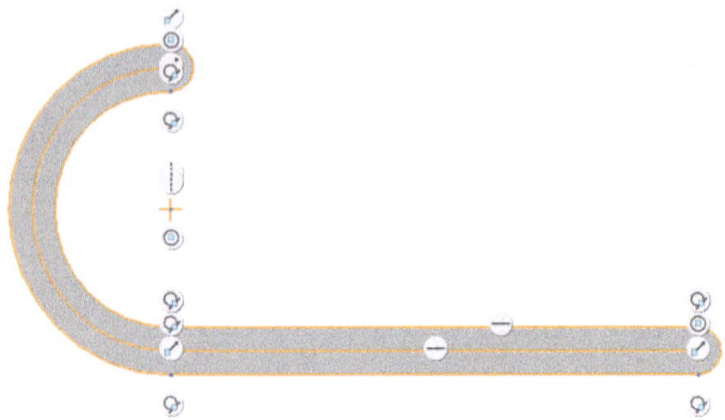

4. Select the elements to offset.
5. Type-in the total offset distance (both sides combined). Click the green check.
6. Type-in the offset distance on the outside. Click the green check.
7. Click **Close** on the **Type** dialog.

Palette

This command displays a palette showing various predefined polygons, shapes, profiles, and stars.

1. On the ribbon, click **Sketch > Sketching > Palette**.
2. On the **Palette** dialog, click the **Polygons** tab.
3. Under the **Polygons** tab, select **6-Sided Hexagon**.
4. Drag it into the graphics window.
5. Use the handles available on the polygon to move, rotate, and scale it.

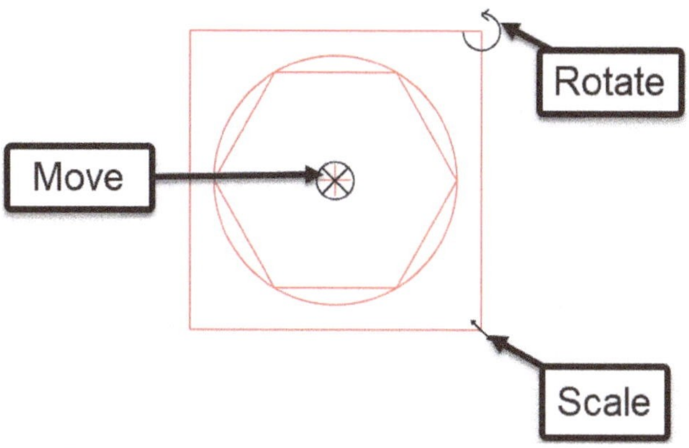

6. Click the green check on the Dashboard.
7. You can modify the dimensions to change the size and location of the polygon.

Likewise, you can insert other predefined shapes using the tabs available on the **Palette** dialog.

Text

Texts are used to provide information on the models, such as company name, model, and specifications.

1. Start a new sketch.
2. Activate the **Construction Mode** icon on the **Sketching** panel of the ribbon.
3. Create the circle, as shown.

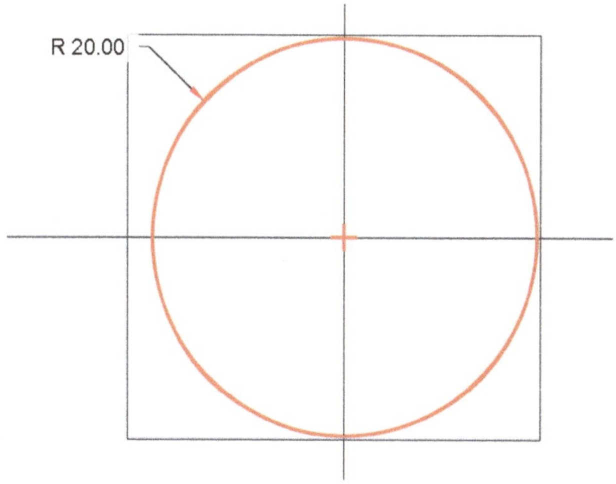

4. Deactivate the **Construction Mode** icon.
5. On the **Sketching** tab of the ribbon, click the **Text** tool.
6. Select the origin point of the sketch.
7. Move the pointer upward up to a small distance and click to specify the text height.

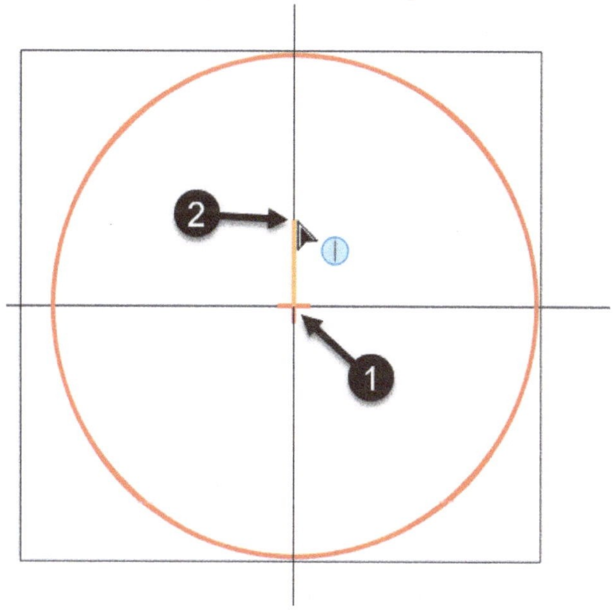

8. On the **Text** dialog, type **150** in the **Enter text** box.

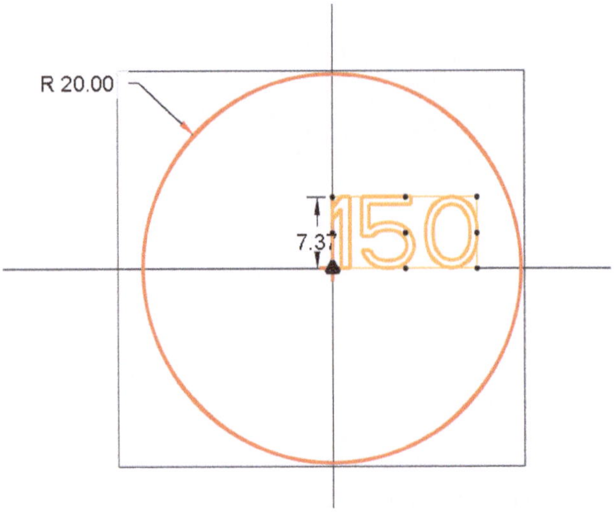

9. In the **Alignment** section, select **Horizontal > Center**.
10. Select **Vertical > Middle**.

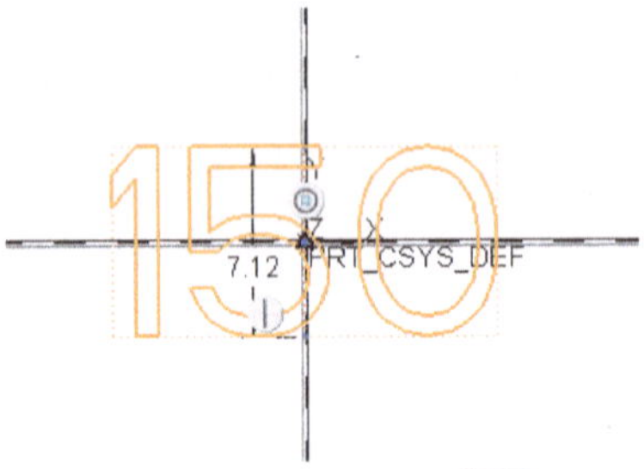

11. Click the **Text Symbol** button next to the **Enter text** box.
12. On the **Text Symbol** dialog, click the **Angle** icon.

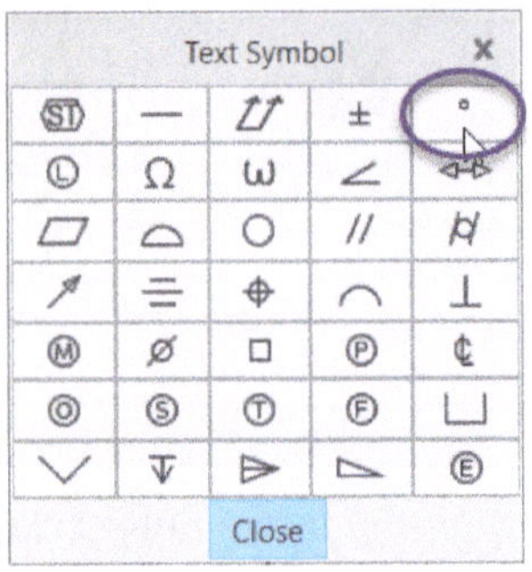

13. Close the **Text Symbol** dialog.
14. Check the **Place along curve** option and select the construction circle.
15. Click the **Flip Text** button next to the **Place along curve** option.
16. Click **OK**.

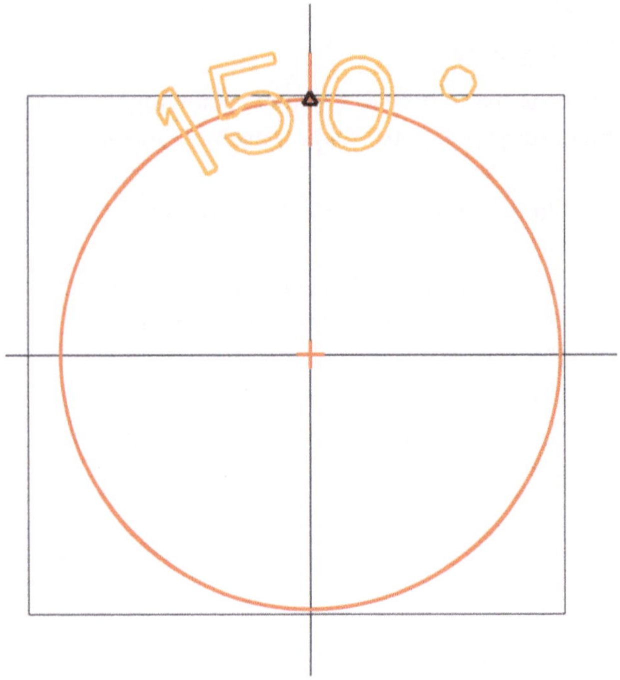

Examples

Example 1

In this example, you will draw the sketch shown below.

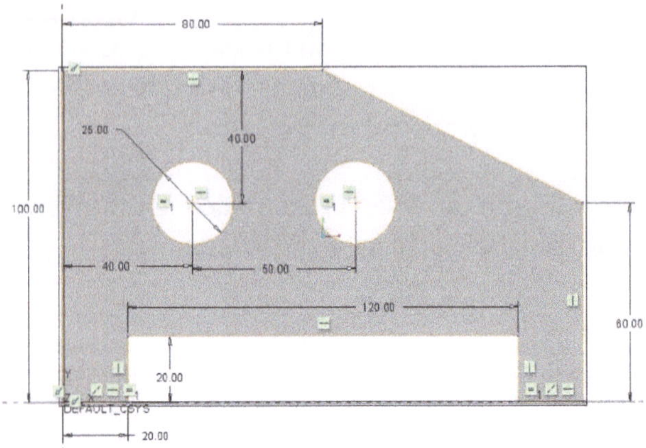

1. Start **Creo Parametric 11.0** by clicking the **Creo Parametric 11.0** icon on your desktop.
2. Create a new folder with the name *Creo Parametric 11.0 Basics* on your drive.
3. On the ribbon, click **Home** tab > **Data** panel > **Select Working Directory**.
4. Go to the *Creo Parametric 11.0 Basics* folder and click **Organize > New Folder**.

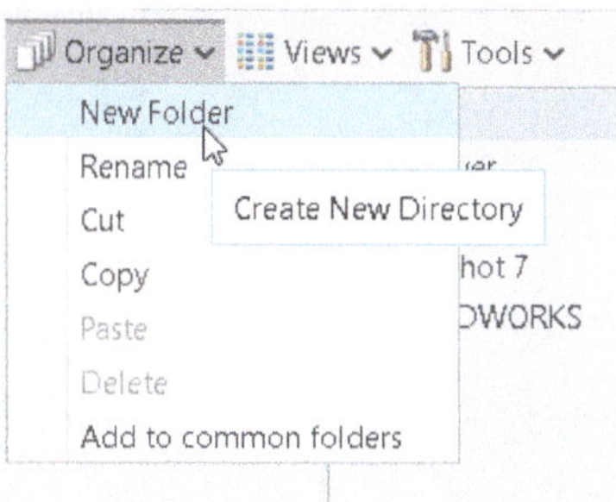

5. Type-in **Sketching** in the **New Folder** dialog and click **OK**.

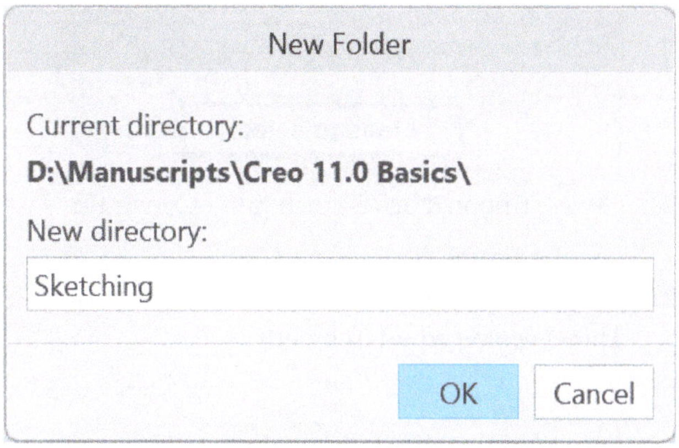

6. Again, click **OK** to set the *Sketching* folder as the working directory.
7. On the ribbon, click **Home** tab > **Data** panel > **New**.
8. On the **New** dialog, select **Type > Part** and **Sub-type > Solid**.
9. Type-in **Example1** in the **File name** box.
10. Uncheck the **Use default template** option and click **OK**.
11. On the **New File Options** dialog, select **solid_part_mmks_abs**, and click **OK**.
12. On the ribbon, click **Model** tab > **Datum** panel > **Sketch** .
13. Click on the Front plane.

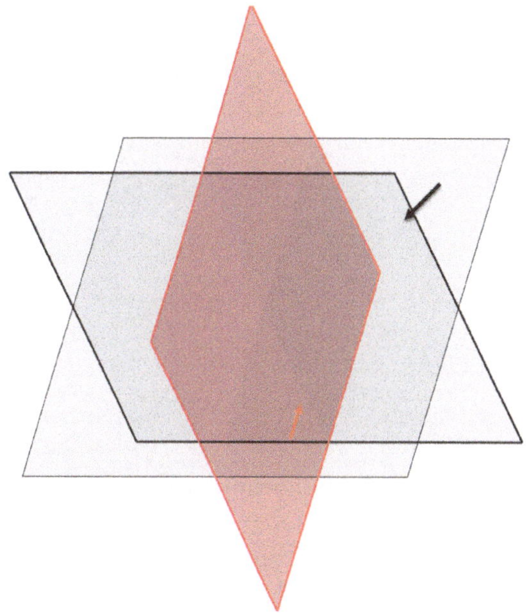

14. Accept the default values on the **Sketch** dialog and click **Sketch**.
15. On the **Graphics** toolbar, click the **Sketch View** icon to orient the sketch plane parallel to the screen.

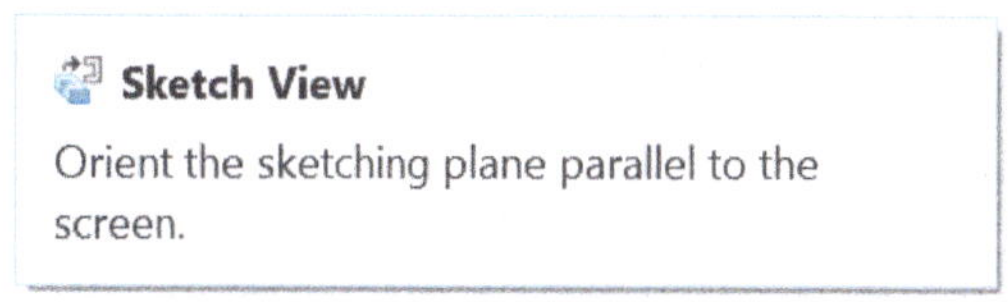

16. On the ribbon, click **Sketch** tab > **Sketching** panel > **Line** .
17. Click on the origin point to define the first point of the line.
18. Move the pointer rightwards and click when the horizontal symbol appears on the line.

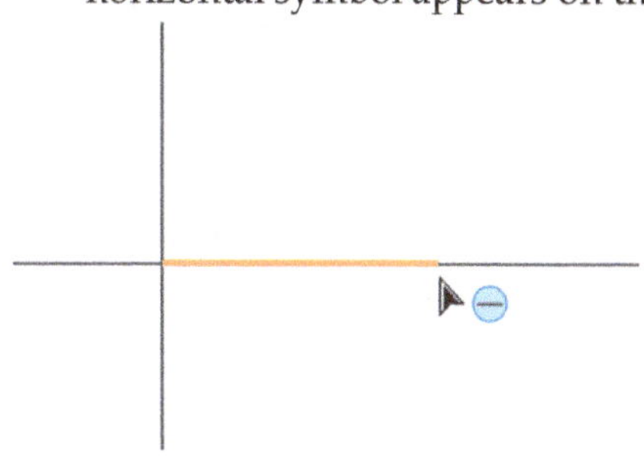

19. Move the pointer upwards and click when the vertical symbol appears. It creates a vertical line.

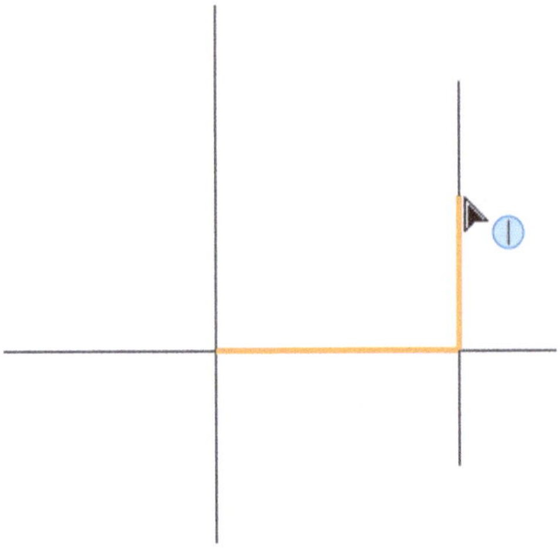

20. Move the pointer rightwards and click to create a horizontal line.

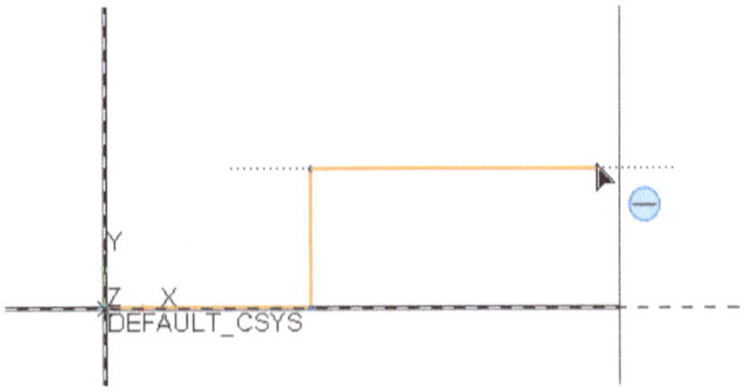

21. Create a closed-loop by selecting points, as shown below. On the ribbon, click **Sketch** tab > **Operations** panel > **Select** icon to deactivate the **Line Chain** command.

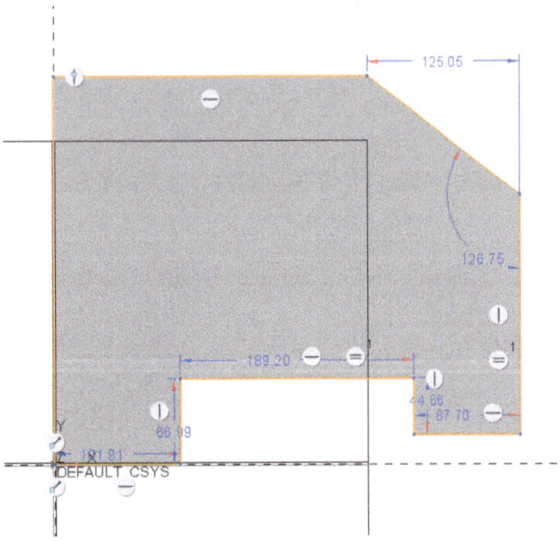

22. On the ribbon, click **Sketch** tab > **Constrain** panel > **Coincident** .
23. Click on the two horizontal lines at the bottom; they become coincident.

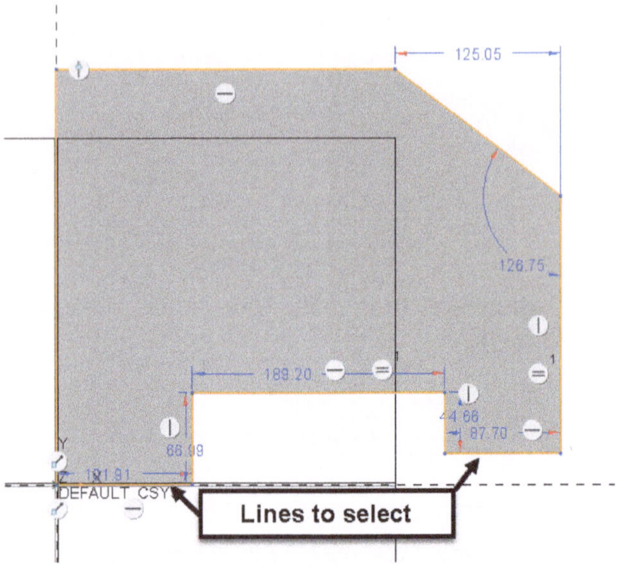

24. On the ribbon, click **Sketch** tab > **Constrain** panel > **Equal** = .
25. Click on the two horizontal lines at the bottom. They become equal in length.

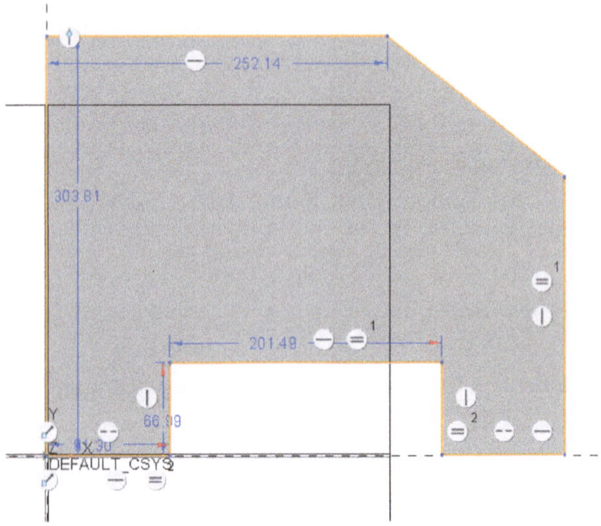

26. On the ribbon, click **Sketch** tab > **Operations** panel > **Select** drop-down > **One by One**.
27. On the ribbon, click **Sketch** tab > **Editing** panel > **Modify** .
28. Click on the horizontal dimension, as shown in the figure.

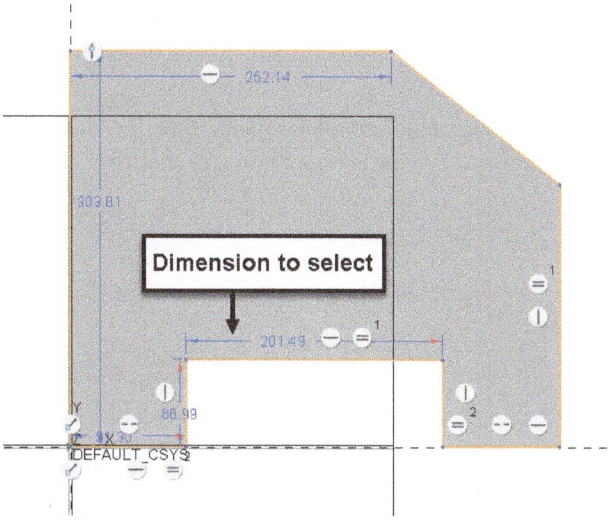

29. Type-in **120** on the **Modify Dimensions** dialog. Click **OK**.

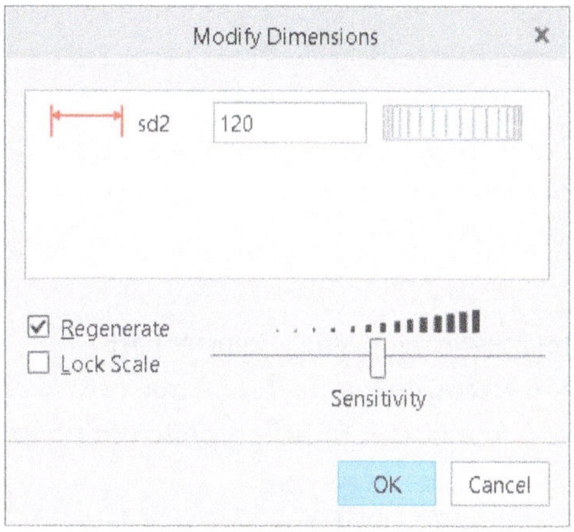

30. Likewise, activate the **Modify** command and change the other-dimensional values. You can also select all the dimensions at a time by dragging a crossing window.

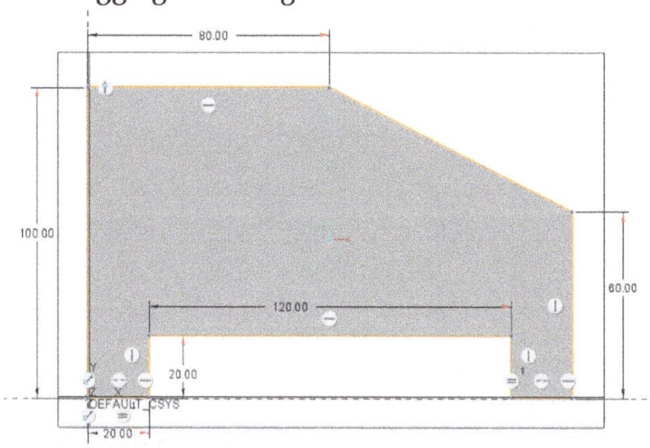

31. Click **OK** on the **Modify** dialog.

32. On the ribbon, click **Sketch** tab > **Sketching** panel > **Circle** drop-down **> Center and Point** .

33. Click inside the sketch region to define the center point of the circle. Move the pointer and click to define the diameter.

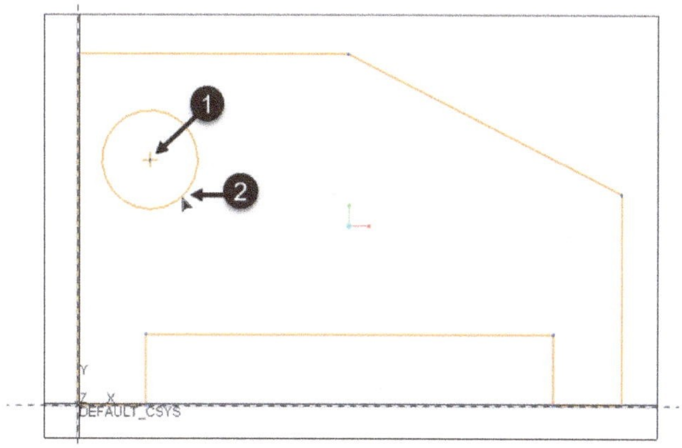

34. Likewise, create another circle.

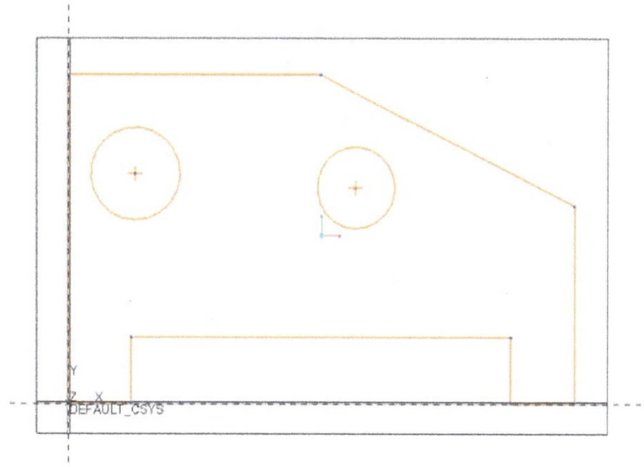

35. On the ribbon, click **Sketch** tab > **Constraint** panel > **Horizontal** .

36. Select the centerpoints of the circles.

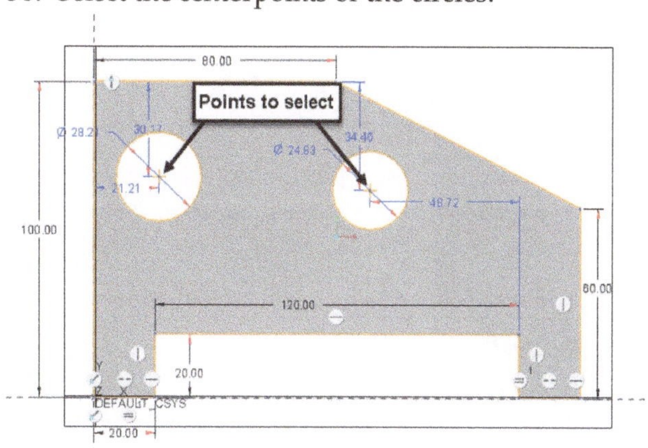

37. Apply the **Equal** constraint between the two circles if there is not equal.
38. Activate the **Modify** command and modify the dimension values of the circles and their positioning dimensions. Click **OK** on the dialog.

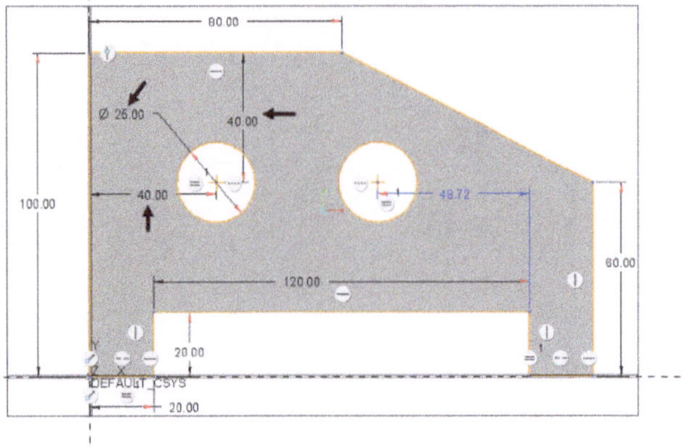

39. Press and hold the Ctrl key and select the center points of the circles.
40. Click the right mouse button.
41. On the shortcut menu, click **Horizontal**.

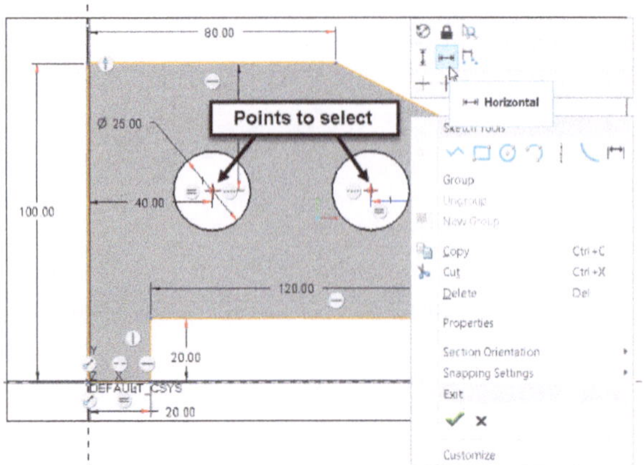

42. Type-in **50** in the value box and press Enter.

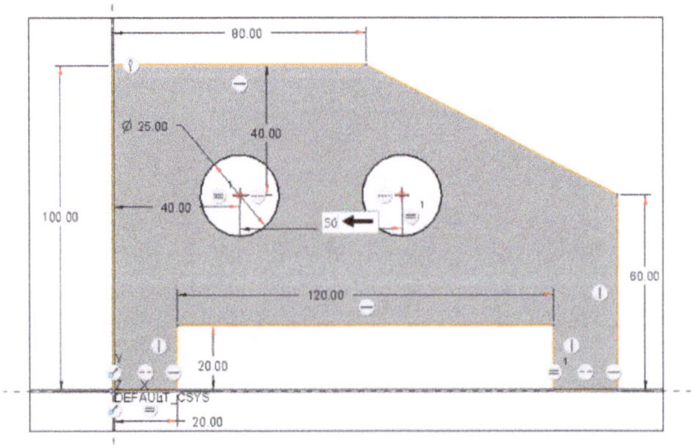

43. On the ribbon, click **Sketch** tab > **Close** panel > **OK** .
44. On the **Quick Access Toolbar**, click the **Save** icon (or) click **File > Save** on the Menu.
45. Click **OK** to save the part file.
46. Click **File > Close.**

Example 2

In this example, you will draw the sketch shown below.

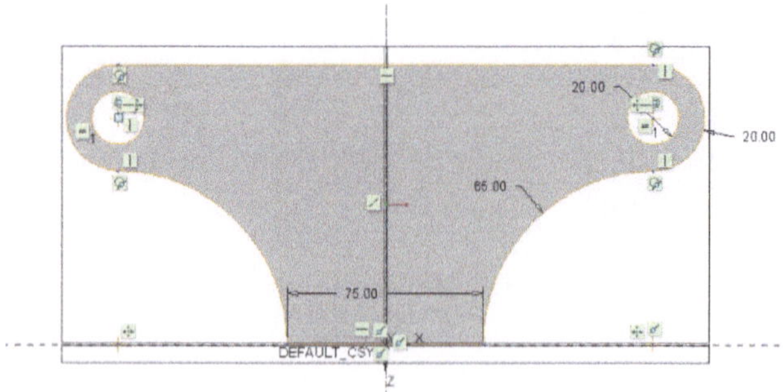

1. Start **Creo Parametric 11.0** by clicking the **Creo Parametric 11.0** icon on your desktop.
2. On the **Quick Access Toolbar**, click the **New** icon.
3. On the **New** dialog, click **Type > Part.**
4. Type-in **Example2** in the **File name** box.
5. Uncheck the **Use default template** option and click **OK.**
6. On the **New File Options** dialog, select **solid_part_mmks_abs**, and click **OK.**
7. To start a new sketch, click the **Sketch** icon on the **Datum** panel.
8. Click on the Top Plane, and then click **Sketch** to start the sketch.

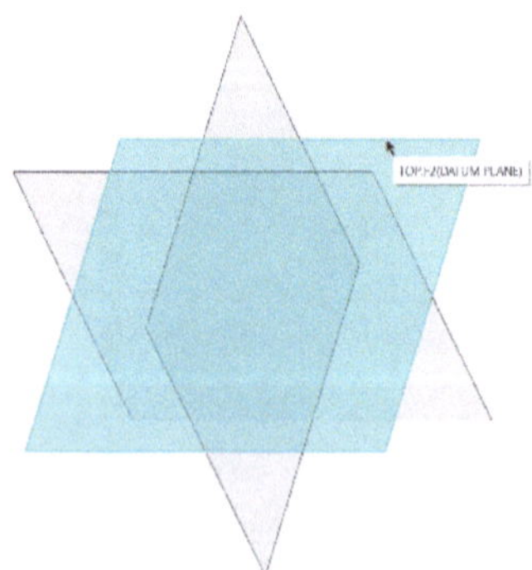

9. On the **Graphics** toolbar, click the **Sketch View** icon.

10. On the ribbon, click **Sketch** tab > **Sketching** panel > **Line Chain** .
11. Click in the second quadrant of the coordinate system to define the start point of the profile. Drag the pointer horizontally and click to define the endpoint.

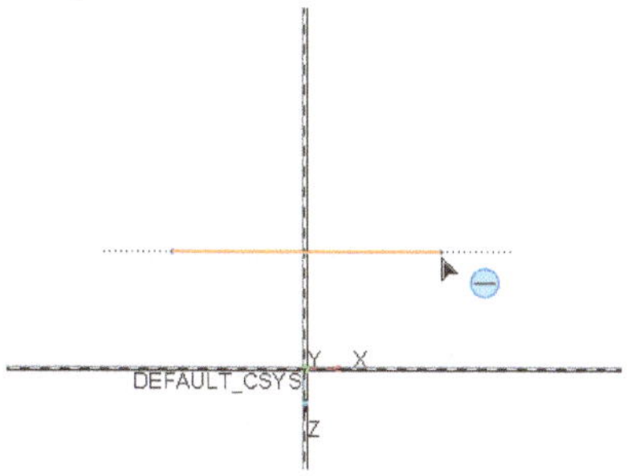

12. On the ribbon, click **Sketch** tab > **Sketching** panel **>** **Arc** drop-down **>** **3-Point/Tangent End** .
13. Select the right endpoint of the line.
14. Move the pointer upwards right and click to define the second point of the arc.

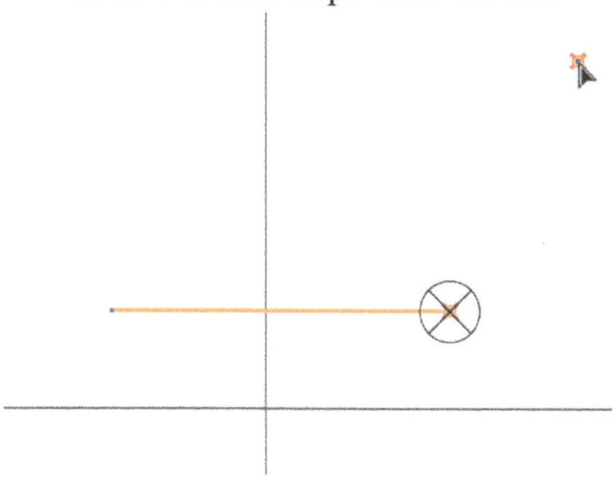

15. Move the pointer and click to define the third point of the arc.

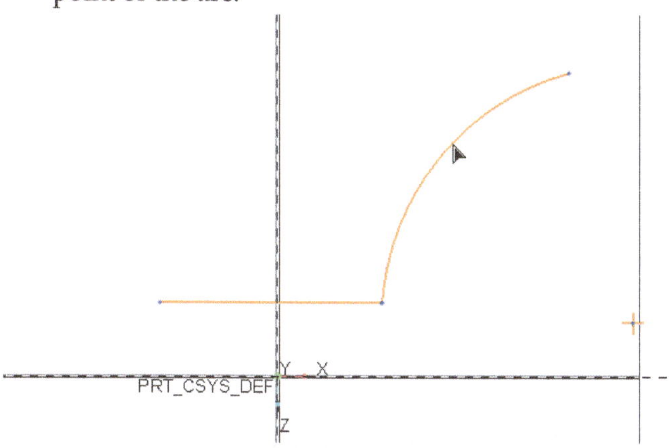

16. Select the endpoint of the arc.
17. Move the pointer rightwards and upwards, and then click to create an arc tangent to the previous arc.

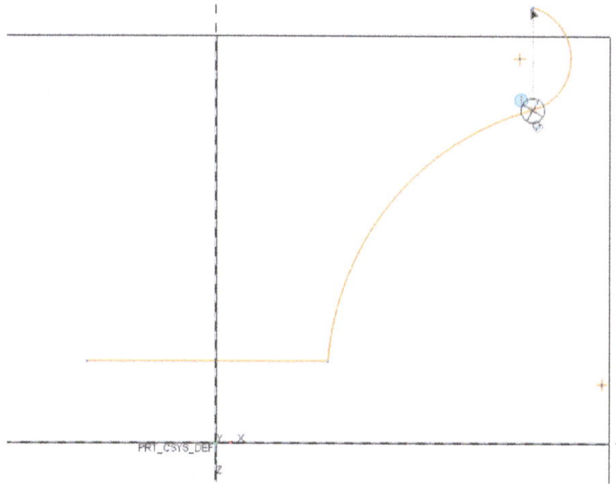

18. On the ribbon, click **Sketch** tab > **Sketching** panel **>** **Line Chain** .
19. Select the endpoint of the arc.
20. Move the pointer toward the left and click to create a horizontal line.

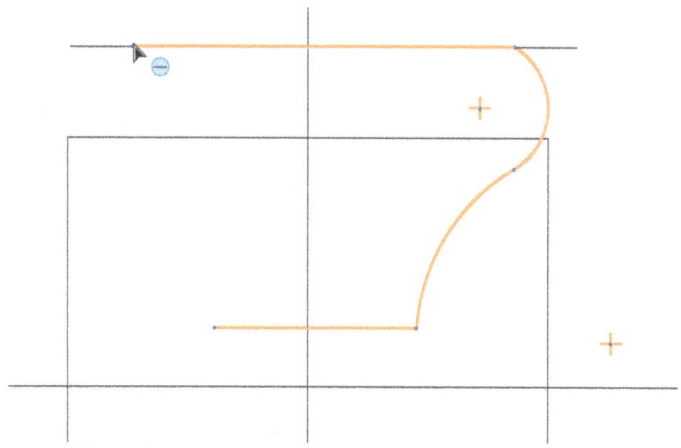

21. Click the **3-Point/Tangent End** icon on the **Sketching** panel.
22. Select the endpoint of the horizontal line.
23. Move the pointer leftwards and downwards, and then click when a vertical dotted line appears, as shown below.

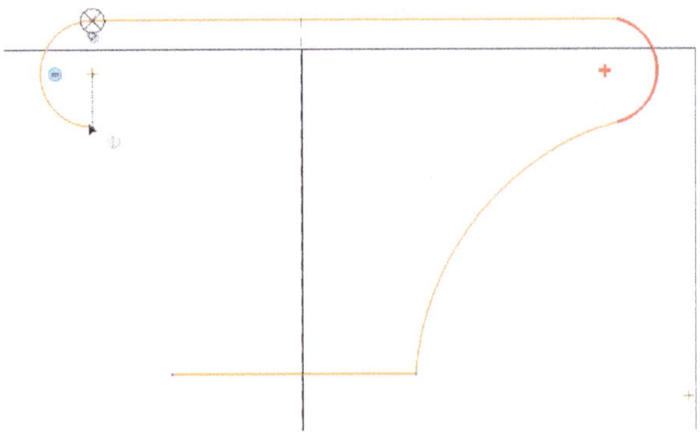

24. Select the endpoint of the arc. Move the pointer toward down and right, and then click on the start point to close the sketch.

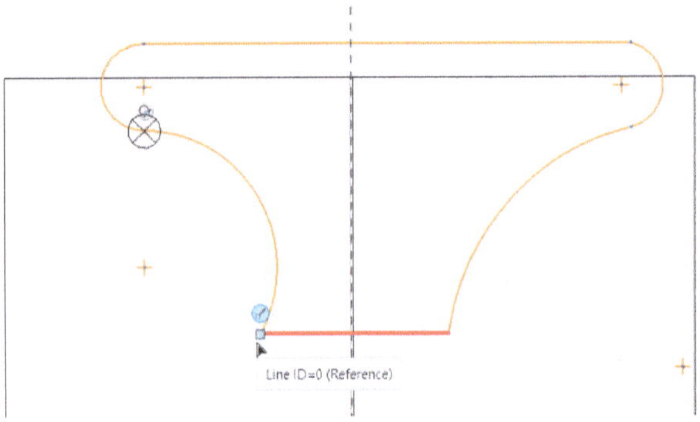

25. Click the **Select** icon on the ribbon to deactivate the command.
26. On the ribbon, click **Sketch** tab > **Sketching** panel > **Circle** drop-down > **Concentric** .
27. Select the top right arc to define the center of the circle.

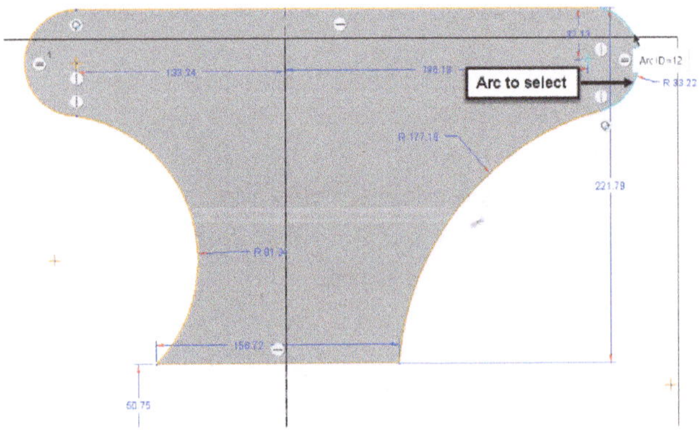

28. Move the pointer and click to create the circle.

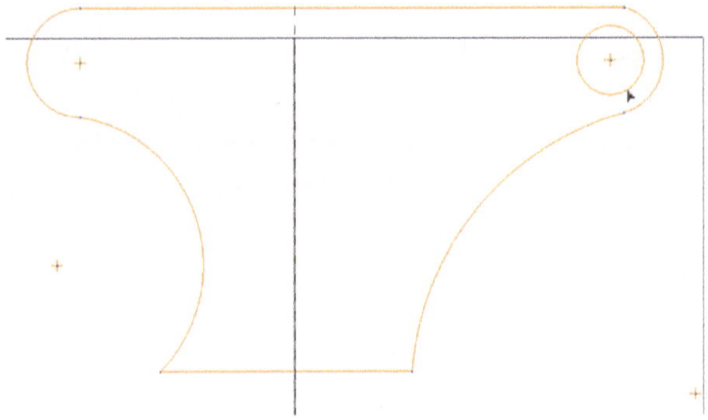

29. Click the **Select** icon on the ribbon to deactivate the command.
30. Again, activate the **Concentric** command and create another circle, as shown below.

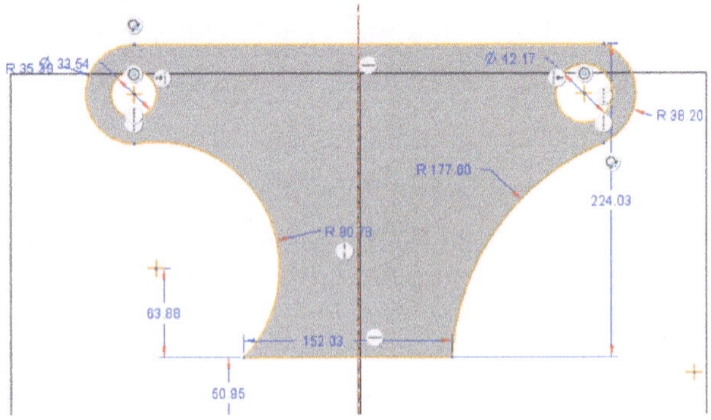

31. On the ribbon, click **Sketch** tab > **Sketching** panel > **Centerline** .
32. Select the origin of the sketch.
33. Move the pointer vertically upward and click to create a vertical centerline.

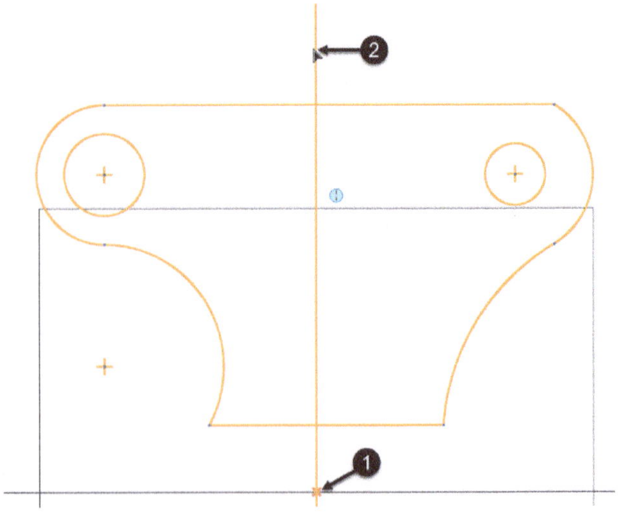

34. On the ribbon, click **Sketch** tab > **Constrain** panel > **Symmetric** .

35. Select the centerline to define the symmetry line.
36. Select the centerpoints of the circles to make them symmetric.

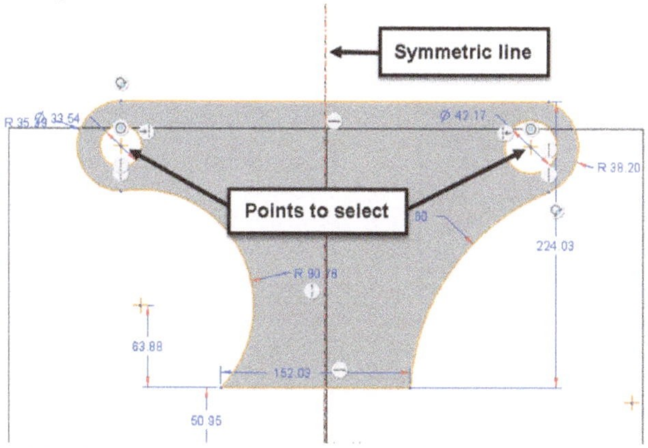

37. Select the centerline and then the center points of the arcs.

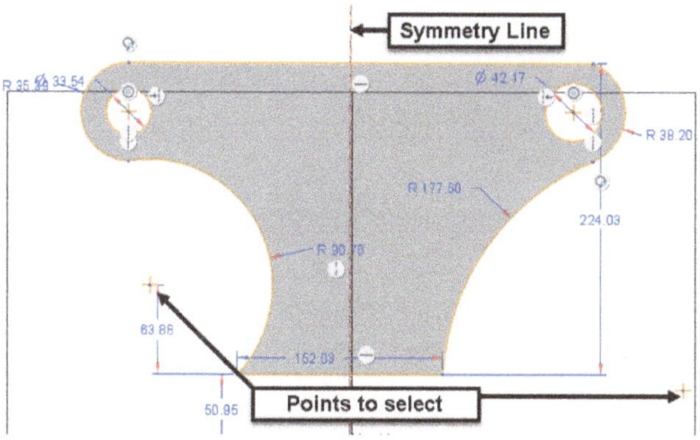

38. Activate the **Coincident** command, and then click on the bottom horizontal line and the arc's centerpoint. The selections will be made coincident.

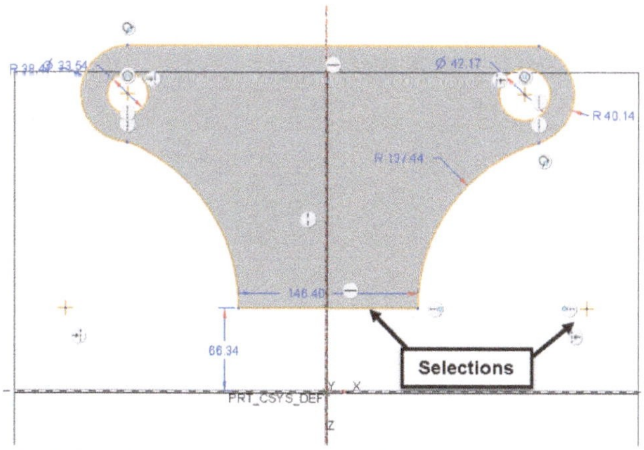

39. Likewise, make the bottom horizontal line coincident with the origin.

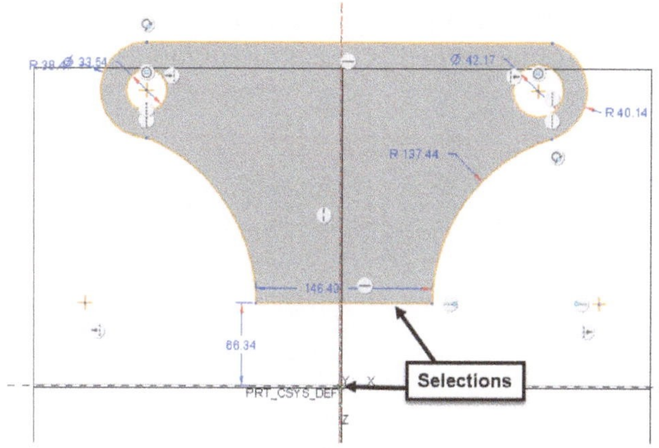

40. Click the **Tangent** icon on the **Constrain** panel.
41. Select the top horizontal line and the right arc. A tangent constraint is created between the selections.

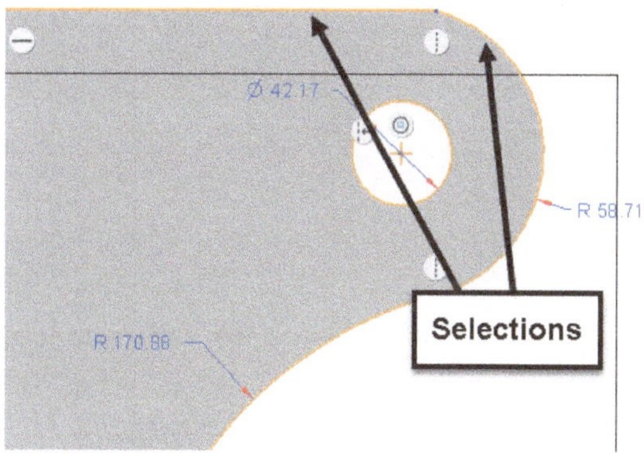

42. Apply the **Equal** constraint between the two circles.

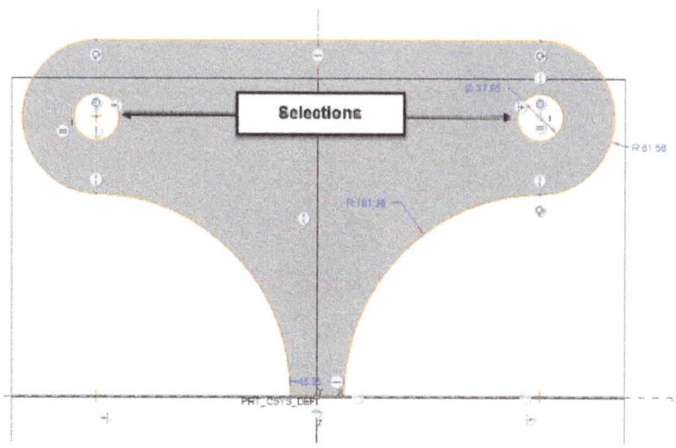

43. On the ribbon, click **Sketch** tab > **Editing** panel > **Modify** .
44. Click on the diameter value of the circle.

45. On the **Modify Dimension** dialog, uncheck the **Regenerate** option and type-in **20** in the value box.

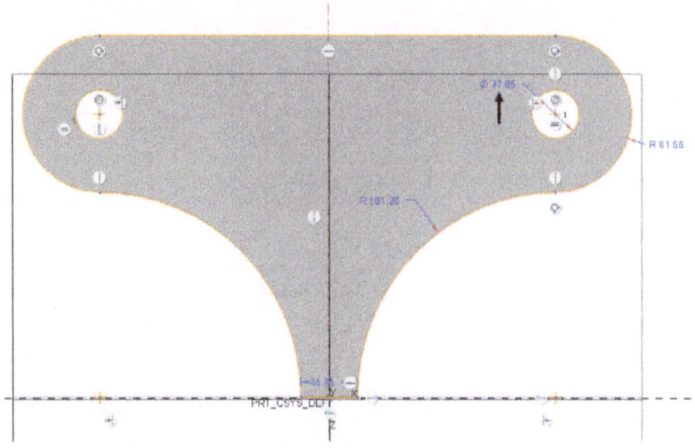

46. Likewise, select the other dimensions and change their values. Click **OK** to regenerate the dimensions.

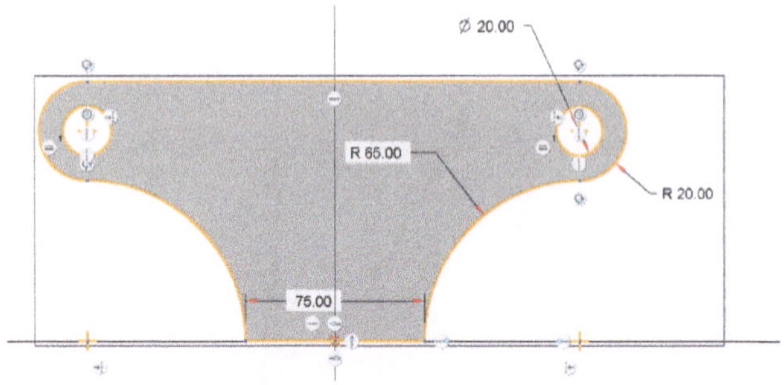

47. Click **OK** on the ribbon to complete the sketch.
48. To save the file, click **File > Save**. Next, click **OK**.
49. To close the file, click **File > Close**.

Questions

1. What is the procedure to create sketches in Creo Parametric?
2. List any two sketch constraints in Creo Parametric.
3. How to create constraints automatically?
4. Describe the methods to create an ellipse.
5. How do you define the shape and size of a sketch?
6. How do you create a tangent arc?
7. Which command is used to apply different types of dimensions to a sketch?
8. List any two methods to create circles.
9. How do you create fillet?

Exercises

Exercise 1

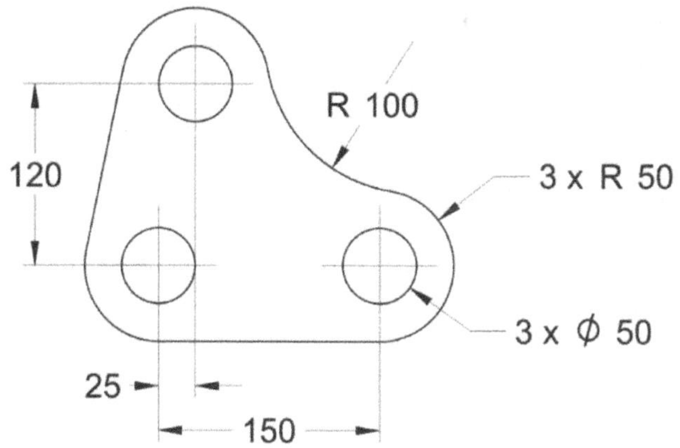

Exercise 2

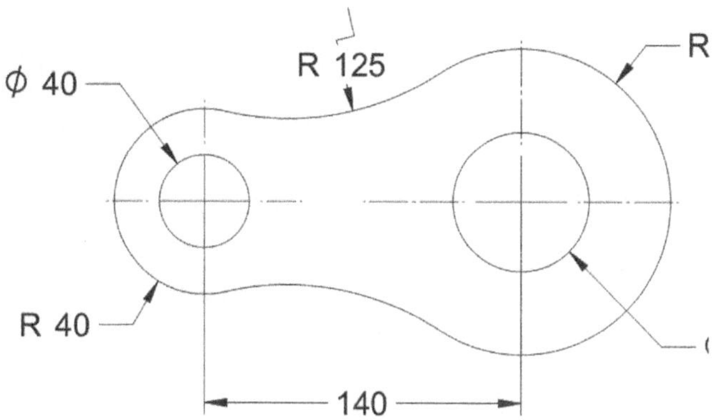

Exercise 3

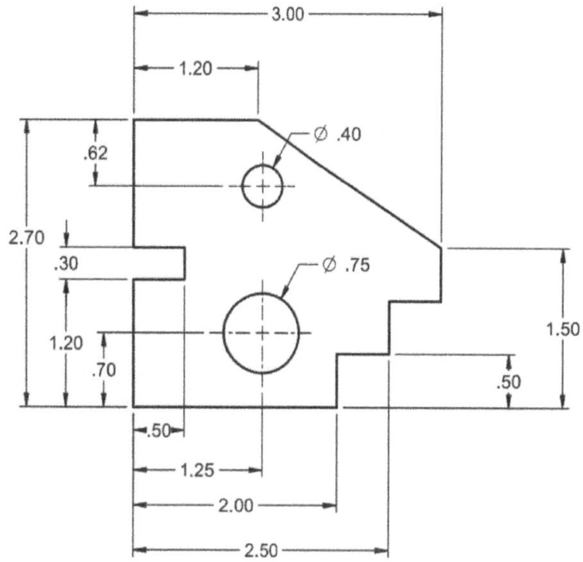

Chapter 3: Basic Features

Basic features are used to create basic and simple parts. Most of the time, they form the base for complex parts as well. These features are easy to create and require a single sketch. Now, you will learn the commands to create these features.

The topics covered in this chapter are:

- *Extrude Features*
- *Revolve Features*
- *Datum planes*
- *More Options in the Extrude and Revolve commands*
- *View commands*

Extrude

Extrusion is the process of taking a two-dimensional profile and converting it into 3D by giving it some thickness. A simple example of this would be taking a circle and converting it into a cylinder.

1. Once you have created a sketch profile or profiles you want to *Extrude*, activate the **Extrude** command (On the ribbon, click **Model** tab > **Shapes** panel > **Extrude**).
2. Click on the sketch profile to add thickness to it.

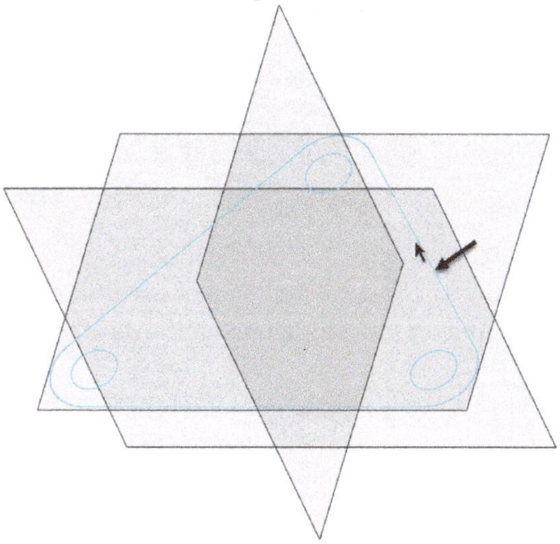

3. On the **Extrude** dashboard, type-in a value in the **Depth** box.

You can also click and drag the Extrude handle that appears on the preview. It changes the extrude thickness

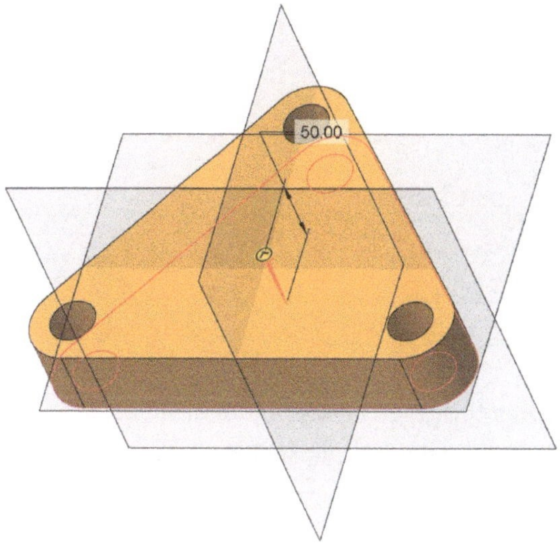

(or) Double-click in the value box that appears on the preview and type-in the Extrude depth.

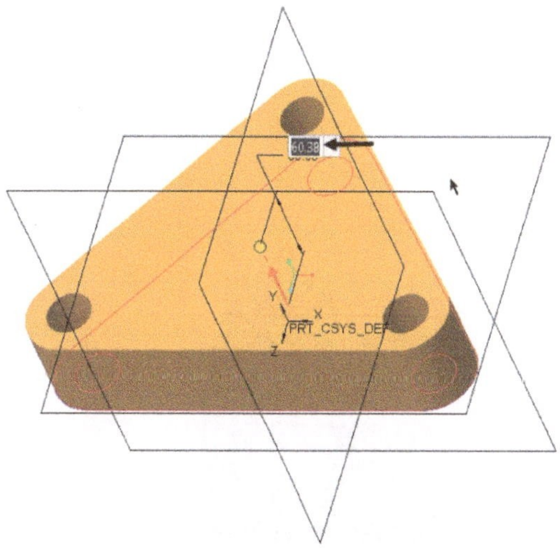

4. Click the **Reverse direction** button next to the **Depth** box if you want to reverse the extrusion direction.
5. If you want to add equal thickness on both sides of the sketch, select the **Symmetric** option from the drop-down next to the **Depth** box.

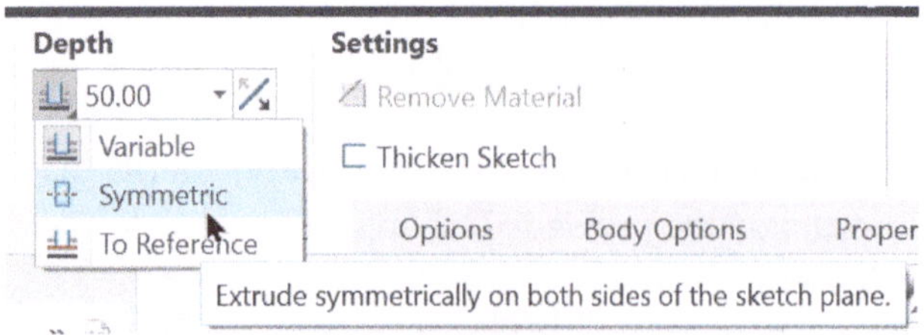

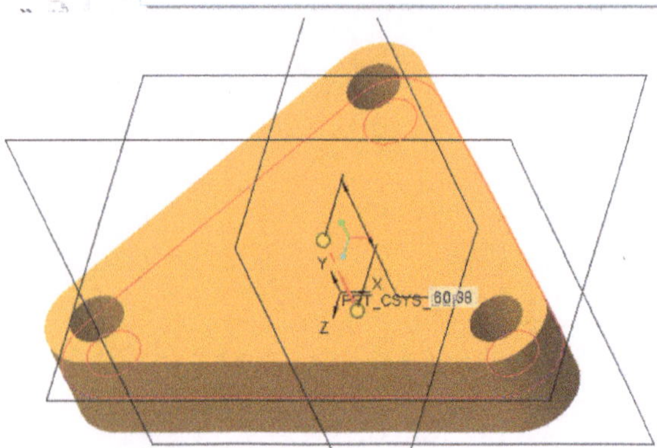

6. Click the green check on the dashboard to complete the *Extrude* feature.

Revolve

Revolving is the process of taking a two-dimensional profile and revolving it about a centerline to create a 3D geometry (axially symmetric shapes). While creating a sketch for the *Revolved* feature, it is important to think about the cross-sectional shape defining the 3D geometry once it revolves around an axis. For instance, the following geometry has a hole in the center.

It could be created with a separate *Cut* or *Hole* feature. But to make that hole part of the *Revolved* feature, you need to sketch the centerline of revolution so that it leaves a space between the profile and the centerline.

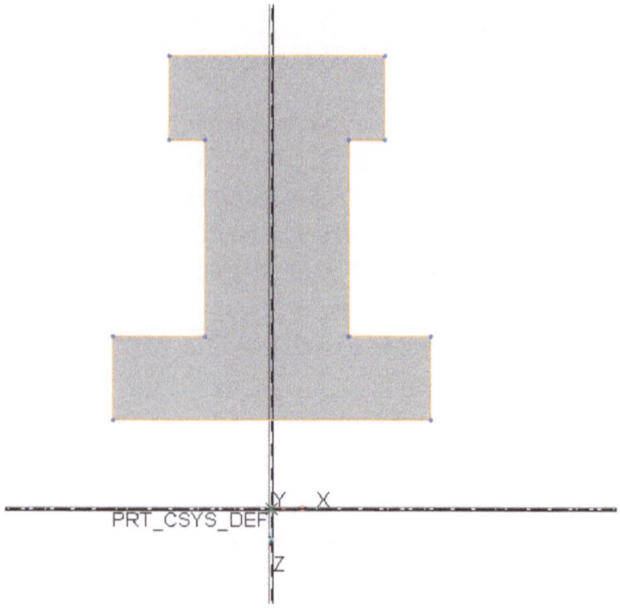

1. After completing the sketch, activate the **Revolve** command (On the ribbon, click **Model** tab > **Shapes** panel > **Revolve**).
2. Select the sketch, if not already selected. The sketch will be revolved by full 360 degrees.

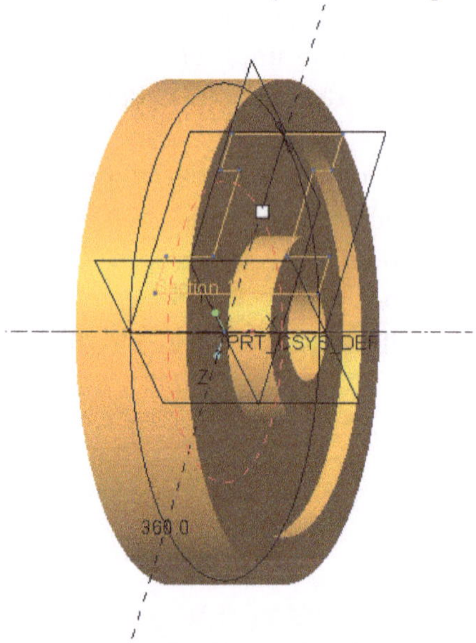

3. If you want to enter an angle of revolution, type-in a value in the **Angle** box on the dashboard.

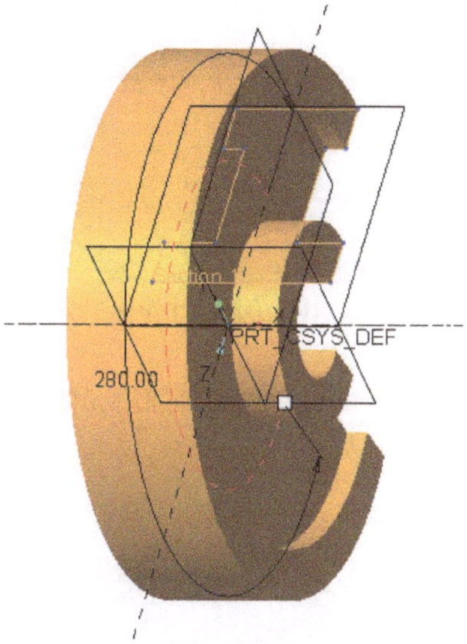

4. On the dashboard, click the green check to complete the *Revolved* feature.

Project

This command projects the edges of a 3D geometry onto a sketch plane.

1. Activate the **Sketch** mode by selecting a plane or model face.
2. On the ribbon, click **Sketch** tab > **Sketching** panel > **Project**.
3. Click on the edges of the model geometry to project them onto the sketch plane.

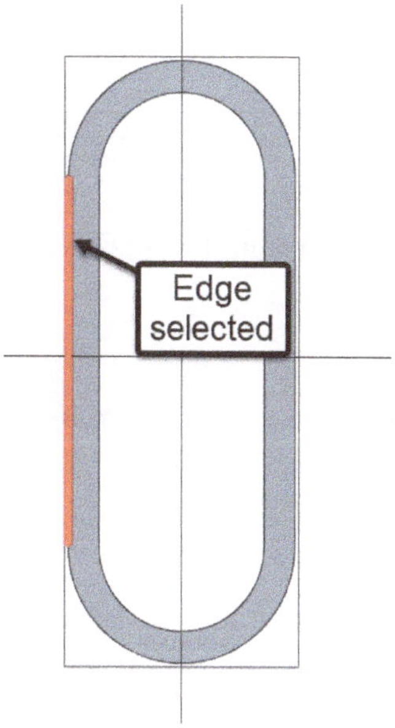

4. Click the green check on the toolbar.

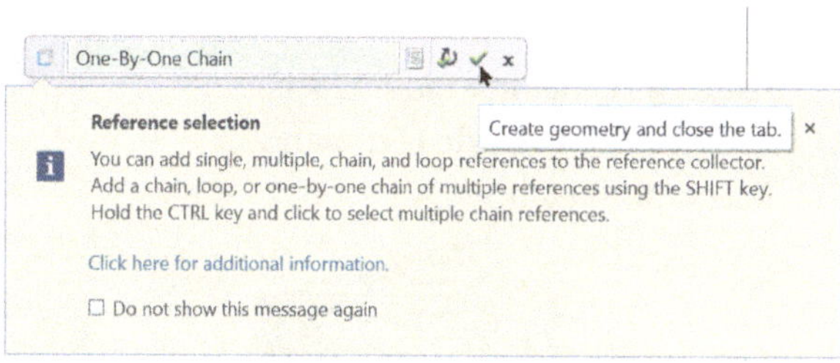

The projected element will be orange in color and fully constrained.

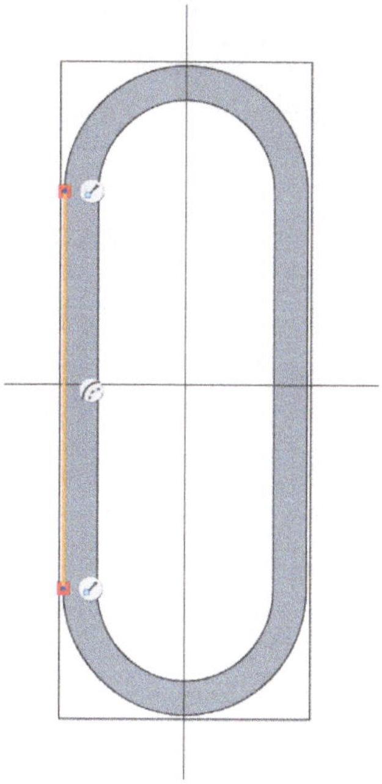

5. Complete the sketch and exit the Sketch mode.

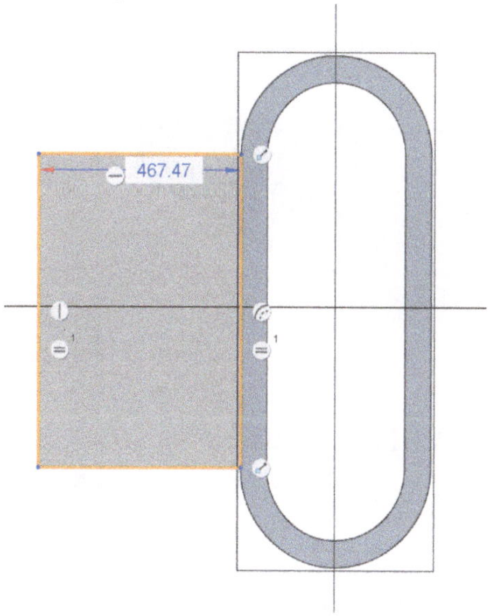

Creating Extruded Cuts

Creating Extruded cuts is similar to extruded features.

1. Sketch a plane or a model face.
2. Activate the **Extrude** command.
3. Select the sketch.

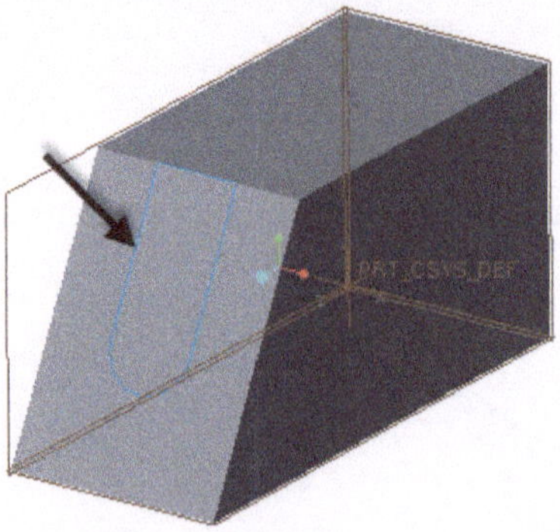

4. On the **Extrude** dashboard, click the **Remove Material** button.

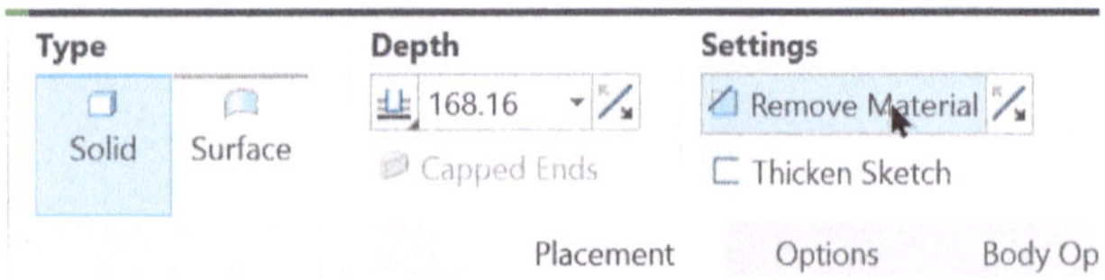

5. Type-in a value in the **Depth** box and click the **Reverse direction** button next to it.
6. Click the green check to complete the cut feature.

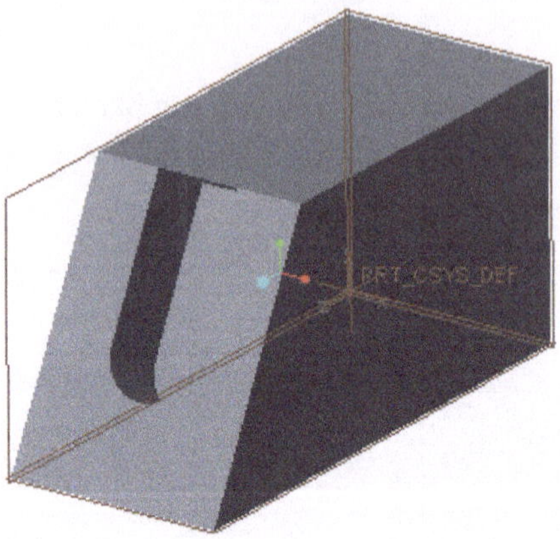

Creating Revolved Cuts

Revolved cuts are created by revolving a sketch about an axis.

1. Sketch a plane or a model face. Also, draw a centerline using the **Centerline** command.

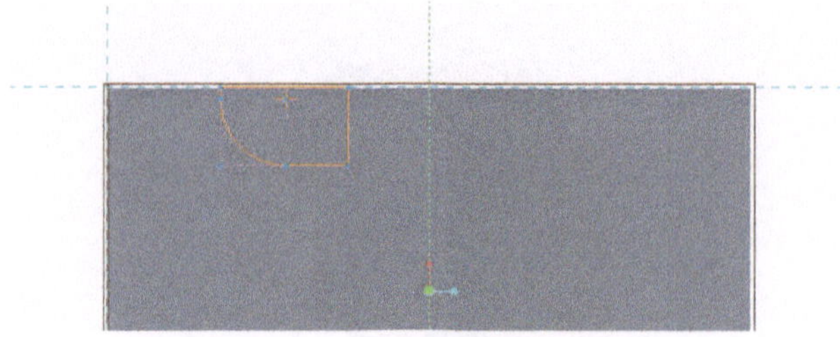

2. On the ribbon, click **Model** tab > **Shapes** panel > **Revolve**.
3. Select the sketch. If you have created the centerline, a revolved cut will be created automatically.

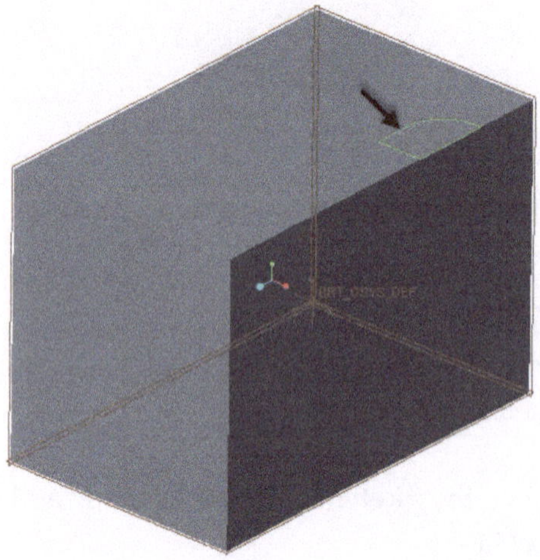

4. On the **Revolve** dashboard, click the **Remove Material** button.

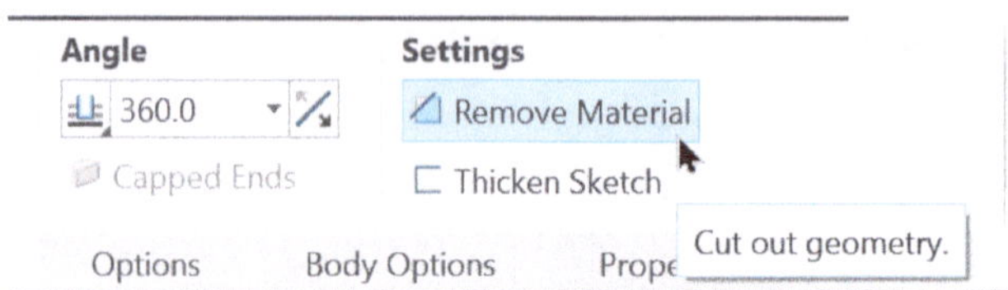

5. Click the green check to complete the revolve cut feature.

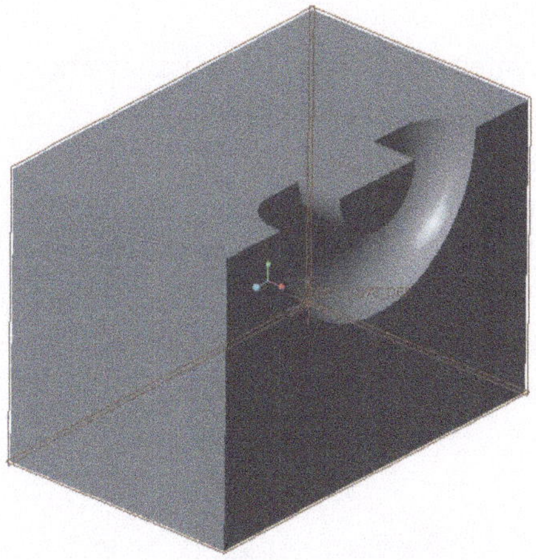

The Plane command

Each time you start a new part file, Creo Parametric automatically creates default datum planes. Planes are a specific type of element in Creo Parametric, known as Datum features. These features act as supports to your 3D geometry. In addition to the default datum features, you can create your additional planes. Until now, you have known to create sketches on any of the default datum planes (XY, YZ, and XZ planes). If you want to create sketches and geometry at locations other than default datum planes, you can manually create new data planes. You can do this by using the **Plane** command.

Offset from plane

This method creates a datum plane, which will be parallel to a face or another plane.

1. Activate the **Plane** command (On the ribbon, click **Model > Datum > Plane**).
2. Select a flat face/plane.

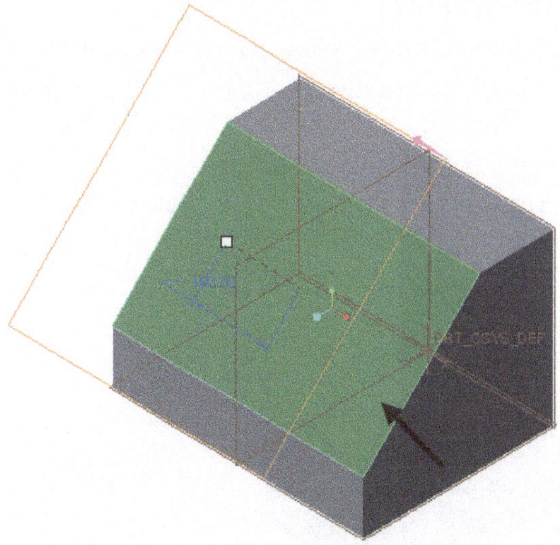

3. On the **Datum Plane** dialog, select **Offset** from the drop-down in the **References** section.
4. Drag the Offset handle that appears on the plane (or) type-in a value in the **Translation** box to define the offset distance.

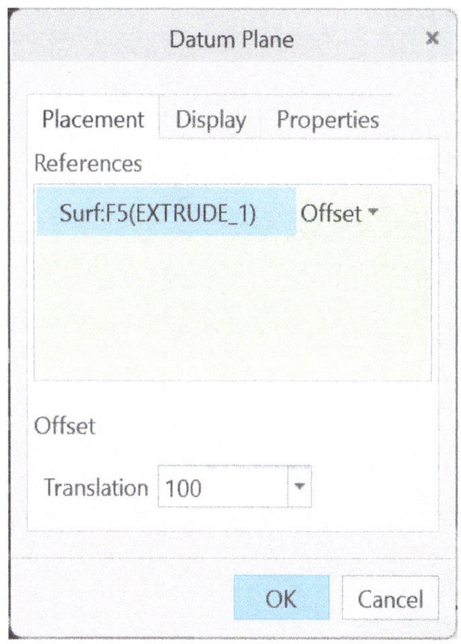

You can type a negative value in the **Translation** box to create the plane on the other side of the model face/plane on the dialog.

5. Click **OK** to create the offset plane.

Plane and Point

This method creates a plane parallel/normal to a flat face at a selected point.

1. Activate the **Plane** command.
2. Press the Ctrl key and select a flat face and point.

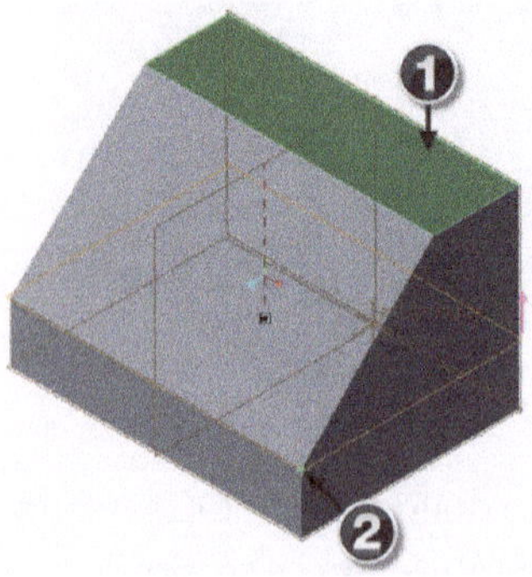

3. On the **Datum Plane** dialog, select the **Normal** option from the drop-down next to the plane reference. The datum plane is created normal to reference flat face and passing through the selected point.

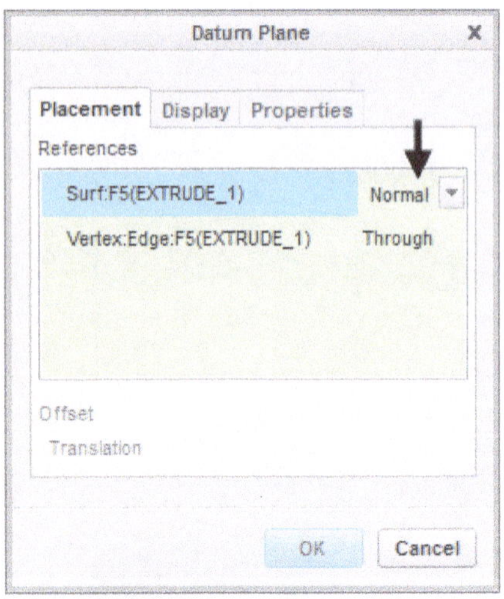

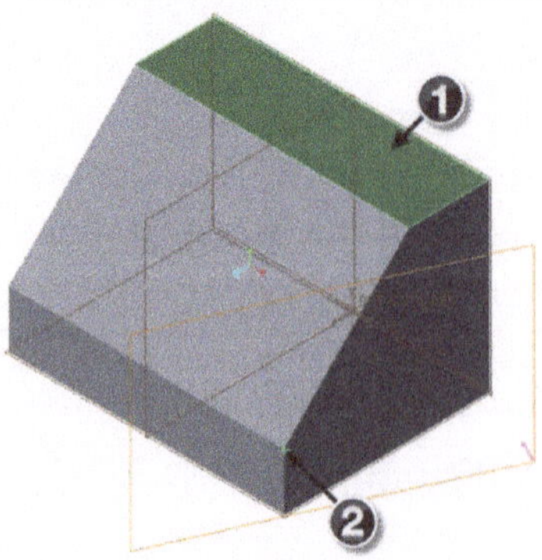

Plane and Edge

This method creates a plane positioned at an angle or parallel or normal to a face or plane.

1. Activate the **Plane** command.
2. Select a flat face or plane to define the reference.
3. Press the Ctrl key and click on the edge of the part geometry to define the rotation axis.
4. Type-in a value in the **Rotation** box.

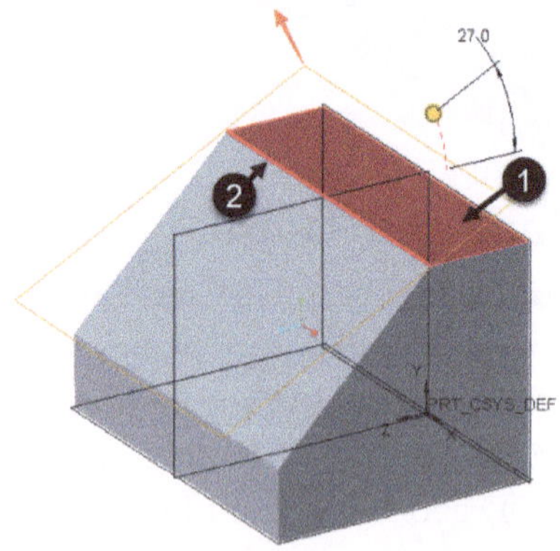

5. On the **Datum Plane** dialog, select the **Normal** option from the drop-down next to the plane reference. The datum plane is created normal to reference flat face and passing through the selected edge.

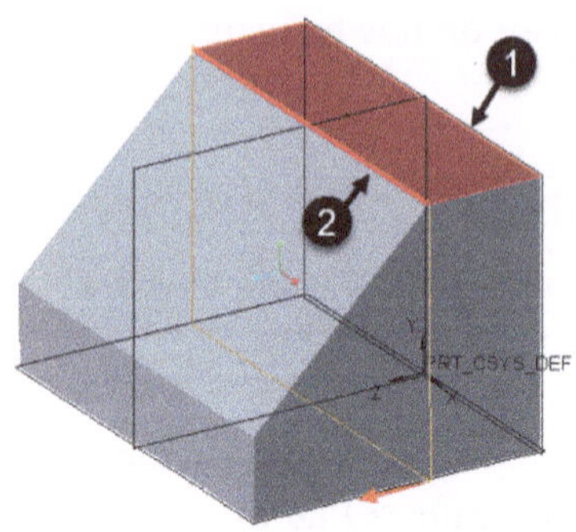

6. On the **Datum Plane** dialog, select the **Parallel** option from the drop-down next to the plane reference. The datum plane is created parallel to the flat reference face and passing through the selected edge.

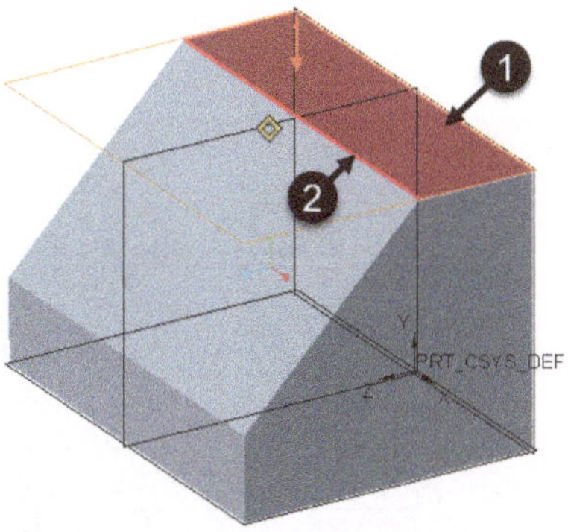

Through three points

This method creates a plane by selecting three points.

1. Activate the **Plane** command.
2. Press the Ctrl key and select three points from the model geometry.
3. Click **OK** to create a plane passing through the points.

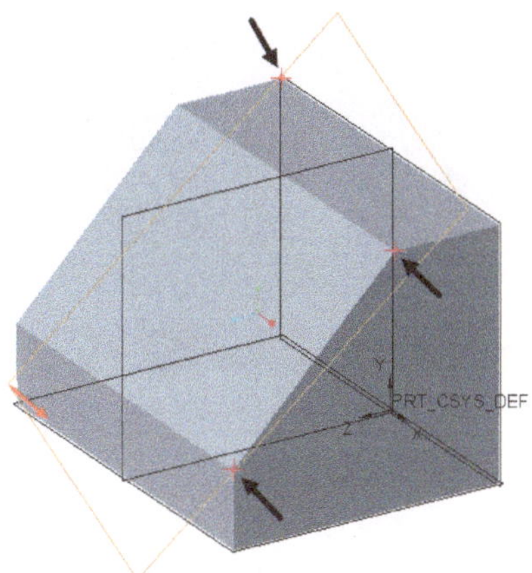

Through two Edges/lines

This method creates a plane by selecting two edges/lines.

1. Activate the **Plane** command.
2. Press the Ctrl key, select two parallel edges/lines from the model geometry.
3. Click **OK**. A plane is created passing through the selected lines/edges.

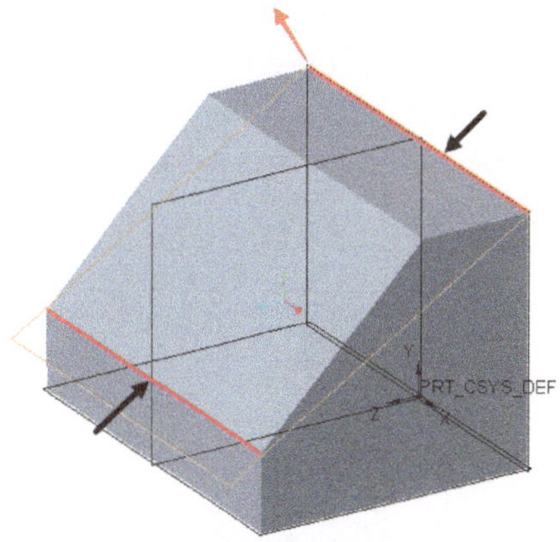

Point and Line/Curve/Edge

This method creates a datum plane, which will be normal (perpendicular) to a line, curve, or edge.

1. Activate the **Plane** command.
2. Press the Ctrl key and select an edge, line, curve, arc, or circle.
3. Click on the point of the selected element to define the location of the plane.
4. On the **Datum Plane** dialog, select the **Normal** option from the drop-down next to the curve reference. The datum plane is created normal to the reference curve and passing through the selected point.

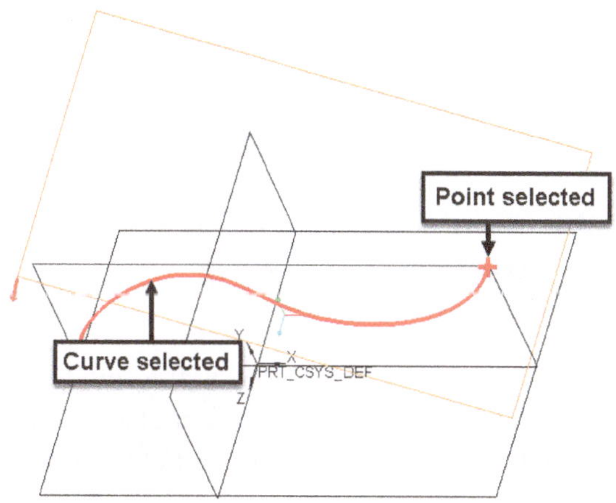

Tangent to surface

This method creates a plane tangent to a curved face.

1. Activate the **Plane** command.
2. Select a curved face.
3. Press the Ctrl key and select an edge.

4. On the **Datum Plane** dialog, select the **Tangent** option from the drop-down next to the surface reference. The datum plane is created tangent to the reference surface and passing through the selected edge.

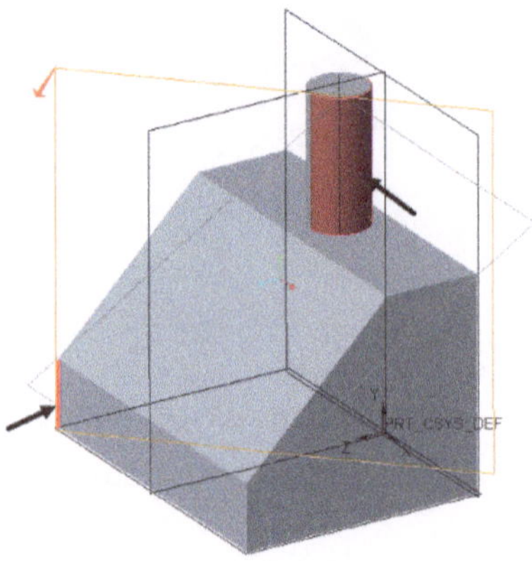

Mid Plane

This method creates a plane, which lies at the midpoint between two selected faces. Activate the **Plane** command. Press hold the Ctrl key, and then select two faces of the model geometry parallel to each other. Click **OK** to create the midplane.

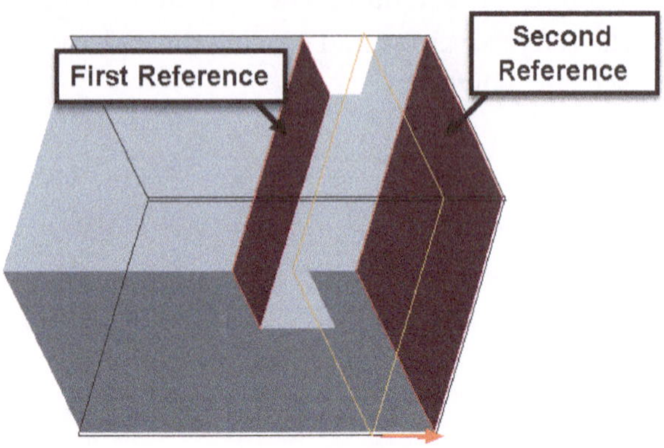

You can also create a plane passing through the intersection point of the two selected planes or faces. Activate the **Plane** command. Press hold the Ctrl key and then select two intersecting surfaces. On the **Datum Plane** dialog, select the **Bisector1** or **Bisector 2** option from the drop-down located next to the second surface. Click **OK** to create the passing through the intersection of selected surfaces.

Bisector 1

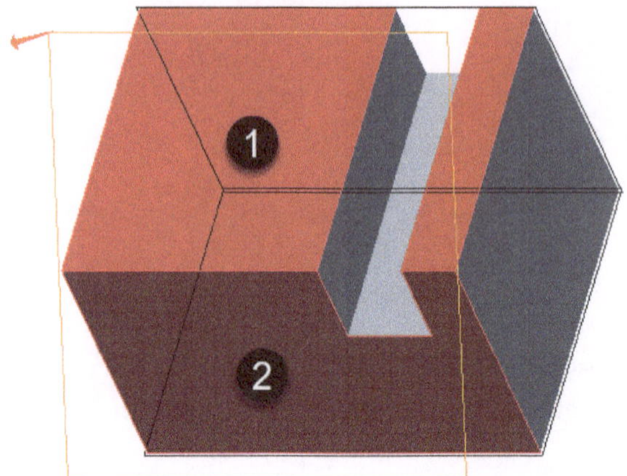

Bisector 2

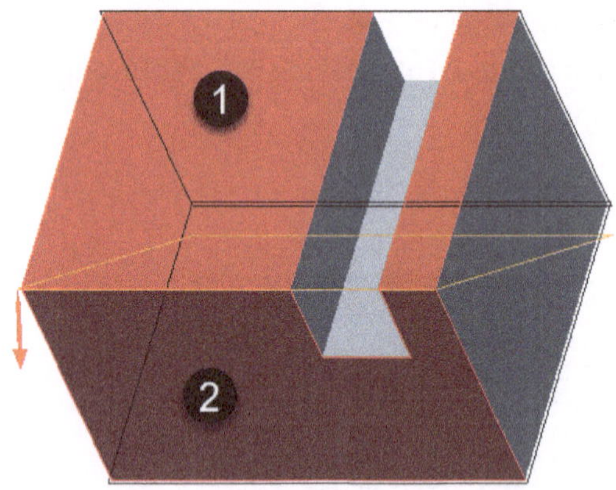

Axis

The **Axis** command (On the ribbon, click the **Model > Datum > Axis**) creates an axis in the 3D space. The methods to create an axis using this command are explained next.

Point-Point

Press the Ctrl Key and select two points.

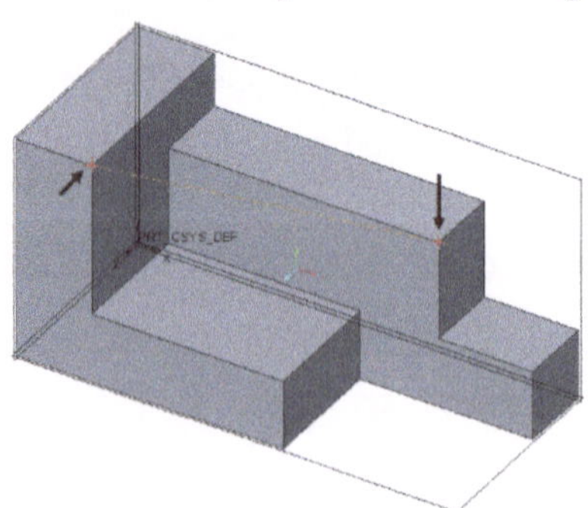

Point and Edge/line

Press the Ctrl Key and select a point and edge.

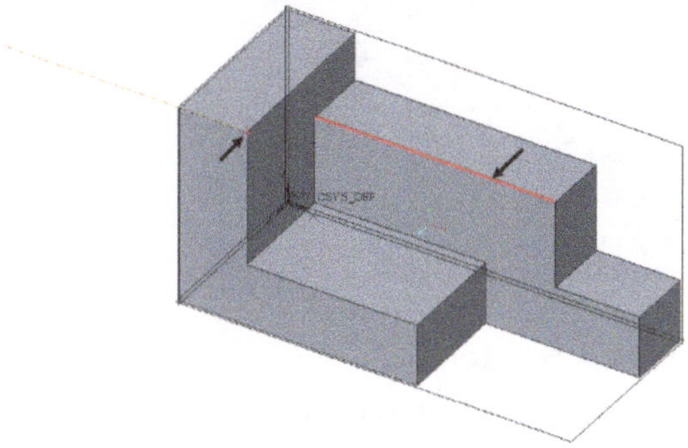

On the **Datum Plane** dialog, select the **Normal** option from the drop-down next to the edge reference. The datum axis is created normal to reference the edge and passing through the selected point.

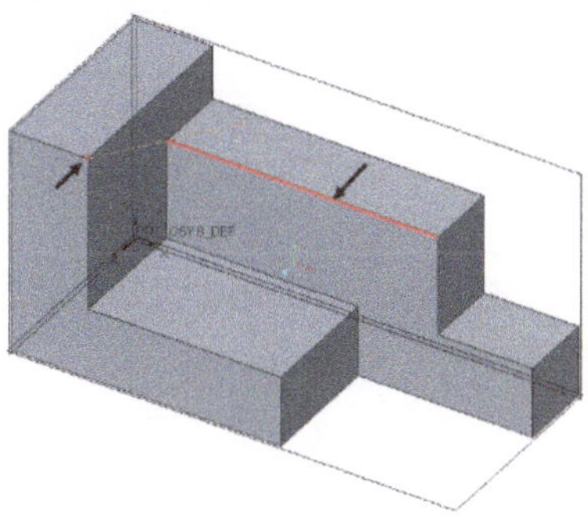

On a planar face

1. Click on a planar face. An axis appears with two reference handles.
2. Click the right mouse button and select the Offset Reference.
3. Press the Ctrl key and select two faces that are perpendicular to the placement face.
4. On the **Datum Plane** dialog, type the values in the Offset references section.

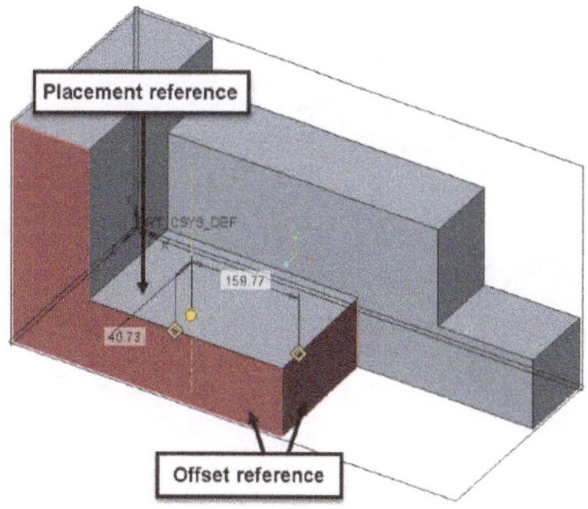

Additional options of the Extrude command

The **Extrude** command has some additional options to create 3D geometry and complex features. These options are also available on the **Revolve** dashboard.

Depth

On the **Extrude** dashboard, the **Options** tab has options to define the Extrude feature's start and end depths. These options are **Blind, Symmetric, To Next, Through All, Through Until,** and **To Selected**.

The **To Next** option extrudes the sketch through the face next to the sketch plane.

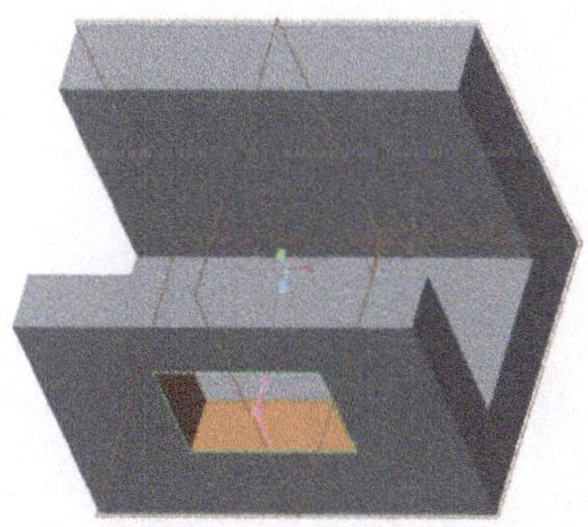

The **Through Until** option extrudes the sketch up to a selected surface. Activate the **Extrude** command and select the sketch to be extruded. On the **Extrude** dashboard, select **Through Until** from the drop-down, and then click on a surface. The sketch will be extruded up to the selected surface.

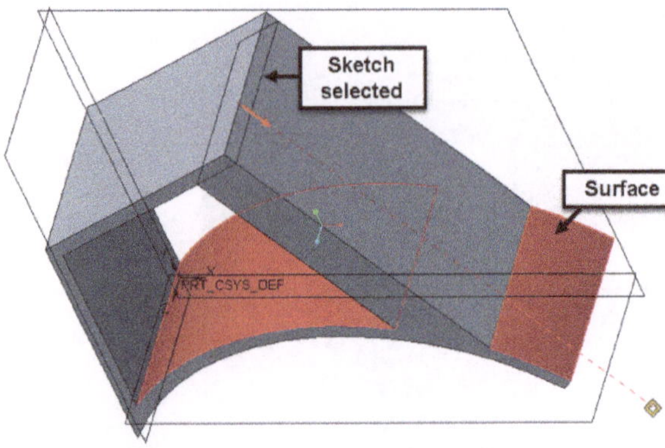

The **To Selected** option extrudes the sketch from the sketch plane up to a selected planar face, point, curve, and surface.

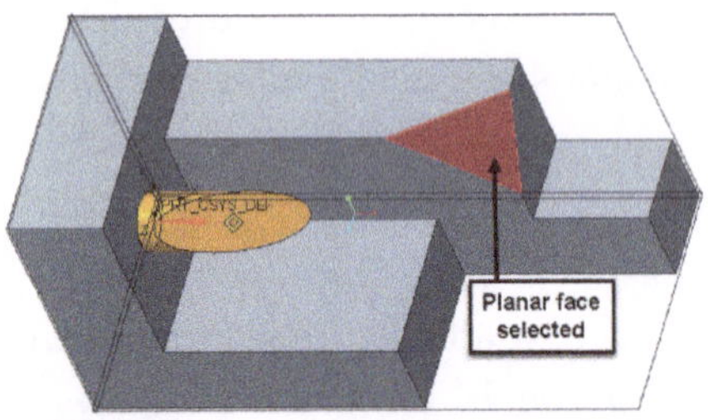

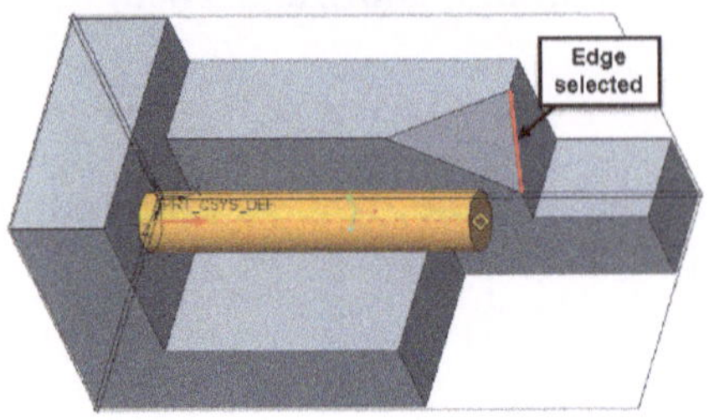

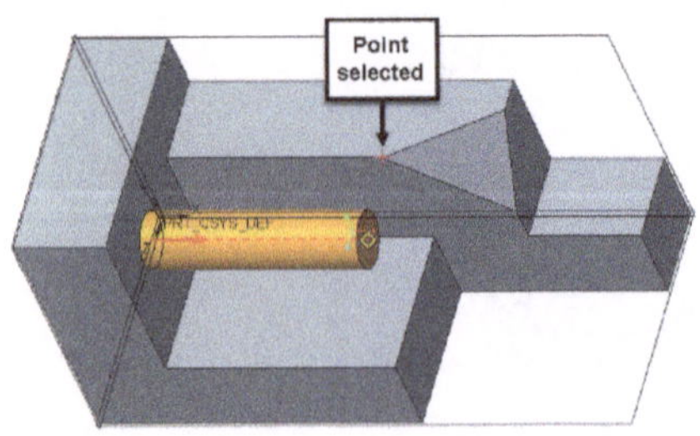

The **Through All** option extrudes the sketch throughout the 3D geometry.

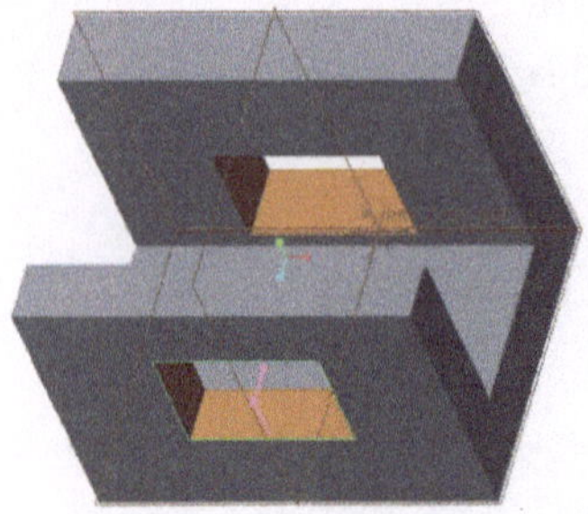

Thicken Sketch

The **Thicken Sketch** icon will help you to add thickness to the selected sketch. Click this icon on the **Extrude** or **Revolve** dashboard to add thickness to the sketch. Type-in thickness value in the box located next to this icon. Click the **Flip** icon next to the box to change the thickness side. You can add thickness to the inside, outside, or both sides of the sketch using this icon.

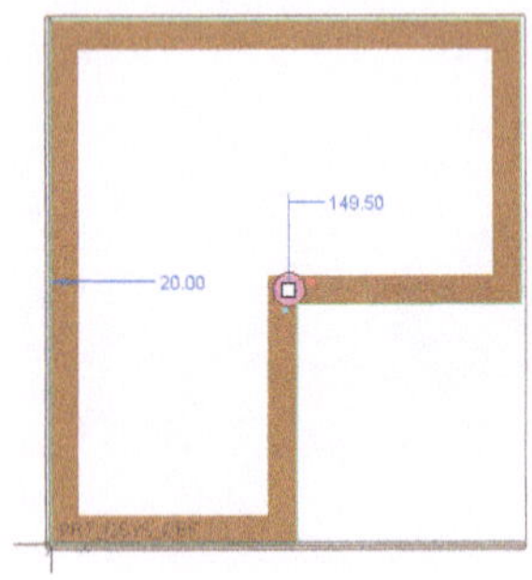

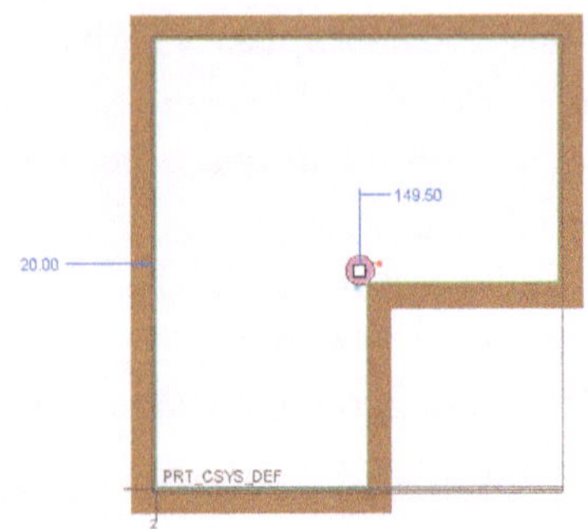

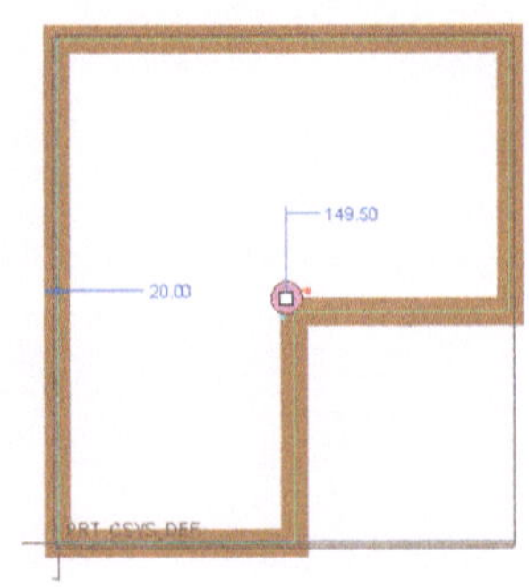

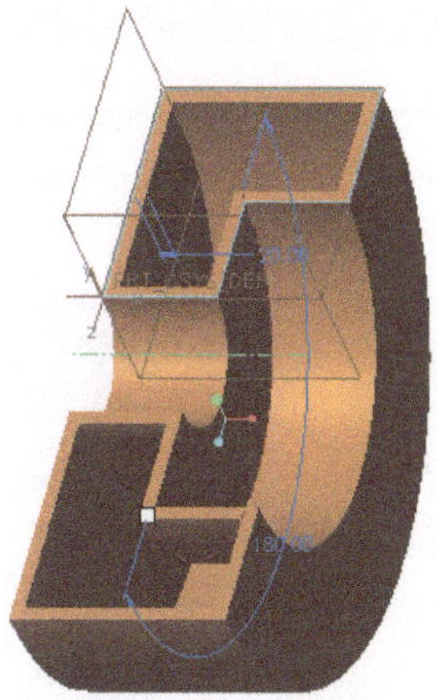

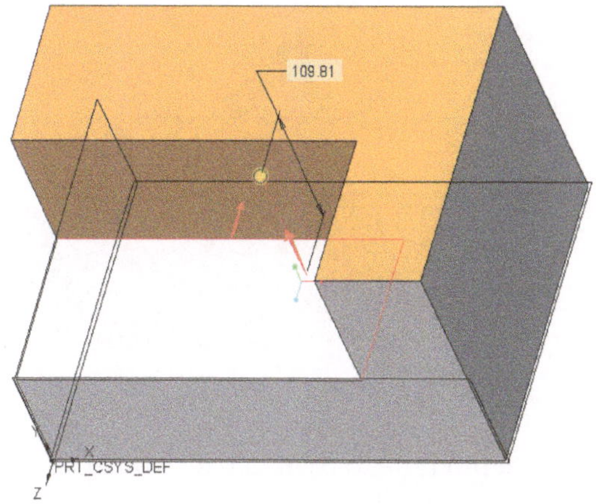

Extruding Open Profile

The **Extrude** command can also create a feature using an open profile. It uses the adjacent edges of the open profile to form a closed loop. Activate the **Extrude** command and select the open sketch.

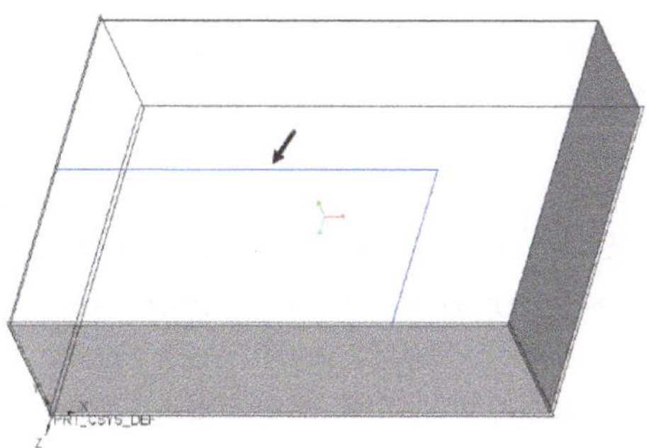

A preview of the *Extrude* feature appears. Click on the horizontal arrow to change the material side. On the dashboard, type-in a value in the **Depth** box located on the **Extrude** ribbon, and then press Enter.

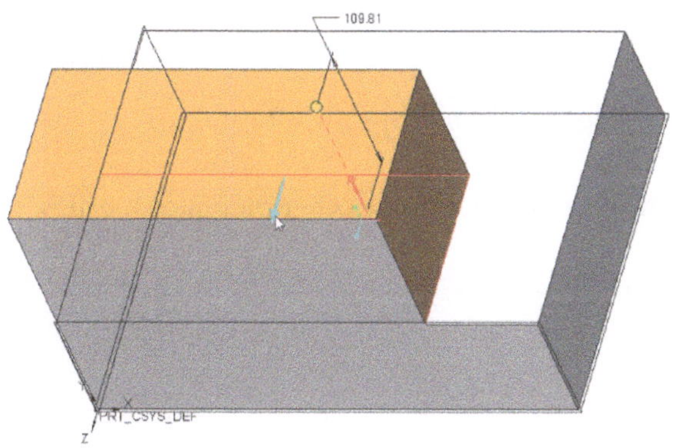

Use the **Remove Material** icon to create cutouts.

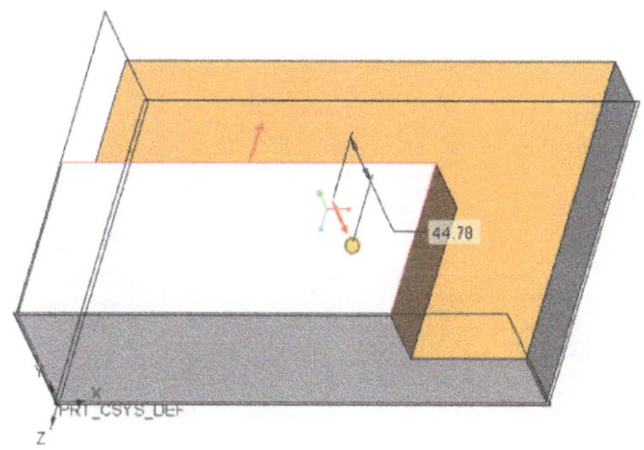

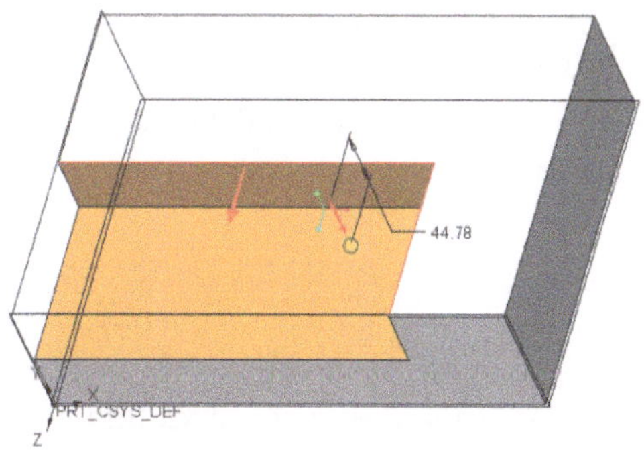

Add taper

The **Add taper** option will help you to apply the draft to the extrusion. It applies a draft to the extrusion from the sketch plane.

1. Activate the **Extrude** command and select the sketch.
2. Click the **Options** tab on the Dashboard and check the **Add taper** option.
3. Type the taper angle in the angle box.

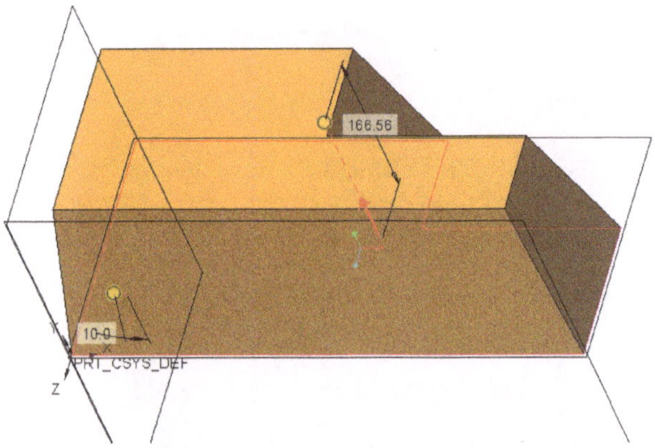

4. Set the depth type to **Symmetric**. Notice that the taper angle is applied with reference to the sketch plane.

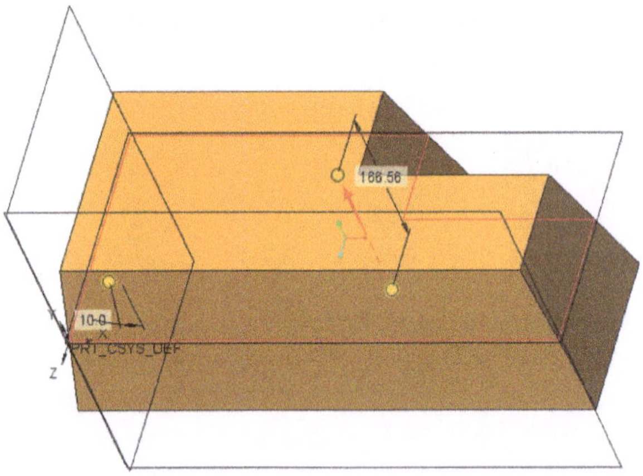

Editing Model Properties

Creo Parametric allows you to edit the model properties such as material and units.

1. Click **File > Prepare > Model Properties.** The **Model Properties** dialog displays the physical properties, parameters, and features properties.
2. On the **Model Properties** dialog, click the **change** link located next to the **Material** property.
3. On the **Materials** dialog, double-click on any one of the folders available in the list box.

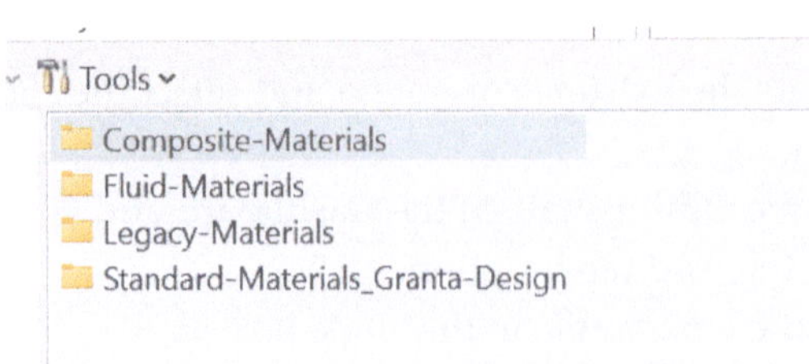

4. On the **Materials** dialog, select the material from the list and click the arrow icon pointing toward the right. The selected material appears in the **Materials in Model** section.

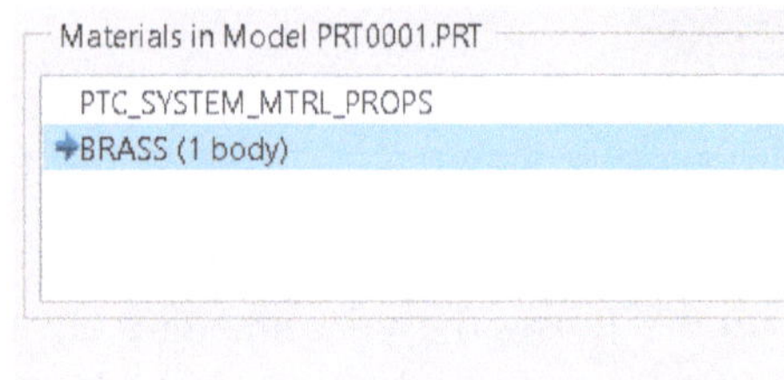

5. Click **OK** to assign the material to the geometry.
6. Click the 'i' icon located next to **Mass Properties**. The **Mass Properties Report** shows physical properties such as density, mass, and volume. If you want to change the mass properties, click the **Change** button located at the bottom right corner. The **Mass Properties** dialog appears. On this dialog, change the density value and click **OK** to change all the properties.

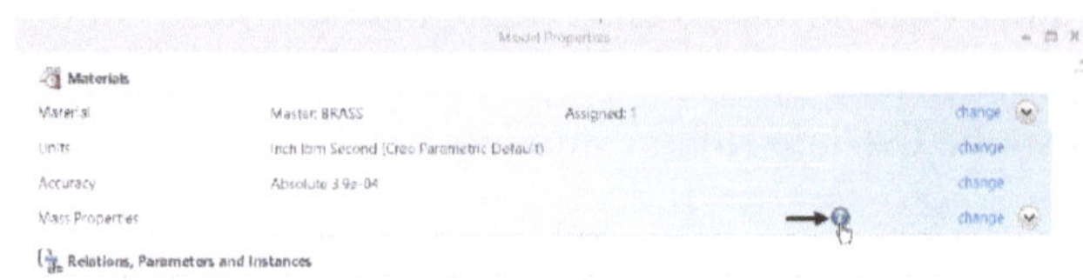

7. Close the **Mass Properties Report**.

Likewise, you can change other model properties.

8. Click **Close** on the **Model Properties** dialog.

View commands

The model display in the graphics window can be determined using various view commands. Most of these commands are located on the **Graphics** toolbar or the **View** ribbon tab. The following are some of the main view commands:

	Refit	The model will be fitted in the graphics window's current size to be completely visible.
	Pan	Activate this command and press the left mouse button. Drag the pointer to move the model view on the plane parallel to the screen.
	Orient mode	Activate this command (Expand the **Orientation** panel on the **View** ribbon tab and click the **Orient mode** icon) and press the middle mouse button. Drag the pointer to rotate the model view.
	Zoom In	Activate this command and create a box by specifying its corners. The area inside the box is magnified.
	Zoom Out	Click this icon to zoom out of the geometry.
	Sketch View	Click this icon to orient the sketch plane parallel to the screen.
	Shading with Reflections	This option represents the geometry with shades and reflections 

	**Shading with Edges**	This option represents the model with shades along with visible edges.	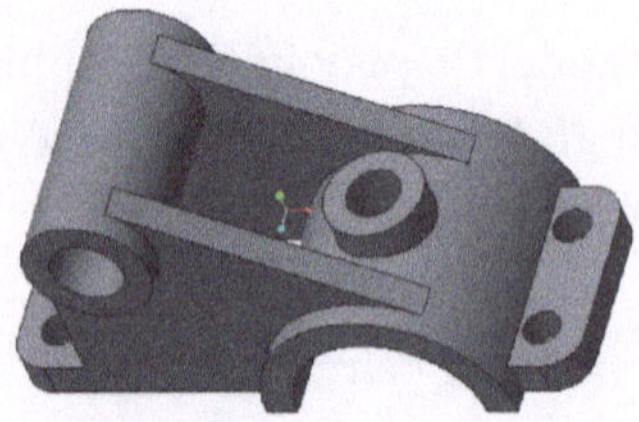
	Shading	This option represents the model with shades without visible edges.	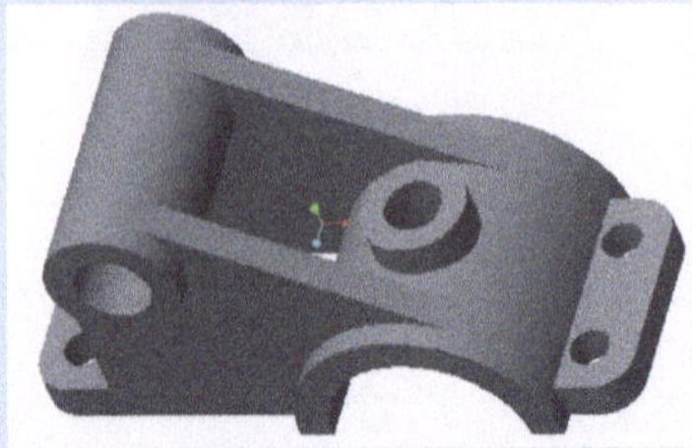
	**No Hidden**	This option represents the model in wireframe without any hidden lines	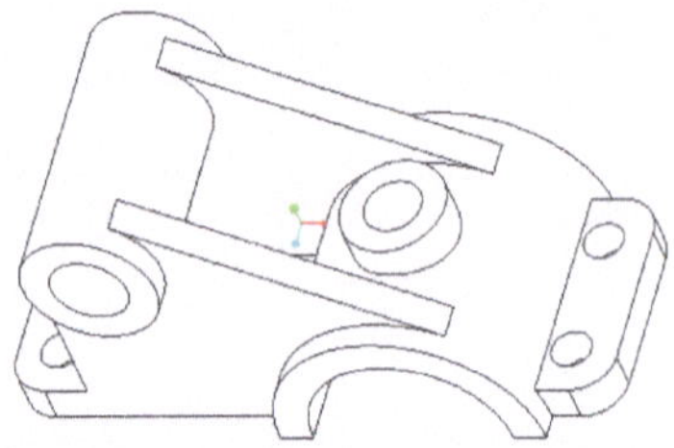
	**Wireframe**	This option represents the model in wireframe.	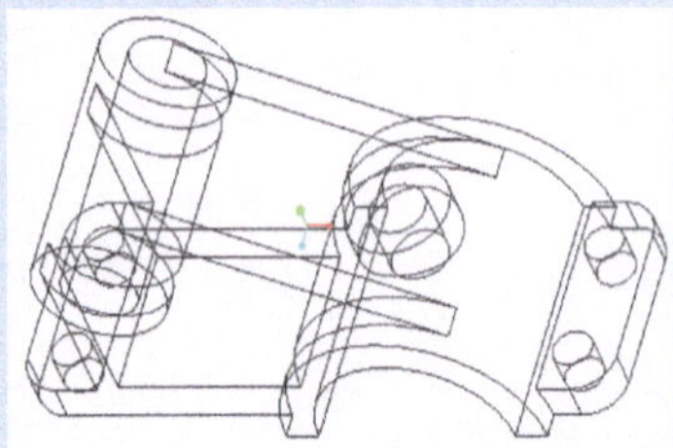
	**Hidden Line**	It represents the model in wireframe along with hidden edges greyed out	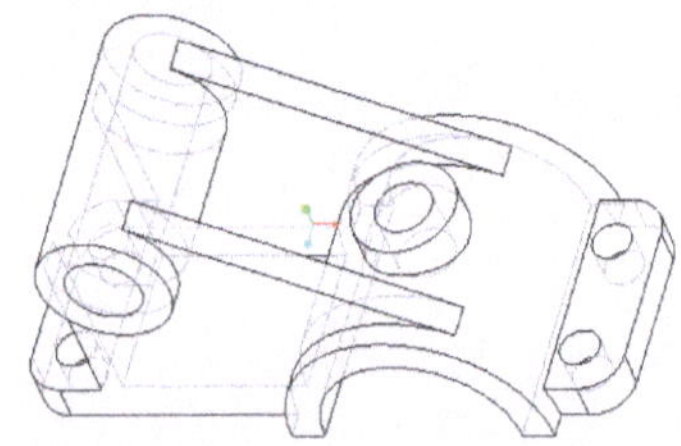
	Saved Orientation Drop-down	Use this drop-down to change the model view orientation.	

Measure Commands

The measure commands help you to measure the physical properties of geometry. These commands are explained next.

Summary

This command displays the measurements of the selected element based on the element type. For example, if you select a face, it displays the area and perimeter.

1. On the ribbon, click the **Analysis** tab > **Measure > Summary**.
2. Click on an element to display its measurements.

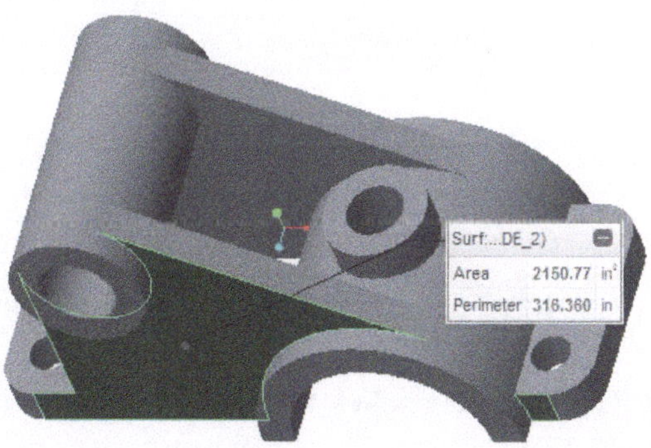

3. Press the Ctrl Key and select another element. A summary appears showing the measurements of both the elements.

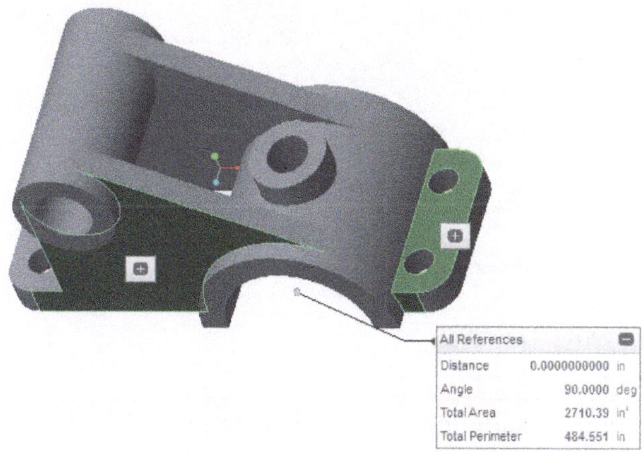

4. Click the right mouse button and click **Clear**.

Length

This command measures the length of the selected edge or curve.

1. On the ribbon, click the **Analysis > Measure > Length**.
2. Click on the edge. The curve length of the edge will appear.
3. Click the right mouse button and select **Clear**.

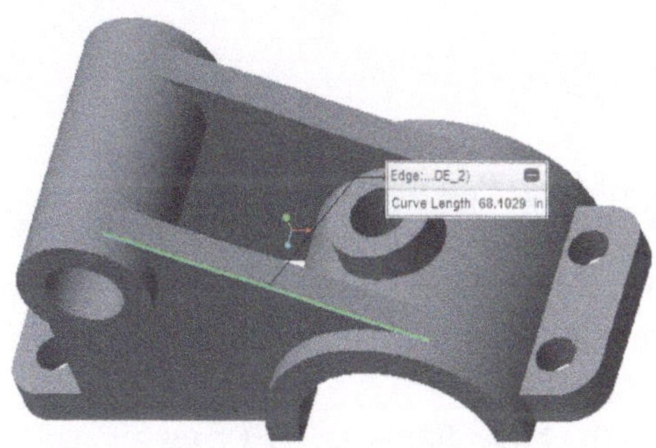

Distance

This command measures the distance between two elements.

1. On the ribbon, click the **Analysis > Measure > Distance**.
2. Press the Ctrl key and click on two elements. The distance between the two elements will appear.
3. Click the right mouse button and select **Clear**.

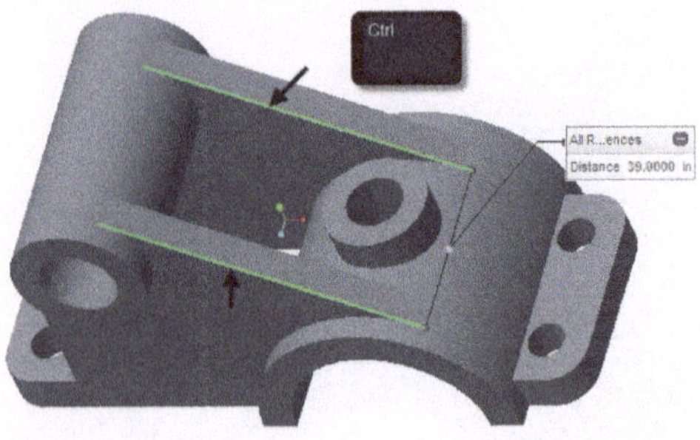

Examples

Example 1

In this example, you will create the part shown below.

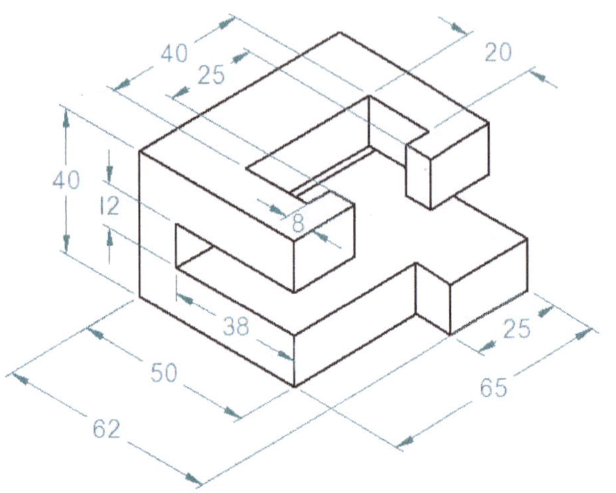

1. Start **Creo Parametric 11.0**.
2. Create the *Basic Features* folder and set it as the current working folder.
3. On the Quick Access Toolbar, click the **New** button.
4. On the **New** dialog, select **Types > Part**, and then type-in **C03-Example1**.
5. Uncheck the **Use default template** option and click **OK**.
6. On the **New File Options** dialog, select **solid_part_mmks_abs**, and click **OK**.
7. On the ribbon, click **Model** tab > **Datum** panel > **Sketch**.
8. Select the Front plane and click the **Sketch** button.
9. On the ribbon, click **Sketch** tab > **Sketching** panel > **Rectangle** drop-down > **Corner Rectangle**.
10. Click the origin point to define the first corner of the rectangle.
11. Move the pointer toward the top right and click to define the second corner.
12. On the ribbon, click **Sketch** tab > **Operations** panel > **Select** drop-down > **One by One**.
13. On the ribbon, click **Sketch** tab > **Editing** panel > **Modify**.
14. Modify the rectangle dimensions (refer to the **Modify** section of Chapter 2 to learn how to modify dimensions).

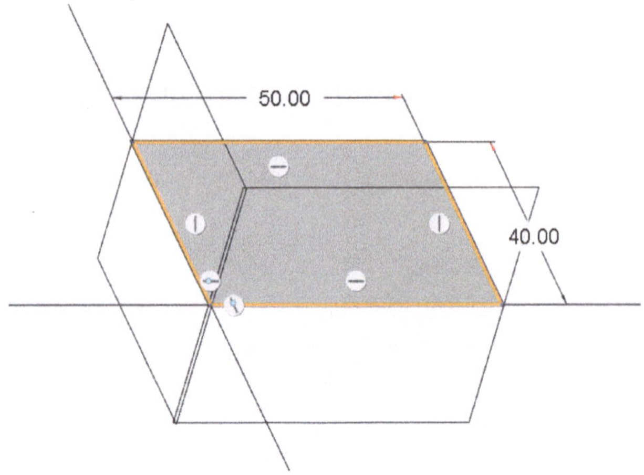

15. On the ribbon, click **Sketch** tab > **Close** panel > **OK**.
16. On the ribbon, click **Model** tab > **Shapes** panel > **Extrude**.
17. On the **Extrude** dashboard, type-in **65** in the **Depth** box.
18. Select the **Symmetric** option from the drop-down next to the **Depth** box.
19. Click the green check on the dashboard.

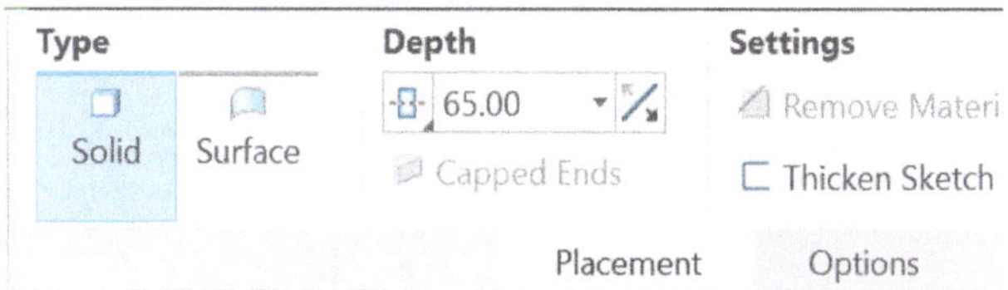

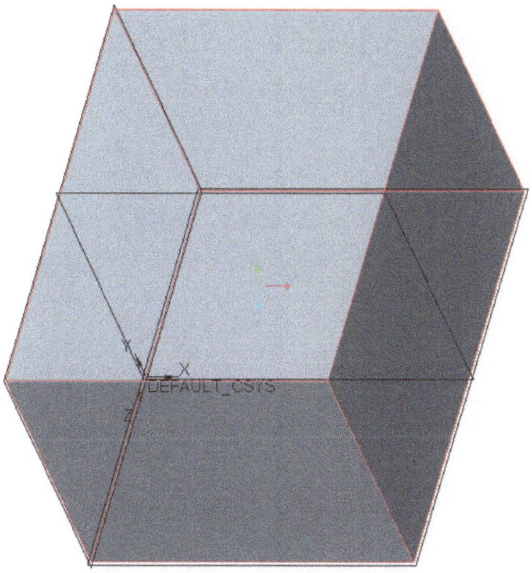

20. On the ribbon, click **Model** tab > **Datum** panel > **Sketch**.
21. Click on the front face of the model geometry.
22. On the **Sketch** dialog, click in the **Reference** box and select the right face of the model.

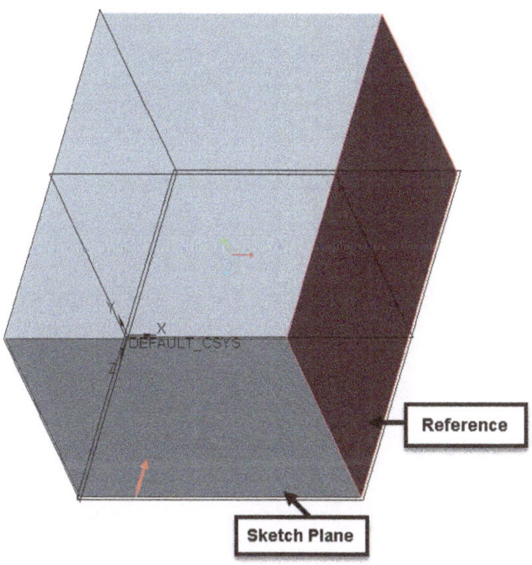

23. Click the **Sketch** button.
24. On the **Graphics** toolbar, click the **Sketch View** icon. It orients the sketch parallel to the screen.
25. On the ribbon, click **Sketch** tab > **Sketching** panel > **Rectangle** drop-down **> Corner Rectangle**.
26. Modify the dimensions, as shown below (refer to the **Modify** section of Chapter 2 to learn how to modify dimensions).

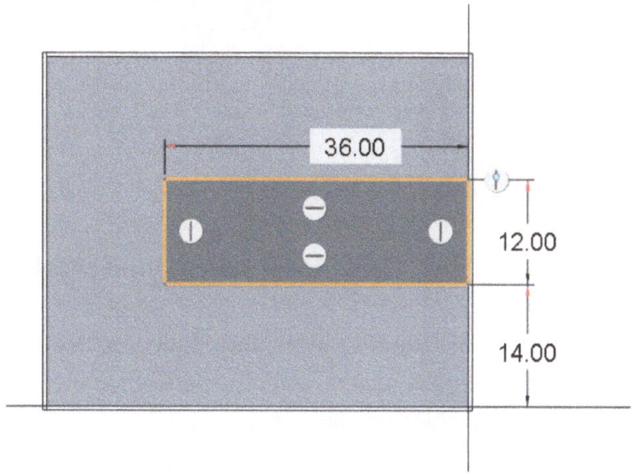

27. On the ribbon, click **Sketch** tab > **Close** panel > **OK**.
28. On the **Graphics** toolbar, click **Saved Orientations** drop-down > **Standard Orientation**.

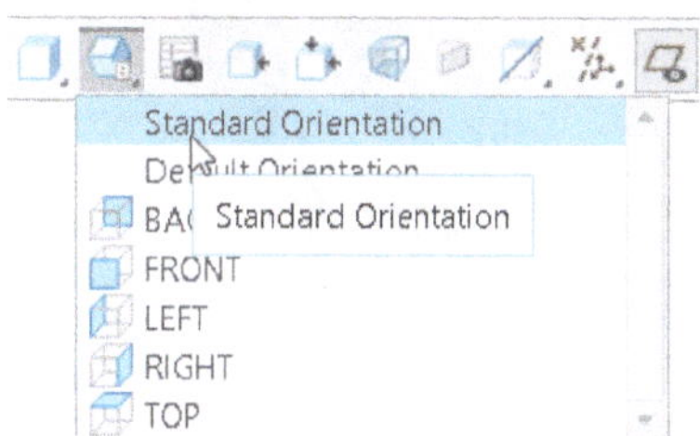

29. On the ribbon, click **Model** tab > **Shapes** panel > **Extrude**.
30. Select the sketch.
31. On the ribbon, click the **Remove Material** button.
32. Click the **Reverse Direction** button next to the **Depth** box.
33. Select the **Through All** option from the drop-down next to the **Depth** box.
34. Click the green check on the dashboard.

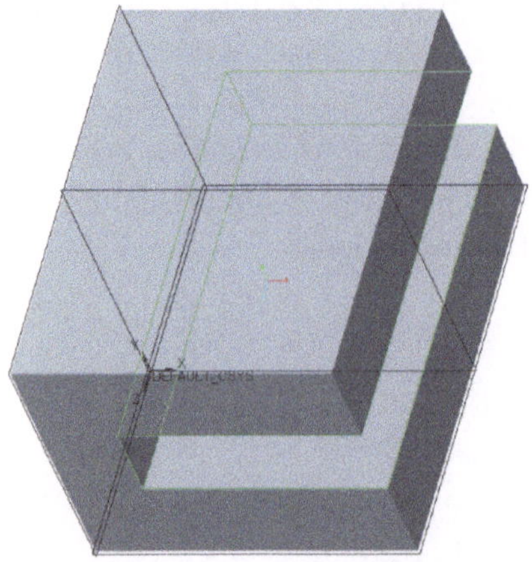

35. On the ribbon, click **Model** tab > **Datum** panel > **Sketch**.
36. Click on the top face of the model geometry.
37. On the **Sketch** dialog, click in the **Reference** box and select the right face of the model.

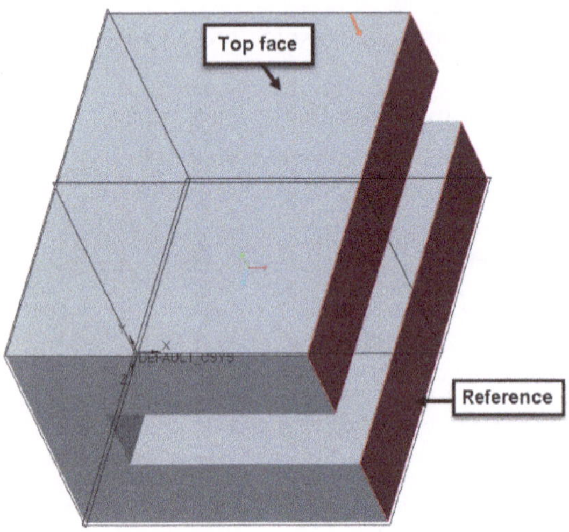

38. Click the **Sketch** button.
39. On the **Graphics** toolbar, click the **Sketch View** icon. It orients the sketch parallel to the screen.
40. On the ribbon, click **Sketch** tab > **Sketching** panel > **Line Chain** .
41. Draw the sketch, as shown below.

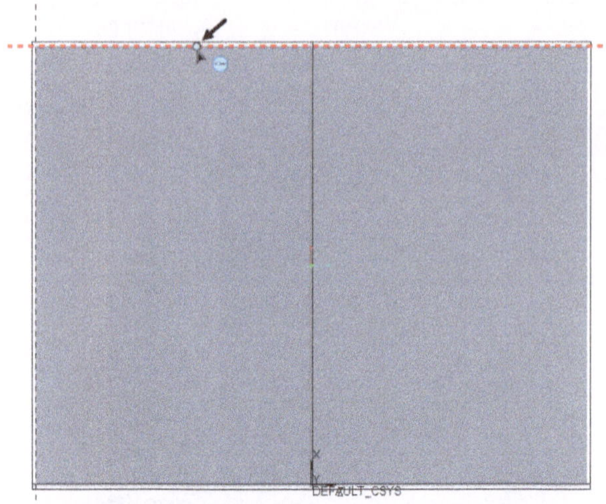

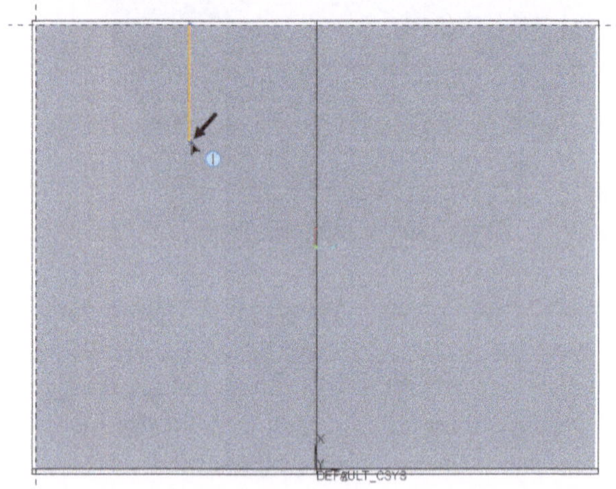

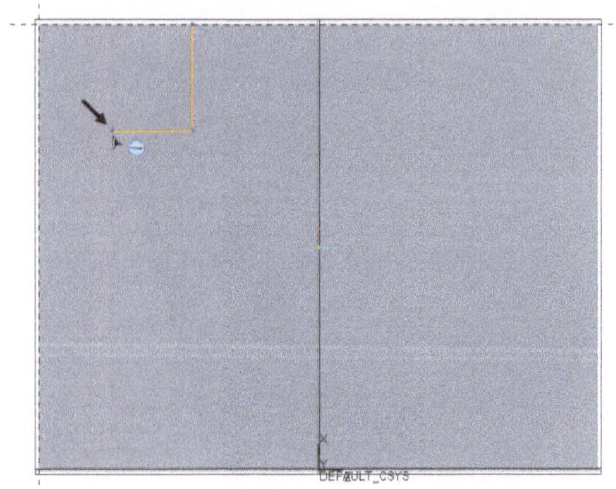

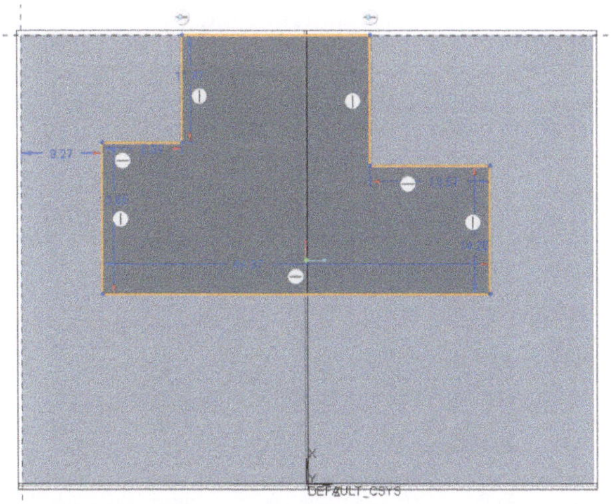

42. On the ribbon, click **Sketch** tab > **Constrain** panel > **Equal** .
43. Select the two vertical lines, as shown below.

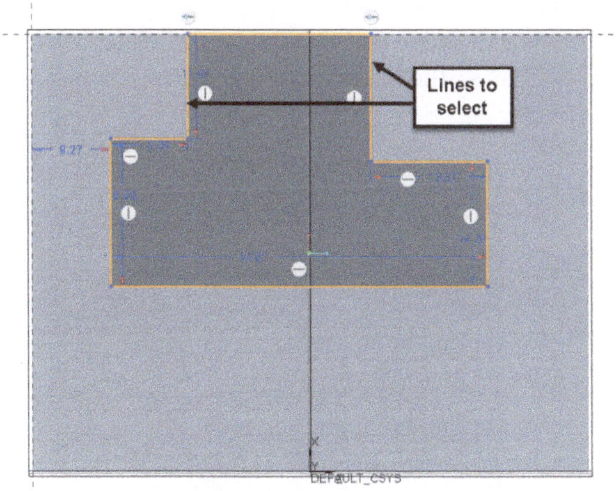

44. Likewise, apply the **Equal** constraint to the horizontal lines.

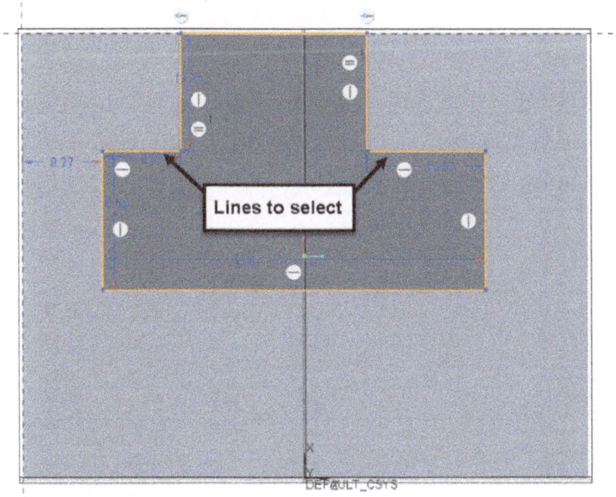

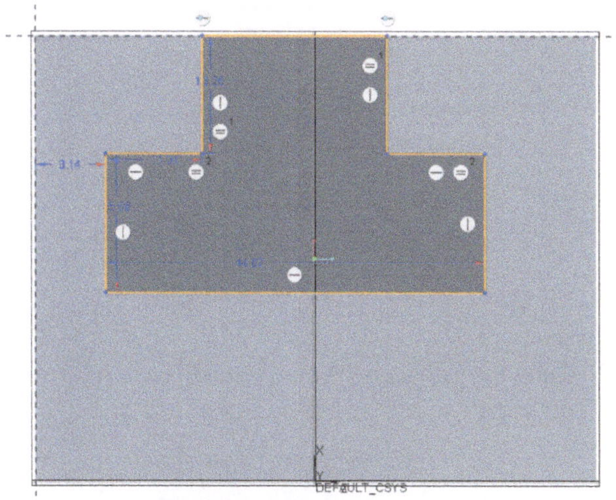

45. Modify the sketch's dimensions, as shown below (refer to the **Modify** section of Chapter 2 to learn how to modify dimensions).

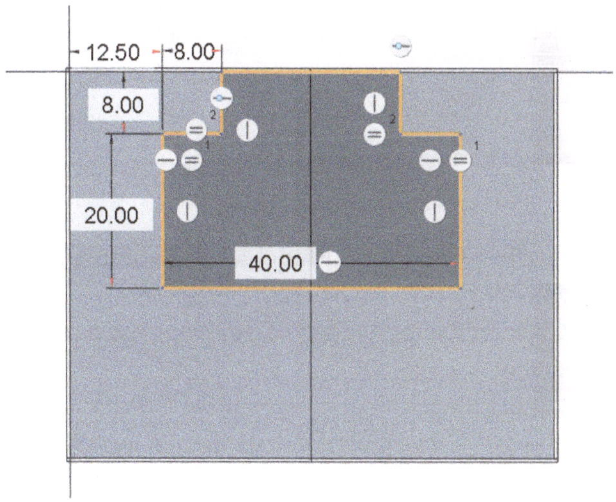

46. Click **OK** on the ribbon.
47. Change the view to **Standard Orientation.**
48. On the ribbon, click **Model** tab > **Shapes** panel > **Extrude.**
49. Select the sketch and click the **Remove Material** button on the dashboard.
50. Click the **Reverse Direction** button next to the **Depth** box.
51. Select **To next** option from the drop-down next to the **Depth** box.

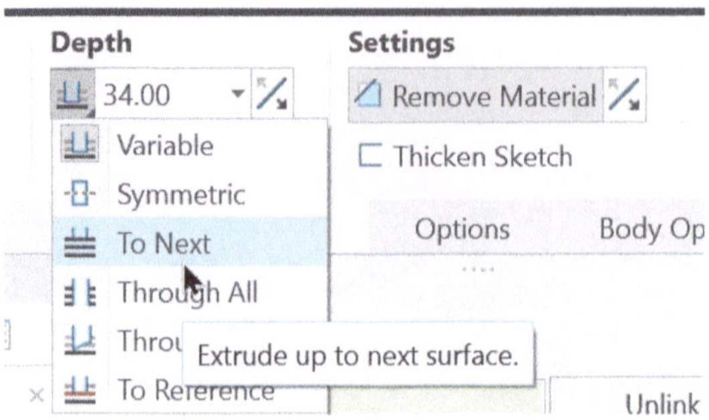

52. Click the green check on the dashboard to create the cut.

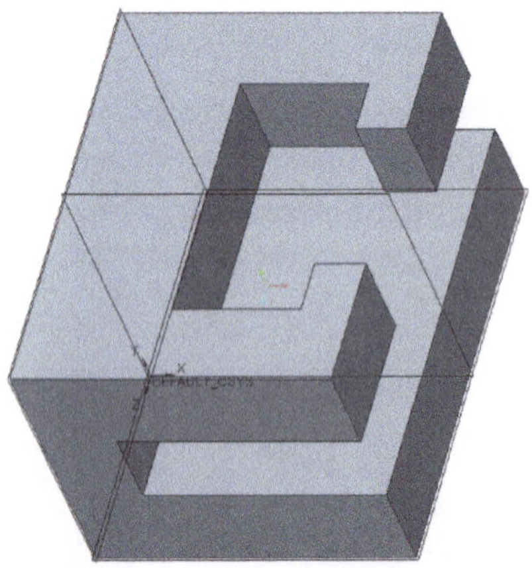

53. On the ribbon, click **Model** tab > **Datum** panel > **Sketch**.
54. Click on the top plane to define the sketching plane.
55. On the **Sketch** dialog, click in the **Reference** box and select the right face of the model geometry.

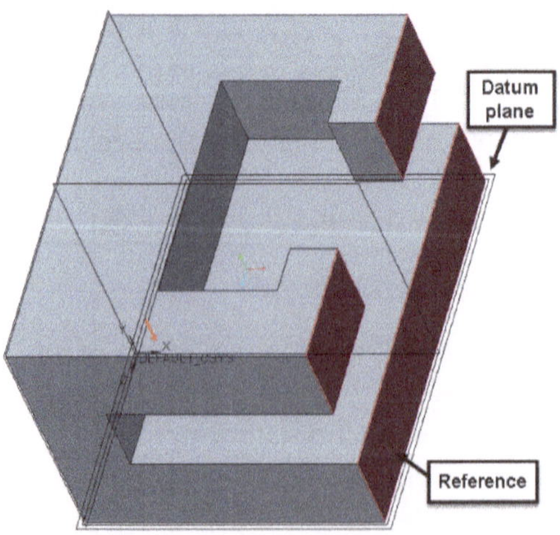

56. Click the **Sketch** button.
57. On the **Graphics** toolbar, click the **Sketch View** icon. It orients the sketch parallel to the screen.
58. Create a sketch, as shown below.

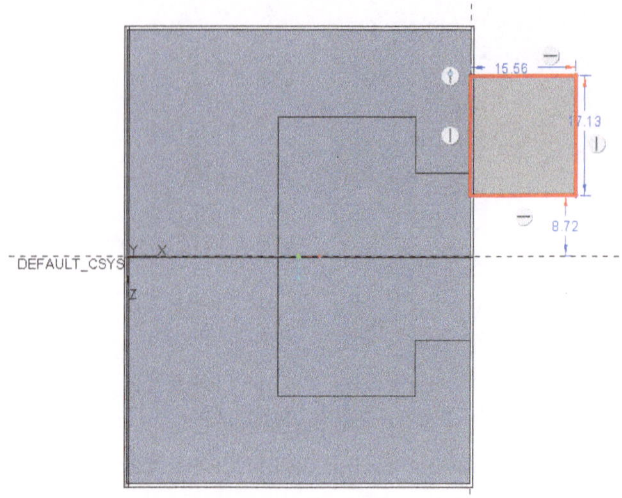

59. On the ribbon, click **Sketch** tab > **Constrain** panel > **Coincident** .
60. Select the edge and the line, as shown below. It will make the selections coincident with each other.

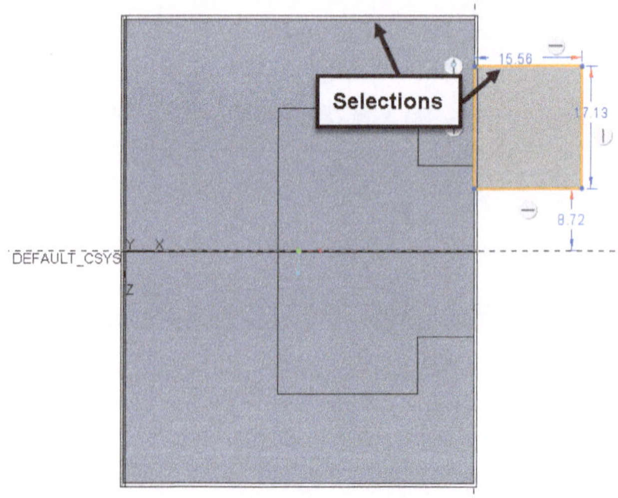

61. Modify the dimensions, as shown below (refer to the **Modify** section of Chapter 2 to learn how to modify dimensions).

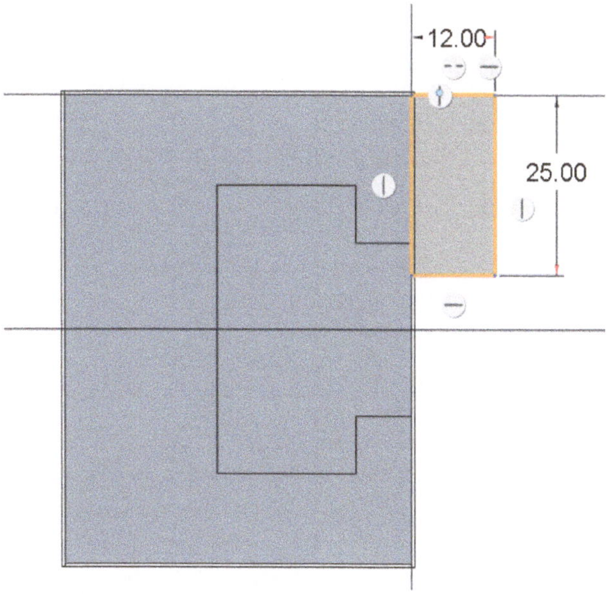

62. Click **OK** on the ribbon.
63. Change the view to **Standard Orientation.**
64. Activate the **Extrude** command and select the sketch.
65. On the **Extrude** dashboard, select the **To Reference** option from the drop-down next to the **Depth** box.

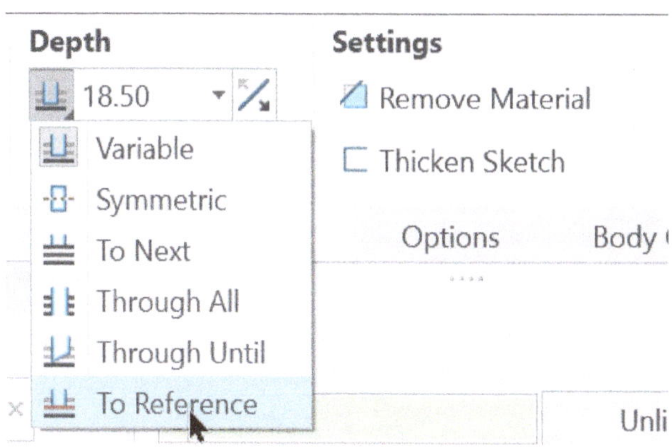

66. Select the horizontal face of the part geometry, as shown in the figure.

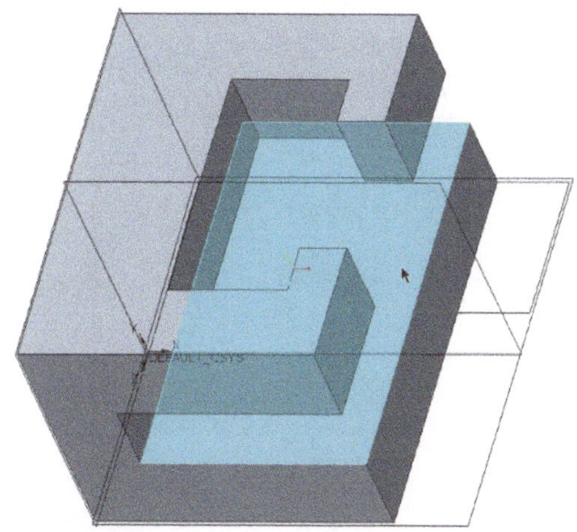

67. Click the green check to complete the part.

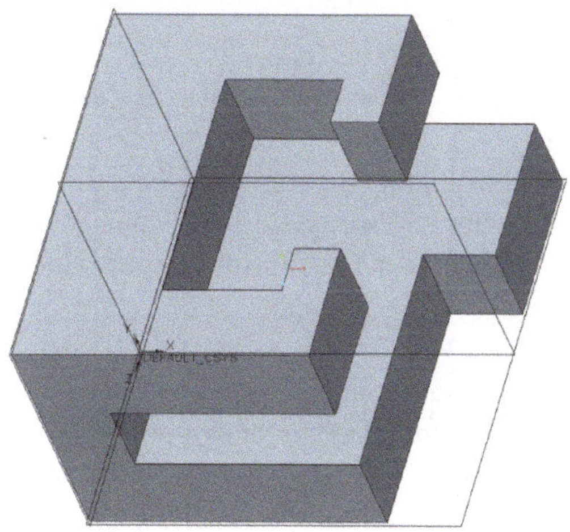

68. Save and close the file.

Example 2

In this example, you will create the part shown below.

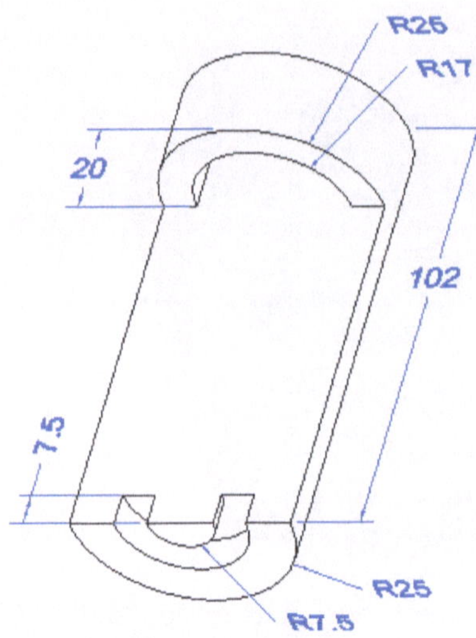

1. Start **Creo Parametric 11.0**.
2. On the Quick Access Toolbar, click the **New** button.
3. On the **New** dialog, select **Types > Part**, and then type-in **C03-Example2** in the **Name** box.
4. Uncheck the **Use default template** option and click **OK**.
5. On the **New File Options** dialog, select **solid_part_mmks**, and click **OK**.
6. Sketch on the top plane, as shown below.

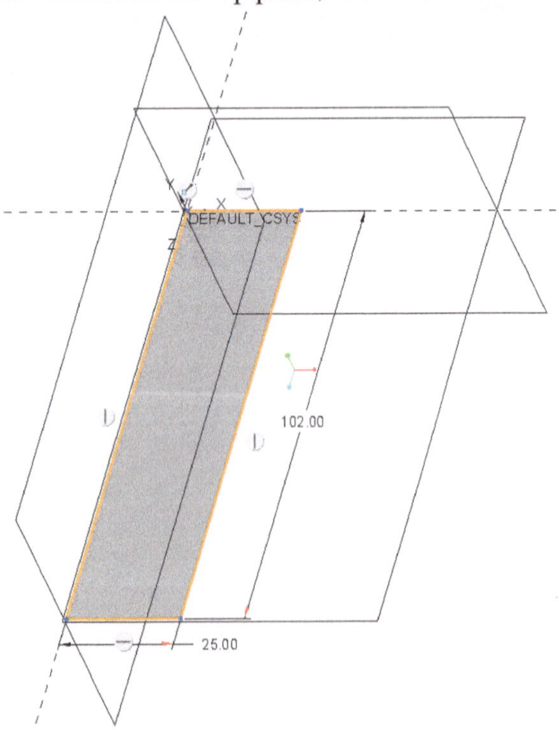

7. On the ribbon, click **OK** to exit the **Sketch** mode.
8. On the ribbon, click **Model** tab > **Shapes** panel > **Revolve** .
9. Select the sketch.
10. Click on the line passing through the origin.

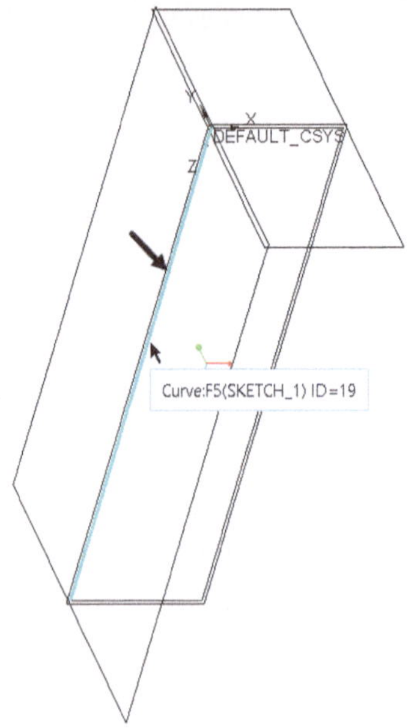

11. On the **Revolve** dashboard, type-in **180** in the **Angle** box and click the **Reverse Direction** button.

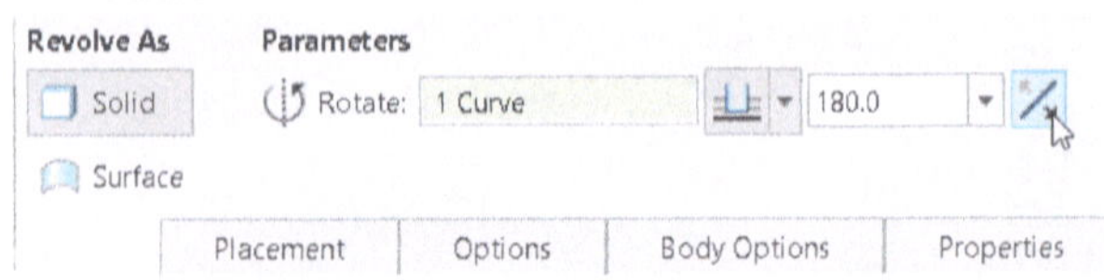

12. Click the green check to create the *Revolved* feature.

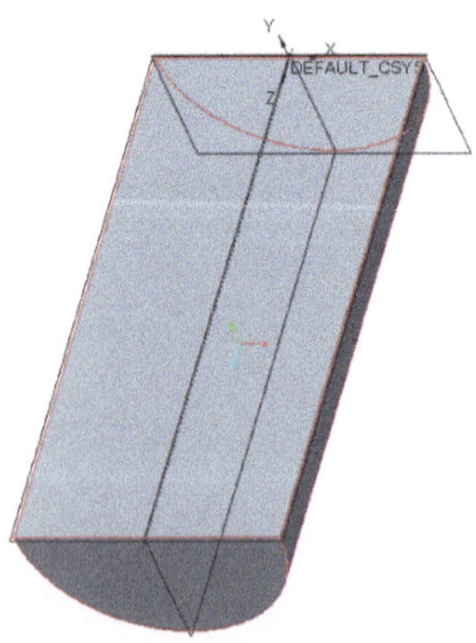

13. On the ribbon, click **Model** tab > **Datum** panel > **Sketch**.

14. Click on the top face of the model geometry.
15. On the **Sketch** dialog, click in the **Reference** box and select the front face of the model.
16. Click the **Sketch** button to start the sketch.
17. Draw the sketch and create a centerline, as shown below.

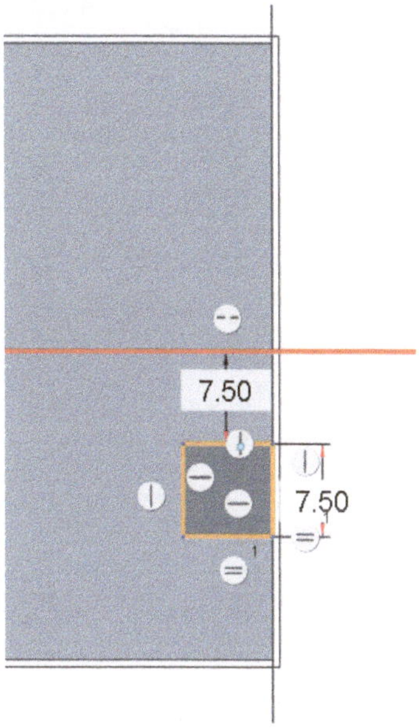

18. Click **OK** on the ribbon.
19. Activate the **Revolve** command and select the sketch, if not already selected.
20. On the **Revolve** dashboard, click the **Remove material** button.
21. Click the green check to complete the revolved cut.

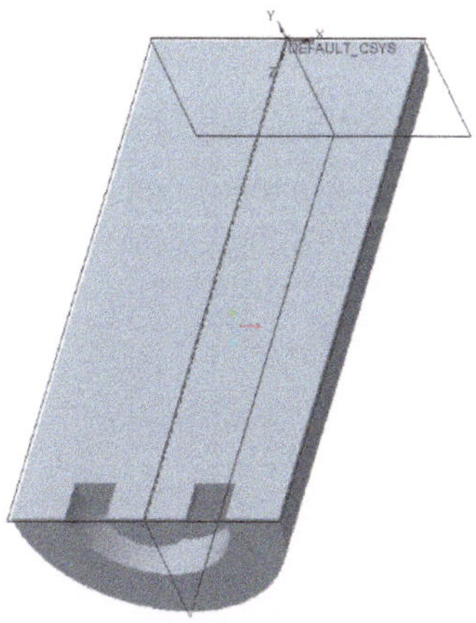

22. Activate the **Sketch** command and click on the top face of the model.
23. On the **Sketch** dialog, click in the **Reference** box and select the back face of the model.
24. Click the **Sketch** button to start the sketch.
25. On the ribbon, click **Sketch > Setup > References**.
26. Click the side edges of the geometry and click **Close**.
27. Create the sketch and centerline, as shown below.

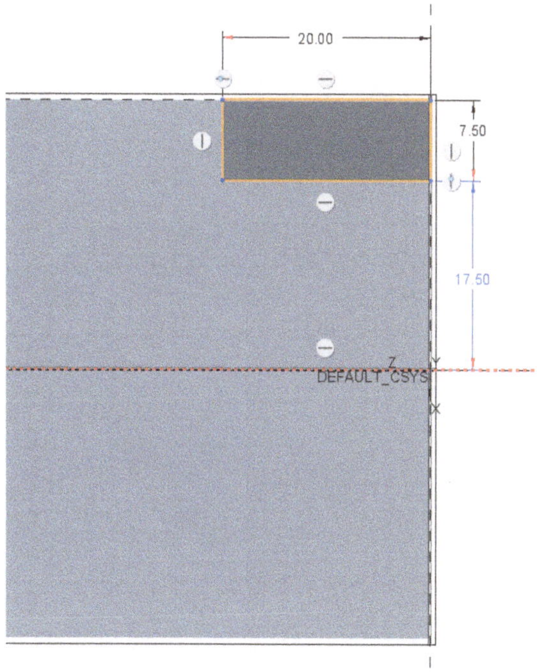

28. Click **OK** on the ribbon.
29. Activate the **Revolve** command and select the sketch, if not already selected.
30. Type-in **180** in the **Angle** box on the dashboard.
31. Click the green check on the dashboard.

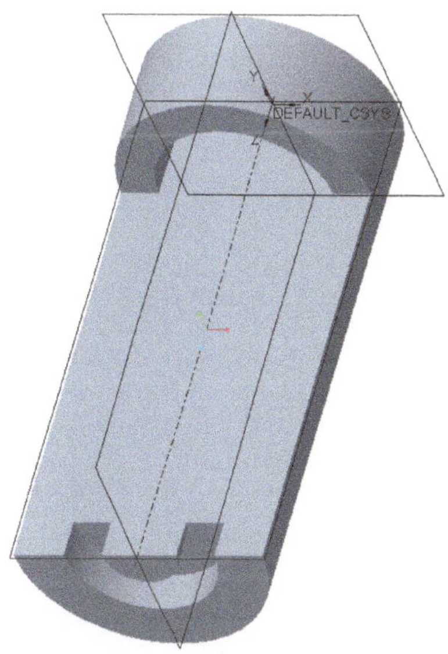

32. Save and close the file.

Questions

1. How do you create parallel planes in Creo Parametric?
2. List any two depth types available on the **Extrude** dashboard.
3. List the commands to create basic features.
4. How do you create angled planes in Creo Parametric?

Exercises

Exercise 1

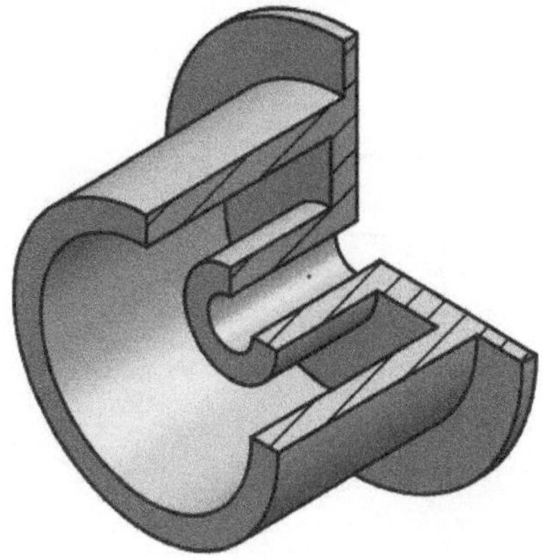

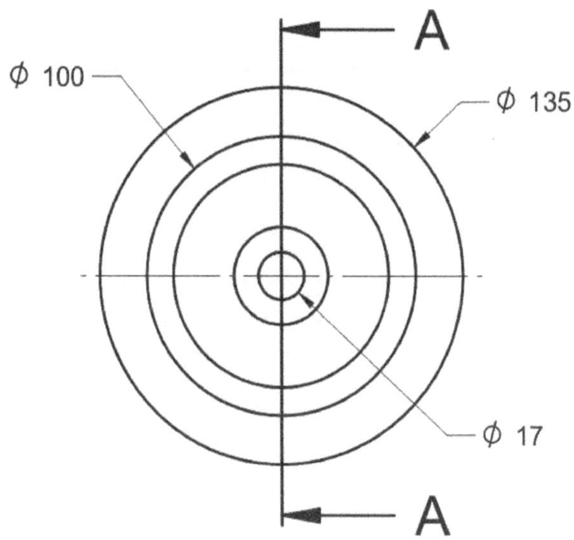

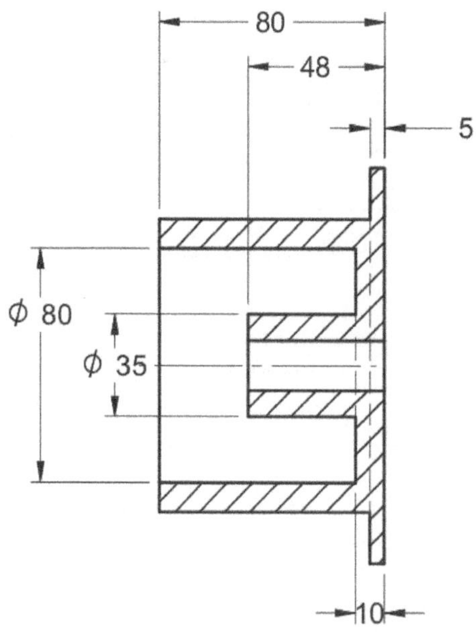

SECTION A-A

Exercise 2

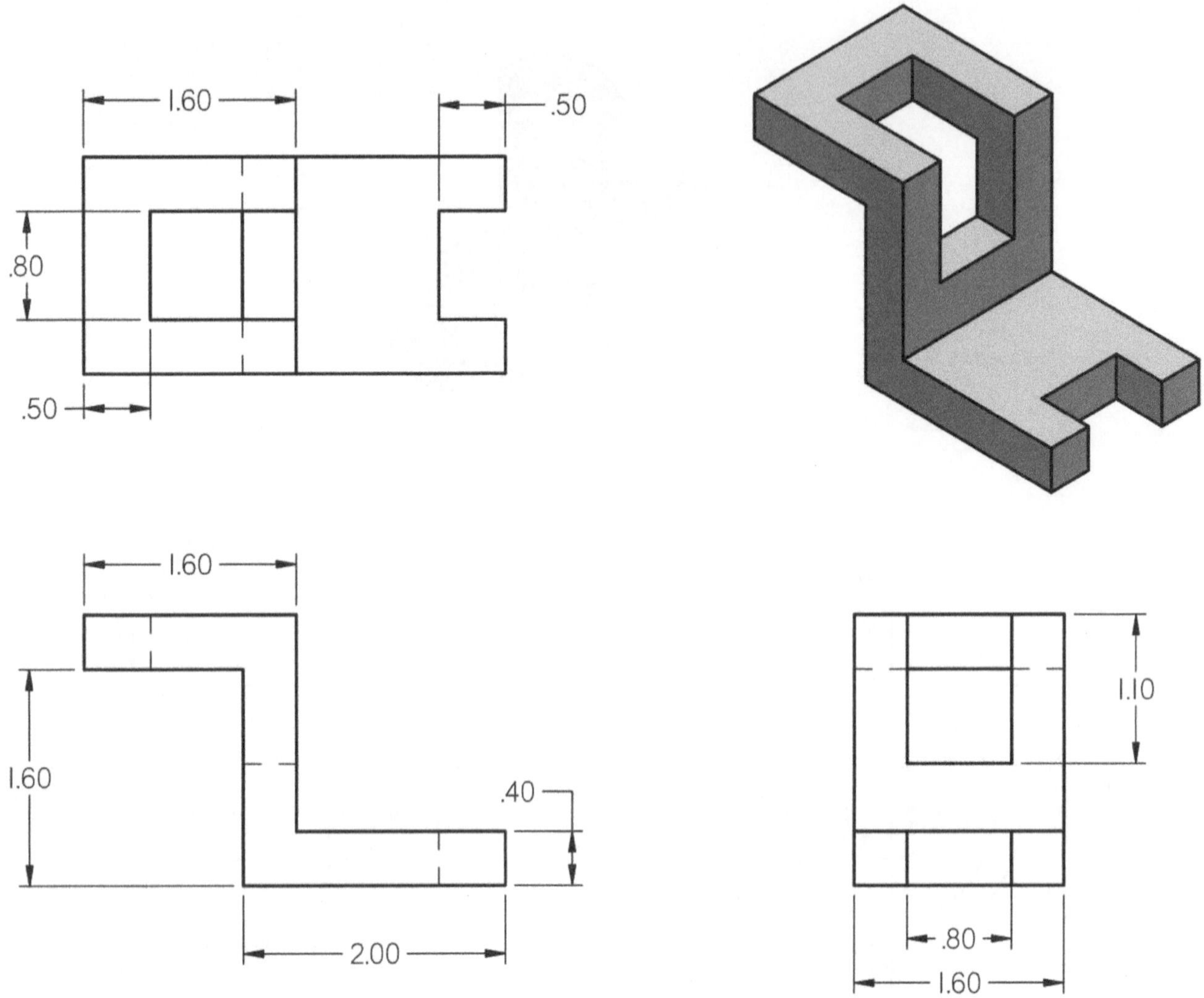

Exercise 3

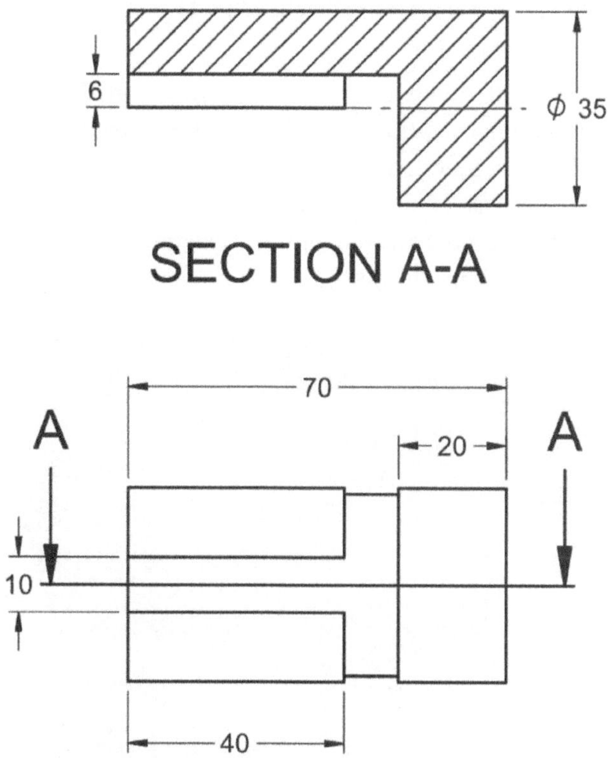
6
Ø 35
SECTION A-A
70
A
20
A
10
40

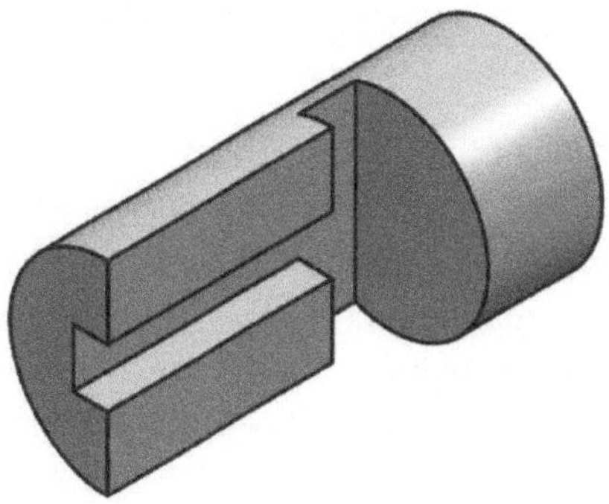

Chapter 4: Holes and Placed Features

So far, all of the features that were covered in the previous chapter were based on two-dimensional sketches. However, there are certain features in Creo Parametric that do not require a sketch at all. Features that do not require a sketch are called placed features. You can simply place them on your models. However, you must have some existing geometry to add these features. Unlike a sketch-based feature, you cannot use a placed feature for a model's first feature. For example, to create a *Round* feature, you must have an already existing edge. In this chapter, you will learn how to add Holes and placed features to your design.

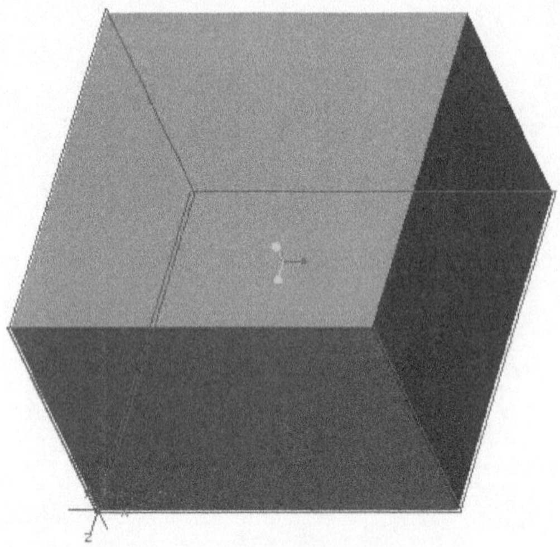

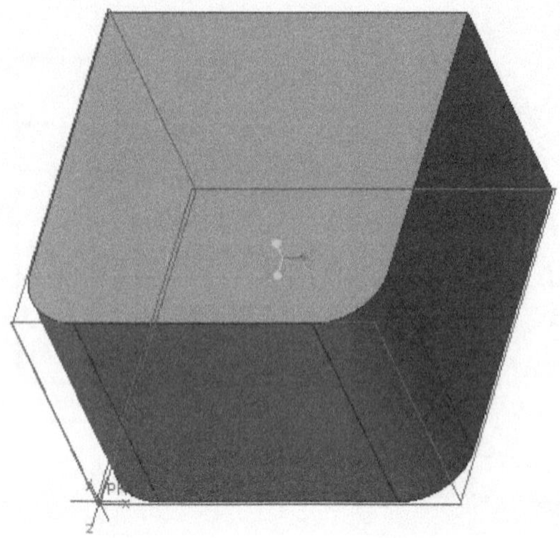

The topics covered in this chapter are:

- *Holes*
- *Threads*
- *Rounds*
- *Chamfers*
- *Drafts*
- *Shells*

Hole

As you know, it is possible to use the *Extrude* command to create cuts and remove material. But, if you want to drill holes of standard sizes, the **Hole** command is a better way to do this. The reason for this is that it has many hole types already predefined for you. All you have to do is choose the correct hole type and size. The other benefit is when you create a 2D drawing, Creo Parametric can automatically place the correct hole annotation. Activate this command (On the ribbon, click **Model > Engineering > Hole**) and click on a face to add a hole. You can select a flat or cylindrical face. You will notice that the **Hole** dashboard appears. There are options on this dashboard that make it easy to create different types of holes. The procedures to create various types of holes are explained next.

Simple Hole

1. To create a simple hole feature, click the **Simple** icon on the **Hole** dashboard.
2. On the **Hole** dashboard, type-in a value in the **Diameter** ⌀ box.
3. If you want a through-hole, click **Depth** drop-down > **Through All**. If you want a blind hole, then select **Blind** from the **Depth** drop-down. Next, type-in a value in the **Depth** box.

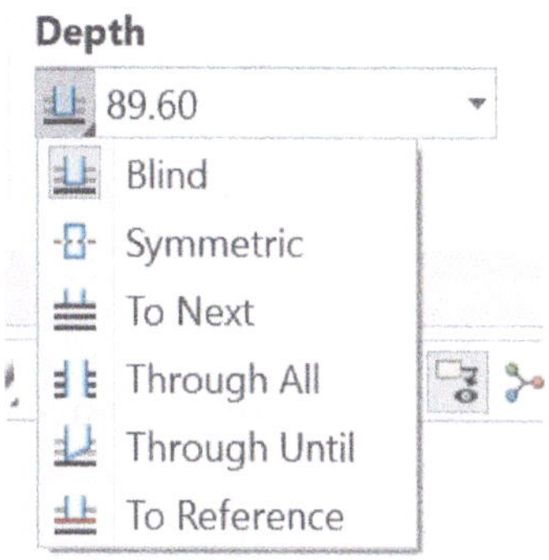

4. If you want a V-bottom hole, then click the **Drilled** icon on the dashboard.
5. Click the **Shape** tab and type-in a value in the **Angle** box. You can define the drill depth up to the shoulder or tip of the hole using the **Shoulder** or **Tip** options, respectively.

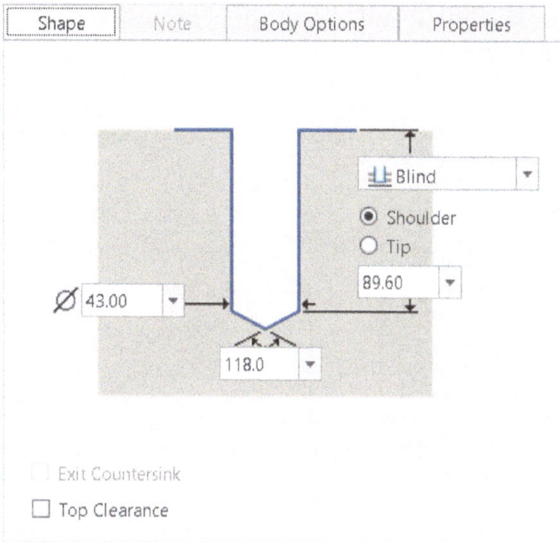

You can also create Counterbored or Countersunk holes using the **Counterbore** or **Countersunk** icons.

A counterbore hole is a large diameter hole added at the opening of another hole. It is used to accommodate a fastener below the level of the workpiece surface. Click the **Counterbore** icon on the dashboard and edit the dimensions on the **Shape** tab.

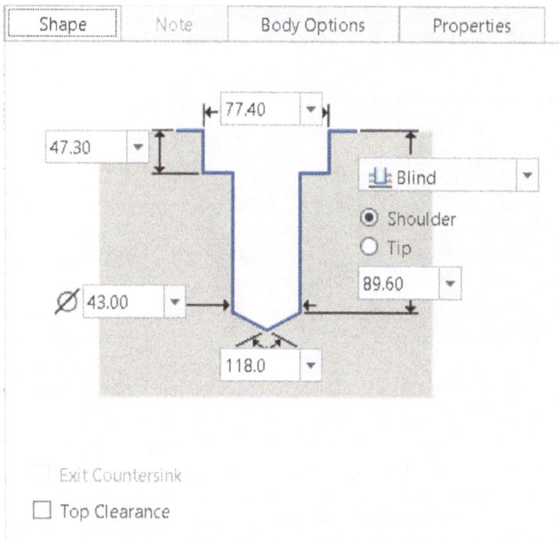

A countersunk hole has an enlarged V-shaped opening to accommodate a fastener below the workpiece surface level. Click the **Countersink** icon on the dashboard and edit the dimensions on the **Shape** tab.

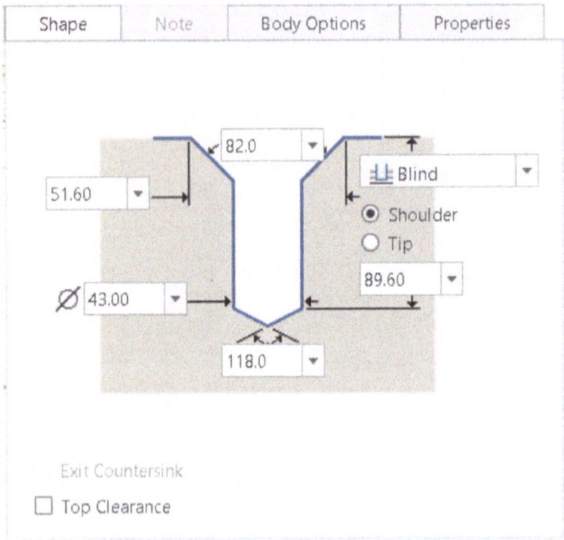

6. Click and drag any one of the red handles attached to the holes onto the model's side face.
7. Likewise, drag another handle onto the side face perpendicular to the previous face.

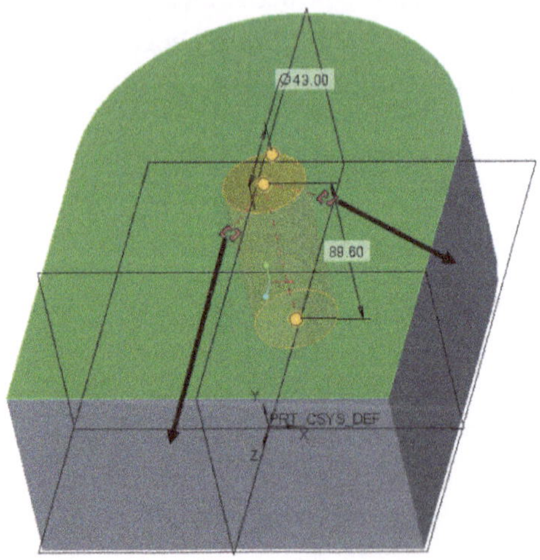

8. Modify the offset dimensions to define the hole position.

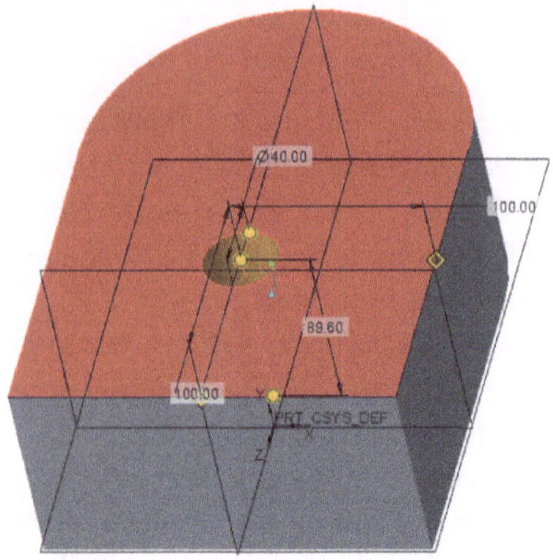

9. Click the green check on the dashboard to create the hole.

Coaxial Hole

You can create holes coaxial to a cylindrical face.

1. Create a datum axis by activating the **Axis** command and selecting the edge of a cylindrical face.

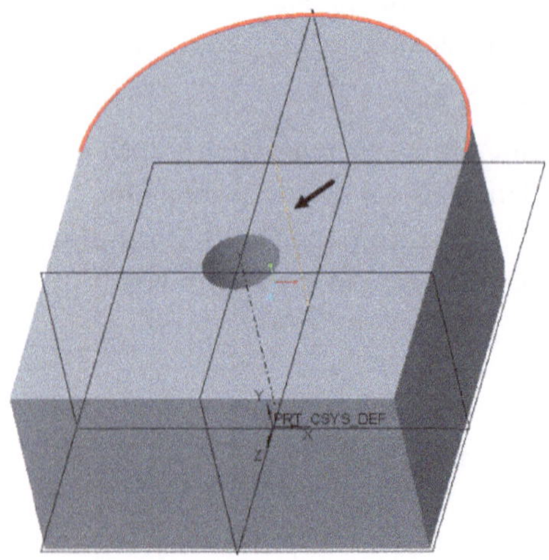

2. Activate the **Hole** command.
3. Press the Ctrl key and click on the datum axis and the face on which the hole is to be placed.

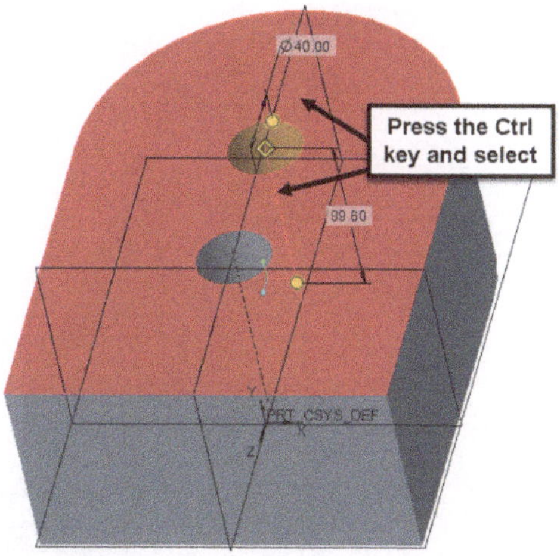

4. Set the other options on the dashboard and click the green check.

Radial and Diameter Holes

You can create a hole on a planar or cylindrical face at a radial distance from an axis. To do this, you need to make three selections: placement face, an axis to define the radial offset, a plane to define the angular offset.

Radial or diameter hole on a planar face

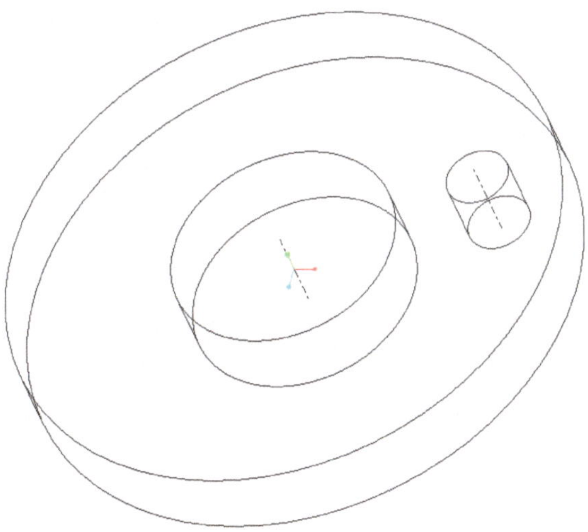

Radial or diameter hole on a cylindrical face

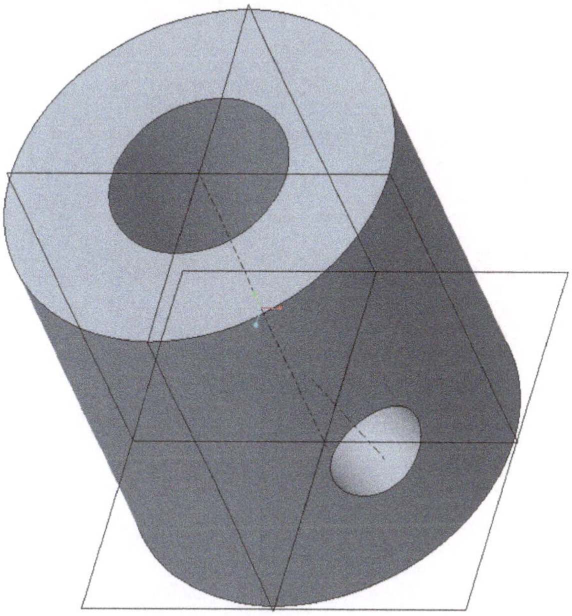

1. Activate the **Hole** command and click on the placement face.
2. On the **Hole** dashboard, click the **Placement** tab and select **Type > Radial.**
3. Click in the **Offset References** section on the **Placement** tab.
4. Press the Ctrl key and select an axis and plane. The axis is used to define the radial distance, and the plane is used to define the angle.

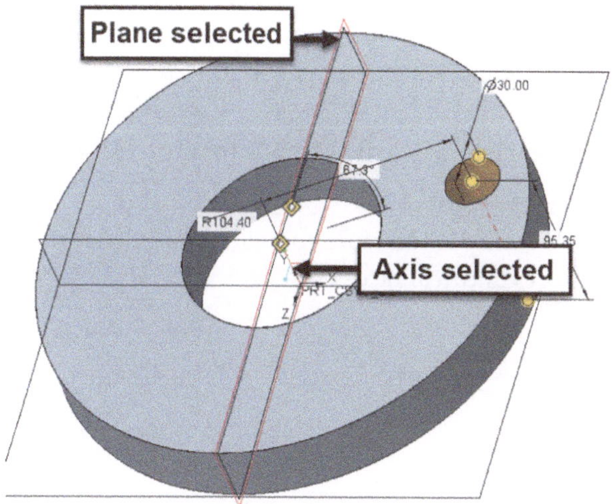

5. Modify the radial and angle values to define the location of the hole.

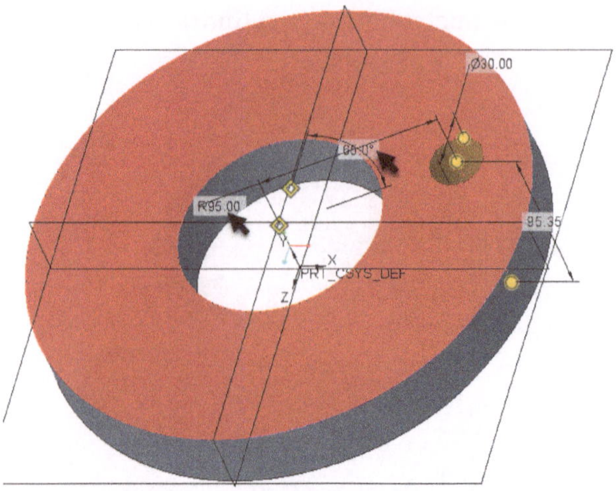

6. Click the green check.

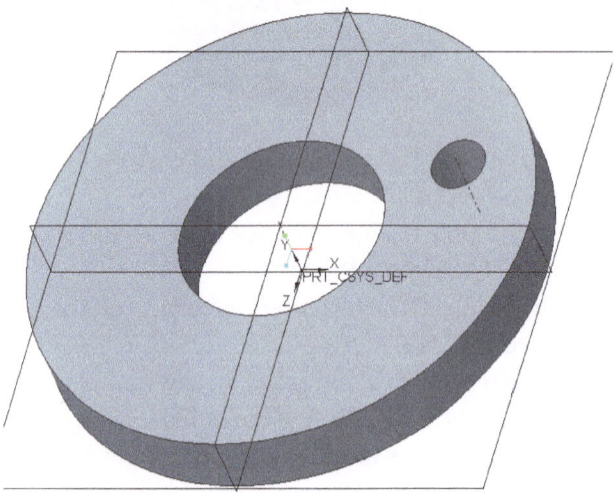

Likewise, you can create a hole by specifying the diameter distance from an axis.

Creating a Radial or Diameter Hole on a Cylindrical face.

1. Activate the **Hole** command and click on a cylindrical face.

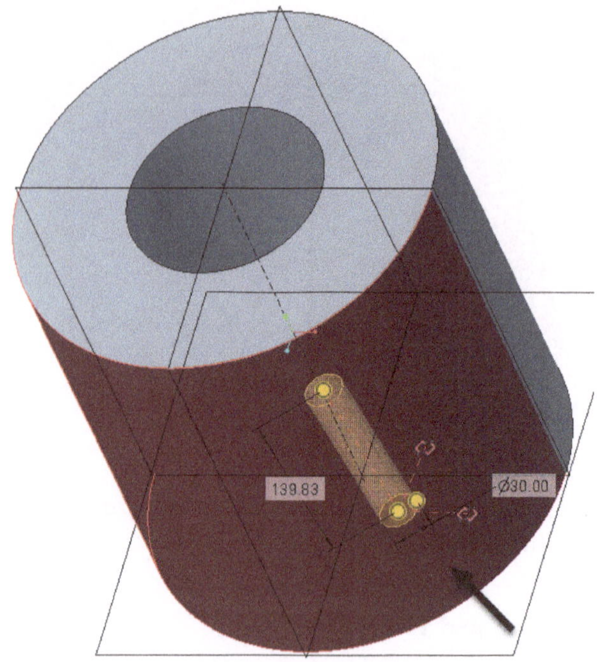

2. Click in the **Offset Reference** selection box.
3. Press and hold the CTRL key and select the Right plane and top face. The Right plane is used as the angular reference. At the same time, the top face is used as the offset reference.

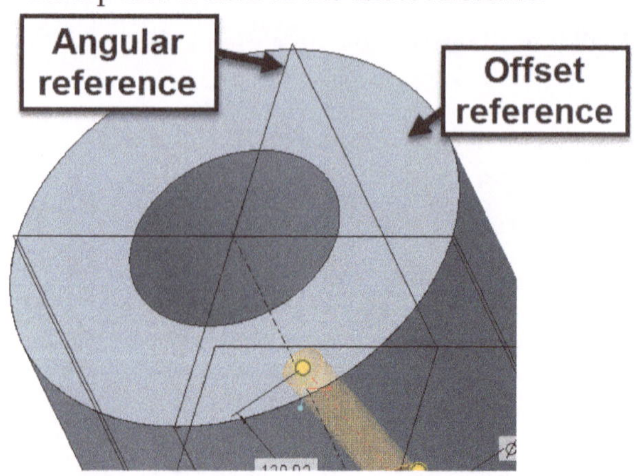

You can also select the references by dragging and placing the reference handles.

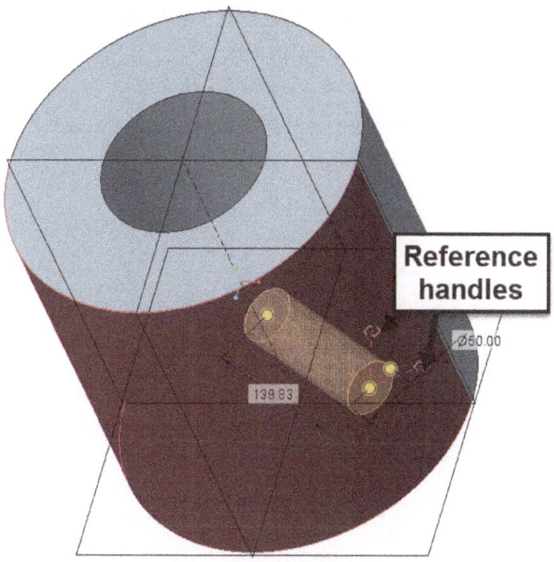

4. On the **Placement** tab of the dashboard, change the **Angle** and **Axial** distance values.

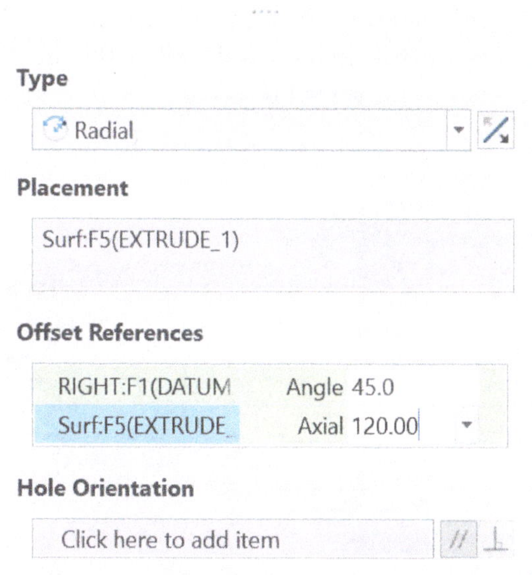

5. Change the **Diameter** value on the Dashboard.
6. Click **OK**.

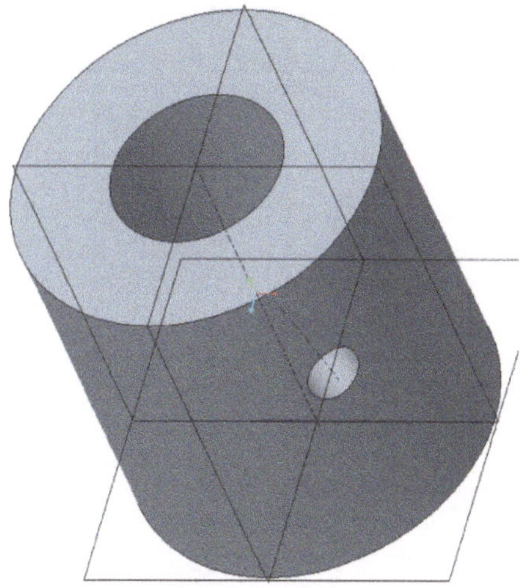

Standard Hole

Creo Parametric allows you to create holes based on UNF, ISO, and UNC standards. You can create a thread, clearance, or tapered hole using the standard charts.

1. Activate the **Hole** command and click the **Standard** icon on the **Hole** dashboard.
2. Select the standard from the **Thread type** drop-down.
3. Select the screw size from the **Screw size** drop-down.
4. Define the hole depth on the dashboard. You can also use the **Countersink** and **Counterbore** options to create countersink or counterbored holes.

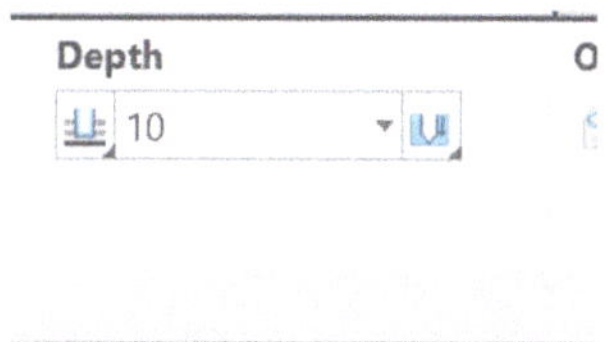

5. Click on the placement face and position the hole.

Likewise, you can add a clearance hole to the model.

1. Activate the **Hole** command and click the **Standard** icon on the **Hole** dashboard.
2. Click the **Clearance** icon on the Dashboard.
3. Set the standard and screw size on the Dashboard.

4. Click the **Shape** tab on the Dashboard.
5. Select the type of **Fit** from the drop-down.

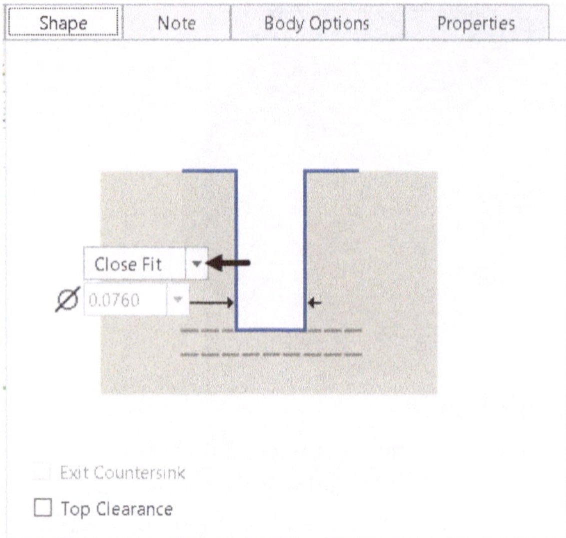

6. Define the hole depth.
7. Click on the placement face and position the hole.

Tapered Hole

Tapering is the process of decreasing the hole diameter toward one end. A tapered hole has a smaller diameter at the bottom.

1. Activate the **Hole** command and click the **Standard** icon on the **Hole** dashboard.
2. Activate the **Tapped** icon.
3. Click the **Tapered** icon on the Dashboard.
4. Set the **Thread type** and screw size on the Dashboard.
5. Define the hole depth.
6. Click on the placement face and position the hole.

The Cosmetic Thread command

This command adds a cosmetic thread/tap feature to a cylindrical face. A thread is added to the outer cylindrical face, whereas a tap is added to the inner cylindrical face (holes). You add thread/tap features to a 3D geometry so that when you create a 2D drawing, Creo Parametric can automatically place the correct thread annotation.

1. On the ribbon, click **Model > Engineering > Cosmetic Thread.**

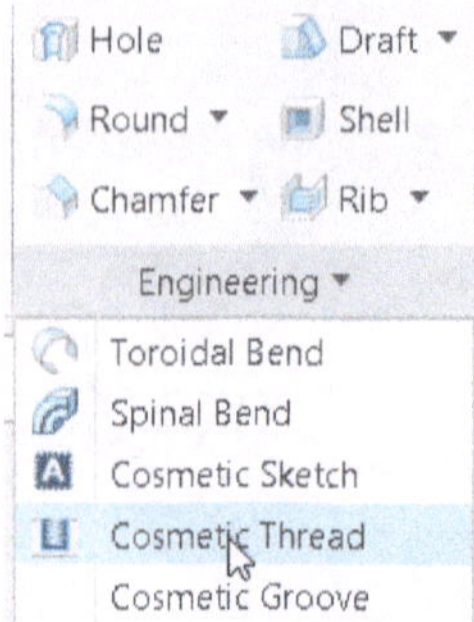

2. To create a thread, click on the outer cylindrical face of the part geometry.
3. Click on the end face of the cylindrical feature to define the limiting face.
4. On the **Cosmetic Thread** Dashboard, type-in the thread diameter, thread depth, and pitch values.
5. Use the arrow that is displayed on the preview to change the thread direction.

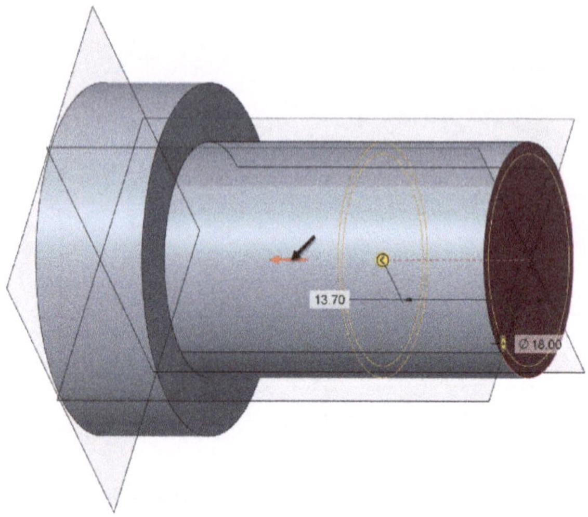

6. On the **Cosmetic Thread** Dashboard, click the **Properties** tab to view the thread properties. You can use the **Open** button to import the thread properties (or) use the **Save** button to save future use properties.

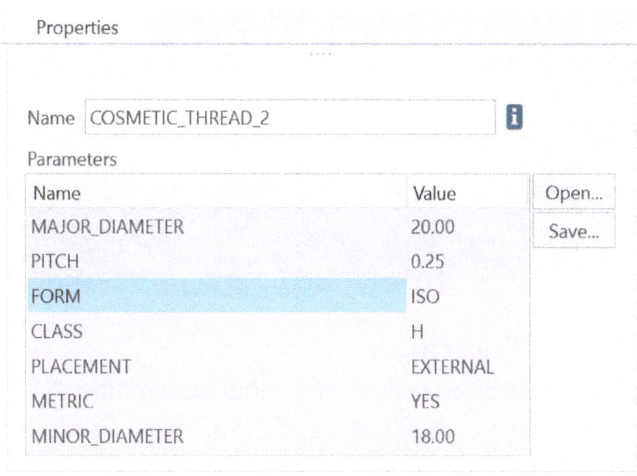

You can also create a standard thread.

1. On the **Cosmetic Thread** Dashboard, click the **Define standard thread** icon.
2. Set the standard and thread size.
3. Click the **Properties** tab to view and modify the thread properties.

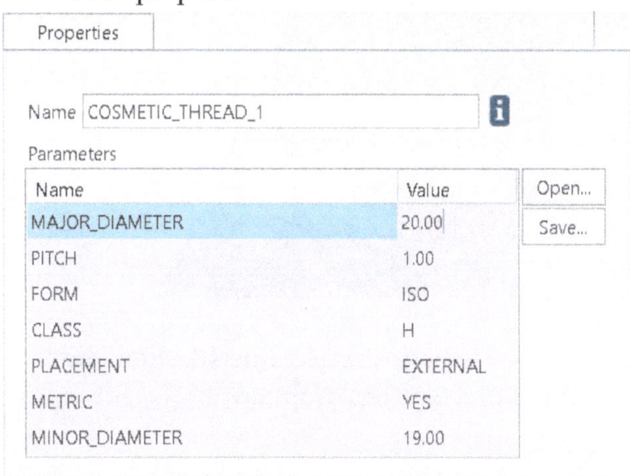

4. Click the green check on the dashboard.

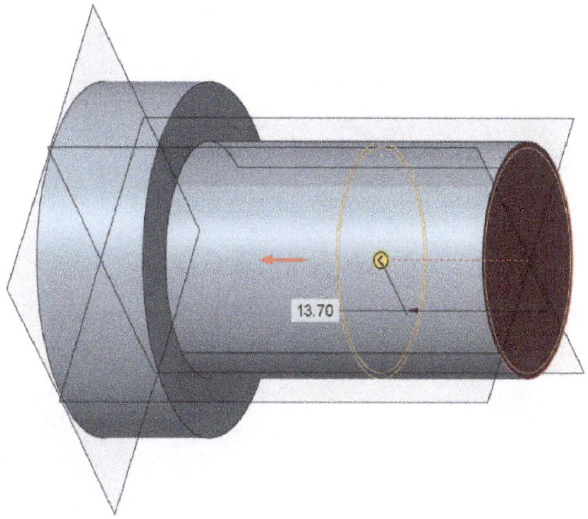

The Round command

This command breaks the sharp edges of a model and rounds them. It does not need a sketch to create a round. All you need to have is model edges.

1. On the ribbon, click **Model > Engineering > Round**.
2. Select the edge to round if you want to create multiple rounds with the same radius, press Ctrl and select multiple edges. By mistake, if you have selected a wrong edge, you can deselect it by pressing Ctrl and selecting the edge again.

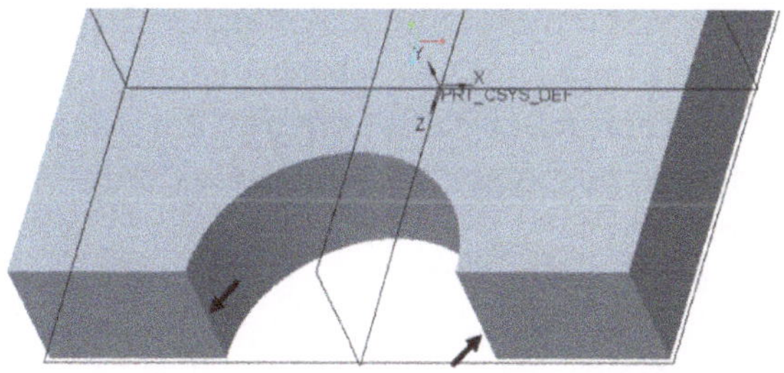

3. You can change the radius by typing a value in the **Radius** box available on the **Round** Dashboard. As you change the radius, all the selected edges will be updated. This is because they are all part of one instance. If you want the edges to have different radii, you must select edges without pressing the Ctrl key.
4. Click **OK** to finish this feature. The *Round* feature will be listed in the Model Tree.

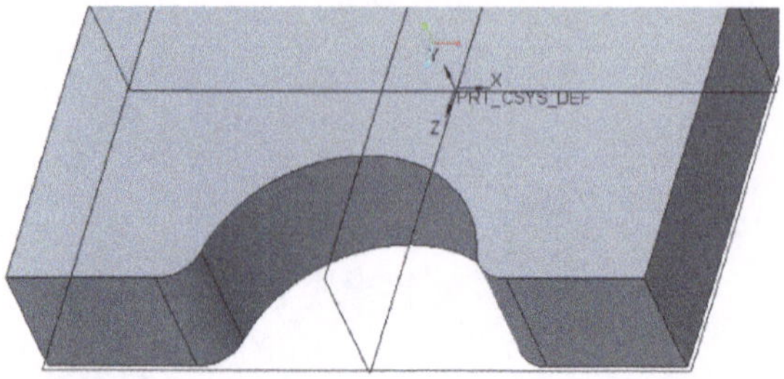

If you want to select all the edges that are tangentially connected, then simply click on any one of the tangentially connected edges.

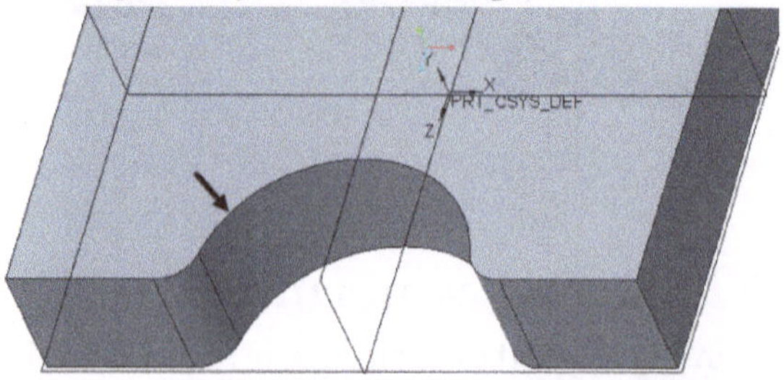

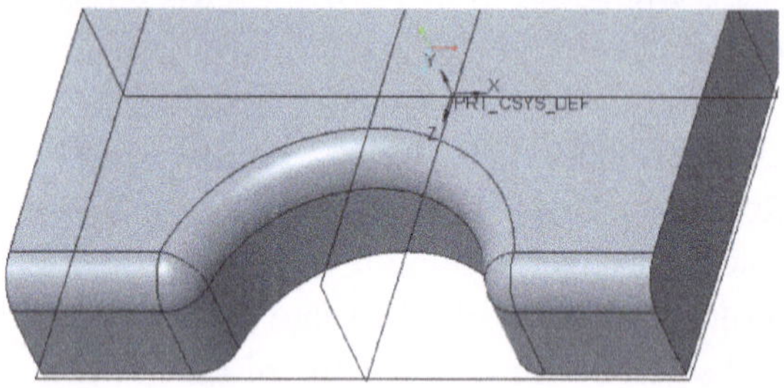

Conic Rounds

By default, the rounds have a circular arc profile. However, if you want to create a round with a conical arc profile, click the **Sets** tab on the Dashboard and select **Conic** from the **Cross-section** drop-down. Next, type-in a value in the **Conic parameter** box.

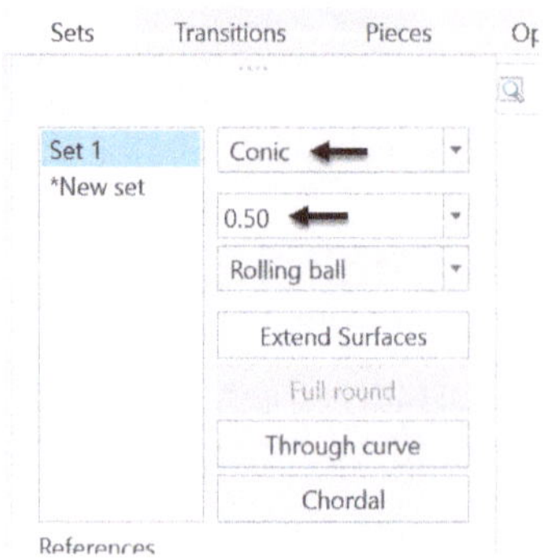

The rounds with different conic parameters are shown below.

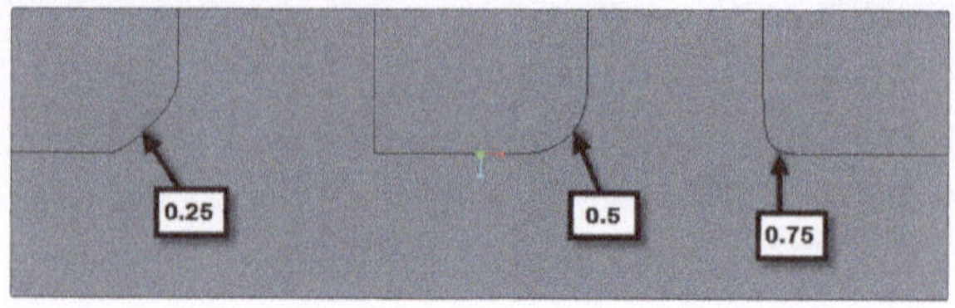

Corner Transition

If you create a round on three edges that come together at a corner, you have the option to control how these three rounds are blend together.

1. Activate the **Round** command and select the three edges that meet together at a corner.
2. On the **Round** dashboard, click the **Transitions** icon.
3. Click on the corner segment.

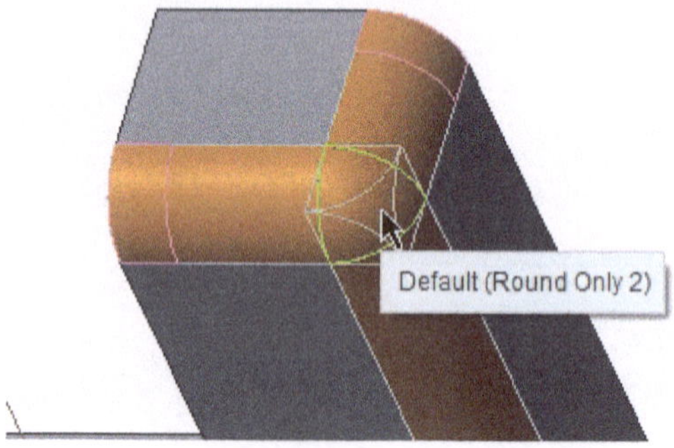

4. On the Dashboard, select **Intersect** from the **Transition Settings** drop-down.

5. Click the **Preview** icon.

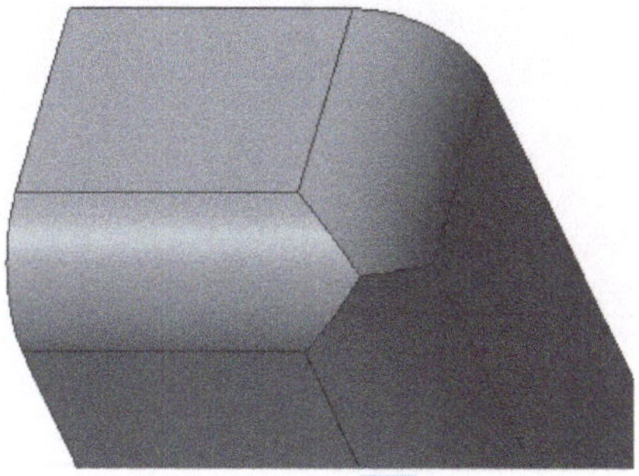

6. Click the **Resume**  icon.
7. On the Dashboard, select **Corner Sphere** from the **Transition Settings** drop-down.
8. Type-in 0.4 in the **R** box and press Enter. Notice the L1, L2, and L3 boxes on the Dashboard. You can type-in the setback distances in these boxes.

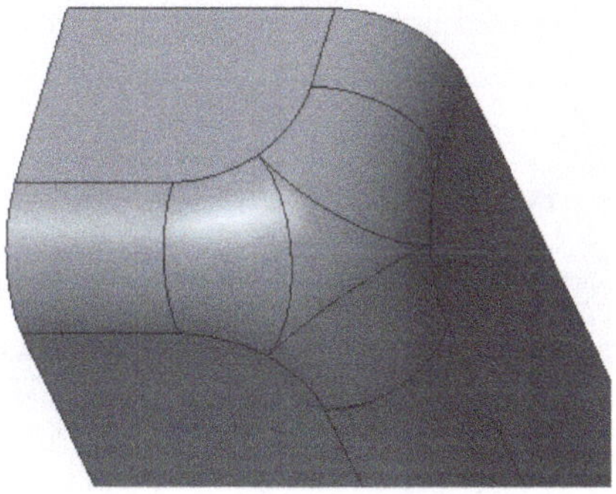

Likewise, you can create other transitions at the corners.

Variable Radius Rounds

Creo Parametric allows you to create a round with a varying radius along the selected edge.

1. Activate the **Round** command.
2. Click on the edge to round.
3. Click the right mouse button and drag the cursor downwards.
4. Select the **Make variable** icon. Two separate radii are added at the ends.

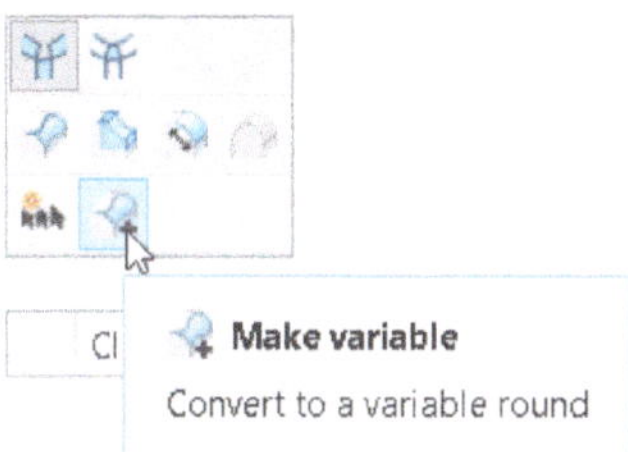

5. On the dashboard, click the **Sets** tab.
6. Click the right mouse button on the table available at the bottom of the **Sets** tab and select **Add radius**. A new radius is added to the round.

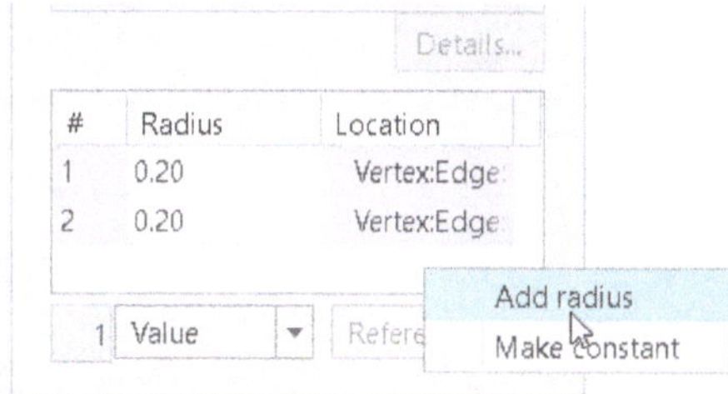

7. Click and drag the radius handle to move it to the center.

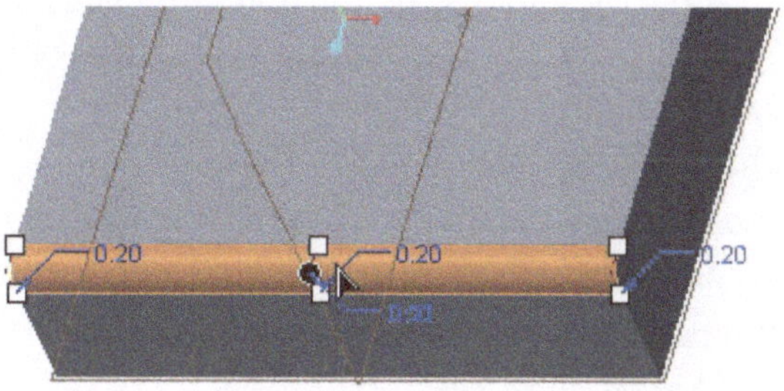

8. Type-in the radii values in the table available at the bottom of the **Sets** tab. You can also modify the radii by dragging the radii handles.

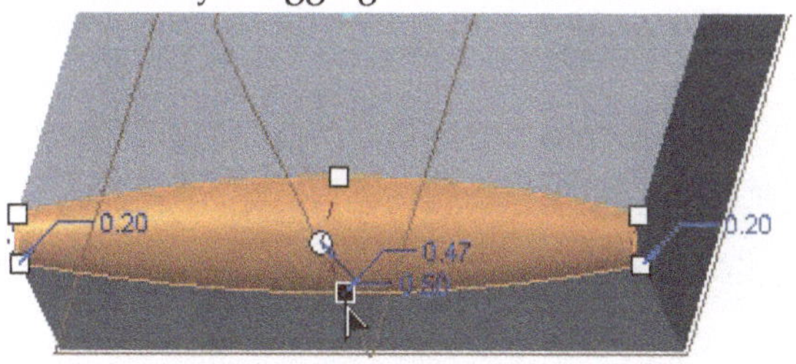

You can also convert the variable radius round to constant radius by clicking the right mouse button and selecting **Make constant**.

9. Click the green check to complete the feature.

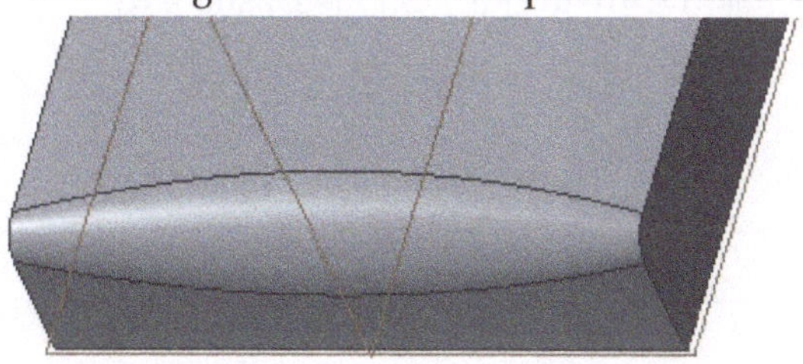

Chordal Round

You can create a round by specifying the chord length of the round instead of a radius. The chord length is the distance between the endpoints of the round profile.

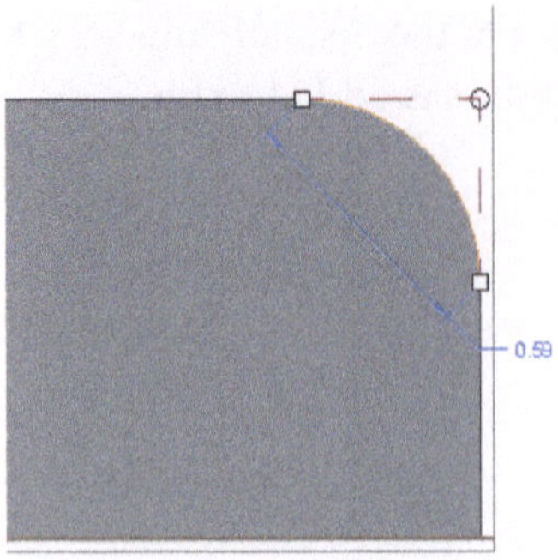

1. Activate the **Round** command and click on the edge to round.
2. Click the right mouse button and select **Chordal**.
3. Type-in a value in the **Chordal Length** box on the dashboard.
4. Click the green check on the dashboard.

Face-Face Round

The **Round** command also allows you to create a round between two faces.

1. Activate the **Round** command.
2. Press the Ctrl key and click on two faces connected.

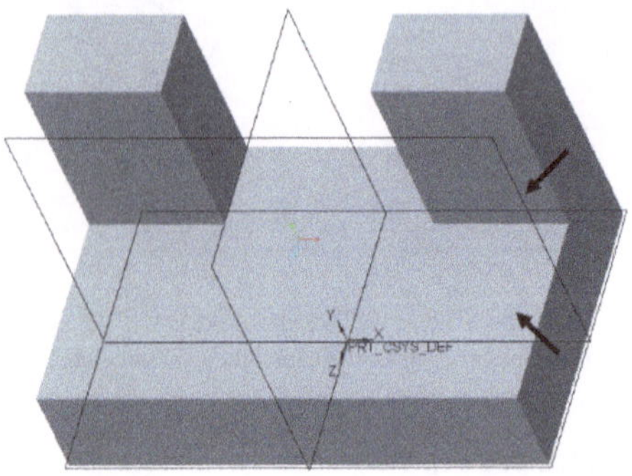

3. Type-in a value in the **Radius** box.
4. Click the green check on the Dashboard.

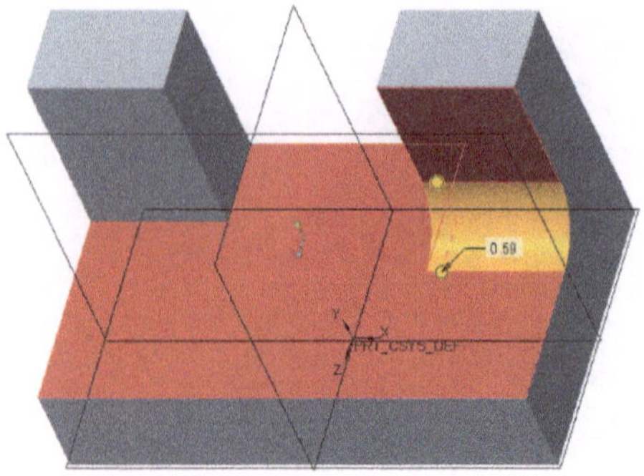

Face-Edge round

The **Round** command also allows you to create a round by selecting a face and a limiting edge.

1. Activate the **Round** command.
2. Press the Ctrl key and click on a face and edge. A round is created between the face and edge.

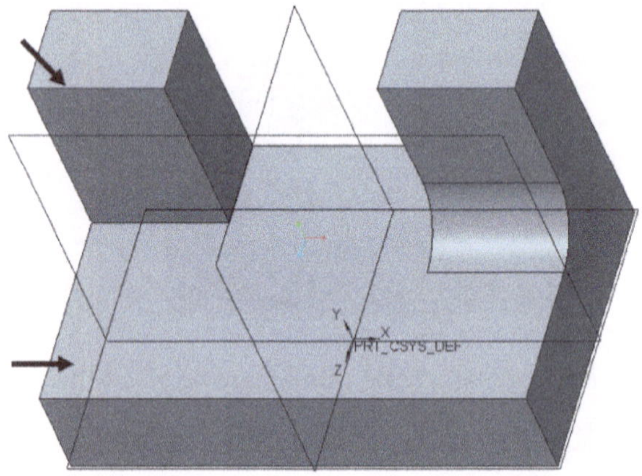

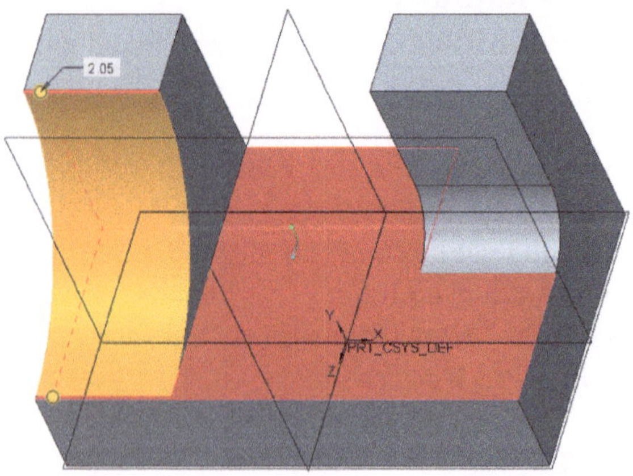

3. Click the green check on the Dashboard.

Full round

This option creates a full round between two selected edges.

1. Activate the **Round** command.
2. Press the Ctrl key and click on two edges having a common face.
3. Click the right mouse button and select **Full round**.

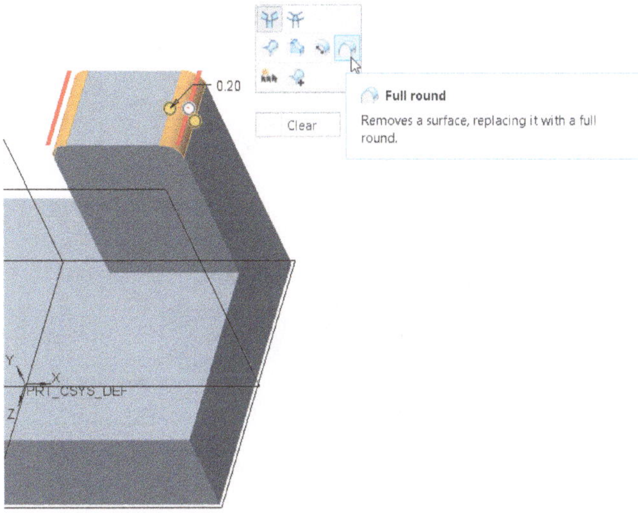

A round appears, replacing the common face.

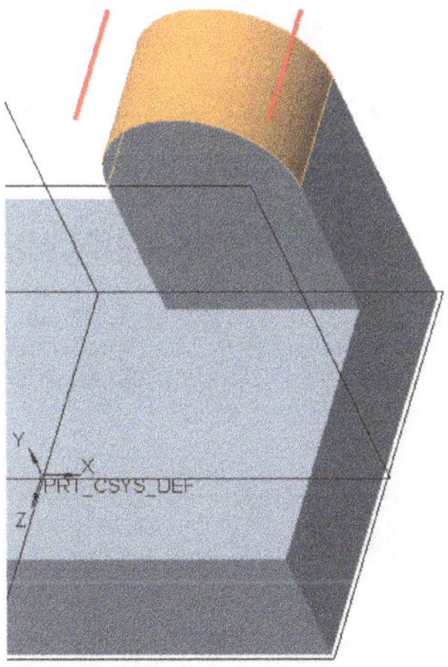

4. Click the green check on the Dashboard.

Auto Round

This command allows you add rounds automatically to all edges of the geometry. It recognizes edges of a geometry where rounds can be added. On the ribbon, click **Model > Engineering > Round** drop-down **> Auto Round**. The geometry in the graphics window is selected. On the **Auto Round** dashboard, you can find the **Convex** and **Concave** options under the **Settings** section. The **Concave** option adds rounds only to edges that are inwardly curved.

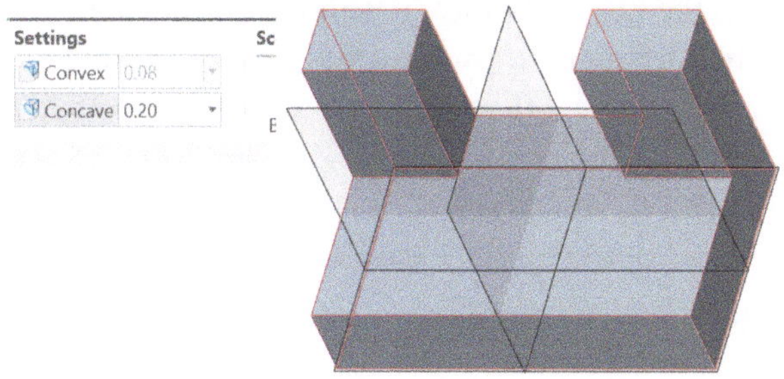

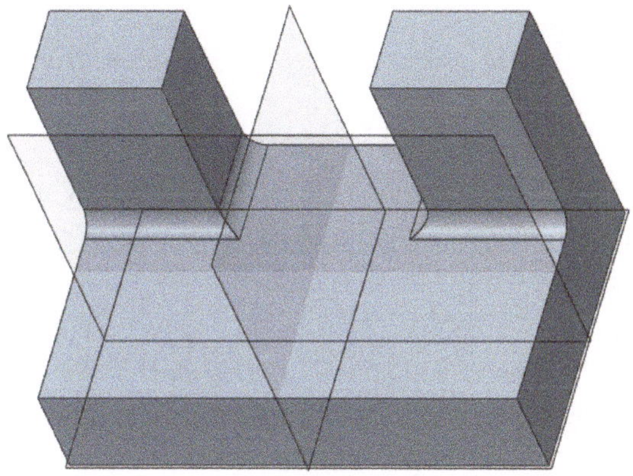

The **Convex** option rounds the outwardly curved edges.

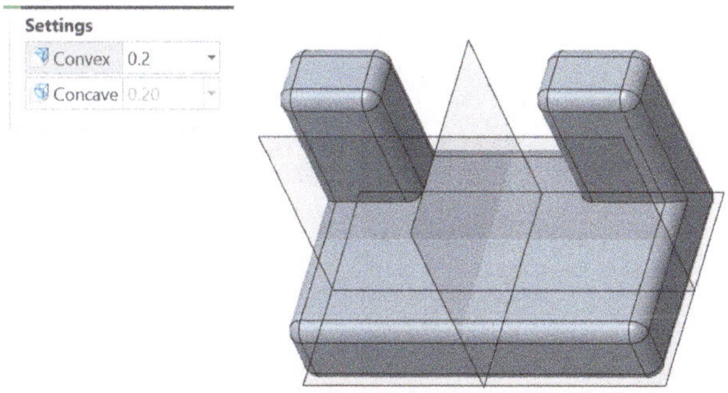

After selecting the appropriate option, enter the desired radius values in the **Radius** boxes next to each option. Next, click **OK** to create the rounds.

The Edge Chamfer command

The **Edge Chamfer** and **Round** commands are commonly used to break sharp edges. The difference is that the **Edge Chamfer** command adds a bevel face to the model. A chamfer is also a placed feature.

1. On the ribbon, click **Model > Engineering > Chamfer**.
2. On the **Edge Chamfer** dashboard, select the chamfer mode from the drop-down. You can select **D x D, D1 x D2, Angle x D, 45 x D, O x O,** or **O1 x O2**.

The **D x D** option defines the chamfer size by using a single distance value.

The **D1 x D2** option defines the chamfer size by using vertical and horizontal distances.

The **Angle x D** option defines the chamfer size by using angle and distance values

The **45 x D** option defines the chamfer size by using the distance specified at a 45-degree angle. You can use this type only for perpendicular faces.

3. If you select **Angle x D**, then type-in the angle and distance values of the chamfer.
4. Click on the edge(s) to chamfer.
5. Click the green check.

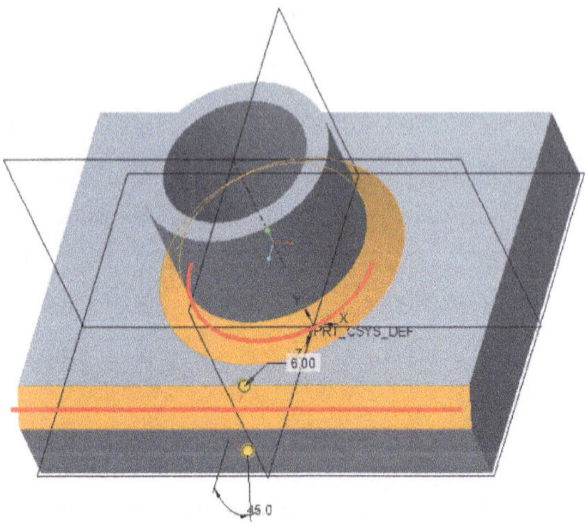

Draft

When creating cast or plastic parts, you are often required to add a draft on them so that they can be molded. A draft is an angle or taper applied to parts' faces to make it easier to remove them from a mold.

1. On the ribbon, click **Model > Engineering > Draft**.
2. Press the Ctrl key and click on the faces to draft. You can select all the tangentially connected faces by clicking on any single face.
3. On the Dashboard, click in the **Draft hinges** box and select a flat face or plane. It defines the draft hinge. The draft angle will be measured with reference to this face.

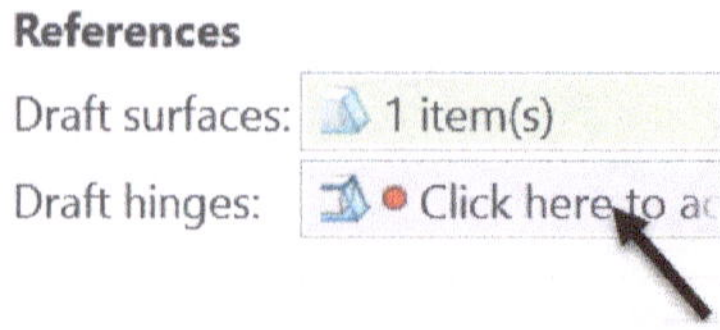

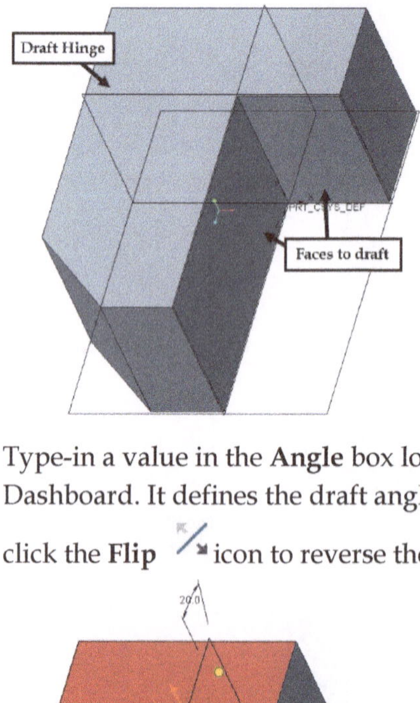

4. Type-in a value in the **Angle** box located on the Dashboard. It defines the draft angle. You can click the **Flip** icon to reverse the draft angle.

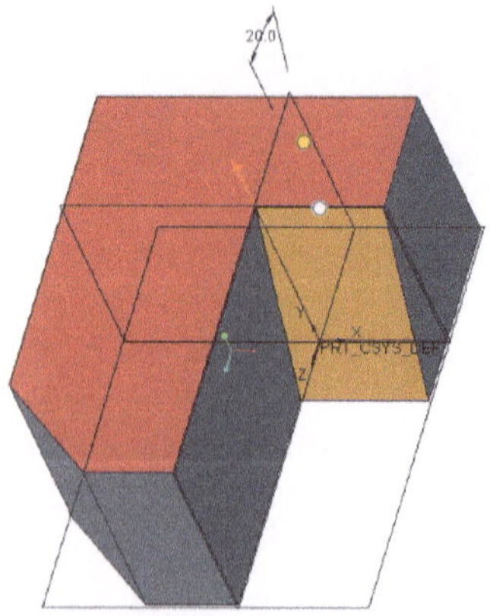

5. Click in the **Draft hinges** box and select the plane located at an offset from the bottom face.

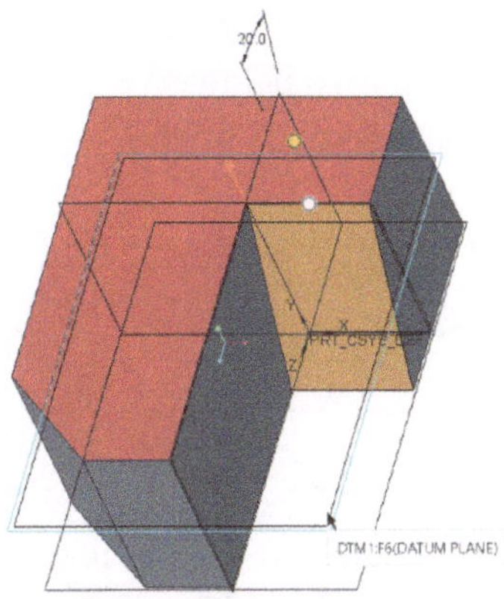

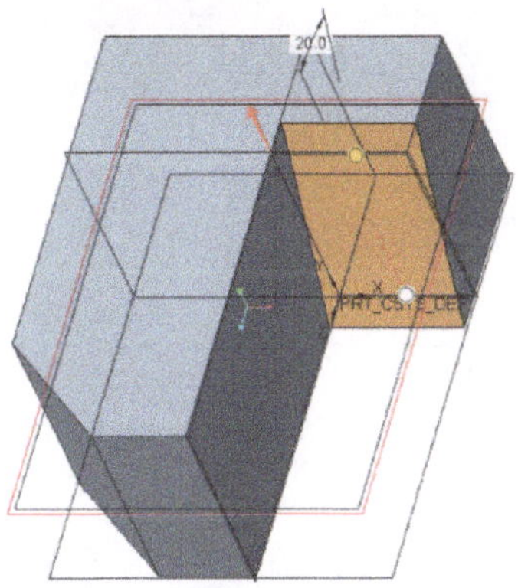

Split Drafts

If you want to add a draft-only up to a certain height, then create a plane at that height. Activate the **Draft** command and select the faces to draft.

Click in the **Draft hinges** box and select the plane. On the Dashboard, click the **Split** tab and select **Split options > Split by draft hinge**. Select the plane perpendicular to the draft faces.

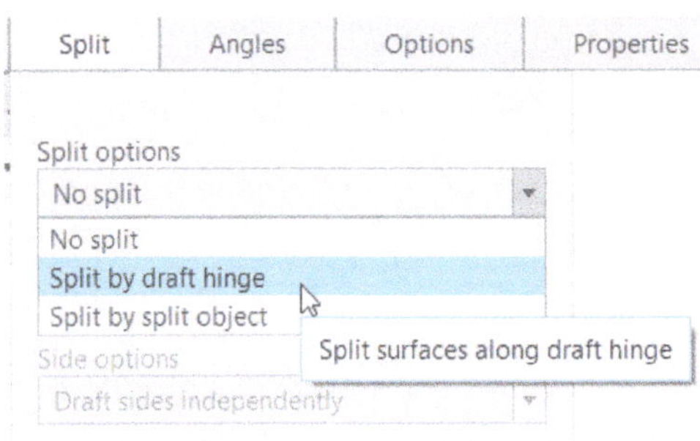

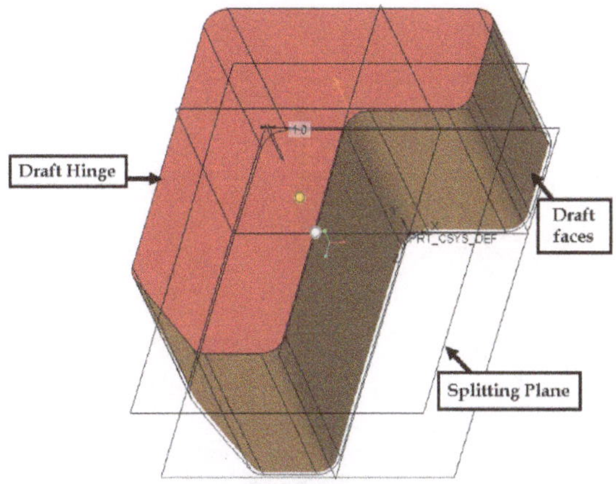

On the **Split** tab, select **Side options > Draft sides independently**. Enter different draft angles for each side.

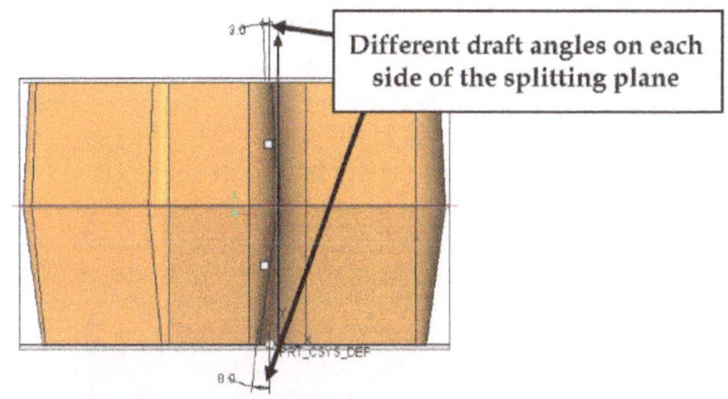

On the **Split** tab, select **Side options > Draft sides dependently**. Enter a single draft angle for both sides about a splitting plane.

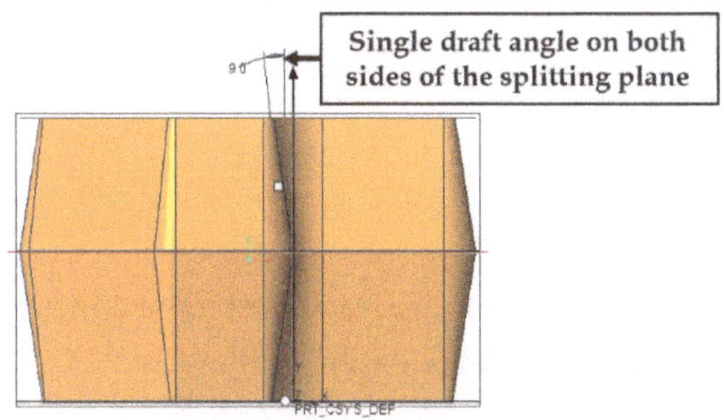

On the **Split** tab, select **Side options > Draft first side only**. Draft the first side only.

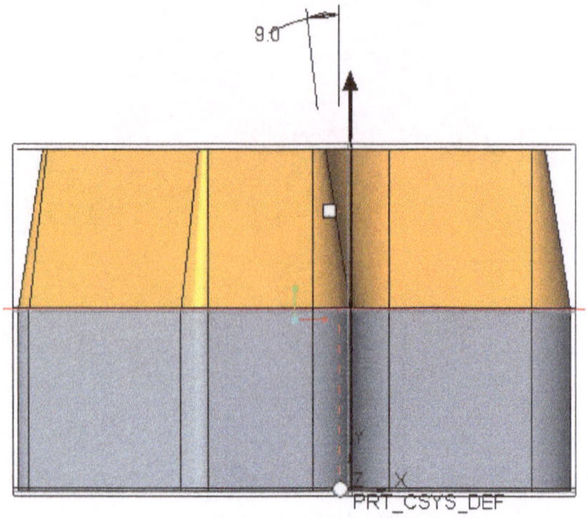

On the **Split** tab, select **Side options > Draft second side only**. Draft the second side only.

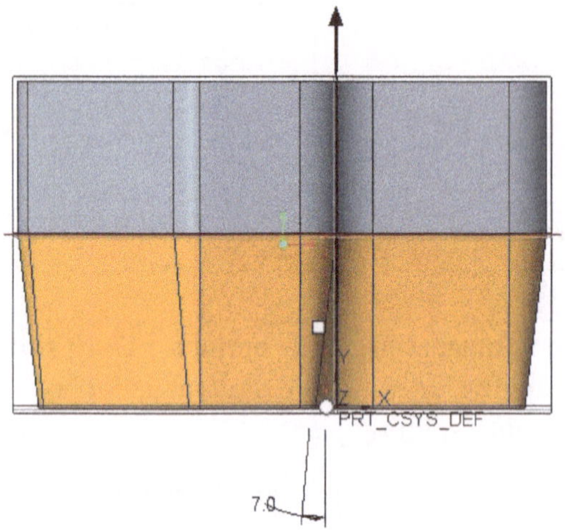

Variable Pull Direction Draft

This command creates a variable pull direction draft.

1. On the ribbon, click **Model > Engineering > Draft > Variable Pull Direction Draft** .

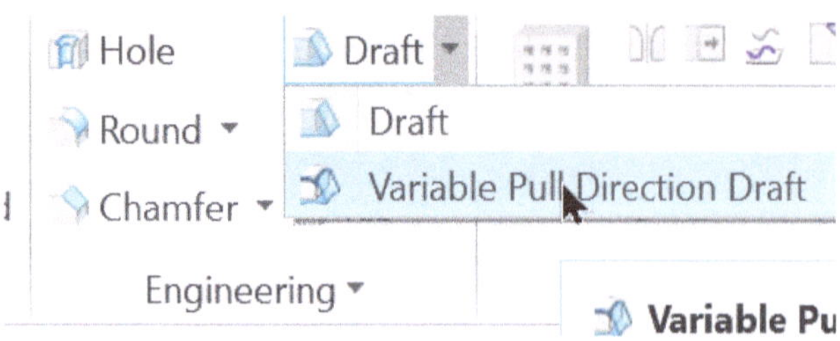

2. Click on the top face to define the draft reference.
3. On the Dashboard, click in the **Draft hinges** box and select the edge, as shown below.
4. Type-in a value in the **Angle** box on the Dashboard.

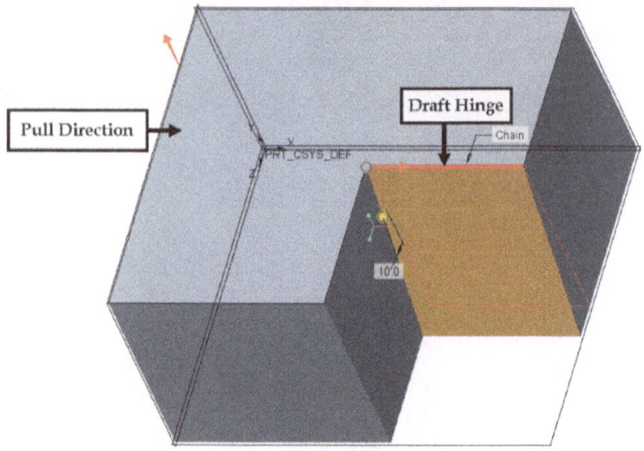

5. On the Dashboard, click the **References** tab and click the **New set** option.
6. Select a new draft hinge and type-in a new angle value.

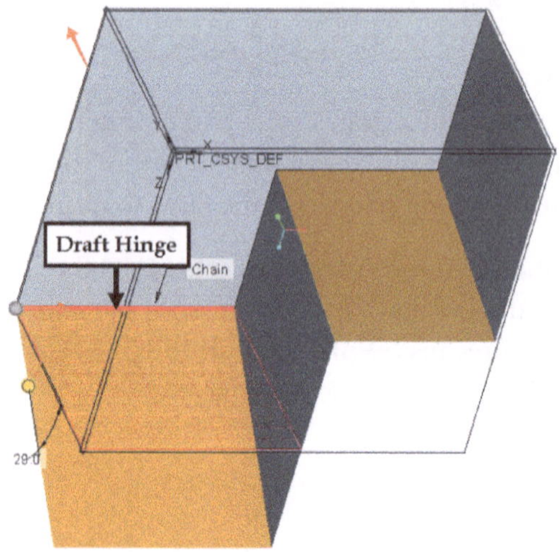

7. Click the green check to complete the feature.

Shell

The **Shell** command is another useful feature that can be applied directly to a solid model. It allows you to take a solid geometry and make it hollow. It can be a powerful and time-saving technique when designing parts that call for thin walls such as bottles, tanks, and containers. This command is easy to use.

1. You should have a solid part and activate this command by clicking **Model > Engineering > Shell** on the Ribbon.
2. Select the faces to remove.
3. Type-in the wall thickness in the **Thickness** box.
4. If you want to add different thickness to some faces, click the **Reference** tab on the Dashboard. Next, click in the **Non-default thickness** box, and then select the faces to add different thicknesses. You will notice that a thickness value appears in the Non-default thickness box. Double-click on the value and change it.

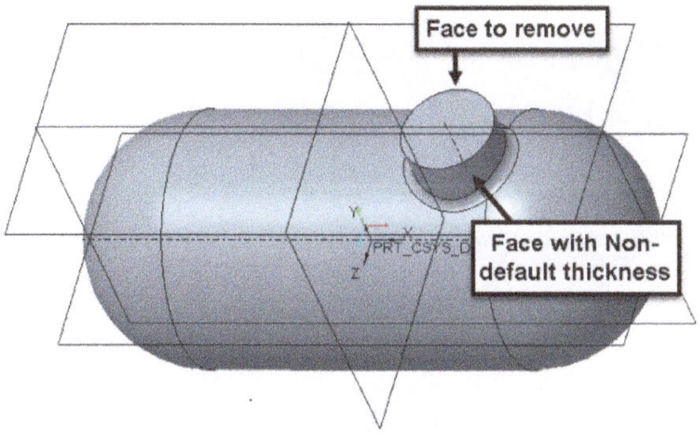

5. Click **OK** to finish the feature.

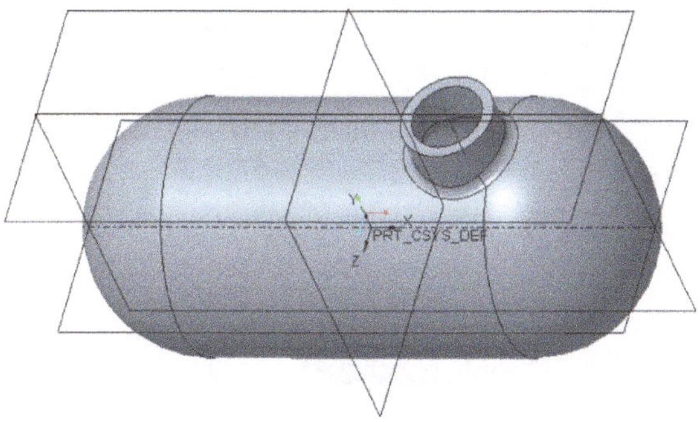

Suppose you want to shell the solid body without removing any faces, then simply type-in a value in the **Thickness** box without selecting any face. Next, click the green check. It creates the shell without removing any faces. Change the **Display style** to **Wireframe** or **Hidden Lines** to view the shell.

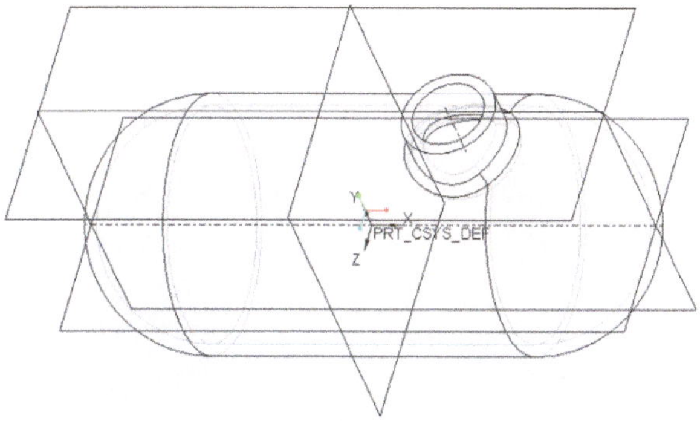

Profile Rib

This command creates stiffening ribs to add structural stability, strength, and support to your designs. Just like any other sketch-based feature, a rib feature requires a two-dimensional sketch.

1. On the ribbon, click **Model > Engineering > Rib** drop-down **> Profile Rib**.
2. Click on a datum plane to define the sketch location.

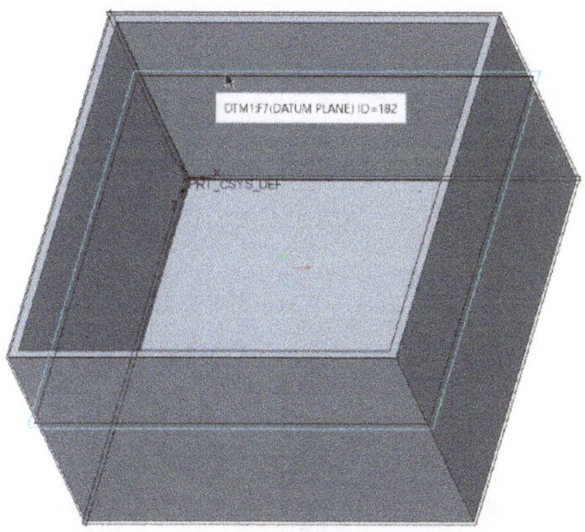

3. Create a sketch, as shown in the figure.

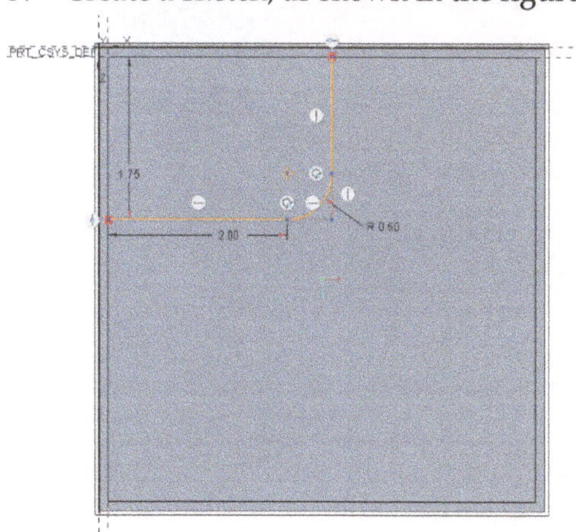

4. Click **OK** on the ribbon. A preview of the geometry appears.

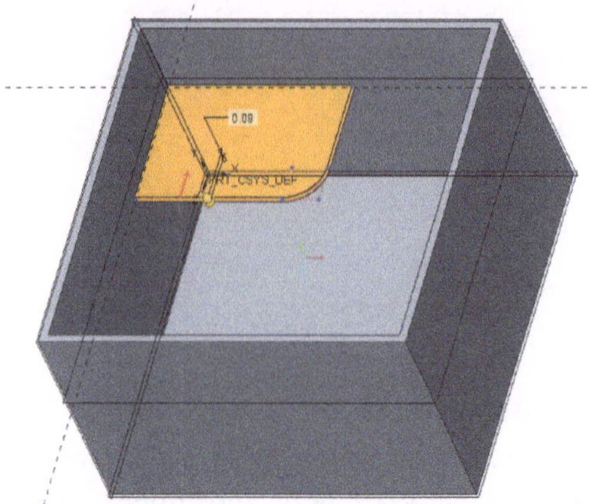

You can add material to either side of the sketch line or evenly to both sides using the **Flip** icon located on the Dashboard.

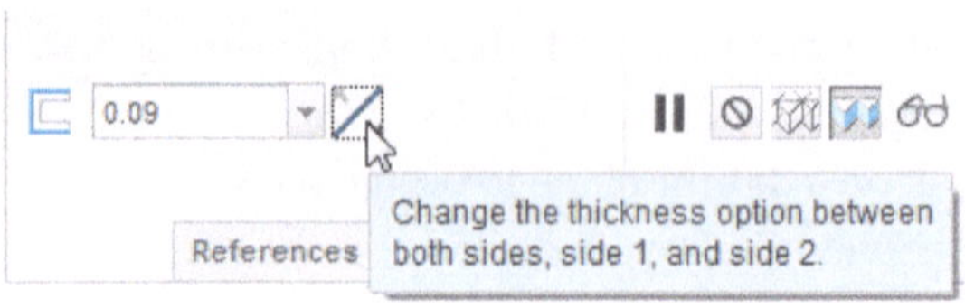

5. Click the **Flip** icon and see that the preview changes.
6. Type-in the thickness value of the rib feature in the **Thickness** box (or) drag the thickness handle.
7. On the Dashboard, click the **References** tab and click **Flip** to reverse the material side.

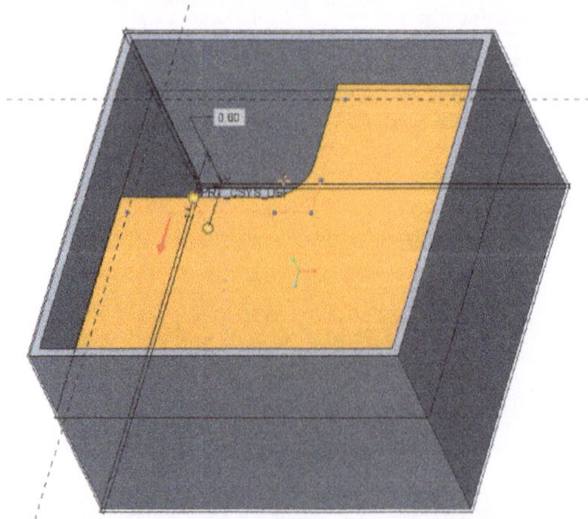

8. Again, click the **Flip** button on the **References** tab.
9. Click the green check to complete the feature.

Trajectory Rib

This command is similar to the **Profile Rib** command but creates ribs perpendicular to the sketch.

1. On the ribbon, click **Model > Engineering > Rib** drop-down **> Trajectory Rib**.
2. Click on the face to define the sketch plane.

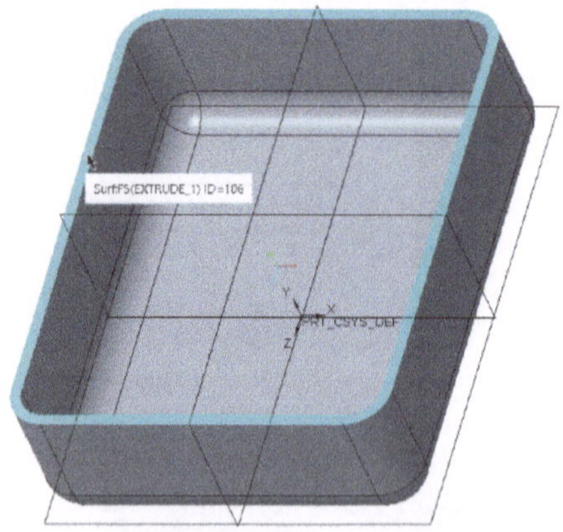

10. Create a sketch, as shown in the figure.

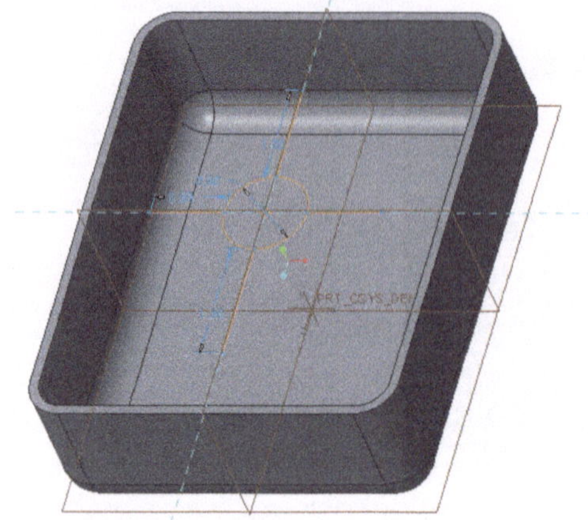

11. Click **OK** on the ribbon. A preview of the geometry appears.

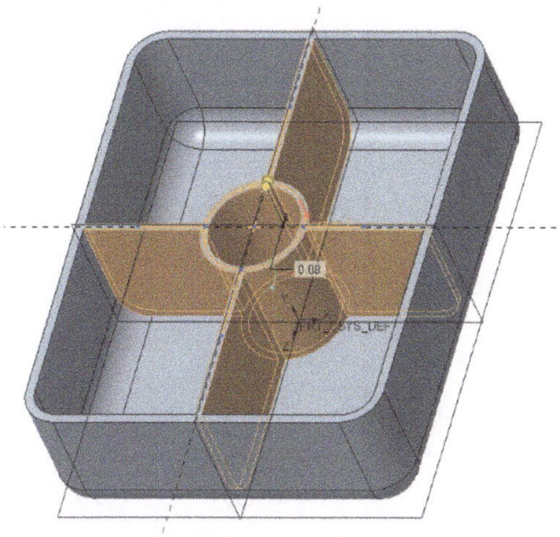

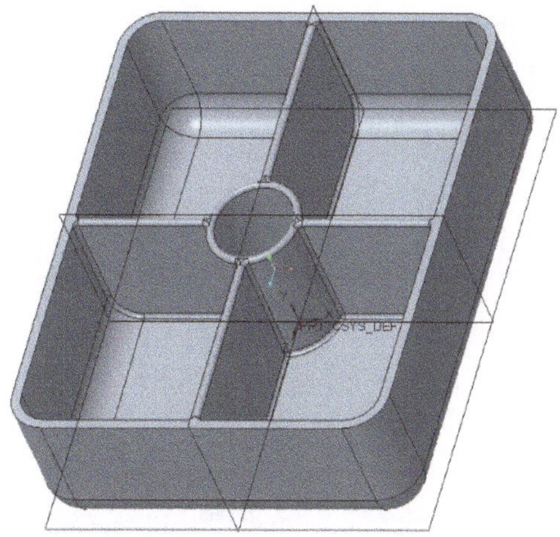

12. Type-in the thickness value of the rib feature in the **Width** box (or) drag the thickness handle.
13. On the Dashboard, click the **Add draft** icon.
14. Click the **Round internal Edges** icon.
15. Click the **Rounds Exposed Edges** icon.
16. On the Dashboard, click the **Shape** tab and modify the shape dimensions (thickness, draft angle, and round radius).

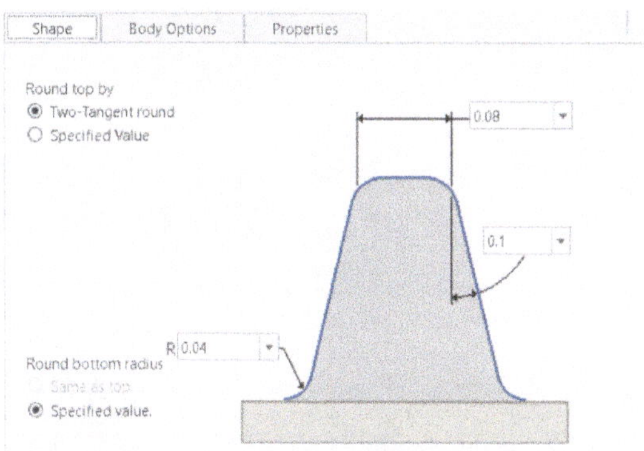

17. Click the green check to complete the feature.

Examples

Example 1

In this example, you will create the part shown below.

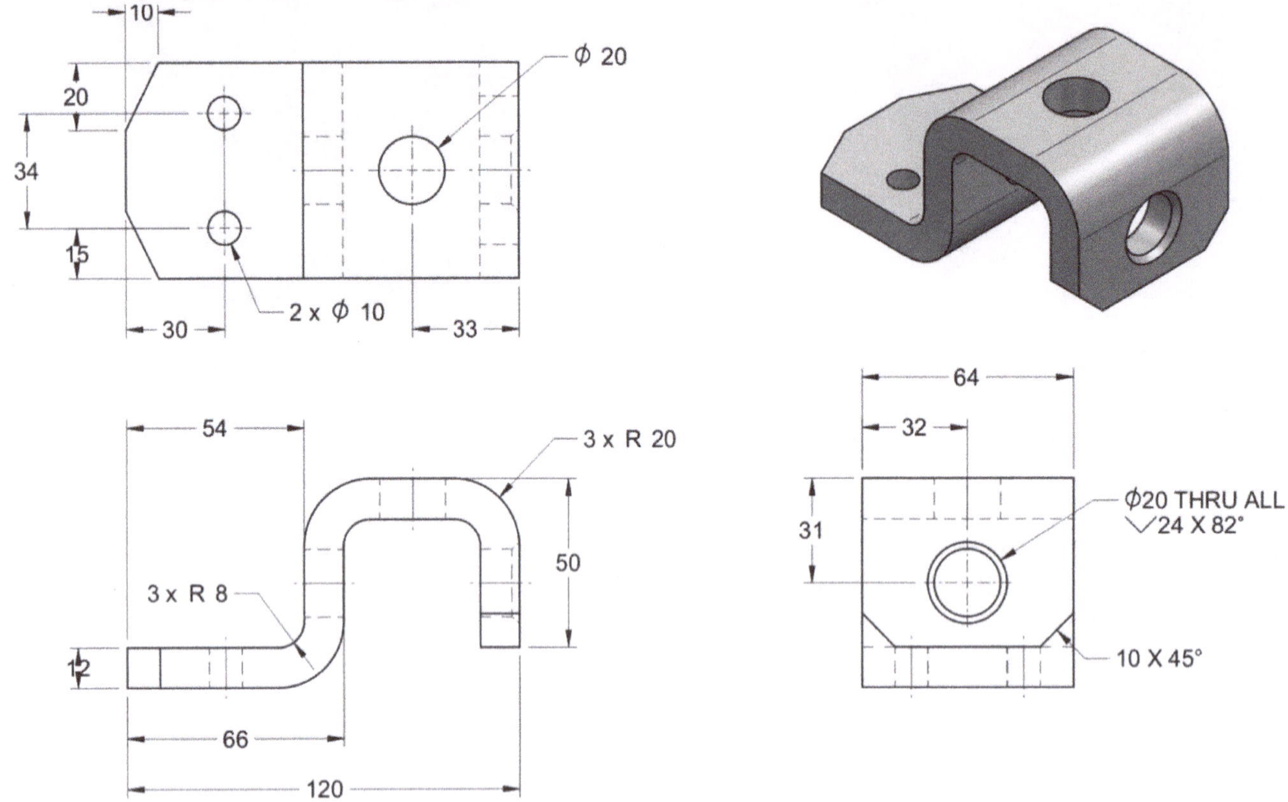

1. Start **Creo Parametric 11.0.**
2. Create the *Placed Features* folder and set it as the current working folder.
3. On the Quick Access Toolbar, click the **New** button.
4. On the **New** dialog, select **Types > Part**, and then type-in **C04-Example1**.
5. Uncheck the **Use default template** option and click **OK**.
6. On the **New File Options** dialog, select **solid_part_mmks_abs**, and click **OK**.
7. On the ribbon, click **Model** tab > **Shapes** panel > **Extrude**.
8. Click on the Front plane.
9. Draw the sketch and modify dimensions, as shown in the figure (refer to the **Modify** section of Chapter 2 to learn how to modify dimensions).

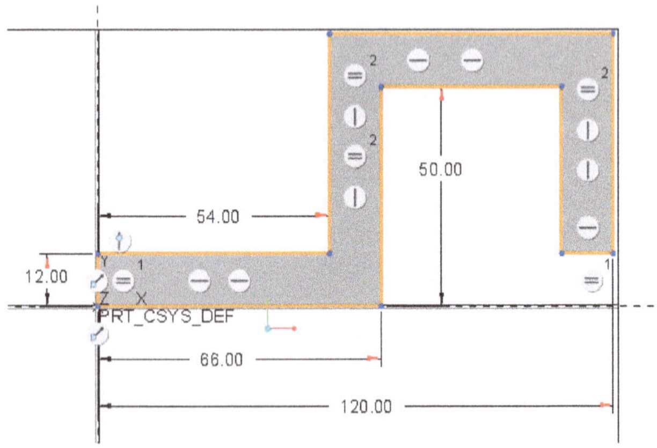

10. Extrude the sketch up to 64 mm depth.

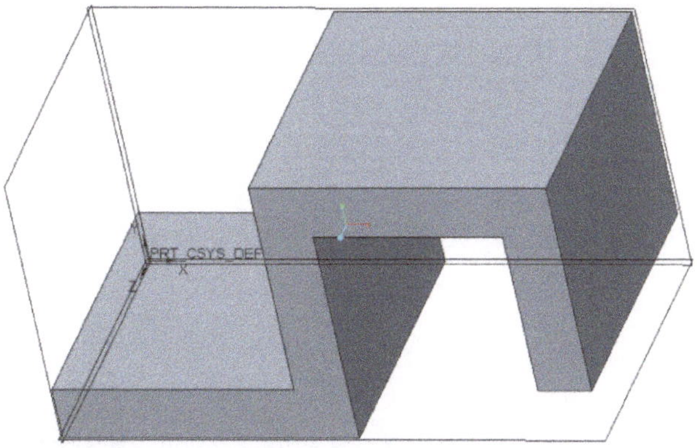

11. On the ribbon, click **Model** tab > **Engineering** panel > **Hole** .
12. Select the right-side face of the model geometry.

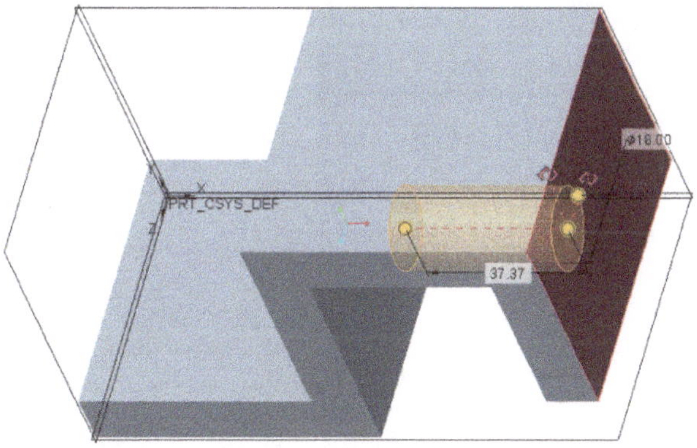

You will notice that there are two red handles attached to the hole. These handles are used to define the location of the hole.

13. Click on the horizontal red handle and align it with the vertical edge of the model.
14. Likewise, align the vertical red handle to the top horizontal edge.

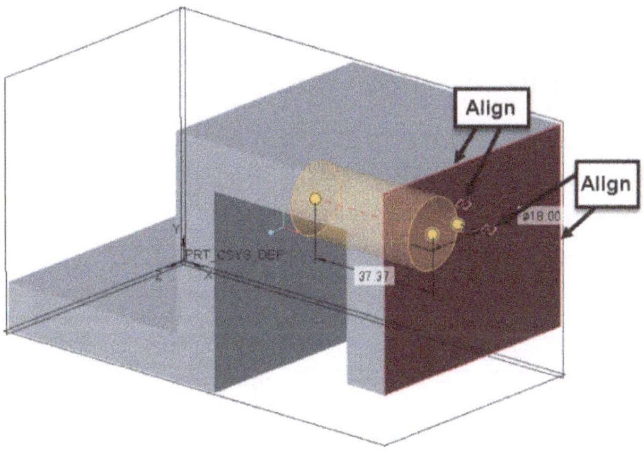

15. On the **Hole** dashboard, click the **Placement** tab.
16. On the **Placement** tab, type-in 31 and 32 in the vertical and horizontal offset boxes, respectively.

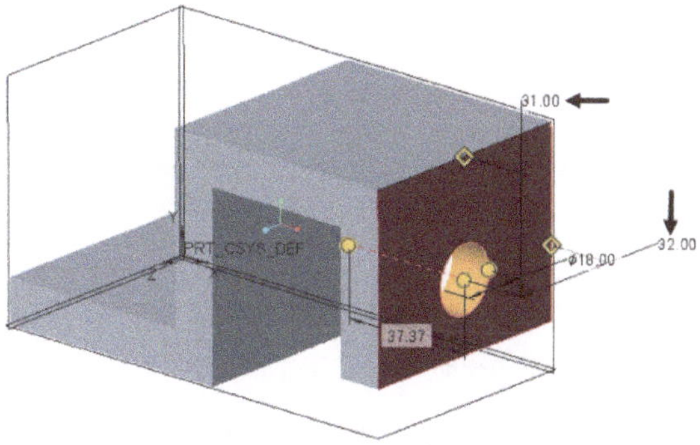

17. On the dashboard, click the **Standard** icon.
18. Click the **Countersink** button.
19. On the dashboard, set the hole standard to ISO.
20. Set the screw size to M20x1.5.
21. Select the **Through all** option from the drop-down.

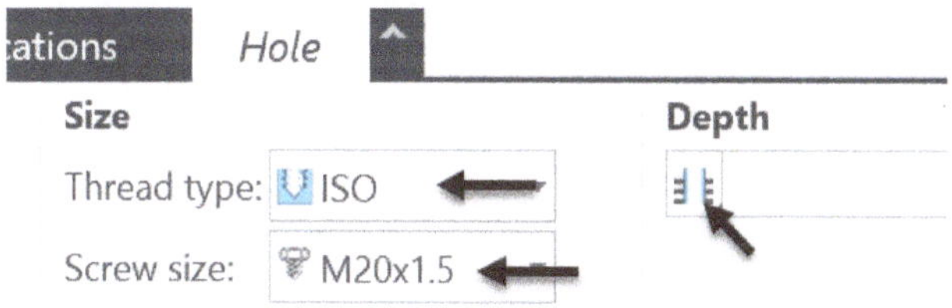

22. Click on the **Shape** tab and set the angle and countersink diameter to 82 and 24, respectively.
23. Select the **Thru Thread** option. It creates the thread throughout the hole.

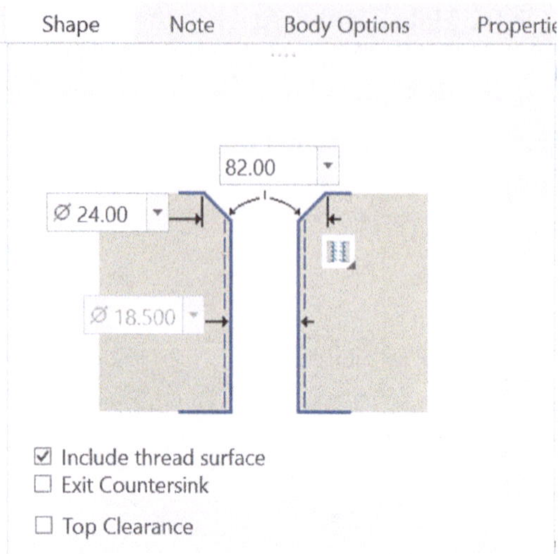

24. Click the green check on the dashboard to create the hole.

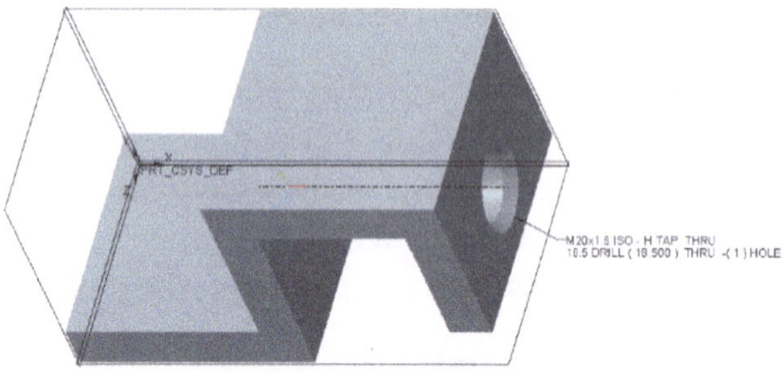

25. Activate the **Hole** command and click on the top face of the part geometry.
26. Align the red handles of the hole to the horizontal and vertical edges of the face.

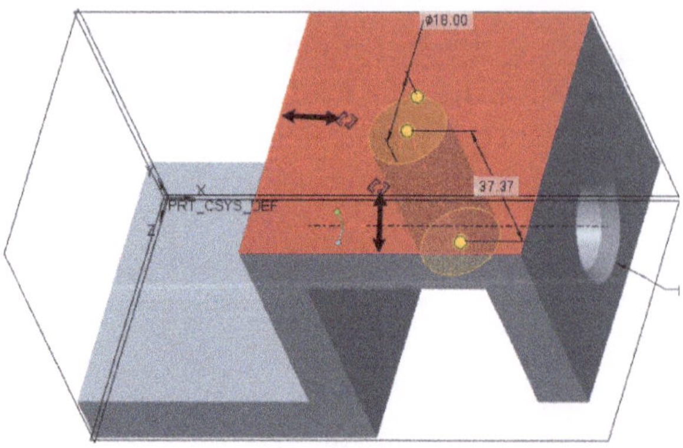

27. Change the horizontal and vertical offset distances of the hole to 33 and 32, respectively.
28. Type-in **20** in the **Diameter** box.
29. Select the **To Next** option from the drop-down.

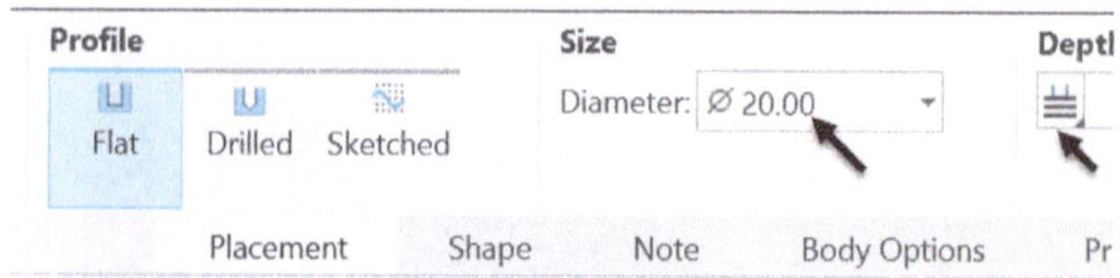

30. Click the green check on the dashboard to create the hole.

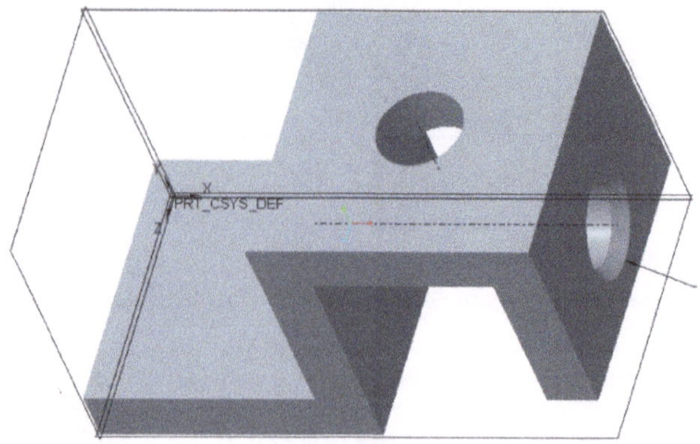

31. Likewise, create two more holes of 10 mm diameter each. Refer to the dimensions given at the starting of the example.

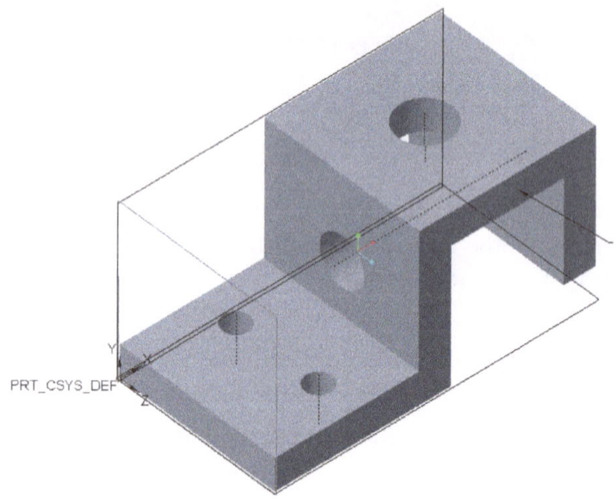

Chamfer Edges

1. On the ribbon, click **Model** tab > **Engineering** panel > **Chamfer**  .
2. On the **Edge Chamfer** dashboard, select **D1 x D2** from the drop-down.
3. Set the **D1** and **D2** values to **10** and **20**, respectively.
4. Press the Ctrl key and click on the side vertical edges as shown.

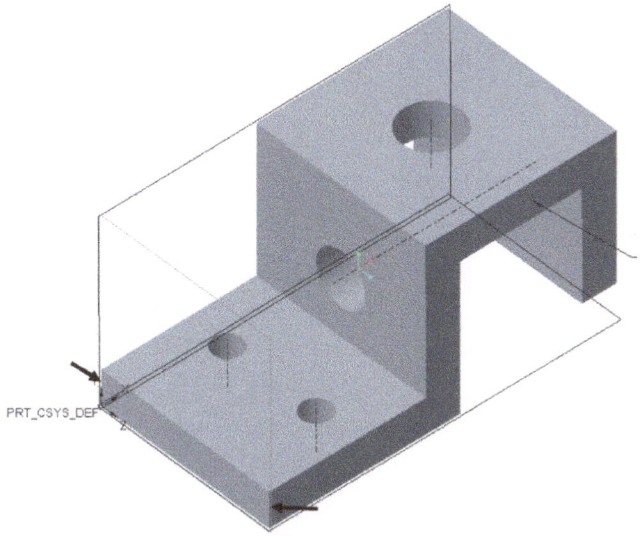

5. Click the green check to apply chamfers.

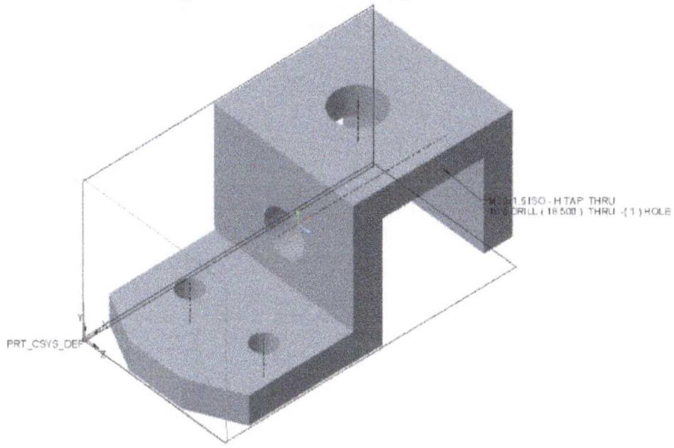

Round Edges

1. On the **Graphics** toolbar, click **Display Style** drop-down > **Wireframe**.

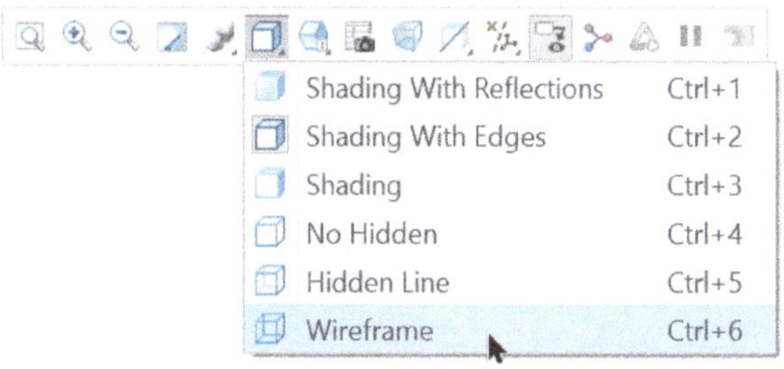

2. On the ribbon, click **Model** tab > **Engineering** panel > **Round** .
3. On the ribbon, type-in 8 in the **Radius** box. Press Enter.

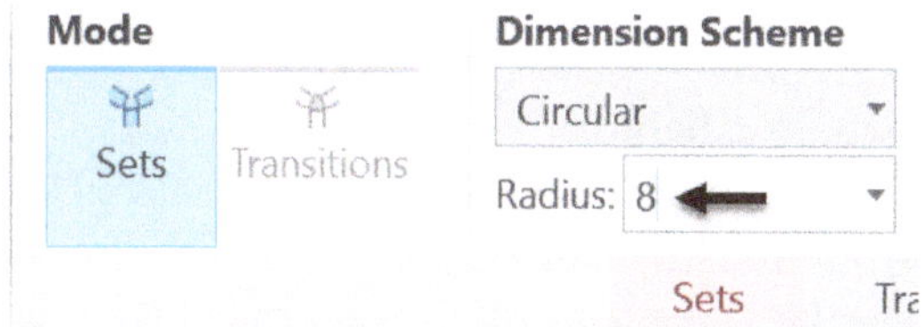

4. Click on the horizontal edges of the geometry, as shown below.

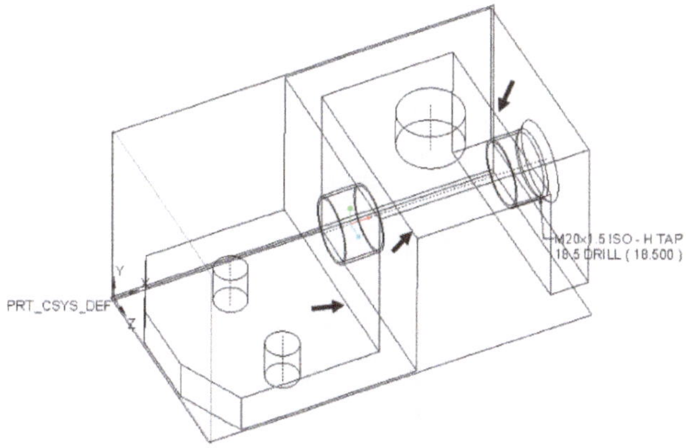

5. Click the green check to add rounds.
6. Activate the **Round** command and type-in 20 in the **Radius** box. Press Enter.
7. Click on the outer edges of the model, as shown below. Click the green check to complete the round feature.

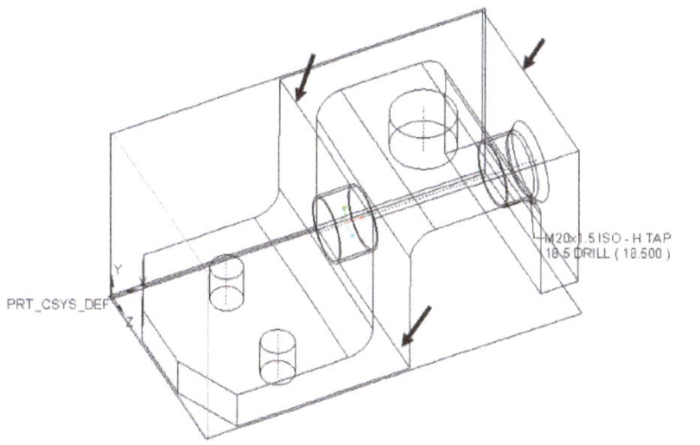

8. On the **Graphics** toolbar, click **Display Style** drop-down > **Shading**.

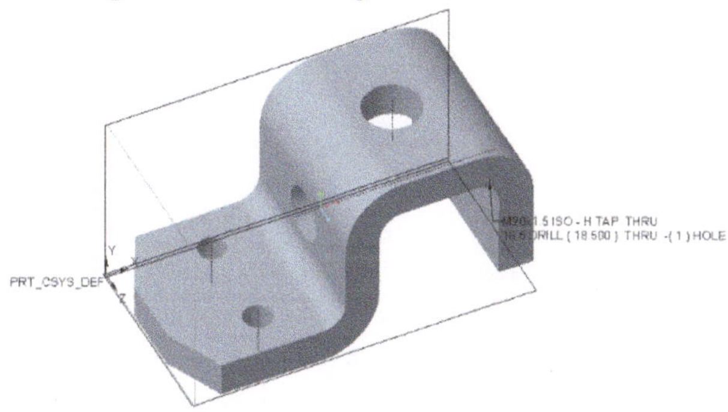

9. On the ribbon, click **Model** tab > **Engineering** panel > **Chamfer** .
10. On the **Edge Chamfer** dashboard, select **D x D** from the drop-down.
11. Set the **D** value to **10.**
12. Click on the lower corners of the part geometry.

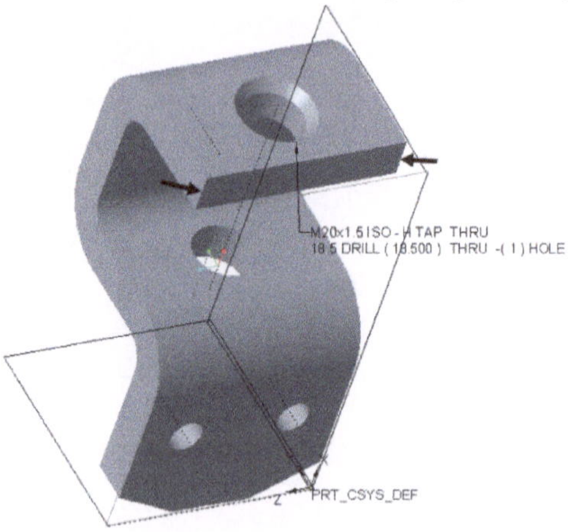

13. Click the green check to chamfer the edges.

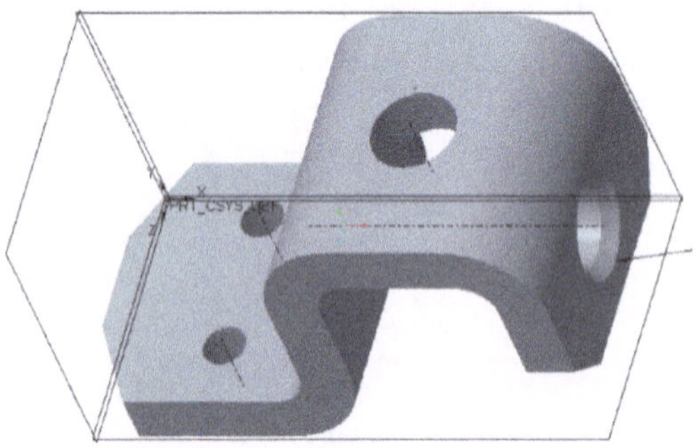

14. On the **Graphics** toolbar, click **Saved Orientations** drop-down **> Standard Orientation.**
15. Save and close the file.

Example 2

In this example, you will create the part shown next.

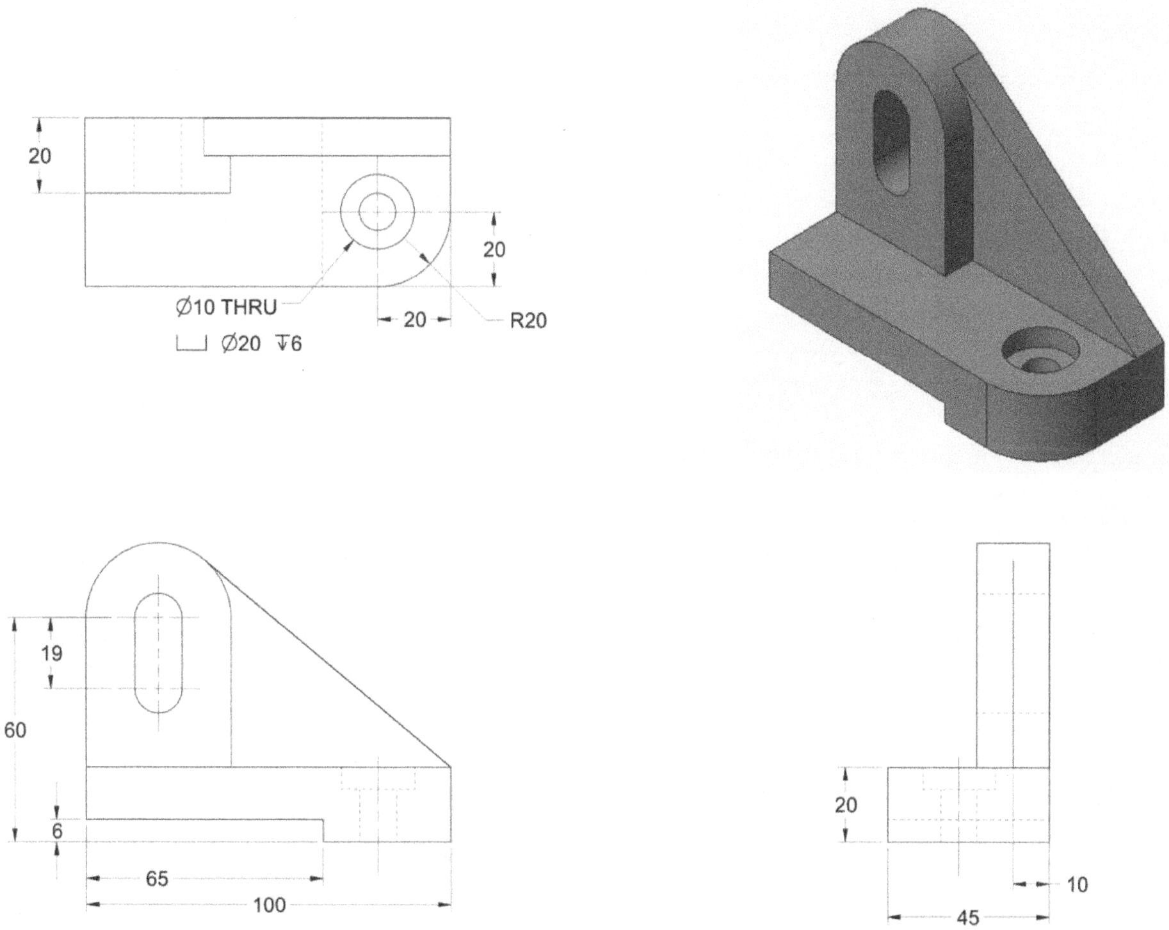

1. Start **Creo Parametric 11.0**.
2. Create the *Placed Features* folder and set it as the current working folder.
3. On the Quick Access Toolbar, click the **New** button.
4. On the **New** dialog, select **Types > Part**, and then type-in **C04-Example2**.
5. Uncheck the **Use default template** option.
6. Click **OK**.
7. On the **New File Options** dialog, select the **solid_part_mmks_abs** template. Click **OK** to start the file.
8. Activate the **Extrude** command and click on the top plane.
9. On the ribbon, click **Sketch** tab > **Sketching** panel > **Rectangle** drop-down > **Corner Rectangle**.
10. Select the origin point to define the first corner of the rectangle.
11. Move the pointer toward the bottom right corner, and then click to create the rectangle.
12. Modify the rectangle dimensions, as shown (refer to the **Modify** section of Chapter 2 to learn how to modify dimensions).

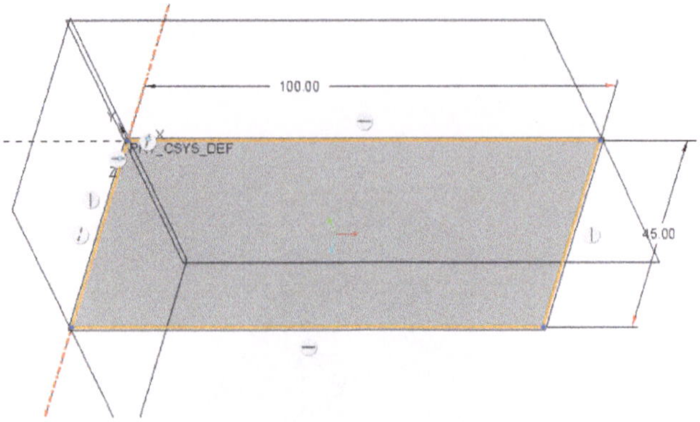

13. Extrude the rectangle up to a depth of 20 mm.

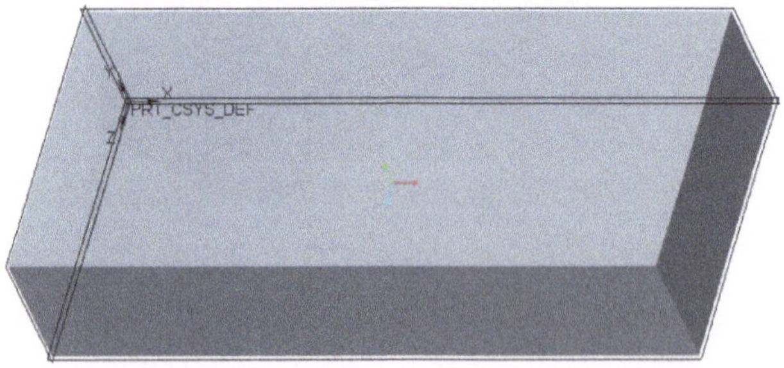

14. Activate the **Extrude** command, and then click on the Front Datum plane.

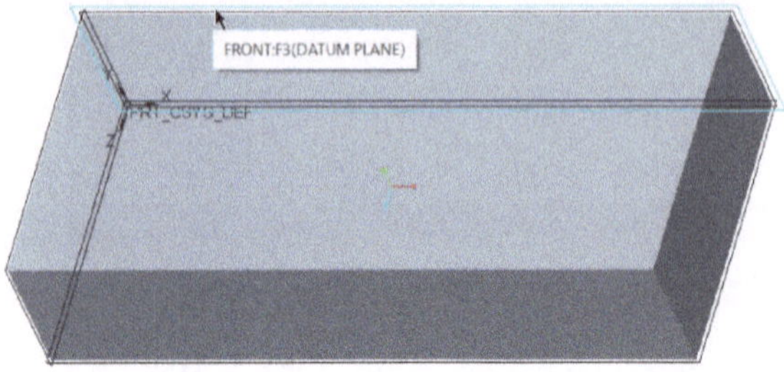

15. Click **Sketch View** on the Graphics toolbar.
16. Create the sketch, as shown.

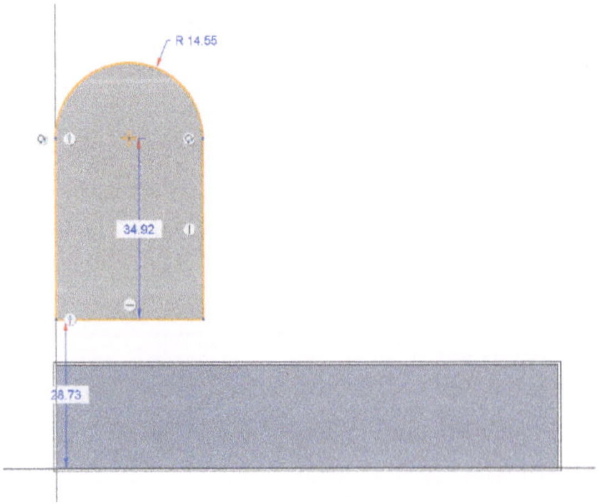

17. Make the horizontal line coincident with the top horizontal edge.
18. Modify the sketch dimensions (refer to the **Modify** section of Chapter 2 to learn how to modify dimensions).

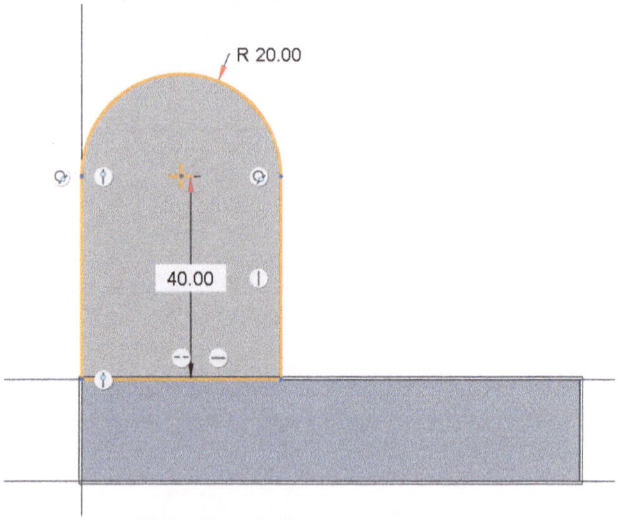

19. Click **OK** on the **Sketch** tab of the ribbon.
20. Type 20 in the **Depth** box of the **Extrude** Dashboard, and then click the green check.

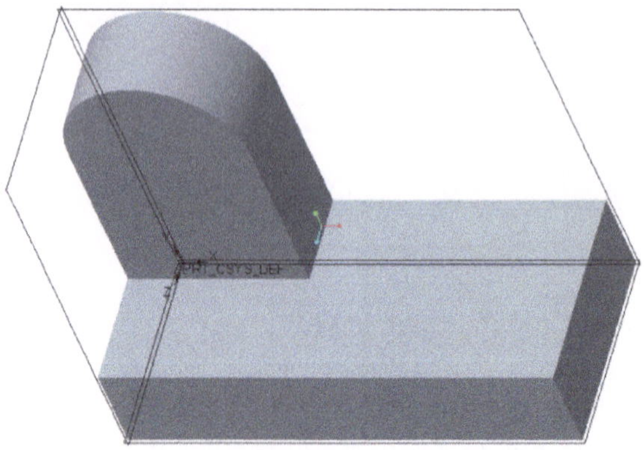

21. Activate the **Sketch** command and select the Front datum plane.
22. Click in the **Reference** box and select the right face of the model.

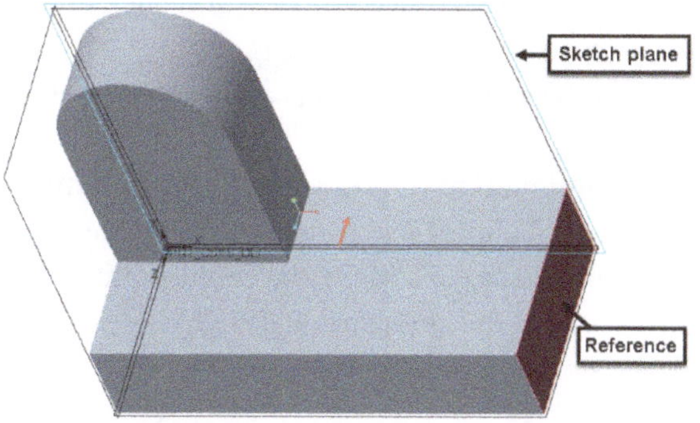

23. Click the **Sketch** button to start the sketch.
24. On the ribbon, click **Sketch** tab > **Setup** panel > **References** .
25. Select the top face of the first feature, right and curved faces of the second feature.

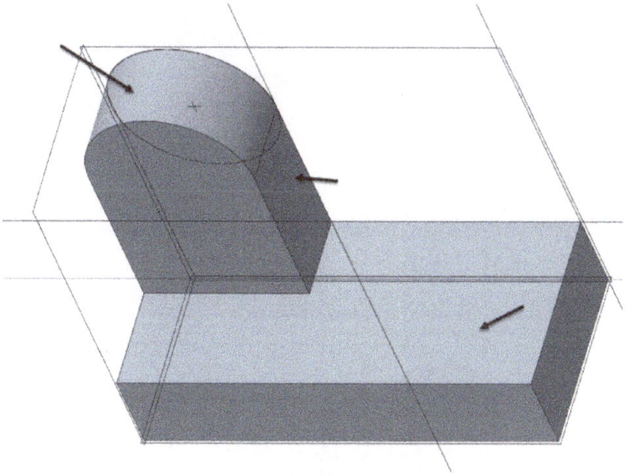

26. Close the **References** dialog.
27. Activate the **Line** command and click on the curved edge.

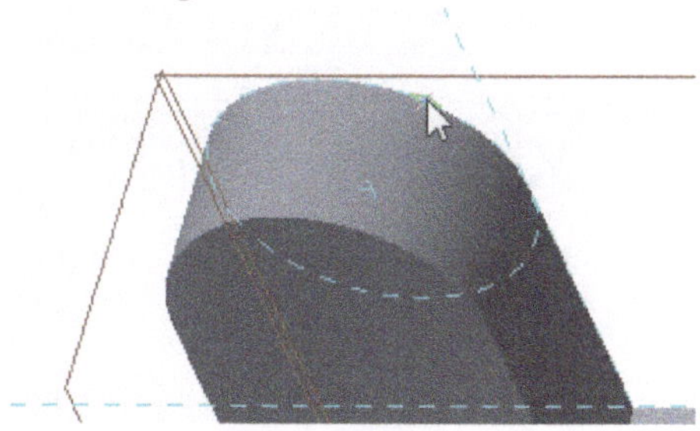

28. Move the pointer and click to create a line.

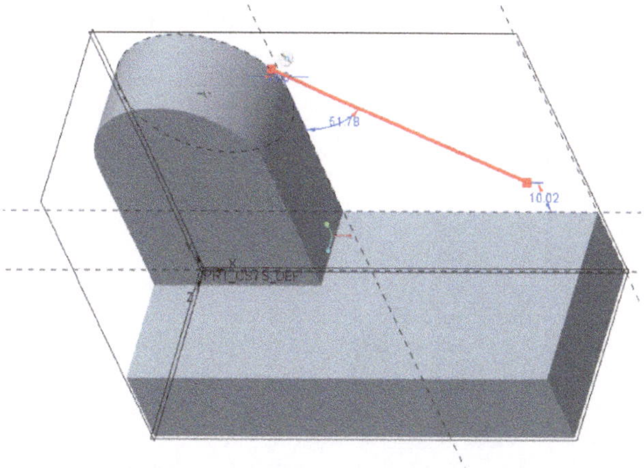

29. On the ribbon, click **Sketch** tab > **Constrain** panel > **Coincident** .
30. Select the bottom endpoint of the line.
31. Select the horizontal reference line; the line's endpoint is made coincident with the horizontal reference line.

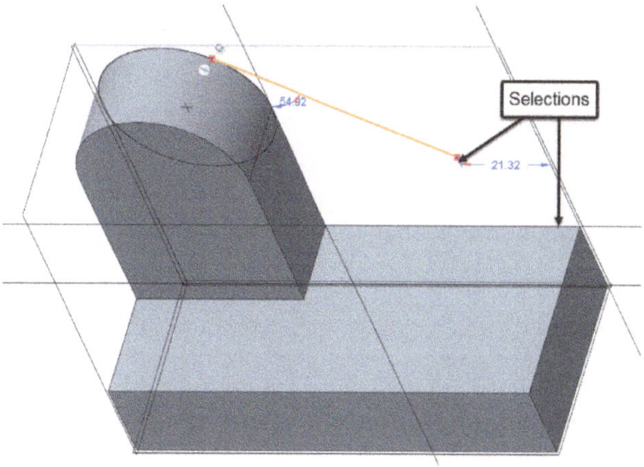

32. Likewise, make the endpoint of the line coincident with the vertical reference line.

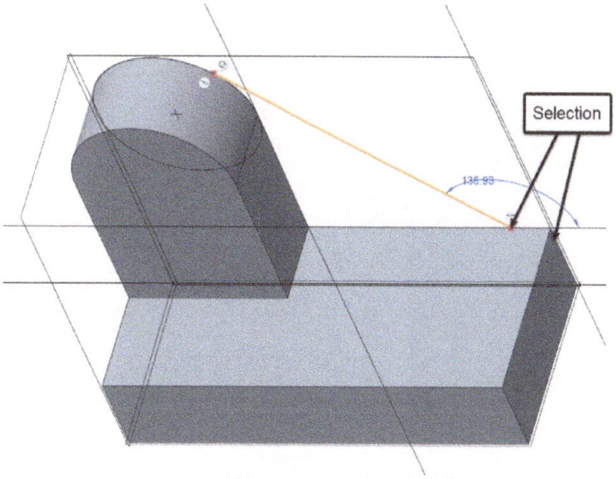

33. On the ribbon, click **Sketch** tab > **Constrain** panel > **Tangent**.
34. Select the line and the second feature's curved face; the line is made tangent to the curve face.

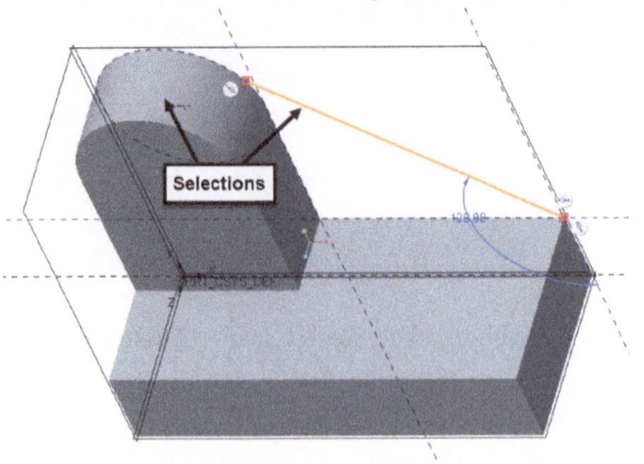

35. Click **OK** on the ribbon.
36. On the ribbon, click **Model** tab > **Engineering** panel > **Rib** drop-down > **Profile Rib**.
37. Select the sketch line, if not selected.
38. On the **Profile Rib** dashboard, click the **References** tab, and then click the **Flip** button. You can also click the arrow that appears on the sketch line. It changes the rib direction.

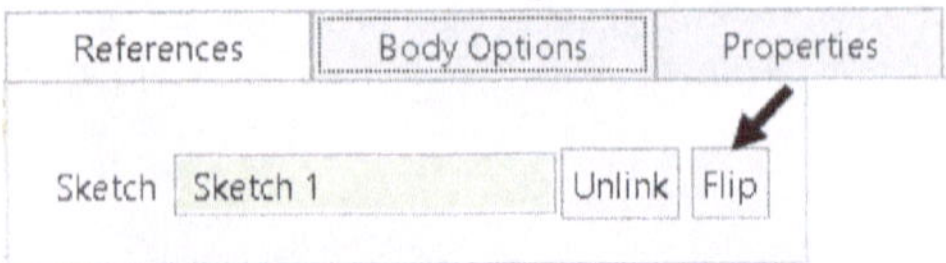

39. On the dashboard, type-in 10 in the Width box.
40. Click the **Change thickness option** button until the thickness side is changed, as shown.

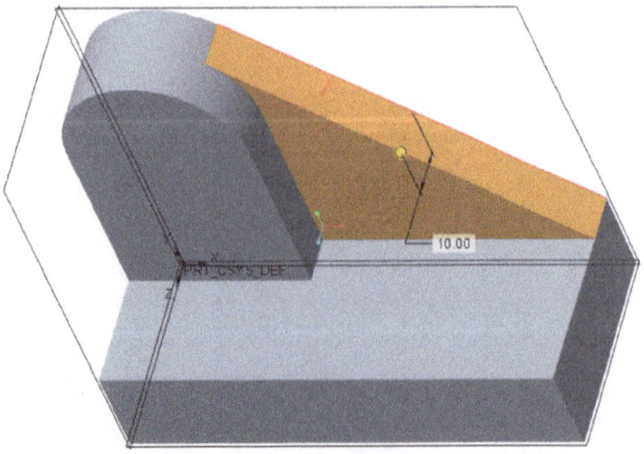

41. Click the green check to complete the rib feature.
42. Activate the **Extrude** command and click on the front face of the second feature.
43. Sketch the slot feature. You can use the **Palette** command to do this (refer to the **Palette** section of Chapter 2 to learn how to create predefined shapes). Make the centerpoint of the upper arc of the slot concentric to the centerpoint of the circular edge.

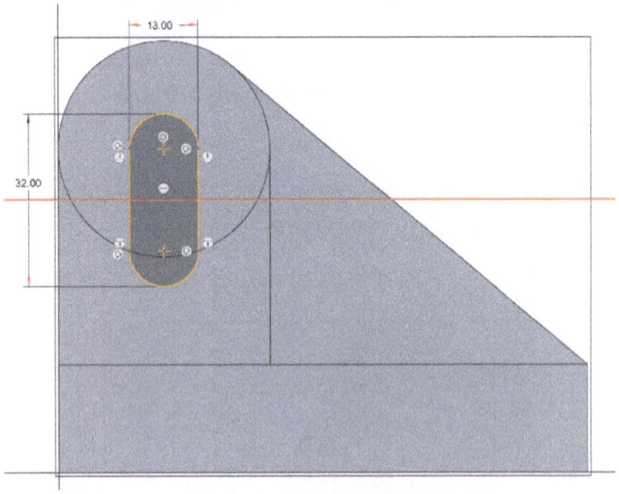

44. Exit the sketch and create the *Extrude cut* feature.

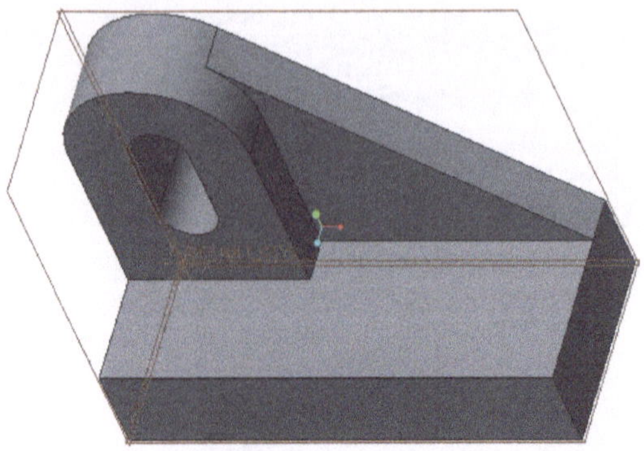

45. Create a sketch on the front face of the base.

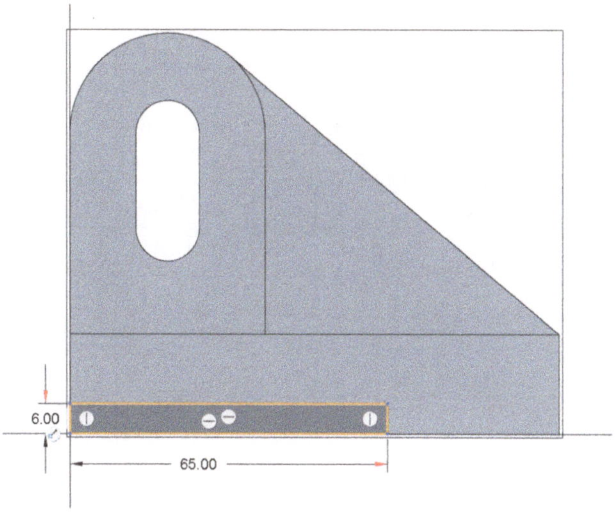

46. Create another *Extrude cut* feature throughout the model.

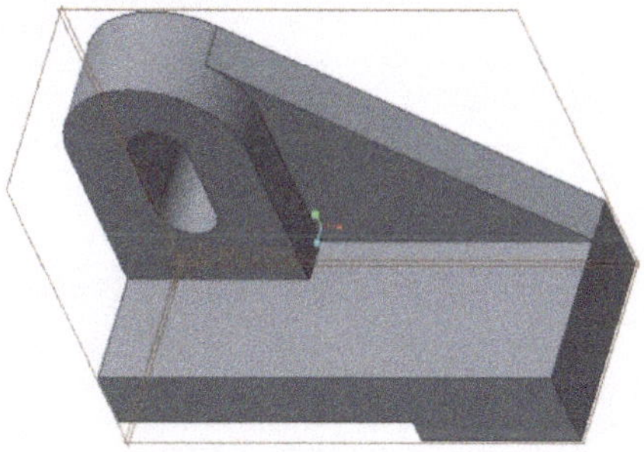

47. On the ribbon, click **Model** tab > **Engineering** panel > **Round** .
48. Select the lower right corner edge of the first feature.

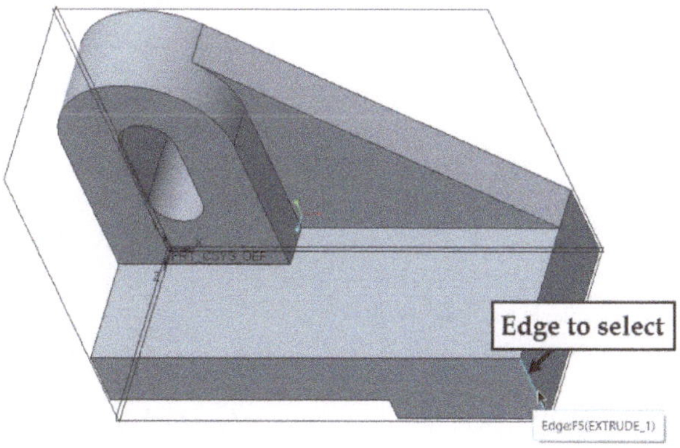

49. Type 20 in the **Radius** box on the **Round** dashboard.
50. Click the green check.

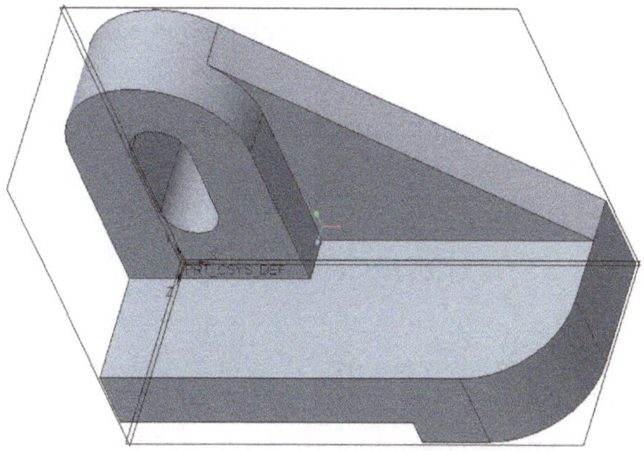

51. On the ribbon, click **Model** tab > **Datum** panel > **Axis** .
52. Select the round face of the model, as shown.

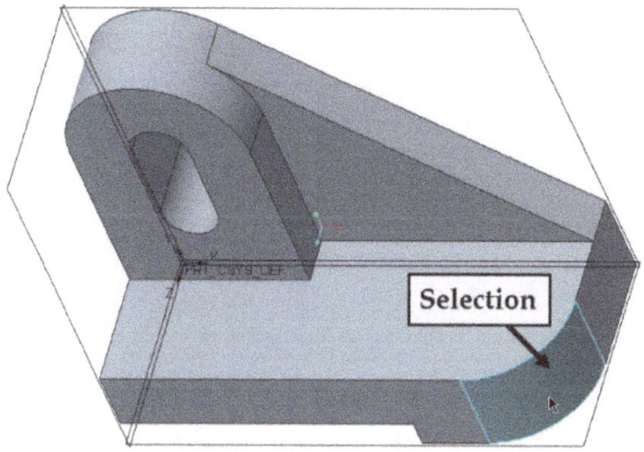

53. Click **OK** on the **Datum Axis** dialog to create the axis at the center point of the selected round face.
54. On the ribbon, click **Model** tab > **Engineering** panel > **Hole** .
55. Press hold the Ctrl key and then click on the first feature's top face and the axis.

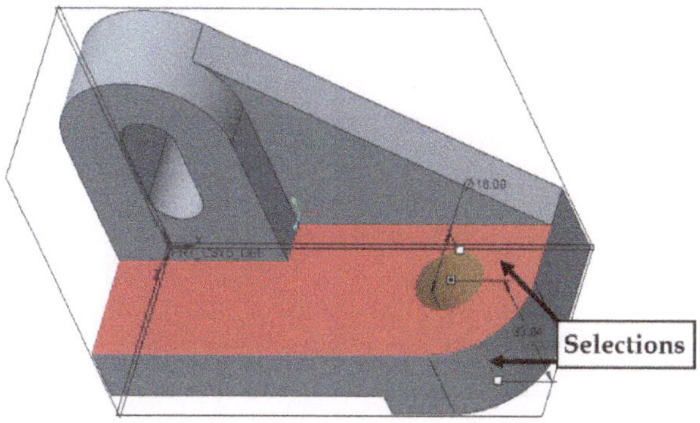

56. On the **Hole** dashboard, click the **Standard** icon.
57. Click the **Counterbore** button on the **Hole** dashboard.
58. Set the **Thread Type** to **ISO**.
59. Select **M10X1.25** from the **Screw Size** drop-down.
60. Select the **Through All** from the **Depth** drop-down.
61. Click the **Shape** tab on the **Hole** dashboard, and then specify the settings, as shown.

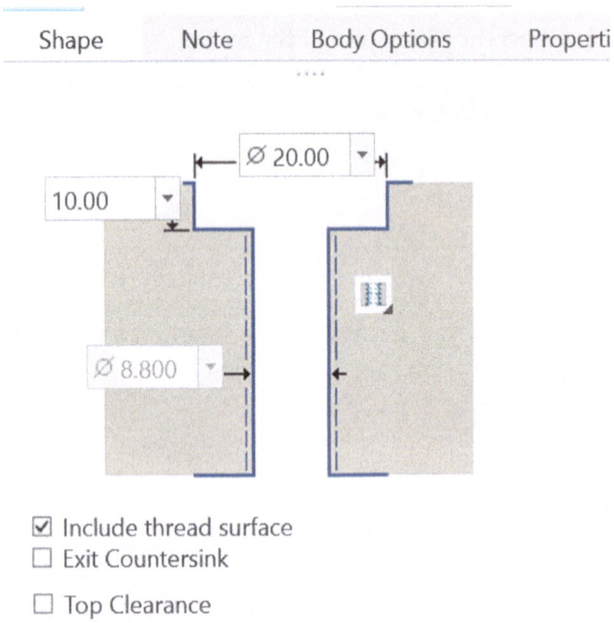

Example 3

In this example, you will create the part shown below.

62. Click the green check .

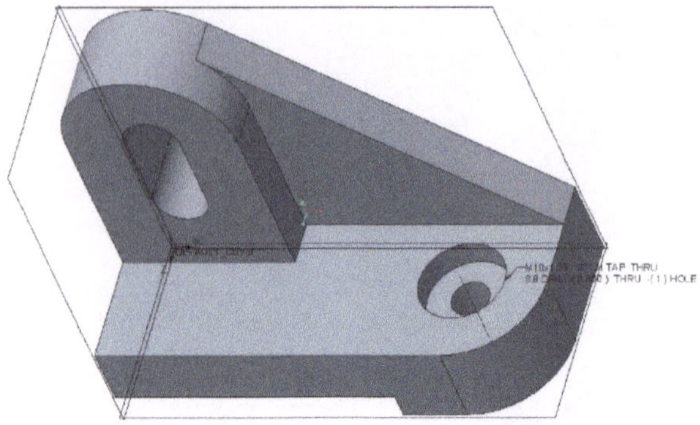

63. Save and close the file.

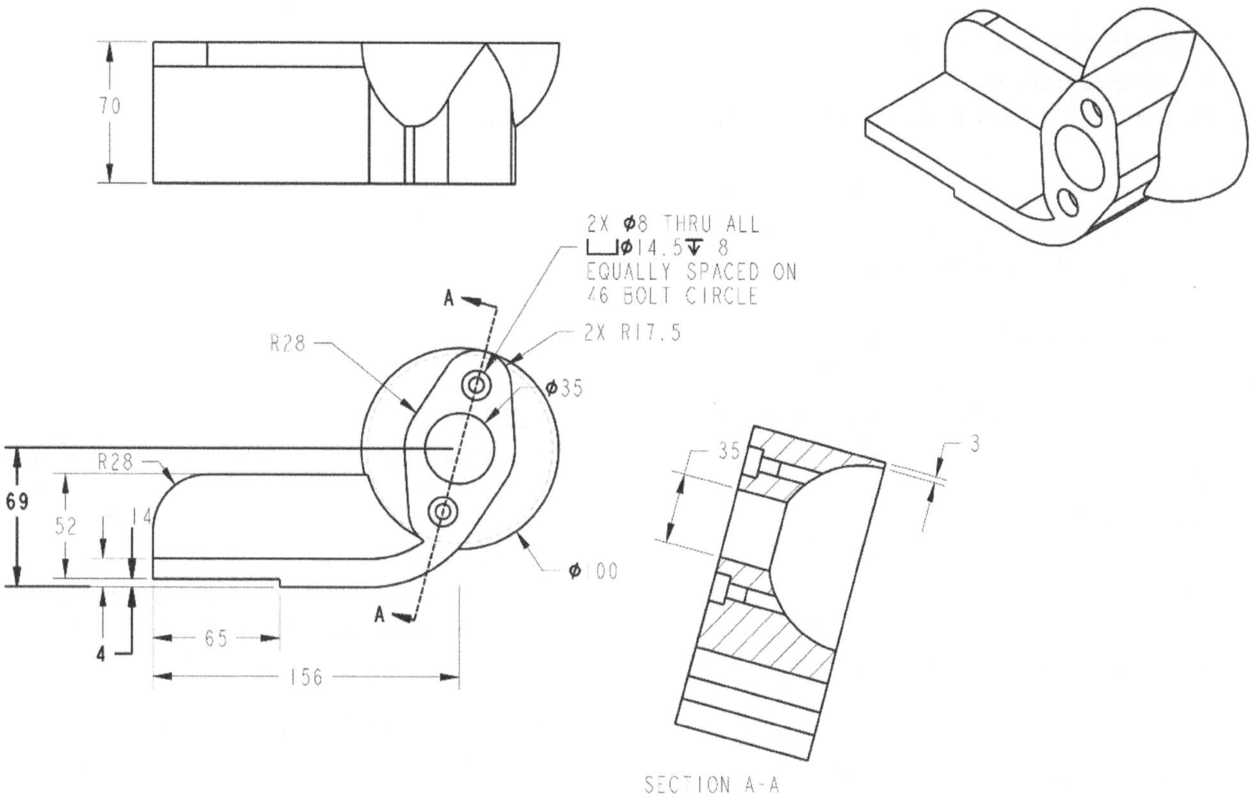
70
2X ⌀8 THRU ALL
⌴⌀14.5↧ 8
EQUALLY SPACED ON
46 BOLT CIRCLE
2X R17.5
R28
⌀35
A
R28
69
52
14
4
65
156
⌀100
35
3
SECTION A-A

Creating the First Feature

1. Start **Creo Parametric 11.0.**
2. On the Quick Access Toolbar, click the **New** button.
3. On the **New** dialog, select **Types > Part**, and then type-in **C05-Example2** in the **Name** box.
4. Uncheck the **Use default template** option and click **OK**.
5. On the **New File Options** dialog, select **mmns_part_solid_abs**, and click **OK**.
6. On the ribbon, click **Model** tab > **Datum** panel > **Sketch** .
7. Click on the Front plane.
8. Accept the default values on the **Sketch** dialog and click **Sketch**.
9. On the **Graphics** toolbar, click the **Sketch View** icon to orient the sketch plane parallel to the screen.
10. On the ribbon, click **Sketch** tab > **Sketching** panel > **Circle** drop-down **> Center and Point**.
11. Click on the origin point to define the centerpoint.
12. Move the pointer outward and click.
13. On the ribbon, click **Sketch** tab > **Sketching** panel > **Line Chain**.
14. Select the top and bottom quadrant points of the circle.
15. On the ribbon, click **Sketch** tab > **Editing** panel > **Delete Segment**.
16. Click on the elements to trim.

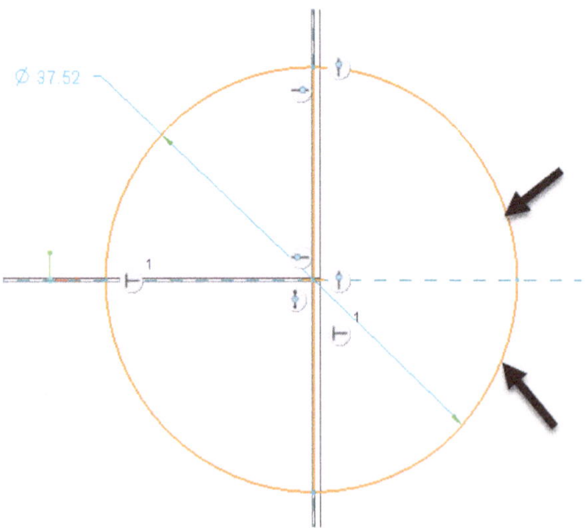

17. Add dimension to the vertical line, as shown.

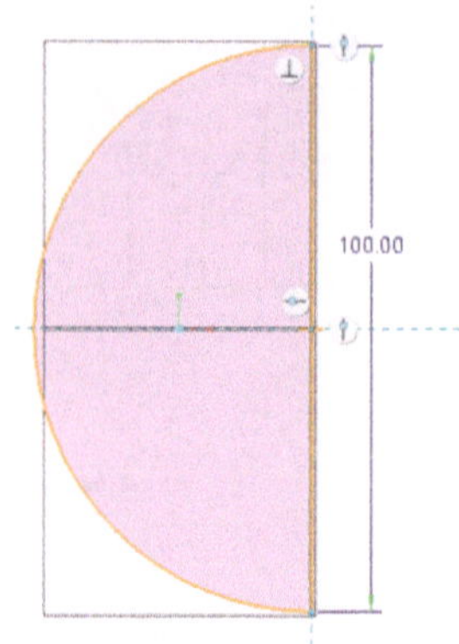

18. Click **OK**.
19. On the ribbon, click **Model** tab > **Shapes** panel > **Revolve** .
20. Select the sketch.
21. Click on the line passing through the origin.
22. On the **Revolve** dashboard, type-in 180 in the **Angle** box and press ENTER.
23. Click the green check to create the *Revolved* feature.

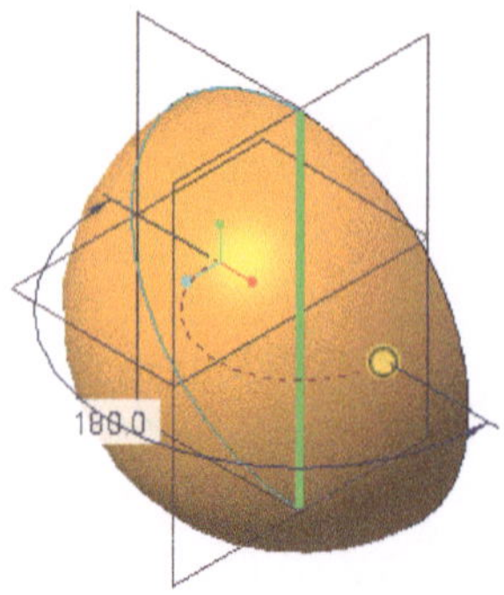

Creating the Extruded Features

1. On the ribbon, click **Model** tab > **Shapes** panel > **Extrude**.
2. Click on the Front plane.
3. On the **Graphics** toolbar, click the **Sketch View** icon to orient the sketch plane parallel to the screen.
4. Create three circles, as shown.
5. Apply the **Equal** constraint between the two circles, as shown.

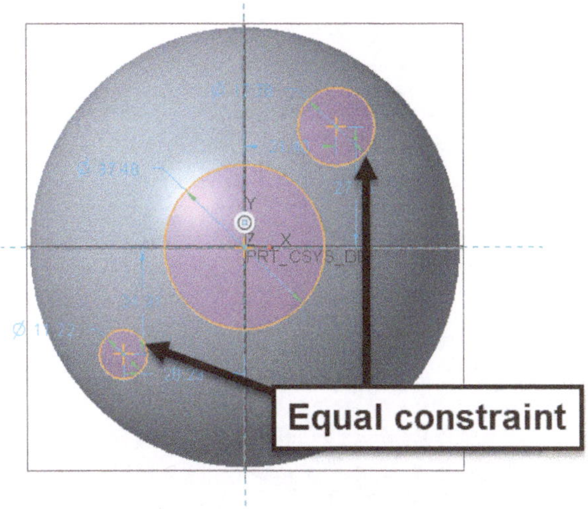

6. On the ribbon, click **Sketch** tab > **Sketching** panel > **Construction Mode**.
7. On the ribbon, click **Sketch** tab > **Sketching** panel > **Line Chain**.
8. Select the centerpoints of the two circles, as shown.

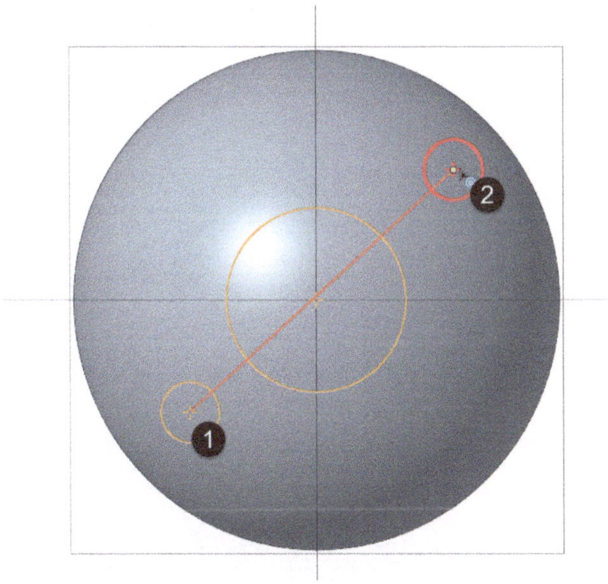

9. Press ESC.
10. On the ribbon, click **Sketch** tab > **Constrain** panel > **Mid-point**.
11. Select the centerpoint of the large circle.
12. Select the construction line.

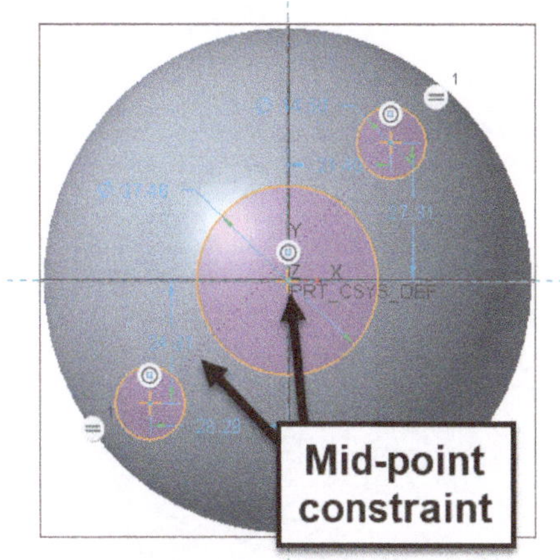

13. On the ribbon, click **Sketch** tab > **Constrain** panel > **Tangent** .
14. Select the small circle and the circular edge; the two ent6ities are made tangent to each other.

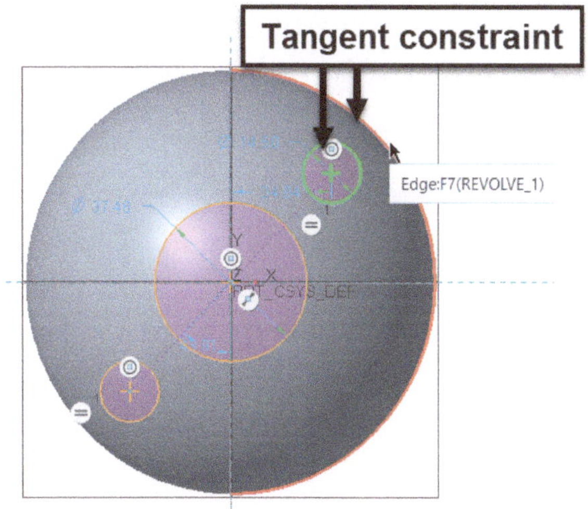

15. On the ribbon, click **Sketch** tab > **Dimension** panel > **Dimension**.
16. Create the dimensions, as shown.

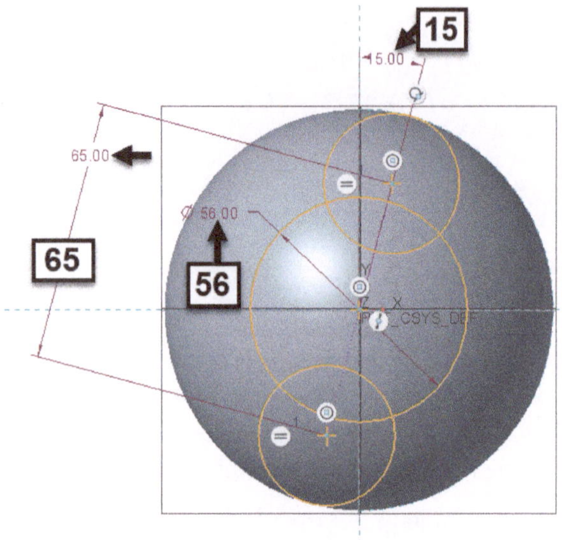

17. Deactivate the **Construction Mode** icon on the **Sketching** panel of the **Sketch** tab.
18. On the ribbon, click **Sketch** tab > **Sketching** panel > **Line** drop-down > **Line Tangent**.

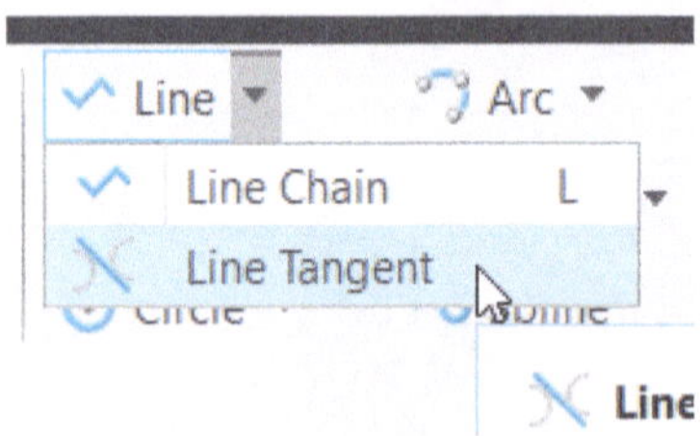

19. Select the two circles, as shown.

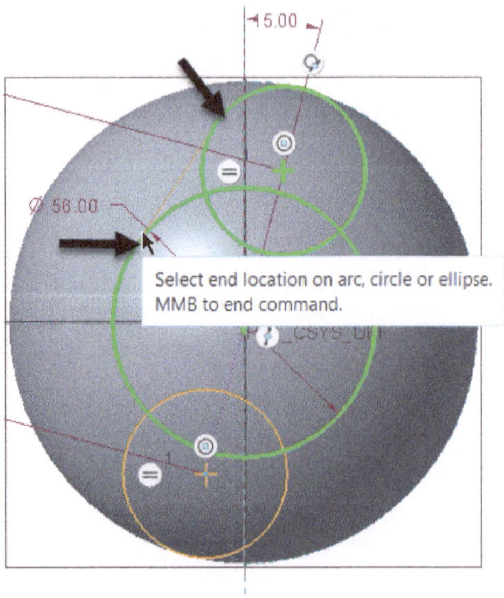

20. Likewise, create three more tangent lines, as shown.

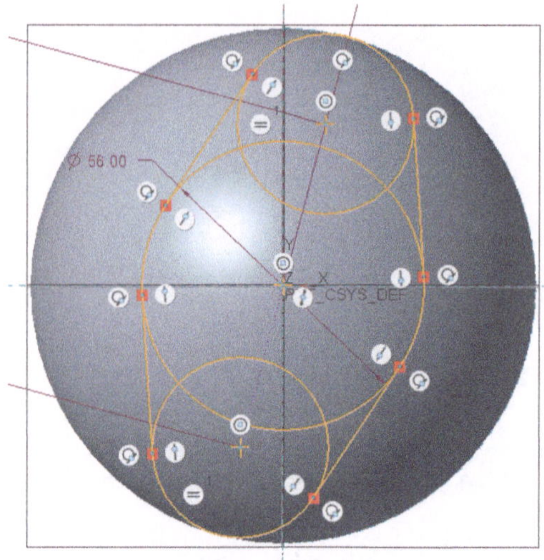

21. On the ribbon, click **Sketch** tab > **Editing** panel > **Delete Segment**.
22. Select the inner segments of the circles, as shown.

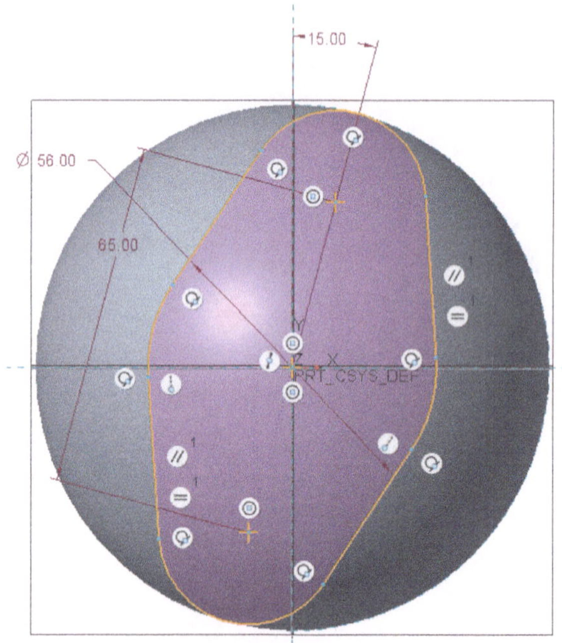

23. Click **OK** on the **Sketch** tab of the ribbon.
24. On the **Extrude** Dashboard, type **70** in the **Depth** box.
25. Click **OK** on the **Extrude** Dashboard.

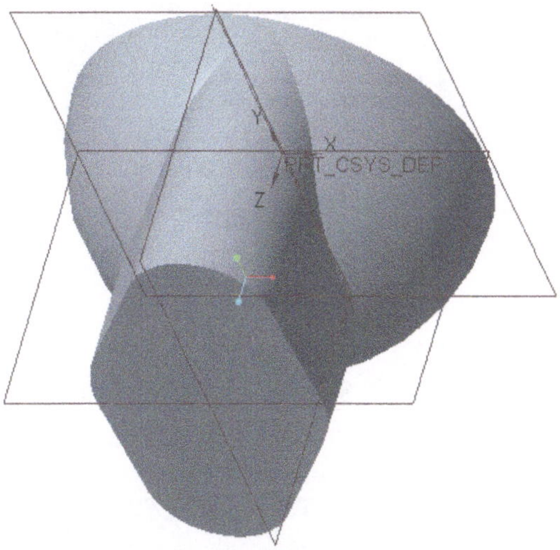

26. On the ribbon, click **Model** tab > **Shapes** panel > **Extrude**.
27. Click on the Front plane.
28. On the **Graphics** toolbar, click the **Sketch View** icon to orient the sketch plane parallel to the screen.
29. On the ribbon, click **Sketch** tab > **Sketching** panel > **Line** drop-down > **Line Chain**.
30. Create four lines, as shown.

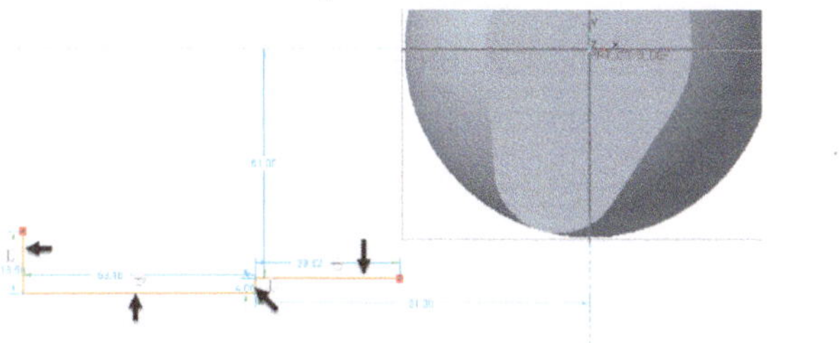

31. On the ribbon, click **Sketch** tab > **Sketching** panel > **Arc** drop-down > **3-Point/Tangent End**.
32. Select the endpoint of the right horizontal line.
33. Select the circular edge of the model, as shown.

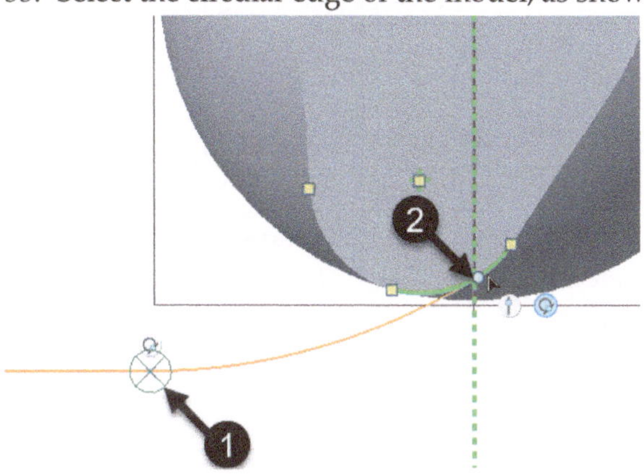

34. On the ribbon, click **Sketch** tab > **Constrain** panel > **Tangent** .
35. Select the newly created arc and the circular edge.

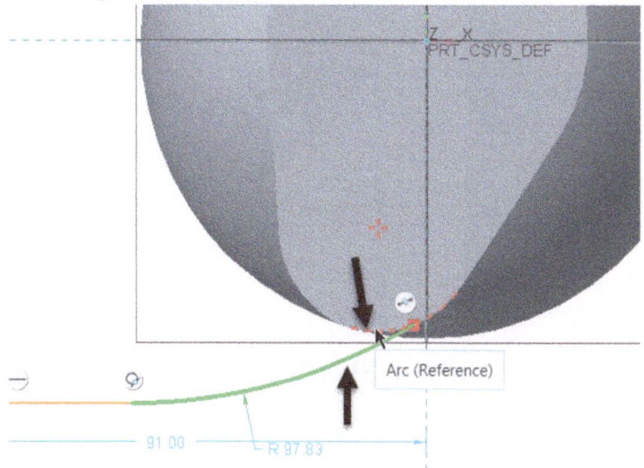

36. On the ribbon, click **Sketch** tab > **Sketching** panel > **Offset**.
37. Select the arc.
38. Press and hold the SHIFT key and horizontal line, as shown.

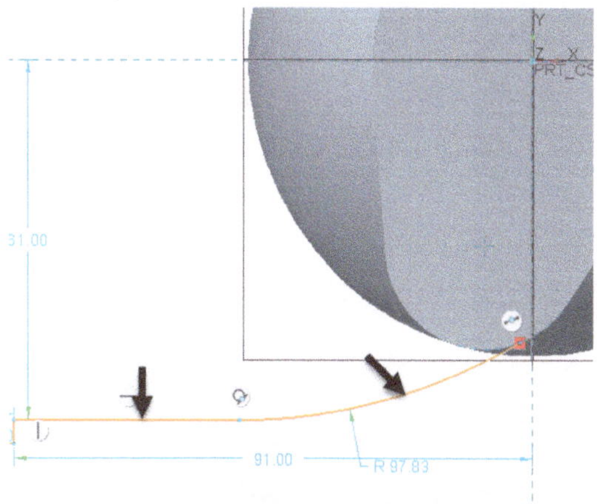

39. Type-in the offset distance value and click the green check.

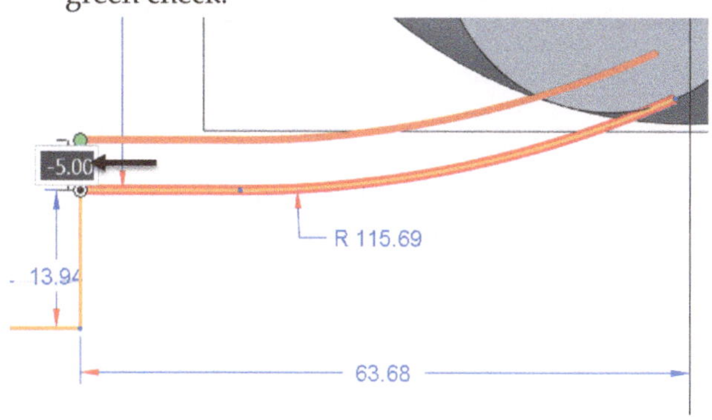

40. Click **OK** on the toolbar.

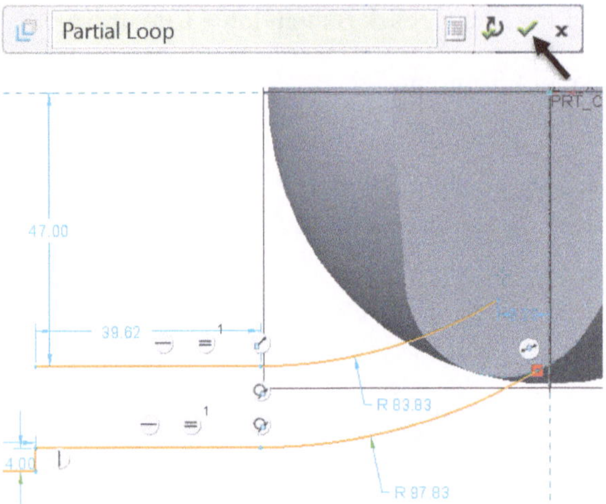

41. On the ribbon, click **Sketch** tab > **Editing** panel > **Corner**.

42. Select vertical and horizontal lines, as shown.

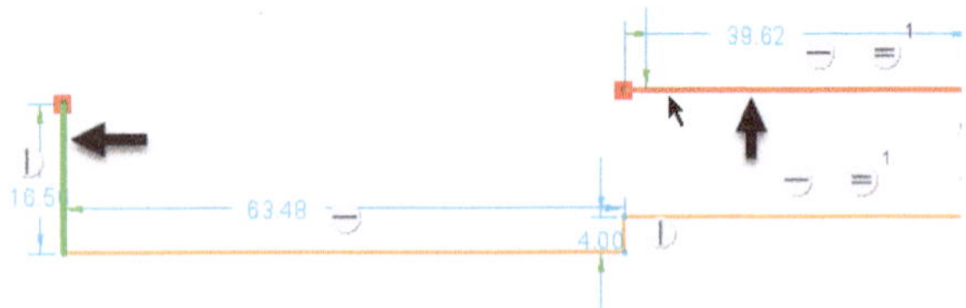

43. Create a line connecting the endpoints of the arcs, as shown.

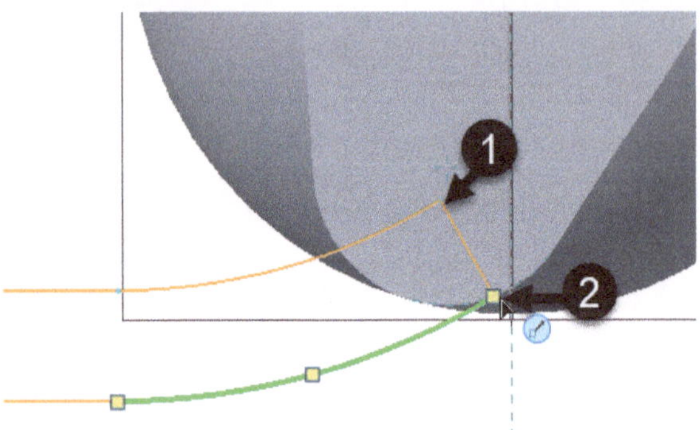

44. On the ribbon, click **Sketch** tab > **Constrain** panel > **Coincident**.
45. Select the endpoint of the arc and the quadrant point of the circular edge.

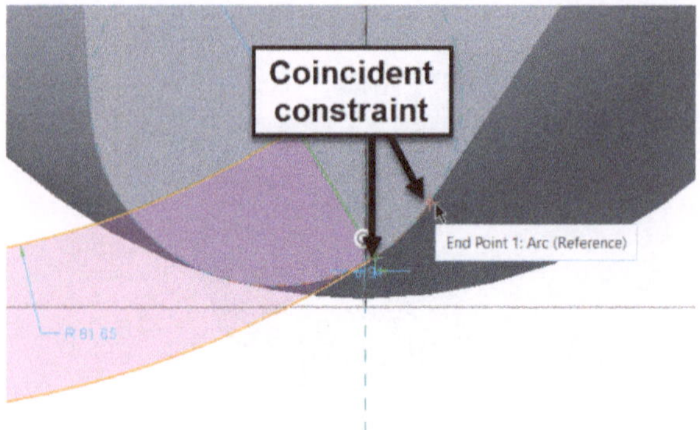

46. On the ribbon, click **Sketch** tab > **Constrain** panel > **Perpendicular**.
47. Select the arc and the line, as shown.

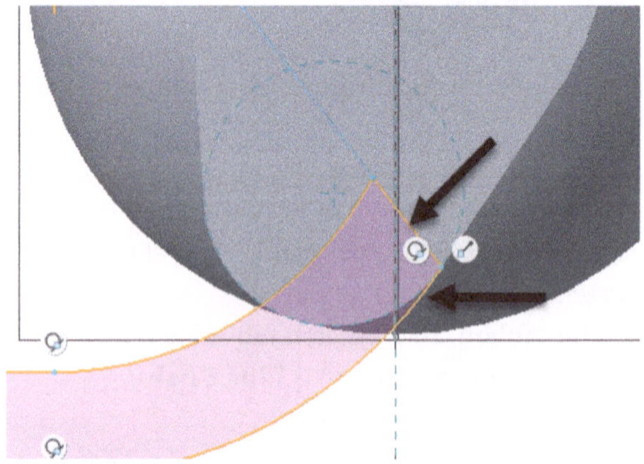

48. Add dimensions to the sketch, as shown.

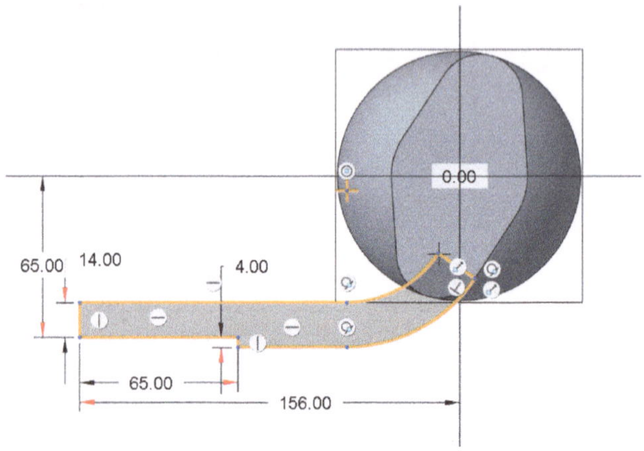

49. Click **OK** on the ribbon.
50. On the **Extrude** Dashboard, select **To Reference** from the **Depth** drop-down.
51. Select the flat end face of the extruded feature, as shown.

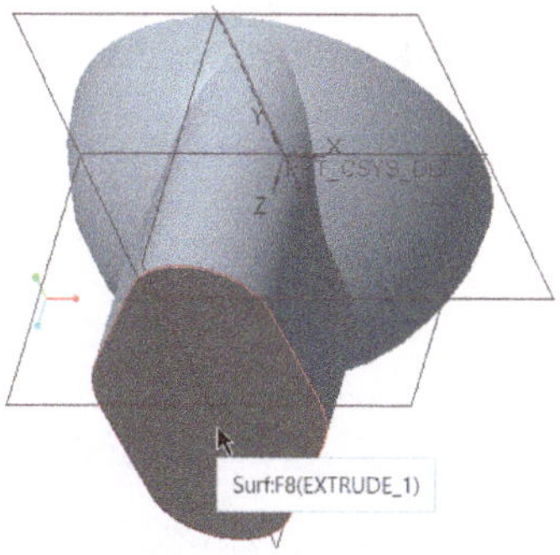

52. Click **OK** on the **Extrude** Dashboard.

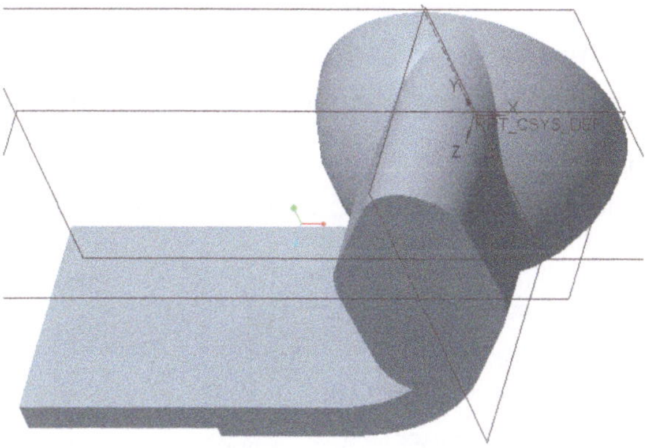

53. On the ribbon, click **Model** tab > **Shapes** panel > **Extrude**.
54. Click on the Front plane.
55. On the **Graphics** toolbar, click the **Sketch View** icon to orient the sketch plane parallel to the screen.
56. On the ribbon, click **Sketch** tab > **Sketching** panel > **Line** drop-down > **Line Chain**.
57. Create two lines, as shown.

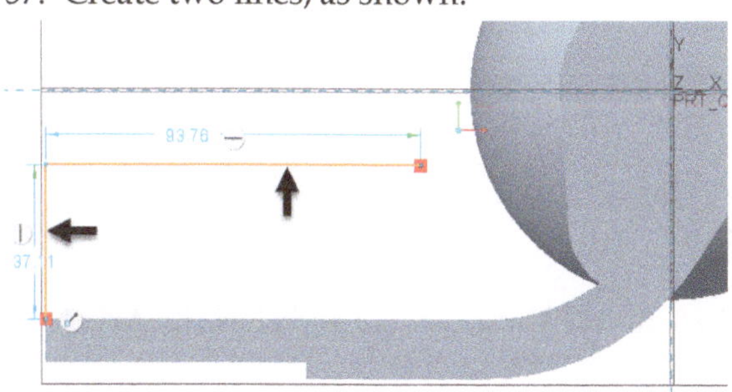

58. On the ribbon, click **Sketch** tab > **Sketching** panel > **Project**.
59. Select the horizontal.
60. Press and hold the SHIFT key and select the curved edge, as shown.

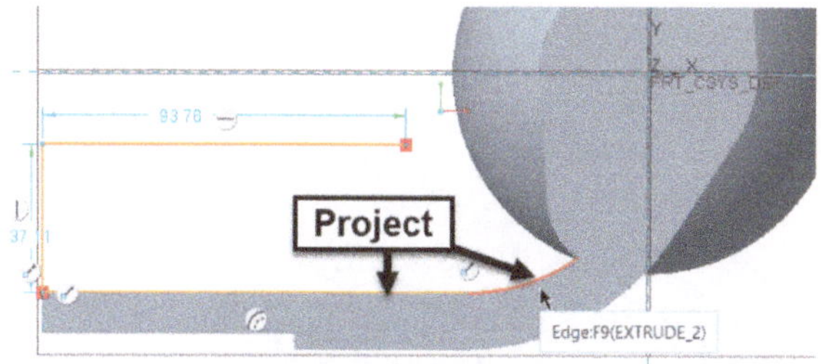

61. Click **OK** on the toolbar.
62. On the ribbon, click **Sketch** tab > **Editing** panel > **Corner**.
63. Select the end portion of the horizontal and arc.

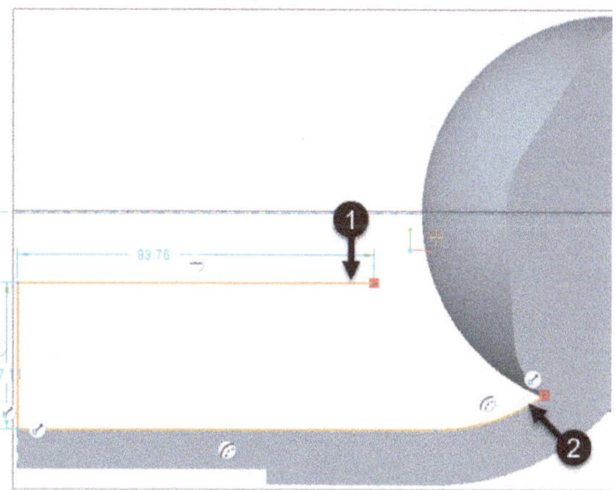

64. Add a fillet and dimensions to the sketch, as shown.

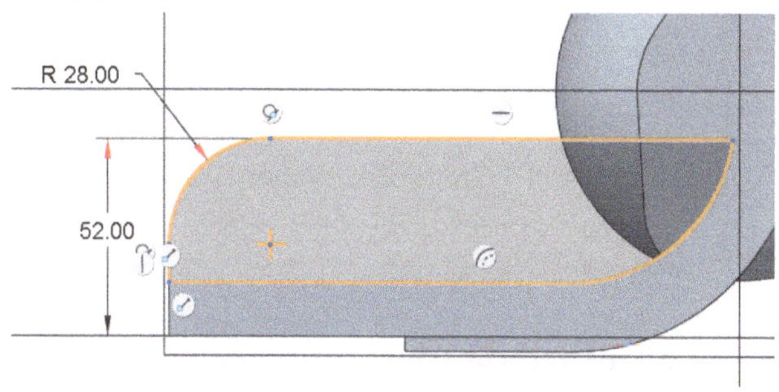

65. Click **OK** on the ribbon.
66. On the **Extrude** Dashboard, type **12** in the **Depth** box.
67. Click **OK** on the **Extrude** Dashboard.

Creating the Revolved Cut Feature

1. On the ribbon, click **Model** tab > **Shapes** panel > **Revolve**.
2. Select the Front plane.
3. On the **Graphics** toolbar, click the **Sketch View** icon to orient the sketch plane parallel to the screen.

4. Create an arc and line, as shown.

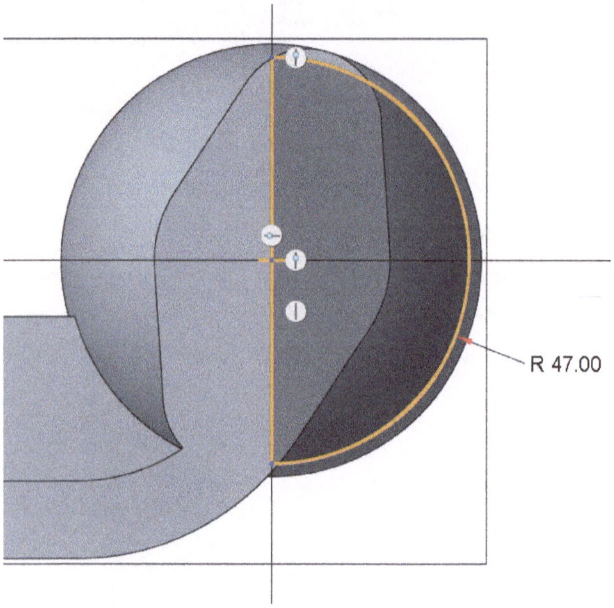

5. Click **OK** on the ribbon.
6. On the **Graphics** toolbar, click the **Datum Display Filters drop-**down and check the **Axis Display** option.

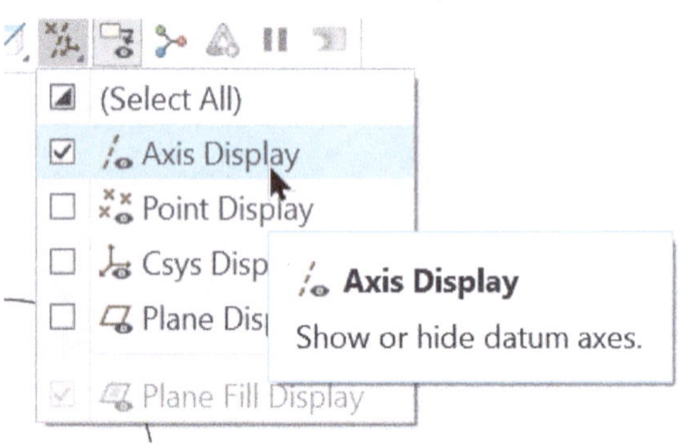

7. Select the vertical axis to define the revolution axis.

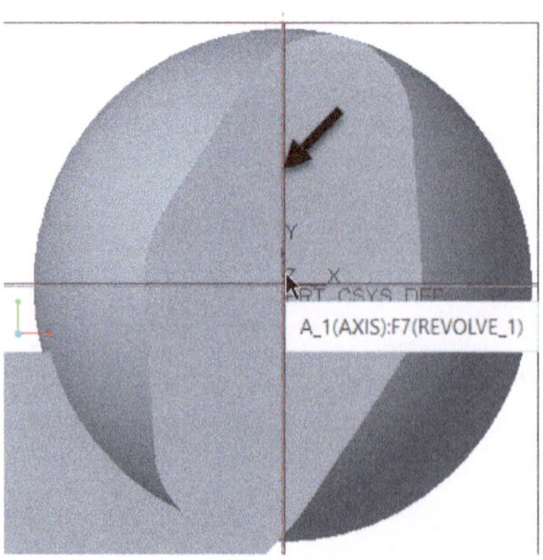

8. Click the **Remove material** button.
9. Click **OK** on the **Revolve** Dashboard.

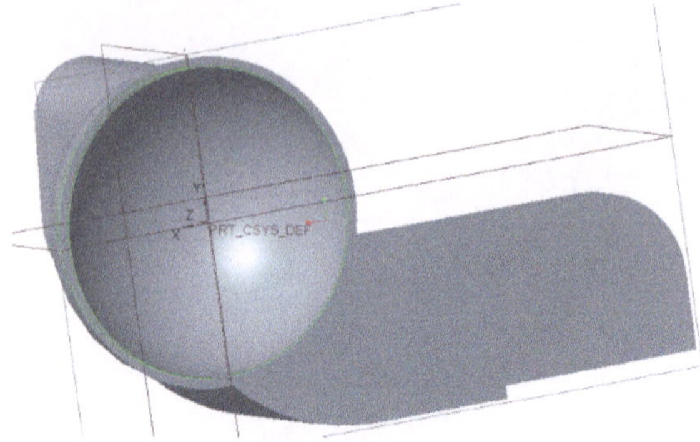

Creating the Hole Features

1. On the ribbon, click **Model** tab > **Engineering** panel > **Hole** .
2. Select the front face of the model geometry.

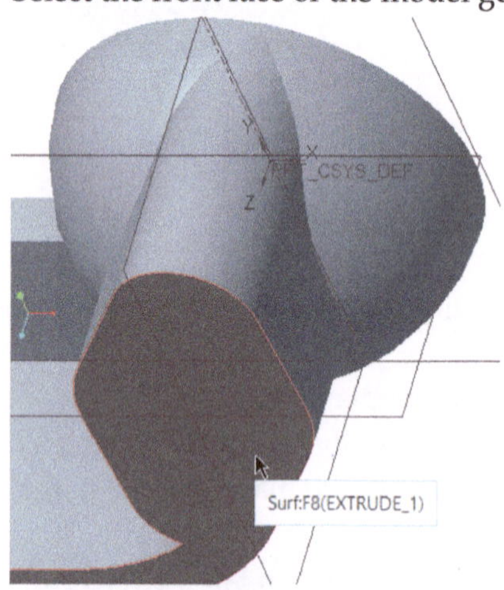

3. Expand the Dashboard by clicking the arrow button on the right-side.

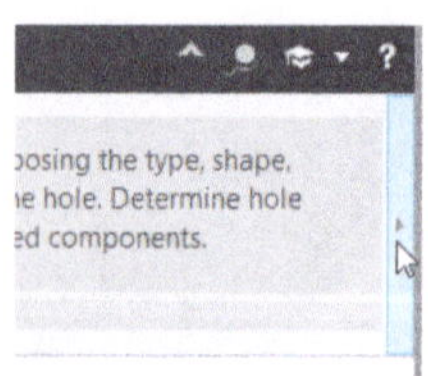

4. Expand the **Datum** panel and click the **Axis** button.

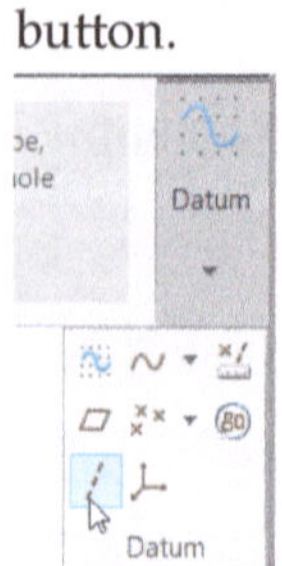

5. Select the curved face of the model, as shown.

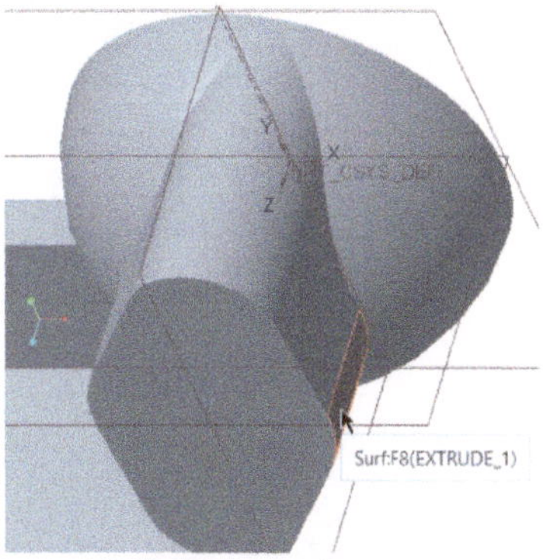

6. Click **OK** on the **Datum Axis** dialog.
7. Click **Resume** on the Dashboard.
8. Select **Through All** from the **Depth** drop-down.
10. Type **35** in the **Diameter** box.
11. Click **OK** on the Dashboard.

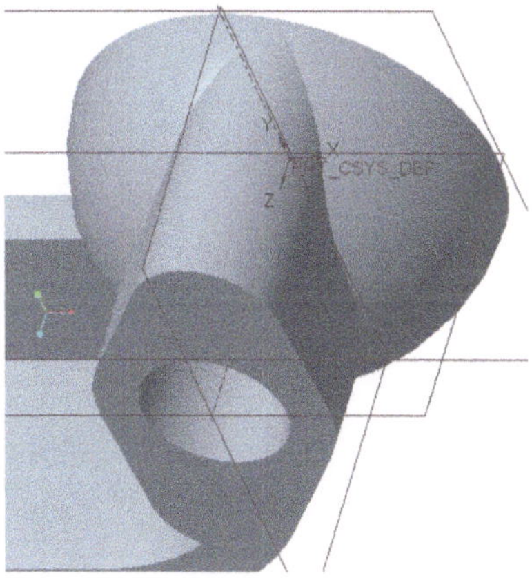

12. On the ribbon, click **Model** tab > **Datum** panel > **Axis** .
13. Select the round face of the model, as shown.

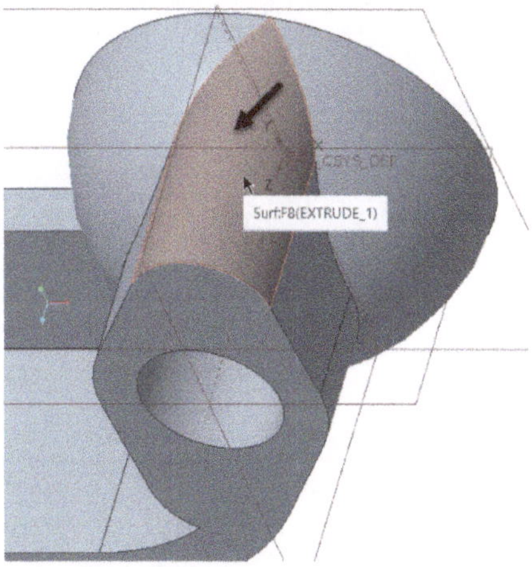

14. Click **OK** on the **Datum Axis** dialog.
15. On the ribbon, click **Model** tab > **Datum** panel > **Axis** .
16. Select the curved edge, as shown.

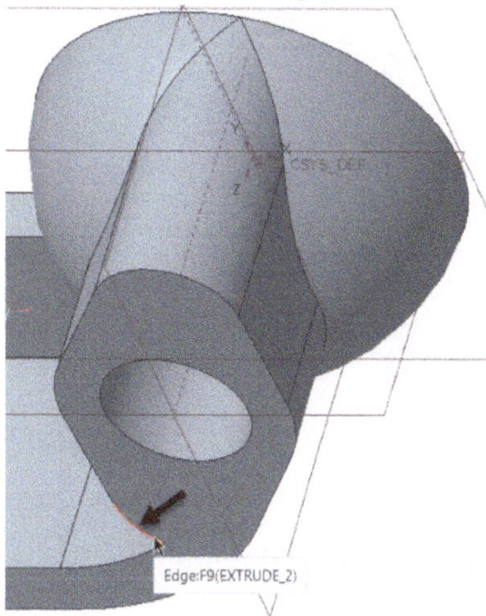

17. Click **OK** on the **Datum Axis** dialog.
18. On the ribbon, click **Model** tab > **Engineering** panel > **Hole** .
19. On the **Hole** dashboard, click the **Standard** icon.
20. Click the **Counterbore** button on the **Hole** dashboard.
21. Set the **Thread Type** to **ISO**.
22. Select **M8X.5**from the **Screw Size** drop-down.
23. Select the **Through All** from the **Specify drill depth type** drop-down.
24. Press and hold the CTRL key and select the front face and the axis, as shown.

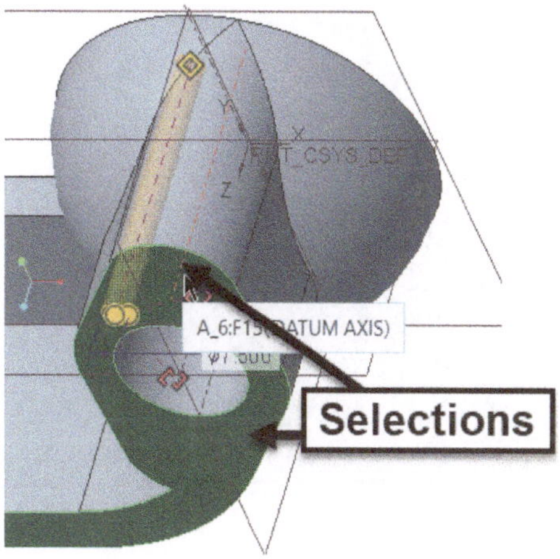

25. Click the green check.
26. Likewise, create another hole, as shown.

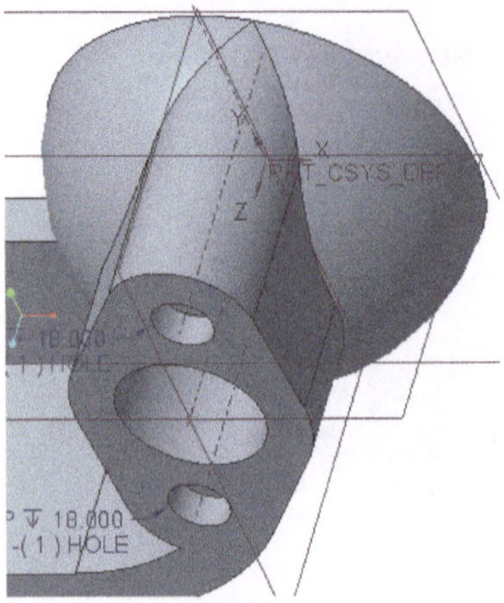

Creating the Rounds

1. On the ribbon, click **Model > Engineering > Round**.
2. Type **4** in the **Radius** box,
3. Select the edges in the sequence, as shown.

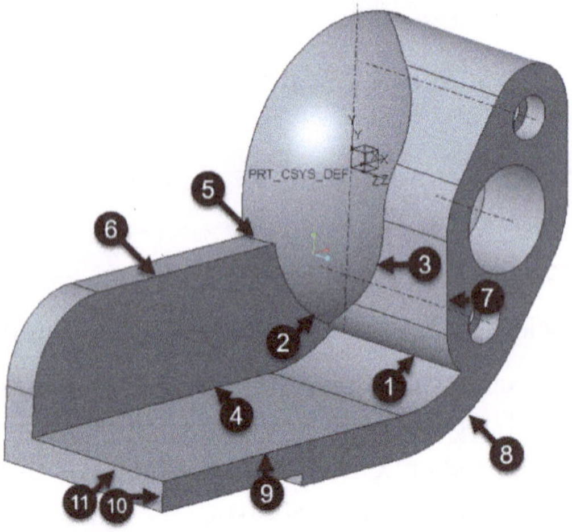

4. Click **OK**.
5. Save and close the file.

Questions

1. What are Placed features?
2. Which option allows you to create a chamfer with unequal setbacks?
3. Which command allows you to create a variable radius blend?
4. When you create a thread on a cylindrical face, the thread diameter will be calculated automatically or not.

Exercises

Exercise 1

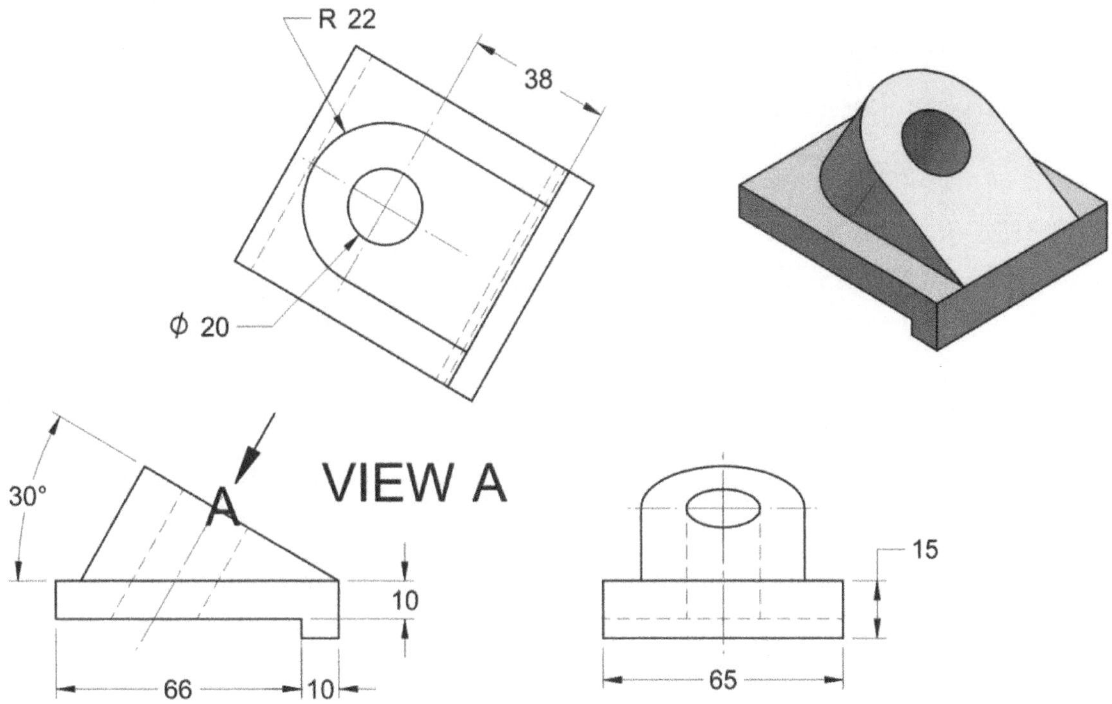

Exercise 2

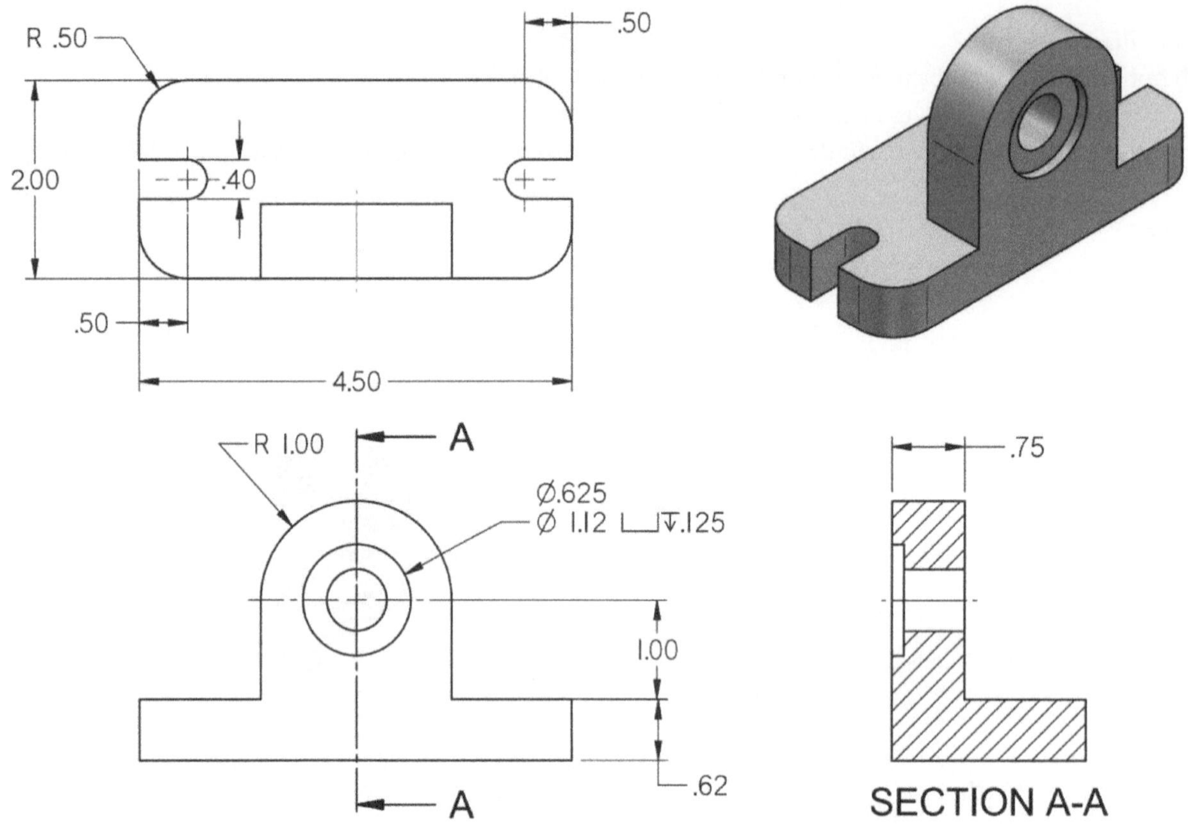

Exercise 3

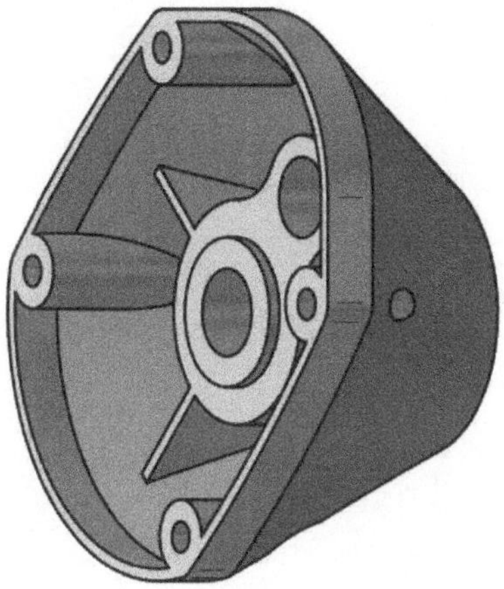

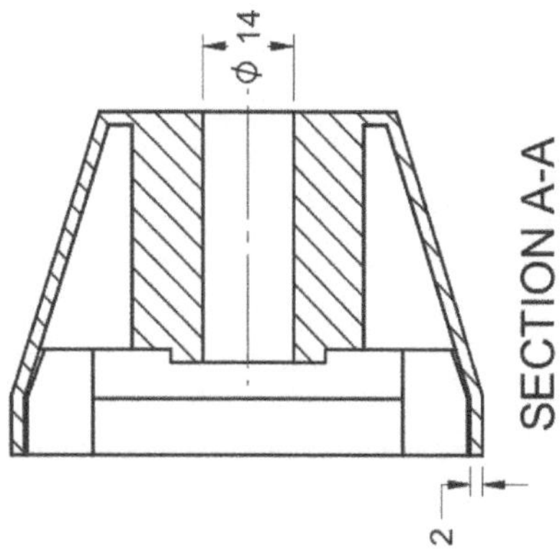
ϕ 14
2
SECTION A-A

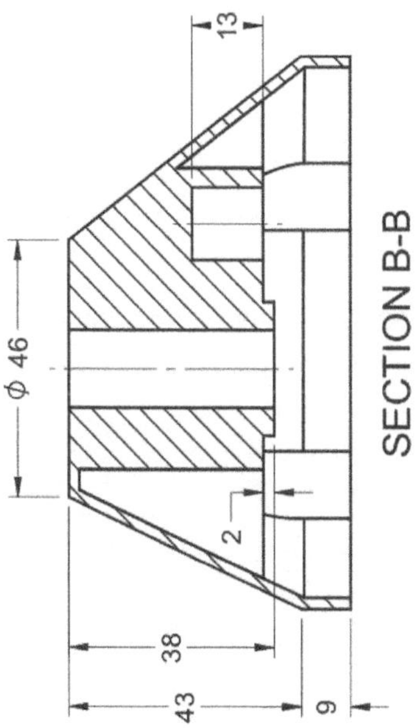
13
ϕ 46
2
38
43
9
SECTION B-B

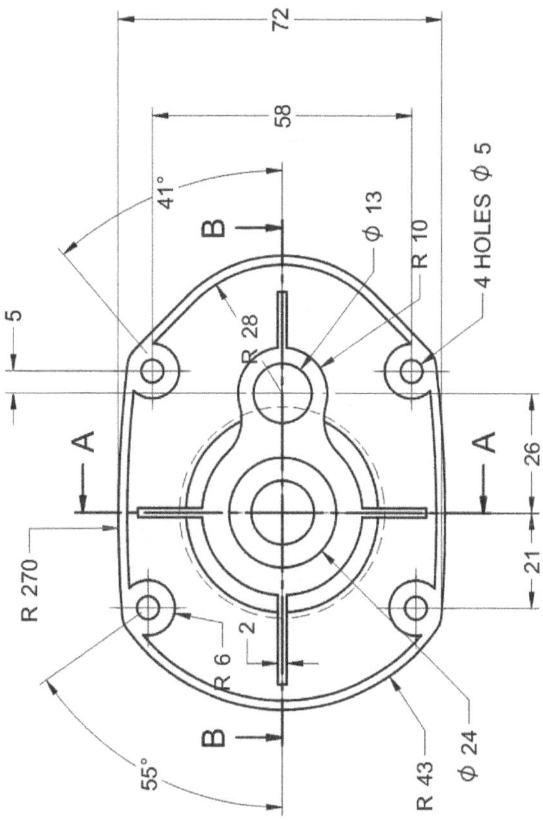
72
58
41°
B
ϕ 13
R 10
4 HOLES ϕ 5
5
R 28
R 2
A
A
26
21
R 270
2
R 6
B
55°
R 43
ϕ 24

Exercise 4

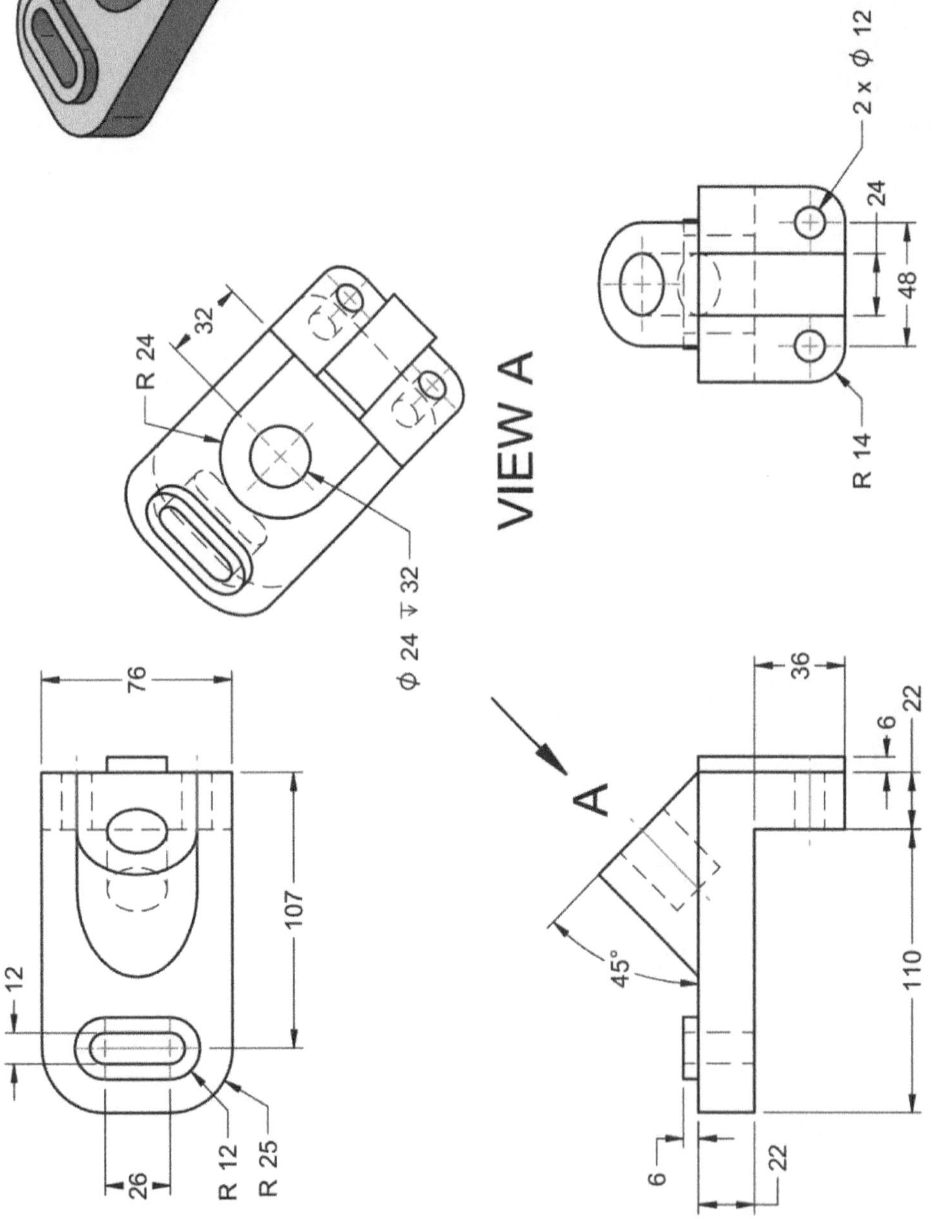

2 x Φ 12
24
48
R 14
VIEW A
R 24
32
Φ 24 ↧ 32
76
107
12
26
R 12
R 25
A
36
6
22
110
45°
6
22

Chapter 5: Patterned Geometry

When designing a part geometry, there are often symmetry elements in each part or at least a few repeated features multiple times. In these situations, Creo Parametric offers you some commands that save you time. For example, you can use mirror features to design symmetric parts, making the part quicker. This is because you only have to design a portion of the part and use the mirror feature to create the remaining geometry.

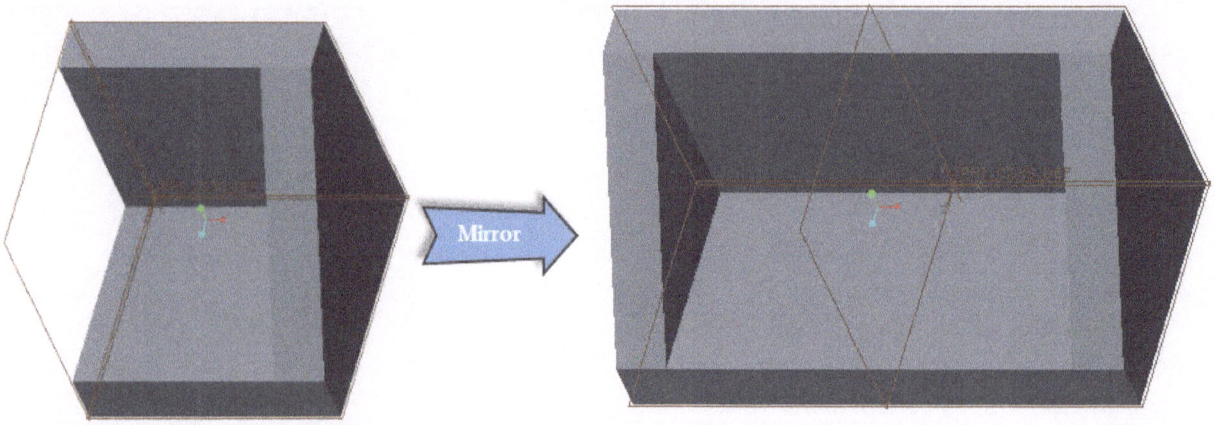

Also, there are some transformation commands to replicate a feature throughout a part quickly. They save you time from creating additional features individually and help you modify the design easily. If the design changes, you only need to change the first feature, and the rest of the pattern features will update automatically. In this chapter, you will learn to create mirrored and pattern geometries using the commands available in Creo Parametric.

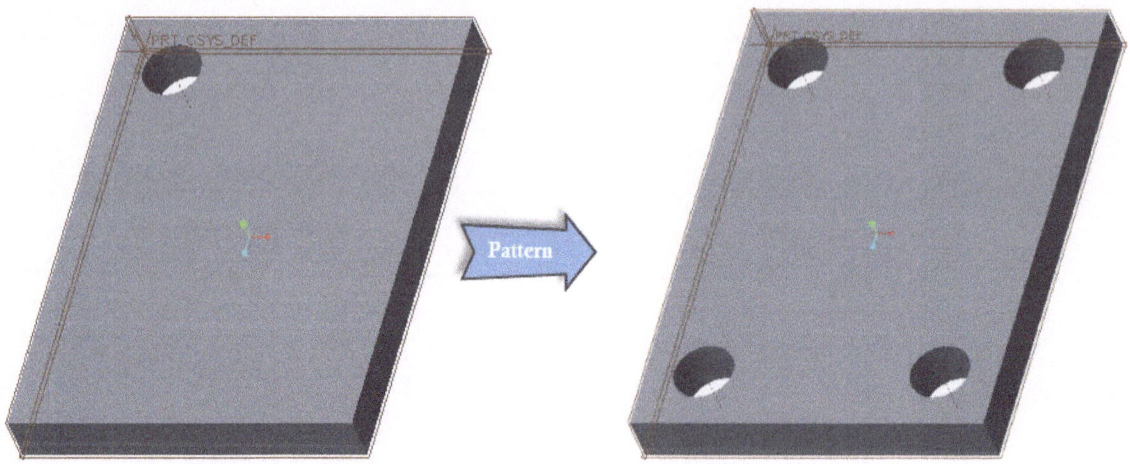

The topics covered in this chapter are:

- *Mirror features*
- *Mirror the entire body*
- *Save a mirrored copy of the part*
- *Direction Patterns*
- *Axis Patterns*
- *Reference Patterns*
- *Curve Patterns*
- *Point Patterns*

The Mirror command

If you are designing a symmetric part, you can save time by using the **Mirror** command. Using this command, you can replicate individual features or the entire body. To mirror features (3D geometry), you need to have a face or plane to use as a mirroring element. You can use a model face, default plane, or create a new plane if it does not exist where it is needed.

1. Press and hold the Ctrl key and select the features to mirror from the Model Tree.

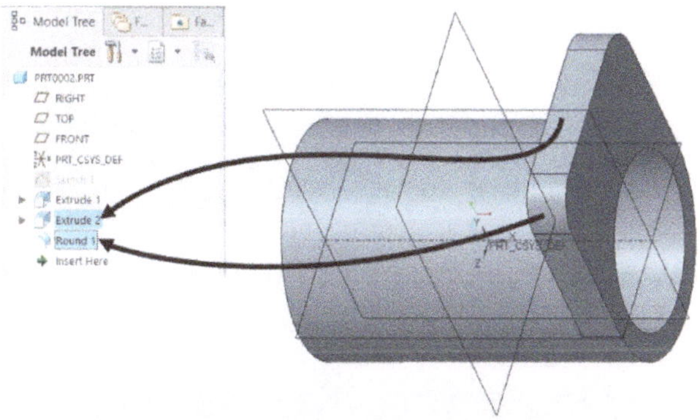

2. On the ribbon, click **Model > Editing > Mirror** .
3. Select the plane/face about which the features are to be mirrored.

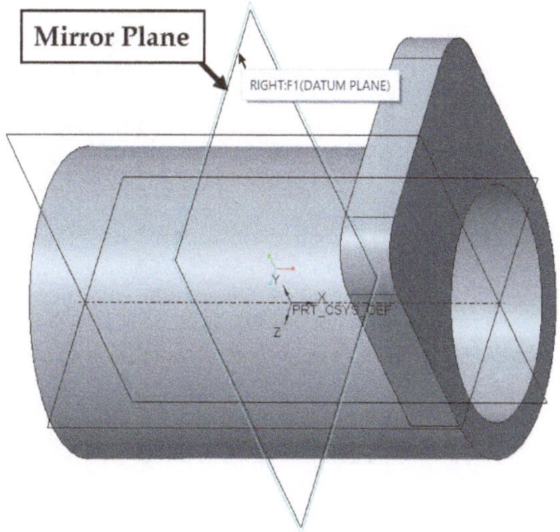

4. Click the green check on the **Mirror** dashboard.

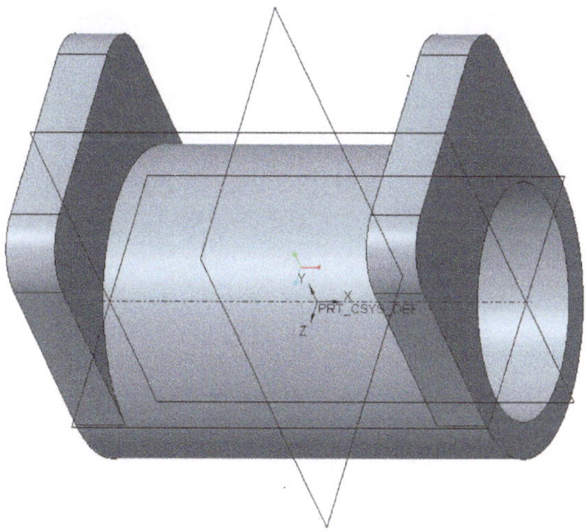

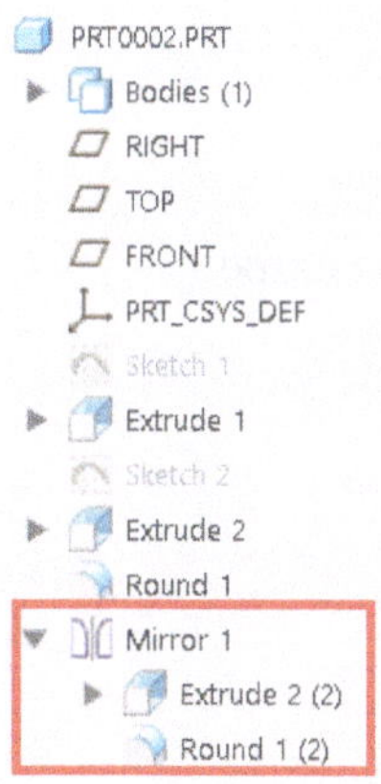

Now, if you make changes to the original feature, the mirror feature will be updated automatically.

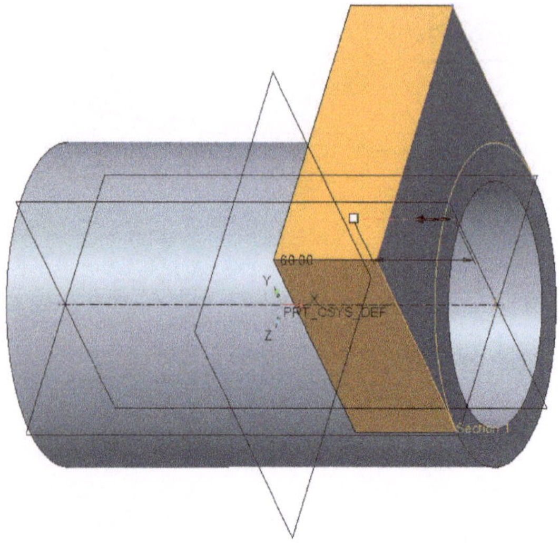

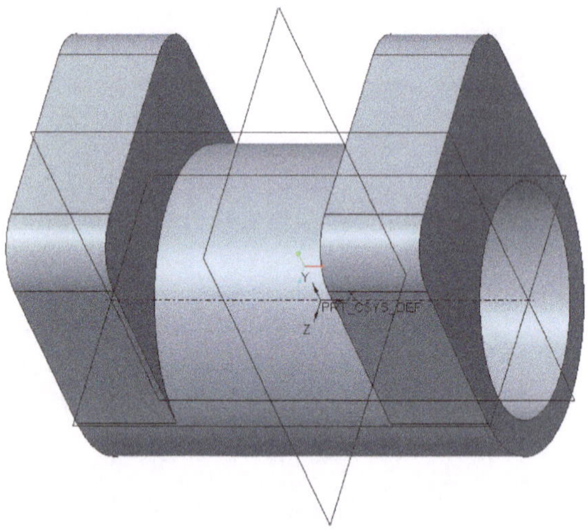

Mirror the entire body

If the part you are creating is completely symmetric, you can save more time by creating half of it and mirroring the entire geometry rather than individual features.

1. In the Model Tree, click the part name.

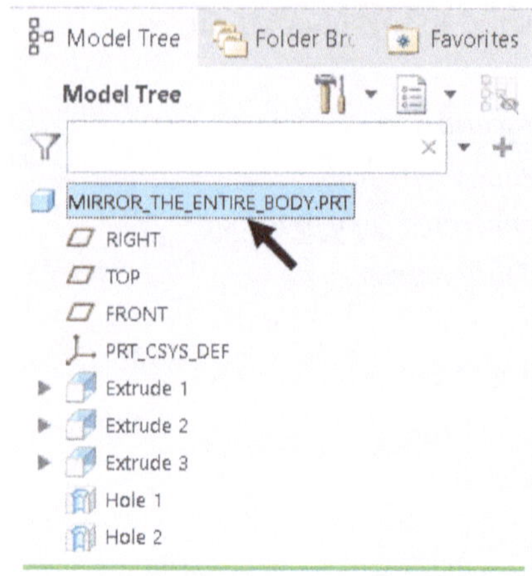

2. Activate the **Mirror** command and click on the mirror plane.

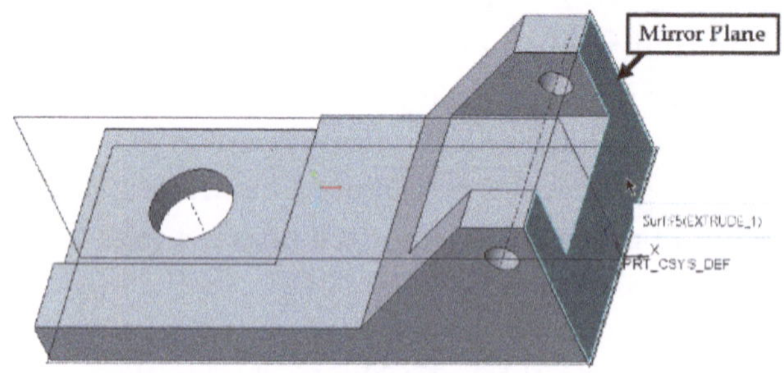

3. Click the green check on the **Mirror** dashboard to mirror the complete body.

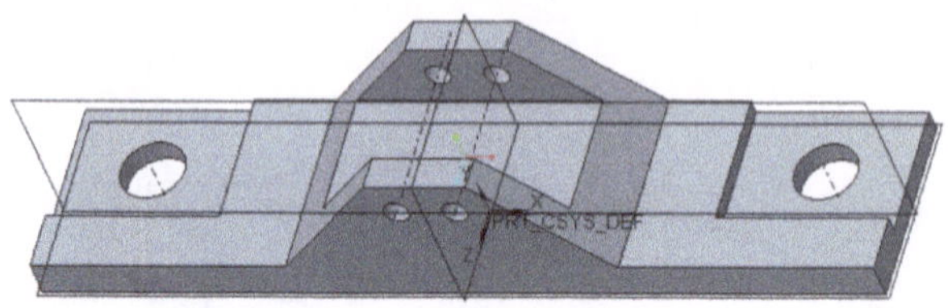

Save a Mirrored copy of the Part

Creo allows you to save a mirror copy of the part.

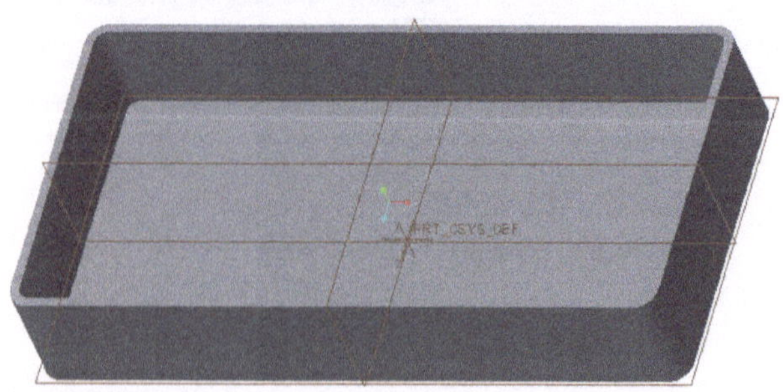

1. On the **File** menu, click **Save As > Mirror Part**.

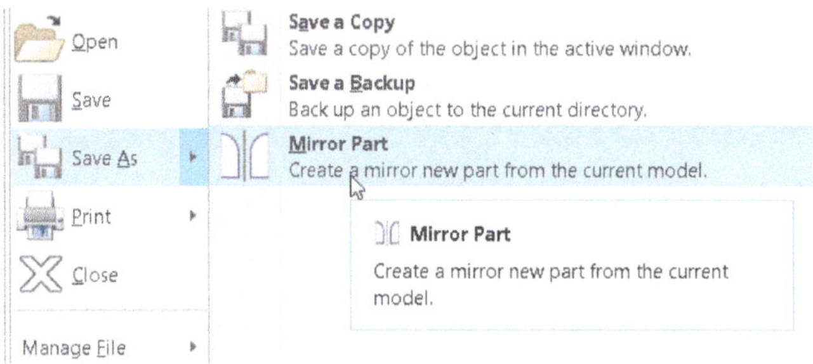

2. On the **Mirror Part** dialog, select **Geometry only** to mirror only the part geometry. You cannot edit the individual features of the geometry. The **Geometry with features** option allows you to edit the features of the mirrored part.
3. Examine the other options and check the **Preview** option. The preview of the mirrored part appears. Note that you cannot define the mirror plane as the program defines it automatically.

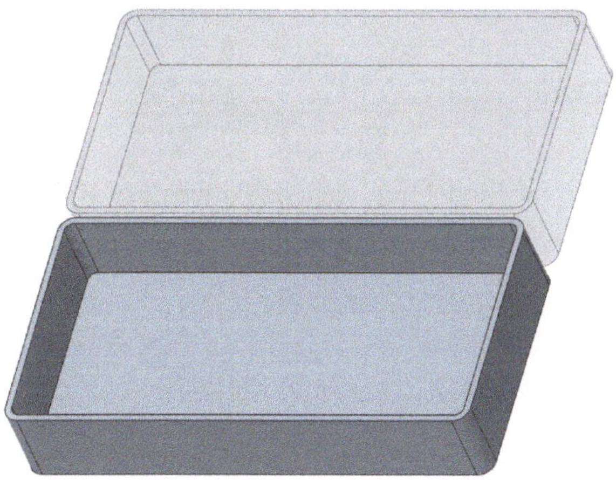

4. Type the name of the mirrored copy and click **OK**.

The Pattern command

This command replicates a feature using different references such as direction, axis, surface boundary, dimension, an existing pattern, table, curve, and randomly arranged points. On the ribbon, click **Model > Editing > Pattern** to activate this command. The different types of patterns that can be created using this command are explained next.

Direction

This option replicates a feature using a directional reference such as plane, face, edge, or axis.

1. Select the feature to pattern.

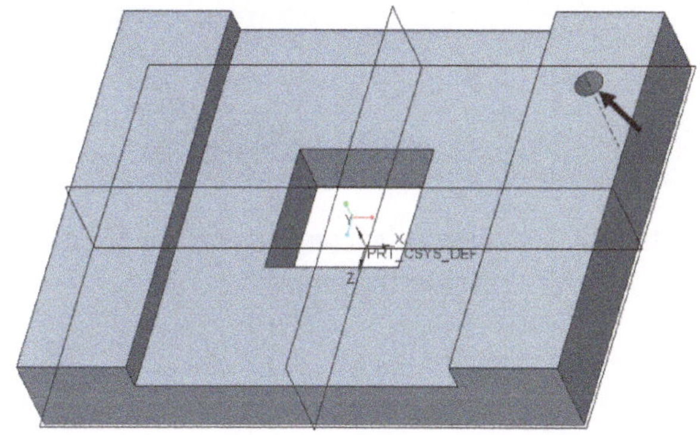

2. On the ribbon, click **Model > Editing > Pattern**.
3. On the **Pattern** dashboard, select **Direction** from the **Type** drop-down available on the left side.
4. Select the edge along the Z-axis to define the first direction of the pattern.

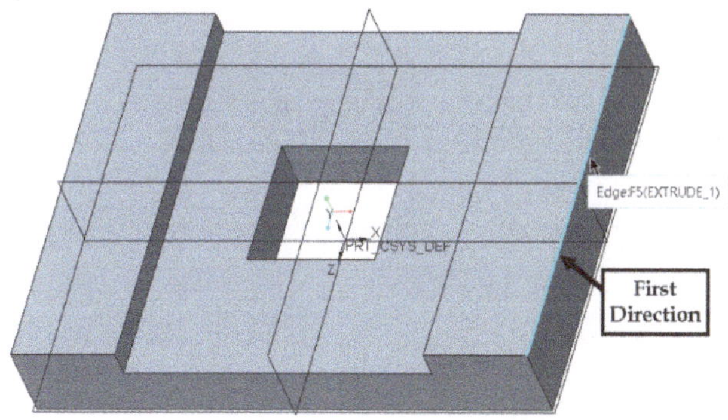

5. Specify the **Members** as **4** and **Spacing** as **30**.

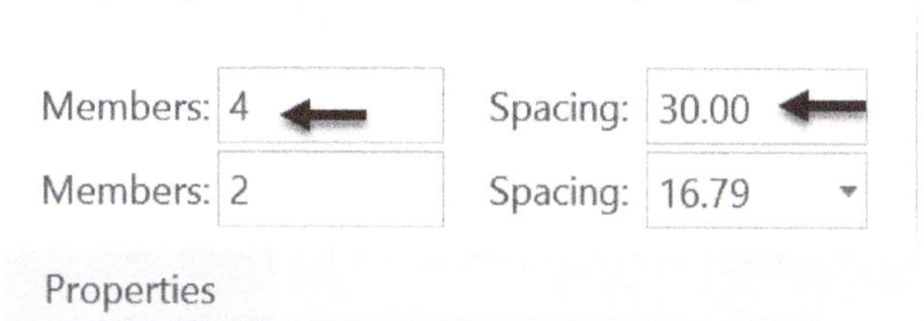

6. Use the **Flip** icon to correct the pattern direction, if required.
7. Click the green check on the dashboard to create the direction pattern.

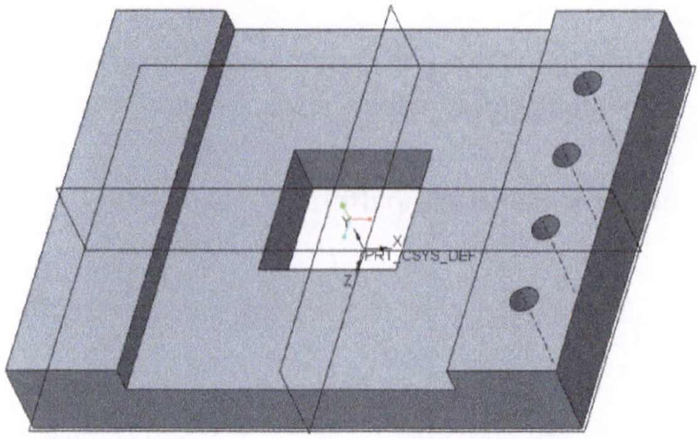

8. In the Model tree, click on **Pattern 1 of Hole 1** and select **Edit Definition**.

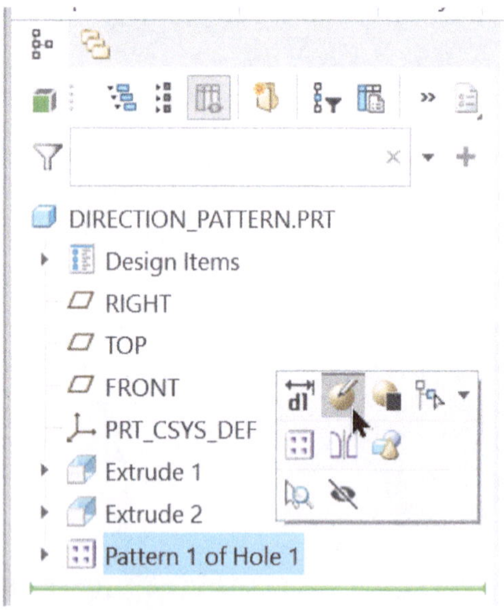

9. On the **Pattern** dashboard, click the **Dimensions** tab.
10. Under the **Direction 1** section, click in the **Dimension** field and select the diameter of the hole.

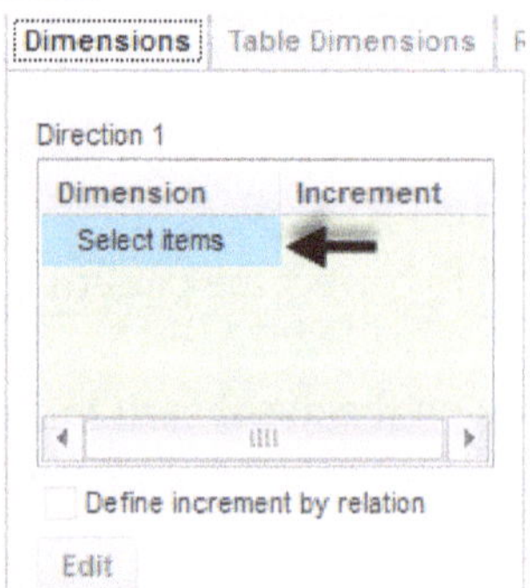

11. Type-in 2 in the **Increment** box in the **Direction 1** section. The diameter of the hole is increased by 2 for each increment.

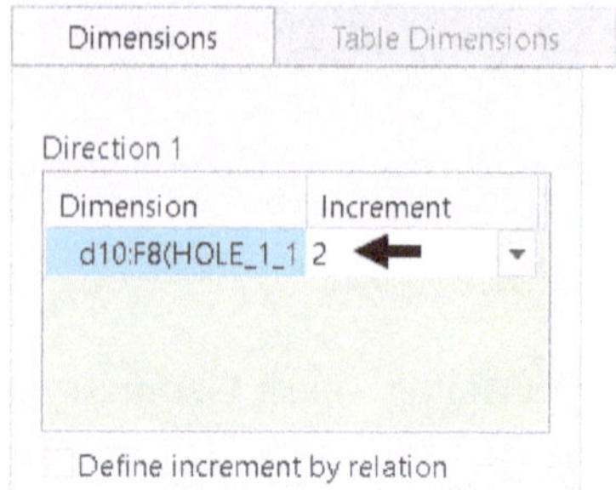

12. Click the green check to update the pattern.

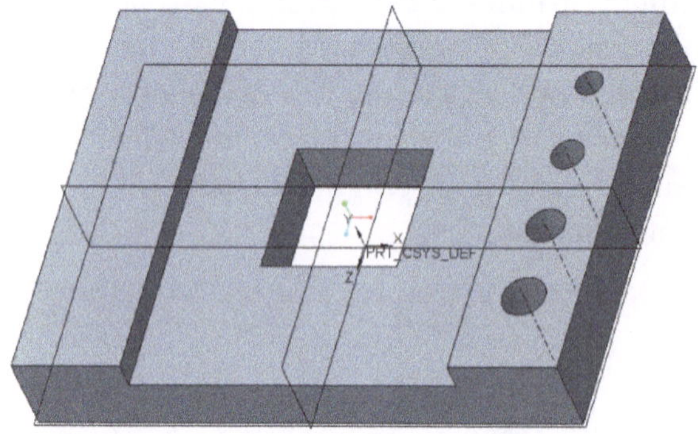

13. In the Model tree, click on **Pattern 1 of Hole 1** and select **Edit Definition**.

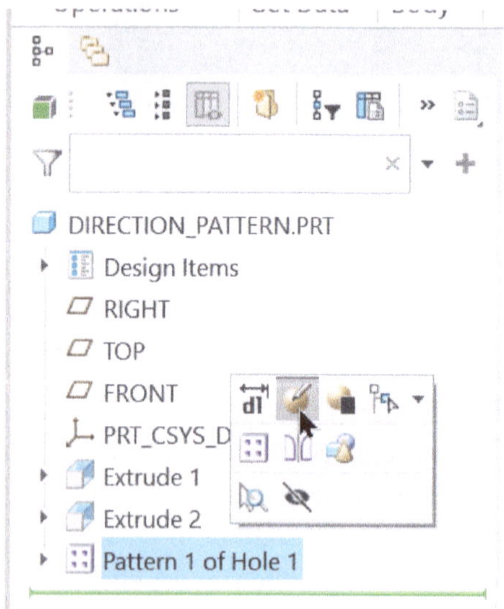

14. Click in the **Second Direction** box on the **Pattern** dashboard.

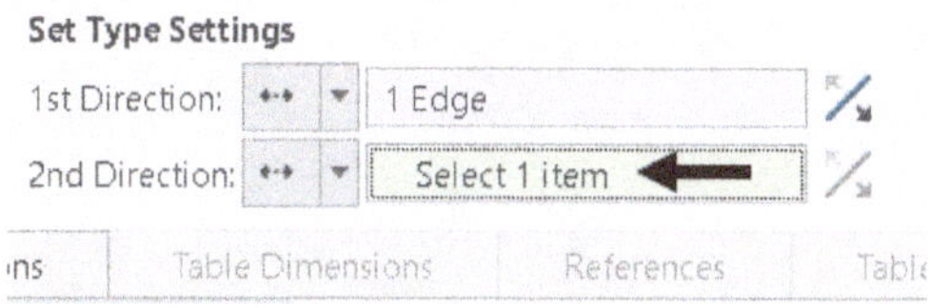

15. Select the edge along the X-axis to define the second direction.

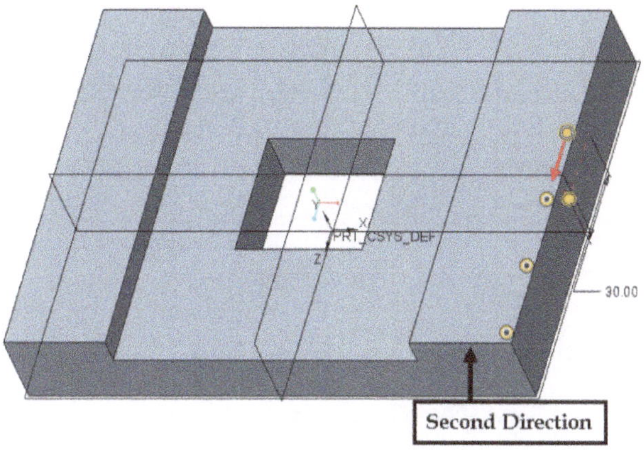

16. Specify the number of instances as **5** and spacing between them as **40**.

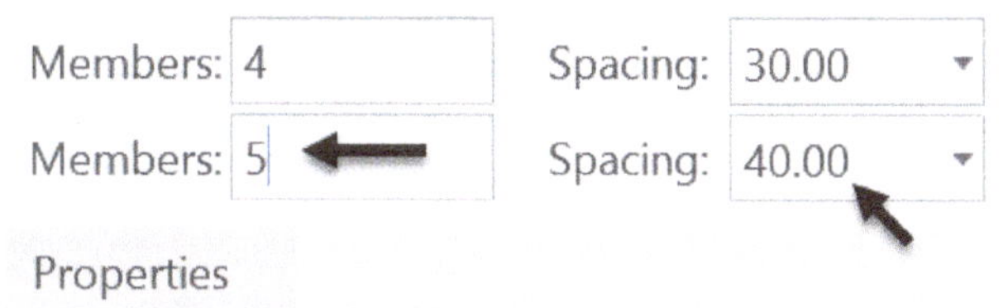

17. Use the **Flip** icon available next to the 2nd **direction** box to correct the pattern direction, if required.

18. Click the green check to update the pattern.

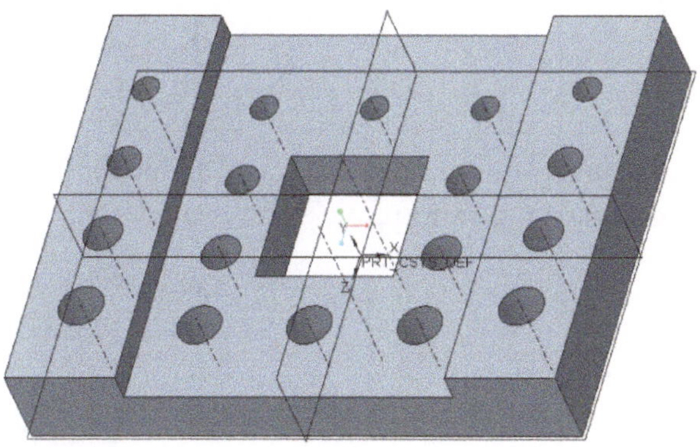

19. In the Model tree, click the right mouse button on **Pattern 1 of Hole 1** and select **Edit Definition.**

20. On the **Pattern** dashboard, click the **Dimensions** tab.

21. Under the **Direction 2** section, click in the **Dimension** field and select the diameter of the hole.

22. Type-in -1 in the **Increment** box under the **Direction 2** section. The diameter of the hole is decreased by **1** for each increment along the second direction.

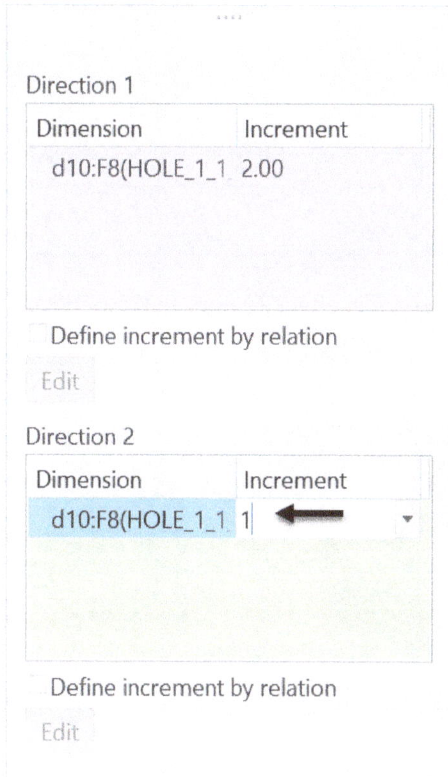

23. Click the green check to update the pattern.

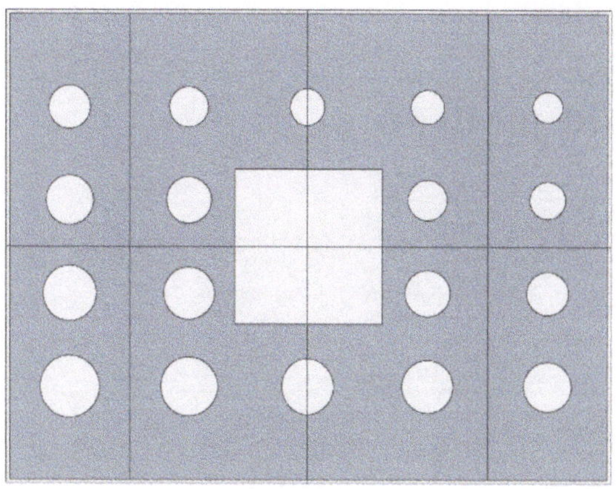

24. In the Model tree, click the right mouse button on **Pattern 1 of Hole 1** and select **Edit Definition**.
25. On the pattern preview, click the black dots at the center to suppress them.

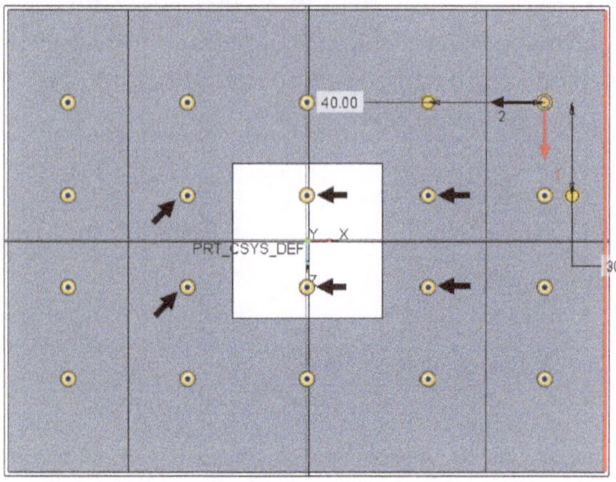

26. Click the green check to update the pattern.

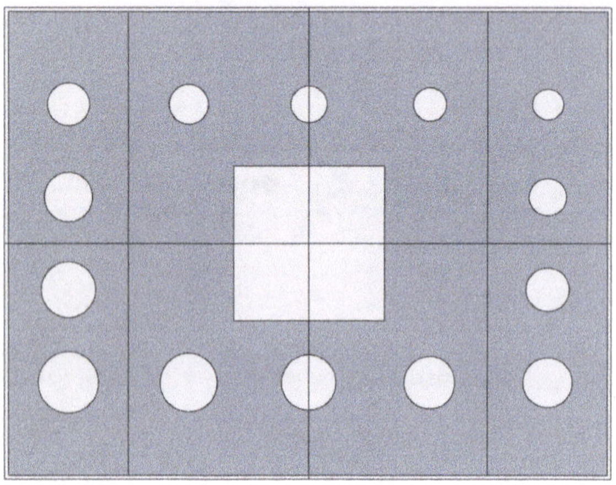

Axis

This option circularly patterns the selected features.

1. On the **Graphics** toolbar, make sure that the **Axis Display** is turned ON.

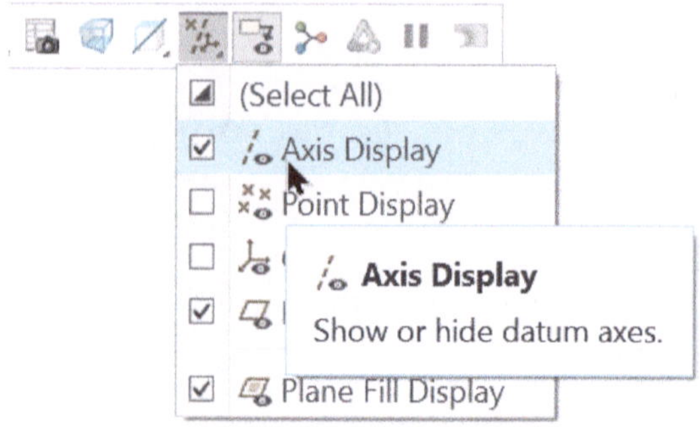

2. Select the feature to pattern and activate the **Pattern**  command.

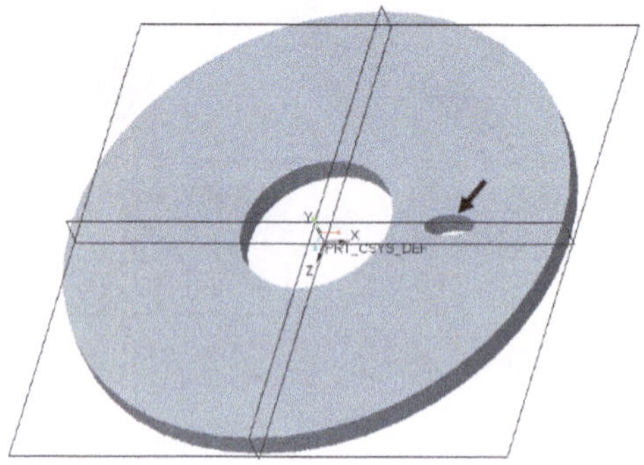

3. On the **Pattern** dashboard, select **Axis** from the **Type** drop-down available on the left side.

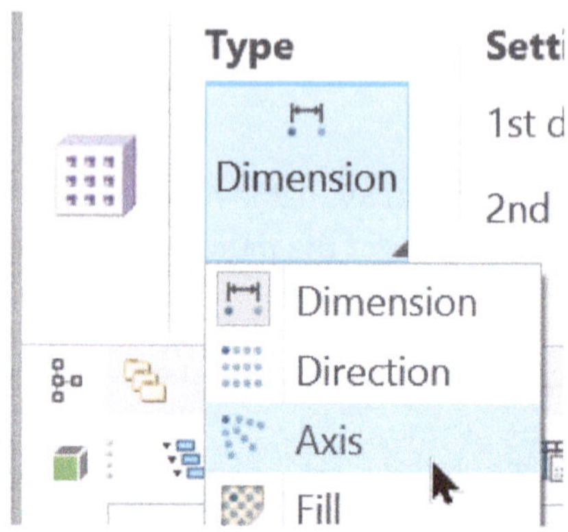

4. Select a Datum axis or Csys axis to define the center of the pattern.

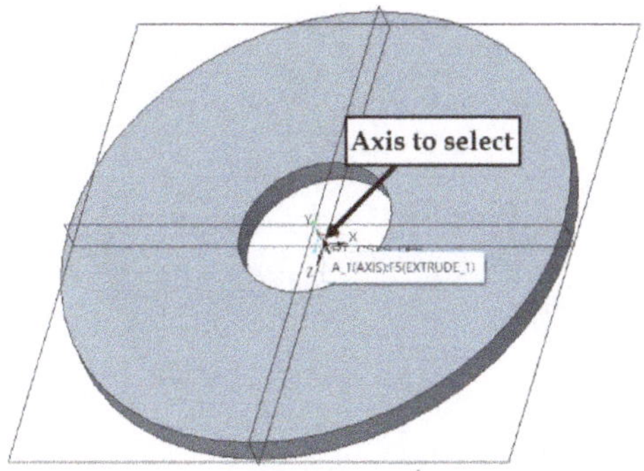

5. Type in the 1st **direction members** value on the Dashboard.

Deactivate the **Angular Extent** icon if you want to type-in the **Angle between members** box.

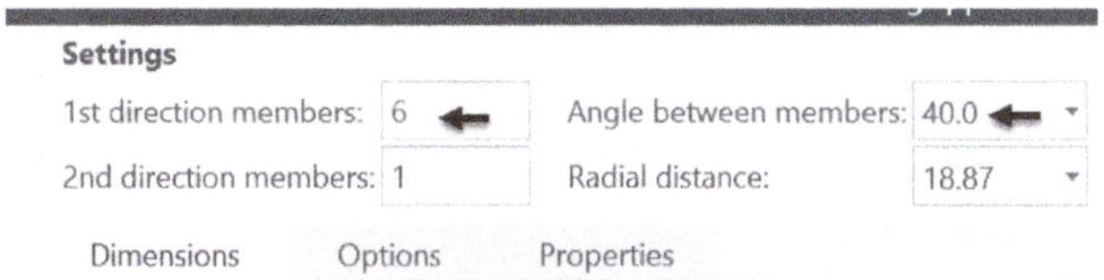

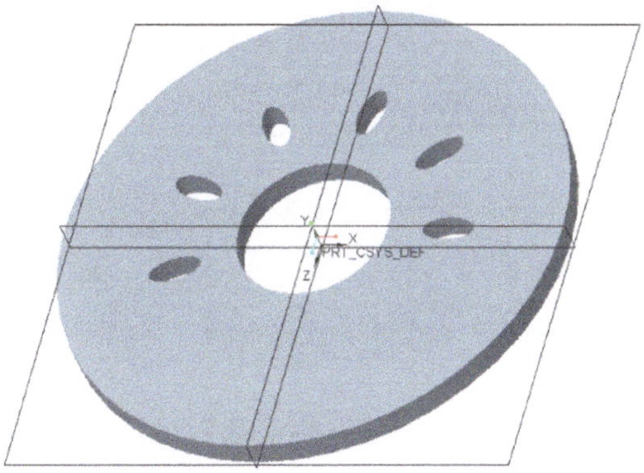

Activate the **Angular extent** icon if you want to type-in the **1st direction members** and **Extent angle**. The Angle between the members value will be calculated automatically. For example, enter **5** in the **1st direction members** box and **360** in the **Angular Extent** box. It creates five instances, including the original one. The angle between members will be 72 (360/5).

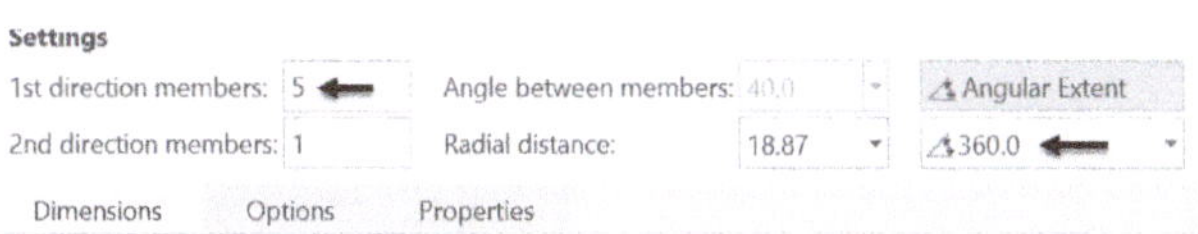

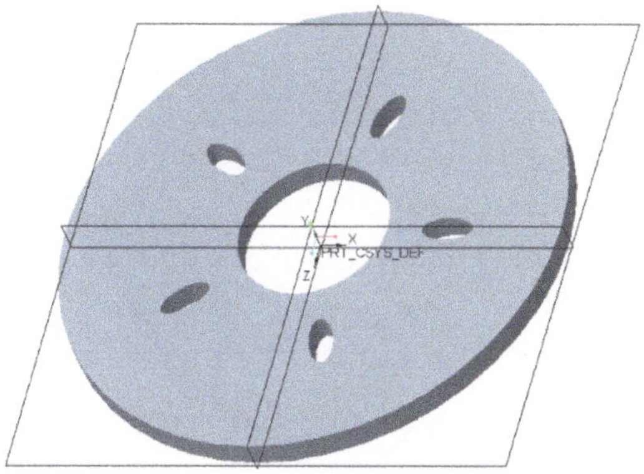

On the **Options** tab, uncheck **Follow axis rotation** to pattern the feature with the original orientation.

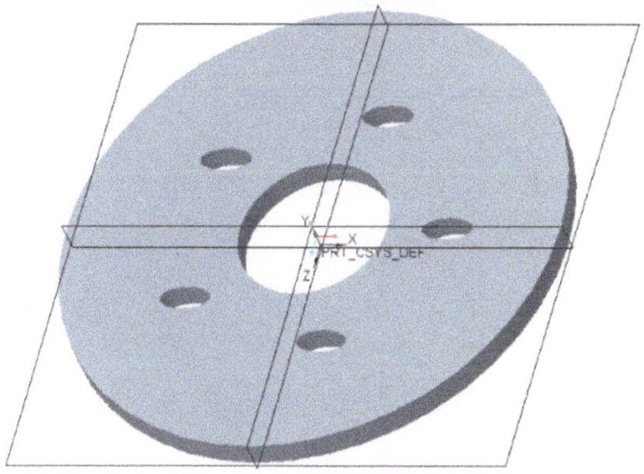

You can check the **Use alternate origin** option and select a datum point, coordinate system, curve end, or vertex to define the origin of the pattern.

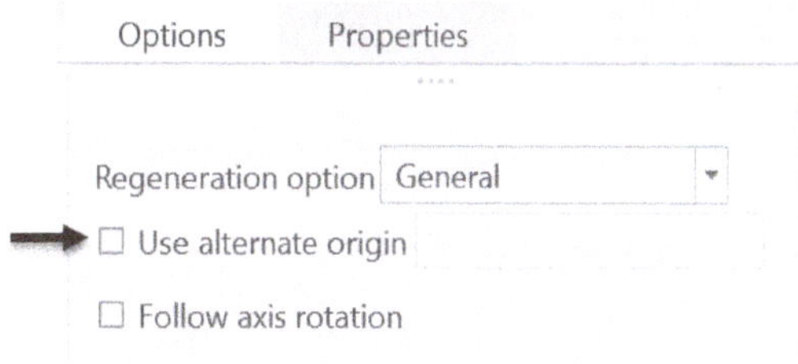

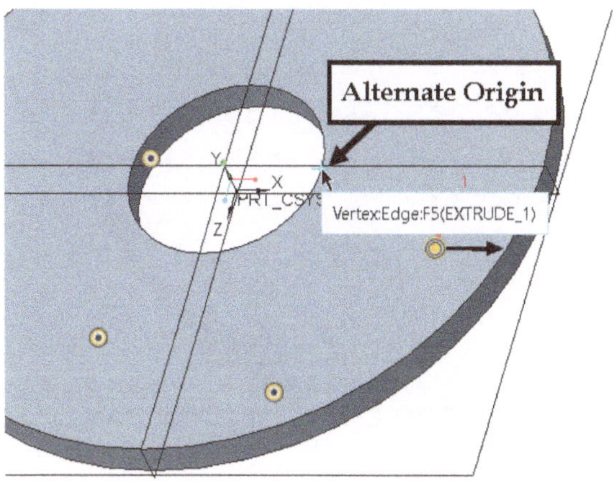

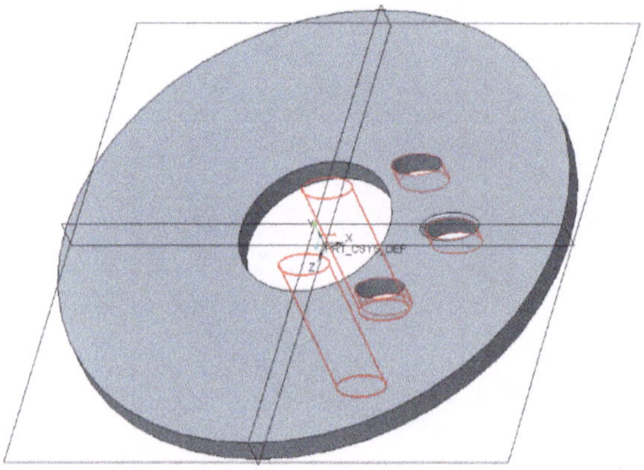

Check the **Follow axis rotation** option to change the instances' orientation, as they are patterned circularly.

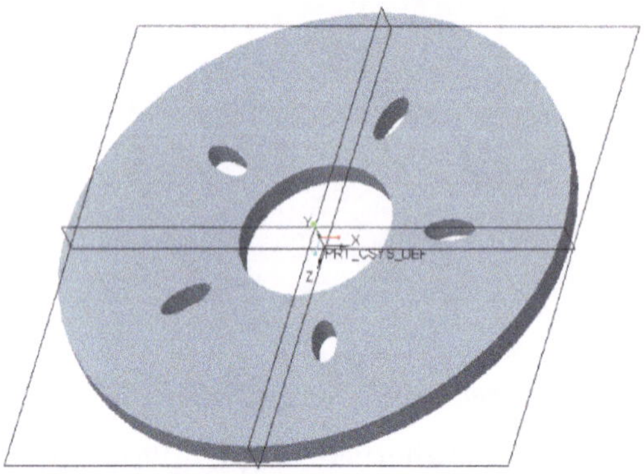

You can also create pattern instances in the second direction. Specify the **2nd direction members** and **Radial distance** values on the Dashboard.

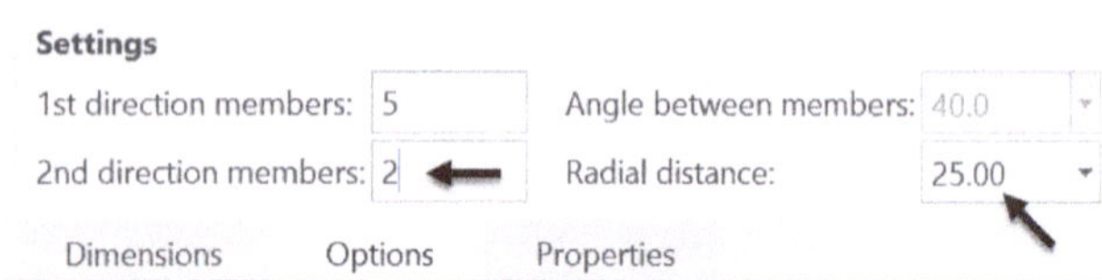

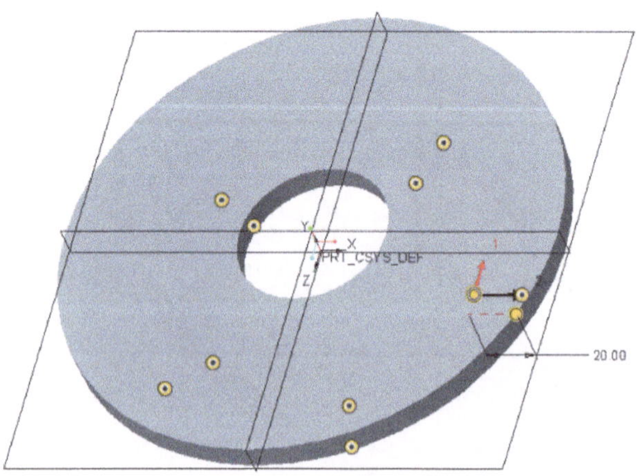

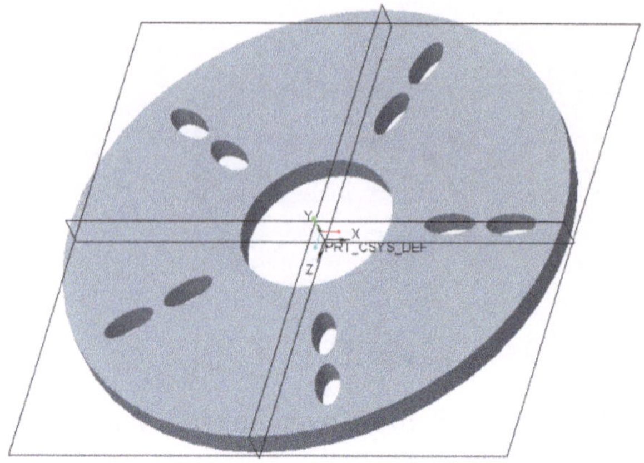

Reference

This option patterns a feature using an existing pattern. The feature should be associated with the feature of the existing pattern.

1. Select the feature associated with an existing pattern.

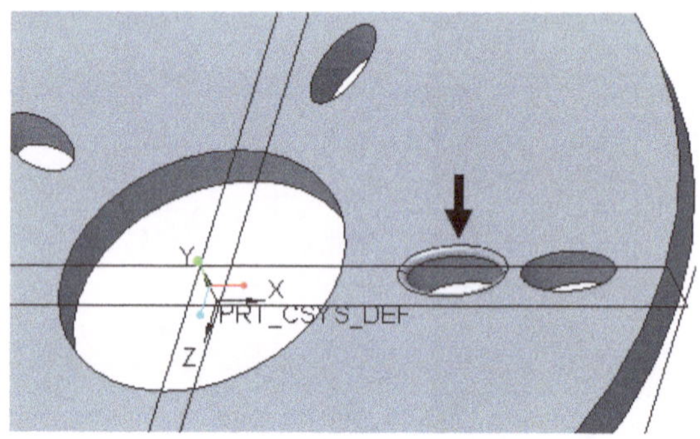

2. Activate the **Pattern** command. The **Reference** option is active on the **Pattern** dashboard.
3. Click the green check to create the reference pattern.

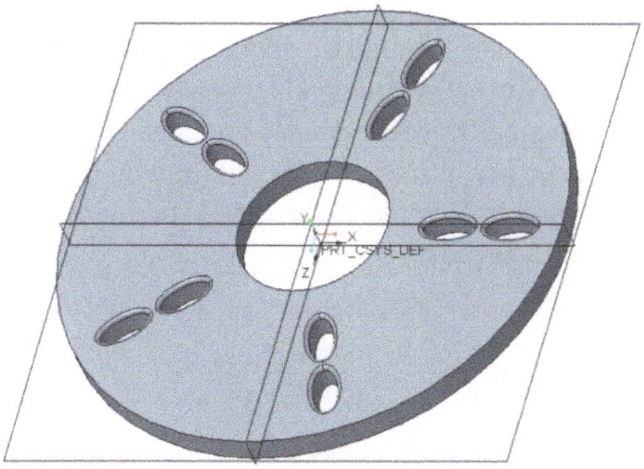

Curve

The **Curve** option creates a pattern along a selected curve.

1. Select the feature to pattern and activate the **Pattern** command.

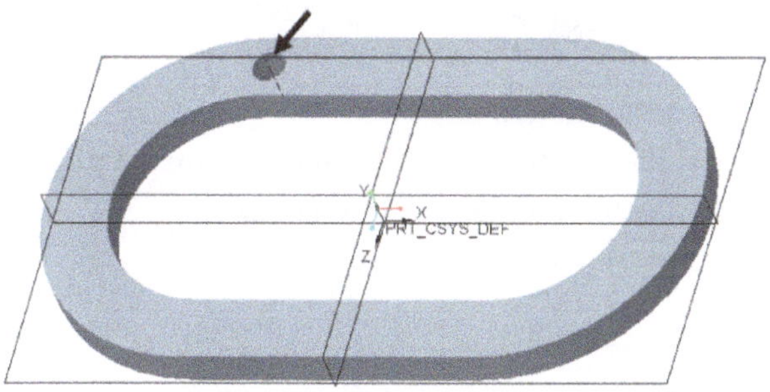

2. On the **Pattern** dashboard, select **Curve** from the **Type** drop-down available on the left side.

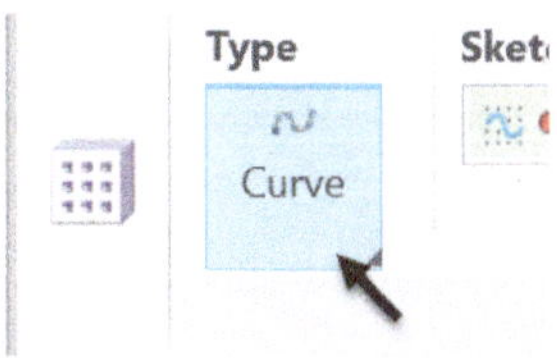

3. On the **Pattern** dashboard, click the **References** tab, and then click the **Define** button.
4. Click on the top face of the model and click the **Sketch** button.
5. On the **Sketch** ribbon, click **Sketching > Offset** .
6. Select the inner horizontal edge of the model.

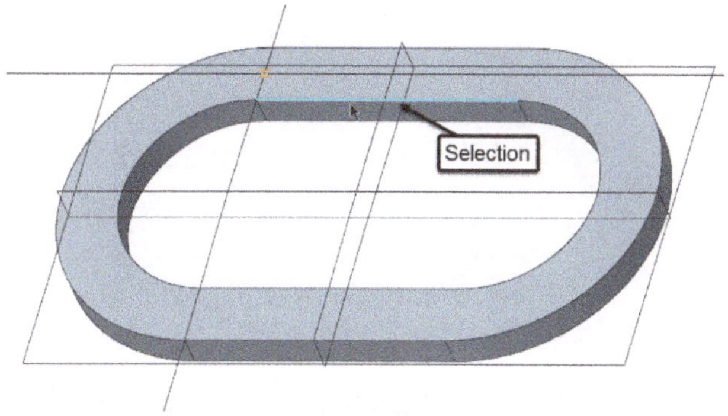

7. Press and hold the SHIFT key and select the curved edge next to it. The edge loop is selected.

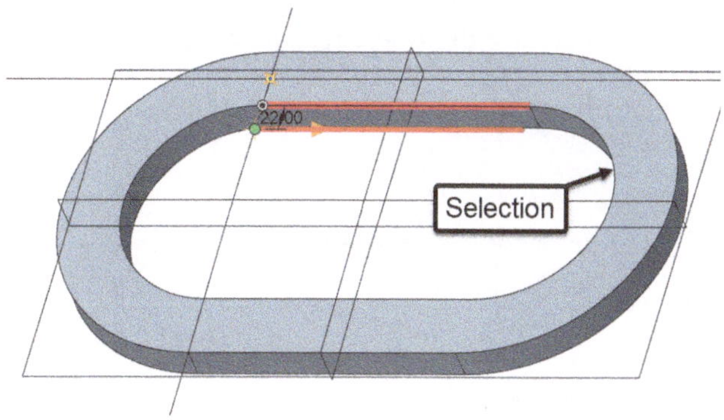

-

8. Type -25 in the offset box, and then press ENTER.

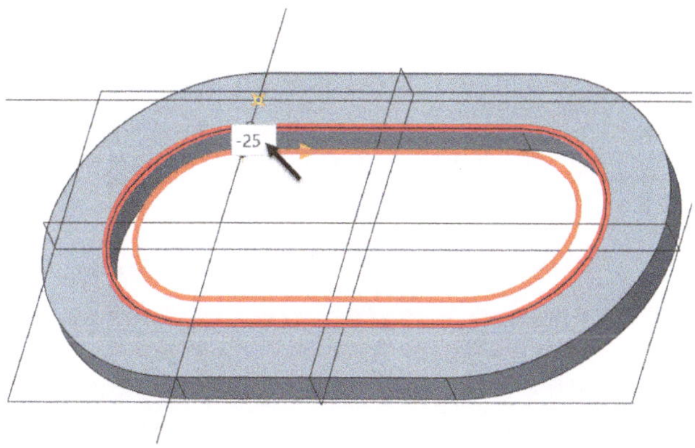

9. Click the green check on the toolbar.

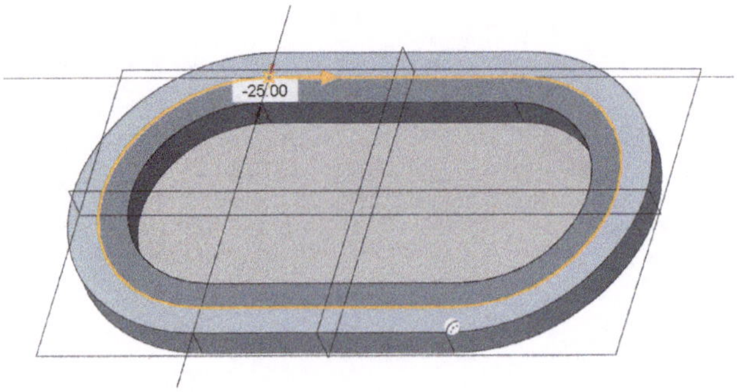

10. Click **OK** on the **Sketch** ribbon. The pattern preview appears, and the sketch origin is used as pattern origin. However, you can change the origin of the pattern by clicking the **Options** tab and checking the **Use alternate origin** option.

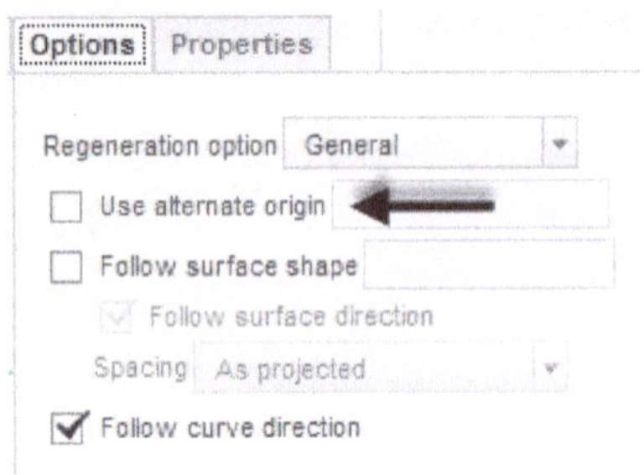

11. On the **Pattern** dashboard, click the **Number of members** icon and type 12 in the **Quantity** box.

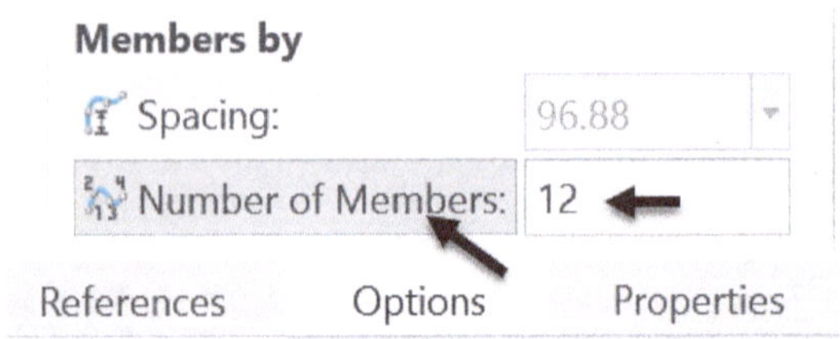

12. Click the green check to complete the pattern.

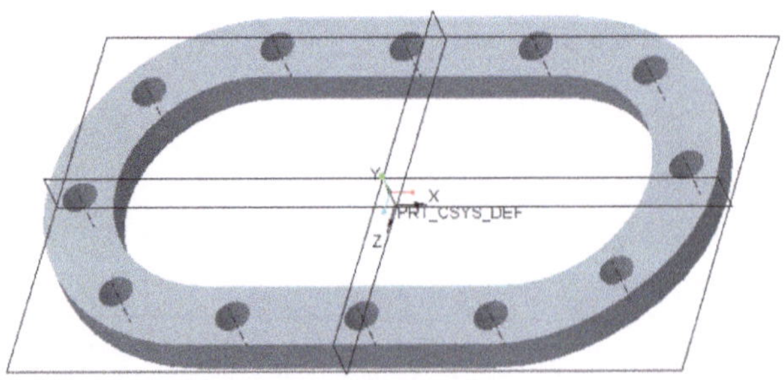

Point

This option patterns the selected features by using user-defined points.

1. Start a sketch and place datum points, as shown below. You need to divide the sketch entities by using the **Divide** command and then place the datum points (refer to **The Divide command** section in Chapter 2 to learn how to divide sketch entities).

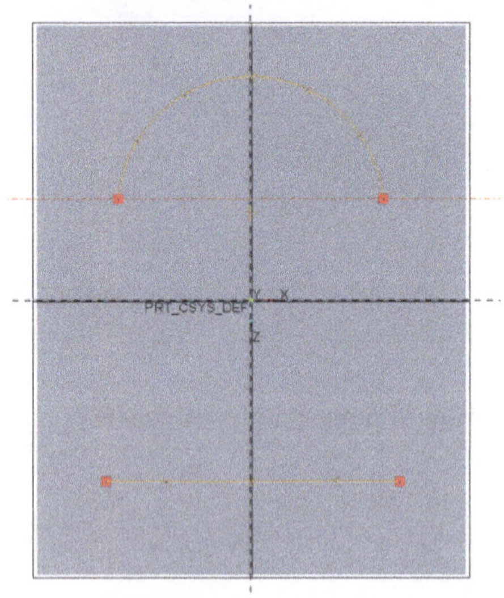

2. Exit the sketch.
3. On the ribbon, click **Model > Datum > Point**, and place points, as shown below.

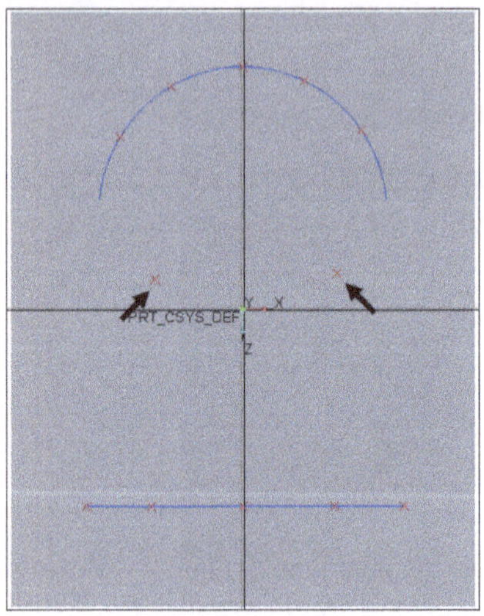

4. Create a hole or any other feature to pattern.

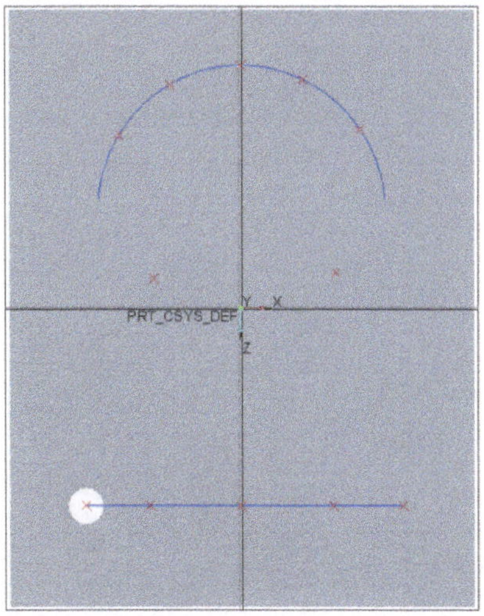

5. Select the feature to pattern and activate the **Pattern** command.
6. On the **Pattern** dashboard, select **Point** from the **Type** drop-down available on the left side.

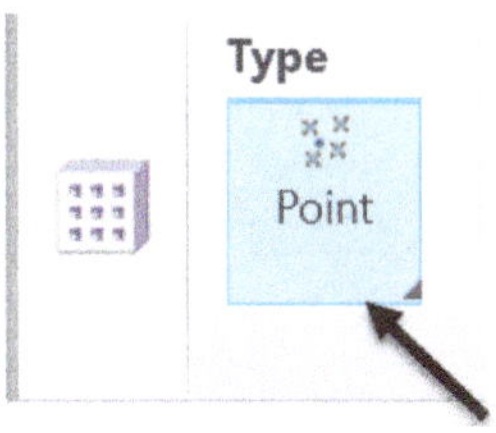

7. Click the **From Sketch** icon on the dashboard and select the sketch.
8. Click the green check.

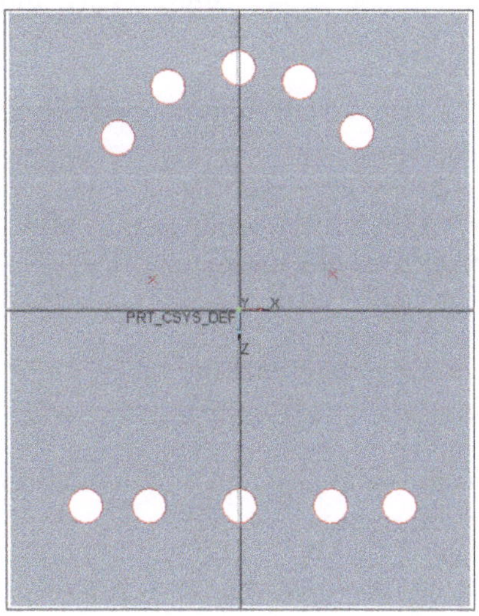

9. In the model tree, click the right mouse button on the Pattern and select **Edit Definition**.
10. On the **Pattern** dashboard, click the **From Feature** icon, and select the datum points.
11. Click the green check.

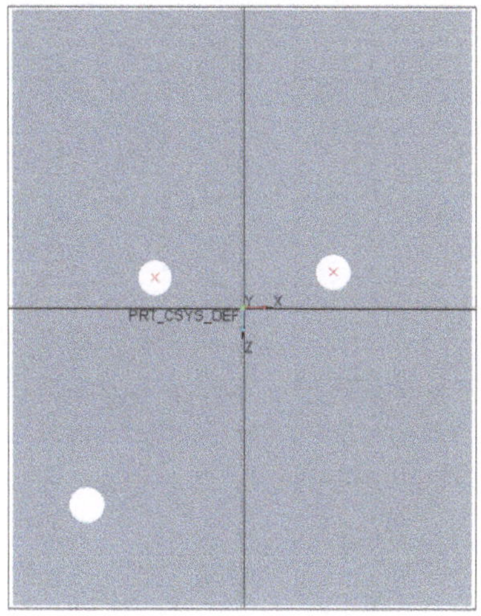

Examples

Example 1

In this example, you will create the part shown below.

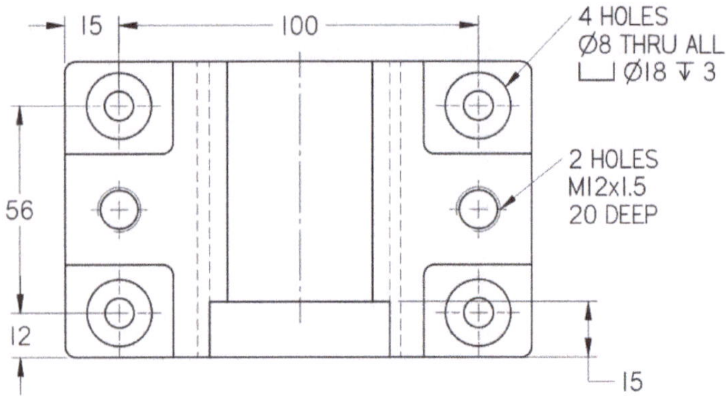

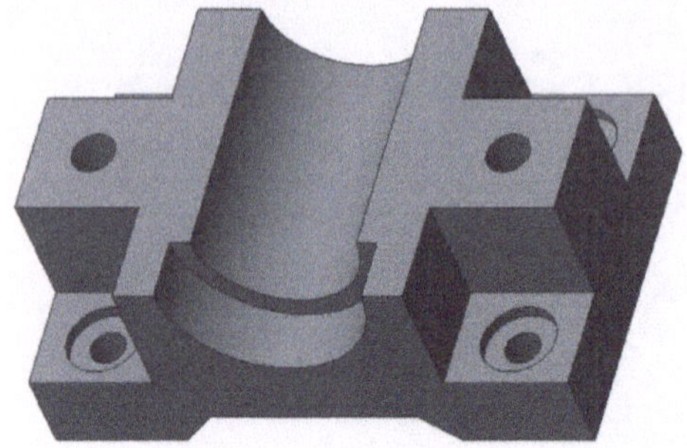

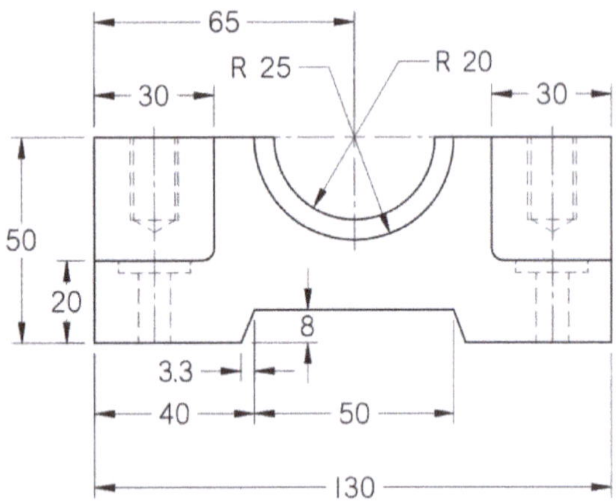

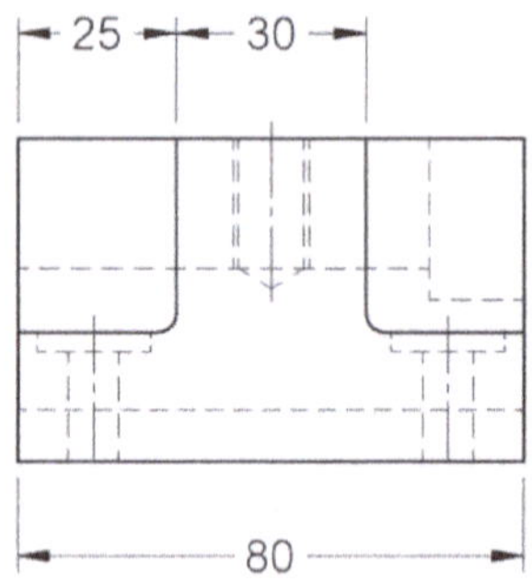

1. Start **Creo Parametric 11.0**.
2. Create the *Patterned Geometry* folder.
3. On the ribbon, click **File > Manage Session > Select Working Directory**.

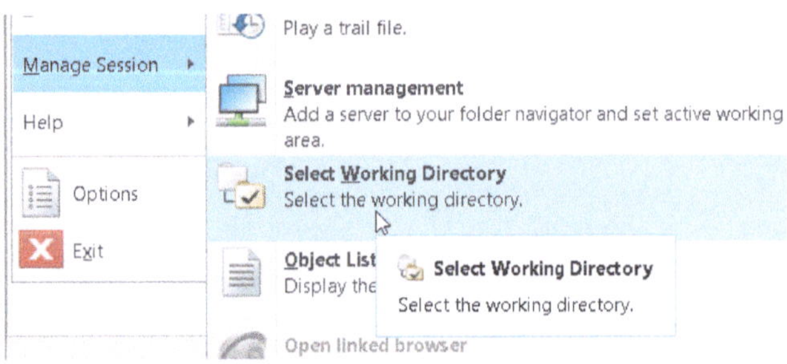

4. Browse to the location of the *Patterned Geometry* folder, and then click **OK**.
5. On the Quick Access Toolbar, click the **New** button.
6. On the **New** dialog, select **Types > Part**, and then type-in **C05-Example1**.
7. Uncheck the **Use default template** option and click **OK**.
8. On the **New File Options** dialog, select the **solid_part_mmks_abs** template. Click **OK** to start the file.
9. Activate the **Extrude** command and click on the Front plane.
10. Create a rectangular sketch using the **Center Rectangle** command.
11. Modify the dimensions, and then click **OK** on the ribbon.

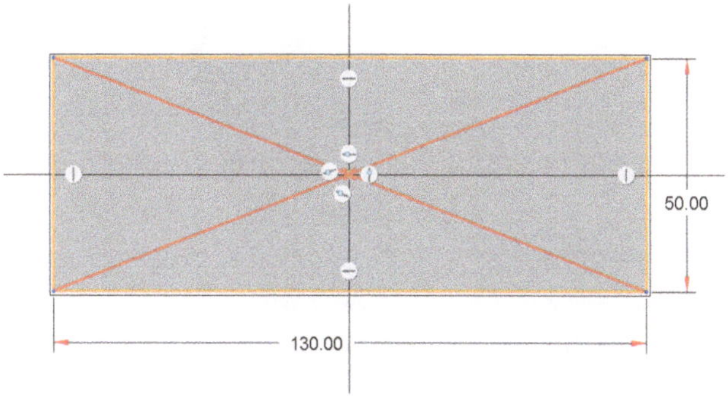

12. On the dashboard, type-in **80** in the **Depth** box.
13. Select the **Symmetric** option from the **Depth** drop-down.
14. Click the green check to complete the *Extrude* feature.

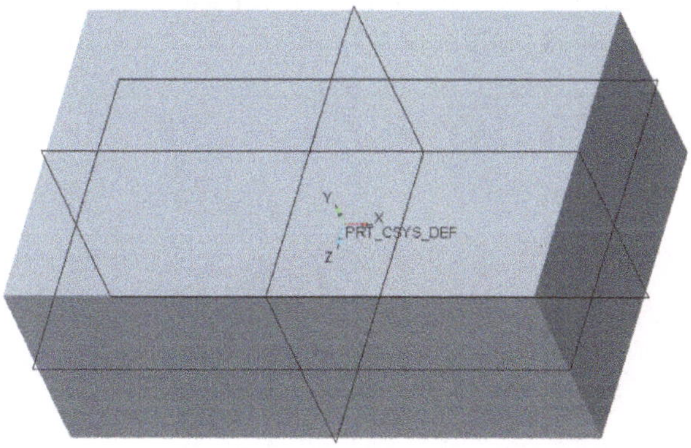

15. On the ribbon, click **Model** tab > **Datum** panel > **Sketch**.
16. Click on the top face of the part geometry.
17. On the **Sketch** dialog, click in the **Reference** box and select the right face of the model.
18. Click **Sketch** to start the sketch.
19. Create a rectangular sketch and click **OK**.

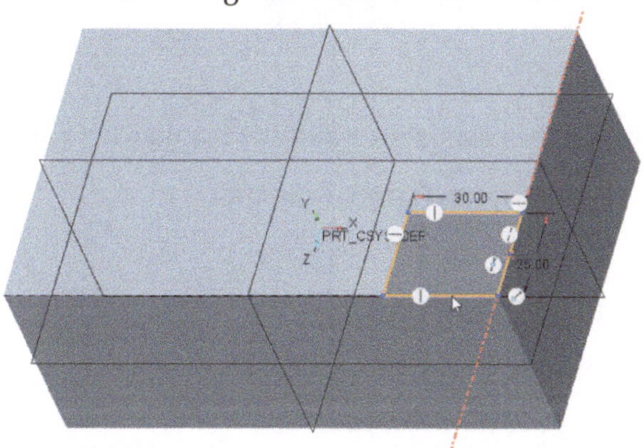

20. Activate the **Extrude** command.
21. Create the *Extruded cut* feature of **30 mm** depth.

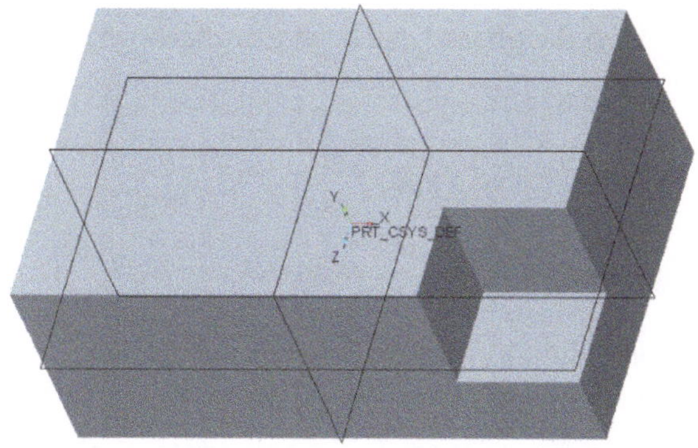

22. Activate the **Hole** command and click on the bottom face of the *Extruded cut* feature.

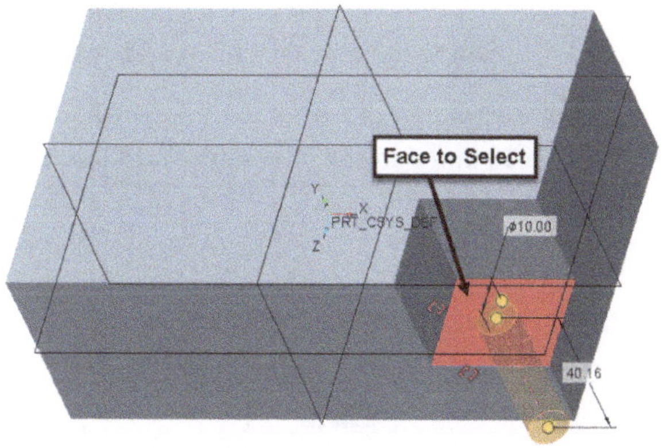

23. Align the red handles of the hole to the horizontal and vertical edges of the placement face.
24. Change the horizontal and vertical offset distances of the hole to 15 and 12, respectively.

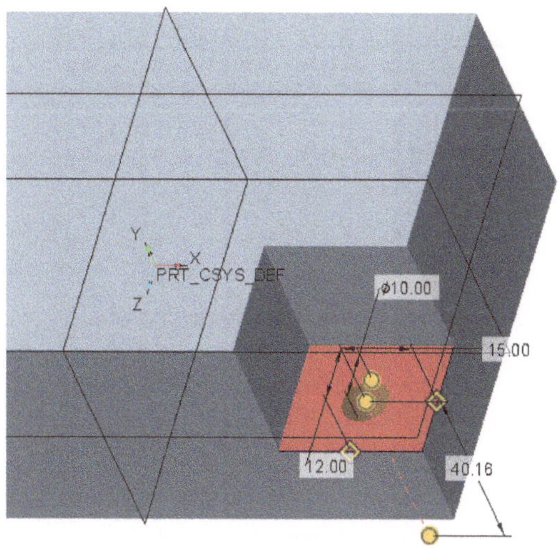

25. On the dashboard, click the **Standard**  icon.

26. On the dashboard, click the **Counterbore** icon.
27. Set the **Thread Type** to **ISO**.
28. Set the **Screw Size** to **10x1.5**.
29. Select the **Through all** option from the **Depth** drop-down.

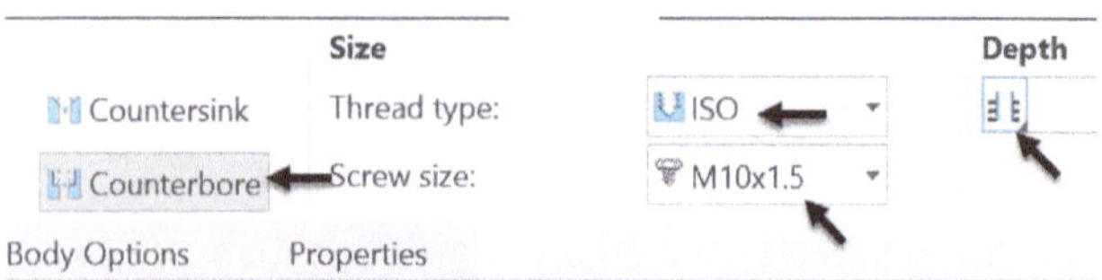

30. Click the **Shape** tab and select **Thru Thread** option.
31. Type-in **18** and **3** in the **Diameter** and **Depth** boxes, respectively.

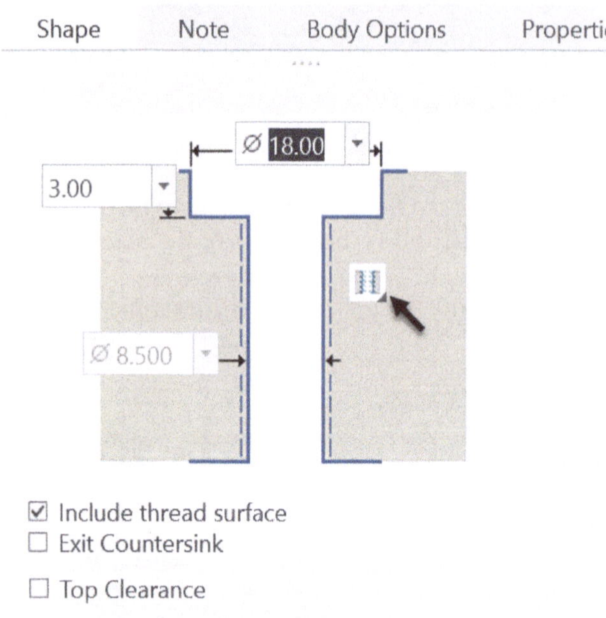

32. Click the green check to create the hole.

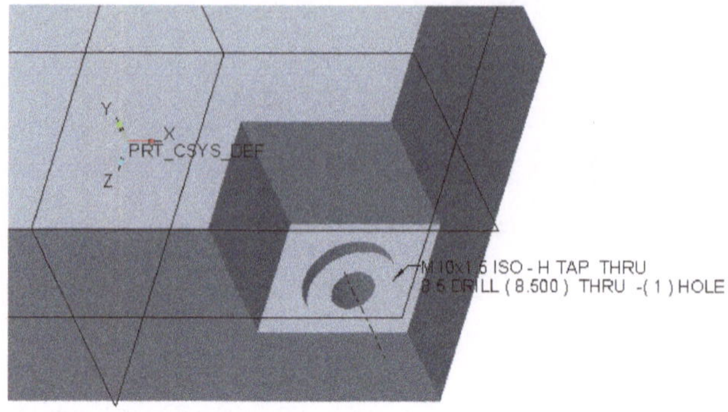

33. Activate the **Hole** command and click on the top face of the model.
34. Align the green handles of the hole to the horizontal and vertical edges of the face.
35. Change the horizontal and vertical offset distances of the hole to **15** and **40**, respectively.

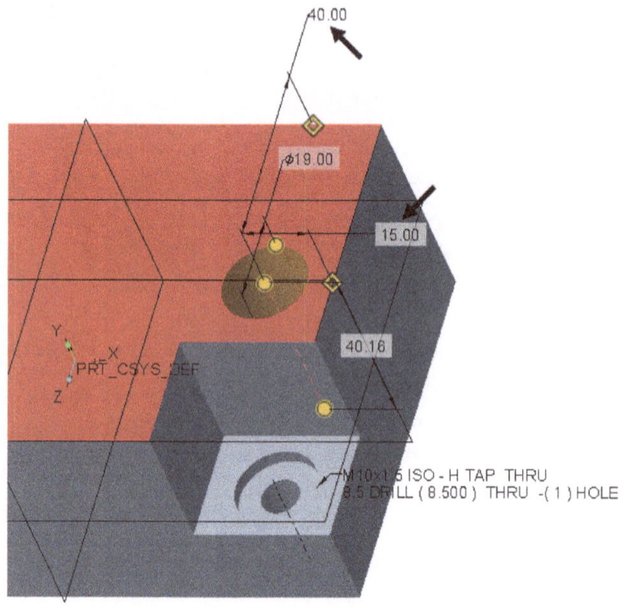

36. On the dashboard, select the **Standard** icon.
37. Set the thread standard to **ISO**.
38. Set the screw size to **12x1.5**.
39. Select the **Blind** option from the **Depth** drop-down.
40. Type 20 in the **Depth** box.
41. Select **Shoulder** from the drop-down located next to the depth drop-down.

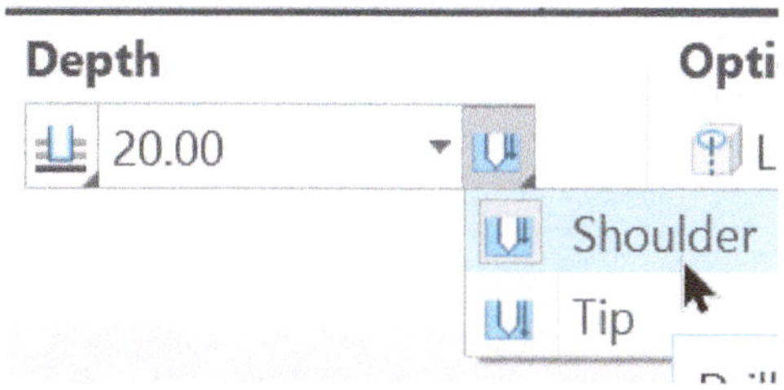

42. Click the **Shape** tab on the dashboard and select **Thru Thread** option.

43. Click the green check to create the hole.

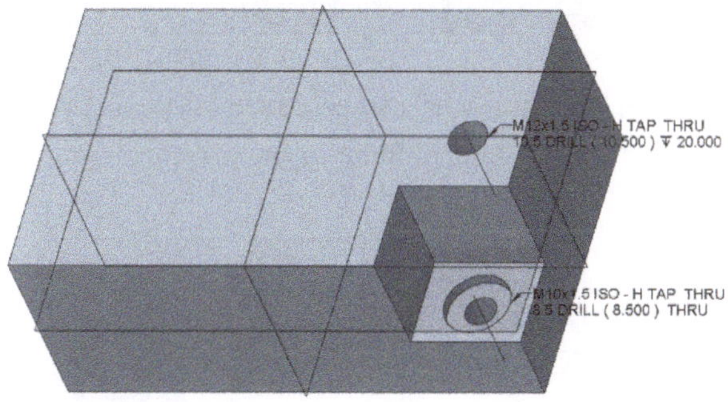

44. Select the *Extruded cut* feature from the Model Tree.

45. On the ribbon, click **Model** tab > **Editing** panel > **Pattern** drop-down **> Pattern** .

46. On the dashboard, select the **Direction** option from the **Type** drop-down located on the left side.

47. Click on the top front edge of the part geometry to define the first direction of the pattern.

48. Click in the **2nd Direction** reference box and select the top-right edge of the part geometry. It defines the second direction.

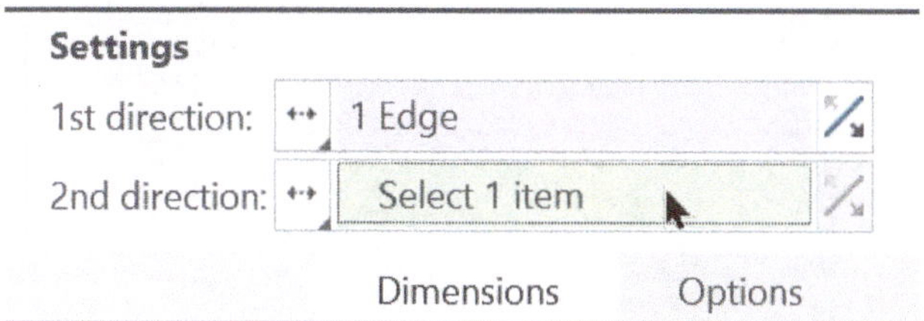

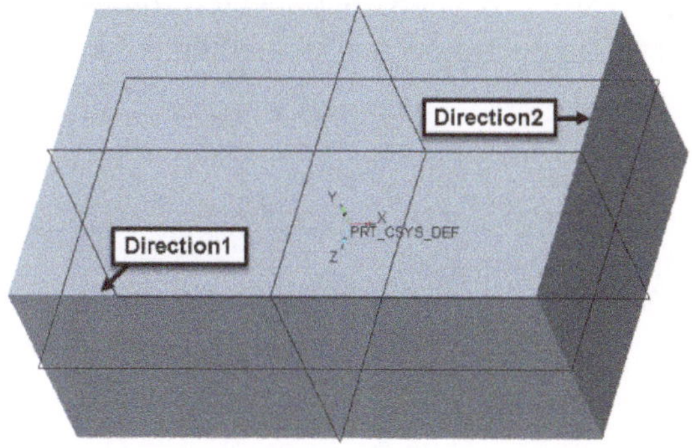

49. Enter members in the first direction as **2** and spacing value as **100**.

50. Enter members in the second direction as **2** and spacing value as **55**.

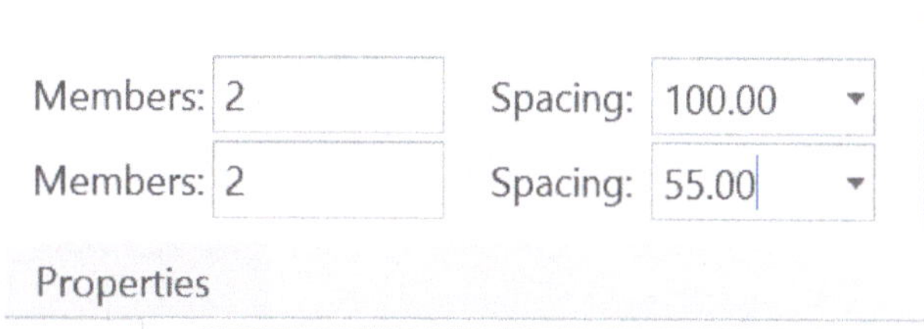

51. Click the **Flip the second direction** button on the dashboard.

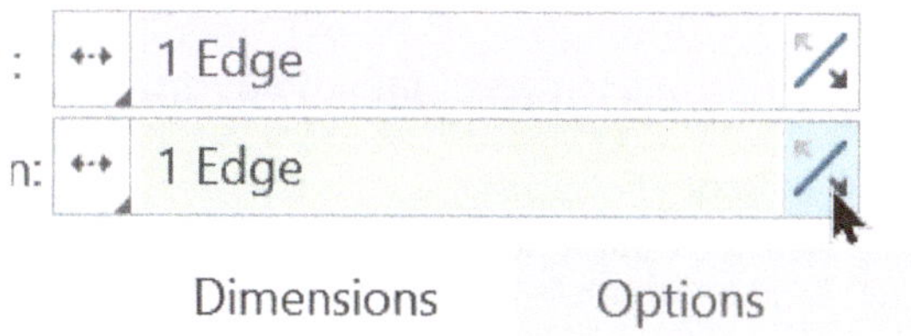

52. Click the green check to complete the pattern.

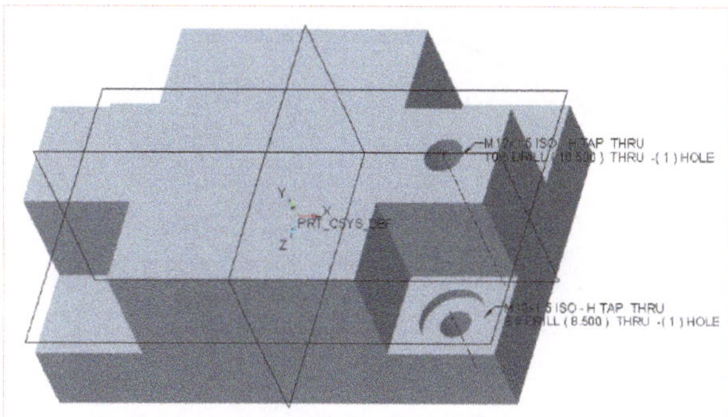

53. Select the counterbore hole and click the **Pattern** icon on the ribbon.

54. On the **Pattern** dashboard, select **Reference** from the **Type** drop-down located on the left side.

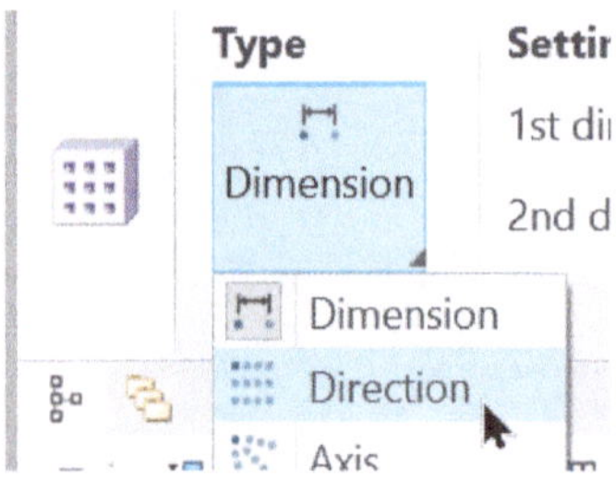

55. Specify the same parameters used in the previously created pattern.

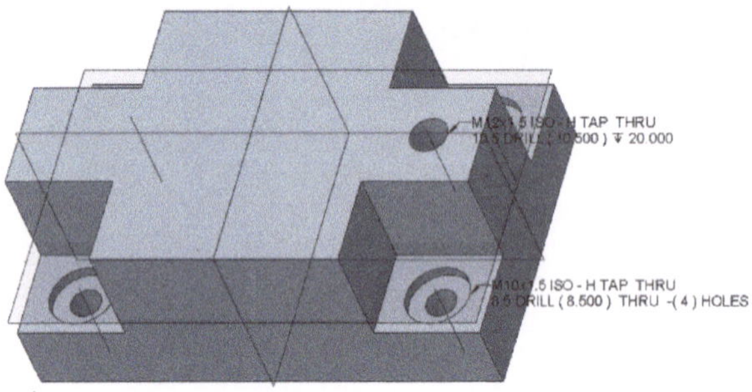

56. Click **OK.**
57. Select the simple threaded hole from the Model Tree.
58. On the ribbon, click the **Model** tab > **Editing** panel > **Mirror** .
59. Select the Right plane to define the mirroring plane.
60. Click the green check on the dashboard to mirror the hole.

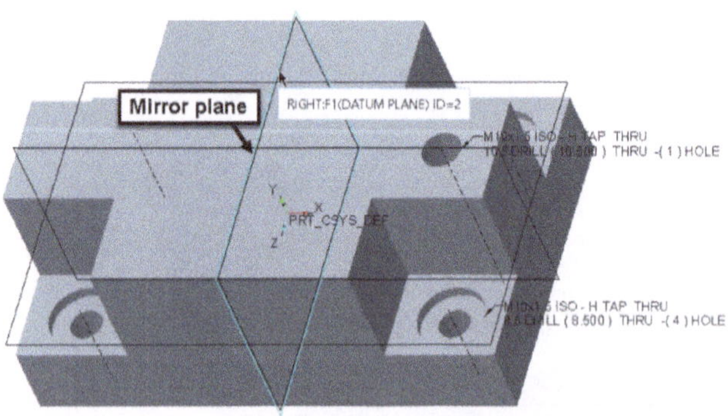

61. On the **Model** ribbon tab, click **Datum** panel > **Axis**.
62. Press the Ctrl key and click on the top face of the model and the right plane.

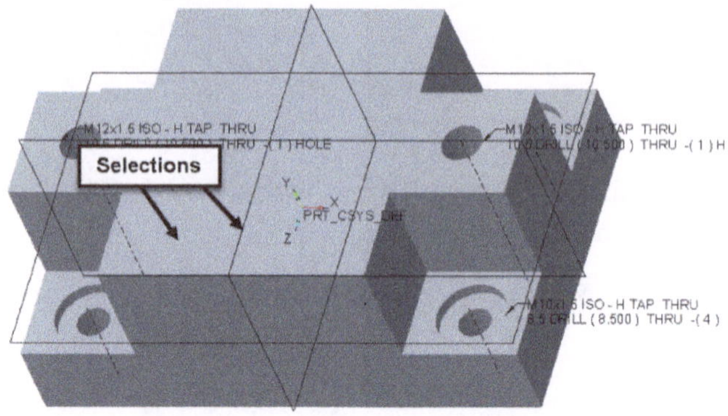

63. Click **OK** to create the axis at the intersection of the two selected planes.

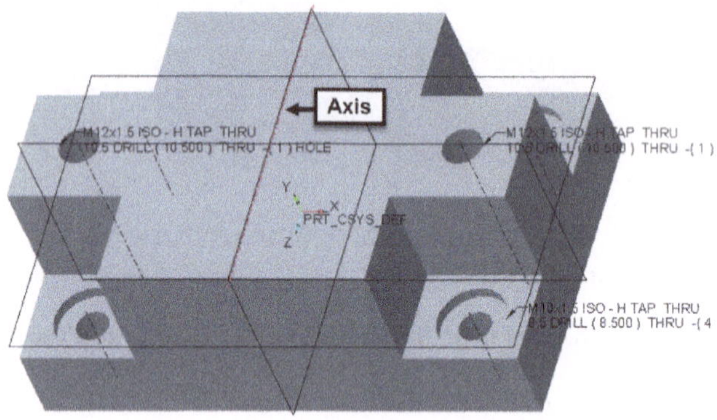

64. On the ribbon, click the **Model** tab > **Engineering** panel > **Hole**.
65. Press and hold the CTRL key and select the model's front face and the newly created axis; the hole preview appears on the axis.

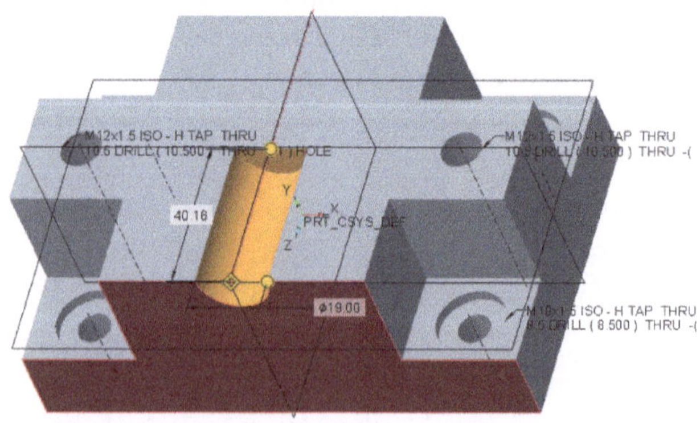

66. Click the **Simple** icon under the **Type** section on the **Hole** dashboard.

67. Click the **Drilled** icon under the **Profile** section on the dashboard.

68. Click **Counterbore** icon on the **Hole** dashboard.

69. Type 40 in the Diameter box.

70. Click the **Shape** tab and specify the parameters, as shown.

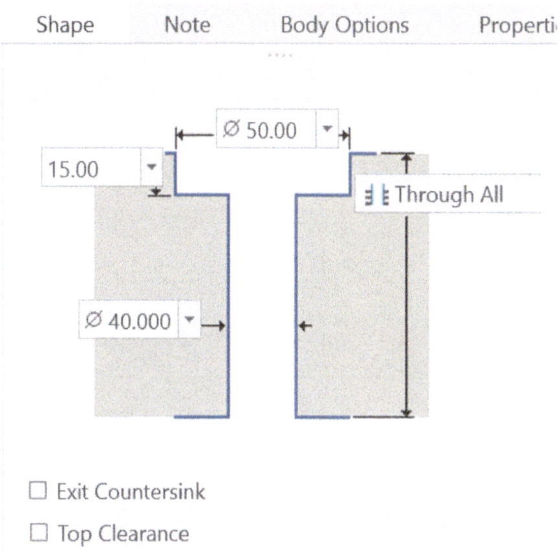

71. Click **OK** to create the counterbore hole.

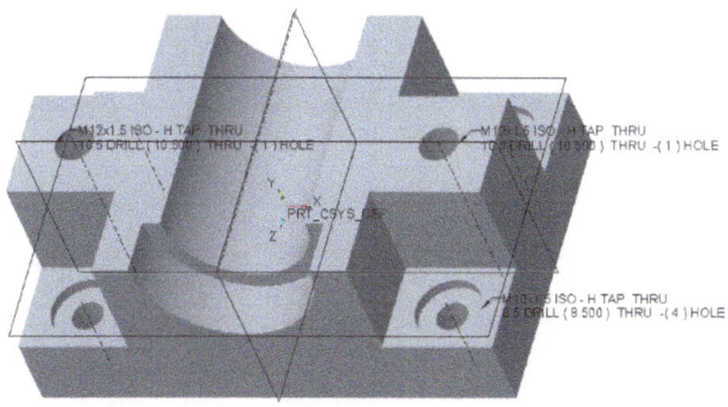

72. Activate the **Sketch** command and click on the front face of the model.

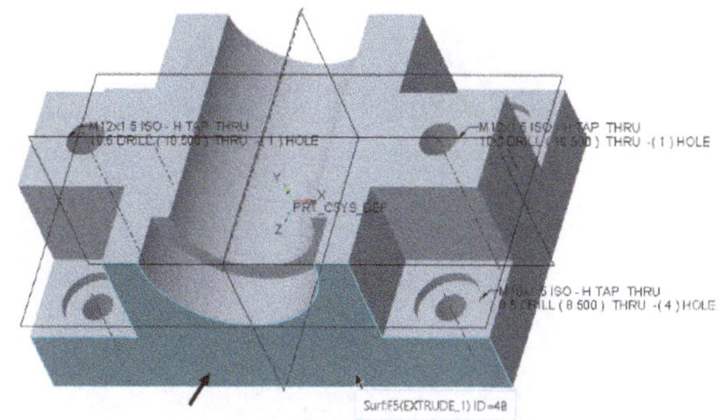

73. On the **Sketch** dialog, click in the **Reference** box and select the bottom face of the model.

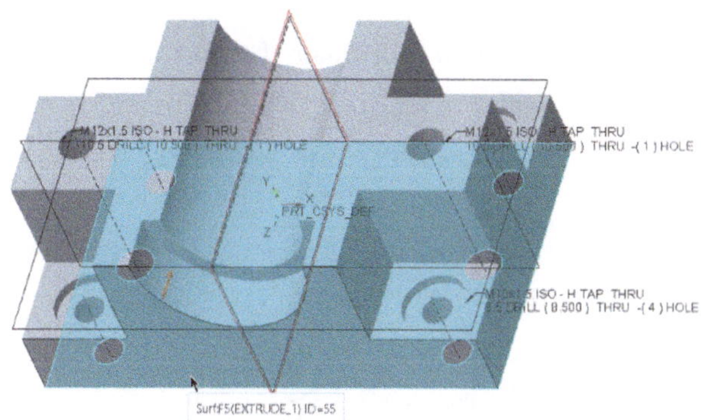

74. Click **Sketch** on the **Sketch** dialog.

75. Create the sketch, as shown below.

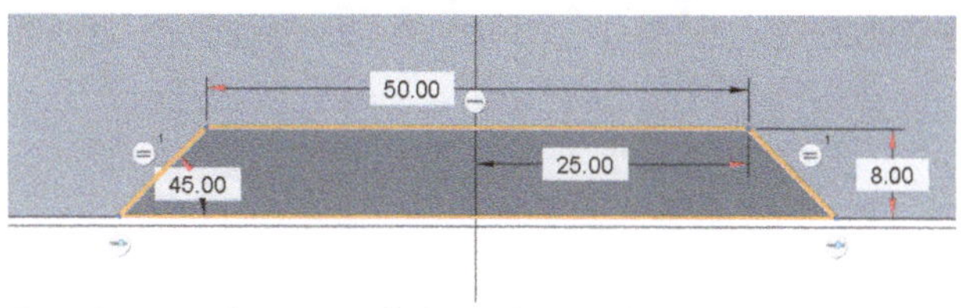

76. Create the *Extruded cut* throughout the model geometry.

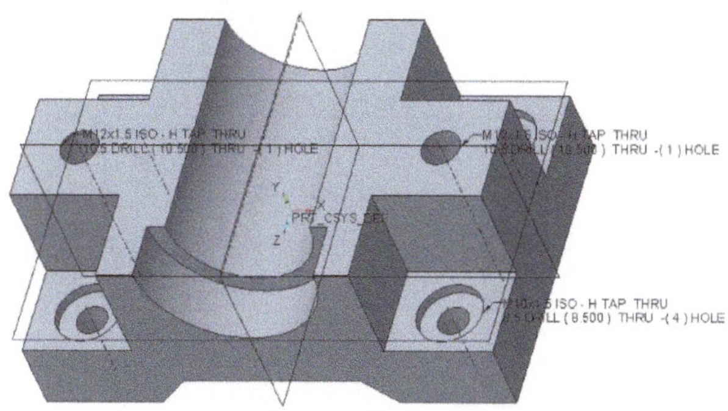

77. Round the sharp edges of the *Extrude cut* features. The round radius is 2 mm.

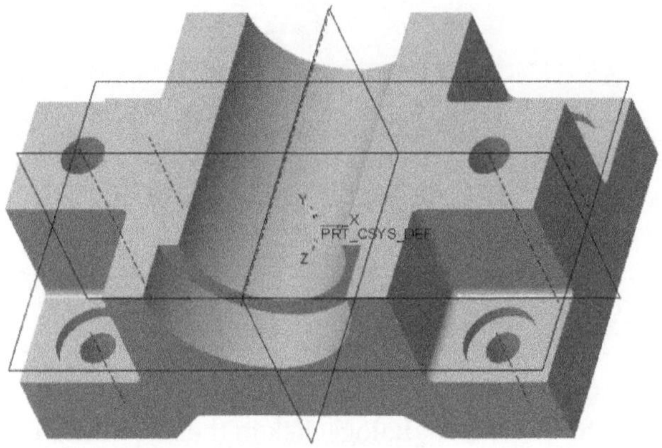

78. Save and close the part file.

Example 2

In this example, you will create the part shown below.

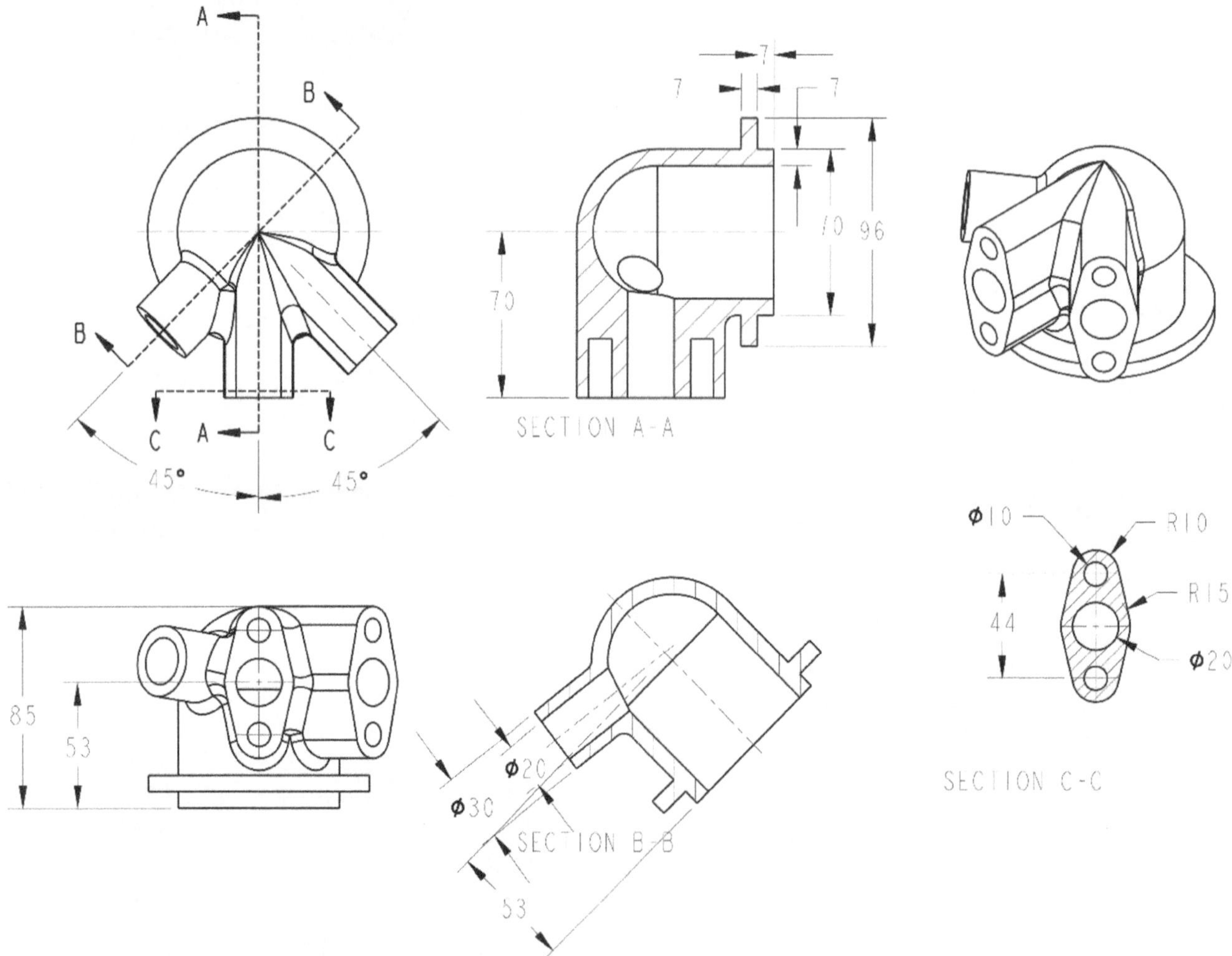

Creating the First Feature

1. Start **Creo Parametric 11.0**.
2. On the Quick Access Toolbar, click the **New** button.
3. On the **New** dialog, select **Types > Part**, and then type-in **C05-Example2** in the **Name** box.
4. Uncheck the **Use default template** option and click **OK**.
5. On the **New File Options** dialog, select **solid_part_mmks_abs**, and click **OK**.
6. On the ribbon, click **Model** tab > **Datum** panel > **Sketch** .
7. Click on the Front plane.

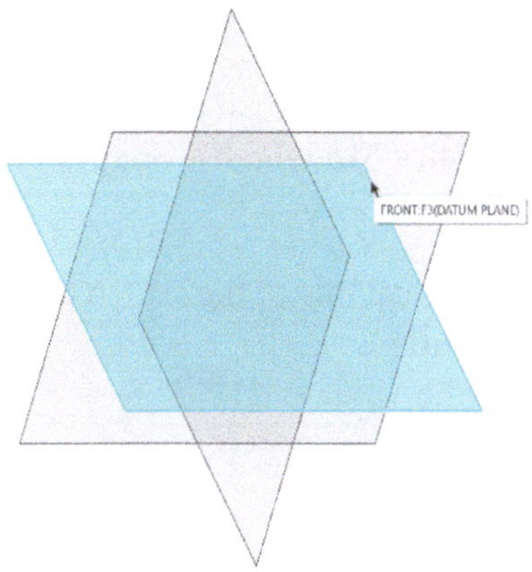

8. Accept the default values on the **Sketch** dialog and click **Sketch**.
9. On the **Graphics** toolbar, click the **Sketch View** icon to orient the sketch plane parallel to the screen.

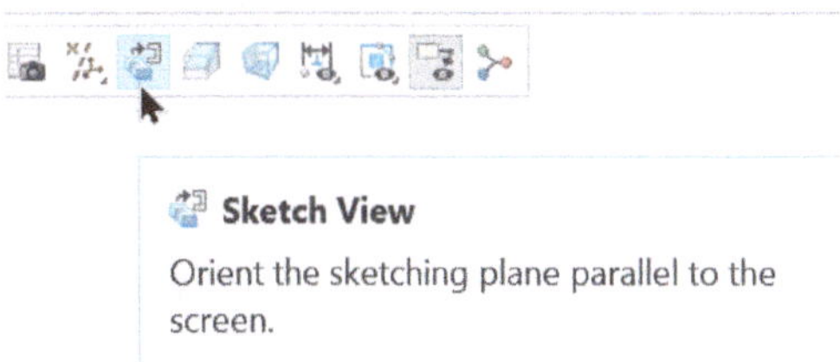

10. On the ribbon, click **Sketch** tab > **Sketching** panel > **Line Chain**.
11. Specify the start point of the line on the vertical reference.
12. Click on the origin point to define the second point.
13. Move the pointer horizontally toward the right and click on the horizontal reference.
14. Move the pointer vertically up to a small distance and click.
15. Move the pointer horizontally toward the right up to a small distance and click.
16. Move the pointer vertically up to a small distance and click.
17. Move the pointer horizontally toward the left up to a small distance and click.
18. Move the pointer vertically upward and click.

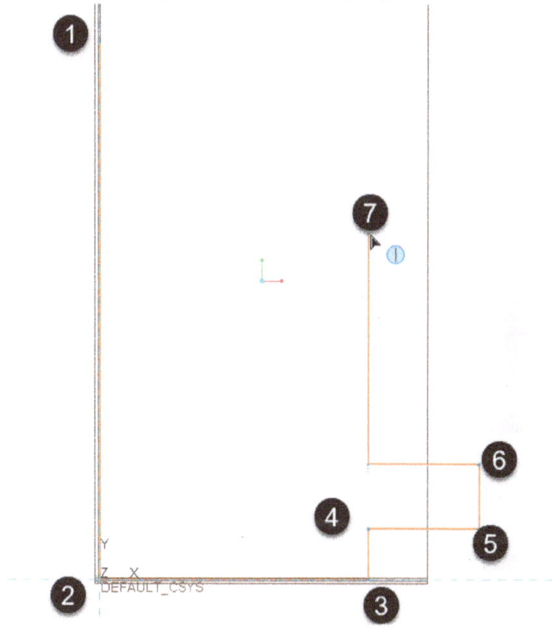

19. On the ribbon, click **Sketch** tab > **Sketching** panel > **Arc** drop-down > **3-Point/Tangent End**.

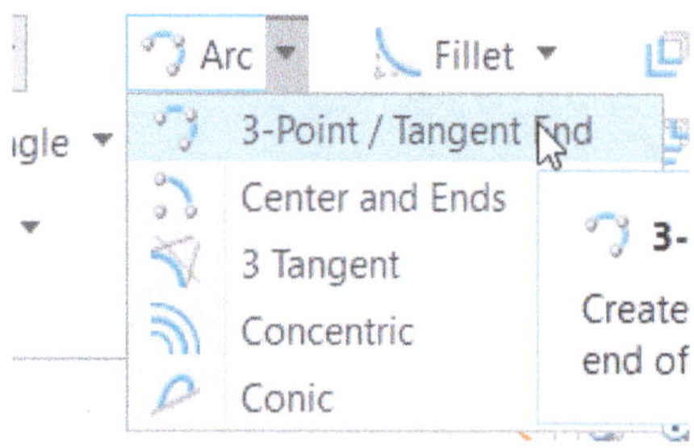

20. Select the endpoint of the right vertical line.
21. Move the pointer in-line with the right vertical line.
22. Select the endpoint of the left vertical line.

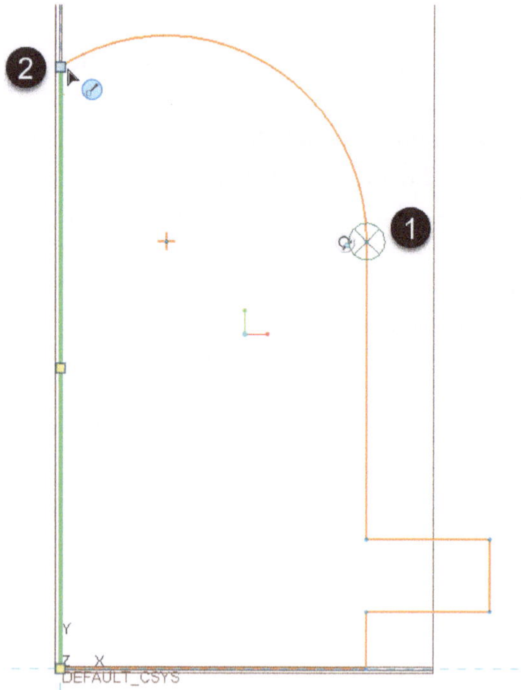

23. Apply the Coincident constraint between the centerpoint of the arc and the left vertical line.

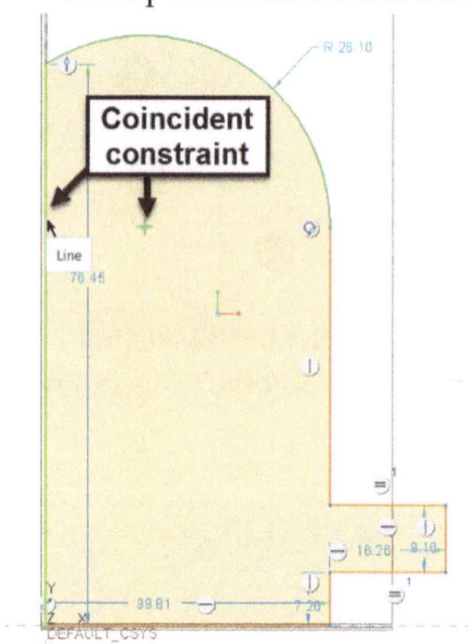

24. Add dimensions to the sketch, as shown.

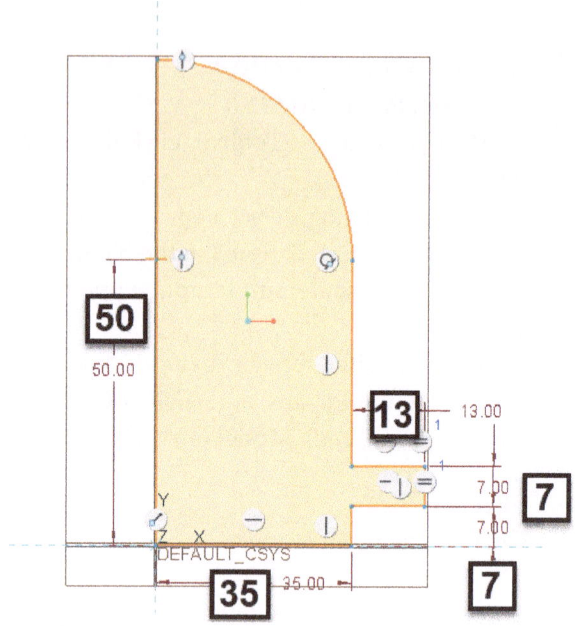

25. On the ribbon, click **OK** to exit the **Sketch** mode.
26. On the ribbon, click **Model** tab > **Shapes** panel > **Revolve** .
27. Select the left vertical line of the sketch to define the axis of revolution.

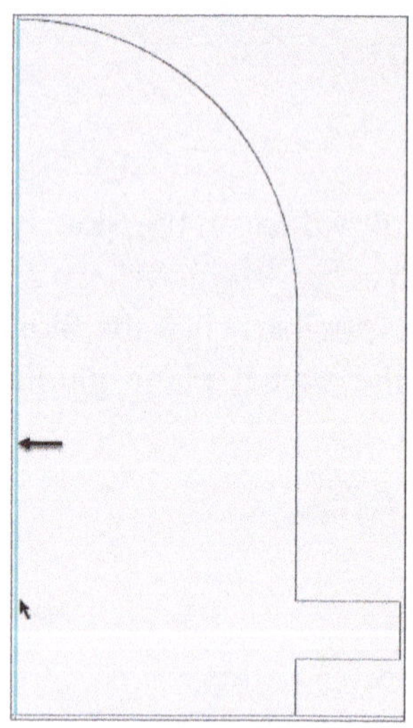

28. On the **Revolve** dashboard, type-in 360 in the **Angle** box.
29. Click the green check to create the *Revolved* feature.

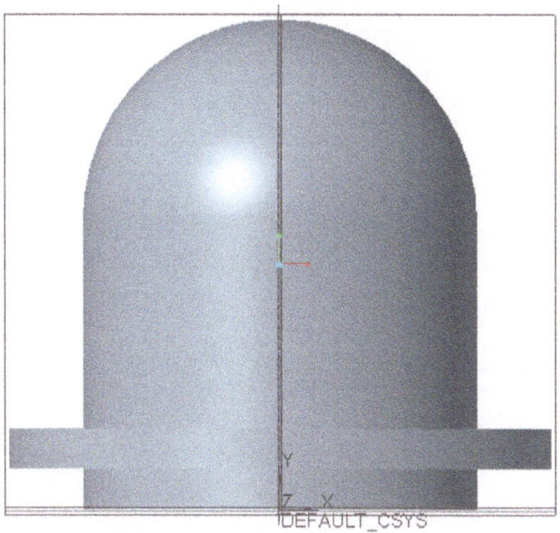

Creating the Second Feature

1. On the ribbon, click **Model** tab > **Datum** panel > **Sketch** .
2. Click on the Front plane.
3. Click the **Sketch** button on the **Sketch** dialog.
4. On the **Graphics** toolbar, click the **Sketch View** icon to orient the sketch plane parallel to the screen.
5. Create three circles, as shown.
6. Apply the **Equal** constraint between the two circles, as shown.

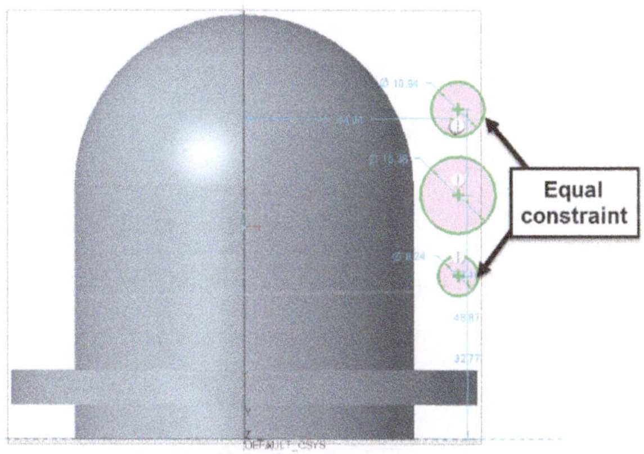

7. Apply the **Vertical** constraint between the center points of the circles.
8. On the ribbon, click **Sketch** tab > **Constrain** panel > **Coincident** .
9. Select the centerpoint of any one of the circles.
10. Select the vertical reference line.

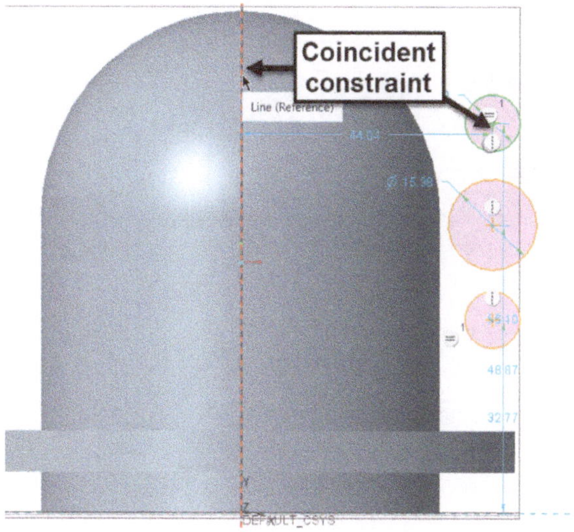

11. On the ribbon, click **Sketch** tab > **Constrain** panel > **Tangent** .
12. Select the top circle and the curve edge, as shown.

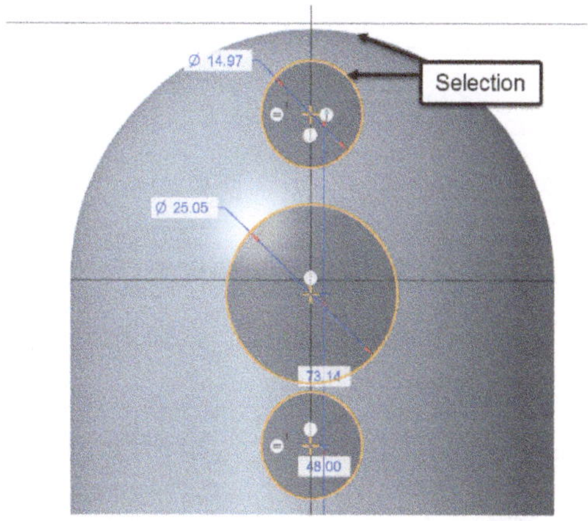

13. On the ribbon, click **Sketch** tab > **Dimension** panel > **Dimension**.
14. Create the dimensions, as shown.

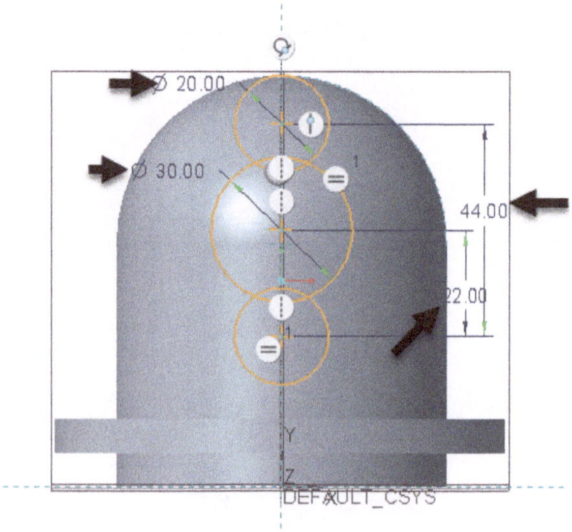

15. On the ribbon, click **Sketch** tab > **Sketching** panel > **Line** drop-down > **Line Tangent**.

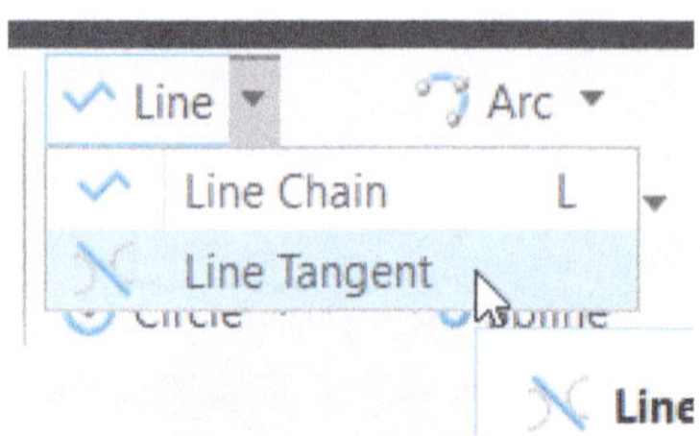

16. Select the two circles, as shown.

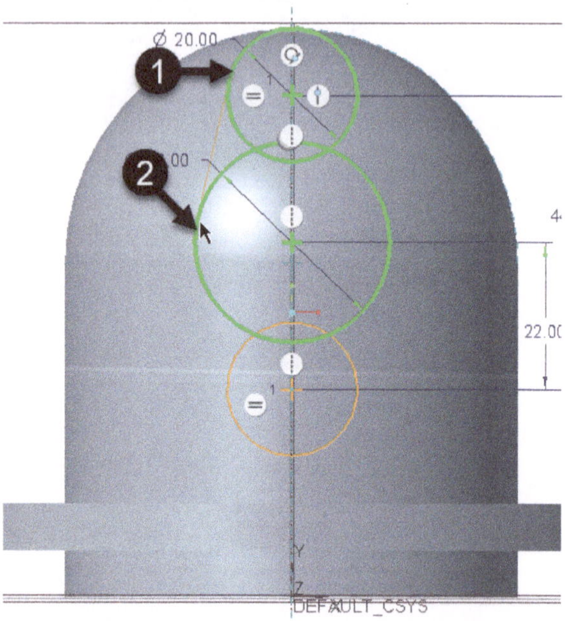

17. Likewise, create three more tangent lines, as shown.

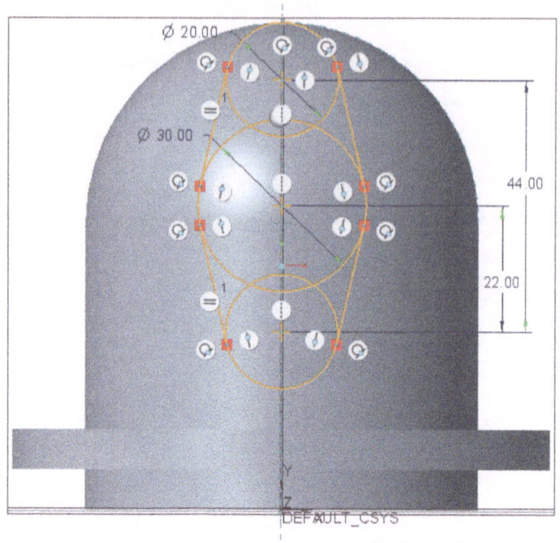

18. On the ribbon, click **Sketch** tab > **Editing** panel > **Delete Segment**.
19. Select the inner segments of the circles, as shown.

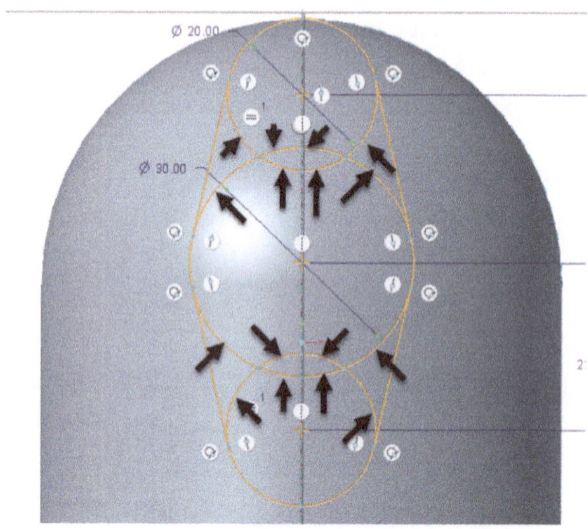

20. Click **OK** on the **Sketch** tab of the ribbon.

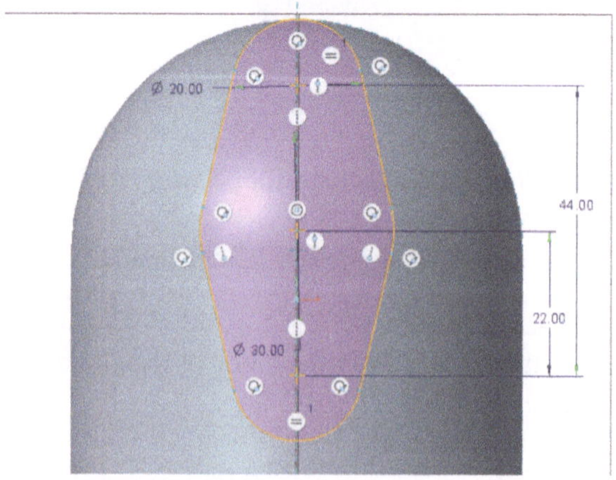

21. On the **Graphics** toolbar, click the **Orientation** drop-down > **Standard Orientation.**

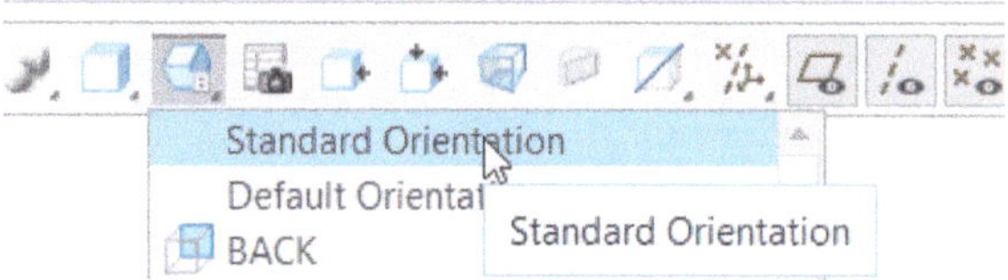

22. On the ribbon, click **Model** tab > **Shapes** panel > **Extrude.**
23. On the **Extrude** Dashboard, type **70** in the **Depth** box.
24. Click the **Options** tab, and select **Side 2 > Through Until.**

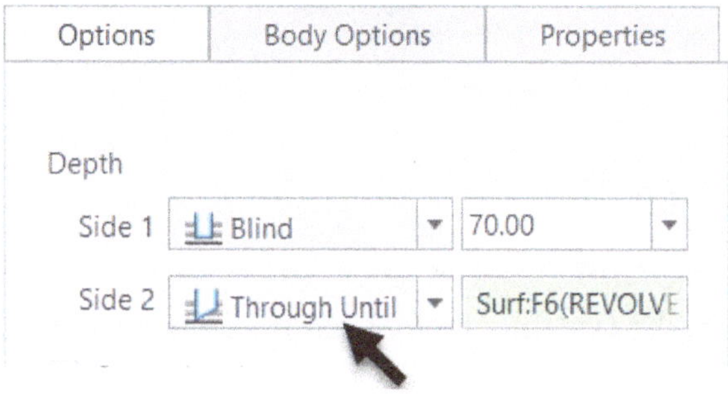

25. Select the cylindrical face of the model, as shown.

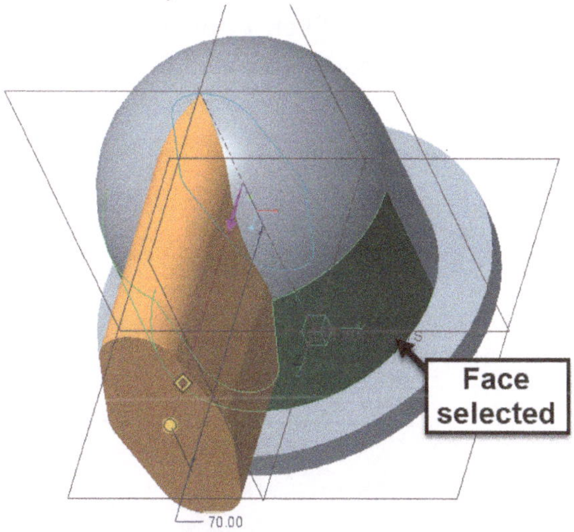

26. Click **OK** on the **Extrude** Dashboard.

Creating the Circular Pattern

1. On the **Graphics** toolbar, click **Datum Display Filters** drop-down and check the **Axis Display** option.

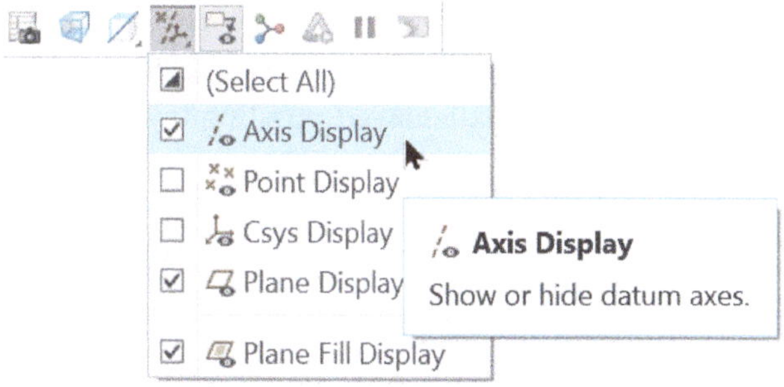

2. In the Model Tree, right-click on the **Extrude 1** feature and select the **Pattern** icon.

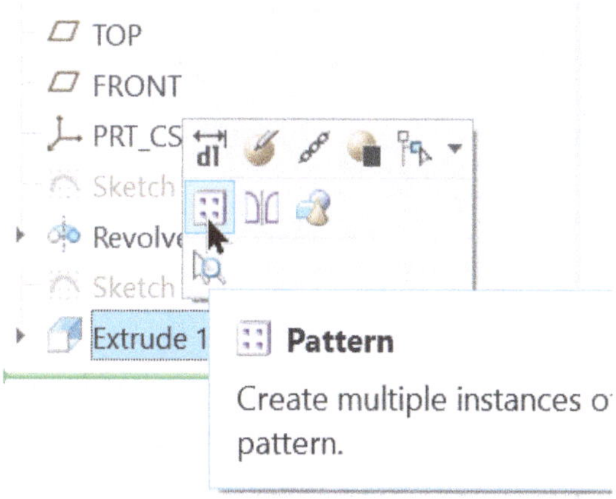

3. On the **Pattern** Dashboard, select **Axis** from the **Type** drop-down.

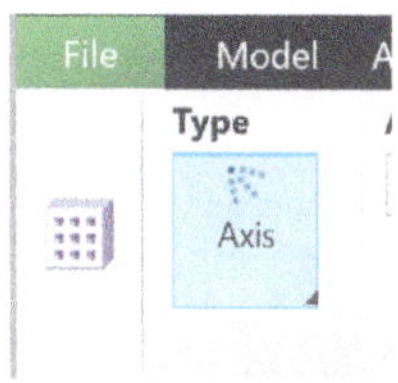

4. Select the axis passing through the origin.

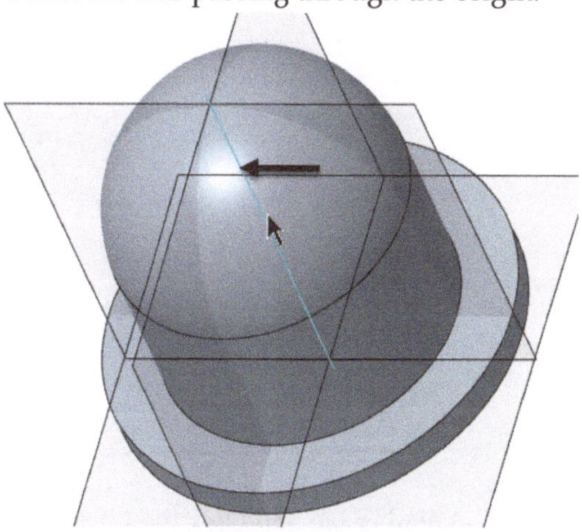

5. Type **2** in the **1st direction members** box.

6. Type **45** in the **Angle between members** box.
7. Click the **Flip** icon next to the Axis selection box, if the arrows are displayed pointing toward the left.
8. Click **OK**.

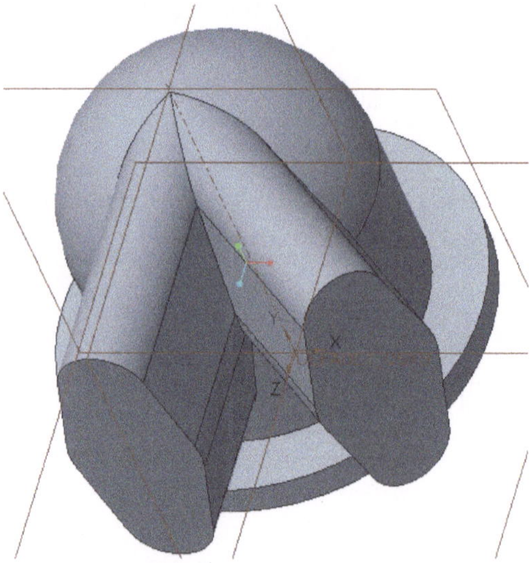

Creating the Inclined Boss

1. On the ribbon, click **Model > Datum > Plane**.
2. Press and hold the Ctrl key and select the Front and Right planes.

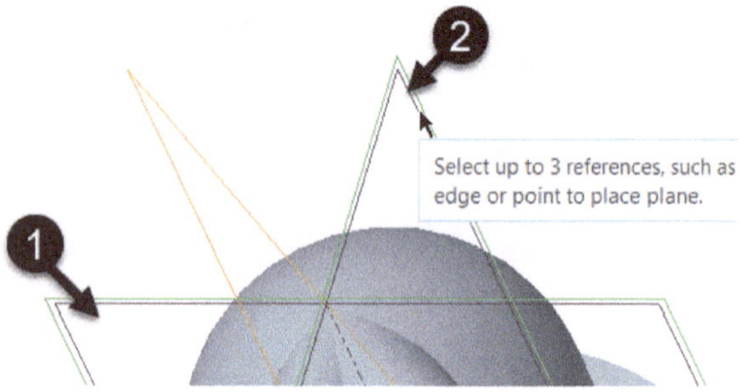

3. On the **Datum Plane** dialog, select the **Bisector 1** option from the drop-down next to the Right Plane.

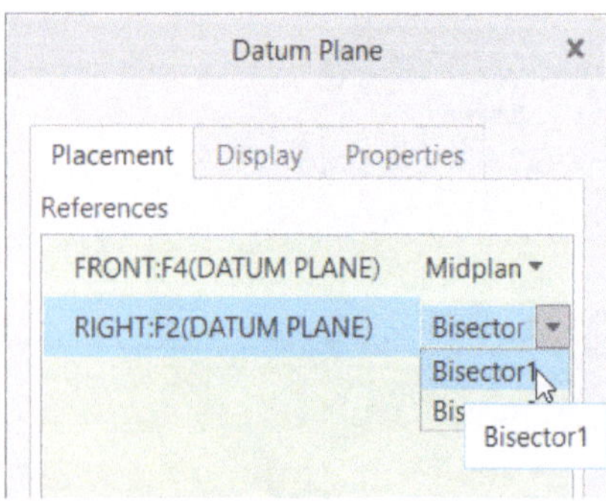

4. Click the **Display** tab and click the **Flip** button next to the **Normal Direction** option.
5. Click **OK**.

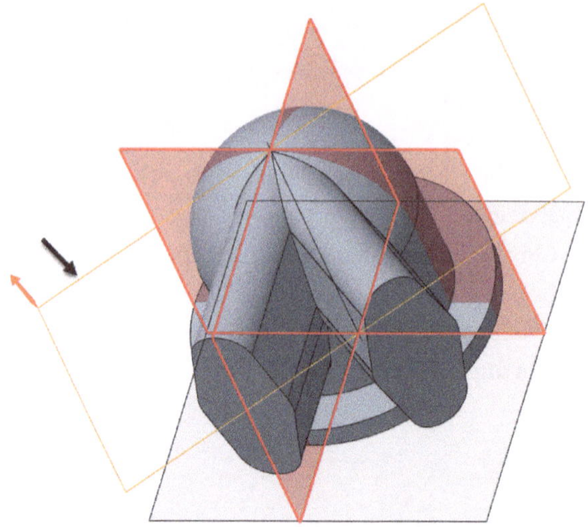

6. On the ribbon, click **Model > Datum > Sketch**.
7. Select the newly created plane, if not already selected.
8. On the **Graphics** toolbar, click the **Sketch View** icon to orient the sketch plane parallel to the screen.
9. On the ribbon, click **Sketch > Sketching > Rectangle** drop-down > **Slanted Rectangle**.

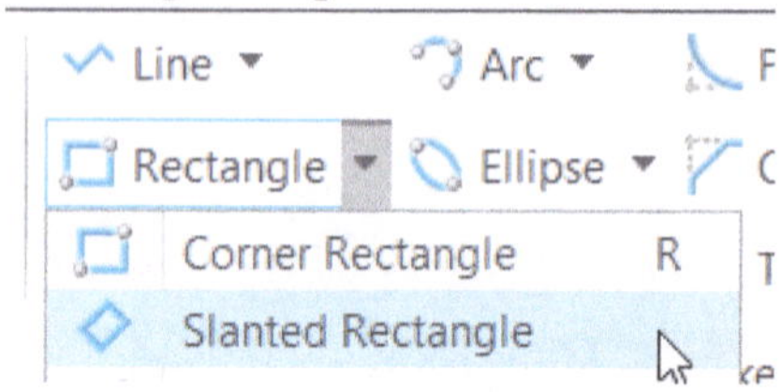

10. Select the two points, as shown.
11. Move the pointer upward and click.

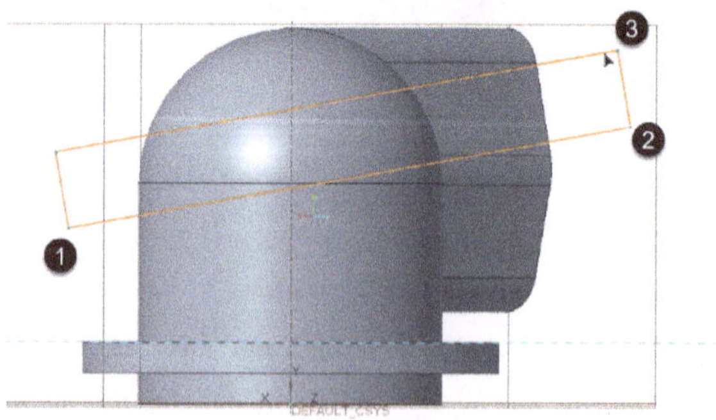

12. Add dimensions to the sketch, as shown.

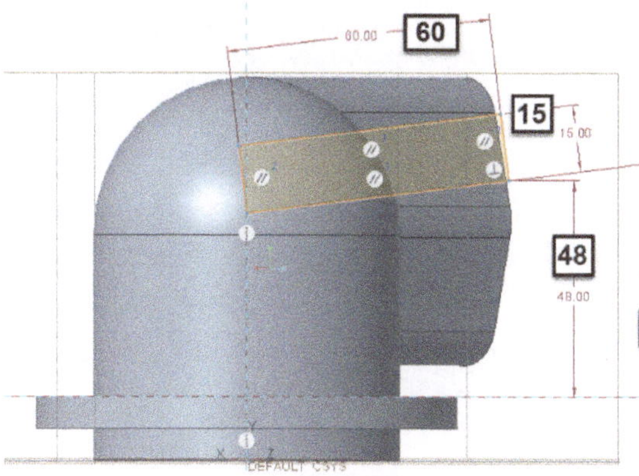

13. Click **OK** on the ribbon.
14. On the ribbon, click **Model > Shapes > Revolve**.
15. Select the newly created sketch.
16. Select the lower inclined line to define the axis.
17. Click **OK**.

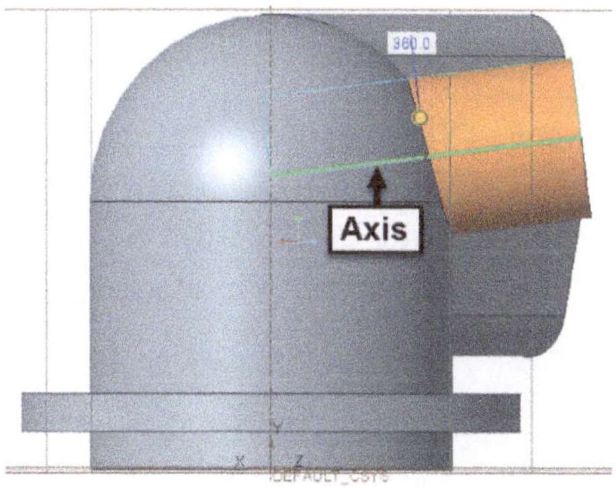

18. On the ribbon, click **Model** tab > **Shapes** panel > **Extrude**.
19. Click on the flat face of the inclined boss.

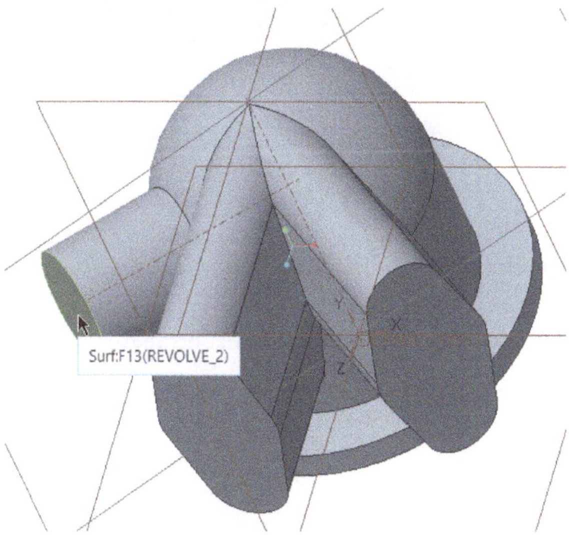

20. On the ribbon, click **Sketch** tab > **Sketching** panel > **Circle** drop-down > **Concentric**.
21. Select the cylindrical face of the inclined boss.

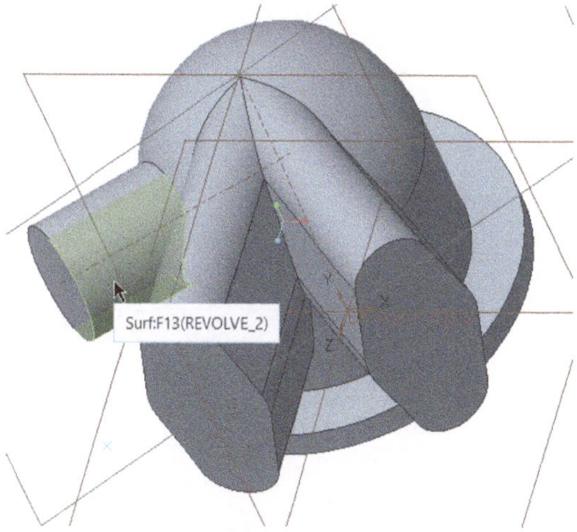

22. Move the pointer outward and click.
23. Press ESC twice.
24. Change the diameter dimension to **20**.
25. Click **OK** on the **Sketch** ribbon.
26. On the **Extrude** Dashboard, click the **Remove Material** icon.
27. Type **60** in the **Depth** box.
28. Click the **Change Direction** button next to the **Depth** box.
29. Click **OK**.

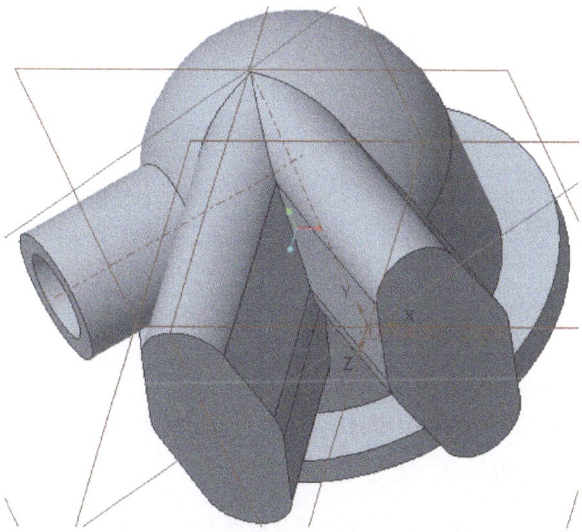

Creating the Extruded Cut Features

1. On the ribbon, click **Model** tab > **Shapes** panel > **Extrude**.
2. Click on the flat face of the second feature.

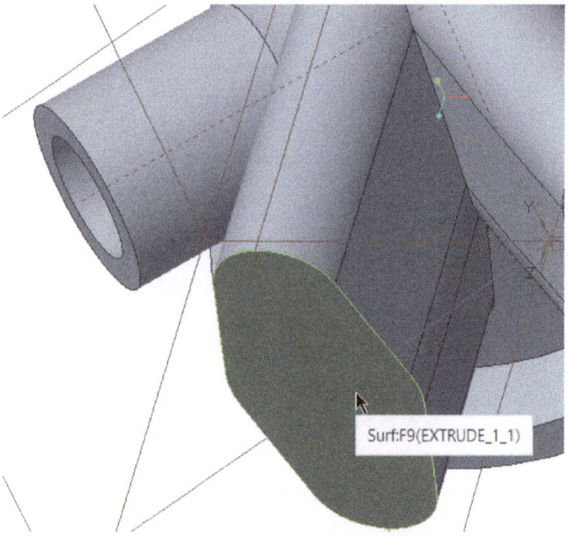

3. On the ribbon, click **Sketch** tab > **Sketching** panel > **Circle** drop-down > **Concentric**.

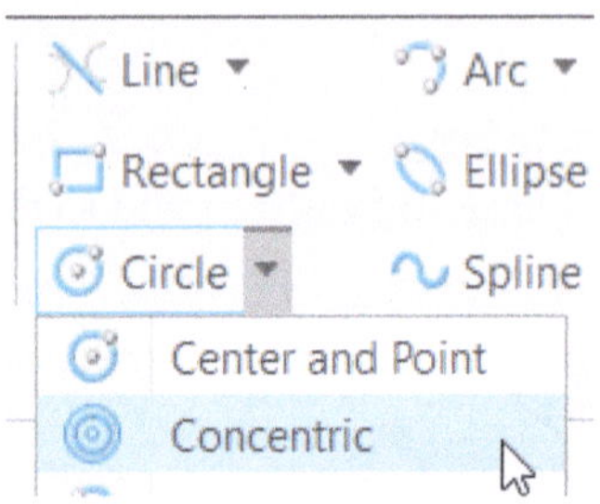

4. Select the curved face of the second feature.

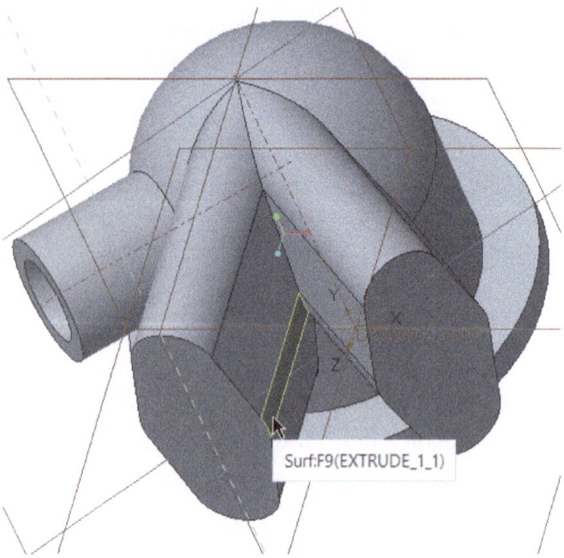

5. Move the pointer outward and click.
6. Press ESC twice.
7. Double-click on the diameter dimension.
8. Change the diameter value to 20.

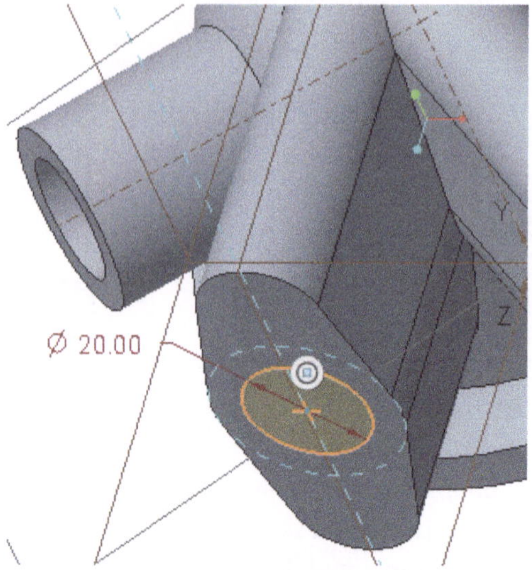

9. Click **OK** on the ribbon.
10. On the **Extrude** Dashboard, click the **Remove Material** icon.
11. Type **70** in the **Depth** box.
12. Click the **Change Direction** button next to the **Depth** box.
13. Click **OK** on the **Extrude** Dashboard.

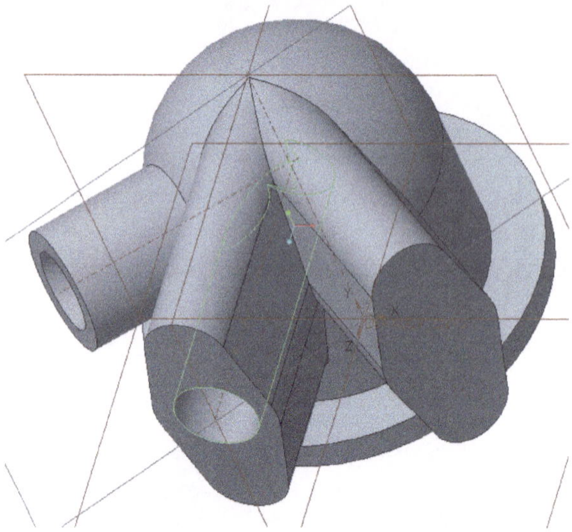

14. On the ribbon, click **Model** tab > **Shapes** panel > **Extrude**.
15. Click on the flat face of the second feature.

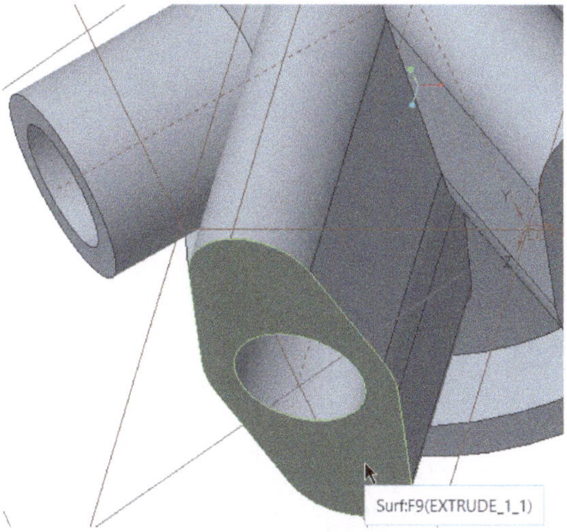

16. On the ribbon, click **Sketch** tab > **Sketching** panel > **Circle** drop-down > **Concentric**.

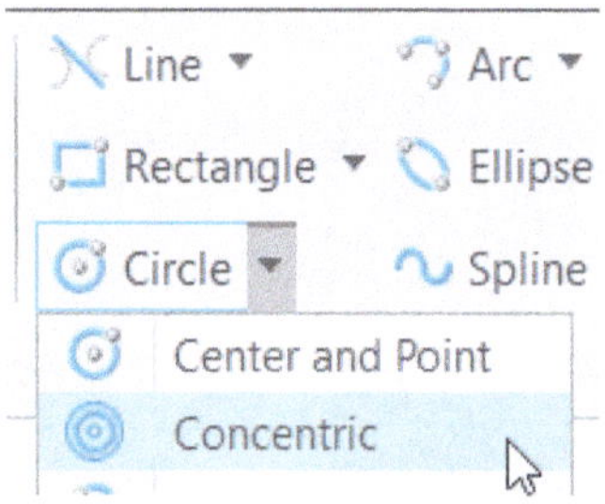

17. Select the curved face of the second feature.

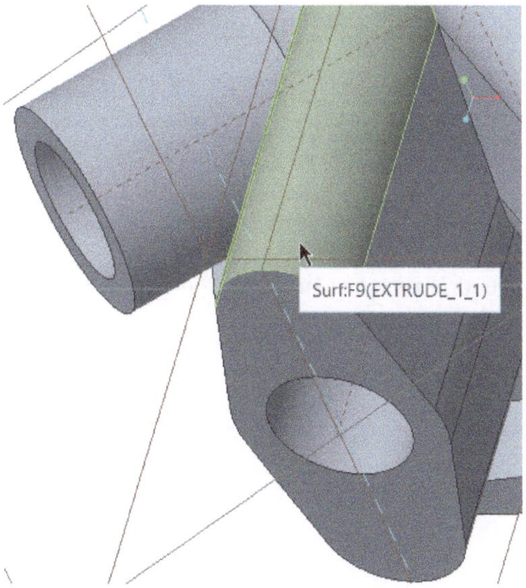

18. Move the pointer outward and click.
19. Press ESC.
20. Select the lower curved edge of the second feature.

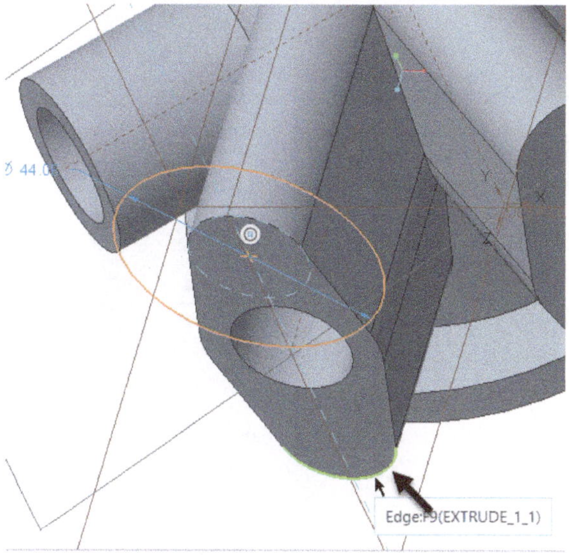

21. Move the pointer outward and click.
22. Press ESC twice.
23. Apply the **Equal** constraint between the two circles.
24. Change the Diameter of the circle to 10.

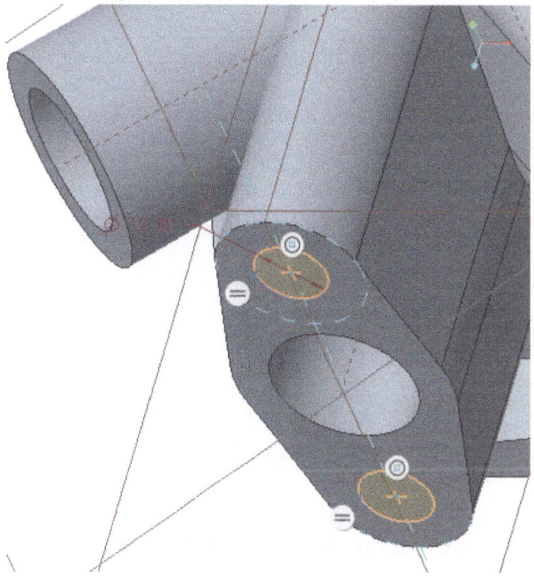

25. Click **OK** on the ribbon.
26. On the **Extrude** Dashboard, click the **Remove Material** icon.
27. Type **25** in the **Depth** box.
28. Click the **Change Direction** button to reverse the direction of the extrusion.
29. Click **OK**.

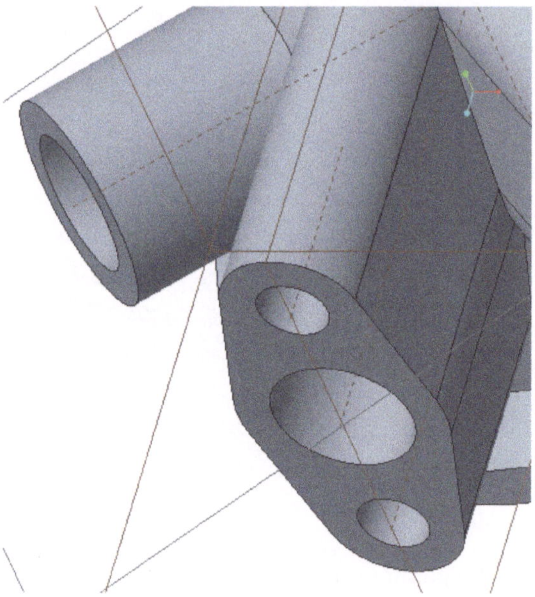

30. Create the circular patterns of the extruded cut features (refer to the **Creating Circular Pattern** section of this Example).

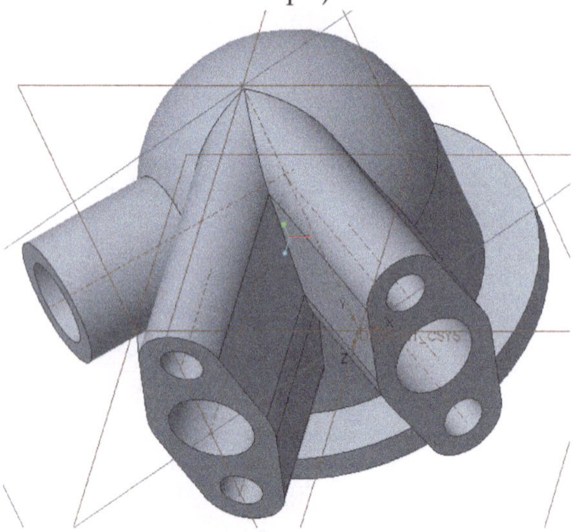

Creating the Revolved Cut Feature

1. On the ribbon, click **Model > Shapes > Revolve**.
2. Select the Front plane.
3. On the **Graphics** toolbar, click the **Sketch View** icon to orient the sketch plane parallel to the screen.
4. Create the sketch, as shown.

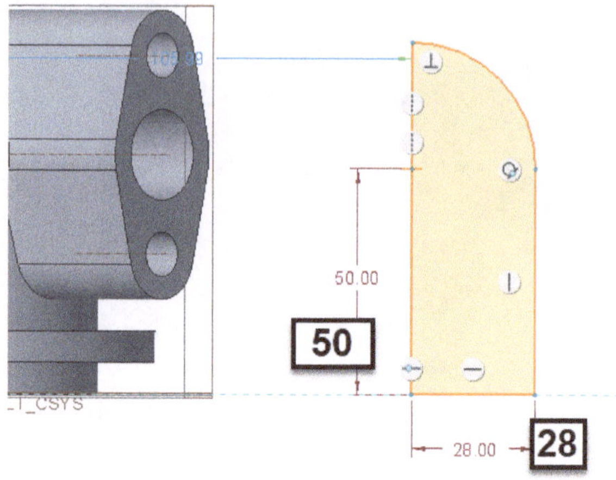

5. Apply the **Coincident** constraint between the lower right corner of the sketch and the vertical reference.

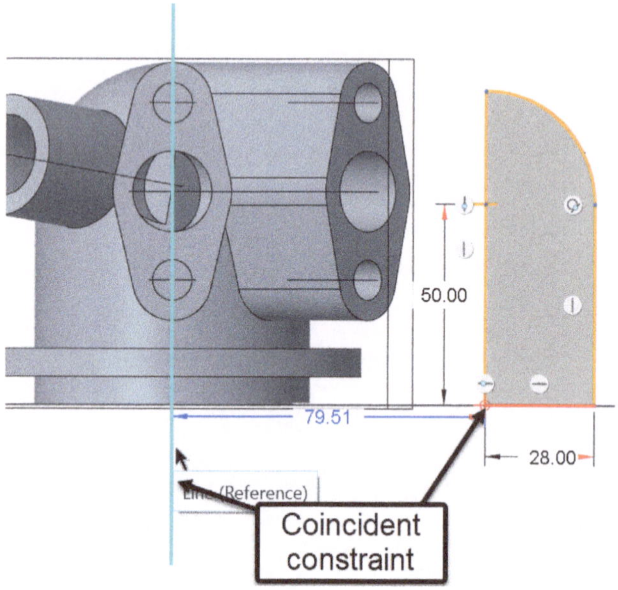

6. Click **OK** on the ribbon.
7. Select the axis passing through the origin to define the axis of revolution.

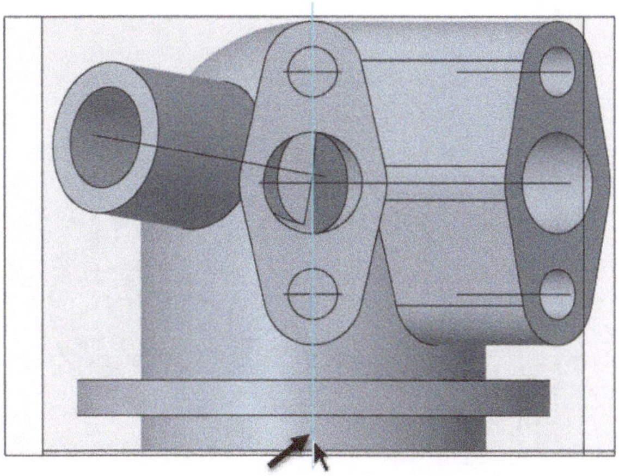

8. Click the **Remove Material** button.
9. Click **OK** on the **Revolve** Dashboard.

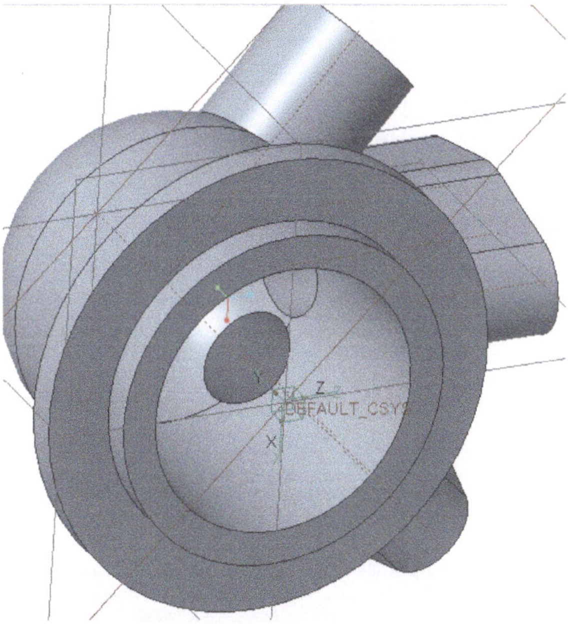

Creating the Rounds

1. On the ribbon, click **Model > Engineering > Round**.
2. On the **Round** dashboard, type **5** in the **Radius** box.
3. Select the edges between the main body and its features, as shown.

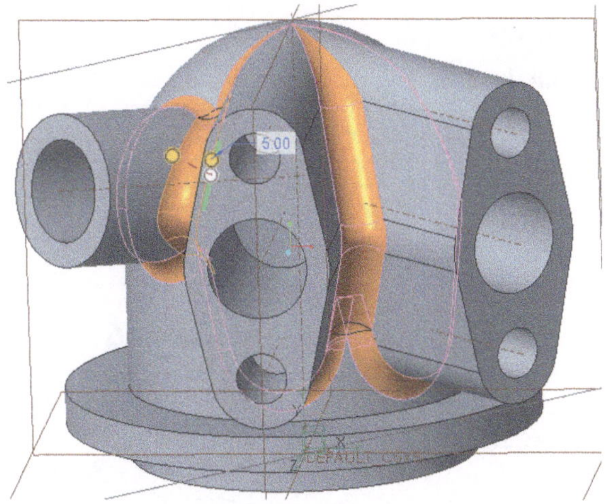

4. Click **OK**.
5. Save and close the file.

Questions

1. Describe the procedure to create a mirror feature.
2. List any two types of patterns.
3. Describe the procedure to create a curve pattern
4. List the methods to define spacing in a directional pattern.

Exercises

Exercise 1

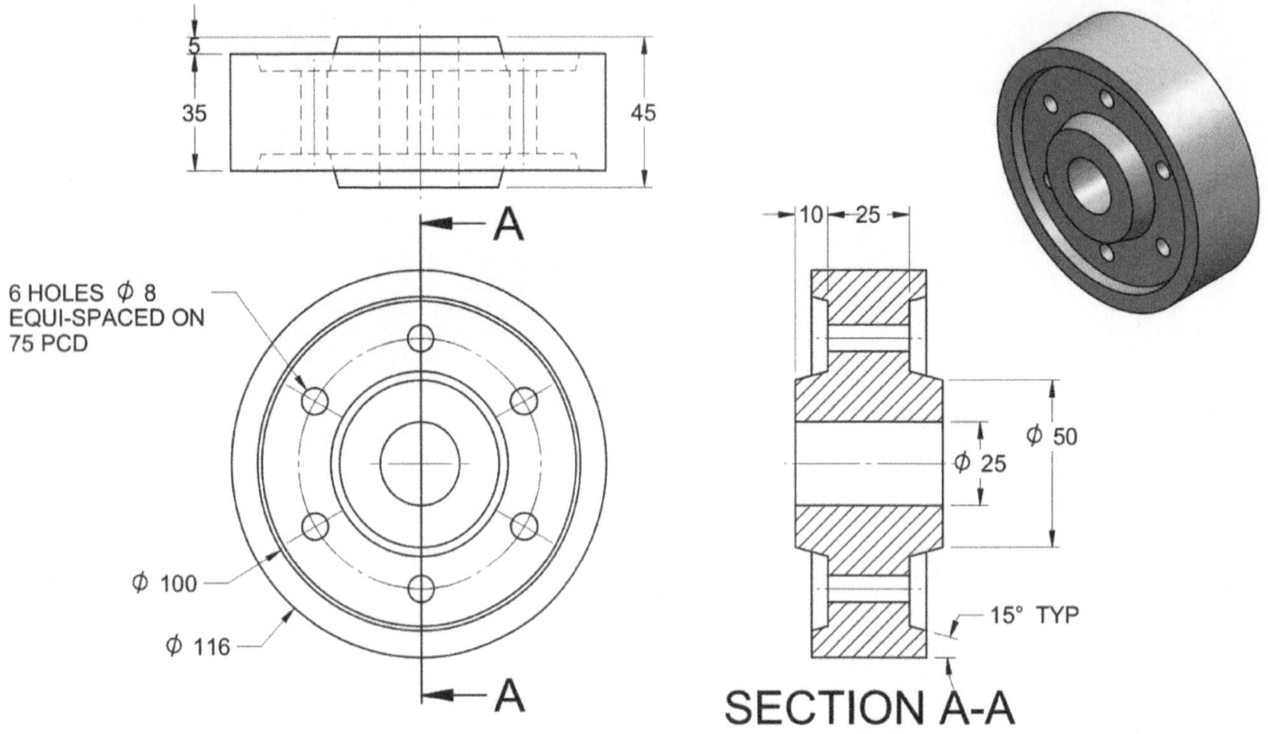

Exercise 2

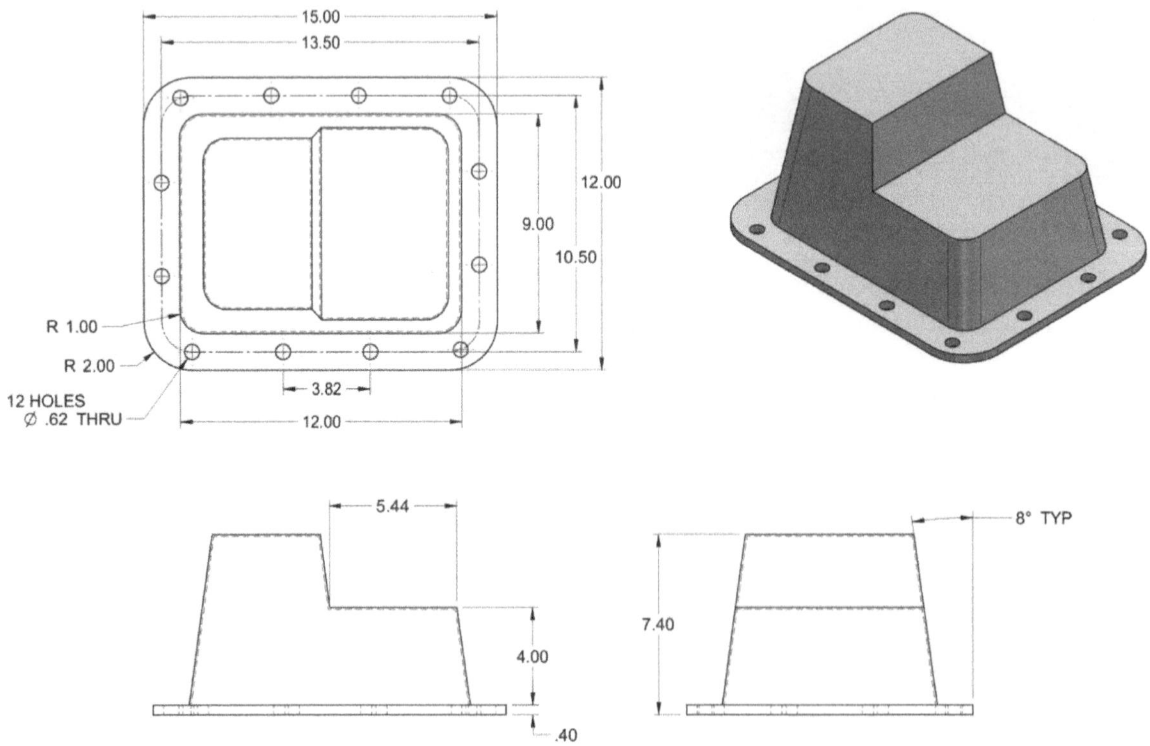

SHEET THICKNESS = 0.079 in

Exercise 3 (Inches)

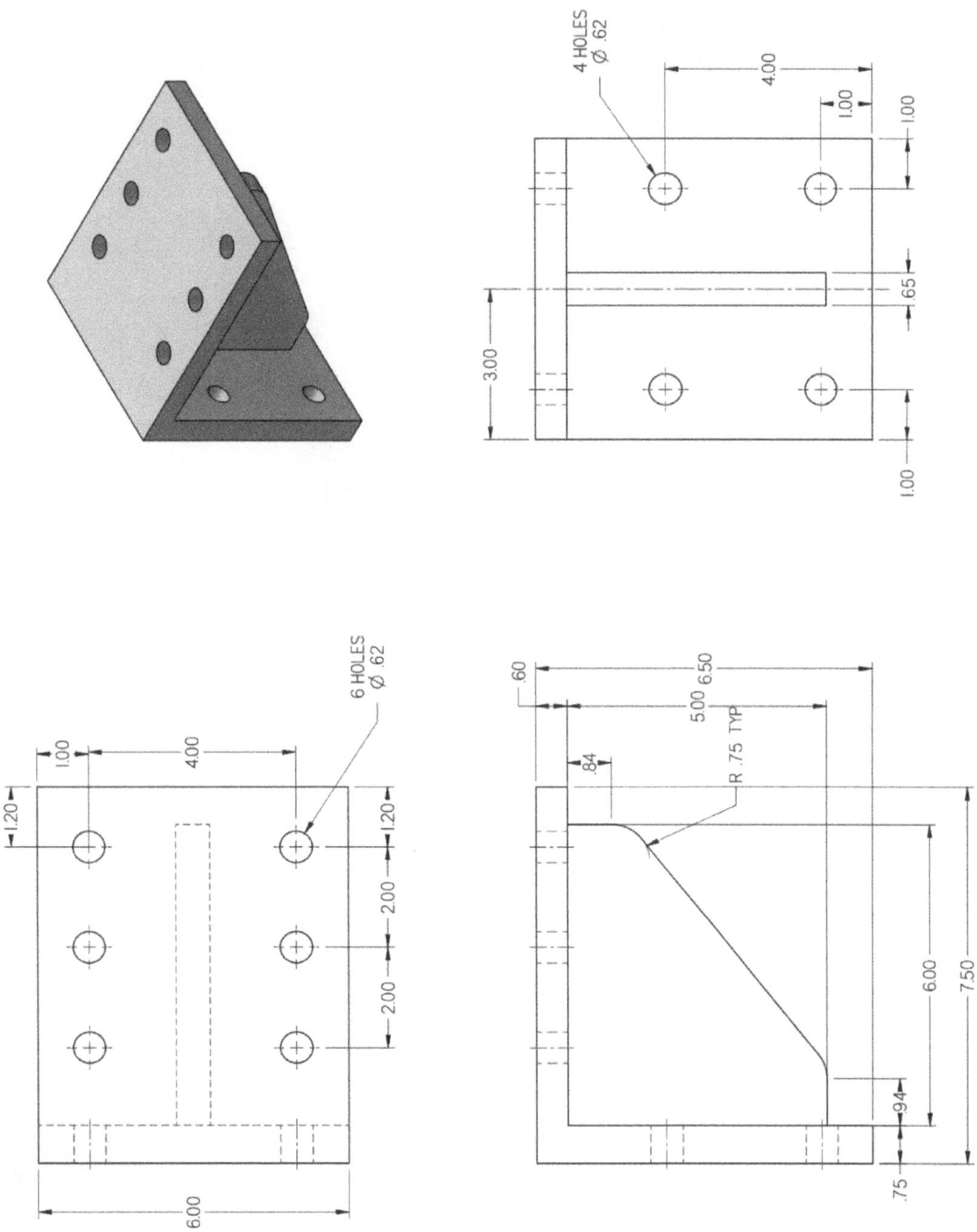

Chapter 6: Sweep Features

The Sweep feature is one of the basic features available in Creo Parametric that allow you to generate a solid geometry. It can be used to create simple geometry as well as complex shapes. A sweep is composed of two items: a cross-section and a trajectory. The cross-section controls the shape of the sweep while the trajectory controls its direction. For example, look at the angled cylinder shown in the figure. It is created using a simple sweep with the circle as the profile and an angled line as the trajectory.

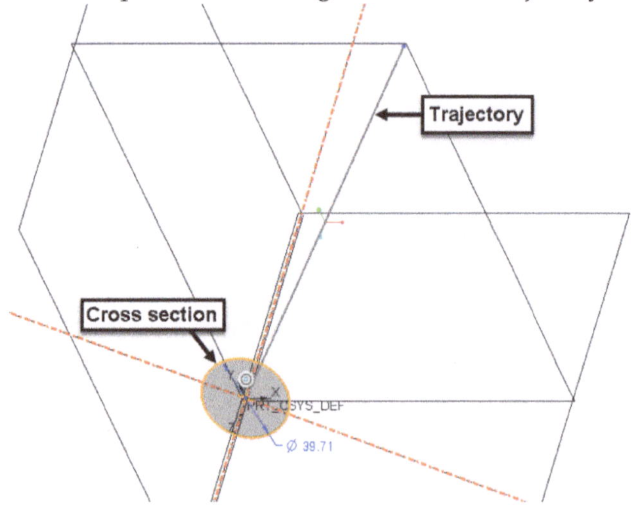

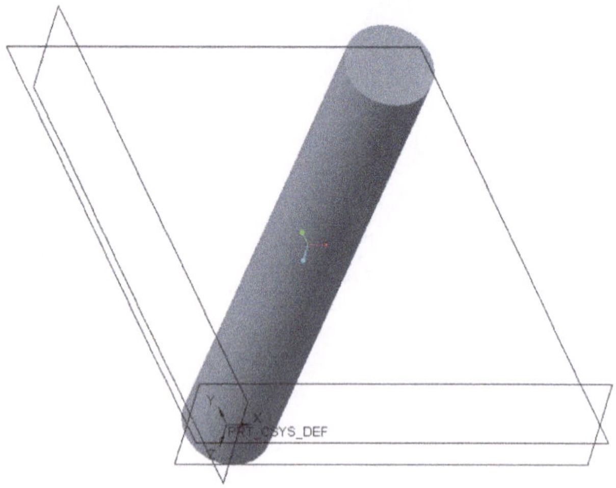

By making the path a bit more complex, you can see that a sweep allows you to create the shape you would not be able to create using commands such as Extrude or Revolve.

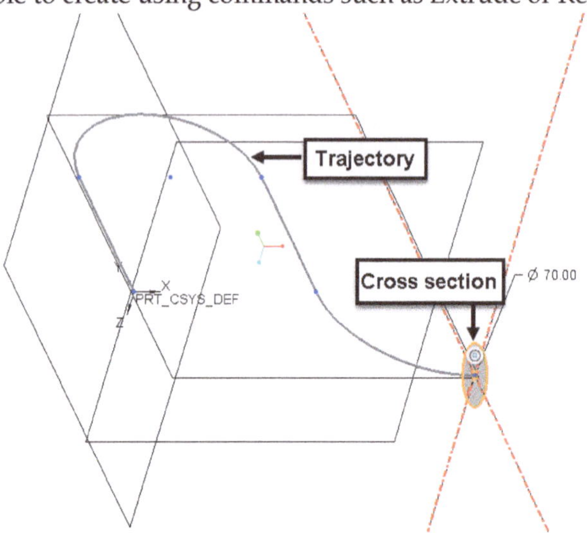

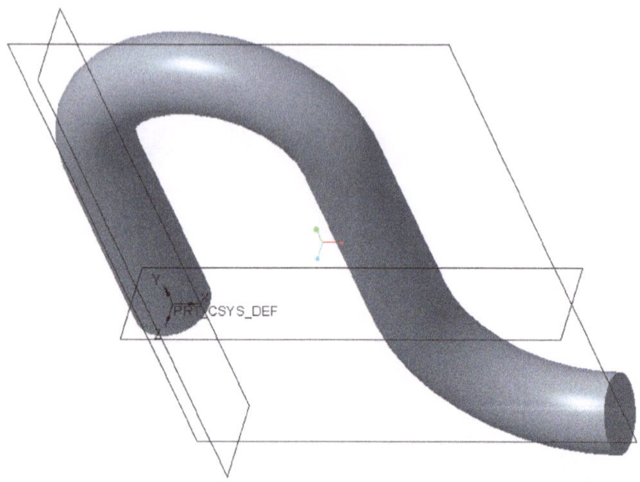

The topics covered in this chapter are:

- *Creating sweep features*
- *Avoiding errors and intersections*
- *Various types of trajectories that can be used to create sweep features*
- *Merging end faces of the sweep*
- *Swept cutouts*

The Sweep command

The sweep feature requires two elements: a trajectory and cross-section. The cross-section defines the shape of the sweep along the trajectory. A trajectory is used to control the cross-section's direction, and it can be a sketch or an edge.

1. To create a sweep, you must first create a trajectory.
2. Create a trajectory by drawing a sketch. It can be an open or closed sketch.

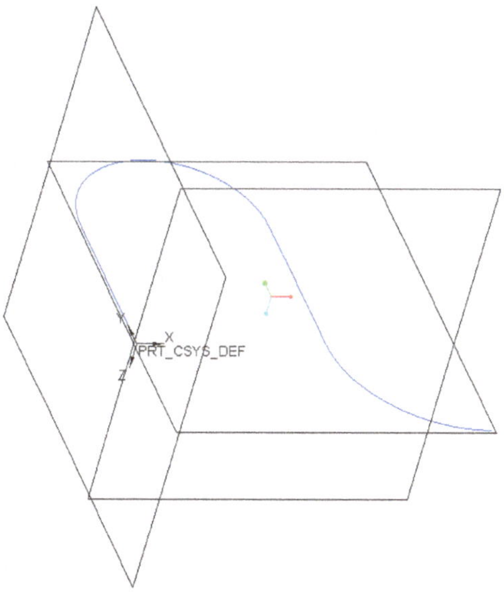

3. On the ribbon, click **Model > Shapes > Sweep**.
4. Select trajectory and click the **Sketch** icon on the Dashboard.
5. Sketch the cross-section on the plane normal to the trajectory.

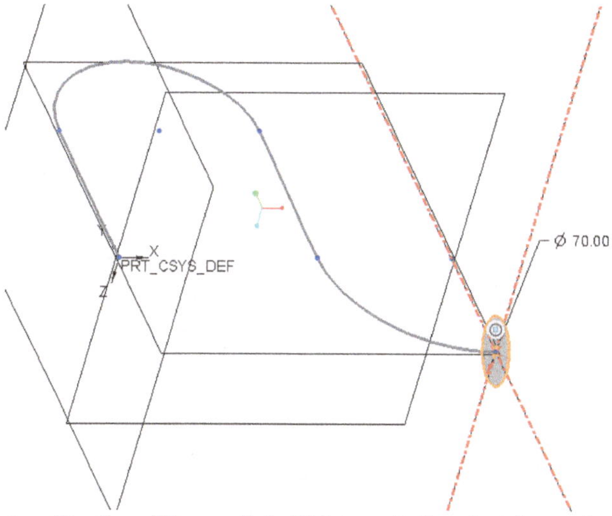

6. On the ribbon, click **OK** to exit the sketch mode. The preview of the sweep feature appears.
7. Click the green check to complete the feature.

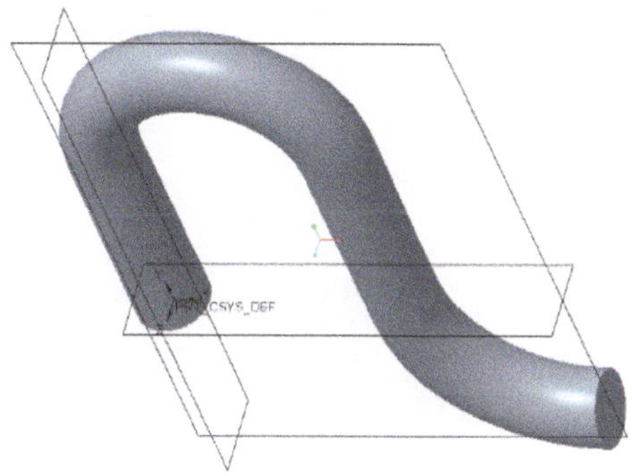

Creo Parametric will not allow the sweep to result in a self-intersecting geometry. As the cross-section is swept along a trajectory, it cannot come back and cross itself. For example, if the sweep's cross-section is larger than the trajectory, the resulting geometry will intersect, and the sweep will fail.

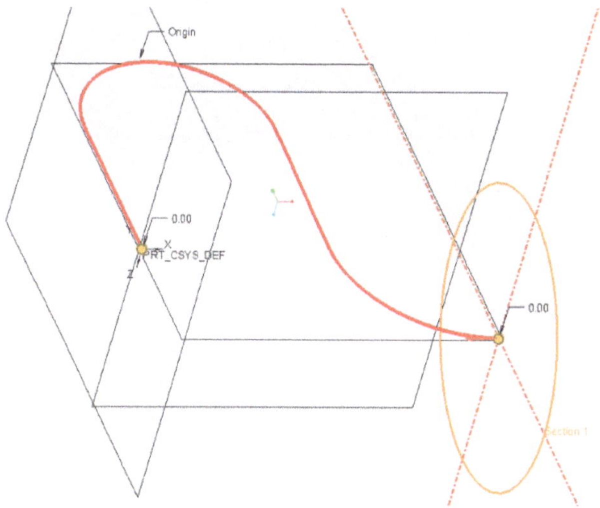

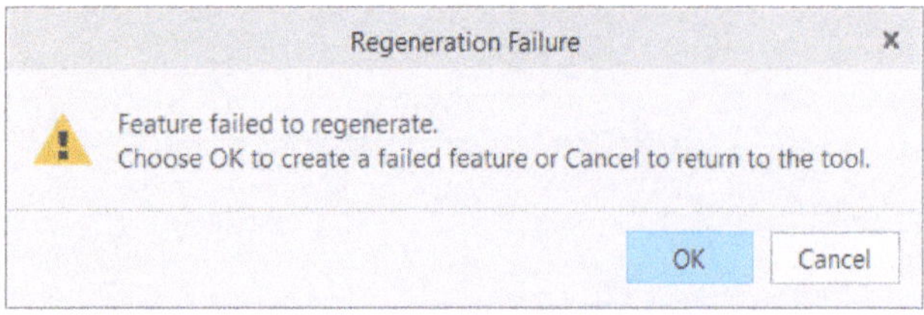

A sweep cross-section must be created as a sketch. However, a trajectory can be a sketch, curve, or edge. The following illustrations show various types of center curves and resultant sweep features.

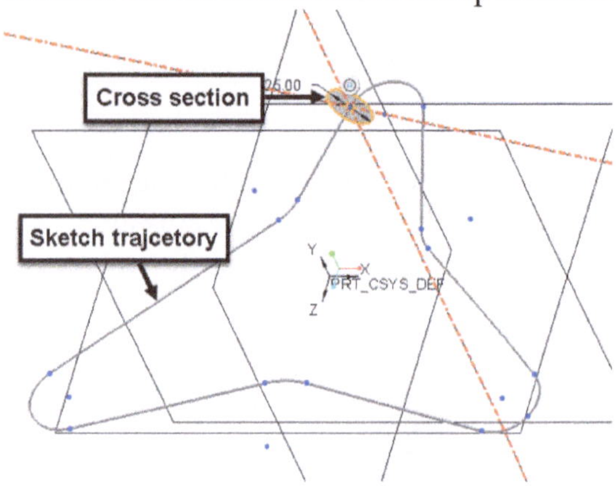

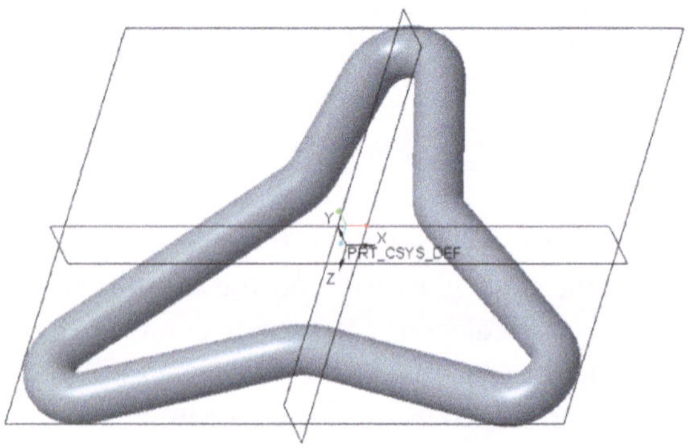

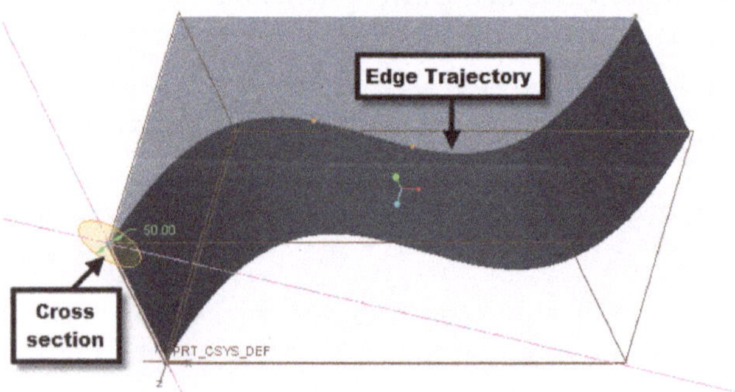

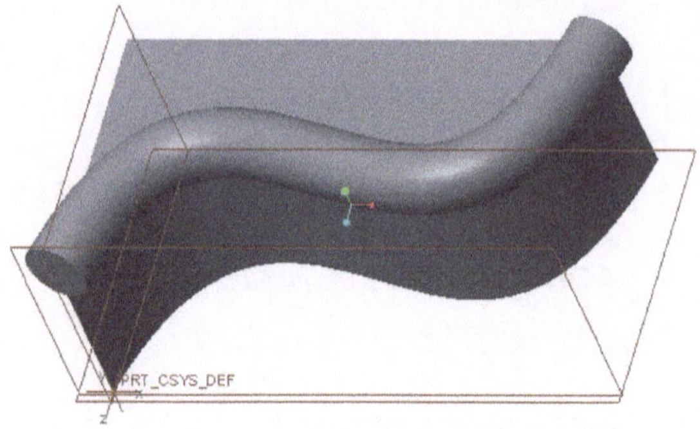

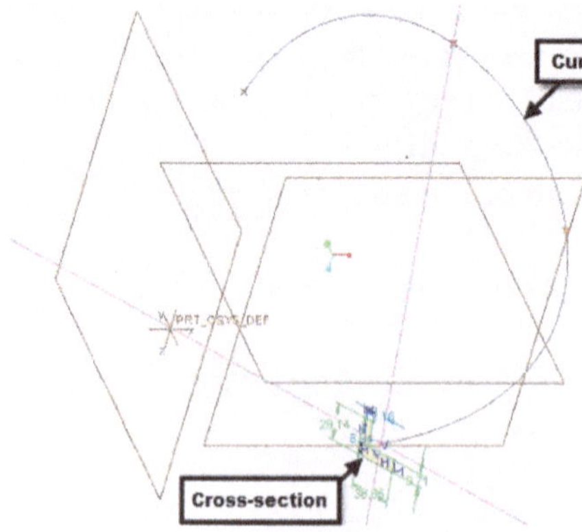

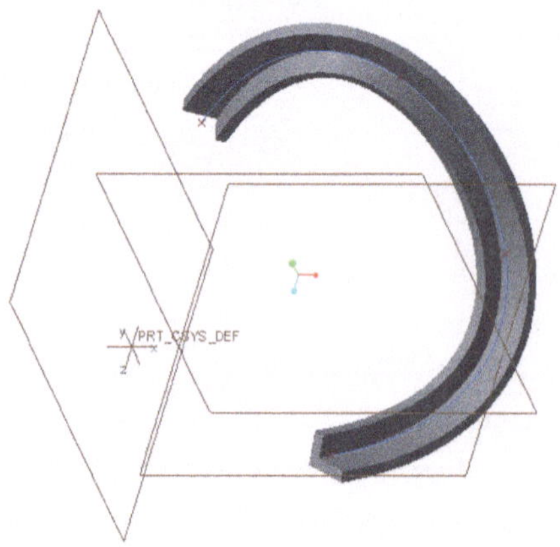

Thin Sweep feature

You can create a thin sweep feature by using the **Create a thin feature** icon. After defining the trajectory and cross-section, click the **Thicken Sketch** icon on the Dashboard and type-in a thickness value.

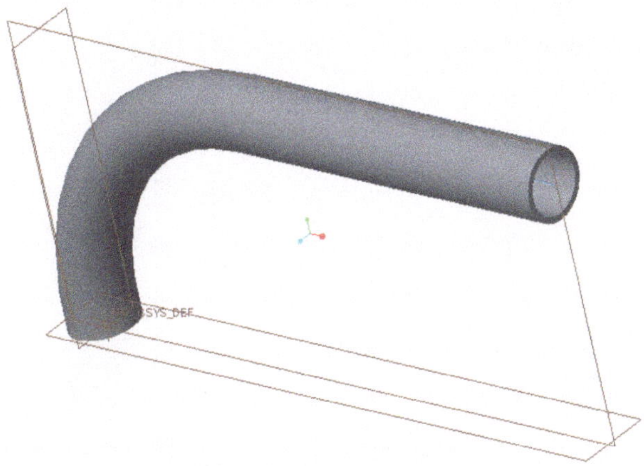

Remove Material

In addition to adding sweep features, Creo Parametric allows you to remove geometry using the **Remove material** option.

1. Activate the **Sweep** command and select the edge to define the trajectory.

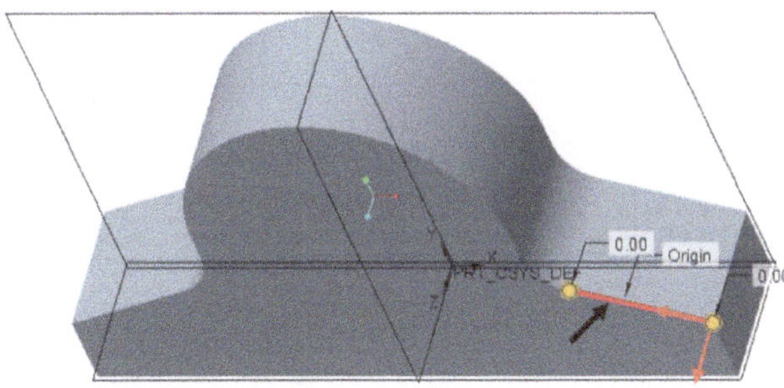

2. If you want to select tangentially connected edges, click the **References** tab on the Dashboard and click the **Details** button.
3. On the **Chain** dialog, select the **Rule-based** option, and then select the **Tangent** rule.
4. Click **OK** to close the dialog. The tangentially connected edges are selected.

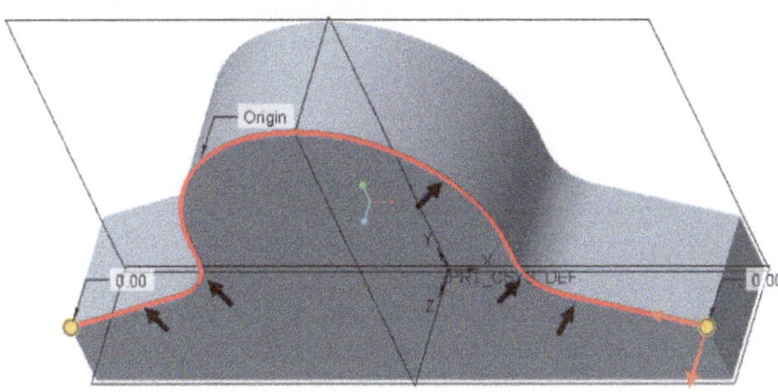

5. Click the **Sketch** icon on the Dashboard.
6. Sketch the cross-section and click **OK**.

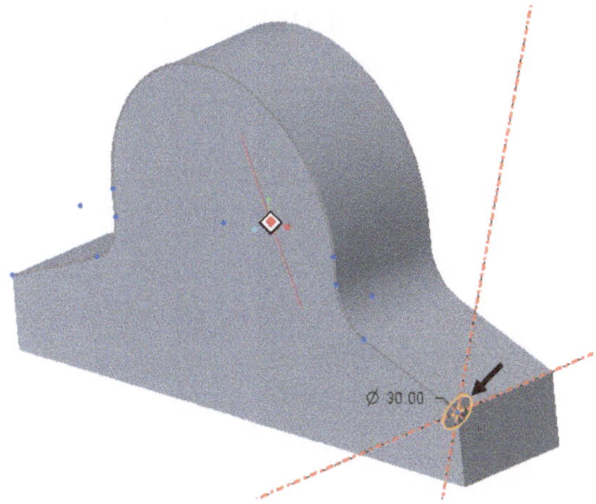

7. On the Dashboard, click the **Remove Material** icon.
8. Click **Preview** on the Dashboard. You will notice that sweep is not created throughout the geometry.

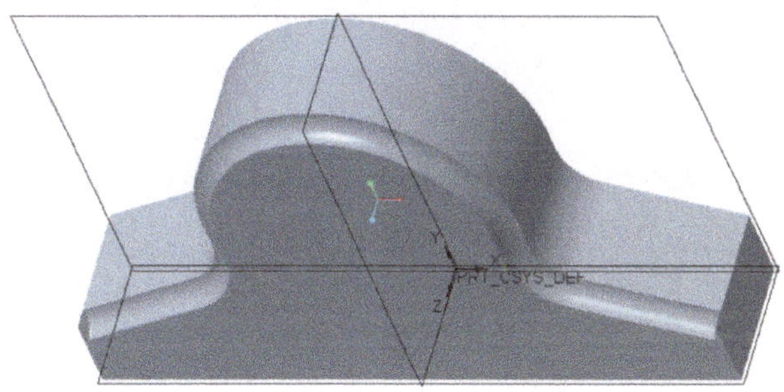

Notice that the swept cut is not created up to the end of the model geometry.

9. Click the **Resume** icon.
10. On the Dashboard, click the **References** tab and select **Horizontal/Vertical Control > Automatic**.

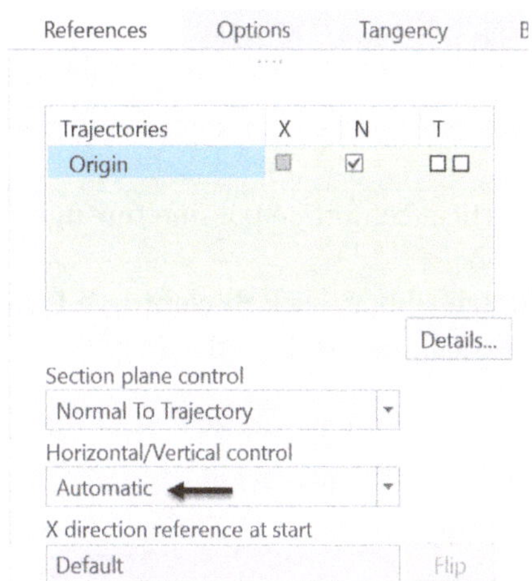

11. On the Dashboard, click the **Options** tab and check the **Merge ends** option. The resultant swept cutout will be throughout the geometry.

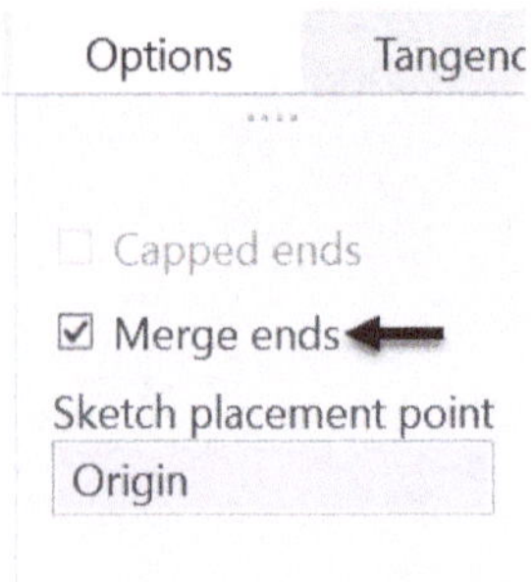

12. Click the green check to complete the feature.

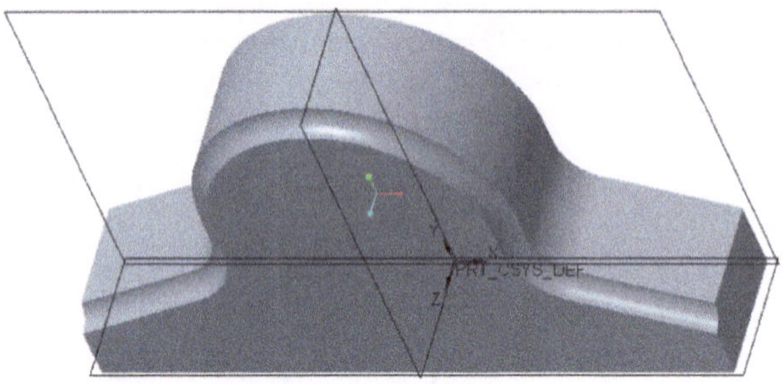

Helical Sweep

This command creates a spring shape feature.

1. On the ribbon, click **Model > Shapes > Sweep > Helical Sweep**.
2. On the **Helical Sweep** Dashboard, click the **References** tab.
3. Click the **Define** button next to the **Helical sweep profile** box.
4. Select the Front datum plane and click **Sketch**.
5. Click the **Sketch View** icon on the **Graphics** toolbar.
6. On the **Sketch** ribbon, click **Sketching > Centerline**.
7. Create a vertical centerline passing through the sketch origin.
8. On the **Sketch** ribbon, click **Sketching > Line**.
9. Create a vertical line on the left side of the centerline.
10. Change the distance between the centerline and line to 2.
11. Change the length of the line to 5.

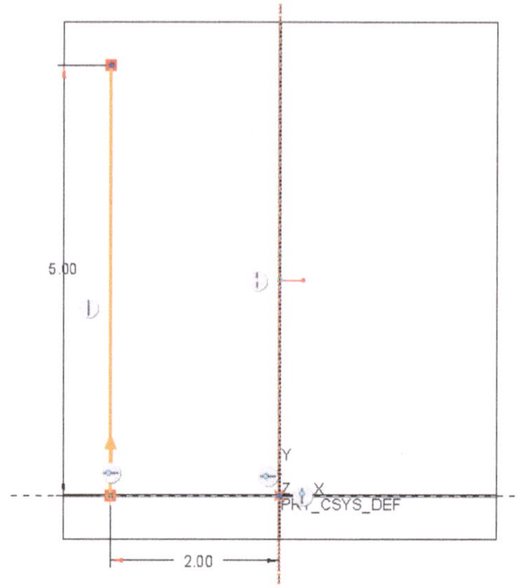

12. Click **OK** on the ribbon.
13. Click the **Sketch** icon on the Dashboard.
14. Create a circle of 0.75 diameter at the intersection of construction lines.

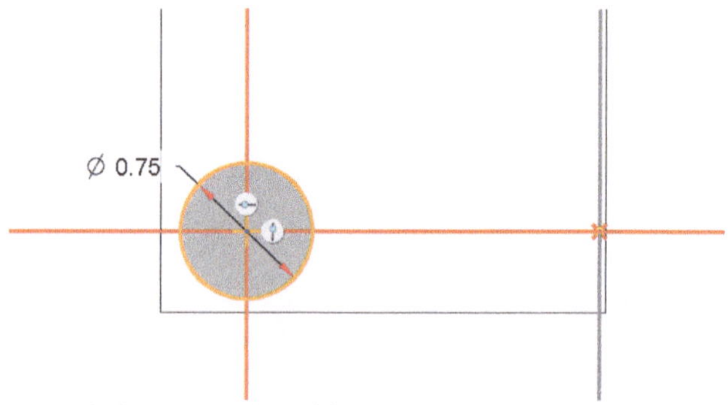

15. Click **OK** on the ribbon.
16. Type-in 1 in the **Pitch Value** box located on the Dashboard.
17. Use the **Left handed rule** or **Right handed rule** icon to define the helix direction.
18. Click the green check to complete the feature.

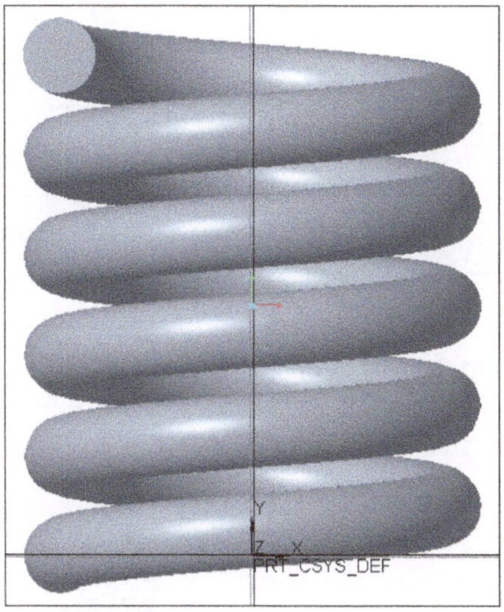

You can add hooks and other extensions to the ends using the **Sweep** command.

Helical Sweep cutout

The **Helical Sweep** command can also be used for creating cutouts.

1. Create a cylinder with diameter and length as 3 and 5, respectively.
2. Activate the **Helical Sweep** command.
3. On the **Helical Sweep** Dashboard, click the **References** tab.
4. Click the **Define** button next to the **Helical profile** box.
5. Select the Front datum plane and click **Sketch**.

   Click the **Sketch View** icon on the **Graphics** toolbar.
6. On the **Sketch** ribbon, click **Sketching > Centerline**.
7. Create a vertical centerline passing through the sketch origin.
8. On the **Sketch** ribbon, click **Sketching > Line**.
9. Create a vertical line on the right side of the centerline.
10. Modify the dimensions of the line, as shown below.

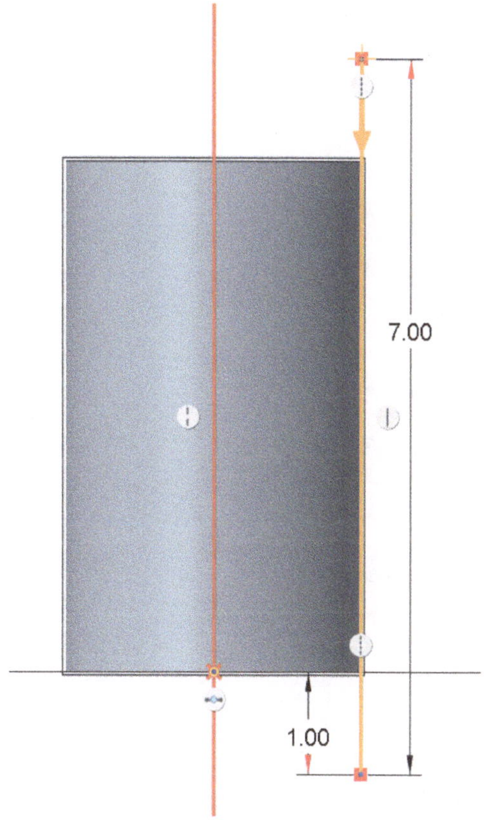

19. Click **OK** on the ribbon.
20. Click the **Sketch** icon on the Dashboard.
21. Create the cross-section and click **OK**.

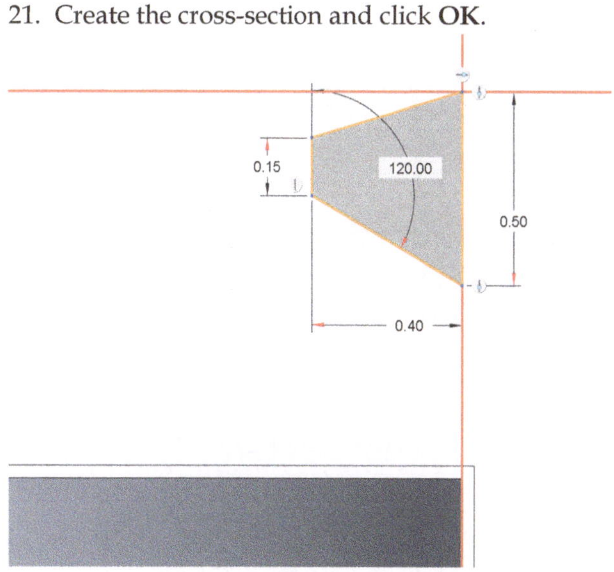

22. On the Dashboard, click the **Remove Material** icon.
23. Type-in 0.7 in the **Pitch Value** box located on the Dashboard.

24. Define the helix direction and click the green check.

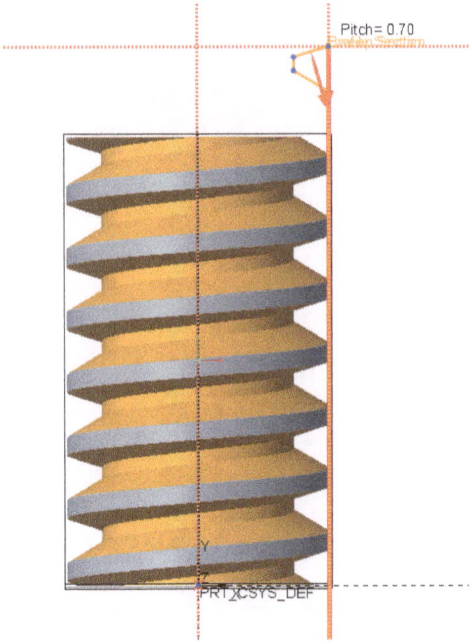

Volume Helical Sweep

This command removes material by sweeping the volume of a 3D sweep object along a helical curve. First, to sweep a volume, create the target object, and then create the 3D sweep object.

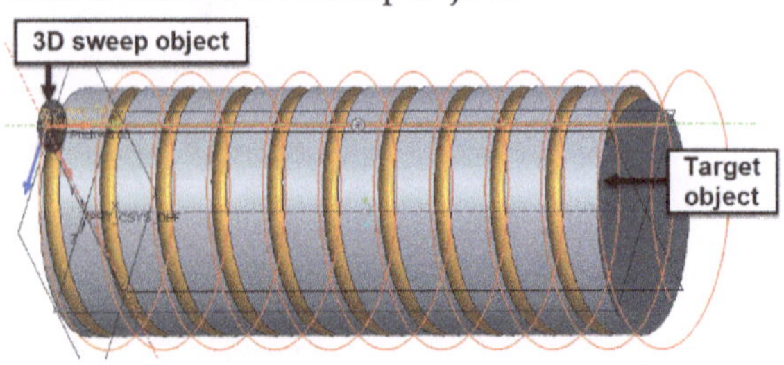

The 3D sweep object should be convex shaped. Examples of tool bodies are shown in the figure below.

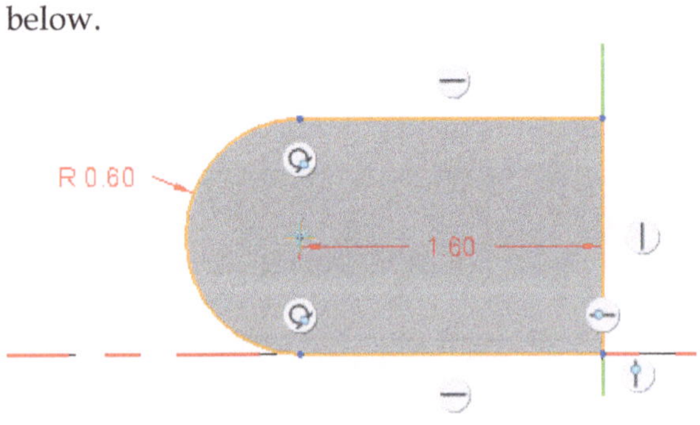

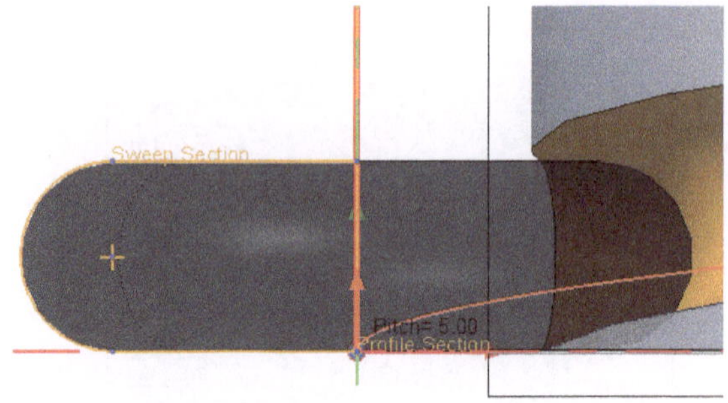

1. Create the target object, as shown.

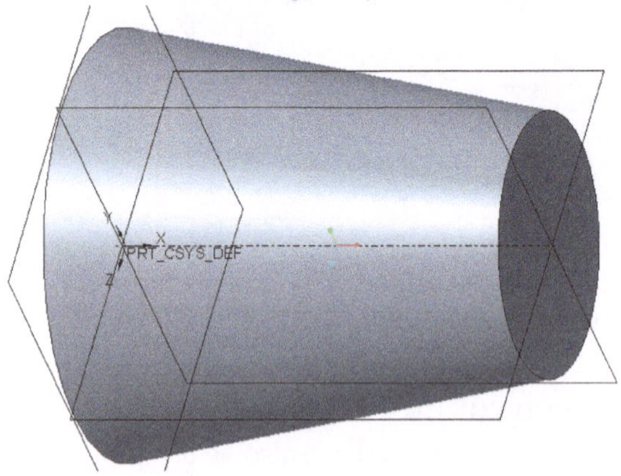

2. On the ribbon, click **Model** tab > **Shapes** panel > **Sweep** drop-down > **Volume Helical Sweep**.

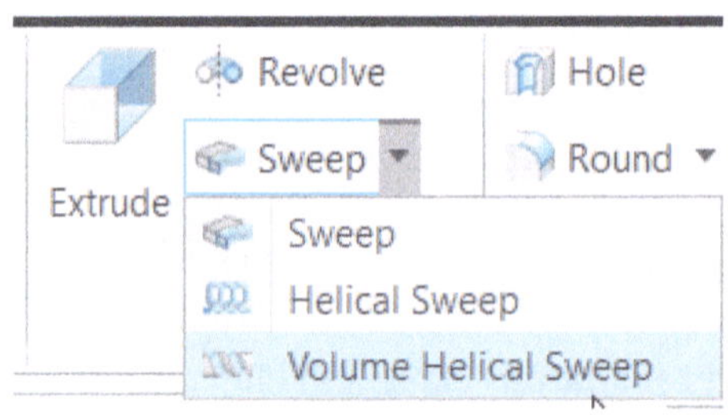

3. On the **Volume Helical Sweep** Dashboard, click the **References** tab.
4. On the **References** tab, click the **Define** button next to the **Helix profile** selection box.
5. Select the Front plane and click the **Sketch** button.
6. Click the **Sketch View** icon on the **Graphics** toolbar.
7. Create the line, as shown.

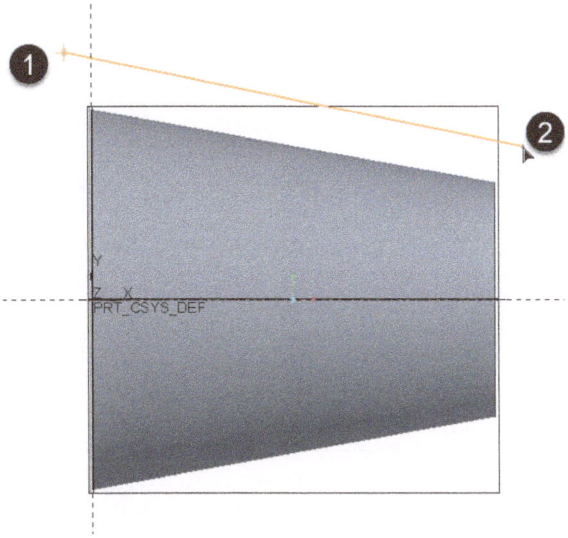

8. Apply the **Parallel** constraint between the inclined line and the silhouette edge of the target model.

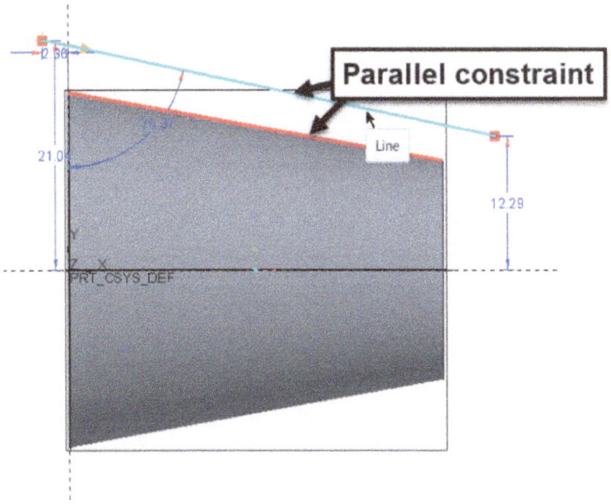

9. Click **OK** on the ribbon.
10. Select the axis of the helical sweep, as shown.

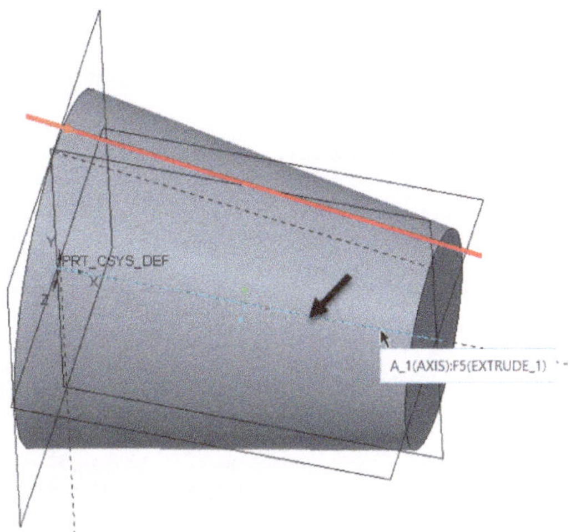

11. Click the **Section** tab and select the **Sketched section** option.
12. Click the **Create/Edit section** button.
13. Click the **Sketch View** icon on the **Graphics** toolbar.
14. Create the section, as shown.

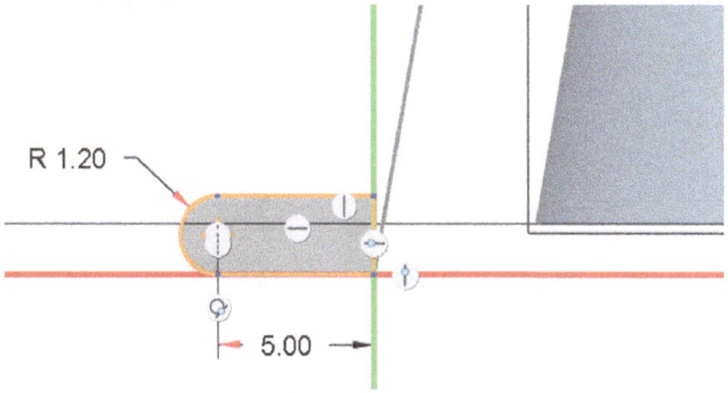

15. Click **OK** on the **Sketch** ribbon.
16. Type **5** in the **Pitch value** box.
17. Select the **Right-handed rule** button from the **Settings** section.
18. Click the **Helix and orientation** button to display the helix.
19. Click the **3D Object** button to display the 3D object.

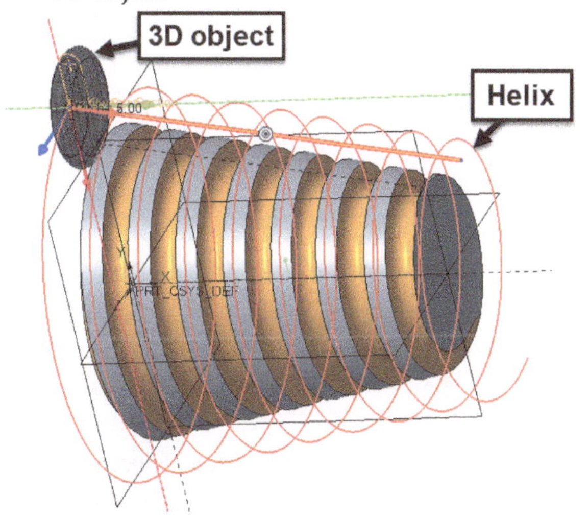

20. Click **OK** on the Dashboard.

Examples

Example 1

In this example, you will create the part shown below.

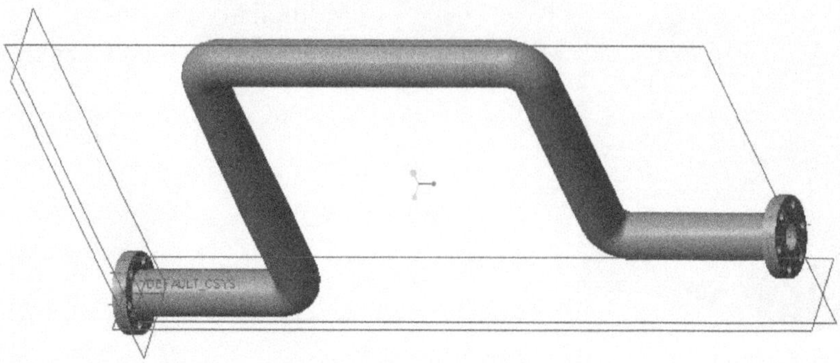

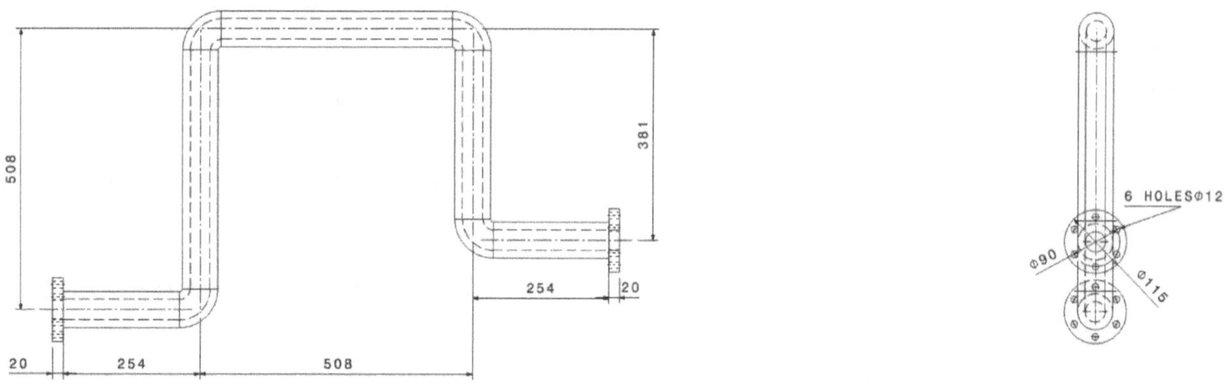

PIPE I.D. 51

PIPE O.D. 65

1. Start **Creo Parametric 11.0.**
2. Create the *Swept Features* folder and set it as the current working folder.
3. On the Quick Access Toolbar, click the **New** button.
4. On the **New** dialog, select **Types > Part**, and then type-in **C06-Example1.**
5. Uncheck the **Use default template** option;
6. Click **OK**.
7. On the **New File Options** dialog, select the **solid_part_mmks_abs** template. Click **OK** to start the file.
8. On the Front plane, create the sketch shown below.

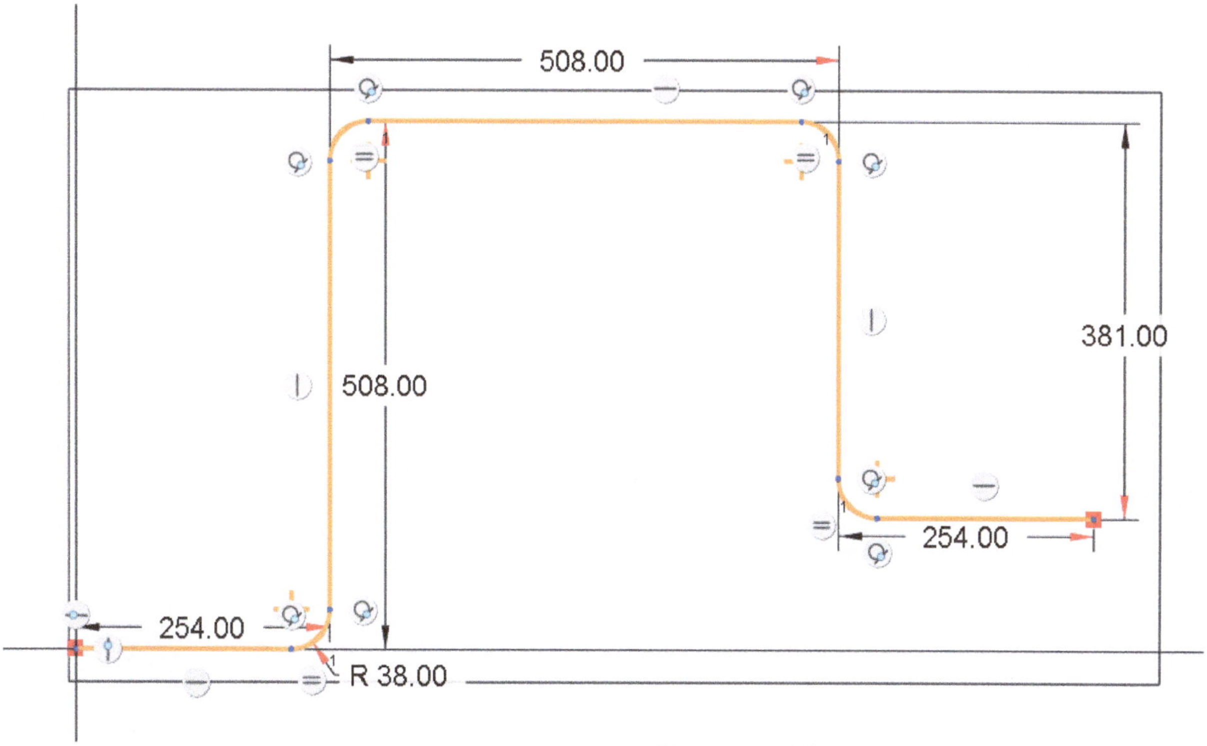

9. Exit the sketch mode and change the orientation to Standard.
10. On the ribbon, click **Model** tab > **Shapes** panel > **Sweep** drop-down > **Sweep** .
11. Select the sketch.

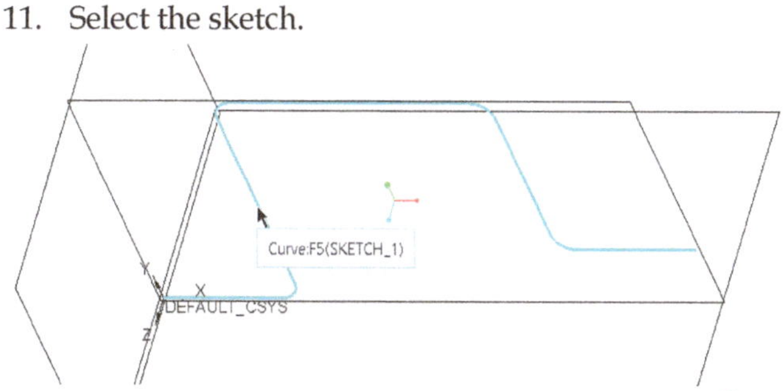

12. On the **Sweep** dashboard, click the **Sketch** icon.
13. On the ribbon, click **Sketch** tab > **Sketching** panel > **Circle** drop-down > **Center and Point**.
14. Create a circle of 65 mm diameter at the origin.

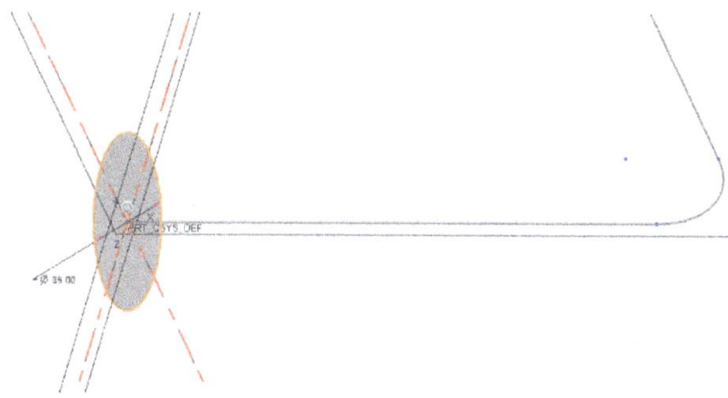

15. Click the **OK** button on the **Sketch** tab.
16. On the **Sweep** dashboard, click the **Thicken Sketch** icon.
17. Type-in **14** in the thickness value box.
18. Click the **Change direction** icon next to thickness value box if the preview of the sweep feature is not displayed.
19. Click the green check to create the sweep feature.

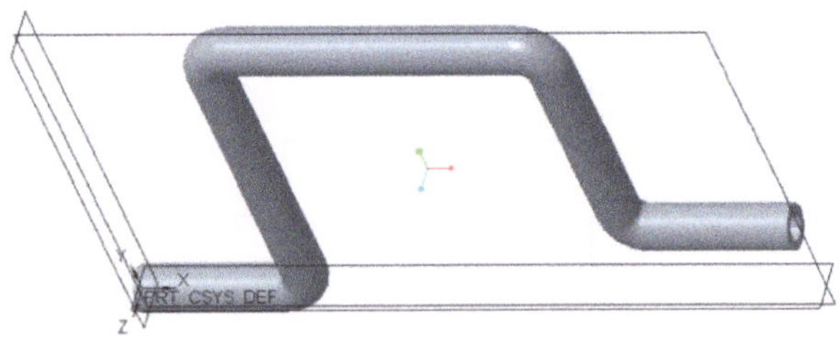

20. Activate the **Extrude** command and click on the front-end face of the *Sweep* feature.

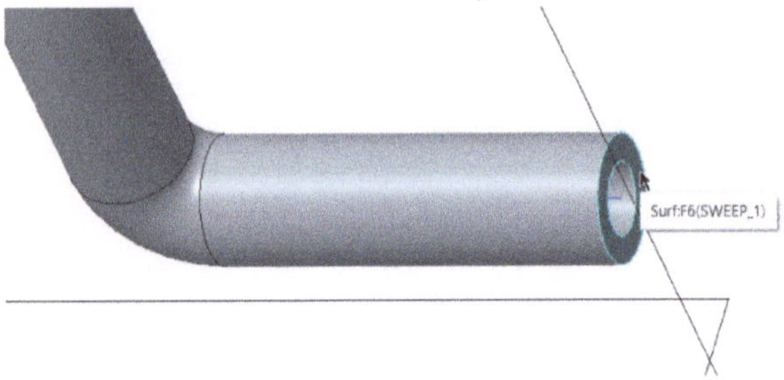

21. On the **Sketch** dashboard, click the **Sketching** panel > **Project** icon.
22. Click on the inner edge of the front-end face.
23. Press and hold the SHIFT key and select another inner edge.

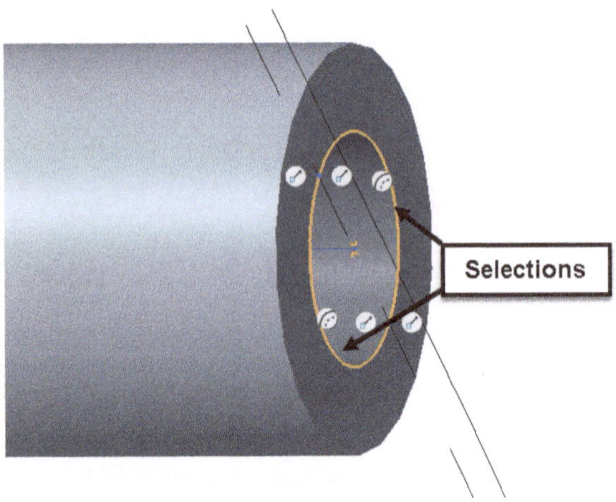

24. Click **OK** on the toolbar.
25. Draw a circle of 115 diameter.

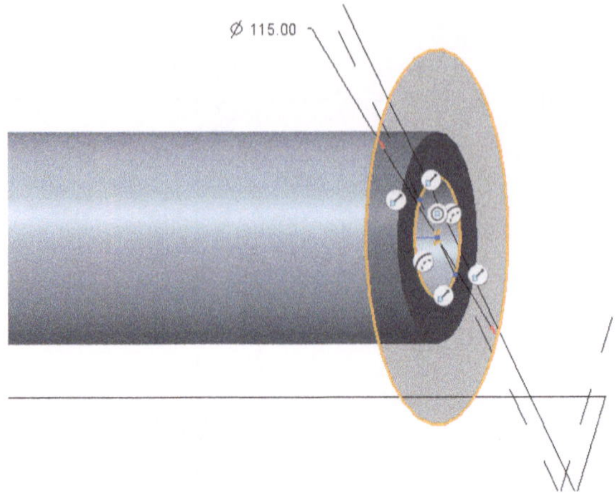

26. Click **OK** to complete the sketch.
27. Type-in **20** in the **Length** box and click the green check to complete the *Extrude* feature.

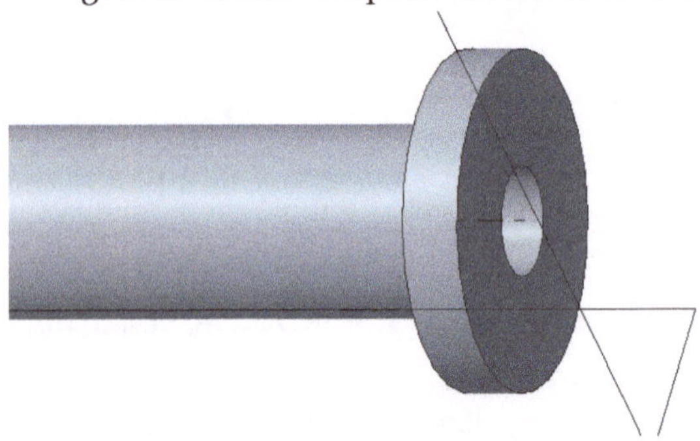

28. Activate the **Hole** command and click on the front face of the *Extrude* feature.
29. Set the hole diameter to 12.
30. On the Dashboard, click the **Placement** tab and select **Type > Radial**.
31. Click in the **Offset References** box and select the axis of the cylindrical face.
32. Press the Ctrl key and select the Front plane.

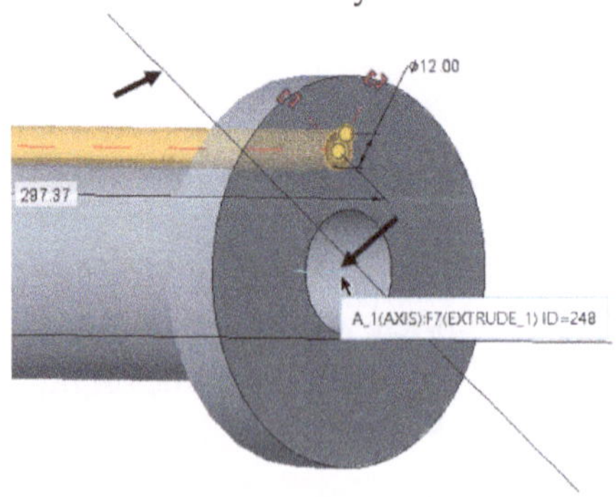

33. Specify the angle as 0 and the radius dimension as 45.

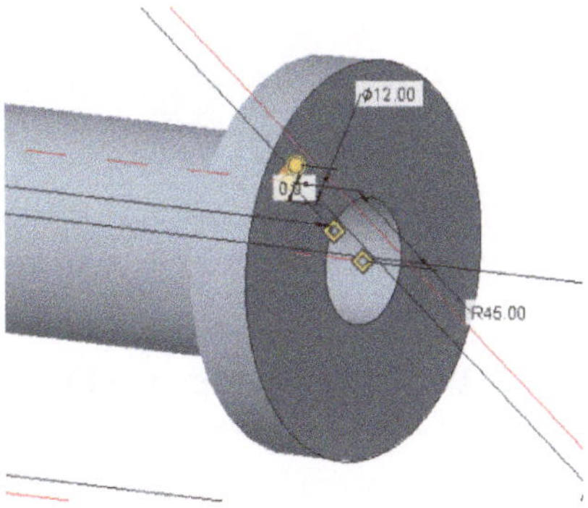

34. Select the **To Next** option from the drop-down located next to the diameter box.
35. Click the green check to create the hole.

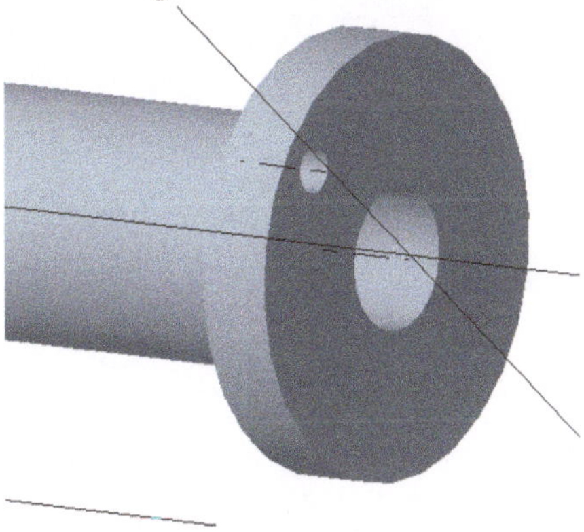

36. Select the small hole from the part geometry.
37. On the ribbon, click **Model** tab > **Editing** panel > **Pattern** drop-down > **Pattern** .
38. On the dashboard, select the **Axis** option from the **Type** drop-down located on the left side.

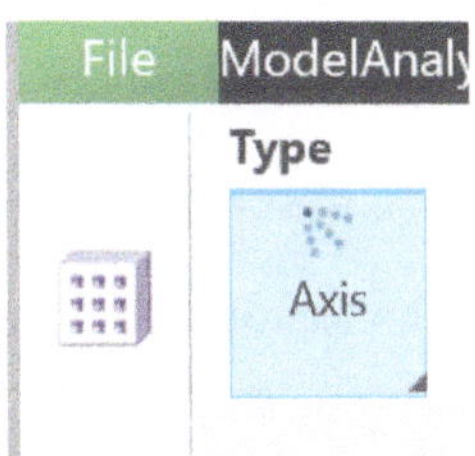

39. Select the axis of the *Extruded* feature, as shown below.

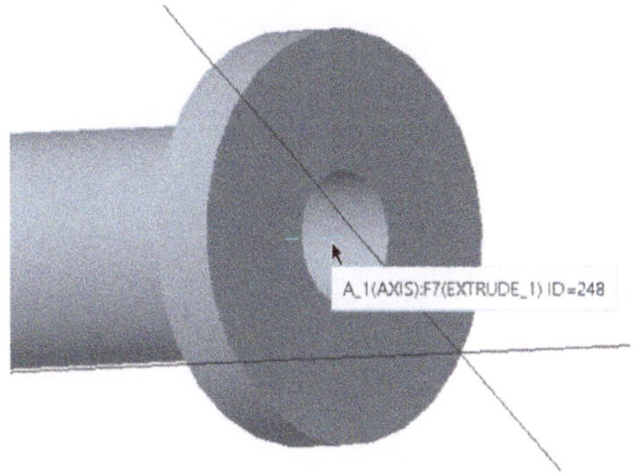

40. On the dashboard, click the Angular Extent button and set the angular extent to 360.
41. Set the 1st direction members to 6.

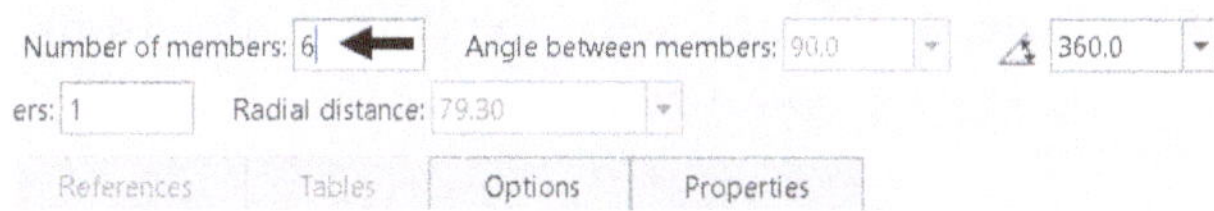

42. Click the green check to complete the pattern.

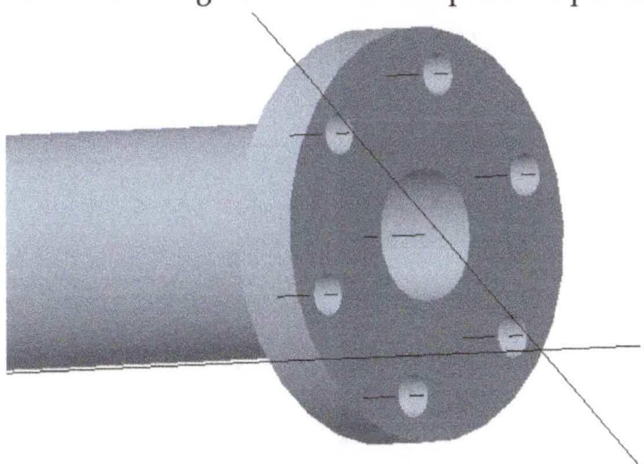

43. On the **Graphics** toolbar, click **Datum Display Filters** drop-down > **Csys Display**.

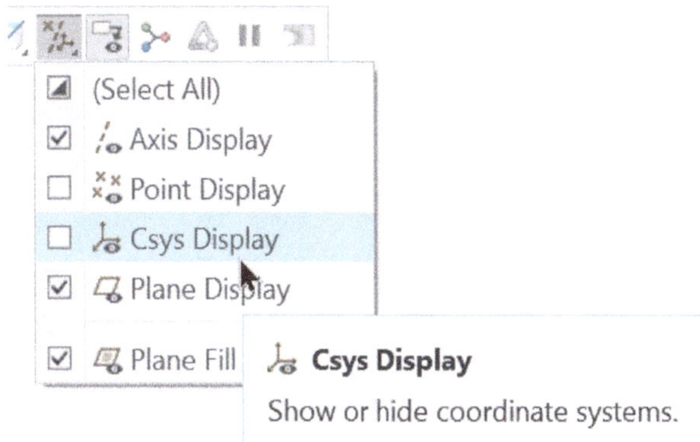

44. Select the *Extrude* feature and activate the **Pattern** command.

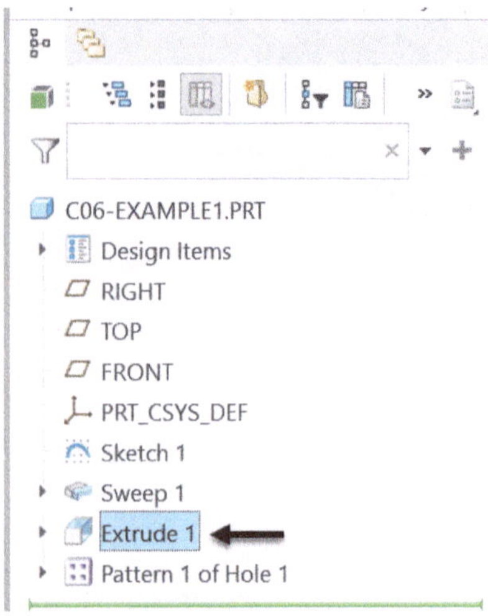

45. On the dashboard, select the **Point** option from the **Type** drop-down located on the left side.

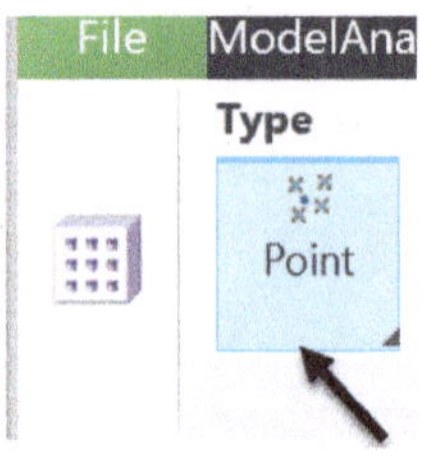

46. Click the **From Feature** icon.

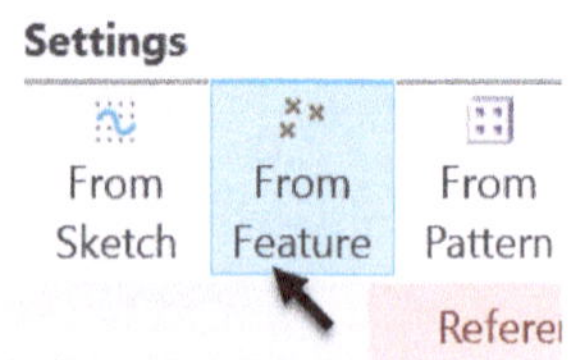

47. On the dashboard, at the right-side, click **Datum** drop-down > **Point** drop-down > **Offset Coordinate system**.

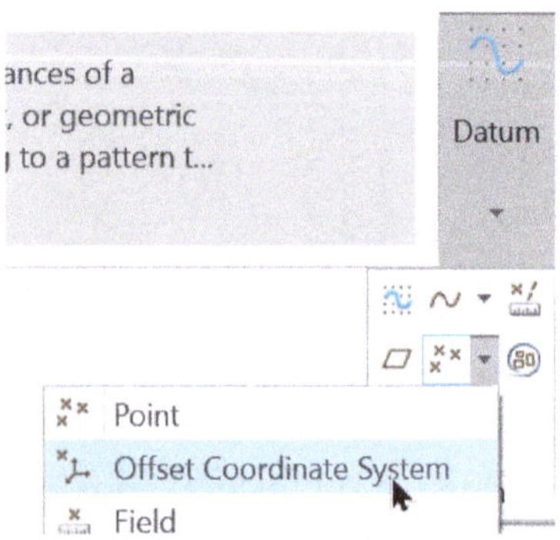

48. Select the Default Coordinate system.

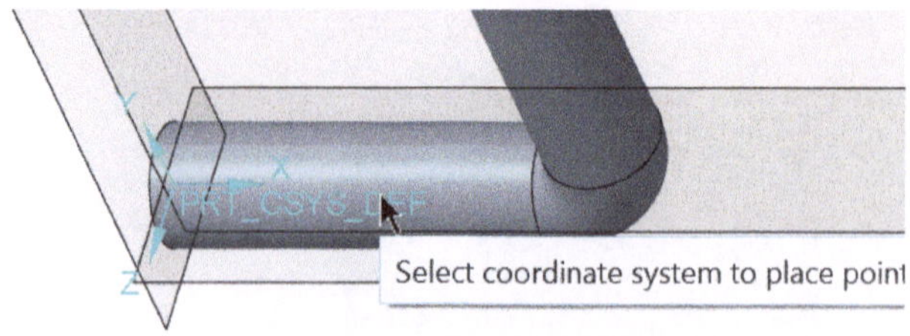

49. On the **Datum Point** dialog, type-in **-10** in the **X Axis** box.

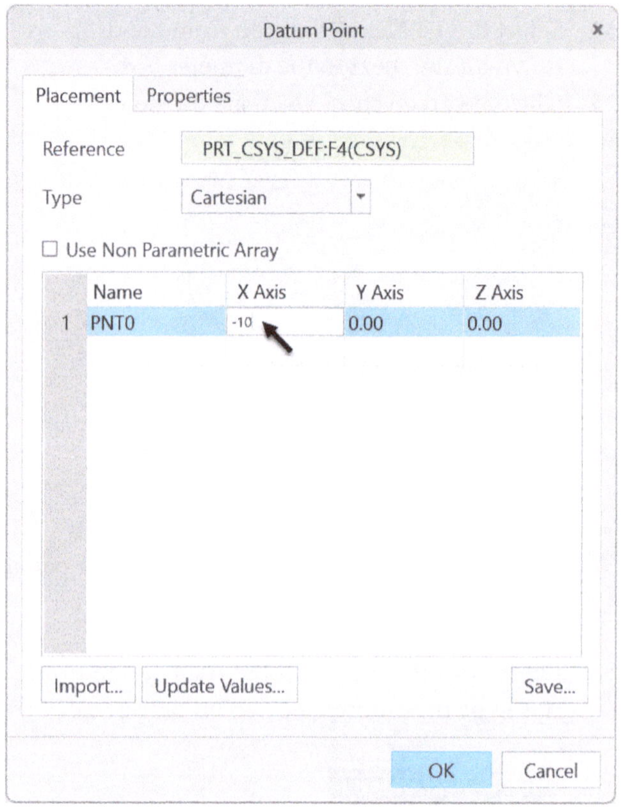

50. Click **OK** to create a new datum point.

51. On the dashboard, click the **Resume**  icon.

52. Click the green check to create the pattern.

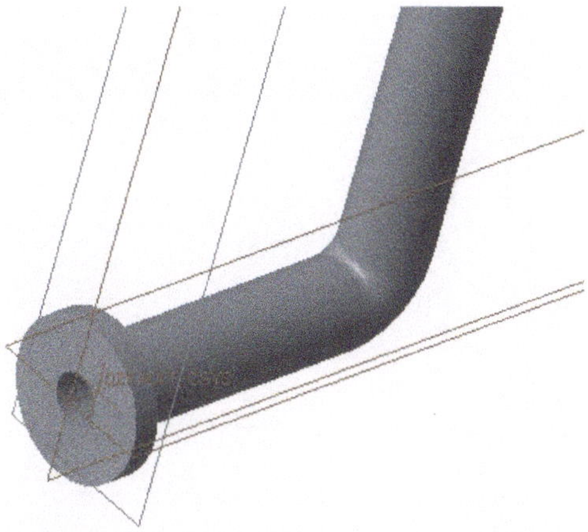

53. Select the circular pattern of the holes from the Model tree.

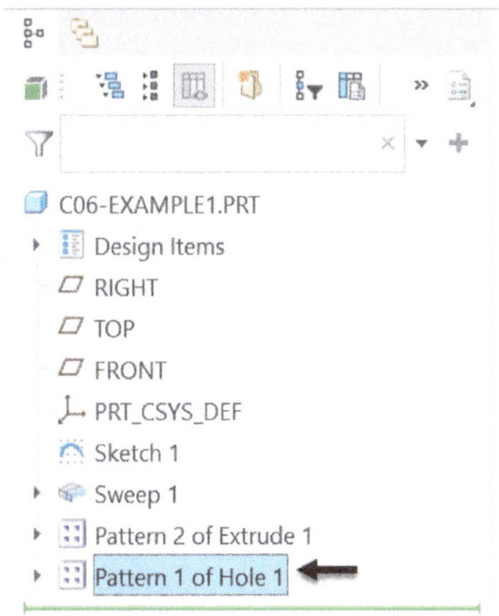

Example 2

In this example, you will create the part shown below.

54. Activate the **Pattern** command.
55. Make sure that the **Reference** option is selected in the **Type** drop-down.

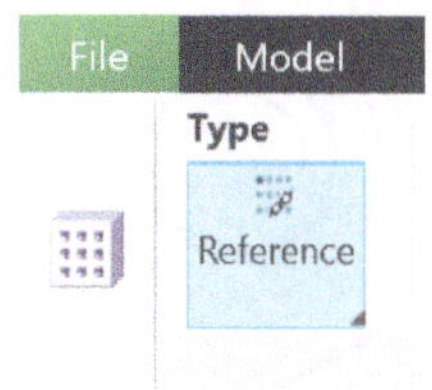

56. Click the green check to create the reference pattern.

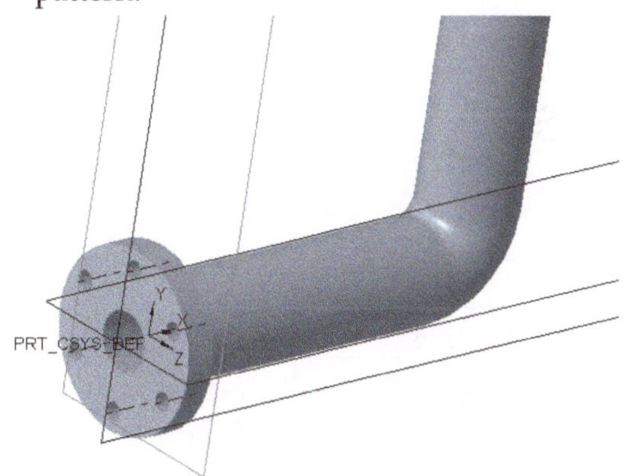

57. Save and close the part file.

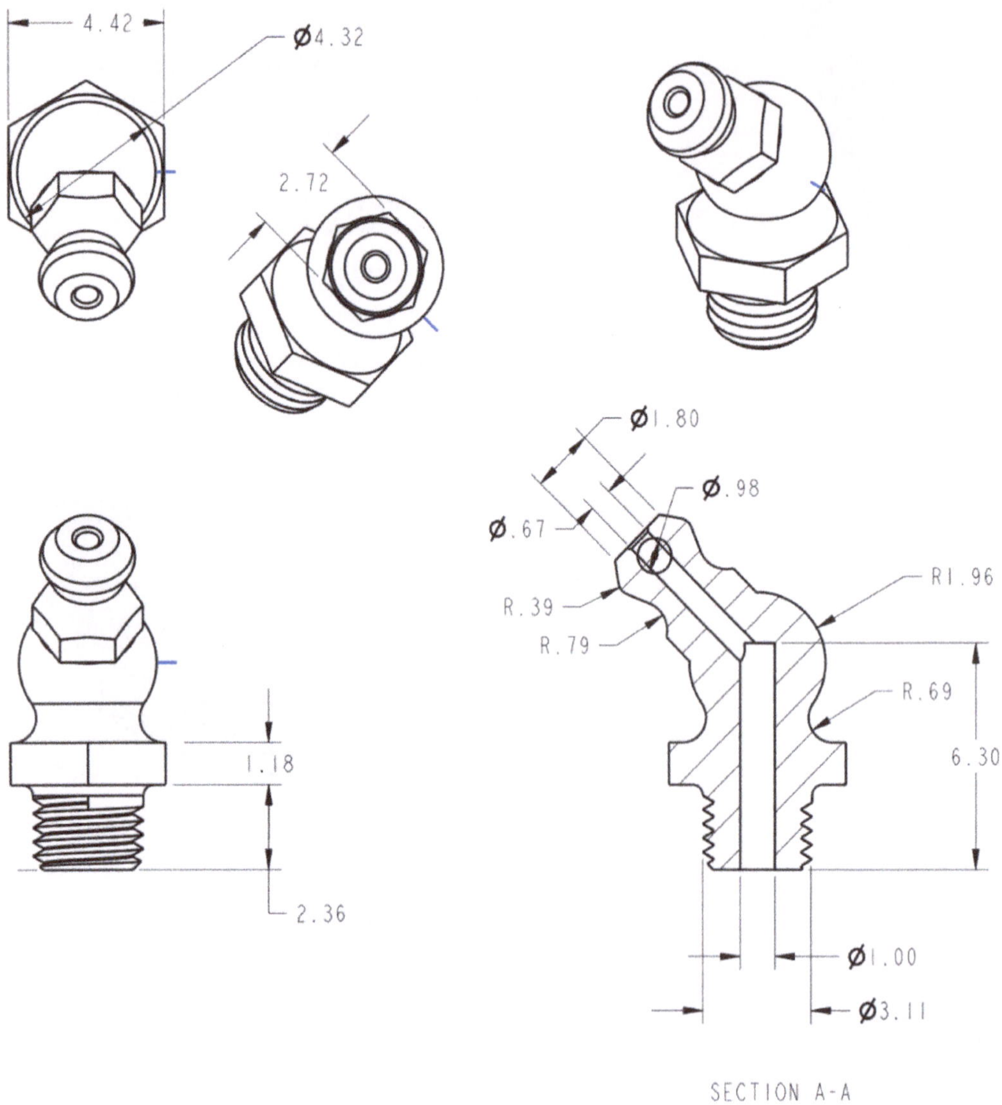

Creating the First Feature

1. Start **Creo Parametric 11.0**.
2. On the Quick Access Toolbar, click the **New** button.
3. On the **New** dialog, select **Types > Part**, and then type-in **C05-Example2** in the **Name** box.
4. Uncheck the **Use default template** option and click **OK**.
5. On the **New File Options** dialog, select **inlbs_part_solid_abs**, and click **OK**.
6. On the ribbon, click **Model** tab > **Datum** panel > **Sketch** .
7. Click on the Front plane.
8. Accept the default values on the **Sketch** dialog and click **Sketch**.
9. On the **Graphics** toolbar, click the **Sketch View** icon to orient the sketch plane parallel to the screen.
10. On the ribbon, click **Sketch** tab > **Sketching** panel > **Line Chain**.
11. Specify the start point of the line on the vertical reference.
12. Click on the origin point to define the second point.
13. Move the pointer horizontally toward the right and click on the horizontal reference.

14. Move the pointer vertically up to a small distance and click.
15. Move the pointer horizontally toward the right up to a small distance and click.
16. Move the pointer vertically up to a small distance and click.
17. Move the pointer horizontally toward the left up to a small distance and click.

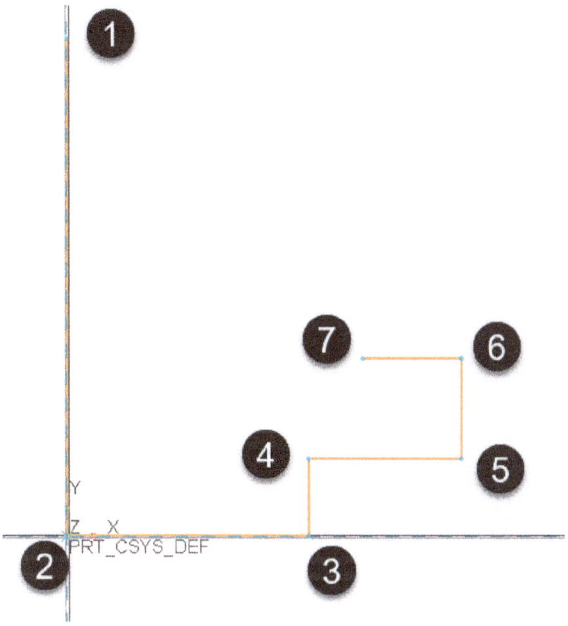

18. Add dimensions to the lines, as shown.

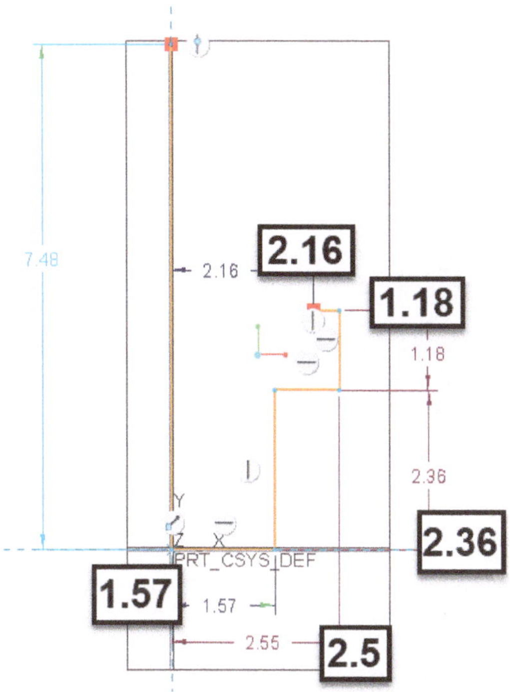

19. On the ribbon, click **Sketch** tab > **Sketching** panel > **Arc** drop-down > **Center and Ends**.
20. Click on the vertical line passing through the origin to specify the centepoint of the arc.
21. Select the end point of the horizontal line to specify the start point of the arc.
22. Move the pointer toward left and click on the vertical reference line to specify the endpoint of the arc.

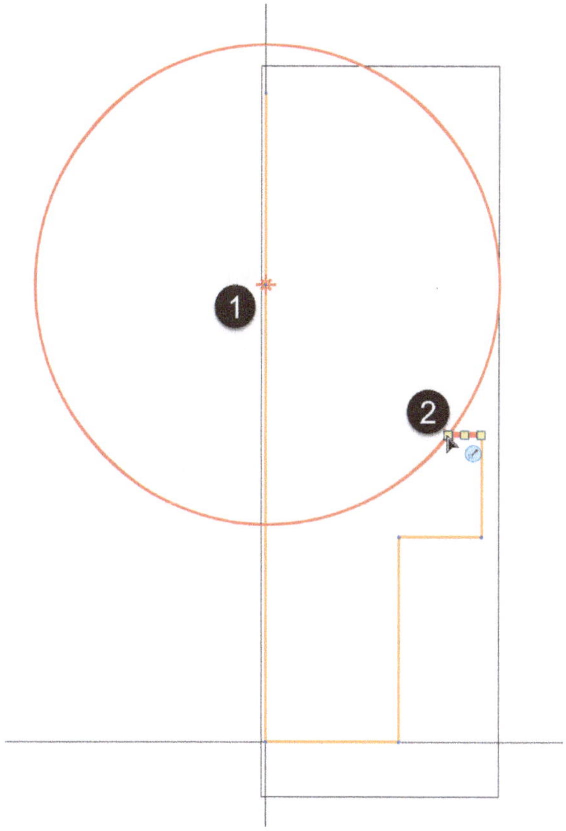

23. Apply the **Coincident** constraint between the endpoint of the arc and the endpoint of the vertical line, as shown.

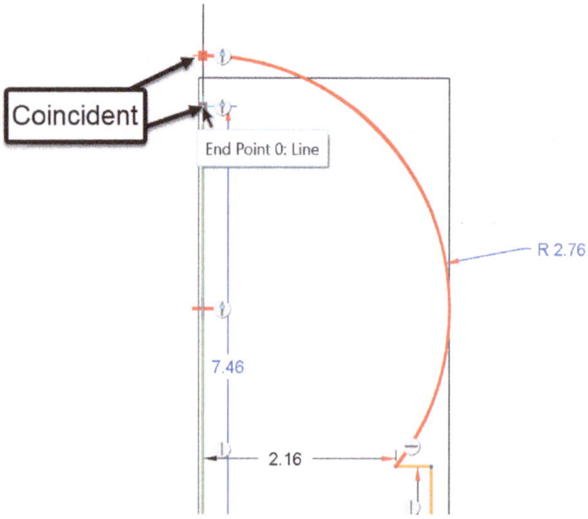

24. Select the **Point On Entity** constraint related to the vertical line and click the **Delete** button on the **Resolve Sketch** dialog.

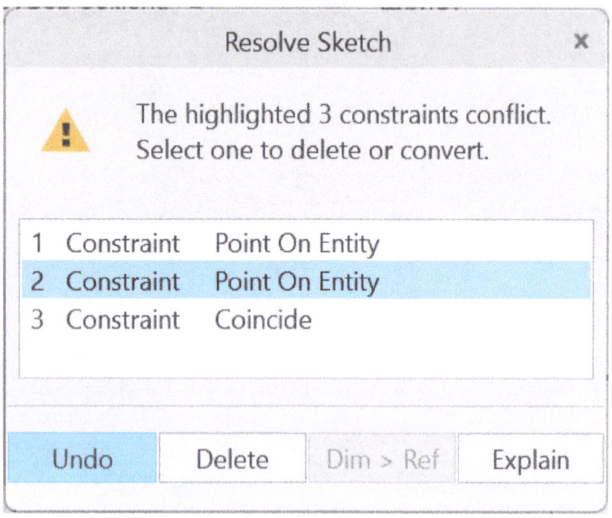

25. On the ribbon, click **Sketch** tab > **Sketching** panel > **Fillet** drop-down > **Circular Trim**.

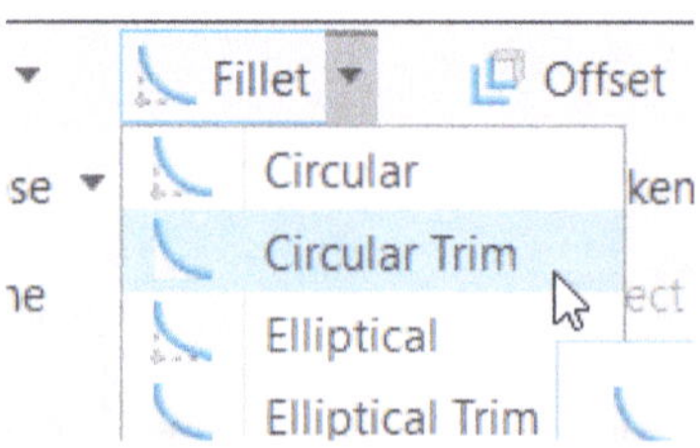

26. Select the horizontal line and the arc.

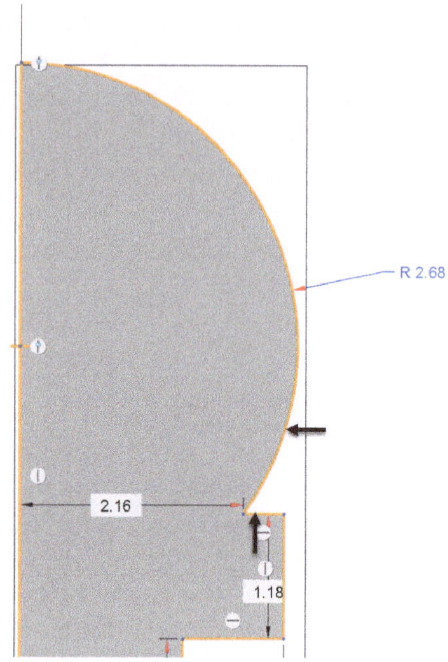

27. Add dimensions to the sketch, as shown.

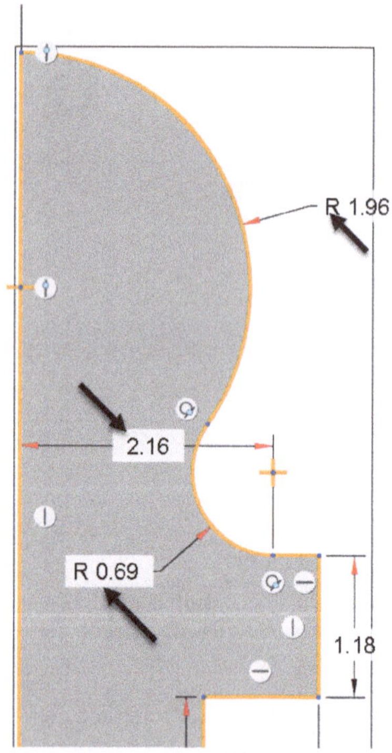

28. Click **OK** on the ribbon.
29. On the ribbon, click **Model** tab > **Shapes** panel > **Revolve** .
30. Select the left vertical line to define the axis of revolution.
31. Click the green check to create the *Revolved* feature.

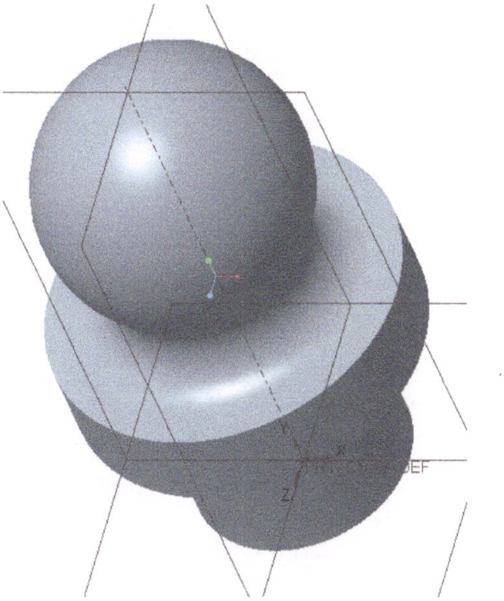

Creating the Extruded Cut Features

1. On the ribbon, click **Model** tab > **Shapes** panel > **Extrude**.
2. Click on the flat face of the model, as shown.

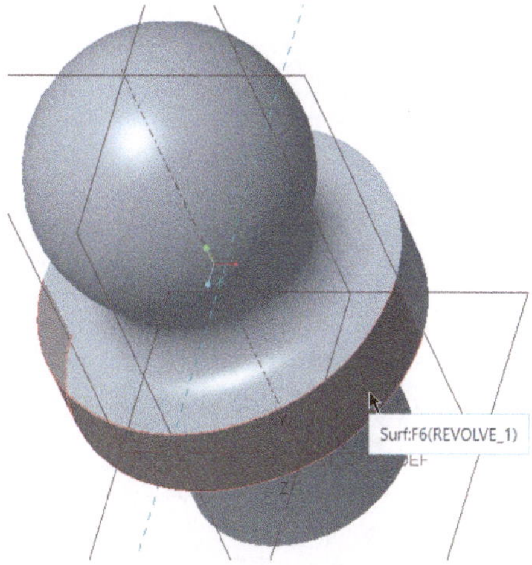

3. On the ribbon, click **Sketch** tab > **Sketching** panel > **Circle** drop-down > **Concentric**.
4. Select the cylindrical face of the inclined boss.

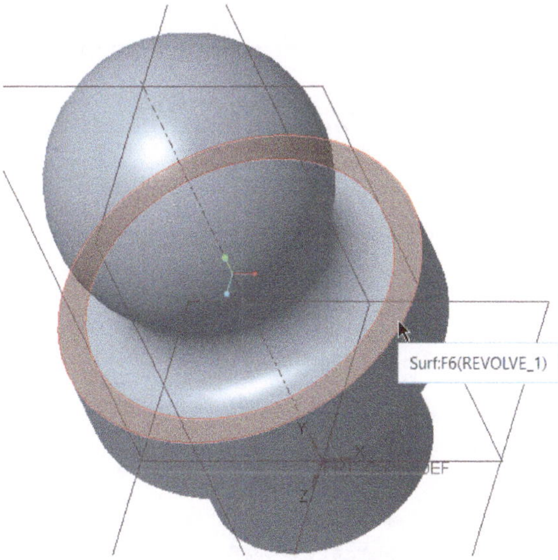

5. Move the pointer outward and click.
6. Press ESC twice.
7. Change the diameter dimension to **5.9**.
8. On the ribbon, click **Sketch** tab > **Sketching** panel > **Palette**.

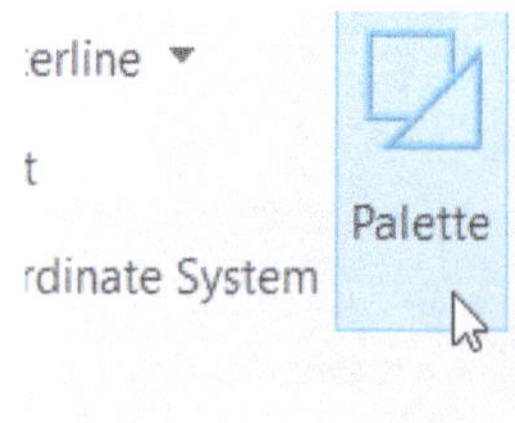

9. On the **Sketcher Profile** dialog, click the **Polygons** tab.
10. Click and drag the **6-Sided Hexagon**.

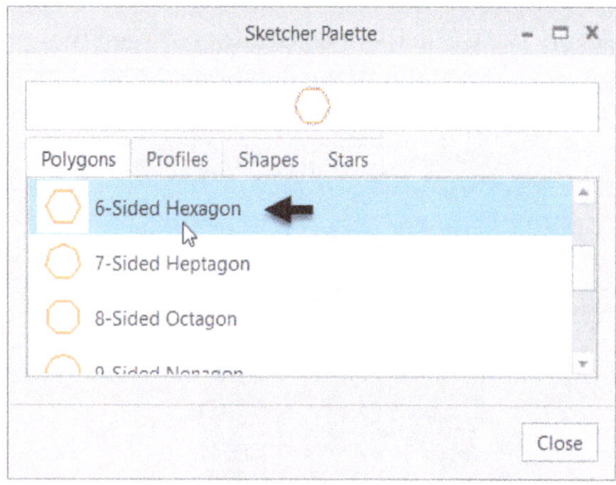

11. Release it into the graphics window.

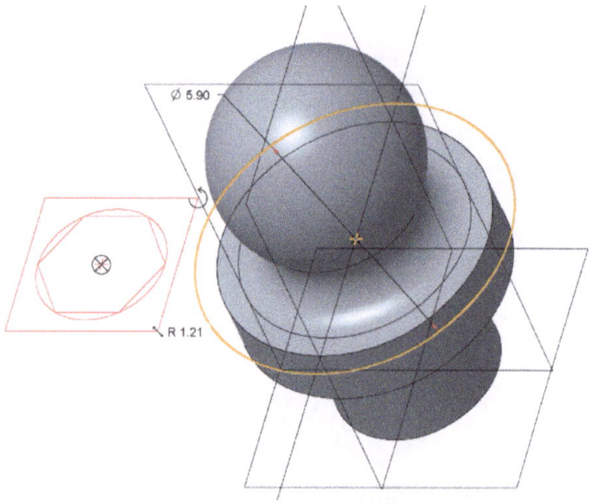

12. Type **90** in the **Angle** box and click **OK**.
13. Apply the **Coincident** constraint between the centerpoint of the polygon and the origin.

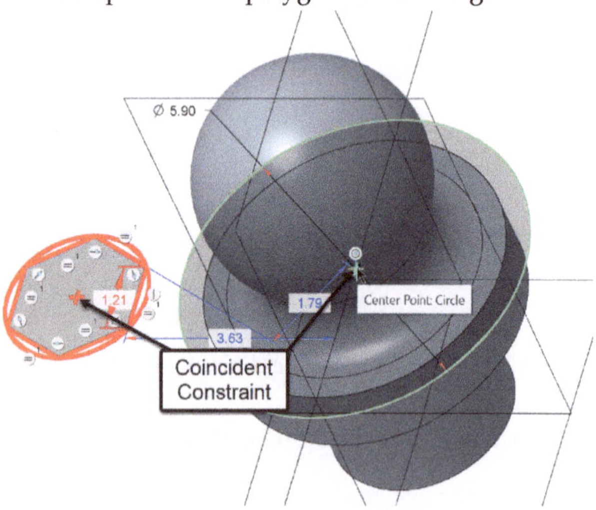

14. Apply the **Coincident** constraint between the lower corner point of the polygon and the circular edge.

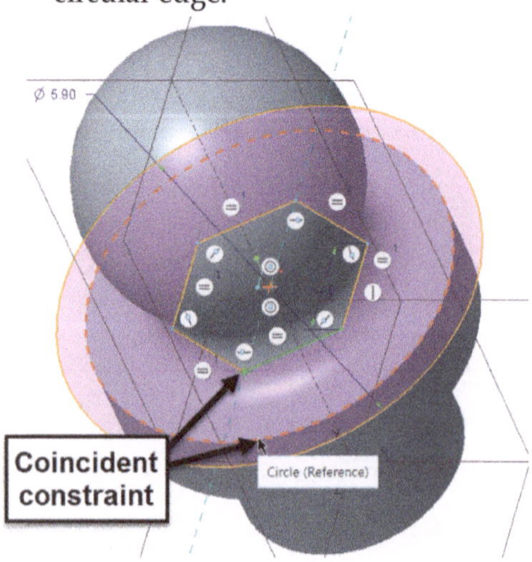

15. On the **Resolve Sketch** dialog, select the **1.40** dimension and click the **Delete** button.

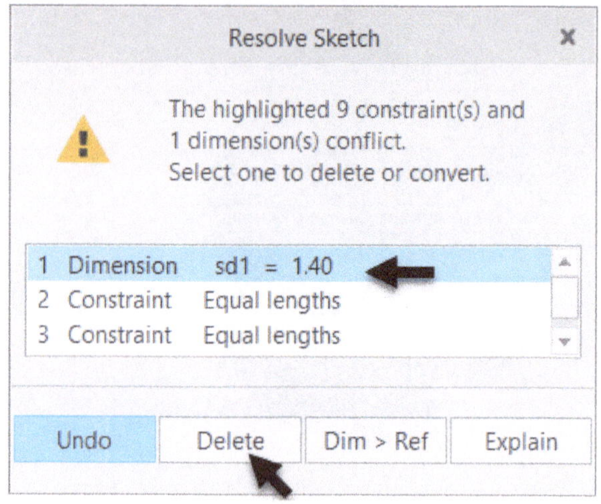

16. Click **OK** on the ribbon.
17. On the **Extrude** Dashboard, click the **Remove Material** icon.
18. Select the **Through all** option from the **Depth** drop-down.
19. Click the **Change Direction** button next to the **Depth** box.
20. Click **OK**.

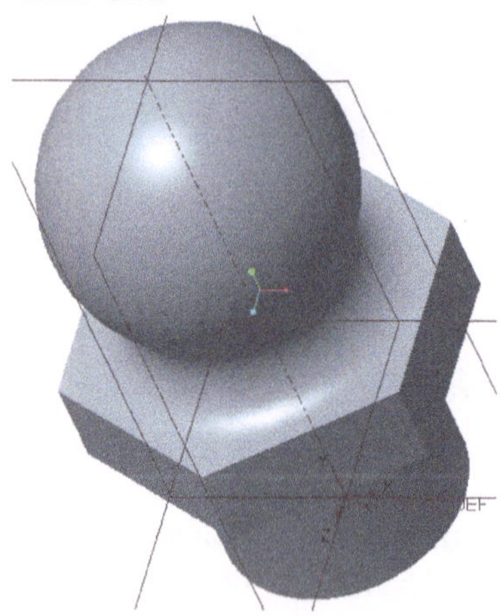

21. On the ribbon, click **Model** tab > **Shapes** panel > **Extrude**.
22. Click on the bottom face of the model, as shown.

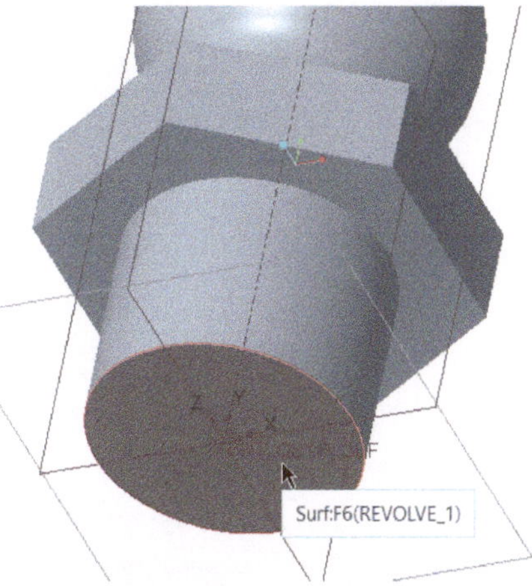

23. On the ribbon, click **Sketch** tab > **Sketching** panel > **Circle** drop-down > **Concentric**.
24. Select the cylindrical face of the inclined boss.

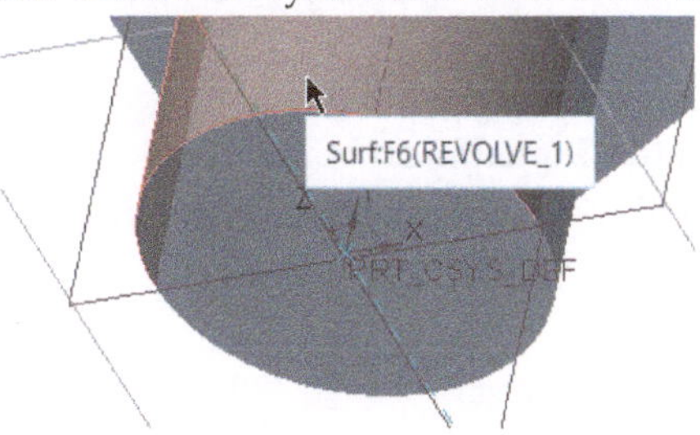

25. Move the pointer outward and click.
26. Press ESC twice.
27. Change the diameter dimension to **1**.

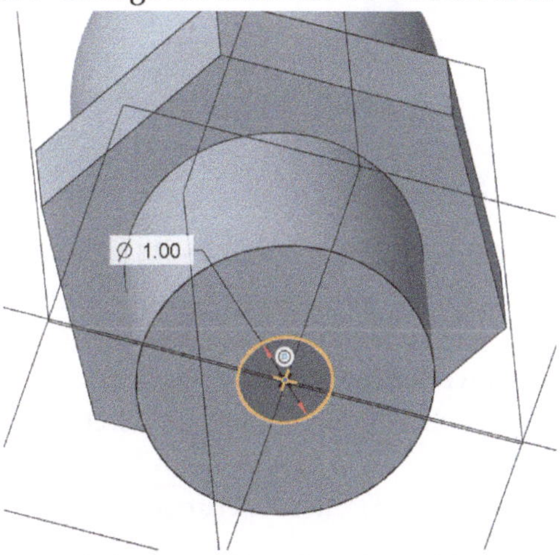

28. Click **OK** on the **Sketch** Dashboard.
29. On the **Extrude** Dashboard, click the **Remove Material** icon.
30. Type **6.3** in the **Depth** box.
31. Click the **Change Direction** button next to the **Depth** box.
32. Click **OK**.

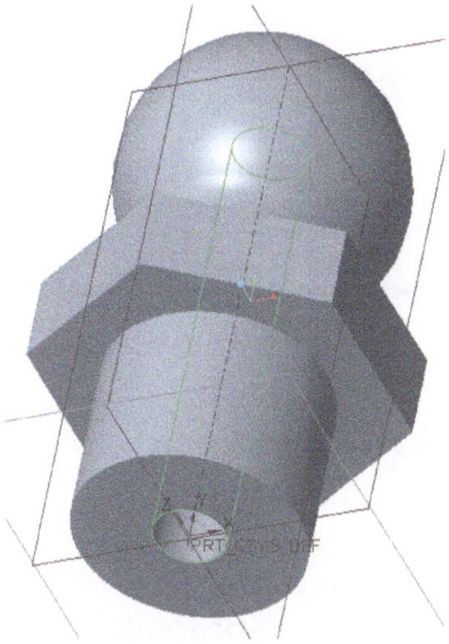

33. On the ribbon, click **Model** tab > **Datum** panel > **Sketch** .
34. Click on the Front plane.
35. Accept the default values on the **Sketch** dialog and click **Sketch**.
36. On the **Graphics** toolbar, click the **Sketch View** icon to orient the sketch plane parallel to the screen.
37. On the ribbon, click **Sketch > Setup > References**.
38. Click the silhouette edge of the sphere and click **Close**.

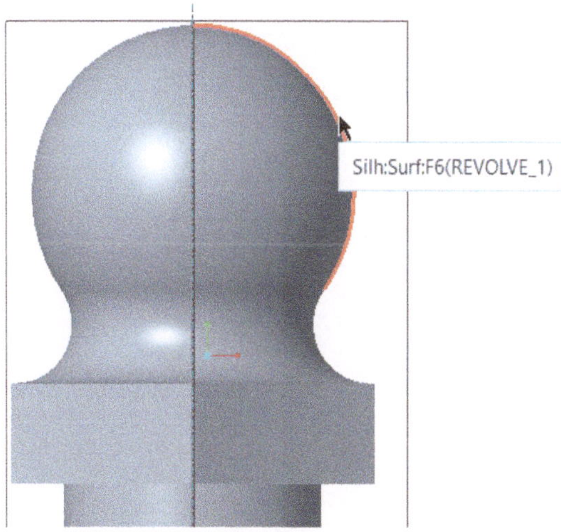

39. On the ribbon, click **Sketch** tab > **Sketching** panel > **Line Chain**.
40. Select the centerpoint of the circular reference edge.
41. Move the pointer horizontally toward the right and click.

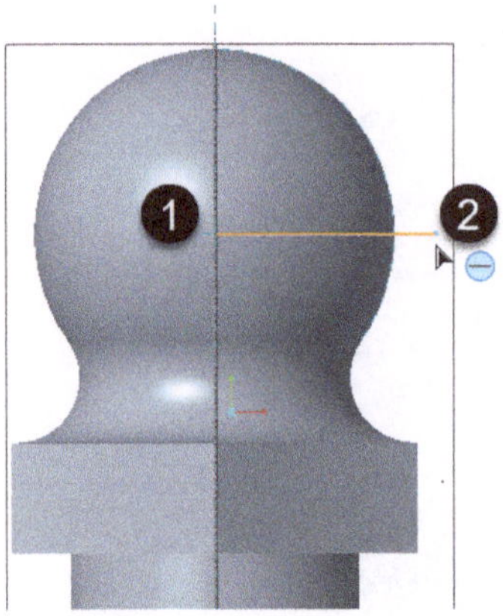

42. Press ESC.
43. Click **OK** on the ribbon.
44. On the **Graphics** toolbar, click **Saved Orientations** drop-down **> Standard Orientation**.
45. On the ribbon, click **Model** tab > **Datum** panel > **Plane**.
46. Press and hold the CTRL key and select the newly created line and the Front plane.

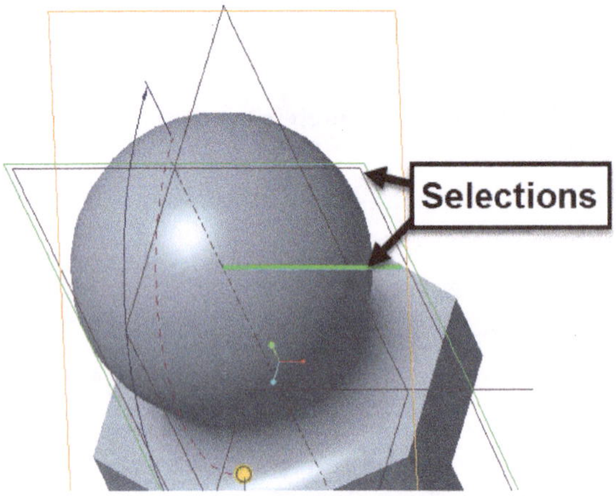

47. Type 135 in the **Rotation** box and click **OK**.

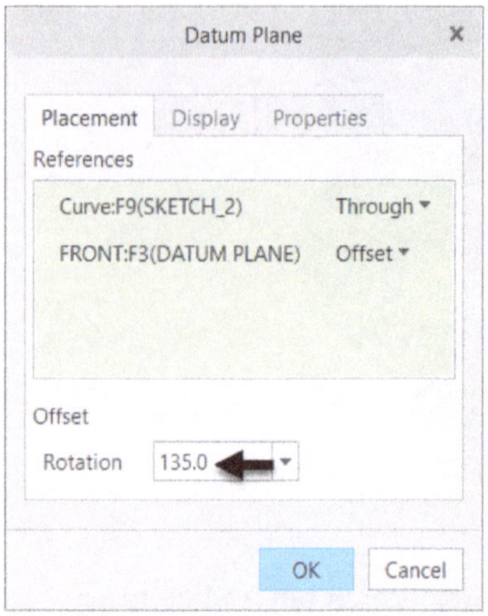

48. On the ribbon, click **Model** tab > **Datum** panel > **Plane**.
49. Select the newly created plane.
50. Type **-1.37** in the **Translation** box.
51. Click the **Display** tab and click the **Flip** button next to the **Normal Direction** option.
52. Click **OK**.

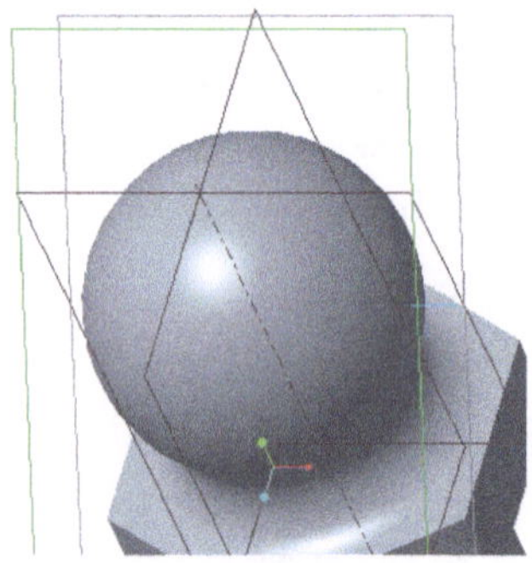

53. On the ribbon, click **Model** tab > **Datum** panel > **Sketch**.
54. Select the newly created plane.
55. Click the **Sketch** button.
56. On the ribbon, click **Sketch > Setup > Sketch View**.
57. On the ribbon, click **Sketch > Setup > References**.
58. Select the horizontal line, as shown.

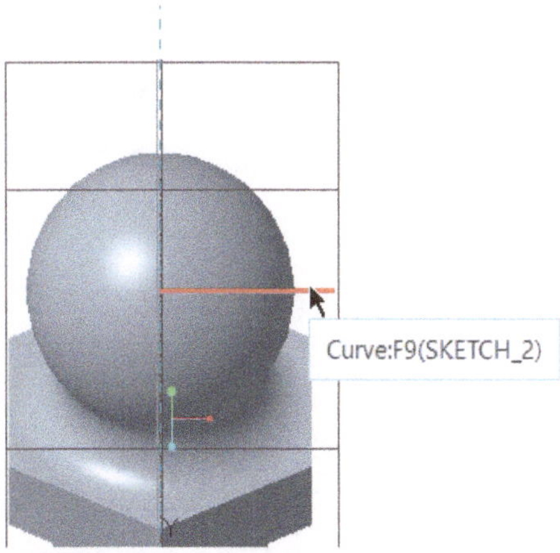

59. Click **Close**.
60. On the ribbon, click **Sketch** tab > **Sketching** panel > **Circle** drop-down > **Center and Point**.
61. Select the left endpoint of the reference line.
62. Move the pointer outward and click.

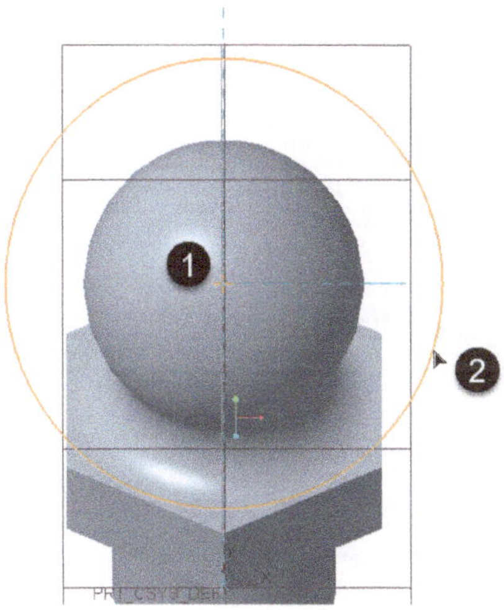

63. Change the diameter dimension to **3.5**.

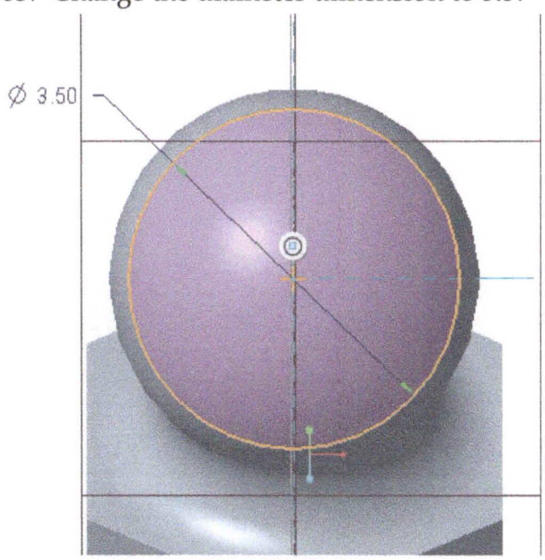

64. Click **OK** on the ribbon.

65. On the ribbon, click **Model** tab > **Shapes** panel > **Extrude**.
66. Select the newly created sketch.
67. On the **Extrude** Dashboard, click the **Remove Material** icon.
68. Select the **Through all** option from the **Depth** drop-down.
69. Click **OK**.

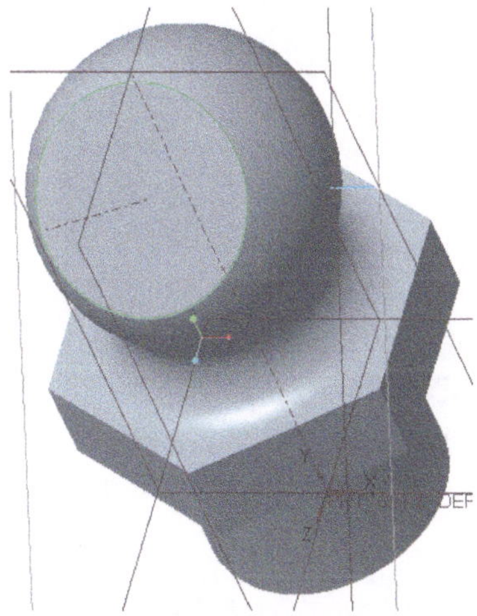

Creating the Revolved Feature

1. On the ribbon, click **Model** tab > **Shapes** panel > **Revolve**.
2. Select the right plane.

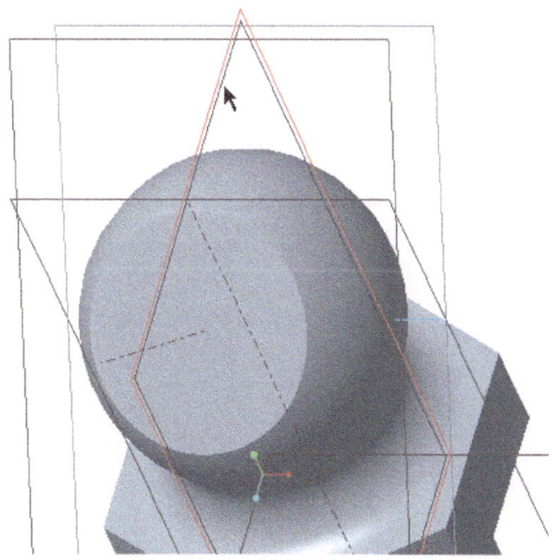

3. On the **Graphics** toolbar, click the **Sketch View** icon to orient the sketch plane parallel to the screen.
4. Create the sketch, as shown.

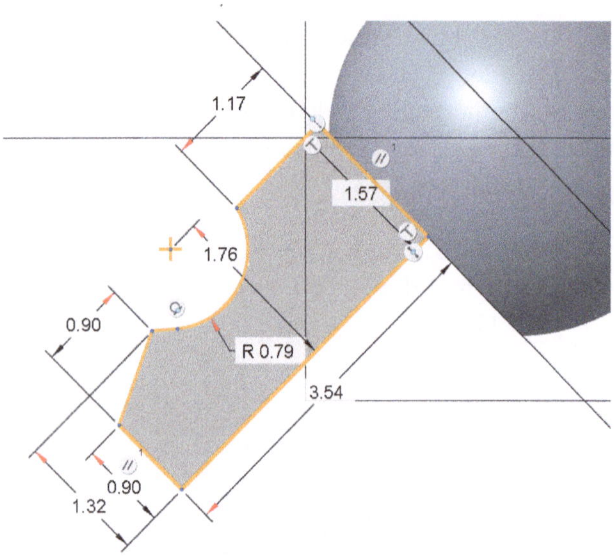

5. On the ribbon, click **Sketch > Sketching > Fillet** drop-down **> Circular**.
6. Select the two inclined lines.
7. Add and change the sketch dimensions, as shown.

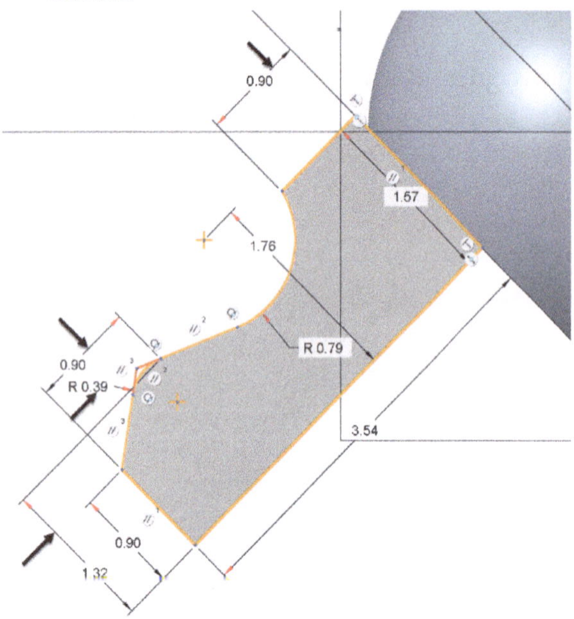

8. Click **OK** on the ribbon.
9. Select the axis of revolution, as shown.

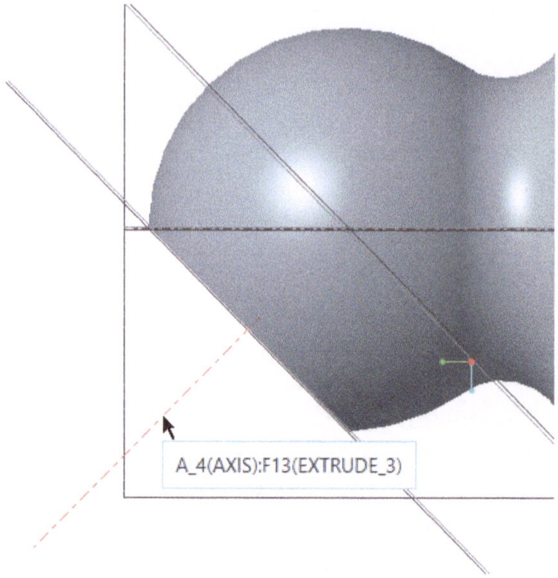

10. Click **OK** on the **Revolve** dashboard.

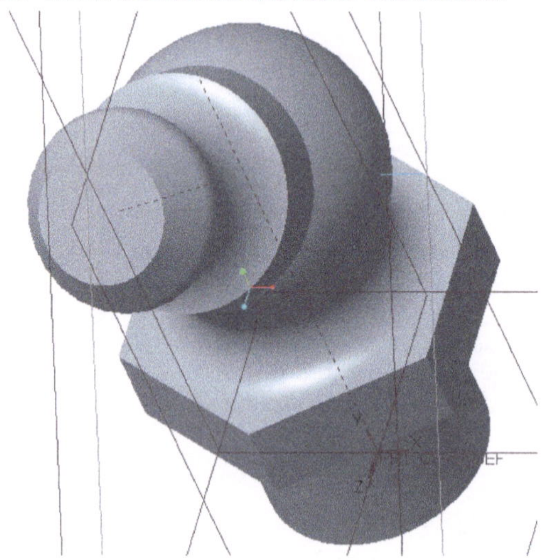

Creating the Extruded Cut Features

1. On the ribbon, click **Model** tab > **Shapes** panel > **Extrude**.
2. Rotate the model and click on the flat face of the revolved feature, as shown.

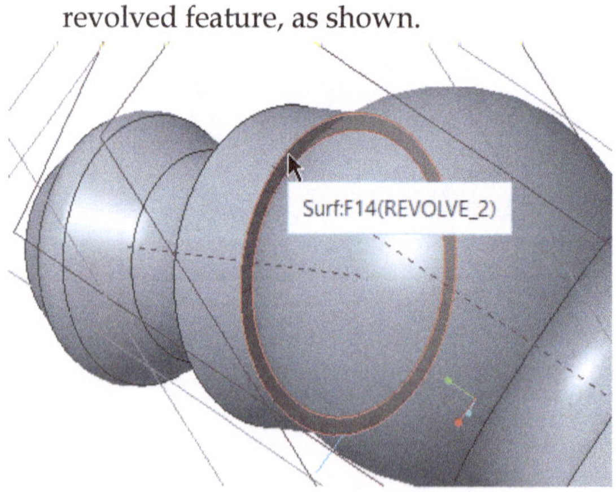

3. Create the sketch, as shown.

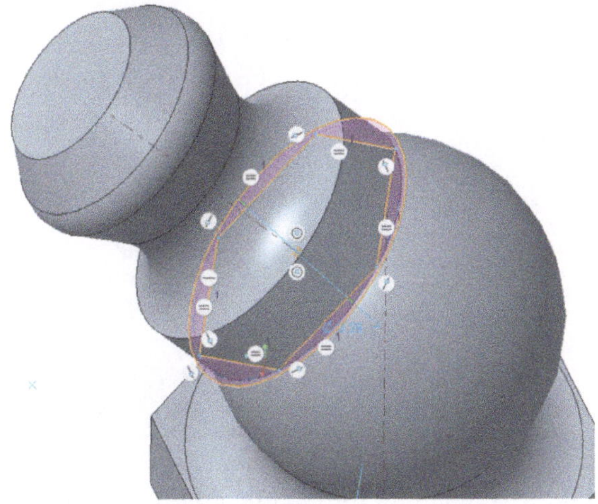

4. Click **OK** on the ribbon.
5. On the **Extrude** Dashboard, click the **Remove Material** icon.
6. Select the **Through all** option from the **Depth** drop-down.
7. Click the **Change Direction** button next to the **Depth** box.
8. Click **OK**.

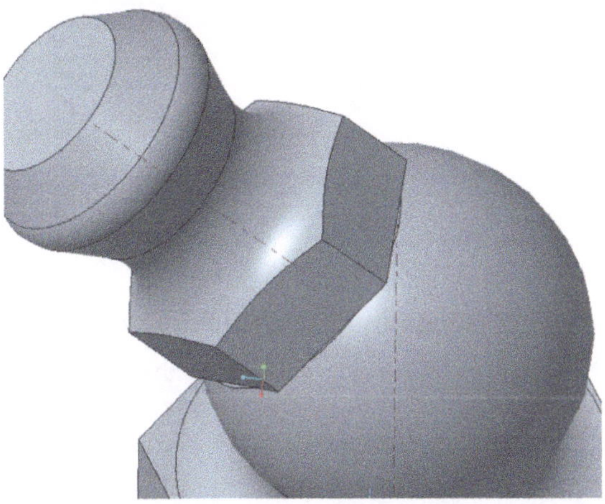

9. On the ribbon, click **Model** tab > **Shapes** panel > **Extrude**.
10. Rotate the model and click on the flat face of the revolved feature, as shown.

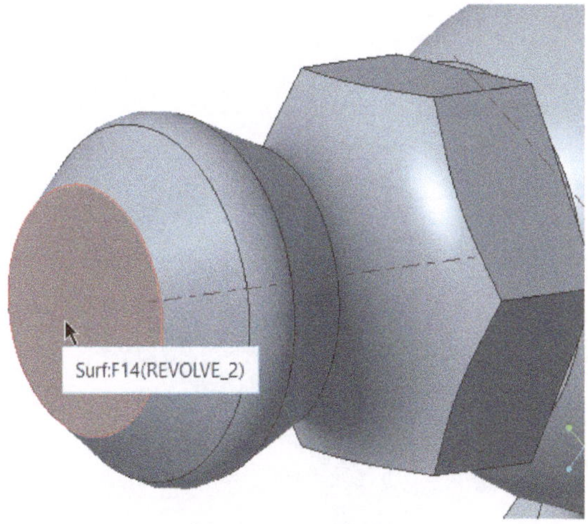

11. Create a circle of 0.67 diameters.
12. Click OK on the ribbon.
13. On the **Extrude** Dashboard, click the **Remove Material** icon.
14. Type **5.11** in the **Depth** box.
15. Click the **Change Direction** button next to the **Depth** box.
16. Click **OK**.

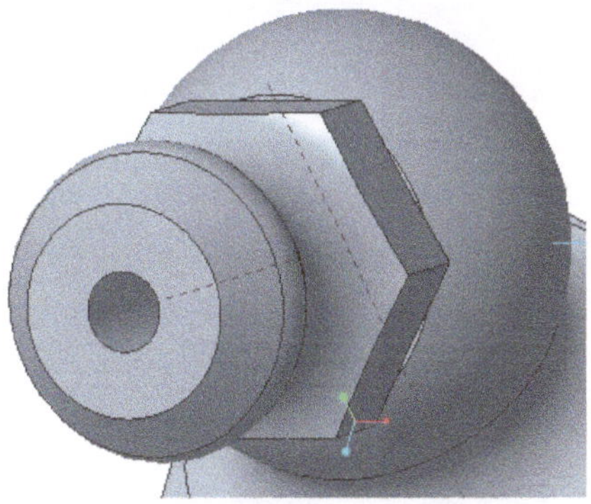

Creating the Ball

1. On the ribbon, click **Model** tab > **Shapes** panel > **Revolve**.
2. Select the right plane.
3. On the **Graphics** toolbar, click the **Sketch View** icon to orient the sketch plane parallel to the screen.
4. Create the sketch, as shown.

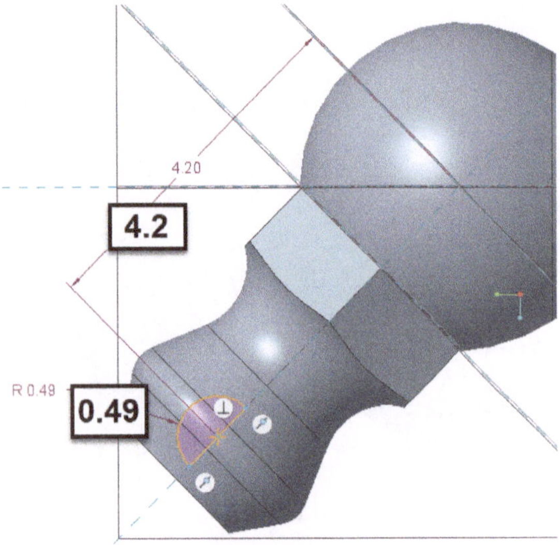

5. Click **OK** on the ribbon.
6. Select the axis of revolution, as shown.

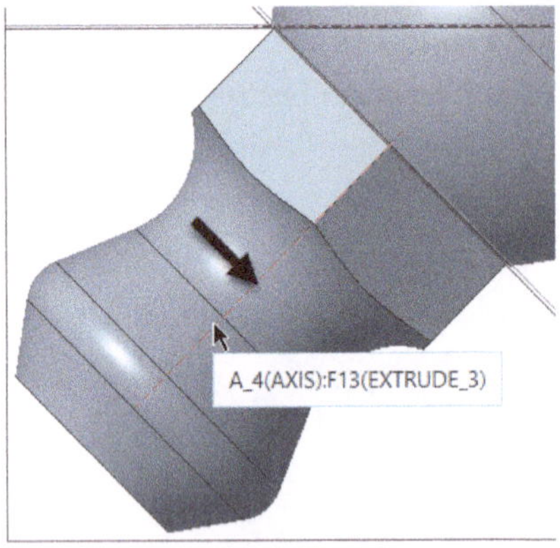

7. Click **OK** on the **Revolve** dashboard.

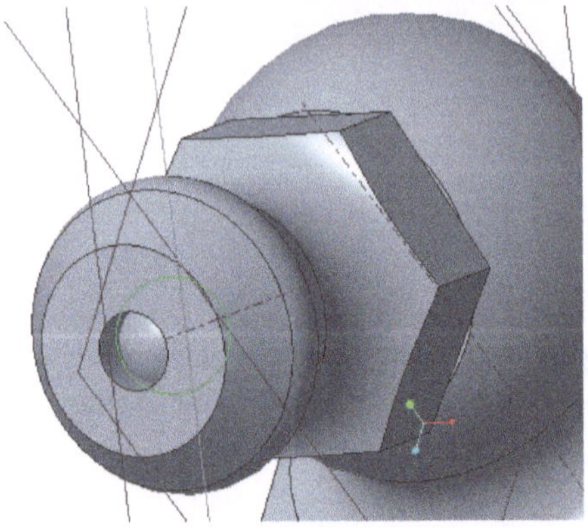

Creating the Chamfers and Rounds

1. On the ribbon, click **Model** tab > **Engineering** panel > **Chamfer** drop-down **> Edge Chamfer** .
2. On the **Edge Chamfer** dashboard, select **D x D** from the drop-down.
3. Set the **D** value to **0.1**.
4. Select the circular edge, as shown.

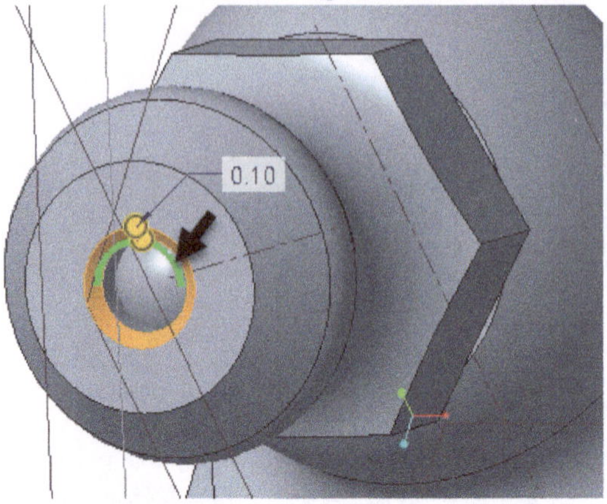

5. Click **OK**.
6. Likewise, chamfer the circular edge of the bottom face, as shown. The chamfer distance is **0.3**.

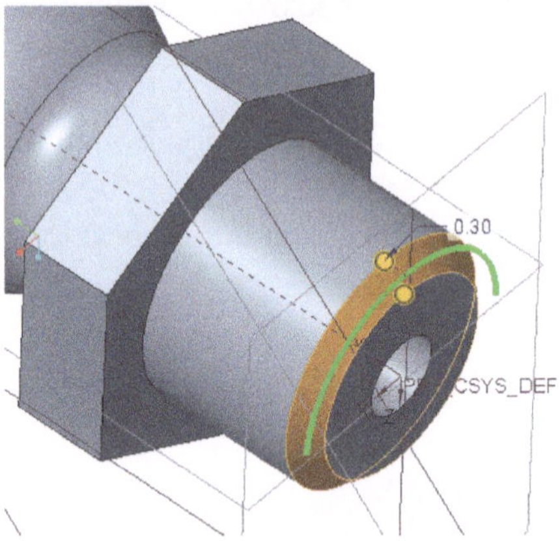

7. On the ribbon, click **Model** tab > **Engineering** panel > **Round** .
8. Select the circular edge, as shown.
9. Type **0.3** in the **Radius** box on the **Round** dashboard.
10. Click **OK**.

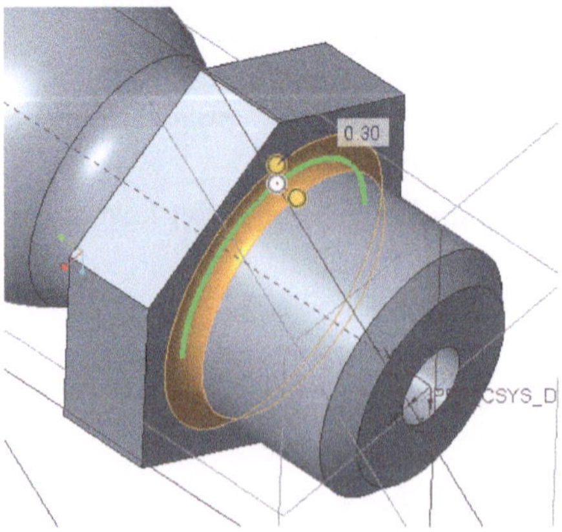

Creating the Helical Swept Cut

1. Activate the **Helical Sweep** command.

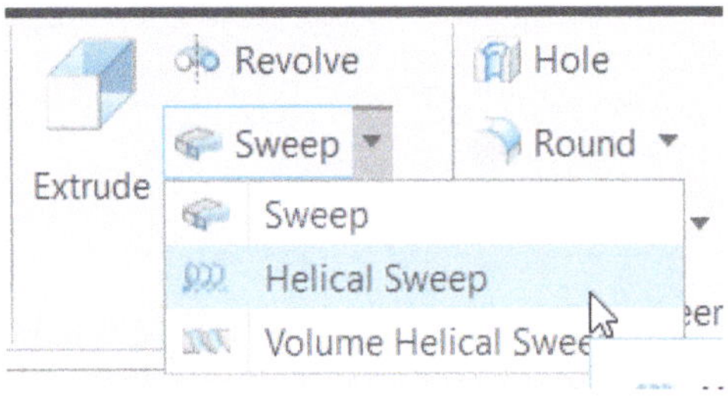

2. On the **Helical Sweep** Dashboard, click the **References** tab.
3. Click the **Define** button next to the **Helical profile** box.
4. Select the Right datum plane and click **Sketch**.

   Click the **Sketch View** icon on the **Graphics** toolbar.
5. On the **Sketch** ribbon, click **Sketching > Centerline**.
6. Create a horizontal centerline passing through the sketch origin.

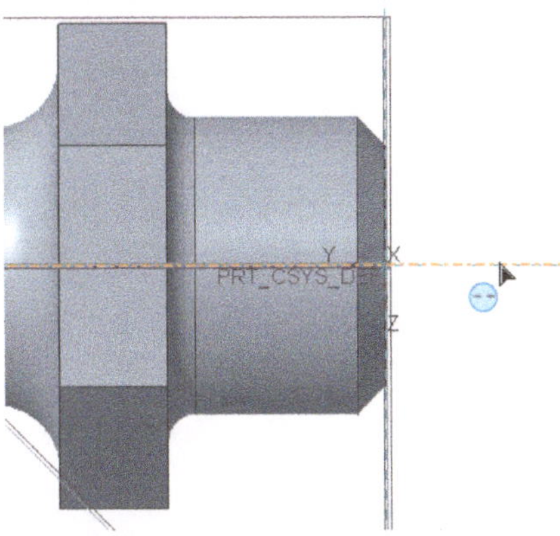

7. On the ribbon, click **Sketch** tab > **Sketching** panel > **Line Chain**.
8. Specify the start and endpoints of the line, as shown.

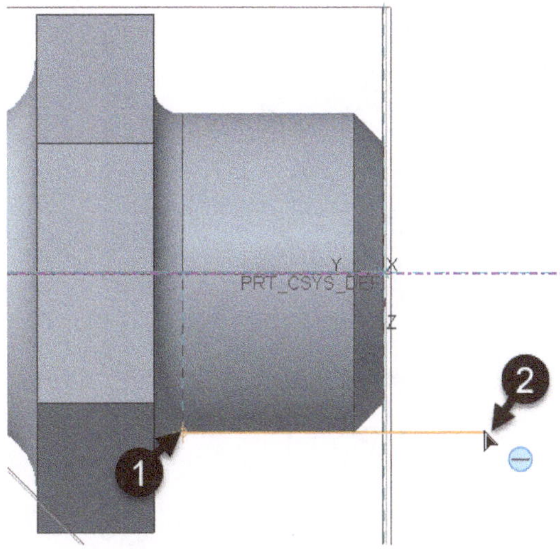

9. Click **OK** on the ribbon.
10. Click the **Sketch** icon on the Dashboard.
11. Create the cross-section and click **OK**.

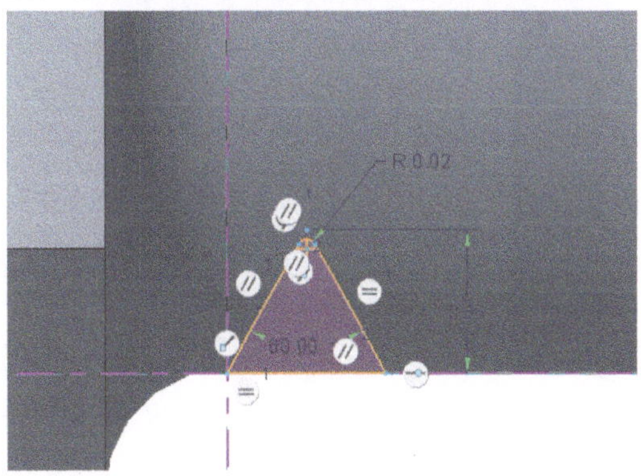

12. On the Dashboard, click the **Remove Material** icon.
13. Type-in 0.394 in the **Pitch Value** box located on the Dashboard.
14. Click **OK**.

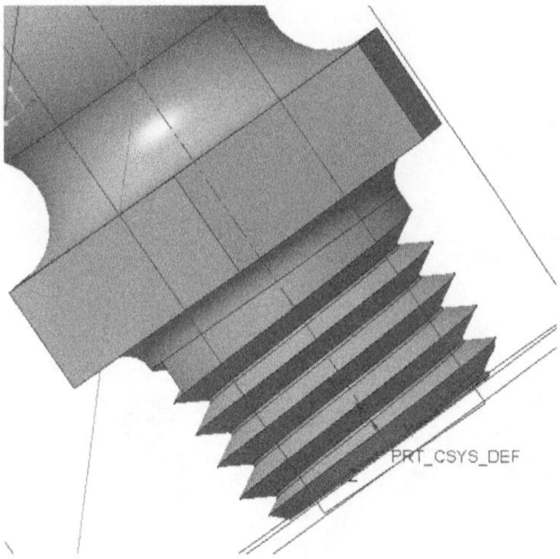

Questions

1. List the types of trajectories that can be used to create *Sweep* features.
2. What is the use of the **Merge ends** option?
3. List the options to define the helix direction.

Exercises

Exercise1

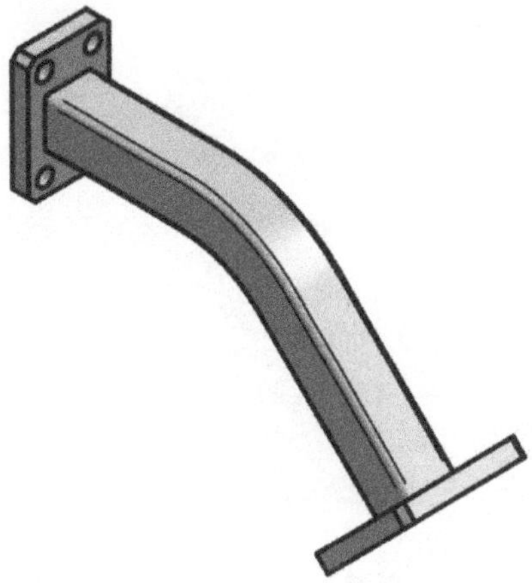

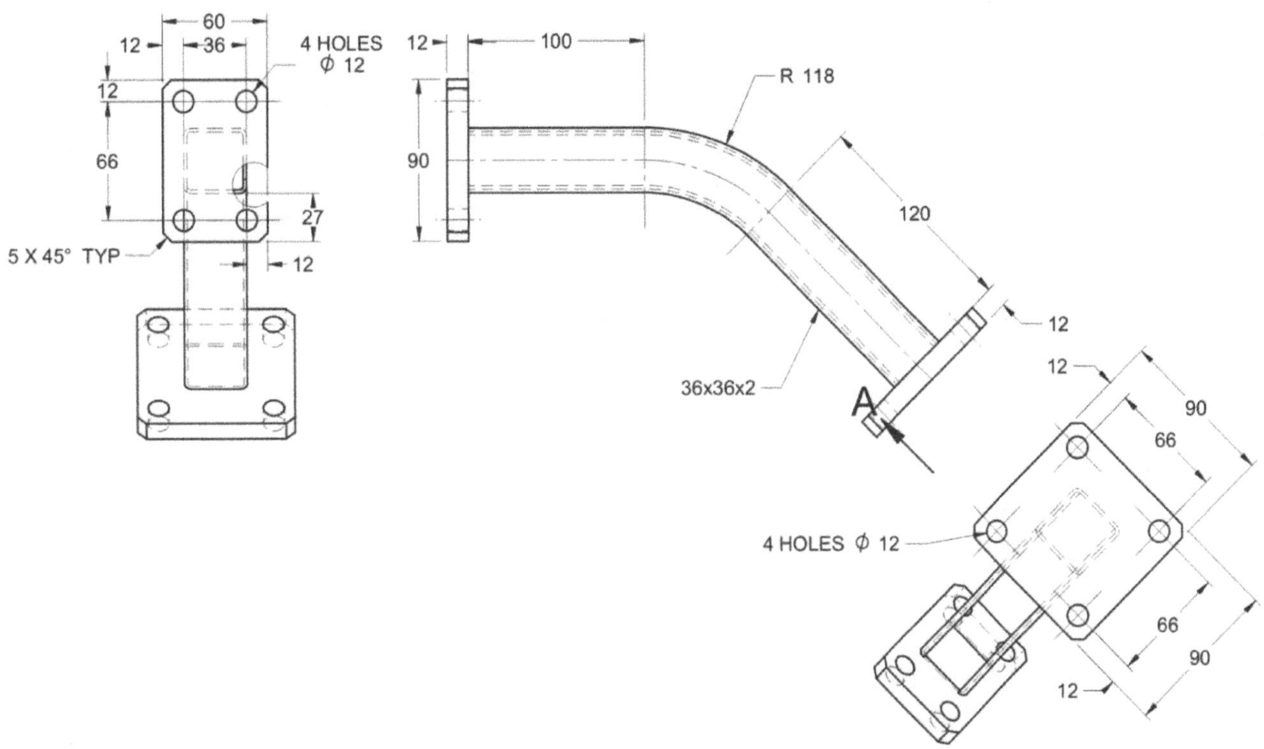

Chapter 7: Blend Features

A blend feature is one of the advanced features available in Creo Parametric that allows you to create simple and complex shapes. A basic blend feature is created by defining two cross-sections and joining them together. For example, if you create a blend feature between a circle and a square, you can easily change the solid's cross-sectional shape. This ability is what separates the solid blend feature from the sweep feature.

The topics covered in this chapter are:

- *Blend features*
- *Blend Cutouts*
- *Types of Cross-sections*
- *Rotational Blends*
- *Swept Blends*

The Blend command

This command creates a feature between different cross-sections.

1. To create this type of feature, first, create two or more sections on different planes. The planes can be parallel or perpendicular to each other.
2. On the ribbon, click **Model > Shapes > Blend**.

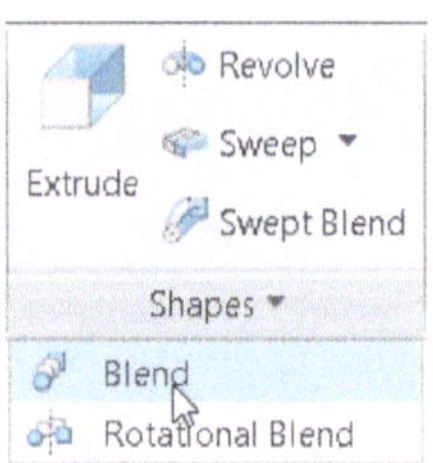

3. On the **Blend** Dashboard, click the **Selected Sections** icon.
4. Select the first cross-section.
5. On the **Sections** tab, click the **Add** button and select the second cross-section.

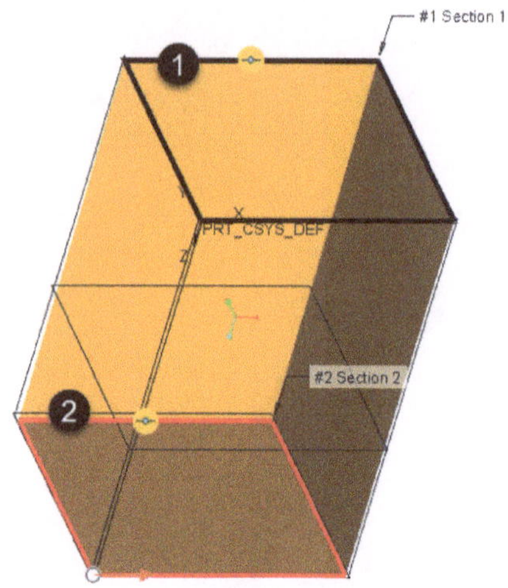

6. Again, click **Add** and select the third cross-section.

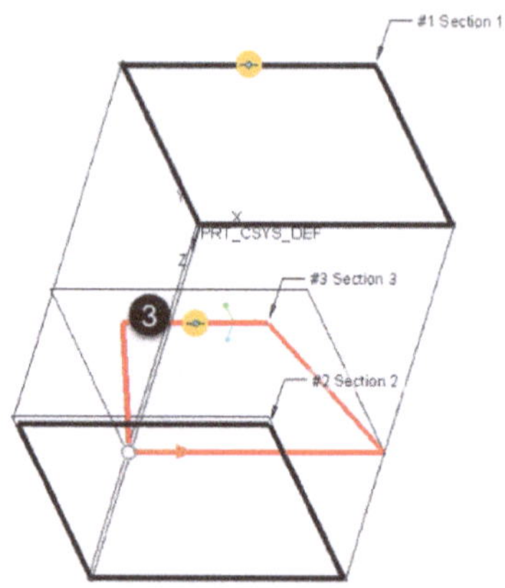

7. On the **Sections** tab, select the third section from the **Sections** list, and then click the **Move Up** button. The third section is moved to the middle, and the preview changes.

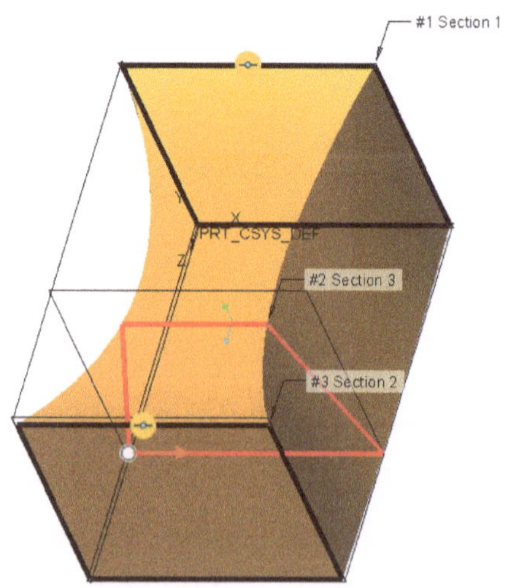

8. Click and drag the origin of the third section. Notice that the blend is twisted.

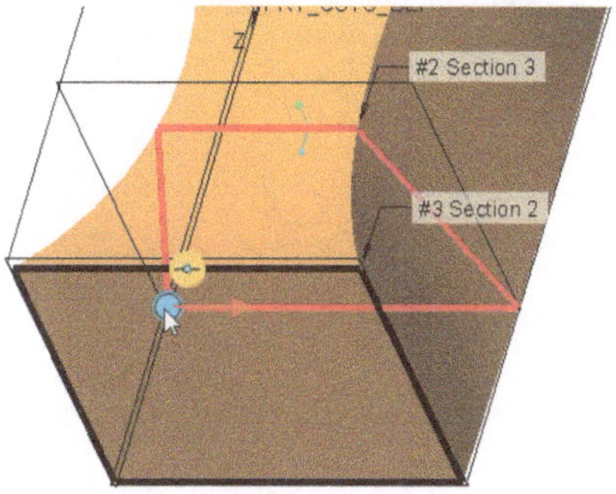

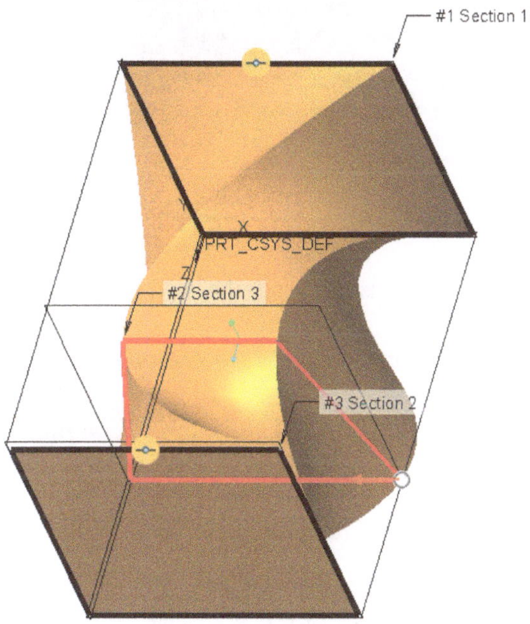

9. Drag the origin back to its initial position.

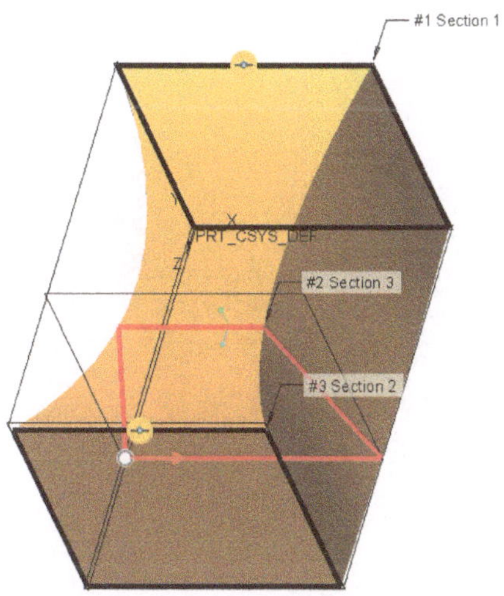

10. On the Dashboard, click the **Options** tab and set the **Blended surfaces** to **Straight**. Notice that the transition between the sections is changed to straight.

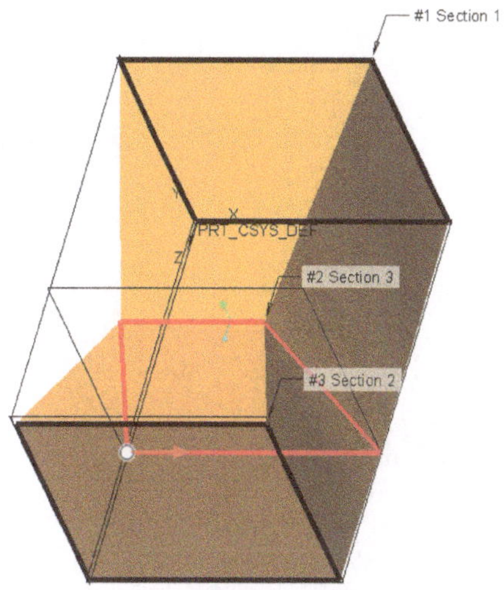

11. Again, set the **Blended surfaces** to **Smooth**. Click the green check to complete the feature.

Creating Blend Cut-outs

Like other standard features such as extrusion, revolve, and sweep, the blend feature can add or remove material.

1. Activate the **Blend** command.
2. On the **Blend** Dashboard, click the **Sections** tab.
3. With the **Sketched sections** option selected, click the **Define** button next to the **Sketch** box.
4. Click on the front face of the model.

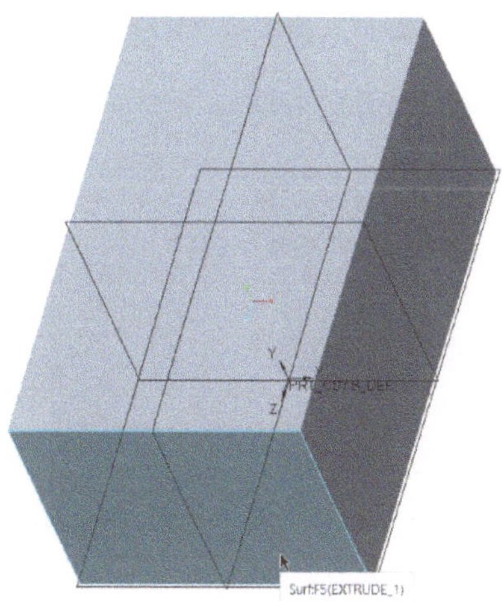

5. Click the **Sketch** button.
6. Create the first cross-section and click **OK** on the ribbon.

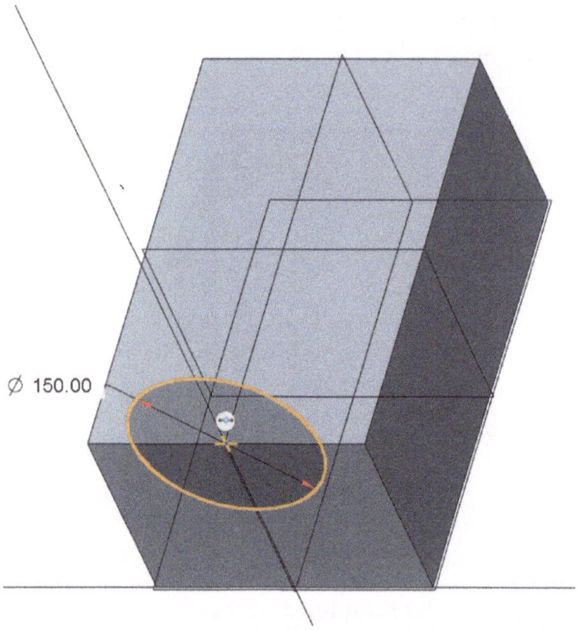

7. On the Dashboard, click the **Sections** tab. Notice that the **Section 2** definition is activated. Also, the **Offset dimension** option is selected to define the sketch plane by an offset value. You can type in the offset value in the **Offset from** box.
8. On the **Sections** tab, select the **Reference** option to define the sketch plane manually.
9. Select the Front datum plane and click the **Sketch** button.

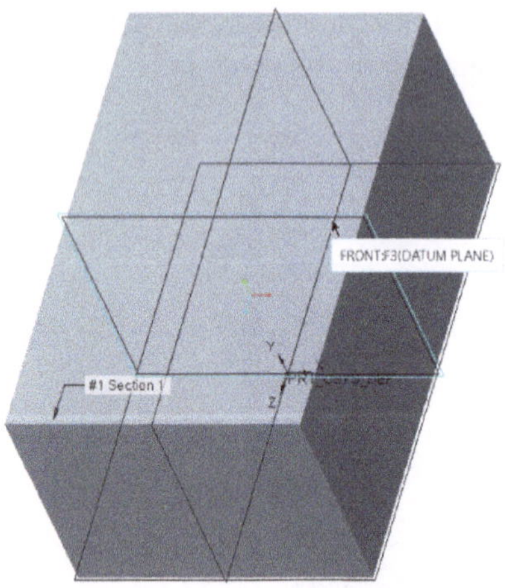

10. Create the second section and click **OK** on the ribbon.

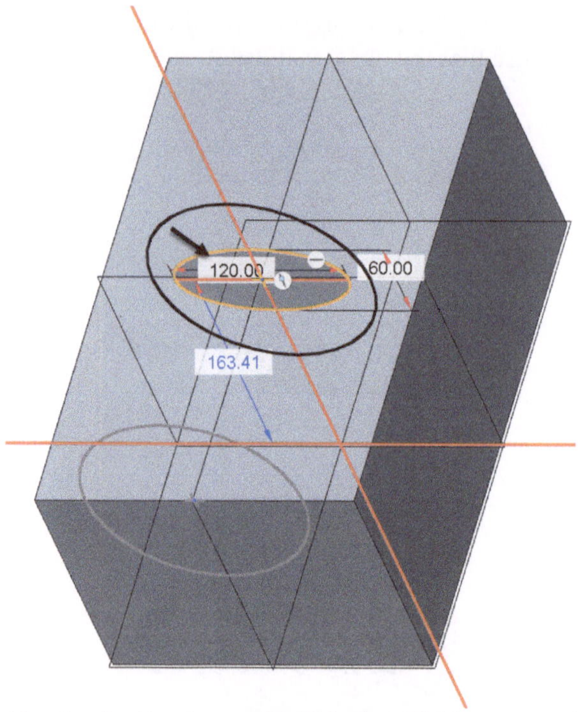

11. On the **Sections** tab, click the **Add** button and select the **Reference** option.
12. Select the back face of the geometry and click **Sketch**.
13. Create the third section and click **OK** on the ribbon.

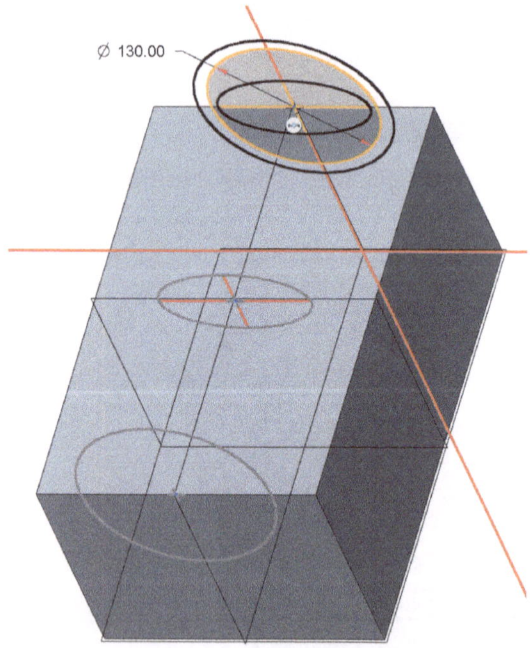

14. Click the **Remove material** icon on the Dashboard.
15. Click the green check to complete the feature.

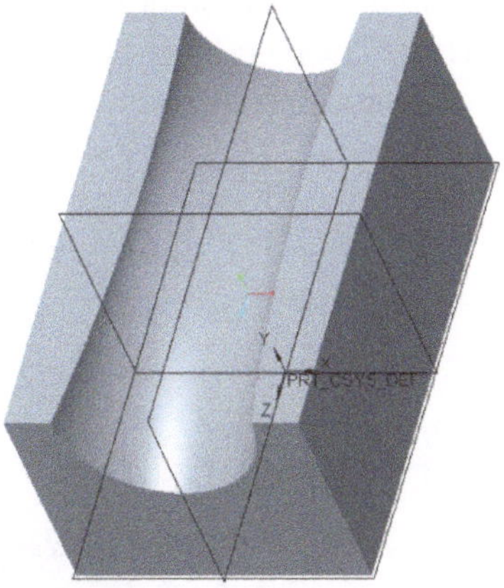

Types of the Cross-sections

In addition to 2D sketches, you can also use different element types to define cross-sections using different element types. For instance, you can use existing model faces, surfaces, and curves.

Blends between existing model faces

The **Blend** command can be used to join two solids.

1. Activate the **Blend** command.
2. On the **Blend** Dashboard, click the **Selected Sections** icon.
3. Click on the edge of the solid as shown.

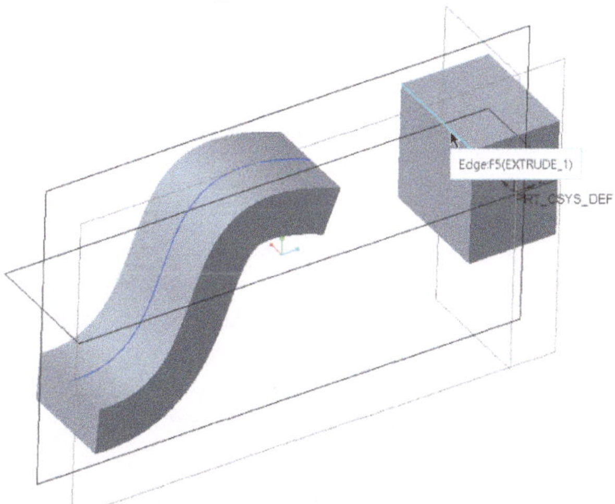

4. On the **Sections** tab, click the **Details** button.
5. On the **Chain** dialog, select the **Rule-based** option and set the **Rule** to **Complete Loop**.
6. Click in the **Loop Reference** box and click on the end face of the solid. Click **OK** on the **Chain** dialog.

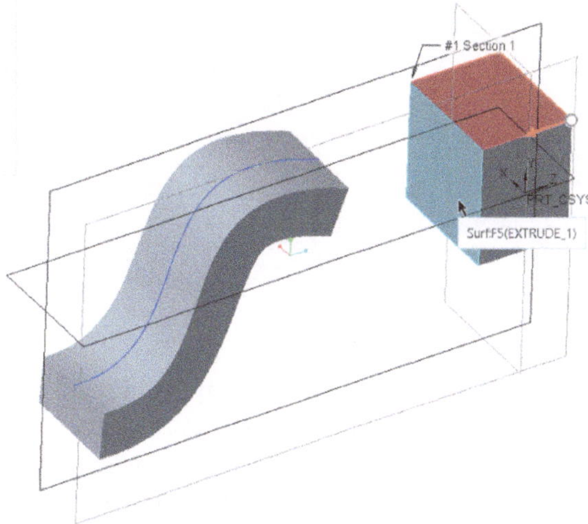

7. On the **Sections** tab, click the **Add** button to define the second section.
8. Likewise, select the edge chain of the other solid as shown.
9. On the **Sections** tab, click the **Details** button.
10. On the **Chain** dialog, select the **Rule-based** option and set the **Rule** to **Complete Loop**.
11. Click on the end face of the solid. Click **OK** on the **Chain** dialog.

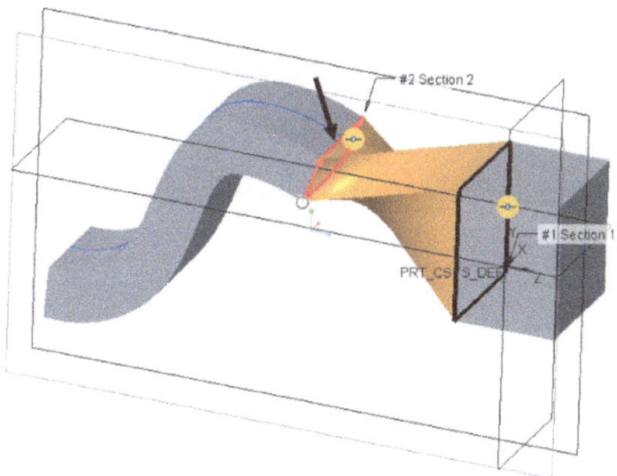

12. Click and drag the origin of the second cross-section. The twist is removed.

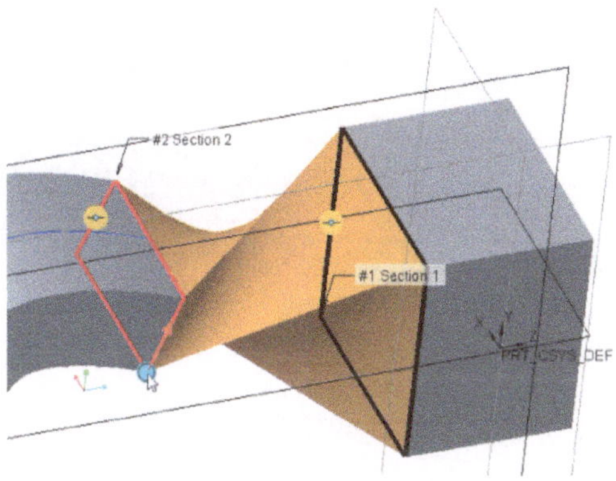

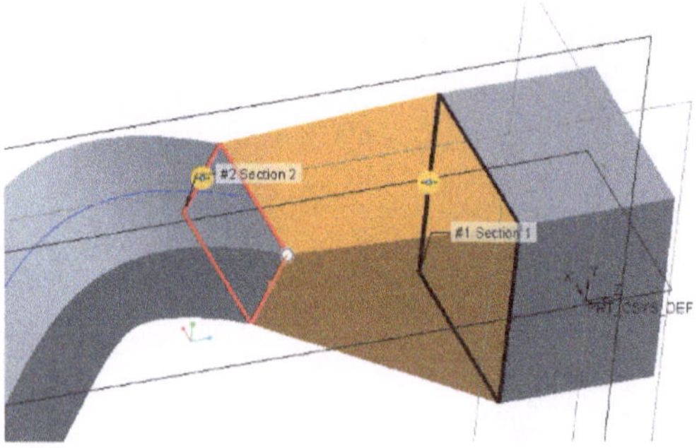

13. On the Dashboard, click the **Options** tab and make sure that the **Blend Surfaces** is set to **Smooth**.
14. On the Dashboard, click the **Tangency** tab.
15. Set the boundary condition of the **Start Section** to **Tangent**. An edge is highlighted.
16. Click on the face associated with the highlighted edge.

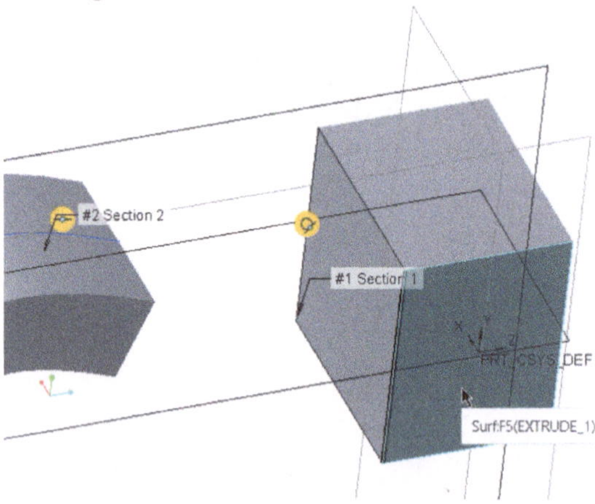

17. Likewise, select the faces associated with other highlighted edges. The blend faces at the start section become tangent to the side faces of the start section.

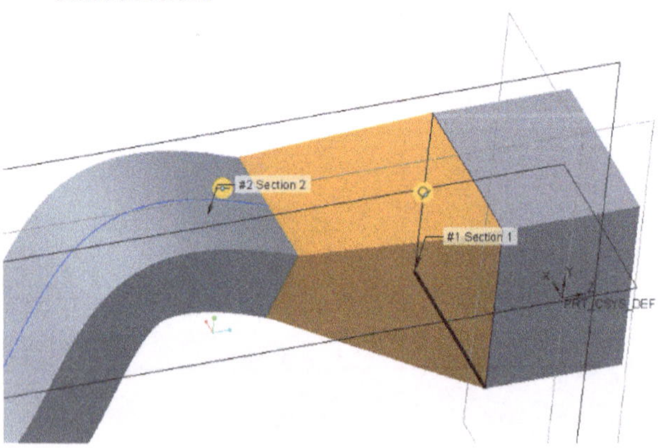

18. Change the boundary condition of the **End Section** to **Normal**. The blend faces become normal to the end section face.

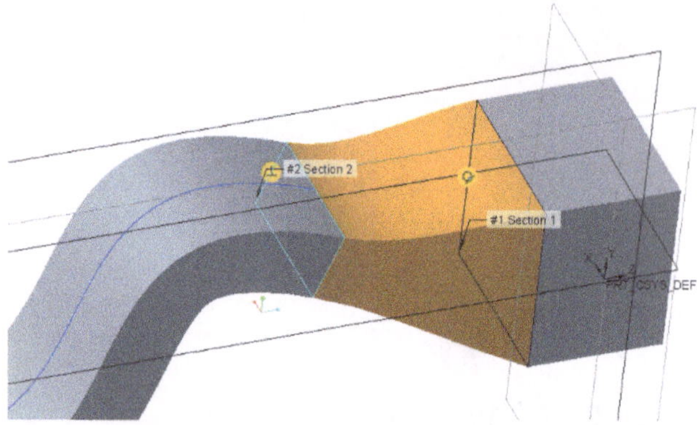

19. Click the green check to complete the model.

Cross Sections with different number of sides

Sections used for creating the blend feature should have a matching number of segments. For example, a three-sided section will blend nicely with another three-sided section despite the individual segments' shape differences. The **Blend** command does a good job of generating smooth faces to join them.

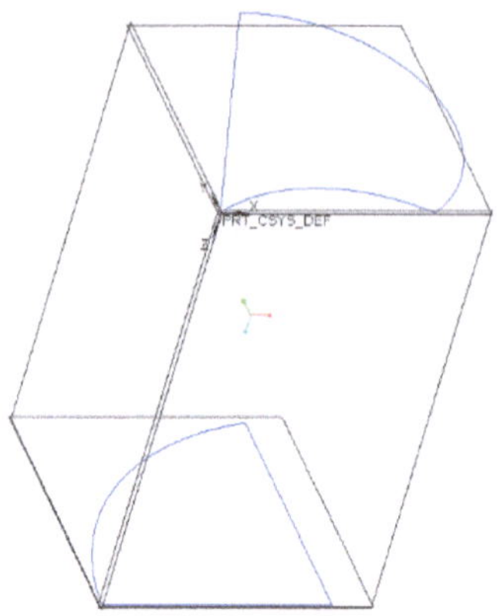

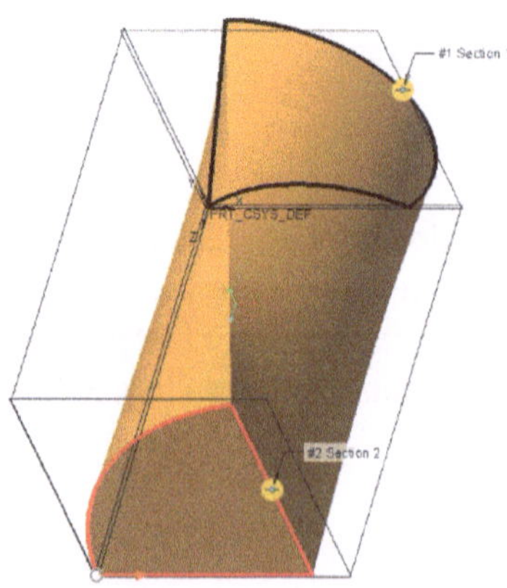

On the other hand, a four-sided section and two-sided section will result in an error.

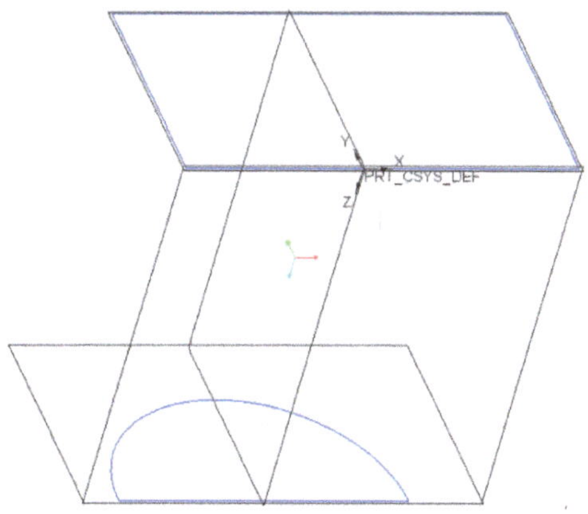

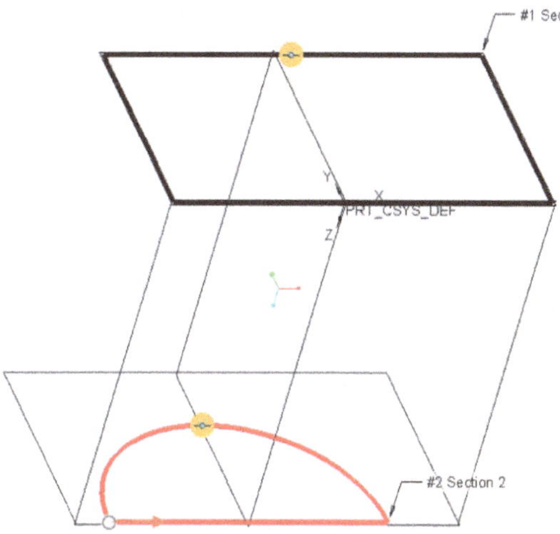

To get the desired result, you have to break one of the sections to have an equal number of segments.

1. Click **Cancel** on the **Blend** dashboard.
2. Click **Yes** on the **Confirm Cancel** dialog.
3. Click the right mouse button on the arc sketch in the Model tree. Select **Edit Definition** to activate the sketch.
4. Activate the **Divide** command (click **Sketch > Editing > Divide** on the ribbon) and break the arc into three segments (refer to **The Divide command** section of Chapter 2 to learn how to divide segments). You can also use dimensions to define the exact location of the breakpoints.

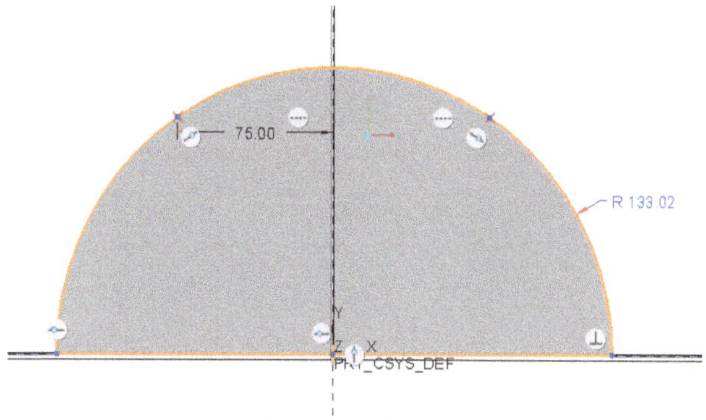

5. Now, exit the **Sketch** mode and activate the **Blend** command.
6. Create a blend by selecting sections.

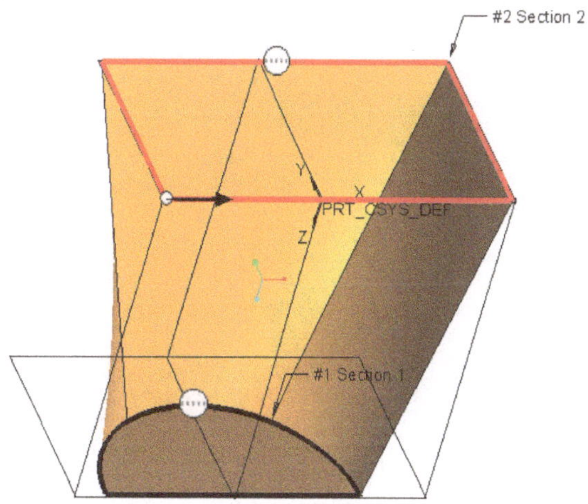

7. Click the green check to complete the feature.

Rotational Blend

The **Rotational Blend** command creates a blend feature through cross-sections having a common axis. The difference between the **Rotational Blend** and **Blend** command is shown in the figure. The **Blend** command simply blends the cross-sections, whereas the **Rotational Blend** command blends the cross-sections by rotating them about a common axis.

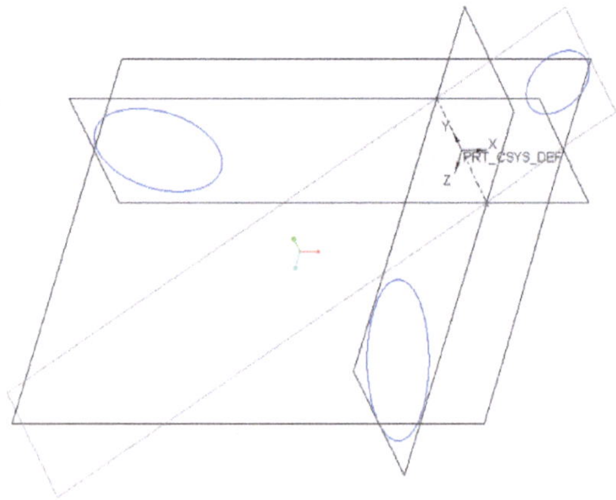

Blend feature

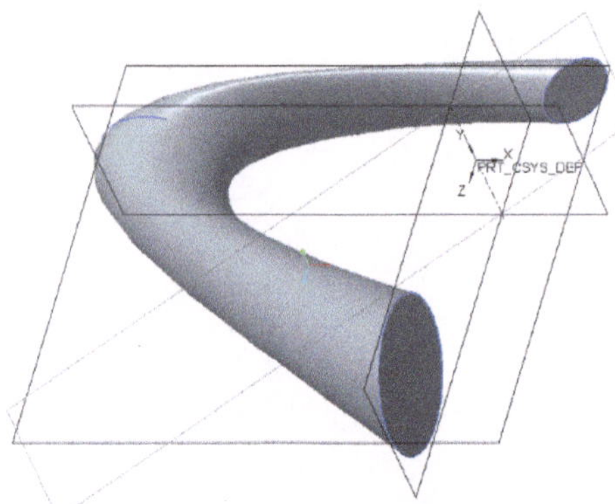

Rotational Blend feature

1. On the ribbon, click **Model > Shapes > Rotational Blend** .
2. On the **Rotational Blend** Dashboard, click the **Selected Sections** icon.
3. Select the first cross-section.
4. Click the **Sections** tab and click the **Add** button.
5. Select the second cross-section.
6. Likewise, select the third cross-section.

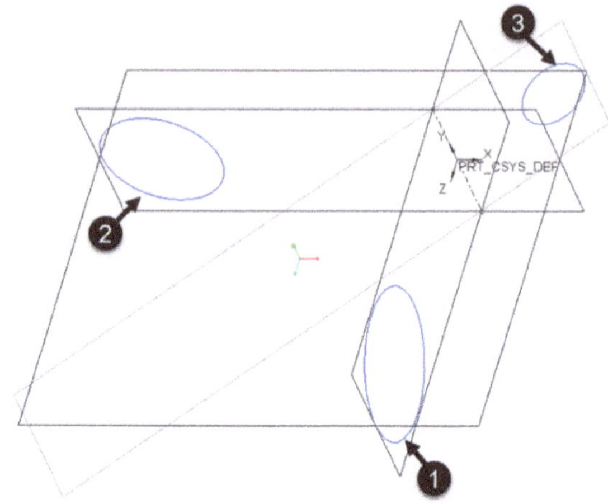

7. Click and drag the origin point of the third cross-section. A smooth blend is created between the sections.

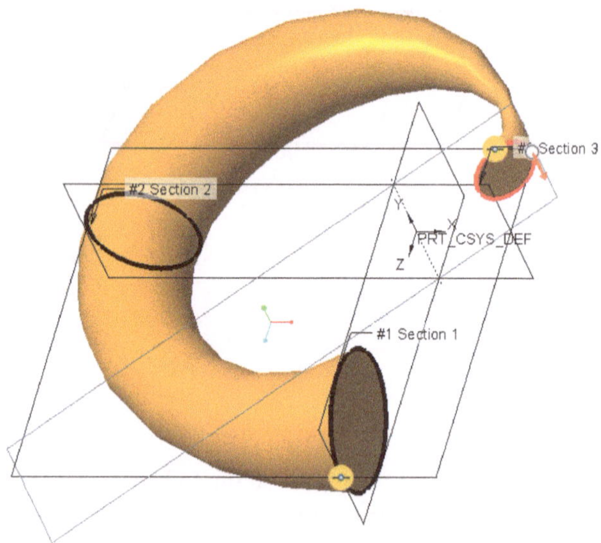

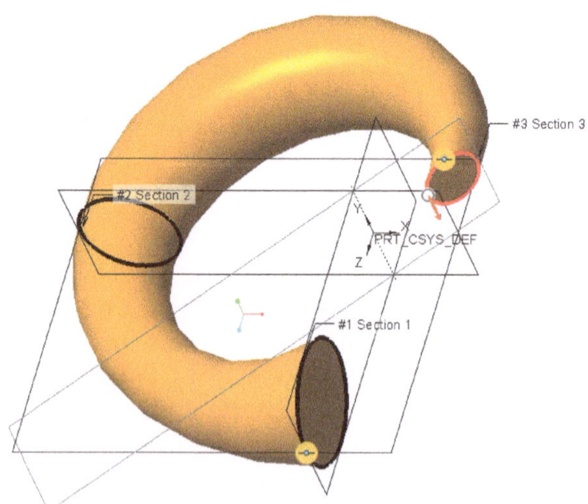

8. On the Dashboard, click the **Options** tab and set the **Blended surfaces** to **Straight**. Notice that the transition between the sections is changed to straight.

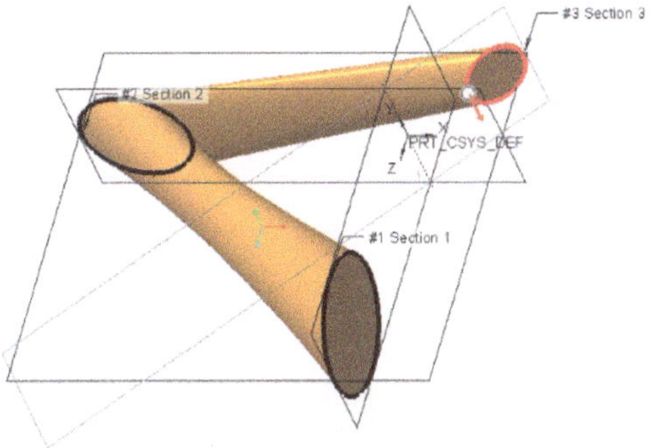

Likewise, you can change the boundary condition between sections using the **Tangency** options.

9. On the **Options** tab, check the **Connect end and start sections** option. Notice that the blend is closed.

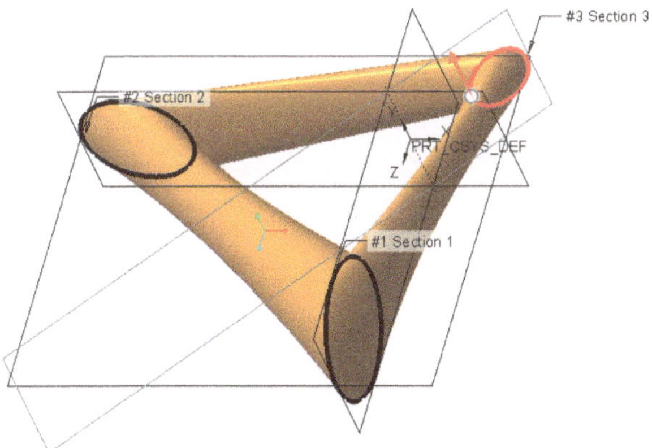

10. Set the **Blended surfaces** to **Smooth**.

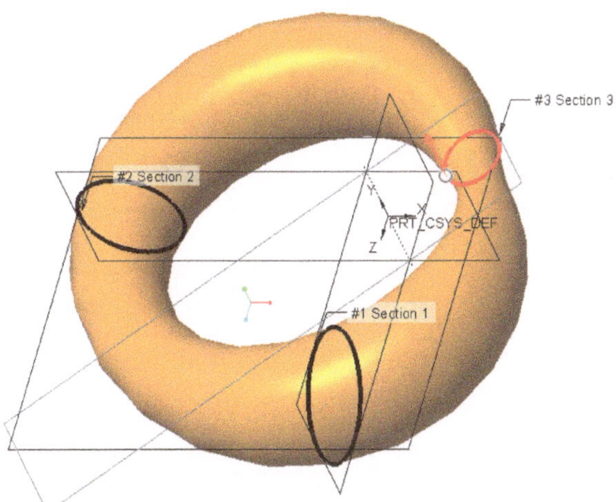

11. Click the green check to complete the feature.

Swept Blend

When you create a **Blend** feature, the material is added between the cross-sections. The shapes of the cross-sections control the blend feature. You do not have much control over the direction of the blend feature. The **Swept Blend** command allows you to control the direction by adding a trajectory. The trajectory controls the way the blend features are transformed between the sections. You can define the trajectory using a curve or sketch.

1. Create three sections and a trajectory, as shown.

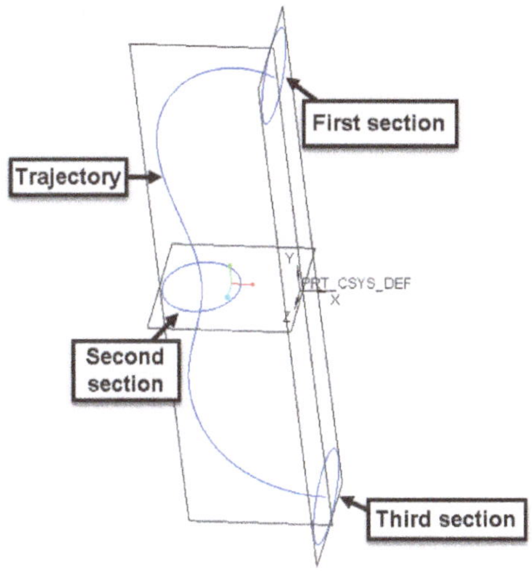

2. On the ribbon, click **Model > Shapes > Swept Blend** .
3. Select the trajectory passing through the sections.
4. On the dashboard, click the **Sections** tab.
5. Select the **Selected Sections** option
6. Select the first section.
7. Click the **Insert** button on the **Sections** tab.
8. Select the third section. The preview of the swept blend appears.

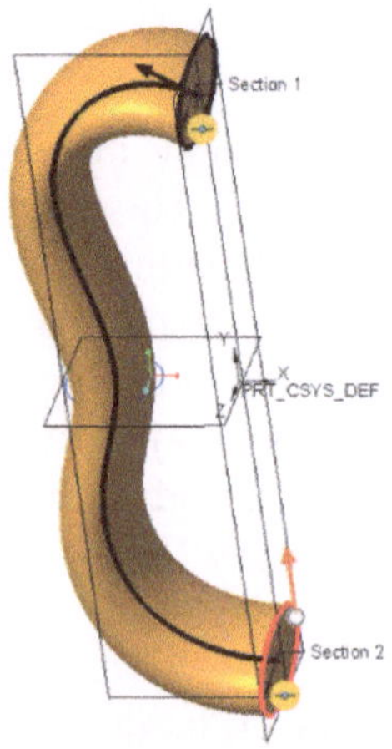

9. On the **Sections** tab, select **Section 1**, and then click the **Insert** button.

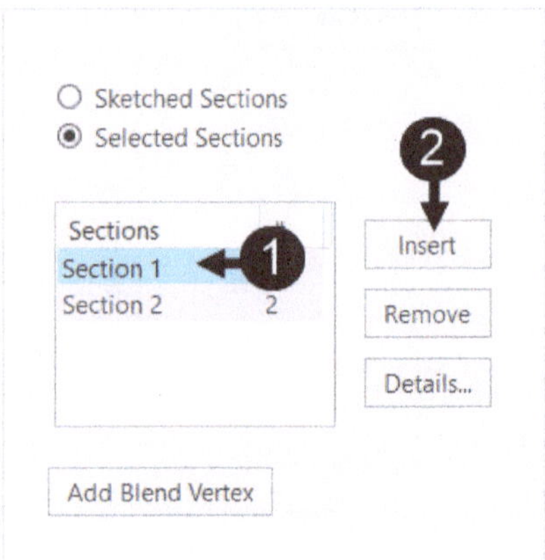

10. Select the second section. The preview of the swept blend changes as shown.

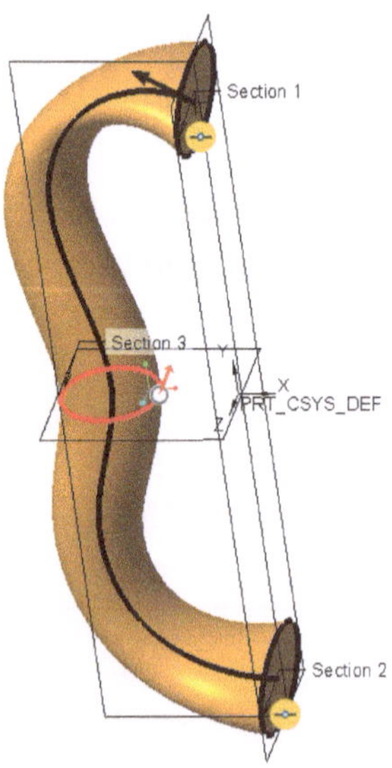

You can use the **Tangency** tab to control the continuity at the start and end sections.

11. Click the green check to complete the feature.

Examples

Example 1

In this example, you will create the part shown below.

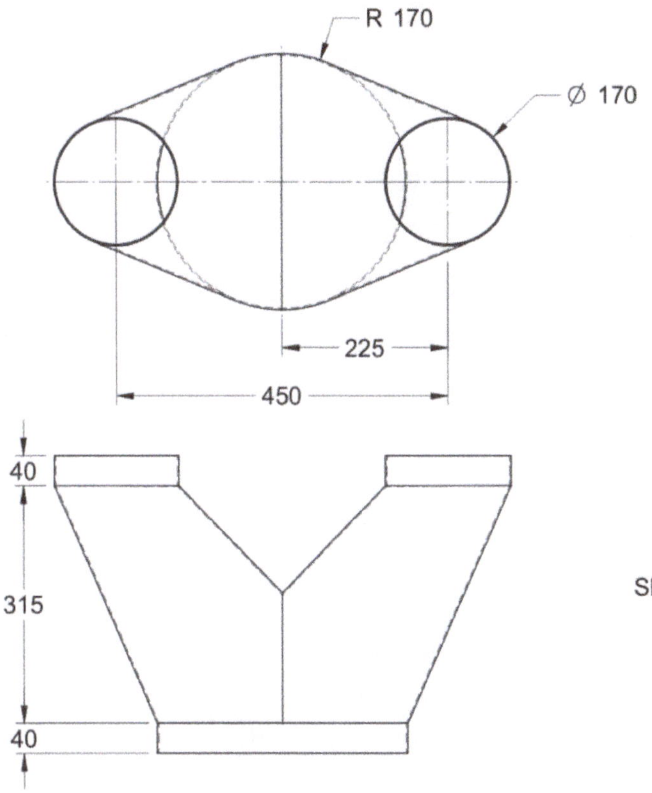

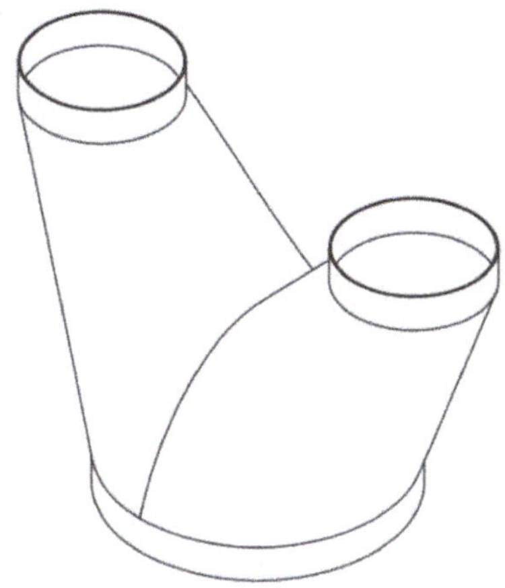

SHELL INSIDE TO 2 mm

1. Start **Creo Parametric 11.0**.
2. Create the *Blend Features* folder and set it as the current working folder.
3. On the Quick Access Toolbar, click the **New** button.
4. On the **New** dialog, select **Types > Part**, and then type-in **C07-Example1**.
5. Uncheck **Use default template** option.
6. Click **OK**.
7. On the **New File Options** dialog, select the **solid_part_mmks_abs** template. Click **OK** to start the file.
8. Start a new sketch on the Top plane and draw a circle of 340 mm in diameter.

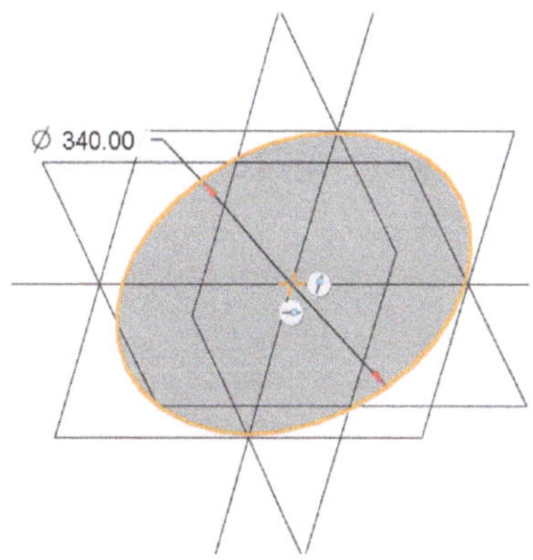

9. Exit the sketch.
10. Create the *Extrude* feature with 40 mm depth.

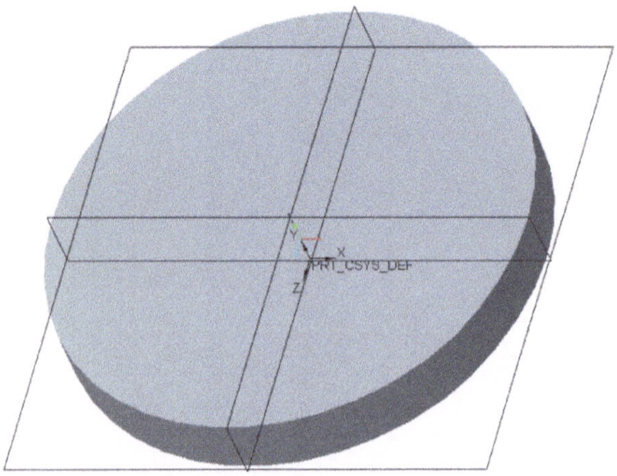

11. On the ribbon, expand the **Shapes** panel and click the **Blend** icon.
12. On the **Blend** dashboard, click the **Sections** tab.
13. Click the **Define** button and select the top face of the model.

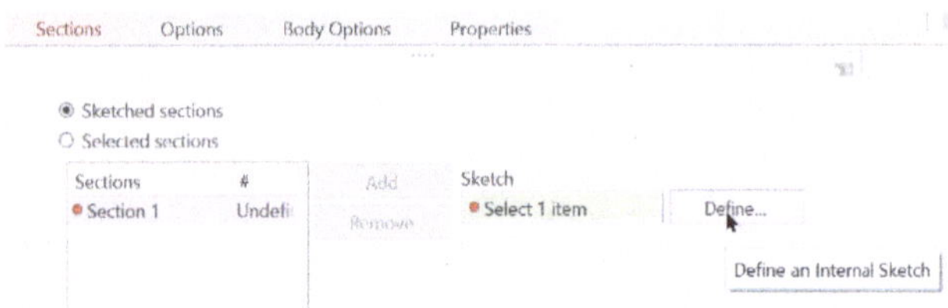

14. On the **Sketch** dialog, click the **Sketch** button.
15. On the ribbon, click **Sketch** tab > **Sketching** panel > **Circle** drop-down > **Concentric**.
16. Create a circle of 340 diameters concentric to the *Extrude* feature.
17. Click **OK** on the ribbon. Now, you need to create the second section.
18. On the **Blend** dashboard, type-in 315 in the offset box and click the edit icon next.

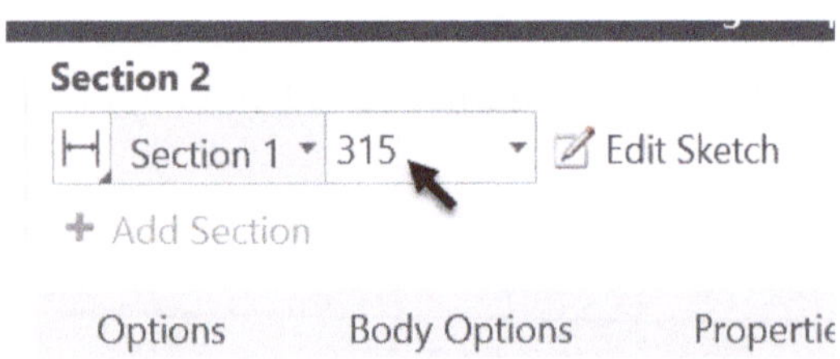

19. Create a sketch, as shown below. Click **OK** on the ribbon to complete the sketch.

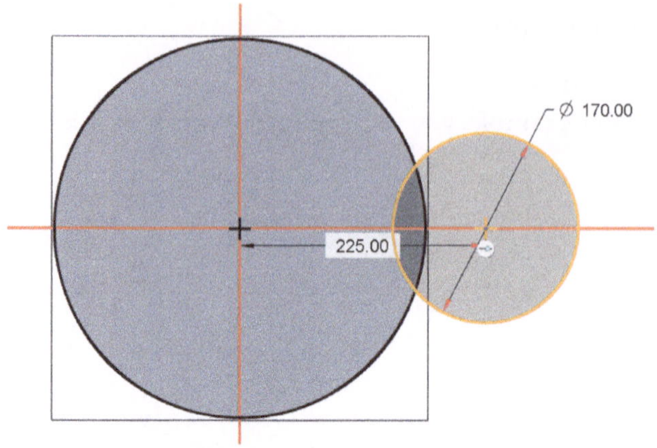

20. On the **Blend** dashboard, click the green check to create the blend feature.

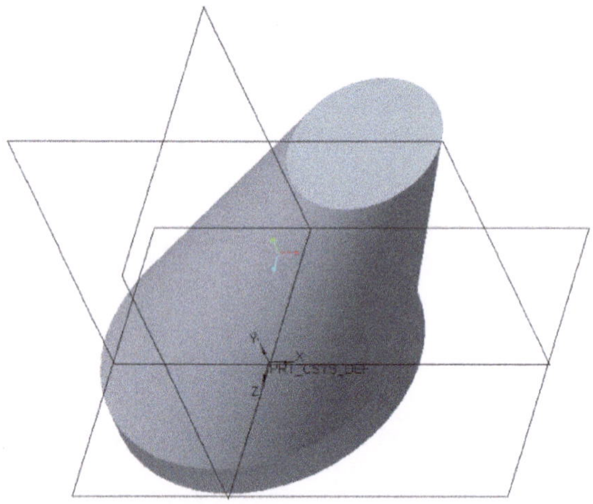

21. Activate the **Extrude** command and click on the top face of the blend feature.
22. Draw a circle of 170 mm diameter and add dimensions to it. Exit the sketch.
23. Create an *Extrude* feature of the 40 mm depth.

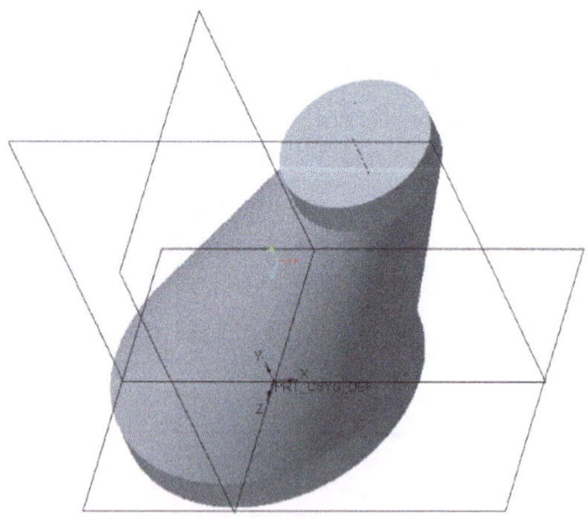

24. Press the Ctrl key and select the Blend feature and the Extrude feature on top of it.

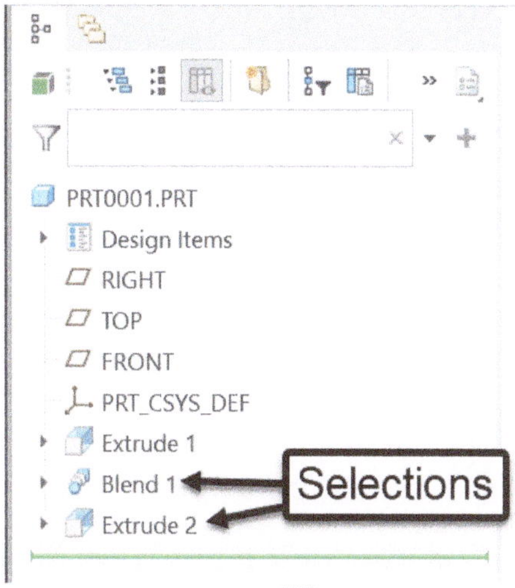

25. Activate the **Mirror** command.
26. Select the right plane to define the mirroring plane.
27. Click the green check to mirror the selected feature.

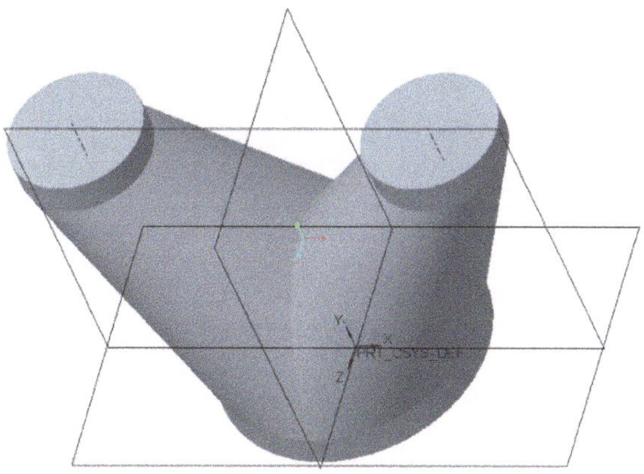

28. On the ribbon, click the **Model** tab > **Engineering** panel > **Shell** .
29. Press the Ctrl key and click on the flat faces of the model geometry.

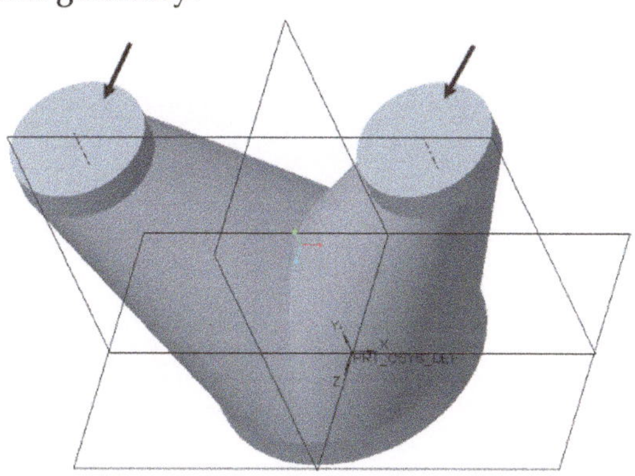

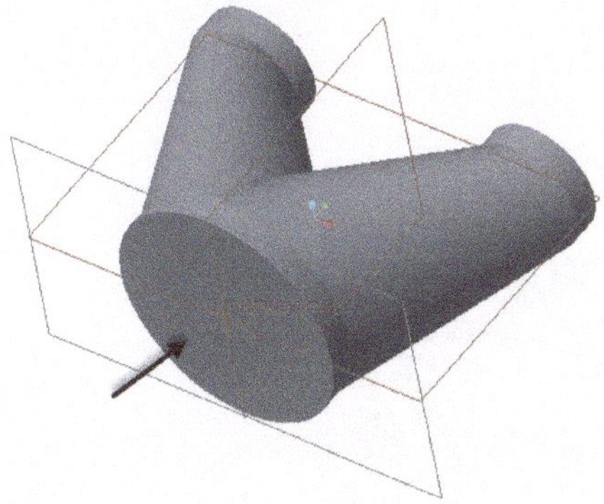

30. On the **Shell** dashboard, type-in 2 in the **Thickness** box.
31. Click **OK**. The part geometry is shelled.

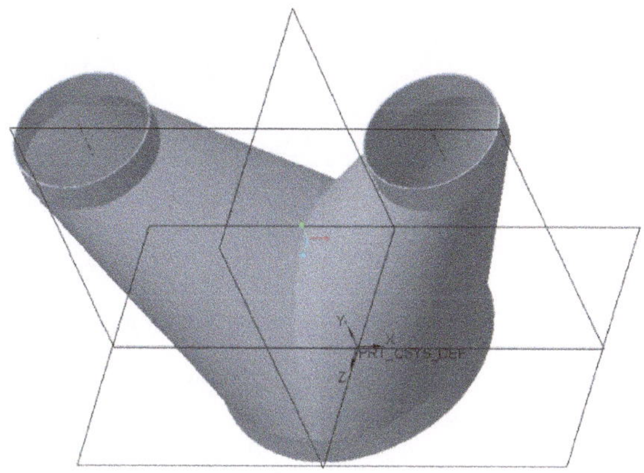

32. Save and close the part file.

Questions

1. Describe the procedure to create a *Blend* feature.
2. List the **Tangency** options.
3. List the type of elements that can be selected to create a *Blend* feature.

Exercises

Exercise 1

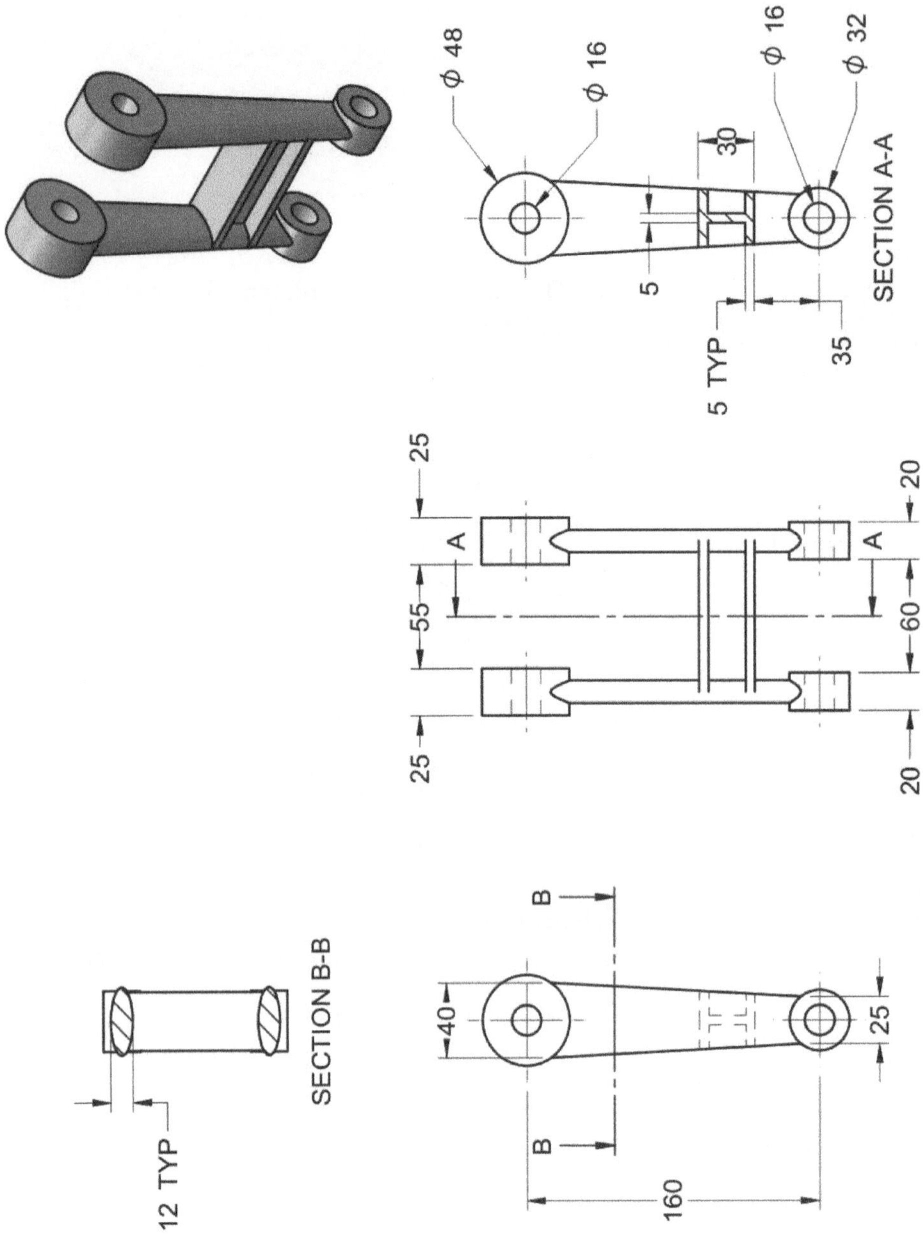

Chapter 8: Modifying Parts

In the design process, it is not required to achieve the final model in the first attempt. There is always a need to modify the existing parts to get the desired part geometry. In this chapter, you will learn various commands and techniques to make changes to a part.

The topics covered in this chapter are:

- *Edit Sketches*
- *Edit Feature Parameters*
- *Edit Feature definition*
- *Suppress and Resume features*

Edit Sketches

Sketches form the base of a 3D geometry. They control the size and shape of the geometry. If you want to modify the 3D geometry, most of the time, you are required to edit sketches.

1. In the Model Tree, expand the feature and click on the sketch.

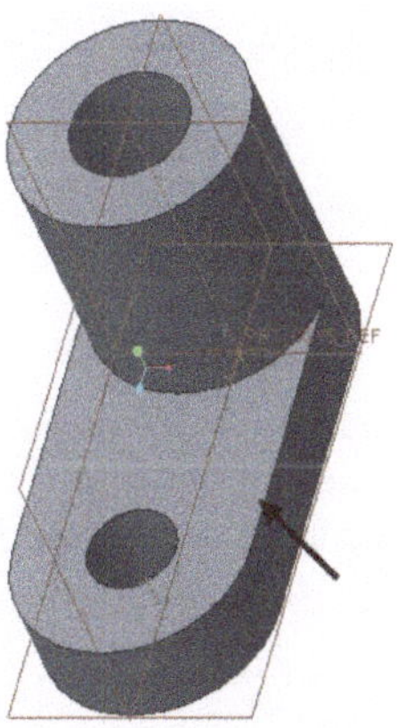

2. Select **Edit Definition** from the menu.

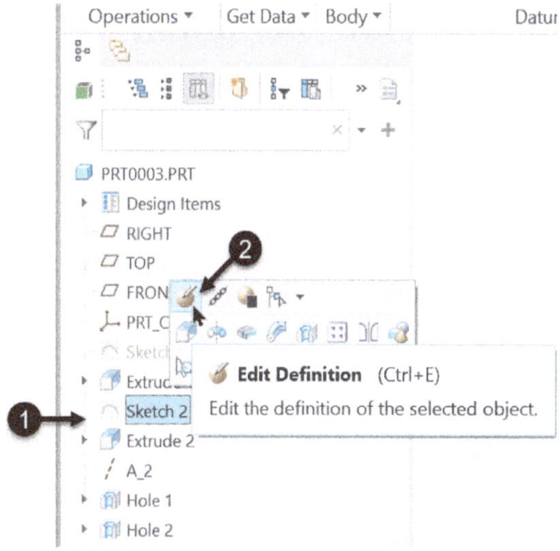

3. Now, modify the sketch and click **OK**. You will notice that the part geometry updates immediately.

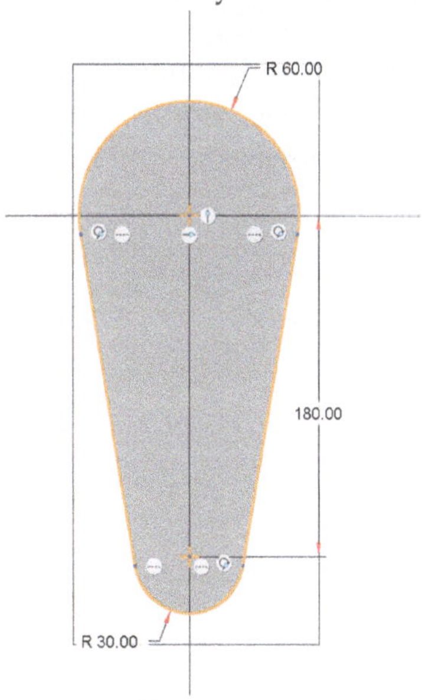

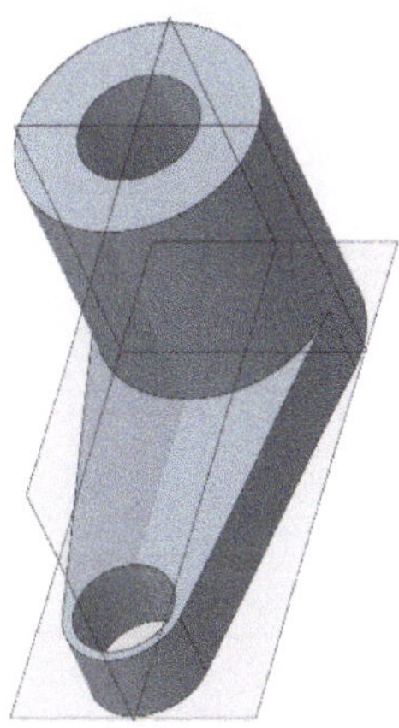

Editing Feature Definition

Features are the building blocks of model geometry. You can edit a feature by following the steps given next.

1. Select the feature to edit.
2. Select **Edit Definition**. The Dashboard related to the feature appears.

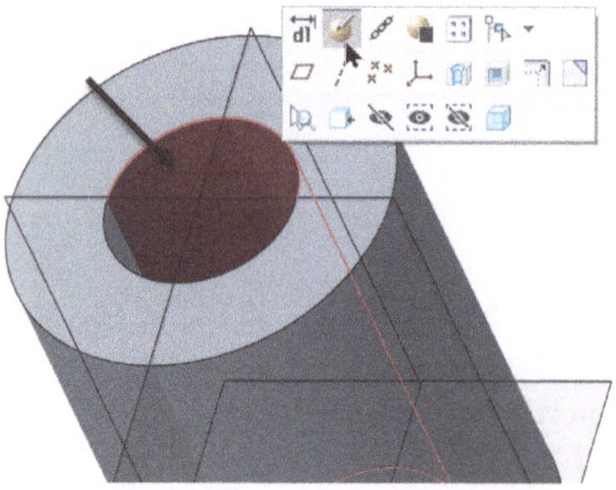

3. On this Dashboard, modify the parameters of the feature and click the green check. The changes take place instantaneously.

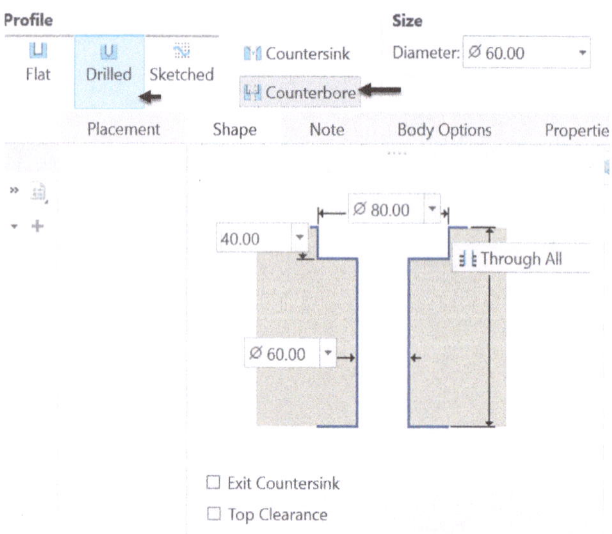

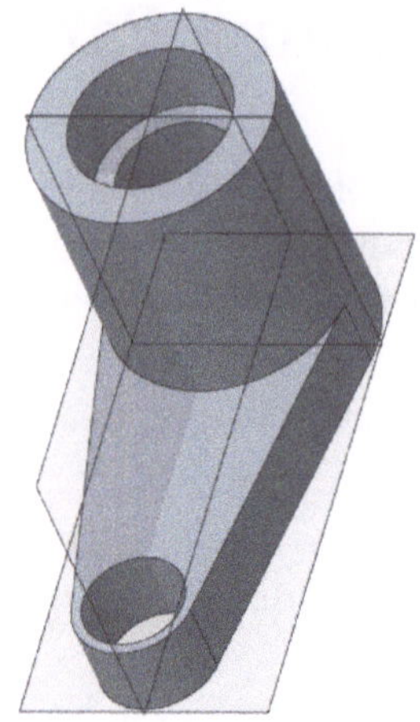

Edit Feature Dimensions

Creo Parametric allows you to modify a feature by editing its parametric dimensions.

1. Select the feature to edit.
2. Select **Edit Dimensions**. The parameters of the feature appear.

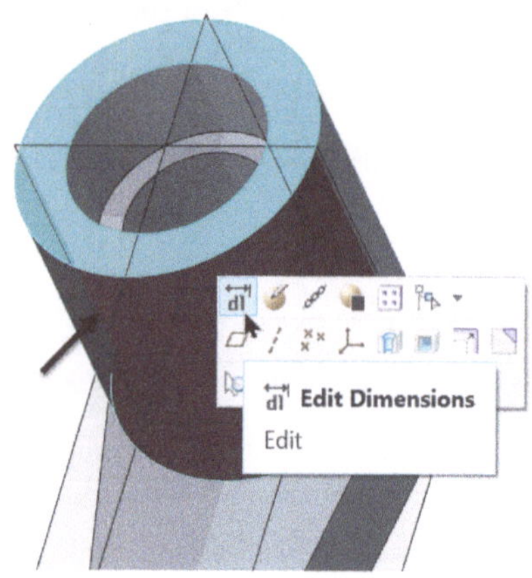

3. To edit a parameter, double-click on it and type-in a new value in the box. Press Enter.

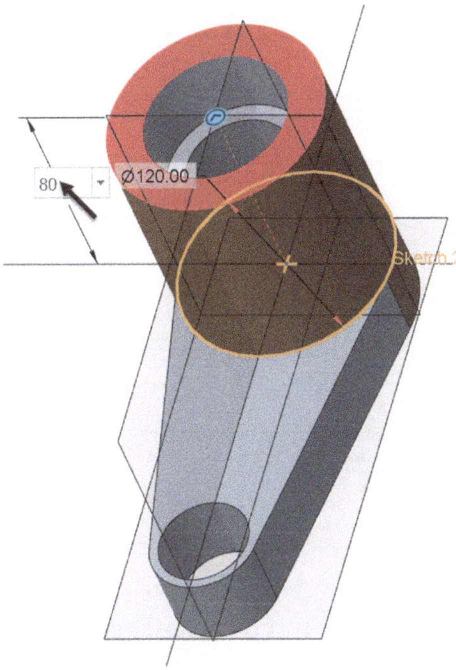

4. Double-click in the graphics window to update the feature.

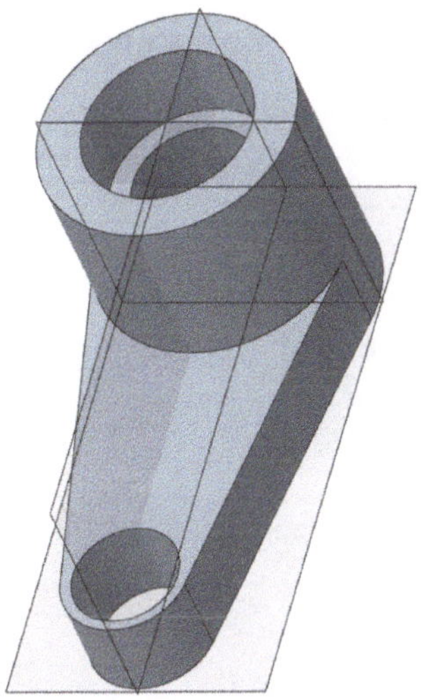

Suppress Features

Sometimes you may need to suppress some features of model geometry.

1. Select the feature to suppress.
2. Select **Suppress**.

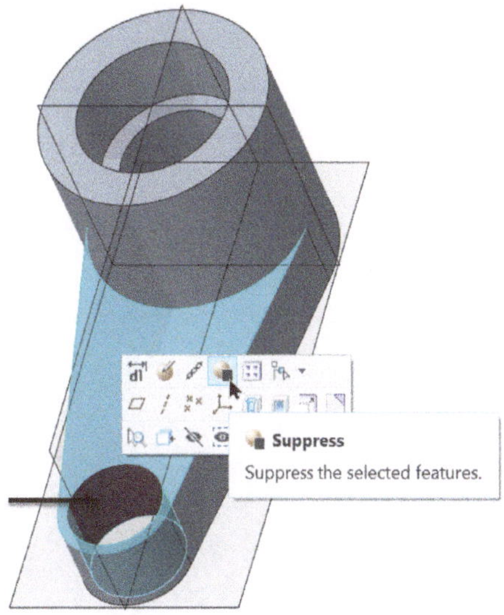

3. Click **OK** to suppress the feature.

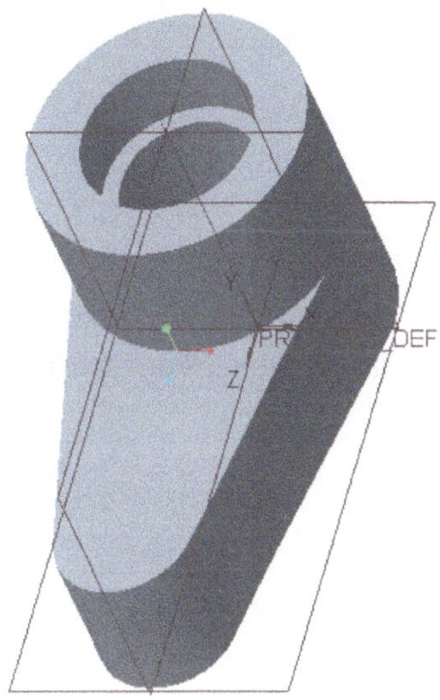

Resume Suppressed Features

1. If you want to resume the suppressed features, click the **Tree Filters** icon in the Model Tree.

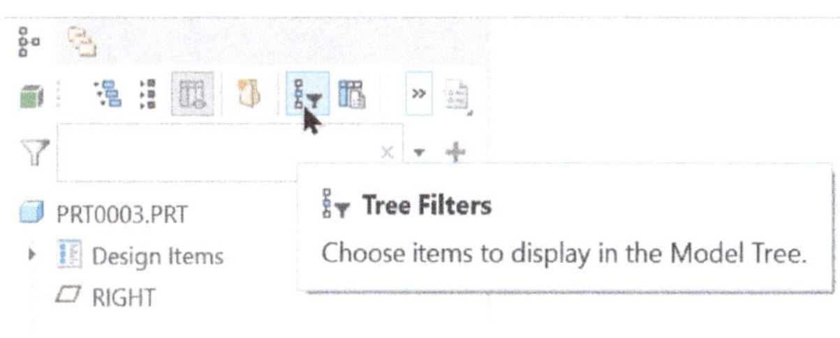

2. On the **Model Tree Items** dialog, check the **Suppressed** option in the **Items by State** section. Click **OK** to close the dialog. The suppressed feature appears with a square dot.

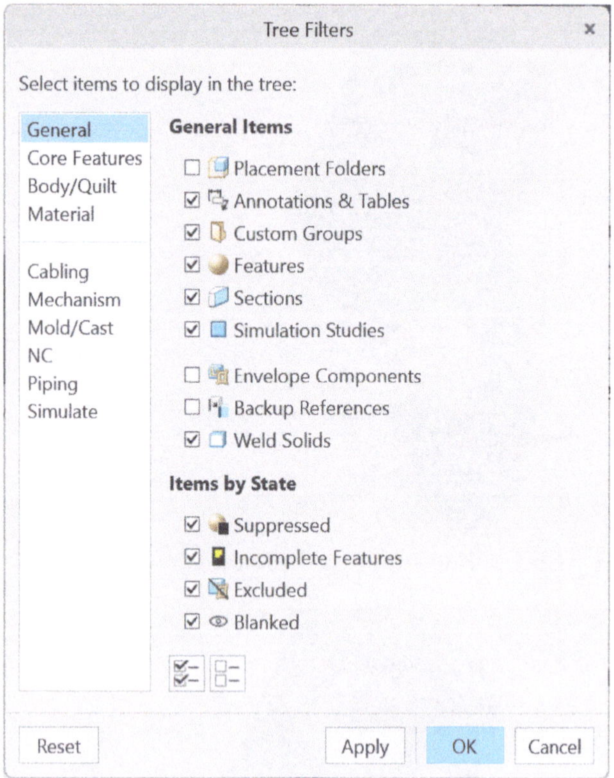

3. In the Model Tree, click on the suppressed feature and select **Resume**. The feature is resumed.

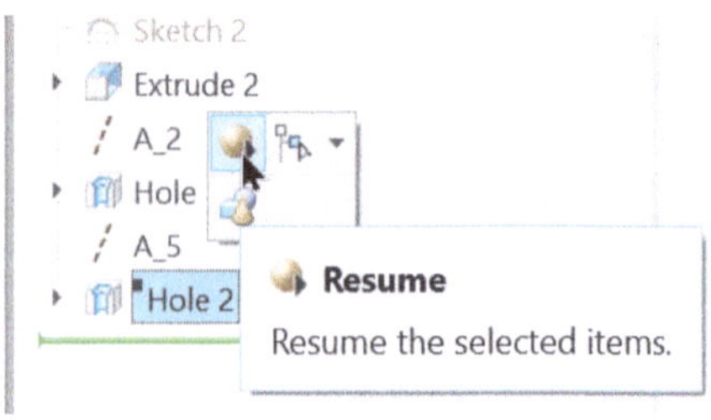

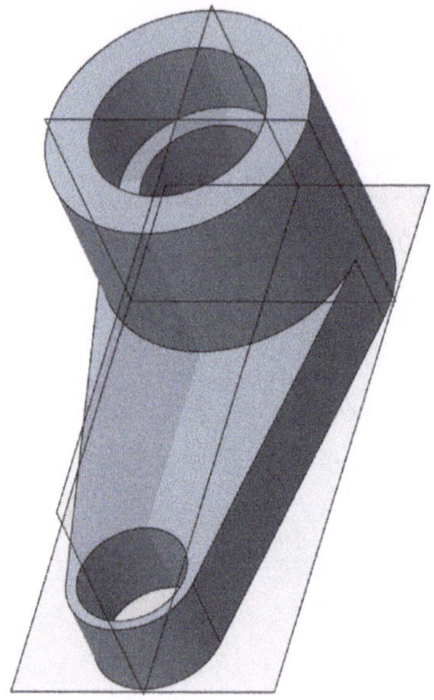

Changing the Feature References

Creo Parametric allows you to change the reference of a feature.

1. In the Model Tree, click on the feature and select **Edit Reference** .

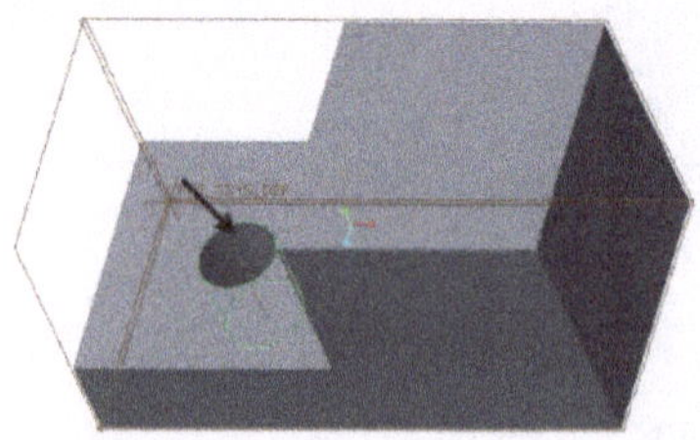

2. Change the first reference of the feature.

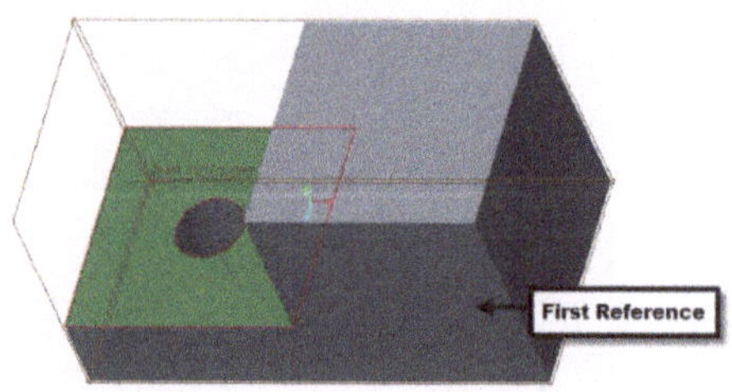

3. Change the second and third reference of the feature.

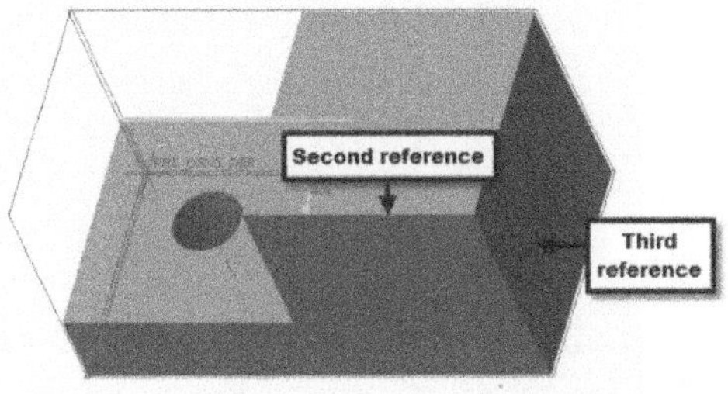

4. On the **Edit References** dialog, click the **Preview** button to view the result. You can also reset the references by selecting them in the **Edit References** dialog and clicking the **Reset** button.
5. Click **OK** to close the dialog.

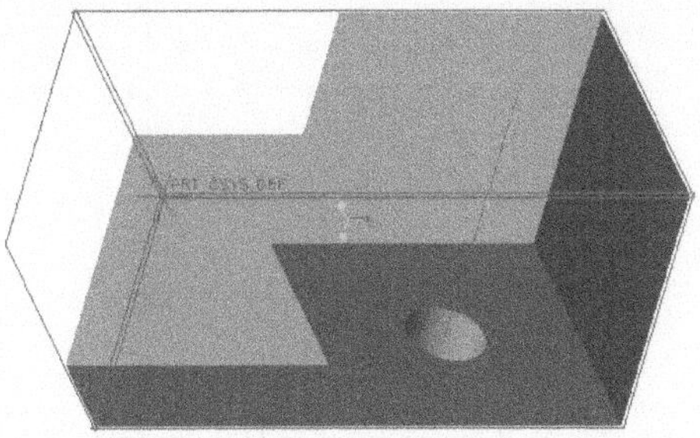

If there are any sketches or features on the geometry, it may show some warnings and error messages. You have to manually solve these problems or avoid changing the sketch support when the model becomes complex. It is recommended that you select the correct plane initially based on the design intent.

Examples

Example 1

In this example, you will create the part shown below and then modify it.

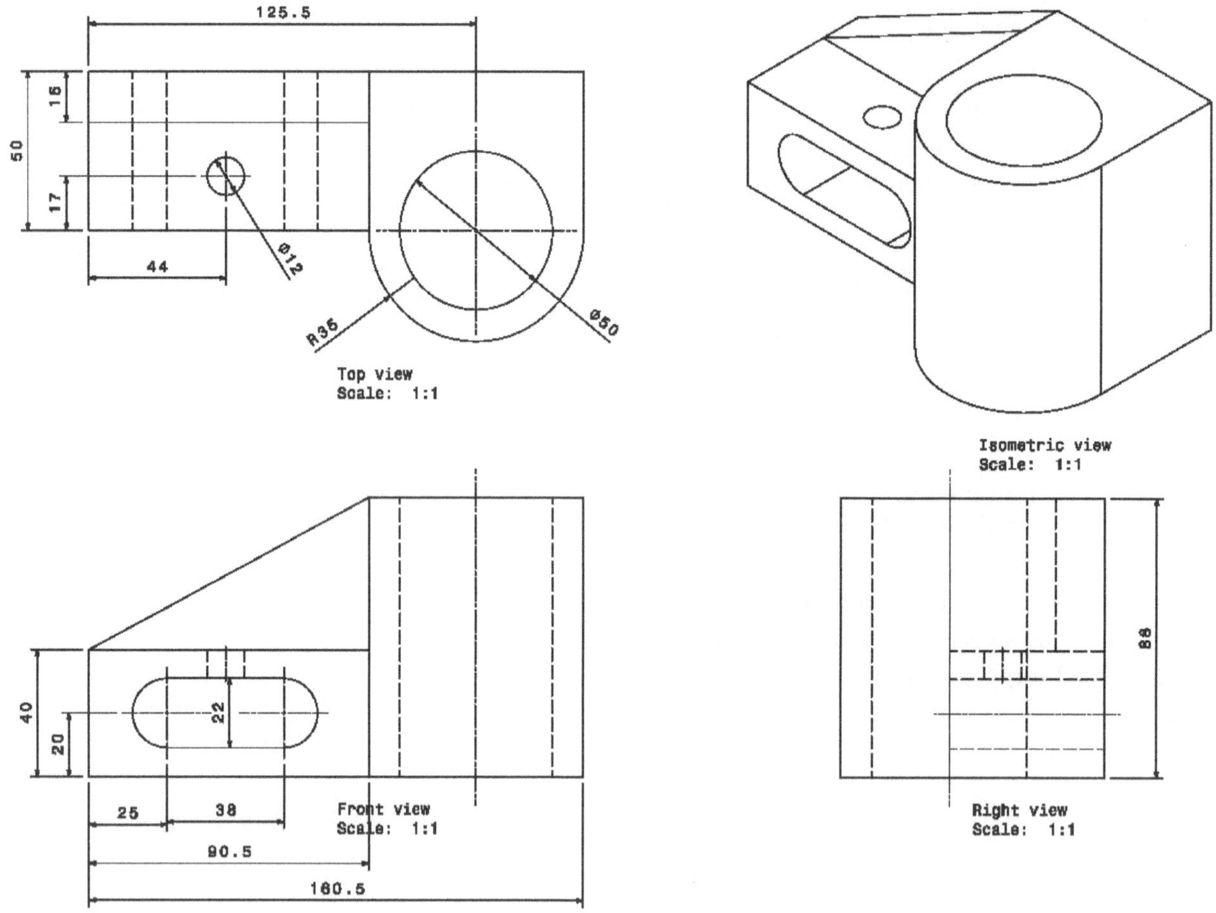

1. Start **Creo Parametric 11.0**.
2. Create the *Modify Parts* folder and set it as the current working folder.
3. On the Quick Access Toolbar, click the **New** button.
4. On the **New** dialog, select **Types > Part**, and then type-in **C08-Example1**.
5. Uncheck the **Use default template** option and click **OK**.
6. On the **New File Options** dialog, select the **solid_part_mmks_abs** template. Click **OK** to start the file.
7. Create the part file, as shown below. If you cannot create it, you can download it from our companion website.

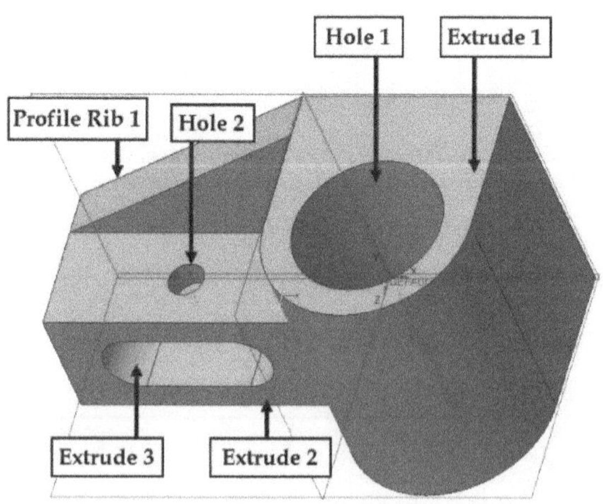

The Model Tree of the part is given next.

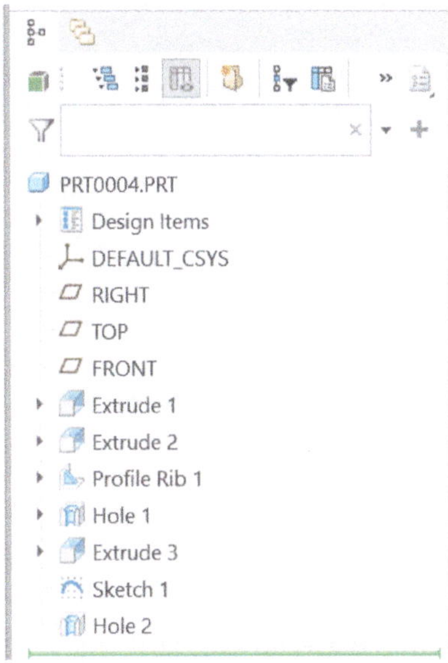

8. Select the 50 mm diameter hole.
9. Select the **Edit definition** icon.

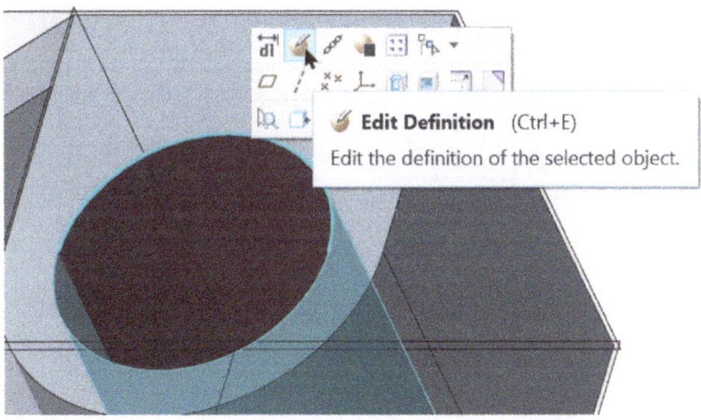

10. On the **Hole** dashboard, click the **Standard** button.
11. Deactivate the **Tapped** button.
12. Click the **Clearance** button.
13. Click the **Counterbore** button.
14. Set the **Screw Size** to **M36x4.**
15. Click the **Shape** tab and define the parameters, as shown below.

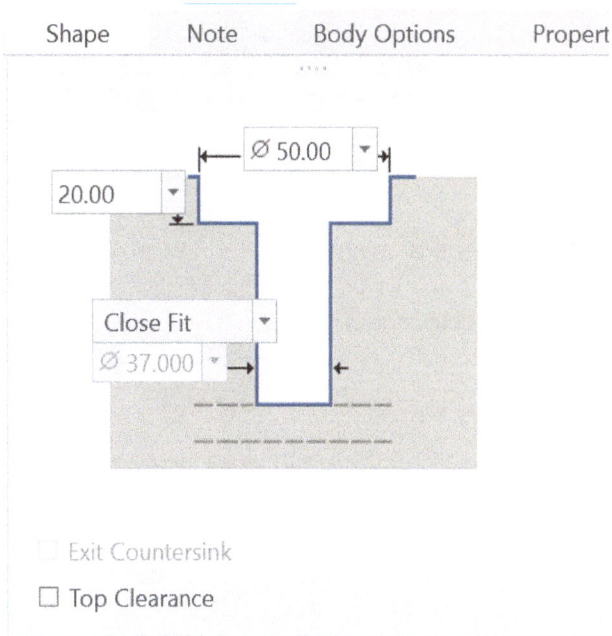

16. Click the green check to complete the modification.

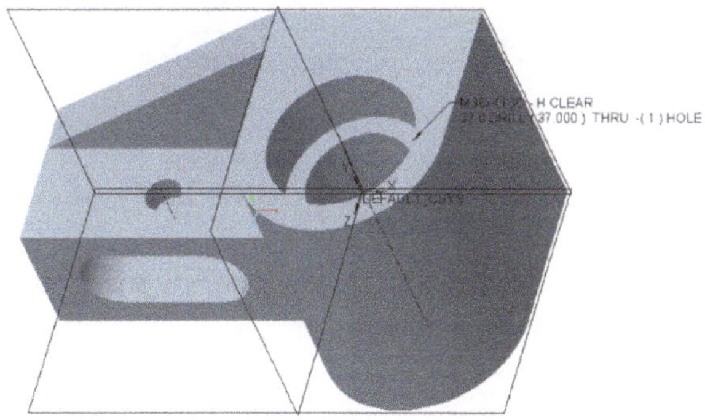

17. Select the rectangular extrude feature from the model.
18. Select **Edit Dimensions** from the shortcut menu.

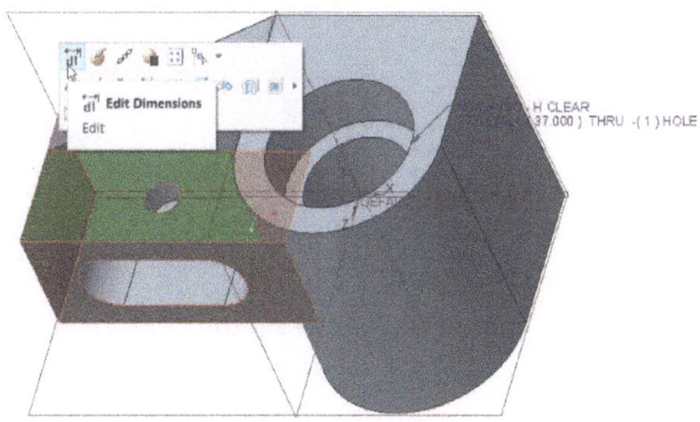

19. Double-click on the horizontal dimension.
20. Type-in 125 in the dimension box and press Enter.

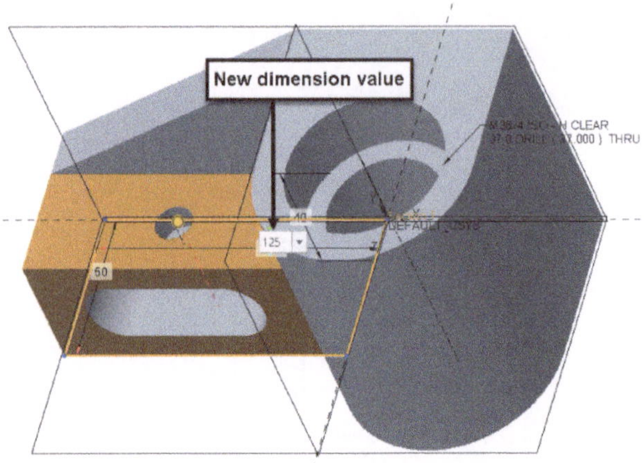

21. Double-click in the graphics window to modify the extrude feature.

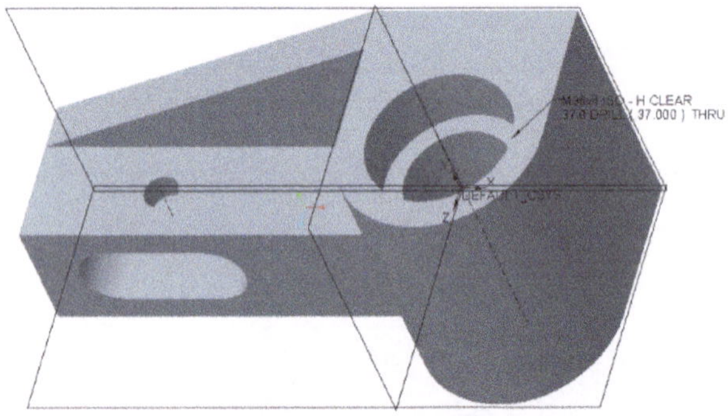

22. In the Model Tree, expand the third extrude feature and click on Section1.
23. Select the **Edit definition** option from the menu. It activates the sketch mode.

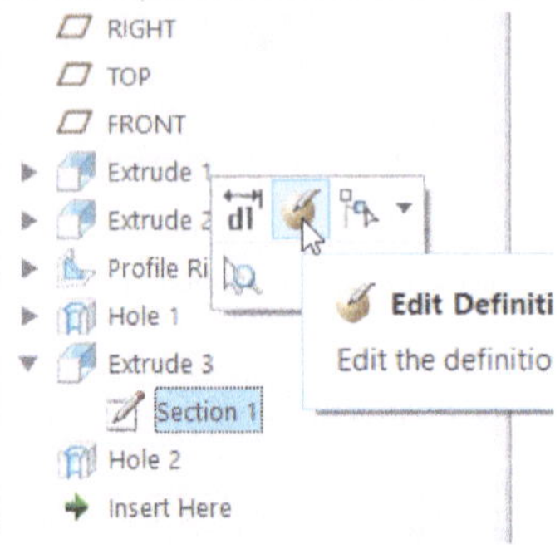

24. On the ribbon, click **Sketch** tab > **Setup** panel > **References** .
25. Create a reference by selecting the left face of the first feature.

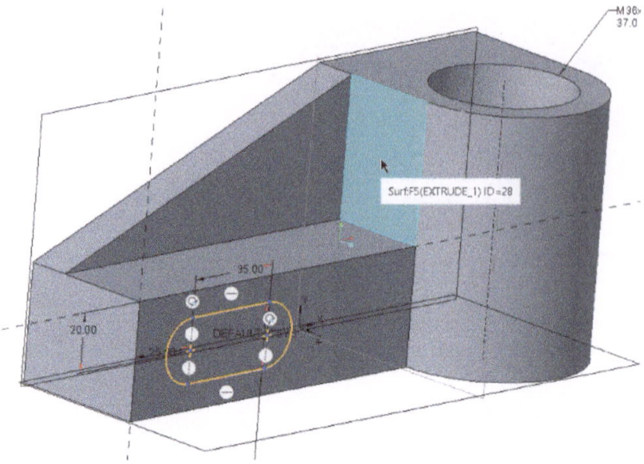

26. Click **Close** on the **References** dialog.
27. Delete the length dimension of the slot, and then add a new dimension between the right-side arc and right vertical edge.

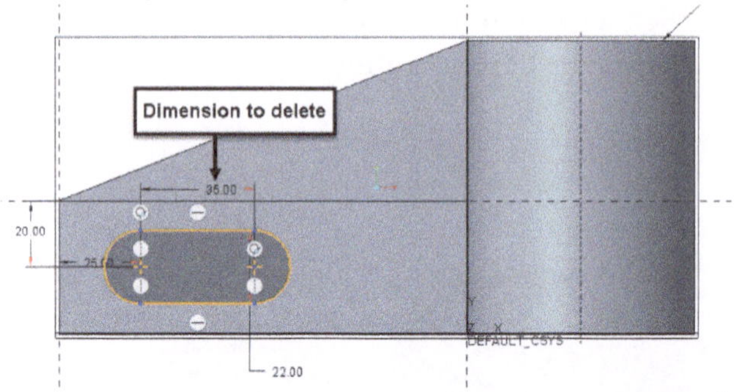

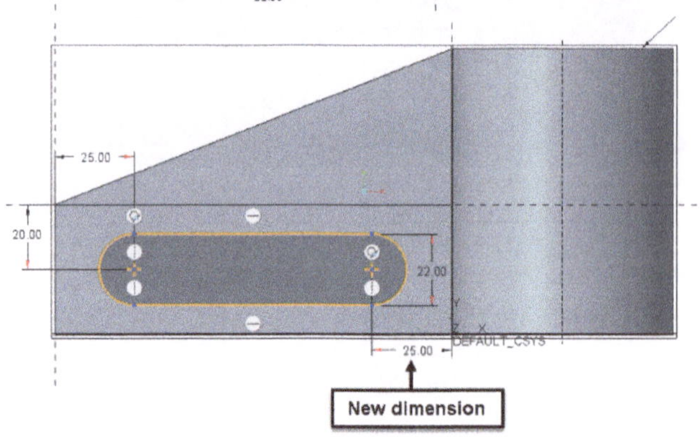

28. Exit the sketch.
29. Select the small hole from the model geometry.
30. Select the **Edit definition** icon.

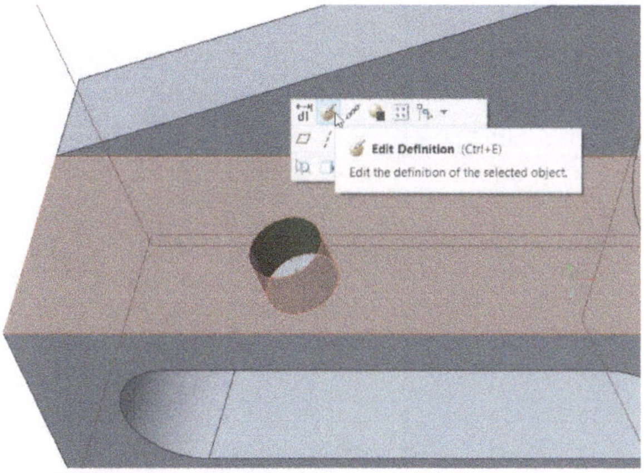

31. On the **Hole** dashboard, click **Datum** drop-down > **Axis**.

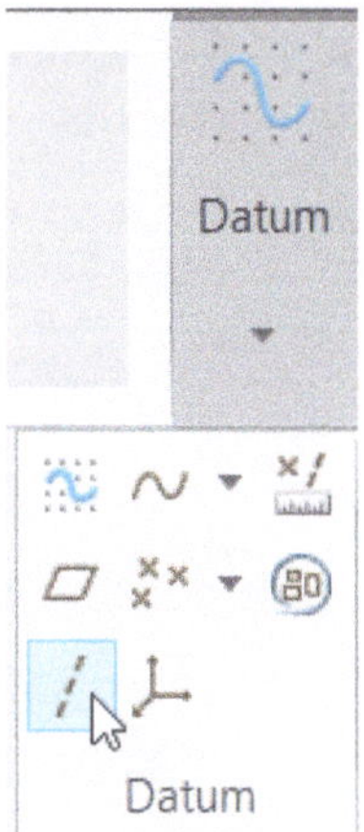

32. Click on the top face of the second extrude feature.

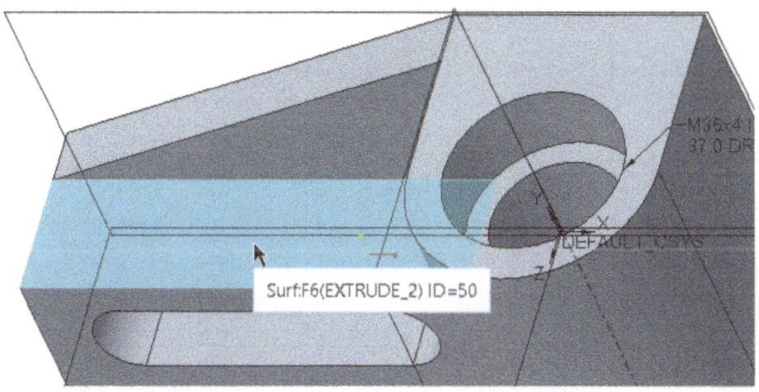

33. Click **Sketch**.
34. Create a line connecting the corners of the top face, as shown.

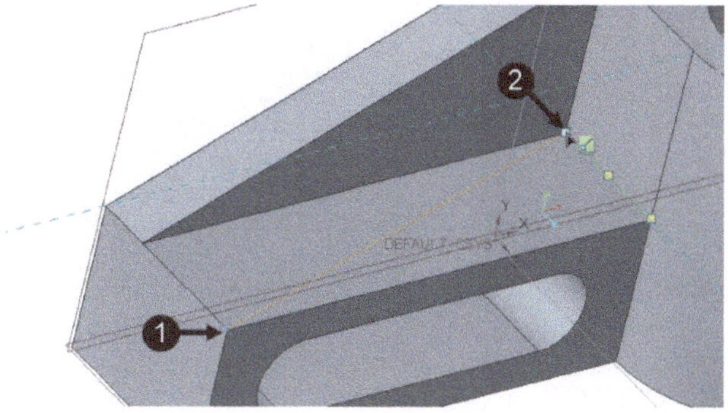

35. On the ribbon, click **Sketch** tab > **Datum** panel > **Point**.

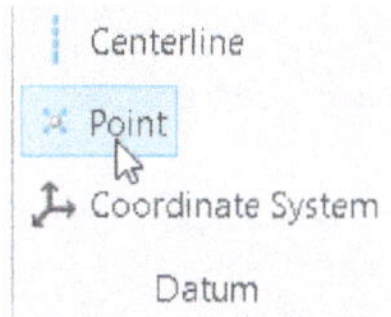

36. Click on the top face of the second extrude feature to place the point.

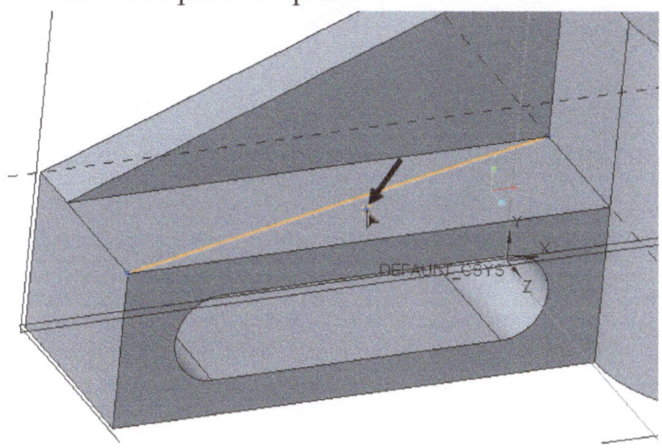

37. Click on the line and select **Toggle Construction**.

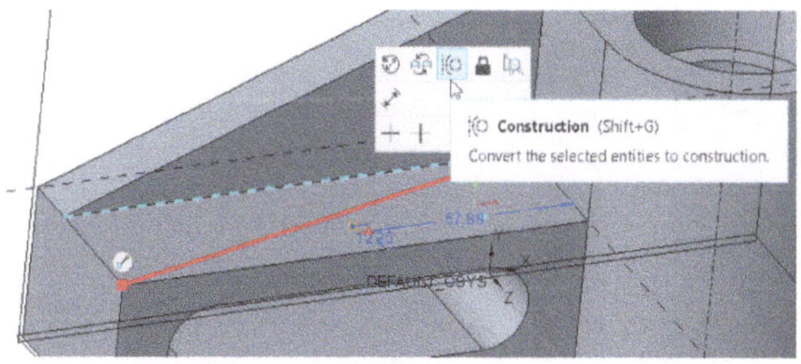

38. On the ribbon, click **Sketch** tab > **Constrain** panel > **Midpoint**.
39. Select the point and the line. The point is made coincident with the midpoint of the line.

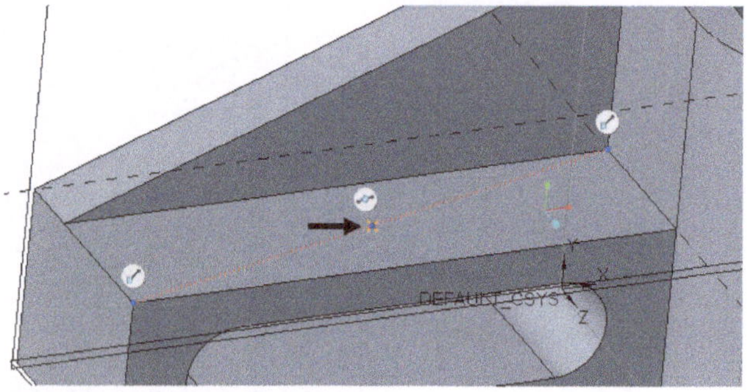

40. Click **OK** on the ribbon.
41. Click the **Resume** icon on the dashboard.
    The hole is placed on the midpoint of the line.
42. Click the green check to complete the modification.

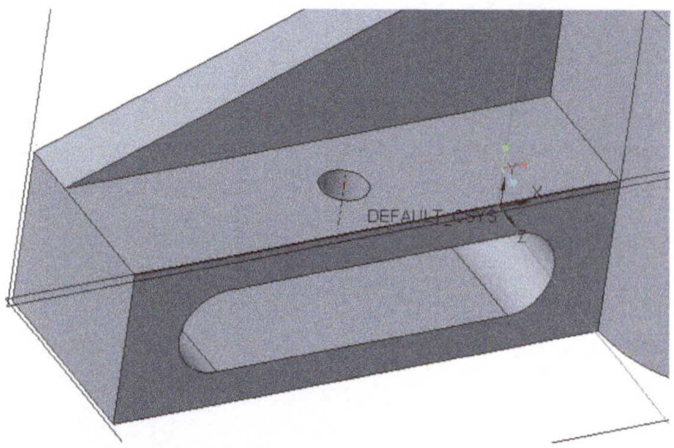

43. Now, change the size of the extrude feature. You will notice that the slot and hole are adjusted automatically.

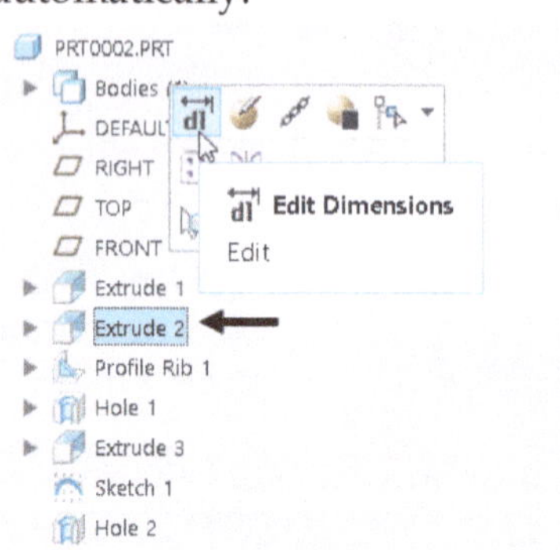

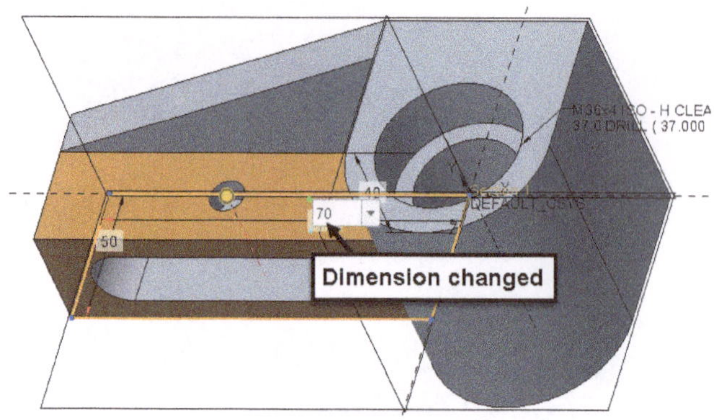

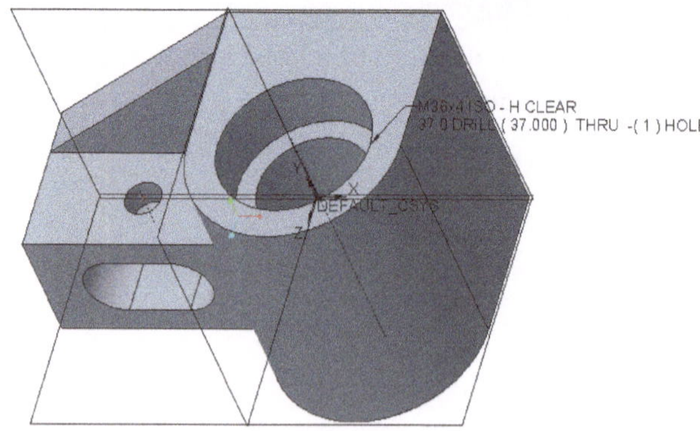

44. Save and close the file.

Questions

1. How do you modify the sketch of a feature?
2. How do you modify a feature directly?
3. How can you change the reference of a feature?

Exercises

Exercise 1

Initial Part

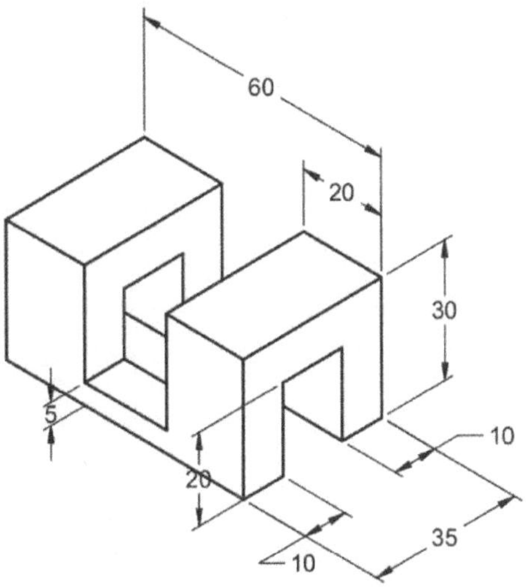

Modified Part

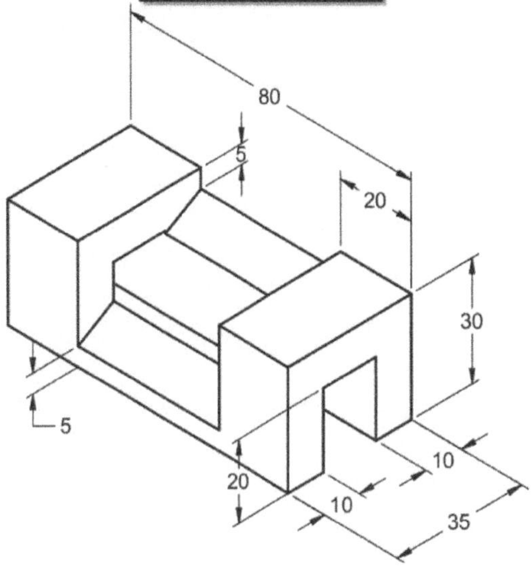

Chapter 9: Assemblies

After creating individual components, you can bring them together into an assembly. By doing so, it is possible to identify incorrect design problems that may not have been noticeable at the part level. In this chapter, you will learn how to bring components into the Assembly environment and position them.

The topics covered in this chapter are:

- *Starting an assembly*
- *Inserting Components*
- *Adding Constraints*
- *Moving components*
- *Collision Detection*
- *Replace Components*
- *Create Subassemblies*
- *Top-down Assembly Design*
- *Create Exploded Views*

Starting an Assembly

To begin an assembly file, you can use the **New** icon and select the **Type > Assembly**. Select **Sub-type > Design** and type-in the name of the file. Click **OK**.

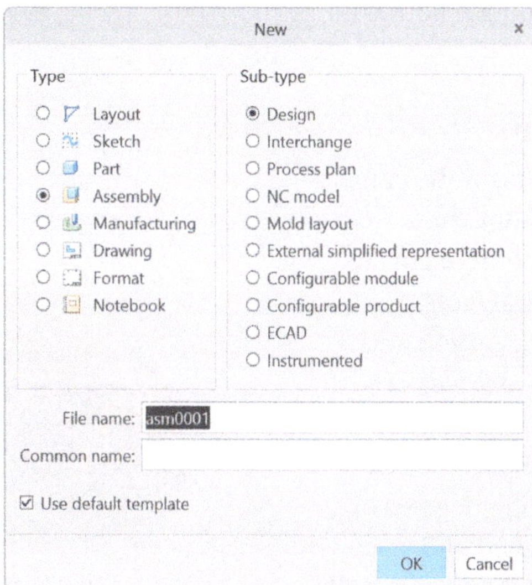

Inserting Components

There are two different methods to insert an existing part into an assembly. The first one is to insert using the **Assemble** command.

1. On the ribbon, click **Model > Component > Assemble** .
2. Browse to the location of the component and select it.
3. Click **Open**. The component appears inside the assembly.

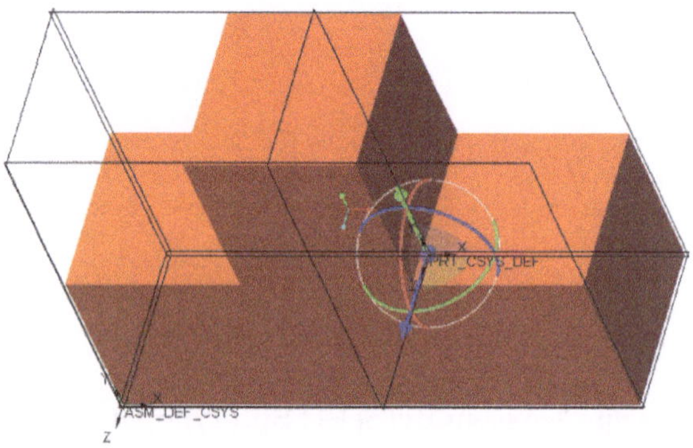

You can also insert a component into the Assembly by dragging it from the windows explorer into the assembly window.

Fixing the first Component

After inserting components into an assembly, you have to define constraints between them. By applying constraints, you can make components to flush with each other or two cylindrical faces concentric with each other, and so on. As you add constraints between components, the degrees of freedom will be removed from them. By default, there are six degrees of freedom for a part (three linear and three rotational). Eliminating degrees of freedom will make components attached and interact with each other as in real life. Now, you will learn to add constraints between components.

After placing the component at the origin, it is free to move. You can check the degrees of freedom by clicking and dragging the 3D Dragger.

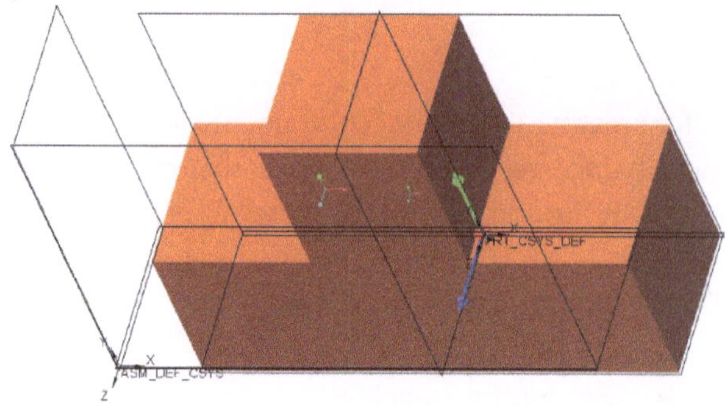

1. To remove the degrees of freedom of the first component, click **Current Constraint > Default** on the **Component Placement** dashboard.

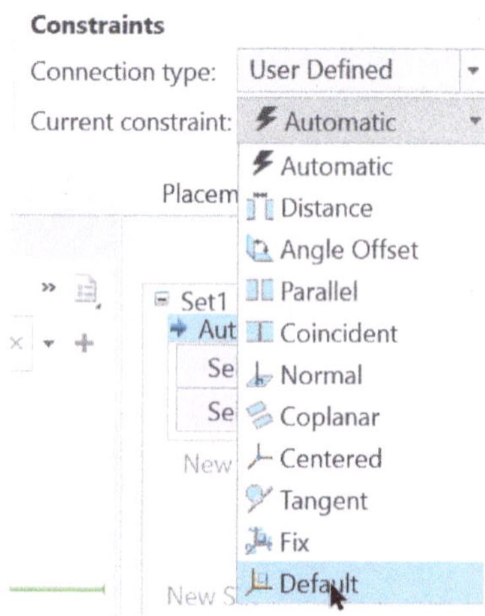

The component is positioned at its default location.

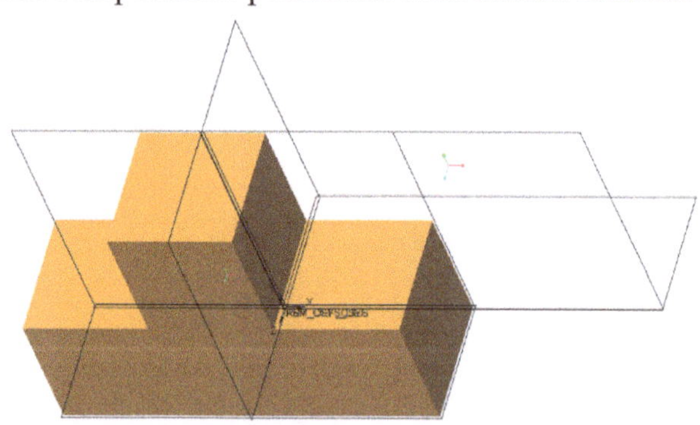

You can also use the **Fix** constraint to position it at its current location.

2. Click the green check.

Inserting the Second Component

1. On the ribbon, click **Model > Component > Assemble** .

2. Go to the location of the second component.
3. Select the component and click **Open**.

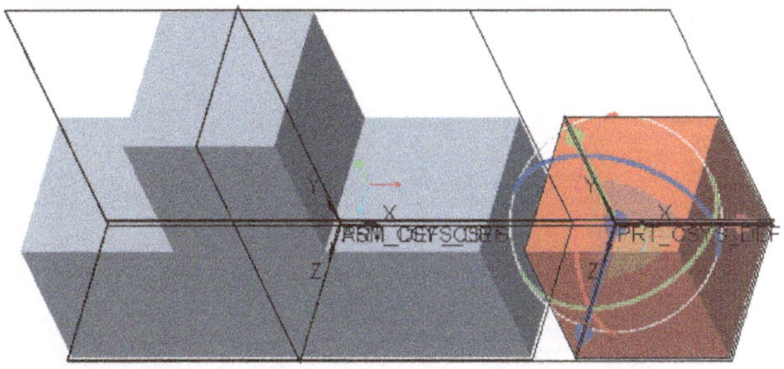

Moving and rotating components

After inserting components into the assembly, you can move or rotate them.

1. On the 3D Dragger, click the **X axis**, and then drag the component along the x-axis.

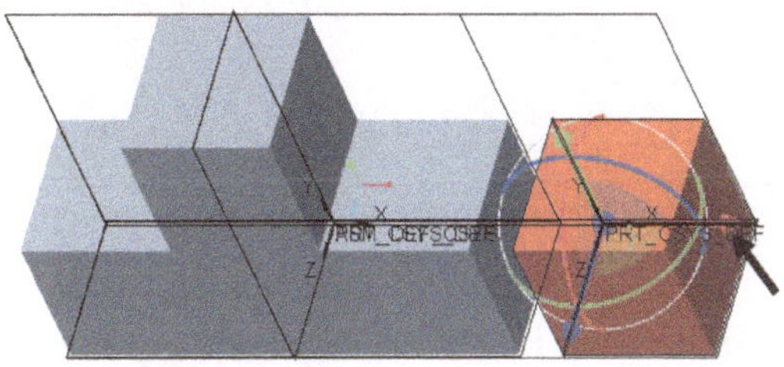

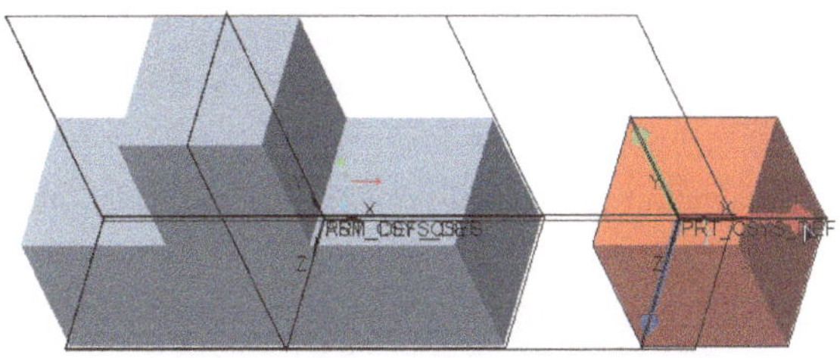

2. Likewise, use the **Y axis, Z axis** to drag the component along the Y and Z axes, respectively.

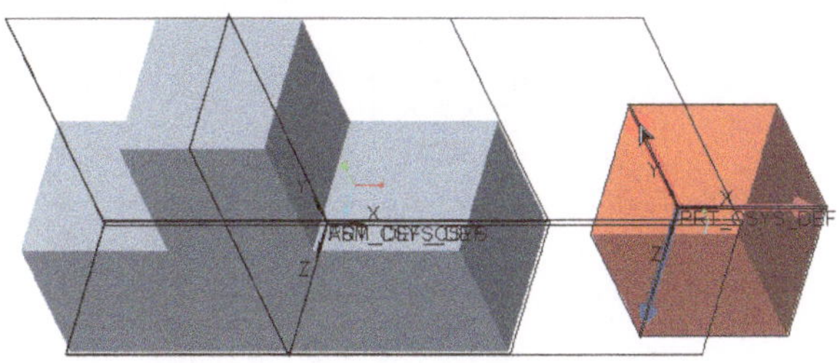

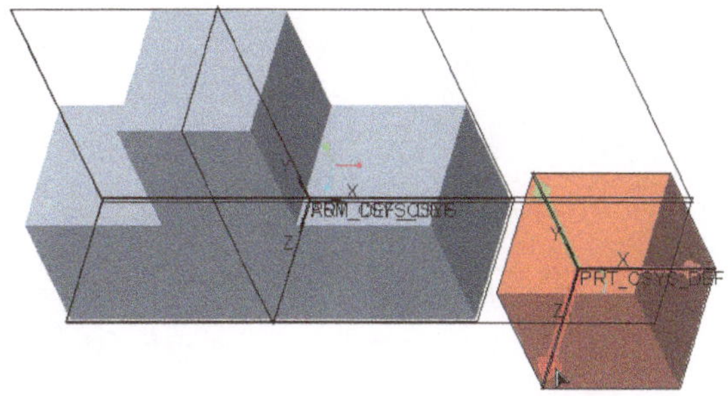

3. Use the **XY plane**, **YZ plane**, or **XZ plane** to move the component on three different planes.

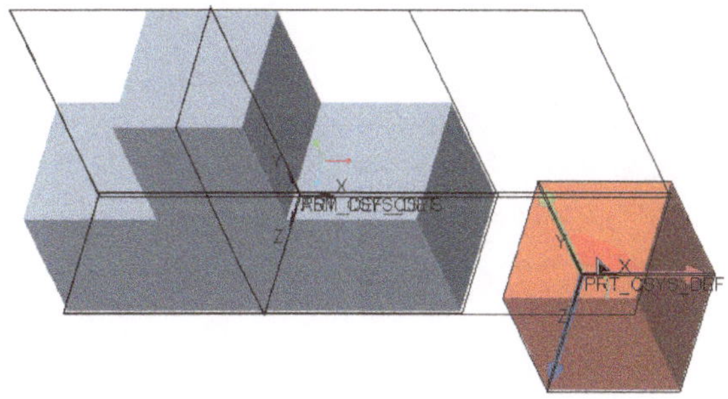

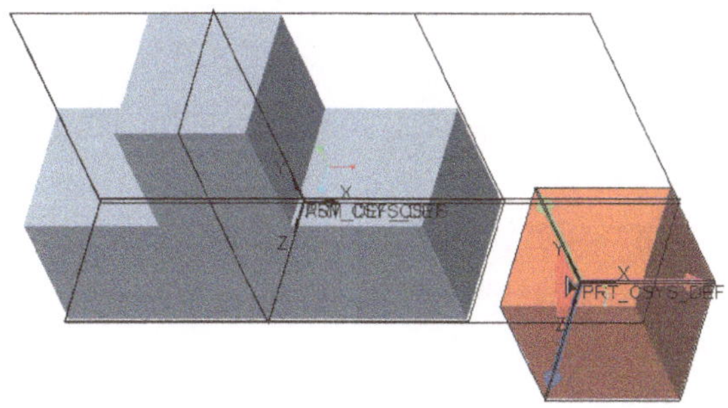

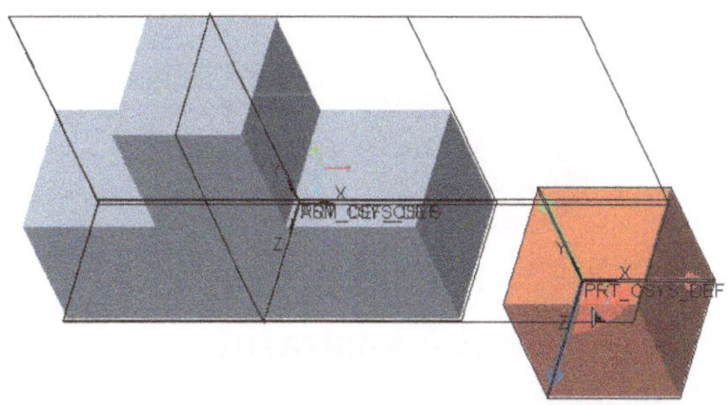

4. Click the sphere of the 3D Dragger and drag the pointer to move the component randomly.

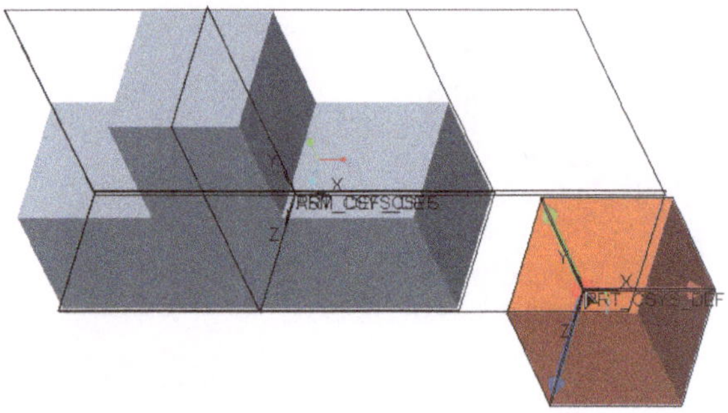

5. Use the torus displayed around the x-axis to rotate the component about the x-axis.

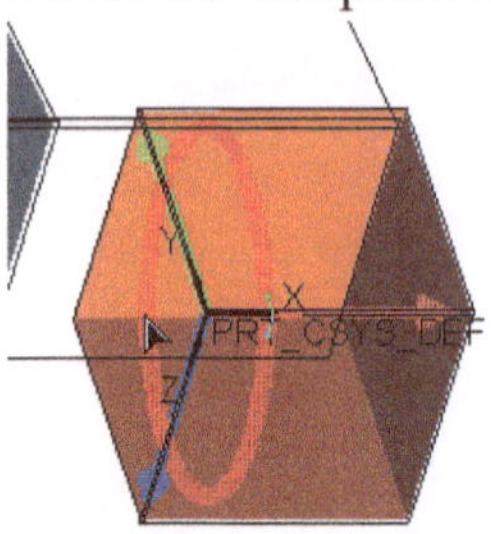

6. Likewise, rotate the component about the Y and Z axis.

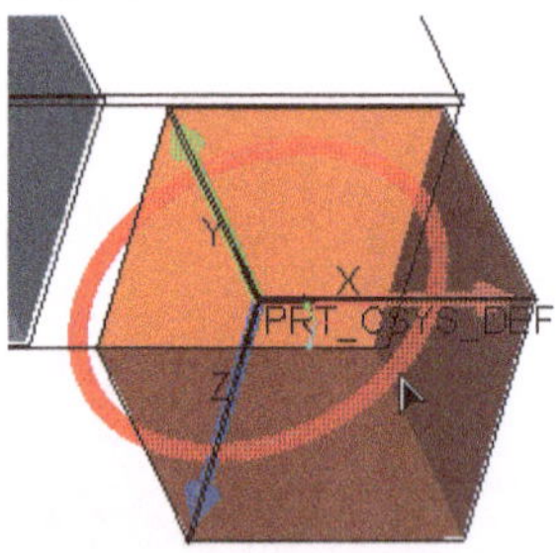

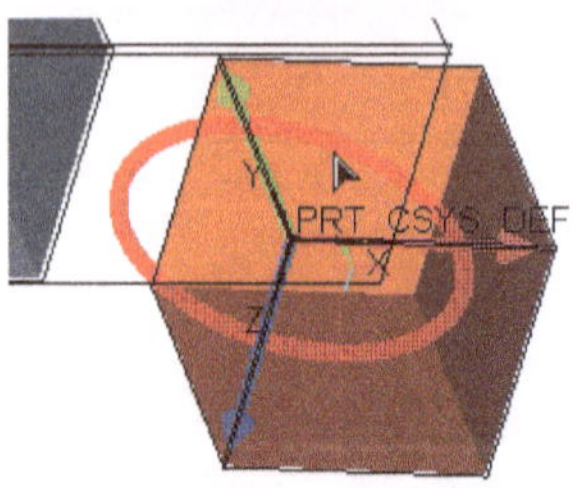

Coincident Constraint

The **Coincident** constraint makes two faces coincident with each other. The selected faces can flush with each other or position opposite to each other.

1. Insert the component into the assembly.
2. Select the face of the first part.
3. Click on a face of the second part.
4. On the Dashboard, click **Current constraint > Coincident**. It creates a coincident constraint between the two faces.

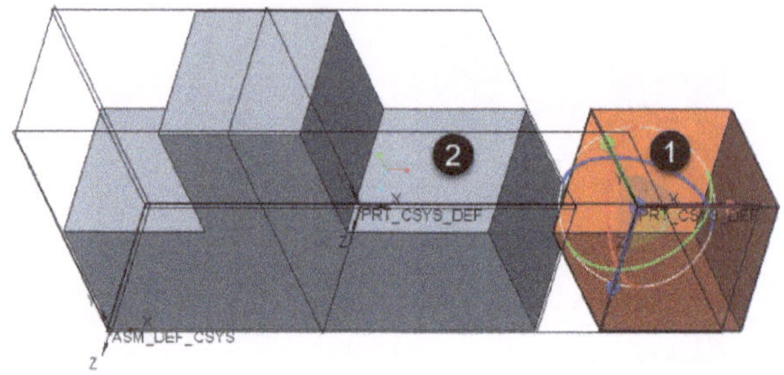

5. On the dashboard, click the **Change orientation** icon to change the orientation of the component.

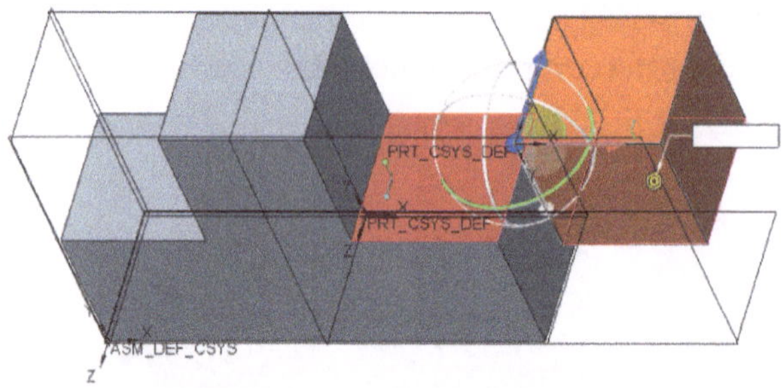

The **Coincident Constraint** also makes the axes of two cylindrical faces coincide with each other.

1. Click on a cylindrical face or axis of the first part.
2. Click on a cylindrical face or axis of the target part.
3. On the Dashboard, click **Current constraint > Coincident** . The two cylindrical axes are aligned together.

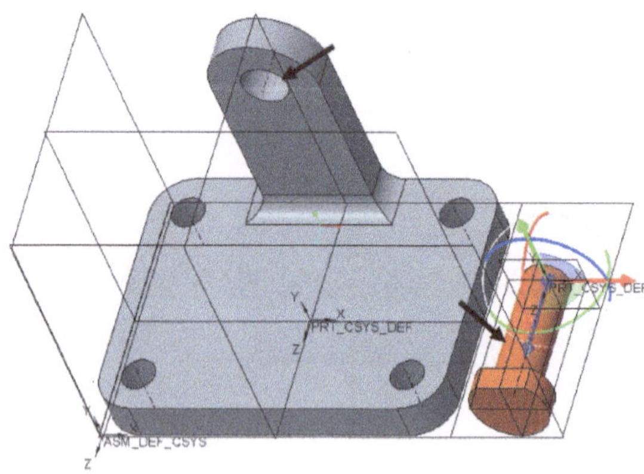

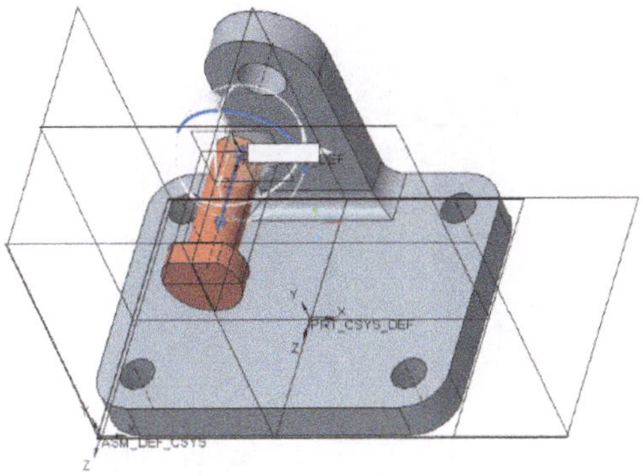

Distance Constraint

The **Distance** constraint creates a distance between two faces. Also, the faces will be parallel to each other.

1. Select the face of the first part.
2. Click on a face of the second part.
3. On the Dashboard, click **Current constraint > Distance**.

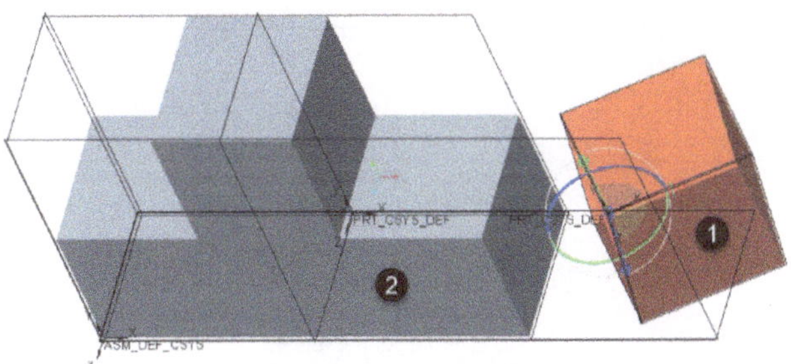

4. On the dashboard, click the **Change orientation** icon to make the selected faces point in the opposite direction.

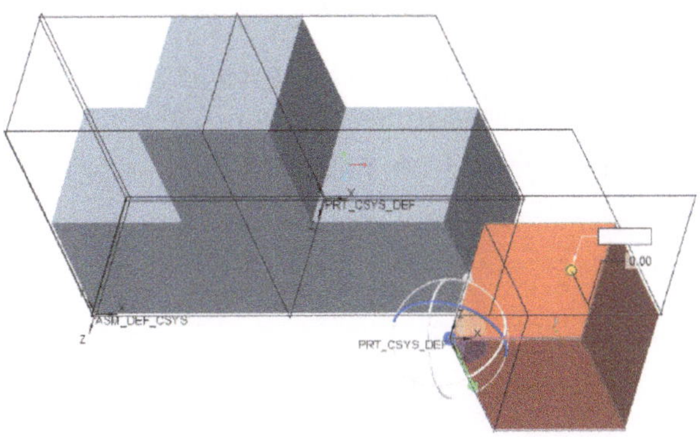

5. Type-in a value in the **Offset** box (or) drag the distance handle to add a distance between the selected faces.

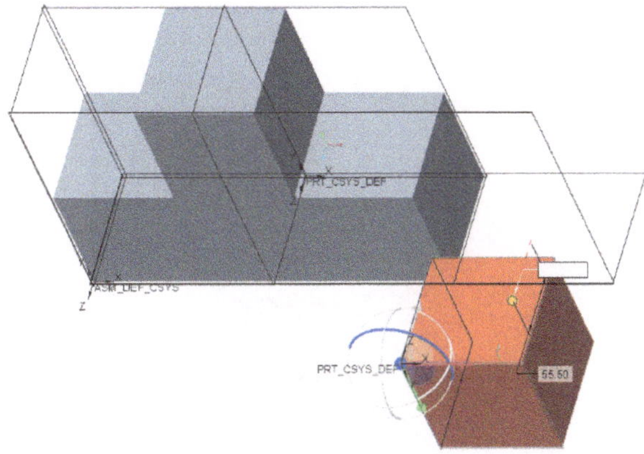

Angle Offset

The **Angle Offset** constraint is used to position faces at a specified angle.

1. Click on a plane or face of the first part.
2. Click on a plane or face of the second part.

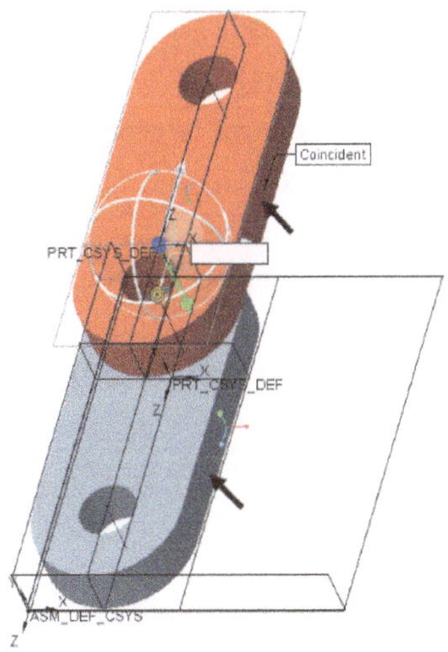

3. On the Dashboard, click **Current constraint > Angle Offset**.
4. Type-in a value in the **Offset** box on the dashboard. Press ENTER.

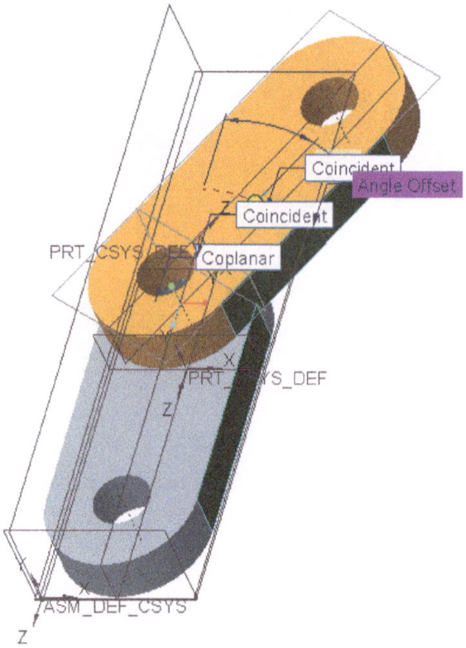

Parallel Constraint

The **Parallel** constraint makes an edge or face of one part parallel to that of another part.

1. Select a planar face or linear edge of the first part.
2. Click on an element of the second part.

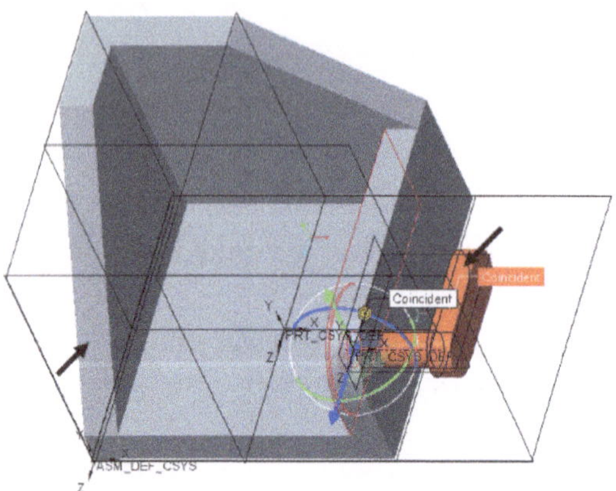

3. On the Dashboard, click **Current constraint > Parallel**. Two selected elements will be parallel to each other.

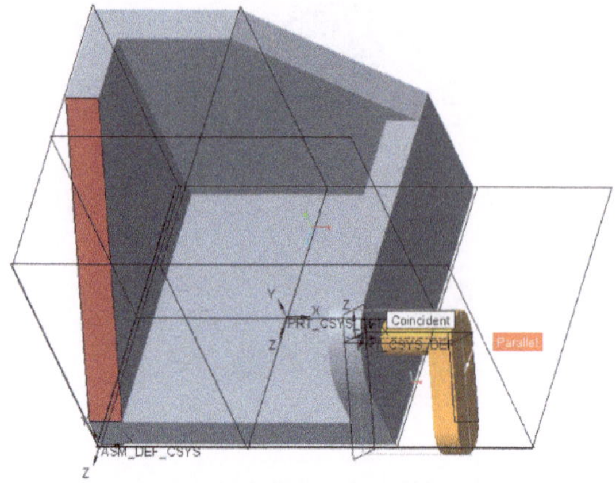

4. On the dashboard, click the **Change orientation** icon to change the orientation of the component.

Normal Constraint

The **Normal** constraint makes a face or edge of one part perpendicular to that of another part.

1. Select a planar face or linear edge of the first part.
2. Click on an element of the second part.

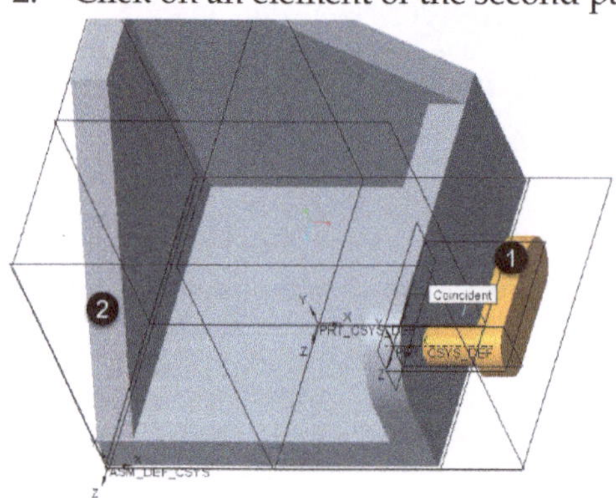

3. On the Dashboard, click **Current constraint > Normal**. Two selected elements will be perpendicular to each other.

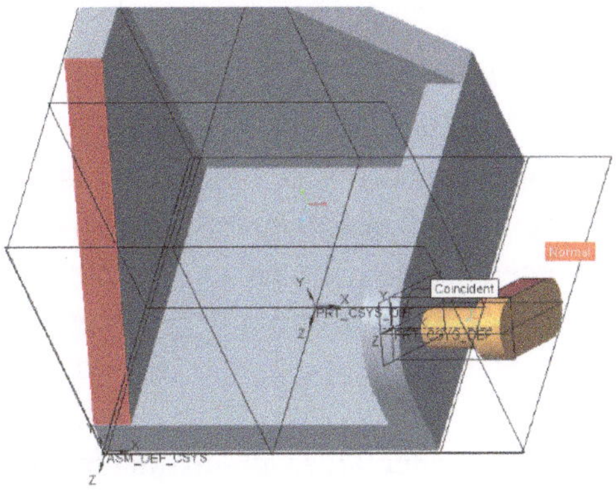

Copying Components with Constraints

If you have an assembly where you need to assemble the same part multiple times, it would be a tedious process. In such cases, the **Copy** and **Paste** commands will drastically reduce or eliminate the time used to assemble commonly used parts. To copy and paste a component, you need first to define a constraint or set of constraints between two parts. For example, define the **Coincident** constraint between the screw axis and the hole, and then make the flat bottom face of the screw head coincident with the top face.

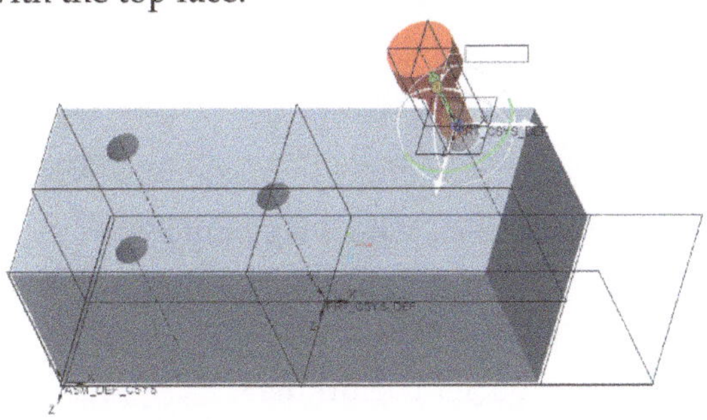

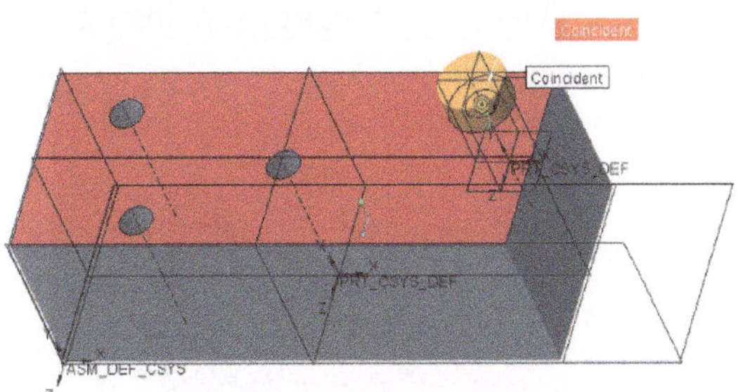

1. Select the screw and click **Model > Operations > Copy** on the ribbon (or) Press Ctrl+C on your keyboard.

2. On the ribbon, click **Model > Operations > Paste** (or) Press Ctrl+V on your keyboard.
3. Select the cylindrical face of another hole and its top face. The screw is pasted into it.

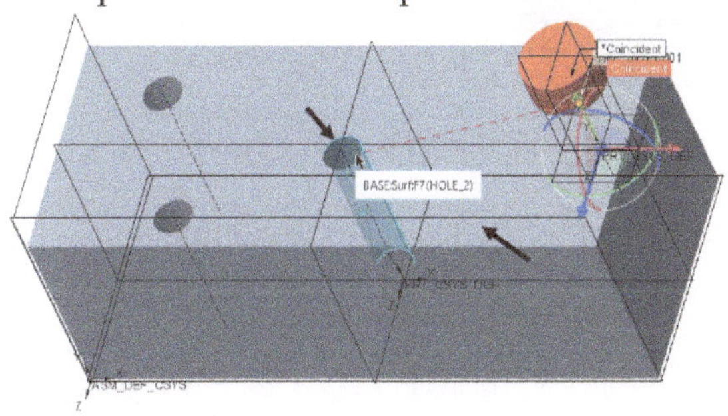

4. Click the green check.

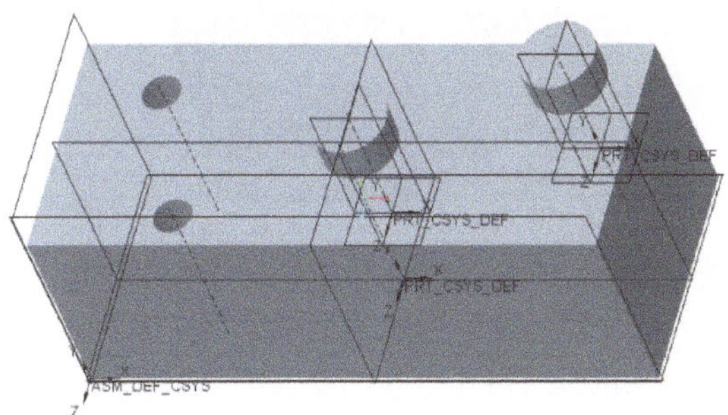

Repeating Components with Constraints

The **Repeat** command provides a more convenient way to insert the repeated components.

1. Select the component to repeat and click **Model > Component > Repeat**.

The **Repeat Component** dialog shows the list of constraints that can be added.

2. On the dialog, select the first Coincident reference and click **Add**.
3. Select the axes of the two holes.

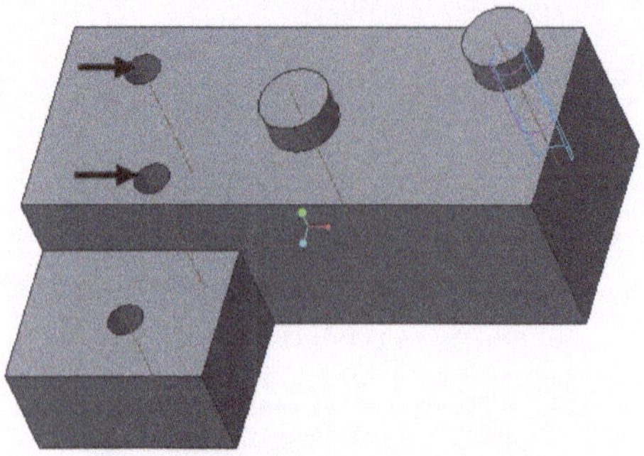

The screw is positioned in both the holes.

4. Press hold the Ctrl key and select both the **Coincident** references from the dialog. Click **Add**.
5. Select the axis and top face of the hole, as shown.

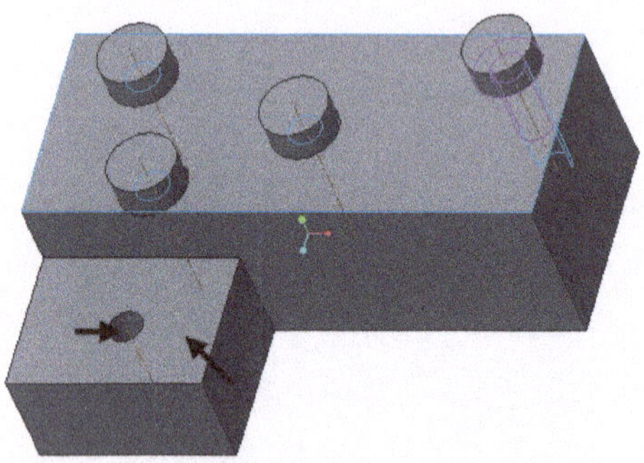

The screw is positioned in the hole, as shown.

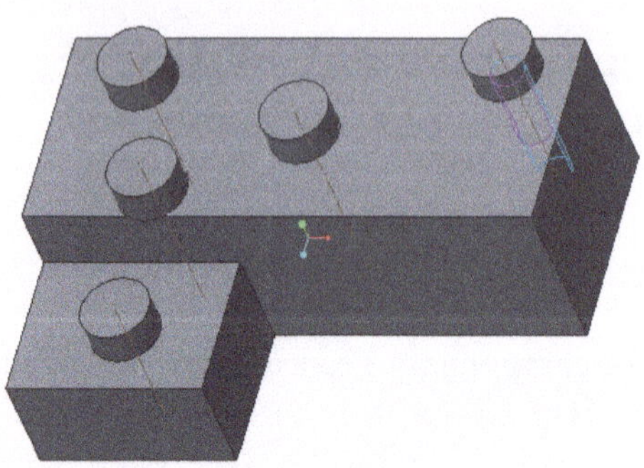

6. Click **OK** on the dialog.

Connections

The Connections between the components control the position and movement. You can define connections between two components by selecting the desired option from the **Connection type** drop-down.

Ball Connection

A ball connection is a mechanical connection consisting of a spherical head (the "ball") that fits into a socket or housing. This design allows for rotational movement in three dimensions: pitch (up and down), yaw (side to side), and roll (twisting motion).

4. Download the **Chapter 9** files and extract to the desired location.
5. Start a new assembly file.
6. On the **Graphics** toolbar, click **Datum Display Filters** drop-down and select the **Axis Display** and **Point Display** options.

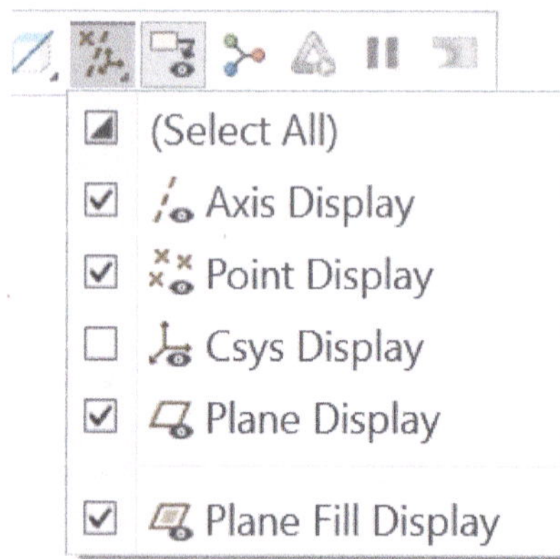

7. On the ribbon, click **Model > Component > Assemble** .
8. Browse to the Ball Connection and select the Ball_connection_female.prt file.
9. Click **Open**. The component appears inside the assembly.

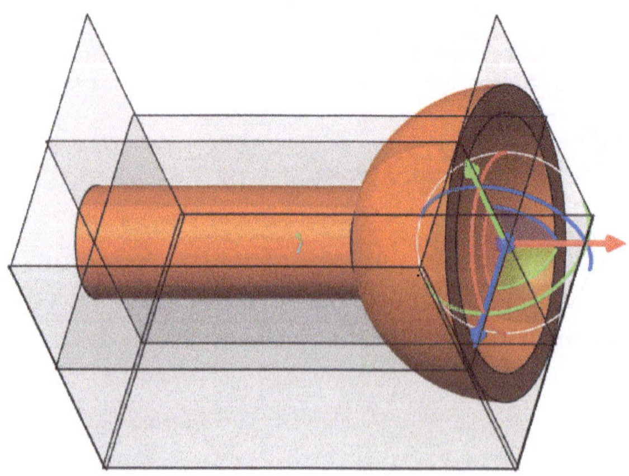

10. Click **Current Constraint > Default** on the **Component Placement** dashboard. The component is positioned at its default location.

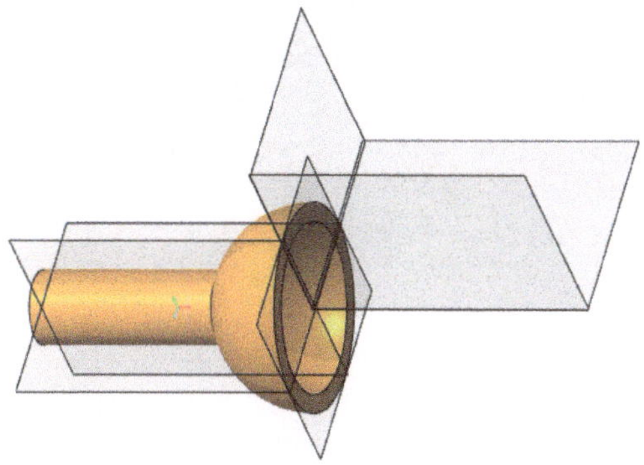

11. Click the green check.
12. On the ribbon, click **Model > Component > Assemble** .
13. Go to the location of the Ball_connection_male.prt.
14. Select the component and click **Open**.

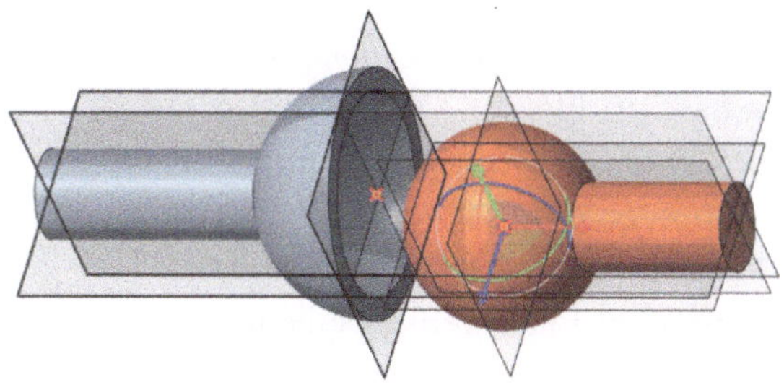

15. Select **Connection type > Ball** on the Dashboard.

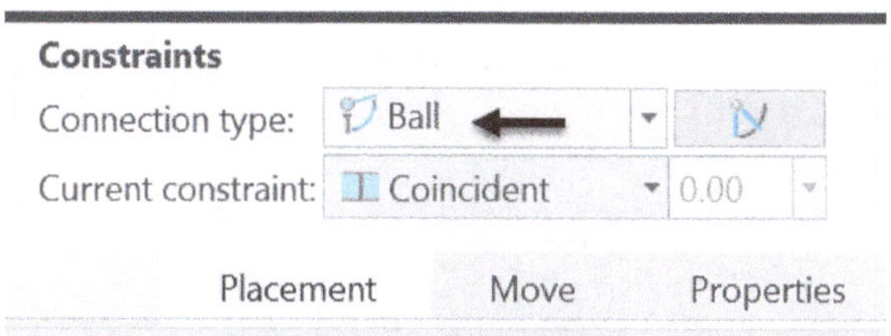

16. Disable the **Display Dragger** icon on the Dashboard; the Dragger is hidden.

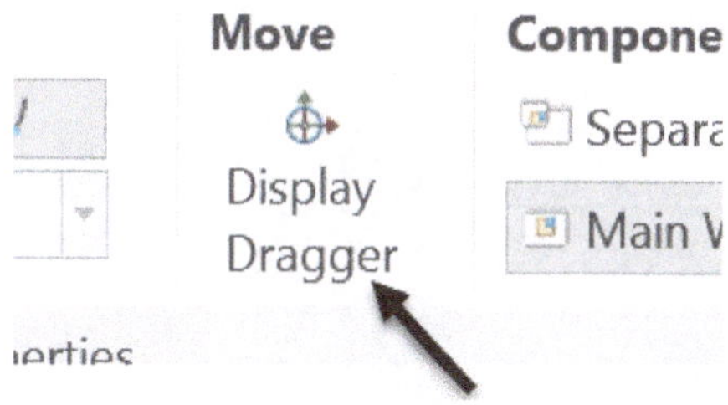

17. Select the point from the Ball_connection_female.prt file, as shown.
18. Select the point from the Ball_connection_male.prt file, as shown.

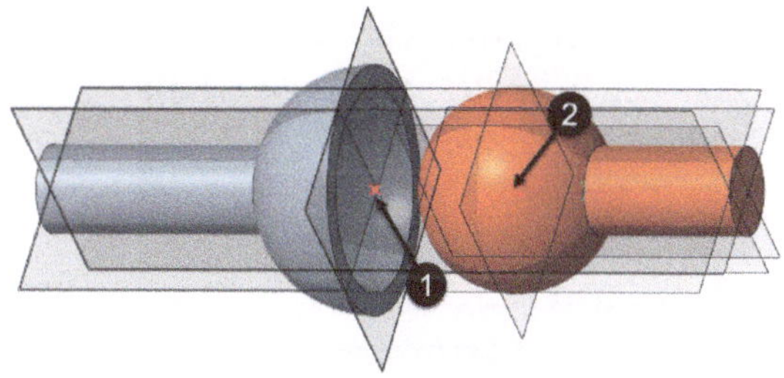

19. Click **OK** on the Dashboard.

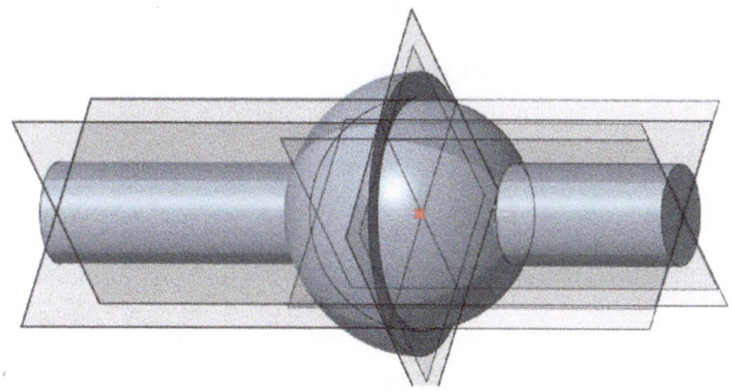

20. On the ribbon, click **Model > Component > Drag Component**.

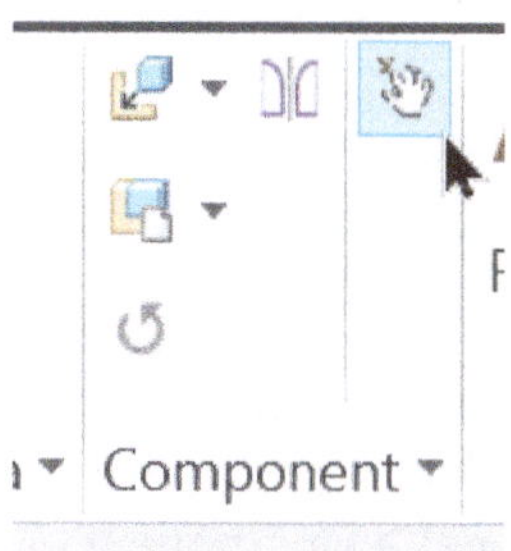

21. Select the **Ball_connection_male** component and move the pointer. You will observe that the selected component moves freely in all directions. Additionally, it interferes with the female component. To prevent this interference, you need to apply constraints that restrict its movement.

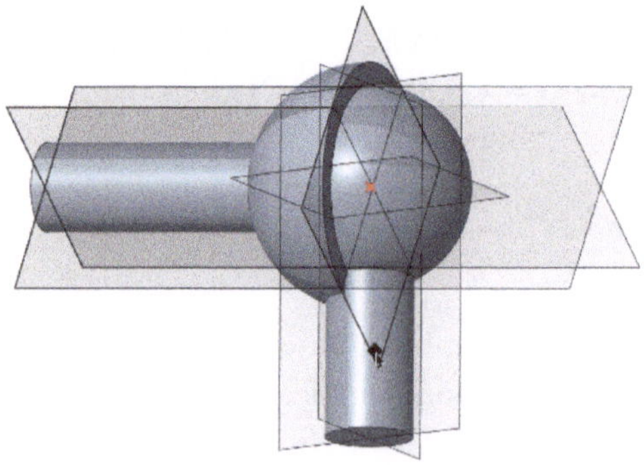

22. Click **Close** on the **Drag** dialog.
23. In the Model Tree, right-click on the Ball_connection_male.prt and select **Edit Definition.**

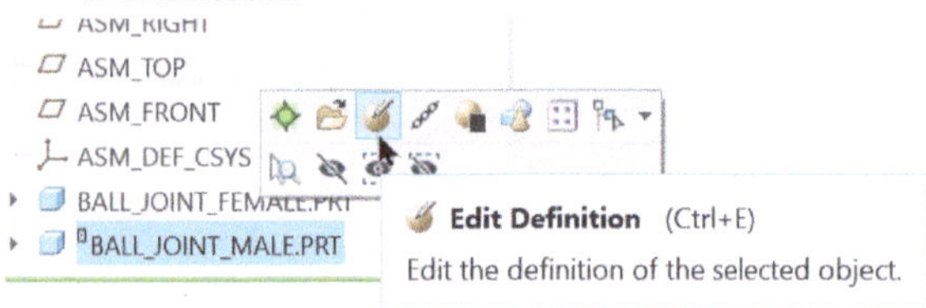

24. On the **Placement** tab of the Dashboard, click the **Cone Axis** option.
25. Select the axes of the two components, as shown.

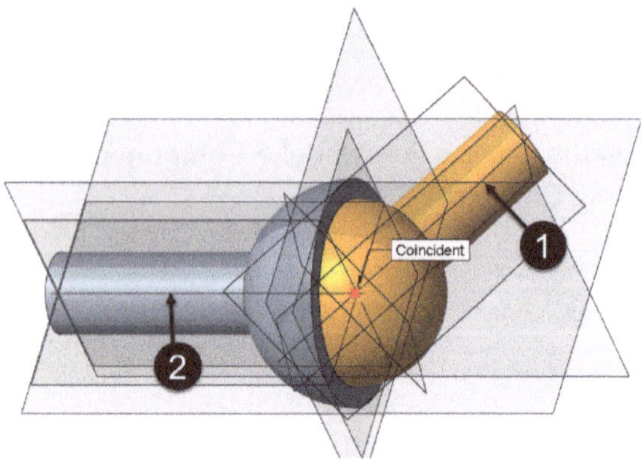

26. Type 52 in the Cone Opening Angle box.
27. Click OK on the Dashboard.
28. On the ribbon, click **Model > Component > Drag Component**.
29. Drag the Ball_connection_male component and notice that the movement is restricted.

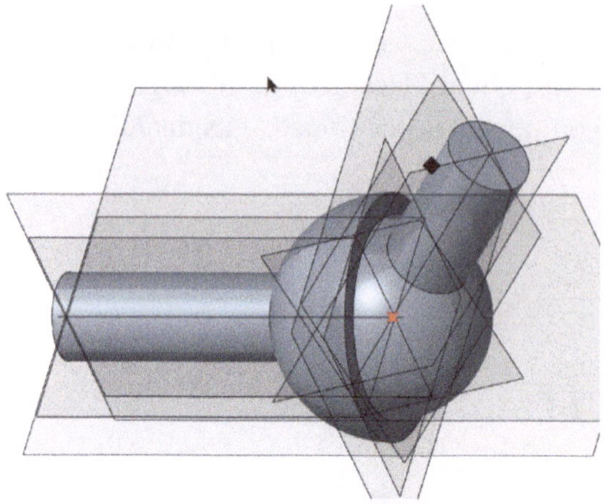

Pin Connection

The **Pin** option creates a pin connection between two cylindrical faces. On creating this connection, all the degrees of the freedom of the component are constrained except the rotational movement.

1. On the ribbon, click **Model > Component > Assemble**.
2. Browse to the *Pin_connection* folder and select the Base.prt file.
3. Click **Open**. The component appears inside the assembly.
4. Click **Current Constraint > Fix** on the **Component Placement** dashboard. The component is fixed at its current location.

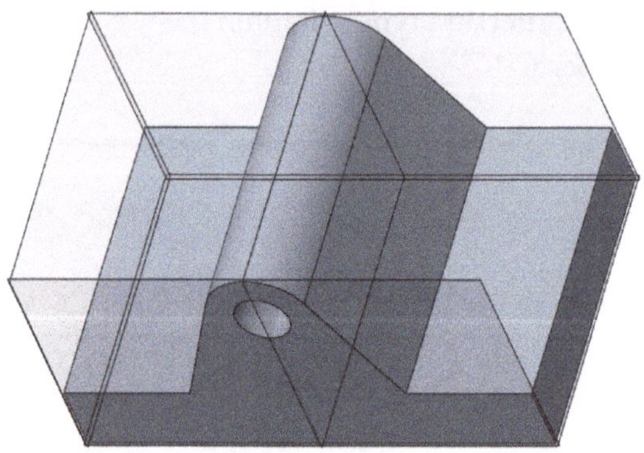

5. Click the green check.
6. On the ribbon, click **Model > Component > Assemble**.
7. Go to the location of the Pin.prt.
8. Select the component and click **Open**.
9. Select **Connection type > Pin** on the Dashboard.

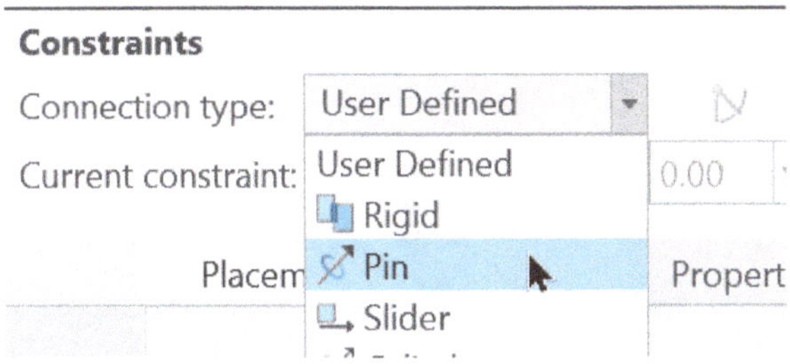

10. Select the cylindrical face of the pin.
11. Select the cylindrical face of the hole of the base component.

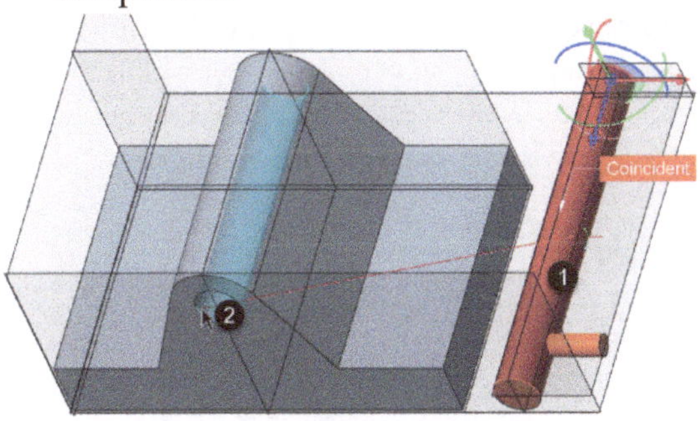

Next, you need to select the planes or points from the components to constrain the translation.

12. Select the planes from the Pin and Base components, as shown.

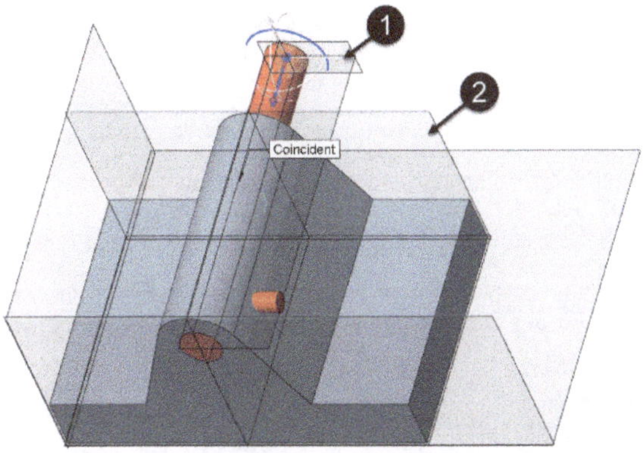

13. Select **Constraint Type > Coincident** from the **Placement** tab.

Optionally, you can the rotation of the pin between two angle limits.

14. Click the **Rotation Axis** option from the **Placement** tab.
15. Select the planes from the Pin and Base components.

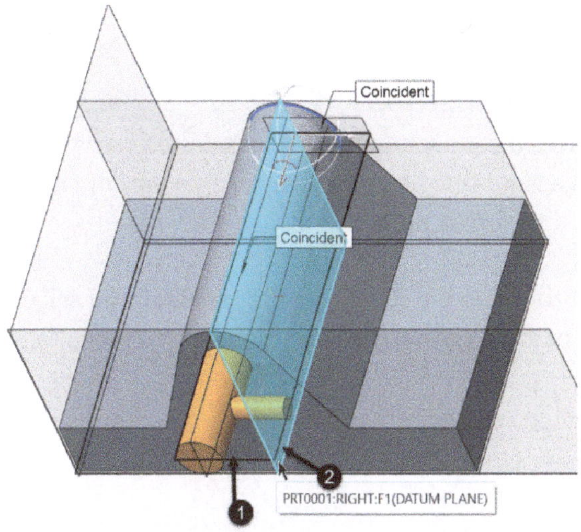

16. Check the **Minimum Limit** and **Maximum Limit** options.
17. Enter values in the **Minimum Limit** and **Maximum Limit** boxes.

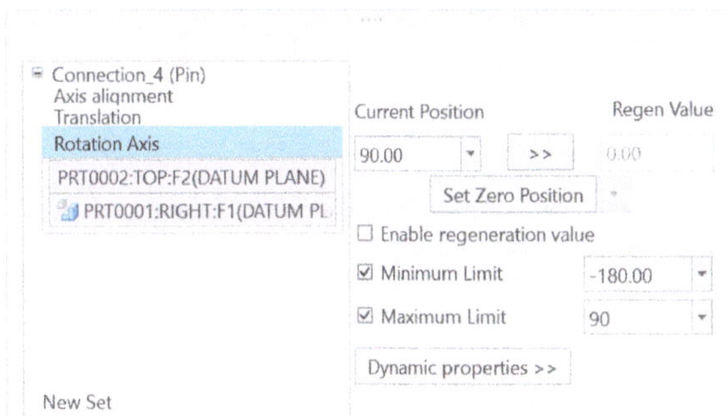

18. Click **OK**.
19. On the ribbon, click **Model > Component > Drag Component**.
20. Select the **Pin** component and move the pointer. You will observe that the selected component rotates between the minimum and maximum limits.

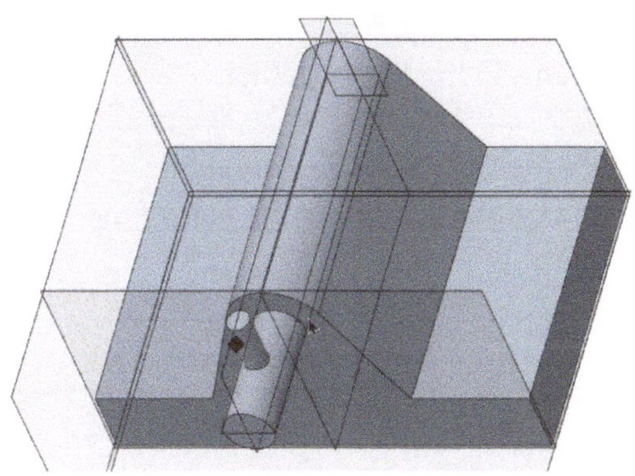

21. Click **Close** on the **Drag** dialog.

Rigid Connection

The **Rigid** connection makes the selected parts to form a rigid set. As you move a single part of a rigid set, all the other parts will also be moved.

1. Browse to the *Rigid_connection* folder and select the Rigi_connection.asm file.

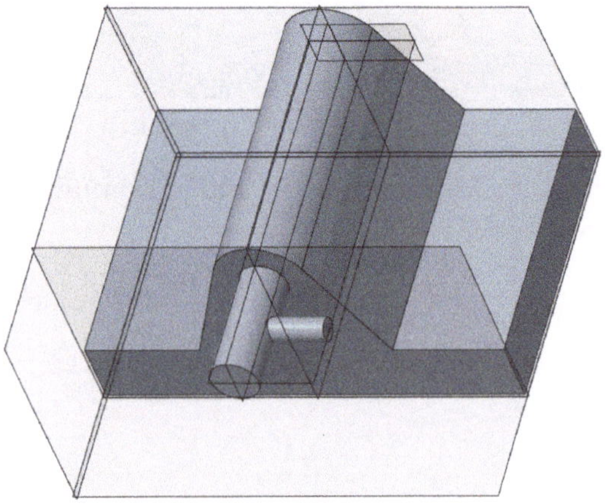

2. On the ribbon, click **Model > Component > Assemble** .
3. Browse to the location of the Sphere.prt file. Next, select it.
4. Click **Open**. The component appears inside the assembly.
5. Select **Connection type > Rigid** on the Dashboard.

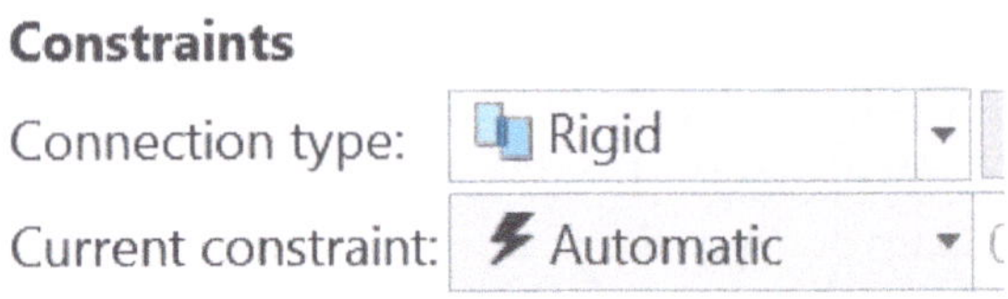

Now, you need to define constraints between the two components to fix them together.

6. Select **Current constraint > Automatic**.
7. Select the cylindrical face of the hole of the Sphere.prt.

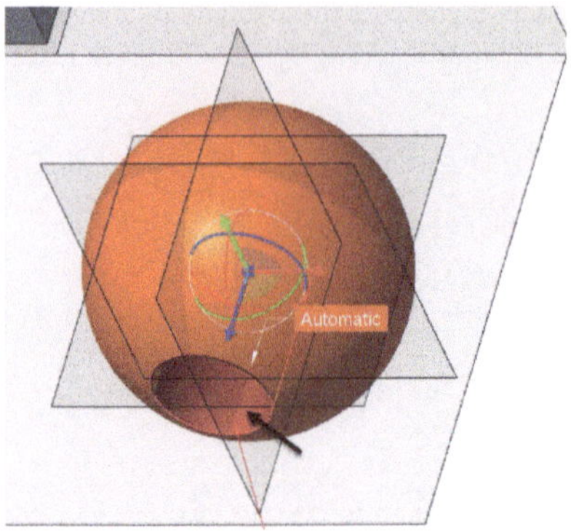

8. Select the cylindrical face of the extruded feature of the pin.
9. Click the **Flip** button, if the Sphere is not oriented properly.

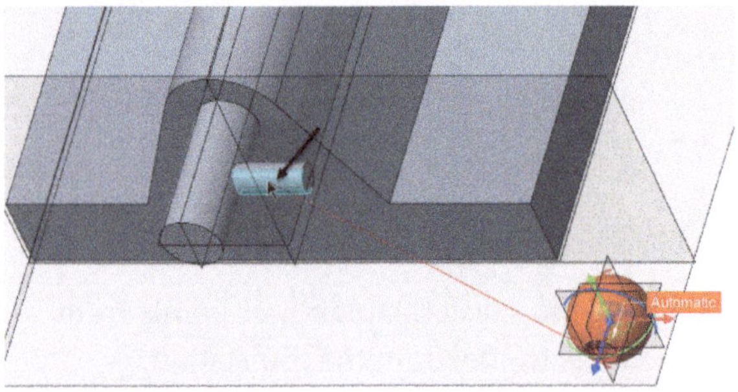

10. Select the **New Constraint** option from the **Placement** tab.
11. Select **Current Constraint > Coincident**.
12. Select the planes of the Sphere and Pin, as shown.

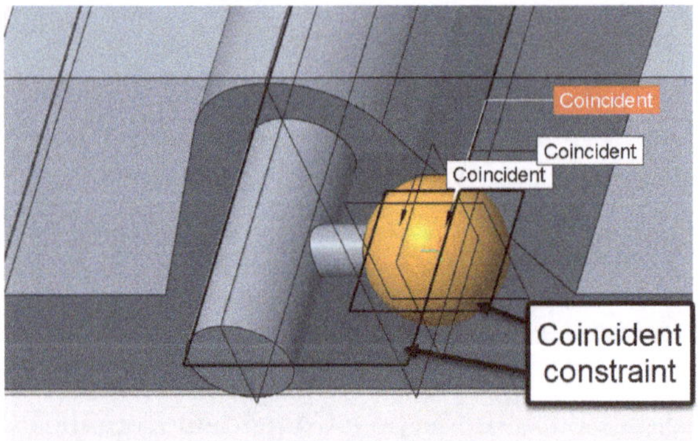

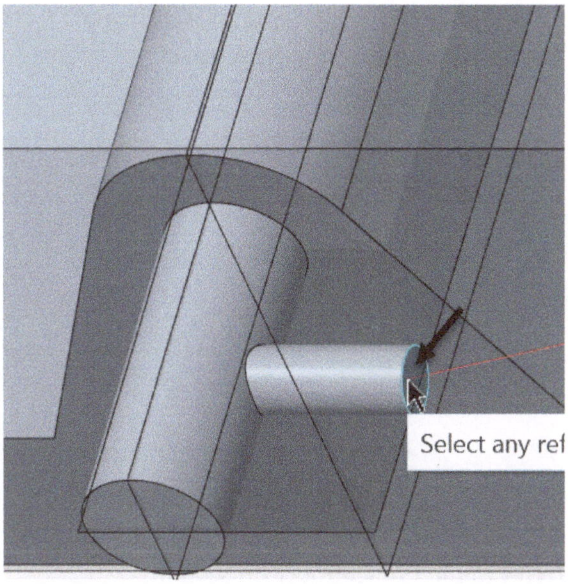

13. Likewise, add one or more constraints until the **Full constrained** status is displayed on the **Placement** tab.

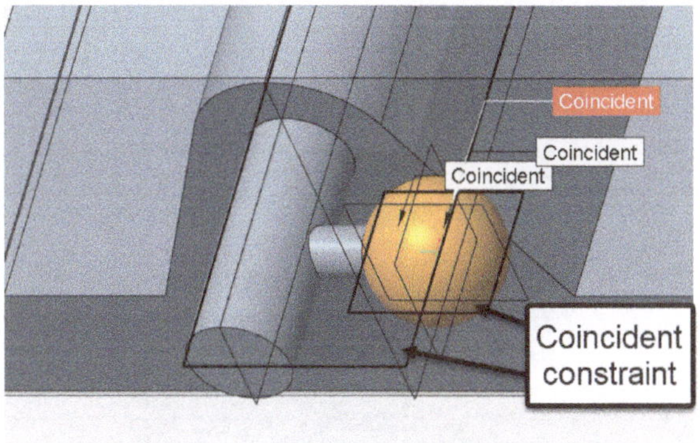

14. Click **OK** on the Dashboard.
15. On the ribbon, click **Model > Component > Drag Component.**
16. Select the **Pin** component and move the pointer. You will observe that the Sphere rotates along with the selected component.

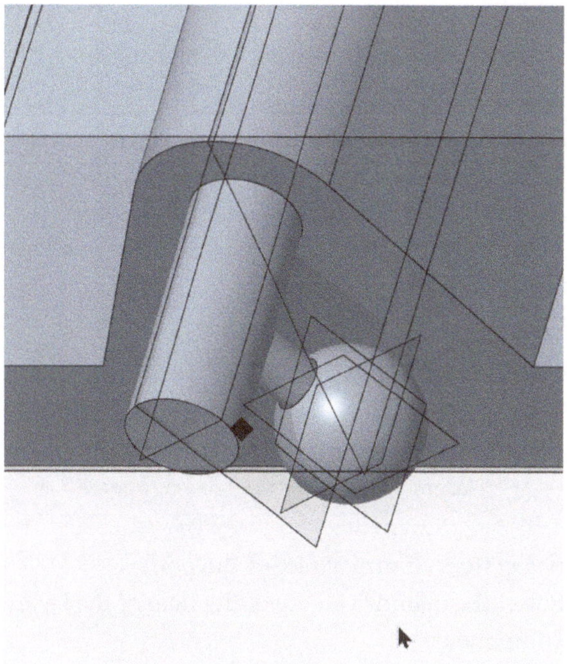

17. Close the **Drag** dialog.

Cylinder Connection

The **Cylinder** option creates a connection with one translational and one rotational degree of freedom.

1. Start a new assembly file.
2. On the ribbon, click **Model > Component > Assemble** .
3. Browse to the Cylinder Connection and select the Base.prt file.
4. Click **Open**. The component appears inside the assembly.
5. Click **Current Constraint > Fix** on the **Component Placement** dashboard. The component is fixed at its location.

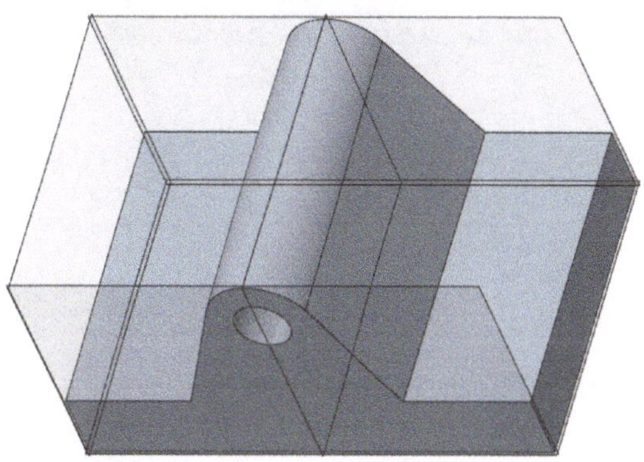

6. Click the green check.
7. On the ribbon, click **Model > Component > Assemble** .
8. Go to the location of the Pin.prt.
9. Select the component and click **Open**.
10. Select **Connection type > Cylinder** on the Dashboard.

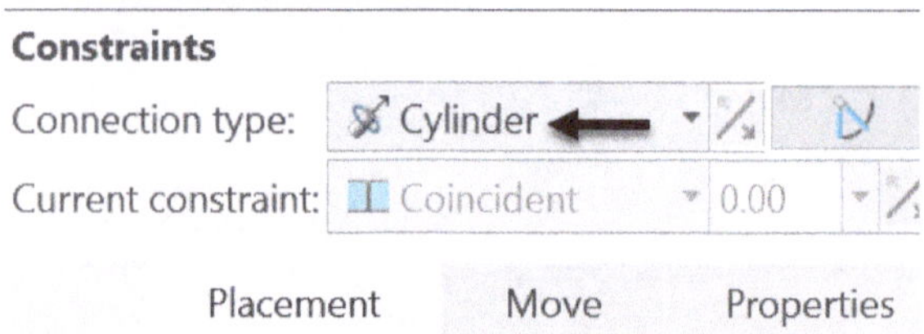

11. Select the cylindrical face of the pin.
12. Select the cylindrical face of the hole of the base component.

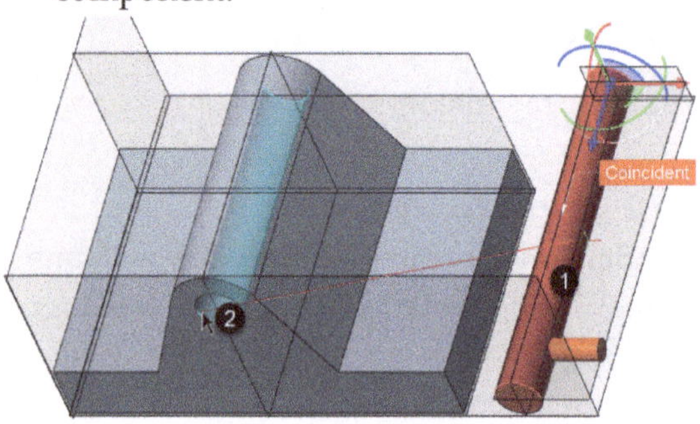

13. Click the **Translation Axis** option from the **Placement** tab.
14. Select the planes from the Pin and Base components.

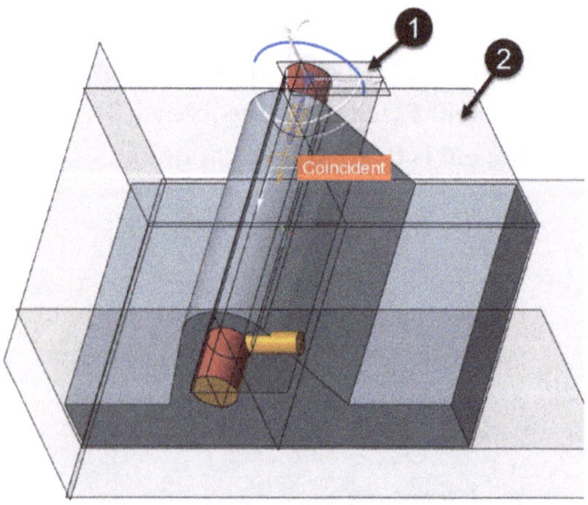

15. Type **0** in the **Current Position** box.
16. Check the **Minimum Limit** and **Maximum Limit** options.
17. Type **0** and **50** in the **Minimum Limit** and **Maximum Limit** boxes, respectively.

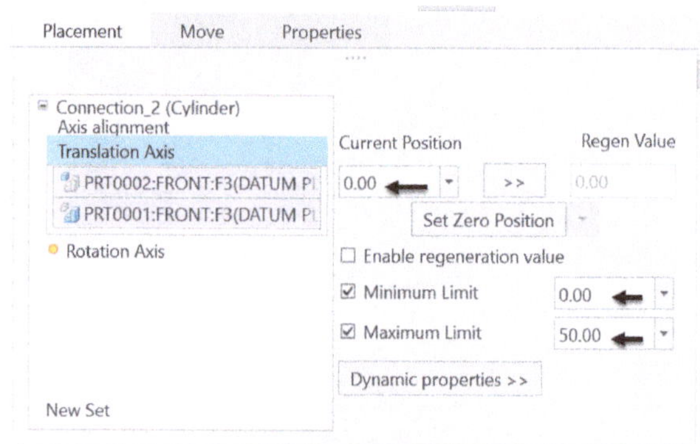

18. Likewise, select the **Rotation Axis** option from the **Placement** tab and define the rotation limits (refer to the **Pin Connection** section).
19. Click **OK** on the Dashboard.
20. On the ribbon, click **Model > Component > Drag Component**.
21. Select the **Pin** component and move the pointer. You will observe that it rotates and translates within the specified limits.
22. Close the **Drag** dialog.

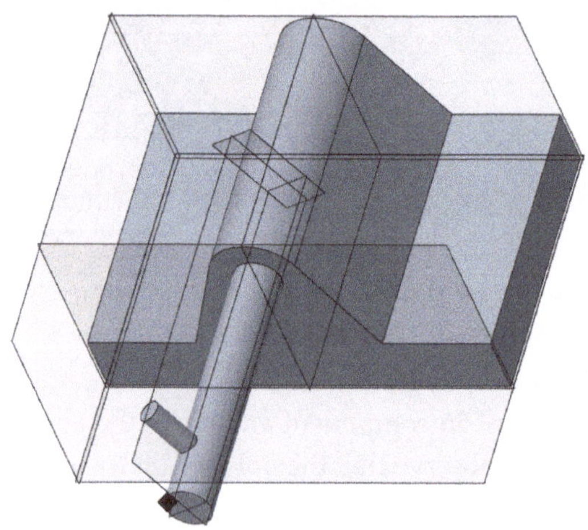

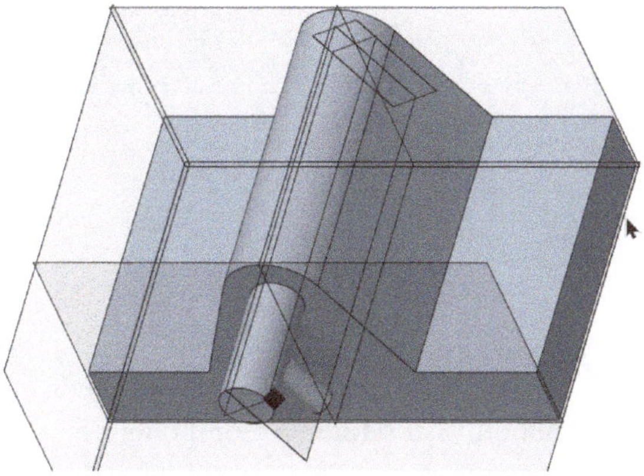

Planar Connection

A **Planar** connection is a restricts movement to a specific plane, allowing two components to move along the plane (X and Y directions) and rotate within it. This is useful for simulating parts that slide or rotate across a surface without moving out of the defined plane.

1. Start a new assembly file.
2. On the ribbon, click **Model > Component > Assemble**.
3. Browse to the Planar Connection and select the Plate.prt file.
4. Click **Open**. The component appears inside the assembly.
5. Click **Current Constraint > Fix** on the **Component Placement** dashboard. The component is fixed at its location.

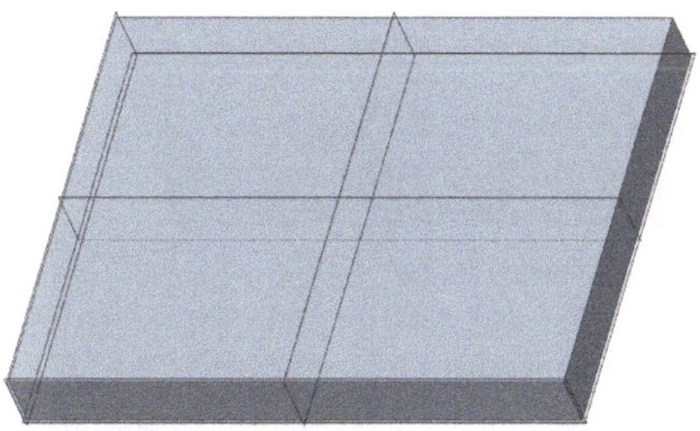

6. Click the green check.
7. On the ribbon, click **Model > Component > Assemble**.
8. Go to the location of the Disc.prt.
9. Select the component and click **Open**.
10. Select **Connection type > Planar** on the Dashboard.

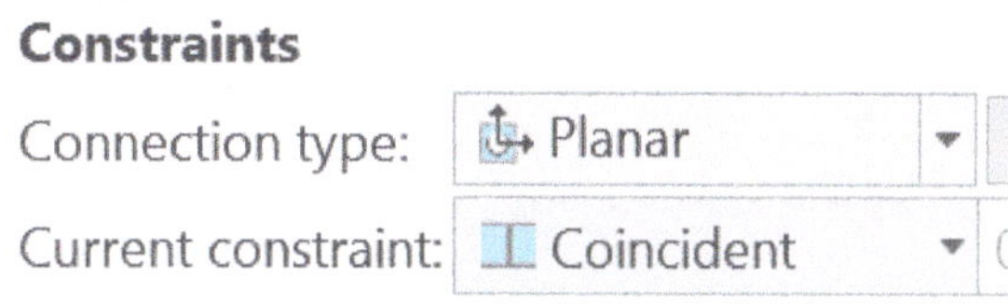

11. Select the bottom face of the Disc.
12. Select the top face of the Plate.

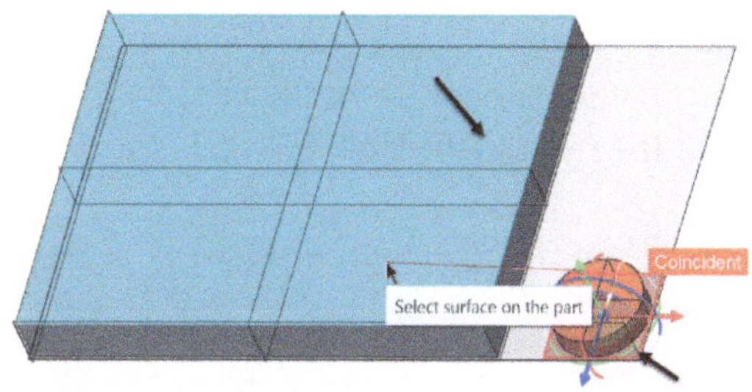

13. Select the **Translation Axis 1** option from the **Placement** tab.
14. Select the right plane from the Disc.
15. Select the right plane from the Plate.

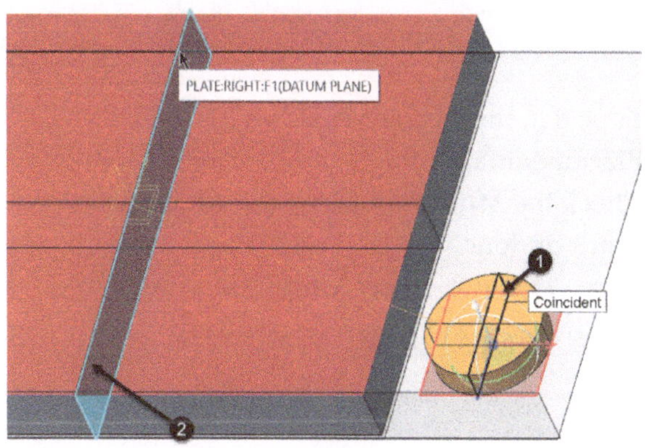

16. Type **0** in the **Current Position** box on the **Placement** tab.
17. Check the **Minimum Limit** and **Maximum Limit** options.
18. Type **-40** and **40** in the **Minimum Limit** and **Maximum Limit** boxes, respectively.

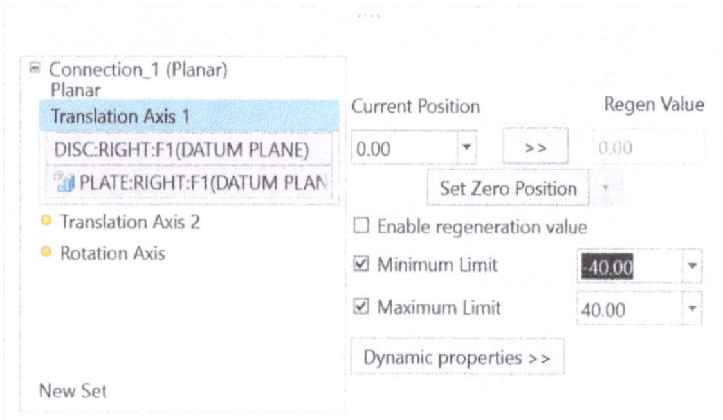

19. Select the **Translation Axis 2** option from the **Placement** tab.
20. Select the front plane from the Disc.
21. Select the front plane from the Plate.

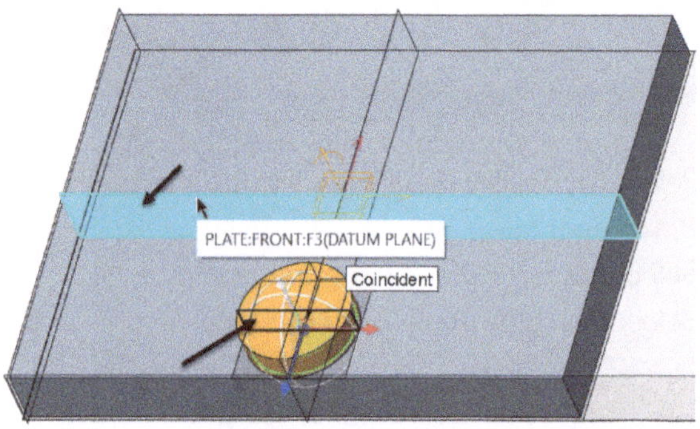

22. Type **0** in the **Current Position** box on the **Placement** tab.
23. Check the **Minimum Limit** and **Maximum Limit** options.
24. Type **-25** and **25** in the **Minimum Limit** and **Maximum Limit** boxes, respectively.

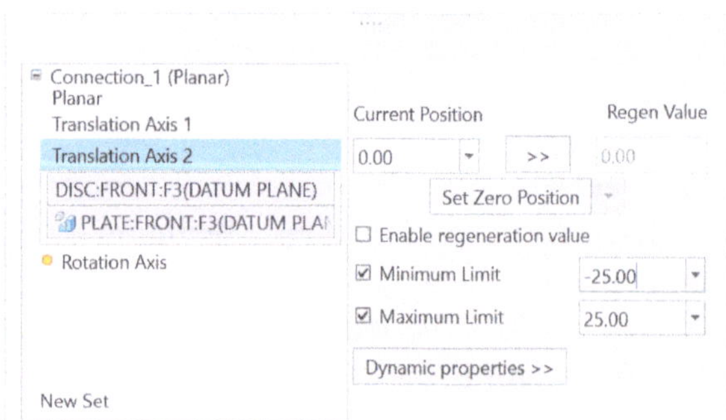

25. Click **OK** on the Dashboard.

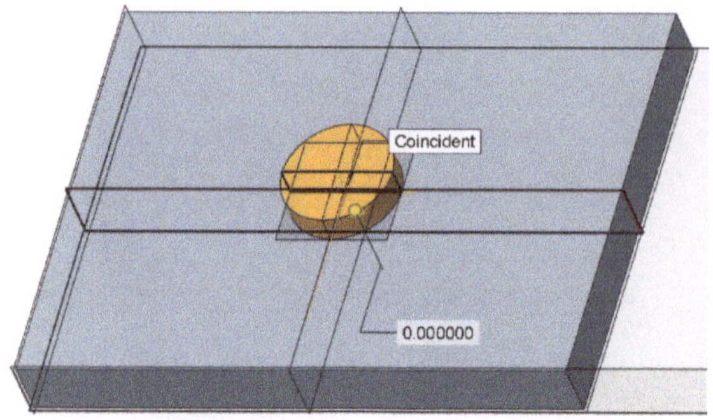

26. On the ribbon, click **Model > Component > Drag Component**.
27. Select the **Disc** component and move the pointer. You will observe that the Disc slides and rotates on the selected plane within the limits defined along the two axes.

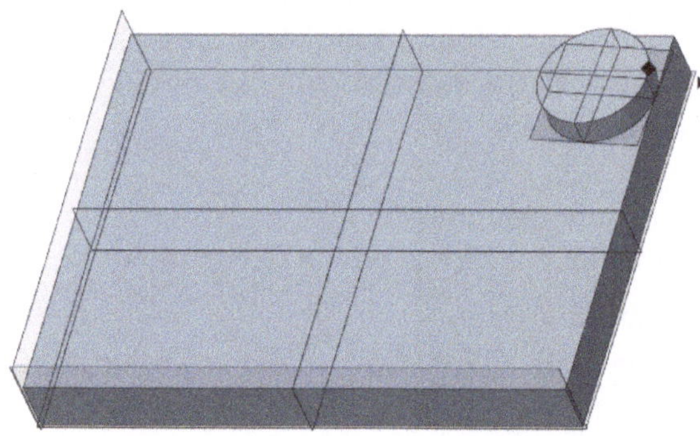

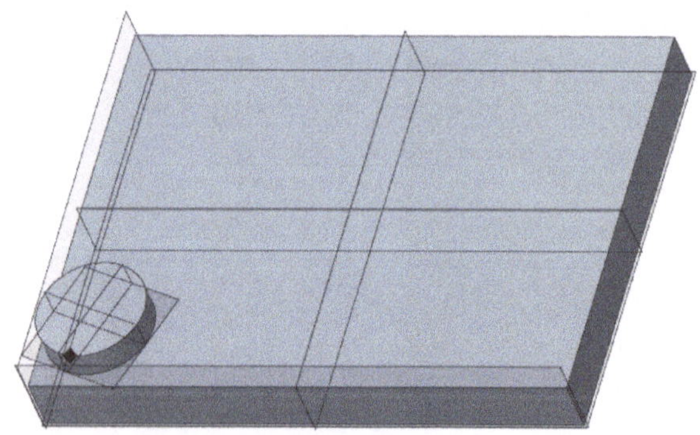

28. Close the **Drag** dialog.

Slider Connection

A **Slider** connection restricts two components to linear movement along a single axis, simulating straight-line motion such as a piston sliding within a cylinder. The connection prevents other forms of motion, like rotation or side-to-side displacement, allowing only sliding along the defined axis.

1. Start a new assembly file.
2. On the ribbon, click **Model > Component > Assemble** .
3. Browse to the **Slider Connection** folder and select the Slot.prt file.
4. Click **Open**. The component appears inside the assembly.
5. Click **Current Constraint > Fix** on the **Component Placement** dashboard. The component is fixed at its location.

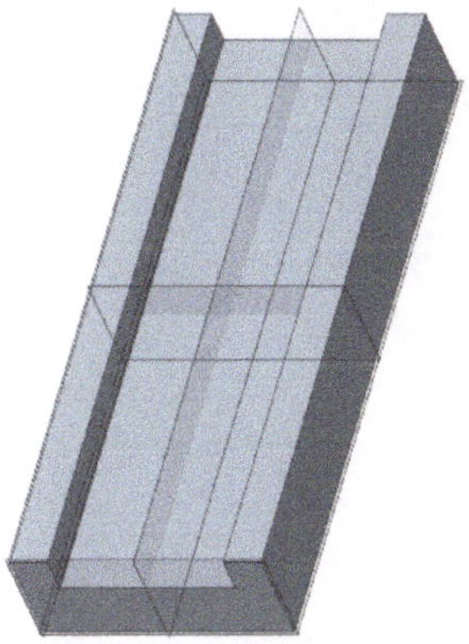

6. Click the green check.
7. On the ribbon, click **Model > Component > Assemble** .
8. Go to the location of the Plate.prt.
9. Select the component and click **Open**.
10. Select **Connection type > Slider** on the Dashboard.

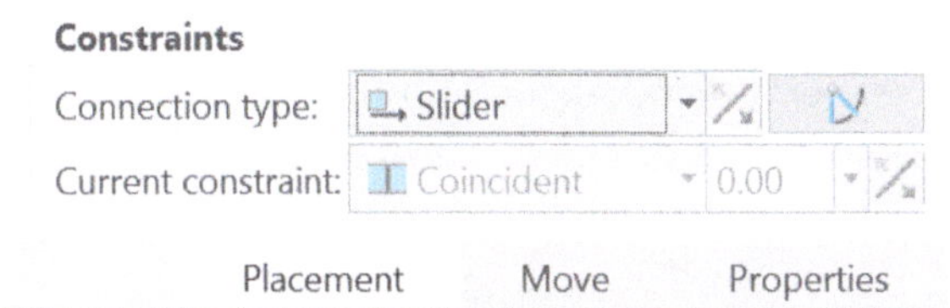

11. Select the edge of the Slot, as shown.
12. Select the edge of the Plate, as shown.

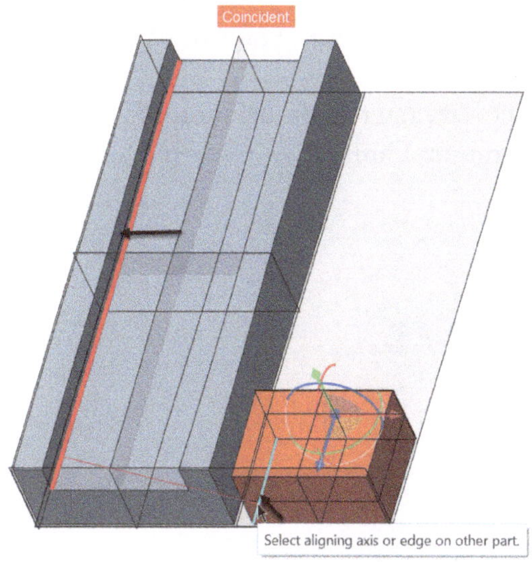

Next, you need to select planes from the two components to constrain the rotation of the Plate.

13. Select the planes from the Slot and Plate, as shown.

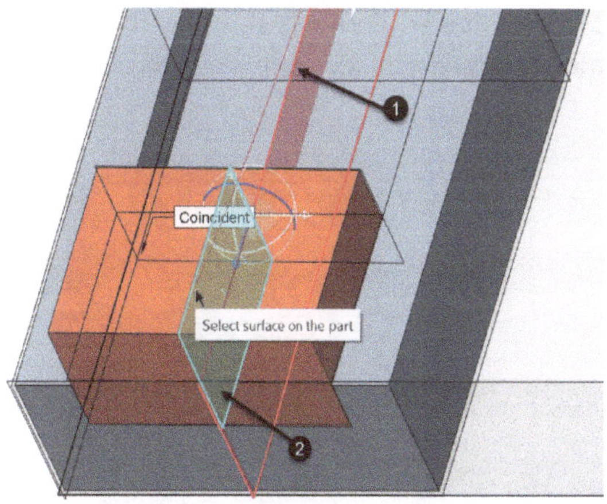

14. Select the **Translation Axis 1** option from the **Placement** tab.
15. Select the faces of the Slot and Plate, as shown.

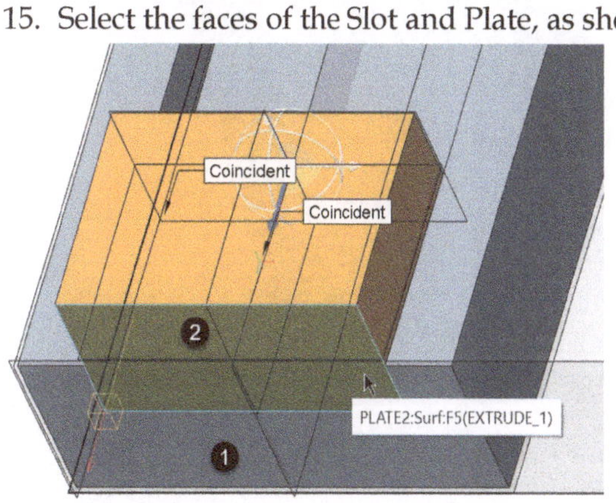

16. Type **0** in the **Current Position** box.
17. Check the **Minimum Limit** and **Maximum Limit** options.
18. Type **-200** and **0** in the **Minimum Limit** and **Maximum Limit** boxes, respectively.

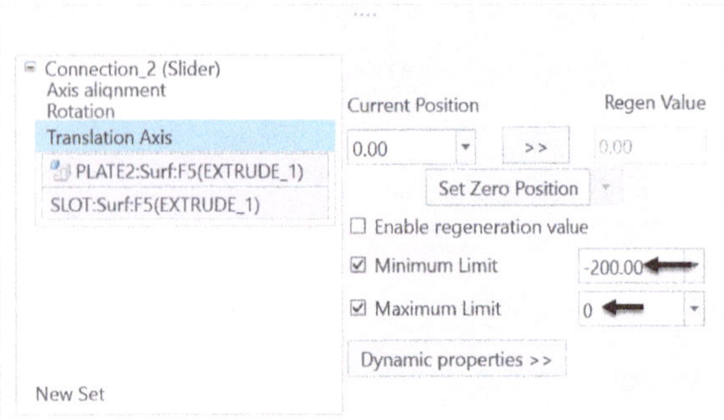

19. Click **OK** on the Dashboard.
20. On the ribbon, click **Model > Component > Drag Component**.
21. Select the **Plate** component and move the pointer. You will observe that the Plate slides along the selected axis within the defined limits.

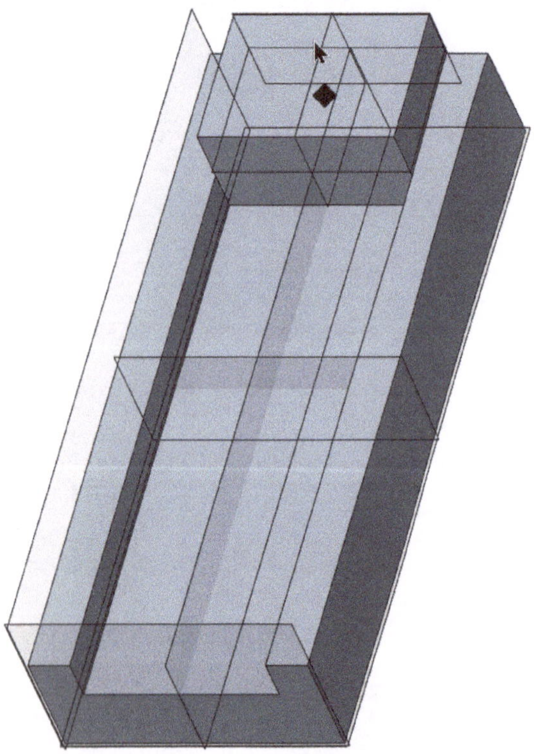

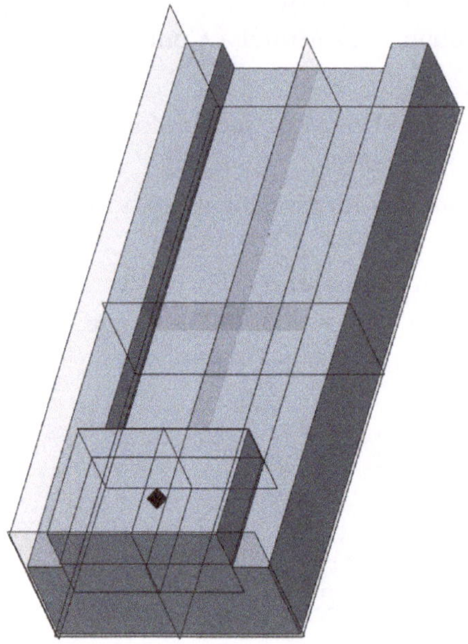

22. Close the **Drag** dialog.

Collision Detection

In an assembly, two or more components can overlap or occupy the same space. However, this would be physically impossible in the real world. When you add constraints between components, Creo Parametric develops real-world contacts and movements between them. However, sometimes clashes can occur. To check such errors, Creo Parametric provides you with an option to identify collision.

1. Insert two components into the assembly, leave the second component unconstrained, and click the green check on the dashboard.

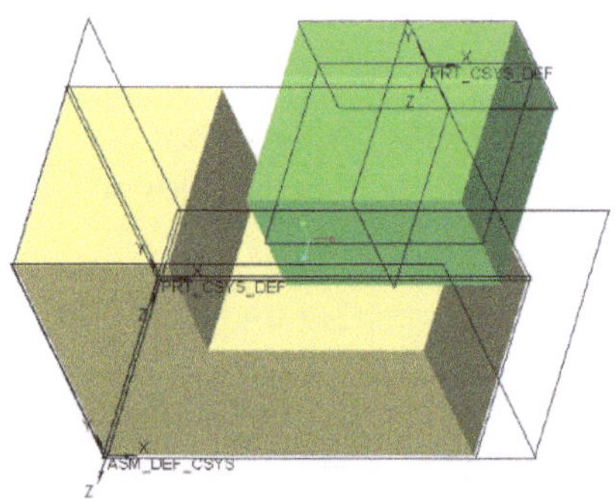

2. Click **File > Prepare > Model Properties**.

3. On the **Model Properties** dialog, under the **Assembly** section, click the **change** option next to **Collision detection**.
4. On the **Collision Detection Settings** dialog, select **Global collision detection** and check the **Sound warning upon collision** option.
5. Click **OK** and close the **Model Properties** dialog.
6. On the ribbon, click **Model > Component > Drag Components**.
7. Select the unconstrained component and move the pointer. The collision between the two components is detected along with a sound.

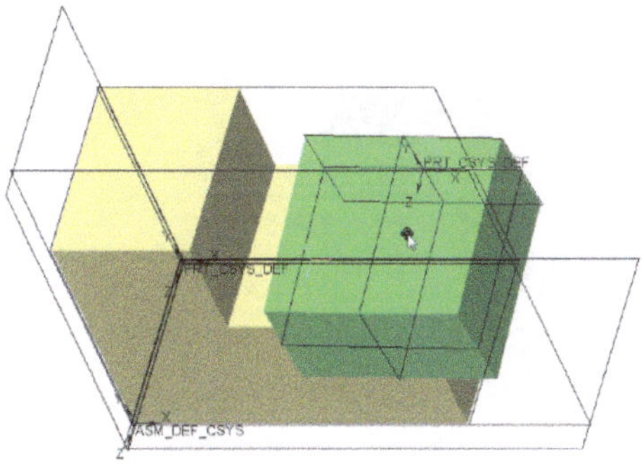

8. Click **Close** on the **Drag** dialog.

Again, you can use the **Drag Components** command to detect the collision between the components.

Editing and Updating Assemblies

During the design process, the correct design is not achieved on the first attempt. There is always a need to go back and make modifications. Creo Parametric allows you to accomplish this process very easily.

1. To modify a part in an assembly, select it from the graphics window.
2. Click the right mouse button and select **Activate** . It activates the **Part** environment. You can also select **Open** to open the part in a separate window.

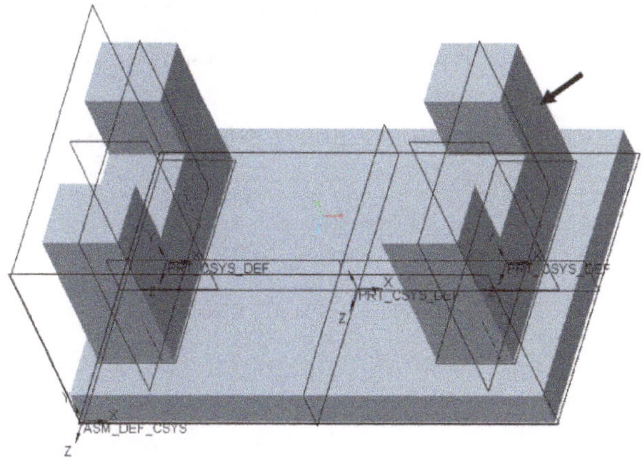

3. Select the feature to edit and select **Edit Definition**.

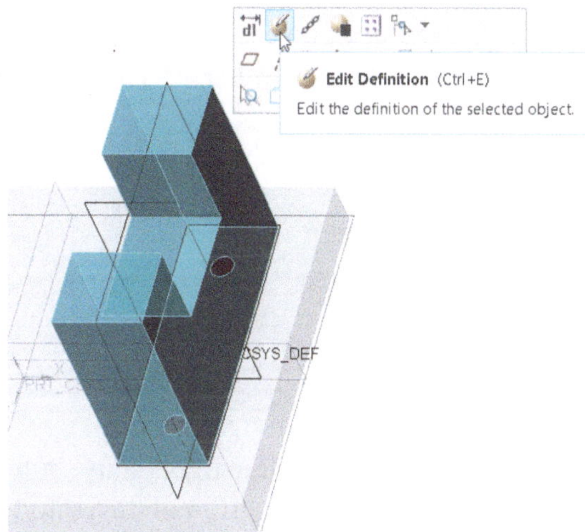

4. To edit the sketch, click the **Placement** tab, and then select the **Edit** button.
5. Click **OK** after editing the sketch.
6. Modify the feature parameters, and then click the green check.

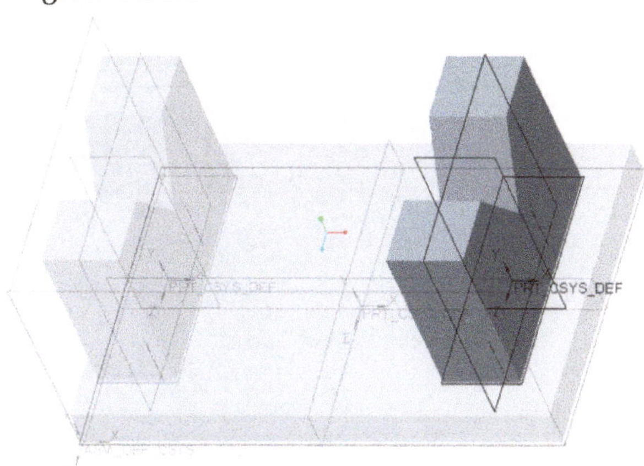

7. In the Model Tree, right-click on **Assembly** and select **Activate** to return to the **Assembly** environment.
8. Right-click in the graphics window and select **Regenerate**.

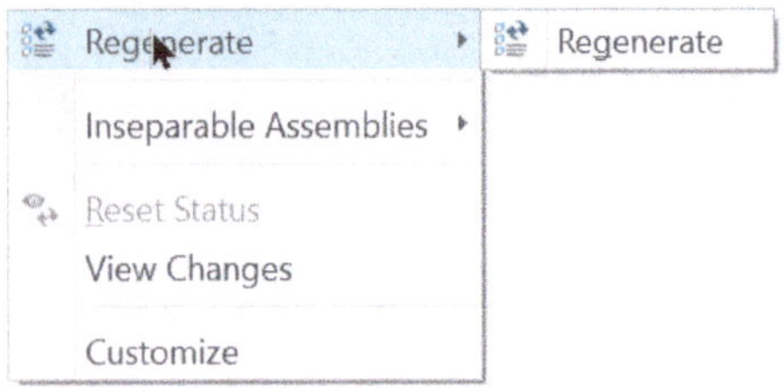

Redefining Constraints

You can also redefine the existing constraints in an assembly. For example, if you want to change the faces that coincide, follow the next steps.

1. In the Model Tree, click the right mouse button on the component to modify, and then select **Edit Definition** . The constraints related to the component appear on the model.
2. Click the right mouse button on the constraint and select **Edit References**.

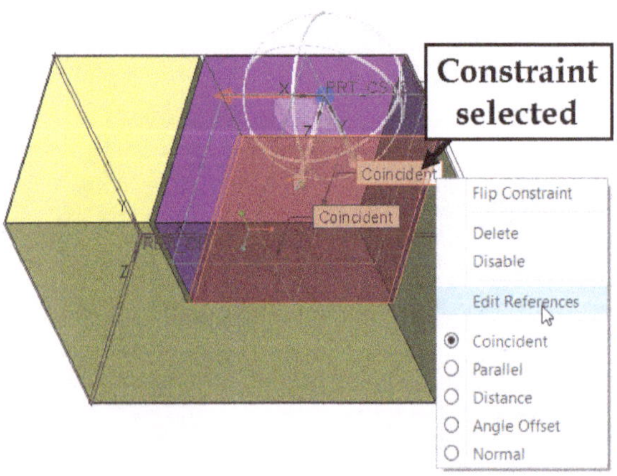

A palette appears on the constraint. You can change the constraint type, orientation, references using this palette.

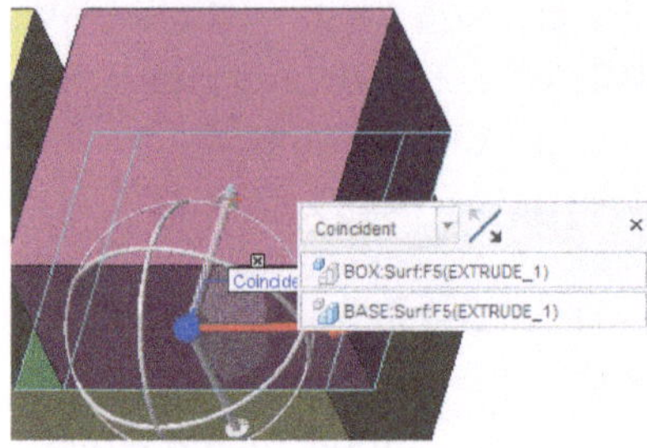

3. Click on the right face of the component.

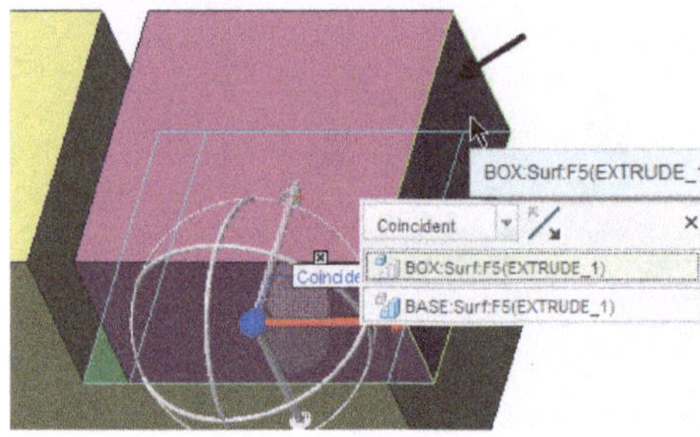

The Coincident constraint is redefined.

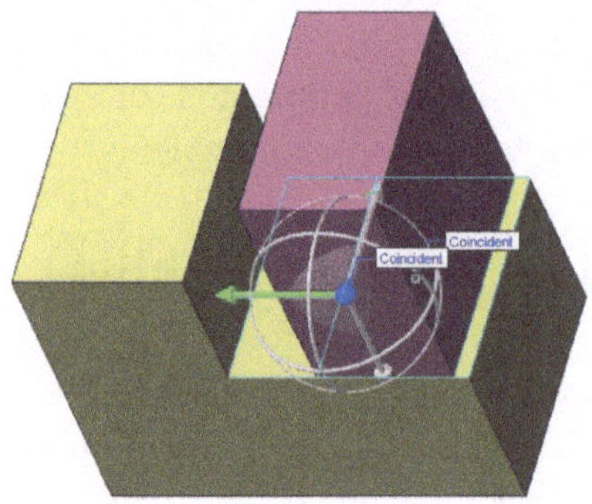

Change Constraint

You can also convert an existing constraint into another type of constraint. For example, if you want to convert the **Coincident** constraint into the **Distance** constraint, follow the next steps.

1. Click the right mouse button on the **Coincident** constraint and select **Distance**.

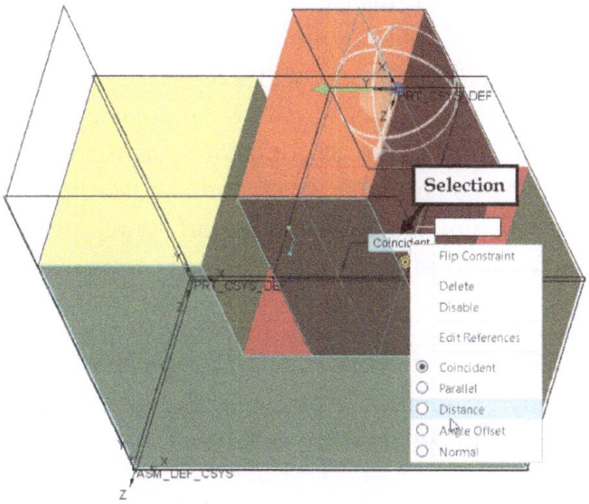

2. Now, drag the Distance handle to change the distance value.
3. Click the green check on the dashboard.

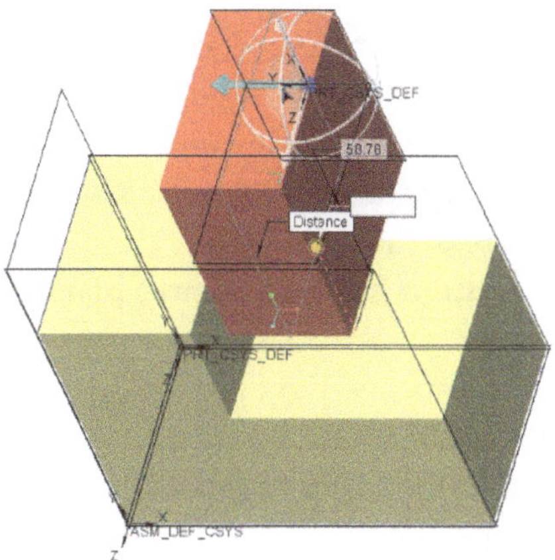

Replace Component

Creo Parametric allows you to replace any component in an assembly. To do this, follow the steps given next.

1. Select the component to replace.
2. Right-click and select **Replace**.

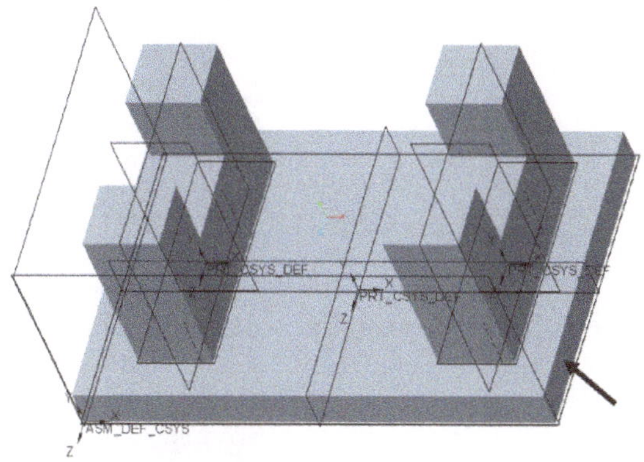

3. On the **Replace** dialog, select **Replace By > Unrelated Component**.
4. Click the folder icon on the dialog and go to the location of the replacement component.
5. Select the component and click **Open**.

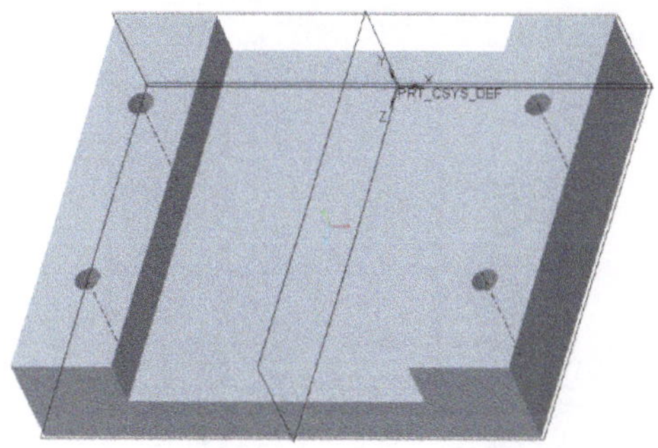

6. Click **OK** to replace the component.

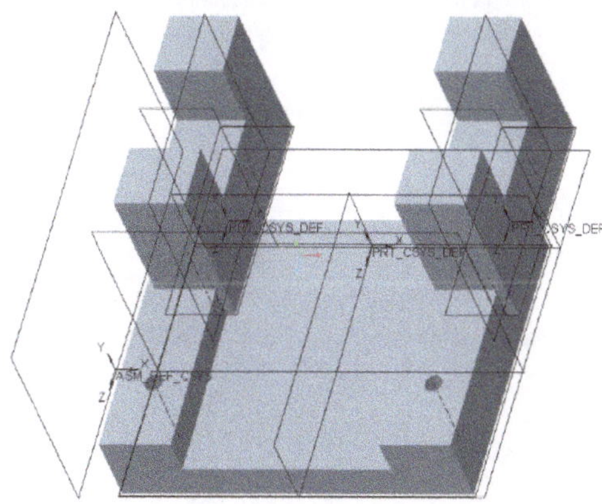

7. Now, you can redefine the existing constraints or delete them and define new constraints. In this case, you can redefine the existing constraints. In the Model Tree, click on the affected component and select **Edit Definition**.

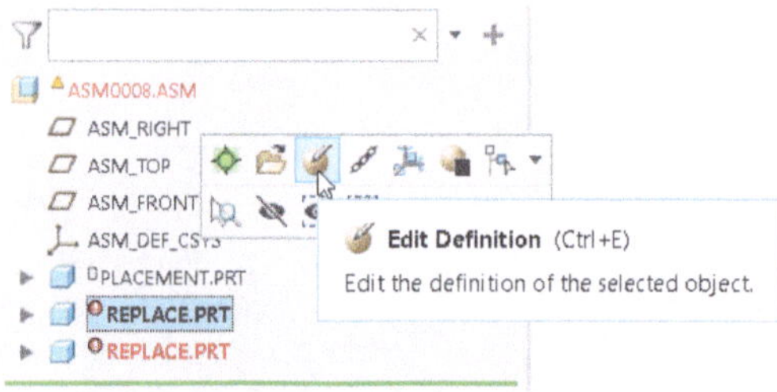

8. Select the references on the replacement part.

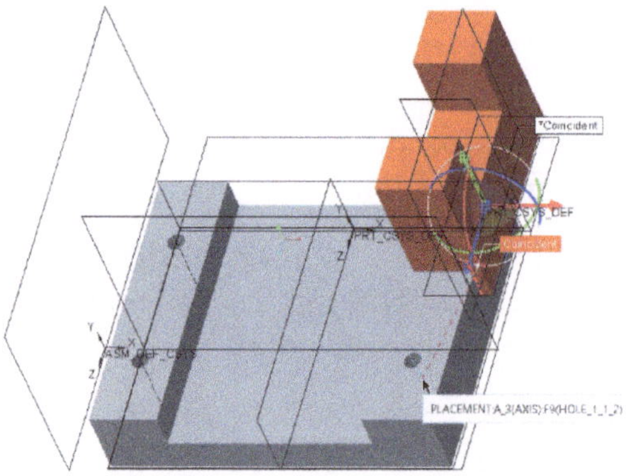

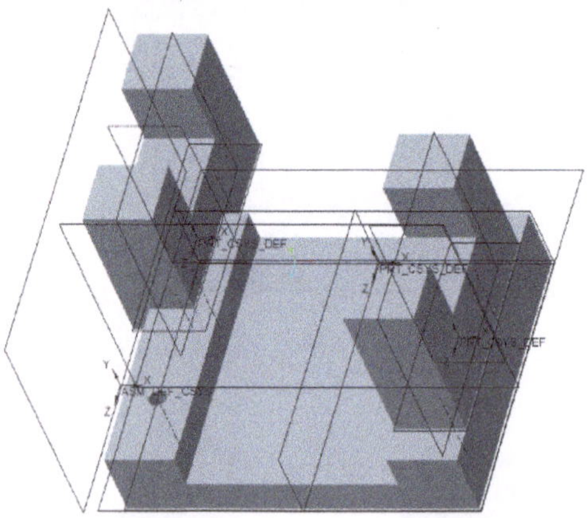

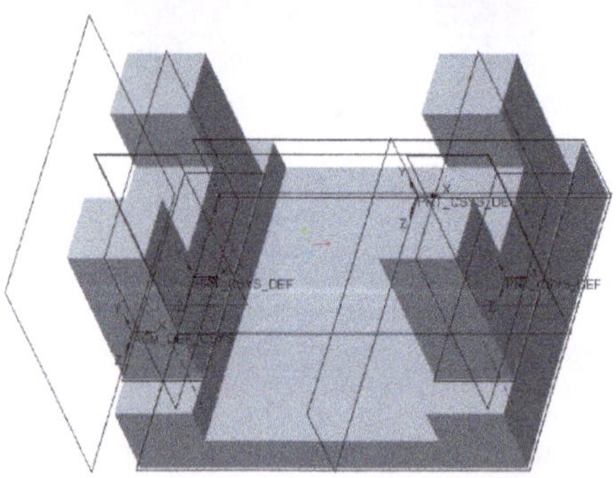

Top-Down Assembly Design

In Creo Parametric, there are two methods to create an assembly. The method you are probably familiar with is to create individual components and then insert them into an assembly. This method is known as Bottom-Up Assembly Design. The second method is called Top-Down Assembly Design. In this method, you will create individual components within the Assembly environment. It allows you to design an individual part while considering how it will interact with other assembly components. There are several advantages to Top-Down Assembly Design. As you design a part within the assembly, you can be sure that it will fit properly. You can also use reference geometry from the other components.

Creating a New Part in the Assembly

Top-down assembly design can be used to add new parts to an already existing assembly.

1. To create a part at the assembly level using the Top-down Design, activate the **Create** command (click the **Create** button on the **Component** panel).
2. In the **Create Component** dialog, click **Type > Part**.
3. Type the name of the component and click **OK**.
4. On the **Creation Options** dialog, select **Creation Method > Locate default datums**.
5. Select **Locate Datums Method > Three planes** and click **OK**.
6. Select the Front, Top, and right planes. A part file is created.
7. Now, use the part modeling commands and create the part geometry.

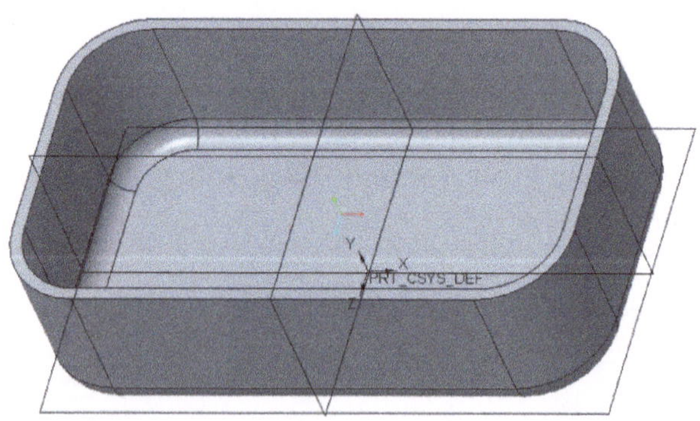

8. In the Model Tree, click on the **Assembly** and select **Activate**.
9. To create the second component, activate the **Create** command and select **Part** on the **Create Component** dialog.
10. Type-in the component name and click **OK**.

11. On the **Creation Options** dialog, select **Create features** and click **OK**.
12. You can now create the part by using the first part's faces and edges as a reference. For example, activate the **Sketch** command and select the top face of the first part.

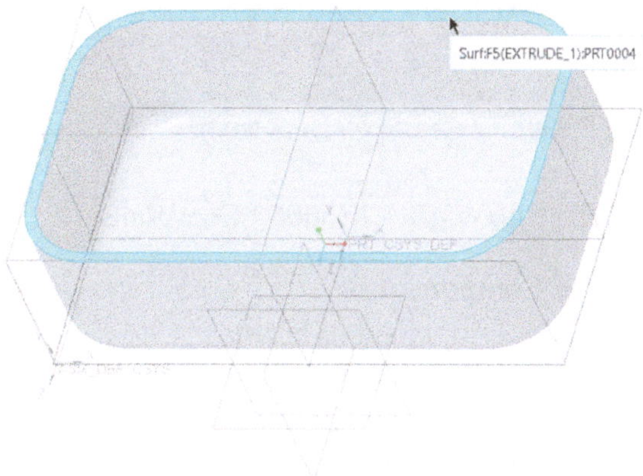

13. Select the Front and Right planes as references and click the **Sketch** button.
14. Activate the **Project** command and project the outer edges of the first component.

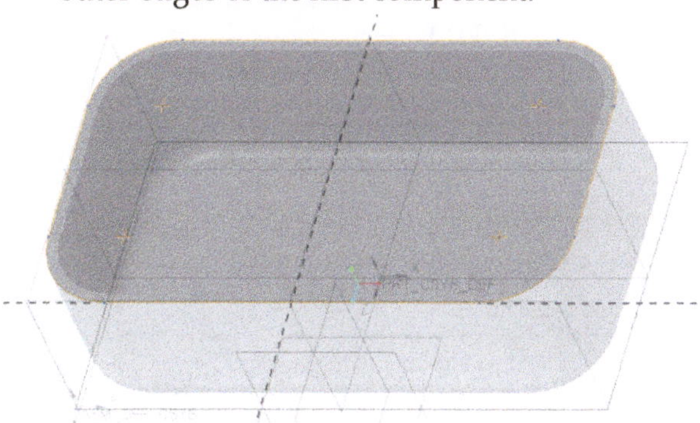

15. Click **OK** on the ribbon.
16. Use the sketch to create an *Extrude* feature.

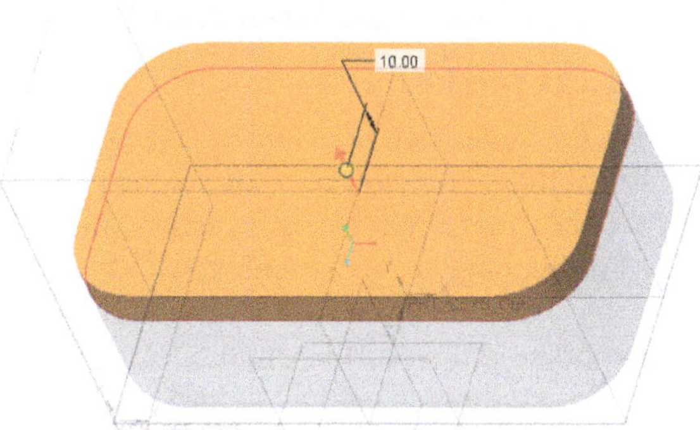

17. Activate the first component and modify the model.

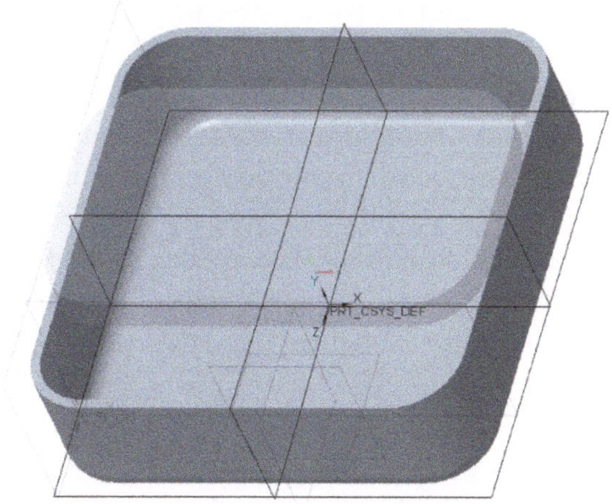

18. At the bottom of the window, click the **Regenerate** button.

19. Return to the **Assembly** environment to see the updated second component.

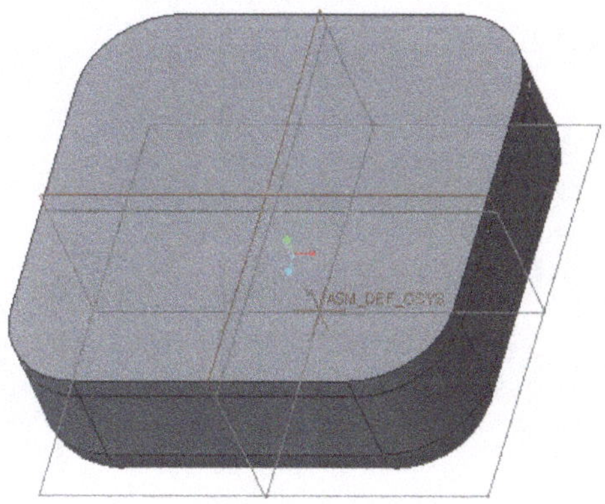

20. To save the assembly and its components, click **Save** on the Quick Access Toolbar.
21. Define the location and file name of the assembly, and then click **OK**. The assembly and its components are saved.

Sub-assemblies

The use of sub-assemblies has many advantages in Creo Parametric. Sub-assemblies make large assemblies easier to manage. They make it easy for multiple users to collaborate on a single large assembly design. They can also affect the way you document a large assembly design in 2D drawings. For these reasons, you need to create sub-assemblies in a variety of ways. The easiest way to create a sub-assembly is to insert an existing assembly into another assembly. Next, apply constraints to constrain the assembly. The process of applying constraints is also simplified. You are required to apply constraints between only one part of a sub-assembly and a part of the main assembly. Also, you can easily hide a group of components with the help of sub-assemblies. To do this, right-click on a sub-assembly in the Model Tree, and then select **Hide** .

Subassembly

Main Assembly

Mirroring Components

When designing symmetric assemblies, Creo Parametric can help you save time and capture design intent. For example, you can mirror the component as shown instead of inserting it again.

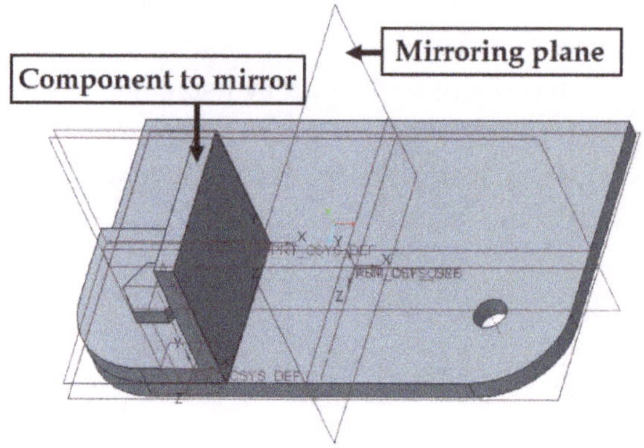

1. On the ribbon, click **Model > Component > Mirror Component** .
2. Select the component to mirror.
3. Select the mirroring plane.
4. On the **Mirror Component** dialog, select **New Component > Create a new model.**
5. Type-in **Mirrored_bracket** in the **Name** box and click **OK.**
6. Select **Mirror > Geometry with features.**
7. Check the **Preview** option to preview the mirrored component.
8. Click **OK** to mirror the component.

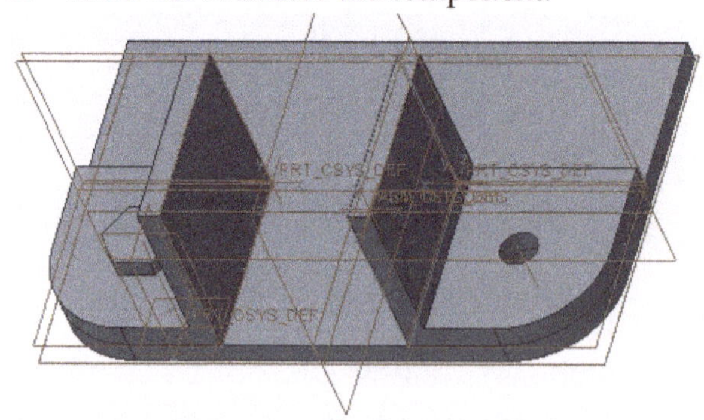

Creating Sub-assemblies from individual parts

In addition to creating sub-assemblies and inserting them into another assembly, you can also take individual parts that already exist in an assembly and convert them into a sub-assembly.

1. Press and hold the **Shift** key and select parts from the assembly from the Model Tree.
2. Click the right mouse button and select **Move to sub-assembly.**

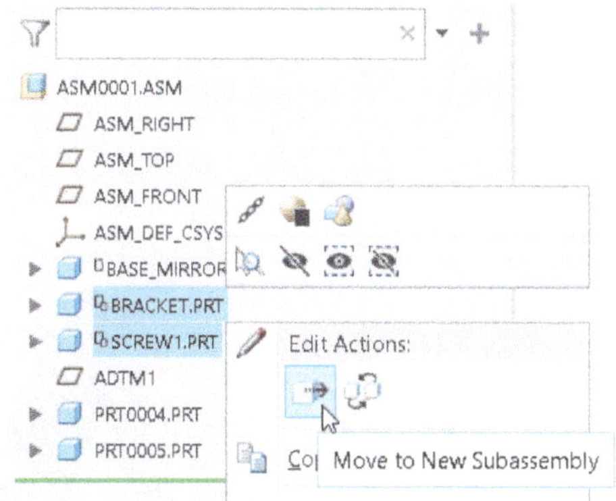

3. On this dialog, type in the name of the sub-assembly and click **OK**.

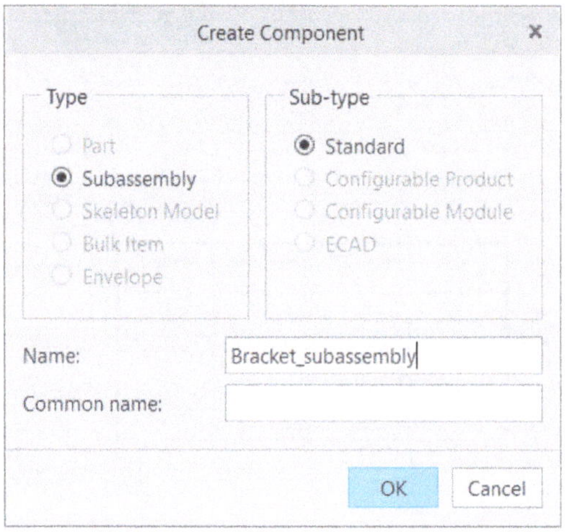

4. On the **Creation Options** dialog, select **Locate default datums** and **Align csys to csys**.

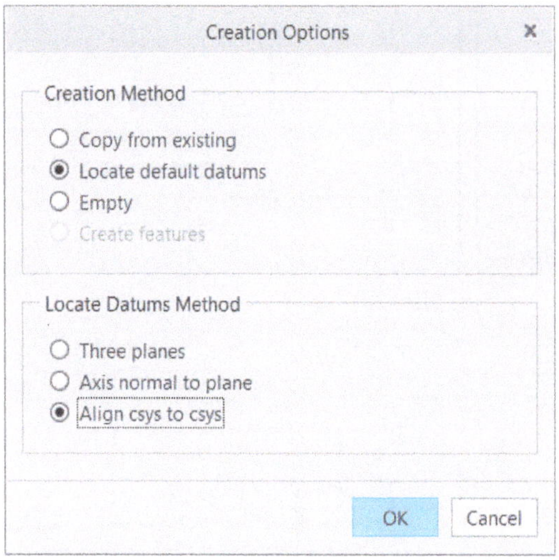

5. Click **OK**.
6. Select the Coordinate system of the assembly. The selected components are moved to the sub-assembly.

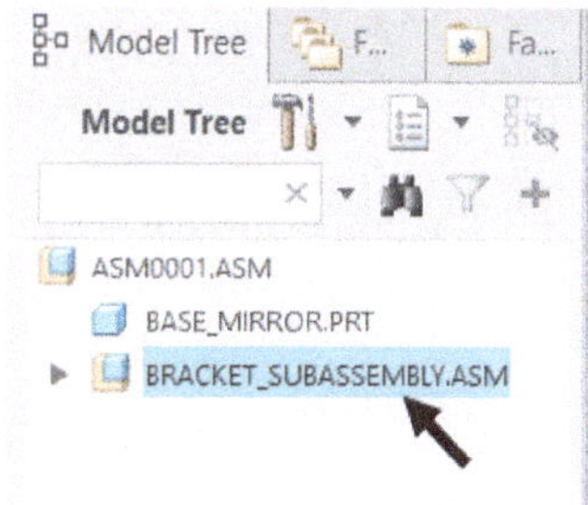

Mirroring Sub-assemblies

Similar to mirroring components, you can also mirror sub-assemblies of an assembly.

1. On the ribbon, click **Model > Component > Mirror Component**.

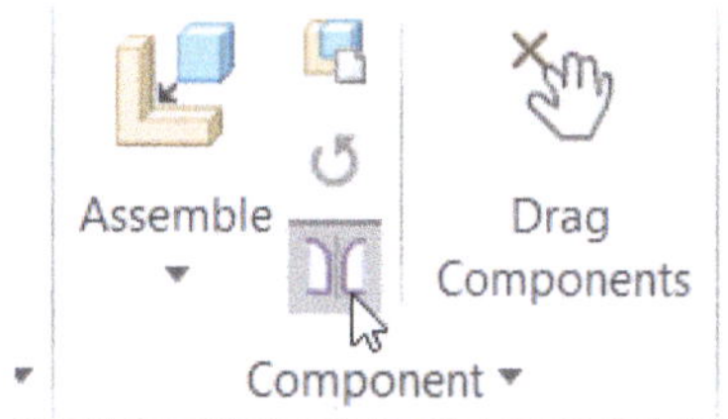

2. On the **Mirror Component** dialog, type in the name of the assembly in the **File name** box.
3. Check the **Geometry dependent** and **Placement dependent** options and select the sub-assembly.

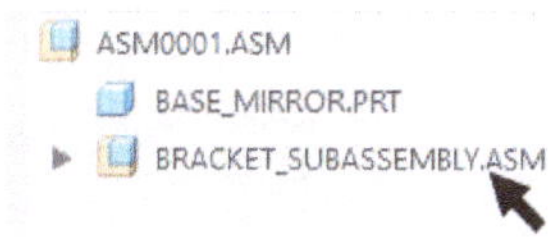

4. Select the right plane.
5. Check the **Preview** option and click **OK** to mirror the subassembly.

Examples

Example 1 (Bottom-Up Assembly)

In this example, you will create the assembly shown next.

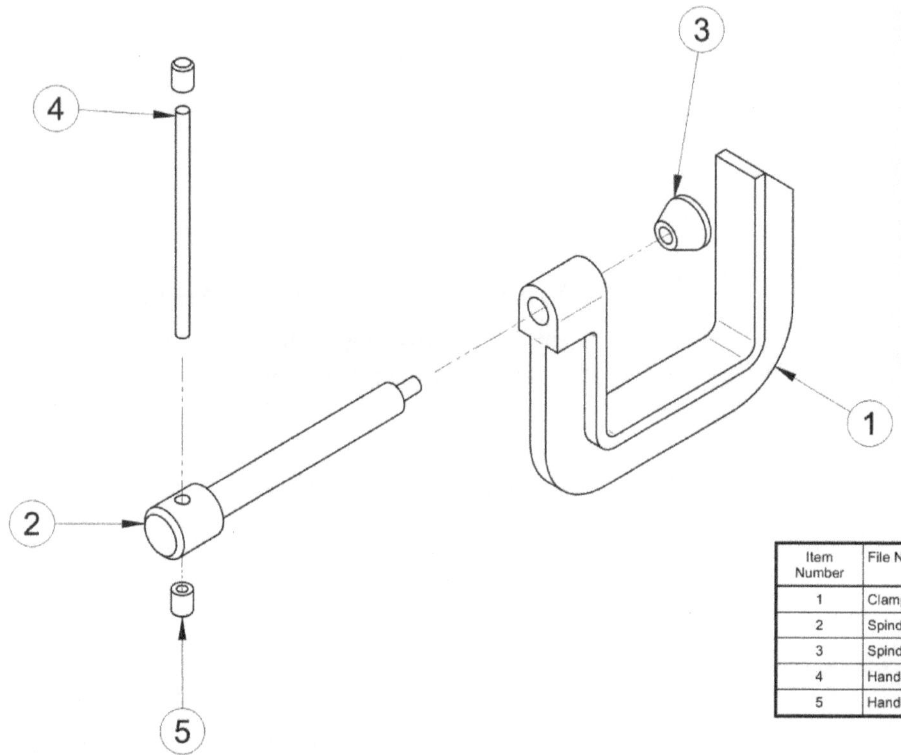

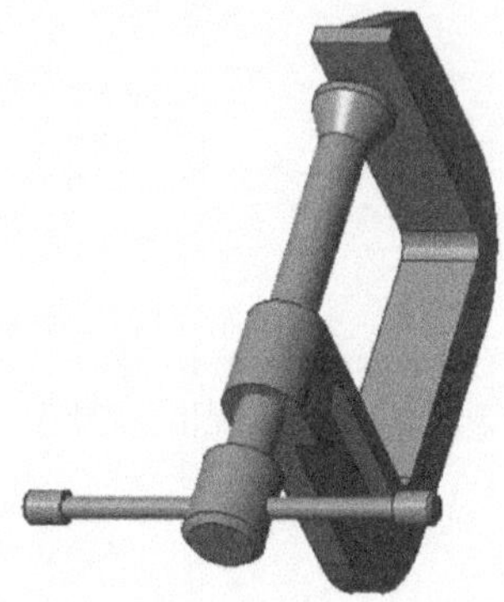

Item Number	File Name (no extension)	Quantity
1	Clamp Jaw	1
2	Spindle	1
3	Spindle Cap	1
4	Handle	1
5	Handle Cap	2

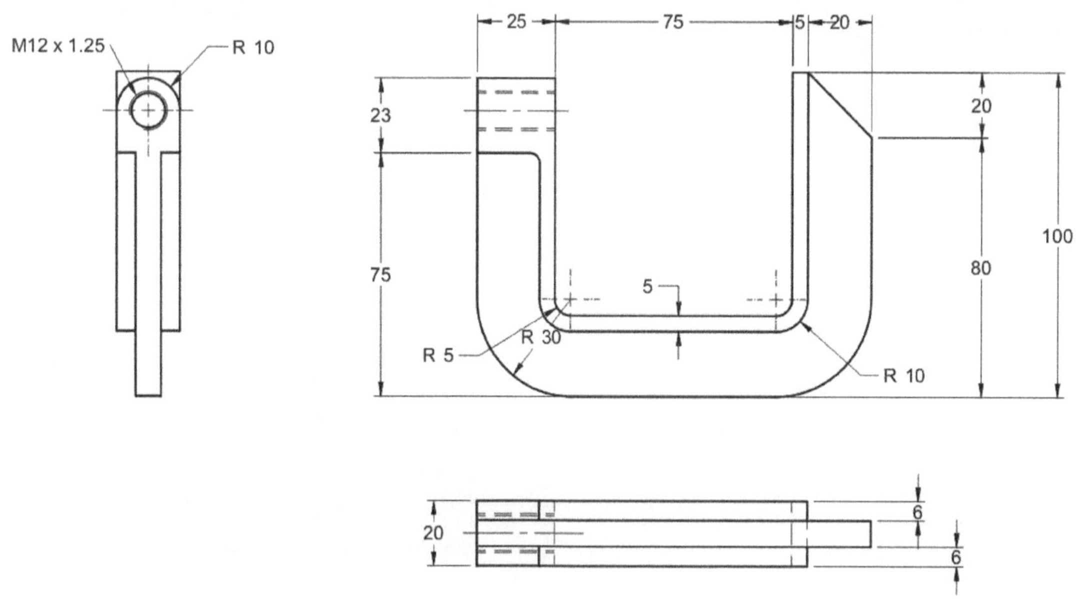

CLAMP JAW

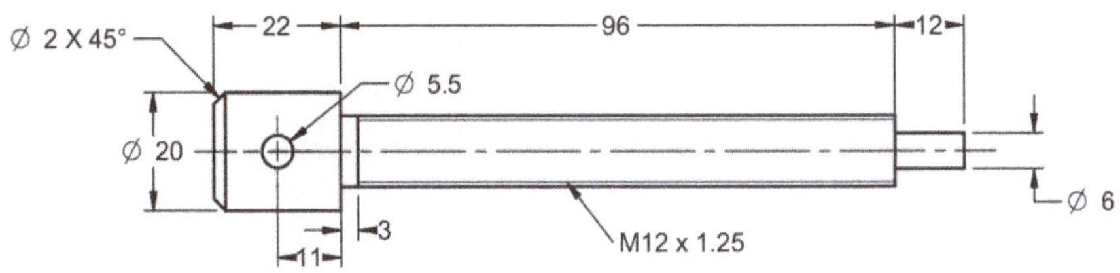

SPINDLE

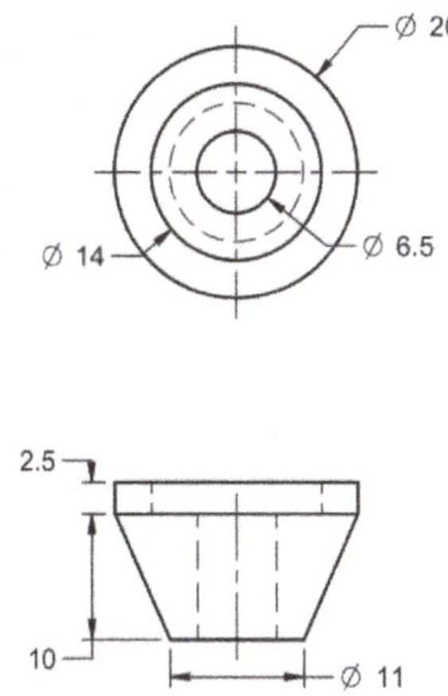

SPINDLE CAP

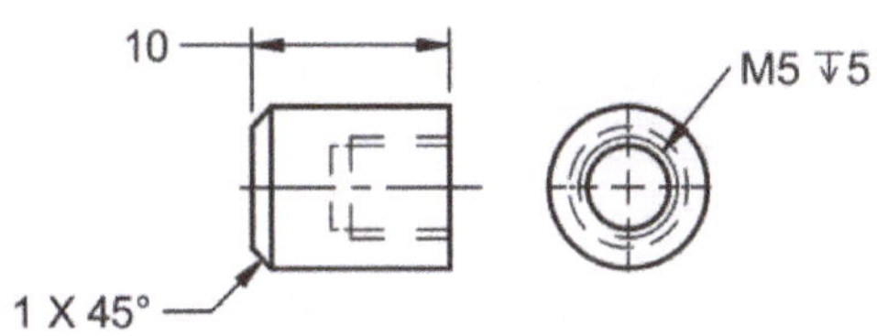

HANDLE CAP

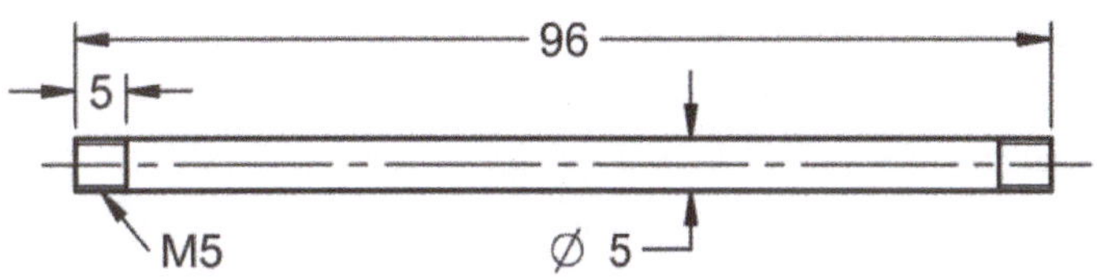

HANDLE

1. Create and save all the components of the assembly in a single folder. Name this folder as *G-Clamp*. Close all the files.

If you cannot create the components, you can download them from the companion website.

2. Start **Creo Parametric 11.0.**
3. Set the *G-Clamp* folder as the current working directory.
4. On the Quick Access Toolbar, click the **New** button.
5. On the **New** dialog, select **Type > Assembly**.
6. Select **Sub-Type > Design**.
7. Type-in *G-Clamp* in the **Name** box and uncheck the **Use default template** option.
8. Click **OK.**
9. On the **New File Options** dialog, select the **mmks_asm_design_abs** option and click **OK.**
10. On the ribbon, click **Model** tab > **Component** panel > **Assemble** drop-down > **Assemble** .
11. Select *Clamp-Jaw.prt* and click **Open**.
12. On the **Component Placement** dashboard, select the **Default** option from the **Current constraint** drop-down.

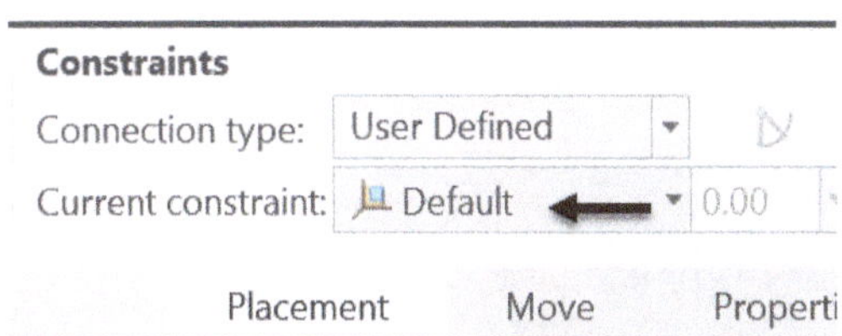

13. Click the green check on the dashboard. It fixes the component at the origin.

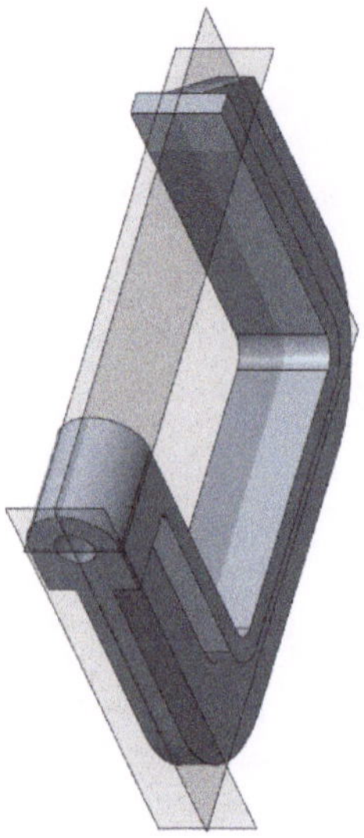

14. On the ribbon, click **Model** tab > **Component** panel > **Assemble** drop-down > **Assemble** .
15. Select *Spindle.prt*, and then click **Open**.
16. Select the cylindrical faces of the spindle and clamp jaw.

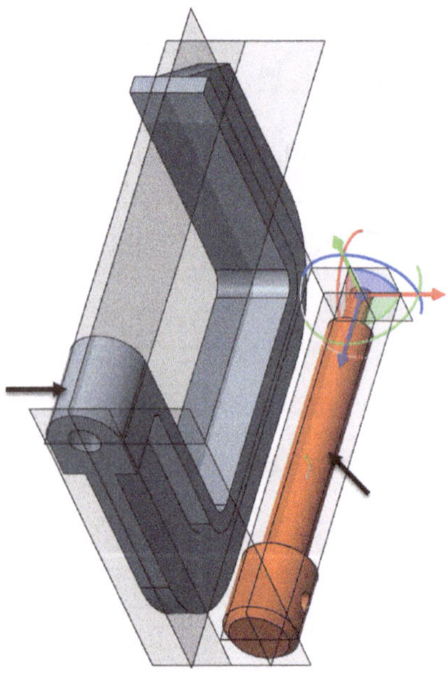

17. On the **Component Placement** dashboard, select the **Coincident** constraint.

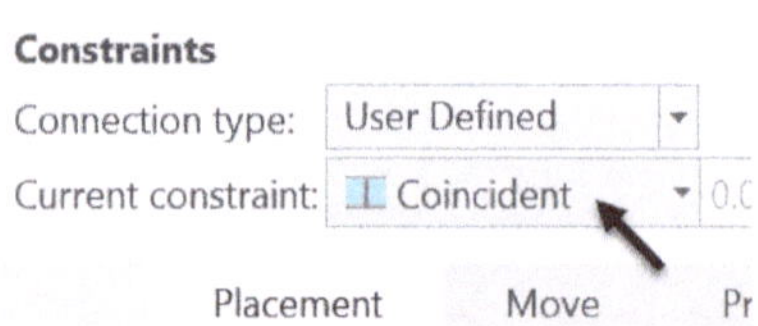

18. Click and drag the blue arrow displayed on the spindle. It will move the spindle forward.

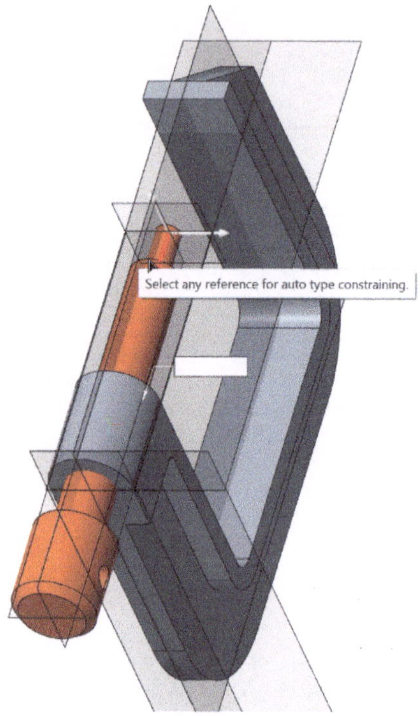

19. Zoom in to the back portion of the spindle and select its horizontal plane.
20. Select the vertical plane of the clamp jaw.

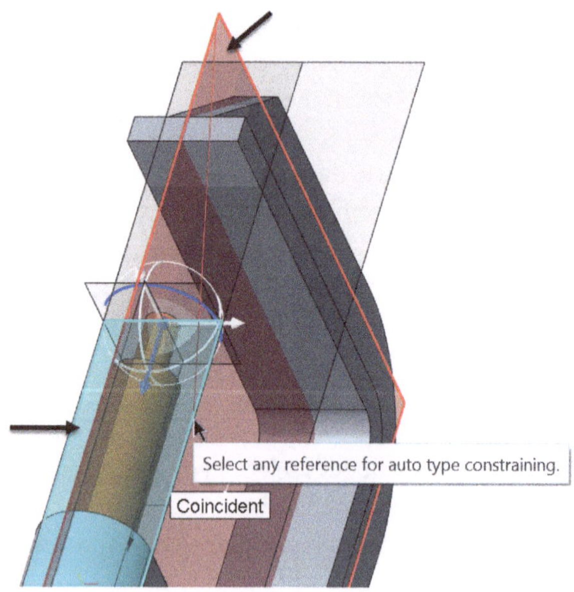

21. On the **Component Placement** dashboard, select the **Parallel** constraint.

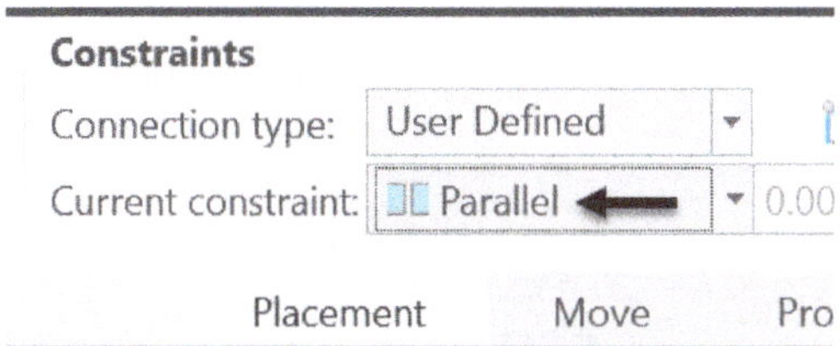

22. Zoom in to the front portion of the spindle and select its front face.
23. Select the front face of the clamp jaw. You will notice that the Coincident constraint is applied between the two faces.

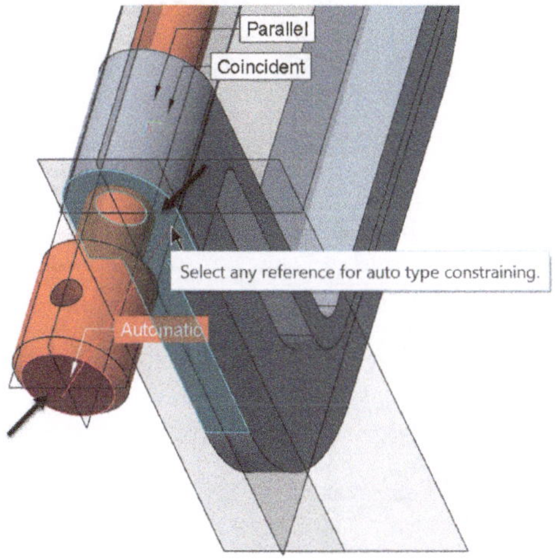

24. Double-click on the **Coincident** constraint.
25. Select the **Distance** option from the drop-down.

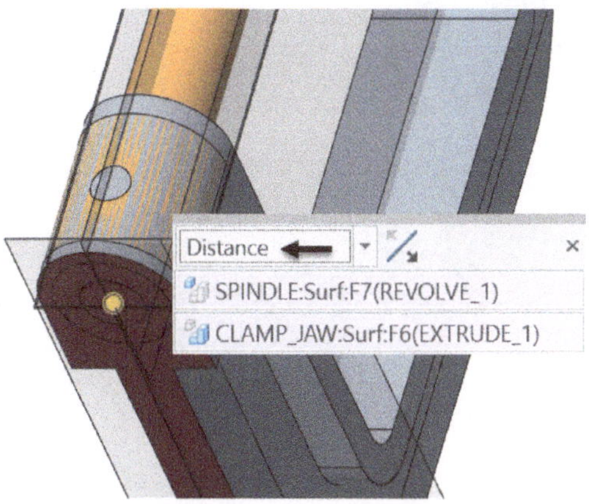

26. On the **Component Placement** dashboard, type-in 40 in the offset box.

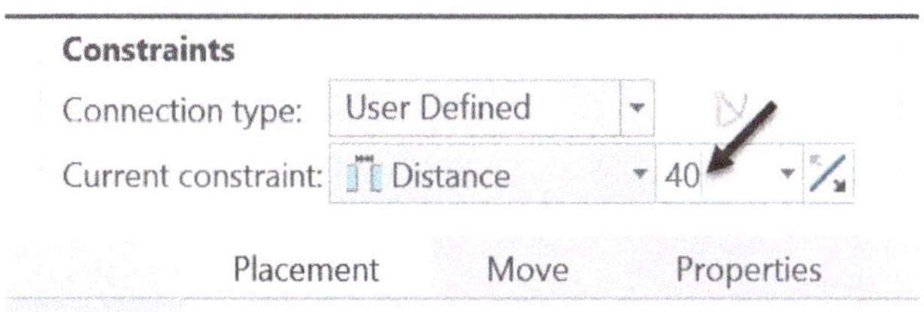

You will notice that the Status on the dashboard changes to Fully Constrained.

27. Click the green check to apply the coincident constraint.

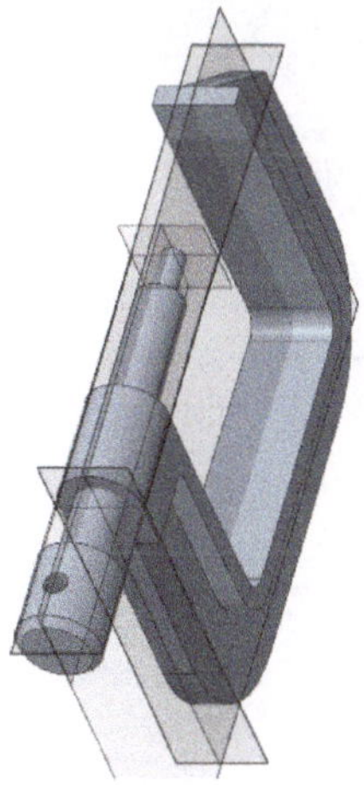

28. On the ribbon, click **Model** tab > **Component** panel > **Assemble** drop-down > **Assemble** .
29. Select *Spindle-Cap.prt*, and then click **Open**.
30. Select the cylindrical faces of the spindle-cap and spindle.

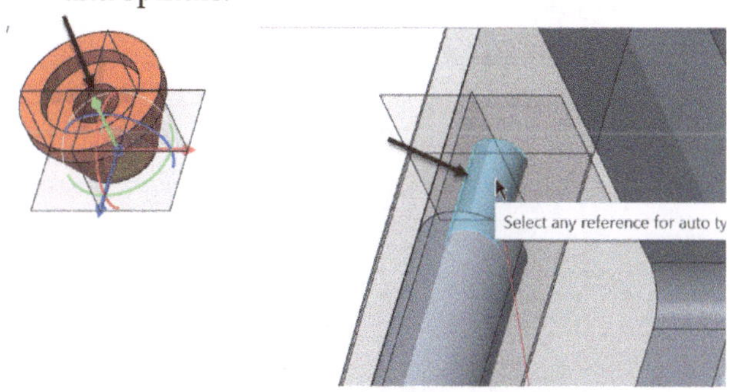

31. On the **Component Placement** dashboard, select the **Coincident** constraint.
32. Click and drag the green handle of the spindle-cap. It moves the spindle-cap.

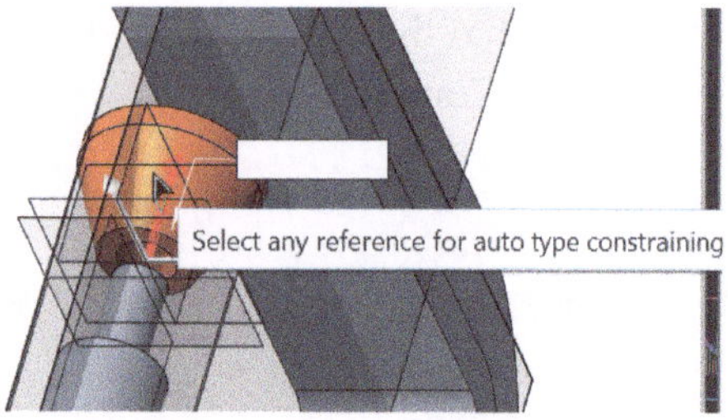

33. Select the flat face of the spindle-cap, as shown below.

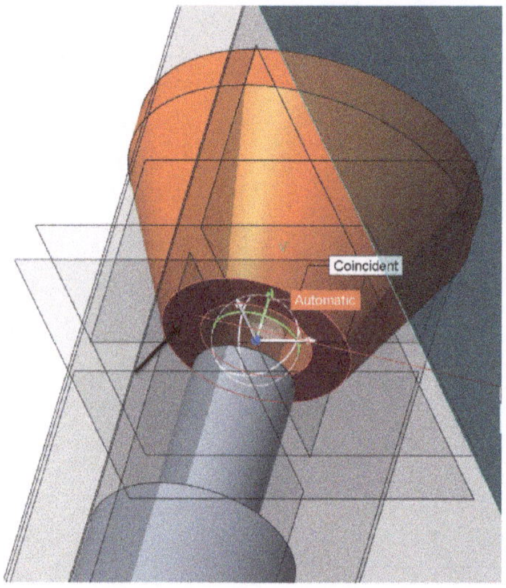

34. Press and hold the middle mouse button and drag the pointer. It rotates the assembly.
35. Select the flat face of the spindle, as shown.

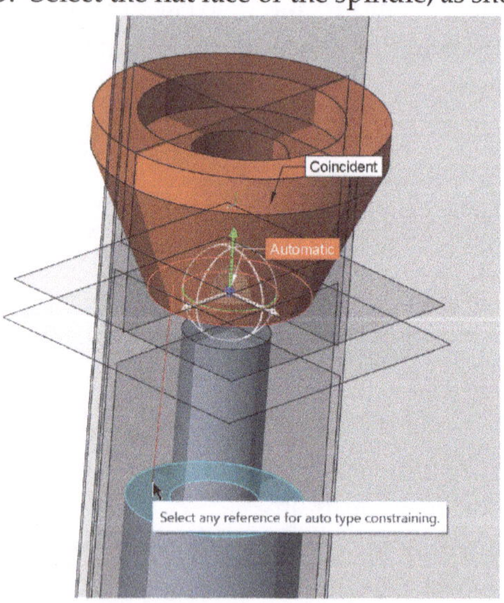

36. On the **Component Placement** tab, select the **Coincident** constraint. It fully-constrains the spindle-cap.

37. Click the green check  on the dashboard.

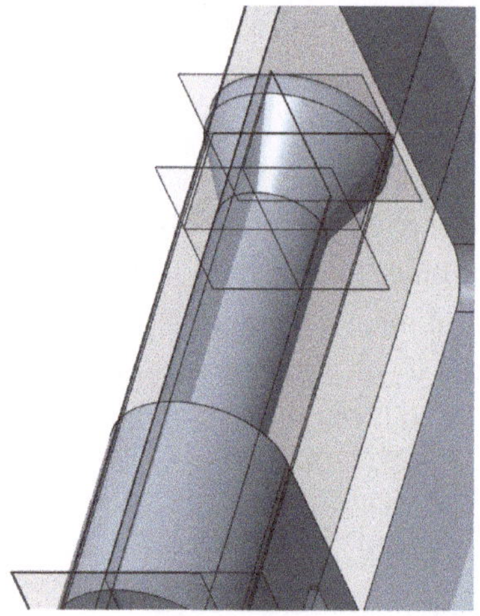

38. Insert the *Handle.prt* into the assembly.

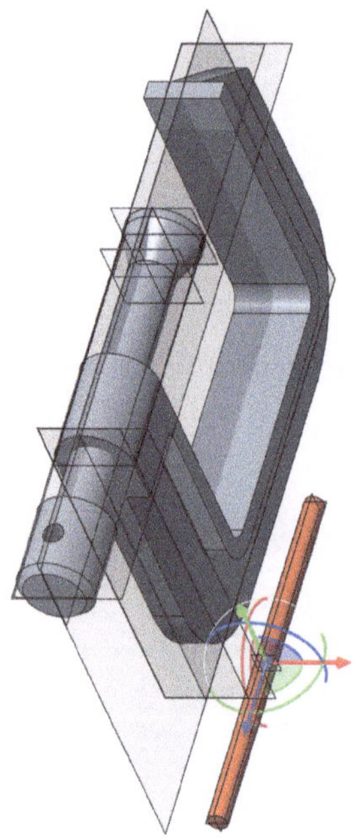

39. Select the cylindrical faces of the handle and the hole on the spindle.

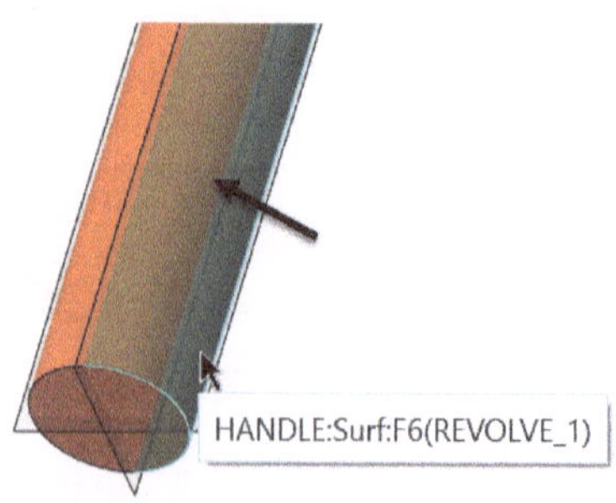

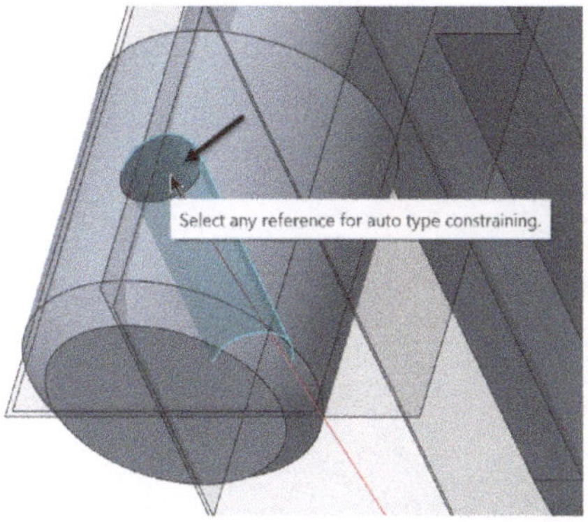

40. Apply the **Coincident** constraint.
41. Zoom in to the handle and select the plane located at the middle of the handle.

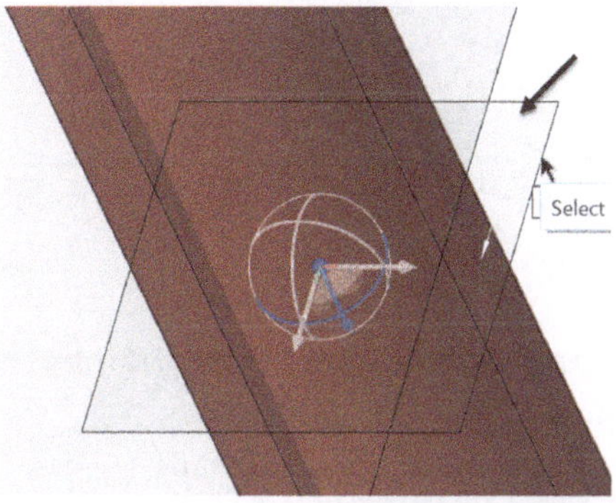

42. Select the vertical plane of the spindle.

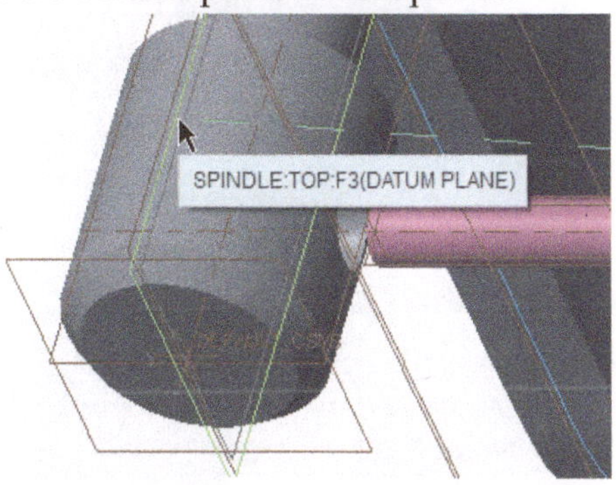

43. Apply the **Coincident** constraint. It fully-constrains the handle.

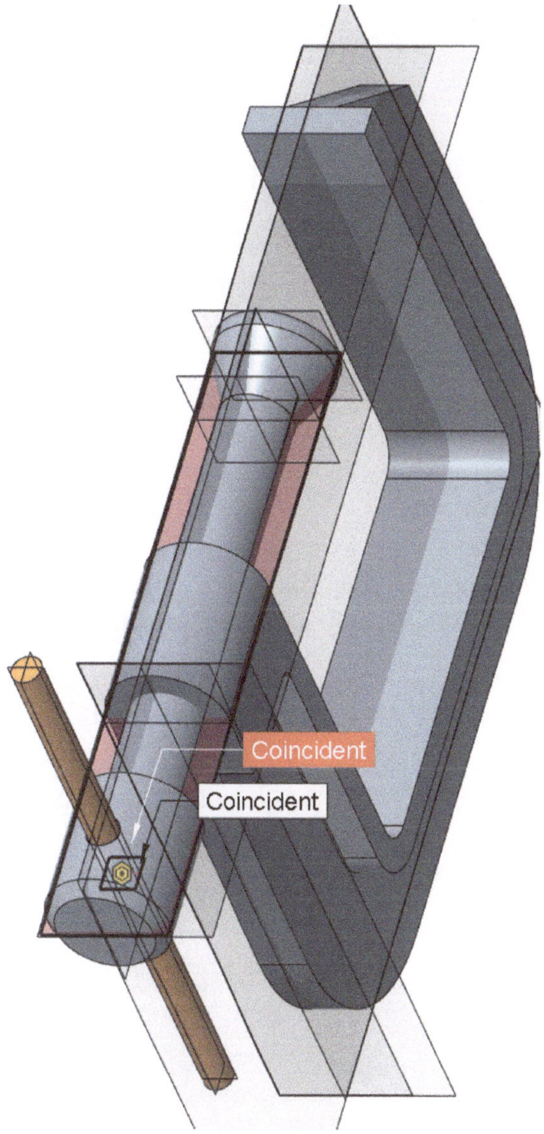

44. Click the green check on the dashboard.
45. Insert the *Handle-cap.prt* into the Assembly window.

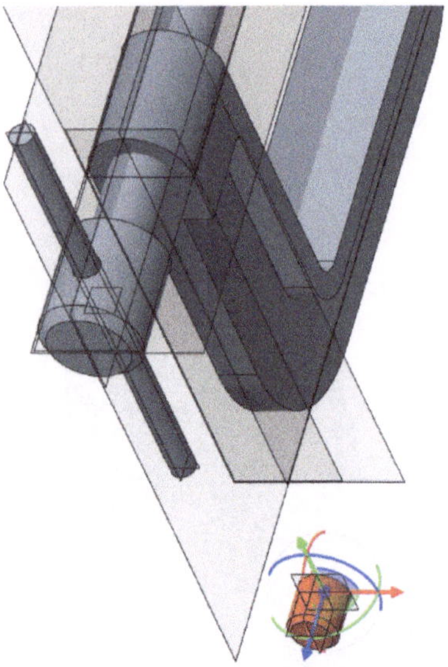

46. Select the cylindrical faces of the handle and handle-cap and apply the **Coincident** constraint.

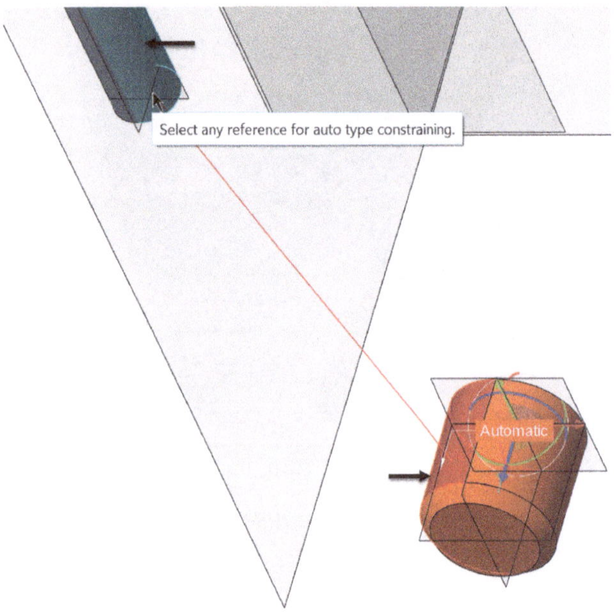

47. Apply the **Distance** constraint between the flat faces of the handle-cap and handle. The offset distance is -5.

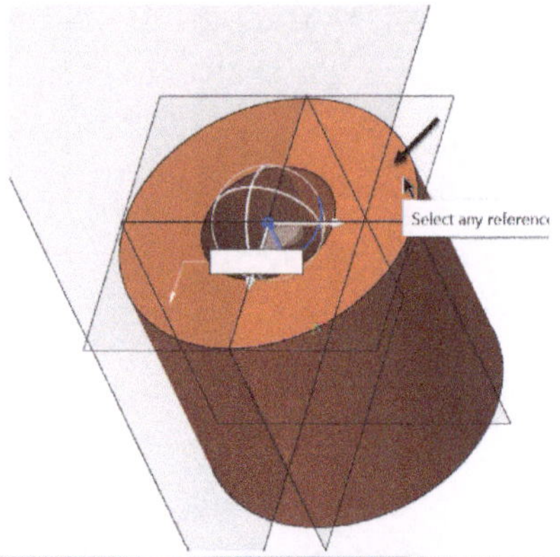

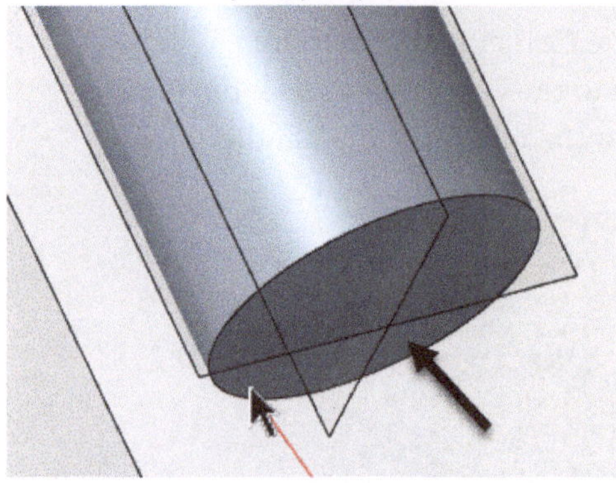

48. Click the **Change orientation of constraint** icon, if required.
49. Click the green check on the dashboard.

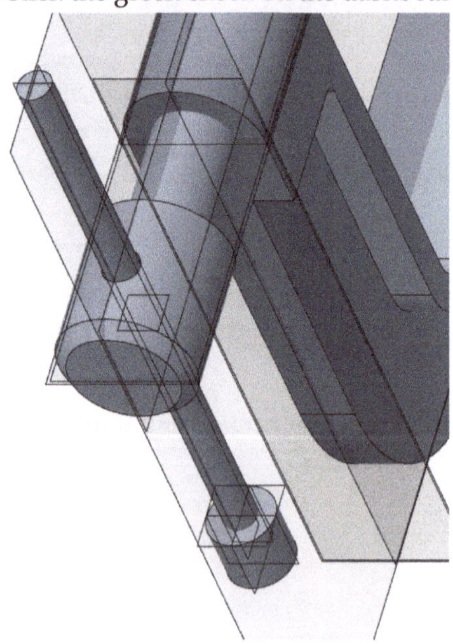

50. Likewise, assemble another instance of the handle cap.

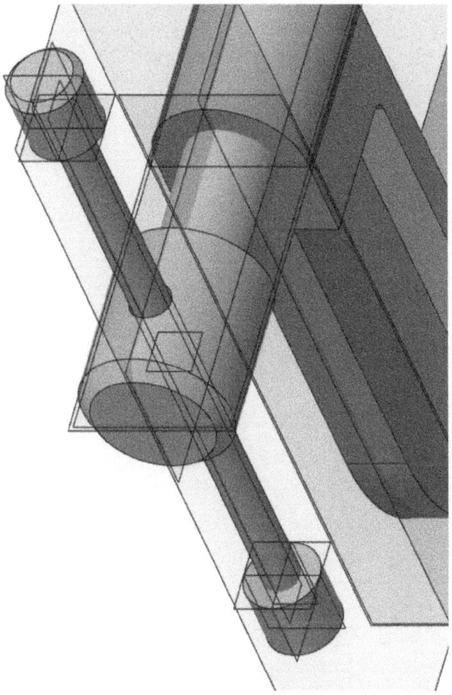

51. Save and close the assembly.

Example 2 (Top-Down Assembly)

In this example, you will create the assembly shown next.

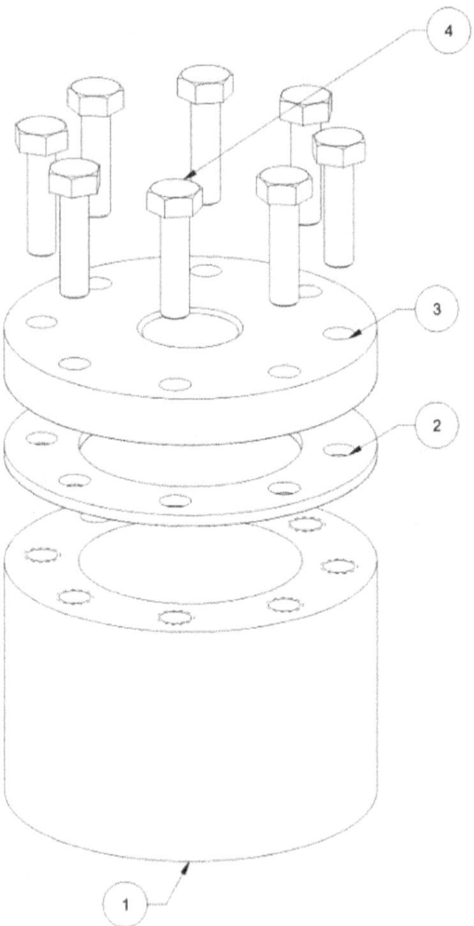

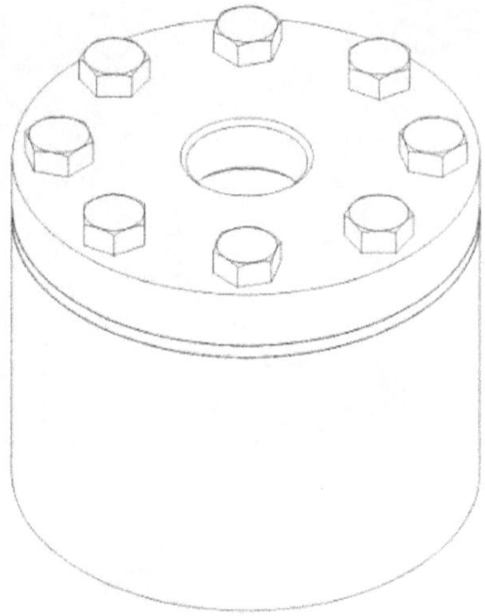

4	HEX BOLT AM,M8X1.25X30	8
3	COVER PLATE	1
2	GASKET	1
1	CYLINDER BASE	1
PC NO	PART NAME	QTY

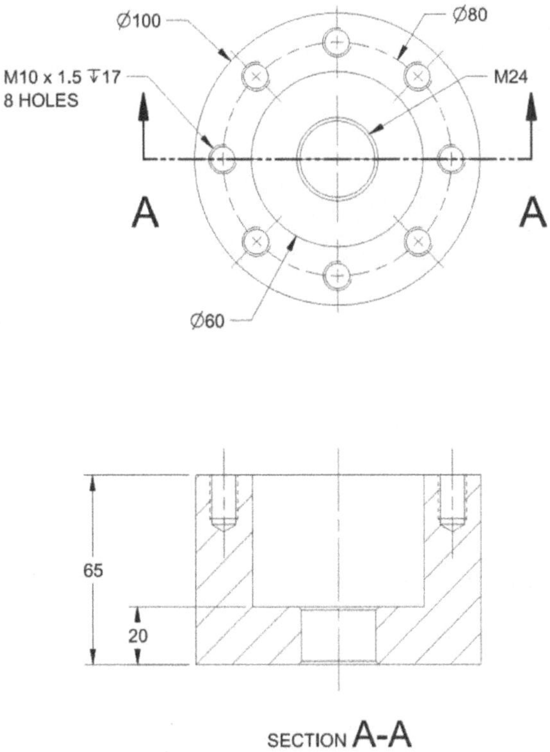

Cylinder Base

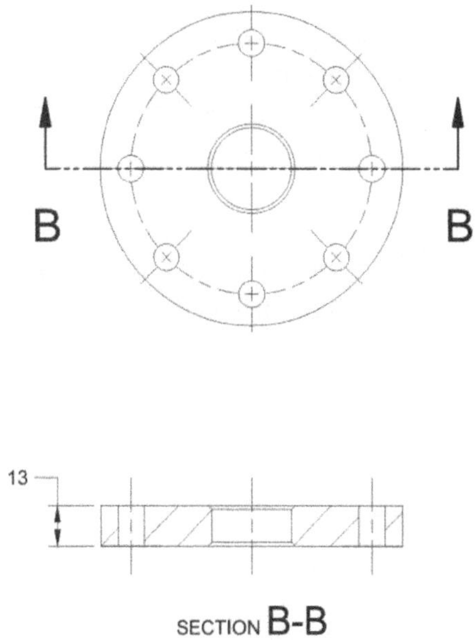

Cover Plate

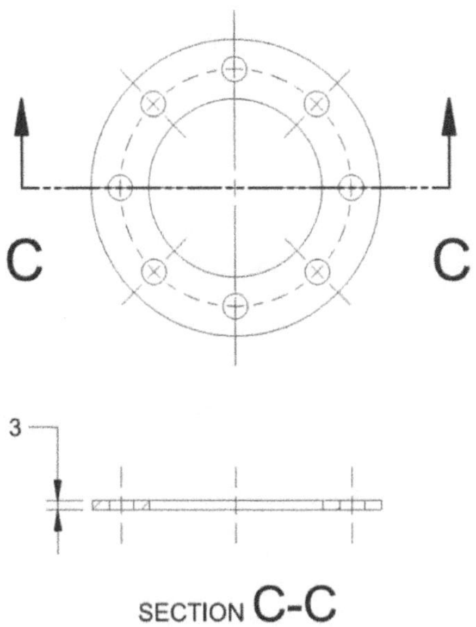

Gasket

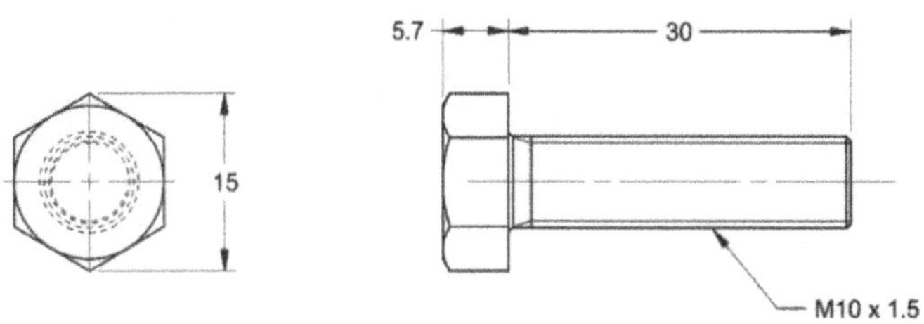

Screw

1. Start **Creo Parametric 11.0.**
2. Create a folder with the name *Pressure Cylinder* and set it as the current working folder.
3. On the Quick Access Toolbar, click the **New** button.
4. On the **New** dialog, select **Type > Assembly**.
5. Select **Sub-Type > Design**.
6. Type-in *Pressure_Cylinder* in the **Name** box and uncheck the **Use default template** option.
7. Click **OK.**
8. On the **New File Options** dialog, select the **mmks_asm_design_abs** template and click **OK.**
9. On the **Graphics** toolbar, click **Datum Display Filters** drop-down and check the **Csys Display** option.

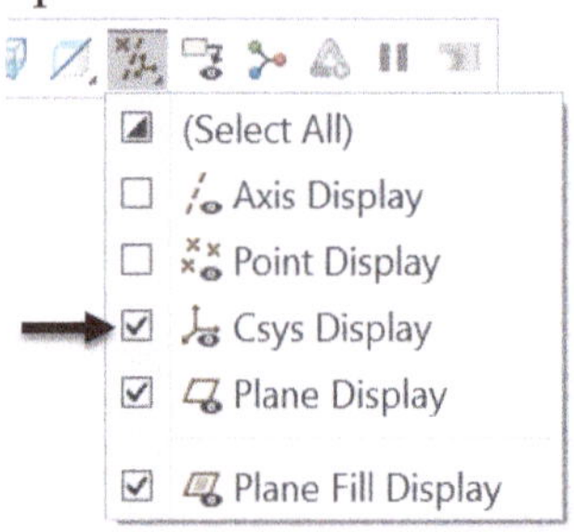

10. On the ribbon, click **Model** tab > **Component** panel > **Create** .
11. Select **Type > Part** from the **Create Component** dialog.
12. Type-in *Cylinder_Base* in the **Name** box and click **OK.**
13. On the **Creation Options** dialog, select **Creation method > Locate default datums.**
14. Select **Locate Datums Method > Align csys to csys.**
15. Click **OK** and select the default coordinate system.

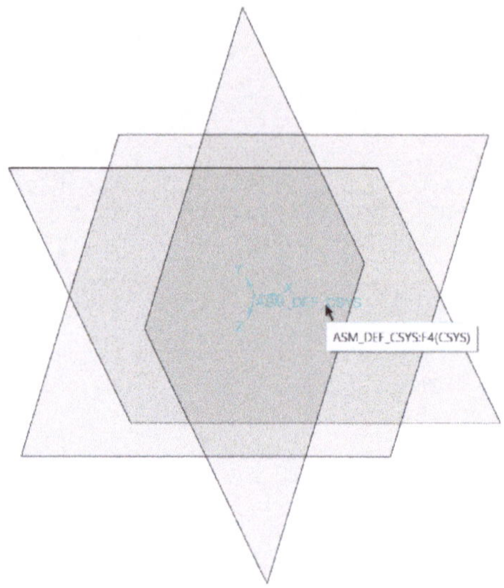

It creates a new part file inside the assembly.

16. Create a sketch on the Front plane and revolve it.

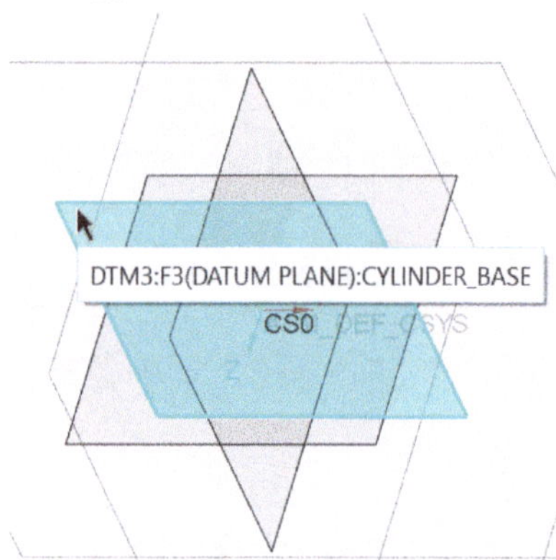

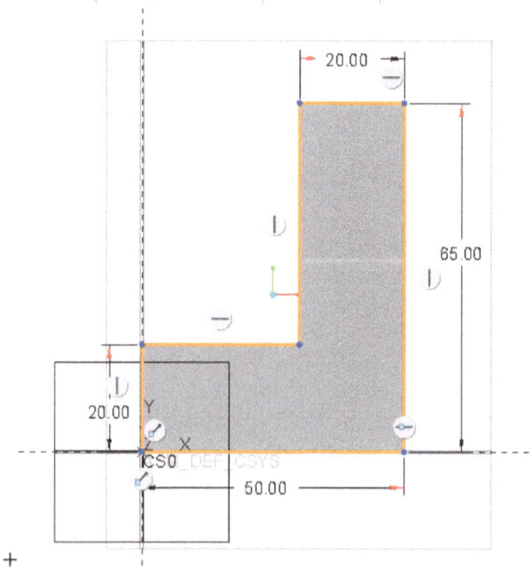

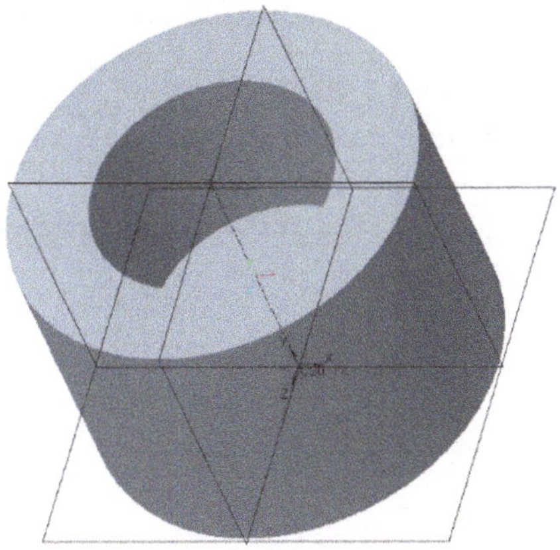

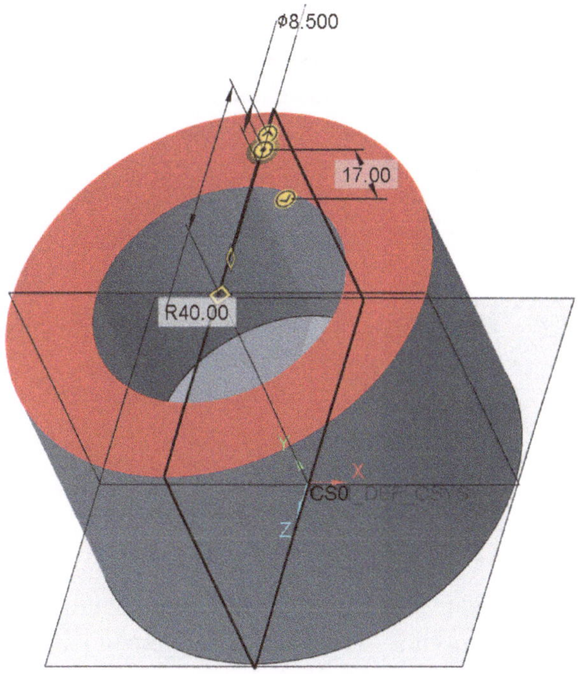

17. Create a threaded hole on the top face of the model.

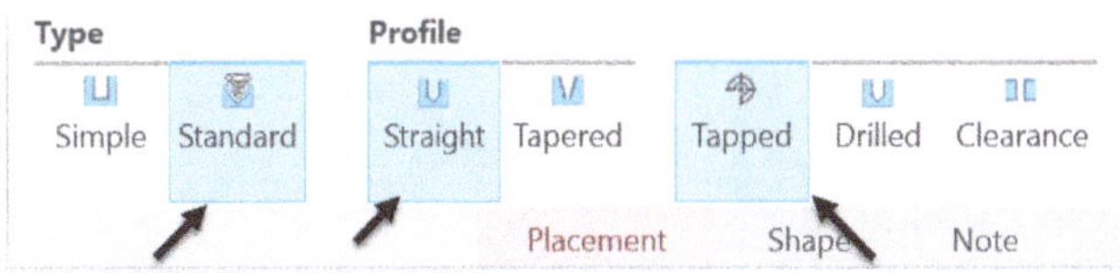

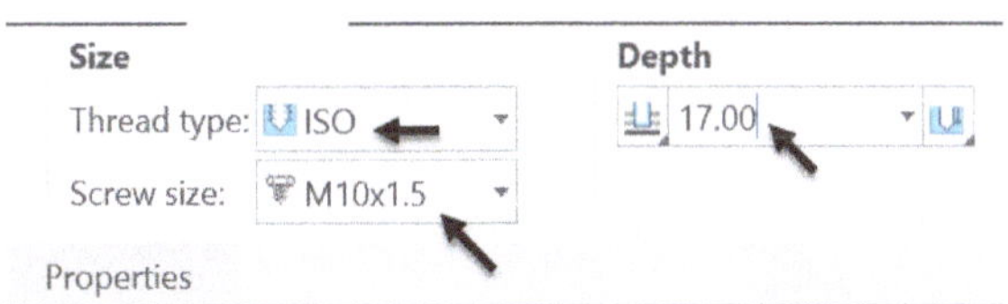

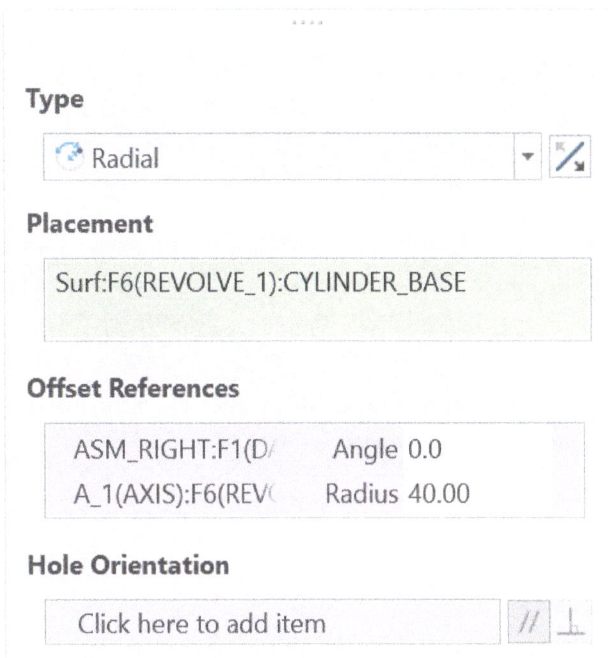

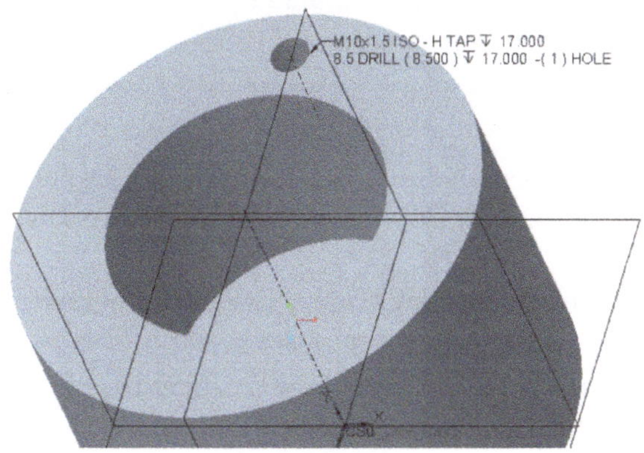

18. Create a Axis pattern of the hole.

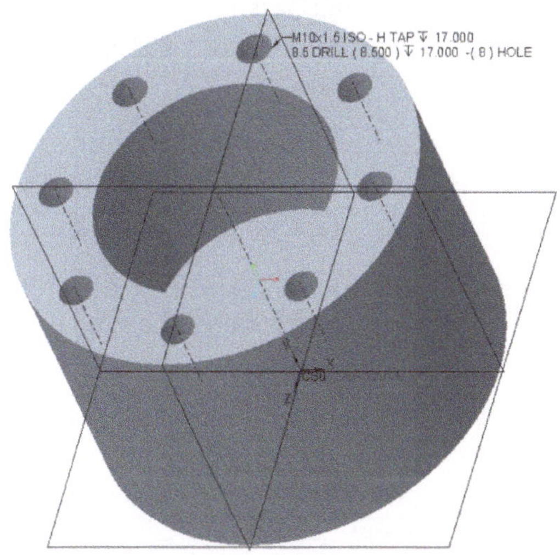

19. In the Model Tree, click on **PRESSURE_CYLINDER.ASM** and select **Activate**. This switches back to the Assembly mode.

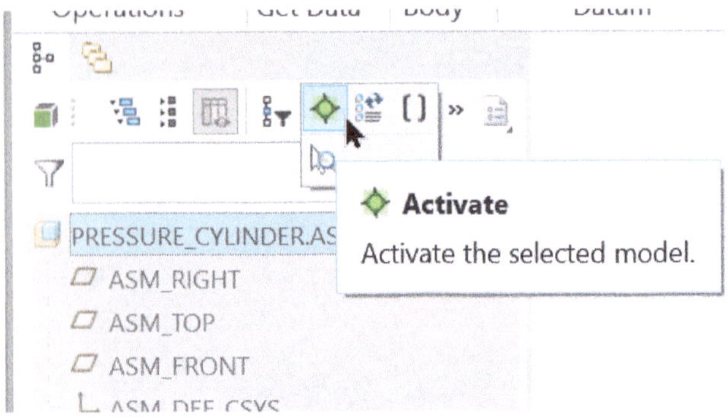

20. Activate the **Create** command (On the ribbon, click **Model** tab > **Component** panel > **Create**).
21. On the **Create Component** dialog, select the **Part** option and type-in *Gasket* in the **Name** box. Click **OK**.
22. On the **Creation Options** dialog, set the **Creation method** to **Locate default datums**.
23. Set **Locate Datums Method** to **Three planes** and click **OK**.
24. Select the front plane of the assembly to define the first plane of the Gasket.
25. Select the top face of the Cylinder base to define the top plane of the Gasket.
26. Select the right plane of the assembly to define the right plane of the Gasket.
27. Activate the **Extrude** command and click on the top plane of the gasket.

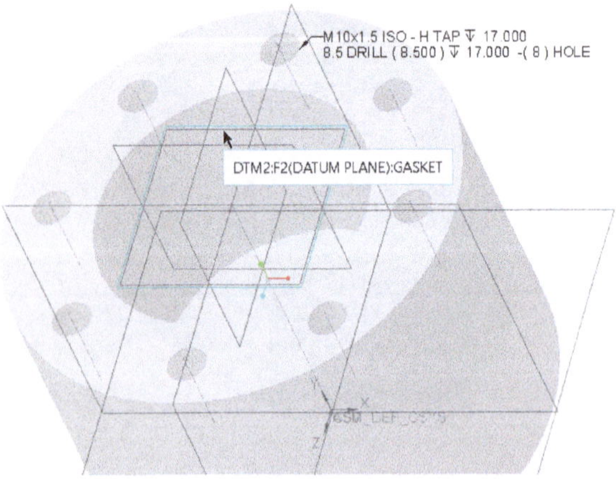

28. On the ribbon, click **Sketch** tab > **Sketching** panel > **Project**.
29. Click on anyone of the outer edges of the top face of the model geometry.
30. Press and hold the SHIFT key and select another outer edge.

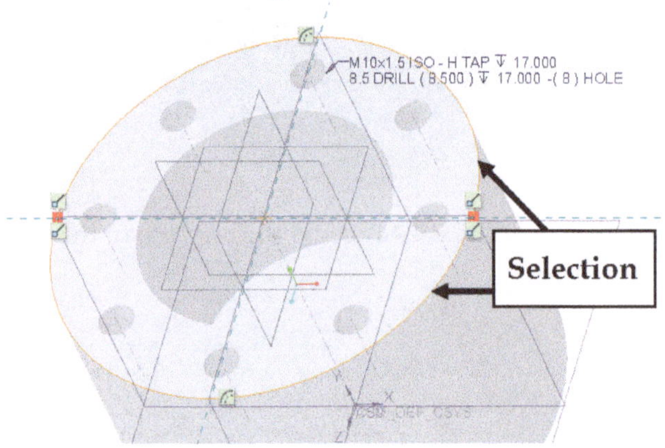

31. Click the green check on the toolbar.
32. Click the **Project** tool on the **Sketching** panel of the **Sketch** ribbon tab.
33. Zoom in to any one of the holes and click its thread edge.

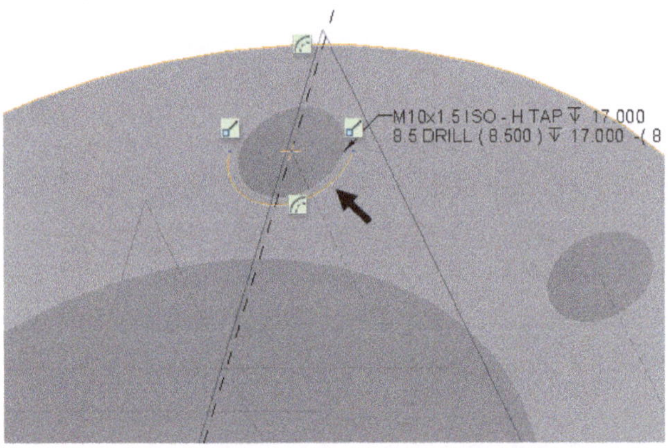

34. Press and hold SHIFT key and select the other edge of the thread.

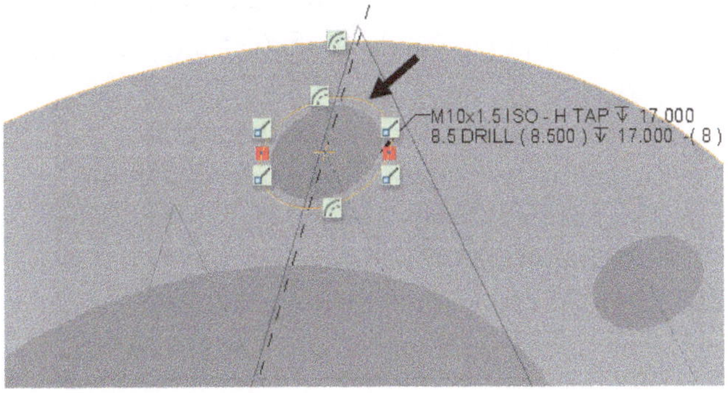

35. Likewise, select the thread edges of other holes, as shown.
36. Click the green check on the toolbar.

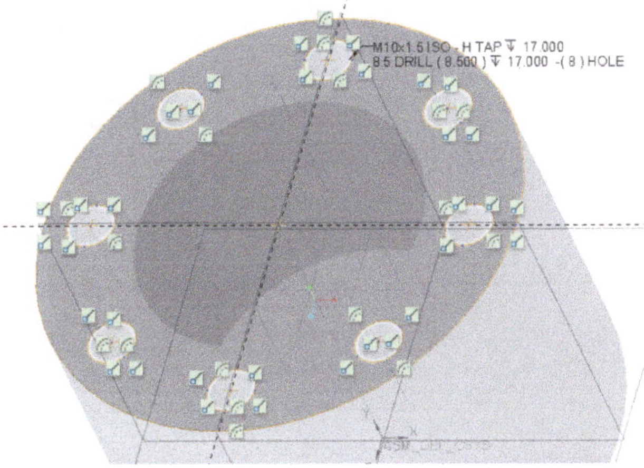

37. Likewise, project the inner circular edges of the top face.

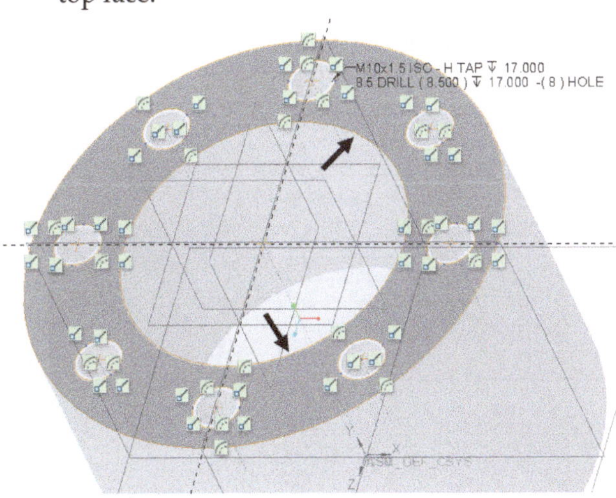

38. Click **OK** on the **Sketch** tab of the ribbon.
39. Extrude the sketch up to 3 mm in length in the upward direction.

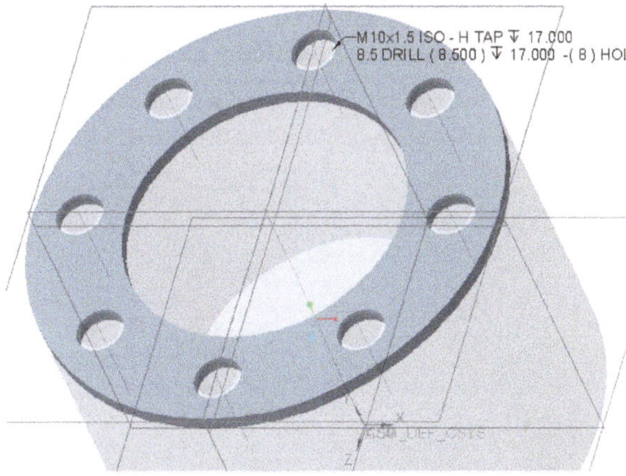

40. In the Model Tree, click on **PRESSURE-CYLINDER.ASM** and select **Activate**. It switches you back to the Assembly mode.
41. Activate the **Create** command.
42. On the **Create Component** dialog, select the **Part** option and type-in *Cover-plate* in the **Name** box. Click **OK**.
43. On the **Creation Options** dialog, set the **Creation method** to **Locate default datums**.
44. Set **Locate Datums Method** to **Three planes** and click **OK**.
45. Select the front plane of the assembly to define the first plane of the Cover-plate.
46. Select the top face of the gasket to define the top plane of the Cover-plate.
47. Select the right plane of the assembly to define the right plane of the Cover-plate.
48. Activate the **Extrude** command and click on the top plane of the gasket.

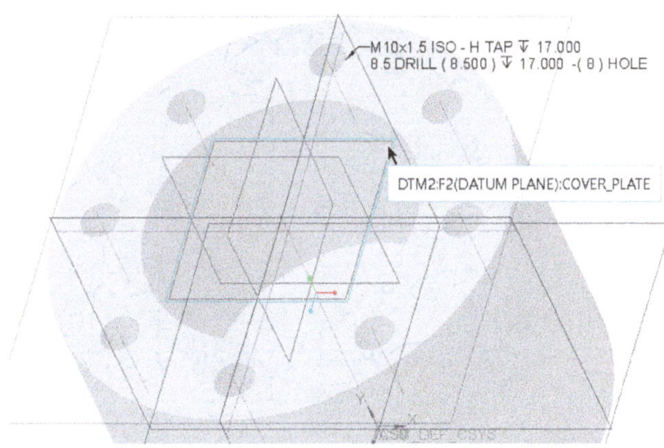

49. On the ribbon, click **Sketch** tab > **Sketching** panel > **Project** .

50. Project the outer edges of the top face of the gasket. Next, click the green check on the toolbar.

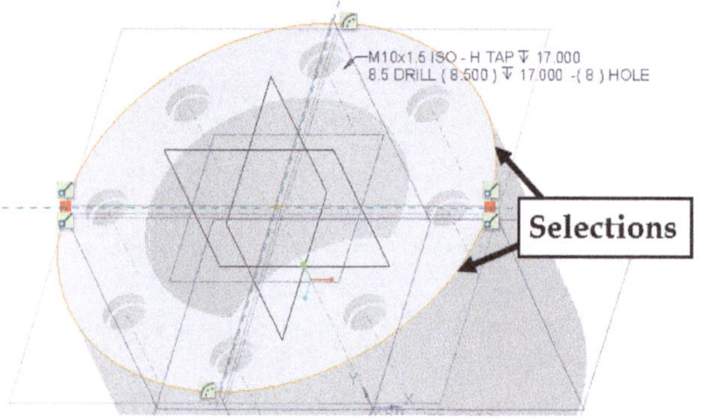

51. Activate the **Project** command and project the edges of the circular hole pattern of the gasket.

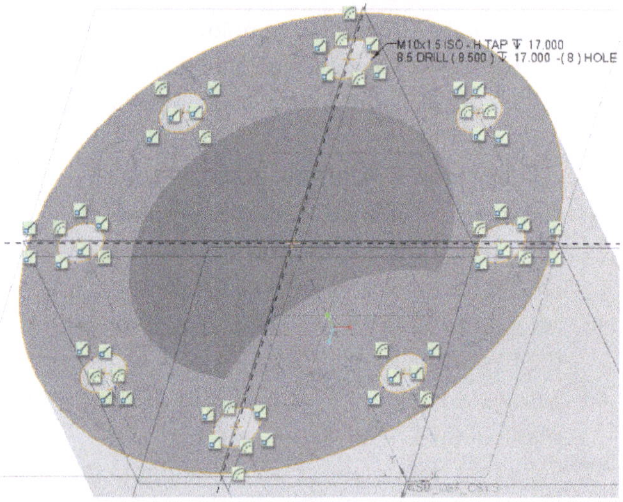

52. Click **OK** on the **Sketch** tab of the ribbon.
53. Create an extruded feature of the 13 mm depth.

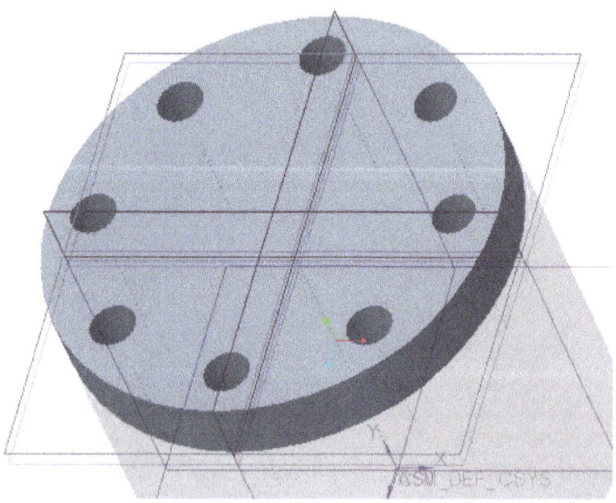

54. Activate the **Assembly** mode.
55. Activate the **Create** command.
56. On the **Create Component** dialog, select the **Part** option and type-in *Screw* in the **Name** box. Click **OK**.
57. On the **Creation Options** dialog, set the **Creation method** to **Locate default datums**.
58. Set **Locate Datums Method** to **Axis normal to plane** and click **OK**.
59. Select the top face of the cover plate.
60. Select the axis of the hole, as shown below.

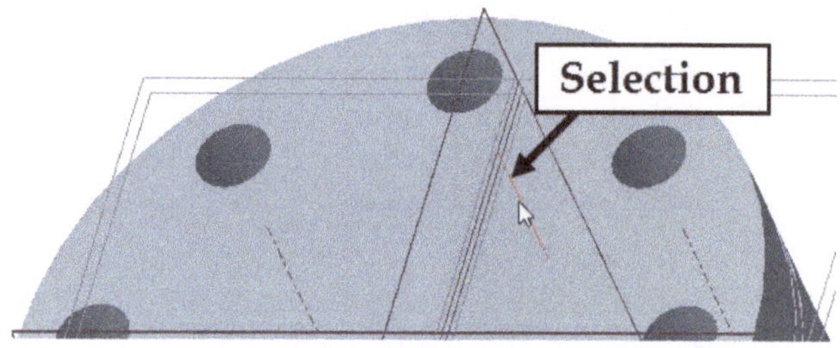

61. Start a sketch on the top plane of the screw.

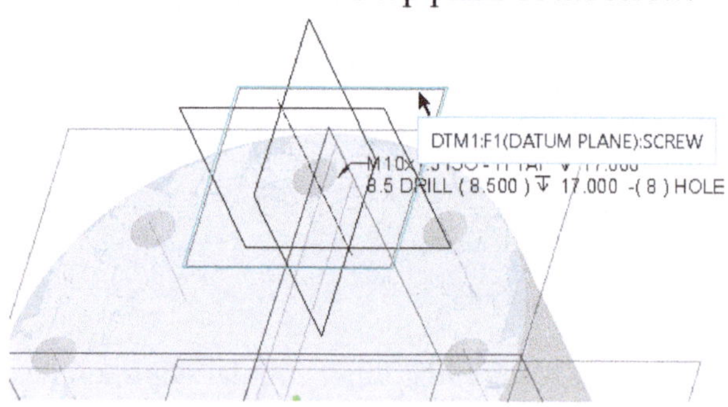

62. Activate the **Project** command.
63. Zoom hole and select anyone of its edges.
64. Press and hold the SHIFT key and select another edge of the hole.

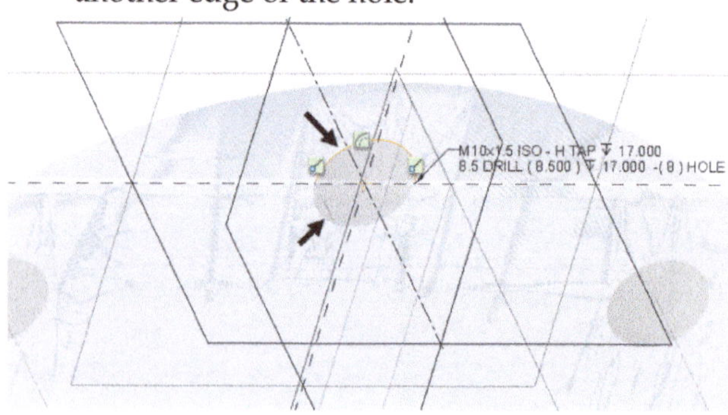

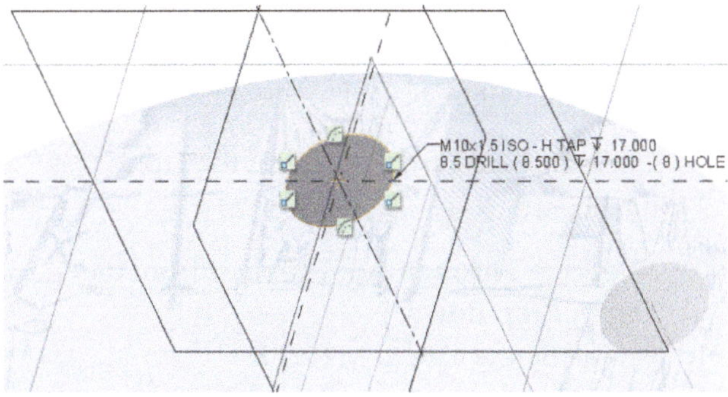

65. Click the green check on toolbar.
66. Click **OK** on the **Sketch** tab of the ribbon.
67. Extrude the sketch up to 30 mm in length in the downward direction.

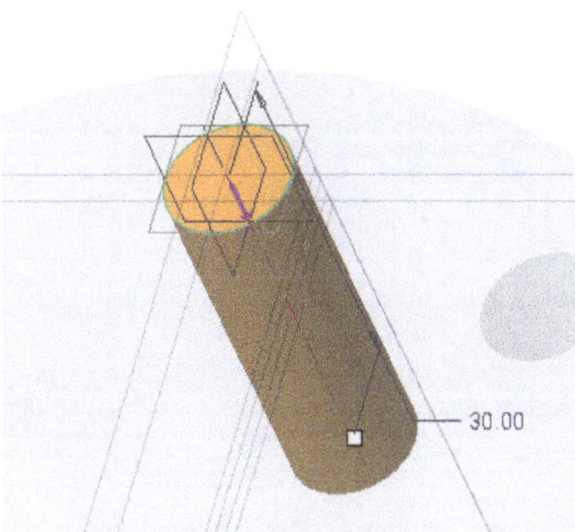

68. Start a sketch on the top face of the extruded feature.
69. On the ribbon, click **Sketch** tab > **Sketching** panel > **Palette** .
70. On the **Sketcher Palette** dialog, click the **Polygons** tab and drag the **6-sided Hexagon** into the sketch.

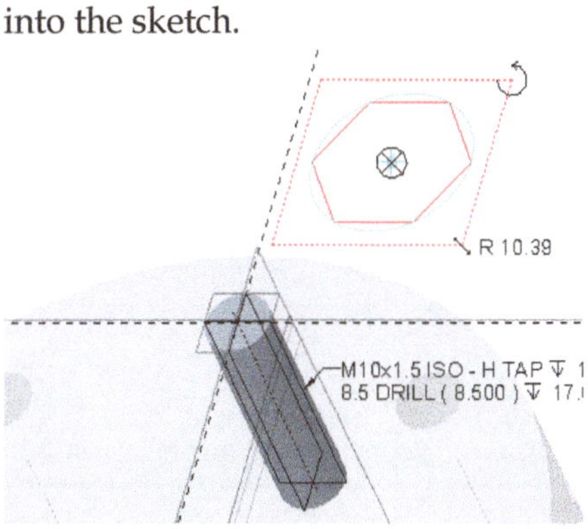

71. Click and drag the center point of the hexagon onto the axis of the extruded feature. Click the green check on the dashboard.

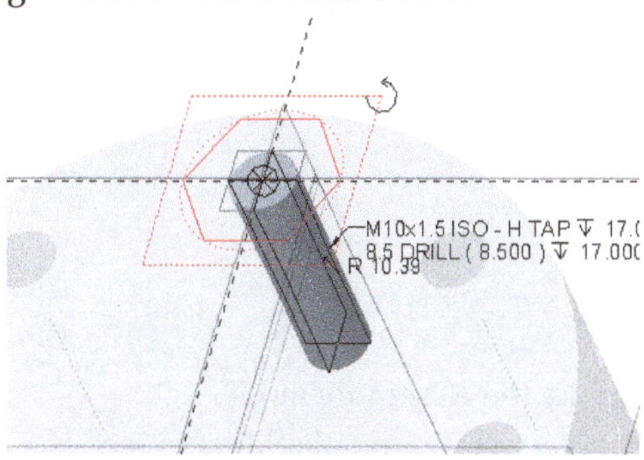

72. Modify the dimension to 8.
73. Make the center point of the hexagon coincident with the sketch origin.

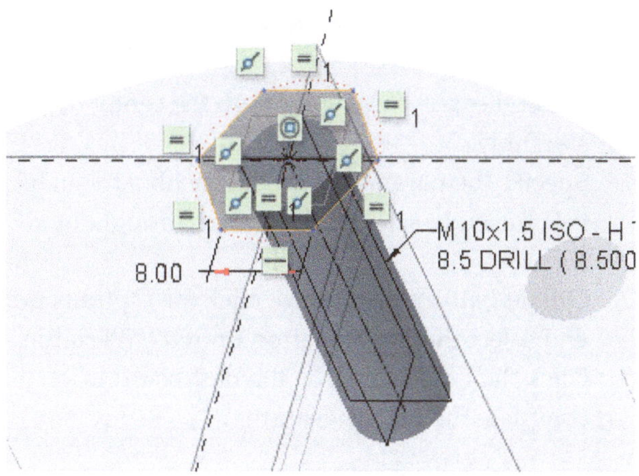

74. Exit the sketch and extrude it up to 5.7 mm in length.

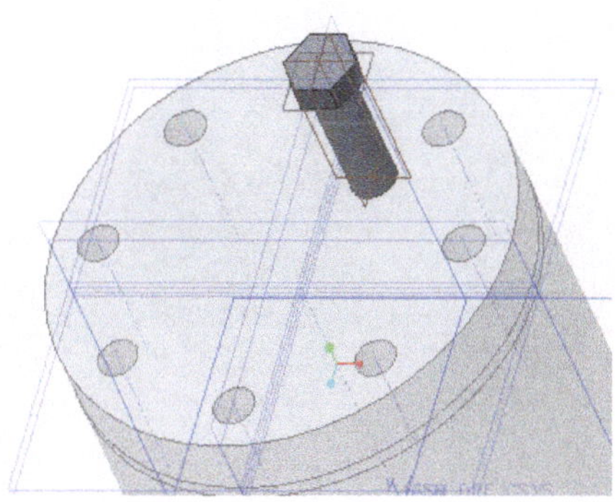

75. Apply Cosmetic Thread M10 x 1.5 to the cylindrical portion of the screw (refer to the **Cosmetic Thread command** section in Chapter 4).

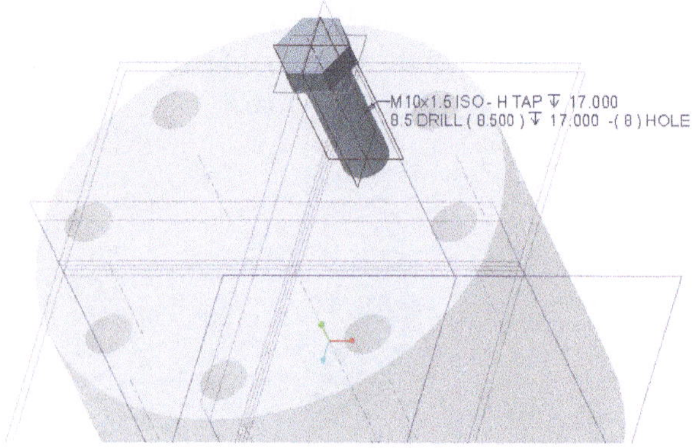

76. Activate the **Assembly** mode.
77. Select the screw from the Model Tree.
78. On the ribbon, click **Model** tab > **Modifiers** panel > **Pattern** drop-down > **Pattern**.
79. On the **Pattern** dashboard, select the **Axis** option from the **Type** drop-down located on the left side.
80. Select the axis passing through the center of the assembly.
81. Specify the parameters on the dashboard such that the eight screws are created throughout 360.
82. On the **Pattern** dashboard, click the **Options** tab and select the **Regeneration option** > **Variable.**
83. Click the green check on the dashboard to complete the pattern feature.

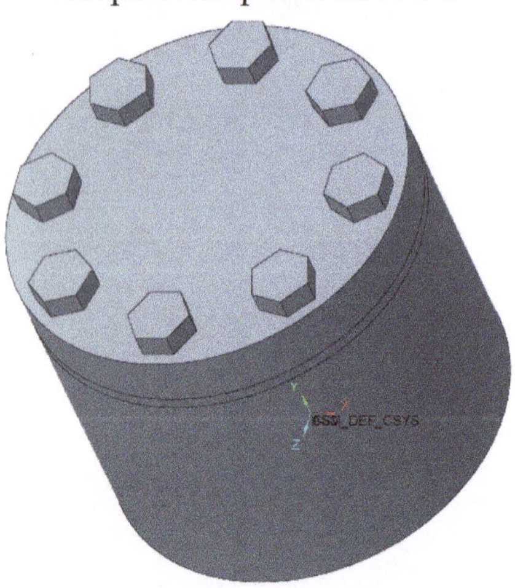

84. On the ribbon, click **Model** tab > **Cut & Surface** panel > **Hole.**
85. Click on the top face of the Cover plate.
86. On the **Hole** dashboard, click **Datum** drop-down >**Axis.**
87. Select the circular edge of the Cover plate and click **OK** on the **Datum Axis** dialog.
88. On the dashboard, click the **Resume** icon. The hole will be placed at the center.
89. Click the **Standard** icon on the **Hole** dashboard.
90. Select the **Through All** option from the **Depth** drop-down.
91. Set the **Screw size** to **M24x1.5**.
92. Click the **Intersection** tab and uncheck the **Automatic Update** option.
93. Click the right mouse button on GASKET and select **Remove.**

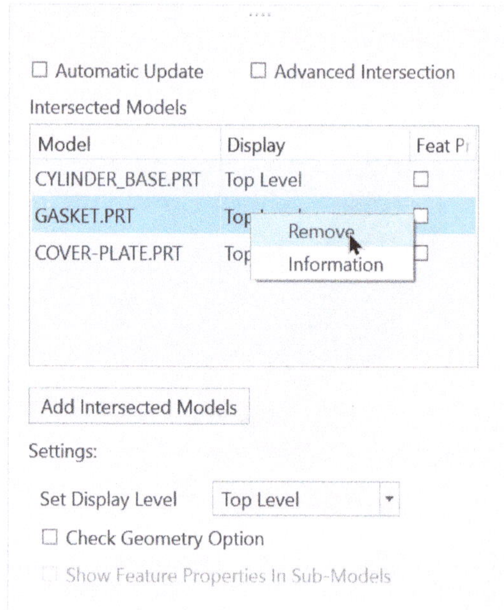

94. Click the **Shape** tab and type-in 81 as the thread distance.
95. Click the green check to create the hole.

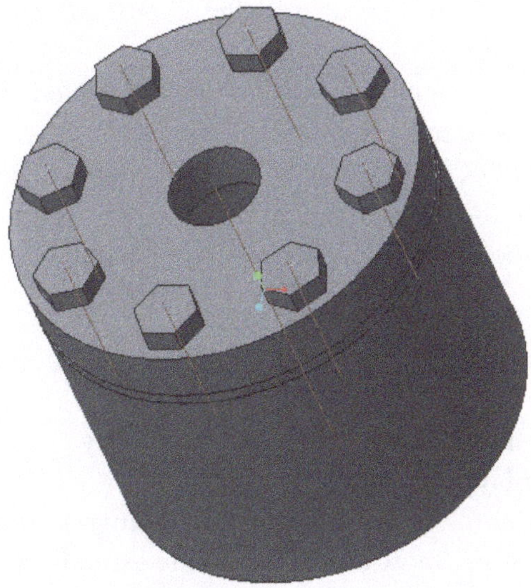

96. On the **Graphics** toolbar, click the **View Manager** button.
97. On the **View Manager** dialog, click the **Explode** tab and click the **New** button.
98. Type-in the name of the explosion and press Enter.
99. Click **Close**.
100. On the ribbon, click **Model** tab > **Model Display** panel > **Edit Position** .
101. On the **Explode Tool** dashboard, make sure that the **Translate** icon is activated.
102. Press and hold the Ctrl key and select all the screws.
103. Click and drag the vertical arrow upward. All the screws will be moved up.

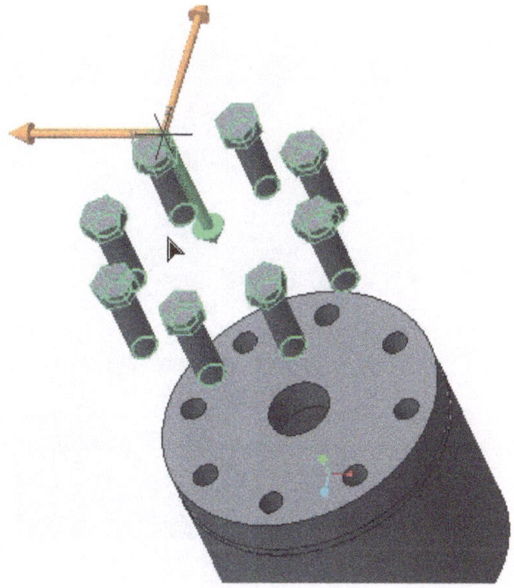

104. Likewise, move the cover plate and gasket upward.

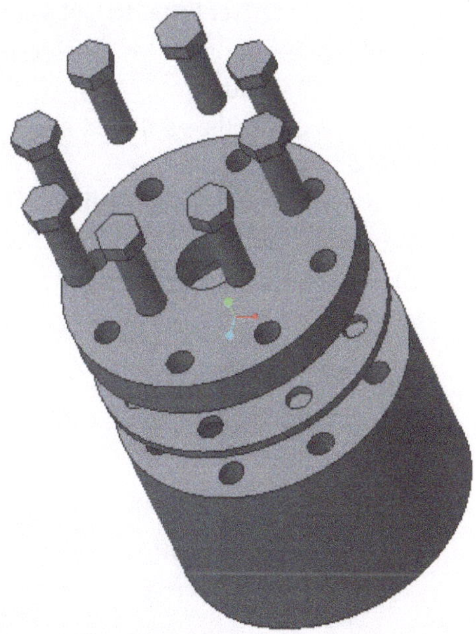

105. On the **Explode Tool** dashboard, click the **Explode Lines** icon.
106. Select the cylindrical face of anyone of the screws.

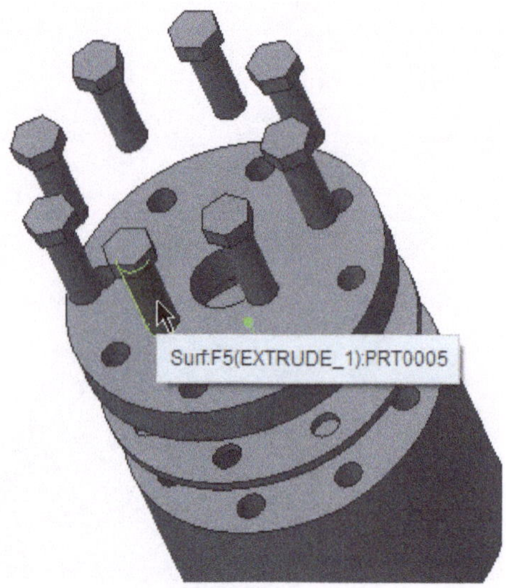

107. Select the cylindrical face of the corresponding hole on the Cylinder base.
108. On the **Cosmetic Offset Line** dialog, select the **Use cylinder axis** option under the **Reference 1** and **Reference 2** sections.
109. Click **Apply** to create the exploded line between the screw and hole.
110. Likewise, create exploded lines between the other screws and holes.
111. Close the **Cosmetic Offset Line** dialog.

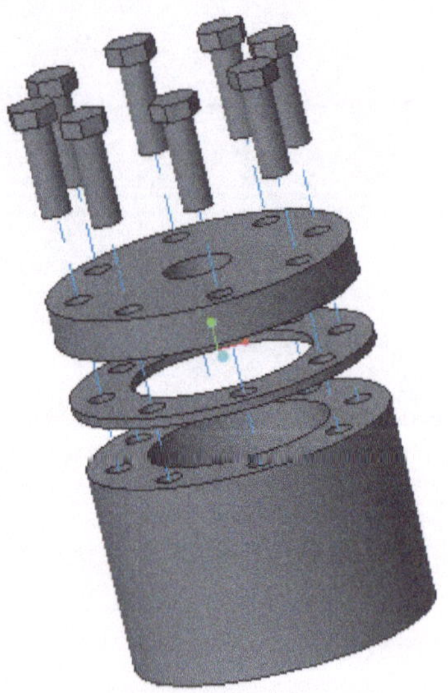

112. Click the green check on the dashboard to complete the explosion.
113. On the **Graphics** toolbar, click the **View Manager** button.
114. On the **View Manager** dialog, click the **Explode** tab.
115. Click the right mouse button on the Exploded view and select **Save**.
116. Click **OK** on the **Save Display Elements** dialog.
117. Close the **View Manager** dialog.
118. On the ribbon, click **Model** tab > **Model Display** panel > **Exploded View** . It collapses the explosion.
119. On the ribbon, click **File > Options**.
120. On the **Options** dialog, click the **Entity Display** category on the left side.
121. Under the **Assembly Display Settings** section, check the **Show animation while exploding the assembly** and **Follow explode sequence** options.
122. Type-in 10 in the **Maximum seconds an animation takes place between explode states** box.
123. Click **OK** and **NO**.
124. On the ribbon, click **Model** tab > **Model Display** panel > **Exploded View**. You will notice that the components of the assembly are exploded in a sequence.
125. Click the **Exploded View** icon to un explode the assembly.
126. Save and close the assembly.

Questions

1. How do you start an assembly?
2. What is the use of the **Repeat** command?
3. List the advantages of the Top-down assembly approach.
4. How do you create a sub-assembly in the Assembly environment?
5. Briefly explain how to edit components in an assembly.
6. What are the results that can be achieved using the **Create** command?
7. How do you redefine constraints in Creo Parametric?
8. What is the use of the **Angle Offset** constraint?

Exercise 1

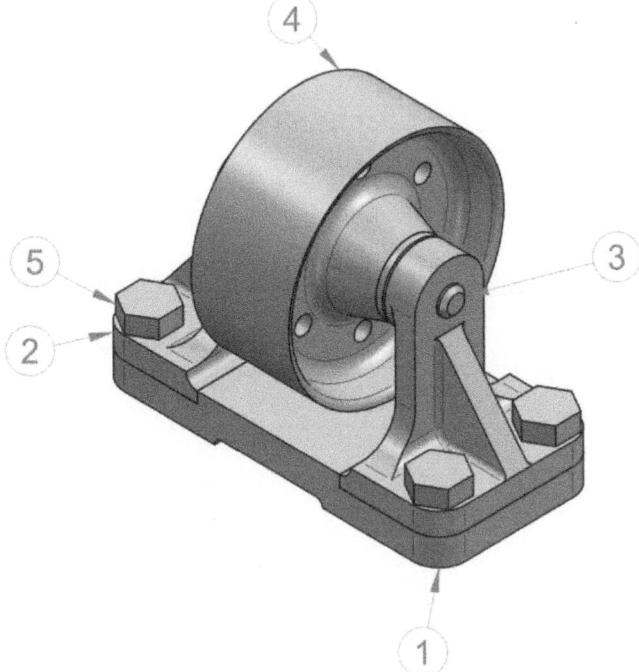

Item Number	File Name (no extension)	Quantity
1	Base	1
2	Bracket	2
3	Spindle	1
4	Roller-Bush assembly	1
5	Bolt	4

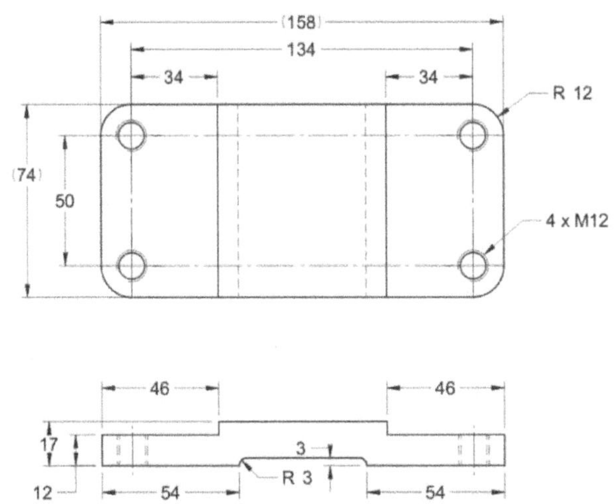

Base

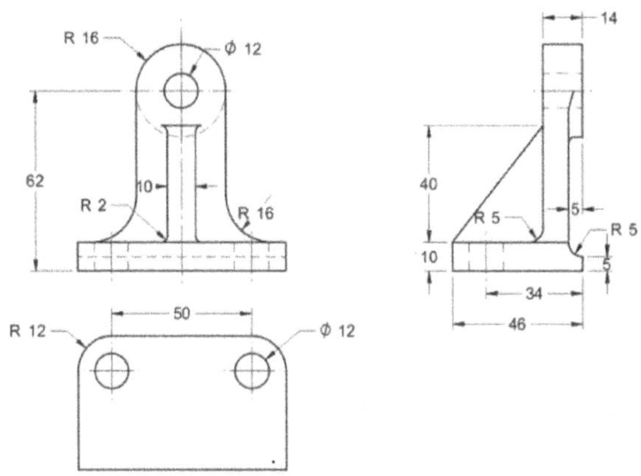

Bracket

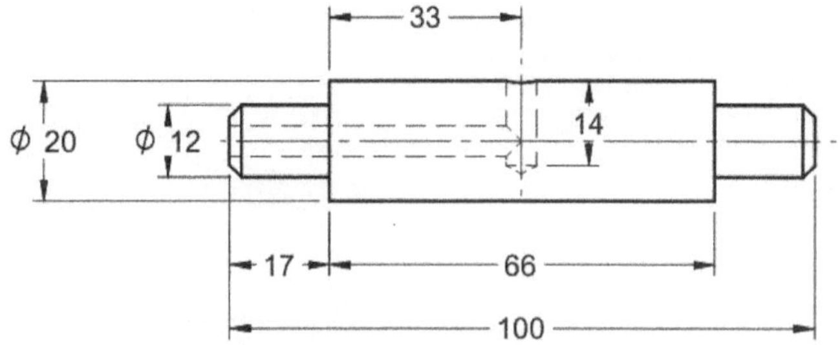

SPINDLE

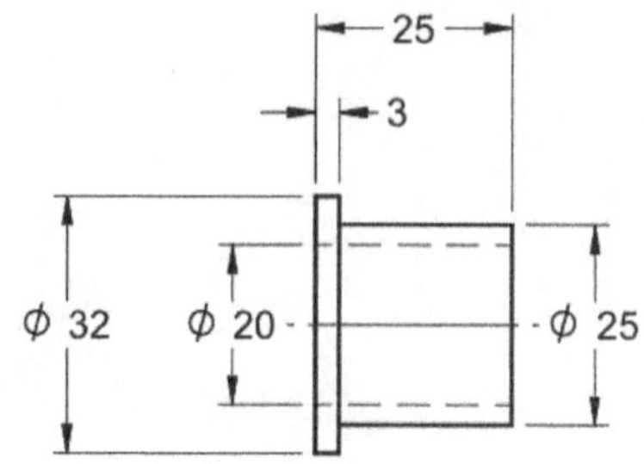

BUSH

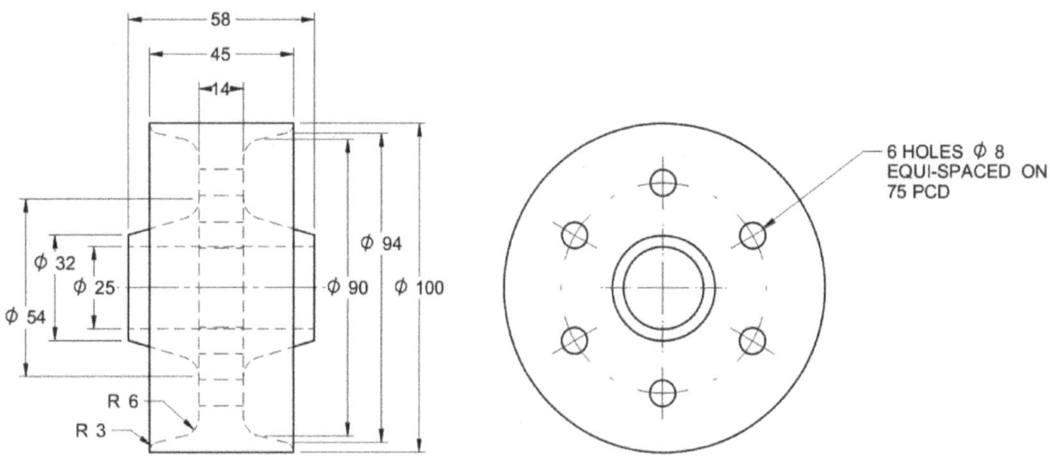

Roller

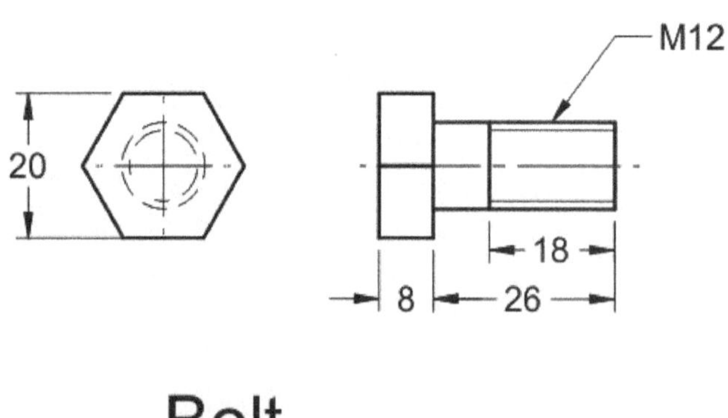

Bolt

Chapter 10: Drawings

Drawings are used to document your 3D models in the traditional 2D format, including dimensions and other instructions useful for the manufacturing purpose. In Creo Parametric, you first create 3D models and assemblies and then use them to generate the drawing. There is a direct association between the 3D model and the drawing. When changes are made to the model, every view in the drawing will be updated. This relationship between the 3D model and the drawing makes the drawing process fast and accurate. Because of the mainstream adoption of 2D drawings in the mechanical industry, drawings are one of the three main file types you can create in Creo Parametric.

The topics covered in this chapter are:

- *Create General views*
- *Projection views*
- *Auxiliary views*
- *Section views*
- *Detail views*
- *Breakout Section views*
- *Broken views*
- *Exploded views*
- *Parts List and Balloons*
- *Generate Dimensions*
- *Dimensions*
- *Axis*
- *Notes*

Starting a Drawing

Follow the steps given next to start a new drawing.

1. On the Quick Access Toolbar, click the **New** icon.
2. On the **New** dialog, select **Type > Drawing**.
3. Type-in the drawing name and click **OK**.
4. On the **New Drawing** dialog, click the **Specify Template > Empty** to start a drawing with an empty sheet.

You can select the **Use template** option and then select a standard template to start a drawing. The standard drawing views are placed on the sheet automatically.

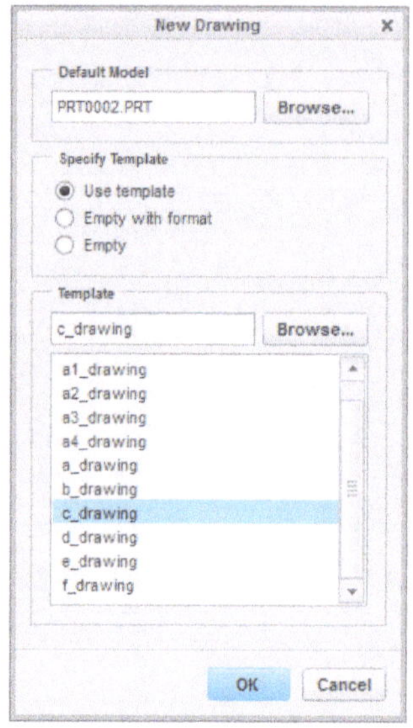

The **Empty with format** option starts a drawing using a standard or user-defined format.

5. Set the drawing orientation to **Portrait** or **Landscape** or **Variable**.
6. Select the sheet size from the **Standard Size** drop-down. The drawing units are defined automatically based on the standard size. You can manually define the units and sheet size by selecting **Variable** orientation.
7. Click the **Browse** button under the **Default Model** section and select the reference 3D model.
8. Click **OK** to start the drawing.

Setting the Drawing Model

A drawing is a 2D representation of a 3D model (part or Assembly). You need to associate a 3D model with the drawing file. In the beginning, you have selected a 3D model while creating the drawing file. However, you can add more models to the drawing after creating the drawing. The **Drawing Model** command helps you add, remove, and set the model to create drawing views. On the ribbon, click **Layout** tab > **Model Views** panel >

Drawing Models. The **DWG MODELS** menu pops up on the top right corner of the screen.

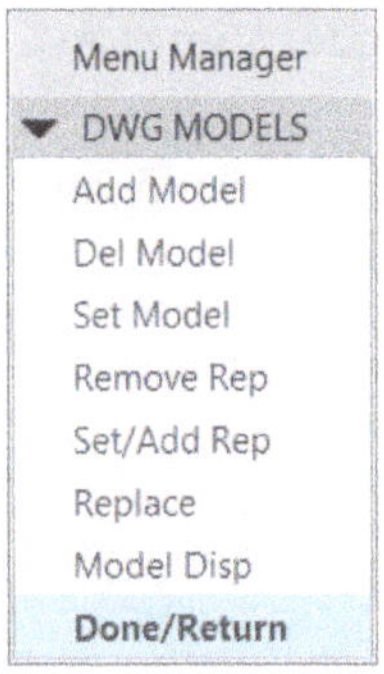

The options on this menu help you add, remove, or set the current drawing model. Click **Done/Return** after selecting the required option.

Drawing Properties

Before creating the drawing, you have to check the sheet properties and modify them as per your requirement.

1. Click **File > Prepare > Drawing Properties**.
2. On the **Drawing Properties** dialog, click the **change** link next to **Detail Options**. The **Options** dialog appears.

In this dialog, you can modify the properties such as the angle of projection and units. For example, if you want to change the angle of projection, type-in projection in the **Option** box and click **Find**. On the **Find Option** dialog, select a value from the **Set value** drop-down, and click **Add/change**. Click **Close** on the **Find Option** dialog. Click **OK** on the **Options** dialog, and then close the **Drawing Properties** dialog.

General View

There are different standard views available in a 3D part, such as front, right, top, and isometric. In Creo Parametric, you can create these views using the **General View** command.

1. On the ribbon, click **Layout > Model Views > General View**.
2. On the **Select Combined State** dialog, click **No combined state**, and click **OK**.
3. Click on the drawing sheet to define the view location.

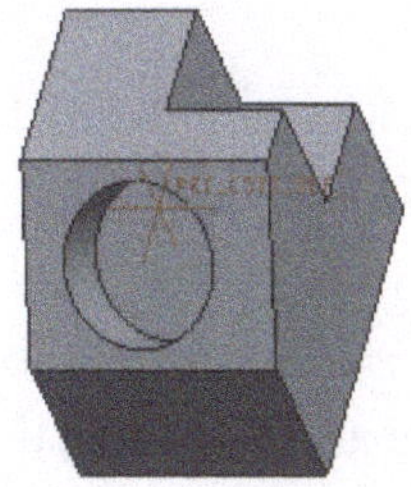

4. On the **Drawing View** dialog, select **Model view names > FRONT**.
5. Type **Front** in the **View name** box, and then click **Apply**.
6. On the dialog, click the **Categories > Scale** and define the view scale. You can use the default scale or define a custom scale. Click **Apply** after making changes.

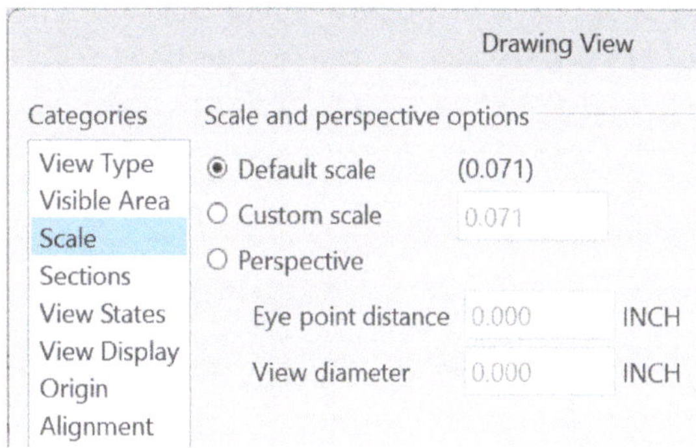

7. Click **Categories > View Display** and set the **Display Style**.

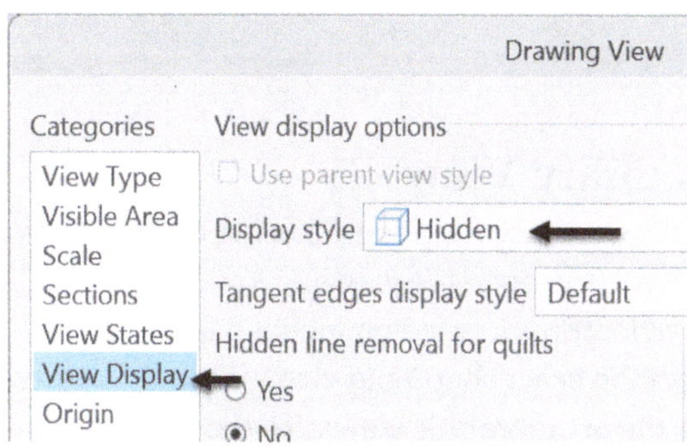

8. Click **OK** to create the view.

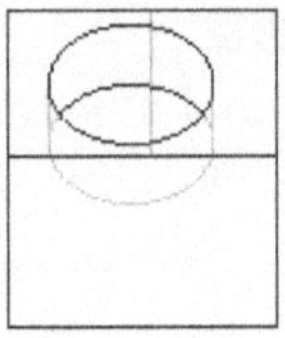

Projection View

After you have created the first view in your drawing, a projection view is one of the simplest views to create. It is an orthographic projection of another view along the vertical or horizontal direction. The orientation of the projection view is 90-degrees from the parent view. Also, the drawing scale is inherited from the parent view. The angle of projection can be the Third angle or First angle.

1. On the ribbon, click **Layout > Model Views > Projection View**.
2. After activating this command, move the pointer in the direction you wish to have the view projected.

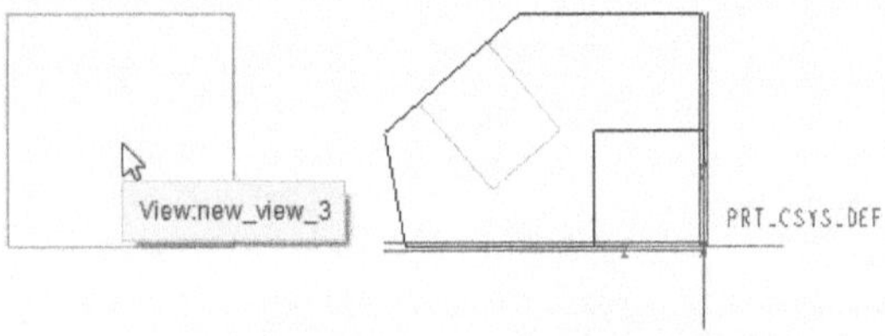

3. Next, click on the sheet to specify the location.

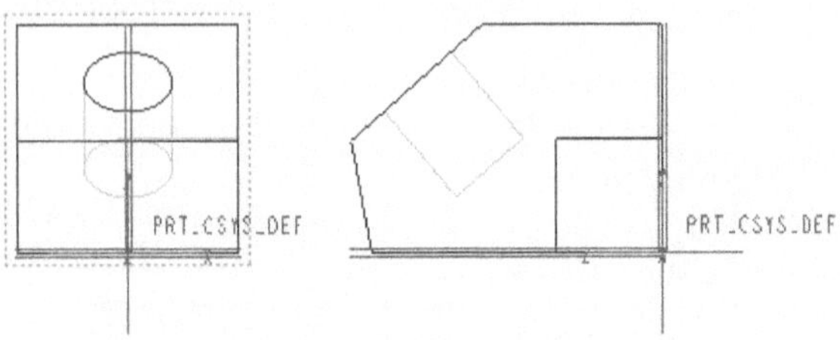

Auxiliary View

Most of the parts are represented using orthographic views (front, top, and side views). However, many parts have features located on inclined faces. You cannot get the exact shape and size for these features by using the orthographic views. To see an accurate size and shape of the inclined features, you need to create an auxiliary view. You create an auxiliary view by projecting the part onto a plane other than horizontal, front, or side planes.

1. On the ribbon, click **Layout > Model Views > Auxiliary View**.
2. Click the angled edge of the model to establish the direction of the auxiliary view.
3. Move the pointer and click.

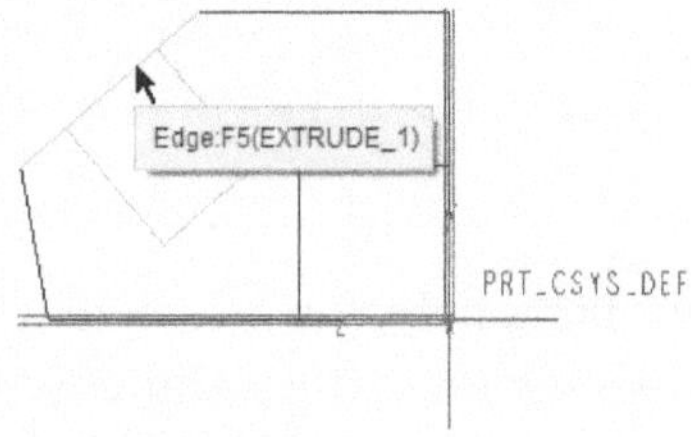

4. Drag the mouse to the desired location. Click to locate the view.

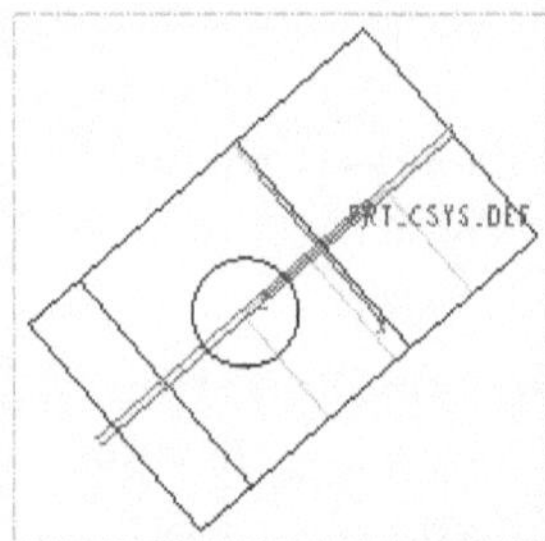

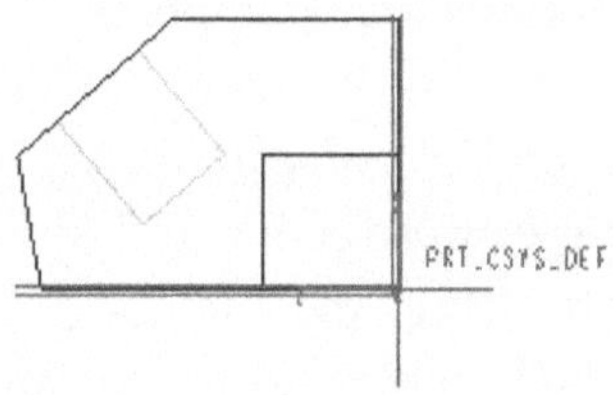

Section Views

One of the standard views used in 2D drawings is the section view. Creating a section view in Creo Parametric is very simple.

1. Create the base view and side view of the model, as shown.
2. On the Graphics toolbar, click **Display Style drop-down > Hidden Line**.
3. On the Graphics toolbar, click **Datum Display Filters > Plane Display**.

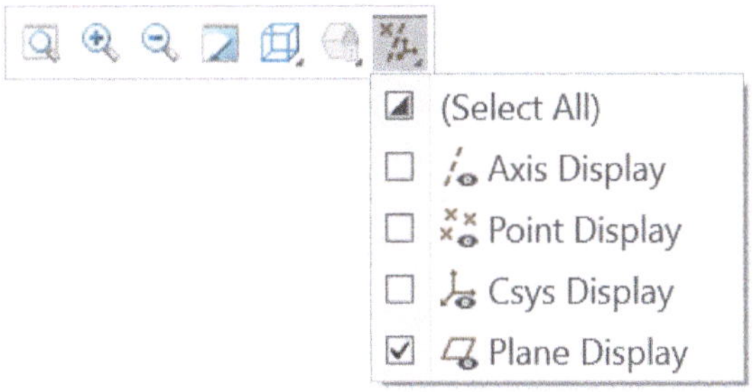

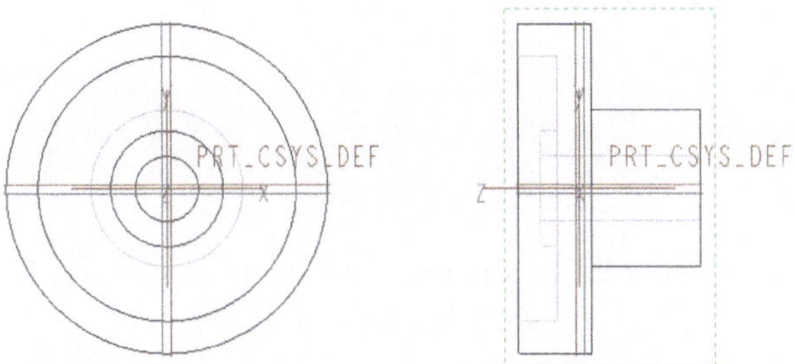

4. Select the side view.
5. Select **Properties** to open the **Drawing View** dialog.

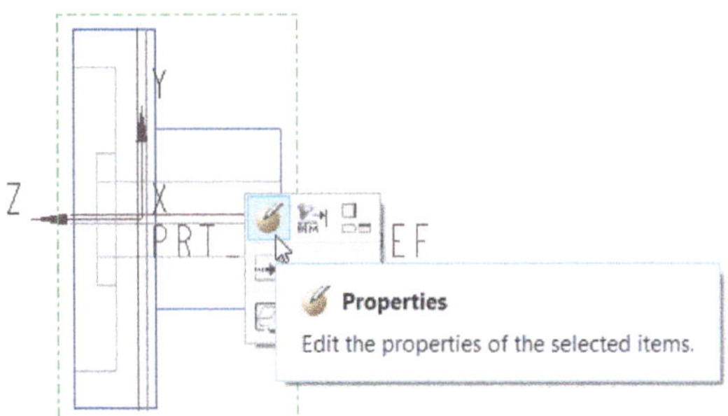

6. Select **Categories > Sections** and click **2D cross-section**.
7. Click the **Add cross-section to view** button.
8. On the **Menu Manager**, select **Planar** and **Single**, and then click **Done**.
9. Enter **A** as the name of the cross-section and click the green check.

10. Select the cutting plane from the base view.

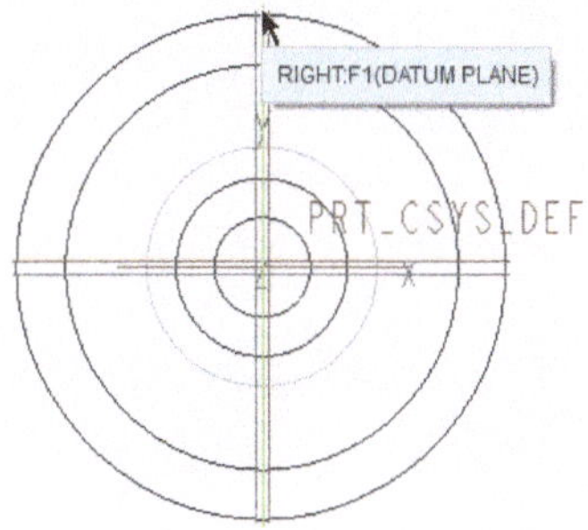

11. On the **Drawing View** dialog, set the **Sectioned Area** to **Full**.

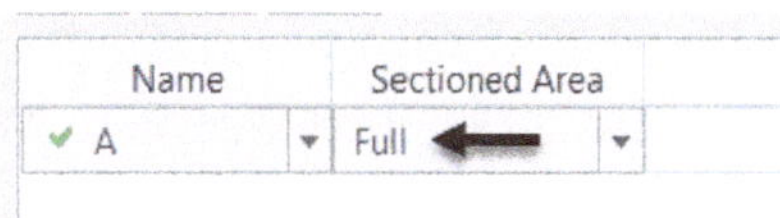

12. Click **OK** to create the section view.

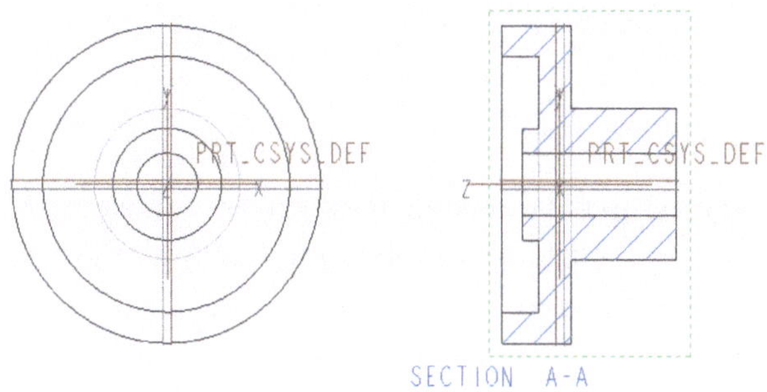

13. On the ribbon, click **Layout > Edit > Arrows**.
14. Select the cross-section and base views.

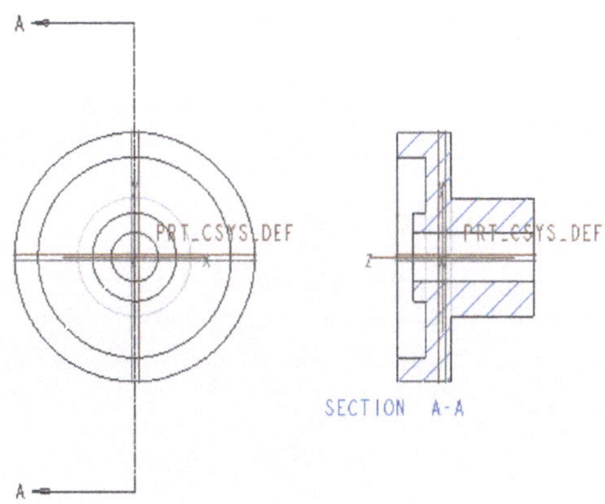

15. Click the middle mouse button to exit the command.
16. Select the section arrows.
17. Press and hold the left mouse button and drag the arrows to reduce their length.

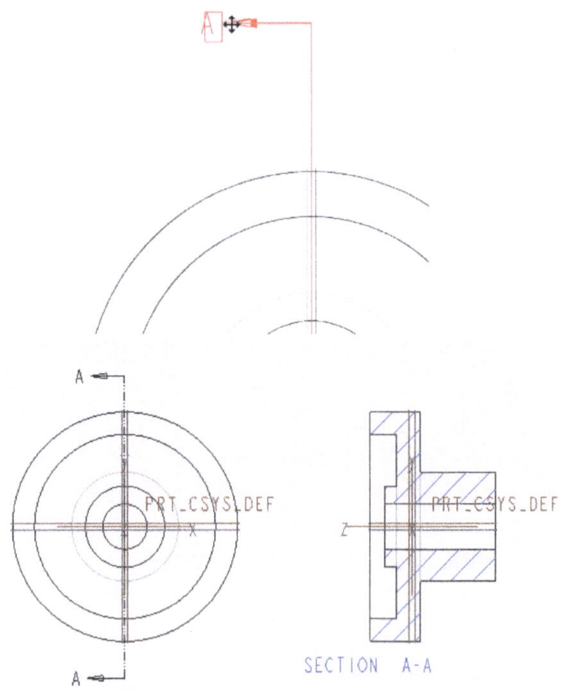

You can flip the direction of the arrows by selecting them, right-clicking, and selecting **Flip Material Removal Side**.

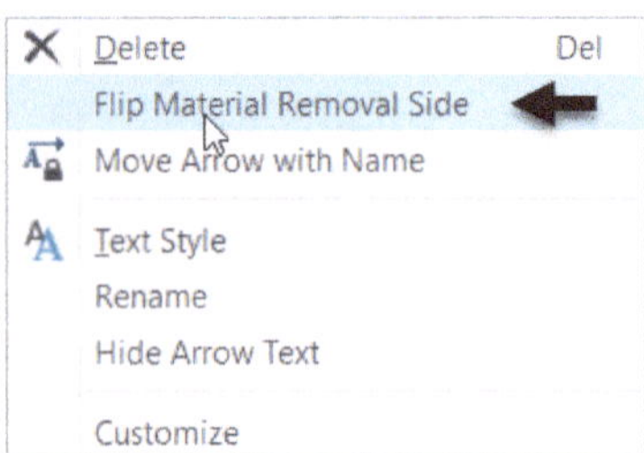

Scaling the Hatch pattern

You can change the spacing between the section view's hatch lines by following the steps given next.

1. Deselect the section view.
2. Select the hatching of the section view.

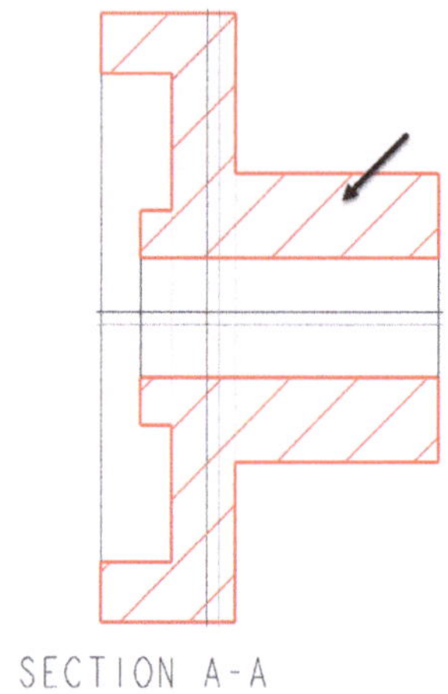

3. On the **Edit Hatching** dashboard, on the **Editing** panel, type **50** in the **Scale** box.

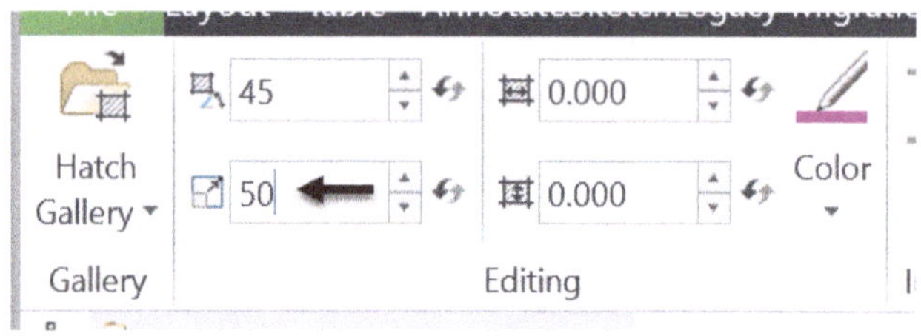

4. Click in the graphics window.

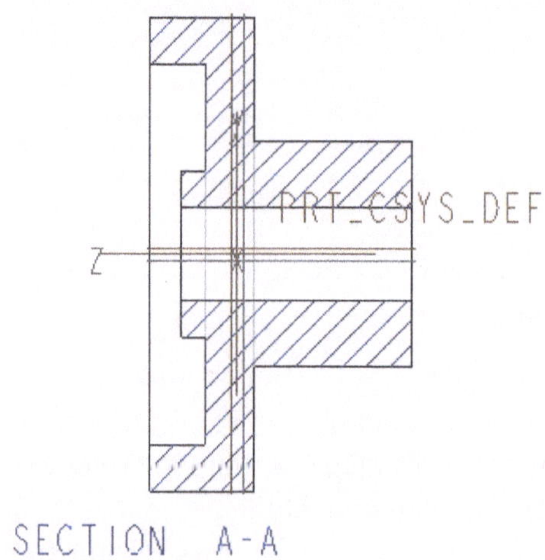

Likewise, you can modify the angle, line style, and other properties of the section view.

Offset Section View

If you want to create a section view using a multi-segment section line, follow the next steps.

1. Create the base and projected views, as shown.

2. Click **View > Model Display > Display Style > Wireframe** on the ribbon.

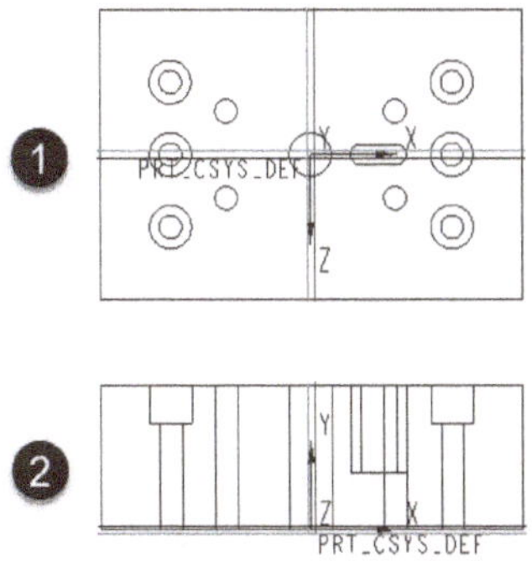

3. Click the right mouse button on the projected view and select **Properties**.
4. Select **Categories > Sections** and click **2D cross-section**.
5. Click the **Add cross-section to view** + button.
6. On the **Menu Manager**, select **Offset** and **Single**, and then click **Done**.

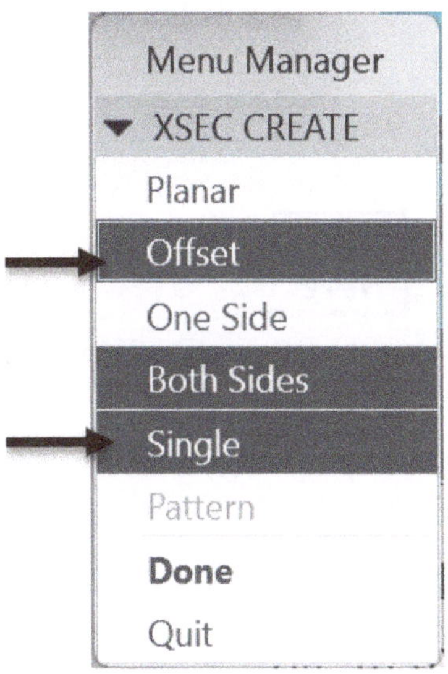

7. Enter **A** as the name of the cross-section and click the green check. A new window appears with the 3D model.
8. Click on the top surface of the model to define the sketching plane.

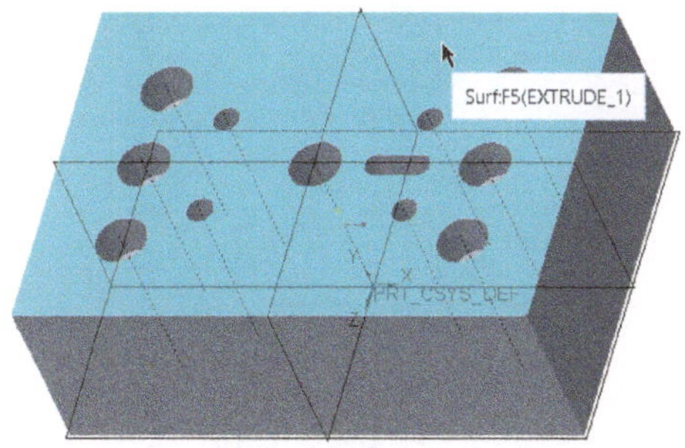

9. Click **Okay** and **Default** on the **Menu Manager**.
10. In the 3D model window, click **View > Orientation > Sketch Orientation**.

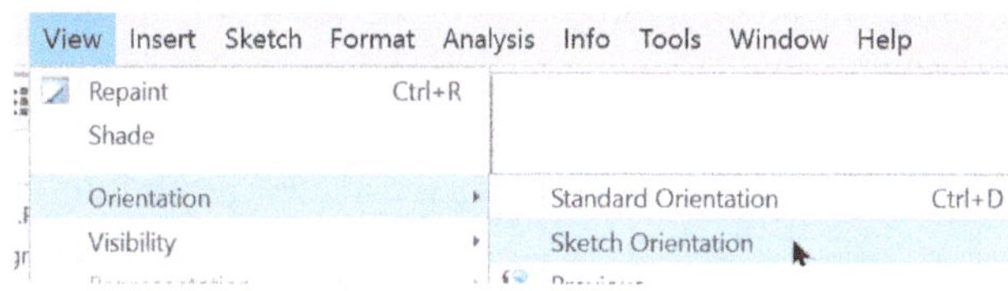

11. Click **Sketch > Line > Line** and draw the cutting plane, as shown.

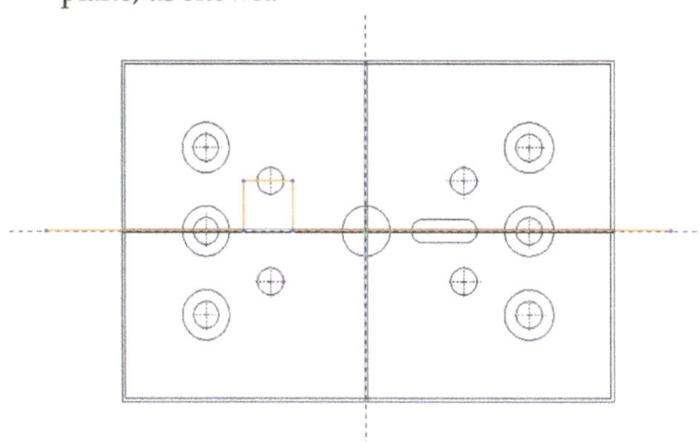

12. Click **Sketch > Done** to close the 3D Model window.
13. On the **Drawing View** dialog, drag the horizontal scroll bar and click in the **Arrow Display** field.
14. Select the base view and click **OK**.

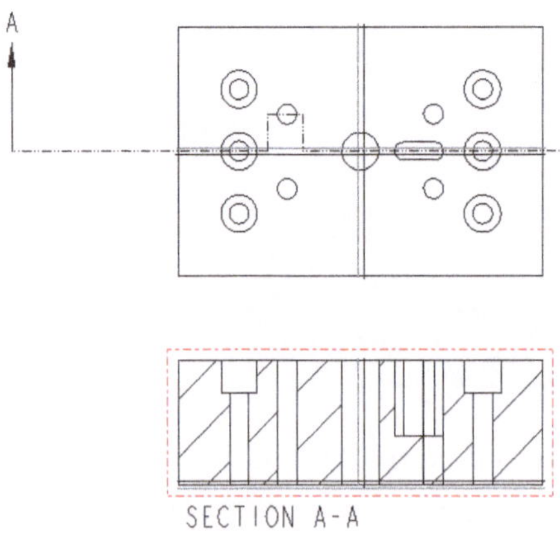

Half Section View

Follow the steps given below to create a half section view.

1. Create the base and projected views, as shown.

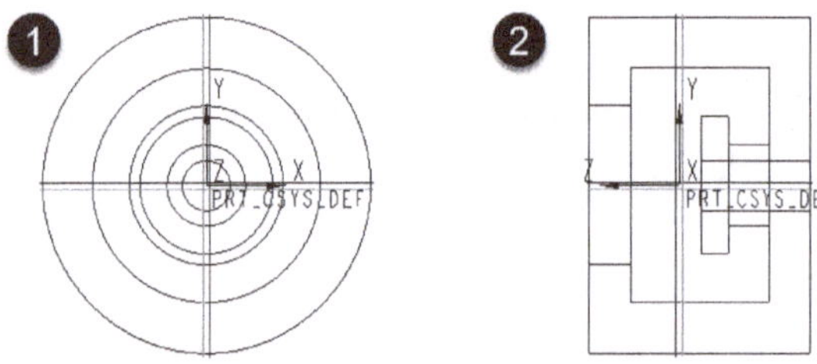

2. Click on the projected view and select **Properties**.
3. Select **Categories > Sections** and click **2D cross-section**.
4. Click the **Add cross-section to view**  button.
5. On the **Menu Manager**, select **Planar** and **Single**, and then click **Done**.
6. Enter **A** as the name of the cross-section and click the green check.
7. Select the cutting plane from the base view.

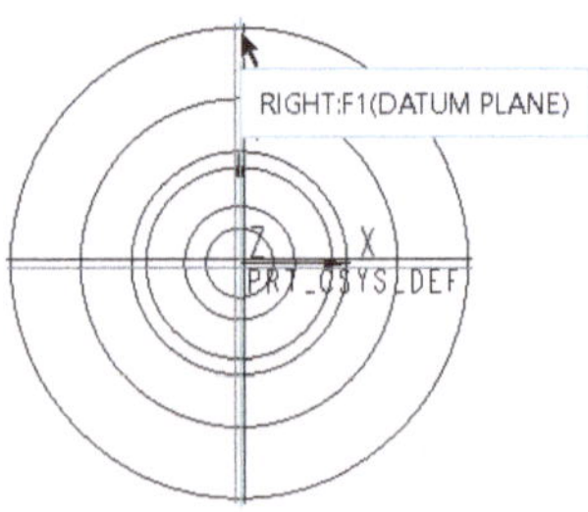

8. On the **Drawing View** dialog, set the **Sectioned Area** to **Half**.

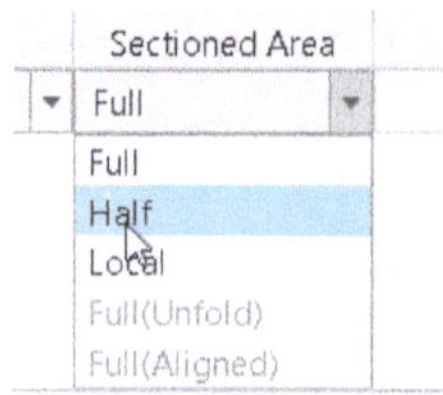

9. Select a plane on the projected view to define the half-section.

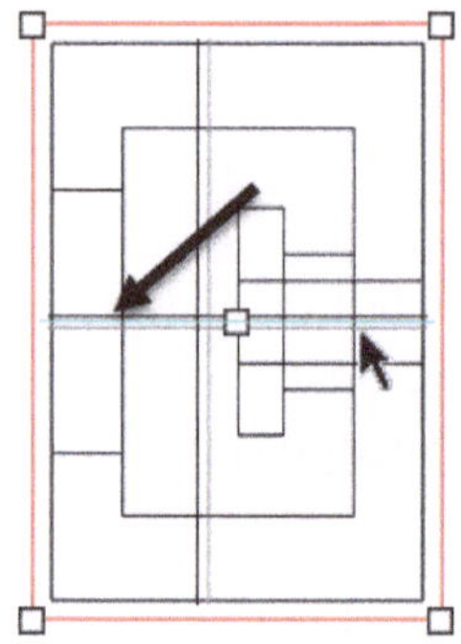

10. Pick a side to display the hatch lines.

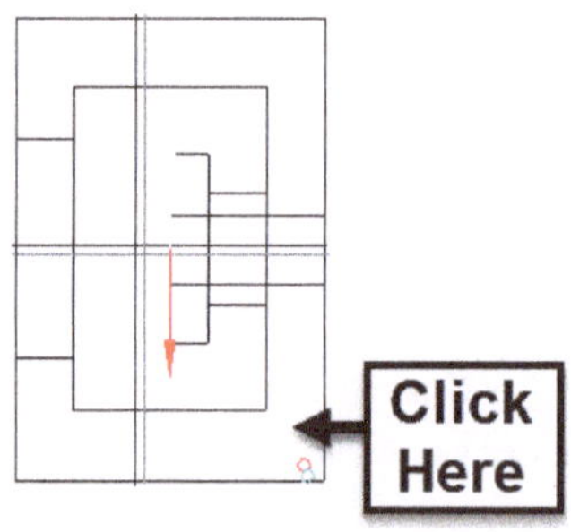

11. Click **OK** to create the half-section view

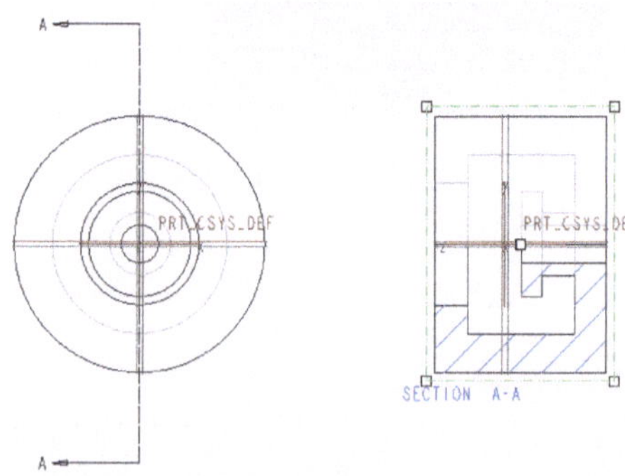

Aligned Section View

Follow the steps given next to create the aligned section view.

1. Create the base and projected views, as shown.

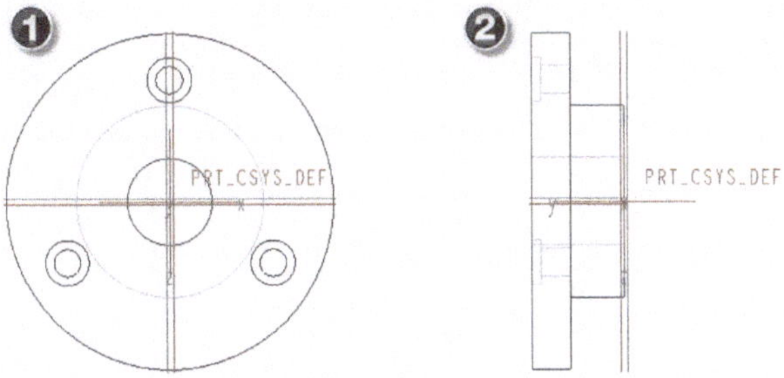

2. On the **Graphics** toolbar, click **Datum Display Filters** drop-down > **Axis Display**.

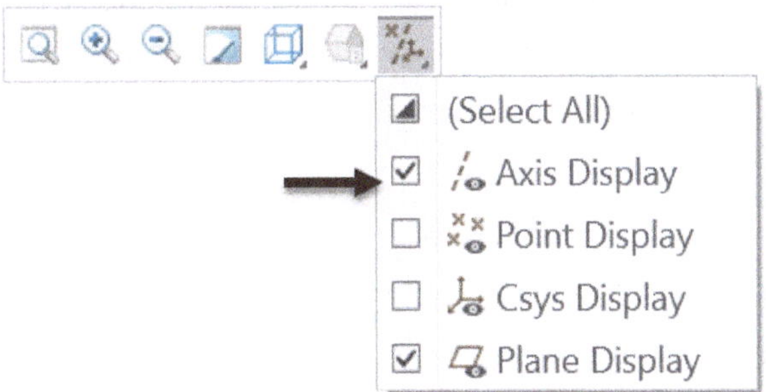

3. Click on the projected view and select **Properties**.
4. Select **Categories > Sections** and click **2D cross-section**.
5. Click the **Add cross-section to view**  button.
6. On the **Menu Manager**, select **Offset** and **Single**, and then click **Done**.
7. Enter **A** as the name of the cross-section and click the green check. A new window appears with the 3D model.
8. Click on the top surface of the model to define the sketching plane.

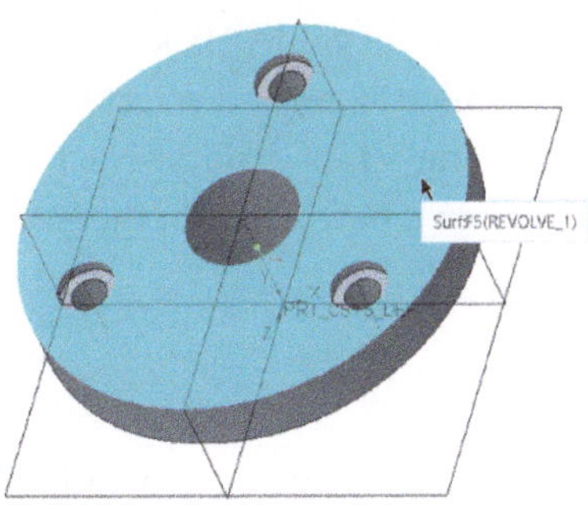

9. Click **Okay** and **Default** on the **Menu Manager**.
10. In the window, click **View > Orientation > Standard Orientation**.
11. Select the axes of the center hole and counterbore hole as the reference.
12. Close the **References** dialog.
13. In the 3D model window, click **View > Orientation > Sketch Orientation**.
14. Click **Sketch > Line > Line** and draw the cutting plane, as shown.

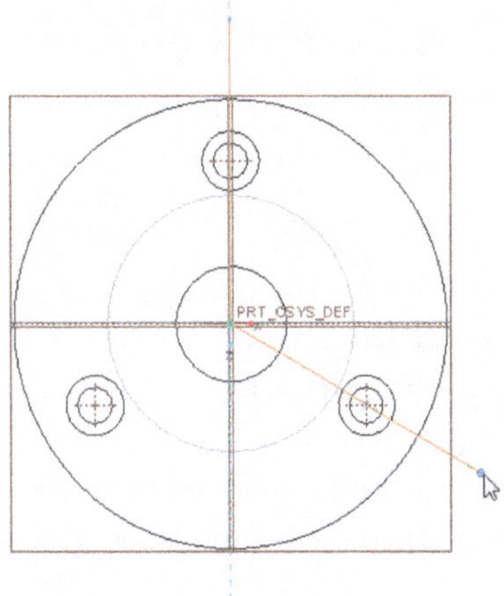

15. Click **Sketch > Done** to close the 3D Model window.
16. On the **Drawing View** dialog, set the **Sectioned Area** to **Full(Aligned)**.

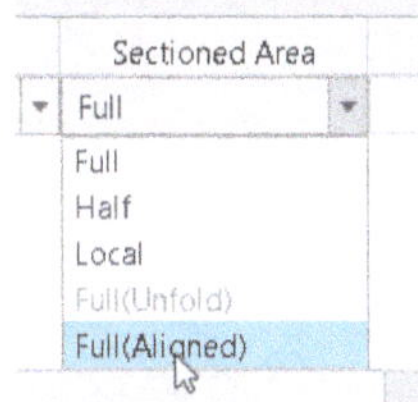

17. Select the axis of the revolved solid, as shown.

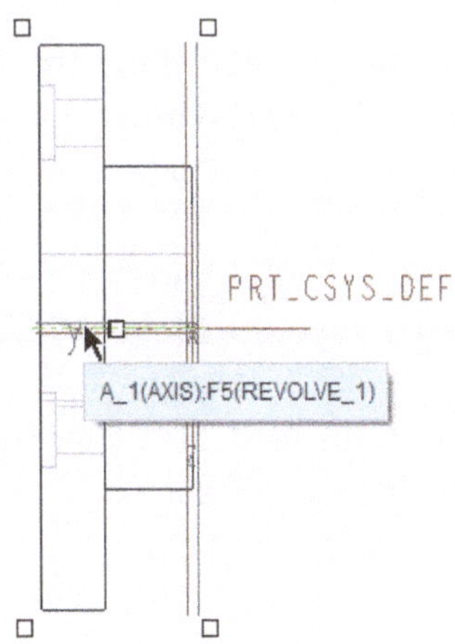

18. On the **Drawing View** dialog, drag the horizontal scroll bar and click in the **Arrow Display** field.
19. Select the base view and click **OK**.

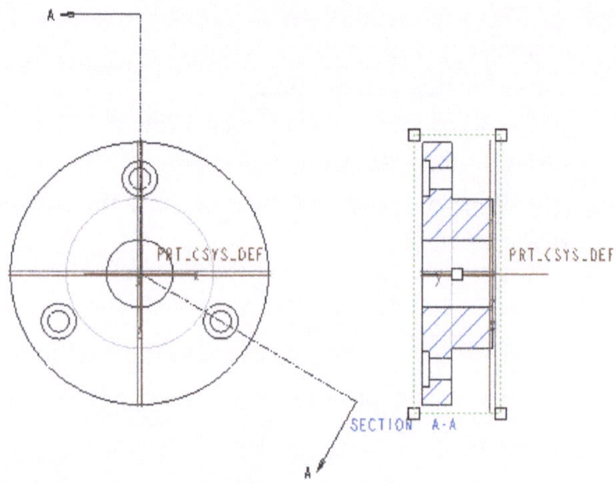

Creating Section Cuts

A section cut displays the surface that is exposed after sectioning. It hides the edges. You can create section cuts by selecting **Model edge visibility > Area** on the **Drawing View** dialog while creating the section view.

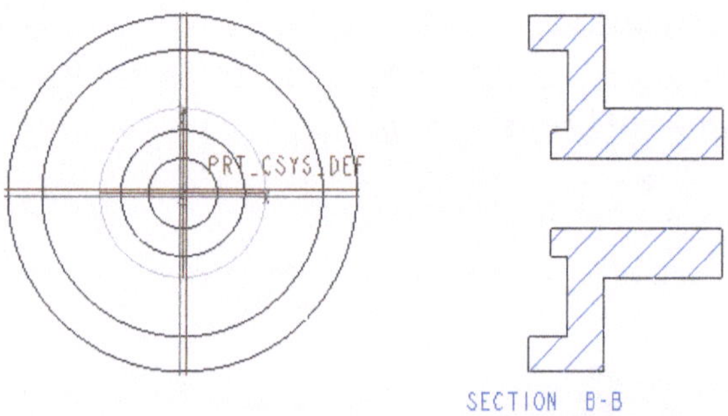

Detailed View

If a drawing view contains small features that are difficult to see, a detailed view can be used to zoom in and clarify. To create a detailed view, follow the steps given next.

1. On the ribbon, click **Layout > Model Views > Detailed View**.
2. Click on the edge of the model to define the center of the detailed view as shown.

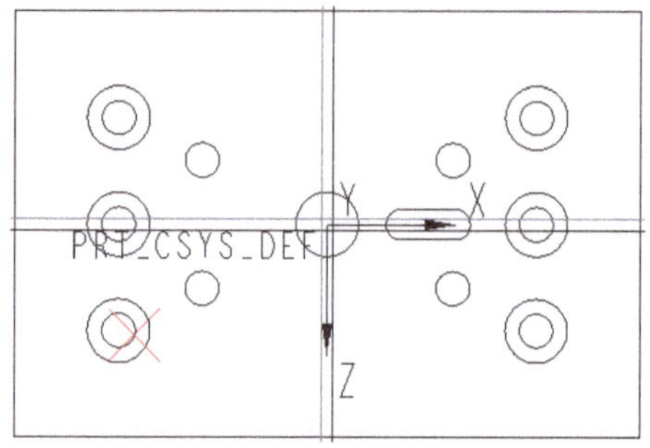

3. Draw a spline to identify the area that you wish to zoom in. It should enclose the center point.

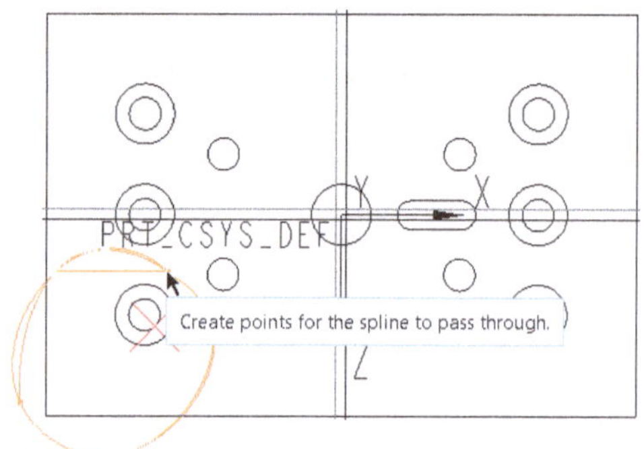

4. Click the middle mouse button once the spline is drawn.
5. Move the pointer and click to locate the view. The detail view will appear with a label.

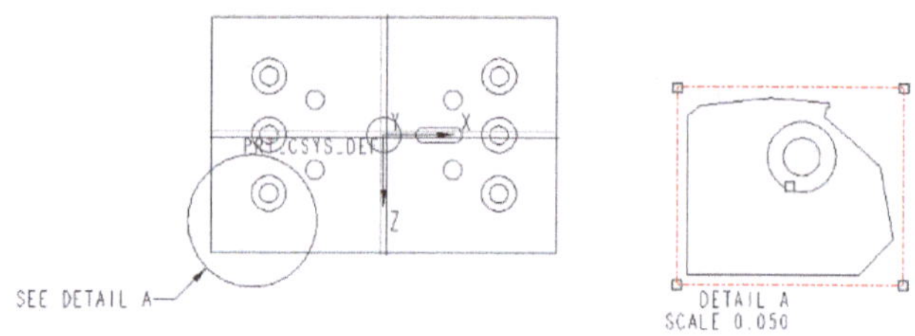

If you want to change the scale value, click the right mouse button on the detailed view and select **Properties**. On the **Drawing View** dialog, select **Categories > Scale**, type-in a new value in the **Scale** box, and click **OK**.

Partial View

Follow the steps given next to create a partial view.

1. Select the view, right-click, and select **Properties**.
2. On the **Drawing view** dialog, click **Categories > Visible Area** and select **View visibility > Partial**

View.

3. Select an edge on the view to define the reference point.

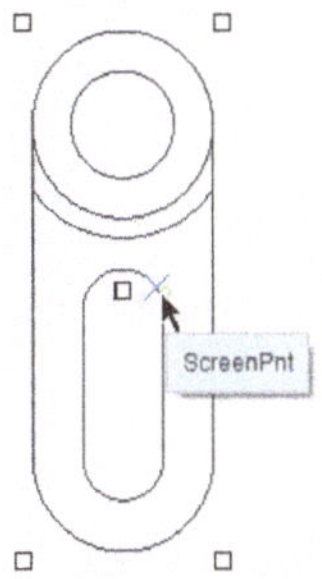

4. Draw a spline enclosing the center point, and then click the middle mouse button.
5. Click **OK**.

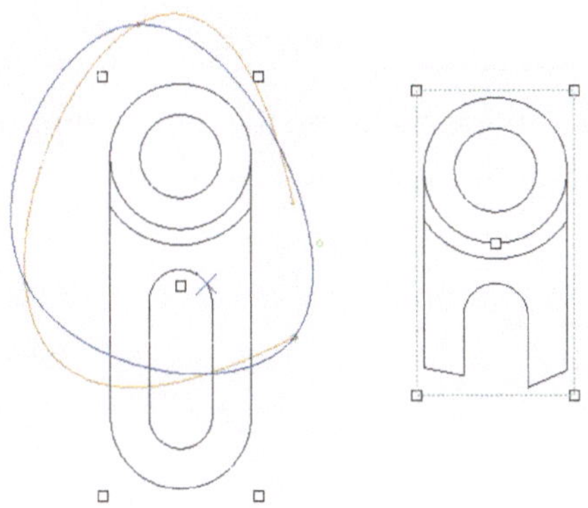

Broken View

You can add break lines to a drawing view, which is too large to fit on the drawing sheet. They break the view so that only important details are shown.

1. Select the view, and select **Properties**.
2. On the **Drawing view** dialog, click **Categories > Visible Area** and select **View visibility > Broken View**.
3. Click the **Add break**  button on the dialog.
4. Click on the edge to locate the beginning of the break.

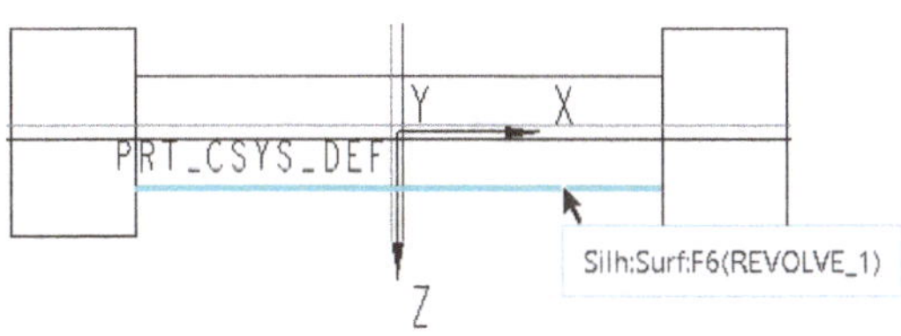

5. Move the pointer in the direction perpendicular to the selected edge.

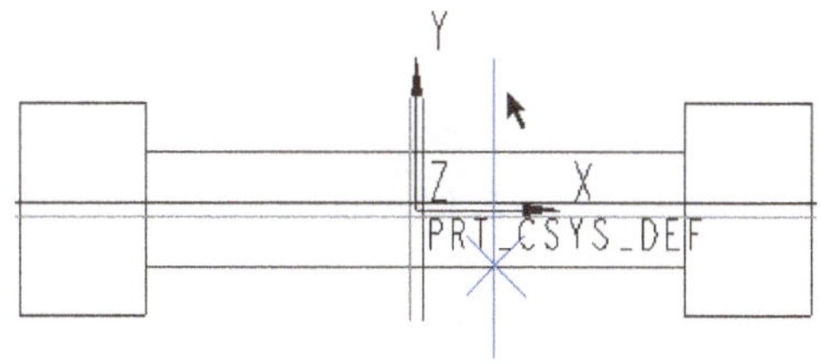

6. Select a point to define the end of the break.

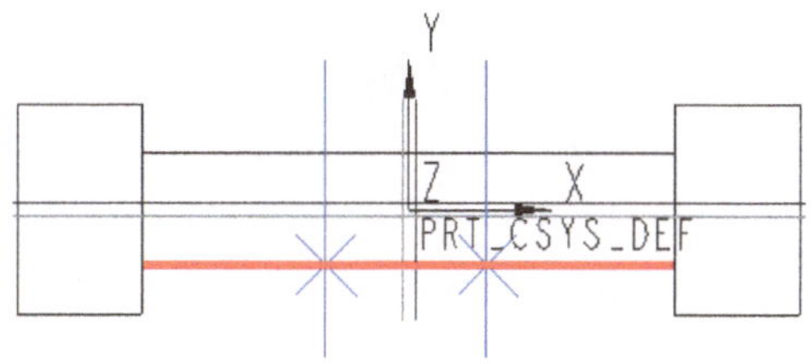

7. Click **OK** to create the broken view.

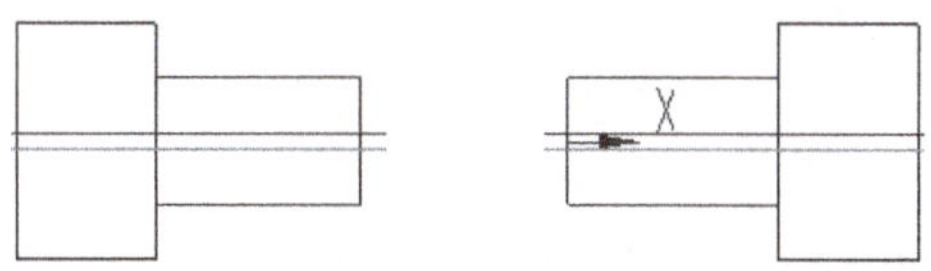

If you want to change the break lines' line type, click the right mouse button on view and select **Properties**. On the **Drawing View** dialog, click **Categories > Visible Area**. Drag the horizontal scroll bar and select a new line type to be applied from the **Break Line Style** drop-down menu. Click **OK** to close the dialog.

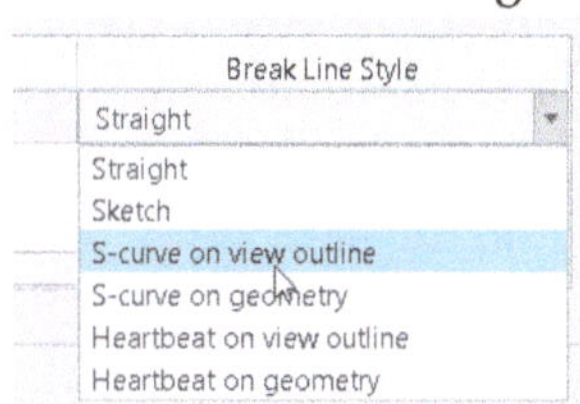

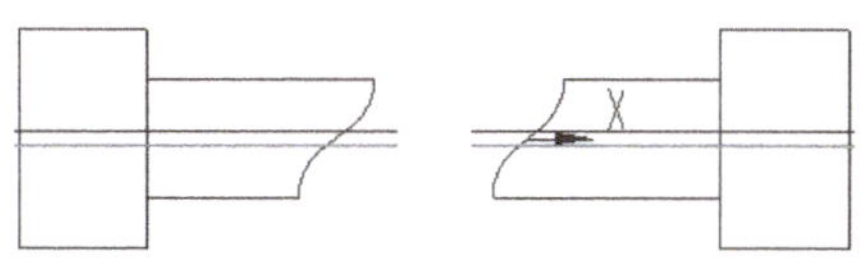

Breakout View

The Breakout View alters an existing view to show the hidden portion of a part or Assembly. This view is very useful to show the parts, which are hidden in an assembly. You need to create a closed profile to breakout a view.

1. Create the base and projected views, as shown.

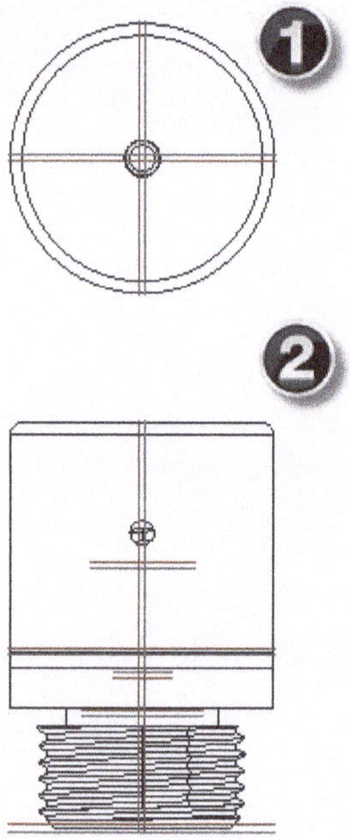

2. Select the view to be broken and select **Properties** .
3. Select **Categories > Sections** and click **2D cross-section**.
4. Click the **Add cross-section to view** button.
5. On the **Menu Manager**, select **Planar** and **Single**, and then click **Done**.
6. Enter **A** as the name of the cross-section and click the green check.
7. Select the cutting plane from the base view.

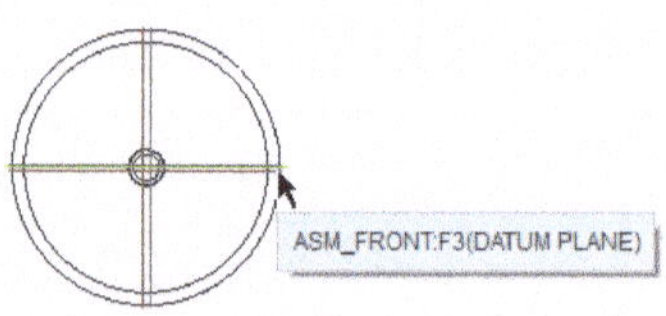

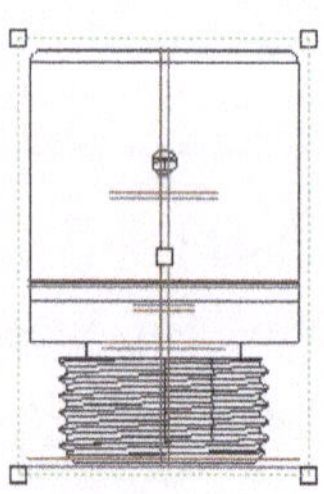

8. On the **Drawing View** dialog, set the **Section Area** to **Local**.

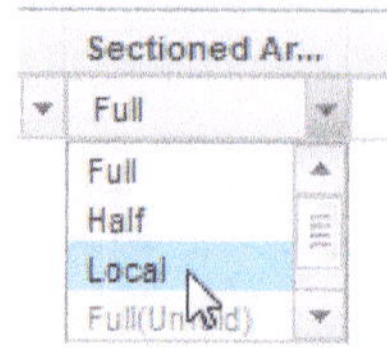

9. Select an edge on the view to define the center point.

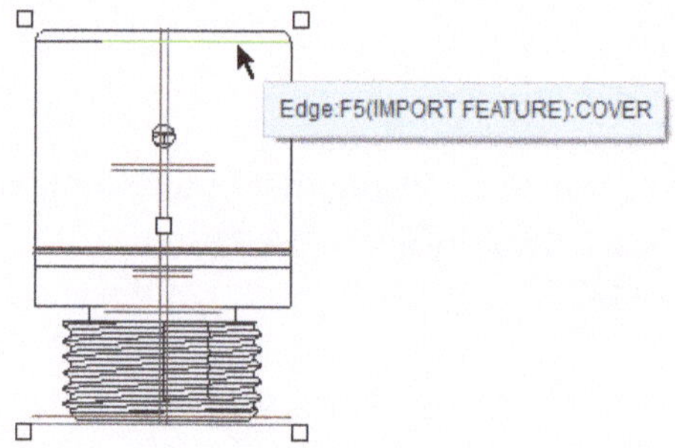

10. Draw a spline enclosing the center point, and then click the middle mouse button.

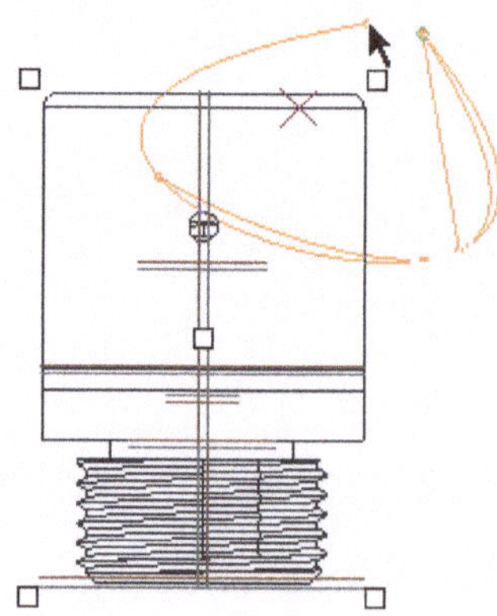

11. Click **OK**.

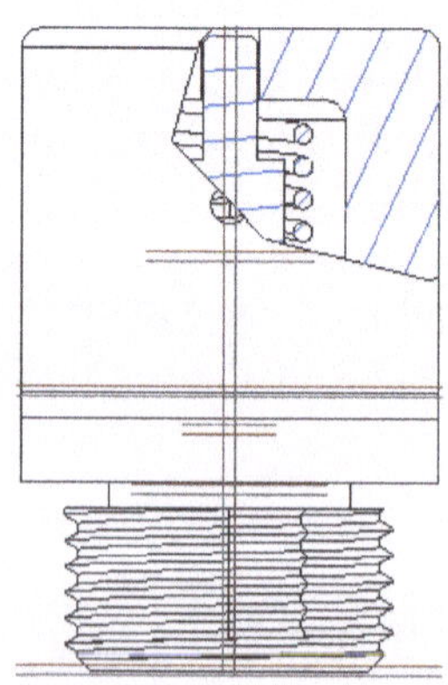

SECTION A-A

Exploded View

You can display an assembly in an exploded state as long as the Assembly already has an exploded view defined. Follow the steps given next to define the exploded view in an assembly.

1. Open the assembly file.
2. On the **Graphics** toolbar, click the **View Manager** icon.
3. On the **View Manager** dialog, click the **Explode** tab and create a new exploded view with the name **Explosion**.
4. Explode the components of the Assembly using the **Edit Position** command.
5. On the **View Manager** dialog, click **Edit > Save**.

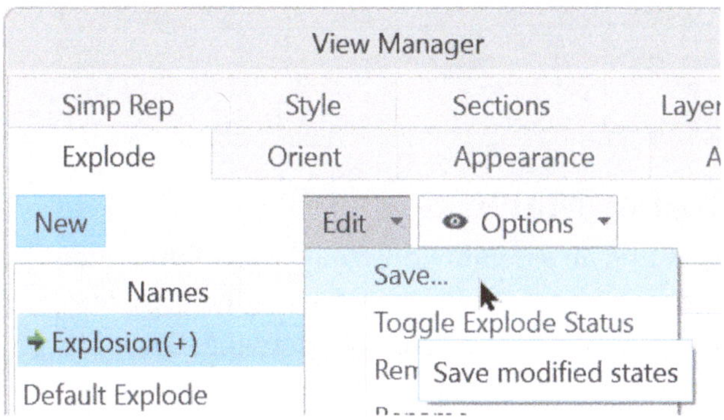

6. Click **OK**.
7. Close the **View Manager** dialog.
8. Save the assembly file.

Follow the steps given next to insert the exploded view in a drawing.

1. Open a drawing file.
2. On the ribbon, click **Layout > Model Views > General View**.
3. Select **No Combined state** and click **OK**.
4. Click on the drawing sheet to position the view.
5. In the **Drawing View** dialog, click **Categories > View States** and check the **Explode components in view** option.
6. Select **Assembly explode state > EXPLOSION**.
7. Click **OK** to generate the exploded view of the Assembly.

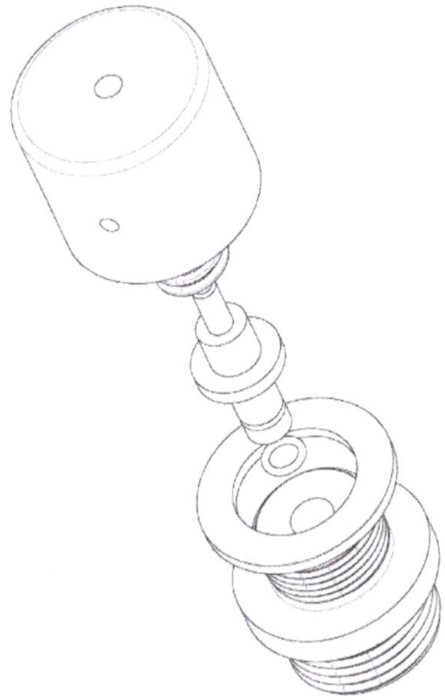

View Display

When working with Creo Parametric drawings, you can control how a model view appears using the **Drawing View** dialog. For example, if you want to show or hide the hidden lines, follow the next steps.

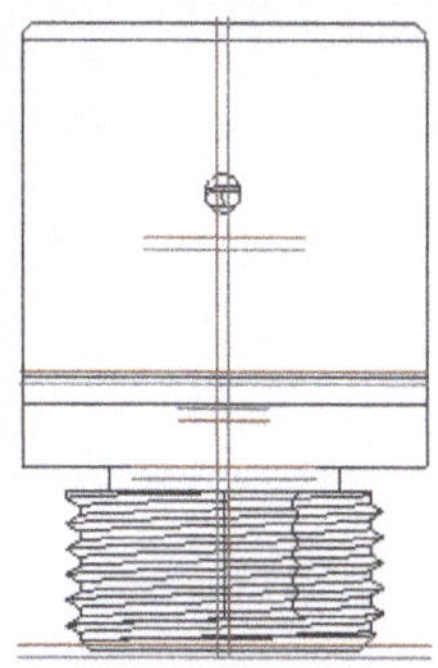

1. Click the right mouse button on the view and select **Properties** .
2. On the **Drawing View** dialog, under the **View Display** section, select **Display Style > Hidden**.
3. Click **OK** to apply the changes.

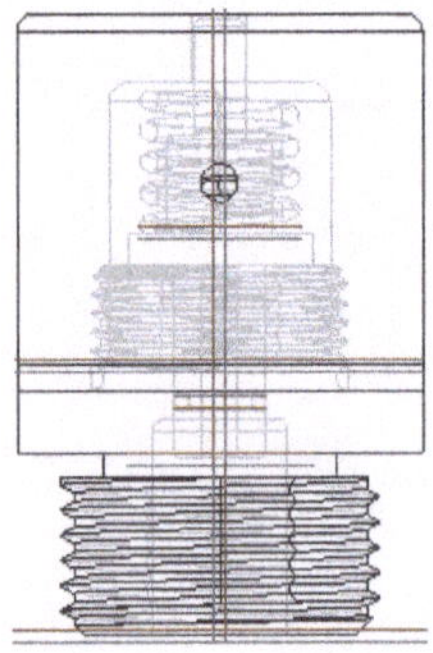

View Movement

Creo Parametric locks the drawing views to their original positions and restricts you from moving them. If you want to move a drawing view, click the right mouse button on it and deactivate **Lock View Movement**.

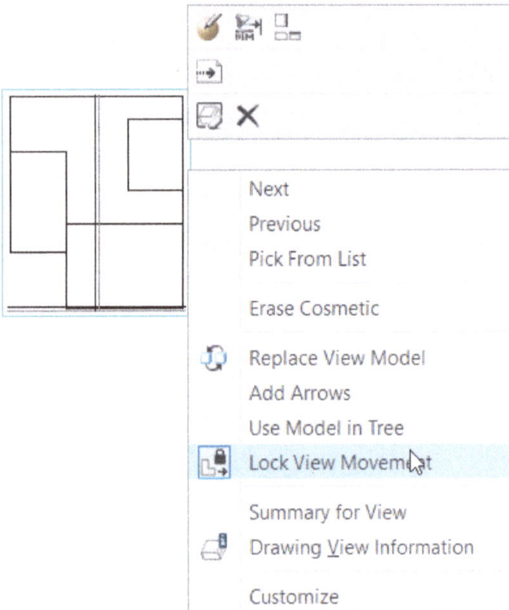

Now, you can move the drawing view.

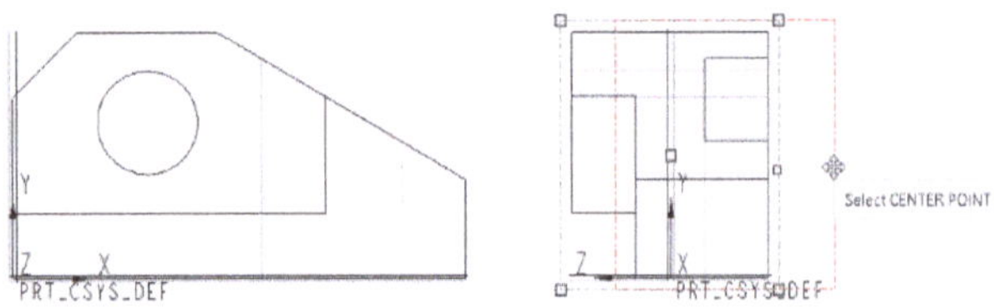

View Alignment

Several types of views are automatically aligned to their parent view. These include projected views, auxiliary views, and section views. For example, if you want to move any view, the movement is constrained along the parent view. You can make the view independent of its parent view by breaking the link between them. To do this, click the right mouse button on the view – select **Properties**.

On the **Drawing View** dialog, click **Categories > Alignment**. Uncheck the **Align this view to other view** option and click **OK**. Now, you can move the view independently.

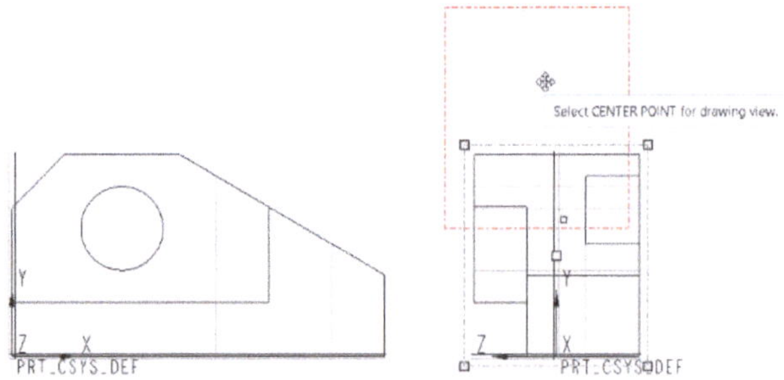

Bill of Material

Creating an assembly drawing is very similar to creating a part drawing. However, there are few things unique in an assembly drawing. One of them is creating a parts list. A parts list identifies the different components in an assembly. Generating a parts list is very easy in Creo Parametric. First, you need to have a view of the Assembly.

1. On the ribbon, click **Table > Table > Table > Quick Tables >Assembly > bom description down**.

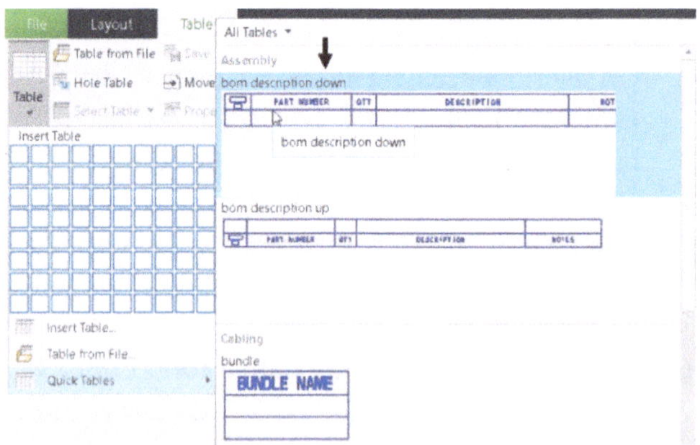

2. Click on the drawing sheet to position the bill of materials.

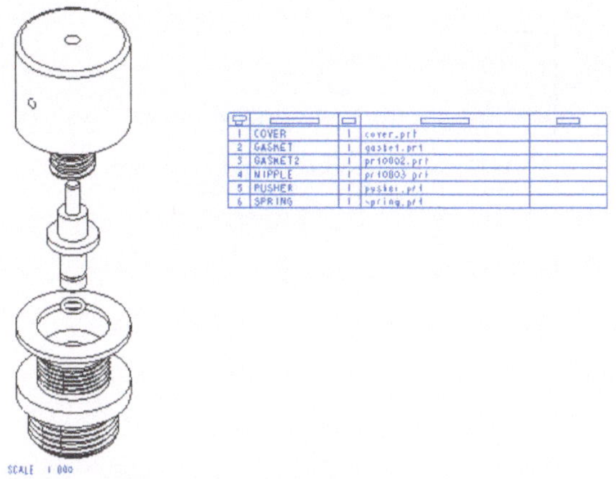

If you want to modify the bill of material, click the right mouse button on the material bill. Select **Properties** to open the **Table Properties** dialog. On the **Table Properties** dialog, click on the **Height and Width** tab and change the table's direction using the buttons available in the **Direction** section. Next, change the **Row** and **Column** properties, if required. Next, click **OK** to apply the changes.

Balloons

To add balloons to the assembly drawing, click **Table > Balloons > Create Balloons > Create Balloons - All** on the ribbon.

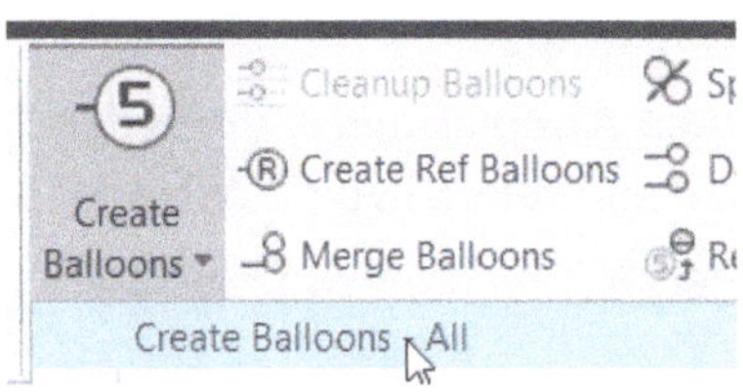

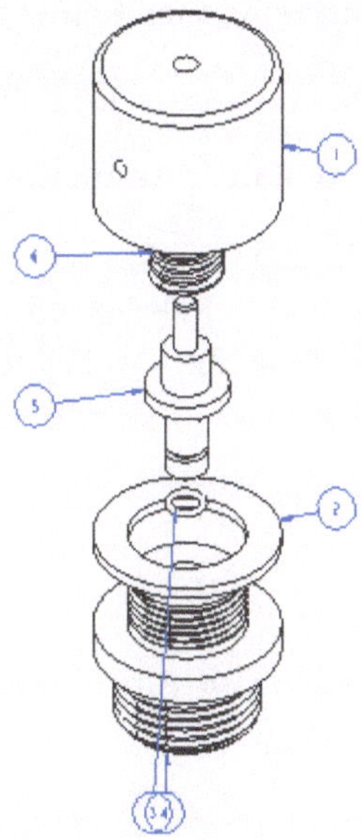

Select the overlapping balloon and drag it to a new location.

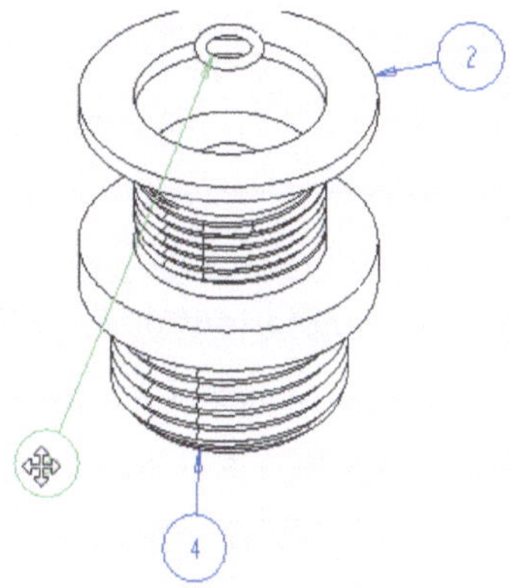

To change the balloon properties, click on the Bill of Materials table and select the Properties option. Next, click the **BOM Balloons** tab and select the balloon-type (**Simple Circle**, **Quantity Split Circle**, **Custom**, **As Is**) from the **Type** drop-down. Next, click **OK**.

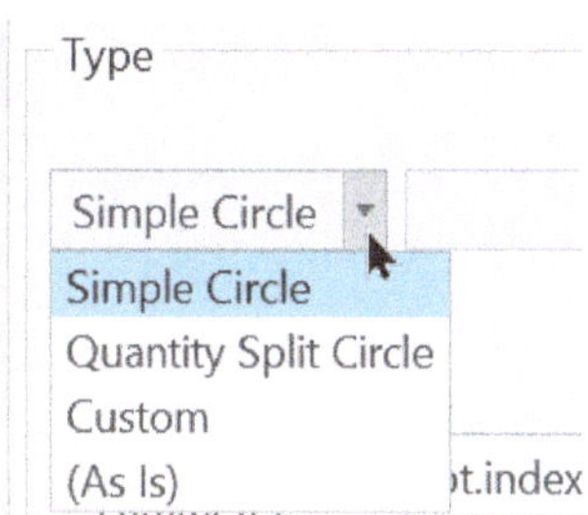

Centerlines

Centerlines are used in engineering drawings to denote hole centers and lines. If you want to display the centerlines of a drawing view, then follow the steps given next.

1. On the ribbon, click **Annotate > Annotations > Show Model Annotations**.
2. Select a drawing view having holes by clicking on the view boundary. Press the Ctrl key to select multiple views.

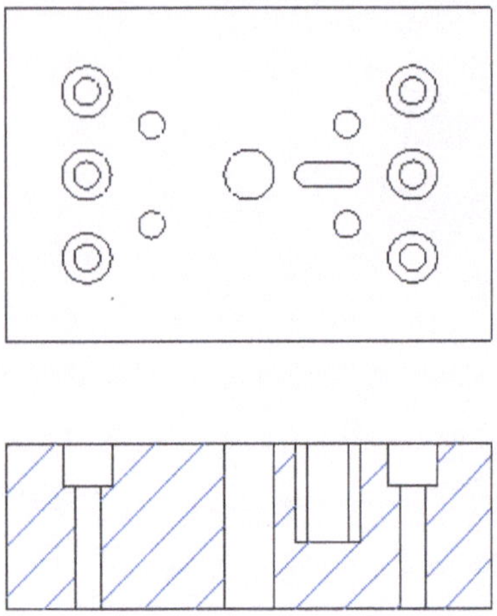

SECTION A-A

3. On the **Show Model Annotations** dialog, click the **Datums** tab and select **Type > Axes**. The axes appear on the drawing view(s).
4. Select the axes to include and click **OK**.

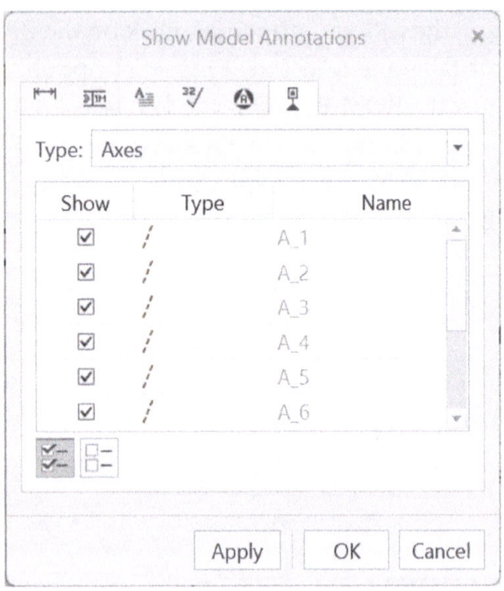

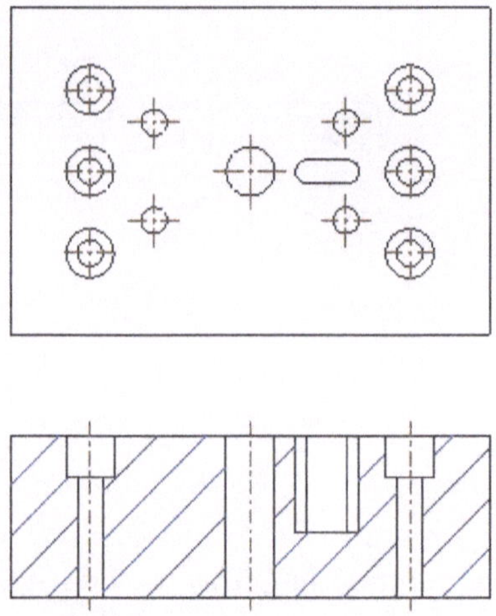

SECTION A-A

Dimensions

Creo Parametric provides you with different types of commands to add dimensions to the drawing.

Show Model Annotations

One way to add dimensions to the drawing is to retrieve the dimensions that are already contained in the 3D part file. The **Show Model Annotations** command helps you to do this.

1. On the ribbon, click **Annotate > Annotations > Show Model Annotations**.
2. On the **Show Model Annotations** dialog, click the **Dimension** tab and select **Type > All**.
3. Select the drawing view by clicking on its view boundary.

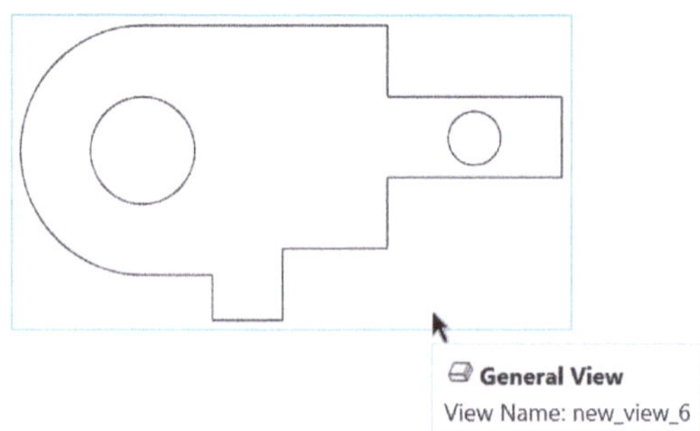

4. Click the **Select All** icon on the **Show Model Annotations** dialog, and then click **OK**.

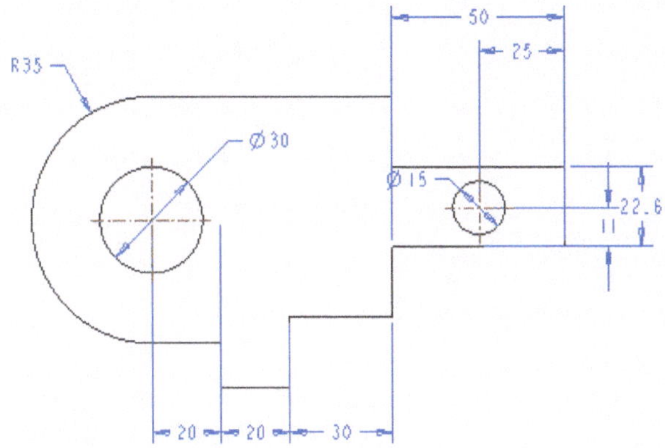

You can erase a dimension by selecting it, right-clicking, and selecting **Erase**.

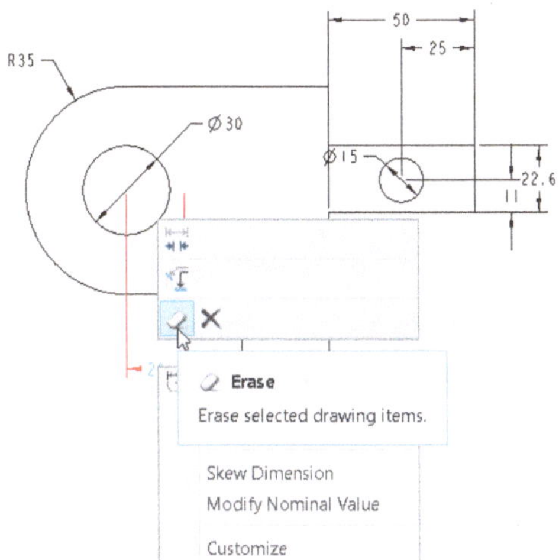

To unerase the erased dimension, expand **Annotations** in the Drawing Tree. Click the right mouse button on the erased dimension and select **Unerase**.

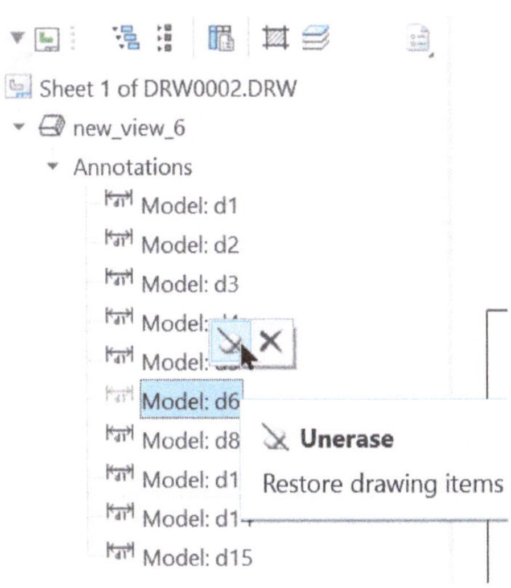

You can delete the dimension permanently by selecting it and pressing **Delete**.

Move to View

The **Move to View** command moves a dimension from one view to another.

1. Select the dimension to move.
2. On the ribbon, click **Annotate > Edit > Move to View**.

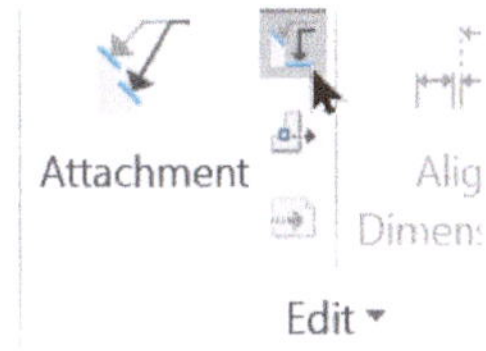

3. Select the destination view.

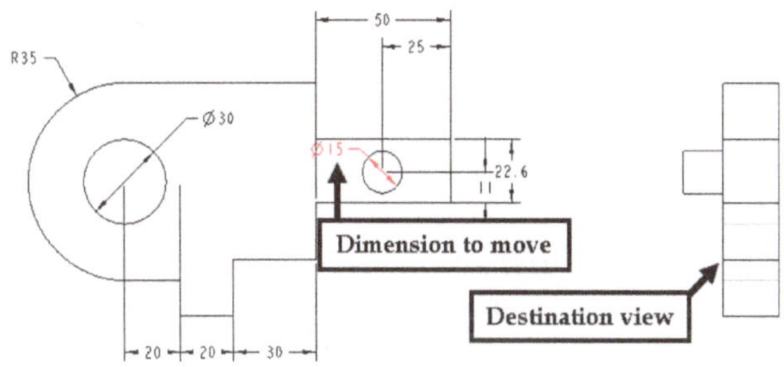

The dimension is moved to the destination view.

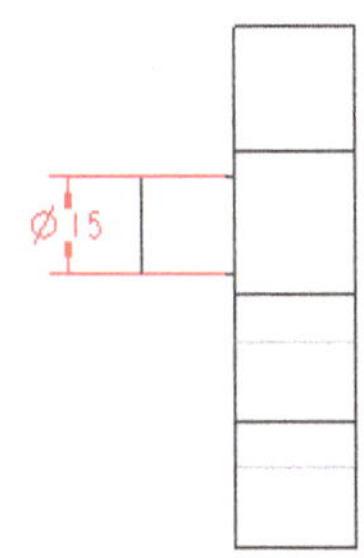

Adding Dimensions

If you want to add some more dimensions necessary to manufacture a part, use the **Dimension** command (on the ribbon, click **Annotate > Annotations > Dimension**) to create linear, radial, or any type of dimension. As you activate this command, the **Select Reference** dialog appears.

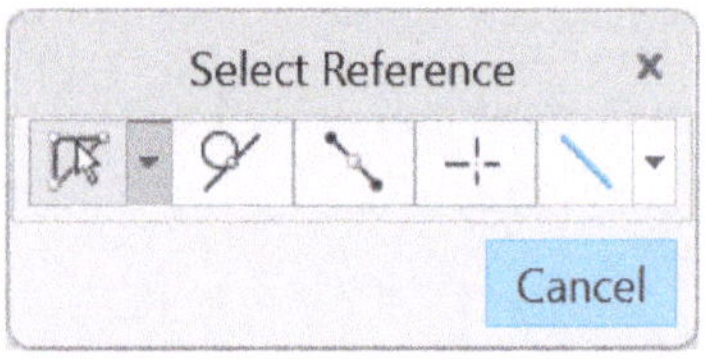

You can use the options on this dialog to define the type of dimension reference. For example, click the **Tangent** icon, press the Ctrl key, and select two arcs. A dimension appears between the tangent points of the arcs. Move the pointer and middle click to position the dimension.

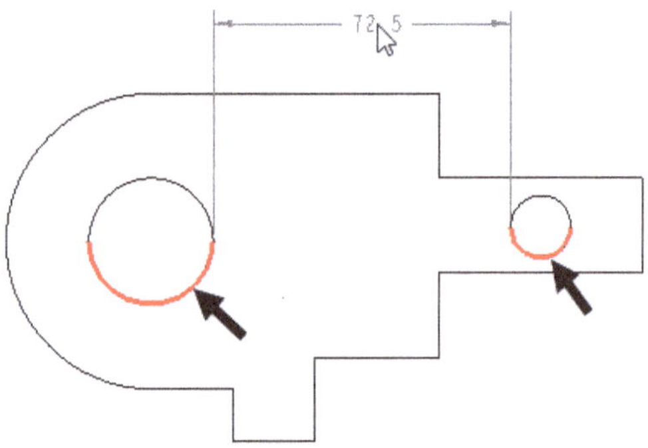

Linear Dimensions

To create a linear dimension, activate the **Dimension** command, and click the **Select an entity** icon on the **Select References** dialog. Next, select a straight edge of the drawing view. Move the pointer and middle click to position the dimension.

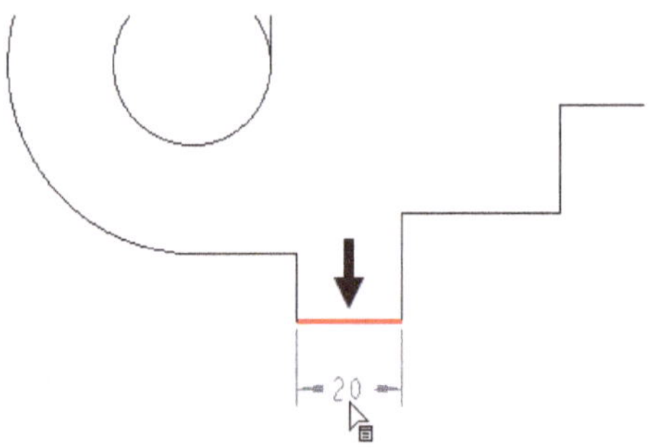

Radial Dimensions

To add a radial dimension, activate the **Dimension** command, and select a circular edge. Click the right mouse button to view a menu. Use the options on this menu to create four different types of radial dimensions

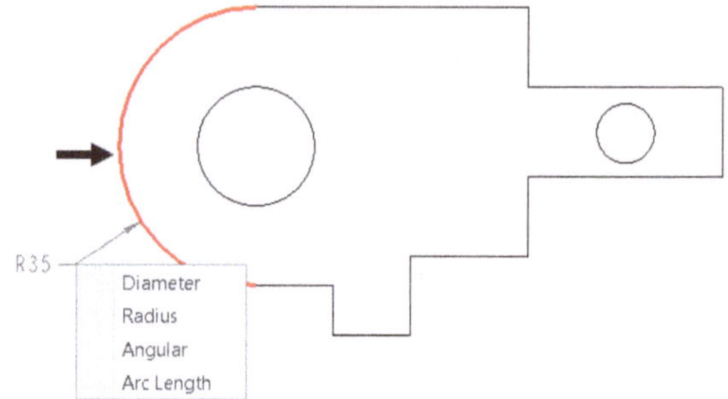

Move the pointer and middle click to position the dimension. You can change the dimension type using the **Orientation** drop-down on the **Display** panel of the **Dimension** tab.

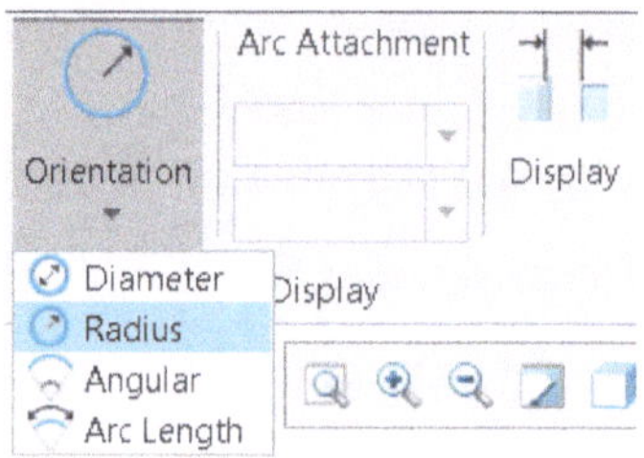

Baseline Dimensions

The **Dimension** command can also be used to create baseline dimensions.

1. Activate the **Dimension** command.
2. Press the Ctrl key and select the parallel edges, as shown.
3. Move the pointer and middle-click to create the baseline dimensions.

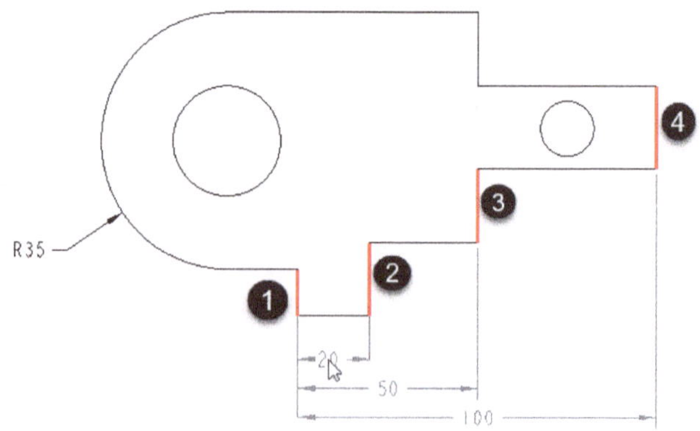

Align Dimensions

This command aligns the dimensions horizontally or vertically.

1. Press the Ctrl key and select two or more dimensions.

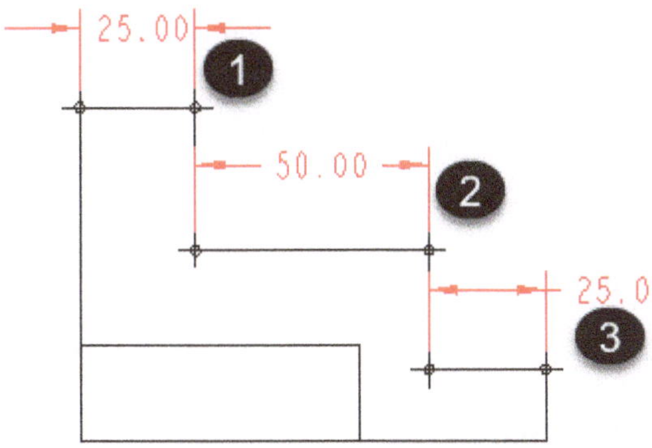

2. On the ribbon, click **Annotate > Edit > Align Dimensions.**

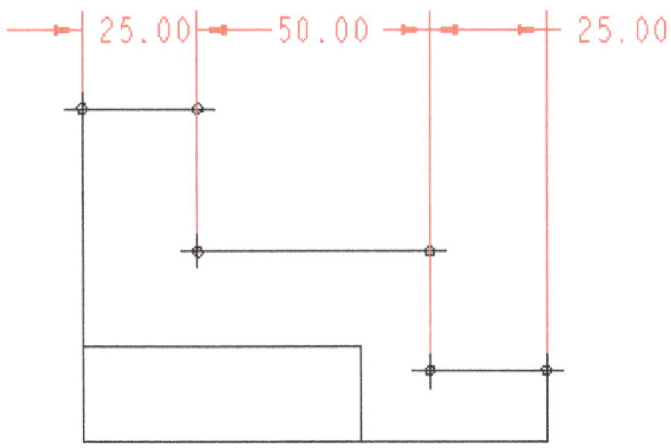

Ordinate Dimension

Ordinate dimensions are another type of dimension that you can add to a drawing.

1. On the ribbon, click **Annotate > Annotations > Ordinate Dimension.**

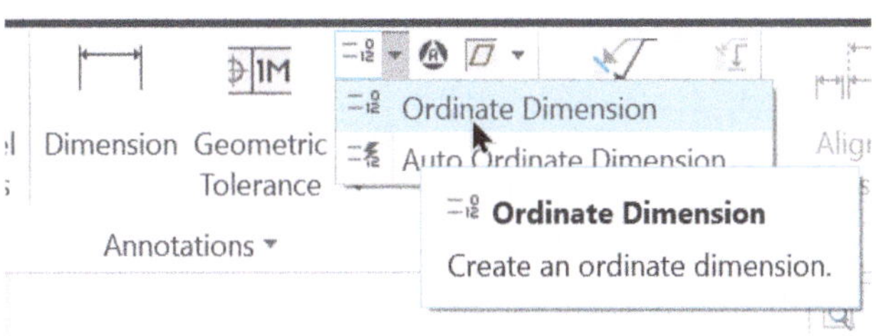

2. Click on any edge of the drawing view to define the zero reference.
3. Now, press the Ctrl key and click on the edge of the drawing view.
4. Likewise, click on other edges parallel to the zero references.

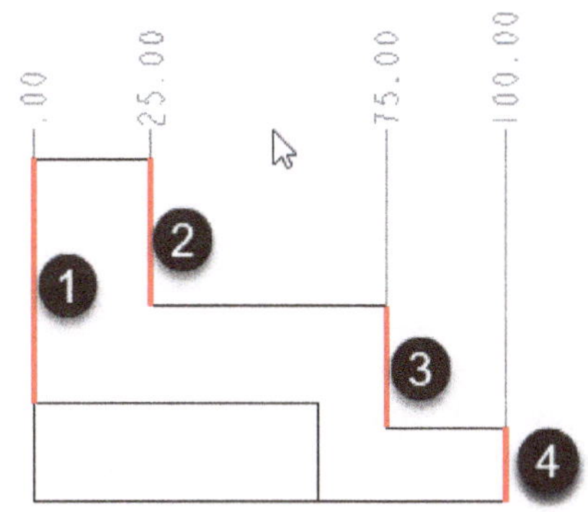

5. Move the pointer and middle click to place the ordinate dimension.

Auto Ordinate Dimension

This command creates ordinate dimensions automatically.

1. On the ribbon, click **Annotate > Annotations > Ordinate Dimension > Auto Ordinate Dimension.**

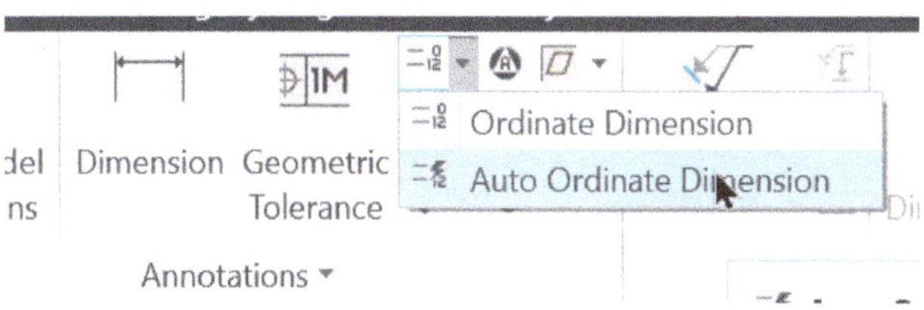

2. Select the surface that has the edges to be dimensioned.

3. Click the middle mouse button.

4. Select the zero reference of the ordinate dimensions.

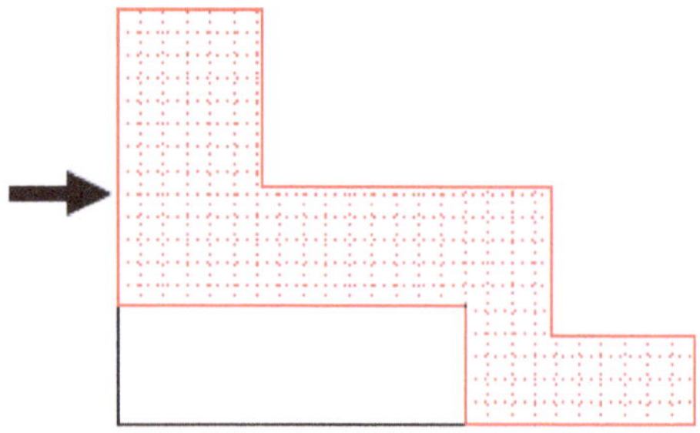

5. Click **Done/Return** on the **Menu Manager**.

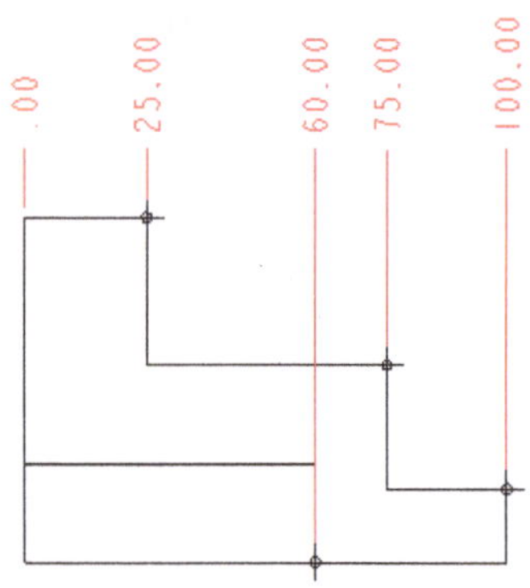

You can also convert baseline dimensions into ordinate dimensions. Press the Ctrl key and select the baseline dimensions. Click the right mouse button and select **Toggle Ordinate/Linear**.

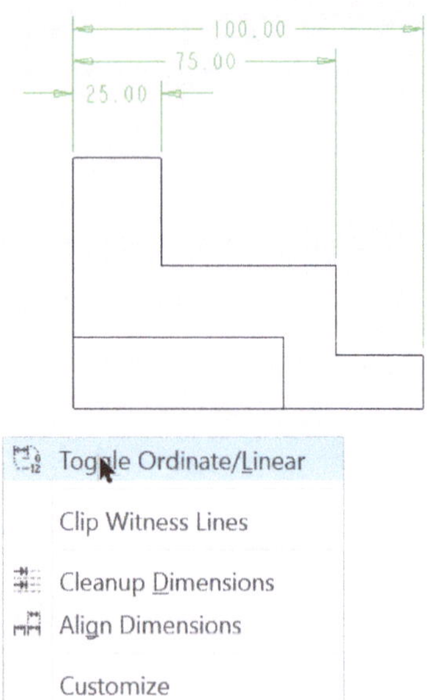

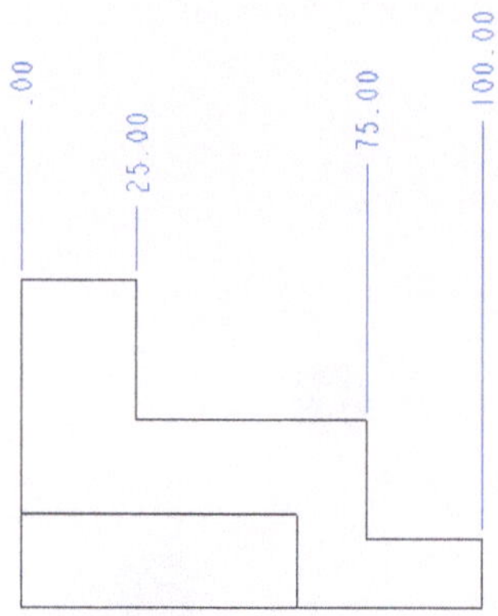

Angle Dimensions

The **Dimension** command can be used to create angle dimensions.

1. On the ribbon, click **Annotate > Annotations > Dimension**.
2. Press the Ctrl key and select two lines, which are positioned at an angle to each other.

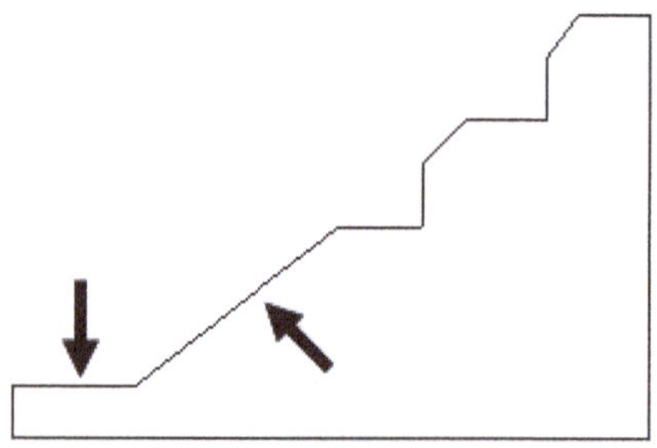

3. Click the right mouse and select any angle sector.

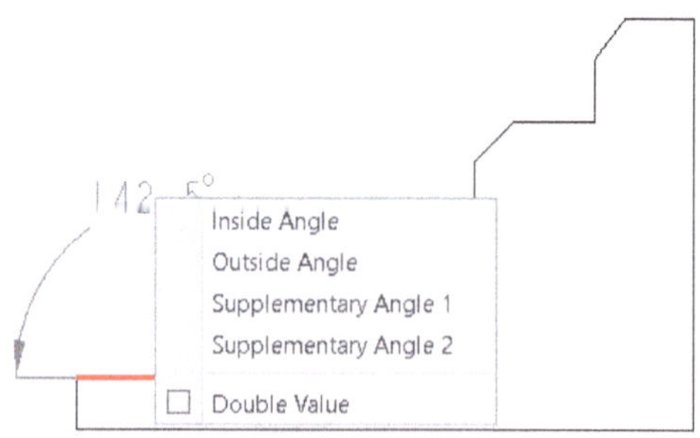

4. Middle-click to position the dimension.

Unattached Note

Notes are an essential part of a drawing. You add notes to provide additional details, which cannot be done using dimensions and annotations.

1. On the ribbon, click **Annotate > Annotations > Note > Unattached Note**.

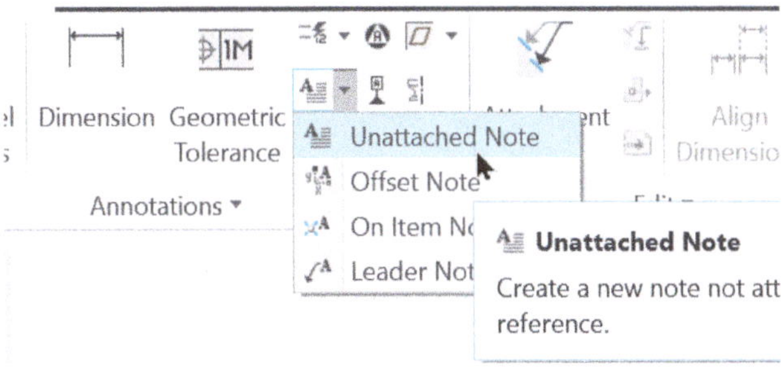

2. Click on the drawing sheet to define the location of the note.
3. Type in the text and click the middle mouse button.

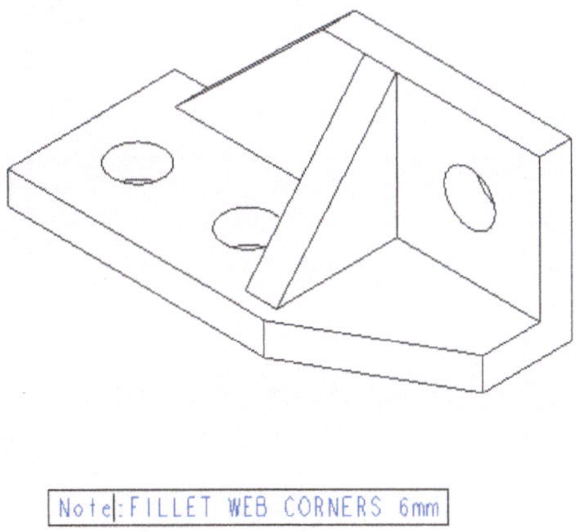

Leader Note

Leader notes are an essential element in creating drawings.

1. On the ribbon, click **Annotate > Annotations > Note > Leader Note**.

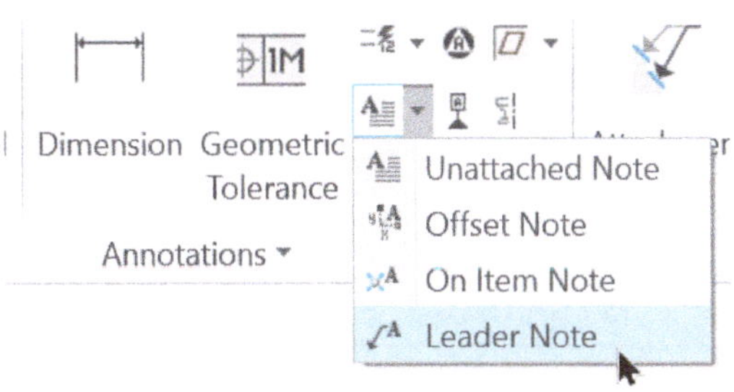

2. Click on the edge to add a leader. Press the Ctrl key and select multiple edges to add a single leader to multiple edges.

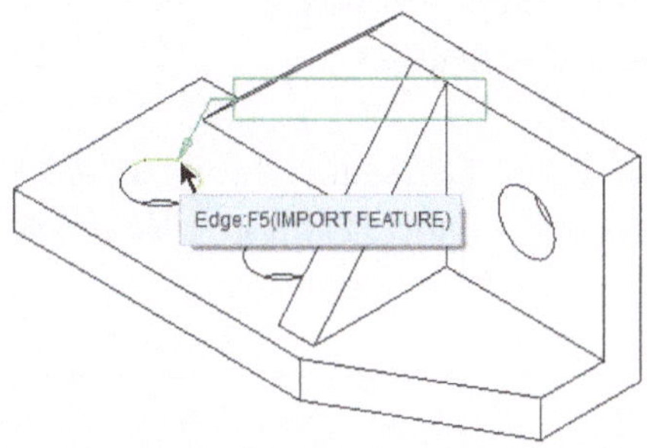

3. Move the pointer and middle click to position the leader.

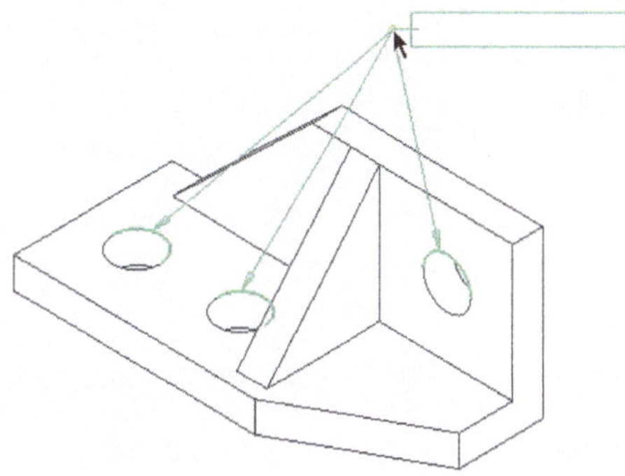

4. Type-in the leader text and middle-click. You can also use the options on the **Format** tab of the ribbon to format the text.

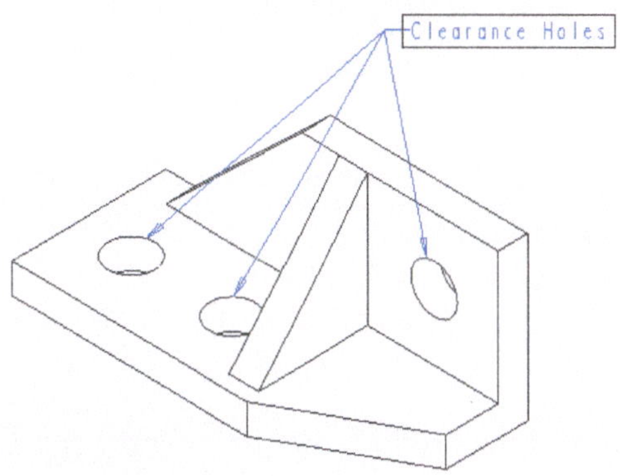

Examples

Example 1

In this example, you will create a drawing format file.

1. Start **Creo Parametric 11.0.**
2. Create the *Drawings* folder and set it as the current working folder.
3. On the **Home** tab, click the **New** button.
4. On the **New** dialog, select **Type > Format**.

5. Type-in *Sample-Format* in the **Name** box and click **OK**.
6. Select **Empty** from the **Select Template** section.
7. Set the **Orientation** to **Landscape**.
8. Set the **Standard Size** to **A3**.
9. Click **OK**.
10. On the ribbon, click **Table** tab > **Table** panel > **Table** drop-down > **Quick Tables** > **title block**. The table is attached to the pointer.

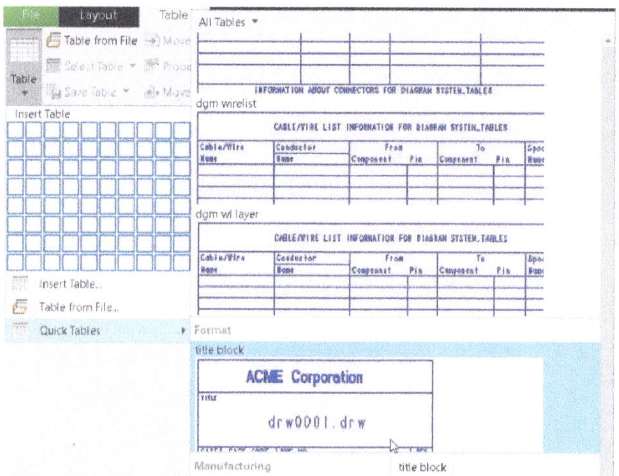

11. On the **Select Point** dialog, click the **Select a point on drawing object or entity** button.

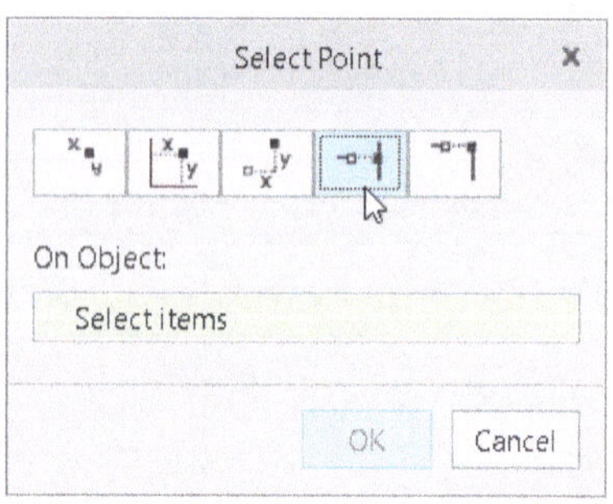

12. Select the lower right corner point of the sheet.

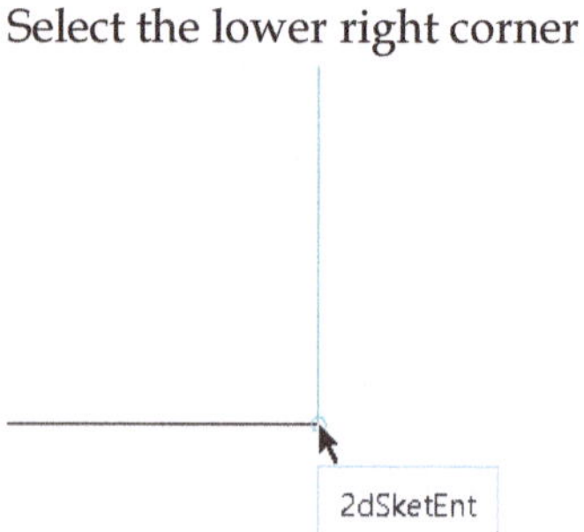

13. Click **OK**. The title block is placed at the selected point.
14. Double-click in the top row of the title block, and then type in the company name.
15. Save and close the format file.

Example 2

In this example, you will create the 2D drawing of the part, as shown.

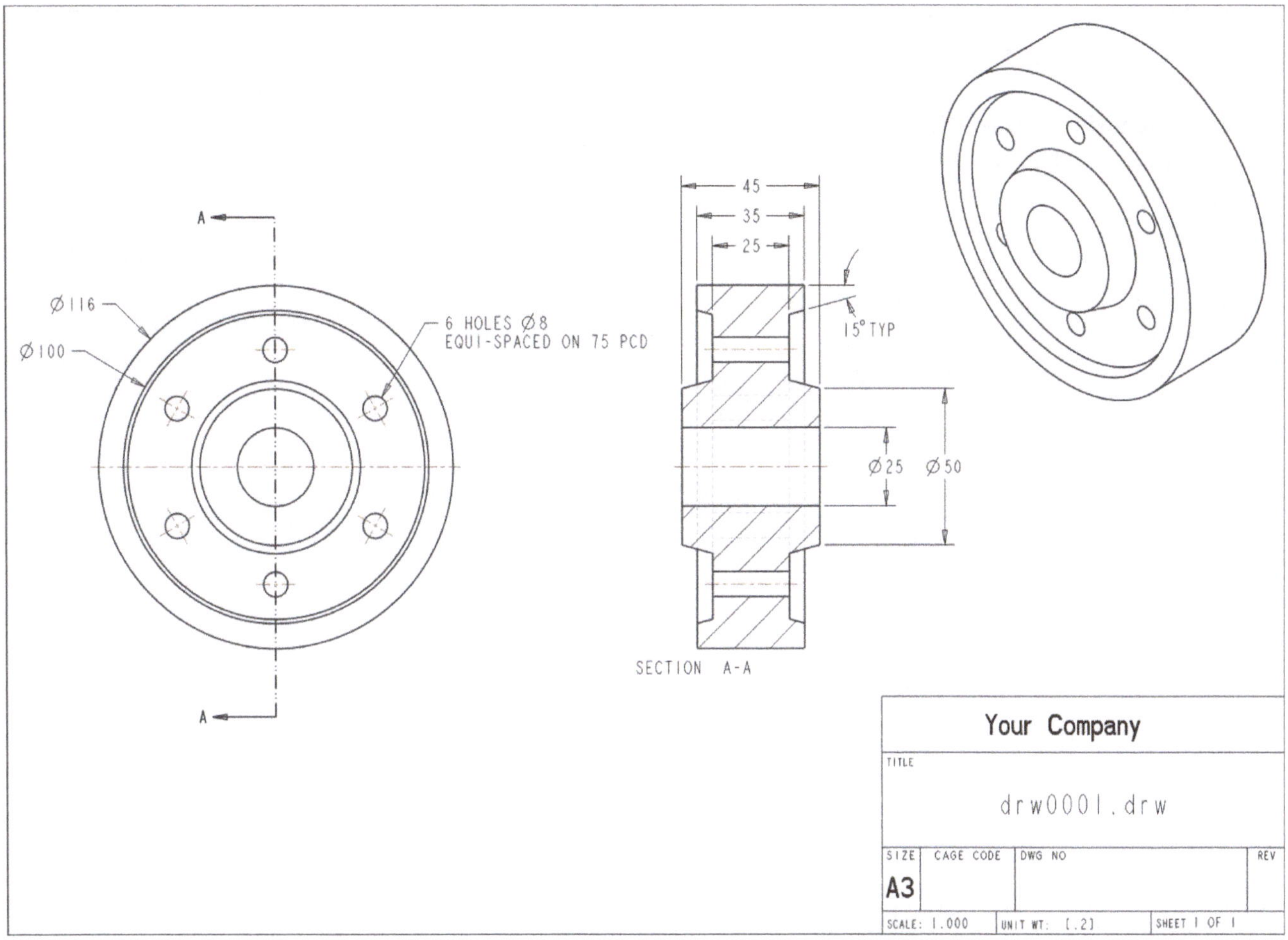

Starting a New Drawing

1. Start **Creo Parametric 11.0**.
2. Set the *Drawings* folder as the current working folder.
3. Copy the Exercise1.prt file created in Chapter 5 to the *Drawings* folder.
4. On the **Home** tab, click the **New** button.
5. On the **New** dialog, select **Type > Drawing**.
6. Type-in *Example2* in the **File name** box and uncheck the **Use default template** option.
7. Click **OK**.
8. On the **New Drawing** dialog, click the **Browse** button in the **Default Model** section and select the *C05-Exercise1.prt* file.
9. Under the **Select Template** section, select the **Empty with Format** option.
10. Click the **Browse** button in the **Format** section.
11. Go to the Drawings folder and select the *Sample-Format.frm* file.
12. Click **Open**, and then click **OK**. The dialog appears, as shown below.

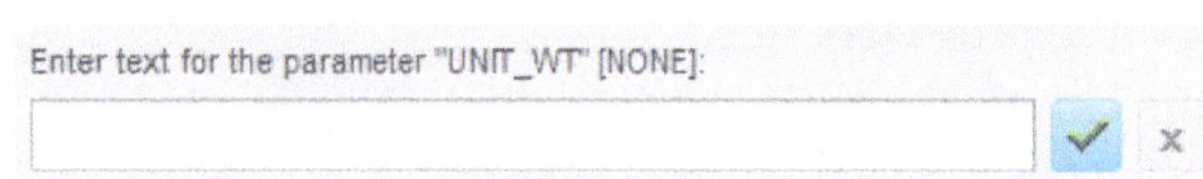

13. Click the green checks to accept the default values.

Generating Drawing Views

1. On the ribbon, click **Layout** tab **> Model Views** panel **> General View** 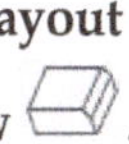.
2. On the **Select Combined State** dialog, select the **No combined State** option and click **OK**.

3. Click on the left side of the drawing sheet to position the view.
4. On the **Drawing View** dialog, select **FRONT** from the **Model view names** list.
5. Type-in **Front** in the **View name** box and click **Apply**.
6. Click **Categories > View Display** and set the **Display style** to **Hidden**.
7. Click **OK**.
8. Select the view and deactivate the **Lock view Movement** icon on the **Document** panel of the ribbon.
9. Move the view to the position, as shown below.

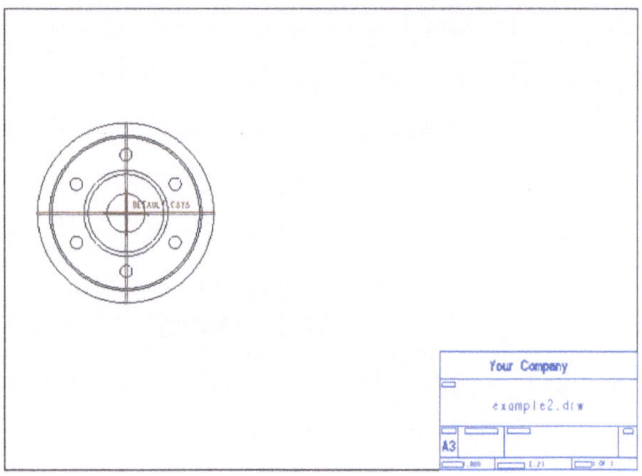

Now, you have to create a projected view.

10. On the ribbon, click **Layout** tab **> Model Views** panel **> Projection View** .
11. Move the pointer rightward and click to position the projected view.
12. On the **Graphics** toolbar, click **Display style** drop-down > **Hidden Line**.

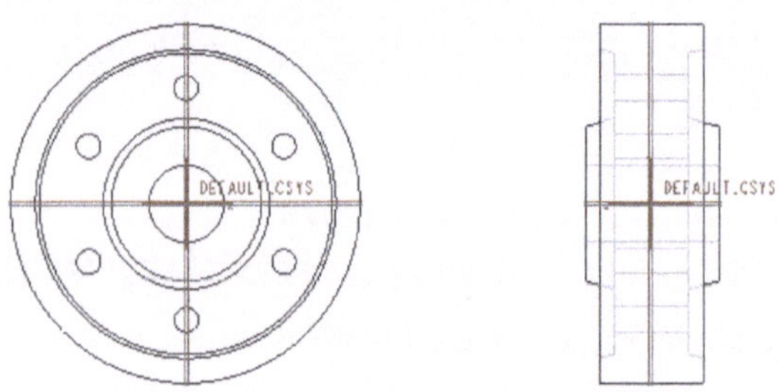

Now, you have to create the section view.

13. Select the right view and click the right mouse button.
14. Select **Properties** from the shortcut menu.
15. On the **Drawing view** dialog, select **Categories > Sections**.
16. Under **Section Options**, select **2D cross-section** and click the **Add cross-section to view** button.
17. Click **Done** on the **Menu Manager**.
18. Enter **A** as the name of the cross-section and click the green check.
19. Select the right plane from the Front view.

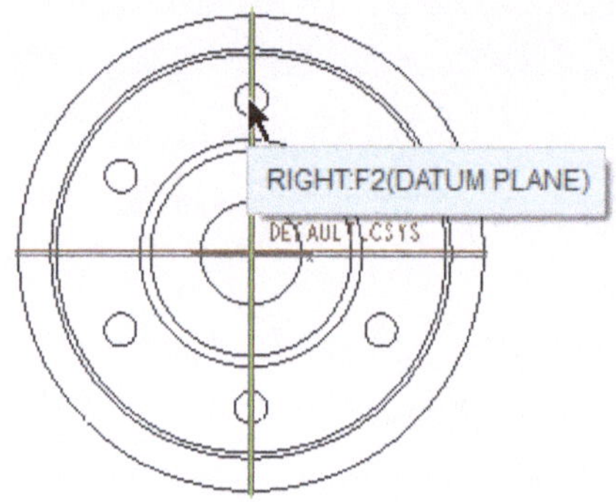

20. Click **OK** to create the section view.

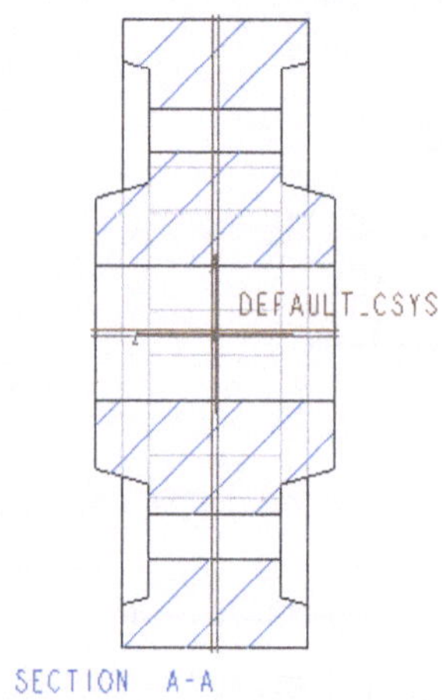

Now, you need to add arrows to the front view.

21. On the ribbon, click **Arrows** on the **Edit** panel.

22. Select the section view.
23. Select the Front view to add arrows to it.

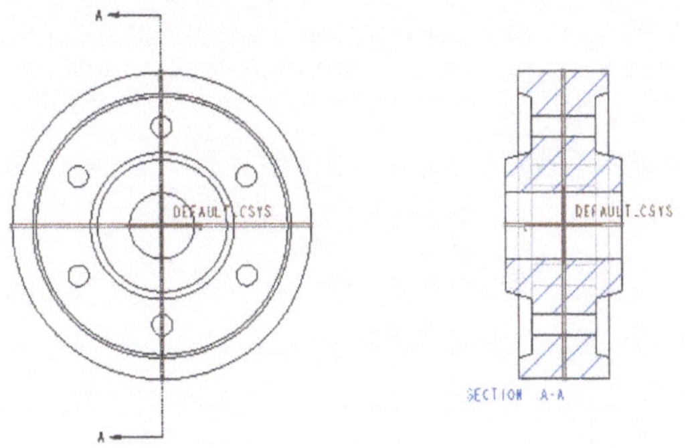

Now, you have to create the Isometric view.

24. On the ribbon, click **Layout** tab > **Model Views** panel > **General View** .
25. Select the **No Combined state** option and click **OK**.
26. Click on the top right corner of the drawing sheet to position the view.
27. On the **Drawing View** dialog, select **Standard Orientation** from the **Model view names** list.
28. Set the **Default Orientation** to **Isometric**.
29. Type-in **Isometric** in the **View name** box and click **Apply**.
30. Select the **View Display** option from the **Categories** list.
31. Set the **Display Style** to **No Hidden**.
32. Click **OK** on the **Drawing View** dialog.
33. Drag the Isometric view and position it, as shown below.

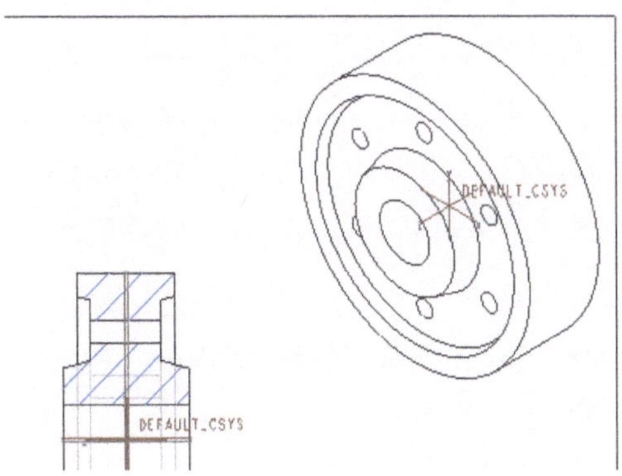

Add Axis lines

1. On the ribbon, click **Annotate** tab > **Annotations** panel > **Show Model Annotations** .
2. On the **Show Model Annotations** dialog, click the **Show Model datums** tab and select **Type > Axes**.
3. Press and hold the Ctrl key and select the holes and revolved feature of the section view.

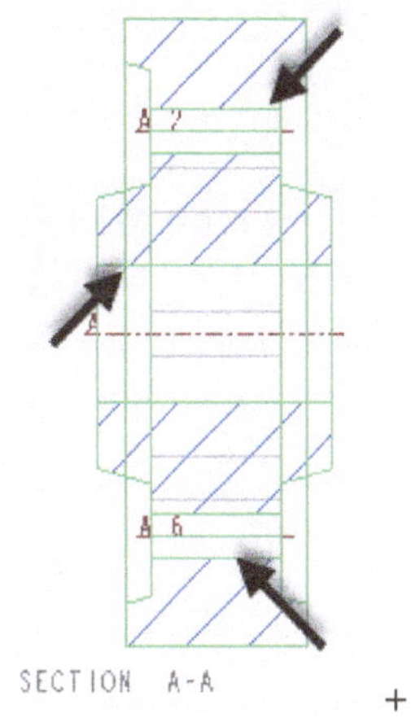

4. Click the **Select All** button located at the bottom-left corner on the **Show Model Annotations** dialog.
5. Click **Apply**.
6. Select the Front view by clicking on its view boundaries.
7. Select the axis lines to be included in the drawing view. Click **OK**.

8. Select the center mark of the hole in the first quadrant.
9. Right-click and select **Edit Attachment**.

10. On the **Menu Manager**, click **Through Geometry** and select the axis line passing through the center.

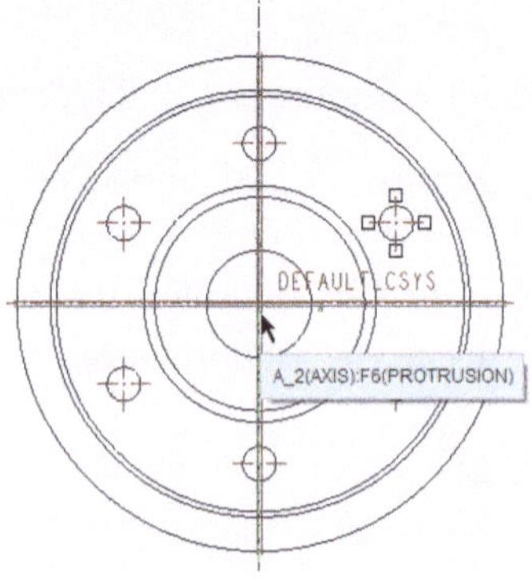

11. Click **Done/Return** on the **Menu Manager**. The orientation of the center mark is changed.

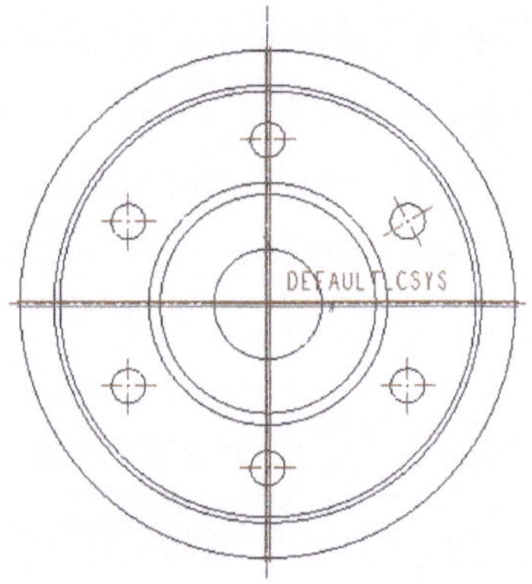

12. Likewise, change the orientation of the other center marks, as shown below.

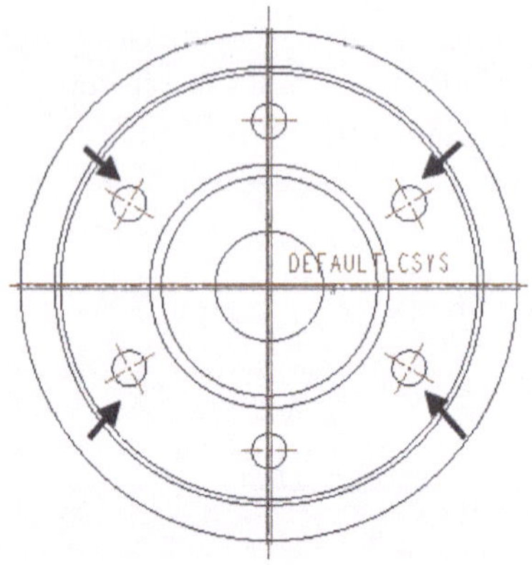

Showing Dimensions of the Geometry

1. On the ribbon, click **Annotate** tab > **Annotations** panel > **Show Model Annotations** .
2. On the **Show Model Annotations** dialog, click the **Show the model dimensions** tab.
3. Select the section view from the drawing sheet. You will notice that the model dimensions appear.
4. Select the dimensions from the section view, as shown below.

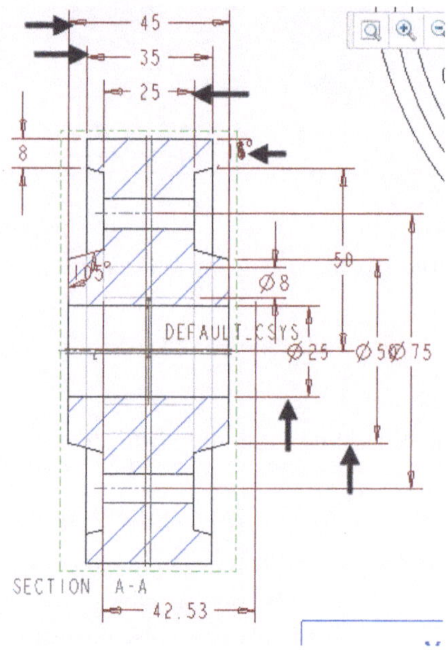

5. Click **OK** on the dialog.
6. Click and drag the diameter 50 dimension.

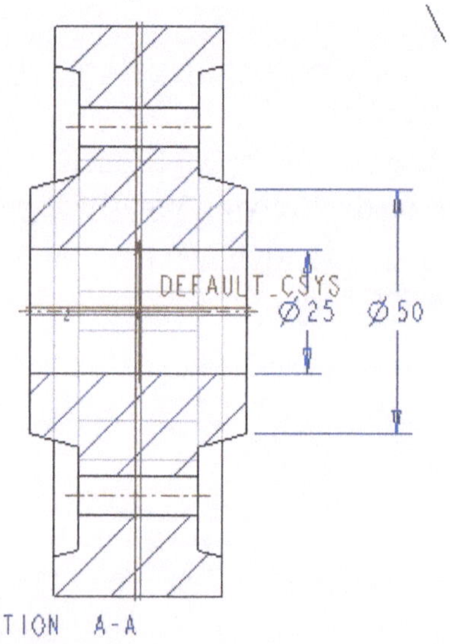

7. Activate the **Show Model Annotations** command.
8. Select the front view.
9. Select the dimensions of the front view, as shown below.
10. Click **OK**.

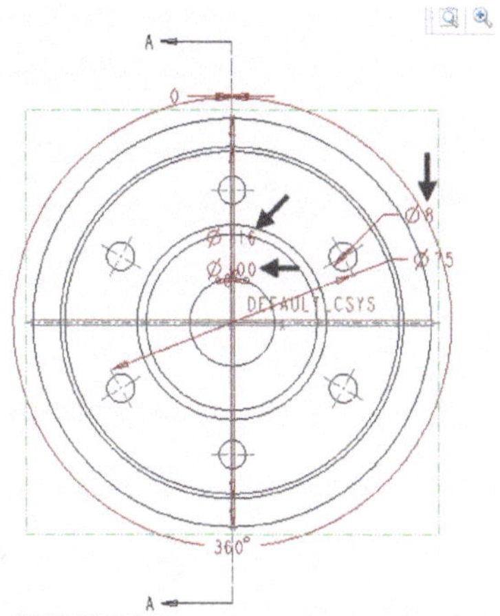

11. Click and drag the diameter dimensions.
12. Select the diameter dimension of the small hole.
13. Click the **Dimension Text** icon on the **Dimension Text** panel.
14. Click before @D.
15. Type-in **6 HOLES**.
16. Click after @D and press ENTER.
17. Type-in **EQUI-SPACED ON 75 PCD** below @D.

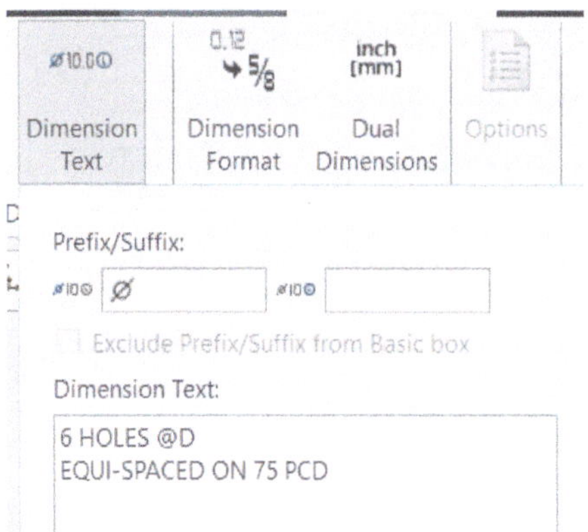

18. Click on the drawing sheet and drag the dimension.
19. Select the hole diameter dimension and select **Flip Arrows**.

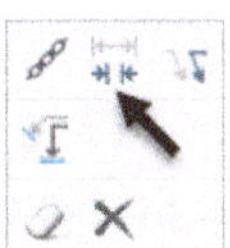

20. Likewise, flip the arrows of the other diameter dimensions.

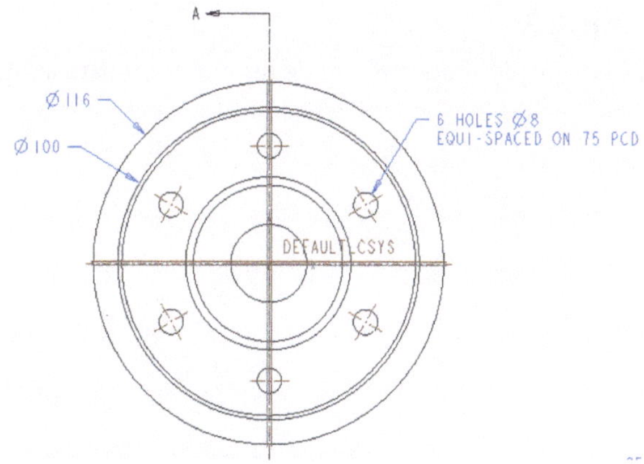

21. Select the angular dimension on the section view.
22. Click the **Dimension Text** icon on the **Dimension Text** panel.
23. Type-in **TYP** in the **Suffix** box.
24. Click on the drawing sheet and drag the dimension.
25. Select the angular dimension.
26. Select **Flip Arrows**.

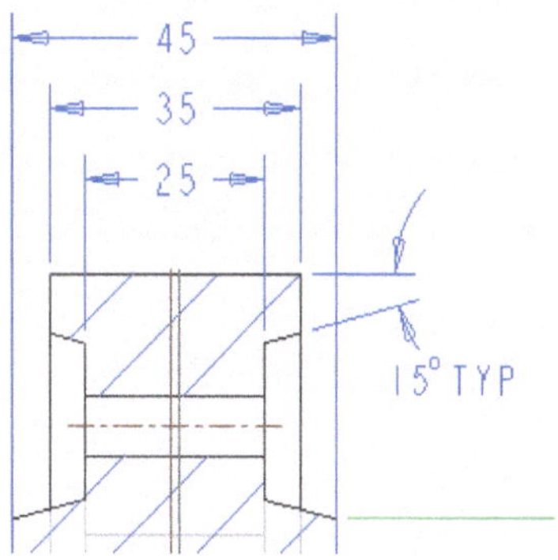

27. Save and close the drawing.

Example 3

In this example, you will create an assembly drawing shown below.

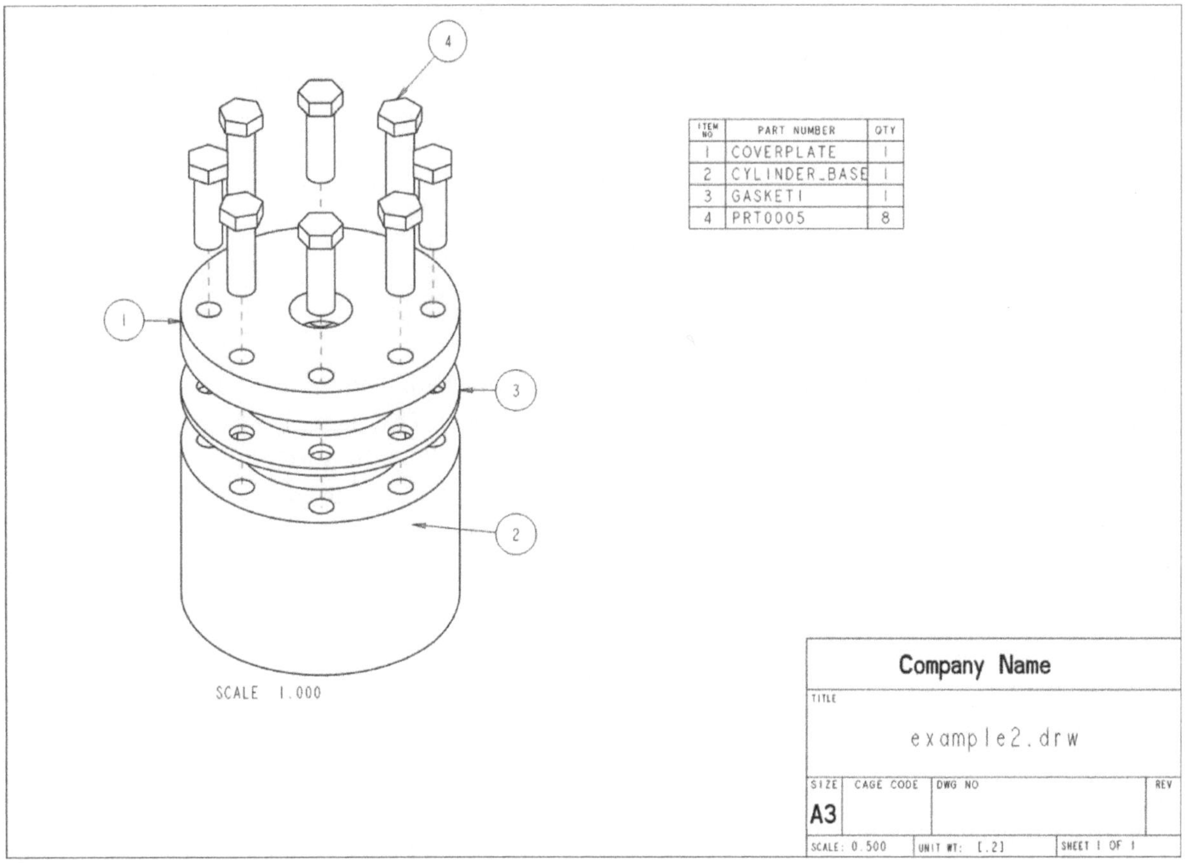

Starting the Drawing

1. Start **Creo Parametric 11.0**.
2. Set the *Drawings* folder as the current working folder.
3. Copy the Pressure-Cylinder.prt file created in Chapter 10 to the *Drawings* folder.
4. On the **Home** tab, click the **New** button.
5. On the **New** dialog, select **Type > Drawing**.
6. Type-in *Example3* in the **File name** box and uncheck the **Use default template** option.
7. Click **OK**.
8. On the **New Drawing** dialog, click the **Browse** button in the **Default Model** section and select the Pressure-Cylinder.asm file.
9. Under the **Select Template** section, select the **Empty with Format** option.
10. Click the **Browse** button in the **Format** section.
11. Go to the Drawings folder and select the *Sample-Format.frm* file.
12. Click **Open**, and then click **OK**. The dialog appears, as shown below.
13. Click the green check to accept the default values.

Generating Exploded View

1. On the ribbon, click **Layout** tab **> Model Views** panel **> General View** .
2. On the **Select Combined State** dialog, select the **No combined State** option and click **OK**.
3. Click on the center of the drawing sheet to position the view.
4. On the **Drawing View** dialog, select **Standard Orientation** from the **Model view names** list.
5. Set the **Default Orientation** to **Isometric**.
6. Type-in **Exploded View** in the **View name** box and click **Apply**.
7. Under the **Categories** section, click the **View**

States option.

8. Under the **Explode view** section, check the **Explode components in view** option.
9. Select the name from the **Assembly explode state** drop-down and click **Apply**.
10. In the **Categories** section, click the **Scale** option.
11. Select **Custom Scale** and type-in **1** in the box next to it.
12. Click **OK**.
13. Change the **Display Style** to **No Hidden**.

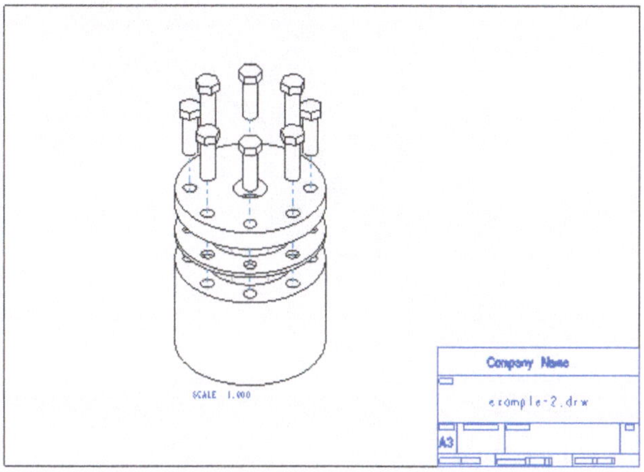

Adding Bill of Materials and Balloons

1. On the ribbon, click **Table** tab > **Table** panel > **Table** drop-down > **Quick Tables** > **Assembly** > **bom description down**.

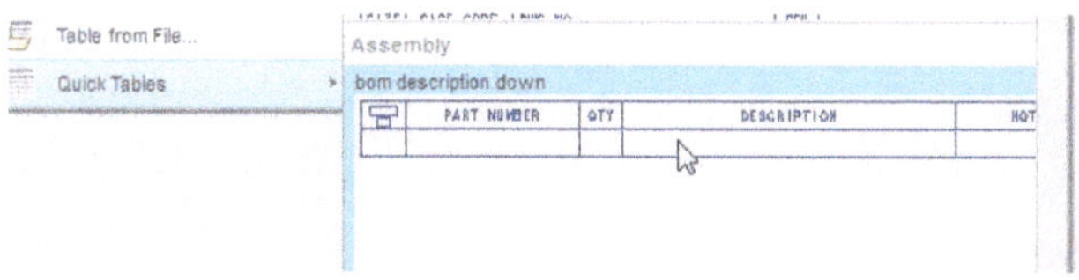

2. Position the table at the top right corner on the drawing sheet.

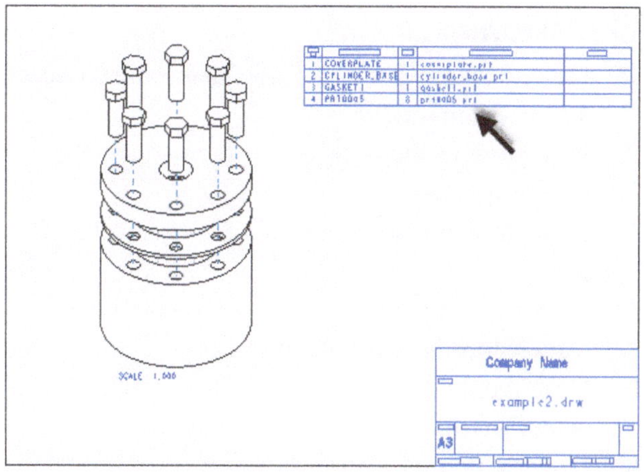

3. Click in the Notes column of the table.
4. On the ribbon, click **Table** tab > **Table** panel > **Select Table** drop-down > **Select Column** .
5. Right-click and select **Delete**.
6. Click **Yes** on the **Confirm** message box.
7. Likewise, delete the **Description** column.

ITEM NO	PART NUMBER	QTY
1	COVERPLATE	1
2	CYLINDER_BASE	1
3	GASKET1	1
4	PRT0005	8

8. On the ribbon, click **Table** tab > **Balloons** panel > **Create Balloons** drop-down > **Create Balloons-All**. It automatically generates the balloons.
9. Select the balloons one-by-one, and then drag them to arrange them properly.

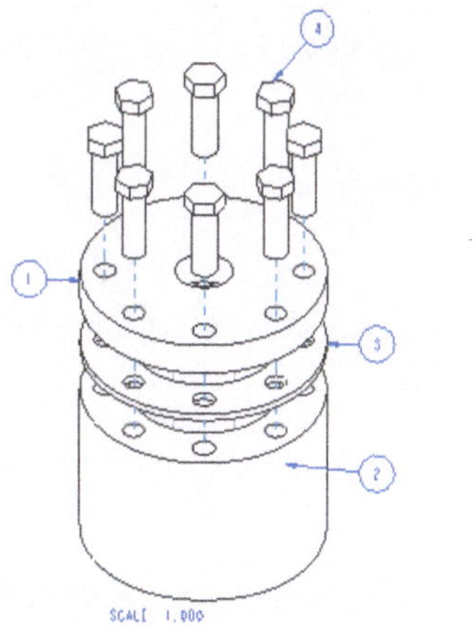

10. Save and close the drawing.

Questions

1. How to create drawing views using the **General View** command?
2. How do you show or hide hidden edges of a drawing view?
3. How do you retrieve the dimensions of the 3D part model?
4. How do you control the properties of dimensions and annotations?
5. Describe the procedure to create centerlines and center marks.
6. How do you add symbols and texts to a dimension?
7. How do you add break lines to the drawing view?
8. How do you create aligned section views?
9. How do you create the exploded view of an assembly?

Exercises

Exercise 1

Create orthographic views of the part model shown next. Add dimensions and annotations to the drawing.

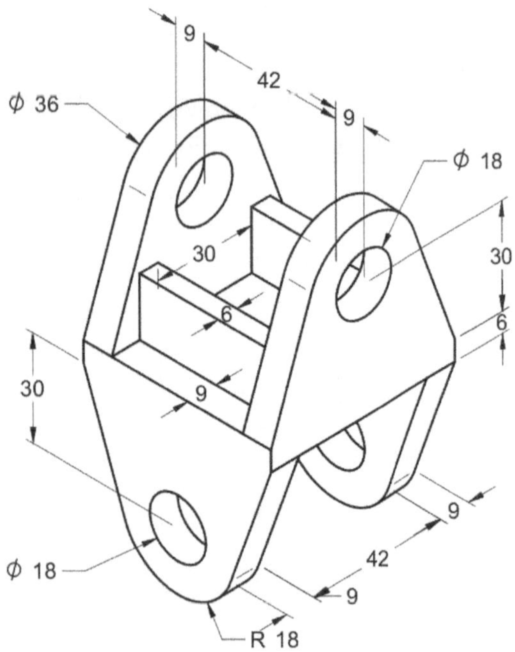

Exercise 2

Create orthographic views and an auxiliary view of the part model shown below. Add dimensions and annotations to the drawing.

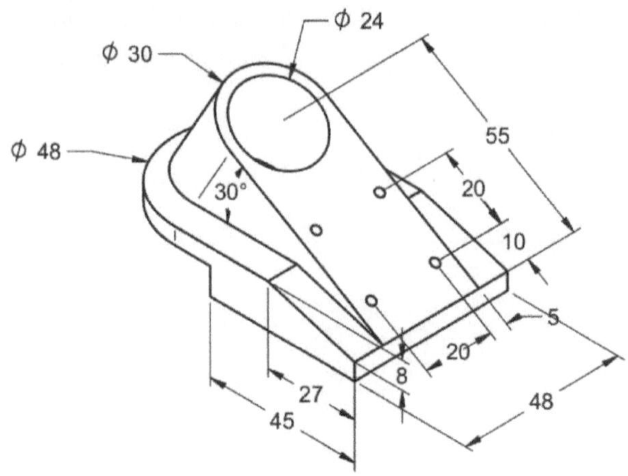

Chapter 11: Sheet Metal Design

You can make sheet metal parts by bending and forming flat sheets of metal. In Creo Parametric, sheet-metal parts can be folded and unfolded, enabling you to show them in the flat pattern as well as their bent-up state. There are two ways to design sheet-metal parts in Creo Parametric. You can either start the sheet-metal part from scratch using sheet-metal features throughout the design process or design it as a regular solid part and later convert it to a sheet-metal part. Most commonly, you design sheet-metal parts in the **Sheetmetal Part** environment from the beginning. In this chapter, you will learn both approaches.

The topics covered in this chapter are:

- *Planar Walls*
- *Flat Walls*
- *Flanges*
- *Extrusions*
- *Bends*
- *Unbend*
- *Bend back*
- *Flat Pattern*
- *Punch and Die Forms*
- *Conversion to Sheet Metal*

Starting a Sheet Metal part

To start a new sheet metal part, follow the steps given next.

1. Click **Home > Data > New** on the ribbon.
2. On the **New** dialog, select **Type > Part** and **Subtype > Sheetmetal**.
3. Type the name of the part and uncheck the **Use template** option.
4. On the **New File Options** dialog, select the required template and click **OK**.

Sheetmetal Model Properties

Sheetmetal Model Properties define the bend allowance, bend size, relief, bend orders, and other design rules. You can define these properties by using the **Model Properties** dialog.

1. On the File menu, click **Prepare > Model Properties**.
2. On the **Model Properties** dialog, click the **change** option next to **Thickness**. The **Sheetmetal Preferences** dialog appears.
3. On the **Sheetmetal Preferences** dialog, type-in the **Thickness** value and click **OK**.
4. On the **Model Properties** dialog, click the **change** option next to **Bend Allowance**.
5. On the **Sheetmetal Preferences** dialog, type-in the K-factor/Y-factor value in the **Factor value** box.

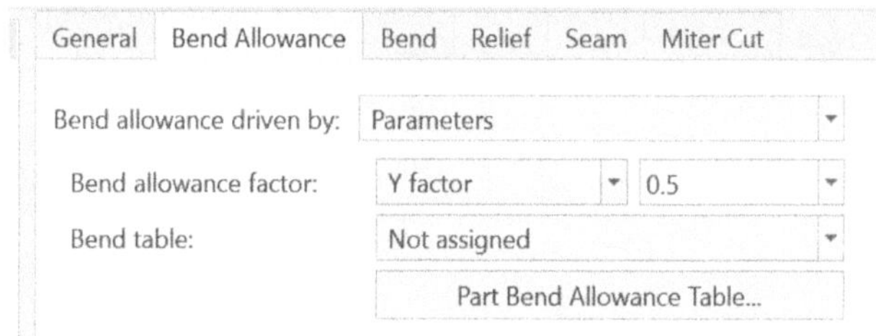

The **K Factor** is the ratio that represents the neutral sheet's location measured from the inside face with respect to the sheet metal part's thickness. The Neutral Factor defines the bend allowance of the sheet metal part. The standard formula that calculates the bend allowance is given below.

$$BA = \frac{\pi(R + KT)A}{180}$$

BA = Bend Allowance

R = Bend Radius

K = Neutral Factor = t/T

T = Material Thickness

t= Distance from inside face to the neutral sheet

A = Bend Angle

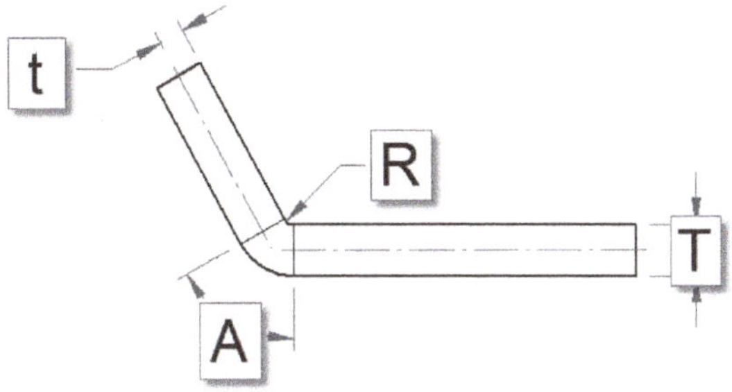

$$Y\ factor\ =\ K\ factor\ *\ (\pi/2)$$

You can also define the bend allowance by using your bend allowance table. Click the **Part Bend Allowances Table** button. On the **Part Bend Allowances Tables** dialog, select a table from the list and click the arrow pointing towards the right. Click **OK** to close the dialog.

6. Click **OK**.
7. Click the **Close** button on the **Model Properties** dialog.

Planar Wall

The planar wall is a basic type of sheet metal feature.

1. To create a wall, create a closed sketch on a plane.

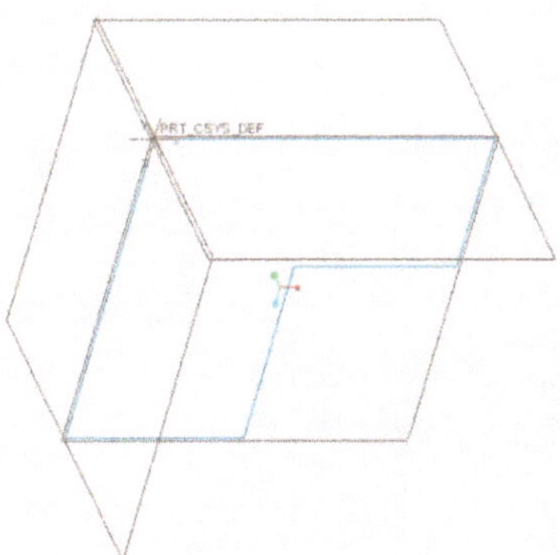

2. On the ribbon, click **Sheetmetal > Shapes > Planar**.
3. Click on the sketch.
4. On the **Planar** dashboard, type-in a value in the **Thickness** box.
5. Click the **Change Direction** button to reverse the direction of the wall.
6. Click **OK**.

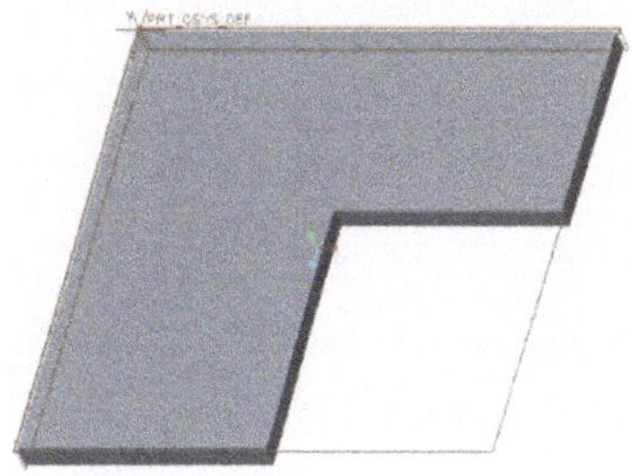

Flat Wall

The second feature after creating a planar wall is a flat wall. You can create this feature using a linear edge of a sheet metal part.

1. On the ribbon, click **Sheetmetal > Shapes > Flat Wall**.
2. Click an edge of the planar wall feature. The wall preview appears on the selected edge.

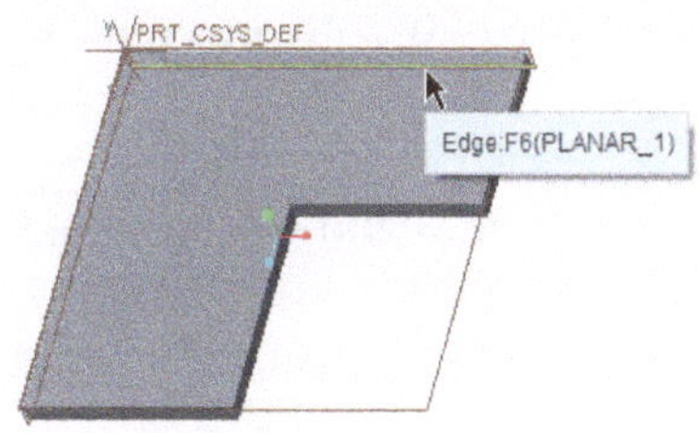

3. On the dashboard, select the wall shape from the **Shape** drop-down available on the left side.

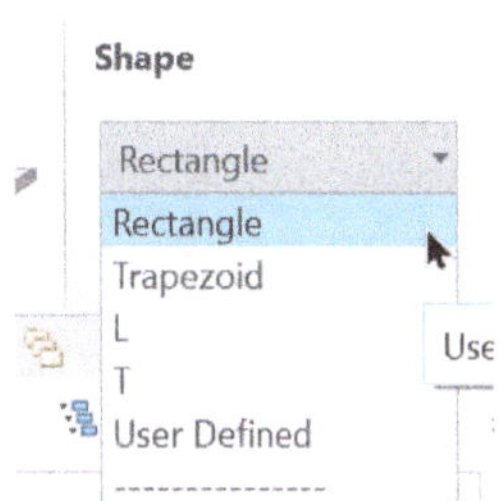

4. On the dashboard, click the **Shape** tab and expand the **Section Preview** to set the shape dimensions. Double-click on the dimension values to edit them.

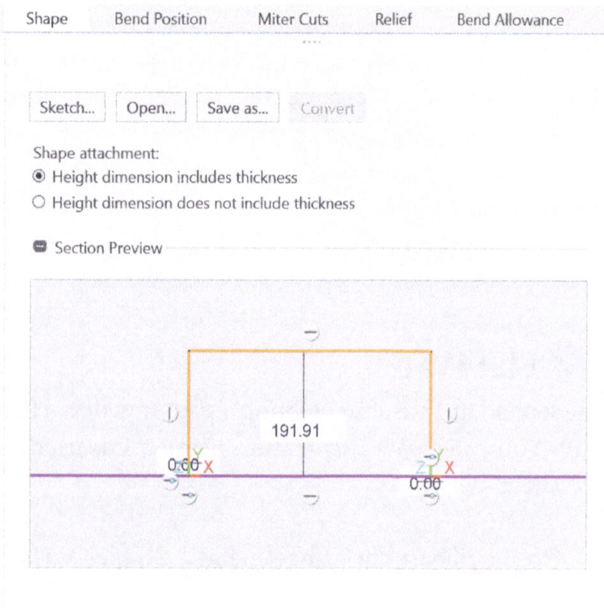

5. Set the method to dimension the radius. The options to dimension radius are given next.

 This option creates the bend by specifying the outer bend radius.

 This option creates the bend by specifying the inner bend radius.

 This option creates the bend by using the default bend side you have specified on the **Model Properties** dialog.

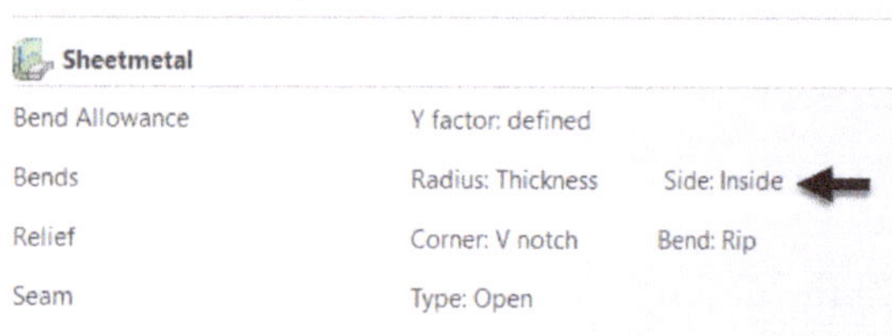

6. Type-in a value in the **Angle** box.
7. Type-in the bend radius or select the **Thickness** or **2.0*Thickness** option.

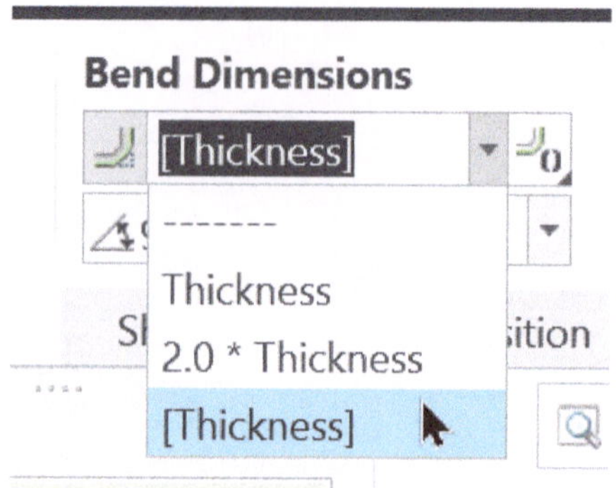

8. Click the **Thickness side**  button if you want to reverse the wall's thickness side.
9. Click the **Relief** tab and select the type of relief to be provided to a bend. The options available in this tab are given next.

Rip: This option rips off the bend extremes.

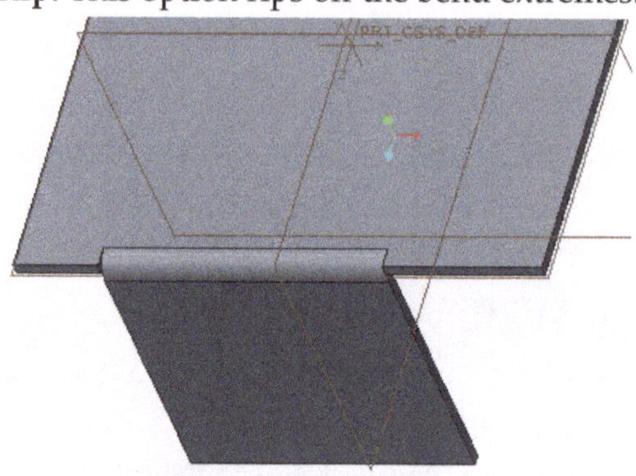

Rectangular: A rectangular relief is applied to bend extremes.

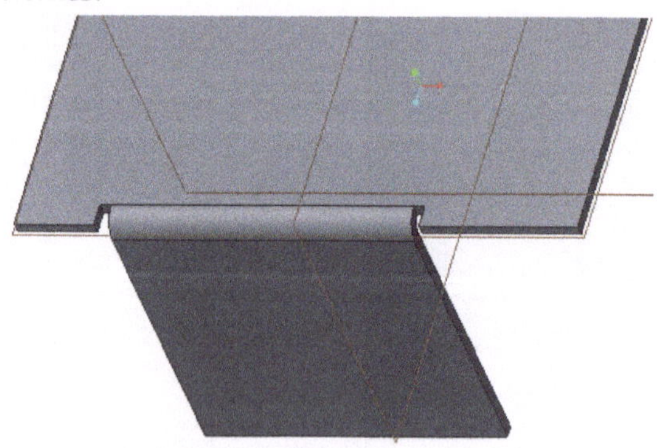

Obround: A round relief is applied to bend extremes.

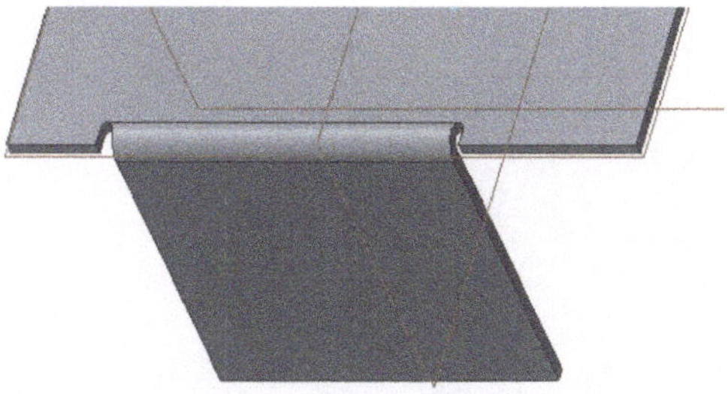

Stretch: The end faces of the bend are stretched at an angle.

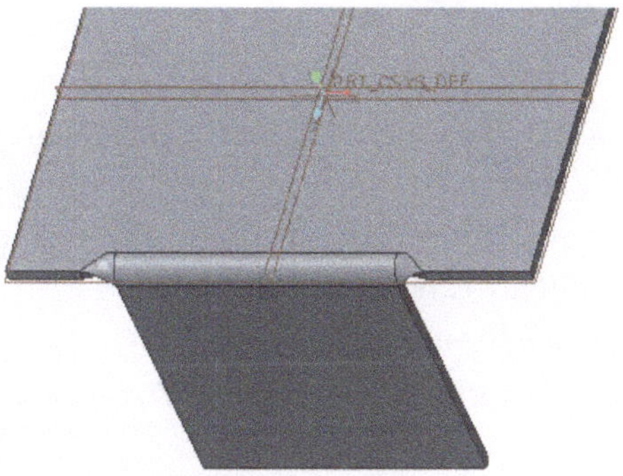

10. Click the green check to complete the flat wall.

Sketch-Based Flat Wall on Edge

1. Activate the **Flat** command and select the edge to add a flat wall.
2. Click the **Shape** tab on the dashboard, and then click the **Sketch** button.
3. Delete unwanted entities of the sketch.
4. Draw the profile of the wall and exit the sketch.

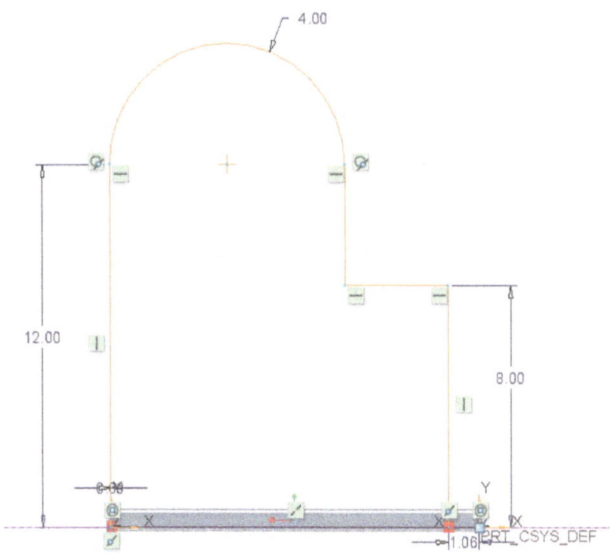

5. Type-in a value in the **Angle** box if you want to create an inclined wall.

6. Click the green check to create the wall.

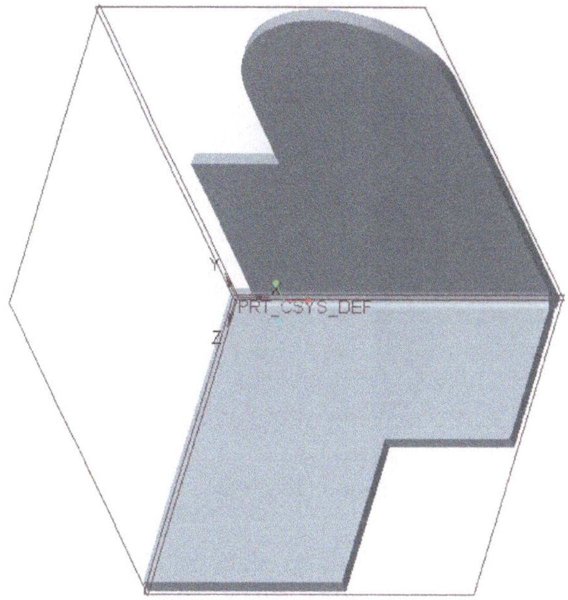

Extrude

The **Extrude** command extrudes an open sketch.

1. Create a sketch on the side face of the sheet metal as shown.

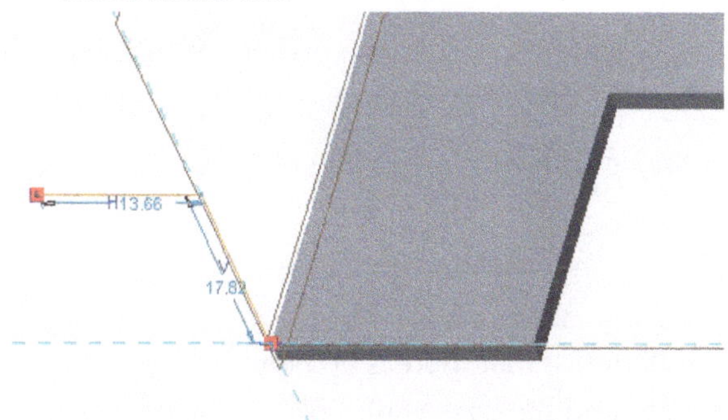

2. Click **OK**.
3. On the ribbon, click **Sheetmetal > Walls > Extrude**.
4. Click the **Depth direction** icon to change the extrude direction.
5. Type-in the extrusion distance on the dashboard or drag the extrude handle.
6. Click the **Change material direction** icon to change the thickness side.

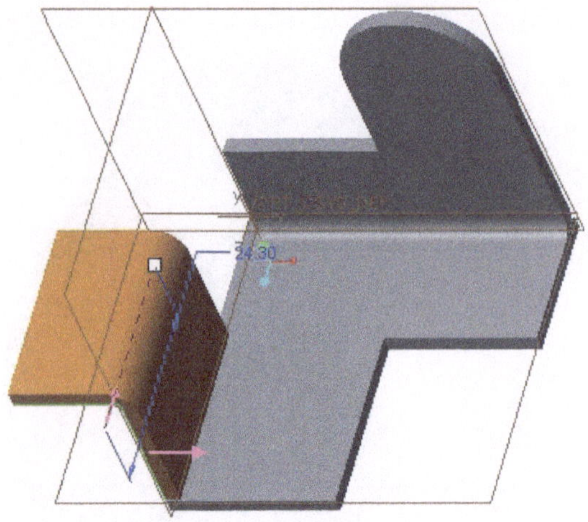

7. Click the **Options** tab on the dashboard.

The **Add bends on sharp edges** option creates bends at the intersections between the sketch elements.

8. Click **OK** to complete the extrusion feature.

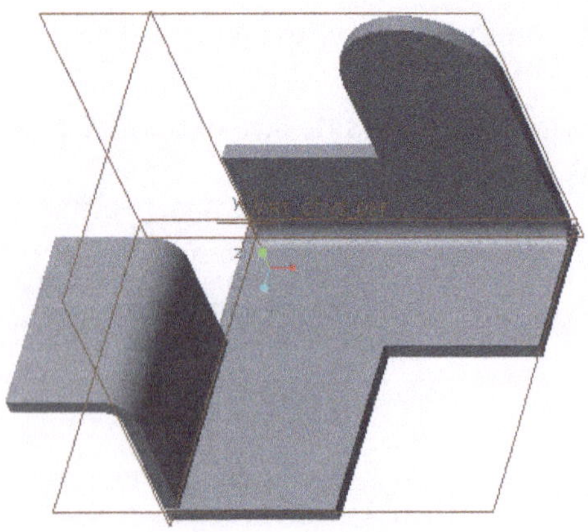

You will notice that there is no bend between the extrusion and the base wall.

Flange

This command creates a flange by sweeping a parametric profile along the selected edge.

1. On the ribbon, click **Sheetmetal > Shapes > Flange**.
2. Click on the edge of the planar wall.

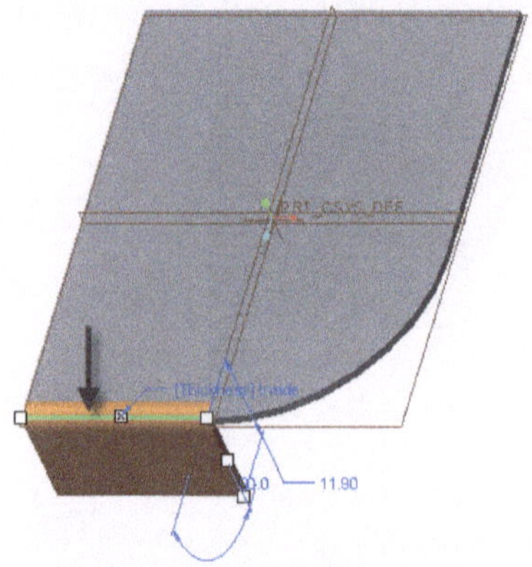

3. Click the **Placement** tab on the dashboard and click **Details**.
4. On the **Chain** dialog, select **Rule-based** and set the **Rule** to **Tangent**.
5. Click **OK** to select the tangentially connected edges. The preview of the flange appears.

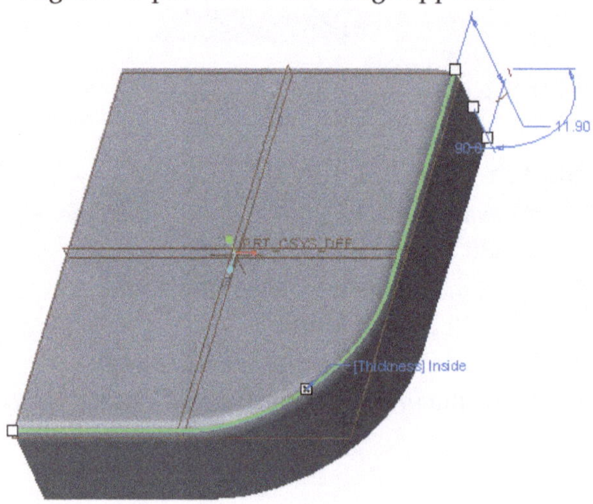

6. On the Dashboard, click the **Shape** tab and select the required **Shape attachment** option. Next, expand the **Sketch Preview** section to view the height and angle dimensions of the flange. You can double-click on them and change their values.

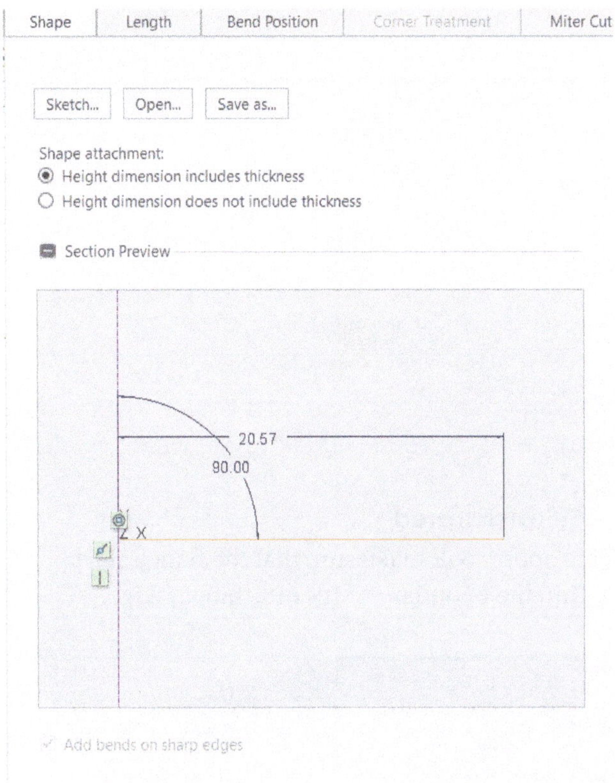

7. Click the **Length** tab and select **Blind** from the first drop-down.

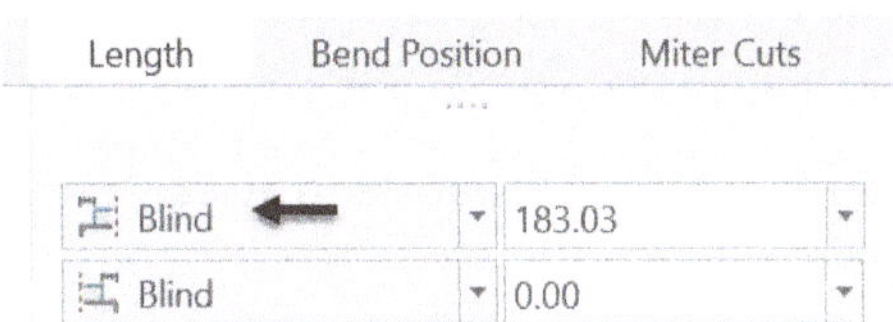

8. Drag the length handle as shown.

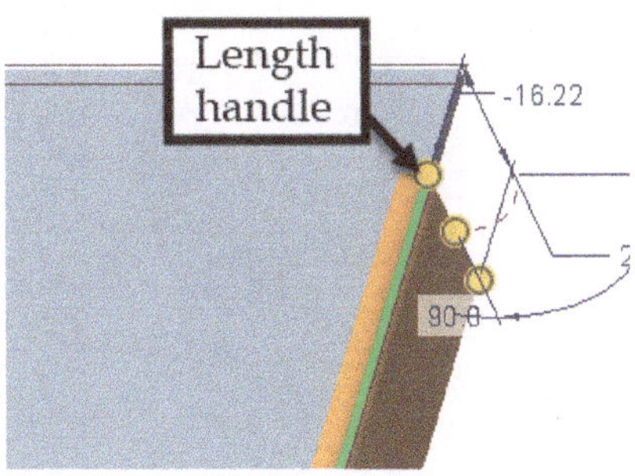

9. On the **Length** tab, select **To selected** from the second drop-down.

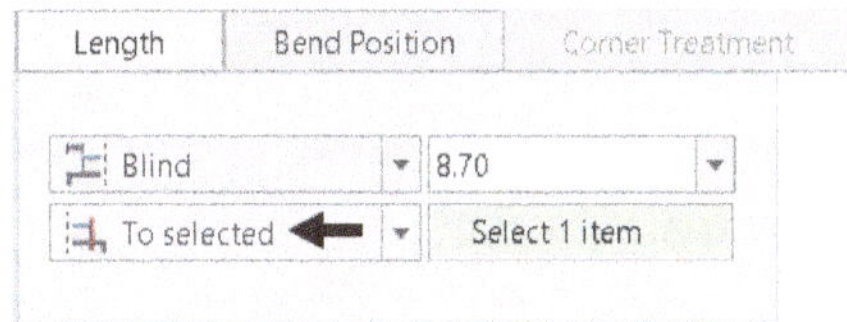

10. Select a plane to define the flange end.

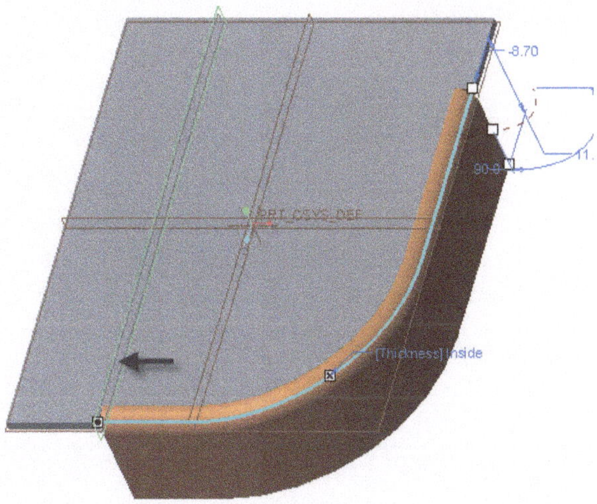

11. On the Dashboard, click the **Bend Position** tab and select the bend position type. There are five bend positions available.

Profile on Edge

This option positions the wall of the bend on the edge selected to create the flange.

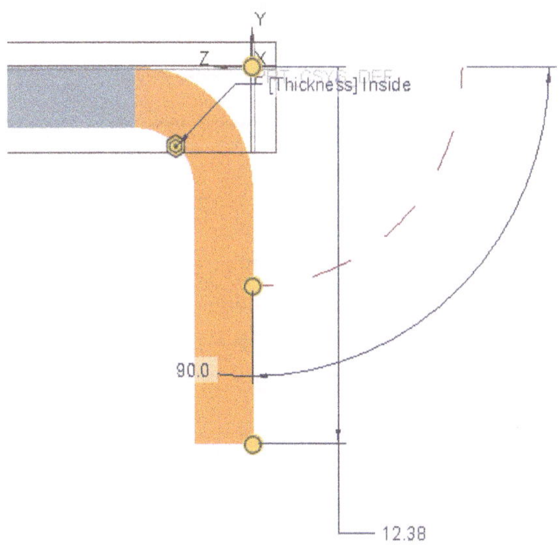

Bend Outside

This option positions the bend line tangent to the edge selected to create the flange.

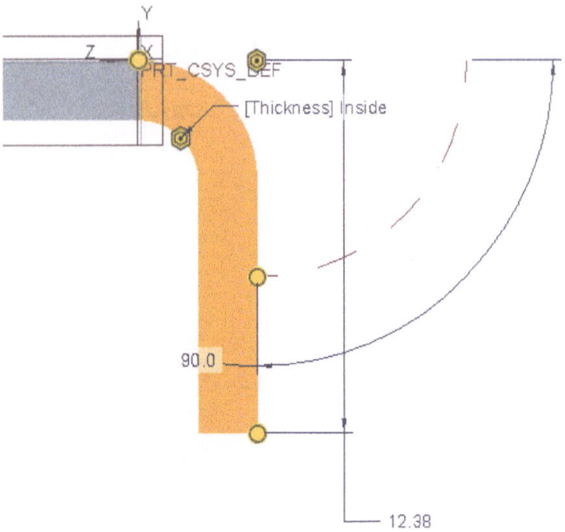

Offset from Bend start

Select this option and enter the offset value in the **Value** box. The bend start will be offset from the attachment edge.

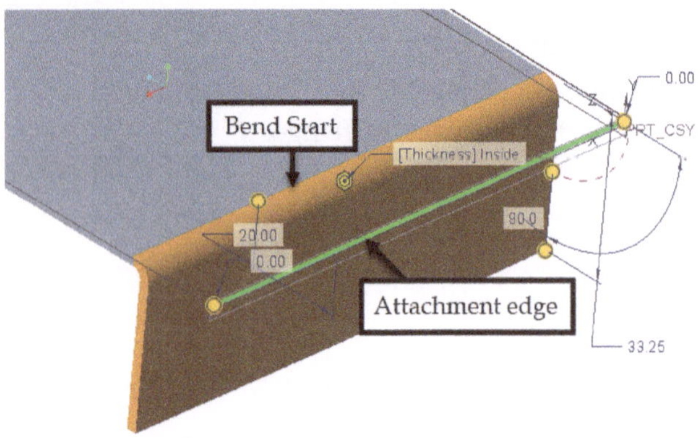

Offset from Bend Apex

Select this option and enter the offset value in the **Value** box. The exterior wall of the flange will be offset from the attachment edge.

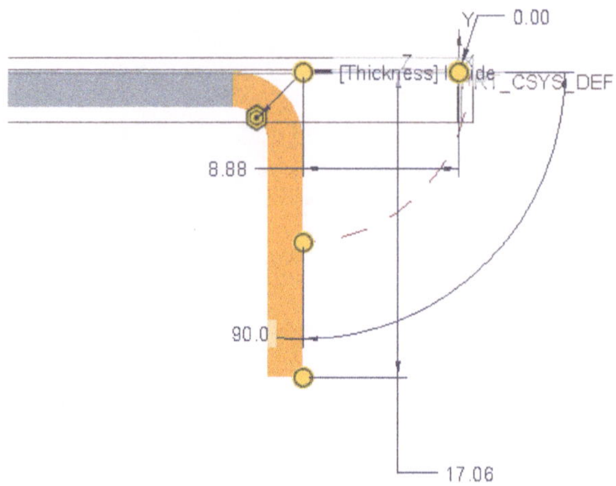

Constrained

This option will make sure that the flange stays within the boundary of the attachment edge.

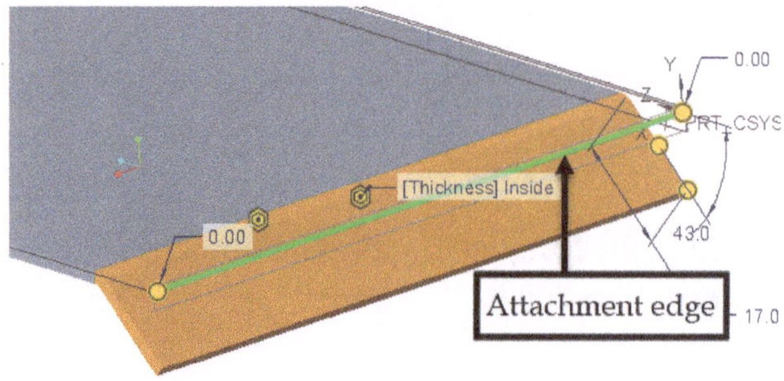

12. Select **Type > Offset from Bend start** and drag the offset handle.

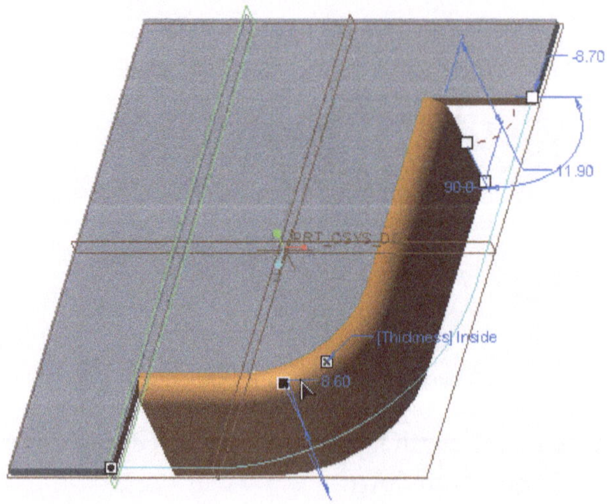

13. On the Dashboard, select **Arc** from the **Shape** drop-down.

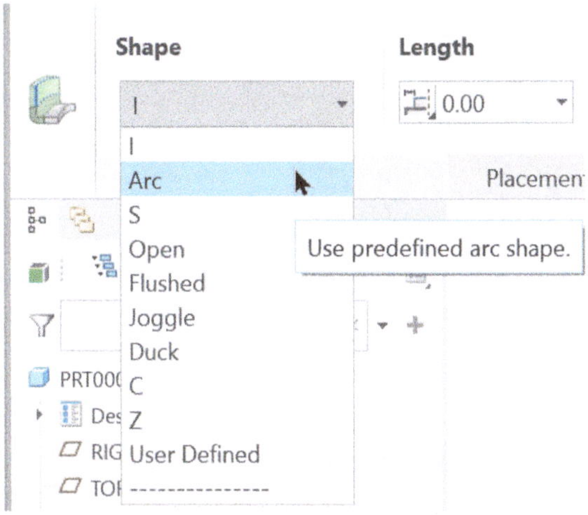

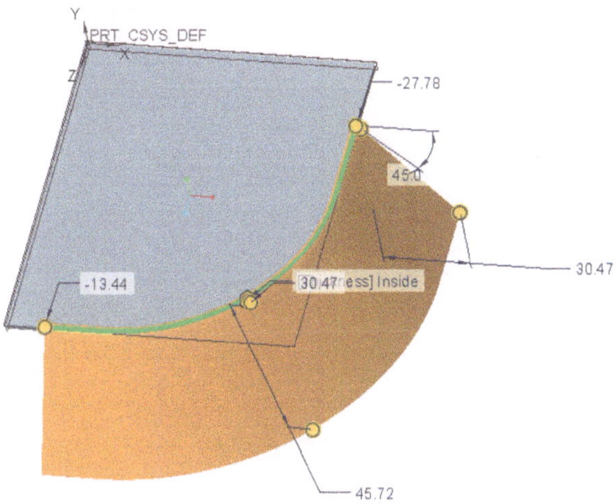

Likewise, you can select other shapes for creating a flange, as shown.

I

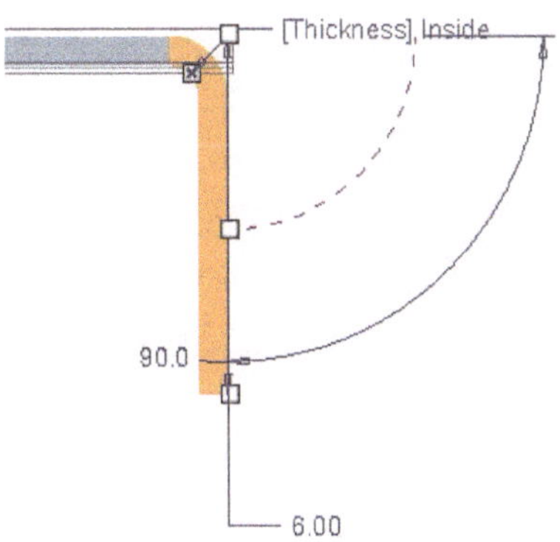

S

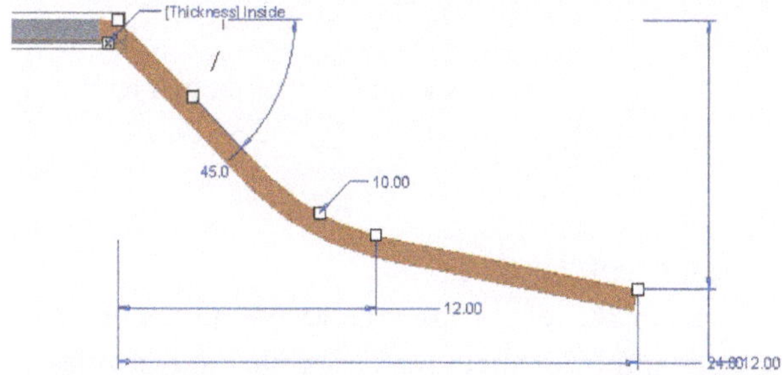

Open

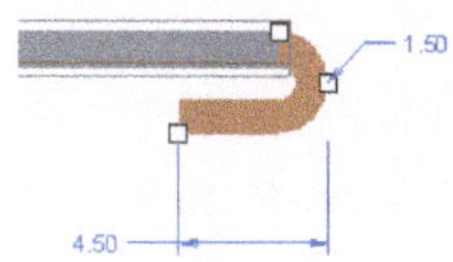

Flushed

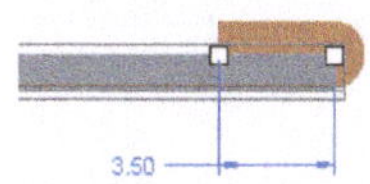

Joggle

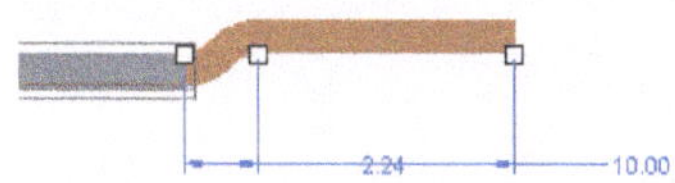

Duck

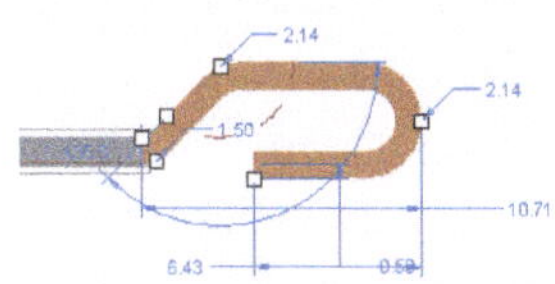

C

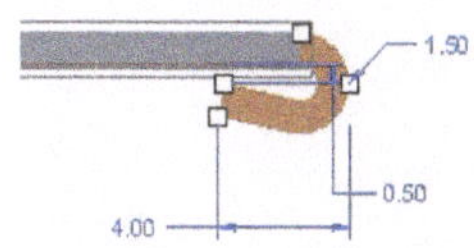

Z

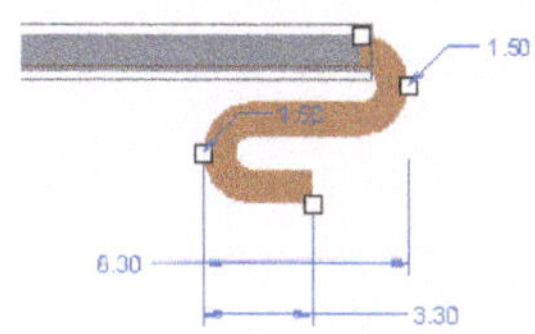

You can also create a user-defined flange by clicking the **Sketch** button on the **Shape** tab.

14. Click the green check on the dashboard to complete the feature.

Corner Relief

The **Corner Relief** command allows you to control the appearance of sheet metal seams. For example, when two flanges meet at a corner, this command allows you to add corner treatment between them.

1. Activate this command (On ribbon, click **Sheetmetal > Engineering > Corner Relief**). The corner point is selected automatically.

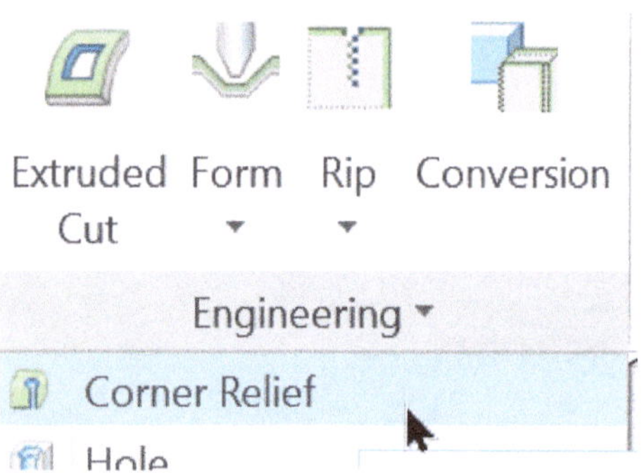

2. On the **Corner Relief** dashboard, select the required corner relief. For example, select the **Circular** corner relief from the drop-down and click the **Placement** tab. The corner relief types available in the drop-down are:

V-notch

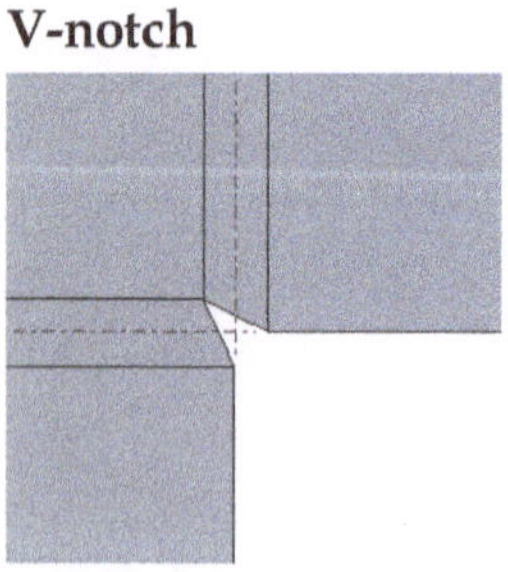

Circular

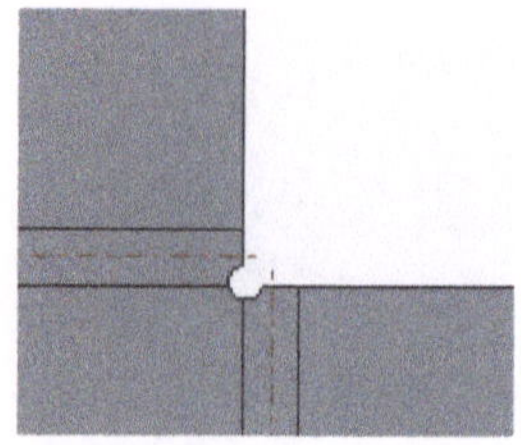

Rectangular

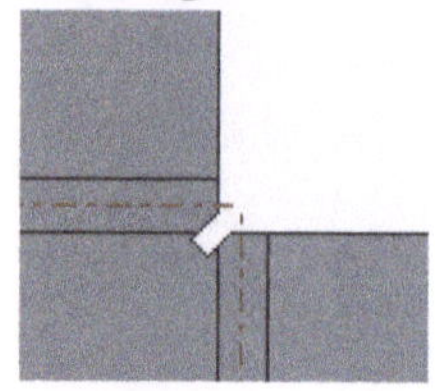

Obround

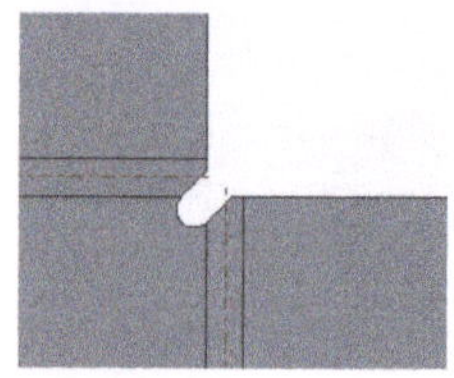

No relief

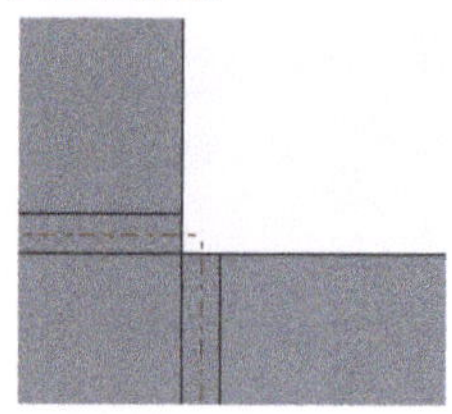

Square

Normal

3. On the **Placement** tab, set the **Origin** type. You can position the anchor point at the Corner Point or Intersection of bend lines.

Corner Point

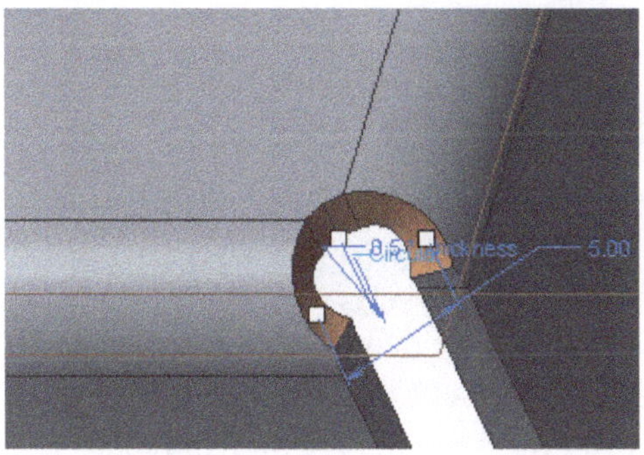

Bend lines intersection

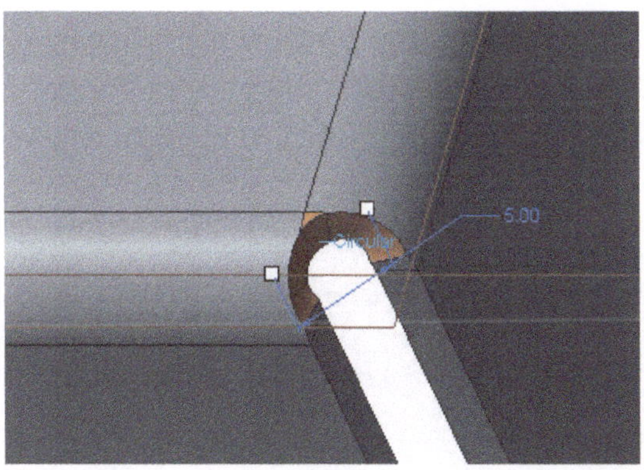

4. Select the Corner relief depth type. You can specify the depth by using the **Blind, Up to bend**, **On Origin** options.

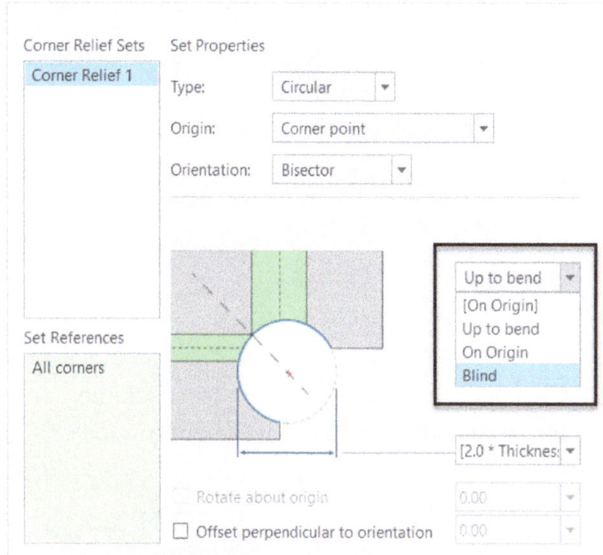

5. Type-in the relief width value.

You can offset the corner relief by checking the **Offset perpendicular to orientation** option and rotate the corner relief by checking the **Rotate by origin** option.

6. Click the green check to complete the corner relief.

Bend

In addition to adding flanges and user flanges, you can also bend a flat sheet using the **Bend** command.

1. Draw a sketched line on the flat sheet and click **OK**.

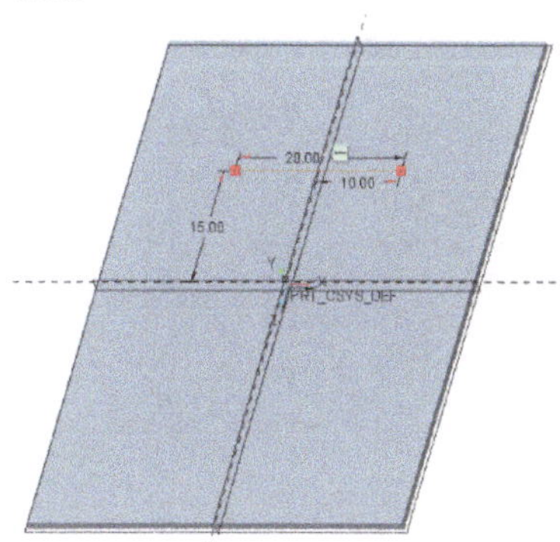

2. On the ribbon, click **Sheetmetal > Bends > Bend**.

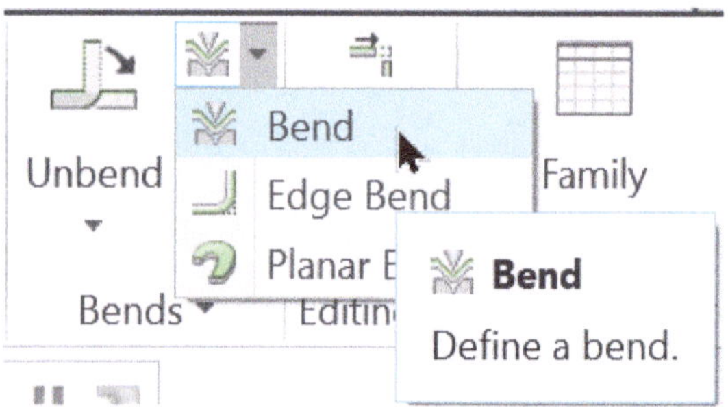

3. Select the sketched line.
4. Click the **Fixed side** icon (or) click the horizontal arrow to change the portion to be fixed.

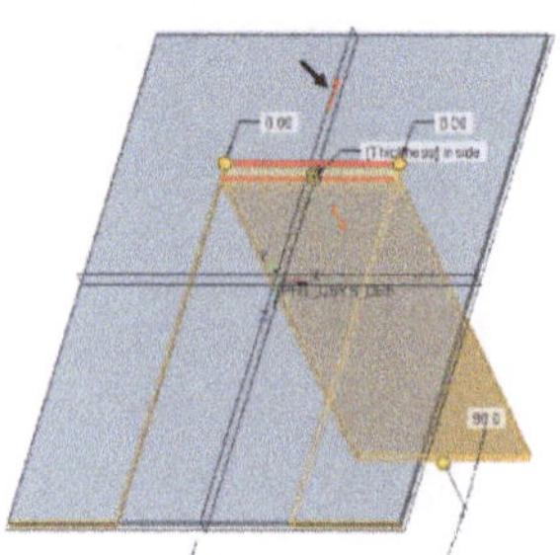

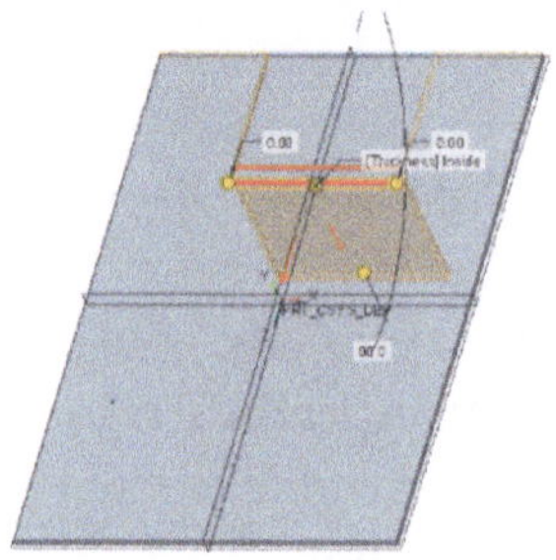

5. Click the vertical arrow that appears on the bend if you want to reverse the bend direction.
6. Type-in a value in the **Angle** box to change the folding angle.
7. Select the option to define the material side of the bend feature. These options are given next.

Centered on Bend Line

This creates the bend with the bend line at its center.

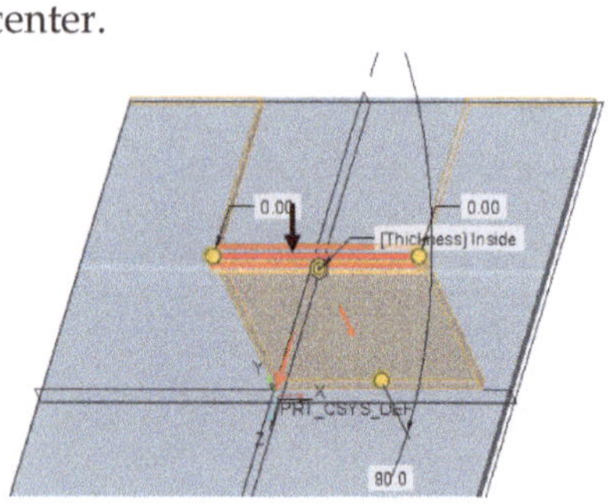

Starts at Bend Line

This creates the bend with the bend line at its starting edge.

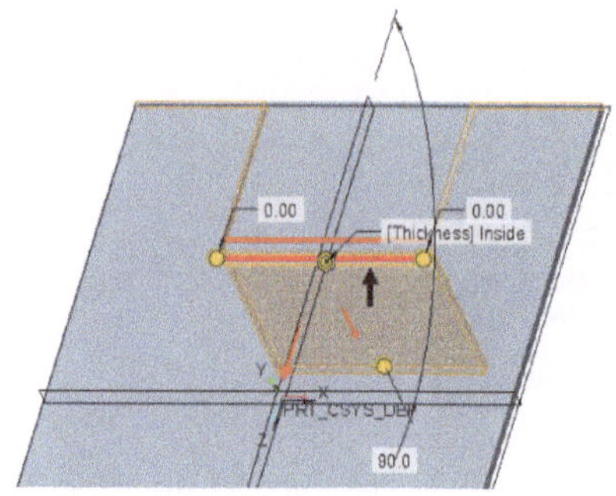

Ends at Bend Line

This creates the bend with the bend line at the intersection of outer faces.

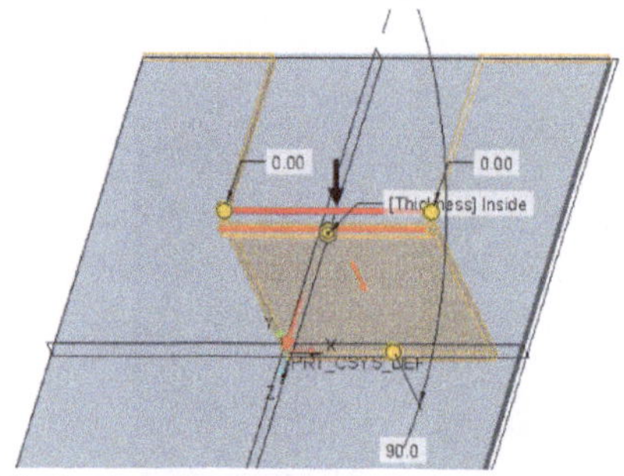

8. Click the **Placement** tab on the dashboard, and then check the **Offset bend line** option. Now, you can drag the bend to offset it from the sketched line.

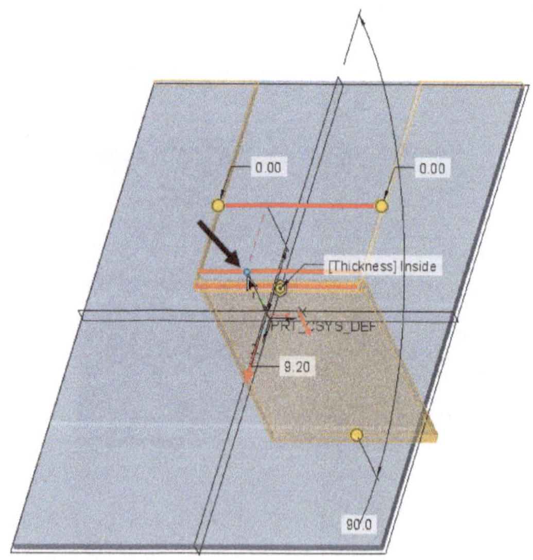

9. Click the green check to complete the bend feature.

Angled Bend

The **Bend** command can also create an angled bend without using any sketched line.

1. Activate the **Bend** command and click on the face to bend.
2. Drag the placement handle onto the side edges of the flat sheet.

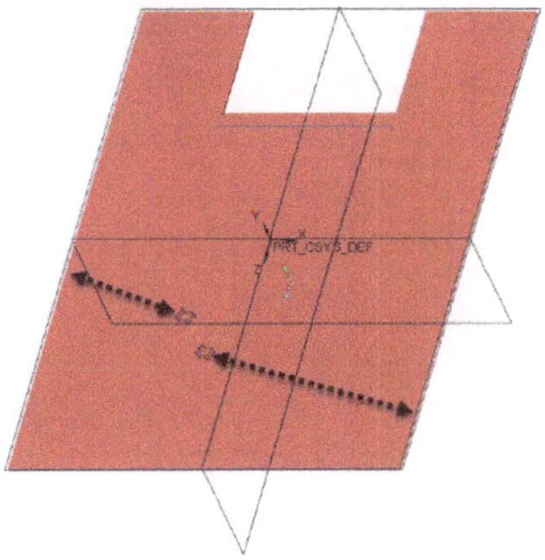

3. Drag the offset handles onto the front edge of the flat sheet.

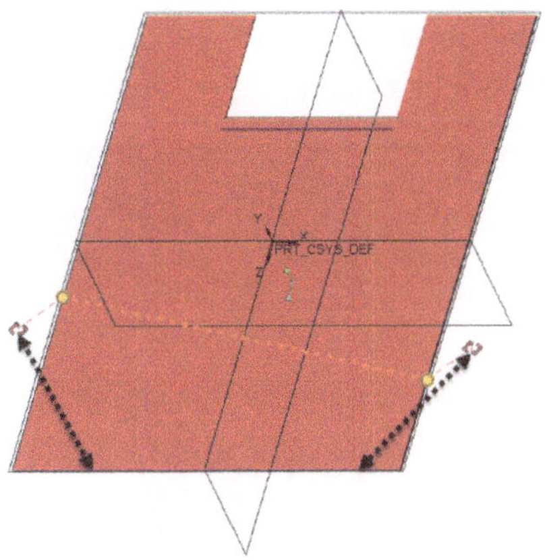

4. Modify the offset dimensions and angle value.

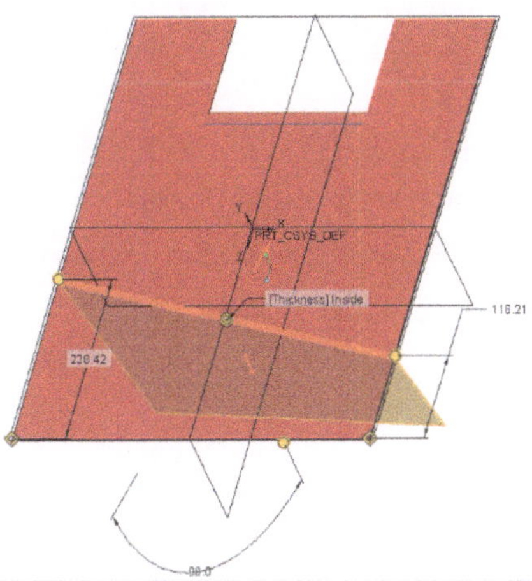

5. On the Dashboard, click the **Relief** tab and select **Type > No relief**.
6. Click the green check to complete the bend feature.

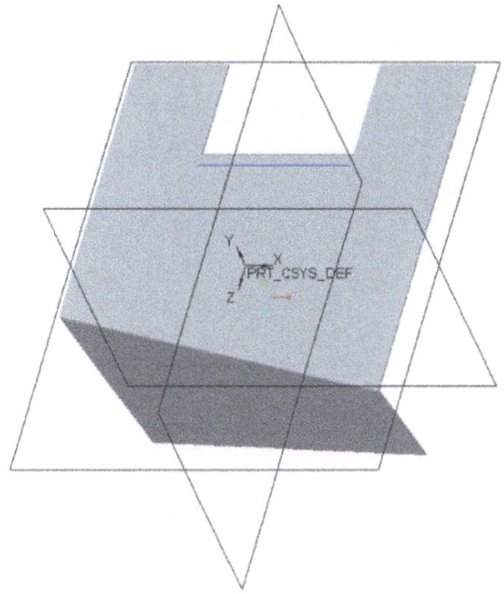

Rolled Bend

The **Bend** command can also bend a sheet by rolling it about a line.

1. Activate the **Bend** command.
2. Click on the flat sheet to be rolled.
3. On the dashboard, click the **Bend Line** tab, and then click the **Sketch** button.
4. Sketch a straight line as shown. Make sure that the endpoints of the line coincide with the adjacent edges of the sheet. Next, click **OK** on the ribbon.

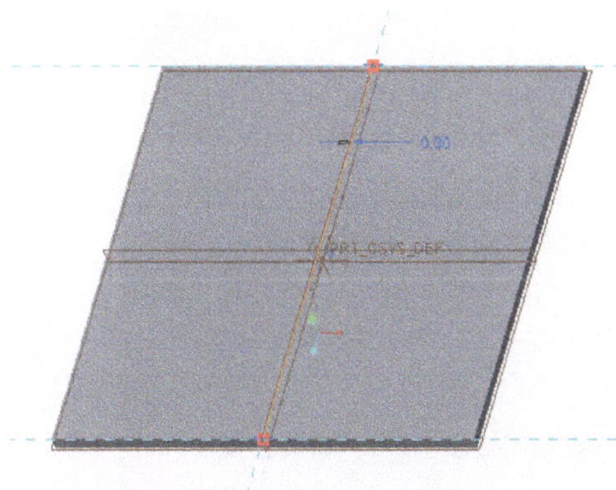

5. On the Dashboard, click the **Roll** icon (or) right-click and select **Rolled Bend**.
6. On the Dashboard, type-in the **Radius** value.

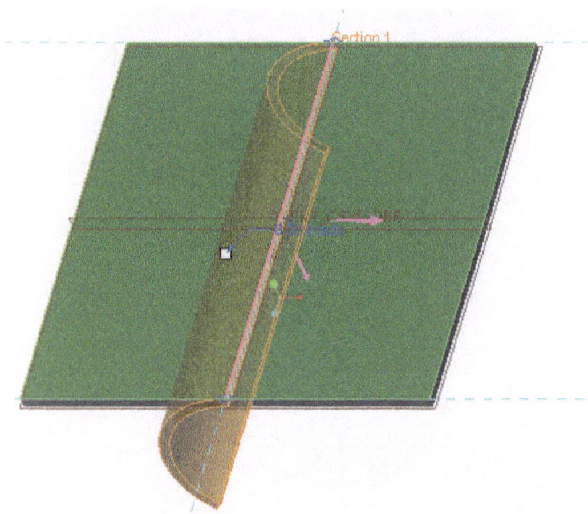

7. On the Dashboard, click the **Ends at Bend line** icon.

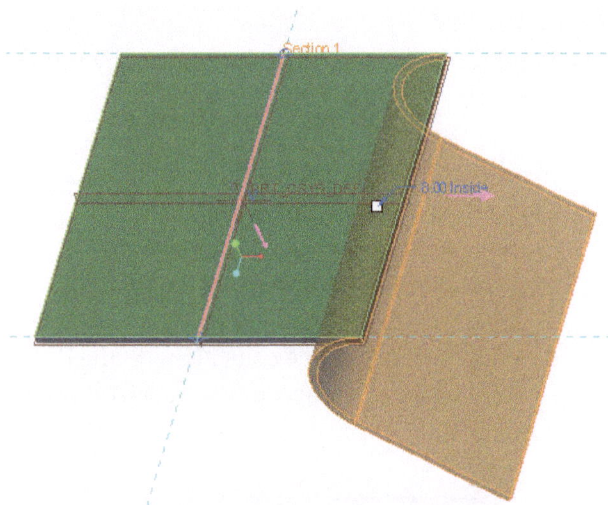

8. Click the **Centered on Bend line** icon.

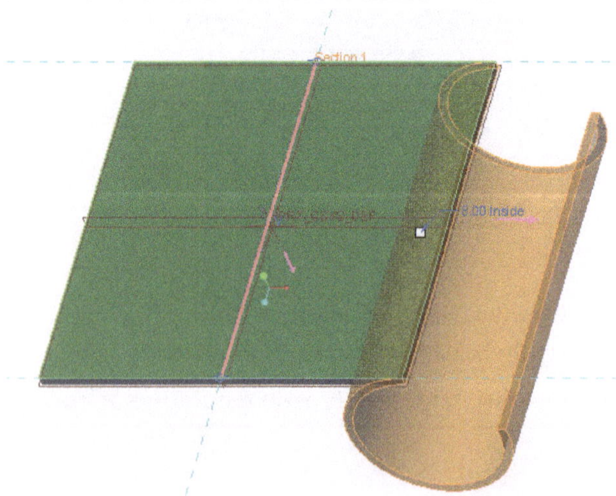

9. Click the green check to complete the feature.

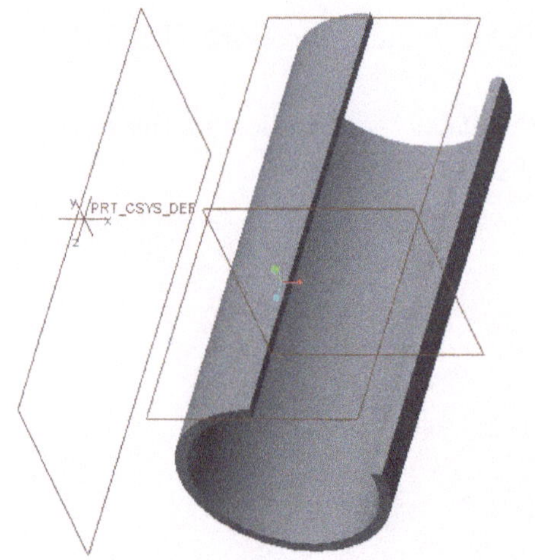

Transition Bend

The **Bend** command allows you to create a transition between the rolled and flat portions of a sheet metal part.

1. Activate the **Bend** command.
2. Select the sketched line to define the bend.

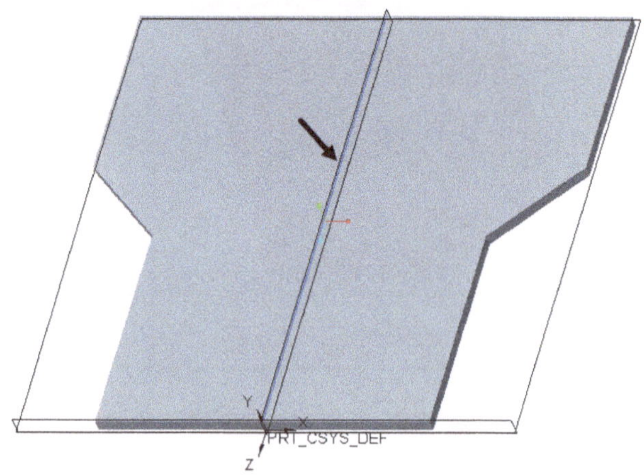

3. On the Dashboard, click the **Roll** icon (or) right-click and select **Rolled Bend**.
4. Click the **Fixed side** icon, if required.

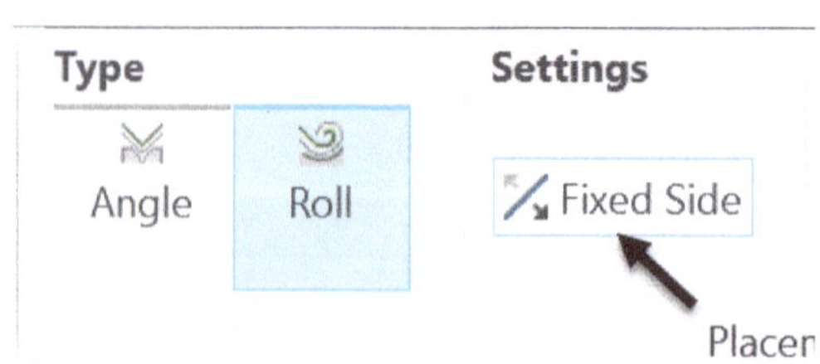

5. On the Dashboard, type-in the **Radius**.

6. Click the **Centered on Bend line** icon.

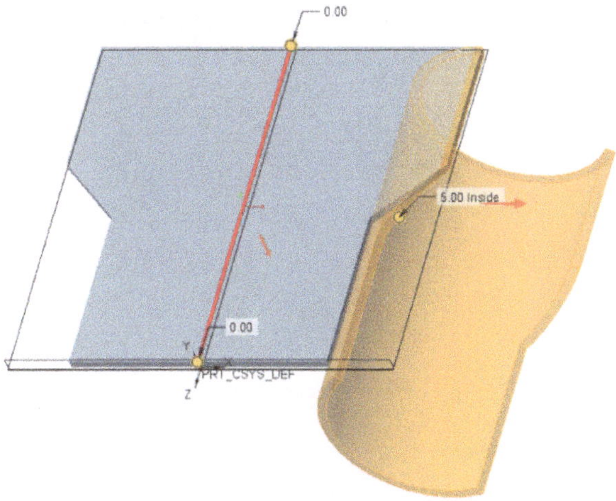

7. On the Dashboard, click the **Transitions** tab and select **Add transition**.
8. Click the **Sketch** button.
9. Sketch the start and end transition line perpendicular to the bend line, and then click **OK** on the ribbon.

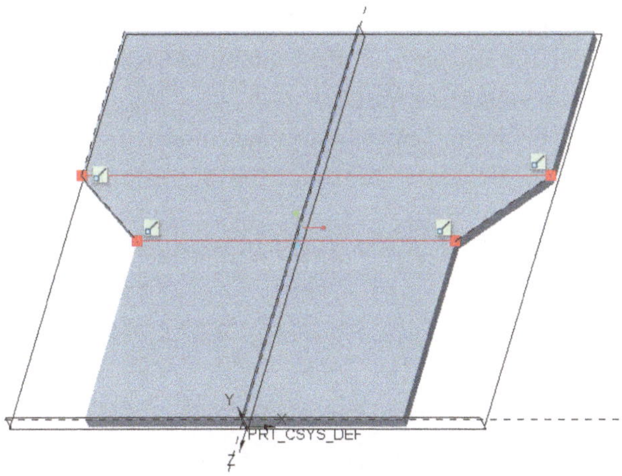

10. Click the **Change bending direction** icon if required.

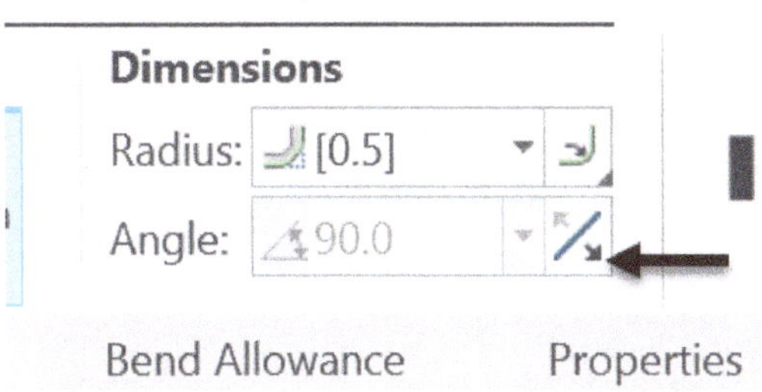

11. Click the green check to complete the feature.

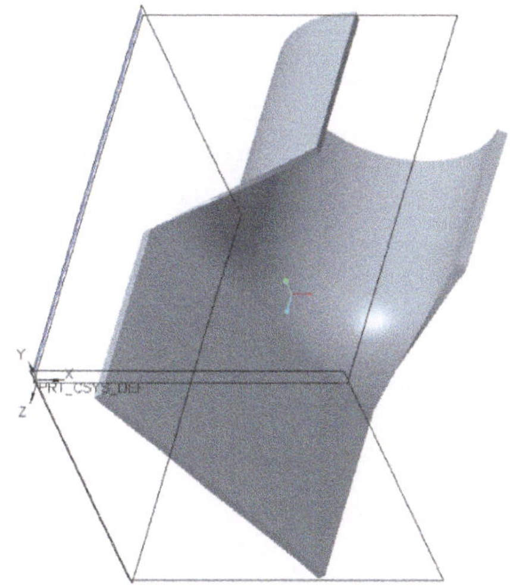

Unbend

This command unfolds a bend to its original position.

1. On the ribbon, click **Sheetmetal > Bends > Unbend**. The preview of the unbent sheet appears.

Notice that the **Automatic** icon is active. As a result, the horizontal portion of the sheet is selected as the fixed geometry automatically.

2. Activate the **Manual** icon on the Dashboard.
3. Select the edges or bends to be unbend.
4. Click in the **Fixed geometry** collector on the Dashboard and select the face to be fixed.

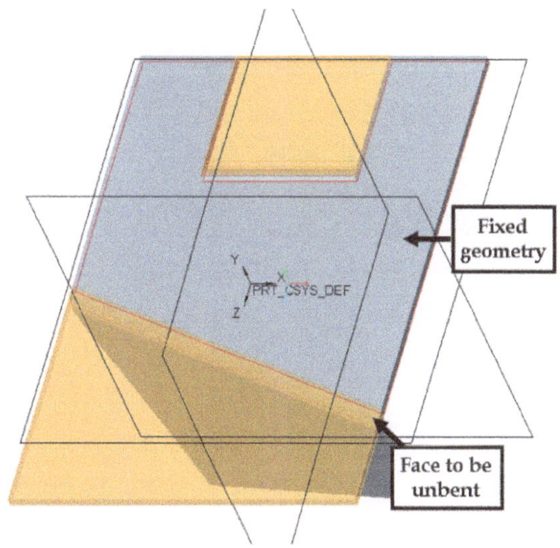

5. Click the green check to unbend the bent faces.

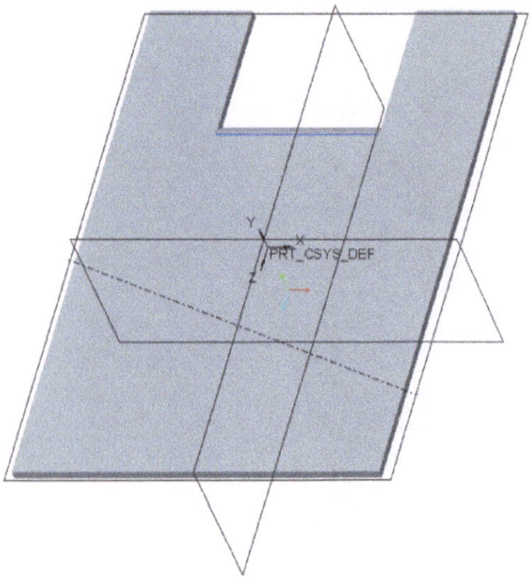

Bend Back

This command refolds the unfolded bend.

1. Create a bend feature, and then unbend it using the **Unbend** command.

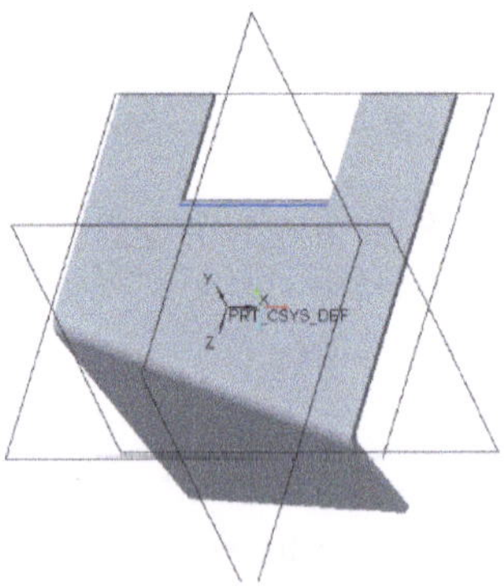

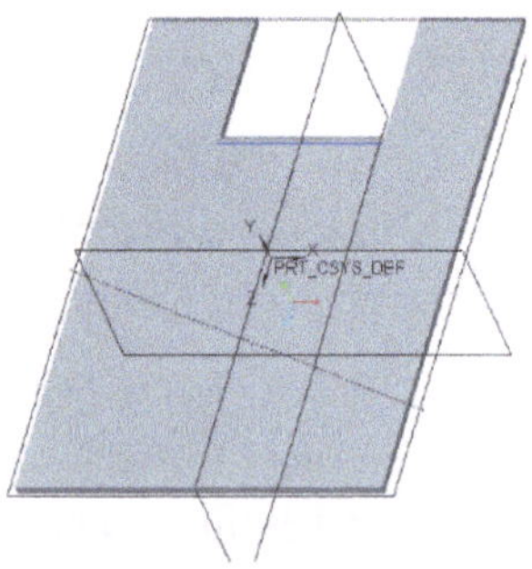

2. Create a sketch on the top face of the flat sheet.

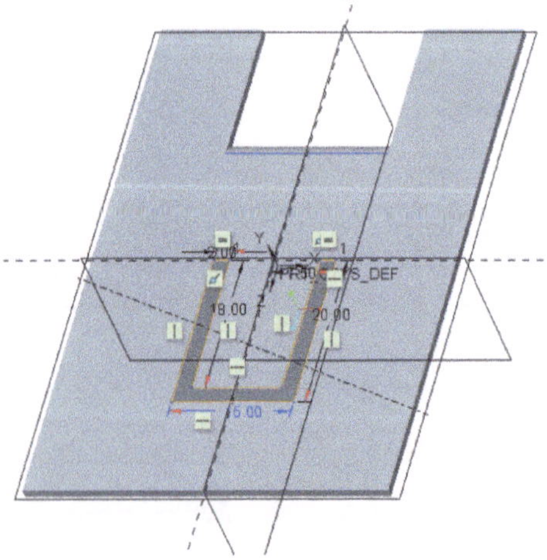

3. Activate the **Extruded Cut** command (on the ribbon, click **Sheetmetal > Engineering > Extruded Cut**) and click **OK**.

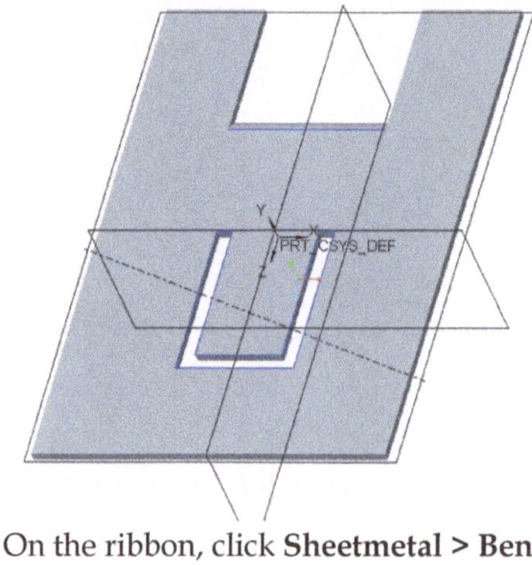

4. On the ribbon, click **Sheetmetal > Bends > Bend Back**. The references are selected automatically.
5. Click the **Preview** icon on the Dashboard.
6. Click the **Resume** icon to disable the preview mode.
7. On the Dashboard, click the **Bend Control** tab and select **Contour 1**.
8. Select **Keep flat** to flatten the contour 1.
9. Click the green check to refold the unfolded bend.

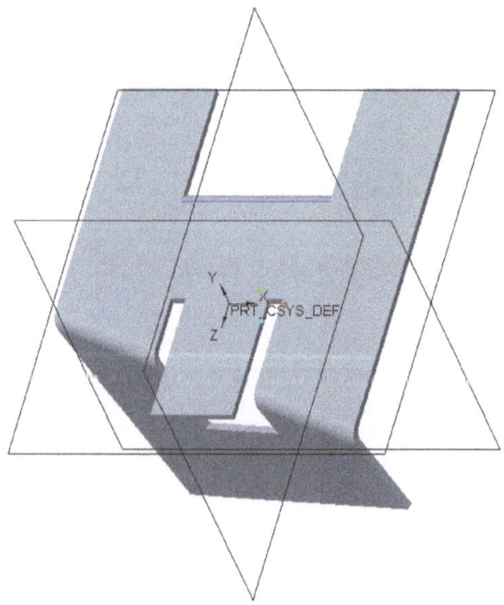

Punch Form

The **Punch Form** command molds a flat sheet using the shape of a reference part. The external surface of the reference part is used to mold a flat sheet. For example, the following figure shows a punch and shape created on the sheet metal part.

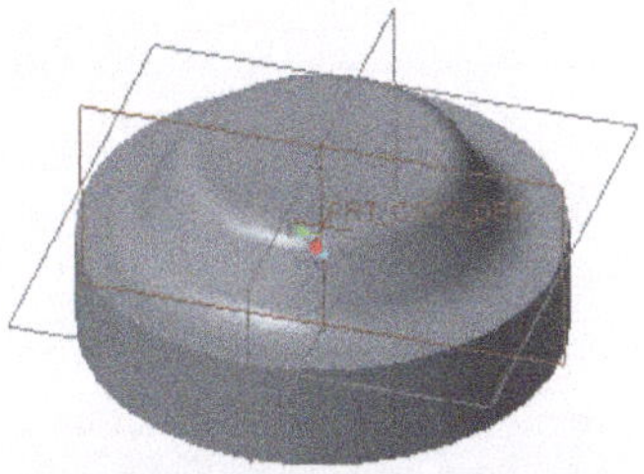

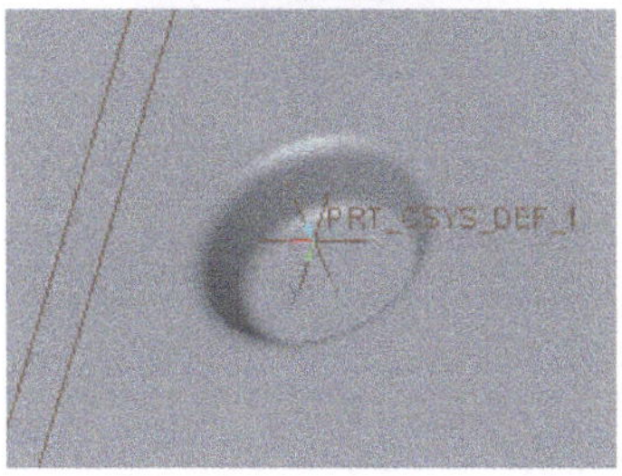

1. On the ribbon, click **Sheetmetal > Engineering > Form > Punch Form**.

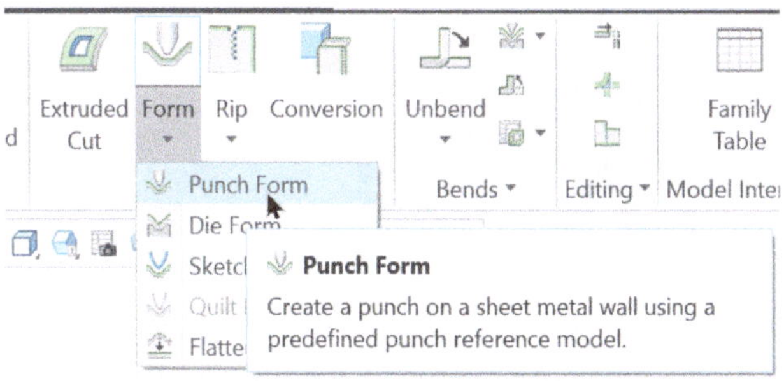

2. On the **Punch Form** Dashboard, select CLOSE_FLAT_LOUVER_FORM_MM from the **Source Model** drop-down.

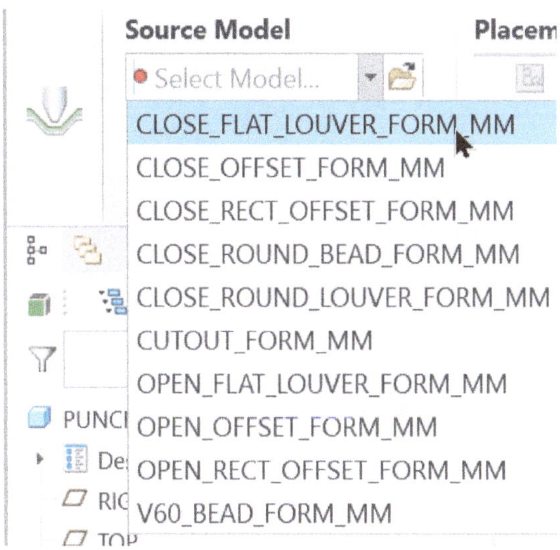

3. Click on the bottom face of the flat sheet to be formed.

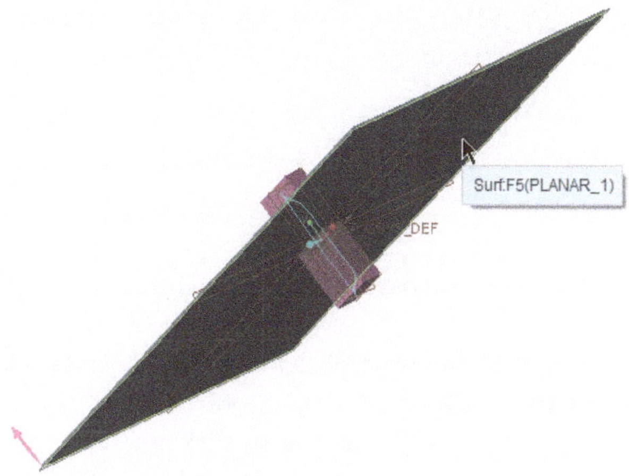

4. Drag the offset handles onto the side edges of the sheet.

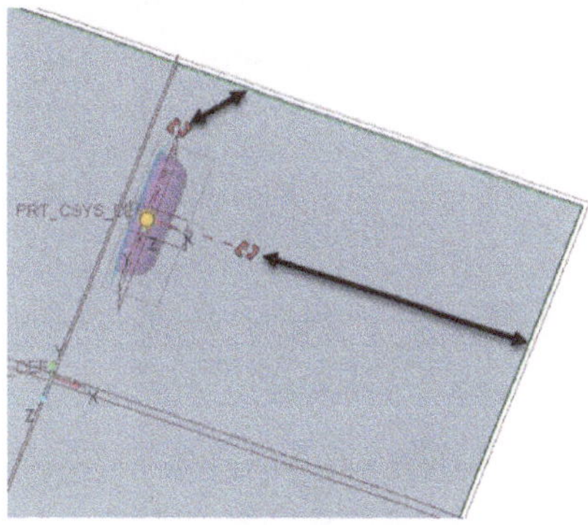

5. Modify the offset dimensions.

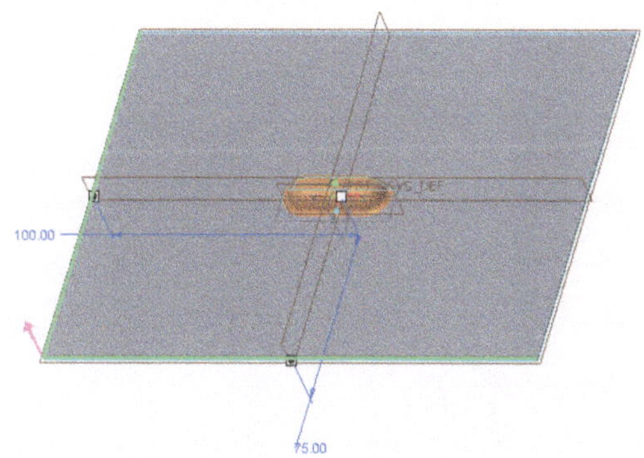

6. On the dashboard, click the **Placement** tab and check the **Add rotation about the first axis** option.
7. Type-in 90 in the **Rotation value** box.

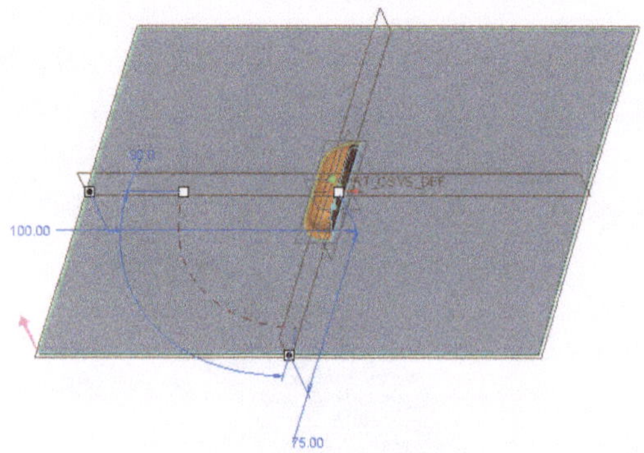

8. On the Dashboard, click the **Use Inheritance** icon.
9. On the Dashboard, click the **Shape** tab and click the **Vary Punch Model** button.
10. On the **Varied Items** dialog, click the **Dimensions** tab and select the + button located at the bottom.
11. In the preview window, select the revolve feature of the reference model as shown.

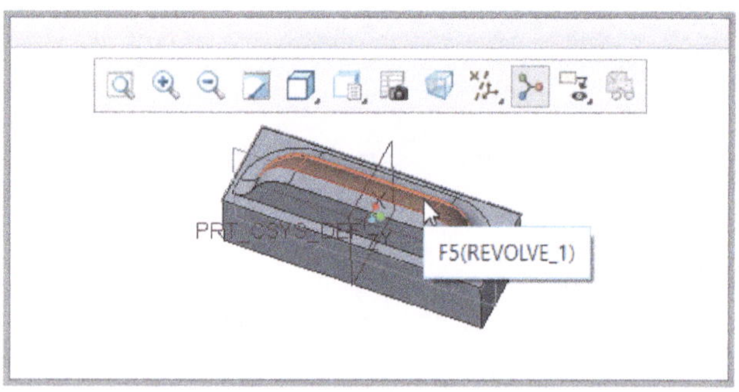

12. Select the dimension as shown.

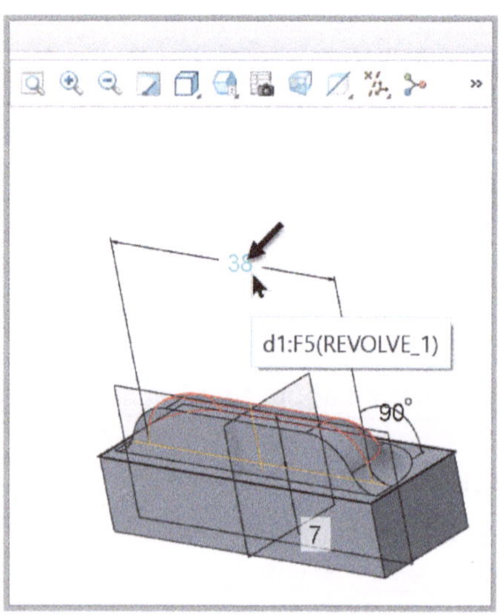

13. On the **Varied Items** dialog, click in the **New value** box and type-in 50.

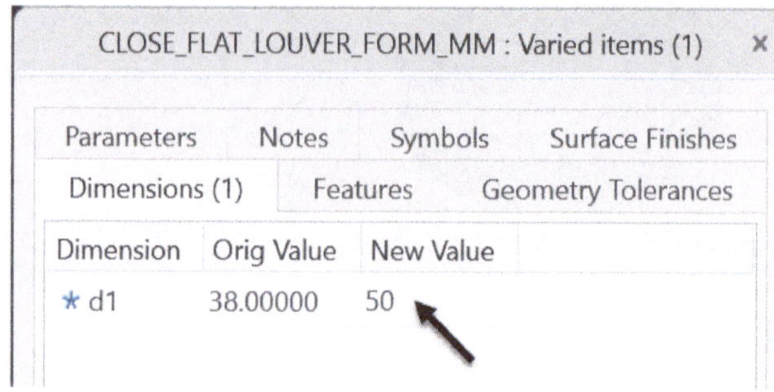

14. Click **OK**.
15. Click the green check to complete the feature.

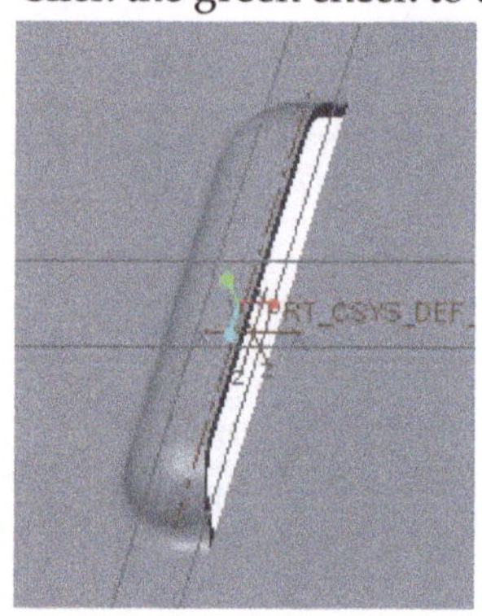

Die Form

The **Die Form** command (on the ribbon, click **Sheetmetal > Engineering > Form > Die Form**) adds a form to a flat sheet using the shape of a reference part. The internal surface of the reference part is used to mold a flat sheet. For example, the following figure shows a die and shape created on the sheet metal part. The procedure to create a die form is the same as that of punch.

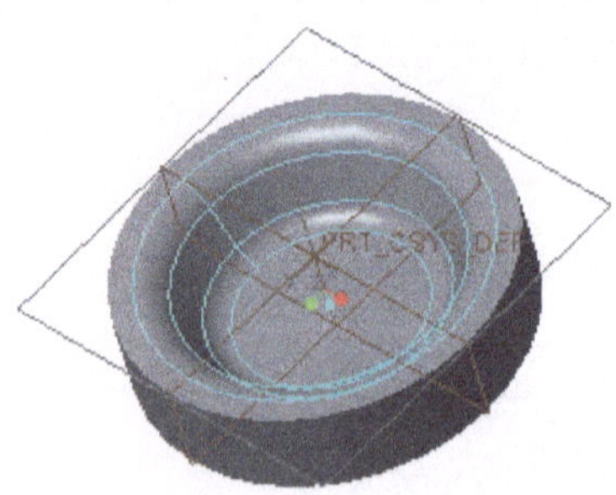

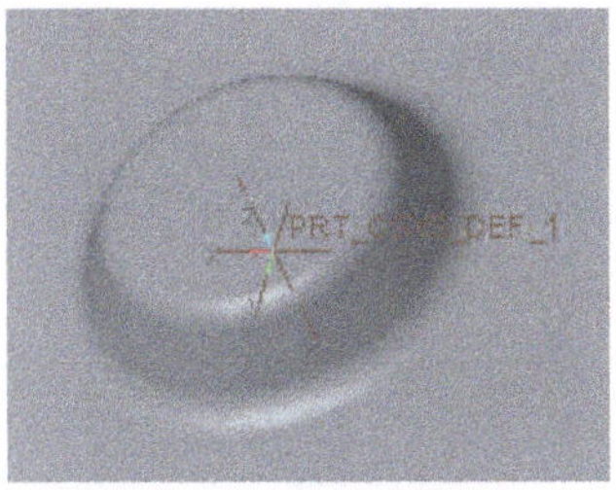

Sketched Form

The **Sketched Form** command adds a form to a flat sheet by using a sketch profile.

1. On the ribbon, click **Sheetmetal >Engineering > Form > Sketched Form.**

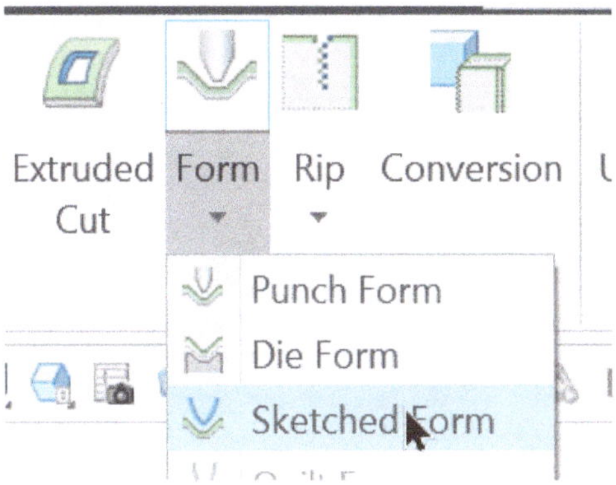

2. On the dashboard, click the **Create a Punch** icon located on the left side.
3. Click on the sketch profile as shown.

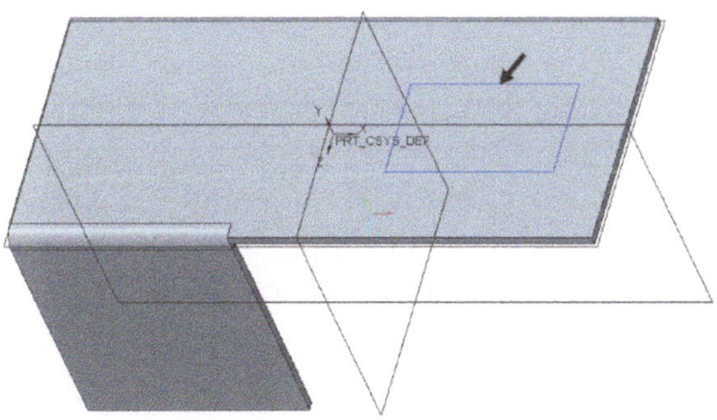

4. Type-in the depth value (or) drag the handle to define the depth.

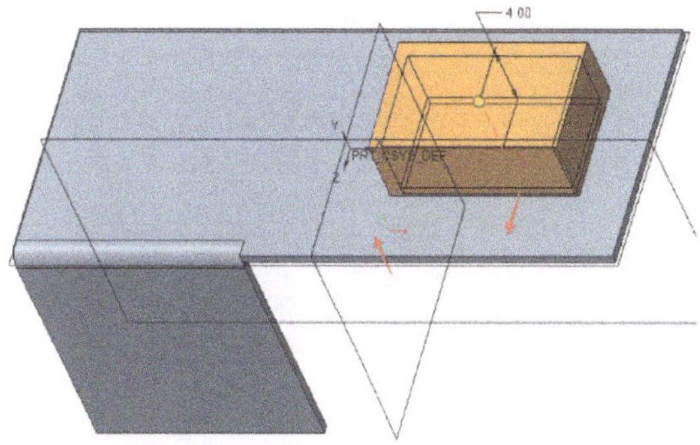

5. On the Dashboard, click the **Options** tab and check the **Add taper** option.
6. Drag the taper handle (or) type a value in the taper box.

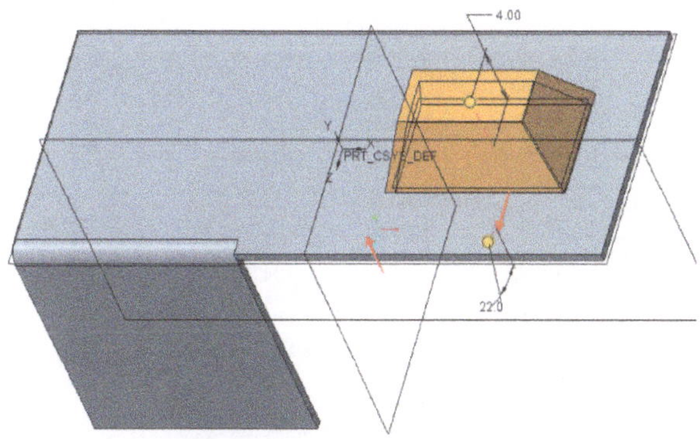

7. On the **Options** tab, check the **Nonplacement edges** option. The side edges are rounded.

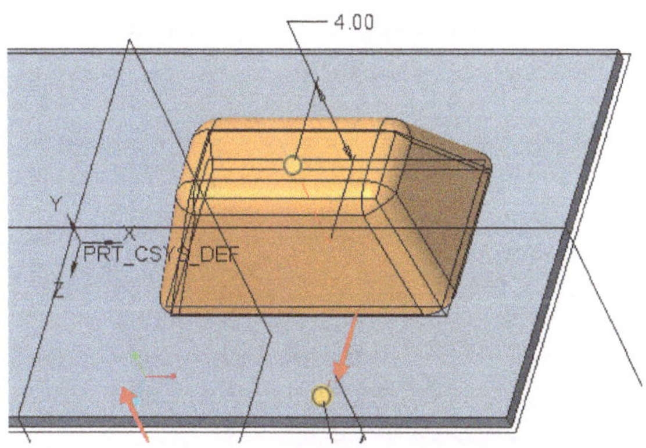

8. On the **Options** tab, check the **Placement edges** option. The placement edges are rounded.

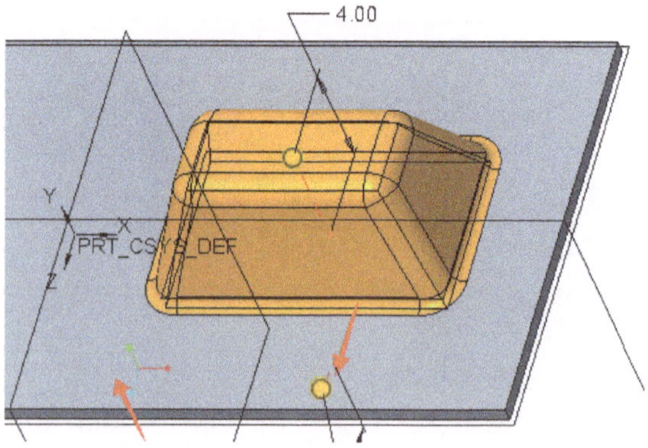

12. On the **Options** tab, click in the **Exclude Surfaces** box and click on the form's front face. The selected face is removed.

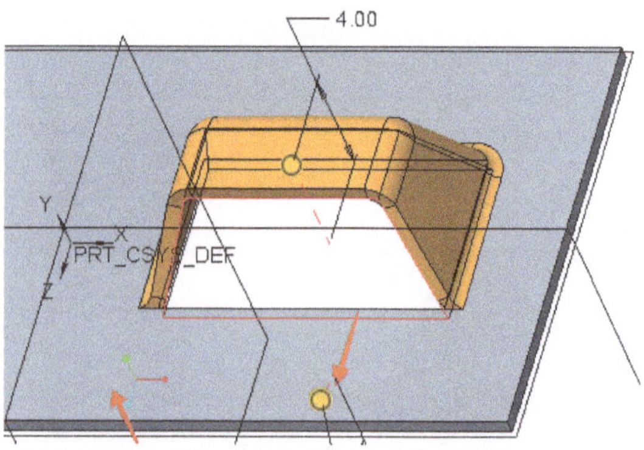

13. Click the right mouse button in the **Exclude Surface** box and select **Remove**.
14. Uncheck the **Capped ends** options to remove the end surface of the form.

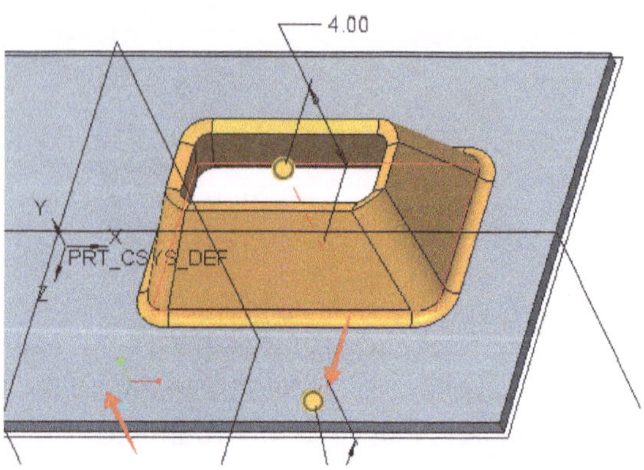

15. On the Dashboard, click the **Change Form Direction** icon next to the depth value box. The form direction is reversed.

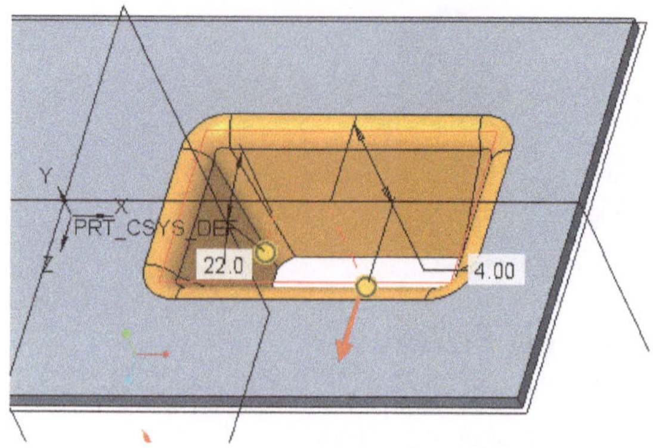

16. On the Dashboard, click the **Change Material Direction** icon next to the **Pause** icon. The material direction is reversed.

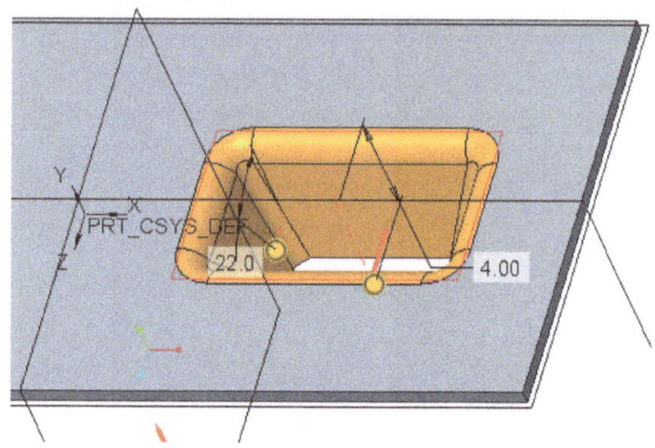

17. Click the green check to complete the feature.

Creating the Pierced Sketched Form

If you click **Create a piercing** icon on the dashboard, the stamp's height will be half of the sheet metal thickness. You can increase the height value up to the sheet metal thickness.

1. Activate the **Sketched Form** command and click on the sheet to add the form.
2. Draw the profile of the form feature and click **OK**.

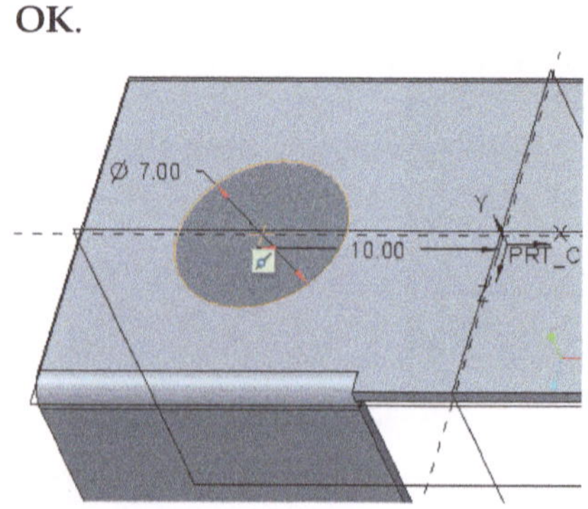

3. On the Dashboard, click the **Piercing** icon.
4. Click the **Change Form Direction** icon next to the **Depth** box.
5. Click the green check.

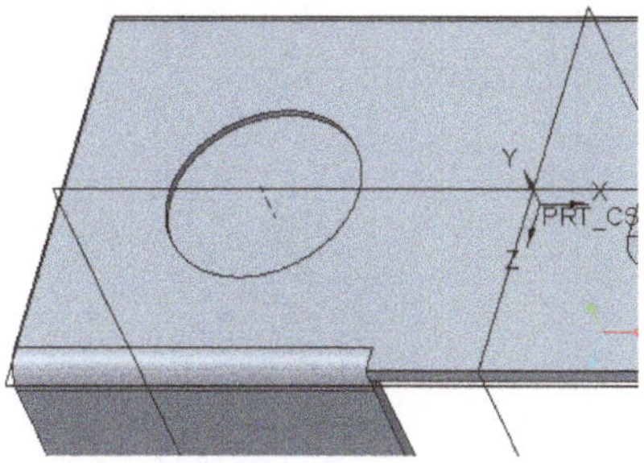

Flat Pattern Preview

The **Flat Pattern Preview** command lets you preview the flattened view in a separate window.

1. On the **Graphics** toolbar, click **Flat Pattern Preview**. A separate window appears with the flattened view.

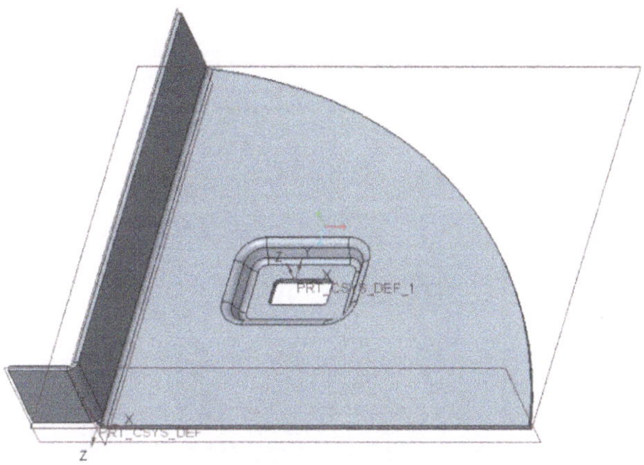

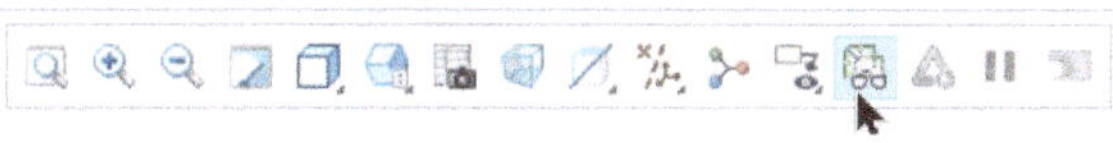

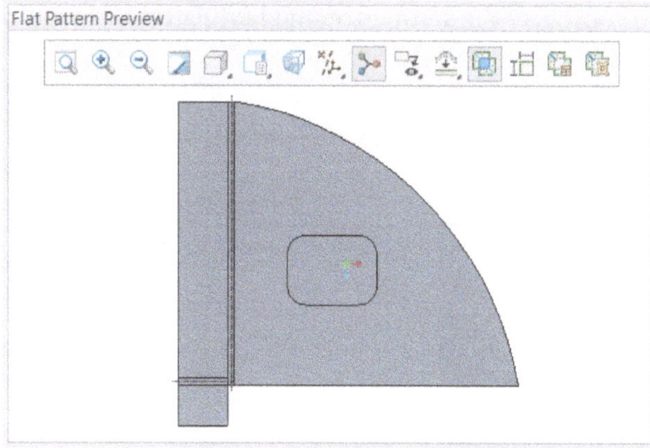

2. Click the **Bounding Box** icon in the **Flat Pattern Preview** window. The program displays the bounding dimensions.

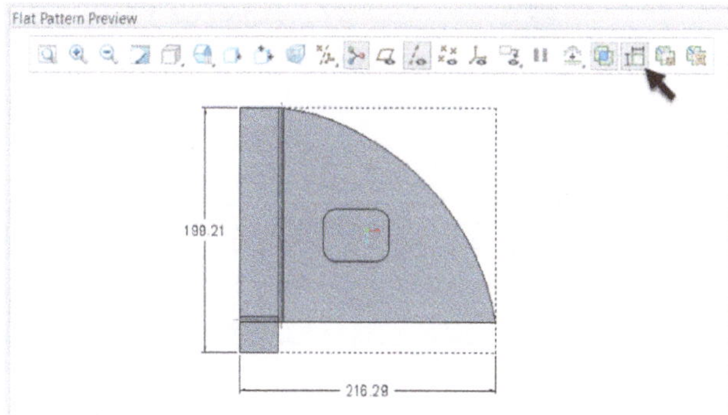

3. Click the **Form Geometry** icon and uncheck the **Flatten Forms** option. The forms are not flattened.

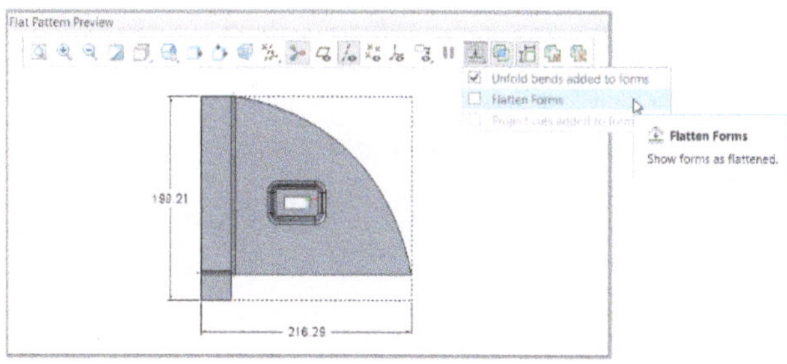

4. Close the **Flat Pattern Preview** window.

Flat Pattern

The **Flat Pattern** command flattens the part so that you can easily display the manufacturing information. Before creating a flat pattern, you need to configure the settings on the **Flat Pattern Preview** window.

1. On the ribbon, click **Sheetmetal > Bends > Flat Pattern**.

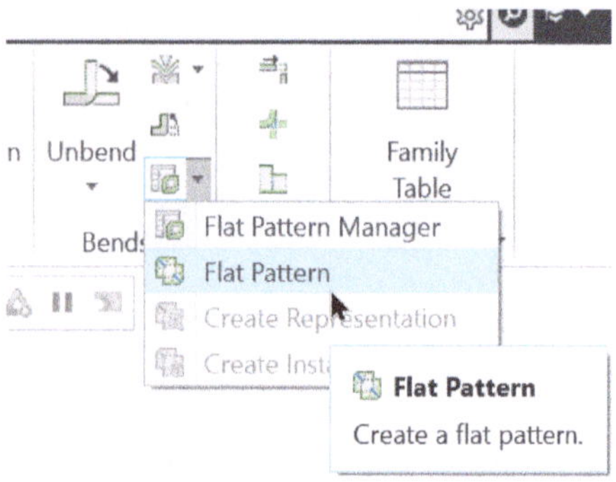

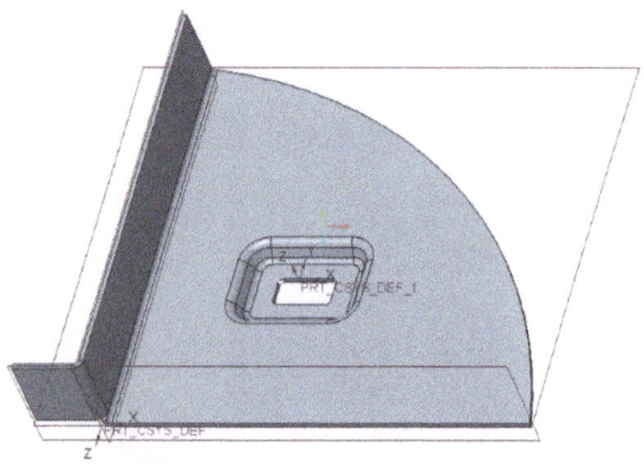

2. Click the green check on the Dashboard. The program flattens the entire sheet metal part. Also, the bend annotations appear on the bends.

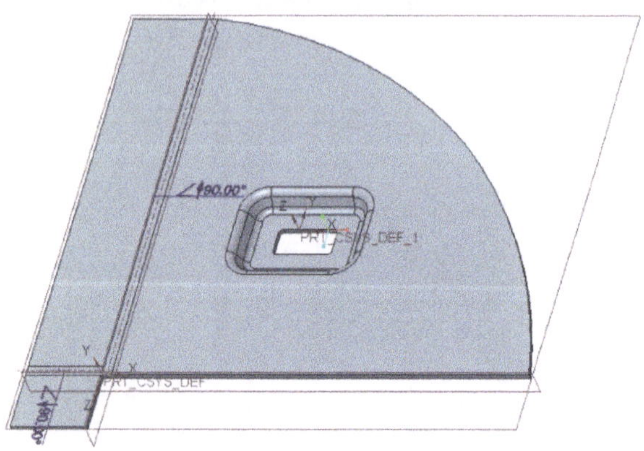

Notice that the form geometry is not flattened as the **Flatten Forms** option is unchecked in the **Flat Pattern Preview** window.

3. Activate a sheet metal command from the ribbon and notice that the flat pattern mode is disabled.

Extruded Cuts

When it is necessary to remove material from a sheet metal part, you must use the **Extruded Cut** command.

1. Draw a sketch, and then click the **Extruded Cut** icon on the **Engineering** panel.
2. Select the sketch, if not selected.

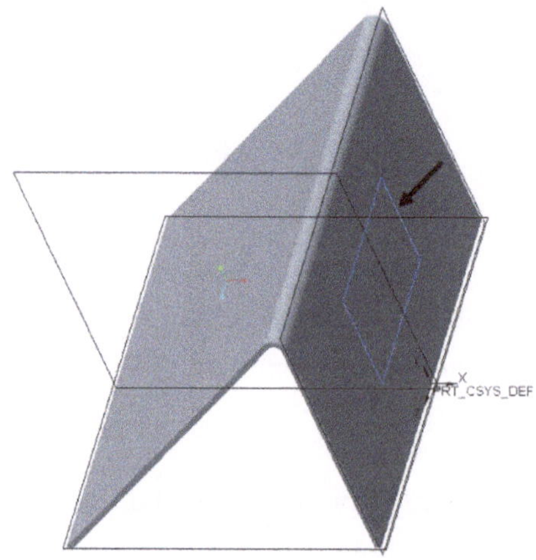

3. On the dashboard, set the **Depth** type to **Through All**.
4. Click the **Preview** icon on the Dashboard.

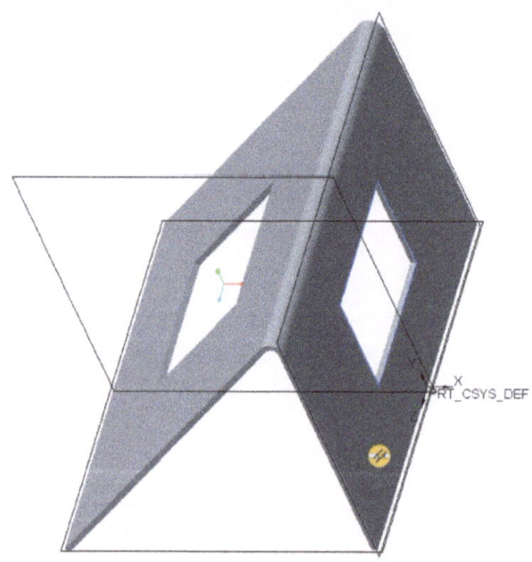

5. Change the **Display Style** to **Wireframe** and **Orientation** to **Front**. Notice that the cut is created normal to the sheet metal surface.

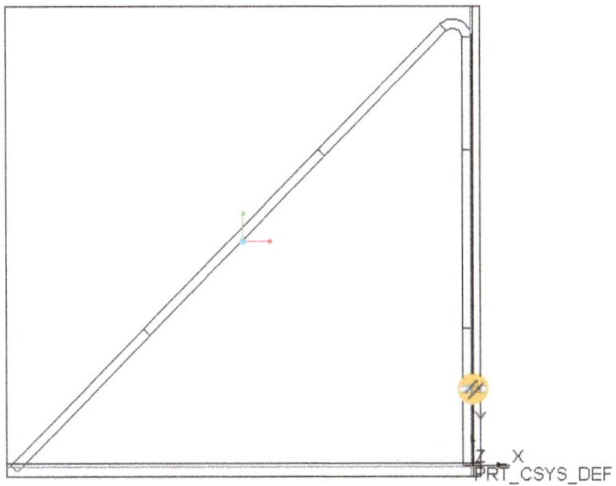

6. Click the **Resume** icon on the Dashboard.
7. On the Dashboard, deactivate the **Normal to surface** icon. Notice that the cut is created normal to the sketch plane.

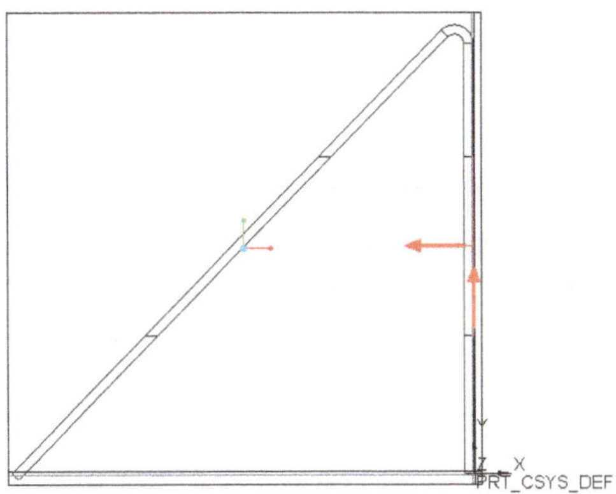

8. Click the green check to complete the feature.

Revolve

This command creates a sheet metal by revolving a profile about an axis.

1. Create an open sketch along with an axis.

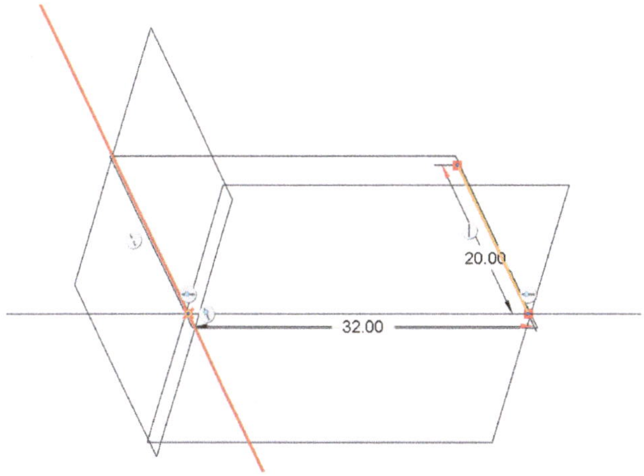

2. On the **Sheetmetal** tab of the ribbon, expand the **Walls** panel and click the **Revolve** icon.

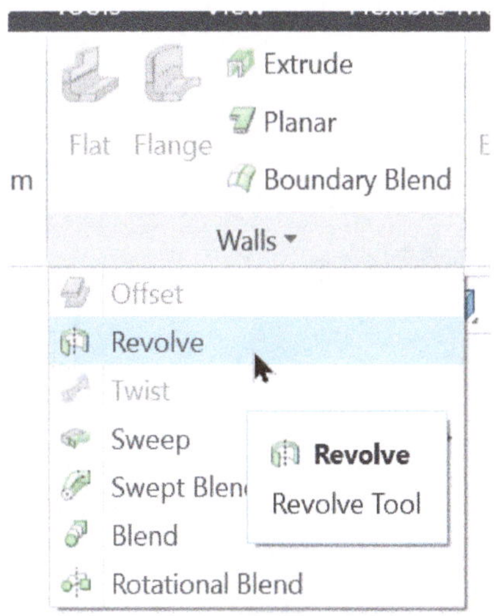

3. Type-in the revolution angle and sheet metal thickness on the Dashboard. Note that the revolution angle should be less than 360 so that you can create a flat pattern.
4. Click the green check to complete the feature.

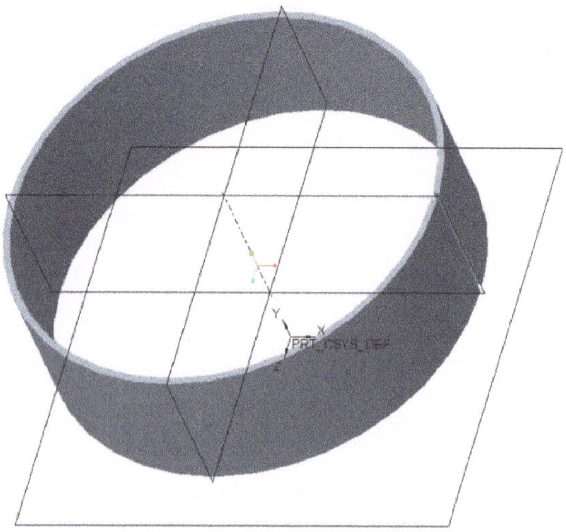

5. Activate the **Flat Pattern** command (on the ribbon, click **Sheetmetal > Bends > Flat Pattern**).
6. Select an edge on the end face of the revolved sheet metal to define the fixed end.

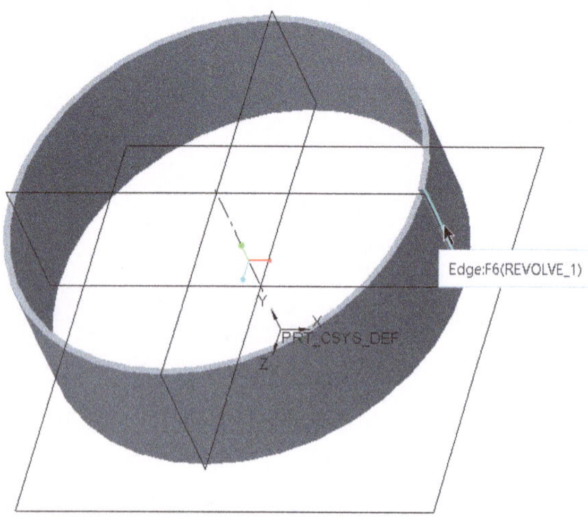

7. Click the green check to create a flat pattern.

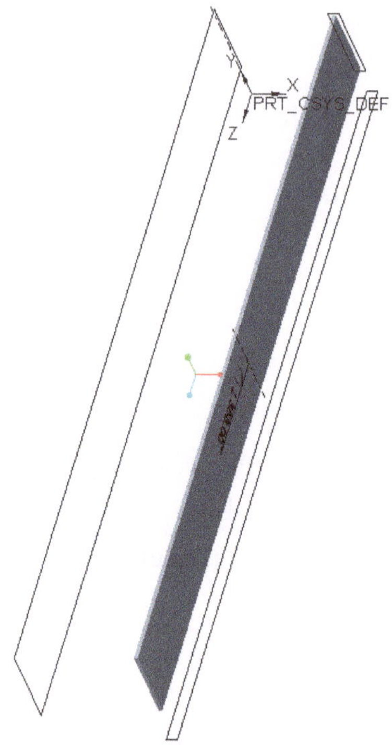

Conversion

Creo Parametric has a special command called **Conversion**, which automates converting an already existing solid part into a sheet metal part.

1. Create a part in the solid **Part** environment.

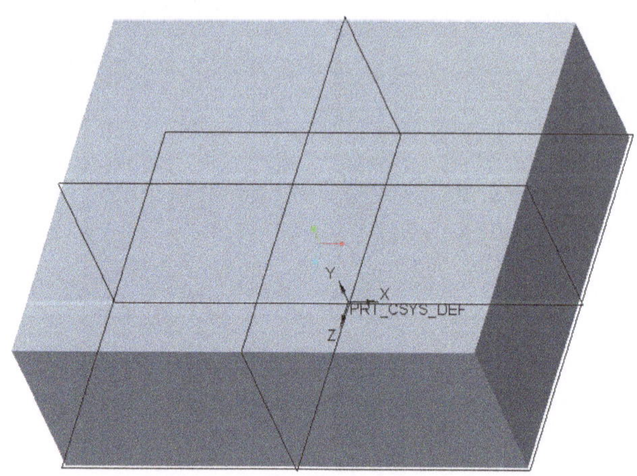

2. On the ribbon, expand the **Operations** panel and select **Convert to Sheetmetal**.

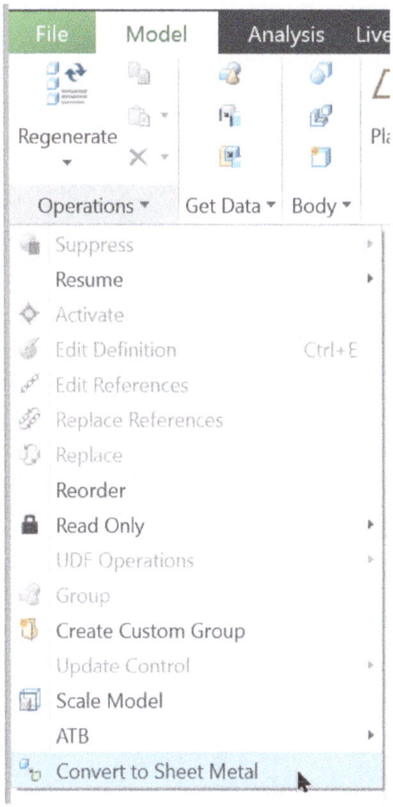

3. On the **Convert** Dashboard, select **ConversionType > Shell**.

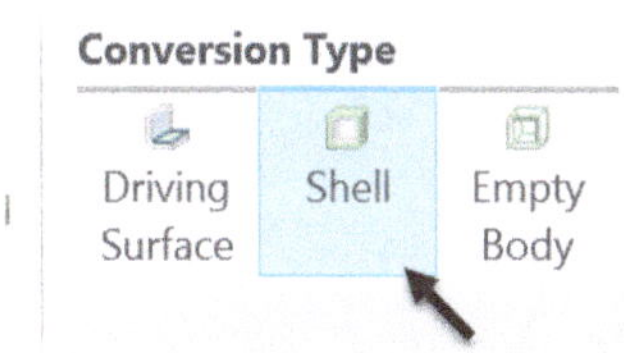

4. Select a face to remove.

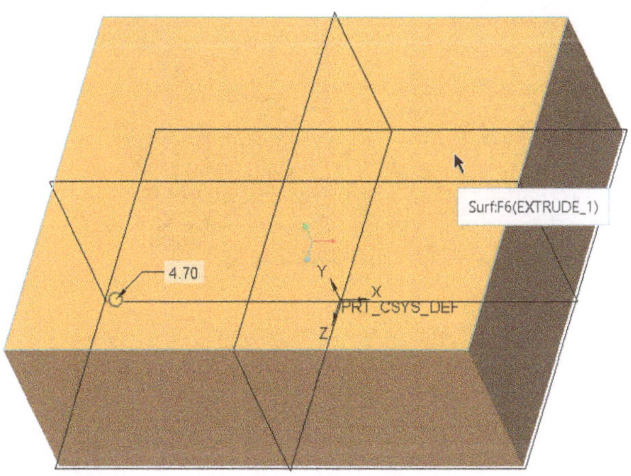

5. Type the thickness value on the Dashboard and click the green check. The solid part is converted into a sheet metal part. Now, you need to make this part developable by using the **Conversion** command.

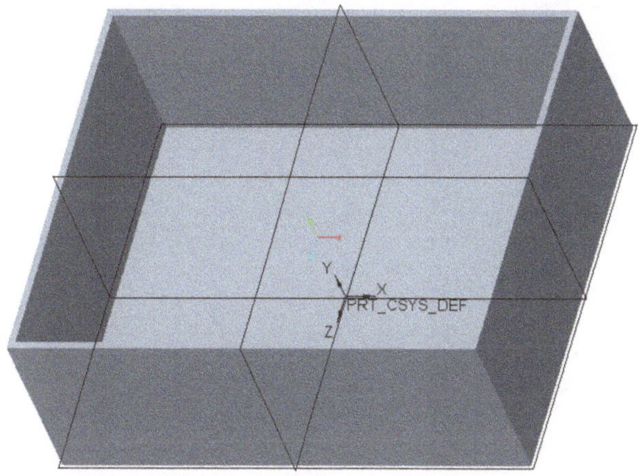

6. On the ribbon, click **Sheetmetal > Engineering > Conversion**.
7. On the **Conversion** Dashboard, click the **Edge Rip** .
8. Click the edges to be ripped.

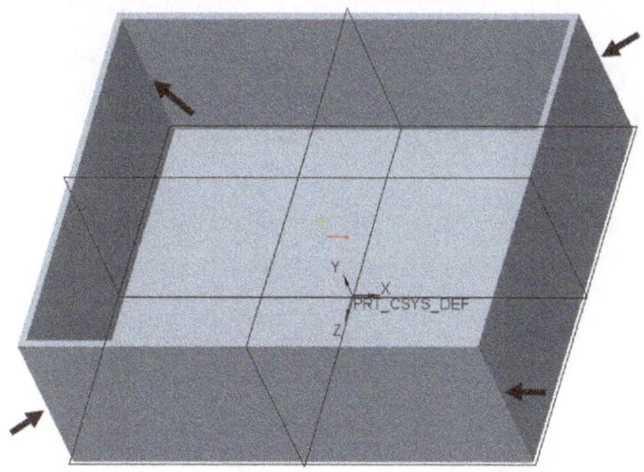

9. On the Dashboard, click the **Placement** tab and select the **Seam type** for each edge.
10. Define the edge treatment parameters on the **Placement** tab and click the green check.

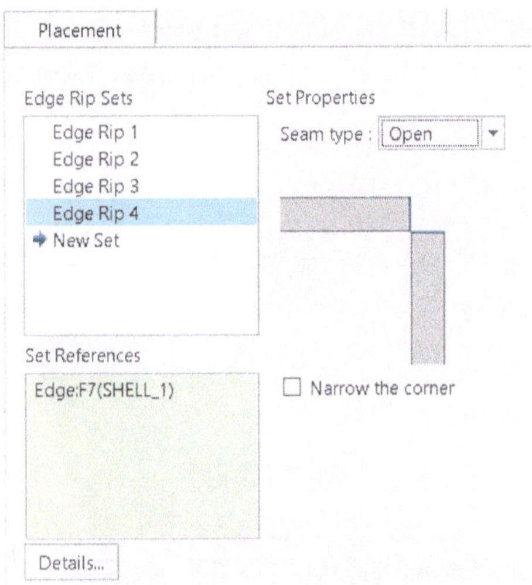

11. Click the green check on the **Conversion** Dashboard. Now, you can perform other sheet metal operations.

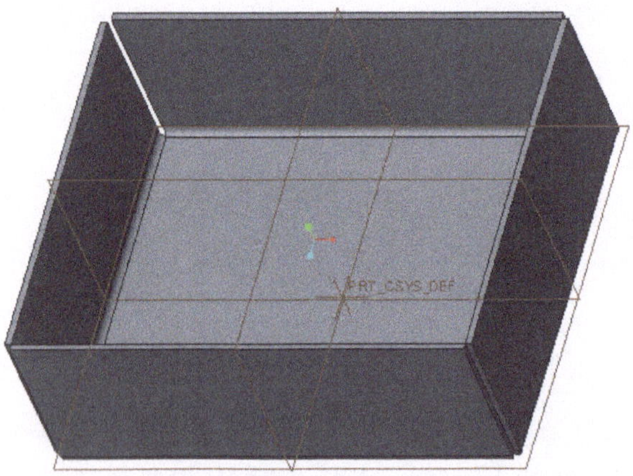

Surface Rip

The **Surface Rip** command in Creo Parametric lets you separate a sheet metal part by selecting specific surfaces to create rips or breaks. This tool is particularly helpful for parts that have been converted into sheet metal and include filleted corners, allowing for more flexibility in design and unfolding operations.

1. Download the Sheetmetal chapter files.
2. Open the Surface_rip.prt file.

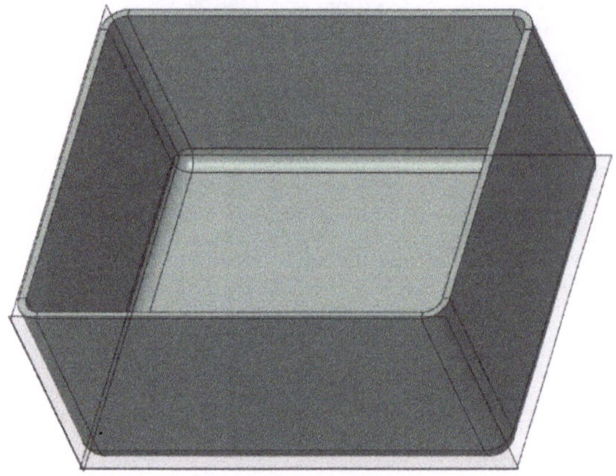

3. On the ribbon, click **Sheet Metal > Engineering > Surface Rip**.

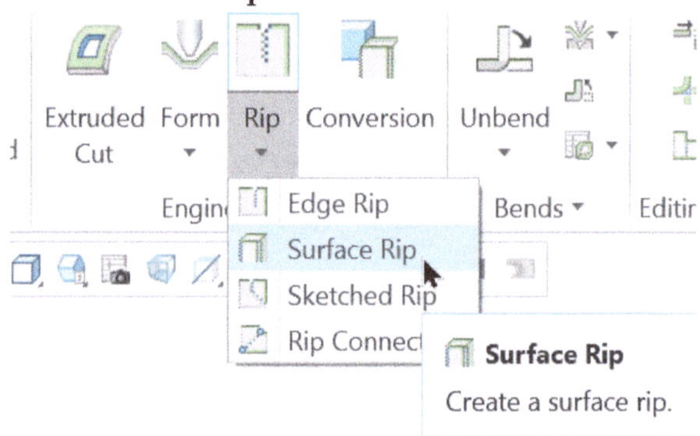

4. Select the faces from the sheetmetal part. You select multiple faces by pressing the CTRL key and clicking on them.

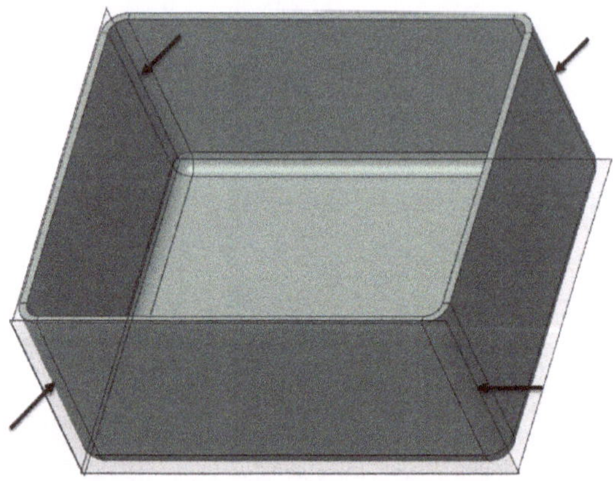

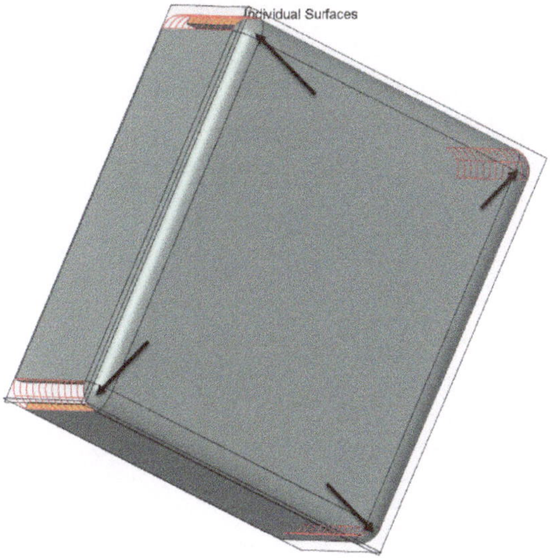

5. Click **OK** on the dashboard to create sheetmetal rips.

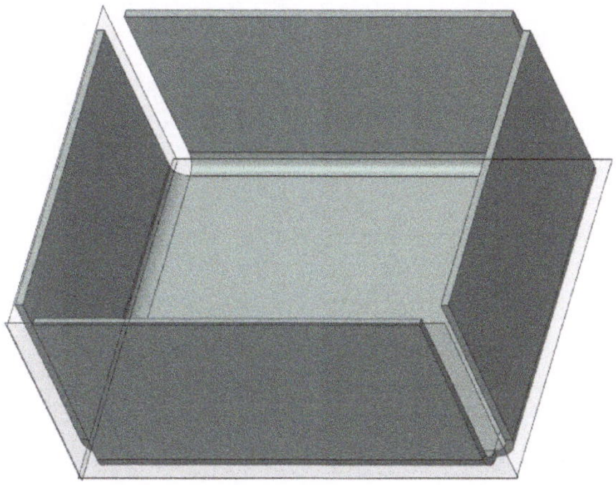

Examples

Example 1

In this example, you will construct the sheet metal part shown below.

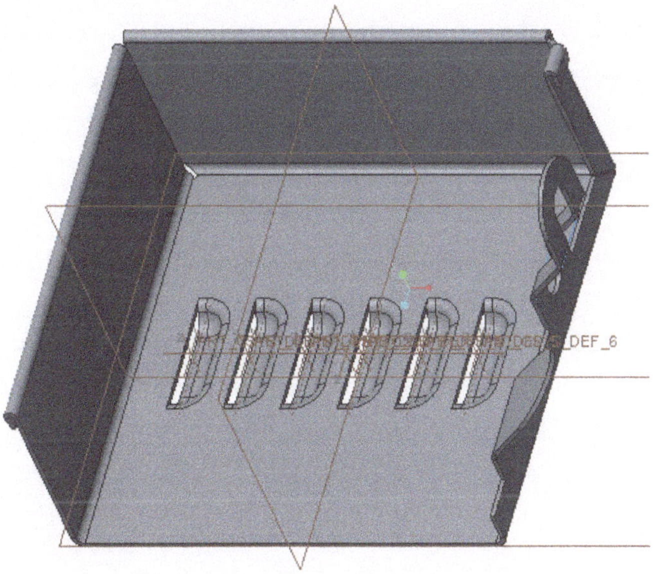

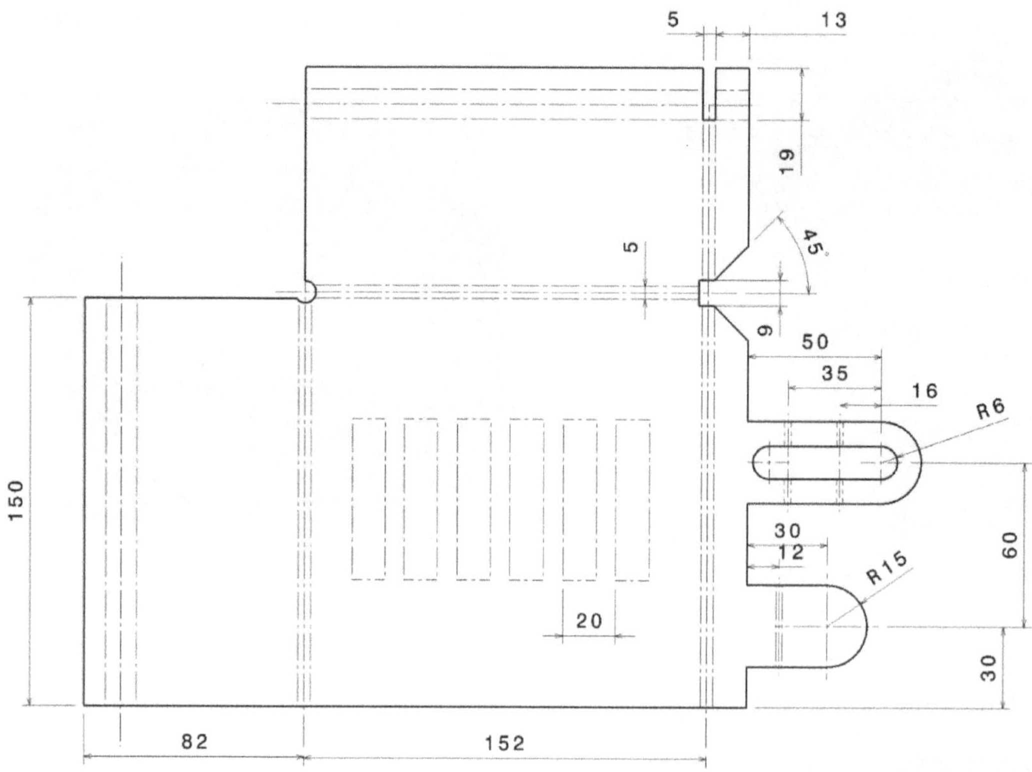

Unfolded view
Scale: 2:3

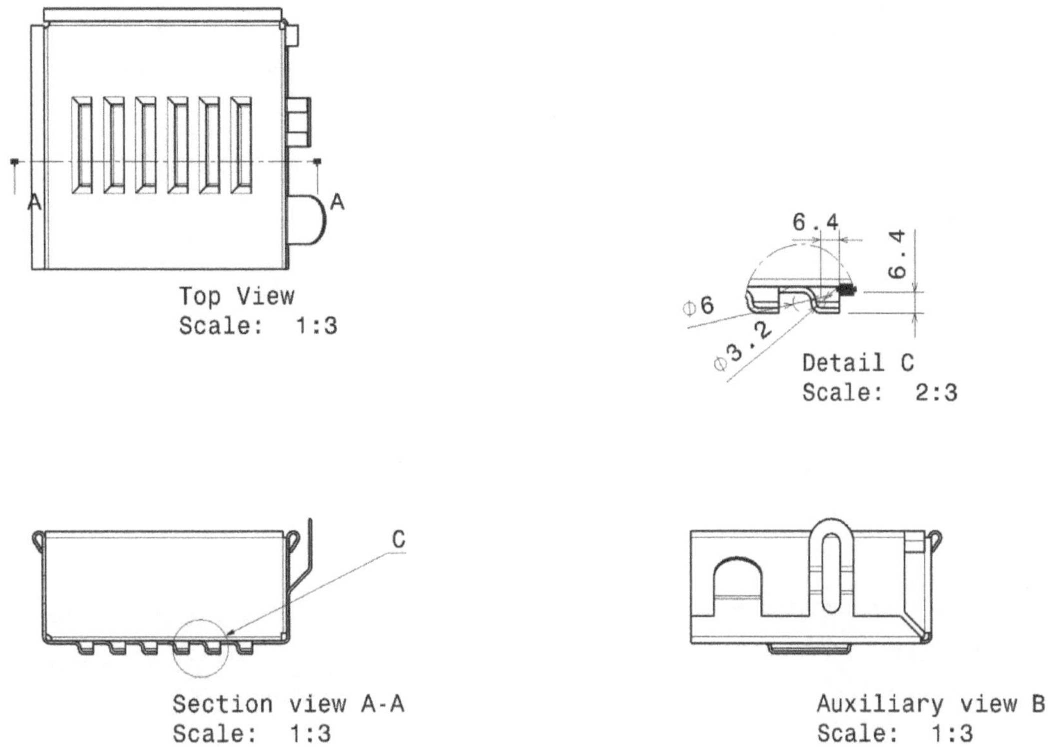

1. Start **Creo Parametric 11.0.**
2. Create a folder with the name *Sheet Metal Design* and set it as the current working folder.
3. On the Quick Access Toolbar, click the **New** button.
4. On the **New** dialog, select **Type > Part**.
5. Select **Sub-Type > Sheetmetal.**
6. Type-in *Example1* in the **Name** box and uncheck the **Use default template** option.
7. Click **OK**.
8. On the **New File Options** dialog, select **mmns_part_sheetmetal_abs** template and click **OK**.
9. Click **File > Prepare > Model Properties**.
10. On the **Model Properties** dialog, click the **change** option next to **Thickness**.
11. Type-in 1.6 in the **Thickness** box and click **OK**.
12. Click the **change** option next to **Bend allowance**.
13. On the **Sheetmetal Preferences** dialog, select the **K factor** option from the **Bend allowance factor** box and type-in 0.33 in the **Factor value** box.
14. Click the **Bends** tab on the dialog and type-in 2.4 in the **Bend radius** box.
15. Click the **Relief** tab on the dialog and select **Rip** from the **Type** drop-down under the **Bend relief settings** section.
16. Leave the other default values, click **OK**, and close the **Model Properties** dialog.
17. Create a sketch on the Top plane and exit the sketch mode.

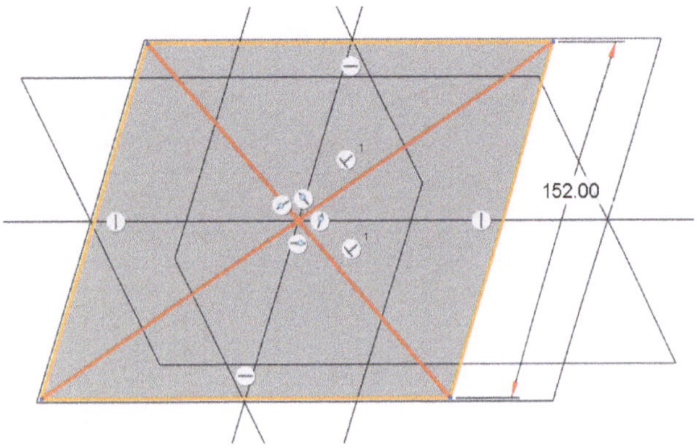

18. On the ribbon, click **Sheetmetal** tab > **Walls** panel > **Planar** .
19. Select the sketch.
20. Click the green check to create the sheet metal wall.

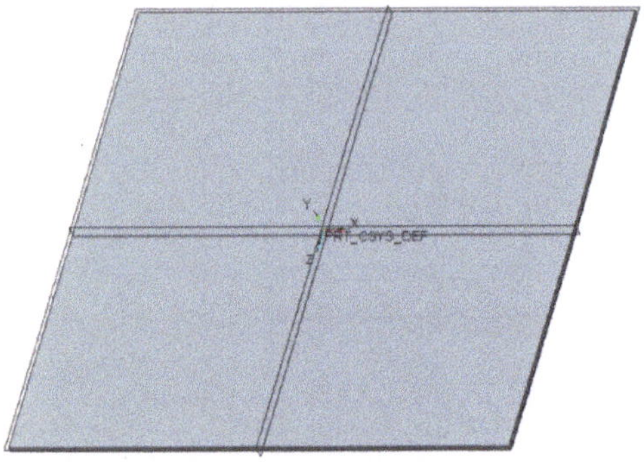

21. On the ribbon, click **Sheetmetal** tab > **Walls** panel > **Flange** .
22. Click on the bottom back edge of the sheet metal wall.

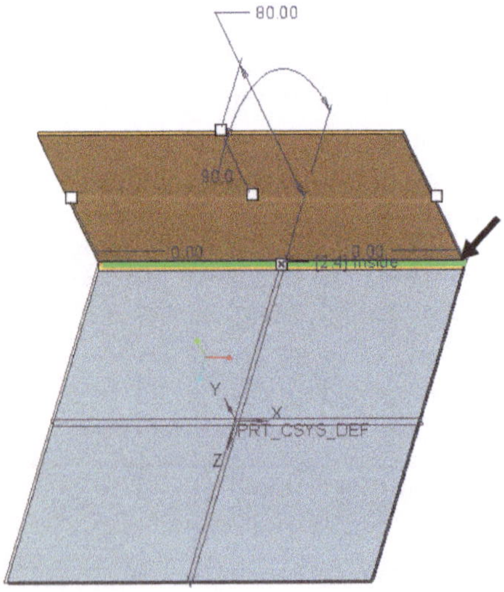

23. On the **Flange** dashboard, click the **Placement** tab, and then click **Details**.
24. On the **Chain** dialog, click the **References** tab.
25. Select the **Rule-based** option and select **Partial Loop** from the **Rule** section.
26. Select the bottom edge of the left side face.

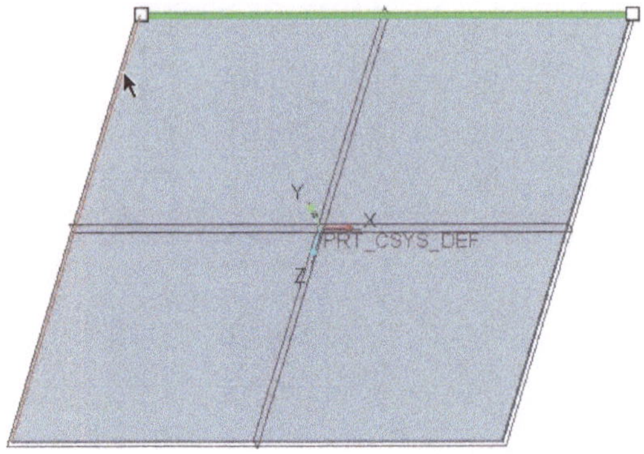

27. Click **OK** on the **Chain** dialog.

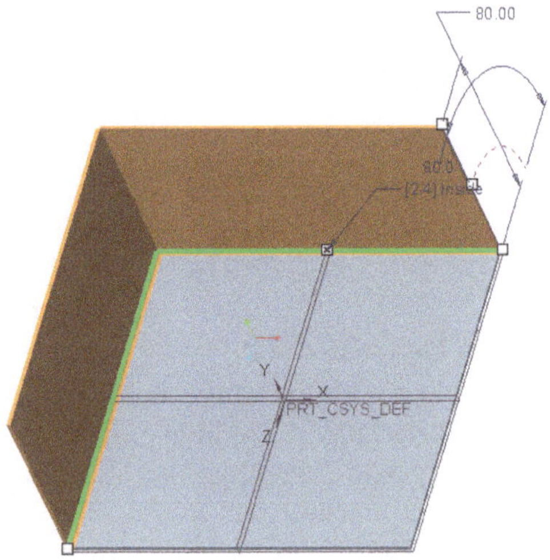

28. On the **Flange** dashboard, click the **Bend Position** tab.
29. On the **Bend Position** tab, click the **Offset from Bend Apex** icon.
30. Type 1.6 in the **Value** box.

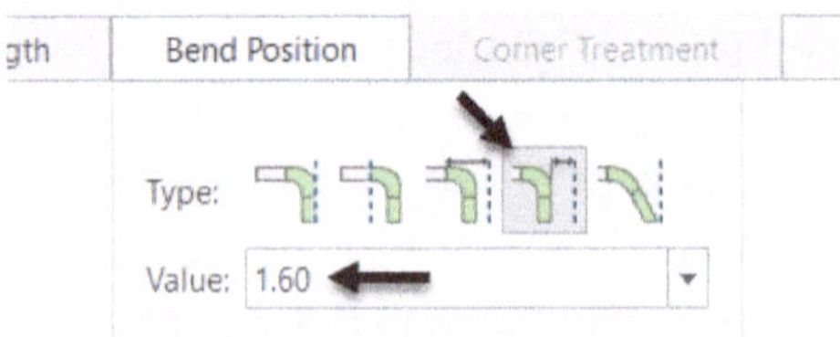

31. On the **Flange** dashboard, click the **Corner Treatment** tab.
32. On the **Corner Treatment** tab, select **Open** from the **Type** drop-down.
33. Check the **Narrow the corner** option.

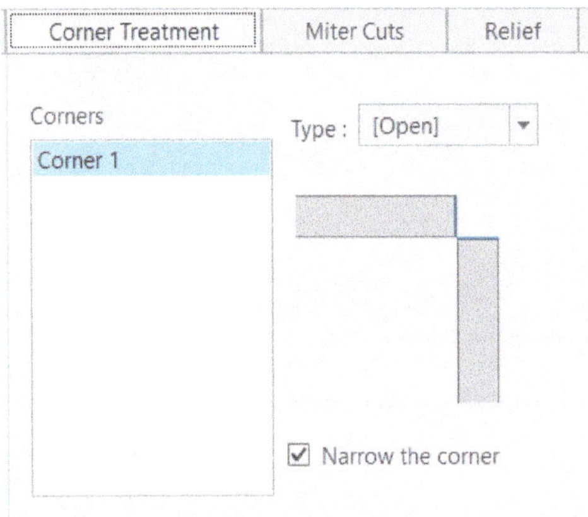

34. On the **Flange** dashboard, click the **Relief** tab.
35. Select the **Corner Relief** option from the list.
36. Select the **Circular** option from the **Type** drop-down.
37. Select the **Bend Lines Intersection** option from the **Origin** drop-down.
38. Type **8** in the **Relief width** box.

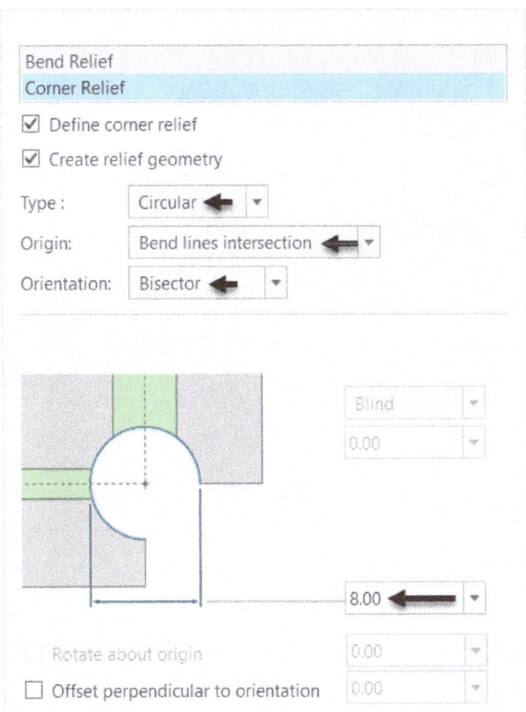

39. Double-click on the length dimension of the flange and type 65. Next, press Enter.

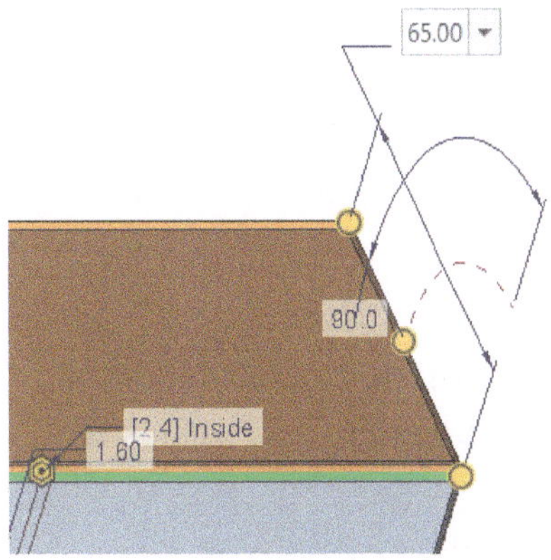

40. Click the green check to create the flange on the selected edges.

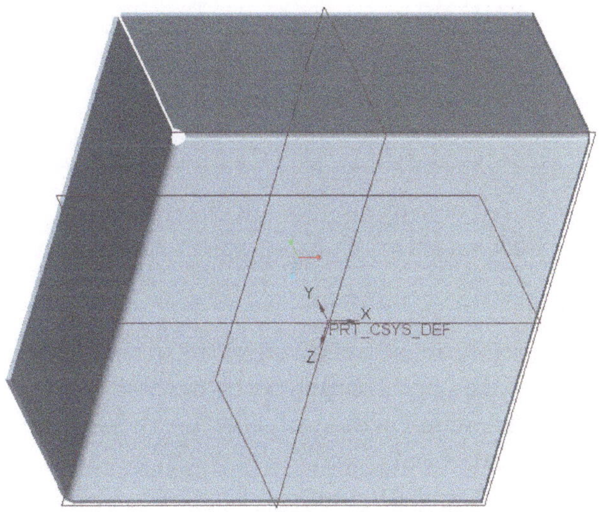

41. Activate the **Flat**  command and click on the right bottom edge of the sheet metal.

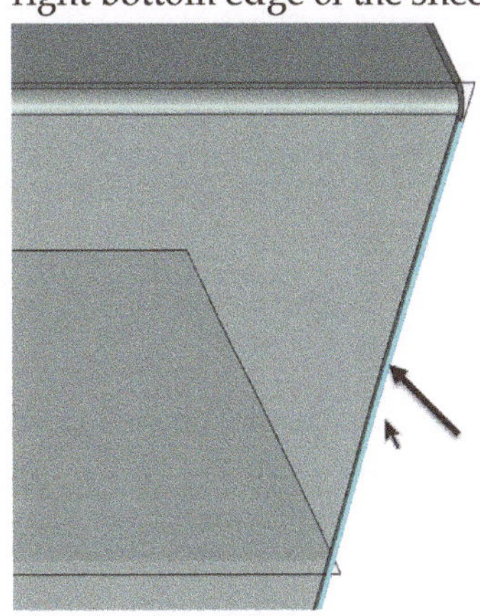

42. On the **Flat** dashboard, select **User Defined** from the **Shape** drop-down located at the left side.

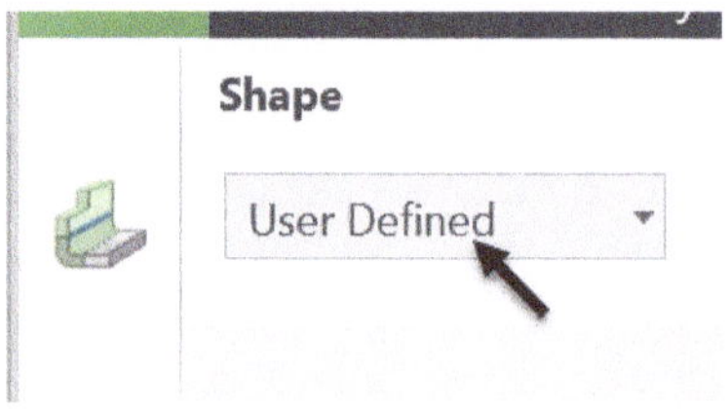

43. On the **Flat** dashboard, click the **Shape** tab, and then click the **Sketch** button.
44. Leave the default settings on the **Sketch** dialog, and then click the **Sketch** button.
45. Click the **Sketch View** icon on the **Graphics** toolbar.
46. Create the sketch, as shown.

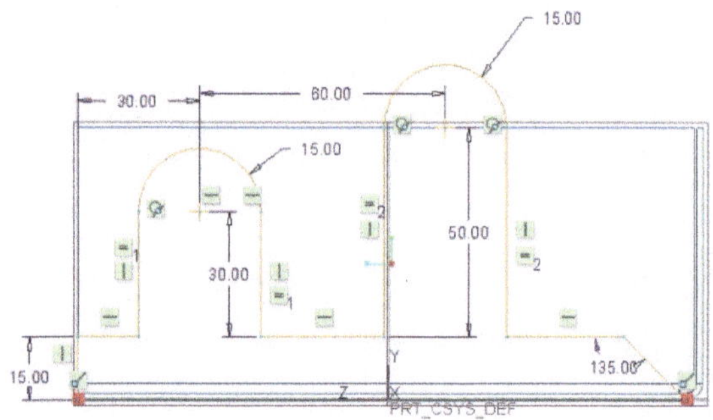

47. Click **OK** on the **Sketch** tab of the ribbon.
48. Click the **Bend Position** tab on the dashboard.
49. On the **Bend Position** tab, click the **Offset from Bend Start** icon.
50. Type 1.6 in the **Value** box.

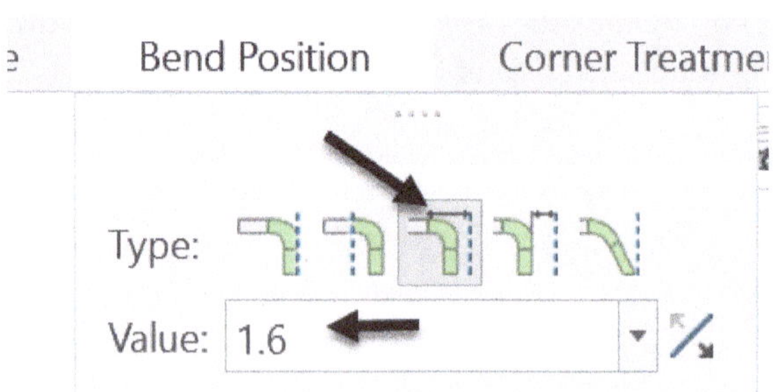

51. Click the green check on the dashboard to create the flat wall.

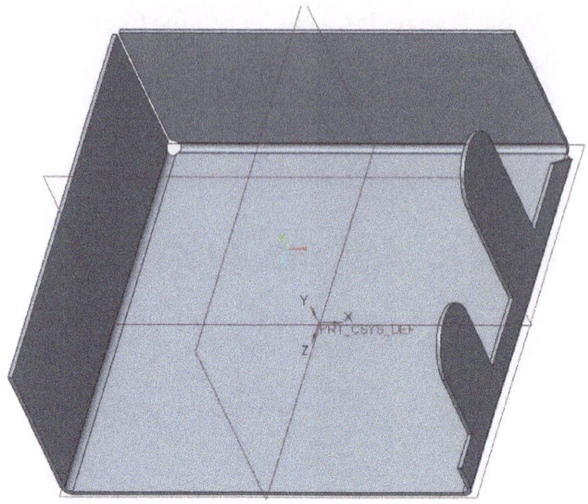

52. On the ribbon, click **Sheetmetal** tab > **Walls** panel > **Flat**.
53. Select the right edge of the flange.

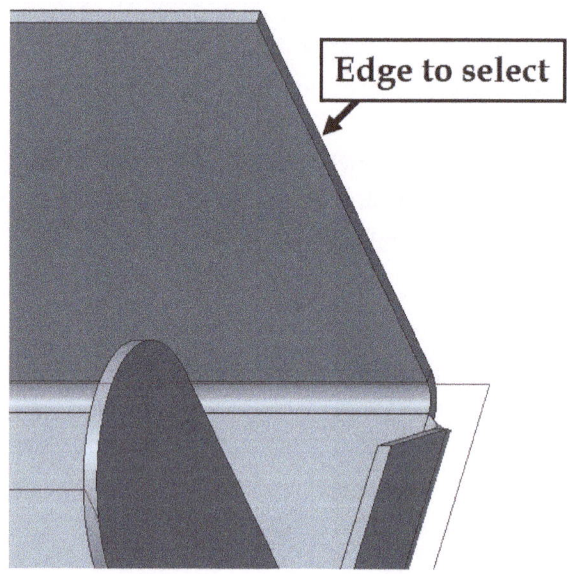

54. On the **Flat** dashboard, select **Trapezoid** from the **Shape** drop-down located at the left side.

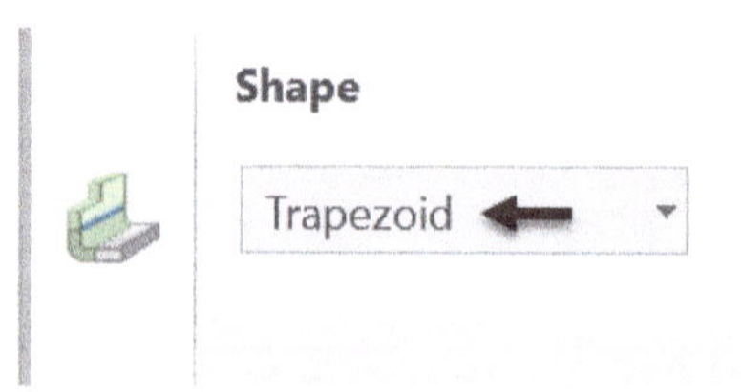

55. On the **Flat** dashboard, click the **Shape** tab, and expand the **Sketch Preview** section.

56. Change the angles and length of the trapezoid, as shown.

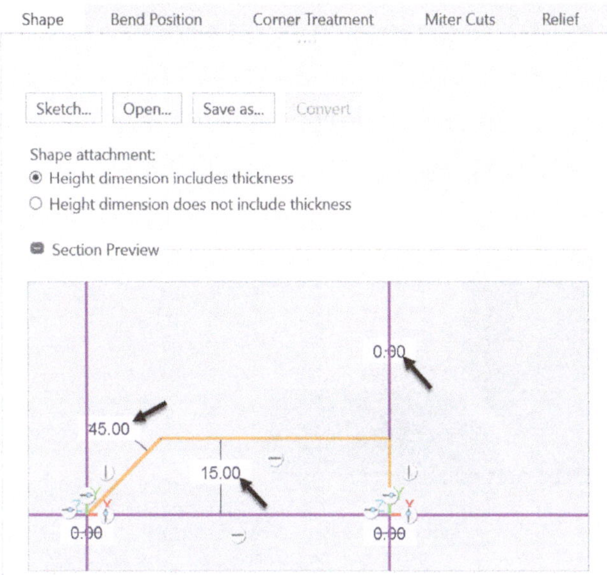

57. Click the **Bend Position** tab.
58. On the **Bend Position** tab, click the **Offset from Bend Start** icon.
59. Type 1.6 in the **Value** box.

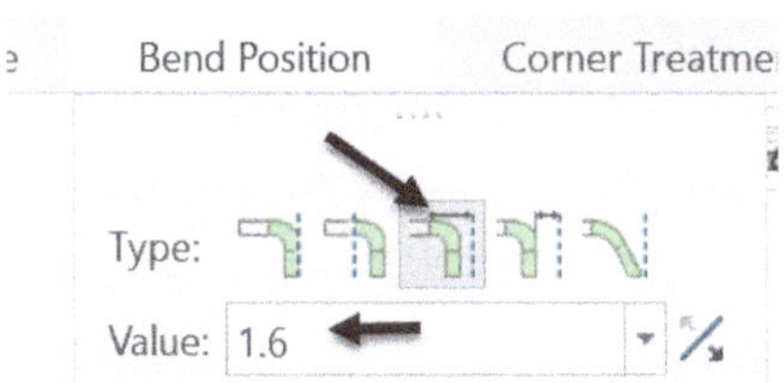

60. Click the green check on the dashboard to create the flat wall.

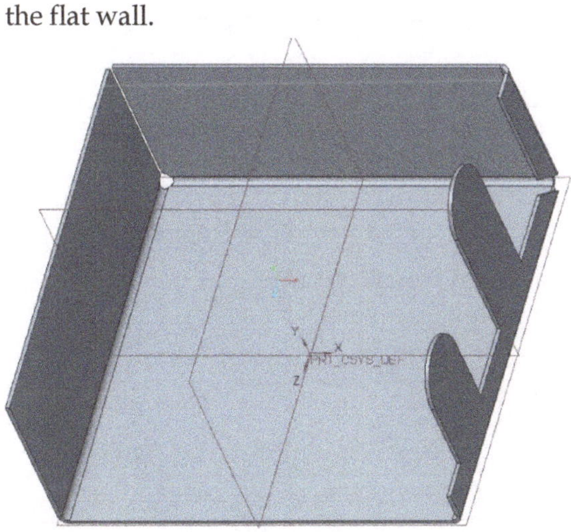

61. Create a sketched line on the outer face of the flat wall, as shown. Next, click **OK** on the **Sketch** tab of the ribbon.

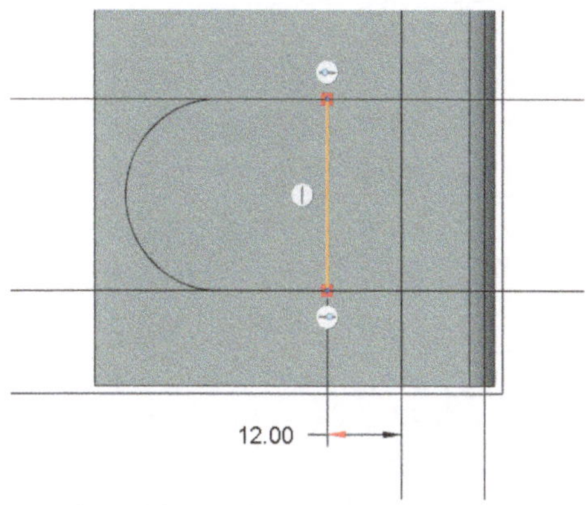

62. On the ribbon, click **Sheetmetal** tab > **Bends** panel > **Bend** drop-down > **Bend**.
63. On the Dashboard, click the **Fixed Side** icon.
64. Click the **Starts at Bend Line** icon under the **Bend Area Position** section.

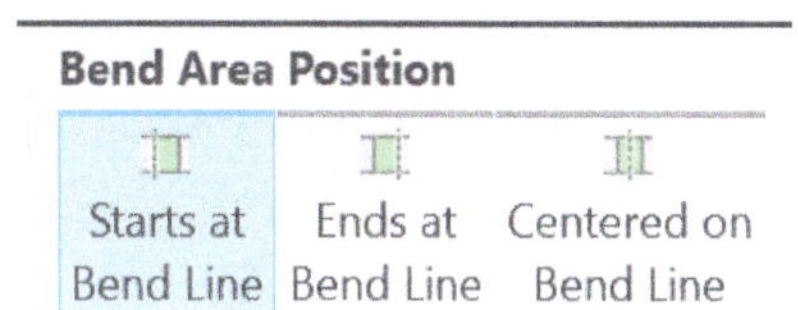

65. Type-in **45** in the **Angle** box.
66. Click the **Change bending direction** icon next to the **Angle** box.
67. Select **External Dimension** from the **Bend angle type** drop-down.
68. Click the green check to complete the feature.

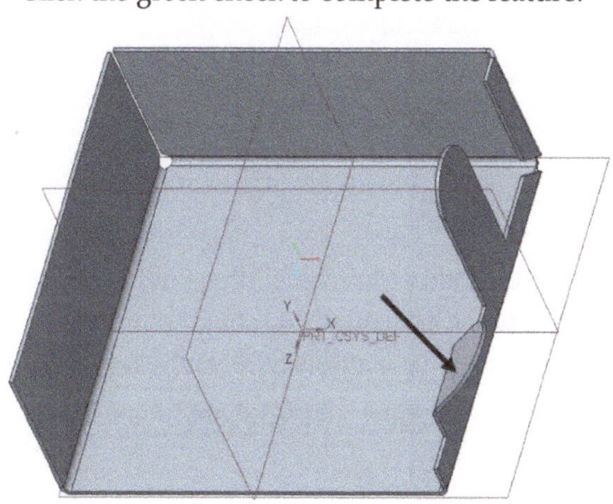

69. Sketch a horizontal line on the vertical wall exit the sketch.

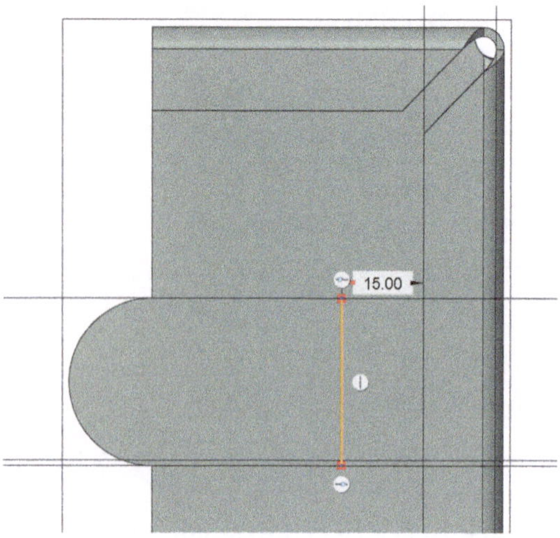

70. Activate the **Bend** command and bend the wall using the sketched line. The bend angle is 45 degrees. Use the **Change bending direction** and **Fixed Side** icons, if required.
71. Click **OK**.

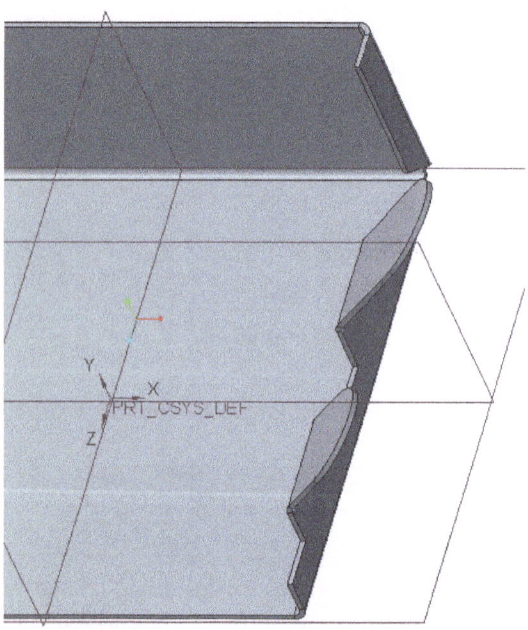

72. Sketch another horizontal line on the inclined face of the wall and bend it in the reverse direction. The bend angle is 45 degrees. Use the **Change location of fixed side** icon, if required.

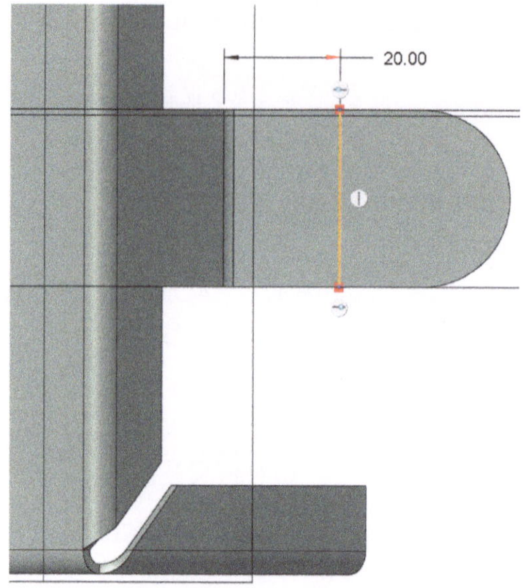

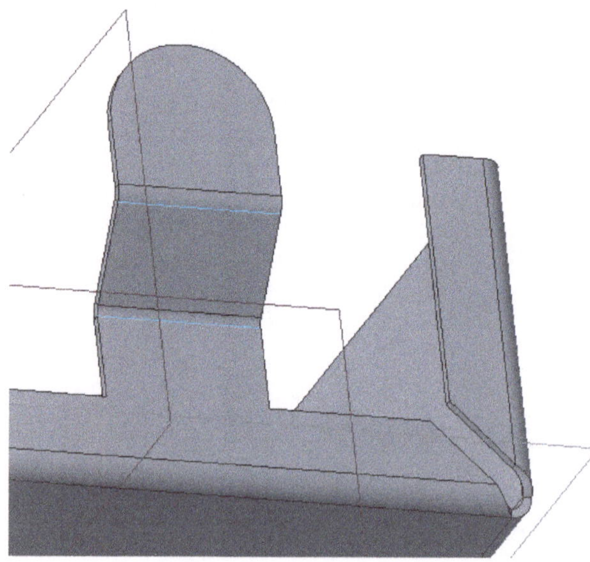

73. On the ribbon, click **Sheetmetal** tab > **Bends** panel > **Unbend** .

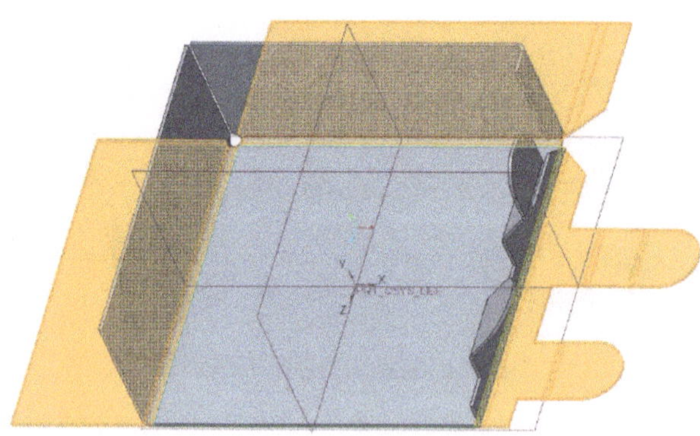

74. Click the green check to unbend the sheet metal part.
75. Sketch the sheet metal part, as shown below.

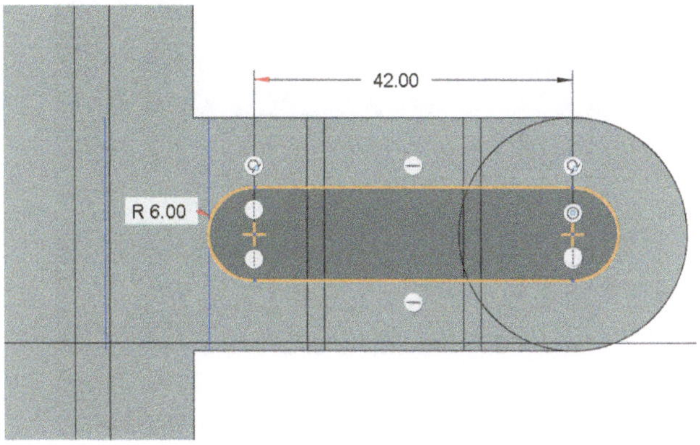

76. Exit the sketch and activate the **Extrude** command (on the ribbon, click **Sheetmetal** tab > **Engineering > Extruded Cut**).
77. Select the sketch, if not already selected.
78. Click **OK**.

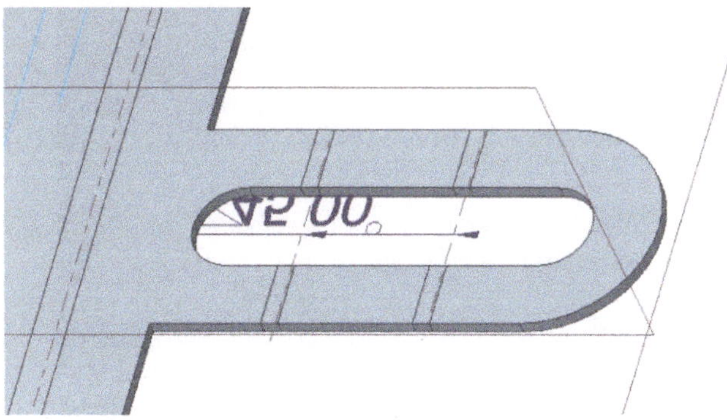

79. On the ribbon, click **Sheetmetal** tab **> Bends** panel **> Bend Back** .
80. Click the green check to unbend the sheet metal part.

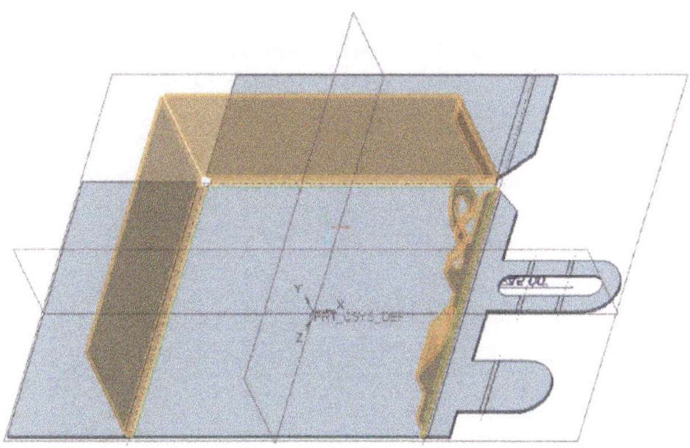

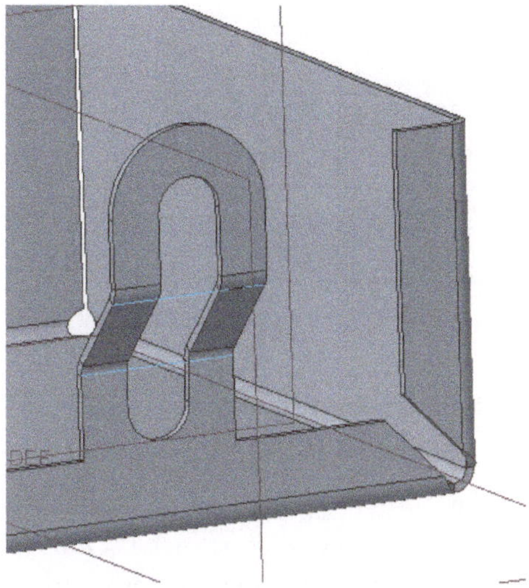

81. On the ribbon, click **Sheetmetal** tab > **Shapes** panel > **Flange** .
82. On the Dashboard, select the **C** option from the **Shape** drop-down located at the left side.
83. Click on the inner edge of the left-side wall.

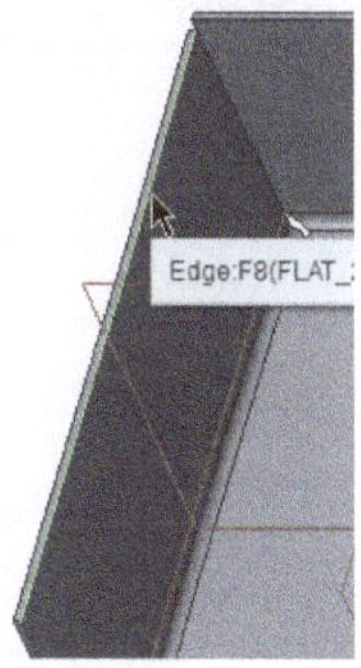

84. Double-click on the length dimension of the flange and enter 8.

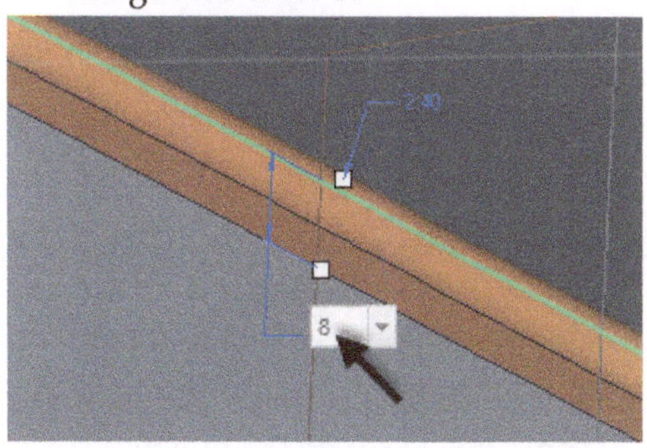

85. Click the green check to create the C-flange.
86. Likewise, create C-flanges on other vertical walls.

87. On the ribbon, click **Sheetmetal** tab > **Engineering** panel > **Form** drop-down > **Punch Form** icon.
88. On the Dashboard, select CLOSE_FLAT_LOUVER_FORM_MM from the **Source Model** drop-down located at the left side.
89. Click on the top face of the horizontal planar wall.
90. Drag and align the placement handles to the left-side wall and front plane.
91. Click the **Placement** tab and specify the settings, as shown.

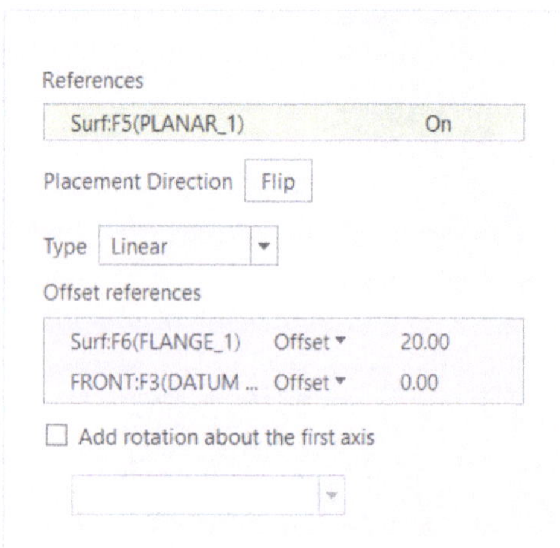

92. Ensure the punch tool is aligned parallel to the left side wall as shown in the diagram. If the punch form is not parallel, check the "**Add rotation about the first axis**" option. Then, input "**90**" in the **Angle** box to rotate the punch form, making it parallel to the left side wall.

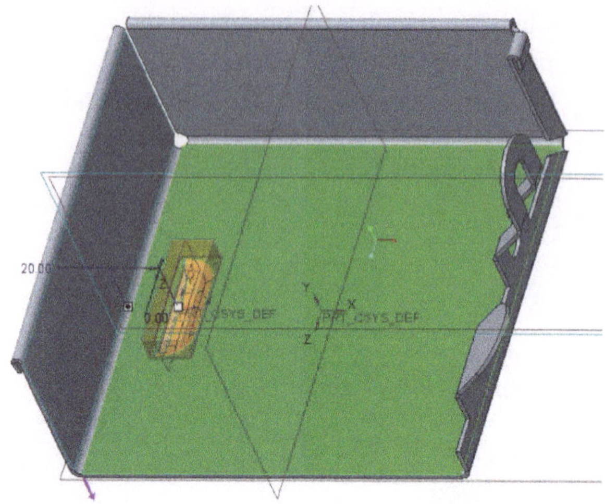

93. On the dashboard, click the **Use Inheritance** option.
94. Click the **Shape** tab, and then click the **Vary Punch Model** button.
95. On the **Varied Items** dialog, click the **Dimensions** tab.
96. In the preview window, click on the features, as shown.

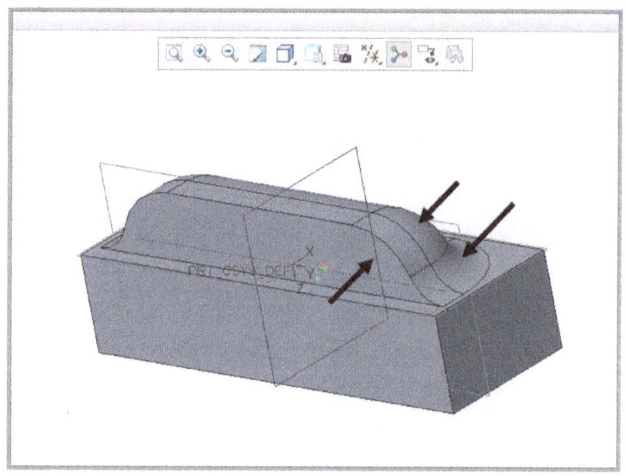

97. Double-click on the dimensions, as shown.

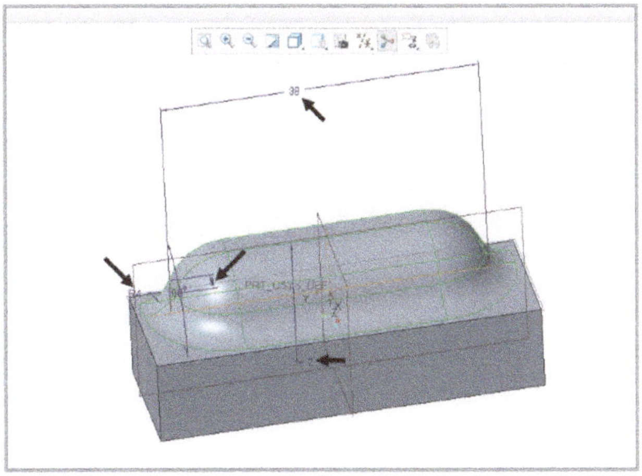

98. Click in the **New Value** box of the first d1 dimension.
99. Type 50 and press Enter.
100. Likewise, change the other values, as shown.

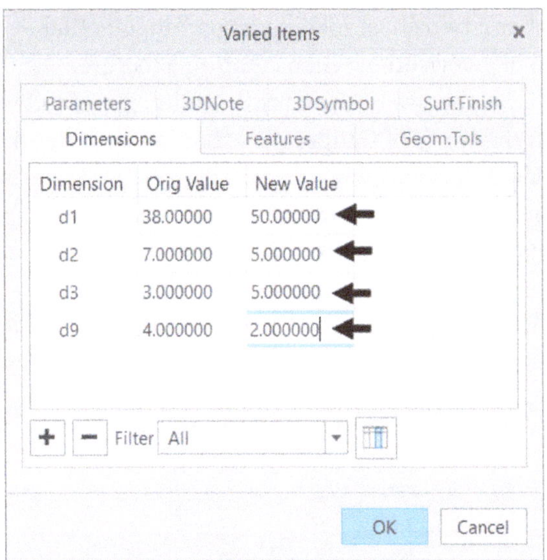

101. Click **OK** on the **Varied Items** dialog.
102. Click the green check to create the louver punch.

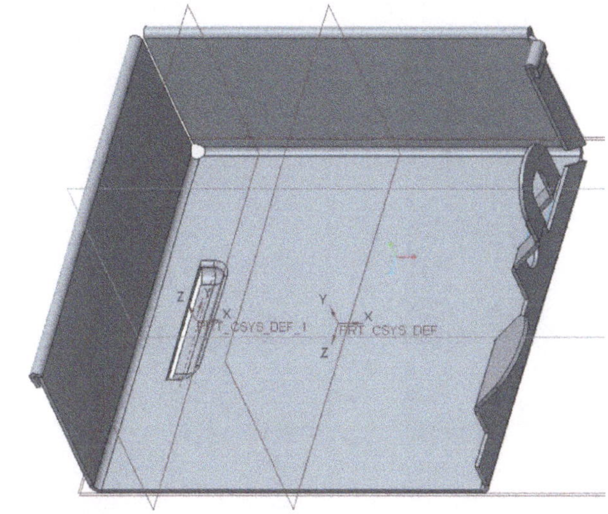

103. Select the louver punch.
104. On the ribbon, click **Model** tab > **Editing** panel > **Pattern** drop-down > **Pattern**.
105. On the Dashboard, select the **Dimension** option from the **Type** drop-down located at the left side.
106. Select the dimension displayed along the x-axis.

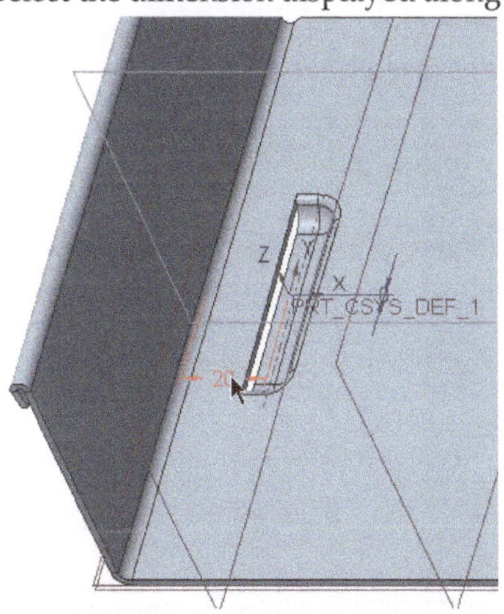

107. Type-in 20 in the value box and press Enter.
108. Type-in 6 as the **Members** box located next to the 1st **direction** selection box.

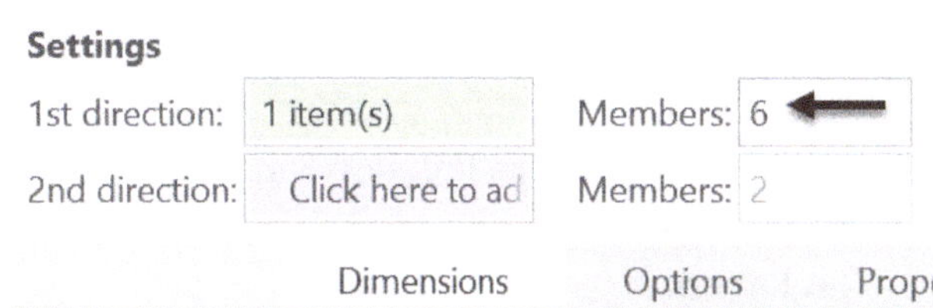

109. Click the green check to create the pattern.

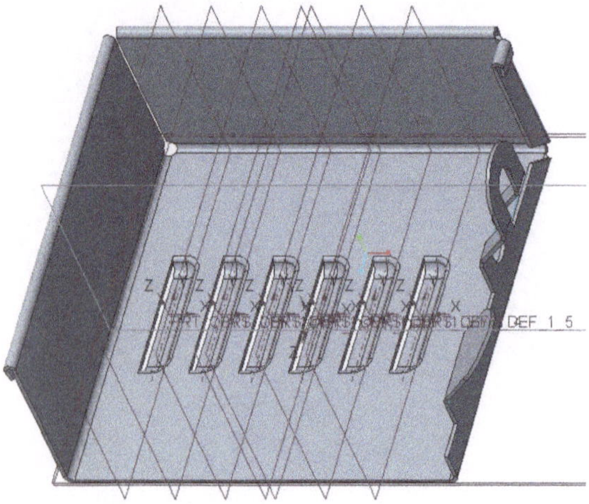

110.On the **Graphics** toolbar, click **Flat Pattern Preview**. It displays the flat pattern preview of the sheet metal part.

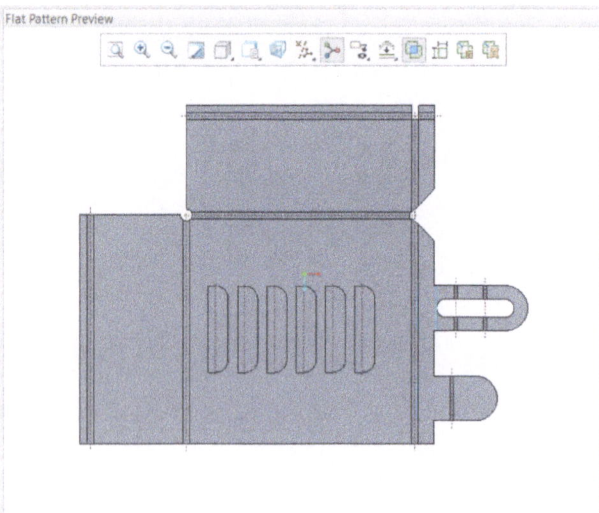

111.In the **Flat Pattern Preview** window, click the **Bounding box** icon to display the bounding box's dimensions.

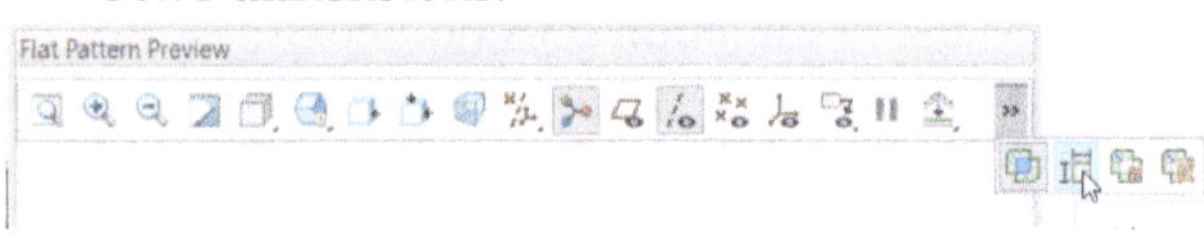

112.Close the **Flat Pattern Preview** window.

113.On the ribbon, click **Sheetmetal > Bends** panel > **Flat Pattern**.

114.Click the green check on the dashboard to create a flat pattern.

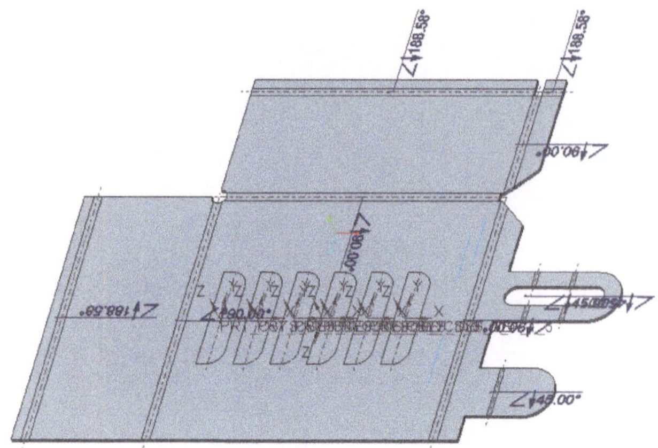

115.Save and close the sheet metal part.

Questions

1. Describe parameters that can be specified on the **Model Properties** dialog.
2. Define the term 'K Factor.'
3. List any two sheet metal part parameters that can be overridden when creating a feature.
4. What is the use of the **Corner Relief** command?
5. List the types of flange walls that can be created in Creo Parametric?
6. How is the **Conversion** command useful?
7. What are the corner relief types available?
8. What is the difference between a punch and die form?

Exercises

Exercise 1

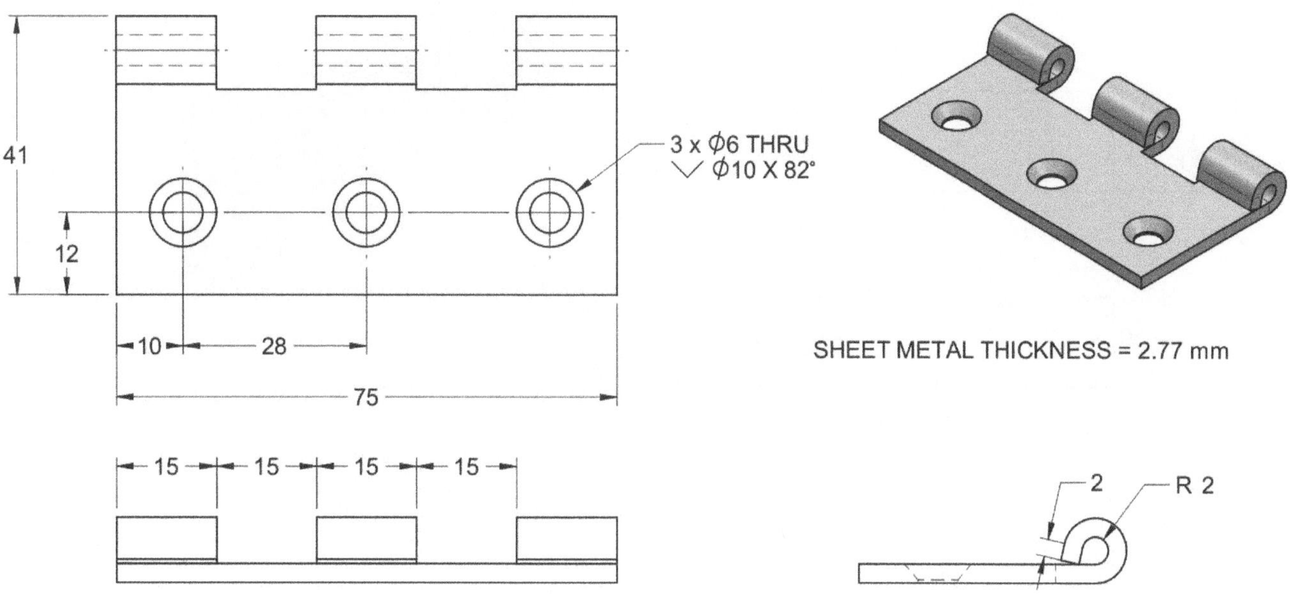

Exercise 2

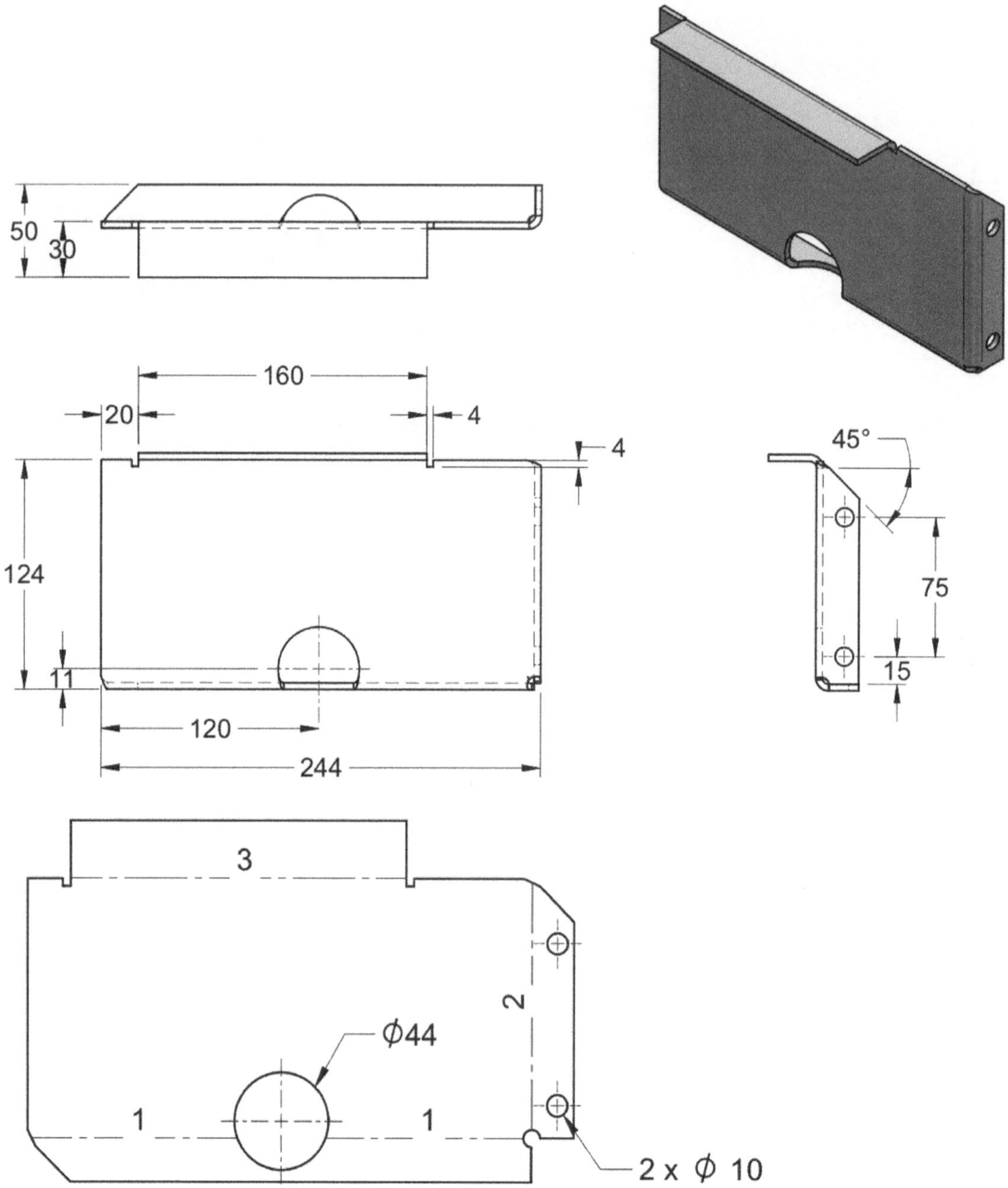

Sequence	Feature	Radius	Angle	Direction	Included Angle
1	Bend 1	3.58 mm	90.00 deg	Down	90.00 deg
2	Bend 2	3.58 mm	90.00 deg	Down	90.00 deg
3	Bend 3	3.58 mm	90.00 deg	Up	90.00 deg

Chapter 12: Surface Design

The topics covered in this chapter are:

- *Basic surfaces*
- *Datum Geometry*
- *Curves*
- *Splines*
- *Boundary Blend*
- *Fill surfaces*
- *Offset Surfaces*
- *Trim*
- *Merge*
- *Solidify*
- *Extend*
- *Mirror*
- *Copy and Paste Surfaces*
- *Mirror*
- *Thicken Surface*

Creo Parametric Surfacing commands can be used to create complex geometries that are very difficult to create using standard extrudes, revolve features, and so on. Surface modeling can also be used to edit and fix the broken imported parts. In this chapter, you learn the basics of surfacing commands that are mostly used. The surfacing commands are available in the **Part** environment.

Creo Parametric offers a rich set of surface design commands. A surface is an infinitely thin piece of geometry. For example, consider a cube shown in the figure. It has six faces. Each of these faces is a surface, an infinitely thin piece of geometry that acts as a boundary in 3D space. Surfaces can be simple or complex shapes.

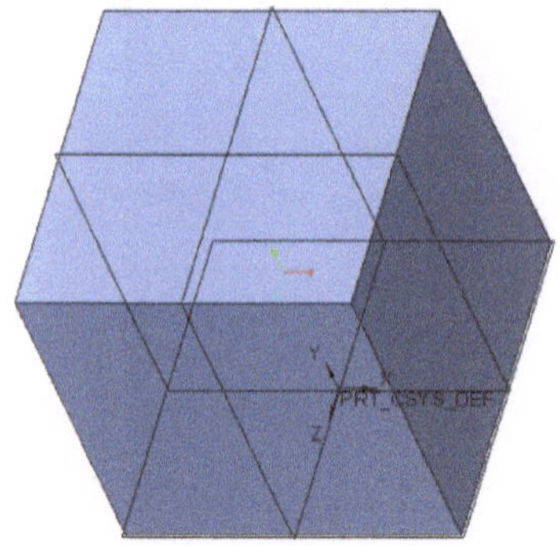

In solid modeling, when you have created solid features such as an extruded feature or a Revolved feature, Creo Parametric creates a set of features (surfaces) that enclose a volume. The airtight enclosure is considered as a solid body. The advantage of using the surfacing commands is that you can design a model with more flexibility.

Extrude

1. To create an extruded surface, first, create an open or closed sketch.

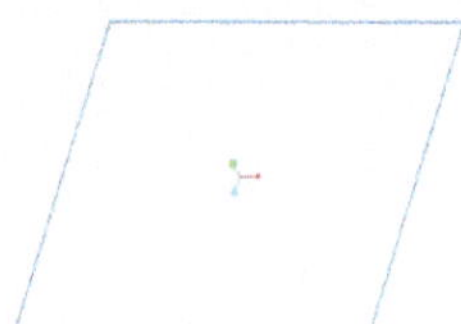

2. On the ribbon, click **Model > Shapes > Extrude**.
3. Select the sketch and click the **Surface** icon on the dashboard.
4. Type-in a value in the **Depth** box available or drag the Depth handle.
5. Click **Preview** to view the extruded surface. You will notice that the extrusion is not capped at the ends.

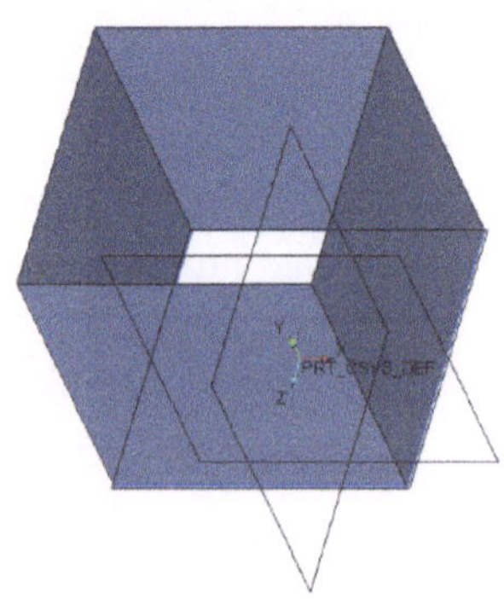

6. Click the **Resume** on the Dashboard.
7. Click the **Capped ends** icon. The ends are capped.
8. Click the green check to complete the feature.

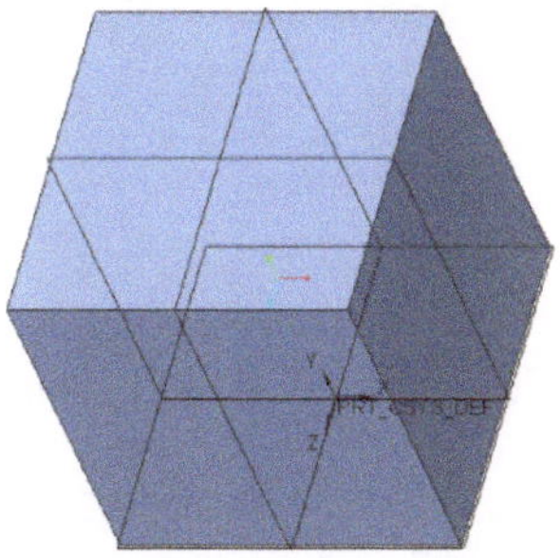

Even if you create an enclosed surface, Creo Parametric will not recognize it as a solid body. You will learn to convert a surface body into a solid later in this chapter.

Revolve

1. To create a revolved surface, first, create an open or closed profile and the axis of revolution.

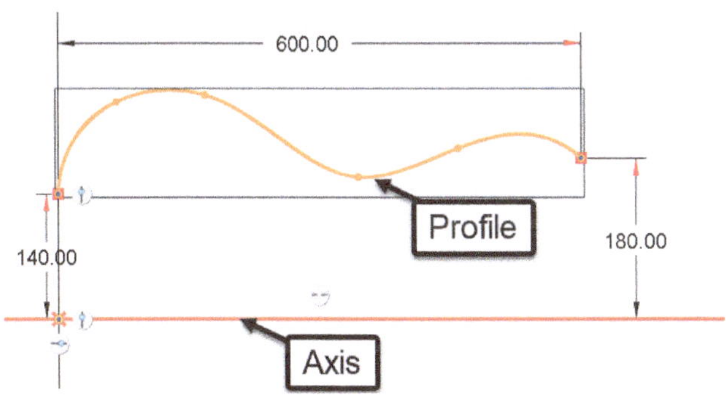

2. On the ribbon, click **Model > Shapes > Revolve**.
3. On the Dashboard, click the **Surface** icon.
4. Select the sketch.
5. Type-in the angle of revolution in the **Angle** box and click the green check.

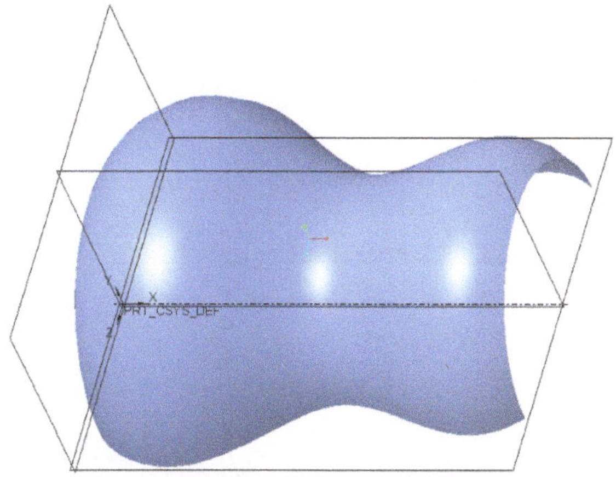

Likewise, you can create a surface using other solid modeling commands such as **Sweep**, **Helical Sweep**, **Swept Blend**, **Blend**, and **Rotational Blend**. These commands are already covered in earlier chapters.

Datum Geometry

Creo Parametric has commands to create three-dimensional curves and datum elements. They help you to create complex surfaces.

Point

This command creates a point in the 3D space.

1. On the ribbon, click **Model > Datum > Point**.
2. Click on a supporting plane or surface.

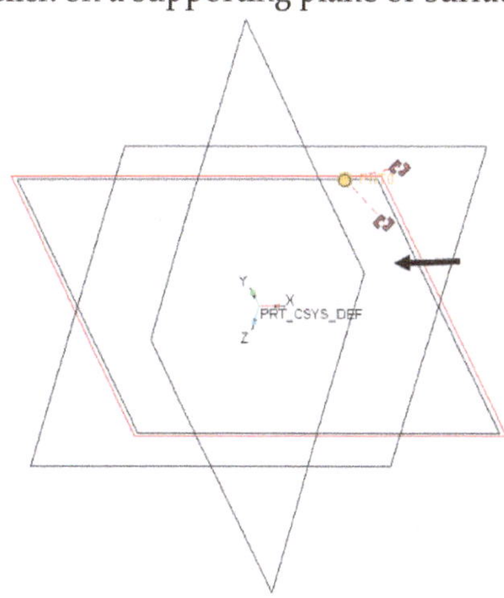

3. Click the right mouse button and select **Offset References**.

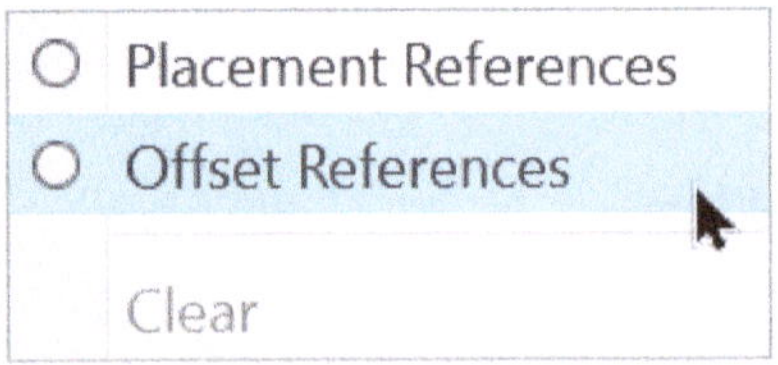

4. Press the Ctrl key and select the offset references.

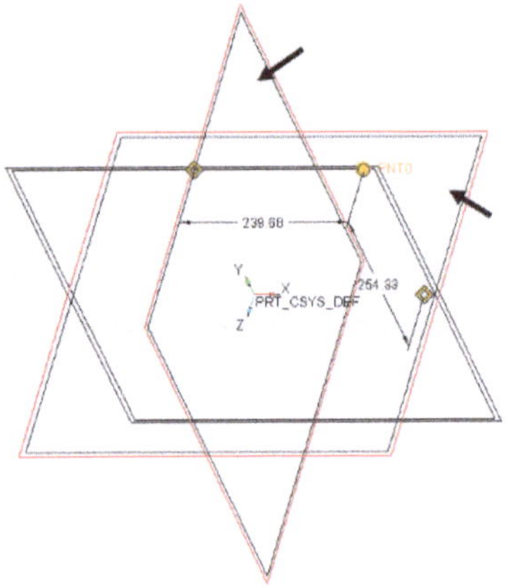

5. Modify the offset reference values on the **Datum Point** dialog and click **OK**.

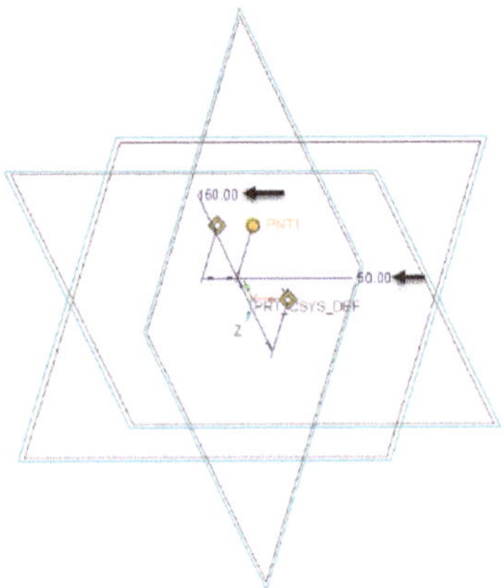

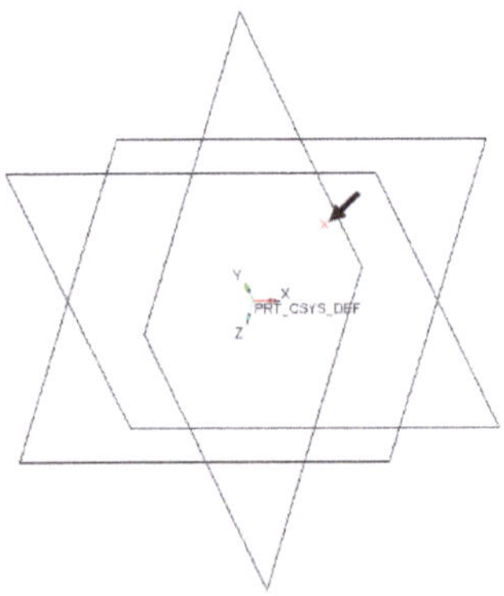

6. Create a new datum plane offset from the Top plane.

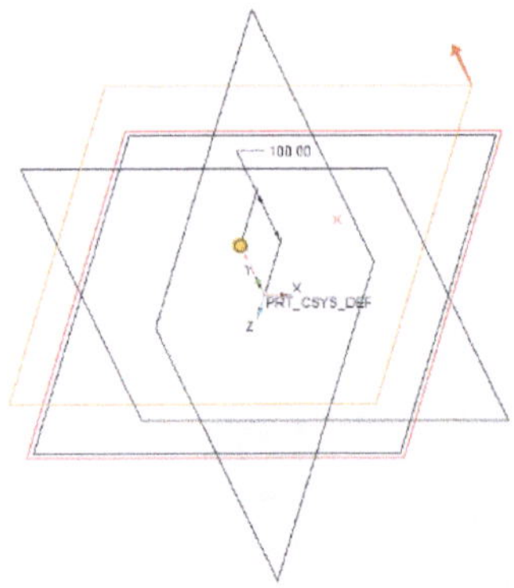

7. Press the Ctrl key and select offset, front and right plane.

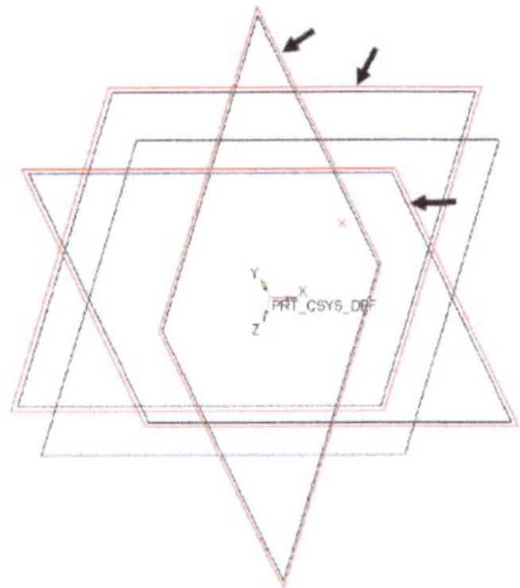

8. Activate the **Point** command (On the ribbon, click **Model > Datum > Point**). A new datum point appears at the intersection of the selected planes.

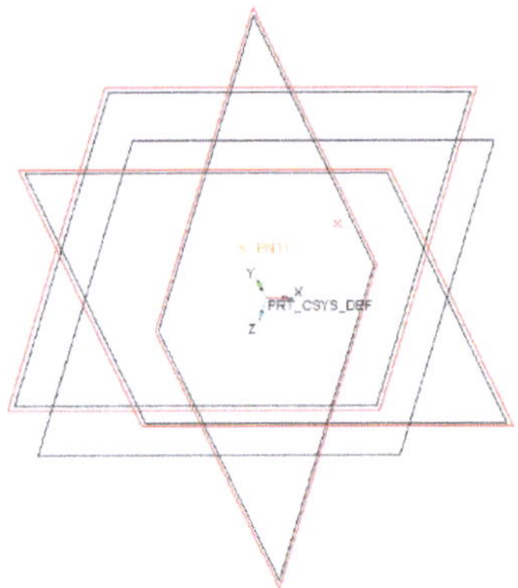

9. Click **OK**.

Offset Coordinate System

This command creates a point by using the offset values from an existing coordinate system. You can specify these values in the Cartesian, Cylindrical, or Spherical coordinate system.

1. On the ribbon, click **Model > Datum > Point >**

Offset Coordinate System.

2. Select an existing coordinate system from the graphics window.

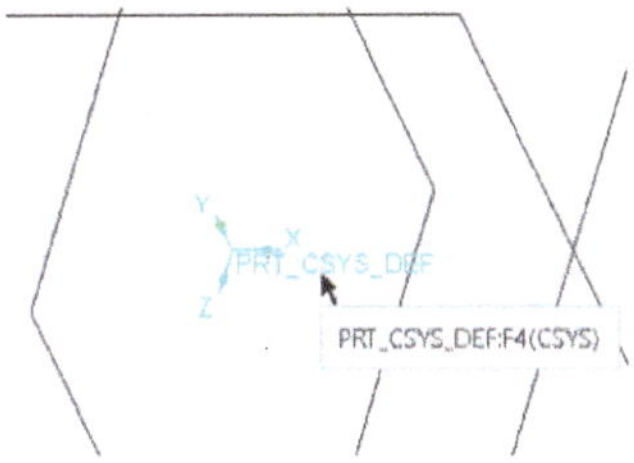

3. On the **Datum Point** dialog, select **Type > Cartesian**.
4. On the **Datum Point** dialog, click in the table and enter the X, Y, and Z values.

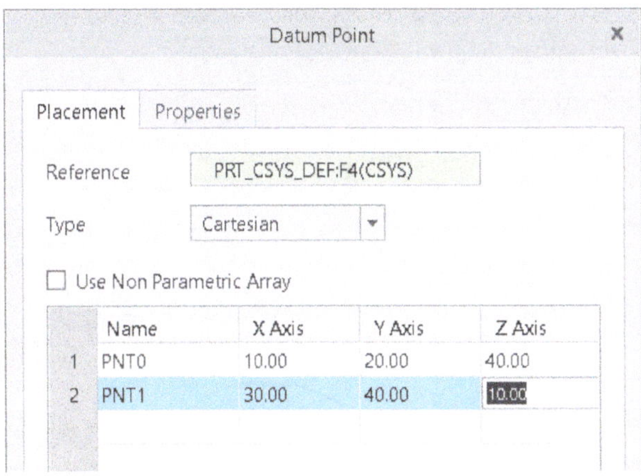

5. Click **OK**.

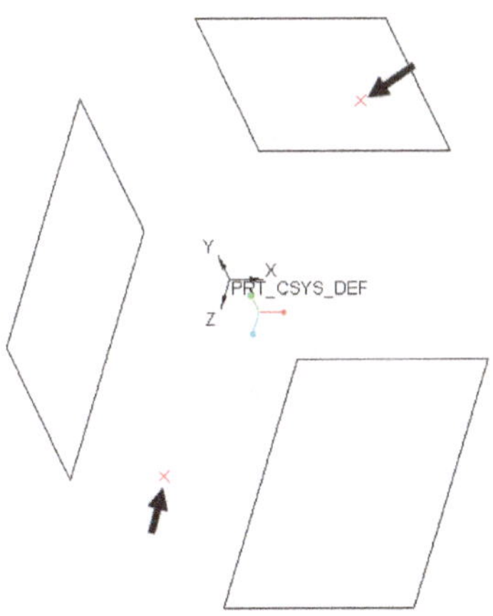

Curve through Points

This command creates a three-dimensional curve through selected points.

1. On the **Model** tab of the ribbon, expand the **Datum** panel and click **Curve > Curve through Points**.

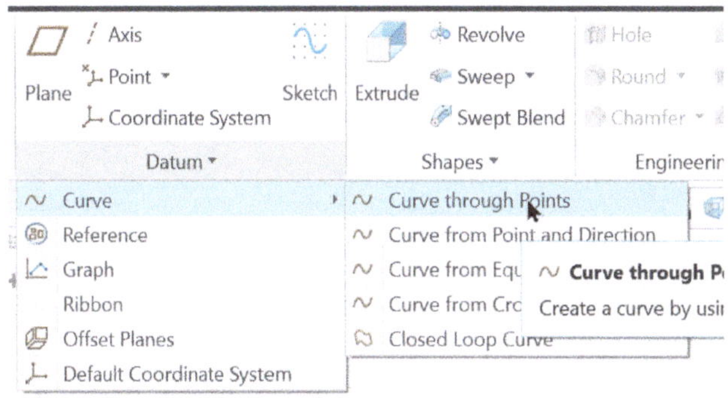

2. Select a point.
3. Likewise, select other points one-by-one.

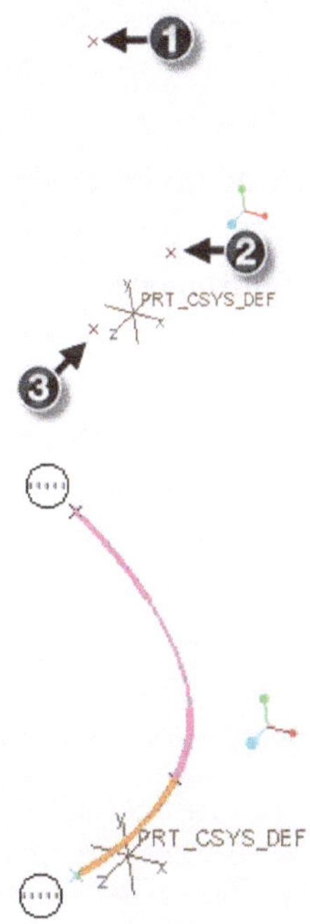

4. On the dashboard, click the **Placement** tab and select **Point 2** from the list.
5. On the **Placement** tab, select the **Straight line** option. A straight line is created between **Point 2** and **Point 1**.

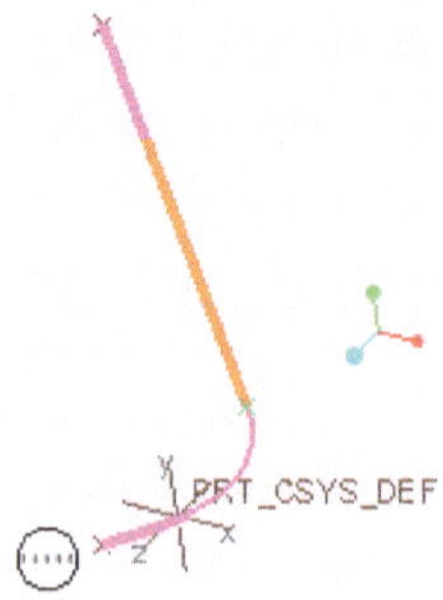

6. Select **Point 3** from the list and select **Straight line**.

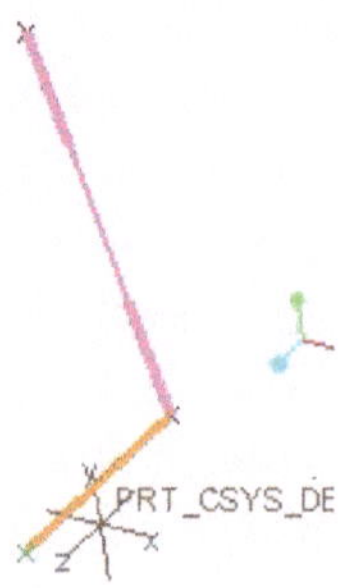

7. Select **Point 2** from the list and check the **Add fillet** option.
8. Type-in a value in the **Radius** box.

9. Click the green check to complete the curve.

Project

This command projects an element onto a supporting surface.

1. On the ribbon, click the **Model > Editing > Project**.
2. Select the element to the project.
3. On the dashboard, click in the **Surfaces** box and select the supporting surface.
4. Select **Project Direction > Normal to surface**. This project the element in the direction normal to the supporting surface. You can select the **Along direction** option to define the direction of projection. You can use a line or plane to define the direction.

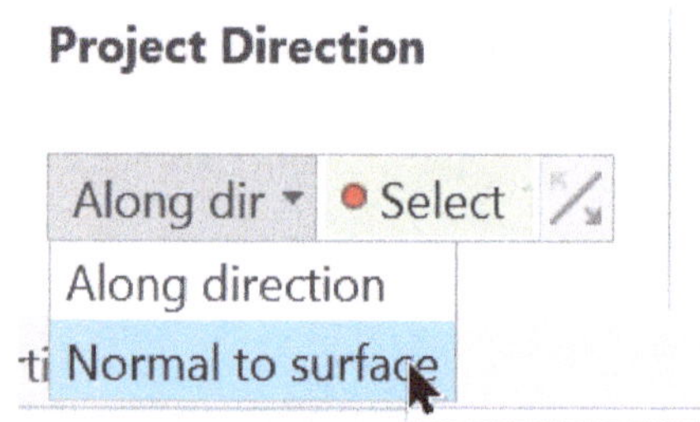

Normal to surface

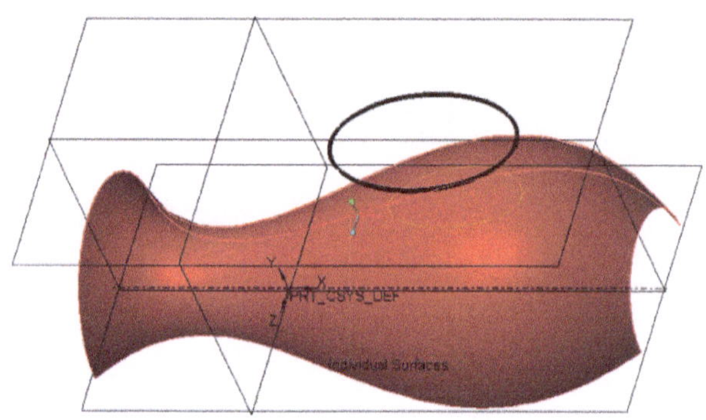

Along direction

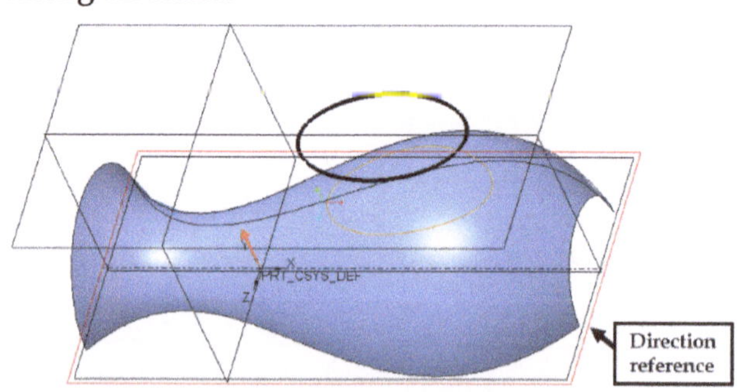

5. Click the green check.

Intersect

This command creates a curve at the intersection of two elements.

1. Press the Ctrl key and select two intersecting elements.

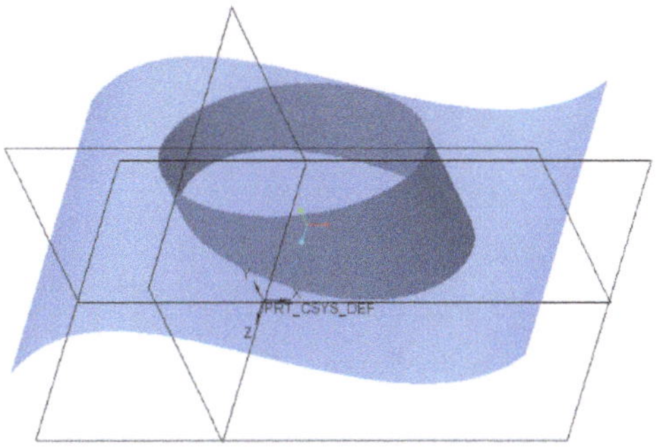

2. On the ribbon, click **Model > Editing > Intersect**. A curve appears at the intersection of the two surfaces.

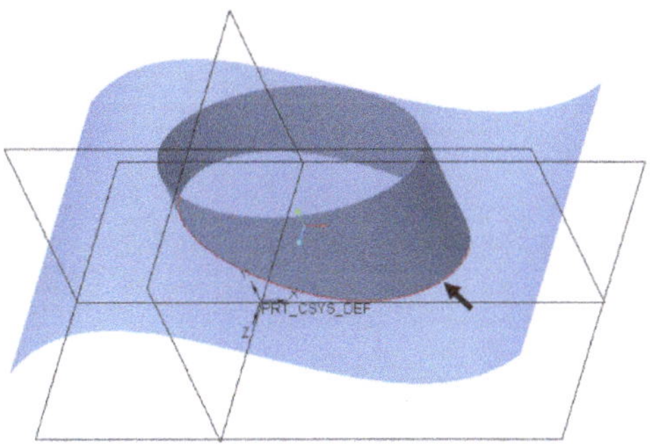

Splines

Splines are non-uniform curves, which are used to create smooth and ergonomic shapes. You have learned to create splines earlier in Chapter 2. Now, you will learn to modify splines.

1. Start a sketch and create a spline as shown.

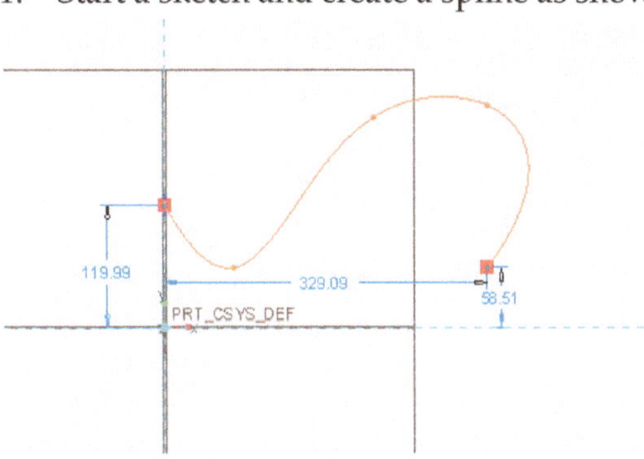

2. On the ribbon, click **Sketch > Operations > Select > One-by-One**.
3. Click on the Interpolation point as shown.

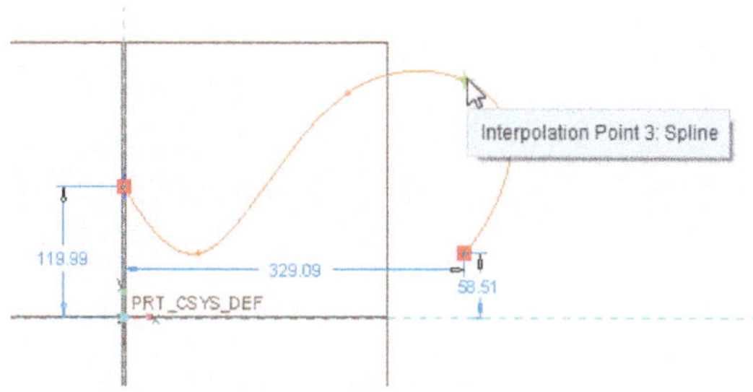

4. Drag the point and notice that the spline is changed.

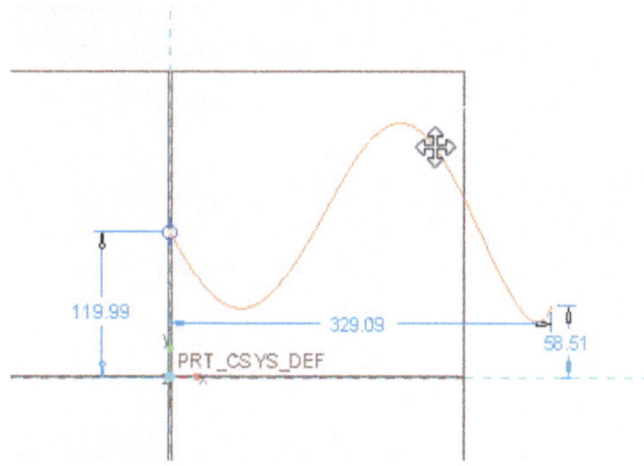

5. Click to release the point.
6. On the ribbon, click **Sketch > Dimension > Dimension** .
7. Click on the Interpolation Point and select the vertical axis of the sketch.

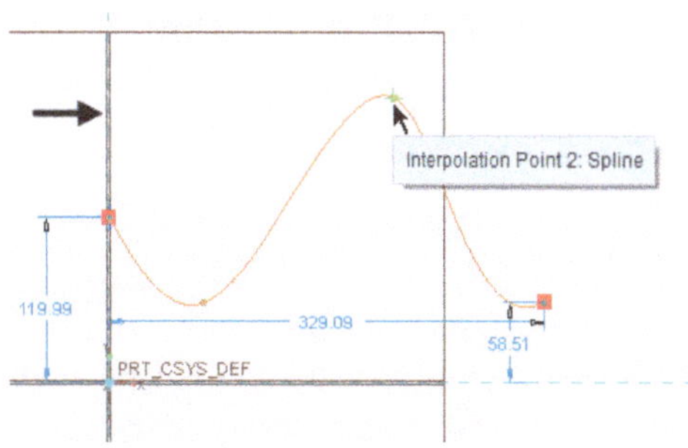

8. Middle-click to place the dimension.
9. On the ribbon, click **Sketch > Operations > Select > One-by-One**, and modify the dimensions.

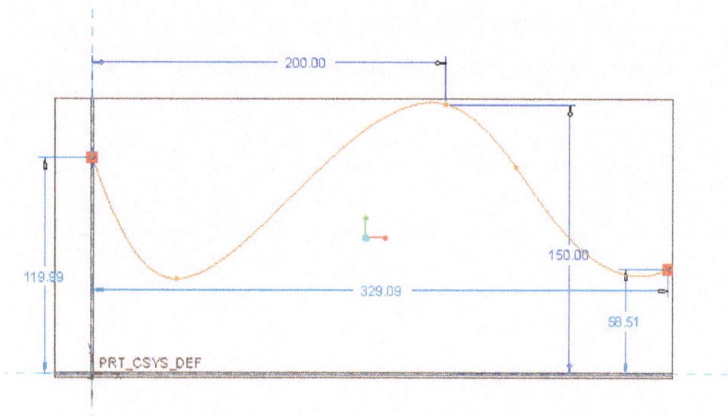

10. Double-click on the spline to activate the edit mode.
11. Click the right mouse button on the spline and select **Add Point**. A new point is added to the spline as shown. You can drag the point or add dimensions to position it.

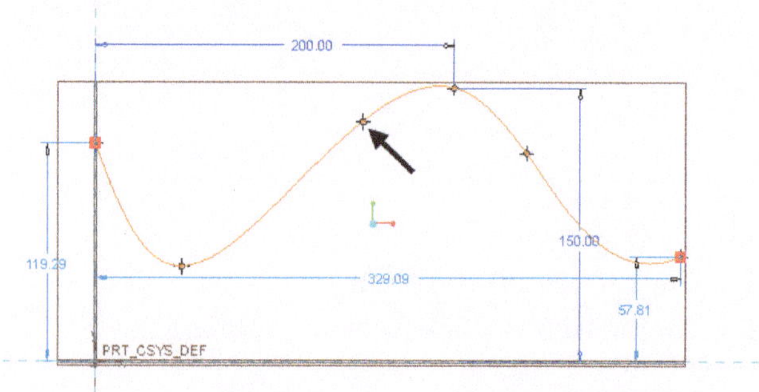

12. On the **Spline** dashboard, click the **Control Points** icon. The **Modify Spline** message appears.

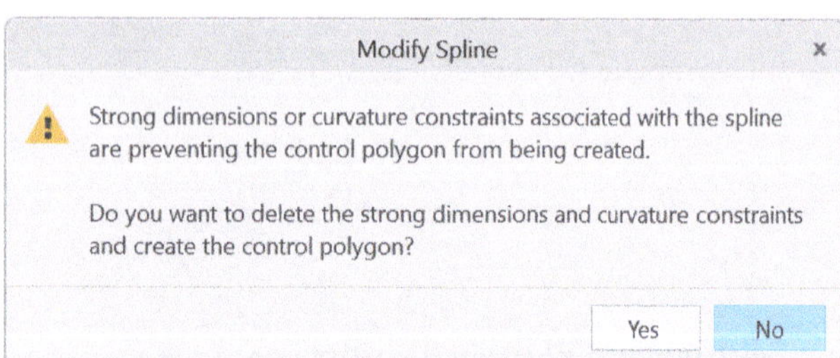

13. Click **Yes** to display control points.
14. Drag the control points of the spline to modify it.

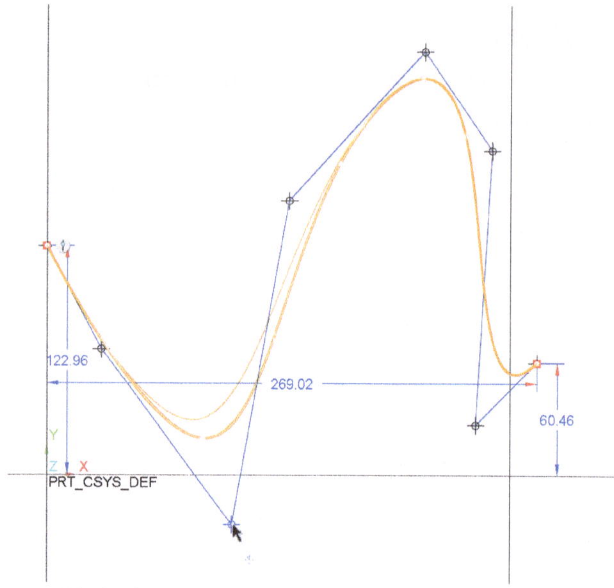

15. Click the right mouse button on a control point and select **Delete Point**. The control point is removed.

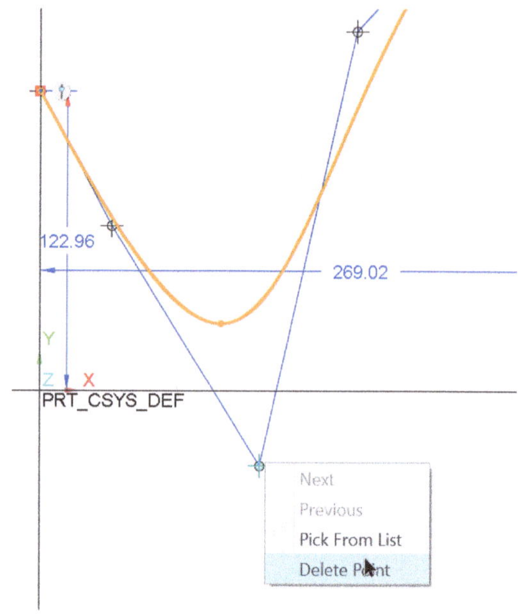

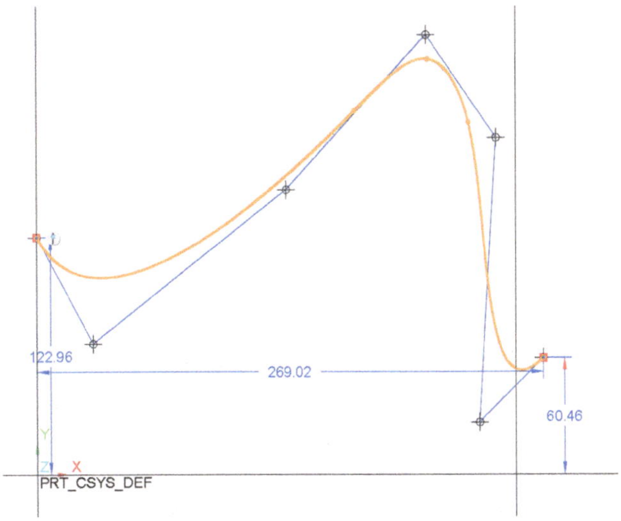

16. On the Dashboard, click **Curvature analysis > Display tools** .
17. On the Dashboard, type 15 in the **Scale** box and press Enter (or) drag the spinner to change the curvature line length.
18. On the Dashboard, type 2 in the **Density** box and press Enter (or) drag the spinner to change the number of curvature lines.

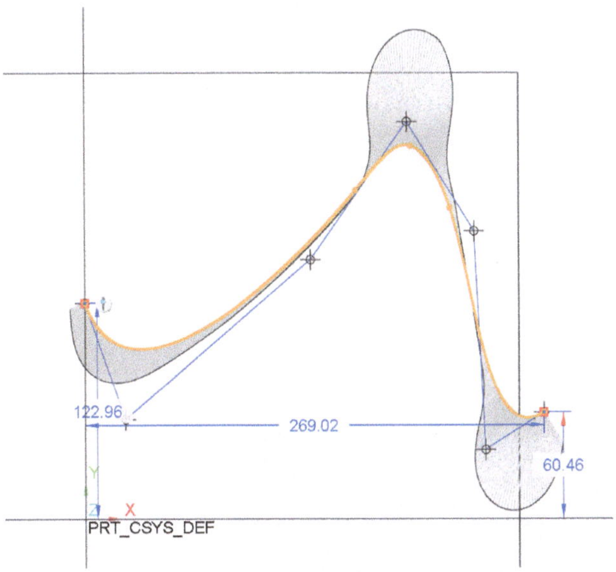

19. Drag the control point and notice the change in curvature length.

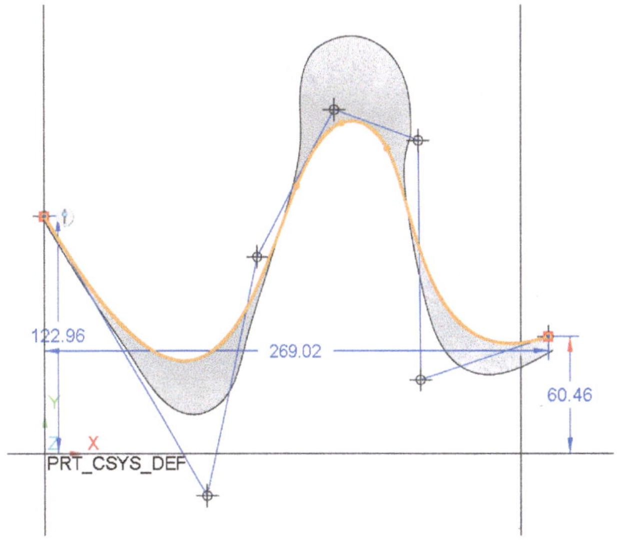

20. On the Dashboard, click the Fit tab and click the **Control Points** icon. Now, you can edit the spline by modifying the dimensions of the control polygon.
21. On the ribbon, click **Sketch > Dimension > Dimension**. The dimensions of the control polygon appear.
22. Change a dimension of the control polygon and notice the change.

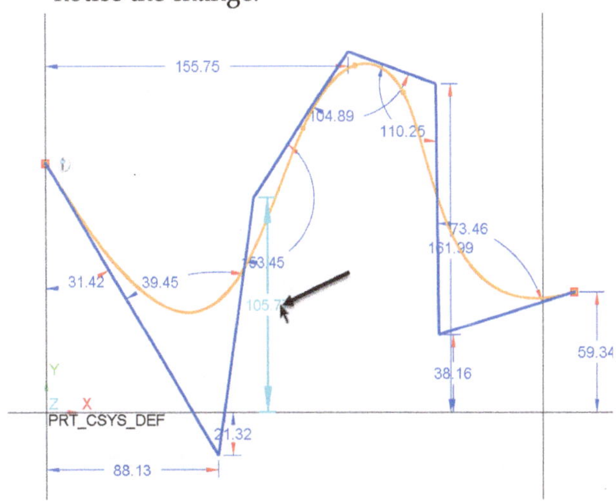

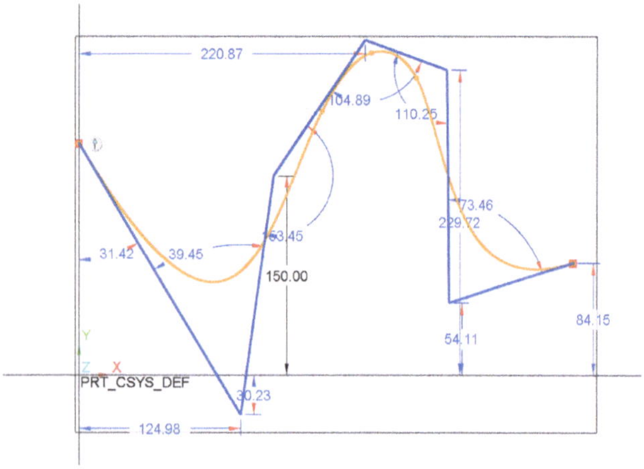

23. Click **OK** on the ribbon.

Boundary Blend

The **Boundary Blend** command creates a surface by using boundary curves in one or two directions. It is a multi-purpose tool, which can be used to achieve a variety of results.

1. Create three boundary curves on different planes, as shown.

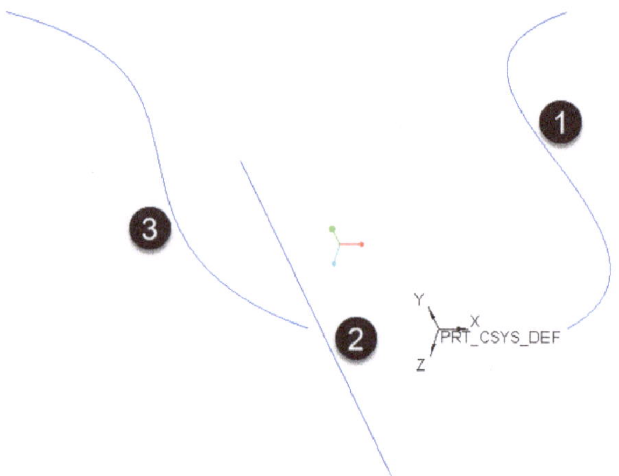

2. On the ribbon, click **Model > Surfaces > Boundary Blend.**
3. Press the Ctrl key and select the first, second, and third boundary curves.

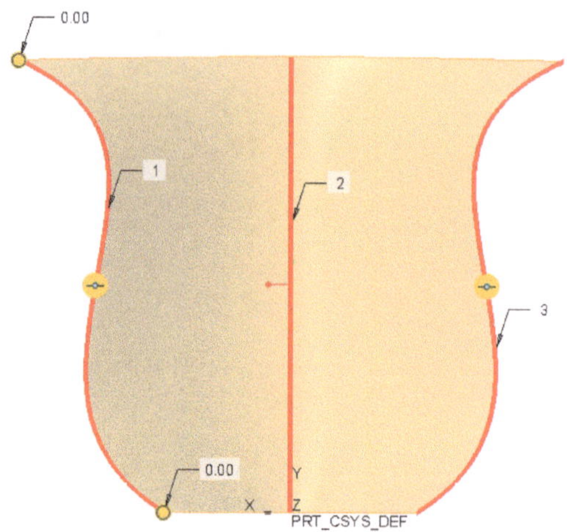

4. On the Dashboard, click the **Constraints** tab. Notice that there are different boundary conditions.

Tangent

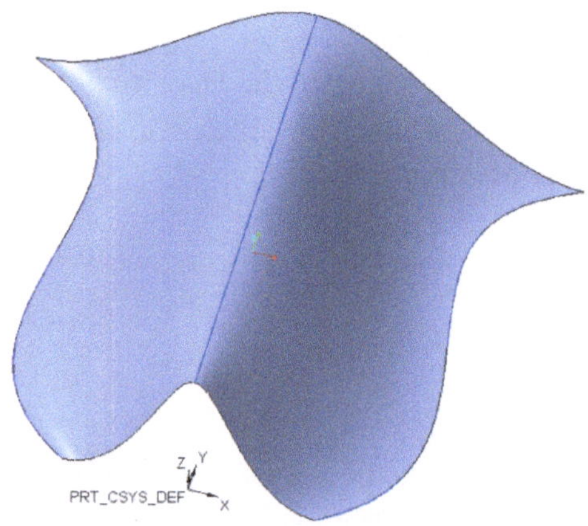

Curvature

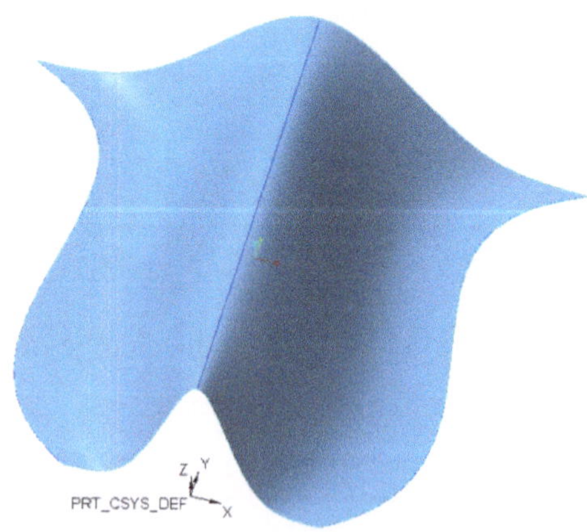

Normal

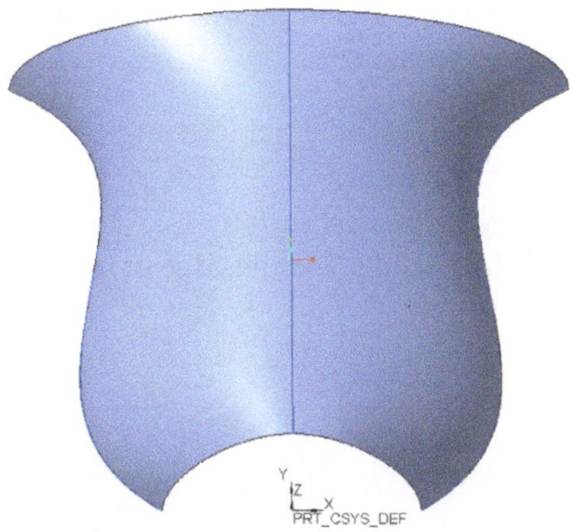

You can adjust the continuity by changing the **Stretch value** on the **Constraints** tab (or) check the **Display drag handles** option and adjust the stretch value.

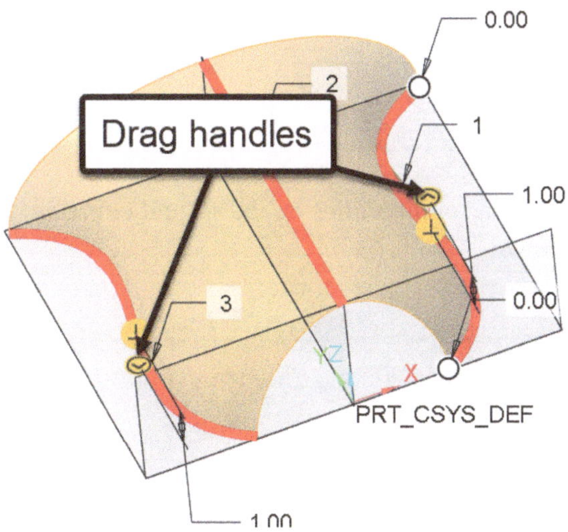

5. Click **Cancel** on the Dashboard.
6. Create three curves, as shown.

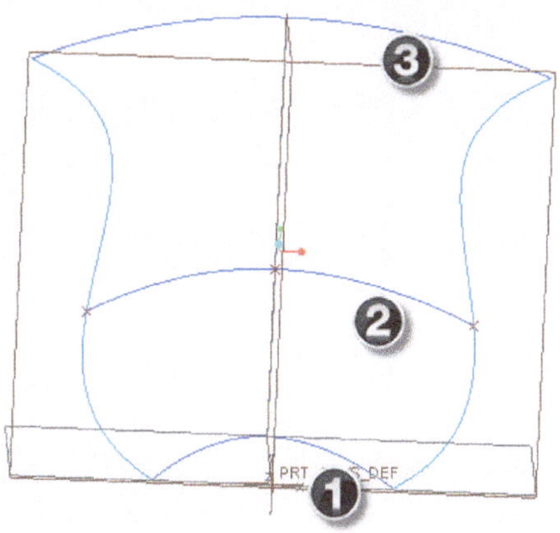

7. Activate the **Boundary Blend** command.
8. Press the Ctrl key and select the three curves as shown.

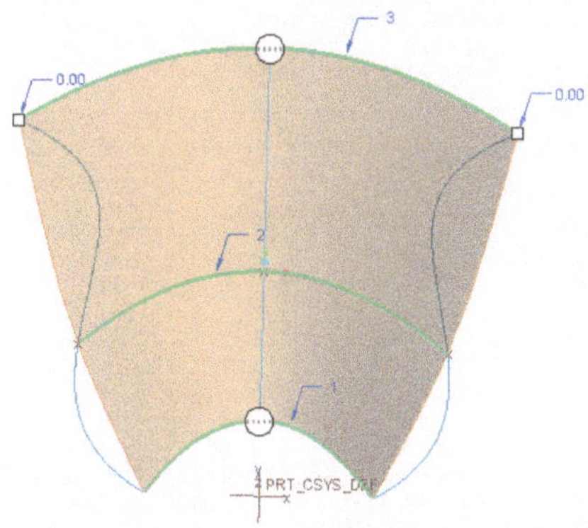

9. On the Dashboard, click in the **2nd direction** box.
10. Press and hold the CTRL key and select the curves as shown.

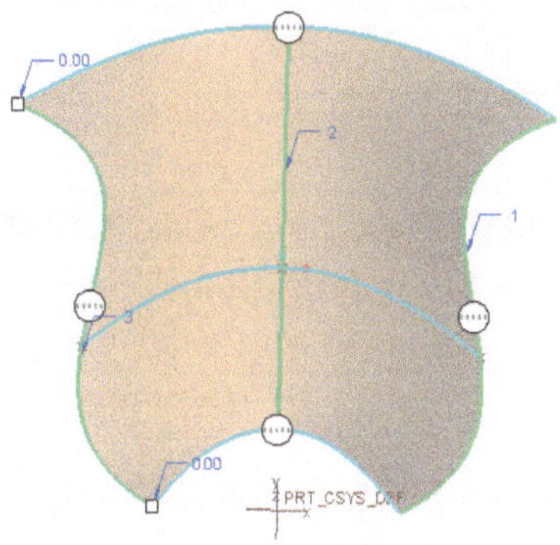

11. Click the green check.

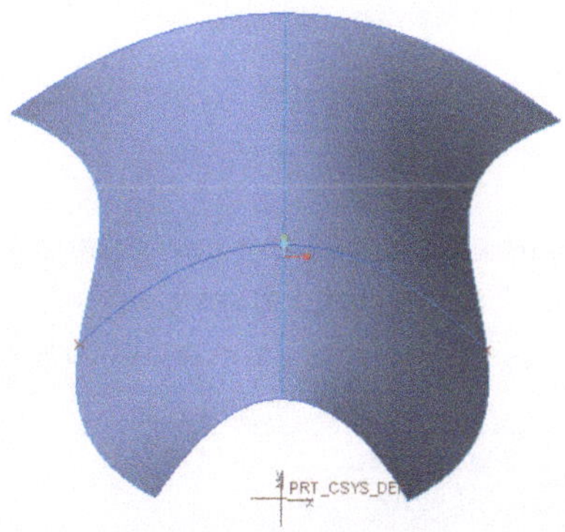

12. Create a sketch as shown.

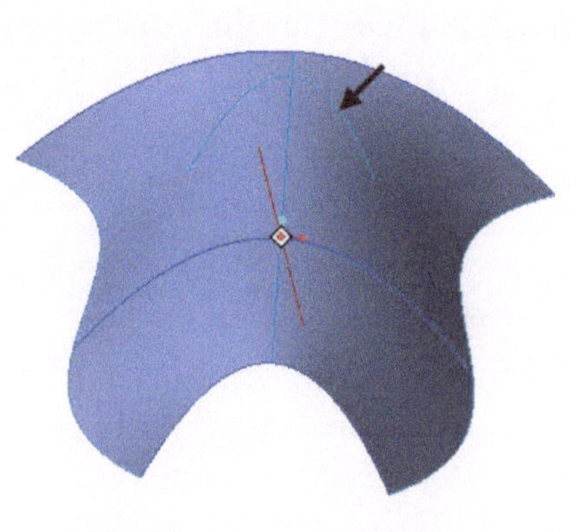

13. In the **Model Tree**, click and drag the sketch above the boundary blend.

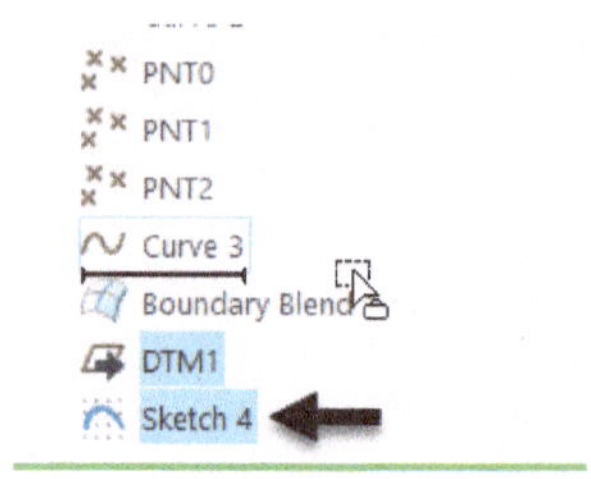

14. Click the right mouse button on the Boundary Blend and select **Edit definition**.

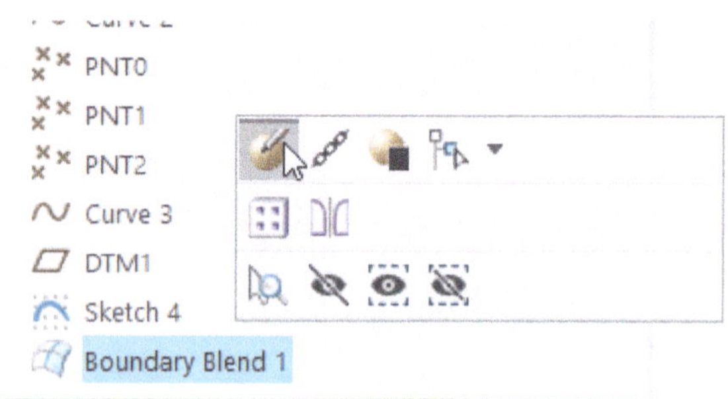

15. On the Dashboard, click the **Options** tab, and then click in the **Influencing curves** box.
16. Select the new sketch and click the green check.

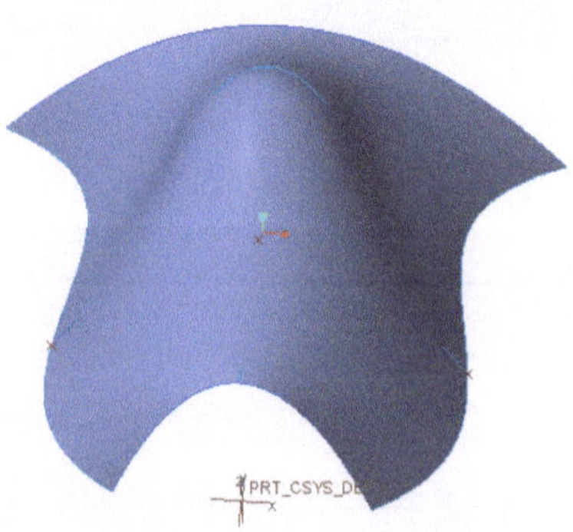

The **Boundary Blend** command creates a surface blending two surfaces. It can be tangent or curvature continuous in both directions.

1. On the ribbon, click **Model > Surfaces > Boundary Blend**.
2. Select the edge of the first surface.
3. Press the Ctrl key and select the edge of the second surface.

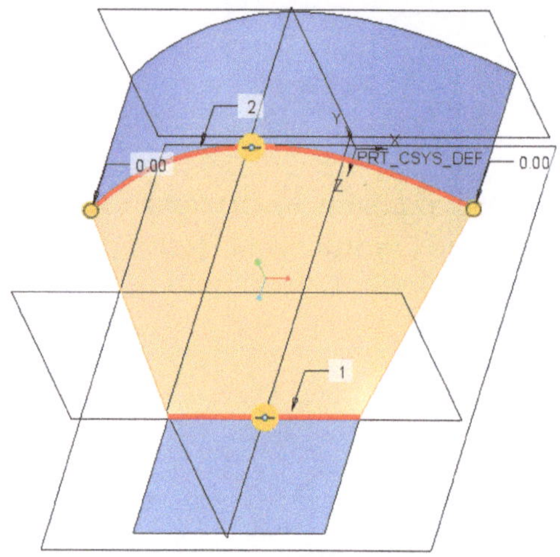

4. Drag the end handles on the second curve as shown.

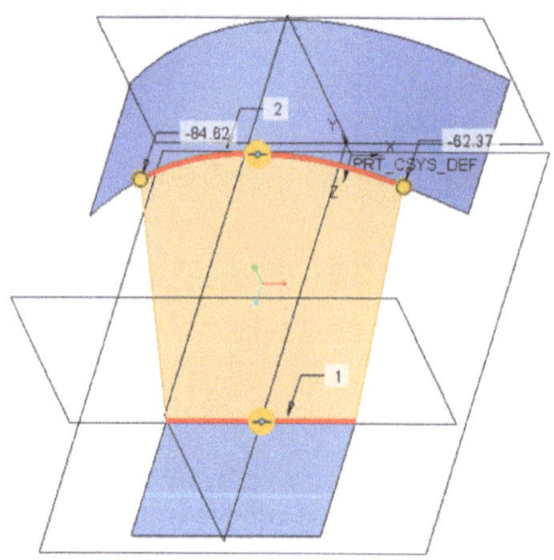

5. Click the right mouse button on the left handle and select **Extend To**.
6. Select the left edge of the surface.

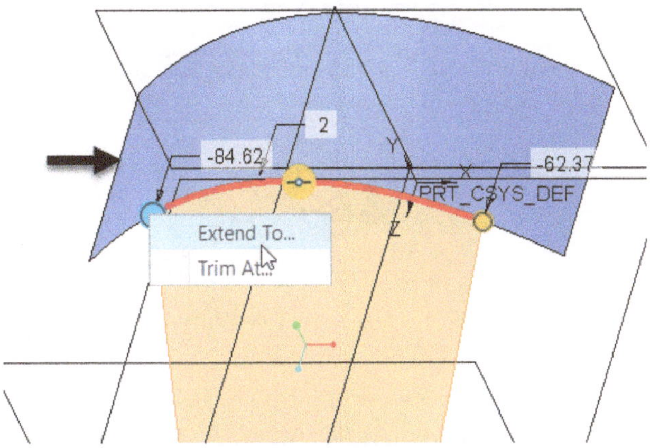

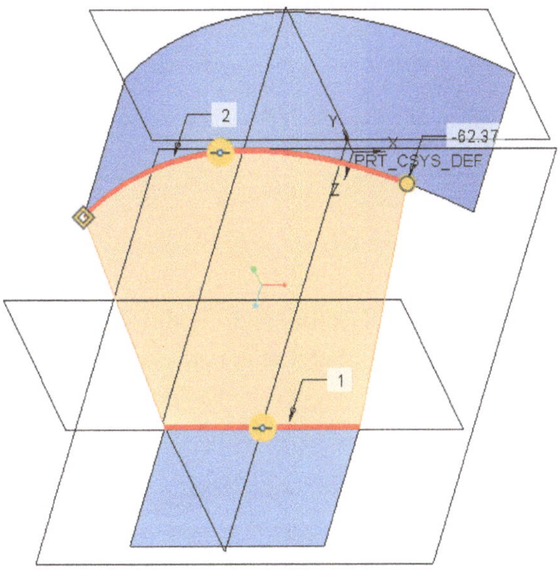

7. Likewise, extend the right edge of the blend surface up to the right edge of the supporting surface.
8. On the Dashboard, click the **Constraints** tab and set the boundary conditions to **Tangent**.

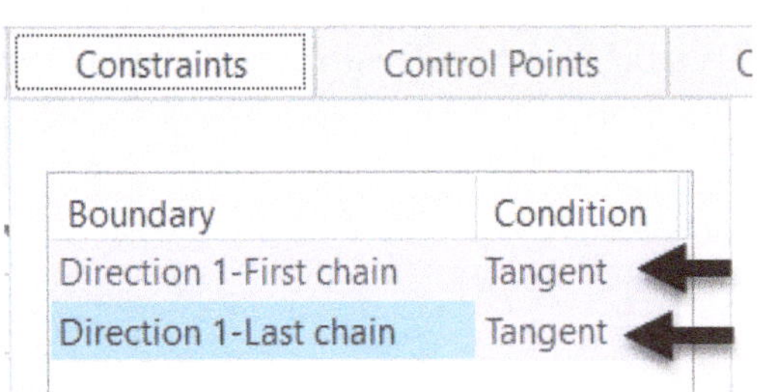

9. Check the **Display drag handles** option.
10. Drag the handles to stretch the surface as shown.

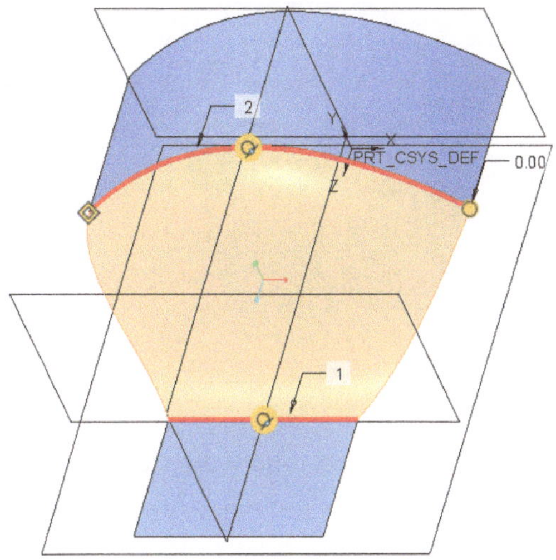

11. Click the green check.

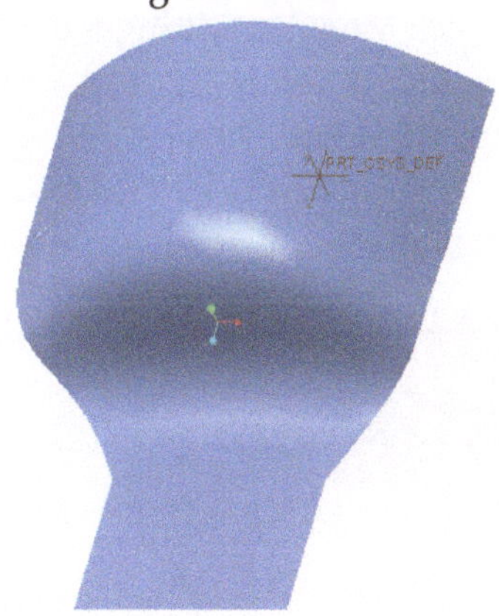

Fill

The **Fill** command can be used to fill the region enclosed by a sketch.

1. On the ribbon, click **Model > Surfaces > Fill**.
2. Click on the closed sketch.

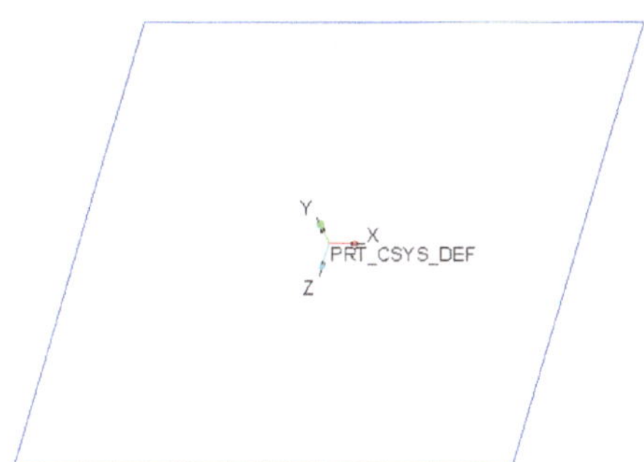

3. Click the green check to fill in the sketch.

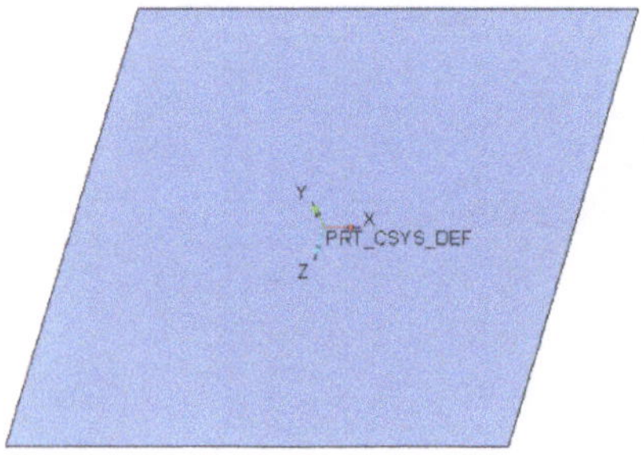

Offset

To create an offset surface, follow the steps given next.

1. Select the surface to offset from the Model Tree.
2. On the ribbon, click **Model > Editing > Offset**.
3. Type-in a value in the **Offset** box (or) drag the handle to change the offset distance.
4. Click the arrow attached to the surface to reverse the offset direction.

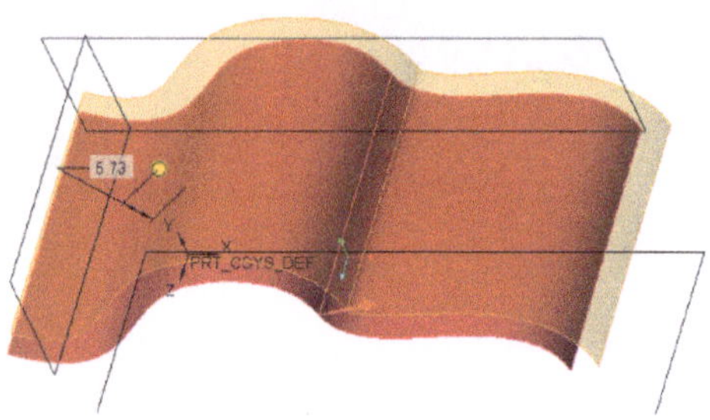

5. Click the **Options** tab on the Dashboard and click in the **Special Handling** box.
6. Select the portion of the surface as shown.

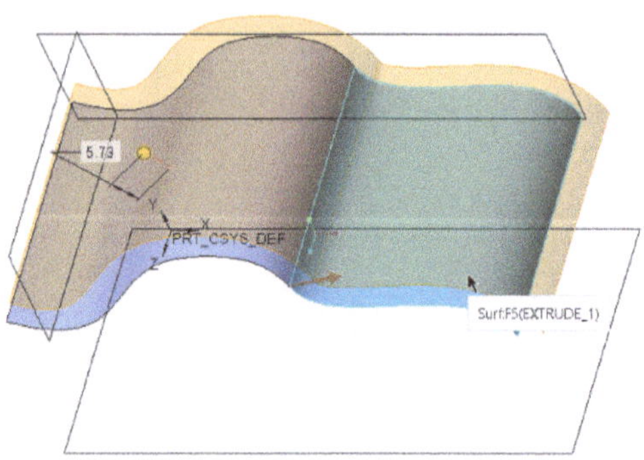

The surface is excluded from the selection.

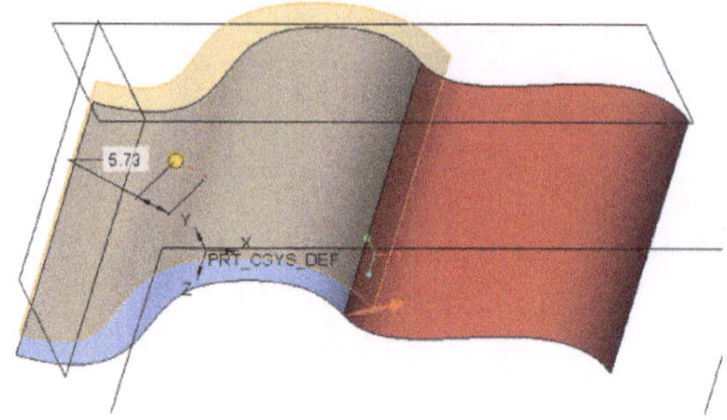

7. On the **Options** tab, select **Automatic Fit** from the drop-down.
8. Change the view orientation to Front.
9. Drag the offset handle and notice the change.

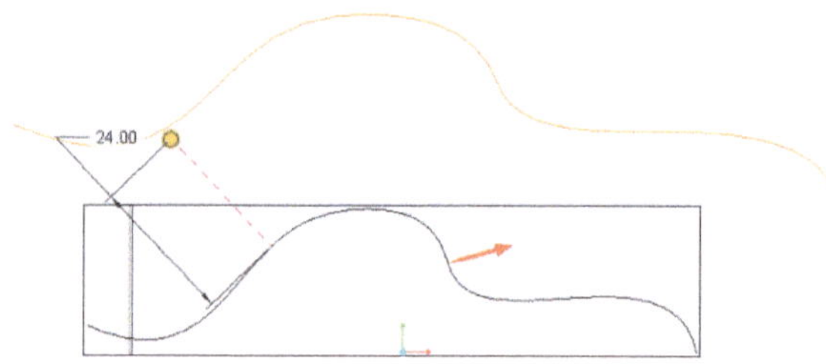

10. Select **Controlled Fit** from the drop-down.
11. Uncheck the **X** option and drag the offset handle. Notice that there is no transition in the X-direction.

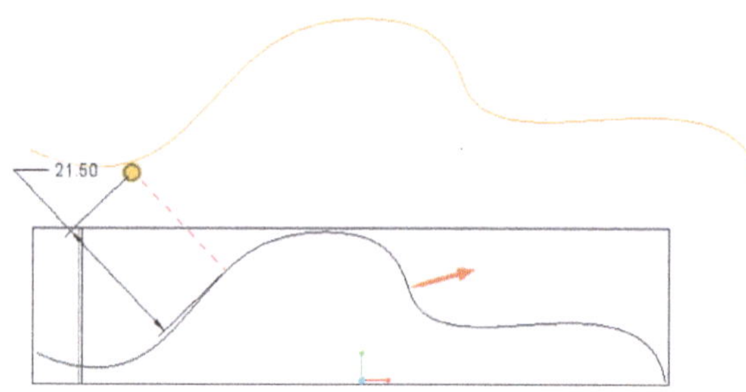

12. Change the view orientation to Default.
13. Check the **Create side surface** option to create side surfaces.

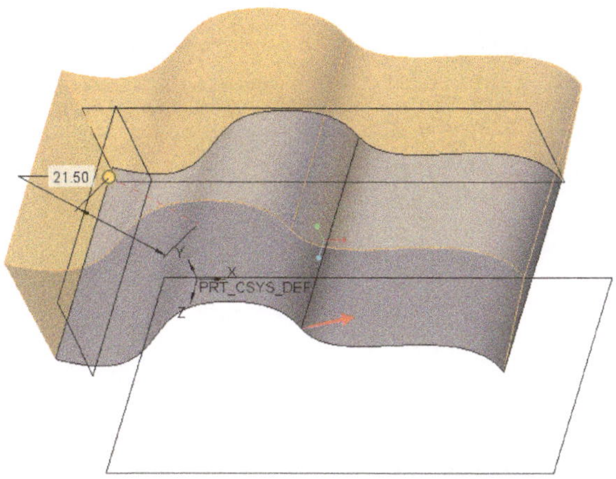

14. Click the green check to complete the feature.

Likewise, you can offset a curve or boundary edges of a surface. To offset a curve, select a curve and click the **Offset** icon on the **Editing** panel. Select a plane/surface to define the offset direction.

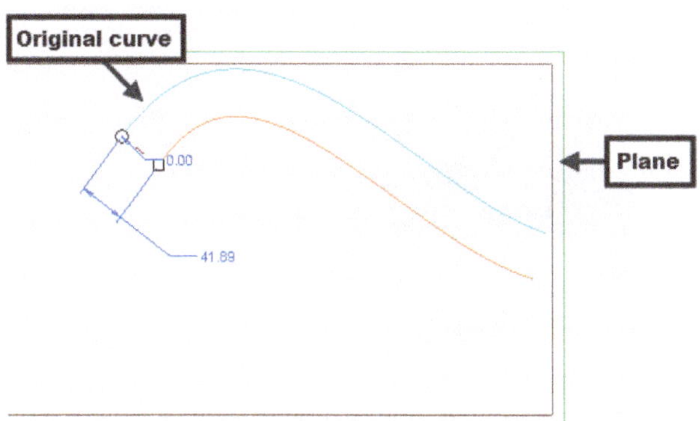

To offset boundary edges of a surface, activate the **Offset** command. Next, click the **Type > Quilt Boundary Chain** on the **Offset** dashboard. Select anyone of the boundary edges of the surface.

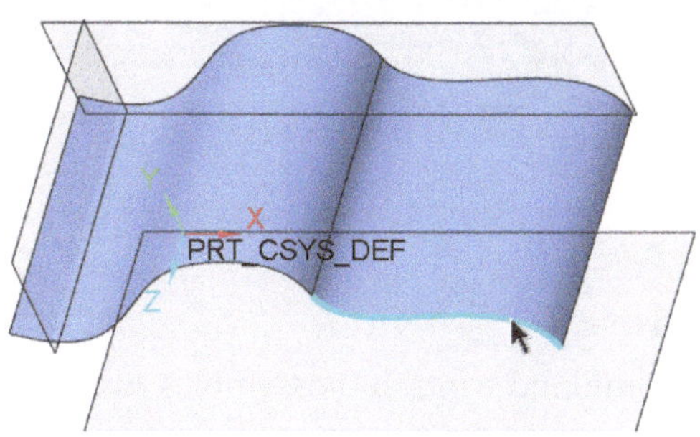

On the **References** tab, click the **Details** button.

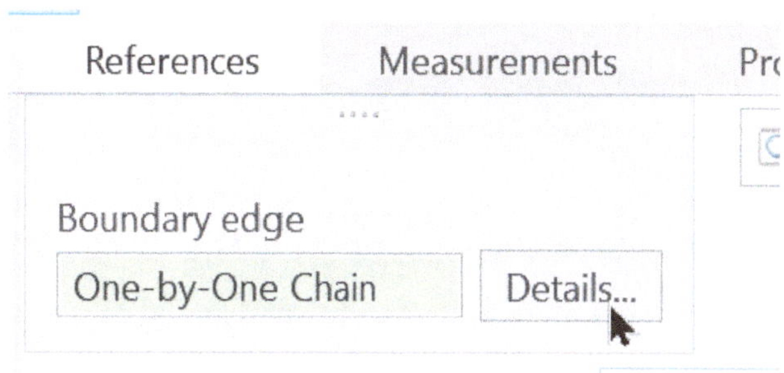

On the **Chain** dialog, select **Rule-based** option. Next, select **Rule > Complete Loop**. Next, click **OK**. Type-in a value in the **Offset** box and click **OK** on the dashboard.

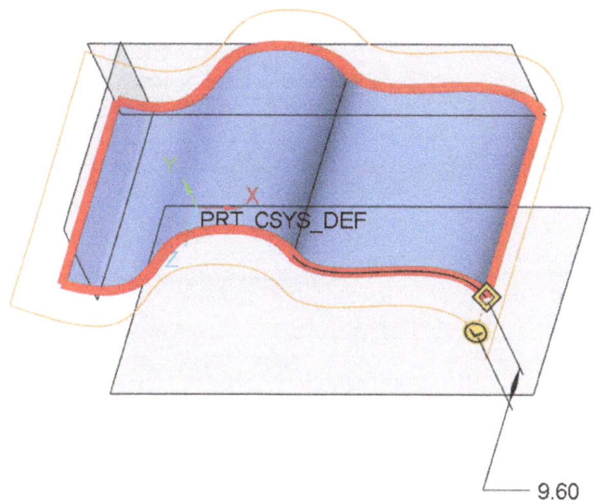

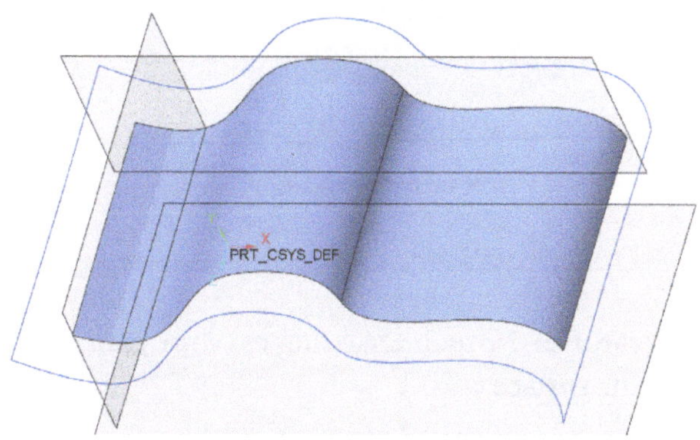

Trim

This command trims a surface using an intersecting element such as plane, curve, and surface.

1. Select the surface to trim.

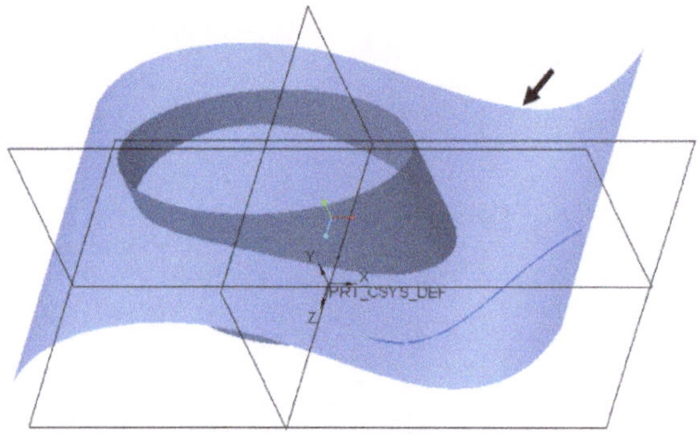

2. On the ribbon, click **Model > Editing > Trim**.
3. Click on the trimming surface.
4. Click the arrow that appears on the trimming surface to change the side to be trimmed.

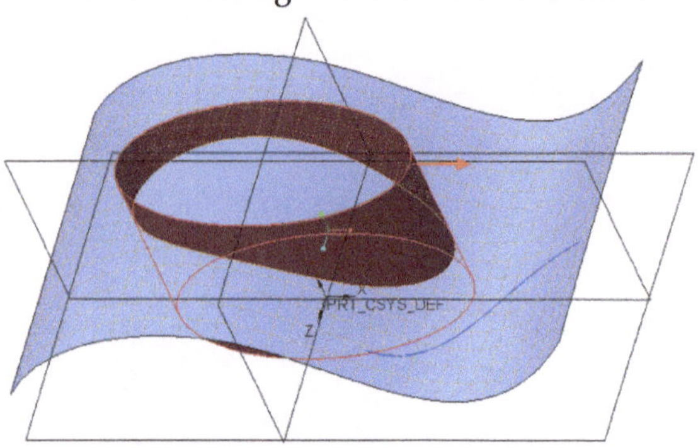

5. Click the green check.

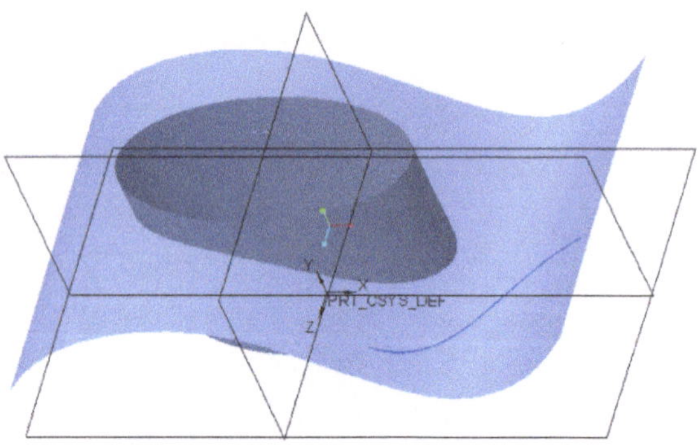

You can also use an intersecting curve or plane to trim the surface.

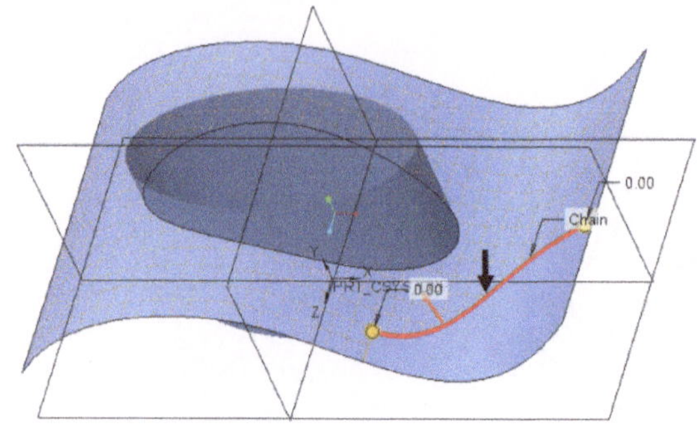

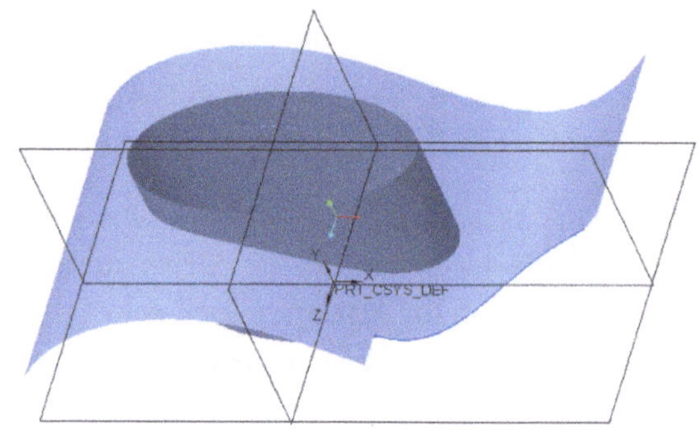

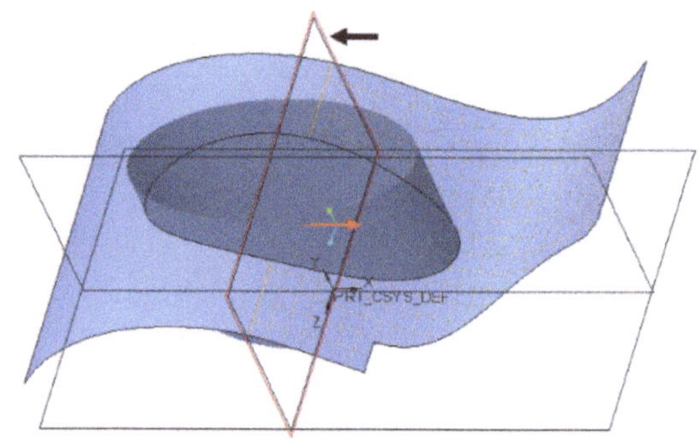

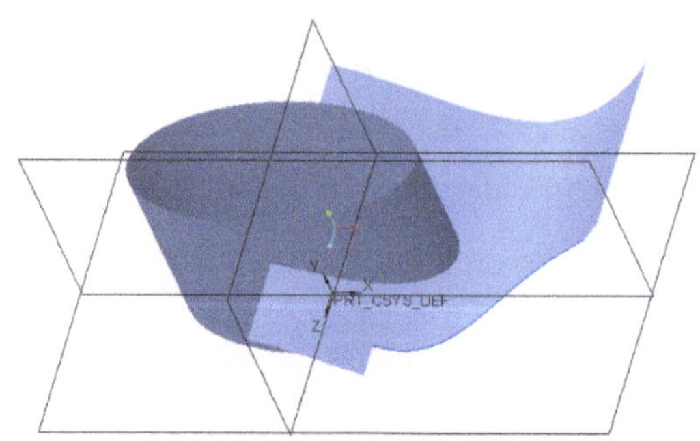

Merge

This command trims and assembles two intersecting surfaces.

1. Press the Ctrl key and select the surfaces to merge
2. On the ribbon, click **Model > Editing > Merge**.

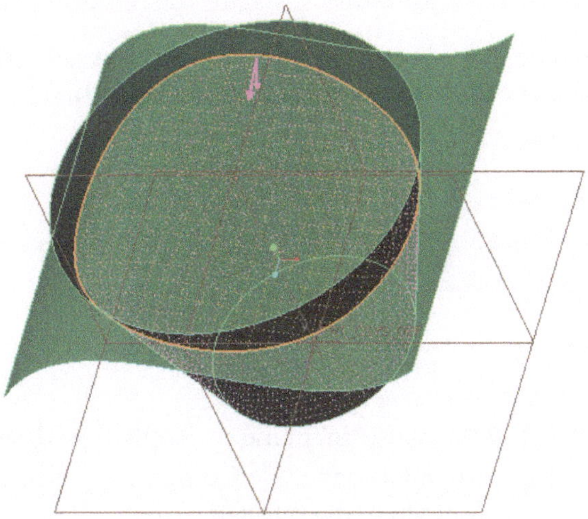

3. Click on the arrows to change the portions to keep.
4. Click the green check.

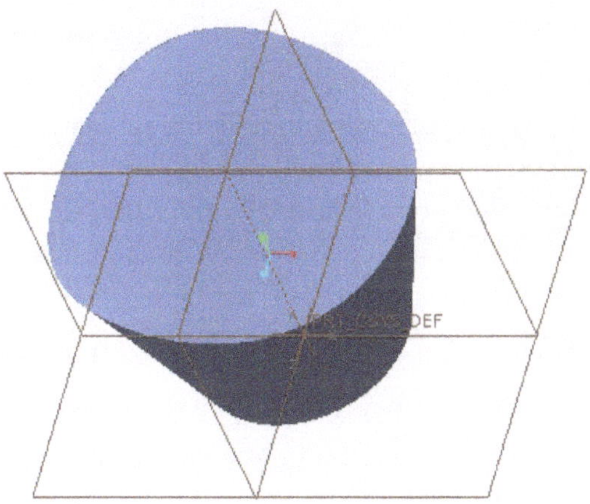

Extend

During the design process, you may sometimes need to extend a surface. You can extend a surface using the **Extend** command.

1. Select the edge of a surface to extend.

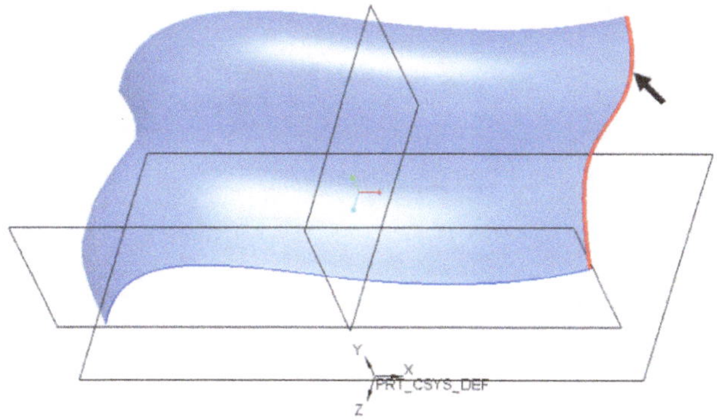

2. On the ribbon, click **Model > Editing > Extend**.
3. Type-in a value in the **Extend by** box or click and drag the limit handle to define the extended portion's length.

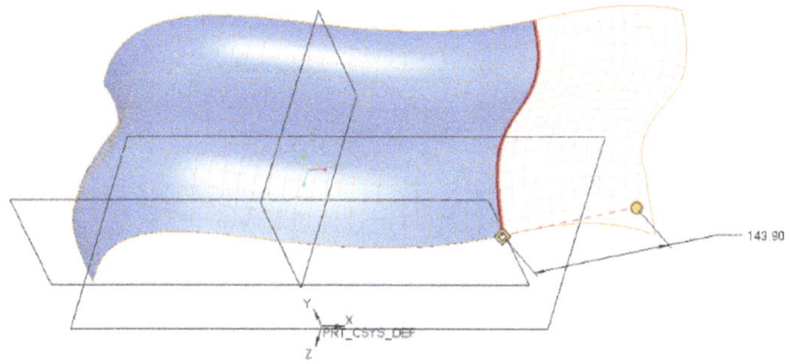

4. Click the **Options** tab and set the extension method. You can extend the surface using three methods: **Same**, **Tangent**, **Approximate, and Extrapolate**.

Same

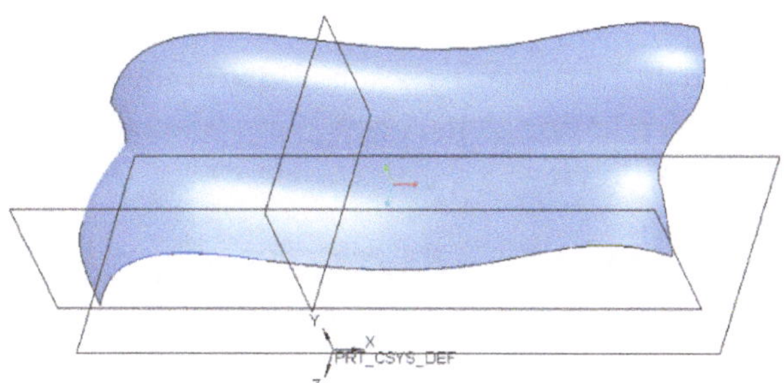

Tangent

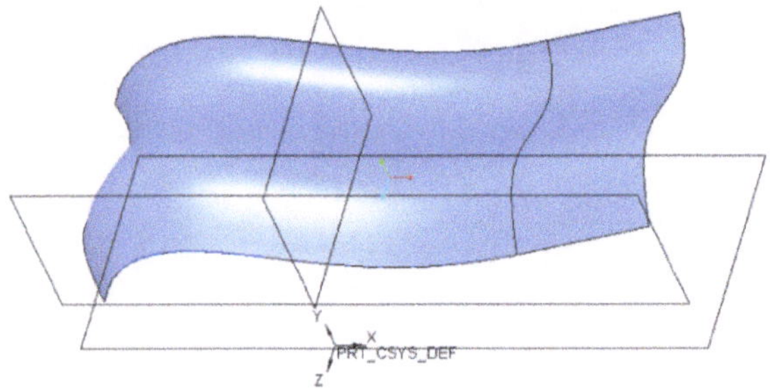

Approximate

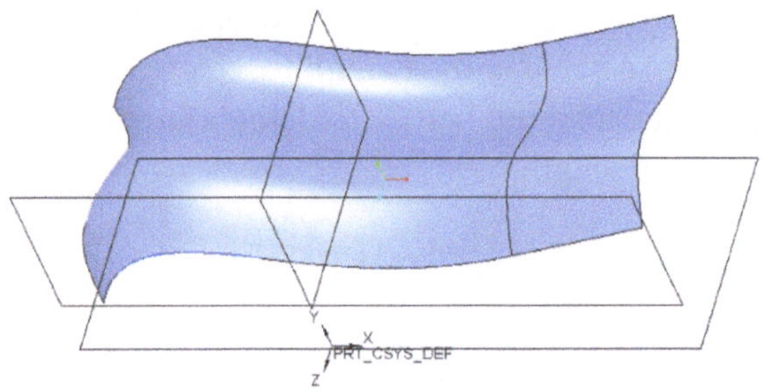

Extrapolate

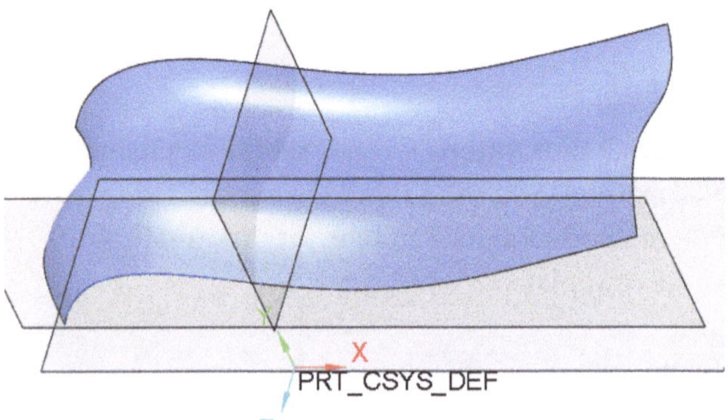

5. On the Dashboard, click the **Up to Plane** icon.
6. Select the horizontal plane.
7. Click **Preview**.

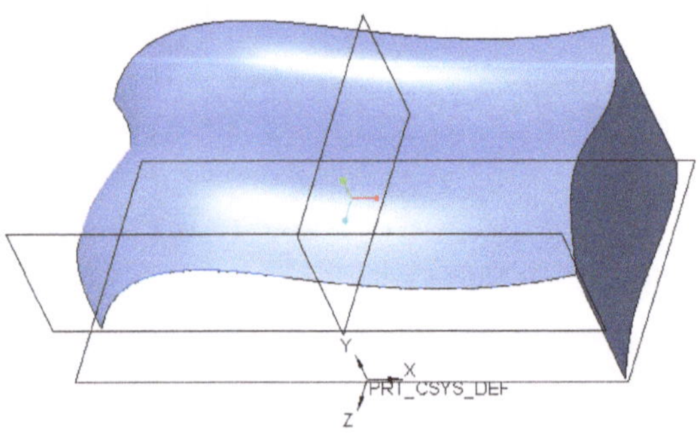

8. Click **Resume**, and then click **Along original surface**.

9. Click the **Measurements** tab and notice that the **Measure in surface** option is selected. The extension distance is measured along the surface.

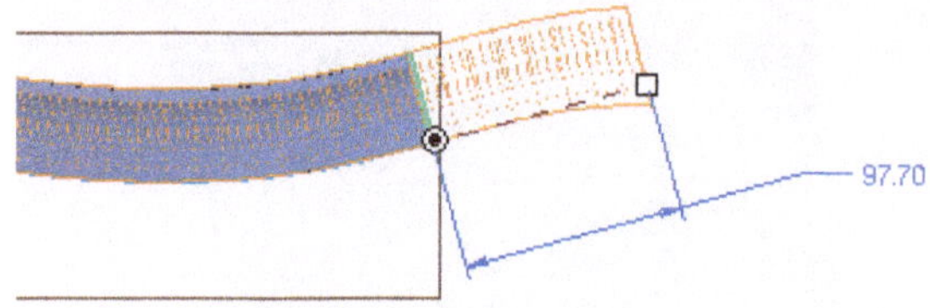

10. Select **Measure in plane** option and select the horizontal plane. Notice that the distance is measured along the selected plane.

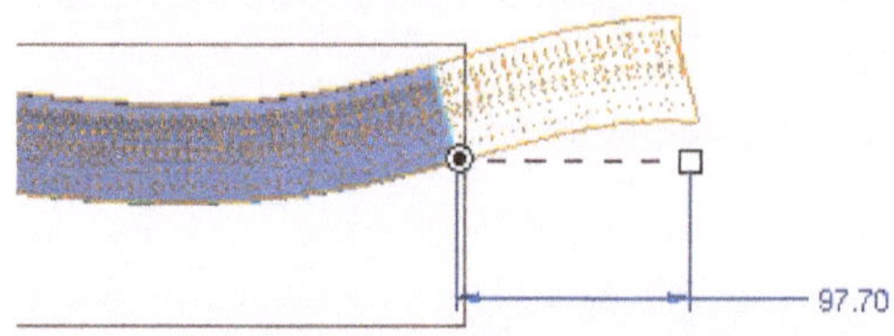

11. On the **Measurements** tab, click the right mouse button on the table and select **Add**. A new measurement point is added to the surface.

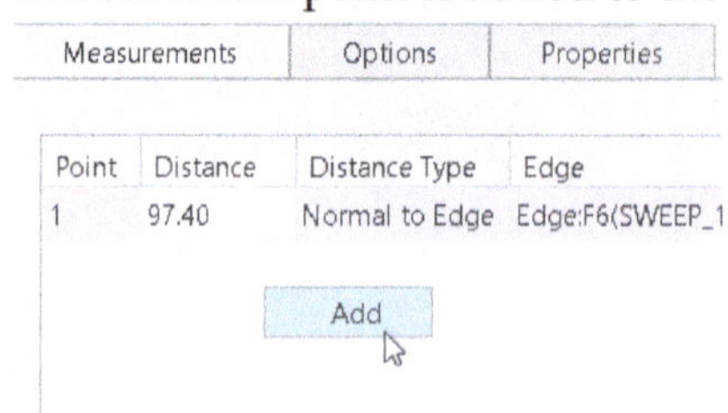

12. Drag the limit handle to define the length of the extended surface at the new point.

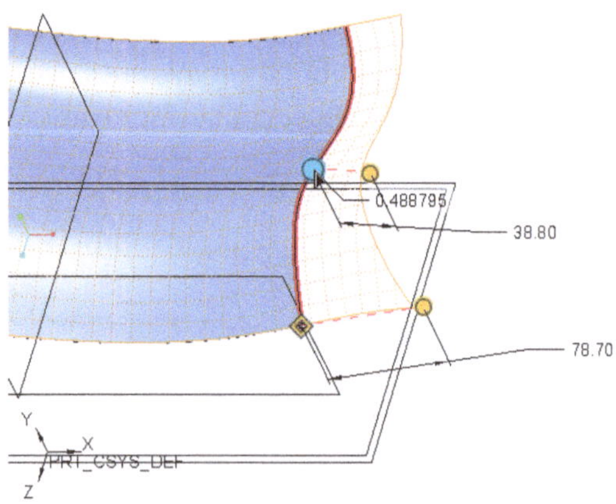

13. Drag the measurement point to change its position.

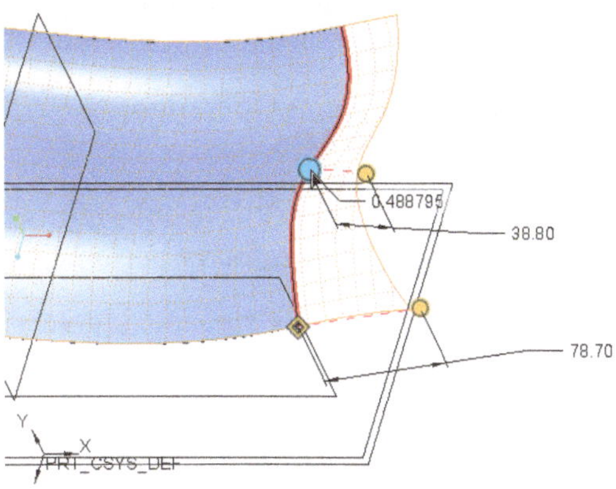

14. Click the green check to complete the feature.

Divide Surface

The **Divide Surface** command enables you to split a single surface into different surfaces without modifying the geometry. It is useful for applying different materials or surface finishes, setting boundary conditions for simulations, or isolating areas for adding new features.

1. On the ribbon, click click **Model > Editing > Separate Surface Region > Divide Surface**.

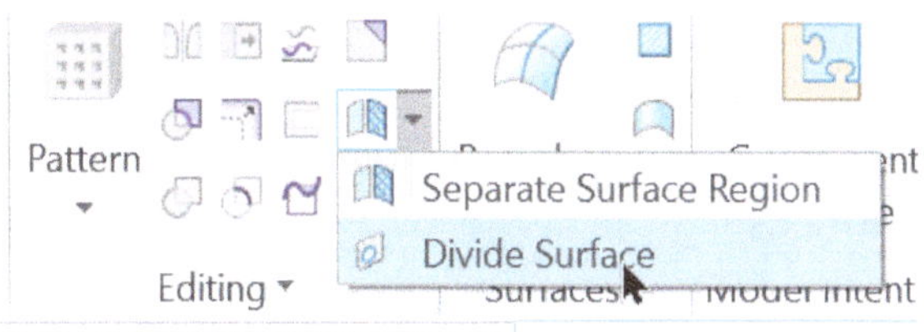

2. Click on the surface to be divided.
3. On the **References** tab, click the **Define** button next to the Sketch selection box.

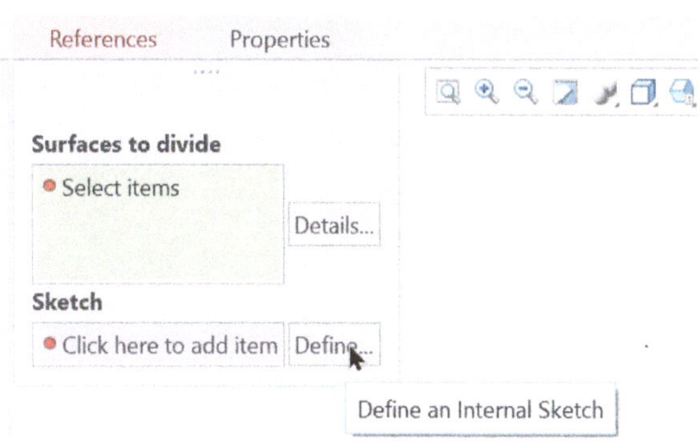

4. Click on a planar surface and click the **Sketch** button.

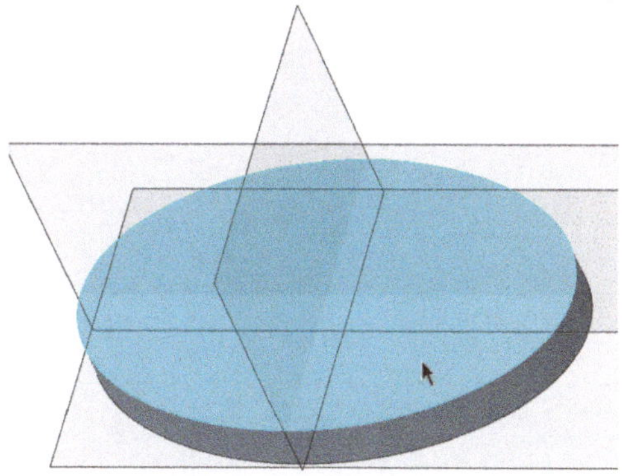

5. Create a sketch that will act as the dividing element. Next, click OK on the Sketch dashboard.

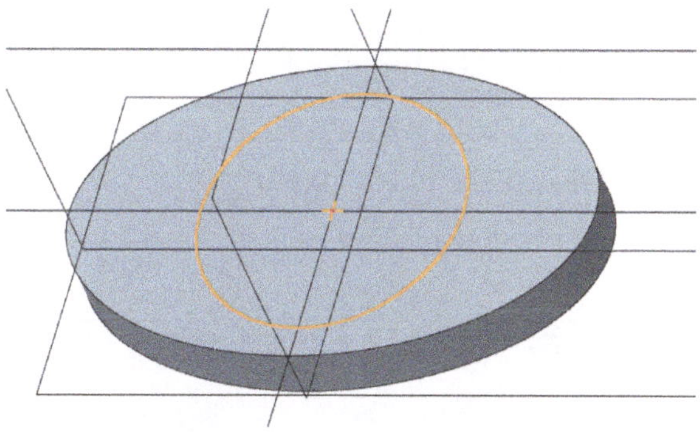

6. Click **OK**.

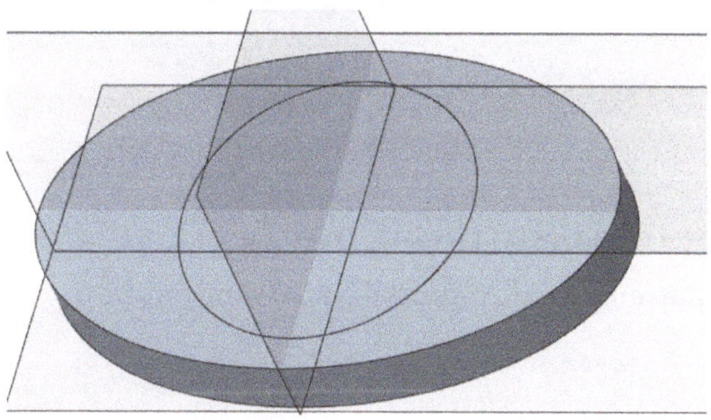

Unify Surfaces

The **Unify Surfaces** command lets you combine two or more surfaces to form a single surface.

1. To unify surfaces, activate the **Unify Surfaces** command (click **3D Model > Editing > Unify Surfaces** on the ribbon) and select the surfaces to combine.

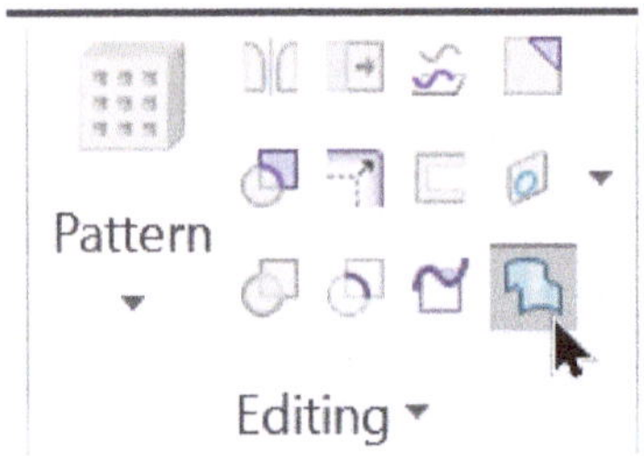

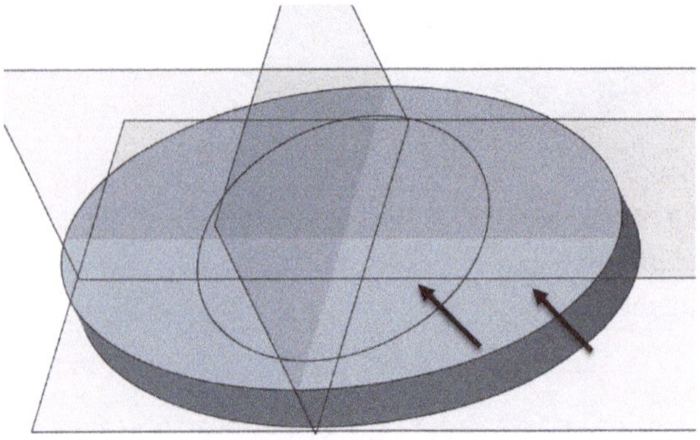

2. Click **OK** on the Dashboard.

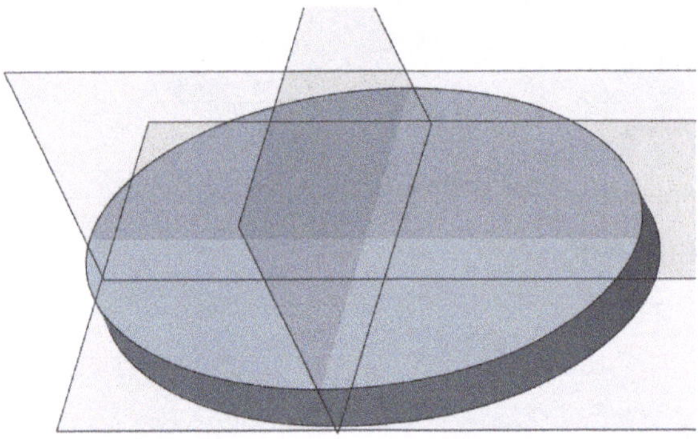

Moving a Surface Copy

The **Paste Special** command moves and copies a surface.

1. Select the surface/element to move.

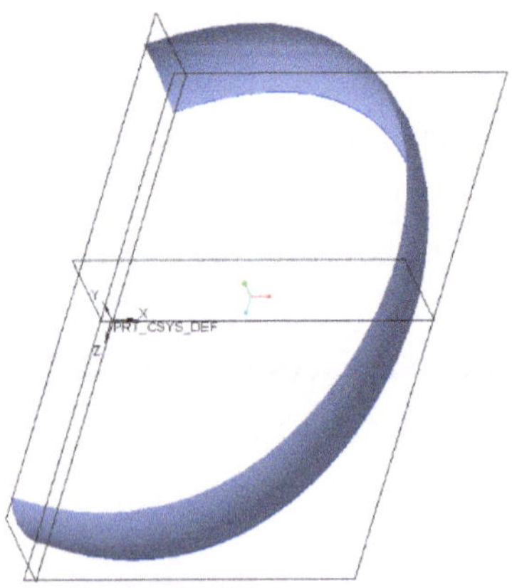

2. On the ribbon, click **Model > Operations > Copy** .
3. On the ribbon, click **Model > Operations > Paste > Paste Special** .
4. On the dashboard, click the **Options** tab and uncheck the **Hide original geometry** option.
5. On the dashboard, click **Translate** .
6. Select a line, axis, or plane to define the translation direction.
7. Type-in a value in the **Distance** box or drag the distance handle (Circle with an arrow).
8. Click the green check to complete the feature.

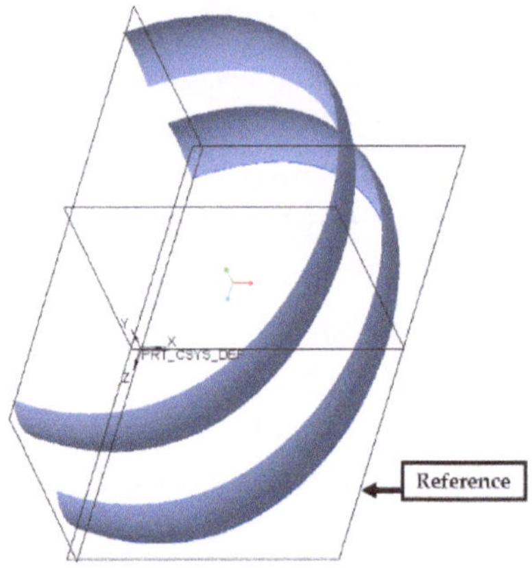

Rotating Surfaces

Creo Parametric allows you to rotate an element about an axis.

1. Select the surface/element to rotate.

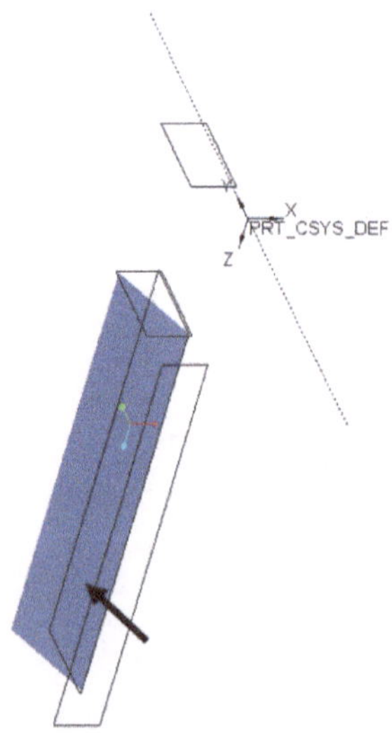

2. On the ribbon, click **Model > Operations > Copy** .

3. On the ribbon, click **Model > Operations > Paste > Paste Special** .
4. On the dashboard, click the **Options** tab and uncheck the **Hide original geometry** option.
5. On the dashboard, click **Rotate** .
6. Select a line or axis to define the rotation axis.
7. Type-in a value in the **Angle** box.
8. Click the green check.

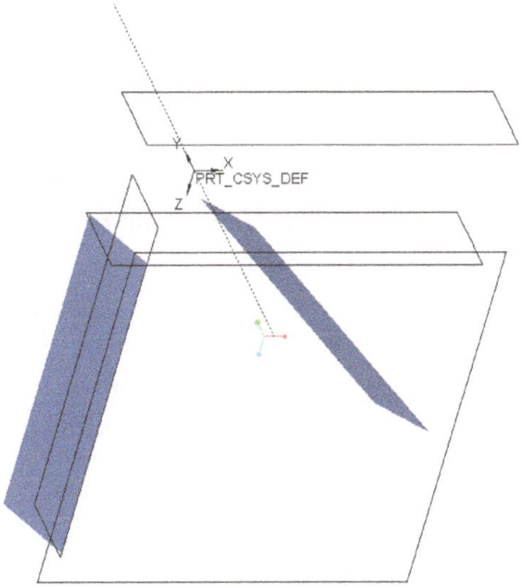

Solidify

This command uses a surface to modify the shape of a solid geometry. You can use a surface to add or remove geometry.

1. Create a solid body and a surface, as shown.

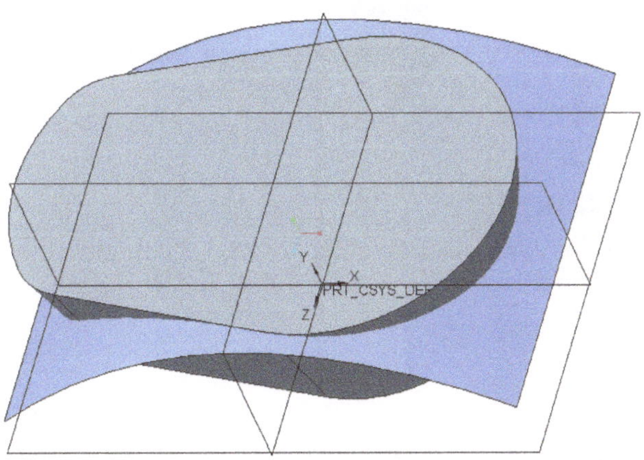

2. Select the surface used to modify the geometry.
3. On the ribbon, click **Model > Editing > Solidify**.
4. On the dashboard, click the **Remove material** icon.

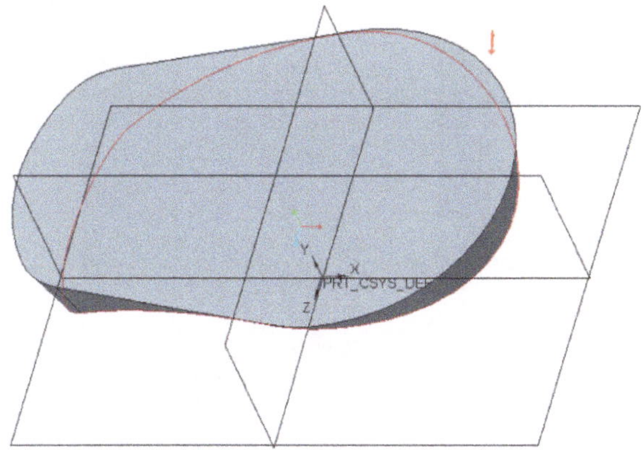

5. Click the arrow that appears in the graphics window to reverse the side to be removed.

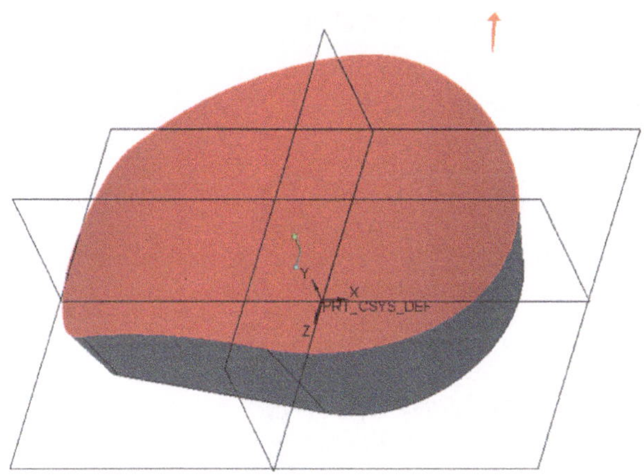

6. Click the green check.

Adding geometry using a surface

1. Create a solid body and an intersecting surface, forming a closed volume.

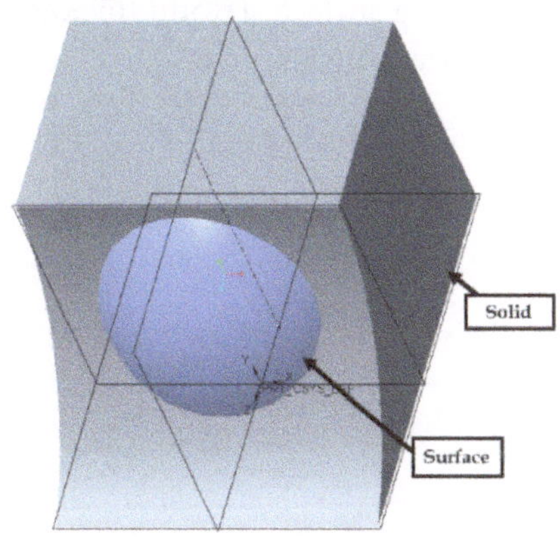

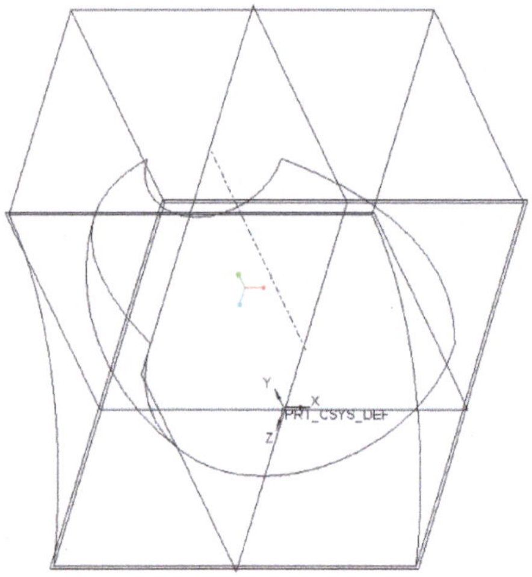

2. Select the surface and activate the **Solidify** command.
3. On the Dashboard, click the **Fill with solid** icon.
4. Click the green check.

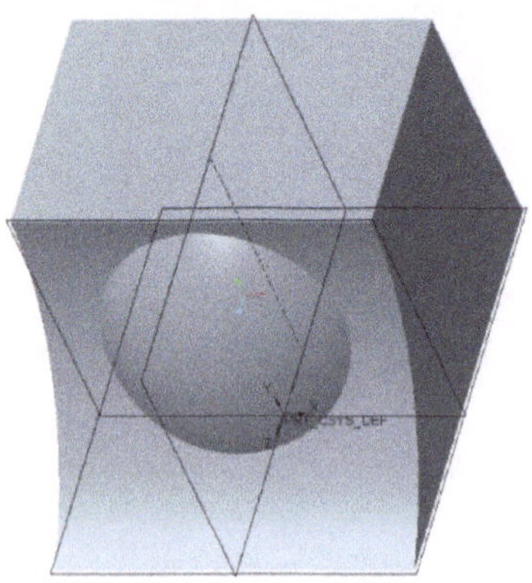

Thicken

Creating a solid from a surface can be accomplished by simply thickening a surface. To add thickness to a surface, follow the steps given next.

1. Select the surface to thicken.

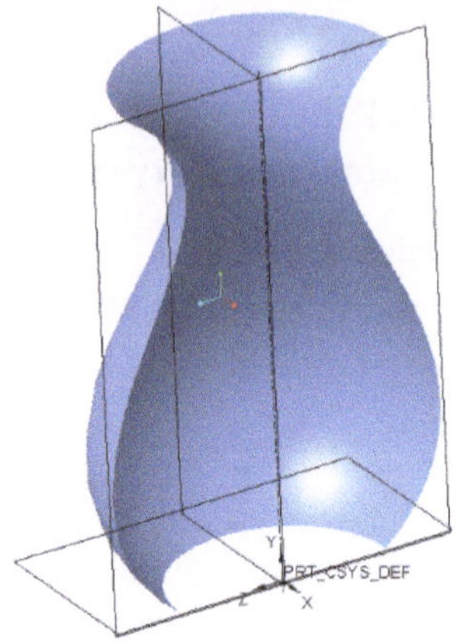

2. On the ribbon, click **Model > Editing > Thicken**.
3. Enter the thickness value in the **Thickness** box (or) drag the offset handle.
4. Click the arrow that appears on the geometry to reverse the side of material addition.
5. Click the **Options** tab and select a method to add thickness. These methods are the same as that available in the **Offset** command.
6. Click the green check.

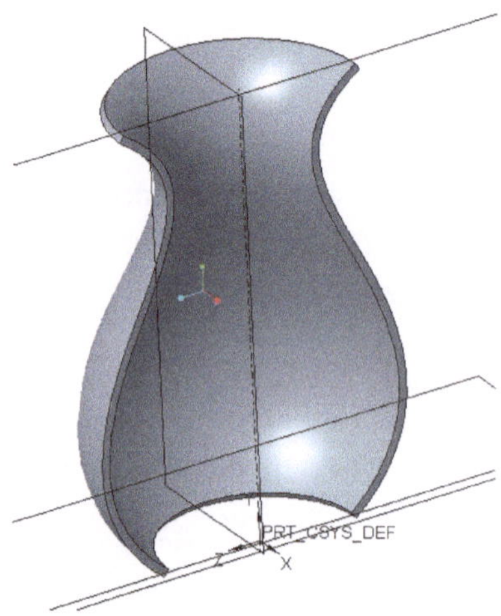

Example

In this example, you will construct the model shown below.

Creating the Layout Curves

1. Start **Creo Parametric 11.0**.
2. Create a folder with the name *Surface Design* and set it as the current working folder.
3. On the Quick Access Toolbar, click the **New** button.
4. On the **New** dialog, select **Type > Part**.
5. Select **Sub-type > Solid**.
6. Type-in *Example1* in the **Name** box and uncheck the **Use default template** option.
7. Click **OK**.
8. On the **New File Options** dialog, select the **mmns_part_solid_abs** option and click **OK**.
9. On the **Graphics** toolbar, click **Display Datum Filters drop-down > (Select All)**.

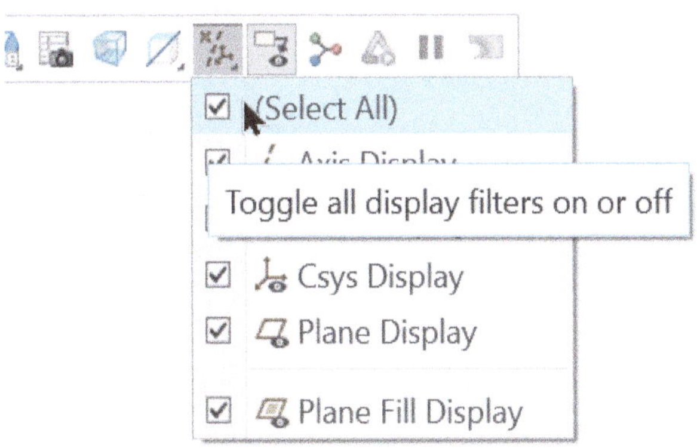

10. On the ribbon, click **Model > Datum > Point > Offset Coordinate System** .
11. Select the default coordinate system.

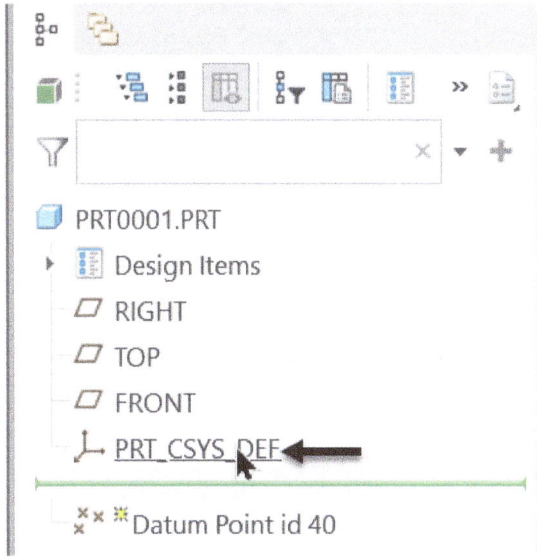

12. On the **Datum Point** dialog, select **Type > Cartesian**.
13. Click in the table and enter the point coordinates as shown. Click **OK**.

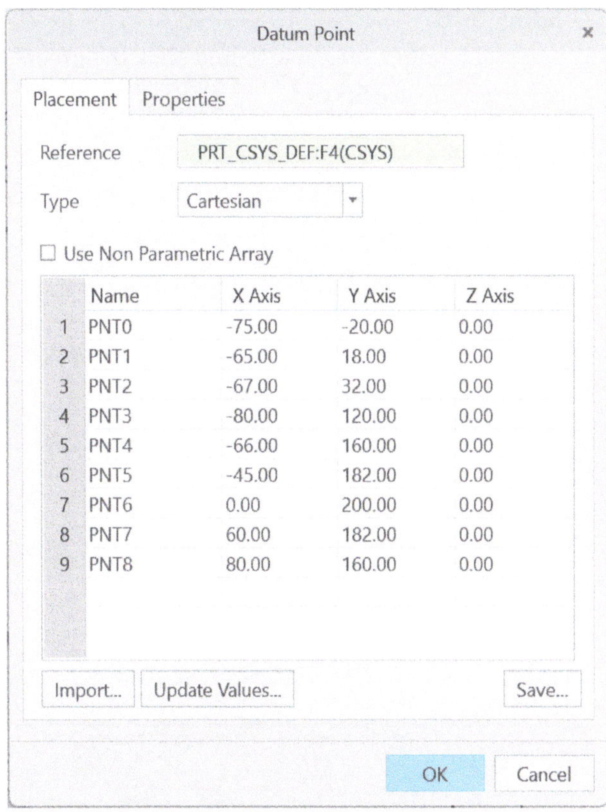

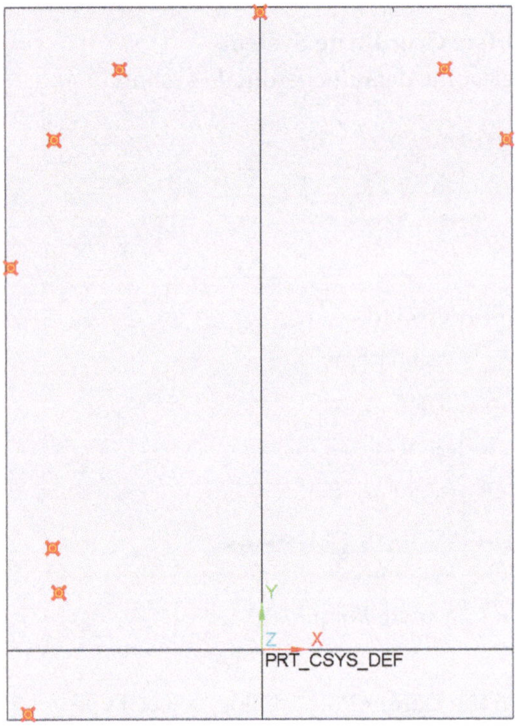

14. On the **Model** tab of the ribbon, expand the **Datum** panel and click **Curve > Curve through point** .
15. Select the points one-by-one and click the green check on the Dashboard.

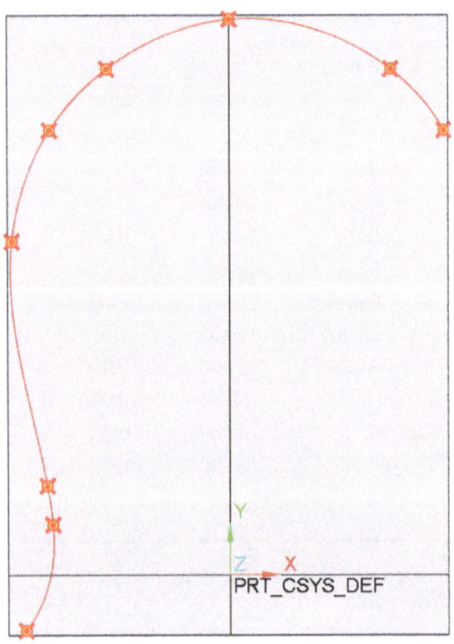

16. Likewise, create the second and third curves as shown.

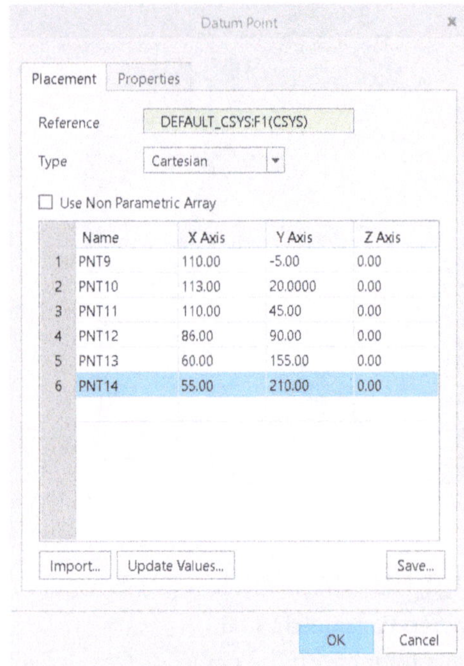

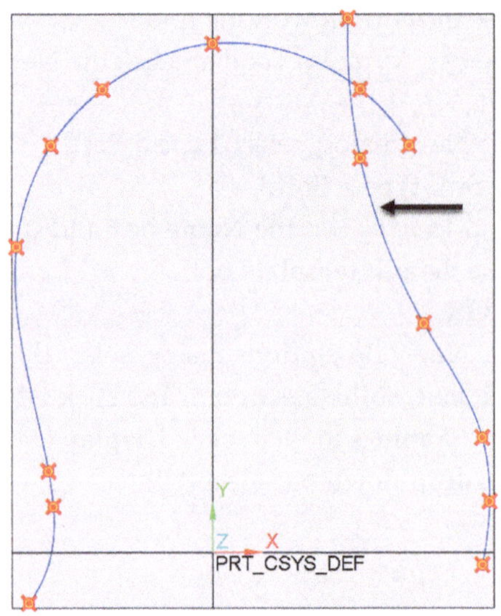

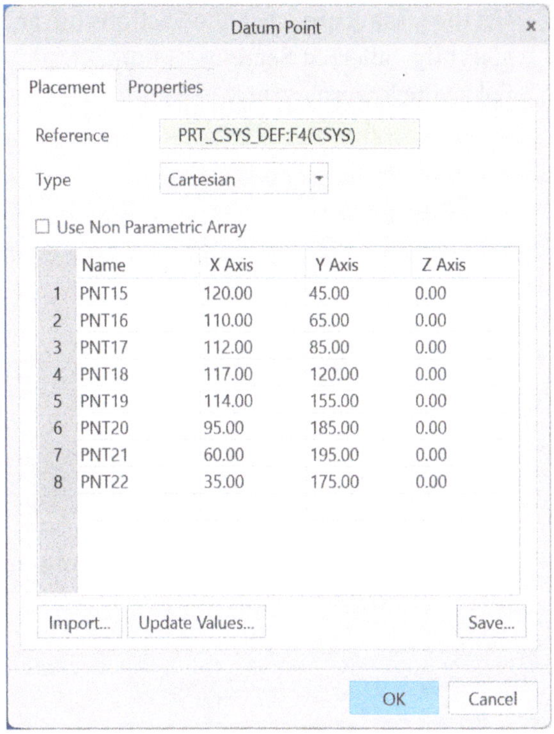

	Name	X Axis	Y Axis	Z Axis
1	PNT15	120.00	45.00	0.00
2	PNT16	110.00	65.00	0.00
3	PNT17	112.00	85.00	0.00
4	PNT18	117.00	120.00	0.00
5	PNT19	114.00	155.00	0.00
6	PNT20	95.00	185.00	0.00
7	PNT21	60.00	195.00	0.00
8	PNT22	35.00	175.00	0.00

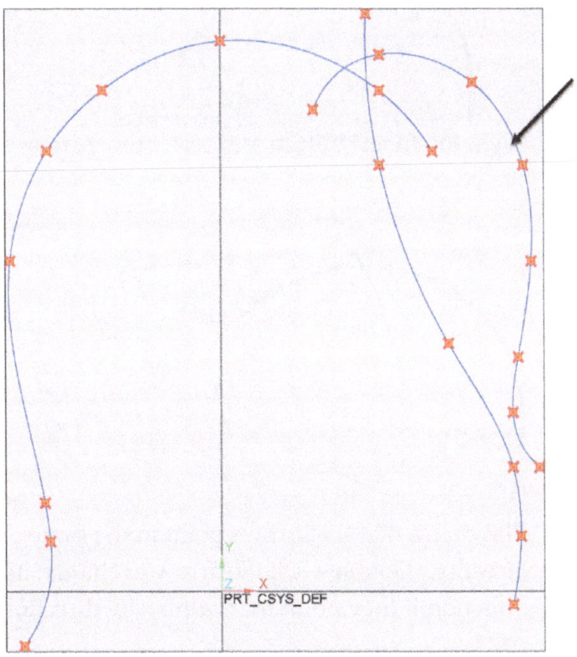

Creating the Front Surface

1. Create an arc on the Top Plane and add dimensions to it. Exit the sketch.

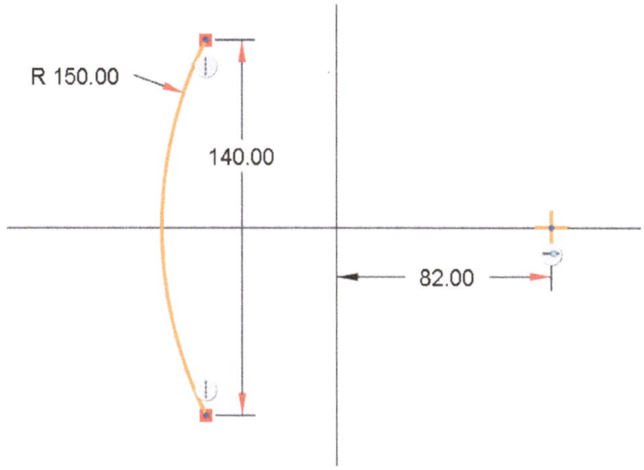

2. Create an arc on the Right Plane and add dimensions to it. Finish the sketch.

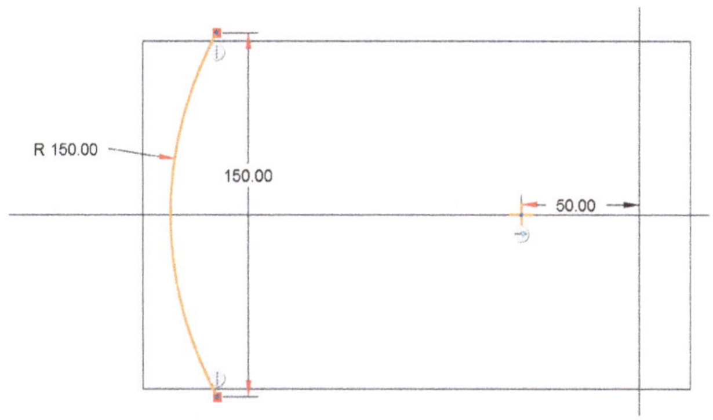

3. Create a datum plane normal to the first curve.

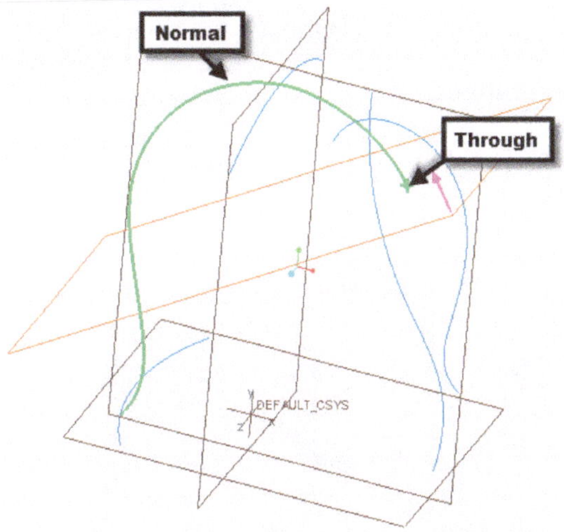

4. Create an arc on the plane normal to the curve.

   Maintain a **Coincident** constraint between the arc and the endpoint of the curve. Finish the sketch.

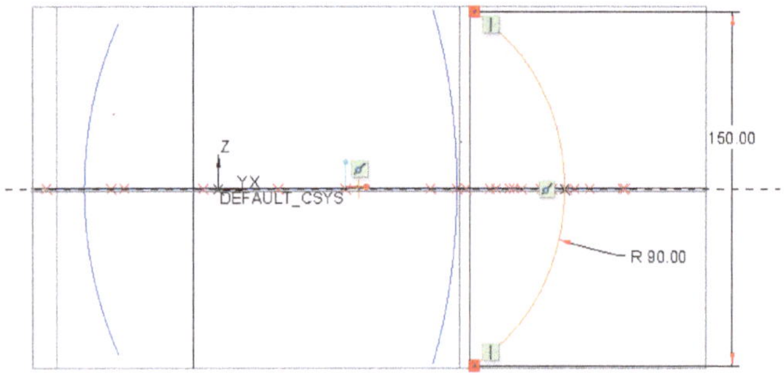

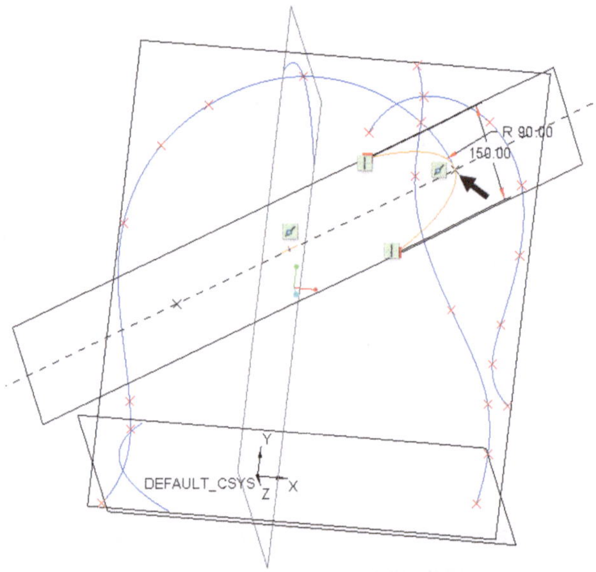

5. On the ribbon, click **Model** tab **>** **Shapes** panel **>** **Swept Blend** .
6. On the Dashboard, click the **Surface** icon.
7. Select the first curve to define the trajectory.

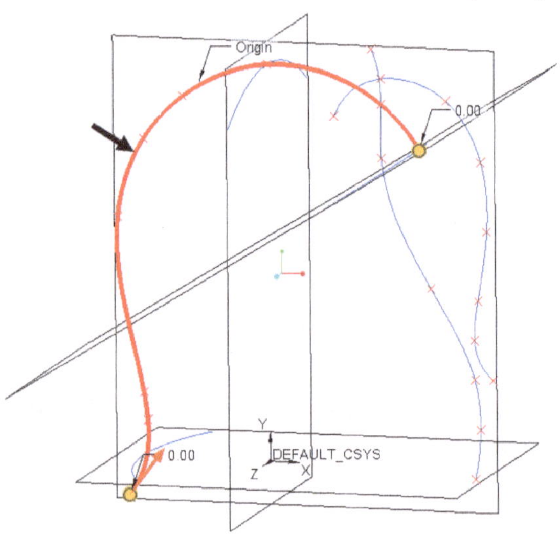

8. On the Dashboard, click the **Sections** tab and select the **Selected Sections** option.
9. Select the lowermost arc.

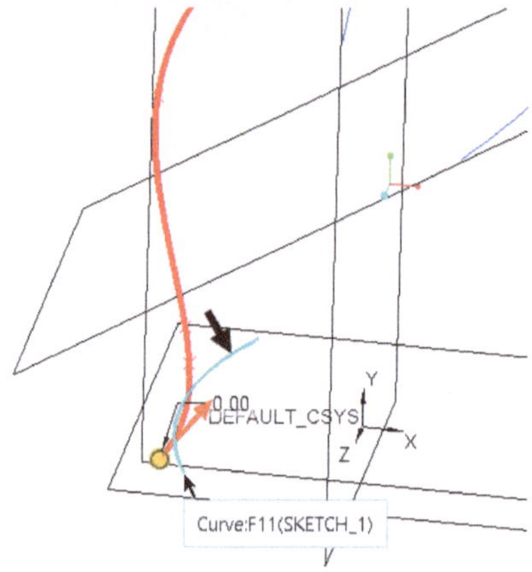

10. Click the **Insert** button on the **Section** tab, and then select the second arc.

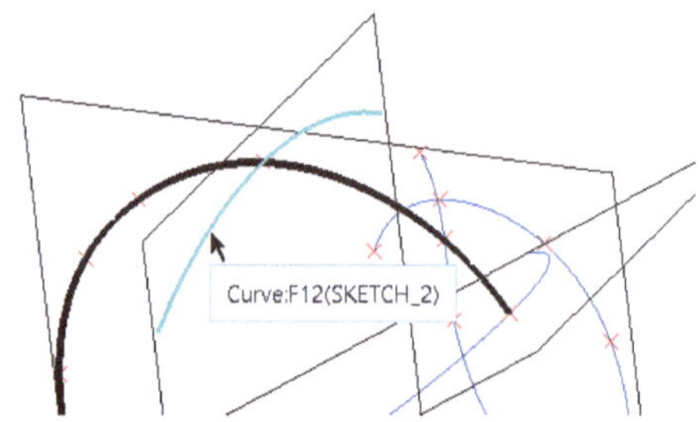

11. Click the **Insert** button and select the third arc.

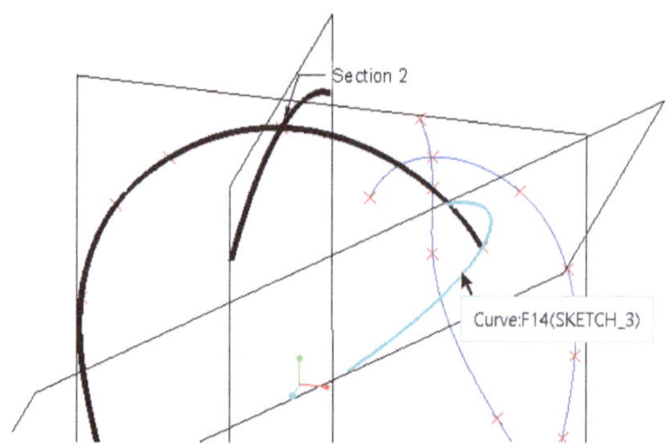

12. Make sure that the arrows point in the same direction. Double-click the arrow to change its direction if they point in the opposite direction.

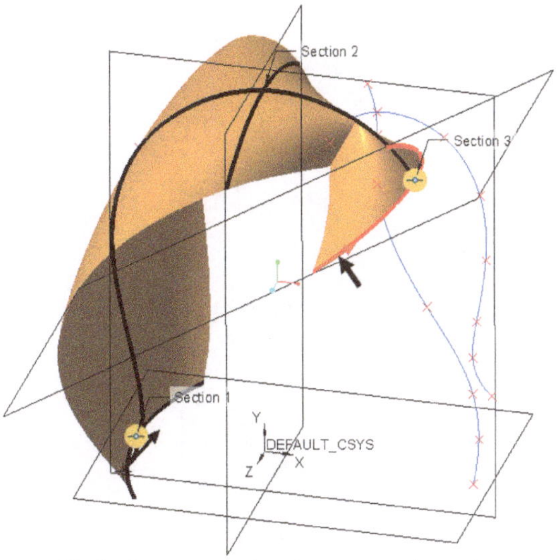

13. Click the green check to complete the swept bend surface.

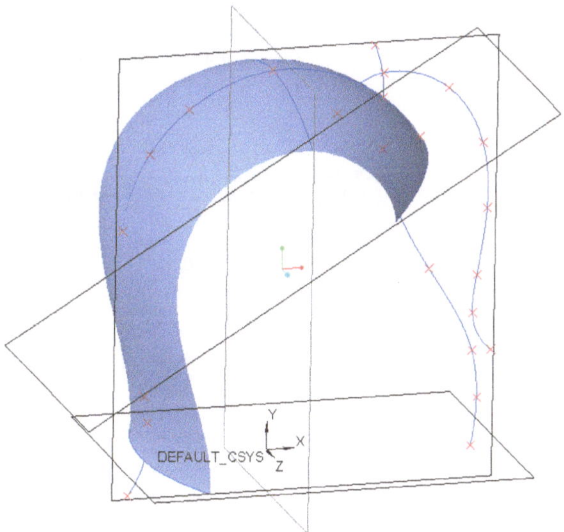

14. Save the file. As you are creating a complex geometry, it is advisable that you save the model after each operation.

Creating the Label surface

1. Create an arc on the top plane. Exit the sketch.

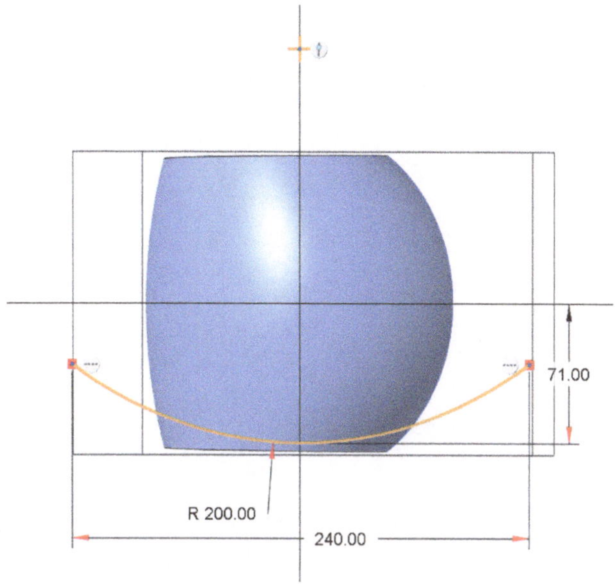

2. On the ribbon, click **Model** tab **>** **Shapes** panel **>** **Extrude**.
3. On the Dashboard, click the **Surface** icon.
4. Extrude the sketch up to **220** distance. Click **OK** on the Dashboard.

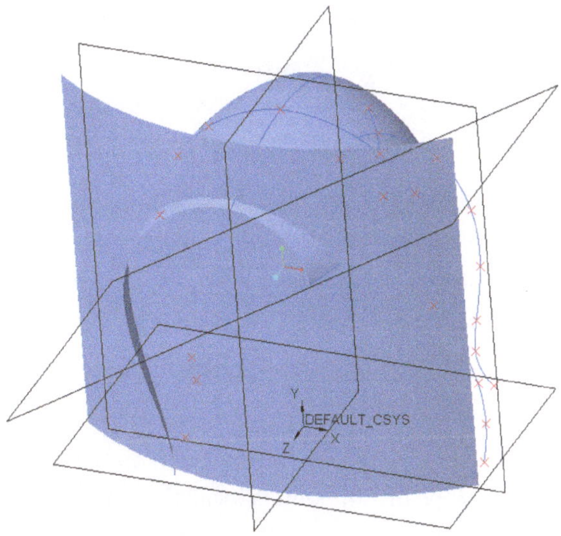

5. Select the extruded surface.
6. On the ribbon, click **Model** tab **>** **Editing** panel **> Mirror**.
7. Select the front plane to define the mirroring plane.
8. Click the green check on the dashboard.

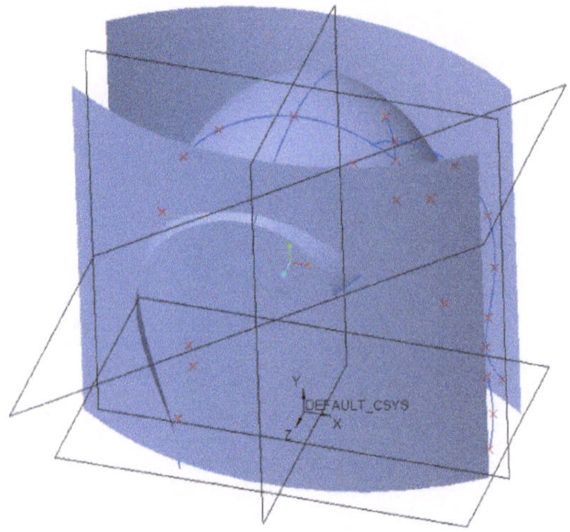

Creating the Back surface

1. On the ribbon, click **Model** tab > **Shapes** panel > **Sweep** .
2. On the Dashboard, click the **Surface** icon.
3. Select the curve, as shown below.

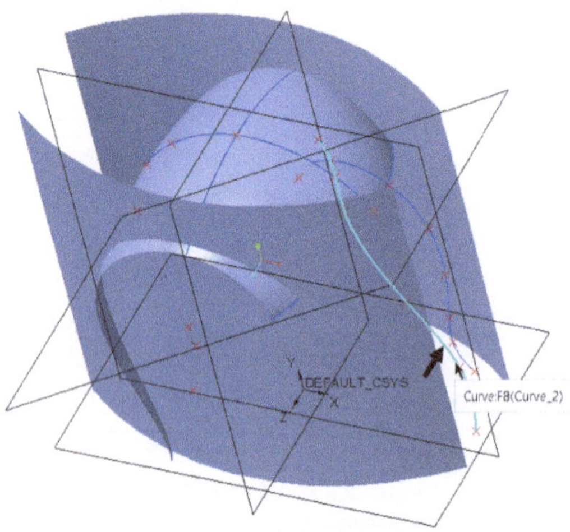

4. Double-click on the arrow displayed on the curve such that the origin point is located at the bottom end of the curve.

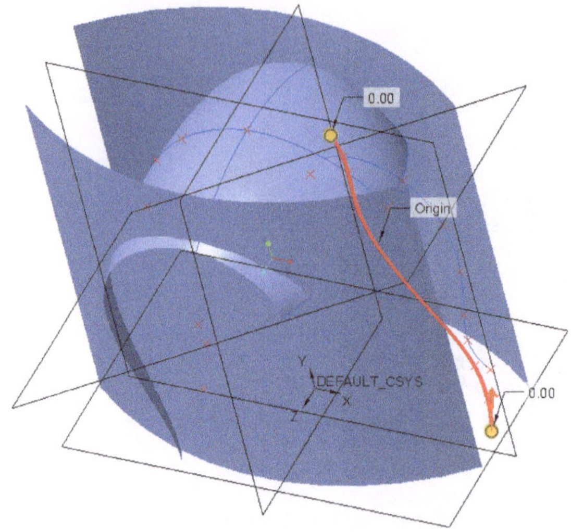

5. On the Dashboard, click the **Sketch** icon.
6. Create an arc and exit the sketch.

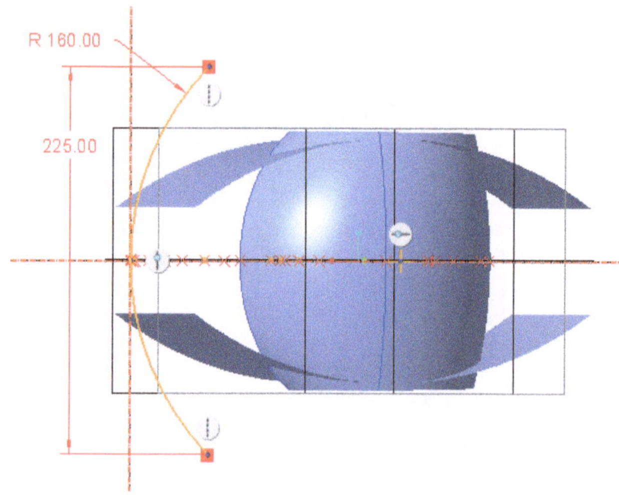

7. Click the green check to create the surface.

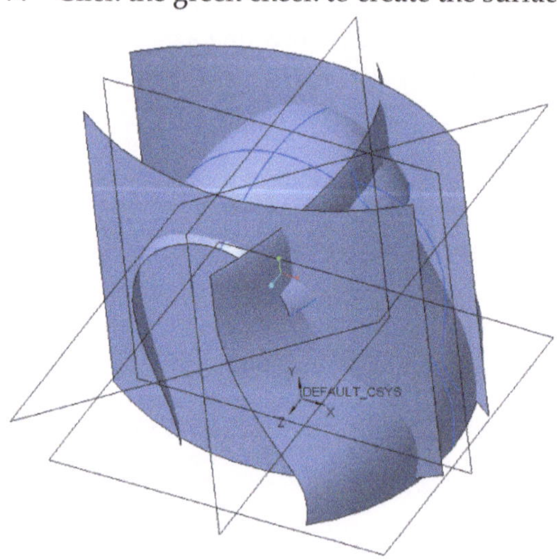

Trimming the Unwanted Portions

1. Press the Ctrl key, select the swept blend and front extruded surface, and click the **Merge** icon on the **Editing** panel.

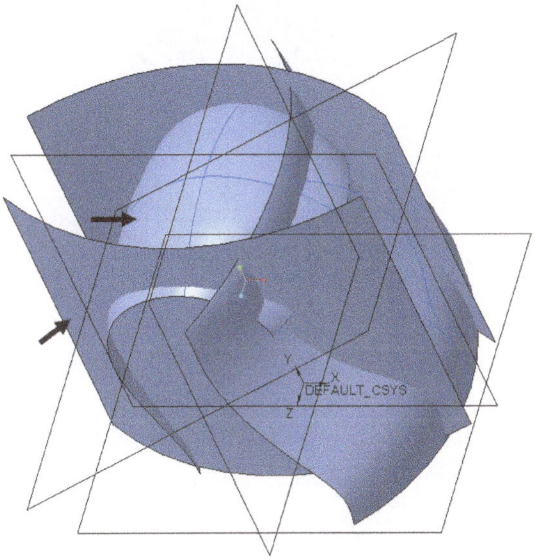

2. Make sure that the arrows point inwards. You can click on them to change the direction.

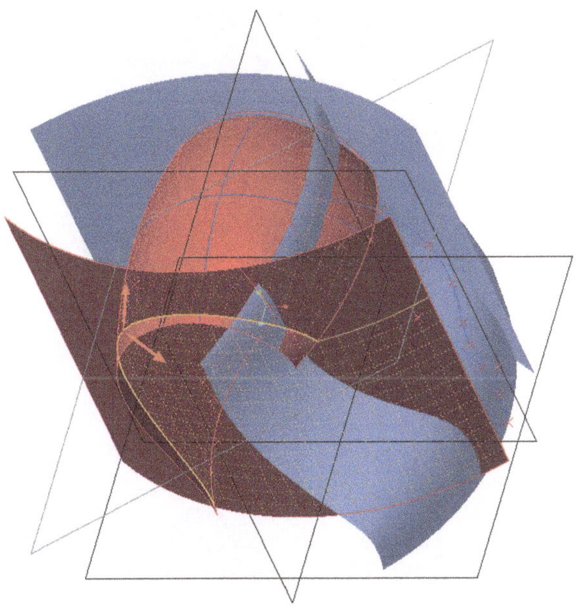

3. Click the green check to merge and trim the swept blend and extrude surfaces.

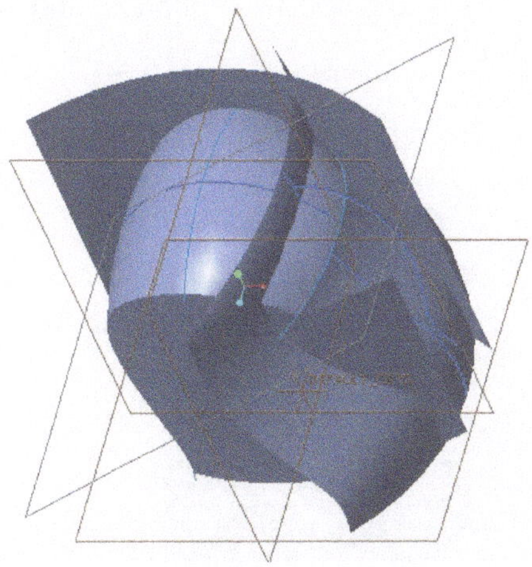

4. Likewise, merge the swept blend and mirror surfaces as shown.

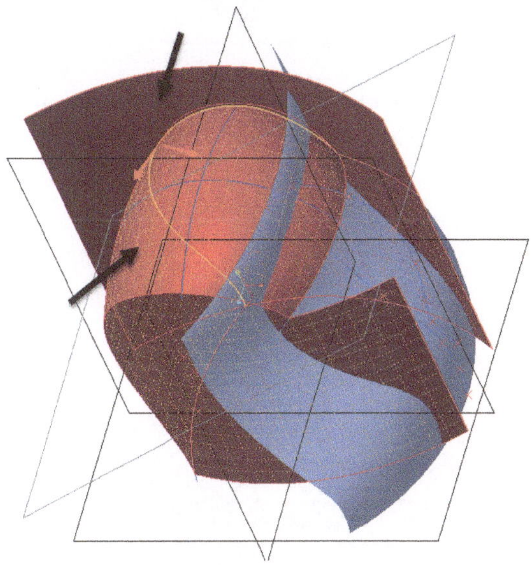

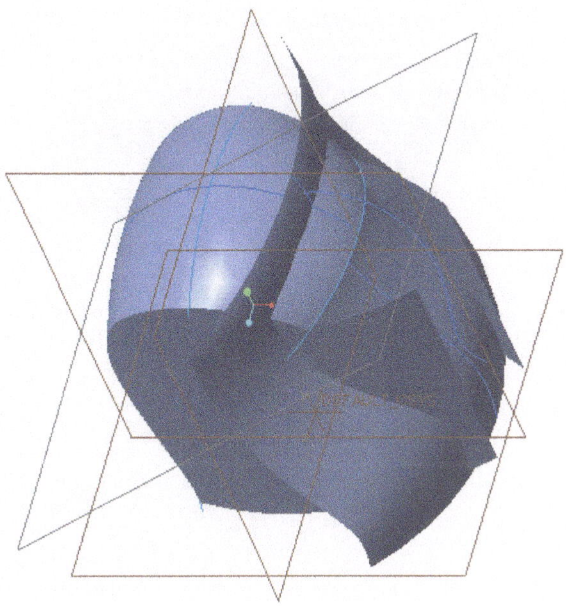

5. Press the Ctrl key and select swept blend and sweep surfaces.

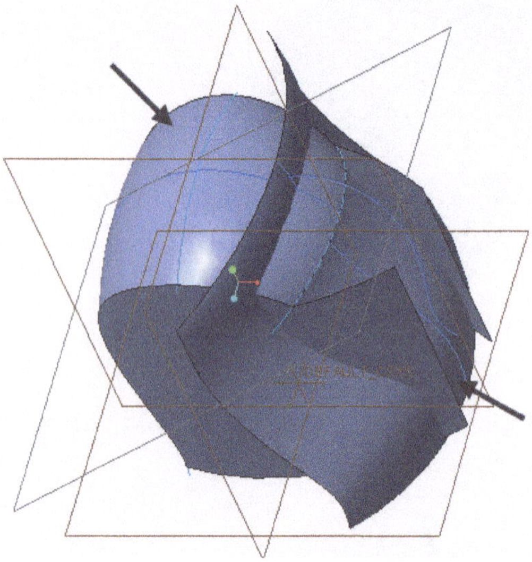

6. On the ribbon, click the **Merge** icon and make sure that the arrows point in the direction as shown.

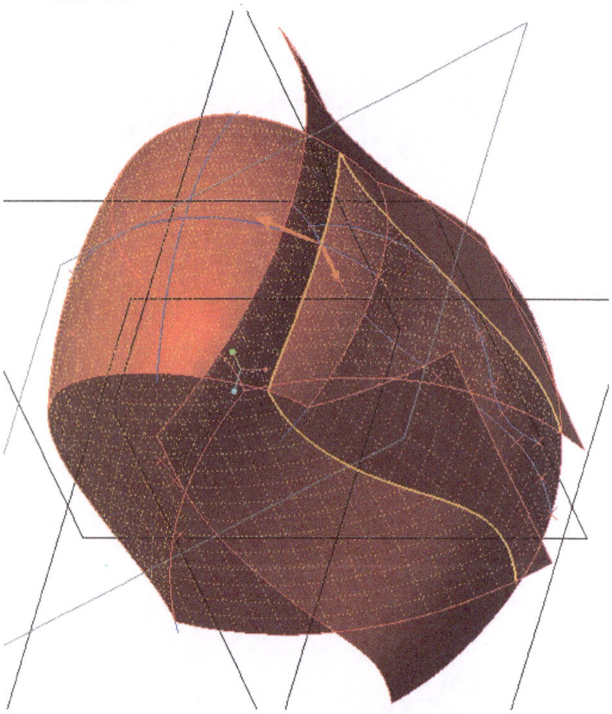

7. Click the green check to merge the surfaces.

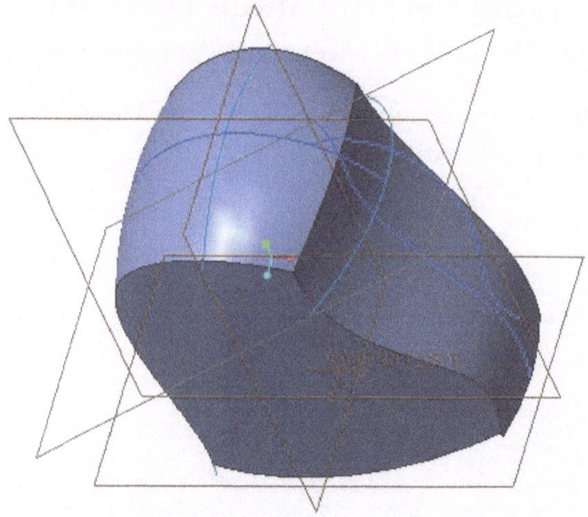

8. Select the sweep surface and click the **Trim** icon on the **Model** ribbon tab's **Editing** panel.
9. Select the Top plane and make sure that the arrow points upwards.

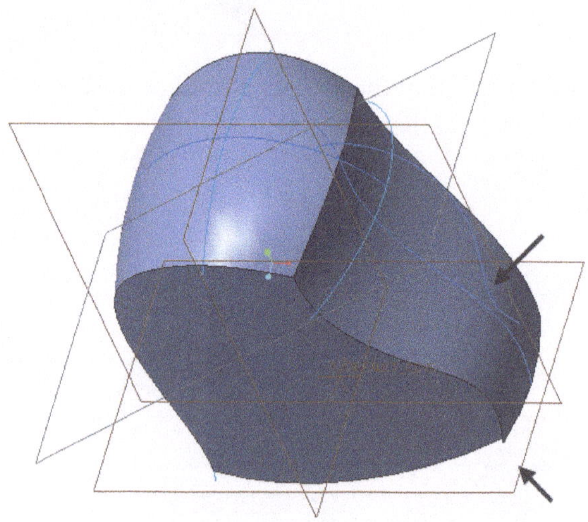

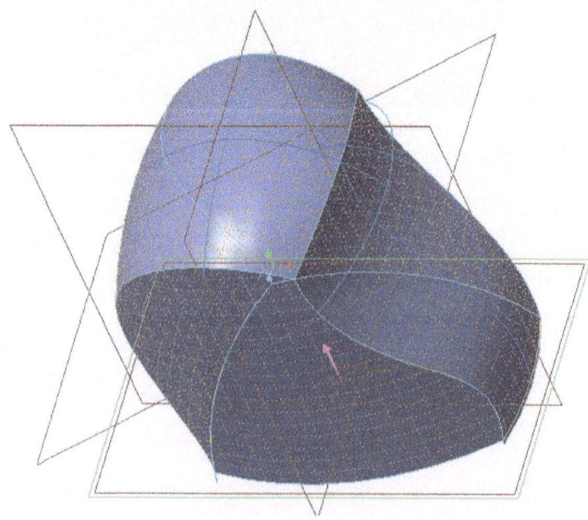

10. Click the green check to trim the unwanted portion of the sweep surface at the bottom.

Creating the Handle Surface

1. Activate the **Sweep** command and select the third curve.
2. Make sure that the origin is located at the bottom.

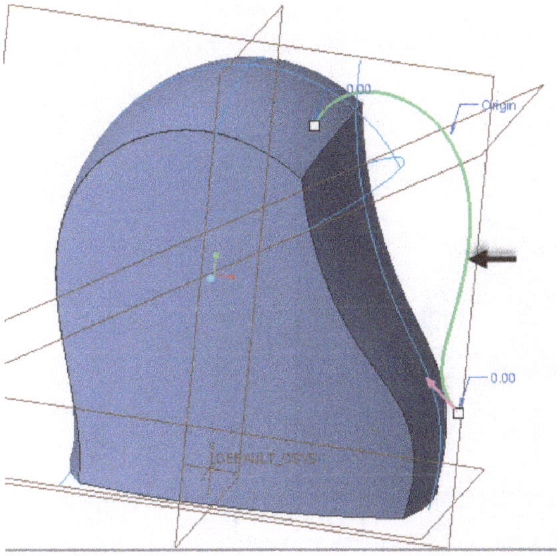

3. On the Dashboard, click the **Sketch** icon.
4. Create an ellipse and make sure that the top quadrant point is coincident with the curve's endpoint.
5. Add dimensions and click **OK** on the ribbon.

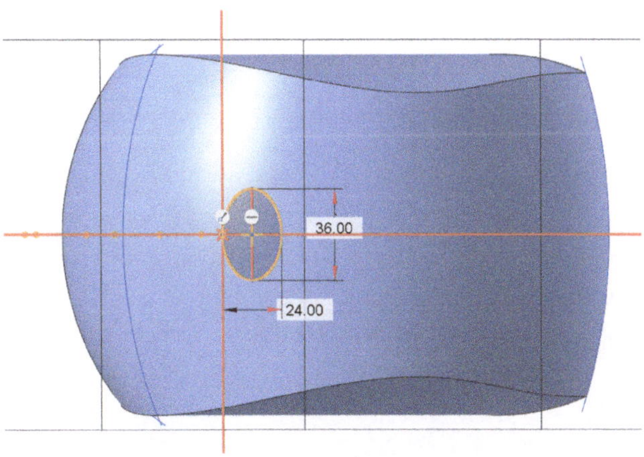

6. On the Dashboard, click the **Surface** icon.
7. Click the green check to complete the swept surface.

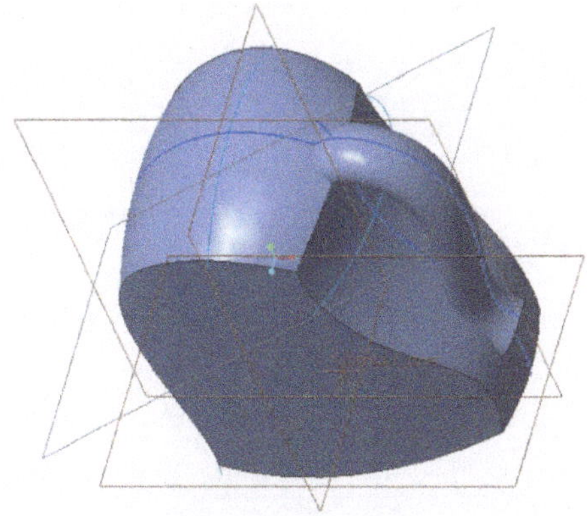

Rounding the intersecting edge

1. On the ribbon, click **Model** tab **> Engineering** panel **> Round** .
2. Click on the edge connecting the front and back faces.

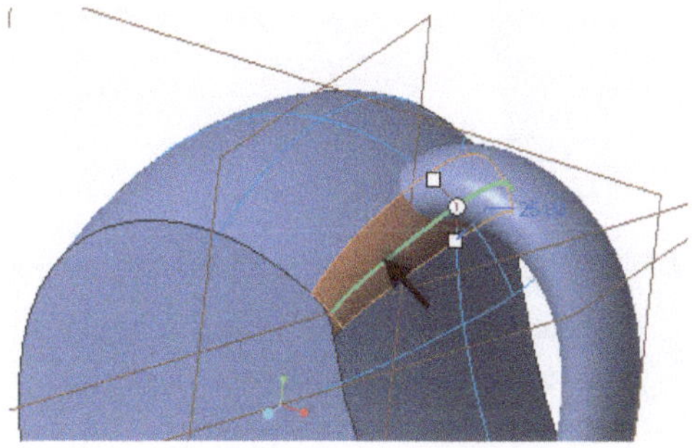

3. On the Dashboard, type-in 25 in the **Radius** box, and then click the green check.

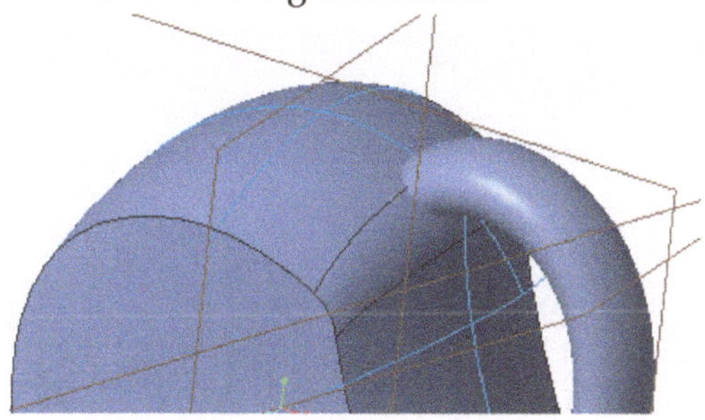

Blending the Bottom handle

1. Start a sketch on the Front plane and select the third layout curve as the sketch reference.

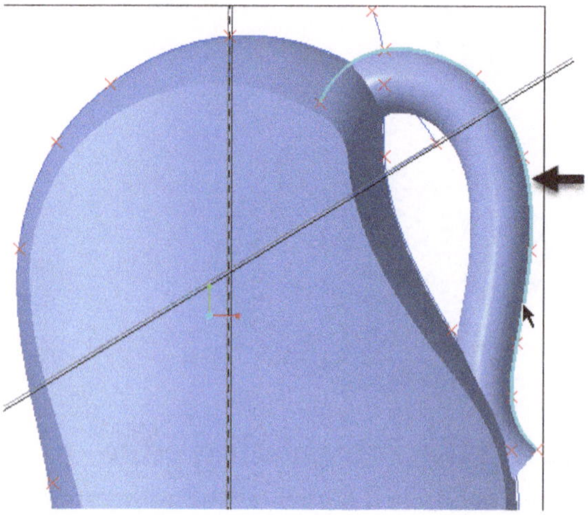

2. Draw a line tangent to the third layout curve, as shown below.

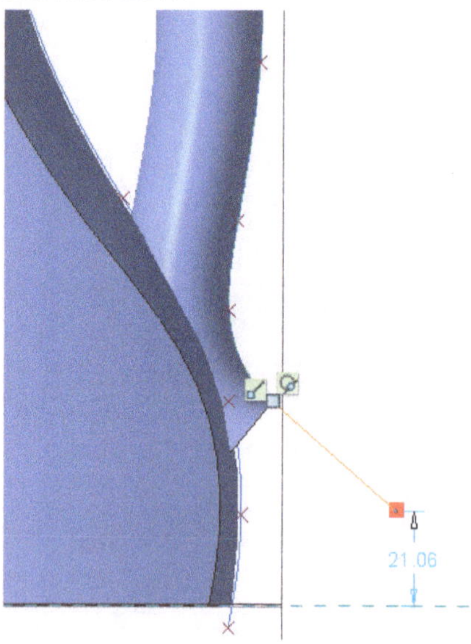

3. Exit the sketch.
4. Activate the **Plane** command.
5. Press and hold the Ctrl key and select the tangent line and Front plane. A new plane appears.
6. Make the plane normal to the Front plane and pass through the tangent line.

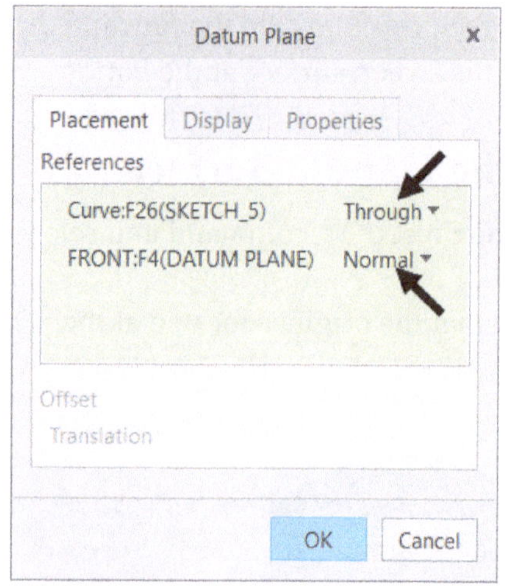

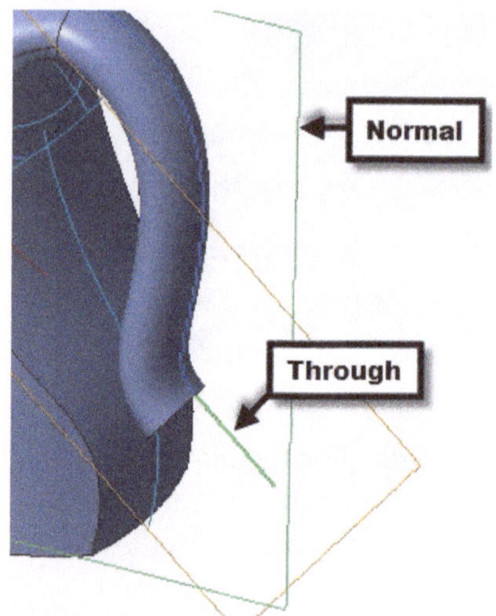

7. Click **OK** to create the datum plane.
8. Draw an ellipse and trim it by half.

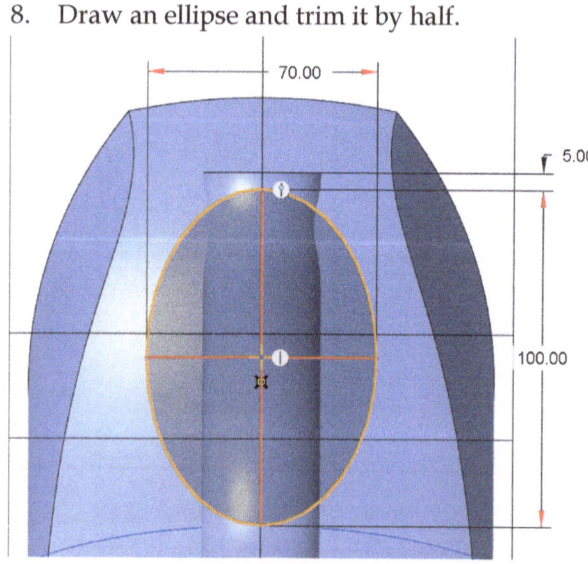

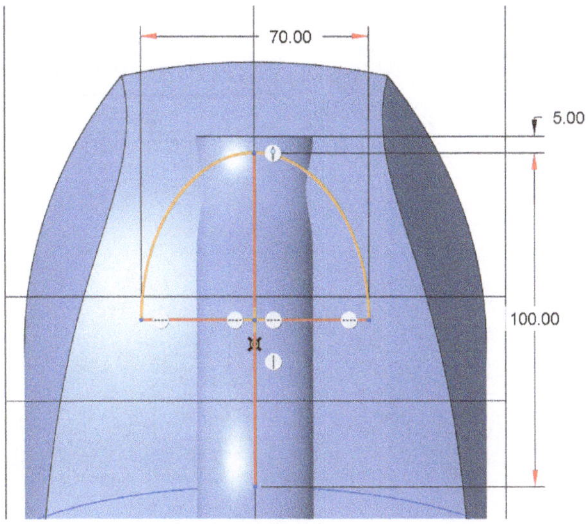

9. Exit the sketch and extrude it in both directions up to an arbitrary distance.

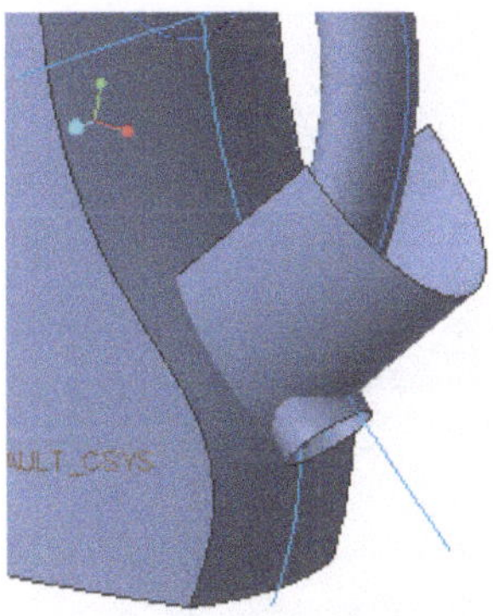

10. Press hold the Ctrl key, and then select the handle and extruded surfaces.
11. Click the **Merge** icon on the **Editing** panel.
12. Make sure that the arrows point in the direction as shown.

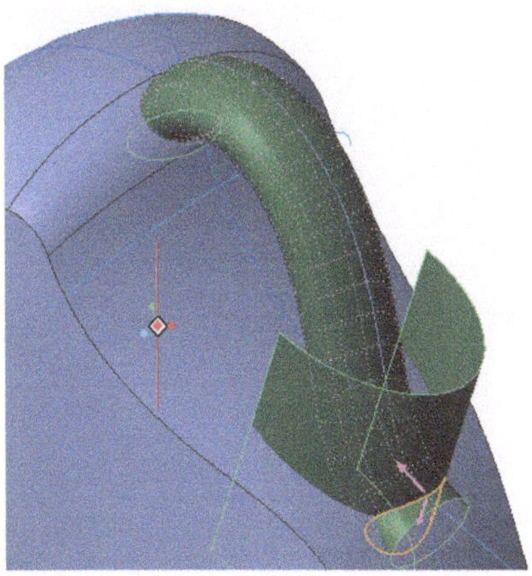

13. Click the green check to merge the two surfaces.

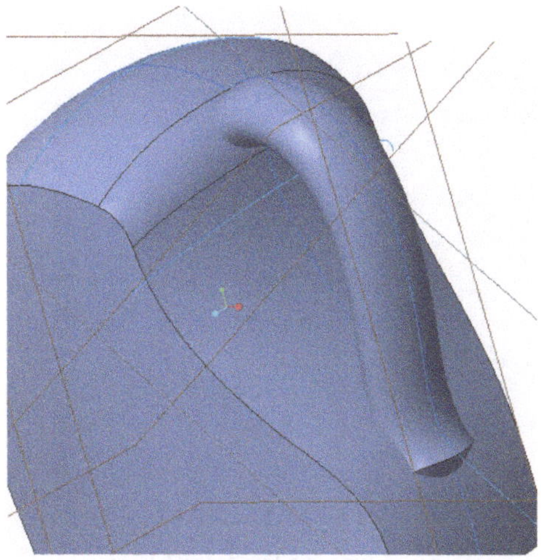

14. Press Ctrl and select the handle surface and main surface body.
15. On the **Editing** panel of the ribbon, click the **Merge** icon.
16. Make sure that the arrows point outward.
17. Click **OK** on the Dashboard.

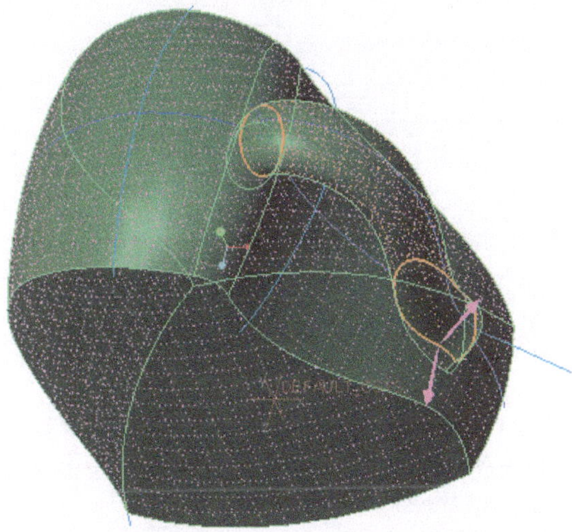

18. Activate the **Round** command and round the edge of the handle. The round radius is 6 mm.

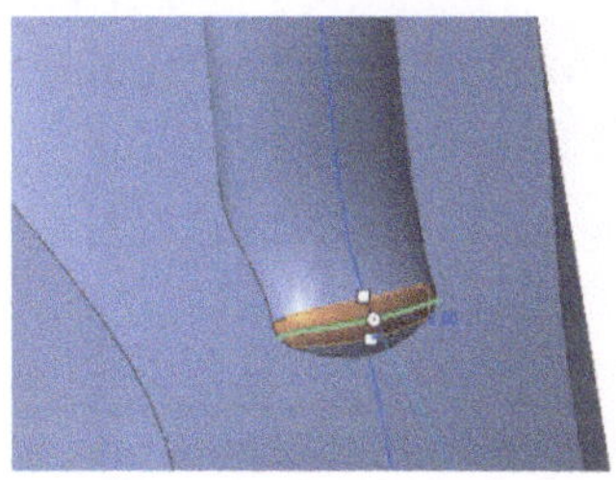

19. Round the intersection between the main surface and handle. The fillet radius is 5 mm.

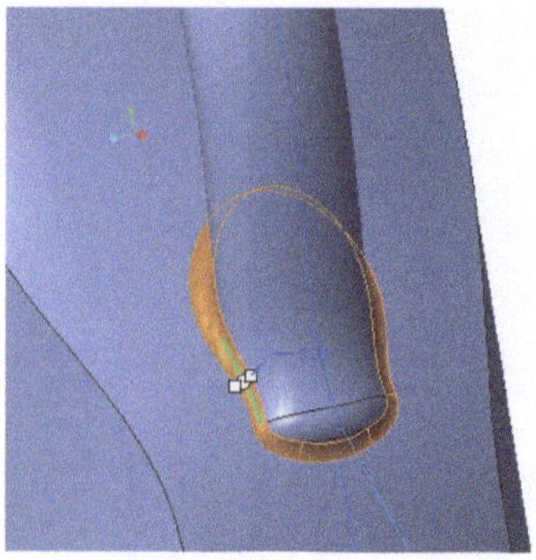

Trimming the Handle

1. Create a vertical line on the Front Plane and finish the sketch.

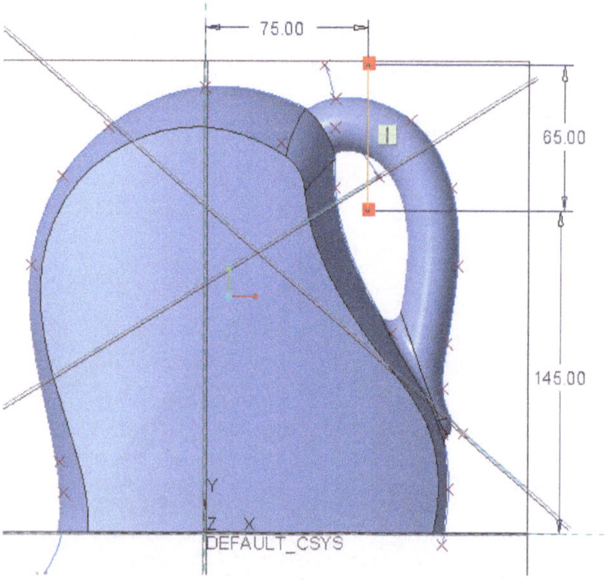

2. Activate the **Project** command (on the ribbon, click **Model** tab > **Editing** panel > **Project**) and click on the sketched line.
3. On the dashboard, click in the **Surfaces** selection box, and then click on the handle surface.
4. On the dashboard, **Direction > Along Direction**.
5. Click in the selection box next to the **Direction** drop-down, and then select the Front plane.

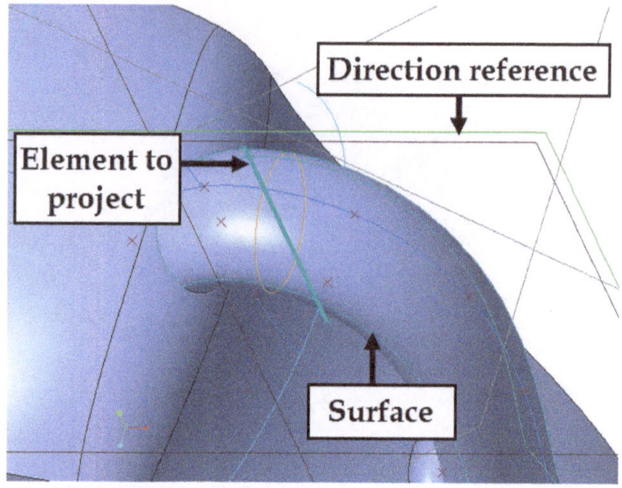

6. Click the green check on the dashboard.
7. Press Esc to deselect the projected curve.
8. Click on the handle surface, and then activate the **Trim** command.
9. Click on the projected curve.

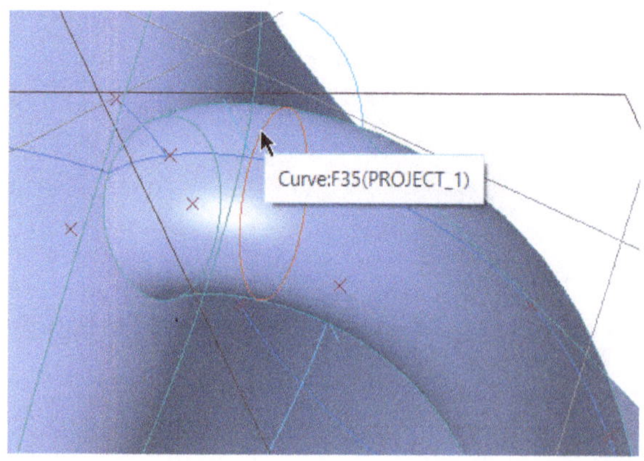

10. Make sure that the arrow points toward the right. Use the **Flip** icon, if required.

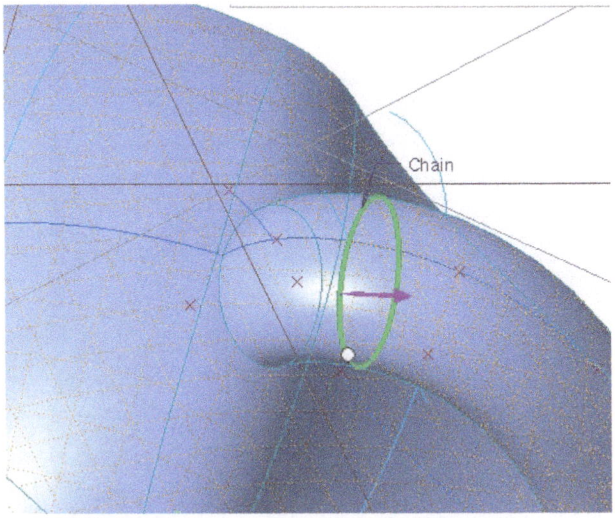

11. Click the green check on the dashboard.

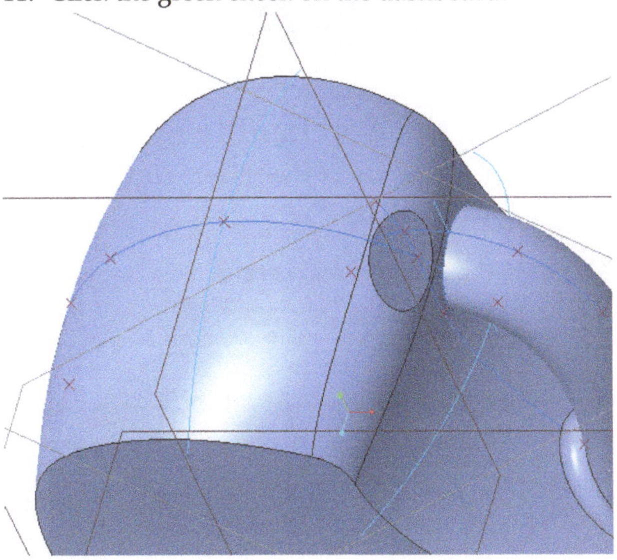

12. On the ribbon, click **Model** tab > **Datum** panel > **Plane.**
13. Press hold the Ctrl key and then click on the handle surface curve and its top endpoint.
14. On the **Datum Plane** dialog, click on the drop-down located next to the selected curve.
15. Select **Normal** from the drop-down.
16. Likewise, select **Through** from the drop-down located next to the selected point, and then click **OK.**

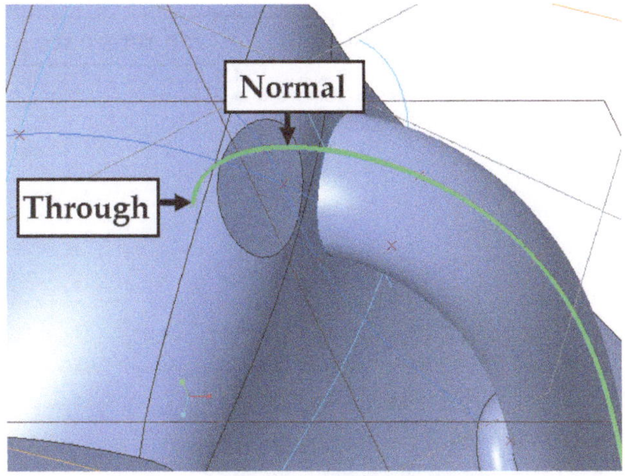

17. Start a sketch on the plane normal to the spline and draw an ellipse. Add dimensions to position the ellipse, and then finish the sketch.

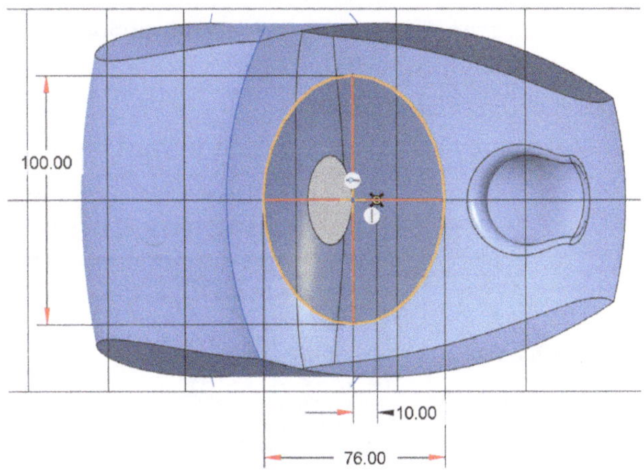

18. Activate the **Project** command (on the ribbon, click **Model** tab > **Editing** panel > **Project**) and click on the sketched ellipse.
19. On the dashboard, click in the **Surfaces** selection box.
20. Press hold the Ctrl key and then click on the three surfaces, as shown.
21. On the dashboard, **Direction > Along Direction**.
22. Click in the selection box next to the **Direction** drop-down, and then select the plane normal to the handle curve.

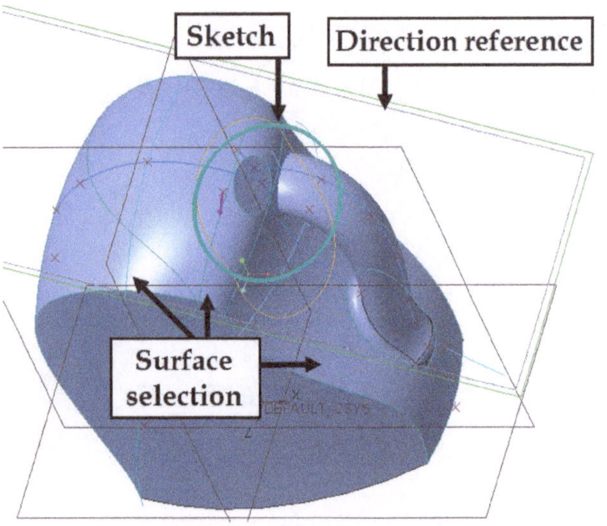

23. Click the green check on the dashboard to project the sketch.
24. Select the surface, as shown.
25. Activate the **Trim** command (on the ribbon, click **Model > Editing > Trim**).
26. Select the projected curve.
27. Make sure that the arrow points toward the left.

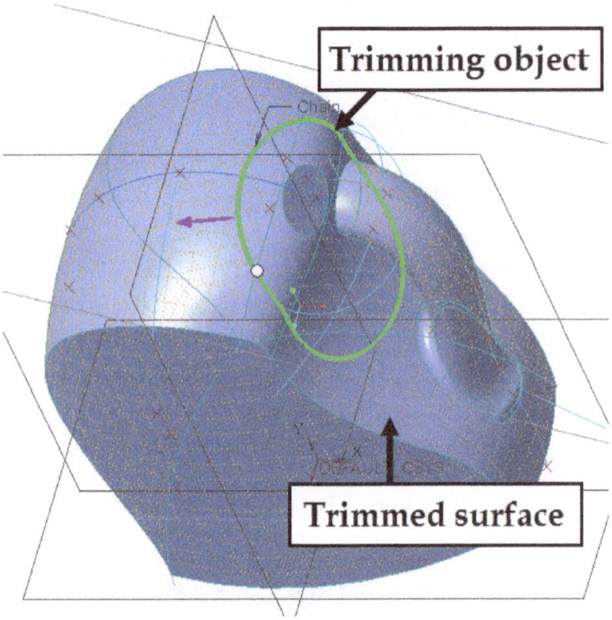

28. Click the green check on the dashboard to trim the surface.

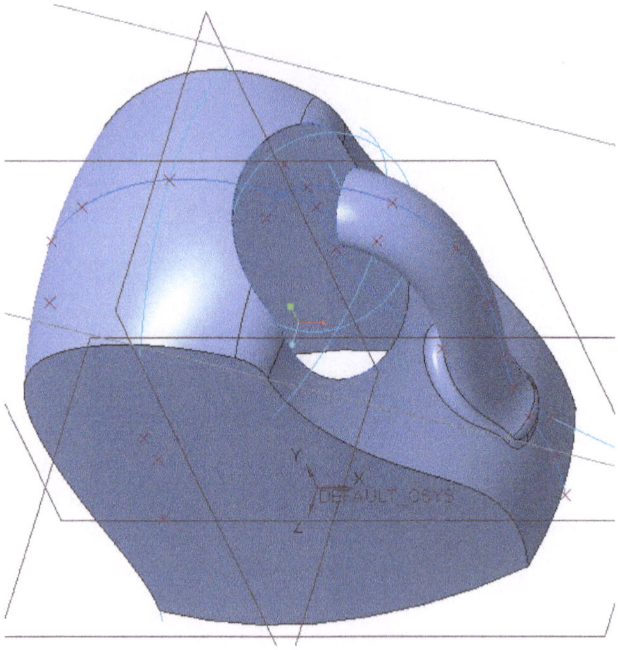

Blending the Top handle

1. On the **Model** tab of the ribbon, click **Datum > Point** .
2. Select the two vertices, as shown.

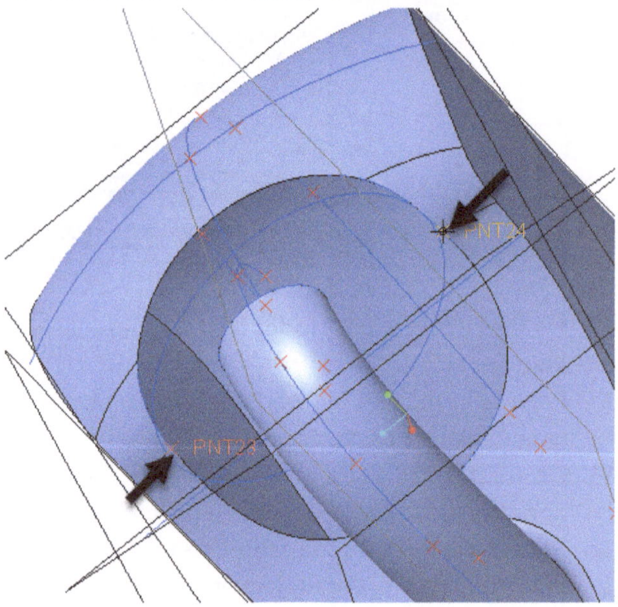

3. Click **OK**.
4. On the **Model** tab of the ribbon, click **Datum > Point** .
5. Select the edge of the handle, as shown.

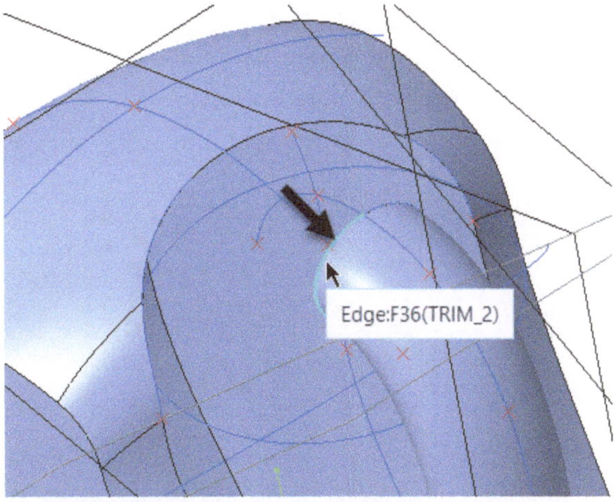

6. On the **Datum Point** dialog, type **0.5** in the **Offset** box.
7. Click **OK**.

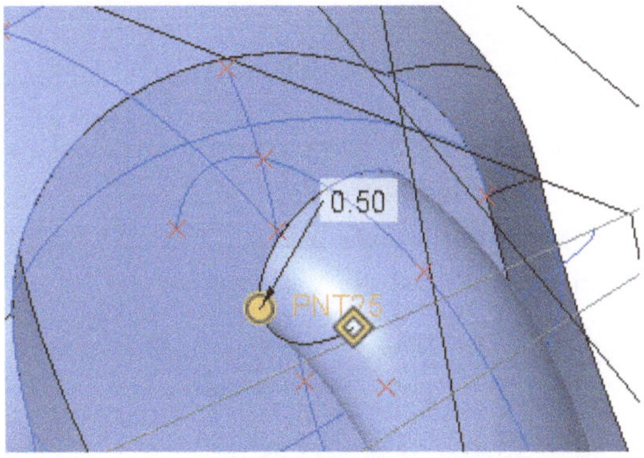

8. On the **Model** tab of the ribbon, click **Datum > Point** .
9. Select the edge of the handle, as shown.

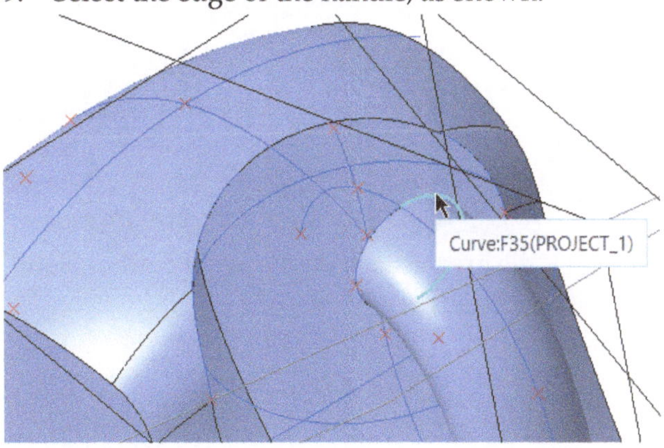

10. On the **Datum Point** dialog, type **0.5** in the **Offset** box.
11. Click **OK**.

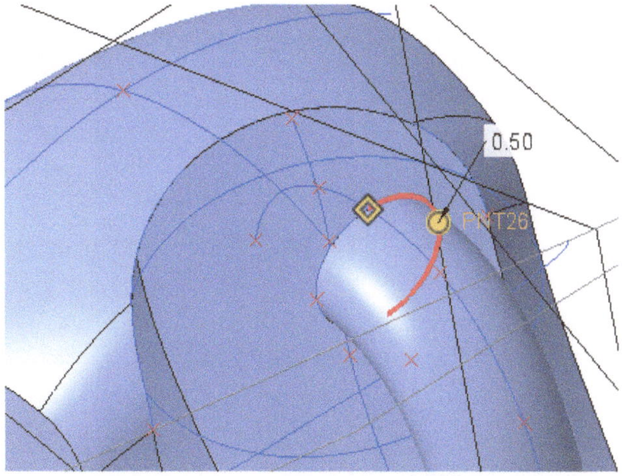

12. Activate the **Boundary Blend** command (on the ribbon, click **Model > Surfaces > Boundary Blend**).
13. Press hold the Ctrl key and click on the edges of the trimmed openings.

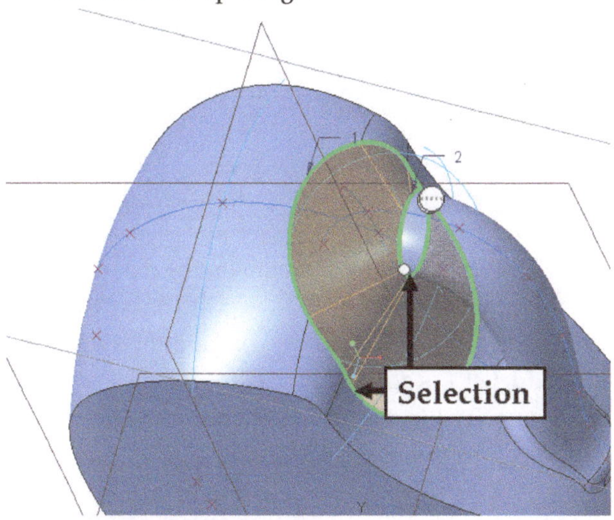

14. On the **Boundary Blend** dashboard, click the **Constraints** tab.
15. On the set the **Condition** of the two boundaries to **Tangent**.
16. Select the **Direction 1-First Chain** and change the **Stretch value** to 1.
17. Select the **Direction 1-Last Chain** and change the **Stretch value** to 2.

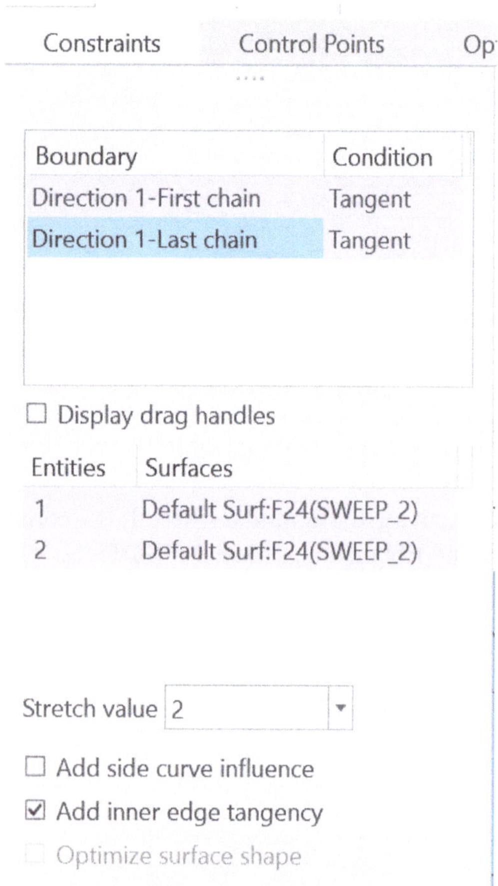

18. Click the **Control Points** tab on the dashboard.
19. Select **Fit > Natural**.
20. Right click in the **Sets** list box, and then select **Add**; Set 1 is added to the list.
21. Select **Set 1** from the Sets list box.
22. Select the points, as shown.

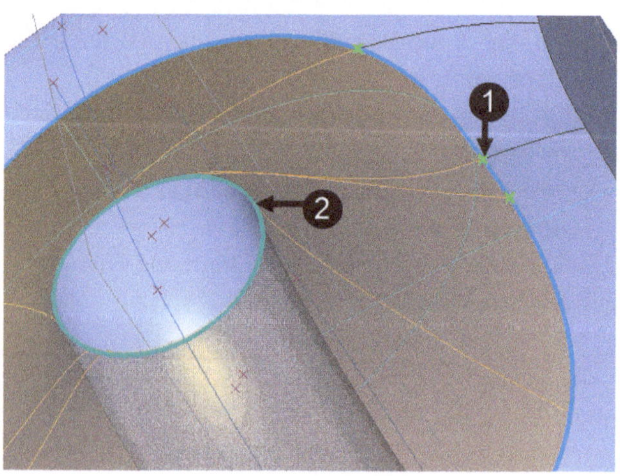

23. Right click in the **Sets** list box, and then select **Add**; Set 2 is added to the list.
24. Select **Set 2** from the **Sets** list box.
25. Select the points from the first and last chain, as shown.

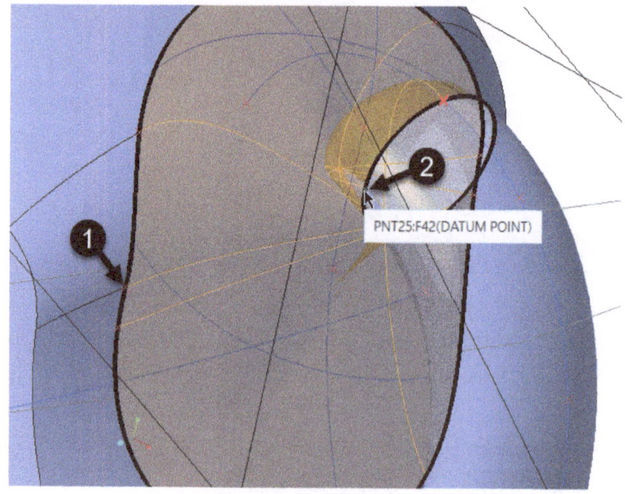

26. Right click in the **Sets** list box, and then select **Add**; **Set 2** is added to the list.
27. Select **Set 2** from the **Sets** list box.
28. Select the points, as shown.

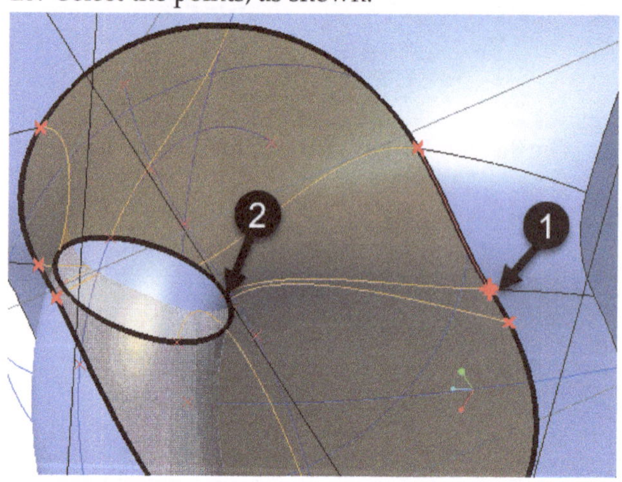

29. Click the green check on the dashboard to blend the handle surface.

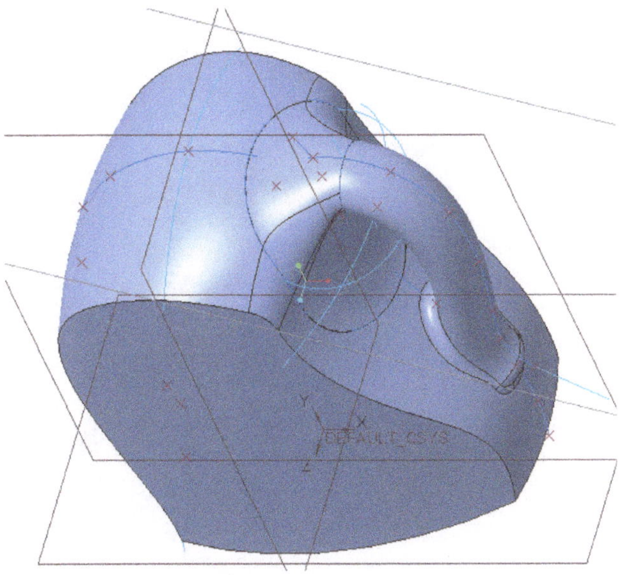

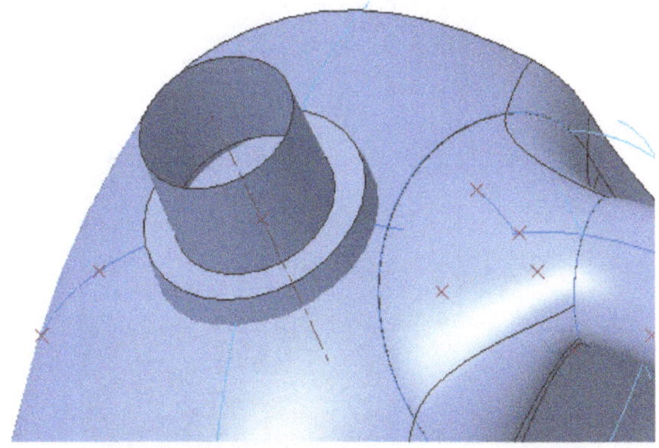

4. Press and hold the Ctrl key and select the main body and boundary blend.
5. Activate the **Merge** command.
6. Click the green check on the dashboard.

Creating the Neck and Spout

1. Start a sketch on the Front Plane and sketch the revolved surface. Exit the sketch.

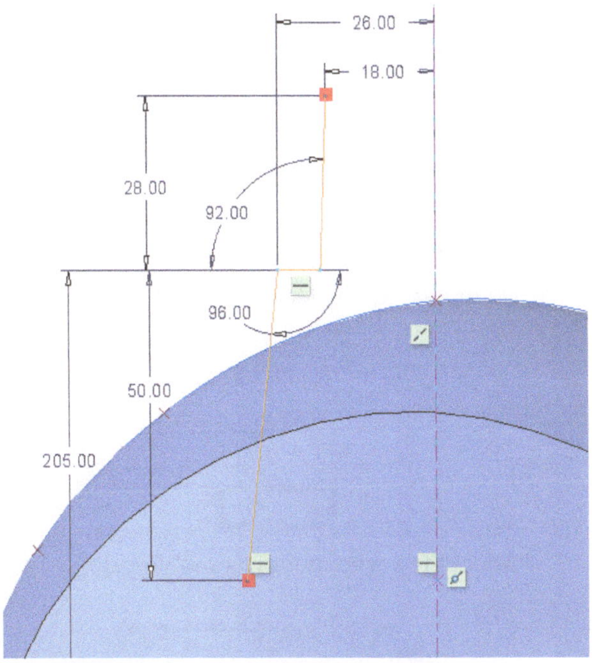

2. On the ribbon, click **Model** tab > **Shapes** panel > **Revolve**.
3. Type-in 360 in the **Angle** box and click the green check.

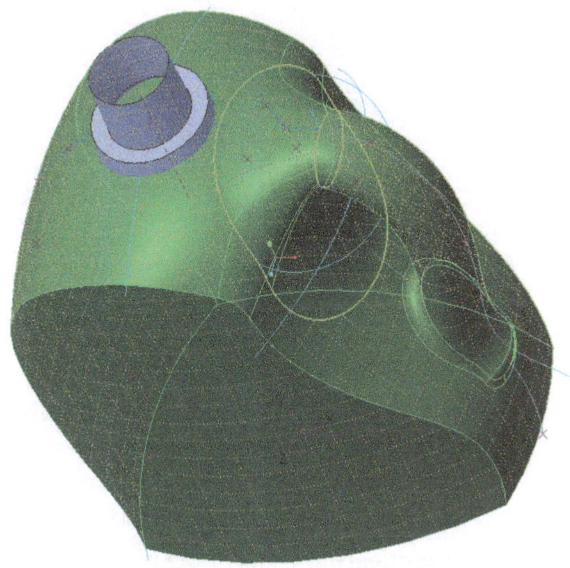

7. Press and hold the Ctrl key and select the main body and neck.
8. Activate the **Merge** command.
9. Make sure that the arrows point in the direction shown below.

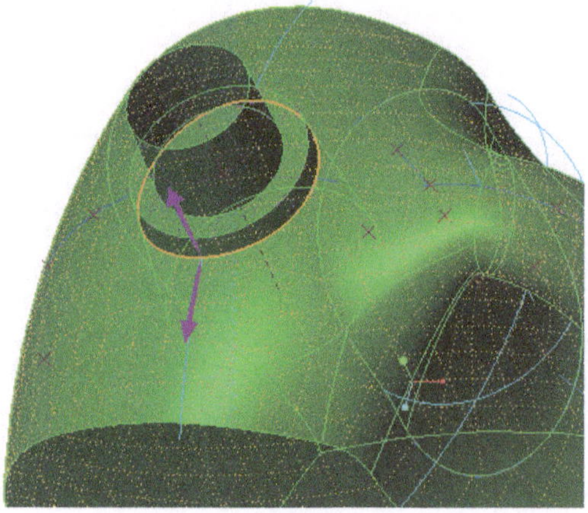

10. Click the green check to trim the unwanted portion.

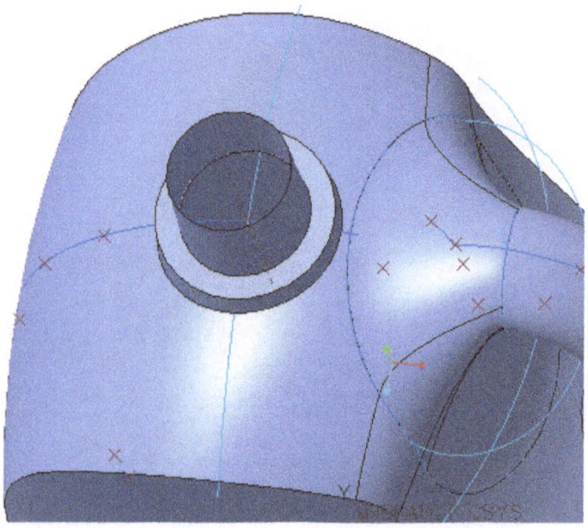

Creating the Variable Radius Round

1. On the **Engineering** panel of the ribbon, click the **Round** icon.
2. Click on the edge of the label surface, as shown below.

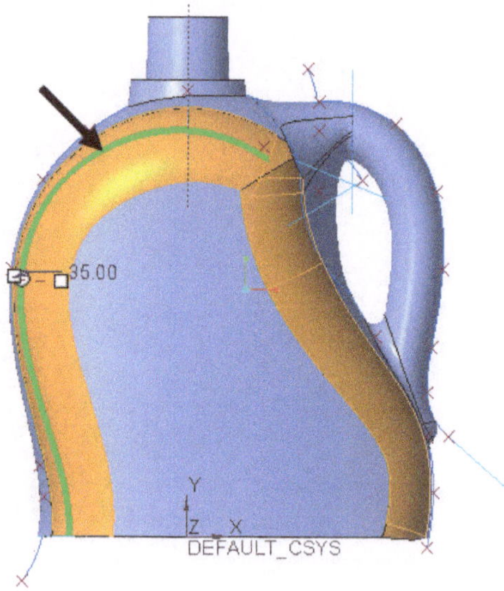

3. On the Dashboard, click the **Sets** tab.
4. In the **Radius** section, click the right mouse button and select **Add Radius**. It adds a radius point at the end of the selected edge chain.

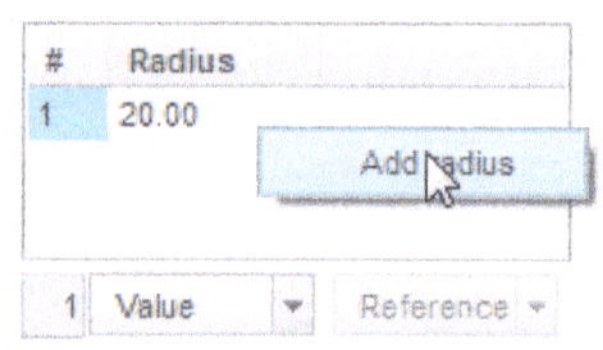

5. Likewise, add another radius point.
6. In the **Radius** section, select the third radius point and set the location type to **Reference**.

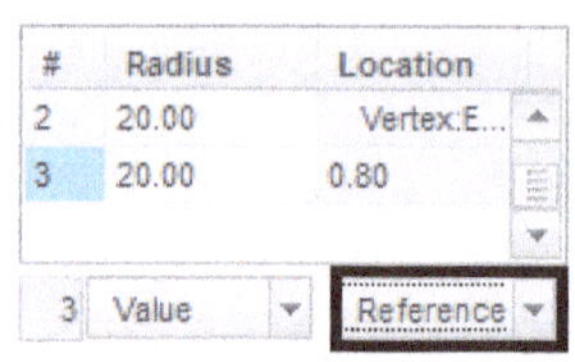

7. Select the vertex point, as shown below.

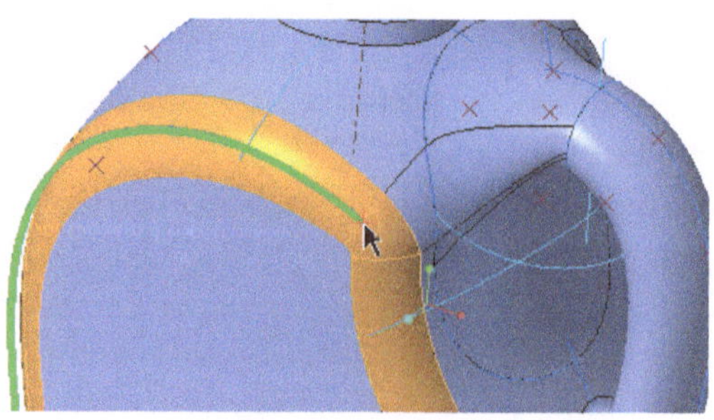

8. In the **Radius** section, set the first and second radius values to 20 and the third to 10.

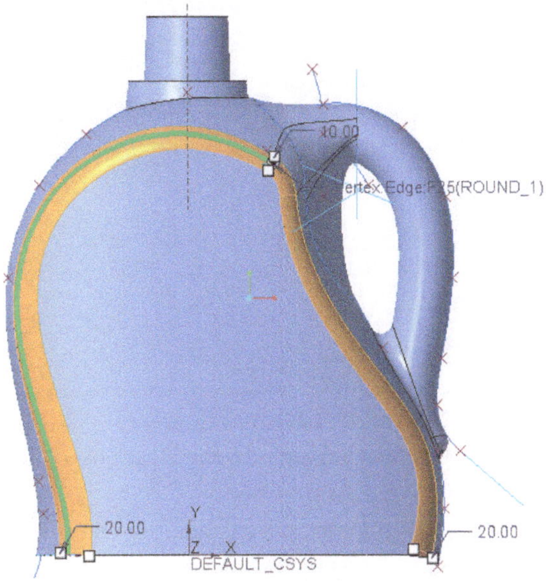

9. Click the green check to complete the variable round.
10. Likewise, create the variable radius round on the other side of the bottle.

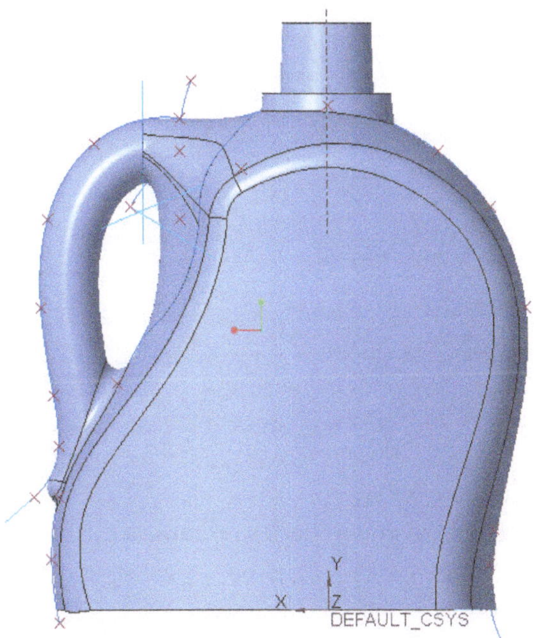

Creating a bump at the bottom

1. Start a sketch on the Top datum plane and project the edge chain at the bottom (refer to the **Project** section in **Chapter 3** to learn how to project edges).

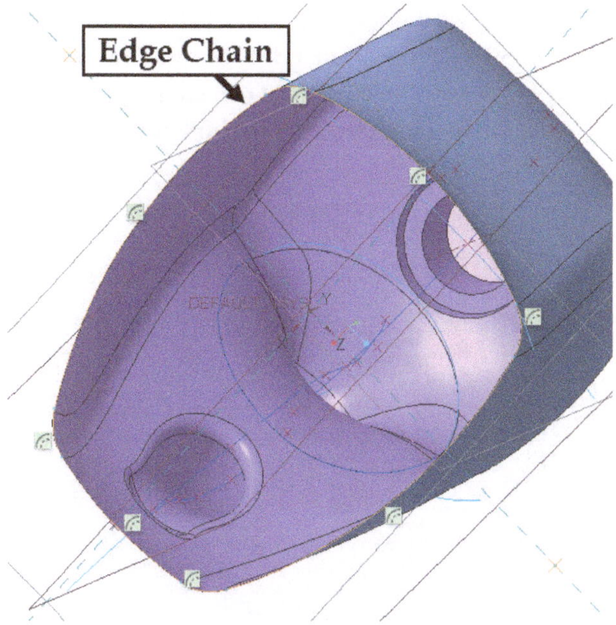

2. Click **OK** on the **Sketch** tab of the ribbon.
3. Create an offset plane from the Top Plane. The offset distance is 10 mm.

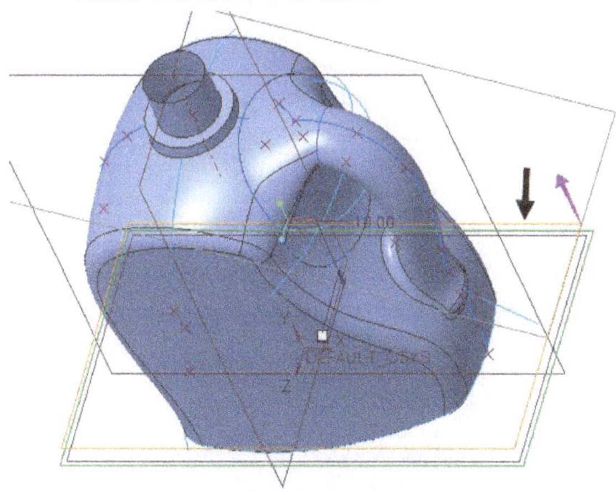

4. Start a sketch on the offset plane.
5. Offset the project edges up to -40 distance (refer to **The Offset Command** section of Chapter 2 to learn how to offset entities).

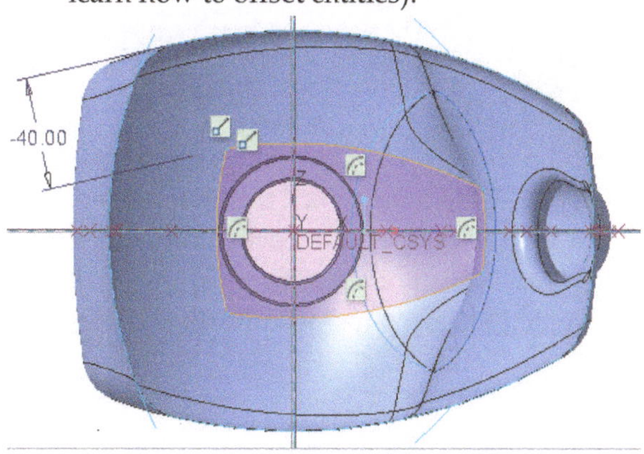

6. Round the corners of the offset sketch using the **Circular Trim** command. The corner radius is 10 (refer to **The Circular Trim command** section in **Chapter 2** to learn how round corners).

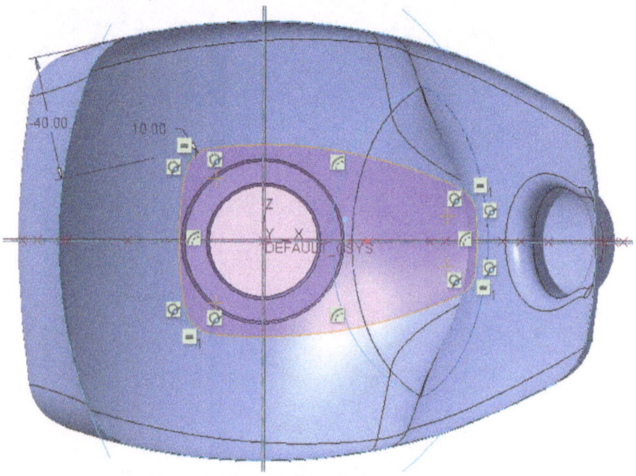

7. Click **OK** on the ribbon and deselect any sketch, if selected.
8. Expand the **Shapes** panel of the ribbon and click the **Blend** icon.
9. On the Dashboard, click the **Surface** icon.
10. Click the **Sections** tab and select the **Selected sections** option.
11. Select the outer loop and click the **Details** button.

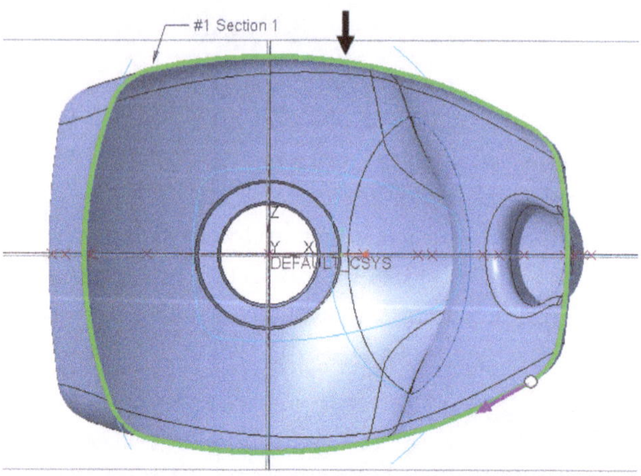

12. On the **Chain** dialog, click the **Options** tab.
13. Click in the **Start Point** selection box and select the curve's endpoint, as shown below. Make sure that the arrow points towards the left.

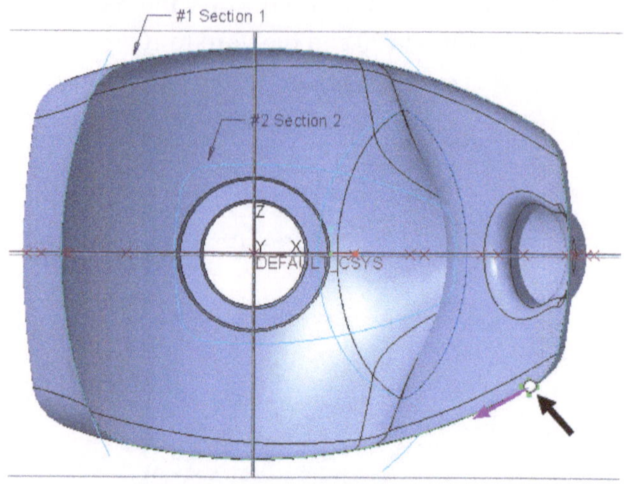

14. Click **OK** on the **Chain** dialog.
15. Click the **Sections** tab on the Dashboard, and then click the **Add** button.
16. Select the inner loop and click the **Details** button.
17. On the **Chain** dialog, click the **Options** tab.
18. Click in the **Start Point** selection box and select the endpoint, as shown below. Make sure that the arrow points towards the left.

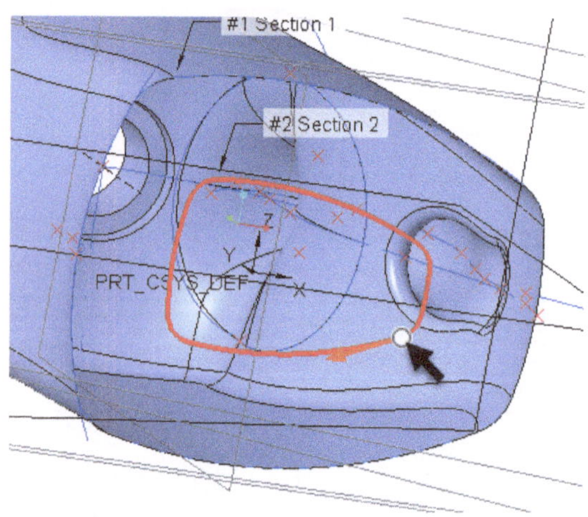

19. Click **OK**.
20. Click the green check to complete the blend.

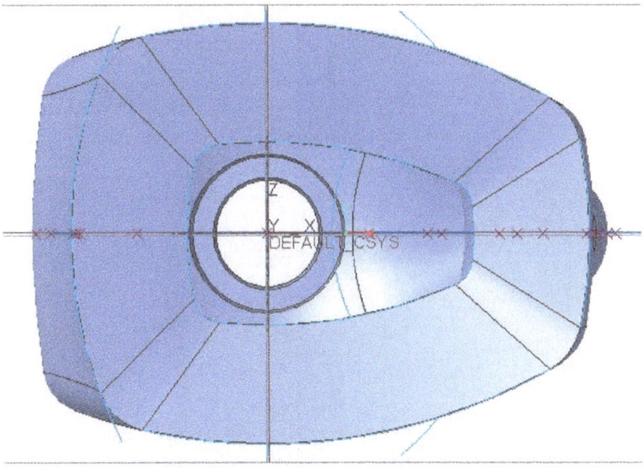

21. On the **Surfaces** panel of the ribbon, click the **Fill** icon.
22. Click on the inner loop, and then click the green check.

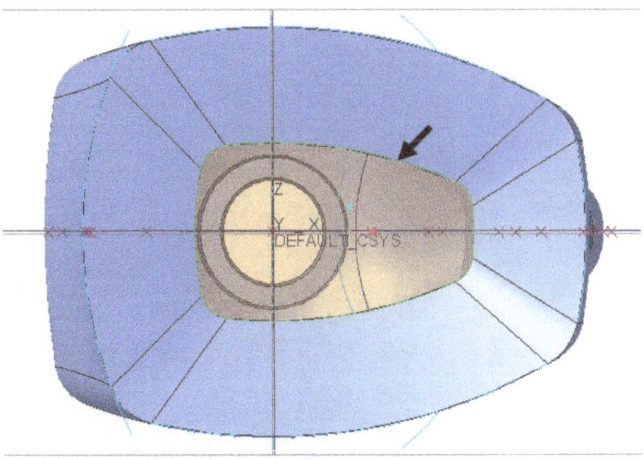

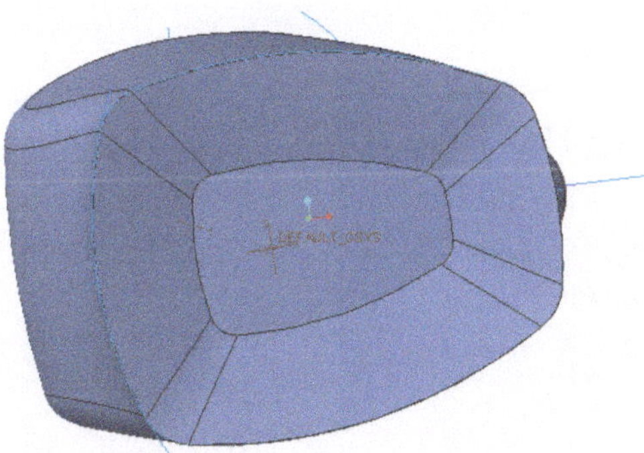

23. Merge the blend and fill surfaces.

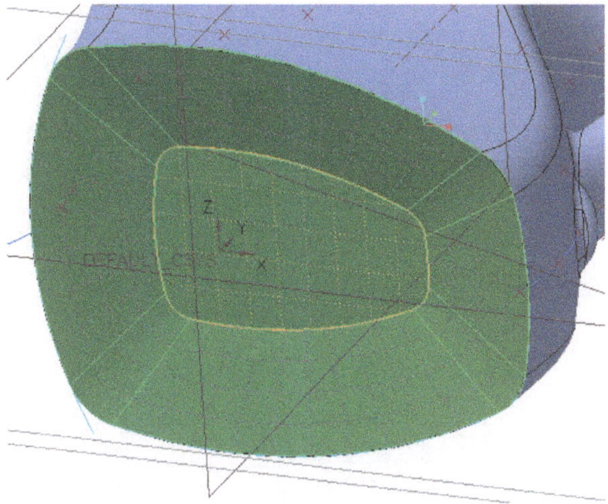

24. Activate the **Round** command.
25. Press and hold the Ctrl key and select the Fill and blend surfaces.
26. Type-in 28 in the **Radius** box, and click the green check.

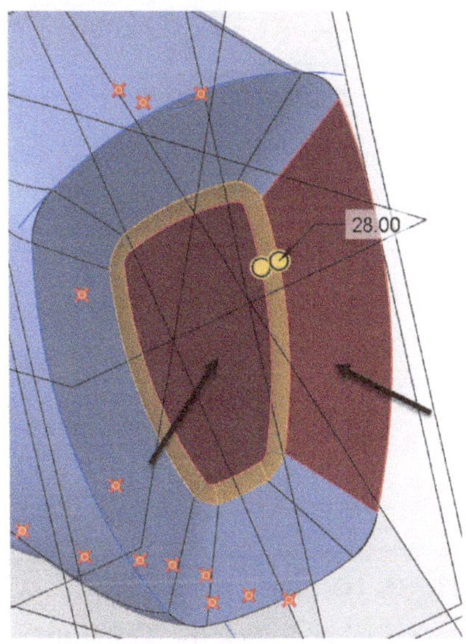

27. Merge the bottom surface with the main surface body.

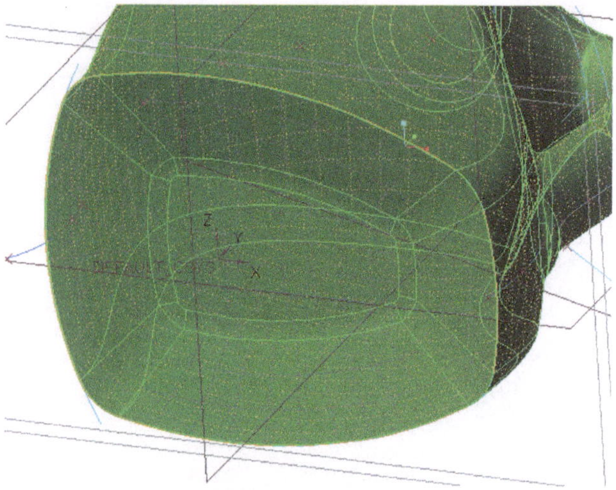

28. Activate the **Round** command.
29. Press and hold the Ctrl key and click on the bottom surface and main body.

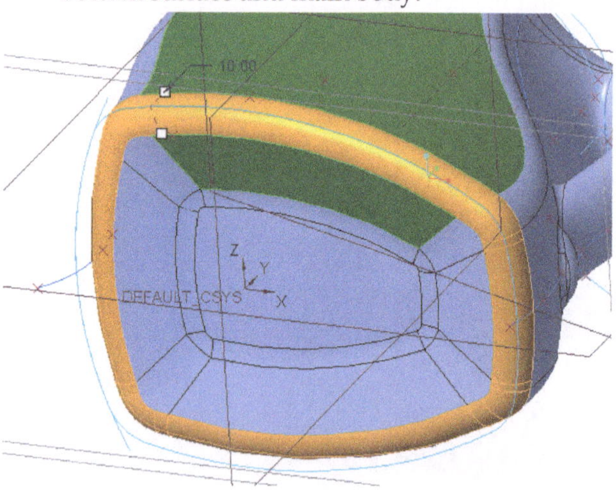

30. Type-in **10** in the **Radius** box and click the green check.

Adding thickness to the model

1. Select the surface model and click the **Thicken** icon on the **Editing** panel.
2. On the Dashboard, type 2 in the **Offset value** box.
3. Make sure that the arrow points outwards.
4. Click the green check to thicken the surface.

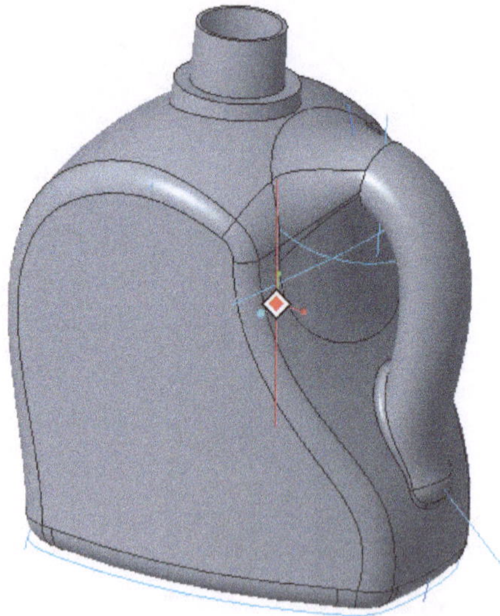

5. Round the sharp edges of the neck. The round radius is 1 mm.

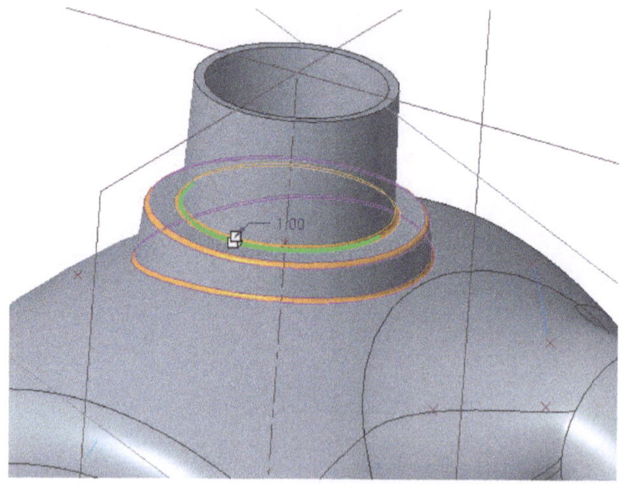

Creating the thread

1. Activate the **Plane** command, and then create a plane offset from the neck surface. The offset distance is 20 mm.

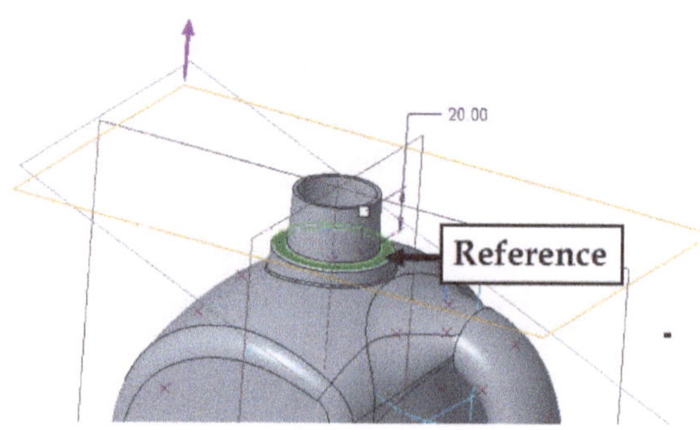

2. On the **Shapes** panel of the ribbon, click **Sweep**

drop-down > **Helical Sweep** .

3. On the Dashboard, click the **References** tab, and then click the **Define** button.
4. Select the front plane. Click the **Sketch** button to activate the sketch.
5. On the **Setup** panel of the ribbon, click the **References** icon.
6. Select the offset plane and silhouette edge of the sprout.
7. Close the **References** dialog.

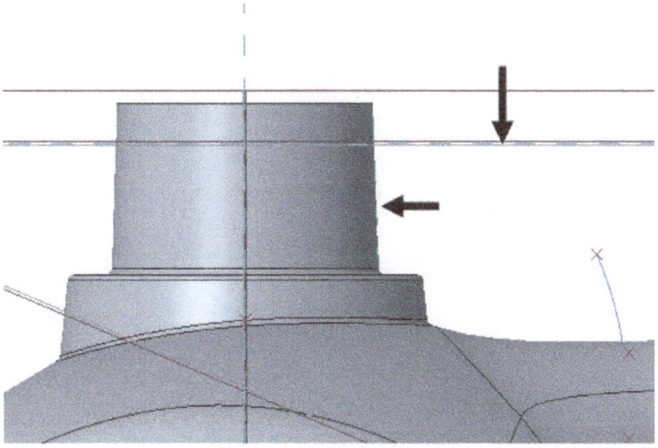

8. Draw a line coinciding with the reference silhouette edge.
9. Draw a centerline passing through the center of the neck, and then click **OK**.

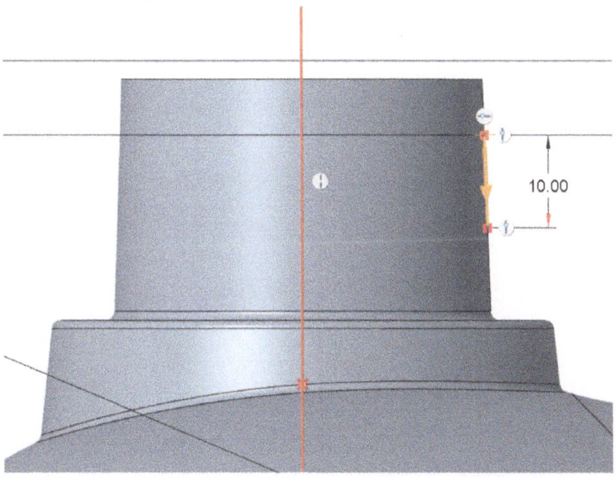

10. On the Dashboard, click the **Sketch** icon.
11. Draw the section, as shown below. Click **OK**.

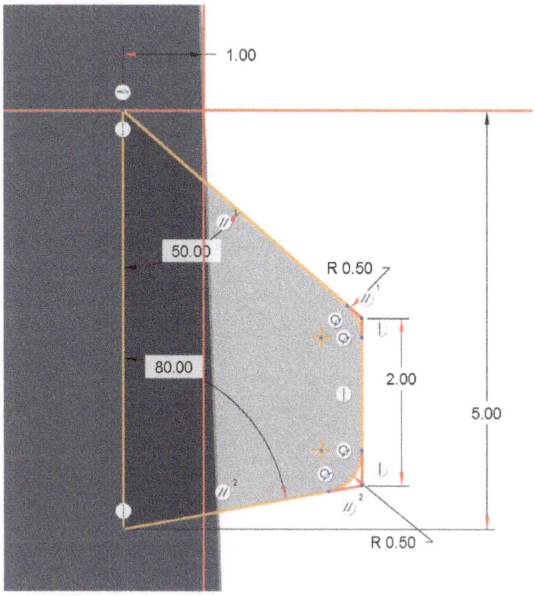

12. On the Dashboard, type-in 5 in the **Pitch** box and click the green check.

13. Save and close the file.

Questions

1. What is the use of the **Merge** command?
2. Why do we use the **Fill** command?
3. What are the commands that can be used to fill the openings on a surface?
4. Which command can be used to bridge the gap between two surfaces?

5. Name the command that can be used to trim and join the surfaces.
6. How do you add thicknesses to a surface body?
7. Which command is used to extend surfaces from an edge?
8. How do you split a solid body?
9. Which command is used to offset a face?

Index

9 788197 342936

Printed at Repro India Ltd.